The Critical Pedagogy Reader

Third Edition

For fifteen years, *The Critical Pedagogy Reader* has established itself as the leading collection of classic and contemporary essays by the major thinkers in the field of critical pedagogy. While retaining its comprehensive introduction, this thoroughly revised third edition includes updated section introductions, expanded bibliographies, and up-to-date classroom questions. The book is arranged topically around issues such as class, racism, gender/sexuality, critical literacies, and classroom issues, for ease of usage and navigation. New to this edition are substantive updates to the selections of contemporary readings, including pieces that reflect issues such as immigrant and refugee students, the role of social justice in teacher education, and an emphasis on practical elements of pedagogy, as well as its significance to forging democratic life. Carefully attentive to theory and practice, this much-anticipated third edition remains the definitive, foundational source for teaching and learning about critical pedagogy.

Antonia Darder holds the Leavey Endowed Chair in Ethics and Moral Leadership at Loyola Marymount University in Los Angeles and is Distinguished Visiting Professor at the University of Johannesburg.

Rodolfo D. Torres is Professor of Urban Planning at the University of California, Irvine.

Marta P. Baltodano is Professor of Education at Loyola Marymount University in Los Angeles.

The Critical Pedagogy Reader

Third Edition

Edited by
Antonia Darder, Rodolfo D. Torres, and Marta P. Baltodano

NEW YORK AND LONDON

Third edition published 2017
by Routledge
711 Third Avenue, New York, NY 10017

and by Routledge
2 Park Square, Milton Park, Abingdon, Oxon, OX14 4RN

Routledge is an imprint of the Taylor & Francis Group, an informa business

First edition published by Routledge 2002

Second edition published by Routledge 2008

Library of Congress Cataloging-in-Publication Data
Names: Darder, Antonia, editor. | Torres, Rodolfo D., 1949– editor. | Baltodano, Marta, editor.
Title: The critical pedagogy reader / edited by Antonia Darder, Rodolfo D. Torres, and Marta Baltodano.
Description: Third edition. | New York : Routledge, 2017. | Previous edition: 2009.
Identifiers: LCCN 2016043208 | ISBN 9781138214569 (Hardback : alk. paper) | ISBN 9781138214576 (Paperback : alk. paper)
Subjects: LCSH: Critical pedagogy.
Classification: LCC LC196 .C758 2017 | DDC 370.11/5—dc23
LC record available at https://lccn.loc.gov/2016043208

ISBN: 978-1-138-21456-9 (hbk)
ISBN: 978-1-138-21457-6 (pbk)

Typeset in Minion
by Apex CoVantage, LLC

Printed and bound in the United States of America by Sheridan

Contents

Acknowledgments

We wish to, once again, acknowledge Catherine Bernard, our dear editor at Routledge, for her brilliance and wise counsel in the production of the three editions of the *Critical Pedagogy Reader*. Her consistent support and commitment to this work has been invaluable.

We also express our appreciation to our outstanding research assistant for this project, Kortney Hernandez, for her untiring and loving support. Also thanks to Krystal Huff for joining us at the end of the project to provide last minute support to its completion. Graduate students like these give us hope for the future of the field.

We also extend our gratitude to our many colleagues and comrades, too many to mention, for their political sustenance and continuing support. We could not move forward with this work, were we not committed to a larger political vision of emancipation and solidarity—a vision we share with so many wonderful comrades.

We wish to similarly acknowledge and express our sincere appreciation to our many students over the years who have struggled with us to learn what it truly means to live a critical pedagogy.

And lastly, we extend our most loving appreciation to our families and friends, who daily extend their patience and love to us in more ways than we can ever name.

Critical Pedagogy: An Introduction

Antonia Darder, Marta P. Baltodano, and Rodolfo D. Torres

A society which makes provision for participation in its good of all members on equal terms and which secures flexible readjustment of its institutions through interaction of the different forms of associated life is in so far democratic. Such a society must have a type of education which gives individuals a personal interest in social relationships and control, and the habits of mind which secure social changes.

John Dewey
Democracy and Education, 1916

The education of any people should begin with the people themselves.

Carter G. Woodson
The Mis-education of the Negro, 1931

We believe that Education leads to action.

Myles Horton
Founder of the Highlander Folk School, 1932

Students live in a historical situation, in a social, political and economic moment. Those things have to be part of what we teach.

Herbert Kohl
Founder of the Open School Movement, 1964

The dual society, at least in public education, seems in general to be unquestioned.

Jonathan Kozol
Death at an Early Age, 1967

If situations cannot be created that enable the young to deal with feelings of being manipulated by outside forces, there will be far too little sense of agency among them. Without a sense of agency, young people are unlikely to pose significant questions, the existentially rooted questions in which learning begins.

Maxine Green
The Dialectics of Freedom, 1988

Many students, especially those who are poor, intuitively know what the schools do for them. They school them to confuse process and substance. Once these become blurred, a new logic is assumed: the more treatment there is, the better are the results; or escalation leads to success. The pupil is thereby "schooled" to confuse teaching with learning, grade advancement with education, a diploma with competence and fluency with the ability to say something new.

Ivan Illich
Deschooling Society, 1971

> Knowledge emerges only through invention and re-invention, through the restless, impatient continuing, hopeful inquiry [we] pursue in the world, with the world, and with each other.
>
> Paulo Freire
> *Pedagogy of the Oppressed*, 1971

> Our analysis of the repressiveness, inequality, and contradictory objectives of contemporary education in America is not only a critique of schools and educators, but also of the social order of which they are a part.
>
> Samuel Bowles and Herbert Gintis
> *Schooling in Capitalist America*, 1976

The words and concerns expressed above illustrate that the struggle for democratic public schooling in America has been a multidimensional enterprise, which for over a century has occupied the dreams, hearts, and minds of progressive educators. These educators were not only firmly committed to the ideal and practice of social justice within schools, but to the transformation of social structures and class conditions within society that thwart the democratic participation of all people.

Hence, critical pedagogy loosely evolved out of a yearning to give some shape and coherence to the theoretical landscape of radical principles, beliefs, and practices that contributed to transformative ideals of democratic schooling in the U.S. during the twentieth century. The development of this school of thought reflected a significant attempt to bring an array of similar and divergent views and perspectives to the table, in order to invigorate the capacity of radical educators to engage critically with the impact of capitalism and gendered, racialized, and homophobic relations on students from historically disenfranchised populations. Moreover, underlying this radical tradition are revolutionary imperatives that are linked to the abolition of class and the social and material reconfiguration of society.

The first textbook use of the term *critical pedagogy* is found in Henry Giroux's *Theory and Resistance in Education,* published in 1983. During the 1980s and 1990s, Giroux's work, along with that of Paulo Freire, Stanley Aronowitz, Michael Apple, Maxine Greene, Peter McLaren, bell hooks, Donaldo Macedo, Michelle Fine, Jean Anyon, and many others, was, inarguably, one of the most central and potent forces in the revitalization of emancipatory educational debates in this country. However, Giroux would be the first to adamantly insist that critical pedagogy emerged from a long historical legacy of radical social thought and progressive educational movements, which aspired to link practices of schooling to democratic principles of society and transformative social action in the interest of oppressed communities.

There is no doubt that in the last two decades monumental historical events have transpired that have intensified the debilitating impact of neoliberal policies in education. These include the 2001 attacks on the Twin Towers, the recalcitrant nature of militarism, financial sector abuses that led to the mortgage collapse of 2007, the expanding economic gap between the rich and the poor, the expansion of the prison industrial complex, the epidemic shooting of unarmed civilian black men and related urban rebellions in places like Baltimore and Ferguson, brown youth killings across the nation, the Black Lives Matter movement, the politics of indigeneity, and climate concerns. These are all concrete material conditions that have challenged critical educators to rethink the meaning of the role of market-driven policies and the politics of schooling in an era of financial crisis that continues to have the world on tenterhooks. This critical process has required the cultivation of greater suppleness and fluidity in defining and expanding the limits of rationality. This was especially apparent in the case of the Donald Trump candidacy during the 2016 presidential campaign.

It is, however, through such awareness that critical theories of education can continue to remain inextricably rooted to the actual material conditions and ideological structures of everyday life and conscious of the historical, political, and economic landscapes that give rise to their formation. In keeping with the spirit of such a commitment, critical pedagogical scholarship has necessitated rigorous examination into societal concerns that inherently give rise to the process of schooling. Included here are aspects of popular culture, media literacy, curricular epistemicides, indigenous struggles, ecological conditions, and the political possibilities of a public pedagogy in the evolution of social movements.

Major Influences on the Formation of Critical Pedagogy

Twentieth Century Educators and Activists

The views of American philosopher and educator John Dewey, often referred to as the *father of the progressive education movement*, had a significant influence on progressive educators concerned with advancing democratic ideals. During the early 1900s, Dewey sought to articulate his pragmatic philosophy and expand on the idea of community to explain the purpose of education in a democratic society. His beliefs centered on a variety of basic principles, including the notion that education must engage with an enlarged experience; that thinking and reflection are central to the act of teaching; and that students must freely interact with their environments in the practice of constructing knowledge. Although there are those who have sharply criticized Dewey's faith in creative intelligence as eminently naïve and accused him of underestimating the sociopolitical and economic forces that shape inequality and injustice, Dewey's work is consistent in "his attempt to link the notion of individual and social (cooperative) intelligence with the discourse of democracy and freedom" (McLaren, 1989, p. 199). By so doing, John Dewey provided "a language of possibility"—a philosophical construct of foremost significance to the evolution of critical pedagogy.

The works of W.E.B. DuBois and Carter G. Woodson, often referred to as the *father of Black History*, rightly merit recognition for their important contributions to the evolution of critical pedagogical thought, particularly with respect to the education of African American students and other racialized inequalities (Graves, 1998). Published in 1902, DuBois's *The Souls of Black Folk* still stands as a poignant treatise on the impact of racism on racialized populations. Woodson's volume, *The Mis-Education of the Negro* published in 1933, boldly speaks to the destructive nature of mainstream education. Ardently convinced that education was essential to liberation, the two men shared a deep desire to transform the social inequalities and educational injustices suffered by African Americans. Moreover, DuBois and Woodson clearly foresaw the importance of an oppressed people regaining access to their own history. They tirelessly championed the right of African American students to a process of schooling that would prepare them to critically challenge socially prevailing notions of the time—notions that denied them their humanity, imprisoned them as a disposable class, and trampled their self-respect as a people. Most importantly, the historical influence of DuBois and Woodson set the stage for many of the contemporary educational struggles associated with anti-racism, multiculturalism, and social justice today.

Myles Horton, considered by some to be one of the sparks that ignited the civil rights movement in the United States, channeled his belief in the political potential of schooling into the founding of the Highlander Folk School (known today as the Highlander Research and Education Center) in Monteagle, Tennessee. His wife, Zilphia Johnson Horton, brought an important cultural dimension to the work, through her integration of singing into the school curriculum and labor organizing activities. The purpose of the school was to provide a place for the education of blacks and whites in defiance of segregation laws. Over the years, Horton and Zilphia's work resulted in the participation of thousands of people, challenging entrenched social, economic, and political structures of a deeply segregated society. One of the most noted among them was the civil rights activist Rosa Parks, who had attended Highlander just a few months prior to her refusal to move to the back of the bus. Key to Horton's political practice was the notion that in order for education or institutional change to be effective, it had to begin with the people themselves—a particularly significant tenet of critical pedagogical thought.

In the early 1960s, the views of educational critic Herbert Kohl provided the impetus for the development of the Open School Movement in the United States. His efforts to challenge and address issues of democratic schooling were fundamentally rooted upon a tradition of radical politics and radical history that could counter the structures of oppression at work in public schools. Kohl's deep commitment to community interactions and his tremendous faith in students set a significant example for the practice of teaching diverse working class students. And although he has been known to take issue with the academic writings of critical educators today, Kohl's uncompromising political views on schooling and activism were significant in helping to lay the groundwork for the development of critical pedagogical practices in the years to come.

Beginning with his first book *Death at an Early Age*, the work of long-time author and social activist, Jonathan Kozol, has consistently examined issues of racism, class, and schooling inequalities, grounding his conclusions upon the actual stories and experiences of dispossessed populations in this country. More importantly, he has sought to address the material conditions and expose the social consequences of poverty and racism to those children and their families who have been relegated to an existence at the margins of American life. For Kozol, questions of education could not only be engaged in terms of the theoretical, programmatic, or technical; they also had to be reconceptualized along human, spiritual, as well as political grounds. In *The Shame of the Nation: The Restoration of Apartheid Schooling in America*, Kozol again exposed the immorality of human oppression, documenting the worsening conditions of schools in poor and racialized communities. During the summer of 2007, both stunned by the U.S. Supreme Court decision that reversed *Brown v. Board of Education* by prohibiting state-ordered integration programs, and in protest of No Child Left Behind, Kozol began a partial fast to call attention to the issue.

The internationally recognized philosopher and educator Maxine Green has played a pivotal role in her work with critical educators in the United States. Often referred to as the *mother of aesthetic education*, Greene was the first woman to be hired at Teachers College as philosopher. In the midst of the hostility she faced as a woman and a Jew within the academy in the early 60s, Greene persevered to become a formidable force in the theoretical arena of aesthetics and its relationship to education and society. Many of her views on education and democracy today still echo thoughts and concerns raised by Dewey, almost a century ago. For Greene, democracy constitutes a way of life that must be practiced within both social and political arenas, made living through our relationships, our educational experiences, as well as our moments of beauty and enjoyment out in the world. Greene's contribution to critical pedagogy is most evident by the manner in which her reflective theories of knowledge, human nature, learning, curriculum, schooling, and society have influenced the practice of progressive educators for over 30 years.

In the arena of schooling and the political economy, the work of such noted theorists as Samuel Bowles and Herbert Gintis, Martin Carnoy, and Michael Apple all contributed significantly to the forging of a critical pedagogical perspective. The work of these scholars consistently upheld the centrality of the economy in the configuration of power and class relations within schools and society. Through their persistent critique of capitalism, these theorists argued, in a variety of ways, that the problems associated with schooling are deeply tied to the reproduction of a system of social relations that perpetuates the existing structures of domination and exploitation. Michael Apple, in particular, linked notions of cultural capital with the school's reproduction of official knowledge—knowledge that primarily functioned to sustain the inequality of class relations within schools and society.

Ivan Illich, who in the 1950s worked as a parish priest among the poor Irish and Puerto Rican communities of New York City, has been considered by many to be one of the most radically political social thinkers in the second half of the twentieth century. His critical writings on schooling and society, including *Deschooling Society* published in 1971, sought to analyze the institutional structures of industrialization and to provide both rigorous criticism and an alternative to what he perceived as the crisis of a society that endorses growth economy, political centralization, and unlimited technology. In very important ways, Illich's views on education and the institutionalization of everyday life inspired critical education theorists and activists during the latter half of the twentieth century to rethink their practice in schools and communities. The most notable among these was the Brazilian educator Paulo Freire.

The Brazilian Influence

While progressive educators and social activists such as Myles Horton, Martin Luther King, Herbert Kohl, Angela Davis, Cesar Chavez, Malcolm X, and many others challenged the disgraceful conditions of oppressed people in the United States, Brazilian educator Paulo Freire and his contemporary Augusto Boal were also involved in challenging the horrendous conditions they found in the cities and countryside of Brazil—a struggle that was historically linked to the emancipatory efforts of many educators and political activists in other countries across Latin America.

Paulo Freire would be forced to live in exile for over 15 years for his writings on education and the dispossessed members of Brazilian society. In the early 1970s, Paulo Freire was extended an invitation to come to Harvard University as a visiting professor. It was his presence in the U.S. during that precise historical moment, along with the translation of *Pedagogy of the Oppressed* into English, that became a watershed for radical educators in schools, communities, and labor organizations, struggling to bring about social change to public health, welfare, and educational institutions across the country.

As a consequence, Paulo Freire is considered by many to be the most influential educational philosopher in the development of critical pedagogical thought and practice. From the 1970s until his death in 1997, Freire continued to publish and speak extensively to educators throughout the United States. Although Freire's writings focused on questions of pedagogy, his thought widely influenced post-colonial theory, ethnic studies, cultural studies, adult education, media studies, and theories of literacy, language, and social development. Most importantly, Freire labored consistently to ground the politics of education within the existing framework of the larger society.

As with so many of the influential educators previously mentioned, Freire's efforts were never simply confined to discussions of methodology or applications of teaching practice. Instead, Freire forthrightly inserted questions of power, culture, and oppression within the context of schooling. In so doing, he reinforced the Frankfurt School's focus on theory and practice as imperative to the political struggles against exploitation and domination. Freire's pedagogical perspective encompassed values that promoted anti-authoritarian, dialogical, and interactive practices, which also sought to critically engage issues of societal power at work in the lives of students and teachers. Through this emancipatory pedagogical vision, Freire made central pedagogical questions related to social agency, voice, and democratic participation—questions that still inform recurrent philosophical and practical expressions of critical pedagogy today.

Augusto Boal's book, *Theatre of the Oppressed,* was released in 1971, the same year as Freire's seminal text, *Pedagogy of the Oppressed.* In the 1960s Boal developed an experimental theatre approach whereby the cast would stop a performance and invite members of the audience to provide or demonstrate new suggestions on stage. By so doing, he unexpectedly discovered an effective pedagogical form of praxis that evolved directly from the audience's participation, collective reflection, and the action generated by participants. Excited and inspired by the process of empowerment he witnessed among participants, Boal began to developed what was to be know the as "spec-actor" (in contrast to spectator) theatre approach.

Seeing the possibilities of his approach as a vehicle for grassroots activism, Boal's work in communities began to give shape to his *Theatre of the Oppressed.* Similar to Freire, Boal's work as a cultural activist was repressed by the military coup that came into power during the 1960s. Similar to Freire, Boal was arrested, tortured, and eventually exiled for his activities. He continued to develop his work in Argentina and later in Paris. He returned to Brazil in 1986, when the military junta was removed from power. Boal's work was first linked to Freire's work in the U.S. at the Pedagogy and Theatre of the Oppressed Conference in 1994. Boal's contribution was to mark a significant turning point for those critical educators and artists who had become frustrated with what they perceived as, on one hand, the deeply theoretical nature of critical pedagogy and, on the other, the absence of more practical and affective strategies to enliven their work. For these critical educators, Boal's *Theatre of the Oppressed* provided a new avenue upon which to build and rethink their educational practice in schools and communities.

Gramsci and Foucault

Although it is impossible to discuss here all the "classical" theorists who influenced the intellectual development of critical pedagogy, the contributions of Antonio Gramsci and Michel Foucault to a critical understanding of education merit some discussion. These philosophers extended existing notions of power and its impact on the construction of knowledge. Their writings also strengthen the theoretical foundation upon which to conduct critical readings of culture, consciousness, history, domination, and resistance.

Antonio Gramsci, imprisoned by Mussolini during World War II for his active membership in the Communist party and public rejection of fascism, was deeply concerned with the manner in which domination was undergoing major shifts and changes within advanced industrial Western societies. In *Prison Notebooks*, Gramsci carefully articulated a theory of hegemony, as he sought to explain how the historical changes of the time were being exercised less and less through brutal physical force. Instead, he argued that the mechanism for social control was exercised through the moral leaders of society (including teachers), who participated and reinforced universal "common sense" assumptions of "truth."

This phenomenon can be understood within the context of schooling in the following way. Through the daily implementation of specific norms, expectations, and behaviors, that incidentally conserve the interest of those in power, students are ushered into consensus. Gramsci argued that by cultivating such consensus through personal and institutional rewards, students could be socialized to support the interest of the ruling elite, even when such actions were clearly in contradiction with the student's own class interests. As such, this reproduction of ideological hegemony within schools functioned to sustain the hegemonic processes that reproduced cultural and economic domination within the society. This process of reproduction was then perpetuated through what Gramsci termed "contradictory consciousness." However, for Gramsci this was not a clean and neat act of one-dimensional reproduction. Instead, domination existed here as a complex combination of thought and practices, in which could also be found the seeds for resistance.

The French philosopher Michel Foucault deeply questioned what he termed "regimes of truth" that were upheld and perpetuated through the manner in which particular knowledge was legitimated within a variety of power relationships within society. However, for Foucault, power did not represent a static entity, but rather an active process constantly at work on our bodies, our relationships, our sexuality, as well as on the ways we construct knowledge and meaning in the world. Power, in Foucault's conceptualization, is not solely at play in the context of domination, but also in the context of creative acts of resistance—creative acts that are produced as human beings interact across the dynamic of relationships, shaped by moments of dominance and autonomy. Such a view of power challenged the tendency of radical education theorists to think of power solely from the dichotomized standpoint of either domination or powerlessness. As such, Foucault's writings on knowledge and power shed light on the phenomenon of student resistance within the classroom and opened the door to a more complex understanding of power relationships within our teaching practice.

The Frankfurt School

Critical educational thought is fundamentally linked to those critical theories of society that emerged from the members of the Frankfurt School and their contemporaries. These theorists sought to challenge the narrowness of traditional forms of rationality that defined the concept of meaning and knowledge in the Western world, during a very critical moment in the history of the twentieth century. As such, their work was driven by an underlying commitment to the notion that theory, as well as practice, must inform the work of those who seek to transform the oppressive conditions that exist in the world.

The Institute for Social Research (*Das Institute fur Sozialforshung*) was officially established in Frankfurt in 1923 and was the home of the Frankfurt School. The institute came under the direction of Max Horkheimer in 1930. Although there were a number of other prominent thinkers who worked under the direction of Horkheimer, those most prominent in the development of critical social theory included Theodor Adorno, Walter Benjamin, Leo Lowenthal, Erich Fromm, and Herbert Marcuse. Herbert Marcuse, in particular, is considered by some as the most prominent scholar of the Frankfurt School to influence critical pedagogical thought. As others in his tradition, Marcuse incorporated the thought of Hegel, Marx, and Heidegger, in his efforts to imagine a society in which all aspects of our humanity—our work, play, love, and sexuality—functioned in sustaining a free society. More recently, the work of Jurgen Habermas has also received much attention within the arena of critical theory.

In the early years, the Frankfurt theorists were primarily concerned with an analysis of bourgeois society's substructure, but with time their interest focused upon the cultural superstructures. This overarching emphasis was, undoubtedly, a result of the disruptions and certain fragmentation experienced in the process of emigration and repeated relocation in the 1930s and 1940s—a process that was precipitated by the threat of Nazism, the member's avowedly Marxist orientation, and the fact that most of them were Jews.

One cannot attempt to understand the foundations of critical theory without considering the historical context that influenced its development and shaped the minds of its foremost thinkers. The Frankfurt School came into being as a response to the important political and historical transformations taking place in the early part of the twentieth century. The political shifts in Germany's governing structure had a significant impact upon its founders. During the early part of the century, Germany had managed to temporarily contain class conflict. But within two years following World War I, the foundations of the German imperial system were undermined and a republic was declared in Berlin (Held, 1980). What followed were thirteen years of chaotic political struggles between the German Communist Party (KPD) and the more conservative forces of the Social Democratic Party (SPD).

As the KPD became increasingly ineffective in their efforts to organize a majority of the working class, the Social Democratic Leadership of the Weimar Republic supervised the destruction of the competing radical and revolutionary movements. In the process, the SDP did not only fail to implement the promised democratization and socialization of production in Germany, but it failed to stop the monopolistic trends of German industrialists and the reactionary elements which eventually paved the way for the emergence of Nazism. As the forces of the Nazis, under Hitler's control, seized power in Germany, Italy and Spain came under the fascist leaderships of Mussolini and Franco. A similar fate befell the workers' struggle in these countries, where all independent socialist and liberal organizations were suppressed.

In light of the Marxist orientation shared by the members of the Frankfurt School, "the emergence of an antidemocratic political system in the country of the first socialist revolution" (Warren, 1984, p. 145), consequently, had a profound impact upon the development of critical theory. Moreover, the Russian revolution had been systematically weakened by foreign interventions, blockades, and civil war; and Lenin's revolutionary vision was rapidly losing ground. After Lenin's death in 1924, Stalin advanced in Russia with the expansion of centralized control and censorship, a process created to maintain European Communist parties under Moscow's leadership. In 1939, the Hitler–Stalin pact was enacted, representing an ironic historical moment for those committed to the struggle of the working class and the socialist principles espoused by Marx.

A final event that strongly influenced the thinking of the Frankfurt School theorists was the nature and impact of unconfined forces of advanced capitalism in the West. The rapid development of science and technology and their persuasive penetration into the political and social systems summoned a new and major transformation in the structure of capitalism. This accelerated development of an advanced industrial-technological society represented a serious area of concern.

The major historical and political developments of capitalist society, as well as the rise of bureaucratic communist orthodoxy affirmed for the founders of critical theory the necessity to address two basic needs: 1) the need to develop a new critical social theory within a

Marxist framework that could deal with the complex changes arising in industrial-technological, postliberal, capitalist society; and 2) the need to recover the philosophical dimensions of Marxism, which had undergone a major economic and materialistic reduction by a new Marxist orthodoxy (Warren, 1984).

The Frankfurt School intended their findings to become a material force in the struggle against domination of all forms. Based upon the conditions they observed, the following questions were central to the work of the Institute (Held, 1980, p. 35):

> The European labor movements did not develop in a unified struggle of workers. What blocked these developments?
>
> Capitalism was a series of acute crises. How could these better be understood? What was the relation between the political and the economic? Was the relation between the political and the economic? Was the relation changing?
>
> Authoritarianism and the development of the bureaucracy seemed increasingly the order of the day. How could these phenomena be comprehended? Nazism and fascism rose to dominate central and southern Europe. How was this possible? How did these movements attain large-scale support?
>
> Social relationships, for example those created by the family, appeared to be undergoing radical social change. In what directions? How were these affecting individual development?
>
> The arena of culture appeared open to direct manipulation. Was a new type of ideology being formed? If so, how was this affecting everyday life?
>
> Given the fate of Marxism in Russia and Western Europe, was Marxism itself nothing other than a state orthodoxy? Was there a social agent capable of progressive change? What possibilities were there for effective socialist practices?

Philosophical Principles of Critical Pedagogy

In response to many of these questions, Horkheimer, Adorno, Marcuse, Fromm, and others wrote seminal essays that were to serve as the building blocks for a critical theory of society. It was this critical perspective that ultimately provided the foundation for the philosophical principles that were to determine the set of heterogeneous ideas that were later to be known as critical pedagogy. We highlight the use of heterogeneous here because it is important to emphasize that there does not exist a formula or homogenous representation for the universal implementation of any form of critical theory or critical pedagogy. In fact, it is precisely this distinguishing factor that supports its critical nature, and therefore its revolutionary potential and transformative possibility.

The philosophical heterogeneity of its array of radical expressions is then only consolidated through an underlying and explicit intent and purpose to the unwavering liberation of oppressed populations—an intent and commitment fundamentally rooted to the abolition of class and the transformation of society. Toward this end, a set of principles tied to the radical belief in the historical possibility of such a transformation can be tentatively fleshed out for the purpose of teaching and to better understand what is implied by a critical perspective of education, society and the world. The following provides a very brief and general introduction to the principles that inform critical pedagogy. However, it is imperative that readers bear in mind that a multitude of both specific and complex expressions of these philosophical ideas has emerged through a variety of historical social processes and within diverse intellectual traditions—traditions that have sought to explore the relationship between human beings, society, and schooling, via a myriad of epistemological, political, economic, cultural, ideological, ethical, historical, aesthetic, and methodological points of reference.

Cultural Politics

Critical pedagogy is fundamentally committed to the development and enactment of a culture of schooling that supports the empowerment of culturally marginalized and economically disenfranchised students. By so doing, this pedagogical perspective seeks to help transform those classroom structures and practices that perpetuate undemocratic life. Of particular importance then is a critical analysis and investigation into the manner in which traditional theories and practices of public schooling thwart or influence the development of a politically emancipatory and humanizing culture of participation, voice, and social action within the classroom. The purpose for this is intricately linked to the fulfillment of what Paulo Freire defined as our "vocation"—to be truly humanized social (cultural) agents in the world.

In an effort to strive for an emancipatory culture of schooling, critical pedagogy calls upon teachers to recognize how schools have historically embraced theories and practices that serve to unite knowledge and power in ways that sustain asymmetrical relations of power. Under the guise of neutral and apolitical views of education, practices of meritocracy, for example, rooted in ideologies of privilege, shaped by power, politics, history, culture, and economics, have prevailed. Schools, thus, function as a terrain of on-going cultural struggle over what is accepted as legitimate knowledge. In response, critical pedagogy seeks to address the concept of cultural politics by both legitimizing, as well as challenging, experiences and perceptions shaped by the histories and socioeconomic realities that give meaning to the everyday lives of students and their constructions of what is perceived as truth.

Political Economy

Critical education contends that, contrary to the traditional view, schools actually work against the class interests of those students who are most politically and economically vulnerable within society. The roles of competing economic interests of the marketplace in the production of knowledge and in the structural relationships and policies that shape public schools are recognized as significant factors, particularly in the schooling of disenfranchised students. From the standpoint of the political economy, public schools serve to position select groups within asymmetrical power relations that replicate the existing cultural values and privileges of the dominant class. It is this uncontested relationship between schools and society that critical pedagogy seeks to challenge, unmasking traditional claims that education provides equal opportunity and access for all.

Hence, what is at issue here is the question of class reproduction and how schooling practices are deceptively organized to perpetuate racialized inequalities. This is to say that within the context of critical pedagogy, the relationship between culture and class is intricate, and they cannot be separated within the context of daily life in schools. The concept of class here refers to the economic, social, ethical, and political relationships that govern particular sectors of the social order. More importantly, critical pedagogy acknowledges the myriad of ways in which social class, within the lives of students and teachers, contributes to their understanding of who they are and how they are perceived within schools and society.

Historicity of Knowledge

Critical pedagogy supports the notion that all knowledge is created within a historical context and it is this historical context that gives life and meaning to human experience.

True to this principle, schools must be understood not only within the boundaries of their social practice but within the boundaries of the historical events that inform educational practice. Along these lines, students and the knowledge they bring into the classroom must be understood as historical—that is, being constructed and produced within a particular historical moment and under particular historical conditions.

As such, critical pedagogy urges teachers to create opportunities in which students can come to discover that "there is no historical reality which is not human" (Freire, 1971, p. 125). By so doing, students come to understand themselves as subjects of history and to recognize that conditions of injustice, although historically produced by human beings, can also be transformed by human beings. This concept of student social agency is then tied to a process of collective and self-determined activity. This historical view of knowledge also challenges the traditional emphasis on historical continuities and historical development. Instead, it offers a mode of analysis that stresses the break, discontinuities, conflicts, differences, and tensions in history, all of which serve in bringing to light the centrality of human agency as it presently exists, as well as within its possibilities for change (Giroux, 1983).

Dialectical Theory

In opposition to traditional theories of education that serve to reinforce certainty, conformity, and technical control of knowledge and power, critical pedagogy embraces a dialectical view of knowledge that functions to unmask the connections between objective knowledge and the cultural norms, values, and standards of the society at large. Within this dialectical perspective, all analysis begins first and foremost with human existence and the contradictions and disjunctions that both shape and make problematic its meaning. Hence, the problems of society are not seen as merely random or isolated events, but rather as moments that arise out of the interaction between the individual and society (McLaren, 1989).

An important emphasis here is that students are encouraged to engage the world within its complexity and fullness, in order to reveal the possibilities of new ways of constructing thought and action beyond how it currently exists. Rooted in a dialectical view of knowledge, critical pedagogy seeks to support dynamic interactive elements, rather than participate in the formation of absolute dichotomies or rigid polarizations of thought or practice. By so doing, it supports a supple and fluid view of humans and nature that is relational; an objectivity and subjectivity that is interconnected; and a coexistent understanding of theory and practice. Most importantly, this perspective resurfaces the power of human activity and human knowledge as both a product and a force in the shaping of the world, whether it is in the interest of domination or the struggle for liberation.

Ideology and Critique

Ideology can best be understood as a societal lens or framework of thought, used in society to create order and give meaning to the social and political world in which we live. Also important here is the notion that ideology be understood as existing at the deep, embedded psychological structures of the personality. Ideology, then, more often than not, manifests itself in the inner histories and experiences that give rise to questions of subjectivity as they are constructed by individual needs, drives, and passions, as well as the changing material conditions and class formations within society. As such, a critical notion of ideology provides the means for not only a critique of educational curricula, texts and practices, but the fundamental ethics that inform their production.

As a pedagogical tool, ideology can be used to interrogate and unmask the contradictions that exist between the mainstream culture of the school and the lived experiences and knowledge that students use to mediate the reality of school life. Ideology in this instance provides teachers with the necessary insight and language to examine how their own views about knowledge, human nature, values, and society are mediated through the commonsense assumptions they employ to structure classroom experiences. In this way, the principle of ideology in critical pedagogy serves as a useful starting point for asking questions that will help teachers to evaluate critically their practice and to better recognize how the culture of the dominant class becomes embedded in the hidden curriculum—a curriculum informed by ideological views that structurally reproduce dominant cultural assumptions and practices that silence and thwart democratic participation.

Hegemony

Hegemony refers to a process of social control that is carried out through the moral and intellectual leadership of a dominant sociocultural class over subordinate groups (Gramsci, 1971). Critical pedagogy incorporates this notion of hegemony in order to demystify the asymmetrical power relations and social arrangements that sustain the interest of the ruling class. This critical principle acknowledges the powerful connection that exists between politics, economics, culture, and pedagogy. By making explicit hegemonic processes in the context of schooling, teachers are challenged to recognize their responsibility to critique and transform those classroom relationships that perpetuate the economic and cultural marginalization of subordinate groups.

What is important to recognize here is that the process of critique must be understood as an on-going phenomenon, for hegemony is never a static or absolute. On the contrary, hegemony must be fought for constantly in order to retain its privileged position as the status quo. As a consequence, each time a radical form threatens the integrity of the status quo, generally this element is appropriated, stripped of its transformative intent, and reified into a palatable form. This process serves to preserve intact the existing power relations. Hence, understanding how hegemony functions in society provides critical educators with the basis for understanding not only how the seeds of domination are produced, but also how they can be challenged and overcome through resistance, critique, and social action.

Resistance and Counter-Hegemony

Critical pedagogy incorporates a theory of resistance in an effort to better explain the complex reasons why many students from subordinate groups consistently fail within the educational system. It begins with the assumption that all people have the capacity and ability to produce knowledge and to resist domination. However, how they choose to resist is clearly influenced and limited by the social and material conditions in which they have been forced to survive and the ideological class formations that have been internalized in the process.

The principle of resistance seeks to uncover, for example, the degree to which oppositional behavior among students is associated with their need to struggle against social and material conditions of oppression in their lives or is inadvertently tied to the perpetuation of their own oppression. As in other aspects of critical pedagogy, the notion of emancipatory interests serves here as a central point of reference in determining when oppositional behavior reflects a moment of resistance that can support counter-hegemonic purposes.

The term counter-hegemony is used within critical pedagogy to refer to those intellectual and social spaces where power relationships are reconstructed to make central the voices and experiences of those who have historically existed at the margins of public institutions. This is achieved whenever a transformative social context is forged out of moments of resistance, through establishing alternative structures and practices that democratize relations of power, in the interest of liberatory possibilities. It is significant to note here that given the powerful and overarching hegemonic political apparatus of advanced capitalist society, there is often great pressure placed upon individuals and groups, who rather than to simply conform to the status quo, seek to enact counter-hegemonic alternatives of teaching and learning that are in sync with revolutionary possibilities.

In response to the stress of this political pressure faced by many critical educators, Freire consistently stressed that it is a political imperative to develop a strong command of one's particular academic discipline. He believed that a solid knowledge of the authorized curriculum was essential, whether one taught in pre-school or primary education, the middle or high school grades, or higher education, or the university, if radical educators were to create effective counter-hegemonic alternatives for their students. By so doing, they could competently teach the current "official transcript" of their field or discipline, while simultaneously creating the opportunities for students to engage critically this content, through their existing knowledge and living history, with an eye toward the future reinvention of a more just world.

Praxis: The Alliance of Theory and Practice

A dialectical view of knowledge supports the notion that theory and practice are inextricably linked to our understanding of the world and the actions we take in our daily lives. In keeping with this view, all theory is considered with respect to the practical intent of challenging asymmetrical relations of power and transforming the fundamental sociopolitical and economic structures that reproduce inequalities. Unlike deterministic notions of schooling practice that focus primarily on an instrumental/technical application of theory, critical praxis is conceived as self-creating and self-generating free human activity in the interest of justice. All human activity is understood as emerging from the on-going interaction of reflection, dialogue, and action—namely praxis—and as praxis, all human activity requires theory to illuminate it and provide a better understanding of the world as we find it and as it might be.

Hence, within critical pedagogy, all theorizing and truth claims are subject to critique, a process that constitutes analysis and questions that are best mediated through human interaction within democratic relations of power. Critical pedagogy places a strong emphasis on this relationship of *question-posing* within the educational process. Freire argued that a true praxis is impossible in the undialectical vacuum driven by a separation of the individual from the object of their study. For within the context of such a dichotomy, both theory and practice lose their power to transform reality. Cut off from practice, theory becomes abstraction or "simple verbalism." Separated from theory, practice becomes ungrounded activity or "blind activism."

Dialogue and Conscientization

The principle of dialogue as best defined by Freire is one of the most significant aspects of critical pedagogy. It speaks to an emancipatory educational process that is above all committed to the empowerment of students through challenging the dominant educational discourse and illuminating the right and freedom of students to become subjects of their world. Dialogue constitutes an educational strategy that centers upon the development of critical social consciousness or what Freire termed "conscientizaçao."

In the practice of critical pedagogy, dialogue and analysis serve as the foundation for reflection and action. It is this educational strategy that supports a problem-posing approach to education—an approach in which the relationship of students to teacher is, without question, dialogical, each having something to contribute and receive. Students learn from the teacher; teachers learn from the students. Hence, the actual lived experiences cannot be ignored nor relegated to the periphery in the process of coming to know. Instead, they must be actively incorporated as part of the exploration of existing conditions and knowledge, in order to understand how these came to be and to consider how they might be different.

Conscientizaçao, or conscientization, is defined as the process by which students, as empowered subjects, achieve a deepening awareness of the social realities that shape their lives and discover their own capacities to recreate them. This constitutes a recurrent, regenerating process of human interaction that is utilized for constant clarification of reflections and actions that arise in the classroom, as students and teachers move freely through the world of their experiences and enter into dialogue anew.

Critiques of Critical Pedagogy

The fundamental purpose of this volume is to provide a starting place for the study of critical pedagogy, through providing a short historical overview of those theoretical perspectives and philosophical principles that inform a critical theory of pedagogy. However, it would be contrary to its philosophical origins and intent to not mention, albeit briefly, some of the fundamental critiques that over the last two decades have fueled major debates within the context of critical pedagogical circles. Many of the critiques raised have effectively served to prompt a deepening consciousness as to our interpretations of critical pedagogical theories and practices within school and society.

Feminist Critiques

Numerous criticisms of critical pedagogy have been rooted in feminist views and articulations of identity, politics, and pedagogy. Some of the most significant critiques that have been issued are by such notable feminist scholars as Elizabeth Ellsworth, Carmen Luke, Jennifer Gore, Patti Lather, and Magda Lewis. As one might instantly recognize in the preceding discussion, the leading recognized scholars considered to have most influenced the development of critical theory and critical pedagogy have all been men, with the exception of Maxine Greene. From this standpoint alone, there has been much suspicion and concern about the failure of critical pedagogy to engage forthrightly questions of women, anchored within the context of female experience and knowledge construction. Moreover, struggles over gender representation persist. A case in point, in a 2016 international conference on critical pedagogy in Mexico, featured ten speakers; nine of the ten were men. As such, critical pedagogy has been accused of only challenging myopically the structures and practices of patriarchy in theory, while conditions of sexism within the field prevail.

Within the context of feminist critiques, questions have been launched against the underlying carte blanche acceptance of the Enlightenment's emphasis on the emancipatory function of cognitive learning that informs the Marxian perspective of reason—a view that underpins critical philosophical views of human beings, knowledge, and the world. Along the same lines, there has been concern with the integration of Freudian analytical views within the work of the Frankfurt School—theories that clearly have served as a guiding light for the evolvement of critical pedagogical thought. Hence, in an effort to challenge the privileging of reason as the ultimate sphere upon which knowledge is constructed, feminists have passionately argued for pedagogical embodiment through the inclusion of personal biography, narratives, a rethinking of authority, and an explicit engagement with the historical and political location of the knowing subject—all aspects essential to challenging patriarchy and reconstructing the sexual politics that obstruct the democratic participation of women as empowered historical subjects of their lives and destinies.

The Language of Critical Pedagogy

In very practical ways, the language of critical pedagogy has often been a serious point of contention not only among feminist scholars but also working class educators, who argue that the theoretical language ultimately functions to create a new form of oppression. Hence, rather than liberate those historically found at the margins of classical intellectual discourse, the language reinscribes power and privilege. Accordingly, the language was not only critiqued in the early days for its incessant use of the masculine pronoun in reference to both male and female subjects, but also for its elitism and consequent inaccessibility to those most affected by social inequalities. On one hand, these critiques challenged critical theorists to rethink the direction of their work and reconsider alternative strategies and approaches to the articulation of theoretical concerns. On another note, they encouraged critical theorists to engage forthrightly with deeper questions being stirred by the debates, in terms of literacy, class, gender, culture, power, and the emancipatory potential of diverse political projects within different traditions of struggle and pedagogy.

Critiques from the Borderlands

As might be expected, similar concerns have been raised among those scholars intimately involved in the struggle against racialized inequalities within schools and society. Although it cannot be denied that the writings of feminist scholars of color, such as Audre Lorde, Toni Morrison, Gloria Anzaldúa, Trinh Minh-Ha, and bell hooks have had a tremendous impact on contemporary perspectives of gender, sexuality, and race in critical pedagogy, much of the work of these scholars remains primarily associated with ethnic, cultural, or feminist studies, with the exception of bell hooks.

Hence, another "obvious" characteristic of these men once again provoked some controversy—the fact that most of them are "white." At moments in the history of critical pedagogy, this factor became a major source of contention, as concerns were raised about the failure of critical pedagogy to explicitly treat questions of race, culture, or indigeneity as central concerns or from the specific location of racialized and colonized populations themselves. When such concerns were raised, they were often silenced by accusations of "essentialism." Hence, questions of voice, agency, and identity politics have fueled massive debates that have often created great suspicion and strife in efforts to work across diverse cultural perspectives.

From such debates sprung the intersectionality argument, grounded in the notion that critical theorists with their link to Marxist analysis and classical European philosophical roots were not only ethnocentric but also reductionist. Feminists and critics of color insisted that questions of race/gender/sexuality be given equal weight in any critical analysis of schooling in the United States. Such efforts were not only focused on the production of different readings of history and society, but on the empowerment of those groups who had existed historically at the margins of mainstream life.

Toward this end, a variety of culturally and racially defined strands of critical pedagogy emerged. Prominent discourses emerged in the field that included, for example, a critical race theory (CRT) of education that made central the issue of race in pedagogical discussions, as well as indigenous and ecological reinterpretations of emancipatory schooling and society. These contributions were significant to the field in that they concretely signaled an organic resistance to reification, inherent in critical pedagogical principles. Hence, critical scholars from a variety of cultural contexts challenged the Western predisposition toward orthodoxy in the field, reinforcing Freire's persistent assertion that critical pedagogical principles exist and remain open to reinvention.

The Postmodern Twist

In many ways, the impact of postmodernist notions such as intersectionality has been considered by some as truly a double-edged sword upon the direction of critical pedagogy. As postmodern theories brought into question many of the philosophical "sacred cows" of Western Enlightenment, they were also thought to stoke the coals of identity politics in ways that unfortunately interfered with solidarity against social class oppression. For some, however, the postmodern "concern for radical plurality" (Biesta, 1995) reflected an important feature, which might potentially infuse critical pedagogy with greater emancipatory possibility. Postmodern theories, however, also sought to move away from meta-narratives, rejecting traditional notions of totality, rationality, and universality of absolute knowledge. As a consequence, the boundaries of traditional configurations of power and their impact on what constitutes legitimate knowledge were suddenly pushed wide open by new methods of deconstruction and reconstruction in the intellectual act of *border crossing*.

Although such a view appeared to hold real promise for a more serious theoretical engagement with developing notions of cultural hybridity, racialized subjects, sexualities, and the politics of difference, its intense fragmenting influence on historically effective organizing strategies across communities of difference led to the dismantling of former political visions of solidarity. Political visions that once offered some unifying direction to diverse political projects were now called into question or simply met wholesale abandonment. As a consequence, the educational left found itself in a disheartening state of disarray, tension, and befuddlement. What is most unfortunate is that this philosophical shift in our understanding of diversity and the multicultural body politic often failed to acknowledge the similar oppressive conditions and human suffering experienced across cultural communities of the same socioeconomic class. This represents an important recognition, in that formerly an anti-imperialist and anti-capitalist international vision had functioned as a significant common ground for politically transformative workers' struggles in the U.S. and around the world.

The Retreat from Class

For almost two decades, a class-blind perspective seemed to dominate much of the debates, as post-civil rights education activists attempted to stave off the impact of the rapidly growing conservative trend of the latter decades of the twentieth century. Critical theorists, who were particularly concerned with the totalizing impact of capitalism, its growing internationalization of capital, and its deleterious impact on working class people in the United States and abroad, lamented the retreat from class in postmodern writings on issues of culture, race, gender, and sexuality. The "postmodern" trend to see "power everywhere and nowhere" (Naiman, 1996) signaled for many a dangerous form of political abstraction, which failed to acknowledge forthrightly the manner in which advanced capitalism whipped wildly across the globe, given well-consolidated neoliberal efforts to perpetuate oppressive structures of economic domination and exploitation.

Without question, there were critical pedagogical theorists who were also tremendously concerned about the destructive impact that this intensified globalization of the economy was having upon the commercialization and appropriation of public schooling by right wing forces that advocated for "choice" and launched a charter school movement that over the last two decades has sought to destroy the nation's commitment to public education for all, replacing it with full-scale efforts to support the growing privatization of education. In light of these growing concerns, critical theorists such as Henry Giroux, Michael Apple, Stanley Aronowitz, Jean Anyon, Peter McLaren, Joel Spring, Alex Molnar, and others urged educators to remain ever cognizant to the centrality of social class oppression in shaping the conditions students experienced within schools and communities. As a consequence, they worked rigorously to draw attention to the continuing significance of class analysis, by challenging the changing nature of the "post-industrial" economy and its consequences on knowledge production and schooling.

However, in the foreground of this concern remained questions of how to engage class as both an analytical and political category, without falling prey to "red-herring" accusations of economic determinism and reductionism. In response, a number of critical educators began to rethink post-civil rights notions of class, race, and gender, in an effort to begin formulating new language for our understanding of gendered and racialized class relations and their impact on education. Hence, at a time in our history when critical educators most needed an economic understanding of schooling, a revived historical materialist approach began to reinvigorate critical pedagogical debates in the age of "globalization." This perspective has challenged the destruction of the "safety-net" once afforded to disenfranchised populations, the politics of privatization, the corporate bureaucratization of society, and the growing impoverishment and pollution of the planet. In so doing, the revolutionary political objectives aimed at the eradication of class and the social and material reformulation of society have gained increasing focus in the work of many critical education theorists today.

The Ecological Critique

Ecological scholars, who question the Western modernizing legacy of progress that anchors much of the theoretical underpinnings of critical pedagogy, have also heavily criticized the field. Here, many of the concerns have been linked to the manner in which the ideas of critical theory structure assumptions and meanings associated with notions of humanity, freedom, and empowerment. As such, critical educators are accused of intensifying or reinscribing dominant values, particularly within contexts where non-Western traditions or indigenous knowledge challenges critical pedagogical definitions of the world. In so doing, critical pedagogical principles tied to knowledge production and dialogical relations are questioned for their potential to essentialize and absolutize knowledge, despite its dialogical and emancipatory intent.

C.A. Bowers (1987, 2004), one of the most strident critics, claims, for example, that the drawback with Freire's perspective of dialogue is not its emphasis on critical reflection, but the manner in which individual reflection is privileged—in the name of empowerment. At issue here are concerns related to the tensions that exist between the privileging of traditional forms of community knowledge and individual knowledge enacted within the praxis of dialogue. Hence, from an ecological standpoint, there has been concern that critical pedagogy, albeit unintentionally, fractures knowledge and supports the further alienation of human beings from nature. Moreover, the lethargic pace at which critical pedagogical scholars have addressed questions of the planet's ecological deterioration has been seen as cause for alarm.

However, in light of such critiques, it is significant to note that, more recently, critical education scholars have begun to seriously engage these critiques, in an effort to explore the manner in which critical pedagogy might become more proactive in the face of the ecological crisis at hand (Kahn, 2010). The Paulo Freire Institute for Ecopedagogy, for example, is expressly committed to "the construction of a planetary citizenship, so that all, with no exception or exclusion, may have healthy conditions, in a planet able to offer life because its own life is being preserved." Rooted in a deep sense of ecological awareness, an ecopedagogy cultivates critical approaches of learning that go beyond mastery and manipulation, encouraging students to develop a sense of kinship with all life, through an integrated commitment to the ecological welfare of the world. Also fundamental to these critical ecological efforts are decolonizing epistemological sensibilities that in theory and practice confront the abyssal divide that both marginalizes indigenous ways of knowing and perpetuates ethnocentric epistemicides, which reproduce banking pedagogies and Eurocentric curricula (Paraskeva, 2011; Santos, 2007).

Critiques on the Right

Despite efforts of critical education theorists to counter the oppressive forces at work in society today, conservative and liberal educators, including public school officials and educational policy makers, adamantly claim that "critical pedagogy is only about politics," dismissing the constitutive role of social movement and political dissent in the making of genuinely democratic life. Hence, it is not uncommon to hear bitter attacks against the political nature of critical pedagogy, as opponents smugly assert the futility and lack of practical value of radical approaches in the classroom. Yet, such expressions of opposition, more often than not, are sly and unjustified proclamations to obstruct the establishment of democratic approaches to teaching and learning within schools—democratic approaches that seek to transform asymmetrical relations of power that sustain class interests and to reconstruct oppressive social and material conditions of hegemonic schooling.

More importantly, such critiques are often generated by the fear, confusion, and hysteria generated among school officials, mainstream educators, and scholars within schools, communities, and universities whenever teachers, students, or parents voice oppositional views that challenge the undemocratic contradictions at work in public schools. Tensions often become heightened at moments when those in power attempt to obstruct efforts by teachers, students, and parents to integrate their voices and participation in the governance of public schools—an act that if successful might signal substantive changes to business as usual. Here we must note that what is brought into question, by those who hold power, is the legitimacy of critical social action among poor, working class, and racialized populations. Hence, overtures for people to conduct themselves in "reasonable" or "civilized" ways are too often a means to silence and derail the expression of legitimate anger, frustration, and concerns. By so doing, opponents of critical pedagogical efforts deflect the possibility of any substantive public dialogue that might potentially lead to the development of new revolutionary possibilities, language, practices, and, most importantly, new relationships and configurations of power within schools and society, which can ultimately move us toward a new society, where social class and oppression become history.

Unfortunately, in efforts to survive conservative assaults, the ideas of critical pedagogy have been, at times, reified into simplistic fetishized methods (Bartolomé, 1994) that are converted into mere instrumentalized formulas for intervention, discouraging us and leaving untouched the ideologies that sustain inequities in schools today. To counter this trend, critical educators must attempt to reach beyond the boundaries of the classroom, into communities, workplaces, and public arenas where people congregate, reflect, and negotiate daily survival. Furthermore, it is within this context, of what Giroux terms a *public pedagogy*, that critical educators can develop their capacity to read power effectively and thus enact political and pedagogical interventions, in the interest of social justice and genuinely democratic life.

Internal Critiques

Since critical pedagogy as a school of thought unfolded in the midst of critique, it is not surprising to discover that a variety of critiques have emerged *within* the field. Yet, no matter how fundamentally useful self-critique has been to the field of critical pedagogy, critique too must be problematized. For example, critique that claims critical pedagogy is "in crisis" (Gur Ze'ev, 2005) can not only be unfortunately overstated but also emanate from what may reflect an epistemological positivism that ignores the inherent unfinishedness (Freire, 1998) of this complex political and pedagogical project, as a counterhegemonic intellectual and practical endeavor.

Accordingly, the complex diversity in the critical pedagogy literature must be understood as emerging, in fact, from "the effects of historical social processes" (Wexler, 2008) that inform how various critical education scholars construct their arguments and their practice. Concerns over this diversity of scholarship in the field, however, must also recognize the contributions to the field as a reflection of multidimensional efforts by critical education theorists to infuse a radical intellectual tradition within traditional and non-traditional educational settings, despite the many contradictions and limitations associated with navigating the cultural hegemony of schooling and the society at large.

What cannot go without saying is that this phenomenon is further complicated by the manner in which contrarian dispositions—some more politically inclined, others more individualistically motivated by careerism—construct claims of missing discourses and the need to move *beyond* critical pedagogy, which only they seem to be able to define and legitimize. This constitutes a major concern in that, wittingly or unwittingly, a more radical or transformational prescription of critical pedagogy can result here in ways that attempt to marginalize and silence some proponents of critical pedagogy with whom critics disagree, while elevating those with whom solidarity has been established. In the process, the use of both hyper-intellectualism and vanguard posturing, at the expense of other ways of knowing, serve to severely thwart dialogue, destroy political solidarity, and stifle the social and material evolution of an educational social movement that must seek to extend this counterhegemonic political project into the arena of revolutionary praxis.

Moreover, to criticize critical pedagogy for "not being critical enough" or framing critical pedagogy as somehow now *fashionable*, and thus inadequate, essentializes the nature of the field and, hence, distorts the fact that critical pedagogy indeed must be engaged as a collective political struggle, which cannot be carried out by solely a handful of theorists, without the democratic participation of teachers, students, parents, and community members. It must, furthermore, be noted that the alienating individualism, brutal competitiveness, and anti-communal values of the capitalist patriarchal and racializing Western intellectual tradition can be inadvertently reflected in critiques launched against critical pedagogy, as well. Accordingly, many critics, most who consider themselves leftists, often devolve in the use of anti-dialogical language that seems more intent on silencing "lesser" voices (or perceived rivals) as either vulgar, insufficiently intellectual, overly humanistic, or simply too romantic. In contrast, we argue that critical pedagogy must be understood as a contested terrain of struggle, where divergent critical educational theorists are positioned across a radical intellectual and epistemological continuum, depending on their cultural histories, class formation, intellectual preparation, political participation on the ground, and the central focus of academic work and/or community activism.

So, rather than simply placing an emphasis on allegiances to particular cognitive identities, albeit critical, what is more important is the capacity of critical educators to move beyond limiting fixations of rightness and divisive rationalizations. Instead, a pedagogical focus on establishing greater openness in our willingness to state our theoretical positions and the rationales that inform these is crucially needed. This would require us to acknowledge the historicity and social production of both individual and collective knowledge, as well as the differences in strategies and tactics employed by different critical theorists to launch transformative pedagogical actions in schools and communities. This also necessitates sobering recognition with respect to political and pedagogical consequences, particularly in terms of their social and material impact on the transformation of social class interests and structural inequalities that bolster the persistence of racism, sexism, heterosexism, disablism, and other forms of oppression.

What can, unfortunately, also be at work in the nature of these internal critiques is a dehumanizing rhetorical style that objectifies theorists with whom the critic disagrees and, therefore, crafts text in ways that seem to lose sight of the central revolutionary task of building solidarity, if we are to genuinely transform disabling conditions that threaten our humanity. As such, many critics on the left become lost in their philosophical proclamations in ways that betray the dialectics of the tradition and render "the other" critical theorists as the enemy, instead of the brutal hegemonic system and its protagonists. So much so, that it led Wexler (2008) to argue, "it is astonishing to me how little the putative heirs of the Frankfurt School can scant description and analysis of both the social conditions of their own discursive self-production and analysis of the larger historical social reality, within which the paradigmatic identity crisis in the development of critical pedagogy takes place" (p. 396). The unfortunate consequence can be the epistemological reascribing of a similar debilitating intellectual idealism and positivism that critical social theory sought to counter in the first place.

This seems the perfect segue to acknowledge that the field of critical pedagogy, as in all fields of study, suffers then from many of the similar problematics of academic intellectuals, but with a twist. Critical educational theorists may seem at times overly concerned with political authenticity or precision of language, to such a degree that we may lose sight of the emancipatory principles that fundamentally underpin our labor as educators, theorists, and activists. This concern should not be confused with crude "political correctness" accusations of the right, but rather speaks to an important political challenge with respect to the intention and purpose of our scholarship and activism, particularly when we fail to enter into sustained and respectful dialogues across our differences—differences from which we must struggle to forge a collective revolutionary educational movement.

Also troubling is the manner in which "camps" are created and students initiated into the field, through exclusionary tactics that, wittingly or unwittingly, belie the liberatory intent of the larger political project. If we are to forge a critical pedagogical project anchored to revolutionary principles, we must support the "revelation, vision, articulation, collective mobilization and the institutionalization of a new lived paradigm" (Wexler, 2008, p. 396) within critical pedagogy. This will demand of us greater intellectual openness and generosity of spirit, "in order to understand not the failure and success of the field, but of the movements to which it belongs, as a clue to the social present and particularly to what is presently socially emergent" (p. 396)—as we struggle to make sense of the world together, in the midst of our diverse efforts to contend with the debilitating social and material forces of oppression that daily impact schools and society.

The Future of Critical Pedagogy

Understanding critical pedagogy within a long tradition of progressive educational movements and on-going struggles of reinvention offers a possible safeguard against the temptation to inadvertently reify and reduce critical pedagogy to a teaching "method" or so-called "best practice" of schooling. This has been particularly at issue in the last two decades, where conservative policies have retained a stronghold on the rigid standardization of the curriculum, championed high-stakes testing, dismantled bilingual education, criminalized working class youth of color, and upheld a conservative national agenda of standardized knowledge (today, under the guise of Common Core) for public schooling practice and educational research. Accordingly, the response of even progressive educators to reactionary policies of No Child Left Behind and Race to the Top, for example, has been to abandon overt liberatory approaches in the classroom or, at best, enact palatable versions of critical pedagogical practice or a pseudo-critical pedagogy. This strategy, unfortunately, has functioned to impede the forthright advancement of an emancipatory educational agenda.

We should, however, not be too surprised, concerned, or discouraged when we find an acceleration of such efforts. Rather, in keeping with the tradition of critical pedagogy, such efforts generally signal for progressive educators the key importance of learning to read the formal and informal power relationships within schools. But even more notably, conservative strategies also serve as a clear reminder that no political struggle in a school or society can be waged by one lone voice in the wilderness, nor are democratic principles of education ever guaranteed. It is precisely for this reason that on-going emancipatory efforts within schools must be linked to collective emancipatory efforts within and across communities.

Although we have included a variety of works by prominent thinkers in the tradition of critical educational theory, critical pedagogy as a school of thought has often been strongly associated with the work of Paulo Freire. Yet, as we have attempted to illustrate here, critical pedagogy does not begin and end with Freire. Nevertheless, it cannot be denied that Freire's influence as a Brazilian or Latin American (that is to say not "white" or European) has played a significant role in the inspiration his writings brought to many radical educators of color in this country and other parts of the world (Darder, 2015). His presence, consciously or unconsciously, legitimated our right to express and define on our own terms the educational needs of working class and racialized students in the U.S.

Moreover, we found in Freire a living politics that defied the iconography of his contribution to the political project of critical pedagogy. As such, his loving ethics of education sought to reinforce the necessity for greater solidarity among critical pedagogical theorists and educators during these difficult and perilous times. In this spirit, Freire's understanding of solidarity challenges critical educators to break with alienating practices of competition, internalized notions of superiority, tendencies to demonize difference, and our "colonized" dependence and yearning to be recognized or legitimated by those who hold official power. For it is only through a revolutionary politics of solidarity that the principles of critical pedagogy can be enacted, in order to affirm and solidly nourish an on-going emancipatory educational movement.

In light of the long-standing historical tradition of progressive and radical educational efforts in the United States and around the world to name societal oppressions and their impact on education, critical pedagogy will and should continue to be reinvented in ways that speak with greater precision to the historical and contemporary conditions of all students, who must also contend with issues of economic privilege, gender, sexuality, physical abilities, religious differences, and so on. Thus, we can safely guarantee that the underlying commitment and revolutionary intent of critical pedagogy will persist, as long as there are those who are forced to exist under conditions of suffering and alienation—and there are educators who refuse to accept such conditions as a "natural" evolution of humankind.

References

Bartolomé, L. (1994). "Beyond the Methods Fetish: toward a Humanizing Pedagogy." *Harvard Educational Review, 62*(1), 173–194.

Biesta, B. (1995). "Postmodernism and the Repoliticization of Education." *Interchange, 26*(2), 161–183.

Boal, A. (1982). *Theatre of the Oppressed*. New York: Routledge.

Bowers, C. A. (1987). *Elements of a Post-liberal Theory of Education*. New York: Teachers College Press.

Bowers, C. A. and Apffel-Marglin, F. (2004). *Re-Thinking Freire: Globalization and the Environmental Crisis*. New York: Lawrence Erlbaum.

Bowles, S. and Gintis, H. (1976). *Schooling in Capitalist America*. New York: Basic Books.

Darder, A. (2015). *Freire and Education*. New York: Routledge.

Dewey, J. (1916). *Democracy and Education*. New York: The Free Press.

DuBois, W. E. B. (1902). *The Souls of Black Folk*. Chicago: A.C. McClurg & Co.

Freire, P. (1971). *Pedagogy of the Oppressed*. New York: Seabury.

Freire, P. (1998). *Pedagogy of Freedom: Ethics, Democracy and Civic Courage*. Lanham, MD: Rowman & Littlefield Publishers.

Giroux, H. (1983). *Theory and Resistance in Education*. South Hadley, MA: Bergin & Garvey.

Gramsci, A. (1971/1992). *Prison Notebooks*. New York: Columbia University Press.

Graves, K. (1998). "Outflanking Oppression: African American Contributions to Critical Pedagogy as Developed in the Scholarship of W. E. B. DuBois and Carter G. Woodson." Paper presented at the *Annual Meeting of the American Educational Research Association*.

Greene, M. (1988). *The Dialectics of Freedom*. Teachers College Press.

Gur Ze'ev, I. (2005). *Critical Theory and Critical Pedagogy Today: Toward a New Critical Language in Education.* Haifa, Israel: University of Haifa.

Held, D. (1980). *Introduction to Critical Theory: Horkheimer to Habermas.* Berkeley and Los Angeles: University of California Press.

Illich, I. (1971). *Deschooling Society.* New York: Harper & Row.

Kahn, R. (2010). *Critical Pedagogy, Ecoliteracy, and Planetary Crisis.* New York: Peter Lang.

Kozol, J. (1967). *Death at an Early Age.* Boston: Houghton Mifflin.

Kozol, J. (2006). *The Shame of the Nation: The Restoration of Apartheid Schooling in America.* New York: Three Rivers Press.

McLaren, P. (1989). *Life in Schools: An Introduction to Critical Pedagogy and the Foundations of Education.* New York: Longman.

Naiman, J. (1996). "Left Feminism and the Return to Class." *Monthly Review, 48*(2), June.

Paraskeva, J. (2011). *Conflicts in Curriculum Theory.* New York: Palgrave Macmillan.

Santos, B. de Sousa (2007). "Beyond Abyssal Thinking." *Eurozine.* See: http://www.eurozine.com/pdf/2007-06-29-santos-en.pdf.

Warren, S. (1984). *The Emergence of Dialectical Theory.* Chicago: University of Chicago Press.

Wexler, P. (2008). "Agonies of Self Criticism in Critical Education." *Studies in Philosophy of Education, 27,* 393–398.

Woodson, C. G. (1933). *The Mis-education of the Negro.* Washington, DC: Associated Publishers.

Part One

Foundations of Critical Pedagogy

Introduction to Part One

As illustrated in the introduction of this volume, the foundations of critical pedagogy have truly emerged from a variety of intellectual traditions. Yet, what has loosely united these traditions has been their uncompromising allegiance to the liberation of oppressed populations and revolutionary efforts to establish emancipatory forms of praxis within schools and communities. In keeping with this underlying commitment, critical pedagogy was founded upon philosophical traditions that critically interrogate the pedagogical interrelationships between culture, economics, ideology, and power. In so doing, critical educational approaches cultivate a process of teaching and learning that deeply nurtures the development of critical consciousness among teachers and their students.

Vital to this critical understanding of the world is the intentional and deliberate development of theoretical faculties, political sensibilities, and practical capacities that challenge educators to define and critique power relations, in ways that promote the transformation of existing educational inequalities and that support the humanity of students and their communities. This entails the ability to read the overt cultural politics at work, as well as the hidden ideologies of power tied to mainstream norms and standards of knowledge, upheld by conserving epistemologies and social arrangements, embedded in the nature and structures of schools and society. Toward this end, a critical theoretical perspective seeks to contest mainstream practices of schooling and explore revolutionary strategies and democratic interventions that can shift relations of power, altering both meaning and consciousness. This is particularly true when working with students from working class, poor, and racialized communities, whose cultural perspectives and histories fundamentally challenge many of the philosophical assumptions of the standardized curriculum. Hence, it is not unusual for critical education theorists to refer to schools as a "terrain of struggle," in that education continues to represent an important political site for the development of democratic voice, participation, and solidarity.

The purpose of critique within critical pedagogy is to serve as a powerful lens of analysis from which social inequalities and oppressive institutional structures can be unveiled, assessed, and, most importantly, transformed through the process of political engagement and social action. This capacity for critique arms educators and students with the language and theoretical organizing principles necessary to disrupt and transgress the hegemonic expectations of the official text and curriculum. In this way, teachers learn to assess inequalities in their lives and to question commonsensical notions of the world that perpetuate our cultural, linguistic, economic, gendered, and sexual subordination.

But, true to the principle of hegemony, critical pedagogy also seeks to assist educators to understand why students who have been oppressed do not necessarily embrace readily the possibility of transformation in the classroom. In an educational context where students from subordinated groups are taught early to believe in their own inherent deficit and to accept the uncompromising authority of standardized knowledge ad neutral, the possibility of transgression can often signal a moment of crisis, anxiety, and intense fear. Hence, an understanding of resistance, within critical pedagogy, encompasses a realization that expressions of resistance are expected, multidimensional, and significant pedagogical moments from which a democratic process of education is forged.

It is precisely for this reason that a critical pedagogy is also founded on the humanizing principle of dialogue, which can only be enacted through on-going, interactive classroom spaces, where teachers and students together can reflect, critique, and act upon their world. This critical dialogical approach seeks to counter the traditional "banking concept" of education, where the teacher functions as the all-knowing subject and students are rendered as passive objects in the dynamics of their own learning. As such, critical educators are engaged in an on-going reconfiguration of oppressive classroom relationships tied to power and authority, knowledge construction, and democratic participation, while simultaneously making central the histories and lived experiences of their students.

Integrating principles of a critical pedagogy in one's teaching practice requires the willingness to seriously interrogate one's ideological understanding of the world. This revolutionary process also necessitates an examination of the underlying consequences of, and alternatives to, traditional curriculum, teaching methods, classroom relationships, and educational policies. However, for teachers to undertake this enormous task effectively necessitates the development of a clear understanding of the theoretical foundations that inform both a revolutionary vision and emancipatory practice of critical pedagogy. The articles featured in this section are meant to assist teachers in beginning this journey.

Summary of Articles

Henry Giroux's seminal work on "Critical Theory and Educational Practice" begins the journey through the evolution of those progressive education ideas which have coalesced into what is today known in the field as critical pedagogy. Without question, Giroux's work is credited with repositioning the education debates of the "New Left" beyond the boundaries of reproduction theories and the hidden curriculum. He presents an analysis that clearly initiates an important turning point in the development of the progressive educational agenda of the 1980s. In this article, Giroux traces the history and development of critical theory back to the members of the Frankfurt School, examining the major themes that informed their work. Namely, rejection of orthodox Marxism, critique of late capitalism, analysis of instrumental reason, deep concerns about the culture industry, and their psychoanalytical view of domination. Giroux's exploration into the historical development of the Frankfurt School provided a strong analytical basis upon which to develop one of the most distinctive features of critical pedagogy—the principle of resistance.

"Critical Pedagogy: A Look at the Major Concepts," by Peter McLaren, a former Canadian schoolteacher and a recognized international leader in the critical educational movement, articulates for the reader the theoretical principles that underscore a critical pedagogical perspective. McLaren's analysis focuses on the significance of dialectical theory, the nature of knowledge, the concepts of hegemony and ideology, and the effects of the hidden curriculum on public schooling. McLaren's discussion of these concepts is intended to assist teachers in considering more closely what ideas inform their teaching practice. Through this interrogation of their daily practice, teachers are encouraged to seek ways in which they might disrupt oppressive tendencies in the process of teaching and learning.

The third article in this section is a chapter from Michael Apple's award winning book, *Official Knowledge*. Apple's work offers a solid foundation for engaging political questions tied to knowledge and legitimation. Moreover, the essay included here, "Cultural Politics and the Text," reflects a key aspect of Apple's many contributions to discussions of ideology in the field of critical pedagogy. Through a careful discussion of cultural politics, Apple posits a critique of mainstream functionalism and neutrality, offering an empowering educational vision of knowledge and culture. His discussion moves to the politics of textbooks, unveiling the ideological intersections that exist *between cultural visions and differential power*—a significant curricular point of departure in the articulation of a critical pedagogical practice.

"Pedagogy of Love: Embodying Our Humanity," by Antonia Darder, is Chapter 2 from her acclaimed book, *Freire and Education*. In her discussion, she speaks to the political significance of love to Freire's political vision for an emancipatory pedagogy. Darder provides a careful analysis of *love as a political force* in concert with Freire's deeply committed practice. The discussion is woven together through the use of critical concepts that speak to the significance of Freirean contributions to our understanding of dialogue, consciousness, struggle, solidarity, and difference. Most importantly, through critically engaging Freire's passionate proclamations of the body and its historical absence within education, Darder asserts the *indispensability of the body* as fundamental to critical pedagogical practice. At the heart of this philosophical engagement with Freire is found a deeply held anti-capitalist commitment, where education exists consistently as a humanizing and decolonizing endeavor for teachers and students alike.

Questions for Reflection and Dialogue

1. Describe the school of thought known as critical theory. What was the role of the Frankfurt School in the development of critical theory?
2. Identify the major themes addressed by the Frankfurt School and why these were important to the development of critical theory.
3. How does McLaren define dialectical thinking and its importance to critical pedagogy?
4. Define hegemony. What role does class, culture, and ideology play in the process of hegemony?
5. How do notions of the "hidden curriculum" and "cultural capital" relate to the standardization of knowledge in schools today?
6. How does Apple define the cultural relationship between knowledge and power? Why is this important to how teachers engage with the curriculum and textbooks?

7. What is official knowledge? Explain what Apple means by the regulation or liberation of the text. How are these linked to the notion of cultural incorporation?
8. In what ways does Paulo Freire's pedagogy of love differ from traditional or mainstream approaches to schooling?
9. Why does Darder argue for the indispensability of the body in critical pedagogy? What are some consequences of ignoring the impact of the body within the pedagogical process?

1

Critical Theory and Educational Practice

Henry A. Giroux

Introduction

This chapter attempts to contribute to the search for a theoretical foundation upon which to develop a critical theory of education. Within the parameters of this task, the notion of critical theory has a two-fold meaning. First, critical theory refers to the legacy of theoretical work developed by certain members of what can be loosely described as "the Frankfurt School." What this suggests is that critical theory was never a fully articulated philosophy shared unproblematically by all members of the Frankfurt School. But it must be stressed that while one cannot point to a single universally shared critical theory, one can point to the common attempt to assess the newly emerging forms of capitalism along with the changing forms of domination that accompanied them. Similarly, there was an attempt on the part of all the members of the Frankfurt School to rethink and radically reconstruct the meaning of human emancipation, a project that differed considerably from the theoretical baggage of orthodox Marxism. Specifically, I argue in this chapter for the importance of original critical theory and the insights it provides for developing a critical foundation for a theory of radical pedagogy. In doing so, I focus on the work of Adorno, Horkheimer, and Marcuse. This seems to be an important concern, especially since so much of the work on the Frankfurt School being used by educators focuses almost exclusively on the work of Jürgen Habermas.

Second, the concept of critical theory refers to the nature of self-conscious critique and to the need to develop a discourse of social transformation and emancipation that does not cling dogmatically to its own doctrinal assumptions. (In other words, critical theory refers to both a "school of thought" and a process of critique.) It points to a body of thought that is, in my view, invaluable for educational theorists; it also exemplifies a body of work that both demonstrates and simultaneously calls for the necessity of ongoing critique, one in which the claims of any theory must be confronted with the distinction between the world it examines and portrays, and the world as it actually exists.

The Frankfurt School took as one of its central values a commitment to penetrate the world of objective appearances to expose the underlying social relationships they often conceal. In other words, penetrating such appearances meant exposing through critical analysis social relationships that took on the status of things or objects. For instance, by examining notions such as money, consumption, distribution, and production, it becomes clear that none of these represents an objective thing or fact, but rather all are historically contingent contexts mediated by relationships of domination and subordination. In adopting such a perspective, the Frankfurt School not only broke with forms of rationality that wedded science and technology into new forms of domination, it also rejected all forms of rationality that subordinated human consciousness and action to the imperatives of universal laws. Whether it be the legacy of Victorian European positivist intellectual thought or the theoretical edifice developed by Engels, Kautsky, Stalin, and other heirs of Marxism, the Frankfurt School argued against the suppression of "subjectivity, consciousness, and culture in history" (Breines 1979–80). In so doing it articulated a notion of negativity or critique that opposed all theories that celebrated social harmony while leaving unproblematic the basic assumptions of the wider society. In more specific terms, the Frankfurt School stressed the importance of critical thinking by arguing that it is a constitutive feature of the struggle for self-emancipation and social change. Moreover, its members argued that it was in the contradictions of society that one could begin to develop forms of social inquiry that analyzed the distinction between *what is* and *what should be*. Finally, it strongly supported the assumption that the basis for thought and action should be grounded, as Marcuse argued just before his death, "in compassion, [and] in our sense of the sufferings of others" (Habermas 1980).

In general terms, the Frankfurt School provided a number of valuable insights for studying the relationship between theory and society. In so doing, its members developed a dialectical framework by which to understand the mediations that link the institutions and activities of everyday life with the logic and commanding forces that shape the larger social totality. The characteristic nature of the form of social inquiry that emerged from such a framework was articulated by Horkheimer when he suggested that members of the Institute for Social Research explore the question of "the interconnection between the economic life of society, the psychic development of the individual, and transformations in the realm of culture . . . including not only the so-called spiritual contents of science, art, and religion, but also law, ethics, fashion, public opinion, sport, amusement, life style, etc." (Horkheimer 1972).

The issues raised here by Horkheimer have not lost their importance with time; they still represent both a critique and a challenge to many of the theoretical currents that presently characterize theories of social education. The necessity for theoretical renewal in the education field, coupled with the massive number of primary and secondary sources that have been translated or published recently in English, provide the opportunity for American- and English-speaking pedagogues to begin to appropriate the discourse and ideas of the Frankfurt School. Needless to say, such a task will not be easily accomplished, since both the complexity of the language used by members of the School and the diversity of the positions and themes they pursued demand a selective and critical reading of their works. Yet their critique of culture, instrumental rationality, authoritarianism, and ideology, pursued in an interdisciplinary context, generated categories, relationships, and forms of social inquiry that constitute a vital resource for developing a critical theory of social education. Since it will be impossible in the scope of this chapter to analyze the diversity of themes examined by the Frankfurt School, I will limit my analysis to the treatment of *rationality, theory, culture*, and *depth psychology*. Finally, I will discuss the implications of these for educational theory and practice.

History and Background of the Frankfurt School

The Institute for Social Research (*Das Institut für Sozialforschung*), officially created in Frankfurt, Germany, in February, 1923, was the original home of the Frankfurt School.

Established by a wealthy grain merchant named Felix Weil, the Institute came under the directorship of Max Horkheimer in 1930. Under Horkheimer's directorship, most of the members who later became famous joined the Institute. These included Erich Fromm, Herbert Marcuse, and Theodor Adorno. As Martin Jay points out in his now-famous history of the Frankfurt School: "If it can be said that in the early years of its history the Institute concerned itself primarily with an analysis of bourgeois society's socio-economic substructure, in the years after 1930 its prime interests lay in its cultural superstructure" (Jay 1973).

The change in the Institute's theoretical focus was soon followed by a shift in its location. Threatened by the Nazis because of the avowedly Marxist orientation of its work and the fact that most of its members were Jews, the Institute was forced to move for a short time in 1933 to Geneva, and then in 1934 to New York City, where it was housed in one of Columbia University's buildings. Emigration to New York was followed by a stay in Los Angeles in 1941, and by 1953 the Institute was re-established in Frankfurt, Germany.

The strengths and weaknesses of the Frankfurt School project become intelligible only if seen as part of the social and historical context in which it developed. In essence, the questions it pursued and the forms of social inquiry it supported represent both a particular moment in the development of Western Marxism and a critique of it. Reacting to the rise of Fascism and Nazism, on the one hand, and to the failure of orthodox Marxism, on the other, the Frankfurt School had to refashion and rethink the meaning of domination and emancipation. The rise of Stalinism, the failure of the European or Western working class to contest capitalist hegemony in a revolutionary manner, and the power of capitalism to reconstitute and reinforce its economic and ideological control forced the Frankfurt School to reject the orthodox reading of Marx and Engels, particularly as developed through the conventional wisdom of the Second and Third Internationals. It is particularly in the rejection of certain doctrinal Marxist assumptions, developed under the historical shadow of totalitarianism and through the rise of the consumer society in the West, that Horkheimer, Adorno, and Marcuse attempted to construct a more sufficient basis for social theory and political action. Certainly, such a basis was not to be found in standard Marxist assumptions such as (a) the notion of historical inevitability, (b) the primacy of the mode of production in shaping history, and (c) the notion that class struggle as well as the mechanisms of domination take place primarily within the confines of the labor process. For the Frankfurt School, orthodox Marxism assumed too much while simultaneously ignoring the benefits of self-criticism. It had failed to develop a theory of consciousness and thus had expelled the human subject from its own theoretical calculus. It is not surprising, then, that the focus of the Frankfurt School's research de-emphasized the area of political economy to focus instead on the issues of how subjectivity was constituted and how the spheres of culture and everyday life represented a new terrain of domination. It is against this historical and theoretical landscape that we can begin to abstract categories and modes of analysis that speak to the nature of schooling as it presently exists, and to its inherent potential for developing into a force for social change.

Rationality and the Critique of Instrumental Reason

Fundamental to an understanding of the Frankfurt School's view of theory and of its critique of instrumental reason is its analysis of the heritage of Enlightenment rationality. Echoing Nietzsche's earlier warning about humanity's unbounded faith in reason, Adorno and Horkheimer voiced a trenchant critique of modernity's unswerving faith in the promise of Enlightenment rationality to rescue the world from the chains of superstition, ignorance, and suffering. The problematic nature of such a promise marks the opening lines of *Dialectic of Enlightenment*: "In the most general sense of progressive thought the Enlightenment has always aimed at liberating men from fear and establishing their sovereignty. Yet the fully enlightened earth radiates disaster triumphant" (Adorno & Horkheimer 1972).

Faith in scientific rationality and the principles of practical judgement did not constitute a legacy that developed exclusively in the seventeenth and eighteenth centuries, when people of reason united on a vast intellectual front in order to master the world through an appeal to the claims of reasoned thought. According to the Frankfurt School, the legacy of scientific rationality represented one of the central themes of Western thought and extended as far back as Plato (Horkheimer 1974). Habermas, a later member of the Frankfurt School, argues that the progressive notion of reason reaches its highest point and most complex expression in the work of Karl Marx, after which it is reduced from an all-encompassing concept of rationality to a particular instrument in the service of industrialized society. According to Habermas:

> On the level of the historical self-reflection of a science with critical intent, Marx for the last time identifies reason with a commitment to rationality in its thrust against dogmatism. In the second half of the nineteenth century, during the course of the reduction of science to a productive force in industrial society, positivism, historicism, and pragmatism, each in turn, isolate one part of this all-encompassing concept of rationality. The hitherto undisputed attempt of the great theories to reflect on the complex of life as a whole is henceforth itself discredited as dogma . . . The spontaneity of hope, the art of taking a position, the experience of relevance or indifference, and above all, the response to suffering and oppression, the desire for adult autonomy, the will to emancipation, and the happiness of discovering one's identity—all these are dismissed for all time from the obligating interest of reason.
>
> (Habermas 1973)

Marx may have employed reason in the name of critique and emancipation, but it was still a notion of reason limited to an overemphasis on the labor process and on the exchange rationality that was both its driving force and ultimate mystification. Adorno, Horkheimer, and Marcuse, in contrast to Marx, believed that "the fateful process of rationalization" (Wellmer 1974) had penetrated all aspects of everyday life, whether it be the mass media, the school, or the workplace. The crucial point here is that no social sphere was free from the encroachments of a form of reason in which "all theoretical means of transcending reality became metaphysical nonsense" (Horkheimer 1974).

In the Frankfurt School's view, reason has not been permanently stripped of its positive dimensions. Marcuse, for instance, believed that reason contained a critical element and was still capable of reconstituting history. As he put it, "Reason represents the highest potentiality of man and existence; the two belong together" (Marcuse 1968a). But if reason was to preserve its promise of creating a more just society, it would have to demonstrate powers of critique and negativity. According to Adorno (1973), the crisis of reason takes place as society becomes more rationalized; under such historical circumstances, in the quest for social harmony, it loses its critical faculty and becomes an instrument of the existing society. As a result, reason as insight and critique turns into its opposite—irrationality.

For the Frankfurt School, the crisis in reason is linked to the more general crises in science and in society as a whole. Horkheimer argued in 1972 that the starting point for understanding "the crisis of science depends on a correct theory of the present social situation." In essence, this speaks to two crucial aspects of Frankfurt School thought. First, it argues that the only solution to the present crisis lies in developing a more fully self-conscious notion of reason, one that embraces elements of critique as well as of human will and transformative action. Second, it means entrusting to theory the task of rescuing reason from the logic of technocratic rationality or positivism. It was the Frankfurt School's view that positivism had emerged as the final ideological expression of the Enlightenment. The victory of positivism represented not the high point but the low point of Enlightenment thought. Positivism became the enemy of reason rather than its agent, and emerged in the twentieth century as a new form of social administration and domination. Friedman sums up the essence of this position:

> To the Frankfurt School, philosophical and practical positivism constituted the end point of the Enlightenment. The social function of the ideology of positivism was to deny the critical faculty of reason by allowing it only the ground of utter facticity to operate upon. By so doing, they denied reason a critical moment. Reason, under the rule of positivism, stands in awe of the fact. Its function is simply to characterize the fact. Its task ends when it has affirmed and explicated the fact. . . . Under the rule of positivism, reason inevitably stops short of critique.
>
> (Friedman 1981)

It is in its critique of positivistic thought that the Frankfurt School makes clear the specific mechanisms of ideological control that permeate the consciousness and practices of advanced capitalist societies. It is also in its critique of positivism that it develops a notion of theory that has major implications for educational critics. But the route to understanding this concept necessitates that one first analyze the Frankfurt School's critique of positivism, particularly since the logic of positivist thought (though in varied forms) represents the major theoretical impetus currently shaping educational theory and practice.

The Frankfurt School defined positivism, in the broad sense, as an amalgam of diverse traditions that included the work of Saint-Simon and Comte, the logical positivism of the Vienna Circle, the early work of Wittgenstein, and the more recent forms of logical empiricism and pragmatism that dominate the social sciences in the West. While the history of these traditions is complex and cluttered with detours and qualifications, each of them has supported the goal of developing forms of social inquiry patterned after the natural sciences and based on the methodological tenets of sense observation and quantification. Marcuse provides both a general definition of positivism as well as a basis for some of the reservations of the Frankfurt School regarding its most basic assumptions:

> Since its first usage, probably in the school of Saint-Simon, the term "positivism" has encompassed (1) the validation of cognitive thought by experience of facts; (2) the orientation of cognitive thought to the physical science as a model of certainty and exactness; (3) the belief that progress in knowledge depends on this orientation. Consequently, positivism is a struggle against all metaphysics, transcendentalisms, and idealisms as obscurantist and regressive modes of thought. To the degree to which the given reality is scientifically comprehended and transformed, to the degree to which society becomes industrial and technological, positivism finds in the society the medium for the realization (and validation) of its concepts—harmony between theory and practice, truth and facts. Philosophic thought turns into affirmative thought; the philosophic critique criticizes within the societal framework and stigmatizes non-positive notions as mere speculation, dreams or fantasies.
>
> (Marcuse 1964)

Positivism, according to Horkheimer, presented a view of knowledge and science that stripped both of their critical possibilities. Knowledge was reduced to the exclusive province of science, and science itself was subsumed within a methodology that limited "scientific activity to the description, classification, and generalization of phenomena, with no care to distinguish the unimportant from the essential" (Horkheimer 1972). Accompanying this view are the ideas that knowledge derives from sense experience and that the ideal it pursues takes place "in the form of a mathematically formulated universe deducible from the smallest possible number of axioms, a system which assures the calculation of the probable occurrence of all events" (ibid).

For the Frankfurt School, positivism did not represent an indictment of science; instead it echoed Nietzsche's insight that "It is not the victory of science that is the distinguishing mark of our nineteenth century, but the victory of the scientific method over science" (Nietzsche 1966). Science, in this perspective, was separated from the question of ends and ethics, which were rendered insignificant because they defied "explication in terms of mathematical structures" (Marcuse 1964). According to the Frankfurt School, the suppression of ethics in positivist rationality precludes the possibility for self-criticism, or, more specifically, for questioning its own normative structure. Facts become separated from values, objectivity undermines critique, and the notion that essence and appearance may not coincide is lost in the positivist view of the world. The latter point becomes particularly clear in the Vienna Circle pronouncement: "The view that thought is a means of knowing more about the world than may be directly observed . . . seems to us entirely mysterious" (Hahn 1933). For Adorno, the idea of value freedom was perfectly suited to a perspective that was to insist on a universal form of knowledge while simultaneously refusing to inquire into its own socio-ideological development and function in society.

According to the Frankfurt School, the *outcome of positivist rationality and its technocratic view of science represented a threat to the notion of subjectivity and critical thinking*. By functioning within an operational context free from ethical commitments, positivism wedded itself to the immediate and "celebrated" the world of "facts." The question of essence—the difference between the world as it is and as it could be—is reduced to the merely methodological task of collecting and classifying facts. In this schema, "Knowledge relates solely to what is, and to its recurrence" (Horkheimer 1972). Questions concerning the genesis, development, and normative nature of the conceptual systems that select, organize, and define the facts appear to be outside the concern of positivist rationality.

Since it recognizes no factors behind the "fact," positivism freezes both human beings and history. In the case of these, the issue of historical development is ignored since the historical dimension contains truths that cannot be assigned "to a special fact-gathering branch of science" (Adorno, quoted in Gross 1979). Of course, positivism is not impervious to history, or to the relationship between history and understanding, at any rate. On the contrary, its key notions of objectivity, theory, and values, as well as its modes of inquiry, are paradoxically a consequence of and a force in the shaping of history. In other words, positivism may ignore history but it cannot escape it. What is important to stress is that fundamental categories of socio-historical development are at odds with the positivist emphasis on the immediate, or more specifically with that which can be expressed, measured, and calculated in precise mathematical formulas. Russell Jacoby (1980) points concisely to this issue in his claim that "the natural reality and natural sciences do not know the fundamental historical categories: consciousness and self-consciousness, subjectivity and objectivity, appearance and essence."

By not reflecting on its paradigmatic premises, positivist thought ignores the value of historical consciousness and consequently endangers the nature of critical thinking itself. That is, inherent in the very structure of positivist thought, with its emphasis on objectivity and its lack of theoretical grounding with regard to the setting of tasks (Horkheimer 1972), are a number of assumptions that appear to preclude its ability to judge the complicated interaction of power, knowledge, and values and to reflect critically on the genesis and nature of its own ideological presuppositions. Moreover, by situating itself within a number of false dualisms (facts *vs.* values, scientific knowledge *vs.* norms, and description *vs.* prescription) positivism dissolves the tension between potentiality and actuality in all spheres of social existence. Thus, under the guise of neutrality, scientific knowledge and all theory become rational on the grounds of whether or not they are efficient, economic, or correct. In this case, a notion of methodological correctness subsumes and devalues the complex philosophical concept of truth. As Marcuse points out, "The fact that a judgement can be correct and nevertheless without truth, has been the crux of formal logic from time immemorial" (quoted in Arato & Gebhardt 1978).

For instance, an empirical study that concludes that native workers in a colonized country work at a slower rate than imported workers who perform the same job may provide an answer that is correct, but such an answer tells us little about the notion of domination or the resistance of workers under its sway. That the native workers may slow down their rate as an act of resistance is not considered here. Thus, the notions of intentionality and historical context are dissolved within the confines of a limiting quantifying methodology.

For Adorno, Marcuse, and Horkheimer, the fetishism of facts and the belief in value neutrality represented more than an epistemological error; more importantly, such a stance served as a form of ideological hegemony that infused positivist rationality with a political conservatism that made it an ideological prop of the status quo. This is not to suggest, however, an intentional support for the status quo on the part of all individuals who work within a positivist rationality. Instead, it implies a particular relationship to the status quo; in some situations this relationship is consciously political, in others it is not. In other words, in the latter instance the relationship to the status quo is a conservative one, but it is not self-consciously recognized by those who help to reproduce it.

The Frankfurt School's Notion of Theory

According to the Frankfurt School, any understanding of the nature of theory has to begin with a grasp of the relationships that exist in society between the particular and the whole, the specific and the universal. This position appears in direct contradiction to the empiricist claim that theory is primarily a matter of classifying and arranging facts. In rejecting the absolutizing of facts, the Frankfurt School argued that in the relation between theory and the wider society mediations exist that give meaning not only to the constitutive nature of a fact but also to the very nature and substance of theoretical discourse. As Horkheimer writes, "The facts of science and science itself are but segments of the life process of society, and in order to understand the significance of facts or of science, generally one must possess the key to the historical situation, the right social theory" (Horkheimer 1972).

This speaks to a second constitutive element of critical theory. If theory is to move beyond the positivist legacy of neutrality, it must develop the capacity of meta-theory. That is, it must acknowledge the value-laden interests it represents and be able to reflect critically on both the historical development or genesis of such interests and the limitations they may present within certain historical and social contexts. In other words, "methodological correctness" does not provide a guarantee of truth, nor does it raise the fundamental question of why a theory functions in a given way under specific historical conditions to serve some interests and not others. Thus, a notion of self-criticism is essential to a critical theory.

A third constitutive element for a critical theory takes its cue from Nietzsche's dictum that "A great truth wants to be criticized, not idolized" (quoted in Arato & Gebhardt 1978). The Frankfurt School believed that the critical spirit of theory should be represented in its unmasking function. The driving force of such a function was to be found in the Frankfurt School's notions of immanent criticism and dialectical thought. Immanent critique is the assertion of difference, the refusal to collapse appearance and essence, the willingness to analyze the reality of the social object against its possibilities. As Adorno wrote:

> Theory . . . must transform the concepts which it brings, as it were, from outside into those which the object has of itself, into what the object, left to itself, seeks to be, and confront it with what it is. It must dissolve the rigidity of the temporally and spatially fixed object into a field of tension of the possible and the real: each one in order to exist, is dependent upon the other. In other words, theory is indisputably critical.
>
> (Adorno et al. 1976)

Dialectical thought, on the other hand, speaks to both critique and theoretical reconstruction (Giroux 1981). As a mode of critique, it uncovers values that are often negated by the social object under analysis. The notion of dialectics is crucial because it reveals "the insufficiencies and imperfections of 'finished' systems of thought. . . . It reveals incompleteness where completeness is claimed. It embraces that which is in terms of that which is not, and that which is real in terms of potentialities not yet realized" (Held 1980). As a mode of theoretical reconstruction, dialectical thought points to historical analysis in the critique of conformist logic, and traces out the "inner history" of the latter's categories and the way in which these are mediated within a specific historical context. By looking at the social and political constellations stored in the categories of any theory, Adorno (1973) believed their history could be traced and their existing limitations revealed. As such, dialectical thought reveals the power of human activity and human knowledge as both a product of and force in the shaping of social reality. But it does not do so to proclaim simply that humans give meaning to the world. Instead, as a form of critique, dialectical thought argues that there is a link between knowledge, power, and domination. Thus it is acknowledged that some knowledge is false, and that the ultimate purpose of critique should be critical thinking in the interest of social change. For instance, as I mentioned earlier, one can exercise critical thought and not fall into the ideological trap of relativism, in which the notion of critique is negated by the assumption that all ideas should be given equal weight. Marcuse points to the connection between thought and action in dialectical thought:

> Dialectical thought starts with the experience that the world is unfree; that is to say, man and nature exist in conditions of alienation, exist as "other than they are." Any mode of thought which excludes this contradiction from its logic is faulty logic. Thought "corresponds" to reality only as it transforms reality by comprehending its contradictory structure. Here the principle of dialectic drives thought beyond the limits of philosophy. For to comprehend reality means to comprehend what things really are, and this in turn means rejecting their mere factuality.

> Rejection is the process of thought as well as of action . . . Dialectical thought thus becomes negative in itself. Its function is to break down the self-assurance and self-contentment of common sense, to undermine the sinister confidence in the power and language of facts, to demonstrate that unfreedom is so much at the core of things that the development of their internal contradictions leads necessarily to qualitative change: the explosion and catastrophe of the established state of affairs.
>
> (Marcuse 1960)

According to the Frankfurt School, all thought and theory are tied to a specific interest in the development of a society without injustice. Theory, in this case, becomes a transformative activity that views itself as explicitly political and commits itself to the projection of a future that is as yet unfulfilled. Thus, critical theory contains a transcendent element in which critical thought becomes the precondition for human freedom. Rather than proclaiming a positivist notion of neutrality, critical theory openly takes sides in the interest of struggling for a better world. In one of his most famous early essays comparing traditional and critical theory, Horkheimer spelled out the essential value of theory as a political endeavour:

> It is not just a research hypothesis which shows its value in the ongoing business of men; it is an essential element in the historical effort to create a world which satisfies the needs and powers of men. However extensive the interaction between the critical theory and the special sciences whose progress the theory must respect and on which it has for decades exercized a liberating and stimulating influence, the theory never aims simply at an increase of knowledge as such. Its goal is man's emancipation from slavery.
>
> (Horkheimer 1972)

Finally, there is the question of the relationship between critical theory and empirical studies. In the ongoing debate over theory and empirical work, we recognize recycled versions of the same old dualisms in which one presupposes the exclusion of the other. One manifestation of this debate is the criticism that the Frankfurt School rejected the value of empirical work, a criticism that is also being lodged currently against many educational critics who have drawn upon the work of the Frankfurt School. Both sets of criticisms appear to have missed the point. It is certainly true that for the Frankfurt School the issue of empirical work was a problematic one, but what was called into question was its universalization at the expense of a more comprehensive notion of rationality. In writing about his experiences as an American scholar, Adorno spelled out a view of empirical studies that was representative of the Frankfurt School in general:

> My own position in the controversy between empirical and theoretical sociology . . . I may sum up by saying that empirical investigations are not only legitimate but essential, even in the realm of cultural phenomena. But one must not confer autonomy upon them or regard them as a universal key. Above all they must terminate the theoretical knowledge. Theory is no mere vehicle that becomes superfluous as soon as data are in hand.
>
> (Adorno 1969)

By insisting on the primacy of theoretical knowledge in the realm of empirical investigations, the Frankfurt School also wanted to highlight the limits of the positivist notion of experience, where research had to confine itself to controlled physical experiences that could be conducted by any researcher. Under such conditions, the research experience is limited to simple observation. As such, abstract methodology follows rules that preclude any understanding of the forces that shape both the object of analysis as well as the subject conducting the research. By contrast, a dialectical notion of society and theory would argue that observation cannot take the place of critical reflection and understanding. That is, one begins not with an observation but with a theoretical framework that situates the observation in rules and conventions that give it meaning while simultaneously acknowledging the limitations of such a perspective or framework. The Frankfurt School's position on the relation between theory and empirical studies thus helps to illuminate its view of theory and practice.

But a further qualification must be made here. While critical theory insists that theory and practice are interrelated, it nonetheless cautions against calling for a specious unity, for as Adorno points out:

> The call for the unity of theory and practice has irresistibly degraded theory to the servant's role, removing the very traits it should have brought to that unity. The visa stamp of practice which we demand of all theory became a censor's place. Yet whereas theory succumbed in the vaunted mixture, practice became nonconceptual, a piece of the politics it was supposed to lead out of; it became the prey of power.
>
> (Adorno 1973)

Theory, in this case, should have as its goal emancipatory practice, but at the same time it requires a certain distance from such practice. Theory and practice represent a particular alliance, not a unity in which one dissolves into the other. The nature of such an alliance might be better understood by illuminating the drawbacks inherent in the traditional anti-theoretical stance in American education, in which it is argued that concrete experience is the great "teacher."

Experience, whether on the part of the researcher or others, contains no inherent guarantees to generate the insights necessary to make it transparent to the self. In other words, while it is indisputable that experience may provide us with knowledge, it is also indisputable that knowledge may distort rather than illuminate the nature of social reality. The point here is that the value of any experience "will depend not on the experience of the subject but on the struggles around the way that experience is interpreted and defined" (Bennett 1980). Moreover, theory cannot be reduced to being perceived as the mistress of experience, empowered to provide recipes for pedagogical practice. Its real value lies in its ability to establish possibilities for reflexive thought and practice on the part of those who use it; in the case of teachers, it becomes invaluable as an instrument of critique and understanding. As a mode of critique and analysis, theory functions as a set of tools inextricably affected by the context in which it is brought to bear, but it is never reducible to that context. It has its own distance and purpose, its own element of practice. The crucial element in both its production and use is not the structure at which it is aimed, but the human agents who use it to give meaning to their lives.

In short, Adorno, Horkheimer, and Marcuse provided forms of historical and sociological analysis that pointed to the promise as well as to the limitations of the existing dominant rationality as it developed in the twentieth century. Such an analysis took as a starting-point the conviction that for self-conscious human beings to act collectively against the modes of technocratic rationality that permeated the workplace and other sociocultural spheres, their behaviour would have to be preceded and mediated by a mode of critical analysis. In other words, the pre-condition for such action was a form of critical theory. But it is important to stress that in linking critical theory to the goals of social and political emancipation, the Frankfurt School redefined the very notion of rationality. Rationality was no longer merely the exercise of critical thought, as had been its earlier Enlightenment counterpart. Instead, rationality now became the nexus of thought and action in the interest of liberating the community or society as a whole. As a higher rationality, it contained a transcendent project in which individual freedom merged with social freedom.

The Frankfurt School's Analysis of Culture

Central to the Frankfurt School's critique of positivist rationality was its analysis of culture. Rejecting the definition and role of culture found in both traditional sociological accounts and orthodox Marxist theory, Adorno and Horkheimer (1972) were noteworthy in developing a view of culture that assigned it a key place in the development of historical experience and everyday life. On the other hand, the Frankfurt School rejected the mainstream sociological notion that culture existed in an autonomous fashion, unrelated to the political and economic life-processes of society. In their view, such a perspective neutralized culture and in so doing abstracted it from the historical and societal context that gave it meaning. For Adorno the conventional view was shot through with a contradiction that reduced culture to nothing more than a piece of ideological shorthand:

> [The conventional view of culture] overlooks what is decisive: the role of ideology in social conflicts. To suppose, if only methodologically, anything like an independent logic of culture is to collaborate in the hypostasis of culture, the ideological *proton pseudos*. The substance of culture . . . resides not in culture alone but in relation to something external, to the material life-process. Culture, as Marx observed of juridical and political systems, cannot be fully "understood either in terms of itself . . . or in terms of the so-called universal development of the mind." To ignore this . . . is to make ideology the basic matter and to establish it firmly.
>
> (Adorno 1967a)

On the other hand, while orthodox Marxist theory established a relationship between culture and the material forces of society, it did so by reducing culture to a mere reflex of the economic realm. In this view, the primacy of economic forces and the logic of scientific laws took precedence over issues concerning the terrain of everyday life, consciousness, or sexuality (Aronowitz 1981a). For the Frankfurt School, changing socioeconomic conditions had made traditional Marxist categories of the 1930s and 1940s untenable. They were no longer adequate for understanding the integration of the working class in the West or the political effects of technocratic rationality in the cultural realm.

Within the Frankfurt School perspective the role of culture in Western society had been modified with the transformation of critical *Enlightenment rationality into repressive forms of positivist rationality*. As a result of the development of new technical capabilities, greater concentrations of economic power, and more sophisticated modes of administration, the rationality of domination increasingly expanded its influence to spheres outside of the locus of economic production. Under the sign of Taylorism and scientific management, instrumental rationality extended its influence from the domination of nature to the domination of human beings. As such, mass-cultural institutions such as schools took on a new role in the first half of the twentieth century as "both a determinant and fundamental component of social consciousness" (Aronowitz 1976). According to the Frankfurt School, this meant that the cultural realm now constitutes a central place in the production and transformation of historical experience. Like Gramsci (1971), Adorno and Horkheimer

(1972) argued that domination has assumed a new form. Instead of being exercised primarily through the use of physical force (the army and police), the power of the ruling classes was now reproduced through a form of ideological hegemony; that is, it was established primarily through the rule of consent, and mediated via cultural institutions such as schools, family, mass media, churches, etc. Briefly put, the colonization of the workplace was now supplemented by the colonization of all other cultural spheres (Aronowitz 1973; Enzenberger 1974; Ewen 1976).

According to the Frankfurt School, culture, like everything else in capitalist society, had been turned into an object. Under the dual rationalities of administration and exchange the elements of critique and opposition, which the Frankfurt School believed inherent in traditional culture, had been lost. Moreover, the objectification of culture did not simply result in the repression of the critical elements in its form and content; such objectification also represented the negation of critical thought itself. In Adorno's words: "... Culture in the true sense did not simply accommodate itself to human beings; ... it always simultaneously raised a protest against the petrified relations under which they lived, thereby honoring them. Insofar as culture becomes wholly assimilated to and integrated into those petrified relations, human beings are once more debased" (Adorno 1975).

As far as the Frankfurt School was concerned, the cultural realm had become a new locus of control for that aspect of Enlightenment rationality in which the domination of nature and society proceeded under the guise of technical progress and economic growth. For Adorno and Horkheimer (1972) culture had become another industry, one which not only produced goods but also legitimated the logic of capital and its institutions. The *term "culture industry" was coined by Adorno as a response to the reification of culture, and it had two immediate purposes*. First, it was coined in order to expose the notion that "culture arises spontaneously from the masses themselves" (Lowenthal 1979). Second, it pointed to the concentration of economic and political determinants that control the cultural sphere in the interest of social and political domination. The term "industry" in the metaphor provided a point of critical analysis. That is, it pointed not only to a concentration of political and economic groups who reproduced and legitimated the dominant belief and value system, it also referred to the mechanisms of rationalization and standardization as they permeated everyday life. In other words, "the expression 'industry' is not to be taken literally. It refers to the standardization of the thing itself—such as the Western, familiar to every movie-goer—and to the rationalization of distribution techniques ... [and] not strictly to the production process" (Adorno 1975).

At the core of the theory of culture advanced by Horkheimer, Adorno, and Marcuse was an attempt to expose, through both a call for and demonstration of critique, how positivist rationality manifested itself in the cultural realm. For instance, they criticised certain cultural products such as art for excluding the principles of resistance and opposition that once informed their relationship with the world while simultaneously helping to expose it (Horkheimer 1972). Likewise, for Marcuse (1978), "the truth of art lies in its power to break the monopoly of established reality (i.e., of those who established it) to define what is real. In this rupture ... the fictitious world of art appears as true reality." The Frankfurt School argued that in a one-dimensional society art collapses, rather than highlights, the distinction between reality and the possibility of a higher truth or better world. In other words, in the true spirit of positivist harmony, art becomes simply a mirror of the existing reality and an affirmation of it. Thus, both the memory of a historical truth or the image of a better way of life are rendered impotent in the ultra-realism of Warhol's Campbell-soup painting or the Stakhanovite paintings of socialist realism.

Dictates of positivist rationality and the attendant mutilation of the power of imagination are also embodied in the techniques and forms that shape the messages and discourse of the culture industry. Whether it be in the glut of interchangeable plots, gags, or stories, or in the rapid pace of the film's development, the logic of standardization reigns supreme. The message is conformity, and the medium for its attainment is amusement, which proudly packages itself as an escape from the necessity of critical thought. Under the sway of the culture industry, style subsumes substance and thought is banished from the temple of official culture. Marcuse states this argument superbly:

> By becoming components of the aesthetic form, words, sounds, shapes, and colors are insulated against their familiar, ordinary use and function; . . . This is the achievement of style, which *is* the poem, the novel, the painting, the composition. The style, embodiment of the aesthetic form, in subjecting reality to another order, subjects it to the laws of beauty. True and false, right and wrong, pain and pleasure, calm and violence become aesthetic categories within the framework of the oeuvre. Thus deprived of their [immediate] reality, they enter a different context in which even the ugly, cruel, sick become parts of the aesthetic harmony governing the whole.
>
> (Marcuse 1972)

Inherent in the reduction of culture to amusement is a significant message which points to the root of the ethos of positivist rationality—the structural division between work and play. Within that division, work is confined to the imperatives of drudgery, boredom, and powerlessness for the vast majority; culture becomes the vehicle by which to escape from work. The power of the Frankfurt School's analysis lies in its exposure of the ideological fraud that constitutes this division of labor. Rather than being an escape from the mechanized work process, the cultural realm becomes an extension of it. Adorno and Horkheimer write:

> Amusement under late capitalism is the prolongation of work. It is sought-after as an escape from the mechanized work process, and to recruit strength in order to be able to cope with it again. But at the same time mechanization has such power over a man's leisure and happiness and so profoundly determines the manufacture of amusement goods, that his experiences are after-images of the work process itself. The ostensible content is merely a faded background; what sinks in is an automatic succession of standardized operations.
>
> (Adorno & Horkheimer 1972)

The most *radical critique of the division of labour* among the three theorists under study finds its expression in the work of *Herbert Marcuse* (1955, 1968b). Marcuse (1968b) claims that Marxism has not been radical enough in its attempt to develop a new sensibility that would develop as "an instinctual barrier against cruelty, brutality, ugliness." Marcuse's (1955) point is that a new rationality taking as its goal the erotization of labour and "the development and fulfillment of human needs" would necessitate new relations of production and organizational structures under which work could take place. This should not suggest that Marcuse abandons all forms of authority or that he equates hierarchical relationships with the realm of domination. On the contrary, he argues that work and play can interpenetrate each other without the loss of either's primary character. As Agger points out:

> Marcuse is . . . saying that . . . work and play converge without abandoning the "work" character of work itself. He retains the rational organization of work without abandoning the Marxian goal of creative praxis. As he notes . . . "hierarchical relationships are not unfree per se." That

> is, it depends upon the kind of hierarchy which informs relationships. . . . Marcuse . . . suggests two things: in the first place, he hints at a theory of work which rests upon the merger of work and play components. His views in this regard are captured in his vision of the "erotization of labor." In the second place, Marcuse hints at a form of organizational rationality which is nondominating.
>
> (Agger 1978)

According to Marcuse (1964) science and technology have been integrated under the imprint of a dominating rationality that has penetrated the world of communicative interaction (the public sphere) as well as the world of work. It is worth mentioning, by contrast, Habermas's (1973) argument that science and technology in the sphere of work are necessarily limited to technical considerations, and that the latter organization of work represents the price an advanced industrial order must pay for its material comfort. This position has been challenged by a number of theorists, including Aronowitz (1981a), who astutely argues that Habermas separates "communications and normative judgments from the labor process" and thus "cede[s] to technological consciousness the entire sphere of rational purposive action (work)." In further opposition to Habermas, Marcuse (1964) argues that radical change means more than simply the creation of conditions that foster critical thinking and communicative competence. Such change also entails the transformation of the labor process itself and the fusion of science and technology under the guise of a rationality stressing cooperation and self-management in the interest of democratic community and social freedom.

While there are significant differences among Adorno, Horkheimer, and Marcuse in their indictment of positivist rationality and in their respective notions about what constitutes an aesthetic or radical sensibility, their views converge on the existing repressiveness underlying positivist rationality and on the need for the development of a collective critical consciousness and sensibility that would embrace a discourse of opposition and non-identity as a precondition of human freedom. Thus, for them, criticism represents an indispensable element in the struggle for emancipation, and it is precisely in their call for criticism and a new sensibility that one finds an analysis of the nature of domination that contains invaluable insights for a theory of education. The analysis, in this case, includes the Frankfurt School's theory of depth psychology, to which I will now briefly turn.

The Frankfurt School's Analysis of Depth Psychology

As I have pointed out previously, the Frankfurt School faced a major contradiction in attempting to develop a critical tradition within Marxist theory. On the one hand, the historical legacy since Marx had witnessed increased material production and the continued conquest of nature in both the advanced industrial countries of the West and the countries of the socialist bloc as well. In both camps, it appeared that despite economic growth the objective conditions that promoted alienation had deepened. For example, in the West the production of goods and the ensuing commodity fetishism made a mockery of the concept of the Good Life, reducing it to the issue of purchasing power. In the socialist bloc, the centralization of political power led to political repression instead of political and economic freedom as had been promised. Yet in both cases the consciousness of the masses failed to keep pace with such conditions.

For the Frankfurt School it became clear that a theory of consciousness and depth psychology was needed to explain the subjective dimension of liberation and domination.

Marx had provided the political and economic grammar of domination, but he relegated the psychic dimension to a secondary status, believing that it would follow any significant changes in the economic realm. Thus it was left to the Frankfurt School, especially Marcuse (1955, 1964, 1968b, 1970), to analyze the formal structure of consciousness in order to discover how a dehumanized society could continue to maintain its control over its inhabitants, and how it was possible that human beings could participate willingly at the level of everyday life in the reproduction of their own dehumanization and exploitation. For answers, the Frankfurt School turned to a critical study of Freud.

For the Frankfurt School, Freud's metapsychology provided an important theoretical foundation for revealing the interplay between the individual and society. More specifically, the value of Freudian psychology in this case rested with its illumination of the antagonistic character of social reality. As a theoretician of contradictions, Freud provided a radical insight into the way in which society reproduced its powers both in and over the individual. As Jacoby puts it:

> Psychoanalysis shows its strength; it demystifies the claims to liberated values, sensitivities, emotions, by tracing them to a repressed psychic, social, and biological dimension.... It keeps to the pulse of the psychic underground. As such it is more capable of grasping the intensifying social unreason that the conformist psychologies repress and forget: the barbarism of civilization itself, the barely suppressed misery of the living, the madness that haunts society.
>
> (Jacoby 1975)

The Frankfurt School theorists believed that it was only in an understanding of the dialectic between the individual and society that the depth and extent of domination as it existed both within and outside of the individual could be open to modification and transformation. Thus, for Adorno, Horkheimer, and Marcuse, Freud's emphasis on the constant struggle between the individual desire for instinctual gratification and the dynamics of social repression provided an indispensable clue to understanding the nature of society and the dynamics of psychic domination and liberation. Adorno points to this in the following comments:

> The only totality the student of society can presume to know is the antagonistic whole, and if he is to attain to totality at all, then only in contradiction.... The jarring elements that make up the individual, his "properties," are invariable moments of the social totality. He is, in the strict sense, a monad, representing the whole and its contradictions, without however being at any time conscious of the whole.
>
> (Adorno 1967b)

To explore the depth of the conflict between the individual and society, the Frankfurt School accepted with some major modifications most of Freud's most radical assumptions. More specifically, Freud's theoretical schema contained three important elements for developing a depth psychology. First, Freud provided a formal psychological structure for the Frankfurt School theorists to work with. That is, the Freudian outline of the structure of the psyche with its underlying struggle between Eros (the life instinct), Thanatos (the death instinct), and the outside world represented a key conception in the depth psychology developed by the Frankfurt School.

Secondly, Freud's studies on psychopathology, particularly his sensitivity to humanity's capacity for self-destructiveness and his focus on the loss of ego stability and the decline of the influence of the family in contemporary society added significantly to the Frankfurt School analyses of mass society and the rise of the authoritarian personality. For the

Frankfurt School, the growing concentration of power in capitalist society, along with the pervasive intervention of the state in the affairs of everyday life, had altered the dialectical role of the traditional family as both a positive and negative site for identity formation. That is, the family had traditionally provided, on the one hand, a sphere of warmth and protection for its members, while, on the other hand, it also functioned as a repository for social and sexual repression. But under the development of advanced industrial capitalism, the dual function of the family was gradually giving way, and it began to function exclusively as a site for social and cultural reproduction.

Finally, by focusing on Freud's theory of instincts and metapsychology, the Frankfurt School devised a theoretical framework for unraveling and exposing the objective and psychological obstacles to social change. This issue is important because it provides significant insights into how depth psychology might be useful for developing a more comprehensive theory of education. Since Adorno shared some major differences with both Horkheimer and Marcuse regarding Freud's theory of instincts and his view of the relationship between the individual and society, I will treat their respective contributions separately.

Adorno (1968) was quick to point out that while Freud's denunciation of "man's unfreedom" over-identified with a particular historical period and thus "petrified into an anthropological constant," it did not seriously detract from his greatness as a theoretician of contradictions. That is, in spite of the limitations in Freudian theory, Adorno—and Horkheimer as well—firmly believed that psychoanalysis provided a strong theoretical bulwark against psychological and social theories that exalted the idea of the "integrated personality" and the "wonders" of social harmony. True to Adorno's (1968) view that "Every image of man is ideology except the negative one," Freud's work appeared to transcend its own shortcomings because at one level it personified the spirit of negation. Adorno (1967b, 1968) clearly exalted the negative and critical features of psychoanalysis and saw them as major theoretical weapons to be used against every form of identity theory. The goals of identity theory and revisionist psychology were both political and ideological in nature, and it was precisely through the use of Freud's metapsychology that they could be exposed as such. As Adorno put it:

> The goal of the well-integrated personality is objectionable because it expects the individual to establish an equilibrium between conflicting forces, which does not obtain in existing society. Nor should it, because these forces are not of equal moral merit. People are taught to forget the objective conflicts which necessarily repeat themselves in every individual instead of helped to grapple with them.
>
> (Adorno 1968)

While it was clear to the Frankfurt School that psychoanalysis could not solve the problems of repression and authoritarianism, they believed that it did provide important insights into how "people become accomplices to their own subjugation" (Benjamin, J. 1977). Yet beneath the analyses put forth on psychoanalysis by Adorno (1967b, 1968, 1972, 1973) and Horkheimer (1972) there lurked a disturbing paradox: while both theorists went to great lengths to explain the dynamics of authoritarianism and psychological domination, they said very little about those formal aspects of consciousness that might provide a basis for resistance and rebellion. In other words, Horkheimer and Adorno, while recognizing that Freudian psychology registered a powerful criticism of existing society in exposing its antagonistic character, failed to extend this insight by locating in either individuals or social classes the psychological or political grounds for a self-conscious recognition of such contradictions and the ability of human agents to transform them. Consequently, they provided a view of Freudian psychology that consigned Freud to the ambiguous status of radical as well as prophet of gloom.

If Adorno and Horkheimer viewed Freud as a revolutionary pessimist, Marcuse (1955) read him as a revolutionary utopian. That is, though he accepts most of Freud's most controversial assumptions, his interpretation of them is both unique and provocative. In one sense, Marcuse's (1955, 1968a&b, 1970) analysis contained an original dialectical twist in that it pointed to a utopian integration of Marx and Freud. Marcuse (1955) accepted Freud's view of the antagonistic relations between the individual and society as a fundamental insight, but he nevertheless altered some of Freud's basic categories, and in doing so situated Freud's pessimism within a historical context that revealed its strengths as well as limitations. In doing so, Marcuse was able to illuminate the importance of Freud's metapsychology as a basis for social change. This becomes particularly clear if we examine how Marcuse (1955, 1968a&b, 1970) reworked Freud's basic claims regarding the life and death instincts, the struggle between the individual and society, the relationship between scarcity and social repression, and, finally, the issues of freedom and human emancipation.

Marcuse (1955, 1964) begins with the basic assumption that inherent in Freud's theory of the unconscious and his theory of the instincts could be found the theoretical elements for a more comprehensive view of the nature of individual and social domination. Marcuse points to this possibility when he writes:

> The struggle against freedom reproduces itself in the psyche of man as the self-repression of the repressed individual, and his self-repression in turn sustains his masters and their institutions. It is this mental dynamic which Freud unfolds as the dynamic of civilization. . . . Freud's metapsychology is an ever-renewed attempt to uncover, and to question, the terrible necessity of the inner connection between civilization and barbarism, progress and suffering, freedom and unhappiness—a connection which reveals itself ultimately as that between Eros and Thanatos.
>
> (Marcuse 1955)

For Marcuse (1955, 1970) Freudian psychology, as a result of its analysis of the relationship between civilization and instinctual repression, posited the theoretical basis for understanding the distinction between socially necessary authority and authoritarianism. That is, in the interplay between the need for social labor and the equally important need for the sublimation of sexual energy, the dynamic connection between domination and freedom, on the one hand, and authority and authoritarianism, on the other, starts to become discernible. Freud presented the conflict between the individual's instinctual need for pleasure and the society's demand for repression as an insoluble problem rooted in a trans-historical struggle; as a result, he pointed to the continuing repressive transformation of Eros in society, along with the growing propensity for self destruction. Marcuse (1970) believed that the "Freudian conception of the relationship between civilization and the dynamics of the instincts [was] in need of a decisive correction." That is, whereas Freud (1949) saw the increased necessity for social and instinctual repression, Marcuse (1955, 1970) argued that any understanding of social repression had to be situated within a specific historical context and judged as to whether such systems of domination exceeded their bounds. To ignore such a distinction was to forfeit the possibility of analyzing the difference between the exercise of legitimate authority and illegitimate forms of domination. Marcuse (1955) deemed that Freud had failed to capture in his analyses the historical dynamic of organized domination, and thus had given to it the status and dignity of a biological development that was universal rather than merely historically contingent.

While Marcuse (1955) accepts the Freudian notion that the central conflict in society is between the reality principle and the pleasure principle, he rejects the position that the latter had to adjust to the former. In other words, Freud believed that "the price of civilization is paid for in forfeiting happiness through heightening of the sense of guilt" (Freud 1949). This is important because at the core of Freud's notion that humanity was forever condemned to diverting pleasure and sexual energy into alienating labor was an appeal to a trans-historical "truth": that scarcity was inevitable in society, and that labor was inherently alienating. In opposition to Freud, Marcuse argued that the reality principle referred to a particular form of historical existence when scarcity legitimately dictated instinctual repression. But in the contemporary period such conditions had been superseded, and as such abundance, not scarcity, characterized or informed the reality principle governing the advanced industrial countries of the West.

In order to add a more fully historical dimension to Freud's analysis, Marcuse (1955) introduced the concepts of the performance principle and of surplus-repression. By arguing that scarcity was not a universal aspect of the human condition, Marcuse (1955, 1970) claimed that the moment had arrived in the industrial West when it was no longer necessary to submit men and women to the demands of alienating labor. The existing reality principle, which Marcuse (1955) labeled the performance principle, had outstripped its historical function, i.e., the sublimation of Eros in the interest of socially necessary labor. The performance principle, with its emphasis on technocratic reason and exchange rationality, was, in Marcuse's (1955) terms, both historically contingent and socially repressive. As a relatively new mode of domination, it tied people to values, ideas, and social practices that blocked their possibilities for gratification and happiness as ends in themselves.

In short, Marcuse (1955) believed that inherent in Marx's view of societal abundance and in Freud's theory of instincts was the basis for a new performance principle, one that was governed by principles of socially necessary labor and by those aspects of the pleasure principle that integrated work, play, and sexuality. This leads us to Marcuse's second important idea, the concept of surplus-repression. The excessiveness of the existing nature of domination could be measured through what Marcuse labeled as surplus-repression. Distinguishing this from socially useful repression, Marcuse claims that:

> Within the total structure of the repressed personality, surplus-repression is that portion which is the result of specific societal conditions sustained in the specific act of domination. The extent of this surplus-repression provides the standard of measurement: the smaller it is, the less repressive is the stage of civilization. The distinction is equivalent to that between the biological and the historical sources of human suffering.
>
> (Marcuse 1955)

According to Marcuse (1955, 1970), it is within this dialectical interplay of the personality structure and historically conditioned repression that the nexus exists for uncovering the historical and contemporary nature of domination. Domination in this sense is doubly historical: first, it is rooted in the historically developed socio-economic conditions of a given society; further, it is rooted in the sedimented history or personality structure of individuals. In speaking of domination as a psychological as well as a political phenomenon, Marcuse did not give a *carte blanche* to wholesale gratification. On the contrary, he agreed with Freud that some forms of repression were generally necessary. What he objected to was the unnecessary repression that was embodied in the ethos and social practices that characterized social institutions like school, the workplace, and the family.

For Marcuse (1964), the most penetrating marks of social repression are generated in the inner history of individuals, in the "needs, satisfactions, and values which reproduce the servitude of human existence." Such needs are mediated and reinforced through the patterns and social routines of everyday life, and the "false" needs that perpetuate toil, misery, and aggressiveness become anchored in the personality structure as second nature; that is, their historical character is forgotten, and they become reduced to patterns of habit.

In the end, Marcuse (1955) grounds even Freud's important notion of the death instinct (the autonomous drive that increasingly leads to self-destruction) in a radical problematic. That is, by claiming that the primary drive of humanity is pleasure, Marcuse redefines the death instinct by arguing that it is mediated not by the need for self-destruction—although this is a form it may take—but by the need to resolve tension. Rooted in such a perspective, the death instinct is not only redefined, it is also politicized as Marcuse argues that in a non-repressive society it would be subordinated to the demands of Eros. Thus, Marcuse (1955, 1964) ends up supporting the Frankfurt School's notion of negative thinking, but with an important qualification. He insists on its value as a mode of critique, but maintains equally that it is grounded in socio-economic conditions that can be transformed. It is the promise of a better future, rather than despair over the existing nature of society, that informs both Marcuse's work and its possibilities as a mode of critique for educators.

Towards a Critical Theory of Education

While it is impossible to elaborate in any detail on the implications of the work of the Frankfurt School for a theory of radical pedagogy, I can point briefly to some general considerations. I believe that it is clear that the thought of the Frankfurt School provides a major challenge and a stimulus to educational theorists who are critical of theories of education tied to functionalist paradigms based on assumptions drawn from a positivist rationality. For instance, against the positivist spirit that infuses existing educational theory and practice, whether it takes the form of the Tyler model or various systems approaches, the Frankfurt School offers an historical analysis and a penetrating philosophical framework that indict the wider culture of positivism, while at the same time providing insight into how the latter becomes incorporated within the ethos and practices of schools. Though there is a growing body of educational literature that is critical of positivist rationality in schools, it lacks the theoretical sophistication characteristic of the work of Horkheimer, Adorno, and Marcuse. Similarly, the importance of historical consciousness as a fundamental dimension of critical thinking in the Frankfurt School perspective creates a valuable epistemological terrain upon which to develop modes of critique that illuminate the interaction of the social and the personal as well as of history and private experience. Through this form of analysis, dialectical thought replaces positivist forms of social inquiry. That is, the logic of predictability, verifiability, transferability, and operationalism is replaced by a dialectical mode of thinking that stresses the historical, relational, and normative dimensions of social inquiry and knowledge. The notion of dialectical thinking as critical thinking, and its implications for pedagogy, become somewhat clear in Jameson's comment that "[D]ialectical thinking is . . . thought about thinking itself, in which the mind must deal with its own thought process just as much as with the material it works on, in which both the particular content involved and the style of thinking suited to it must be held together in the mind at the same time" (Jameson 1971).

What we get here are hints of what a radical view of knowledge might look like. In this case, it would be knowledge that would instruct the oppressed about their situation as a group situated within specific relations of domination and subordination. It would be knowledge that would illuminate how the oppressed could develop a discourse free from the distortions of their own partly mangled cultural inheritance. On the other hand, it would be a form of knowledge that instructed the oppressed in how to appropriate the most progressive dimensions of their own cultural histories, as well as how to restructure and appropriate the most radical aspects of bourgeois culture. Finally, such knowledge would have to provide a motivational connection to action itself; it would have to link a radical decoding of history to a vision of the future that not only exploded the reifications of the existing society, but also reached into those pockets of desires and needs that harbored a longing for a new society and new forms of social relations. It is at this point that the link between history, culture, and psychology becomes important.

It is with regard to the above that the notion of historical understanding in the work of the Frankfurt School makes some important contributions to the notion of radical pedagogy. History, for Adorno and others connected with critical theory, had a two-fold meaning and could not be interpreted as a continuous pattern unfolding under the imperatives of "natural" laws. On the contrary, it had to be viewed as an emerging open-ended phenomenon, the significance of which was to be gleaned in the cracks and tensions that separated individuals and social classes from the imperatives of the dominant society. In other words, there were no laws of history that prefigured human progress, that functioned independently of human action. Moreover, history became meaningful not because it provided the present with the fruits of "interesting" or "stimulating" culture, but because it became the present object of analyses aimed at illuminating the revolutionary possibilities that existed in the given society. For the radical educator, this suggests using history in order "to fight against the spirit of the times rather than join it, to look backward at history rather than 'forward' " (Buck-Morss 1977). To put it another way, it meant, as Benjamin claimed "to brush history against the grain" (Benjamin 1974).

Not only does such a position link historical analysis to the notions of critique and emancipation, it also politicizes the notion of knowledge. That is, it argues for looking at knowledge critically, within constellations of suppressed insights (dialectical images) that point to the ways in which historically repressed cultures and struggles could be used to illuminate radical potentialities in the present. Knowledge in this instance becomes an object of analysis in a two-fold sense. On the one hand, it is examined for its social function, the way in which it legitimates the existing society. At the same time it could also be examined to reveal in its arrangement, words, structure, and style those unintentional truths that might contain "fleeting images" of a different society, more radical practices, and new forms of understanding. For instance, almost every cultural text contains a combination of ideological and utopian moments. Inherent in the most overt messages that characterize mass culture are elements of its antithesis. All cultural artifacts have a hidden referent that speaks to the initial basis for repression. Against the image of the barely clad female model selling the new automobile is the latent tension of misplaced and misappropriated sexual desire. Within the most authoritative modes of classroom discipline and control are fleeting images of freedom that speak to very different relationships. It is this dialectical aspect of knowledge that needs to be developed as part of a radical pedagogy.

Unlike traditional and liberal accounts of schooling, with their emphasis on historical continuities and historical development, critical theory points educators toward a mode of analysis that stresses the breaks, discontinuities, and tensions in history, all of which become valuable in that they highlight the centrality of human agency and struggle while simultaneously revealing the gap between society as it presently exists and society as it might be.

The Frankfurt School's theory of culture also offers new concepts and categories for analysing the role that schools play as agents of social and cultural reproduction. By illuminating the relationship between power and culture, the Frankfurt School provides a perspective on the way in which dominant ideologies are constituted and mediated via specific cultural formations. The concept of culture in this view exists in a particular relationship to the material base of society. The explanatory value of such a relationship is to be found in making problematic the specific content of a culture, its relationship to dominant and subordinate groups, as well as the socio-historical genesis of the ethos and practices of legitimating cultures and their role in constituting relations of domination and resistance. For example, by pointing to schools as cultural sites that embody conflicting political values, histories, and practices, it becomes possible to investigate how schools can be analyzed as an expression of the wider organization of society. Marcuse's (1964) study of the ideological nature of language, Adorno's (1975) analysis of the sociology of music, Horkheimer's (1972) method of dialectical critique and W. Benjamin's (1969, 1977) theory of cognition, all provide a number of valuable theoretical constructs through which to investigate the socially produced nature of knowledge and school experience.

The centrality of culture in the work of the Frankfurt School theorists (despite the differing opinions among its members) points to a number of important insights that illuminate how subjectivities get constituted both within and outside of schools. Though their analysis of culture is somewhat undialectical and clearly underdeveloped, it does provide a foundation for a greater elaboration and understanding of the relationship between culture and power, while simultaneously recognizing the latter as important terrain upon which to analyze the nature of domination and of resistance. By urging an attentiveness to the suppressed moments of history, critical theory points to the need to develop an equal sensitivity to certain aspects of culture. For example, working-class students, women, Blacks, and others need to affirm their own histories through the use of a language, a set of social relations, and body of knowledge that critically reconstructs and dignifies the cultural experiences that make up the tissue, texture, and history of their daily lives. This is no small matter, since once the affirmative nature of such a pedagogy is established, it becomes possible for students who have been traditionally voiceless in schools to learn the skills, knowledge, and modes of inquiry that will allow them to critically examine the role society has played in their own self-formation. More specifically, they will have the tools to examine how this society has functioned to shape and thwart their aspirations and goals, or prevented them from even imagining a life outside the one they presently lead. Thus it is important that students come to grips with what a given society has made of them, how it has incorporated them ideologically and materially into its rules and logic, and what it is that they need to affirm and reject in their own histories in order to begin the process of struggling for the conditions that will give them opportunities to lead a self-managed existence.

While it is true that Adorno, Marcuse, and Horkheimer placed heavy emphasis on the notion of domination in their analyses of culture, and in fact appeared to equate mass culture with mass manipulation, the value of their analyses rests with the mode of critique they developed in their attempt to reconstruct the notion of culture as a political force, as a powerful political moment in the process of domination. There is a paradox in their analyses of culture and human agency—that is, a paradox emerged in their emphasis on the overwhelming and one-sided nature of mass culture as a dominating force, on the one hand, and their relentless insistence on the need for critique, negativity, and critical mediation on the other. It is within this seeming contradiction that more dialectical notions of power and resistance have to be developed, positions that recognize wider structural and ideological determinations while recognizing that human beings never represent simply a reflex of such constraints. Human beings not only make history, they also make the constraints; and needless to say, they also unmake them. It needs to be remembered that power is both an enabling as well as a constraining force, as Foucault (1980) is quick to point out.

It must be stressed that the ideological justification of the given social order is not to be found simply in modes of interpretation that view history as a "natural" evolving process, or in the ideologies distributed through the culture industry. It is also found in the material reality of those needs and wants that bear the inscription of history. That is, history is to be found as "second nature" in those concepts and views of the world that make the most dominating aspects of the social order appear to be immune from historical socio-political development. Those aspects of reality that rest on an appeal to the universal and invariant often slip from historical consciousness and become embedded within those historically specific needs and desires that link individuals to the logics of conformity and domination. There is a certain irony in the fact that the personal and political join in the structure of domination precisely at those moments where history functions to tie individuals to a set of assumptions and practices that deny the historical nature of the political. "Second nature" represents history that has hardened into a form of social amnesia (Jacoby 1975), a mode of consciousness that "forgets" its own development. The significance of this perspective for radical pedagogy is that it points to the value of a *depth psychology* that can unravel how the mechanisms of domination and the possible seeds of liberation reach into the very structure of the human psyche. Radical pedagogy is much too cognitive in its orientation, and it needs to develop a theory of domination that incorporates needs and wants. Radical pedagogy lacks a depth psychology as well as appreciation for a sensibility that points to the importance of the sensual and imaginative as central dimensions of the schooling experience. The Frankfurt School's notion of depth psychology, especially Marcuse's work, opens up new terrain for developing a critical pedagogy. It speaks to the need to fashion new categories of analysis that will enable educators to become more knowledgeable about how teachers, students, and other educational workers become part of the system of social and cultural reproduction, particularly as it works through the messages and values that are constituted via the social practices of the hidden curriculum (Giroux 1981). By acknowledging the need for a critical social psychology, educators can begin to identify how ideologies get constituted, and they can then identify and reconstruct social practices and processes that break rather than continue existing forms of social and psychological domination.

The relevance of Marcuse's analysis of depth psychology for educational theory becomes obvious in the more recent work of Pierre Bourdieu (1977a, 1977b). Bourdieu argues that the school and other social institutions legitimate and reinforce through specific sets of practices and discourses class-based systems of behavior and dispositions that reproduce the existing dominant society. Bourdieu extends Marcuse's insights by pointing to a notion of learning in which a child internalizes the cultural messages of the school not only via the latter's official discourse (symbolic mastery), but also through the messages embodied in the "insignificant" practices of daily classroom life. Bourdieu (1977b) is worth quoting at length on this issue:

> [Schools] . . . set such a store on the seemingly most insignificant details of dress, bearing, physical and verbal manners. . . . The principles embodied in this way are placed beyond the grasp of consciousness, and hence cannot be touched by voluntary, deliberate transformation, cannot even be made explicit. . . . The whole trick of pedagogic reason lies precisely in the way it extorts the essential while seeming to demand the insignificant: in obtaining respect for forms and forms of respect which constitute the most visible and at the same time the best hidden manifestations to the established order.
>
> (Bourdieu 1977b)

Unlike Bourdieu, Marcuse believes that historically conditioned needs that function in the interest of domination can be changed. That is, in Marcuse's view (1955) any viable form of political action must begin with a notion of political education in which a new language, qualitatively different social relations, and a new set of values would have to operate with the purpose of creating a new environment "in which the nonaggressive, erotic, receptive faculties of man, in harmony with the consciousness of freedom, strive for the pacification of man and nature" (Marcuse 1969). Thus the notion of depth psychology developed by the Frankfurt School not only provides new insights into how subjectivities are formed or how ideology functions as lived experience, it also provides theoretical tools to establish the conditions for new needs, new systems of values, and new social practices that take seriously the imperatives of a critical pedagogy.

Conclusion

In conclusion, I have attempted to present selected aspects of the work of critical theorists such as Adorno, Horkheimer, and Marcuse that provide theoretical insights for developing a critical theory of education. Specifically, I have focused on their critique of positivist rationality, their view of theory, their critical reconstruction of a theory of culture, and, finally, on their analysis of depth psychology. It is within the context of these four areas that radical educators can begin the task of reconstructing and applying the insights of critical theory to schooling. Of course, the task of translating the work of the Frankfurt School into terms that inform and enrich radical educational theory and practice will be difficult. This is especially true since any attempt to use such work will have to begin with the understanding that it contains a number of shortcomings and moreover cannot be imposed in grid-like fashion onto a theory of radical pedagogy. For example, the critical theorists I have discussed did not develop a comprehensive theoretical approach for dealing with the patterns of conflict and contradictions that existed in various cultural spheres. To the contrary, they developed an unsatisfactory notion of domination and an exaggerated view of the integrated nature of the American public; they constantly underestimated the radical potential inherent in working-class culture; and they never developed an adequate theory of social consciousness. That is, in spite of their insistence on the importance of the notion of mediation, they never explored the contradictory modes of thinking that characterize the way most people view the world. Of course, the latter selection does not exhaust the list of criticisms that could be made against the work of the critical theorists under analysis here. The point is that critical theory needs to be reformulated to provide the opportunity to both critique and elaborate its insights beyond the constraints and historical conditions under which they were first generated. It must be stressed that the insights critical theory has provided have not been exhausted. In fact, one may argue that we are just beginning to work out the implications of their analyses. The real issue is to reformulate the central contributions of critical theory in terms of new historical conditions, without sacrificing the emancipatory spirit that generated them.

References

Adorno, T. W. 1967a. *Prisms*, trans. Samuel and Shierry Weber. London: Neville Spearman.

——. 1967b. "Sociology and psychology: Part I." *New Left Review*, 46.

——. 1968. "Sociology and psychology: Part II." *New Left Review*, 47.

——. 1969. "Scientific Experiences of a European Scholar in America." In *The Intellectual Migration*, ed. Donald Fleming and Bernard Bailyn. Cambridge, Mass.: Harvard University Press.

Adorno, T. W., and M. Horkheimer, 1972. *Dialectic of Enlightenment*, trans. John Cumming. New York: Seabury Press.

——. 1973. *Negative Dialectics*. New York: Seabury Press.

——. 1975. "The Culture Industry Reconsidered." *New German Critique*, 6 (Fall).

—— 1976. "On the Logic of the Social Sciences." In *The Positivist Dispute in German Sociology*, T. W. Adorno et al. London: Heinemann.

Agger, B. 1978. "Work and Authority in Marcuse and Habermas." *Human Studies*, 2(3) (July).

Aronowitz, S. 1973. *False Promises*. New York: McGraw-Hill.

——. 1976. "Enzenberger on Mass Culture: A Review Essay." *Minnesota Review*, 7 (Fall).

——. 1981a. *The Crisis in Historical Materialism: Class, Politics, and Culture in Marxist Theory*. New York: Bergin.

——. 1981b. "Redefining Literacy." *Social Policy* (Sept.-Oct.).

Benjamin, J. 1977. "The End of Internationalization: Adorno's Social Psychology." *Telos*, 32 (Summer).

Benjamin, W. 1974. In *Über den Begriff der Geschichte: Gesammelte Schriften*, 1(2), ed. Rolf Tiedemann and Hermann Schweppenhauser, Abhandlungen, Suhrkamp Verlag, Frankfurt am Main.

——. 1969. In *Illuminations*, ed. Hannah Arendt. New York: Schocken.

——. 1977. *The Origin of German Tragic Drama*, trans. John Osborne. London: New Left Books.

Bennett, T. 1980. "The Not-So-Good, the Bad, and the Ugly." *Screen Education*, 36 (Autumn).

Bourdieu, P., and J. C. Passeron. 1977a. *Reproduction in Education, Society, and Culture*. Beverly Hills, Cal.: Sage.

——. 1977b. *Outline of Theory and Practice*. Cambridge: Cambridge University Press.

Breines, P. 1979/80. "Toward an Uncertain Marxism." *Radical History Review*, 22 (Winter).

Buck-Morss, S. 1977. *The Origins of Negative Dialectics*. New York: Free Press.

Enzenberger, H. M. 1974. *The Consciousness Industry*. New York: Seabury Press.

Ewen, S. 1976. *Captains of Consciousness: Advertising and the Social Roots of the Consumer Culture*. New York: McGraw-Hill.

Foucault, M. 1980. *Power and Knowledge: Selected Interviews and Other Writings*, ed. C. Gordon. New York: Pantheon.

Freud, S. 1949. *Civilization and Its Discontents*. London: Hogarth Press.

Friedman, G. 1981. *The Political Philosophy of the Frankfurt School*. Ithaca, N.Y.: Cornell University Press.

Giroux, H. A. 1981. *Ideology, Culture, and the Process of Schooling*. Philadelphia: Temple University Press.

Gramsci, A. 1971. *Selections from Prison Notebooks*, ed. and trans. Quinten Hoare and Geoffrey Smith. New York: International Publishers.

Gross, H. 1979. "Adorno in Los Angeles: The Intellectual Emigration." *Humanities in Society*, 2(4) (Fall).

Habermas, J. 1973. *Theory and Practice*. Boston: Beacon Press.

—— 1980. "Psychic Thermidor and the Rebirth of Rebellious Subjectivity." *Berkeley Journal of Sociology*, 25.

Hahn, H. 1933. "Logik Mathematik und Naturerkennen." *In Einheitswissenschaft* ed. Otto Neurath et al. Vienna: n.p.

Held, D. 1980. *Introduction to Critical Theory: Horkheimer to Habermas*. Berkeley: University of California Press.

Horkheimer, M. 1972. *Critical Theory*. New York: Seabury Press.

——. 1974. *Eclipse of Reason*. New York: Seabury Press.

Jacoby, R. 1975. *Social Amnesia*. Boston: Beacon Press.

—— 1980. "What Is Conformist Marxism?" *Telos*, 45 (Fall).

Jameson, F. 1971. *Marxism and Form*. Princeton, N.J.: Princeton University Press.

Jay, M. 1973. *The Dialectical Imagination: A History of the Frankfurt School and the Institute of Social Research 1923–1950*. Boston: Little, Brown.

Lowenthal, L. 1979. "Theodor W. Adorno: An Intellectual Memoir." *Humanities in Society*, 2(4) (Fall).

Marcuse, H. 1955. *Eros and Civilization*. Boston: Beacon Press.

——. 1960. *Reason and Revolution*, Boston: Beacon Press.

——. 1964. *One Dimensional Man*. Boston: Beacon Press.
——. 1968a. *Negations: Essays in Critical Theory.* Boston: Beacon Press.
——. 1968b. *An Essay on Liberation*. Boston: Beacon Press.
——. 1970. *Five Lectures*, trans. Jeremy Shapiro and Sheirry Weber. Boston: Beacon Press.
——. 1969. "Repressive Tolerance." In *A Critique of Pure Tolerance*, ed. Robert Paul Wolff, Benjamin Moor, Jr., and Herbert Marcuse. Boston: Beacon Press.
—— 1972. *Counter-Revolution and Revolt*. Boston: Beacon Press.
——. 1978. "On Science and Phenomenology." In *The Essential Frankfurt School Reader*, ed. Andrew Arato and Eike Gebhardt. New York: Urizen Books.
Nietzsche, F. 1966. "Aus dem Nachlass der Achtzigerjahre." In *Werke*, vol. 3, ed. Karle Schleckta. Munich: Hanser.
Wellmer, A. 1974. *Critical Theory of Society*, trans. John Cumming. New York: Seabury Press.

2

Critical Pedagogy: A Look at the Major Concepts

Peter McLaren

In practice, critical pedagogy is as diverse as its many adherents, yet common themes and constructs run through many of their writings. In what follows, I will outline in more detail the major categories within this tradition. A category is simply a concept, question, issue, hypothesis, or idea that is central to critical theory. These categories are intended to provide a theoretical framework within which you may reread my journal entries and perhaps better understand the theories generated by critical educational research. The categories are useful for the purposes of clarification and illustration, although some critical theorists will undoubtedly argue that additional concepts should have been included, or that some concepts have not been given the emphasis they deserve.

The Importance of Theory

Before we discuss individual categories, we need to examine how those categories are explored. Critical theorists begin with the premise that *men and women are essentially unfree and inhabit a world rife with contradictions and asymmetries of power and privilege*. The critical educator endorses theories that are, first and foremost, *dialectical*; that is, theories which recognize the problems of society as more than simply isolated events of individuals or deficiencies in the social structure. Rather, these problems form part of the *interactive context* between individual and society. The individual, a social actor, both creates and is created by the social universe of which he/she is a part. Neither the individual nor society is given priority in analysis; the two are inextricably interwoven, so that reference to one must by implication mean reference to the other. Dialectical theory attempts to tease out the histories and relations of accepted meanings and appearances, tracing interactions from the context to the part, from the system inward to the event. In this way, critical theory helps us focus *simultaneously on both sides of a social contradiction.*[1]

Wilfred Carr and Stephen Kemmis describe dialectical thinking as follows:

> Dialectical thinking involves searching out . . . contradictions (like the contradiction of the inadvertent oppression of less able students by a system which aspires to help all students to attain their "full potential"), but it is not really as wooden or mechanical as the formula of thesis-antithesis-synthesis. On the contrary, it is an open and questioning form of thinking which demands reflection back and forth between elements like *part* and *whole, knowledge* and *action, process* and *product, subject* and *object, being* and *becoming, rhetoric* and *reality*, or *structure* and *function*. In the process, *contradictions* may be discovered (as, for example,

> in a political *structure* which aspires to give decision-making power to all, but actually *functions* to deprive some of access to the information with which they could influence crucial decisions about their lives). As contradictions are revealed, new constructive thinking and new constructive action are required to transcend the contradictory state of affairs. The complementarity of the elements is dynamic: it is a kind of a tension, not a static confrontation between the two poles. In the dialectical approach, the elements are regarded as mutually constitutive, not separate and distinct. Contradiction can thus be distinguished from paradox: to speak of a contradiction is to imply that a new resolution can be achieved, while to speak of a paradox is to suggest that two incompatible ideas remain inertly opposed to one another. (italics original)[2]

The dialectical nature of critical theory enables the educational researcher to see the school not simply as an arena of indoctrination or socialization or a site of instruction, but also as a cultural terrain that promotes student empowerment and self-transformation. My own research into parochial education for instance, showed that the school functions *simultaneously* as a means of empowering students around issues of social justice and as a means of sustaining, legitimizing, and reproducing dominant class interests directed at creating obedient, docile, and low-paid future workers.[3]

A dialectical understanding of schooling permits us to see schools as sites of *both* domination and liberation; this runs counter to the overdeterministic orthodox Marxist view of schooling, which claims that schools simply reproduce class relations and passively indoctrinate students into becoming greedy young capitalists. This dialectical understanding of schooling also brushes against the grain of mainstream educational theory, which conceives of schools as mainly providing students with the skills and attitudes necessary for becoming patriotic, industrious, and responsible citizens.

Critical educators argue that any worthwhile theory of schooling *must be partisan*. That is, it must be fundamentally tied to a struggle for a qualitatively better life for all through the construction of a society based on nonexploitative relations and social justice. The critical educator doesn't believe that there are two sides to every question, with both sides needing equal attention. For the critical educator, there are *many* sides to a problem, and often these sides are linked to certain class, race, and gender interests.

Let's turn for a moment to an example of critical theorizing as it is brought to bear on a fundamental teaching practice: writing classroom objectives. In this example, I will draw on Henry Giroux's important distinction between *micro* and *macro* objectives.[4]

The common use of behavioral objectives by teachers reflects a search for certainty and technical control of knowledge and behavior. Teachers often emphasize classroom management procedures, efficiency, and "how-to-do" techniques that ultimately ignore an important question: "Why is this knowledge being taught in the first place?" Giroux recasts classroom objectives into the categories of macro and micro.

Macro objectives are designed to enable students to make connections between the methods, content, and structure of a course and its significance within the larger social reality. This dialectical approach to classroom objectives allows students to acquire a broad frame of reference or world view; in other words, it helps them acquire a political perspective. Students can then make the hidden curriculum explicit and develop a critical political consciousness.

Micro objectives represent the course content and are characterized by their narrowness of purpose and their content-bound path of inquiry. Giroux tells us that the importance of the relationship between macro and micro objectives arises out of *having students uncover the connections between course objectives and the norms, values, and structural relationships of the wider society*. For instance, the micro objectives of teaching about the Vietnam war might be to learn the dates of specific battles, the details of specific Congressional debates surrounding the war, and the reasons given by the White House for fighting the war. The micro objectives are concerned with the organization, classification, mastery, and manipulation of data. This is what Giroux calls *productive knowledge*. Macro objectives, on the other hand, center on the relationship between means and ends, between specific events and their wider social and political implications. A lesson on the Vietnam war or the more recent invasion of Grenada, for instance, might raise the following macro questions: What is the relationship between the invasion of Grenada as a rescue mission in the interests of U.S. citizens and the larger logic of imperialism? During the Vietnam era, what was the relationship between the American economy and the arms industry? Whose interests did the war serve best? Who benefited most from the war? What were the class relationships between those who fought and those who stayed home in the university?

Developing macro objectives fosters a dialectical mode of inquiry; the process constitutes a socio-political application of knowledge, what Giroux calls *directive knowledge*. Critical theorists seek a kind of knowledge that will help students recognize the *social function of particular forms of knowledge*. The purpose of dialectical educational theory, then, is to provide students with a model that permits them to examine the underlying political, social, and economic foundations of the larger society.

Critical Pedagogy and the Social Construction of Knowledge

Critical educational theorists view school knowledge as historically and socially rooted and interest bound. Knowledge acquired in school—or anywhere, for that matter—is never neutral or objective but is ordered and structured in particular ways; its emphases and exclusions partake of a silent logic. Knowledge is a *social construction* deeply rooted in a nexus of power relations. When critical theorists claim that knowledge is socially constructed, they mean that it is the product of agreement or consent between individuals who live out particular social relations (e.g., of class, race, and gender) and who live in particular junctures in time. To claim that knowledge is socially constructed usually means that the world we live in is constructed symbolically by the mind through social interaction with others and is heavily dependent on culture, context, custom, and historical specificity. There is no ideal, autonomous, pristine, or aboriginal world to which our social constructions necessarily correspond; there is always a referential field in which symbols are situated. And this particular referential field (e.g., language, culture, place, time) will influence how symbols generate meaning. There is no pure subjective insight. We do not stand *before* the social world; we live *in the midst* of it. As we seek the meaning of events we seek the meaning of the social. We can now raise certain questions with respect to the social construction of knowledge, such as: why do women and minorities often view social issues differently than white males? Why are teachers more likely to value the opinions of a middle-class white male student, for instance, than those of a black female?

Critical pedagogy asks how and why knowledge gets constructed the way it does, and how and why some constructions of reality are legitimated and celebrated by the dominant culture while others clearly are not. Critical pedagogy asks how our everyday commonsense understandings—our social constructions or "subjectivities"—get produced and lived out. In other words, what are the *social functions* of knowledge? The crucial factor here is that some forms of knowledge have more power and legitimacy than others. For instance, in many schools in the United States, science and math curricula are favored over the liberal arts. This can be explained by the link between the needs of big business to compete in world markets and the imperatives of the new reform movement to bring "excellence" back to the schools. Certain types of knowledge legitimate certain gender, class, and racial interests. Whose interests does this knowledge serve? Who gets excluded as a result? Who is marginalized?

Let's put this in the form of further questions: What is the relationship between social class and knowledge taught in school? Why do we value scientific knowledge over informal knowledge? Why do we have teachers using "standard English"? Why is the public still unlikely to vote for a woman or a black for president? How does school knowledge reinforce stereotypes about women, minorities, and disadvantaged peoples? What accounts for some knowledge having high status (as in the great works of philosophers or scientists) while the practical knowledge of ordinary people or marginalized or subjugated groups is often discredited and devalued? Why do we learn about the great "men" in history and spend less time learning about the contributions of women and minorities and the struggles of people in lower economic classes? Why don't we learn more about the American labor movement? How and why are certain types of knowledge used to reinforce dominant ideologies, which in turn serve to mask unjust power relations among certain groups in society?

Forms of Knowledge

Critical pedagogy follows a distinction regarding forms of knowledge posited by the German social theorist Jürgen Habermas.[5] Let's examine this concept in the context of classroom teaching. Mainstream educators who work primarily within liberal and conservative educational ideologies emphasize *technical knowledge* (similar to Giroux's *productive knowledge*): Knowledge is that which can be measured and quantified. Technical knowledge is based on the natural sciences, uses hypothetico-deductive or empirical analytical methods, and is evaluated by, among other things, intelligence quotients, reading scores, and SAT results, all of which are used by educators to sort, regulate, and control students.

A second type, *practical knowledge*, aims to enlighten individuals so they can shape their daily actions in the world. Practical knowledge is generally acquired through *describing and analyzing social situations historically or developmentally*, and is geared toward helping individuals understand social events that are ongoing and situational. The liberal educational researcher who undertakes fieldwork in a school in order to evaluate student behavior and interaction acquires practical knowledge, for instance. This type of knowledge is not usually generated numerically or by submitting data to some kind of statistical instrument.

The critical educator, however, is most interested in what Habermas calls *emancipatory knowledge* (similar to Giroux's *directive knowledge*), which attempts to reconcile and transcend the opposition between technical and practical knowledge. Emancipatory knowledge helps us understand how social relationships are distorted and manipulated by relations of power and privilege. It also aims at creating the conditions under which irrationality, domination, and oppression can be overcome and transformed through deliberative, collective action. In short, it creates the foundation for social justice, equality, and empowerment.

Class

Class refers to the *economic, social, and political relationships that govern life in a given social order*. Class relationships reflect the constraints and limitations individuals and groups experience in the areas of income level, occupation, place of residence, and other indicators of status and social rank. Relations of class are those associated with surplus labor, who produces it, and who is a recipient of it. Surplus labor is that labor undertaken by workers beyond that which is necessary. Class relations also deal with the social distribution of power and its structural allocation. Today there are greater distinctions within the working classes and it is now possible to talk about the new *underclasses* within the American social structure consisting of black, Hispanic, and Asian class fractions, together with the white aged, the unemployed and underemployed, large sections of women, the handicapped, and other marginalized economic groups.

Culture

The concept of *culture*, varied though it may be, is essential to any understanding of critical pedagogy. I use the term "culture" here to signify *the particular ways in which a social group lives out and makes sense of its "given" circumstances and conditions of life*. In addition to defining culture as *a set of practices, ideologies, and values from which different groups draw to make sense of the world*, we need to recognize how cultural questions help us understand who has power and how it is reproduced and manifested in the social relations that link schooling to the wider social order. The ability of individuals to express their culture is related to the power which certain groups are able to wield in the social order. The expression of values and beliefs by individuals who share certain historical experiences is determined by their collective power in society.[6]

The link between culture and power has been extensively analyzed in critical social theory over the past ten years. It is therefore possible to offer three insights from that literature that particularly illuminate the political logic that underlies various cultural/power relations. First, culture is intimately connected with the structure of social relations within class, gender, and age formations that produce forms of oppression and dependency. Second, culture is analyzed not simply as a way of life, but as a form of production through which different groups in either their dominant or subordinate social relations define and realize their aspirations through unequal relations of power. Third, culture is viewed as a field of struggle in which the production, legitimation, and circulation of particular forms of knowledge and experience are central areas of conflict. What is important here is that each of these insights raises fundamental questions about the ways in which inequalities are maintained and challenged in the spheres of school culture and the wider society.[7]

Dominant Culture, Subordinate Culture, and Subculture

Three central categories related to the concept of culture—dominant culture, subordinate culture, subculture—have been much discussed in recent critical scholarship. Culture can be readily broken down into "dominant" and "subordinate" parent cultures. *Dominant culture* refers to social practices and representations that *affirm the central values, interests, and concerns of the social class in control of the material and symbolic wealth of society*. Groups who live out social relations in subordination to the dominant culture are part of the *subordinate culture*. Group *subcultures* may be described as subsets of the two parent cultures (dominant and subordinate). Individuals who form subcultures often use distinct symbols and social practices to help foster an identity outside that of the dominant culture. As an example, we need only refer to punk subculture, with its distinct musical tastes, fetishistic costumery, spiked hair, and its attempt to disconfirm the dominant rules of propriety fostered by the mainstream media, schools, religions, and culture industry. For the most part, working-class subcultures exist in a subordinate structural position in society, and many of their members engage in oppositional acts against the dominant middle-class culture. It is important to remember, however, that people don't inhabit cultures or social classes but *live out class or cultural relations*, some of which may be dominant and some of which may be subordinate.[8]

Subcultures are involved in contesting the cultural "space" or openings in the dominant culture. The dominant culture is never able to secure total control over subordinate cultural groups. Whether we choose to examine British subcultural groups (i.e., working-class youth, teddy-boys, skinheads, punks, rude boys, rastafarians) or American groups (i.e., motorcycle clubs such as Hell's Angels, ethnic street gangs, or middle class suburban gangs), subcultures are more often *negotiated* than truly *oppositional*. As John Muncie points out, this is because they operate primarily in the arena of leisure that is exceedingly vulnerable to commercial and ideological incorporation.[9] Subcultures do offer a symbolic critique of the social order and are frequently organized around relations of class, gender, style, and race. Despite the often ferocious exploitation of the subcultural resistance of various youth subcultures by bourgeois institutions (school, workplace, justice system, consumer industries), subcultures are usually able to keep alive the struggle over how meanings are produced, defined, and legitimated; consequently, they do represent various degrees of struggle against lived subjugation. Many subcultural movements reflect a crisis within dominant society, rather than a unified mobilization against it. For instance, the hippie movement in the 1960s represented, in part, an exercise of petite-bourgeoisie socialism by middle-class radicals who were nurtured both by idealist principles and by a search for spiritual and life-style comfort. This often served to draw critical attention away from the structural inequalities of capitalist society. As Muncie argues, subcultures constitute "a crisis within dominant culture rather than a conspiracy against dominant culture."[10] The youth counterculture of the sixties served as the ideological loam that fertilized my pedagogy. I had learned the rudiments of a middle-class radicalism that was preoccupied with the politics of expressive life and avoided examining in a minded and a critical manner the structural inequalities within the social order.

Cultural Forms

Cultural forms are those symbols and social practices that express culture, such as those found in music, dress, food, religion, dance, and education, which have developed from the efforts of groups to shape their lives out of their surrounding material and political environment. Television, video, and films are regarded as cultural forms. Schooling is also a cultural form. Baseball is a cultural form. Cultural forms don't exist apart from sets of structural underpinnings which are related to the means of economic production, the mobilization of desire, the construction of social values, asymmetries of power/knowledge, configurations of ideologies, and relations of class, race, and gender.

Hegemony

The dominant culture is able to exercise domination over subordinate classes or groups through a process known as *hegemony*.[11] Hegemony refers to the maintenance of domination not by the sheer exercise of force *but primarily through consensual social practices, social forms, and social structures produced in specific sites such as the church, the state, the school, the mass media, the political system, and the family*. By *social practices*, I refer to what people say and do. Of course, social practices may be accomplished through words, gestures, personally appropriated signs and rituals, or a combination of these. *Social forms* refer to the principles that provide and give legitimacy to specific social practices. For example, the state legislature is one social form that gives legitimacy to the social practice of teaching. The term *social structures* can be defined as those constraints that limit individual life and appear to be beyond the individual's control, having their sources in the power relations that govern society. We can, therefore, talk about the "class structure" or the "economic structure" of our society.

Hegemony is a struggle in which the powerful win the consent of those who are oppressed, with the oppressed unknowingly participating in their own oppression. Hegemony was at work in my own practices as an elementary school teacher. Because I did not teach my students to question the prevailing values, attitudes, and social practices of the dominant society in a sustained critical manner, my classroom preserved the hegemony of the dominant culture. Such hegemony was contested when the students began to question my authority by resisting and disrupting my lessons. The dominant class secures hegemony—the consent of the dominated—by supplying the symbols, representations, and practices of social life in such a way that the basis of social authority and the unequal relations of power and privilege remain hidden. By perpetrating the myth of individual achievement and entrepreneurship in the media, the schools, the church, and the family, for instance, dominant culture ensures that subordinated groups who fail at school or who don't make it into the world of the "rich and famous" will view such failure in terms of personal inadequacy or the "luck of the draw." The oppressed blame themselves for school failure—a failure that can certainly be additionally attributed to the structuring effects of the economy and the class-based division of labor.[12]

Hegemony is a cultural encasement of meanings, a prison-house of language and ideas, that is "freely" entered into by both dominators and dominated. As Todd Gitlin puts it,

> both rulers and ruled derive psychological and material rewards in the course of confirming and reconfirming their inequality. The hegemonic sense of the world seeps into popular "common sense" and gets reproduced there; it may even appear to be generated *by* that common sense.[13]

Hegemony refers to the moral and intellectual leadership of a dominant class over a subordinate class achieved not through coercion (i.e., threat of imprisonment or torture) or the willful construction of rules and regulations (as in a dictatorship or fascist regime), but rather through the general winning of consent of the subordinate class to the authority of the dominant class. The dominant class need not impose force for the manufacture of hegemony since the subordinate class actively subscribes to many of the values and objectives of the dominant class without being aware of the source of those values or the interests which inform them.

Hegemony is not a process of active domination as much as an active structuring of the culture and experiences of the subordinate class by the dominant class. The dominant culture is able to "frame" the ways in which subordinate groups live and respond to their own cultural system and lived experiences; in other words, the dominant culture is able to manufacture dreams and desires for both dominant and subordinate groups by supplying "terms of reference" (i.e., images, visions, stories, ideals) against which all individuals are expected to live their lives. The dominant culture tries to "fix" the meaning of signs, symbols, and representations to provide a "common" worldview, disguising relations of power and privilege through the organs of mass media, state apparatus such as schools, government institutions, and state bureaucracies. Individuals are provided with "subject positions," which condition them to react to ideas and opinions in prescribed ways. For instance, most individuals in the United States, when addressed as "Americans," are generally positioned as subjects by the dominant discourse. To be an "American" carries a certain set of ideological baggage. Americans generally think of themselves as lovers of freedom, defenders of individual rights, guardians of world peace, etc.; rarely do Americans see themselves as contradictory social agents. They rarely view their country as lagging behind other industrial economies in the world in providing security for its citizens in such areas as health care, family allowance, and housing subsidy programs. As citizens of the wealthiest country in the world, Americans generally do not question why their government cannot afford to be more generous to its citizens. Most Americans would be aghast at hearing a description of their country as a "terrorist regime" exercising covert acts of war against Latin American countries such as Nicaragua. The prevailing image of America that the schools, the entertainment industry, and government agencies have promulgated is a benevolent one in which the interests of the dominant classes supposedly represent the interests of all groups. It is an image in which the values and beliefs of the dominant class appear so correct that to reject them would be unnatural, a violation of common sense.

Within the hegemonic process, established meanings are often laundered of contradiction, contestation, and ambiguity. Resistance does occur, however, most often in the domain of popular culture. In this case, popular culture becomes an arena of negotiation in which dominant, subordinate, and oppositional groups affirm and struggle over cultural representations and meanings. The dominant culture is rarely successful on all counts. People *do* resist. Alternative groups do manage to find different values and meanings to regulate their lives. Oppositional groups do attempt to challenge the prevailing culture's mode of structuring and codifying representations and meanings. Prevailing social practices are, in fact, resisted. Schools and other social and cultural sites are rarely in the thrall of the hegemonic process since there we will also find struggle and confrontation. This is why schools can be characterized as terrains of transactions, exchange, and struggle between subordinate groups and the dominant ideology. There is a relative autonomy within school sites that allows for forms of resistance to emerge and to break the cohesiveness of hegemony. Teachers battle over what books to use, over what disciplinary practices to use, and over the aims and objectives of particular courses and programs.

One current example of the battle for hegemony can be seen in the challenge by Christian fundamentalists to public schooling. Fundamentalist critics have instigated a debate over dominant pedagogical practices that ranges all the way from textbooks to how, in science classes, teachers may account for the origins of humankind. The important point to remember, however, is that hegemony is always in operation; certain ideas, values, and social practices generally prevail over others.

Not all prevailing values are oppressive. Critical educators, too, would like to secure hegemony for their own ideas. The challenge for teachers is to recognize and attempt to transform those undemocratic and oppressive features of hegemonic control that often structure everyday classroom existence in ways not readily apparent. These oppressive features are rarely challenged since the dominant ideology is so all inclusive that individuals are taught to view it as natural, commonsensical, and inviolable. For instance, subordinate groups who subscribe to an ideology that could be described as right wing are often the very groups hurt most by the Republican government they elect in terms of cutbacks in social services, agricultural aid, etc. Yet the Republican Party has been able to market itself as no-nonsense, get-tough, anti-Communist, and hyper-patriotic—features that appeal to subordinate groups whose cultural practices may include listening to country and western music, following the televangelist programs and crusades, or cheering the pugilistic exploits of Rambo. Those who seek to chart out the ways in which the affluent are favored over subordinate groups are dismissed as wimpish liberals who don't support the "freedom fighters" in Nicaragua. Who needs to use force when ideational hegemony works this well? As Gore Vidal has observed about the United States: "The genius of our system is that ordinary people go out and vote against their interests. The way our ruling class keeps out of sight is one of the greatest stunts in the political history of any country."[14]

Ideology

Hegemony could not do its work without the support of ideology. Ideology permeates all of social life and does not simply refer to the political ideologies of communism, socialism, anarchism, rationalism, or existentialism. Ideology refers to *the production and representation of ideas, values, and beliefs and the manner in which they are expressed and lived out by both individuals and groups.*[15] Simply put, ideology refers to the production of sense and meaning. It can be described as a way of viewing the world, a complex of ideas, various types of social practices, rituals, and representations *that we tend to accept as natural and as common sense.* It is the result of the intersection of meaning and power in the social world. Customs, rituals, beliefs, and values often produce within individuals distorted conceptions of their place in the sociocultural order and thereby serve to reconcile them to that place and to disguise the inequitable relations of power and privilege; this is sometimes referred to as "ideological hegemony."

Stuart Hall and James Donald define ideology as "the frameworks of thought which are used in society to explain, figure out, make sense of or give meaning to the social and political world . . . Without these frameworks, we could not make sense of the world at all. But with them, our perceptions are inevitably structured in a particular direction by the very concepts we are using."[16] Ideology includes both positive and negative functions at any given moment: The *positive function* of ideology is to "provide the concepts, categories, images, and ideas by means of which people make sense of their social and political world, form projects, come to a certain consciousness of their place in the world and act in it;" the *negative function* of ideology "refers to the fact that all such perspectives are inevitably selective. Thus a perspective positively organizes the 'facts of the case' in *this* and makes sense because it inevitably excludes *that* way of putting things."[17]

In order to fully understand the negative function of ideology, the concept must be linked to a theory of domination. *Domination* occurs when relations of power established at the institutional level are systematically asymmetrical; that is, when they are unequal, therefore privileging some groups over others. According to John Thompson, ideology as a negative function works through four different modes: legitimation, dissimulation, fragmentation, and reification. *Legitimation* occurs when a system of domination is sustained by being represented as legitimate or as eminently just and worthy of respect. For instance, by legitimizing the school system as just and meritocratic, as giving everyone the same opportunity for success, the dominant culture hides the truth of the hidden curriculum—the fact that those whom schooling helps most are those who come from the most affluent families. *Dissimulation* results when relations of domination are concealed, denied, or obscured in various ways. For instance, the practice of institutionalized tracking in schools purports to help better meet the needs of groups of students with varying academic ability. However, describing tracking in this way helps to cloak its socially reproductive function: that of sorting students according to their social class location. *Fragmentation* occurs when relations of domination are sustained by the production of meanings in a way which fragments groups so that they are placed in opposition to one another. For instance, when conservative educational critics explain the declining standards in American education as a result of trying to accommodate low income minority students, this sometimes results in a backlash against immigrant students by other subordinate groups. This "divide and rule" tactic prevents oppressed groups from working together to secure collectively their rights. *Reification* occurs when transitory historical states of affairs are presented as permanent, natural and commonsensical—as if they exist outside of time.[18] This has occurred to a certain extent with the current call for a national curriculum based on acquiring information about the "great books" so as to have a greater access to the dominant culture. These works are revered as high status knowledge since purportedly the force of history has heralded them as such and placed them on book lists in respected cultural institutions such as universities. Here literacy becomes a weapon that can be used against those groups who are "culturally illiterate," whose social class, race, or gender renders their own experiences and stories as too unimportant to be worthy of investigation. That is, as a pedagogical tool, a stress on the great books often deflects attention away from the personal experiences of students and the political nature of everyday life. Teaching the great books is also a way of inculcating certain values and sets of behaviors in social groups, thereby solidifying the existing social hierarchy. The most difficult task in analyzing these negative functions of ideology is to unmask those ideological properties which insinuate themselves within reality as their fundamental components. Ideological functions which barricade themselves within the realm of commonsense often manage to disguise the grounds of their operations.

At this point it should be clear that ideology represents a vocabulary of standardization and a grammar of design sanctioned and sustained by particular social practices. All ideas and systems of thought organize a rendition of reality according to their own metaphors, narratives, and rhetoric. There is no "deep structure," totalizing logic, or grand theory pristine in form and innocent in effects which is altogether uncontaminated by interest, value, or judgement—in short, by *ideology*. There is no privileged sanctuary separate from culture and politics where we can be free to distinguish truth from opinion, fact from value, or image from interpretation. There is no "objective" environment that is not stamped with social presence.

If we all can agree that as individuals, we inherit a preexisting sign community, and acknowledge that all ideas, values, and meanings have social roots and perform social functions, then understanding ideology becomes a matter of investigating *which* concepts, values, and meanings *obscure* our understanding of the social world and our place within the networks of power/knowledge relations, and which concepts, values, and meanings *clarify* such an understanding. In other words, why do certain ideological formations cause us to misrecognize our complicity in establishing or maintaining asymmetrical relations of power and privilege within the sociocultural order?

The *dominant ideology* refers to patterns of beliefs and values shared by the majority of individuals. The majority of Americans—rich and poor alike—share the belief that capitalism is a better system than democratic socialism, for instance, or that men are generally more capable of holding positions of authority than women, or that women should be more passive and housebound. Here, we must recognize that the economic system requires the ideology of consumer capitalism to naturalize it, rendering it common-sensical. The ideology of patriarchy also is necessary to keep the nature of the economy safe and secured within the prevailing hegemony. We have been "fed" these dominant ideologies for decades through the mass media, the schools, and through family socialization.

Oppositional ideologies do exist, however, which attempt to challenge the dominant ideologies and shatter existing stereotypes. On some occasions, the dominant culture is able to manipulate alternative and oppositional ideologies in such a way that hegemony can be more effectively secured. For instance, *The Cosby Show* on commercial television carries a message that a social avenue now exists in America for blacks to be successful doctors and lawyers. This positive view of blacks, however, masks the fact that most blacks in the United States exist in a subordinate position to the dominant white culture with respect to power and privilege. The dominant culture secures hegemony by transmitting and legitimating ideologies like that in *The Cosby Show*, which reflect and shape popular resistance to stereotypes, but which in reality do little to challenge the real basis of power of the ruling dominant groups.

The dominant ideology often encourages oppositional ideologies and tolerates those that challenge their own rationale, since by absorbing these contradictory values, they are more often than not able to domesticate the conflicting and contradictory values. This is because the hegemonic hold of the social system is so strong, it can generally withstand dissension and actually come to neutralize it by permitting token opposition. During my teaching days in the suburban ghetto, school dances in the gym often celebrated the values, meanings, and pleasure of life on the street—some of which could be considered oppositional—but were tolerated by the administration because they helped diffuse tension in the school. They afforded the students some symbolic space for a limited amount of time; yet they redressed nothing concrete in terms of the lived subordination of the students and their families on a day-to-day basis.

The main question for teachers attempting to become aware of the ideologies that inform their own teaching is: How have certain pedagogical practices become so habitual or natural in school settings that teachers accept them as normal, unproblematic, and expected? How often, for instance, do teachers question school practices such as tracking, ability grouping, competitive grading, teacher-centered pedagogical approaches, and the use of rewards and punishments as control devices? The point here is to understand that these practices are not carved in stone; but are, in reality, socially constructed. How, then, is the distilled wisdom of traditional educational theorizing ideologically structured? What constitutes the origins and legitimacy of the pedagogical practices within this tradition? To what extent do such pedagogical practices serve to empower the student, and to what extent do they work as forms of social control that support, stabilize, and legitimate the role of the teacher as a moral gatekeeper of the state? What are the functions and effects of the systematic imposition of ideological perspectives on classroom teaching practices?

In my classroom journal, what characterized the ideological basis of my own teaching practices? How did "being schooled" both enable and contain the subjectivities of the students? I am using the word "subjectivity" here to mean forms of knowledge that are both conscious and unconscious and which express our identity as human agents. Subjectivity relates to everyday knowledge in its socially constructed and historically produced forms. Following this, we can ask: How do the dominant ideological practices of teachers help to structure the subjectivities of students? What are the possible consequences of this, for good and for ill?

Prejudice

Prejudice is the negative prejudgment of individuals and groups on the basis of unrecognized, unsound, and inadequate evidence. Because these negative attitudes occur so frequently, they take on a commonsense or ideological character that is often used to justify acts of discrimination.

Critical Pedagogy and the Power/Knowledge Relation

Critical pedagogy is fundamentally concerned with understanding the relationship between power and knowledge. The dominant curriculum separates knowledge from the issue of power and treats it in an unabashedly technical manner; knowledge is seen in overwhelmingly instrumental terms as something to be mastered. That knowledge is always an ideological construction linked to particular interests and social relations generally receives little consideration in education programs.

The work of the French philosopher Michel Foucault is crucial in understanding the socially constructed nature of truth and its inscription in knowledge/power relations. Foucault's concept of "power/knowledge" extends the notion of power beyond its conventional use by philosophers and social theorists who, like American John Dewey, have understood power as "the sum of conditions available for bringing the desirable end into existence."[19] For Foucault, power comes from everywhere, from above and from below; it is "always already there" and is inextricably implicated in the micro-relations of domination and resistance.

Discourse

Power relations are inscribed in what Foucault refers to as *discourse* or a family of concepts. Discourses are made up of discursive practices that he describes as

> a body of anonymous, historical rules, always determined in the time and space that have defined a given period, and for a given social, economic, geographical, or linguistic area, the conditions of operation of the enunciative function.[20]

Discursive practices, then, *refer to the rules by which discourses are formed, rules that govern what can be said and what must remain unsaid, who can speak with authority and who must listen*. Social and political institutions, such as schools and penal institutions, are governed by discursive practices.

> Discursive practices are not purely and simply ways of producing discourse. They are embodied in technical processes, in institutions, in patterns for general behavior, in forms of transmission and diffusion, and pedagogical forms which, at once, impose and maintain them.[21]

For education, discourse can be defined as a "regulated system of statements" that establish differences between fields and theories of teacher education; it is "not simply words but is embodied in the practice of institutions, patterns of behavior, and in forms of pedagogy."[22]

From this perspective, we can consider *dominant* discourses (those produced by the dominant culture) as "regimes of truth," as general economies of power/knowledge, or as multiple forms of constraint. In a classroom setting, dominant educational discourses determine what books we may use, what classroom approaches we should employ (mastery learning, Socratic method, etc.), and what values and beliefs we should transmit to our students.

For instance, neo-conservative discourses on language in the classroom would view working-class speech as undersocialized or deprived. Liberal discourse would view such speech as merely different. Similarly, to be culturally literate within a conservative discourse is to acquire basic information on American culture (dates of battles, passages of the Constitution, etc.). Conservative discourse focuses mostly on the works of "great men." A liberal discourse on cultural literacy includes knowledge generated from the perspective of women and minorities. A *critical* discourse focuses on the interests and assumptions that inform the generation of knowledge itself. A critical discourse is also self-critical and deconstructs dominant discourses the moment they are ready to achieve hegemony. A critical discourse can, for instance, explain how high status knowledge (the great works of the Western world) can be used to teach concepts that reinforce the status quo. Discourses and discursive practices influence how we live our lives as conscious thinking subjects. They shape our subjectivities (our ways of understanding in relation to the world) because it is only in language and through discourse that social reality can be given meaning. Not all discourses are given the same weight, as some will account for and justify the appropriateness of the status quo and others will provide a context for resisting social and institutional practices.[23]

This follows our earlier discussion that knowledge (truth) is socially constructed, culturally mediated, and historically situated. Cleo Cherryholmes suggests that "dominant discourses determine what counts as true, important, relevant, and what gets spoken. Discourses are generated and governed by rules and power."[24] Truth cannot be spoken in the absence of power relations, and each relation necessarily speaks its own truth. Foucault removes truth from the realm of the absolute; truth is understood only as changes in the determination of what can count as true.

> Truth is a thing of this world: it is produced only by virtue of multiple forms of constraint. And it induces regular effects of power. Each society has its regime of truth, its "general politics" of truth: that is, the types of discourse which it accepts and makes function as true; the mechanisms and instances which enable one to distinguish true and false statements, the means by which each is sanctioned; the techniques and procedures accorded value in the acquisition of truth; the status of those who are charged with saying what counts as true.[25]

In Foucault's view, truth (educational truth, scientific truth, religious truth, legal truth, or whatever) must not be understood as a set of "discovered laws" that exist outside power/knowledge relations and which somehow correspond with the "real." We cannot "know" truth except through its "effects." Truth is not *relative* (in the sense of "truths" proclaimed by various individuals and societies are all equal in their effects) but is *relational* (statements considered "true" are dependent upon history, cultural context, and relations of power operative in a given society, discipline, institution, etc.). The crucial question here is that if truth is *relational* and not *absolute*, what criteria can we use to guide our actions in the world? Critical educators argue that *praxis* (informed actions) must be guided by *phronesis* (the disposition to act truly and rightly). This means, in critical terms, that actions and knowledge must be directed at eliminating pain, oppression, and inequality, and at promoting justice and freedom.

Lawrence Grossberg speaks to the critical perspective on truth and theory when he argues

> the truth of a theory can only be defined by its ability to intervene into, to give us a different and perhaps better ability to come to grips with, the relations that constitute its context. If neither history nor texts speak its own truth, truth has to be won; and it is, consequently, inseparable from relations of power.[26]

An understanding of the power/knowledge relationship raises important issues regarding what kinds of theories educators should work with and what knowledge they can provide in order to empower students. *Empowerment* means not only helping students to understand and engage the world around them, but also enabling them to exercise the kind of courage needed to change the social order where necessary. Teachers need to recognize that *power relations correspond to forms of school knowledge that distort understanding and produce what is commonly accepted as "truth"*. Critical educators argue that knowledge should be analyzed on the basis of whether it is oppressive and exploitative, and not on the basis of whether it is "true." For example, what kind of knowledge do we construct about women and minority groups in school texts? Do the texts we use in class promote stereotypical views that reinforce racist, sexist, and patriarchal attitudes? How do we treat the knowledge that working-class students bring to class discussions and schoolwork? Do we unwittingly devalue such knowledge and thereby disconfirm the voices of these students?

Knowledge should be examined not only for the ways in which it might misrepresent or mediate social reality, but also for the ways in which it actually reflects the daily struggle of people's lives. We must understand that knowledge not only distorts reality, but also provides grounds for understanding the actual conditions that inform everyday life. Teachers, then, should examine knowledge both for the way it misrepresents or marginalizes particular views of the world and for the way it provides a deeper understanding of how the student's world is actually constructed. Knowledge acquired in classrooms should help students participate in vital issues that affect their experience on a daily level rather than simply enshrine the values of business pragmatism. School knowledge should have a more emancipatory goal than churning out workers (human capital) and helping schools become the citadel of corporate ideology.[27] School knowledge should help create the conditions productive for student self-determination in the larger society.

Critical Pedagogy and the Curriculum

From the perspective of critical educational theorists, the curriculum represents much more than a program of study, a classroom text, or a course syllabus. Rather, it represents the *introduction to a particular form of life; it serves in part to prepare students for dominant or subordinate positions in the existing society*.[28] The curriculum favors certain forms of knowledge over others and affirms the dreams, desires, and values of select groups of students over other groups, often discriminatorily on the basis of race, class, and gender. In general, critical educational theorists are concerned with how descriptions, discussions, and representations in textbooks, curriculum materials, course content, and social relations embodied in classroom practices benefit dominant groups and exclude subordinate ones. In this regard, they often refer to the *hidden curriculum*.

The Hidden Curriculum

The *hidden curriculum* refers to *the unintended outcomes of the schooling process*. Critical educators recognize that schools shape students both through standardized learning situations, and through other agendas including rules of conduct, classroom organization, and the informal pedagogical procedures used by teachers with specific groups of students.[29] The hidden curriculum also includes teaching and learning styles that are emphasized in the classroom, the messages that get transmitted to the student by the total physical and instructional environment, governance structures, teacher expectations, and grading procedures.

The hidden curriculum deals with the tacit ways in which knowledge and behavior get constructed, outside the usual course materials and formally scheduled lessons. It is a part of the bureaucratic and managerial "press" of the school—the combined forces by which students are induced to comply with dominant ideologies and social practices related to authority, behavior, and morality. Does the principal expel school offenders or just verbally upbraid them? Is the ethos of the office inviting or hostile? Do the administration and teachers show respect for each other and for the students on a regular basis? Answers to these questions help define the hidden curriculum, which refers then, to the *non-subject-related* sets of behaviors produced in students.

Often, the hidden curriculum displaces the professed educational ideals and goals of the classroom teacher or school. We know, for example, that teachers unconsciously give more intellectual attention, praise, and academic help to boys than to girls. A study reported in *Psychology Today* suggests that stereotypes of garrulous and gossipy women are so strong that when groups of administrators and teachers are shown films of classroom discussion and asked who is talking more, the teachers overwhelmingly choose the girls. In reality, however, the boys in the film "out talk" the girls at a ratio of three to one. The same study also suggests that teachers behave differently depending on whether boys or girls respond during classroom discussions. When boys call out comments without raising their hands, for instance, teachers generally accept their answers; girls, however, are reprimanded for the same behavior. The hidden message is "Boys should be academically aggressive while girls should remain composed and passive." In addition, teachers are twice as likely to give male students detailed instructions on how to do things for themselves; with female students, however, teachers are more likely to do the task for them instead. Not surprisingly, the boys are being taught independence and the girls dependency.[30]

Classroom sexism as a function of the hidden curriculum results in the unwitting and unintended granting of power and privilege to men over women and accounts for many of the following outcomes:

- Although girls start school ahead of boys in reading and basic computation, by the time they graduate from high school, boys have higher SAT scores in both areas.
- By high school, some girls are less committed to careers, although their grades and achievement-test scores may be as good as boys. Many girls' interests turn to

marriage or stereotypically female jobs. Some women may feel that men disapprove of women using their intelligence.

- Girls are less likely to take math and science courses and to participate in special or gifted programs in these subjects, even if they have a talent for them. They are also more likely to believe that they are incapable of pursuing math and science in college and to avoid the subjects.
- Girls are more likely to attribute failure to internal factors, such as ability, rather than to external factors, such as luck.

The sexist communication game is played at work, as well as at school. As reported in numerous studies it goes like this:

- Men speak more often and frequently interrupt women.
- Listeners recall more from male speakers than from female speakers, even when both use a similar speaking style and cover identical content.
- Women participate less actively in conversation. They do more smiling and gazing; they're more often the passive bystanders in professional and social conversations among peers.
- Women often transform declarative statements into tentative comments. This is accomplished by using qualifiers ("kind of" or "I guess") and by adding tag questions ("This is a good movie, isn't it?"). These tentative patterns weaken impact and signal a lack of power and influence.[31]

Of course, most teachers try hard not to be sexist. The hidden curriculum continues to operate, however, despite what the overt curriculum prescribes. The hidden curriculum can be effectively compared to what Australian educator Doug White calls the *multinational curriculum*. For White,

> [T]he multinational curriculum is the curriculum of disembodied universals, of the mind as an information-processing machine, of concepts and skills without moral and social judgment but with enormous manipulative power. That curriculum proposed the elevation of abstract skills over particular content, of universal cognitive principles over the actual conditions of life.[32]

White reminds us that no curriculum, policy, or program is ideologically or politically innocent, and that the concept of the curriculum is inextricably related to issues of social class, culture, gender, and power. This is, of course, not the way curriculum is traditionally understood and discussed in teacher education. The hidden curriculum, then, refers to learning outcomes not openly acknowledged to learners. But we must remember that not all values, attitudes, or patterns of behavior that are by-products of the hidden curriculum in educational settings are necessarily bad. The point is to identify the structural and political assumptions upon which the hidden curriculum rests and to attempt to change the institutional arrangements of the classroom so as to offset the most undemocratic and oppressive outcomes.

Curriculum as a Form of Cultural Politics

Critical educational theorists view curriculum as a form of *cultural politics*, that is, as a part of the sociocultural dimension of the schooling process. The term cultural politics permits the educational theorist to highlight the political consequences of interaction between teachers and students who come from dominant and subordinate cultures. To view the curriculum as a form of cultural politics *assumes that the social, cultural, political and economic dimensions are the primary categories for understanding contemporary schooling.*[33]

School life is understood not as a unitary, monolithic, and ironclad system of rules and regulations, but as a cultural terrain characterized by varying degrees of accommodation, contestation, and resistance. Furthermore, school life is understood as a plurality of conflicting languages and struggles, a place where classroom and street-corner cultures collide and where teachers, students, and school administrators often differ as to how school experiences and practices are to be defined and understood.

This curriculum perspective creates conditions for the student's self-empowerment as an active political and moral subject. I am using the term *empowerment* to refer to the process through which students learn to critically appropriate knowledge existing outside their immediate experience in order to broaden their understanding of themselves, the world, and the possibilities for transforming the taken-for-granted assumptions about the way we live. Stanley Aronowitz has described one aspect of empowerment as "the process of appreciating and loving oneself;"[34] empowerment is gained from knowledge and social relations that dignify one's own history, language, and cultural traditions. But empowerment means more than self-confirmation. It also refers to the process by which students learn to question and selectively appropriate those aspects of the dominant culture that will provide them with the basis for defining and transforming, rather than merely serving, the wider social order.

Basing a curriculum on cultural politics consists of linking critical social theory to a set of stipulated practices through which teachers can dismantle and critically examine dominant educational and cultural traditions. Many of these traditions have fallen prey to an *instrumental rationality* (a way of looking at the world in which "ends" are subordinated to questions of "means" and in which "facts" are separated from questions of "value") that either limits or ignores democratic ideals and principles. Critical theorists want particularly to develop a language of critique and demystification that can be used to analyze those latent interests and ideologies that work to socialize students in a manner compatible with the dominant culture. Of equal concern, however, is the creation of alternative teaching practices capable of empowering students both inside and outside of schools.

Critical Pedagogy and Social Reproduction

Over the decades, critical educational theorists have tried to fathom how schools are implicated in the process of *social reproduction*. In other words, they have attempted to explore how schools *perpetuate or reproduce the social relationships and attitudes needed to sustain the existing dominant economic and class relations of the larger society.*[35] Social reproduction refers to the intergenerational reproduction of social class (i.e., working-class students become working-class adults; middle-class students become middle-class adults). Schools reproduce the structures of social life through the colonization (socialization) of student subjectivities and by establishing social practices characteristic of the wider society.

Critical educators ask: How do schools help transmit the status and class positions of the wider society? The answers, of course, vary enormously. Some of the major mechanisms of social reproduction include the allocation of students into private versus public schools, the socioeconomic composition of school communities, and the placement of students into curriculum tracks within schools.[36] A group of social reproduction theorists, known as *correspondence theorists*, have attempted to show how schools reflect wider social inequalities.[37] In a famous study by Bowles and Gintis (1976), the authors argue in deterministic terms that there is a *relatively simple correspondence between schooling, class, family, and social inequalities*. Bowles and Gintis maintain that children of parents with upper socioeconomic standing most often achieve upper socioeconomic status while children of lower socioeconomic parents acquire a correspondingly low socioeconomic standing. However, schooling structures are not always successful in ensuring privilege for the students' advantaged class positions. The correspondence theorists *could not explain why some children cross over from the status of their parents*. Social reproduction, as it turns out, is more than simply a case of economic and class position; it also involves social, cultural, and linguistic factors.

This brings into the debate the *conflict* or *resistance theorists*, such as Henry Giroux and Paul Willis, who pay significantly more attention to the *partial autonomy* of the school culture and to the role of conflict and contradiction within the reproductive process itself.[38] *Theories of resistance* generally draw upon an understanding of the complexities of culture to define the relationship between schools and the dominant society. Resistance theorists challenge the school's ostensible role as a democratic institution that functions to improve the social position of all students—including, if not especially, those groups that are subordinated to the system. Resistance theorists question the processes by which the school system reflects and sustains the logic of capital as well as dominant social practices and structures that are found in a class, race, and gender divided society.

One of the major contributions to resistance theory has been the discovery by British researcher Paul Willis that working-class students who engage in classroom episodes of resistance often implicate themselves even further in their own domination.[39] Willis's group of working-class schoolboys, known as "the lads," resisted the class-based oppression of the school by rejecting mental labor in favor of more "masculine" manual labor (which reflected the shop floor culture of their family members). In so doing, they ironically displaced the school's potential to help them escape the shop floor once they graduated. Willis's work presents a considerable advance in understanding social and cultural reproduction in the context of student resistance. Social reproduction certainly exceeds mobility for each class, and we know that a substantial amount of class mobility is unlikely in most school settings. The work of the resistance theorists has helped us understand how domination works, even though students continually reject the ideology that is helping to oppress them. Sometimes this resistance only helps secure to an even greater degree the eventual fate of these students.

How, then, can we characterize student resistance? Students resist instruction for many reasons. As Giroux reminds us, not all acts of student misbehavior are acts of resistance. In fact, such "resistance" may simply be repressive moments (sexist, racist) inscribed by the dominant culture.[40] I have argued that the major drama of resistance in schools is an effort on the part of students to bring their street-corner culture into the classroom. Students reject the culture of classroom learning because, for the most part, it is delibidinalized (eros-denying) and is infused with a cultural capital to which subordinate groups have little legitimate access. Resistance to school instruction represents a resolve on the part of students not to be dissimulated in the face of oppression; it is a fight against the erasure of their street-corner identities. To resist means to fight against the monitoring of passion and desire. It is, furthermore, a struggle against the capitalist symbolization of the flesh. By this I mean that students resist turning themselves into worker commodities in which their potential is evaluated only as future members of the labor force. At the same time, however, the images of success manufactured by the dominant culture seem out of reach for most of them.

Students resist the "dead time" of school, where interpersonal relationships are reduced to the imperatives of market ideology. Resistance, in other words, is a rejection of their reformulation as docile objects where spontaneity is replaced by efficiency and productivity, in compliance with the needs of the corporate marketplace. Accordingly, students' very bodies become sites of struggle, and resistance a way of gaining power, celebrating pleasure, and fighting oppression in the lived historicity of the moment.

What, then, are the "regimes of truth" that organize school time, subject matter, pedagogical practice, school values, and personal truth? How does the culture of the school organize the body and monitor passion through its elaborate system of surveillance? How are forms of social control inscripted into the flesh? How are students' subjectivities and social identities produced discursively by institutionalized power, and how is this institutional power at the same time produced by the legitimization of discourses that treat students as if they were merely repositories of lust and passion (the degenerative animal instincts)? How is reason privileged over passion so that it can be used to quell the "crude mob mentality" of students? What is the range of identities available within a system of education designed to produce, regulate, and distribute character, govern gesture, dictate values, and police desire? To what extent does an adherence to the norms of the school mean that students will have to give up the dignity and status maintained through psychosocial adaptations to life on the street? To what extent does compliance with the rituals and norms of school mean that students have to forfeit their identity as members of an ethnic group? These are all questions that theorists within the critical tradition have attempted to answer. And the answers are as various as they are important.

Some versions of student resistance are undoubtedly romantic: The teachers are villains, and the students are anti-heroes. I am not interested in teacher-bashing, nor in resurrecting the resistant student as the new James Dean or Marlon Brando. I much prefer the image of Giroux's resisting intellectual, someone who questions prevailing norms and established regimes of truth in the manner of a Rosa Luxemburg or a Jean-Paul Sartre.[41]

I would like to stress an important point. Our culture in general (and that includes schools, the media, and our social institutions) has helped educate students to acquire a veritable passion for ignorance. The French psycho-analyst Jacques Lacan suggests that ignorance is not a passive state but rather an active excluding from consciousness. The passion for ignorance that has infected our culture demands a complex explanation, but part of it can be attributed, as Lacan suggests, to *a refusal to acknowledge that our subjectivities have been constructed out of the information and social practices that surround us.*[42] Ignorance, as part of the very structure of knowledge, can teach us something. But we lack the critical constructs with which to recover that knowledge *which we choose not to know.* Unable to find meaningful knowledge "out there" in the world of prepackaged commodities, students resort to random violence or an intellectual purple haze where anything more challenging than the late night news is met with retreat, or despair; and of course, it is the dominant culture that benefits most from this epidemic of conceptual anesthesia. The fewer critical intellectuals around to challenge its ideals, the better.

What do all these theories of resistance mean for the classroom teacher? Do we disregard resistance? Do we try to ignore it? Do we always take the student's side?

The answers to these questions are not easy. But let me sketch out the bare bones of a possible answer. First of all, schooling should be a process of understanding how subjectivities are produced. It should be a process of examining how we have been constructed out of the prevailing ideas, values, and worldviews of the dominant culture. The point to remember is that if we have been made, then we can be "unmade" and "made over". What are some alternative models with which we can begin to repattern ourselves and our social order? Teachers need to encourage students to be self-reflexive about these questions and to provide students with a conceptual framework to begin to answer them. Teaching and learning should be a process of *inquiry*, of critique; it should also be a process of *constructing*, of building a social imagination that works within a language of hope. If teaching is cast in the form of what Henry Giroux refers to as a "language of possibility," then a greater potential exists for making learning relevant, critical, and transformative. Knowledge is relevant only when it begins with the experiences students bring with them from the surrounding culture; it is critical only when these experiences are shown to sometimes be problematic (i.e., racist, sexist); and it is transformative only when students begin to use the knowledge to help empower others, including individuals in the surrounding community. Knowledge then becomes linked to social reform. An understanding of the language of the self can help us better negotiate with the world. It can also help us begin to forge the basis of *social transformation:* the building of a better world, the altering of the very ground upon which we live and work.

Teachers can do no better than to create agendas of possibility in their classrooms. Not every student will want to take part, but many will. Teachers may have personal problems—and so may students—that will limit the range of classroom discourses. Some teachers may simply be unwilling to function as critical educators. Critical pedagogy does not guarantee that resistance will not take place. But it does provide teachers with the foundations for understanding resistance, so that whatever pedagogy is developed can be sensitive to sociocultural conditions that construct resistance, lessening the chance that students will be blamed as the sole, originating source of resistance. No emancipatory pedagogy will ever be built out of theories of behavior which view students as lazy, defiant, lacking in ambition, or genetically inferior. A much more penetrating solution is to try to understand the structures of mediation in the sociocultural world that form student resistance. In other words, what is the larger picture? We must remove the concept of student resistance from the preserve of the behaviorist or the depth psychologist and insert it instead into the terrain of social theory.

Cultural Capital

Resistance theorists such as Henry Giroux focus on *cultural reproduction* as a function of class based differences in *cultural capital*. The concept of *cultural capital*, made popular by French sociologist Pierre Bourdieu, refers to the general cultural background, knowledge, disposition, and skills that are passed on from one generation to another. Cultural capital represents *ways of talking, acting, modes of style, moving, socializing, forms of knowledge, language practices, and values*. Cultural capital can exist in the embodied state, as long-lasting dispositions of the mind and body; in the objectified state, as cultural artifacts such as pictures, books, diplomas, and other material objects; and in the institutionalized state, which confers original properties on the cultural capital which it guarantees. For instance, to many teachers, the cultural traits exhibited by students—e.g., tardiness, sincerity, honesty, thrift, industriousness, politeness, a certain way of dressing, speaking, and gesturing—appear as natural qualities emerging from an individual's "inner essence". However, such traits are to a great extent culturally inscribed and are often linked to the social class standing of individuals who exhibit them. Social capital refers to the collectively owned economic and cultural capital of a group.[43] Taking linguistic competency as just one example of cultural capital, theorists such as Basil Bernstein contend that class membership and family socialization generate distinctive speech patterns. Working-class students learn "restricted" linguistic codes while middle-class children use "elaborated" codes. This means that the speech of working-class and middle-class children is generated by underlying regulative principles that govern their choice and combination of words and sentence structures. These, according to Bernstein, have been learned primarily in the course of family socialization.[44] Critical theorists argue that schools generally affirm and reward students who exhibit the elaborately coded "middle-class" speech while disconfirming and devaluing students who use restricted "working-class" coded speech.

Students from the dominant culture inherit substantially different cultural capital than do economically disadvantaged students, and schools generally value and reward those who exhibit that dominant cultural capital (which is also usually exhibited by the teacher). Schools systematically *devalue* the cultural capital of students who occupy subordinate class positions. Cultural capital is reflective of material capital and replaces it as a form of symbolic currency that enters into the exchange system of the school. Cultural capital is therefore symbolic of the social structure's economic force and becomes in itself a productive force in the reproduction of social relations under capitalism. Academic performance represents, therefore, not individual competence or the lack of ability on the part of disadvantaged students but *the school's depreciation of their cultural capital.* The end result is that the school's academic credentials remain indissolubly linked to an unjust system of trading in cultural capital which is eventually transformed into *economic* capital, as working-class students become less likely to get high-paying jobs.

When I worked with students in my urban ghetto classroom, those whose cultural capital most closely resembled my own were the students with whom I initially felt most comfortable, spent the most instructional time, and most often encouraged to work in an independent manner. I could relate more readily and positively—at least at the beginning—to those students whose manners, values, and competencies resembled my own. Teachers—including myself—easily spotted Buddy, T. J., and Duke as members of the economically disadvantaged underclass, and this often worked against them, especially with teachers who registered such students as intellectually or socially deficient. Intellectual and social deficiencies had little, if anything, to do with their behavior. Class-specific character traits and social practices did.

Notes

1. The sources for this section are as follows: Bertell Oilman, "The Meaning of Dialectics," *Monthly Review* (1986, November): 42–55; Wilfrid Carr and Stephen Kemmis, *Becoming Critical: Knowing Through Action Research* (Victoria: Deakin University, 1983); Stephen Kemmis and Lindsay Fitzclarence, *Curriculum Theorizing: Beyond Reproduction Theory* (Victoria: Deakin University, 1986); Henry A. Giroux, *Ideology, Culture and the Process of Schooling* (Philadelphia: Temple University Press and London: Falmer Press, Ltd., 1981); Ernst Bloch, "The Dialectical Method," *Man and World* 16 (1983): 281–313.
2. Kemmis and Fitzclarence, *Curriculum Theorizing* 36–37.
3. McLaren, *Schooling as a Ritual Performance*. London: Routledge, 1986.
4. This discussion of micro and macro objectives is taken from Henry A. Giroux, "Overcoming Behavioral and Humanistic Objectives," *The Education Forum* (1979, May): 409–419. Also, Henry A. Giroux, *Teachers as Intellectuals: Towards a Critical Pedagogy of Practical Learning* (South Hadley, MA: Bergin and Garvey Publishers, 1988).
5. See Jürgen Habermas, *Knowledge and Human Interests*, trans. J. J. Shapiro (London: Heinemann, 1972); see also Jürgen Habermas, *Theory and Practice*, trans. J. Viertel (London: Heinemann, 1974). As cited in Kemmis and Fitzclarence, *Curriculum Theorizing*, 70–72.

6. For a fuller discussion of culture, see Enid Lee, *Letters to Marcia: A Teacher's Guide to Anti-Racist Teaching* (Toronto: Cross Cultural Communication Centre, 1985).
7. Henry A. Giroux and Peter McLaren, "Teacher Education and the Politics of Engagement: The Case for Democratic Schooling," *Harvard Educational Review* 56 (1986): 3,232–233. Developed from Giroux's previous work.
8. For this discussion of culture, I am indebted to Raymond A. Calluori, "The Kids are Alright: New Wave Subcultural Theory," *Social Text* 4, 3 (1985): 43–53; Mike Brake, *The Sociology of Youth Culture and Youth Subculture* (London: Routledge and Kegan Paul, 1980); Graham Murdock, "Mass Communication and the Construction of Meaning," in N. Armstead (Ed.) *Reconstructing Social Psychology* (Harmondsworth: Penguin, 1974); Dick Hebidge, *Subculture: The Meaning of Style* (London and New York: Methuen, 1979); Ian Connell, D. J. Ashenden, S. Kessler and G. W. Dowsett, *Making the Difference: Schooling, Families and Social Division* (Sydney, Australia: George Allen and Unwin, 1982). Also: Stuart Hall and Tony Jefferson, *Resistance Through Rituals: Youth Subcultures in Post War Britain* (London: Hutchinson and the Centre for Contemporary Cultural Studies, University of Birmingham, 1980).
9. John Muncie, "Pop Culture, Pop Music and Post-War Youth Subcultures," *Popular Culture.* Block 5 Units 18 and 19/20, The Open University Press (1981): 31–62.
10. Muncie, "Pop Culture," 76.
11. The section on hegemony draws on the following sources: Giroux, *Ideology, Culture and the Process of Schooling*, 22–26; *Popular Culture* (1981), a second level course at The Open University, Milton Keynes, England, published by The Open University Press and distributed in the United States by Taylor and Francis (Philadelphia, PA). Several booklets in this series were instrumental in developing the sections on ideology and hegemony: Geoffrey Bourne, "Meaning, Image and Ideology," *Form and Meaning I*, Open University Press, Block 4, Units 13, 15, and 15, 37–65; see also Tony Bennett, "Popular Culture: Defining Our Terms," *Popular Culture. Themes and Issues I*, Block 1, Units 1 and 2, 77–87; Tony Bennett, "Popular Culture: History and Theory," *Popular Culture: Themes and Issues II*, Block 1, Unit 3, 29–32. Another important source is a booklet for a third level course at The Open University: *The Politics of Cultural Production*, The Open University Press, 1981. Relevant sections include: Geoff Whiny, "Ideology, Politics and Curriculum," 7–52; David Davies, "Popular Culture, Class and Schooling," 53–108. See also P. J. Hills, *A Dictionary of Education* (London: Routledge and Kegan Paul, 1982), 166–167; and Raymond Williams, *Keywords: A Vocabulary of Culture and Society* (London: Fontana, 1983), 144–146.
12. William Ryan, *Blaming the Victim* (New York: Vintage Books, 1976).
13. Todd Gitlin, *The Whole World is Watching: Mass Media in the Making and Unmaking of the New Left* (Berkeley and London: University of California Press, 1980), 253–254.
14. Gore Vidal, *Monthly Review* 19 (1986, October), as cited in Allen Fenichel "Alternative Economic Policies," *The Ecumenist* 25, 4 (1987, May–June): 49.
15. For this section on ideology, I am indebted to Henry A. Giroux, *Theory and Resistance in Education: Pedagogy for the Opposition* (South Hadley, MA: Bergin and Garvey, 1983), 143. See also Stanley Aronowitz and Henry A. Giroux, *Education Under Siege* (South Hadley, MA: Bergin and Garvey, 1985); Douglas Kellner, "Ideology, Marxism, and Advanced Capitalism," *Socialist Review* 8, 6 (1978): 38; Gibson Winter, *Liberating Creation: Foundations of Religious Social Ethics* (New York: Crossroad, 1981), 97. See also: Geoff Whiny, "Ideology, Politics and Curriculum," 7–52 and David Davies, "Popular Culture, Class and Schooling," 53–108; Williams, *Keywords*, 153–157; Tony Bennett, "Popular Culture: Defining our Terms," 77–87; and Geoffrey Bourne, "Meaning, Image and Ideology," 37–53.
16. James Donald and Stuart Hall, "Introduction," in S. Donald and S. Hall (Eds.), *Politics and Ideology* (Milton Keynes: Philadelphia, Open University Press, 1986), ix–x.
17. Donald and Hall, *Politics and Ideology*, x.
18. John Thompson, "Language and Ideology," *The Sociological Review* 35, 3 (1987, Aug.): 516–536.
19. John Dewey, in J. Ratner (Ed.), *Intelligence in the Modern World: John Dewey's Philosophy* (New York: The Modern Library, 1939), 784. See also Michael Foucault *Power/Knowledge*, in C. Gordon (Ed.), (L. Marshall, J. Mepham, and K. Spoer, Trans.), *Selected Interviews and Other Writings 1972–77* (New York: Pantheon, 1980), 187.
20. Michael Foucault, *The Archaeology of Knowledge* (New York: Harper Colophon Books, 1972), 117.
21. Foucault, *Power/Knowledge*, 200.
22. Richard Smith and Anna Zantiotis, "Teacher Education, Cultural Politics, and the Avant-Garde," in H. Giroux and P. McLaren (Eds.), *Schooling and the Politics of Culture* (Albany, NY: SUNY Press, in press), 123.
23. See Chris Weedon, *Feminist Practice and Post-Structuralist Theory* (Oxford: Basil Blackwell, 1987).
24. Cleo Cherryholmes, "The Social Project of Curriculum: A Poststructural Analysis," *American Journal of Education* (in press): 21.
25. Foucault, *Power/Knowledge*, 131.
26. Lawrence Grossberg, "History, Politics and Postmodernism: Stuart Hall and Cultural Studies," *Journal of Communication Inquiry* 10, 2 (1987): 73.
27. For more about the relationship of power and knowledge, see Kathy Borman and Joel Spring, *Schools in Central Cities* (New York: Longman, 1984); Henry Giroux, "Public Education and the Discourse of Possibility: Rethinking the New Conservative and Left Educational Theory," *News for Teachers of Political Science* 44 (1985, Winter): 13–15.

28. See Doug White, "After the Divided Curriculum," *The Victorian Teacher* 7 (1983, March); Giroux and McLaren, "Teacher Education and the Politics of Engagement," 228.
29. See the wide range of articles in H. Giroux and D. Purple (Eds.), *The Hidden Curriculum and Moral Education: Deception or Discovery?* (Berkeley, CA: McCutchen Publishing Corp., 1983).
30. Myra Sadkev and David Sadkev, "Sexism in the Schoolroom of the '80's," *Psychology Today* (1985, March): 55–57.
31. Sadkev and Sadkev, "Sexism in the Schoolroom," 56–57. Also, the 1980 *Nova* television program, *The Pinks and the Blues* (WGBH, Boston), summarized by Anthony Wilden. "In the Penal Colony: The Body as the Discourse of the Other," *Semiotica*, 54, 1/2(1985): 73–76.
32. White, "After the Divided Curriculum," 6–9.
33. Giroux and McLaren, "Teacher Education and the Politics of Engagement," 228–229.
34. Stanley Aronowitz, "Schooling, Popular Culture, and Post-Industrial Society: Peter McLaren Interviews Stanley Aronowitz," *Orbit* (1986): 17, 18.
35. See Kemmis and Fitzclarence, *Curriculum Theorizing*, 88–89. Also, H. A. Giroux, *Ideology, Culture, and the Process of Schooling*.
36. Glenna Colclough and E. M. Beck, "The American Educational Structure and the Reproduction of Social Class," *Social Inquiry* 56, 4 (1986, Fall): 456–476.
37. Samuel Bowles and Herbert Gintis, *Schooling in Capitalist America* (New York: Basic Books, 1976); see also Kemmis and Fitzclarence, *Curriculum Theorizing*, 90; and Colclough and Beck, "The American Educational Structure," 456–476.
38. See, for instance, Peter McLaren, "The Ritual Dimensions of Resistance: Clowning and Symbolic Inversion," *Boston University Journal of Education* 167, 2 (1985): 84–97, and Giroux, *Theory and Resistance*.
39. Paul Willis, *Learning to Labour: How Working Class Kids Get Working Class Jobs* (Westmead, England: Gower, 1977).
40. Giroux, *Theory and Resistance*, 103.
41. Aronowitz and Giroux, *Education under Siege*.
42. Jacques Lacan, "Seminar XX," *Encore* (Paris: Editions du Seuil, 1975): 100. As cited in Constance Penley, "Teaching in Your Sleep: Feminism and Psychoanalysis," in C. Nelson (Ed.), *Theory in the Classroom* (Chicago: University of Chicago Press), 135.
43. Pierre Bourdieu, "Forms of Capital," in John G. Richardson (Ed.), *Handbook of Theory and Research for the Sociology of Education* (New York: Greenwood Press, 1986), 241–258. See also Henry A. Giroux, "Rethinking the Language of Schooling," *Language Arts* 61, 1 (1984, January): 36; and Henry A. Giroux, *Ideology, Culture and the Process of Schooling*, 77.
44. Paul Atkinson, *Language, Structure and Reproduction: An Introduction to the Sociology of Basil Bernstein* (London: Methuen, 1986).

3

Cultural Politics and the Text

Michael W. Apple

Introduction[1]

For most people, literacy has a nonpolitical function. It is there supposedly to help form the intellectual character of a person and to provide paths to upward mobility. Yet, the process of both defining what counts as literacy and how it should be gained has always had links to particular regimes of morality as well. Literacy was often there to produce economic skills and a shared system of beliefs and values, to help create a "national culture." As the author of a recent volume on newly emerging redefinitions of literacy in education has put it, it served as something of a "moral technology of the soul."[2]

An emphasis on literacy as both "moral technology" and economically driven skills is of course not the only way one could and should approach the issue, no matter what the Right keeps telling us. The value of writing, speaking, and listening should not be seen as access to "refined culture" or to "life skills" for our allotted (by whom?) places in the paid and unpaid labor market, but as a crucial means to gain power and control over our entire lives. In responding to the dangers posed by the conservative restoration, I argued that our aim should not be to create "functional literacy," but *critical* literacy, *powerful* literacy, *political* literacy which enables the growth of genuine understanding and control of all of the spheres of social life in which we participate.[3]

This involves a different vision of knowledge and culture. Neither of these concepts refers to a false universality, a pregiven consensus that is divorced from patterns of domination and exploitation. Rather they refer to the utterly complex struggles over who has the right to "name the world."

Take the word "culture." Culture—the way of life of a people, the constant and complex process by which meanings are made and shared—does not grow out of the pregiven unity of a society. Rather, in many ways, it grows out of its divisions. It has to *work* to construct any unity that it has. The idea of culture should not be used to "celebrate an achieved or natural harmony." Culture is instead "a producer and reproducer of value systems and power relations."[4]

The same is true for the way we think about knowledge. Speaking theoretically, John Fiske reminds us of this:

> Knowledge is never neutral, it never exists in an empiricist, objective relationship to the real. Knowledge is power, and the circulation of knowledge is part of the social distribution of power.

> The discursive power to construct a commonsense reality that can be inserted into cultural and political life is central in the social relationship of power. The power of knowledge has to struggle to exert itself in two dimensions. The first is to control the "real," to reduce reality to the knowable, which entails producing it as a discursive construct whose arbitrariness and inadequacy are disguised as far as possible. The second struggle is to have this discursively (and therefore sociopolitically) constructed reality accepted as truth by those whose interests may not necessarily be served by accepting it. Discursive power involves a struggle both to construct (a sense of) reality and to circulate that reality as widely and smoothly as possible throughout society.[5]

Fiske's language may perhaps be a bit too abstract here, but his points are essential. They point to the relationship among what counts as knowledge, who has power and how power actually functions in our daily lives, and, finally, how this determines what we see as "real" and important in our institutions in general and in education in particular. In this chapter, I focus on one particular aspect of education that helps define what "reality" is and how it is connected to critical, powerful, and political literacy in contradictory ways, ways the Right has recognized for years.

Whose Knowledge is of Most Worth?

Reality, then, doesn't stalk around with a label. What something is, what it does, one's evaluation of it—all this is not naturally preordained. It is socially constructed. This is the case even when we talk about the institutions that organize a good deal of our lives. Take schools, for example. For some groups of people, schooling is seen as a vast engine of democracy: opening horizons, ensuring mobility, and so on. For others, the reality of schooling is strikingly different. It is seen as a form of social control, or, perhaps, as the embodiment of cultural dangers, institutions whose curricula and teaching practices threaten the moral universe of the students who attend them.

While not all of us may agree with this diagnosis of what schools do, this latter position contains a very important insight. It recognizes that behind Spencer's famous question about "What knowledge is of most worth?" there lies another even more contentious question, "*Whose* knowledge is of most worth?"

During the past two decades, a good deal of progress has been made on answering the question of whose knowledge becomes socially legitimate in schools.[6] While much still remains to be understood, we are now much closer to having an adequate understanding of the relationship between school knowledge and the larger society than before. Yet, little attention has actually been paid to that one artifact that plays such a major role in defining whose culture is taught: *the textbook*. Of course, there have been literally thousands of studies of textbooks over the years.[7] But, by and large, until relatively recently, most of these remained unconcerned with the politics of culture. All too many researchers could still be characterized by the phrase coined years ago by C. Wright Mills, "abstract empiricists." These "hunters and gatherers of social numbers" remain unconnected to the relations of inequality that surround them.[8]

This is a distinct problem since, as the rightist coalition has decisively shown by their repeated focus on them, texts are not simply "delivery systems" of "facts." They are at once the results of political, economic, and cultural activities, battles, and compromises. They are conceived, designed, and authored by real people with real interests. They are published within the political and economic constraints of markets, resources, and power.[9] And what texts mean and how they are used are fought over by communities with distinctly different commitments and by teachers and students as well.

As I have argued in a series of volumes, it is naive to think of the school curriculum as neutral knowledge.[10] Rather, what counts as legitimate knowledge is the result of complex power relations and struggles among identifiable class, race, gender, and religious groups. Thus, education and power are terms of an indissoluble couplet. It is at times of social upheaval that this relationship between education and power becomes most visible. Such a relationship was and continues to be made manifest in the struggles by women, people of color, and others to have their history and knowledge included in the curriculum. Driven by an economic crisis and a crisis in ideology and authority relations, it has become even more visible in the past decade or so in the resurgent conservative attacks on schooling. Authoritarian populism is in the air, and the New Right has been more than a little successful in bringing its own power to bear on the goals, content, and process of schooling.[11]

The movement to the right has not stopped outside the schoolroom door, as you well know. Current plans for the centralization of authority over teaching and curriculum, often cleverly disguised as "democratic" reforms, are hardly off the drawing board before new management proposals or privatization initiatives are introduced. Similar tendencies are more than a little evident in Britain, and in some cases are even more advanced.

All of this has brought about countervailing movements in the schools. The slower, but still interesting, growth of more democratically run schools, of practices and policies that give community groups and teachers considerably more authority in text selection and curriculum determination, in teaching strategy, in the use of funds, in administration, and in developing more flexible and less authoritarian evaluation schemes is providing some cause for optimism in the midst of the conservative restoration.

Even with these positive signs, however, it is clear that the New Right has been able to rearticulate traditional political and cultural themes. In so doing, it has often effectively mobilized a mass base of adherents. Among its most powerful causes and effects has been the growing feeling of disaffection about public schooling among conservative groups. Large numbers of parents and other people no longer trust either the institutions or the teachers and administrators in them to make "correct" decisions about what should be taught and how to teach it. The rapid growth of evangelical schooling, of censorship, of textbook controversies, and the emerging tendency of many parents to teach their children at home rather than send them to state-supported schools are clear indications of this loss of legitimacy.[12]

The ideology that stands behind this is often very complex. It combines a commitment to both the "traditional family" and clear gender roles with a commitment to "traditional values" and literal religiosity. Also often packed into this is a defense of capitalist economics, patriotism, the "Western tradition," anticommunism, and a deep mistrust (often based on racial undercurrents) of the "welfare state."[13] When this ideology is applied to schooling, the result can be as simple as dissatisfaction with an occasional book or assignment. On the other hand, the result can be a major conflict that threatens to go well beyond the boundaries of our usual debates about schooling.

Few places in the United States are more well known in this latter context than Kanawha County, West Virginia. In the mid-1970s, it became the scene of one of the most explosive controversies over what schools should teach, who should decide, and what beliefs should guide our educational programs. What began as a protest by a small group of conservative parents, religious leaders, and business people over the content and design of the textbooks that had been approved for use in local schools, soon spread to include school boycotts, violence, and a wrenching split within the community that in many ways has yet to heal.

There were a number of important contributing factors that heightened tensions in West Virginia. Schools in rural areas had been recently consolidated. Class relations and country/city relations were increasingly tense. The lack of participation by rural parents (or many parents at all, for that matter) in text selection or in educational decision making in general also led to increasing alienation. Furthermore, the cultural history of the region, with its fierce independence, its fundamentalist religious traditions, and its history of economic depression, helped create conditions for serious unrest. Finally, Kanawha County became a cause celebre for national right-wing groups who offered moral, legal, and organizational support to the conservative activists there.[14]

Though perhaps less violent, many similar situations have occurred since then in a number of districts throughout the country. For instance, the recent experiences in Yucaipa, California—where the school system and largely conservative and fundamentalist protesters have been locked in what at times seemed to be a nearly explosive situation—document the continuing conflict over what schools are for and whose values should be embodied in them. Here, too, parents and community members have raised serious challenges over texts and over cultural authority, including attacks on the material for witchcraft and occultism, a lack of patriotism, and the destruction of sacred knowledge and authority. And here, too, nationally based conservative organizations have entered the fray.

It is important to realize, then, that controversies over "official knowledge" that usually center around what is included and excluded in textbooks really signify more profound political, economic, and cultural relations and histories. Conflicts over texts are often proxies for wider questions of power relations. They involve what people hold most dear. And, as in the cases of Kanawha County and Yucaipa, they can quickly escalate into conflicts over these deeper issues.

Yet, textbooks are surely important in and of themselves. They signify, through their content *and* form, particular constructions of reality, particular ways of selecting and organizing that vast universe of possible knowledge. They embody what Raymond Williams called the *selective tradition*: someone's selection, someone's vision of legitimate knowledge and culture, one that in the process of enfranchising one group's cultural capital disenfranchises another's.[15]

Texts are really messages to and about the future. As part of a curriculum, they participate in no less than the organized knowledge system of society. They participate in creating what a society has recognized as legitimate and truthful. They help set the canons of truthfulness and, as such, also help recreate a major reference point for what knowledge, culture, belief, and morality really *are*.[16]

Yet such a statement, even with its recognition that texts participate in constructing ideologies and ontologies, is basically misleading in many important ways. For it is not a "society" that has created such texts, but specific groups of people. "We" haven't built such curriculum artifacts in the simple sense that there is universal agreement among all of us and this is what gets to be official knowledge. In fact, the very use of the pronoun "we" simplifies matters all too much.

As Fred Inglis so cogently argues, the pronoun "we"

> smooths over the deep corrugations and ruptures caused precisely by struggle over how that authoritative and editorial "we" is going to be used. The [text], it is not melodramatic to declare,

> really is the battleground for an intellectual civil war, and the battle for cultural authority is a wayward, intermittingly fierce, always protracted and fervent one.[17]

Let me give one example. In the 1930s, conservative groups in the United States mounted a campaign against one of the more progressive textbook series in use in schools. *Man and His Changing World* by Harold Rugg and his colleagues became the subject of a concerted attack by the National Association of Manufacturers, the American Legion, the Advertising Federation of America, and other "neutral" groups. They charged that Rugg's books were socialist, anti-American, anti-business, and so forth. The conservative campaign was more than a little successful in forcing school districts to withdraw Rugg's series from classrooms and libraries. So successful were they that sales fell from nearly 300,000 copies in 1938 to only approximately 20,000 in 1944.[18]

We, of course, may have reservations about such texts today, not least of which would be the sexist title. However, one thing that the Rugg case makes clear is that the *politics* of the textbook is not something new by any means. Current issues surrounding texts—their ideology, their very status as central definers of what we should teach, even their very effectiveness and their design—echo the past moments of these concerns that have had such a long history in so many countries.

Few aspects of schooling currently have been subject to more intense scrutiny and criticism than the text. Perhaps one of the most graphic descriptions is provided by A. Graham Down of the Council for Basic Education.

> Textbooks, for better or worse, dominate what students learn. They set the curriculum, and often the facts learned, in most subjects. For many students, textbooks are their first and sometimes only early exposure to books and to reading. The public regards textbooks as authoritative, accurate, and necessary. And teachers rely on them to organize lessons and structure subject matter. But the current system of textbook adoption has filled our schools with Trojan horses—glossily covered blocks of paper whose words emerge to deaden the minds of our nation's youth, and make them enemies of learning.[19]

This statement is made just as powerfully by the author of a recent study of what she has called "America's textbook fiasco."

> Imagine a public policy system that is perfectly designed to produce textbooks that confuse, mislead, and profoundly bore students, while at the same time making all of the adults involved in the process look good, not only in their own eyes, but in the eyes of others. Although there are some good textbooks on the market, publishers and editors are virtually compelled by public policies and practices to create textbooks that confuse students with non sequiturs, that mislead them with misinformation, and that profoundly bore them with pointlessly arid writing.[20]

Regulation or Liberation and the Text

In order to understand these criticisms and to understand both some of the reasons why texts look the way they do and why they contain some groups' perspectives and not others', we also need to realize that the world of the book has not been cut off from the world of commerce. Books are not only cultural artifacts. They are economic commodities as well. Even though texts may be *vehicles of ideas*, they still have to be "peddled on a market."[21] This is a market, however, that—especially in the national and international world of textbook publishing—is politically volatile, as the Kanawha County and Yucaipa experiences so clearly documented.

Texts are caught up in a complicated set of political and economic dynamics. Text publishing often is highly competitive. In the United States, where text production is a commercial enterprise situated within the vicissitudes of a capitalist market, decisions about the "bottom line" determine what books are published and for how long. Yet, this situation is not just controlled by the "invisible hand" of the market. It is also largely determined by the highly visible "political" hand of state textbook adoption policies.[22]

Nearly half of the states—most of them in the southern tier and the "sun belt"—have state textbook adoption committees that by and large choose what texts will be purchased by the schools in that state, a process that is itself contradictory in its history. . . . It too has signified losses and gains at the same time. The economics of profit and loss of this situation makes it imperative that publishers devote nearly all of their efforts to guaranteeing a place on these lists of approved texts. Because of this, the texts made available to the entire nation, and the knowledge considered legitimate in them, are determined by what will sell in Texas, California, Florida, and so forth. This is one of the major reasons the Right concentrates its attention so heavily on these states (though, because of resistance, with only partial success). There can be no doubt that the political and ideological controversies over content in these states, controversies that were often very similar to those that surfaced in Kanawha County, have had a very real impact on what and whose knowledge is made available. It is also clear that Kanawha County was affected by and had an impact on these larger battles over legitimate knowledge.

Economic and political realities structure text publishing not only internally, however. On an international level, the major text-publishing conglomerates control the market of much of the material not only in the capitalist centers, but in many other nations as well. Cultural domination is a fact of life for millions of students throughout the world, in part because of the economic control of communication and publishing by multinational firms, in part because of the ideologies and systems of political and cultural control of new elites within former colonial countries.[23] All of this, too, has led to complicated relations and struggles over official knowledge and the text, between "center" and "periphery," and within these areas as well.[24] Thus, the politics of official knowledge in Britain and the United States, where rightist policies over legitimate content are having a major impact, also can have a significant impact in other nations that also depend on British and U.S. corporate publishers for their material.

I want to stress that all of this is not simply of historical interest, as in the case of newly emerging nations, Kanawha County, or the Rugg textbooks. The controversies over the form and content of the textbook have not diminished. In fact, they have become even more heated in the United States in particular, as Yucaipa demonstrates. The changing ideological climate has had a major impact on debates over what should be taught in schools and on how it should be taught and evaluated. There is considerable pressure to raise the standards of texts, make them more "difficult," standardize their content, make certain that the texts place more stress on "American" themes of patriotism, free enterprise, and the "Western tradition," and link their content to statewide and national tests of educational achievement.

These kinds of pressures are not only felt in the United States. The text has become the center of ideological and educational conflict in a number of other countries as well. In Japan, for instance, the government approval of a right-wing history textbook that retold the story of the brutal Japanese invasion and occupation of China and Korea in a more positive light has stimulated widespread international antagonism and has led to considerable controversy within Japan as well.

Along these same lines, at the very time that the text has become a source of contention for conservative movements, it has stood at the center of controversy for not being progressive enough. Class, gender, and race bias have been widespread in the materials. All too often, "legitimate" knowledge does not include the historical experiences and cultural expressions of labor, women, people of color, and others who have been less powerful.[25]

All of these controversies are not "simply" about the content of the books students find—or don't find—in their schools, though obviously they are about that as well. The issues are also about profoundly different definitions of the common good[26] about our society and where it should be heading, about cultural visions, and about our children's future. To quote from Inglis again, the entire curriculum, in which the text plays so large a part, is "both the text and context in which production and values intersect; it is the twist-point of imagination and power."[27] In the context of the politics of the textbook, it is the issue of power that should concern us the most.

The concept of power merely connotes the capacity to act and to do so effectively. However, in the ways we use the idea of power in our daily discourse, "the word comes on strongly and menacingly, and its presence is duly fearful."[28] This "dark side" of power is, of course, complemented by a more positive vision. Here, power is seen as connected to a people acting democratically and collectively, in the open, for the best ideals.[29] It is this dual concept of power that concerns me here, both at the level of theory (how we think about the relationship between legitimate knowledge and power) and practice (how texts actually embody this relationship). Both the positive and the negative senses of power are essential for us to understand these relationships. Taken together, they signify that arguments about textbooks are really a form of *cultural politics*. They involve the very nature of the connections between cultural visions and differential power.

This, of course, is not new to anyone who has been interested in the history of the relationship among books, literacy, and popular movements. Books themselves, and one's ability to read them, have been inherently caught up in cultural politics. Take the case of Voltaire, that leader of the Enlightenment who so wanted to become a member of the nobility. For him, the Enlightenment should begin with the "grands." Only when it had captured the hearts and minds of society's commanding heights, could it concern itself with the masses below. But, for Voltaire and many of his followers, one caution should be taken very seriously. One should take care to prevent the masses from learning to read.[30]

For others, teaching "the masses" to read could have a more "beneficial" effect. It enables a "civilizing" process, in which dominated groups would be made more moral, more obedient, more influenced by "real culture."[31] We can, of course, hear echoes of this today in the arguments of the cultural conservatives. And for still others, such literacy could bring social transformation in its wake. It could lead to a "critical literacy," one that would be part of larger movements for a more democratic culture, economy, and polity.[32] The dual sense of the power of the text emerges clearly here.

Thus, activities that we now ask students to engage in every day, activities as "simple" and basic as reading and writing, can be at one and the same time forms of regulation and exploitation *and* potential modes of resistance, celebration, and solidarity. Here, I am reminded of Caliban's cry, "You taught me language; and my profit on't is, I know how to curse."[33]

This contradictory sense of the politics of the book is made clearer if we go into the classrooms of the past. For example, texts often have been related to forms of bureaucratic regulation both of teachers' lives and those of students. Thus, one teacher in Boston in 1899 relates a story of what happened during an observation by the school principal in her first year of teaching. As the teacher rather proudly watched one of her children read aloud an assigned lesson from the text, the principal was less than pleased with the performance of the teacher or her pupil. In the words of the teacher:

> The proper way to read in the public school in 1899 was to say, "page 35, chapter 4" and holding the book in the right hand, with the toes pointing at an angle of forty-five degrees, the head held straight and high, the eyes looking directly ahead, the pupil would lift up his voice and struggle in loud, unnatural tones. Now, I had attended to the position of the toes, the right arm, and the nose, but had failed to enforce the mentioning of page and chapter.[34]

Here, the text participates in both bodily and ideological regulation. The textbook in this instance is part of a system of enforcing a sense of duty, morality, and cultural correctness. Yet, historically, the standardized text was struggled *for* as well as against by many teachers. Faced with large classes, difficult working conditions, insufficient training, and even more importantly, little time to prepare lessons for the vast array of subjects and students they were responsible for, teachers often looked upon texts not necessarily as impositions but as essential tools. For young women elementary school teachers, the text helped prevent exploitation.[35] It solved a multitude of practical problems. It led not only to deskilling, but led to time to become more skilled as a teacher as well.[36] Thus, there were demands for standardized texts by teachers even in the face of what happened to that teacher in Boston and to so many others.

This struggle over texts was linked to broader concerns about who should control the curriculum in schools. Teachers, especially those most politically active, constantly sought to have a say in what they taught. This was seen as part of a larger fight for democratic rights. Margaret Haley, for instance, one of the leaders of the first teachers union in the United States, saw a great need for teachers to work against the tendency toward making the teacher "a mere factory hand, whose duty it is to carry out mechanically and unquestioningly the ideas and orders of those clothed with authority of position."[37] Teachers had to fight against the deskilling or, as she called it, "factoryizing" methods of control being sponsored by administrative and industrial leaders. One of the reasons she was so strongly in favor of teachers' councils as mechanisms of control of schools was that this would reduce considerably the immense power over teaching and texts that administrators then possessed. Quoting John Dewey approvingly, Haley wrote, "If there is a single public school system in the United States where there is official and constitutional provision made for submitting questions of methods, of discipline and teaching, and the questions of curriculum, textbooks, etc. to the discussion of those actually engaged in the work of teaching, that fact has escaped my notice."[38]

In this instance, teacher control over the choice of textbooks and how they were to be used was part of a more extensive movement to enhance the democratic rights of teachers on the job. Without such teacher control, teachers would be the equivalent of factory workers whose every move was determined by management.

These points about the contradictory relationships teachers have had with texts and the way such books depower and empower at different moments (and perhaps at the same time) document something of importance. It is too easy to see a cultural practice or a book as totally carrying its politics around with it, "as if written on its brow for ever and a day." Rather, its political functioning "depends on the network of social and ideological relations" it participates in.[39] Text writing, reading, and use can be retrogressive or progressive (and sometimes some combination of both) depending on the social context. Textbooks can be fought against because they are part of a system of moral regulation. They can be fought for both as providing essential assistance in the labor of teaching or as part of a larger strategy of democratization.

What textbooks do, the social roles they play for different groups, is then *very complicated*. This has important implications not only for the politics of how and by whom textbooks are used, but for the politics of the internal qualities, the content and organization, of the text. Just as crucially, it also has an immense bearing on how people actually read and interpret the text, especially in a time of rightist resurgence. It is to these issues that I now turn.

The Politics of Cultural Incorporation

We cannot assume that because so much of education has been linked to processes of gender, class, and race stratification[40] that all of the knowledge chosen to be included in texts simply represents relations of, say, cultural domination, or only includes the knowledge of dominant groups. This point requires that I speak theoretically and politically in this section of my argument, for all too many critical analyses of school knowledge—of what is included and excluded in the overt and hidden curricula of the school—take the easy way out. Reductive analysis comes cheap. Reality, however, is complex. Let us look at this in more detail.

It has been argued in considerable detail elsewhere that the selection and organization of knowledge for schools is an ideological process, one that serves the interests of particular classes and social groups.[41] However, as I just noted, this does not mean that the entire corpus of school knowledge is "a mirror reflection of ruling class ideas, imposed in an unmediated and coercive manner." Instead, "the processes of cultural incorporation are dynamic, reflecting both continuities and contradictions of that dominant culture and the continual remaking and relegitimation of that culture's plausibility system."[42] Curricula aren't imposed in countries like the United States. Rather, they are the products of often intense conflicts, negotiations, and attempts at rebuilding hegemonic control by actually incorporating the knowledge and perspectives of the less powerful under the umbrella of the discourse of dominant groups.

This is clear in the case of the textbook. As disenfranchised groups have fought to have their knowledge take center stage in the debates over cultural legitimacy, one trend has dominated in text production. In essence, little is usually dropped from textbooks. Major ideological frameworks do not get markedly changed. Textbook publishers are under considerable and constant pressure to include more in their books. Progressive *items* are perhaps mentioned, then, but are not developed in depth.[43] Dominance is partly maintained here through compromise and the process of "mentioning." Here, limited and isolated elements of the history and culture of less powerful groups are included in the texts. Thus, for example, a small and often separate section is included on "the contributions of women" and "minority groups," but without any substantive elaboration of the view of the world as seen from their perspectives. Neo-conservatives have been particularly good at doing this today.

Tony Bennett's discussion of the process by which dominant cultures actually become dominant is worth quoting at length here.

> Dominant culture gains a purchase not in being imposed, as an alien external force, onto the cultures of subordinate groups, but by reaching into these cultures, reshaping them, hooking them and, with them, the people whose consciousness and experience is defined in their terms, into an association with the values and ideologies of the ruling groups in society. Such processes neither erase the cultures of subordinate groups, nor do they rob "the people" of their "true culture": what they do do is shuffle those cultures on to an ideological and cultural terrain in which they can be disconnected from whatever radical impulses which may (but need not) have fuelled them and be connected to more conservative or, often, downright reactionary cultural and ideological tendencies.[44]

In some cases, "mentioning" may operate in exactly this way, integrating selective elements into the dominant tradition by bringing them into close association with the values of powerful groups. Thus, for instance, we will teach about AIDS, but only in the context of total abstinence or the sacredness of particular social constructions of the "traditional family." There will be times, however, when such a strategy will not be successful. Oppositional cultures may at times use elements of the dominant culture against such groups. Bennett goes on, describing how oppositional cultures operate, as well.

> Similarly, resistance to the dominant culture does not take the form of launching against it a ready-formed, constantly simmering oppositional culture—always there, but in need of being turned up from time to time. Oppositional cultural values are formed and take shape only in the context of their struggle with the dominant culture, a struggle which may borrow some of its resources from that culture and which must concede some ground to it if it is to be able to connect with it—and thereby with those whose consciousness and experience is partly shaped by it—in order, by turning it back upon itself, to peel it away, to create a space within and against it in which contradictory values can echo, reverberate and be heard.[45]

Some texts may, in fact, have such progressive "echoes" within them. There are victories in the politics of official knowledge, not only defeats.

Sometimes, of course, not only are people successful in creating some space where such contradictory values can indeed "echo, reverberate, and be heard," but they transform the entire social space. They create entirely new kinds of governments, new possibilities for democratic political, economic, and cultural arrangements. In these situations, the role of education takes on even more importance, since new knowledge, new ethics, and a new reality seek to replace the old. This is one of the reasons that those of us committed to more participatory and democratic cultures inside and outside of schools must give serious attention to changes in official knowledge in those nations that have sought to overthrow their colonial or elitist heritage. Here, the politics of the text takes on special importance, since the textbook often represents an overt attempt to help create a new cultural reality. The case of the creation of more democratic textbooks and other educational materials based on the expressed needs of less powerful groups in Granada during the years of the New Jewel Movement provides a cogent example here[46] even though it was partly destroyed by Reagan's invasion of Granada.

New social contexts, new processes of text creation, a new cultural politics, the transformation of authority relations, and new ways of reading texts, all of this can evolve and help usher in a positive rather than a negative sense of the power of the text. Less regulatory and more emancipatory relations of texts to real people can begin to evolve, a possibility made real in many of the programs of critical literacy that have had such a positive impact in nations throughout the world. Here people help create their own "texts," ones that signify their emerging power in the control of their own destinies.

However, we should not be overly romantic here. Such transformations of cultural authority and mechanisms of control and incorporation will not be easy.

For example, certainly, the ideas and values of a people are not directly prescribed by the conceptions of the world of dominant groups and just as certainly there will be many instances where people have been successful in creating realistic and workable alternatives to the culture and texts in dominance. Yet, we do need to acknowledge that the social distribution of what is considered legitimate knowledge *is* skewed in many nations. The social institutions directly concerned with the "transmission" of this knowledge, such as schools and the media, *are* grounded in and structured by the class, gender, sexual, and race inequalities that organize the society in which we live. The area of symbolic production is not divorced from the unequal relations of power that structure other spheres.[47]

Speaking only of class relations (much the same could be said about race, sex and gender), Stuart Hall, one of the most insightful analysts of cultural politics, puts it this way:

> Ruling or dominant conceptions of the world do not directly prescribe the mental content of the illusions that supposedly fill the heads of dominated classes. But the circle of dominant ideas *does* accumulate the symbolic power to map or classify the world for others; its classifications do acquire not only the constraining power of dominance over other modes of thought but also the initial authority of habit and instinct. It becomes the horizon of the taken-for-granted: what the world is and how it works, for all practical purposes. Ruling ideas may dominate other conceptions of the social world by setting the limit on what will appear as rational, reasonable, credible, indeed sayable or thinkable within the given vocabularies of motive and action available to us. Their dominance lies precisely in the power they have to contain within their limits, to frame within their circumference of thought, the reasoning and calculation of other social groups.[48]

In the United States, . . . there has been a movement of exactly this kind. Dominant groups—really a coalition of economic modernizers, what has been called the old humanists, and neo-conservative intellectuals—have attempted to create an ideological consensus around the return to traditional knowledge. The "great books" and "great ideas" of the "Western tradition" will preserve democracy. By returning to the common culture that has made this nation great, schools will increase student achievement and discipline, increase our international competitiveness, and ultimately reduce unemployment and poverty.

Mirrored in the problematic educational and cultural visions of volumes such as Bloom's *The Closing of the American Mind* and Hirsch's *Cultural Literacy*,[49] this position is probably best represented in quotes from former Secretary of Education William Bennett. In his view, we are finally emerging out of a crisis in which "we neglected and denied much of the best in American education." For a period, "we simply stopped doing the right things [and] allowed an assault on intellectual and moral standards." This assault on the current state of education has led schools to fall away from "the principles of our tradition."[50]

Yet, for Bennett, "the people" have now risen up. "The 1980's gave birth to a grass roots movement for educational reform that has generated a renewed commitment to excellence, character, and fundamentals." Because of this, "we have reason for optimism."[51] Why? Because

> the national debate on education is now focused on truly important matters: mastering the basics; . . . insisting on high standards and expectations; ensuring discipline in the classroom; conveying a grasp of our moral and political principles; and nurturing the character of our young.[52]

Notice the use of "we," "our," and "the people" here. Notice as well the assumed consensus on "basics" and "fundamentals" and the romanticization of the past both in schools and the larger society. The use of these terms, the attempt to bring people in under the ideological umbrella of the conservative restoration, is very clever rhetorically. However, as many people in the United States, Britain, and elsewhere— where rightist governments have been very active in transforming what education is about—have begun to realize, this ideological incorporation is having no small measure of success at the level of policy and at the level of whose knowledge and values are to be taught.[53]

If this movement has its way, the texts made available and the knowledge included in them will surely represent a major loss for many of the groups who have had successes in bringing their knowledge and culture more directly into the body of legitimate content in schools. Just as surely, the ideologies that will dominate the official knowledge will represent a considerably more elitist orientation than what we have now.

Yet, perhaps "surely" is not the correct word here. The situation is actually more complex than that, something we have learned from many of the newer methods of interpreting how social messages are actually "found" in texts.

Allan Luke has dealt with such issues very persuasively. It would be best to quote him at length here.

> A major pitfall of research in the sociology of curriculum has been its willingness to accept text form as a mere adjunct means for the delivery of ideological content: the former described in terms of dominant metaphors, images, or key ideas; the latter described in terms of the sum total of values, beliefs, and ideas which might be seen to constitute a false consciousness. For much content analysis presumes that text mirrors or reflects a particular ideological position, which in turn can be connected to specific class interests. . . . It is predicated on the possibility of a one-to-one identification of school knowledge with textually represented ideas of the dominant classes. Even those critics who have recognized that the ideology encoded in curricular texts may reflect the internally contradictory character of a dominant culture have tended to neglect the need for a more complex model of text analysis, one that does not suppose that texts are simply readable, literal representations of "someone else's" version of social reality, objective knowledge and human relations. For texts do not always mean or communicate what they say.[54]

These are important points for they imply that we need more sophisticated and nuanced models of textual analysis. While we should certainly *not* be at all sanguine about the effects of the conservative restoration on texts and the curriculum, if texts don't simply represent dominant beliefs in some straightforward way and if dominant cultures contain contradictions, fissures, and even elements of the culture of popular groups, then our readings of what knowledge is "in" texts cannot be done by the application of a simple formula.

We can claim, for instance, that the meaning of a text is not necessarily intrinsic to it. As poststructuralist theories would have it, meaning is "the product of a system of differences into which the text is articulated." Thus, there is not "one text," but many. Any text is open to multiple readings. This puts into doubt any claim that one can determine the meanings and politics of a text "by a straightforward encounter with the text itself." It also raises serious questions about whether one can fully understand the text by mechanically applying any interpretive procedure. Meanings, then, can be and are multiple and contradictory, and we must always be willing to "read" our own readings of a text, to interpret our own interpretations of what it means.[55] It seems that answering the questions of "whose knowledge" is in a text is not at all simple, though clearly the Right would very much like to reduce the range of meanings one might find.

This is true of our own interpretations of what is in textbooks. But it is also just as true for the students who sit in schools and at home and read (or in many cases don't read) their texts. I want to stress this point, not only at the level of theory and politics as I have been stressing here, but at the level of practice.

We cannot assume that what is "in" the text is actually taught. Nor can we assume that what is taught is actually learned. . . . Teachers have a long history of mediating and transforming text material when they employ it in classrooms. Students bring their own classed, raced, religious, and gendered biographies with them as well. They, too, accept, reinterpret, and reject what counts as legitimate knowledge selectively. As critical ethnographies of schools have shown, . . . students (and teachers) are not empty vessels into which knowledge is poured. Rather than what Freire has called "banking" education going on,[56] students are active constructors of the meanings of the education they encounter.[57]

We can talk about three ways in which people can potentially respond to a text: dominant, negotiated, and oppositional. In the dominant reading of a text, one accepts the messages at face value. In a negotiated response, the reader may dispute a particular claim, but accept the overall tendencies or interpretations of a text. Finally, an oppositional response rejects these dominant tendencies and interpretations. The reader "repositions" herself or himself in relation to the text and takes on the position of the oppressed.[58] These are, of course, no more than ideal types and many responses will be a contradictory combination of all three. But the point is that not only do texts themselves have contradictory elements, but that audiences *construct* their own responses to texts. They do not passively receive texts, but actively read them based on their own class, race, gender and religious experiences—although we must always remember that there are institutional constraints on oppositional readings.

An immense amount of work needs to be done on student (and teacher) acceptance, interpretation, reinterpretation, or partial and/or total rejection of texts. While there is a tradition of such research, much of it quite good, most of this in education is done in an overly psychologized manner. It is more concerned with questions of learning and achievement than it is with the equally as important and prior issues of whose knowledge it is that students are learning, negotiating, or opposing and what the sociocultural roots and effects are of such processes. Yet we simply cannot fully understand the power of the text, what it does ideologically and politically (or educationally, for that matter) unless we take very seriously the way students actually read them—not only as individuals but as members of social groups with their own particular cultures and histories.[59] For every textbook, then, there are multiple texts—contradictions within it, multiple readings of it, and different uses to which it will be put. Texts—be they the standardized, grade-level specific books so beloved by school systems, or the novels, trade books, and alternative materials that teachers either use to supplement these books or simply to replace them—are part of a complex story of cultural politics. They can signify authority (not always legitimate) or freedom. And critical teachers throughout many nations have learned a good deal about how we can employ even the most conservative material into a site for reflexive and challenging activity that clarifies with students the realities they (teachers and students) experience and construct. They can search out, as so many of them have, material and experiences that show the very possibility of alternative and oppositional interpretations of the world that go well beyond mere mentioning.[60] . . .

To recognize this, then, is also to recognize that our task as critically and democratically minded educators is itself a political one. We must acknowledge and understand the tremendous capacity of dominant institutions to regenerate themselves "not only in their material foundations and structures but in the hearts and minds of people." Yet, at the very same time—and especially now with the Right being so powerful and with their increasing attention to politics at the local, county, and state levels—we need never to lose sight of the power of popular organizations, of real people, to struggle, resist, and transform them.[61] Cultural authority, what counts as legitimate knowledge, what norms and values are represented in the officially sponsored curriculum of the school, all of these serve as important arenas in which the positive and negative relations of power surrounding the text will work themselves out . . . And all of them involve the hopes and dreams of real people in real institutions, in real relations of inequality.

From all that I have said here, it should be clear that I oppose the idea that there can be one textual authority, one definitive set of "facts" that is divorced from its context of power relations. A "common culture" can never be an extension to everyone of what a minority mean and believe. Rather, and crucially, it requires not the stipulation and incorporation within textbooks of lists and concepts that make us all "culturally literate," *but the creation of the conditions necessary for all people to participate in the creation and re-creation of meanings and values*. It requires a democratic process in which all people—not simply those who see themselves as the intellectual guardians of the 'Western tradition"—can be involved in the deliberation of what is important.[62] It should go without saying that this necessitates the removal of the very real material obstacles (unequal power, wealth, time for reflection) that stand in the way of such participation.[63] Whether a more "moderate" administration can provide substantial spaces for countering the New Right and for removing these obstacles will take some time to see.

The very idea that there is one set of values that must guide the "selective tradition" can be a great danger, especially in contexts of differential power. Take, as one example, a famous line that was printed on an equally famous public building. It read, "There is one road to freedom. Its milestones are obedience, diligence, honesty, order, cleanliness, temperance, truth, sacrifice, and love of country." Many people may perhaps agree with much of the sentiment represented by these words. It may be of some interest that the building on which they appeared was in the administration block of the concentration camp at Dachau.[64]

We must ask, then, are we in the business of creating dead texts and dead minds? If we accept the title of educator—with all of the ethical and political commitments this entails—I think we already know what our answer should be. Critical literacy demands no less.

These struggles over the politics of official knowledge—over the text as both a commodity and a set of meaningful practices—are grounded in the history of previous conflicts and accords. Here, too, compromises were made. And here, too, dominant groups attempted to move the terms of the compromise in their direction. Yet, once again, the accord had cracks, spaces for action, but ones that were always in danger of being coopted, as this history will show. Perhaps the best way to document this is to go even deeper into the politics of the text by focusing our attention on the growth of the activist state, on how the government—as a site of conflicting power relations and social movements—entered into the regulation of official knowledge. Conservatives (and even some of those upwardly mobile "cosmopolitan elites") may have dominated here, but as we shall see, this is *not* the entire story.

Notes

1. This chapter is an expansion and refinement of the introductory chapter to Michael W. Apple and Linda Christian-Smith, eds., *The Politics of the Textbook* (New York: Routledge, 1991). Many of the essays in that volume are crucial to a more thorough understanding of the issues I raise here.
2. See John Willinsky, *The New Literacy* (New York: Routledge, 1990).
3. Janet Batsleer, Tony Davies, Rebecca O'Rourke, and Chris Weedon, *Rewriting English: Cultural Politics of Gender and Class* (New York: Methuen, 1985), 164–65. For an exceptional treatment of "political literacy" in theory and practice, see Colin Lankshear with Moira Lawler, *Literacy, Schooling and Revolution* (Philadelphia: Falmer, 1988).
4. John Fiske, Bob Hodge, and Graeme Turner, *Myths of Oz: Reading Australian Popular Culture* (Boston: Allen and Unwin, 1987), x.
5. John Fiske, *Reading the Popular* (Boston: Unwin Hyman, 1989), 149–50.
6. See, for example, Michael W. Apple and Lois Weis, eds., *Ideology and Practice in Schooling* (Philadelphia: Temple University Press, 1983).
7. For a current representative sample of the varied kinds of studies being done on the textbook, see Arthur Woodward, David L. Elliot, and Kathleen Carter Nagel eds, *Textbooks in School and Society* (New York: Garland, 1988). We need to make a distinction between the generic use of "texts" (all meaningful materials: symbolic, bodily, physical, etc., created by human, and sometimes "natural," activity) and textbooks. My focus in this chapter is mostly on the latter, though many schools and many teachers are considerably more than standardized textbook material. Also, in passing, I am more than a little concerned that some people have overstated the case that the world is "only a text." See Bryan D. Palmer, *Descent into Discourse* (Philadelphia: Temple University Press, 1990).

8. Fred Inglis, *Popular Culture and Political Power* (New York: St. Martin' s Press, 1988), 9.
9. Allan Luke, Literacy, *Textbooks and Ideology* (Philadelphia: Falmer, 1988), 27–29.
10. Michael W. Apple, *Ideology and Curriculum*, 2nd ed. (New York: Routledge, 1990); Michael W. Apple, *Education and Power* (New York: Routledge , rev. ARK ed., 1985); and Michael W. Apple, *Teachers and Texts: A Political Economy of Class and Gender Relations in Education* (New York and London: Routledge, 1988).
11. Michael W. Apple, "Redefining Equality: Authoritarian Populism and the Conservative Restoration," *Teachers College Record* 90. (Winter 1988): 167–84.
12. See, for example, Susan Rose, *Keeping Them Out of the Hands of Satan* (New York: Routledge, 1988).
13. Allen Hunter, *Children in the Service of Conservatism* (Madison: University of Wisconsin Institute for Legal Studies, 1988).
14. James Moffett, *Storm in the Mountains* (Carbonate: Southern Illinois University Press, 1988).
15. Raymond Williams, *The Long Revolution* (London: Chatto and Windus, 1961). See also Apple, *Ideology and Curriculum.*
16. Fred Inglis, *The Management of Ignorance: A Political Theory of the Curriculum* (New York: Basil Blackwell, 1985), 22–23.
17. Ibid., 23.
18. Miriam Schipper, "Textbook Controversy: Past and Present," *New York University Education Quarterly* 14. (Spring/Summer 1983): 31–36.
19. A. Graham Down, "Preface," in Harriet Tyson-Bernstein, *A Conspiracy of Good Intentions: America's Textbook Fiasco* (Washington, D.C.: The Council for Basic Education, 1988), viii.
20. Harriet Tyson-Bernstein, *A Conspiracy of Good Intentions*, 3.
21. Robert Darnton, *The Literacy Underground of the Old Regime* (Cambridge: Harvard University Press, 1982), 199.
22. The social roots of such adoption policies will be discussed in chapter four.
23. The issues surrounding cultural imperialism and colonialism are nicely laid out in Philip Altback and Gail Kelly, eds., *Education and the Colonial Experience* (New York: Transaction Books, 1984). For an excellent discussion of international relations over texts and knowledge, see Philip Altbach, *The Knowledge Context* (Albany: State University of New York Press, 1988).
24. See the analysis of such power relations in Bruce Fuller, *Growing Up Modern* (New York: Routledge, 1991) and Martin Carnoy and Joel Samoff, *Education and Social Transition in the Third World* (Princeton: Princeton University Press, 1990).
25. For some of the most elegant discussions of how we need to think about these "cultural silences," see Leslie Roman and Linda Christian-Smith with Elizabeth Ellsworth, eds., *Becoming Feminine: The Politics of Popular Culture* (Philadelphia: Falmer, 1988).
26. Marcus Raskin, *The Common Good* (New York: Routledge, 1986).
27. Inglis, *The Management of Ignorance*, 142.
28. Inglis, *Popular Culture and Political Power*, 4.
29. Ibid. I have placed "dark side" in quotation marks in the previous sentence because of the dominant tendency to unfortunately equate darkness with negativity. This is just one of the ways popular culture expresses racism. See Michael Omi and Howard Winant, *Racial Formation in the United States* (New York: Routledge 1986); and Edward Said, *Orientalism* (New York: Pantheon , 1978).
30. Darnton, *The Literary Underground of the Old Regime*, 13.
31. Batsleer, Davies, O'Rourke, and Weedon, *Rewriting English: Cultural Politics of Gender and Class.*
32. Lankshear with Lawler, *Literacy, Schooling and Revolution.*
33. Batsleer et al. *Rewriting English*, 5.
34. James W. Fraser, "Agents of Democracy: Urban Elementary School Teachers and the Conditions of Teaching," in Donald Warren, ed., *American Teachers: Histories of a Profession at Work* (New York: Macmillan, 1989), 128.
35. Apple, *Teachers and Texts.*
36. For further discussion of deskilling and reskilling, see Apple, *Education and Power.*
37. Margaret Haley, quoted in Fraser, "Agents of Democracy," 128.
38. Haley, quoted in Fraser, "Agents of Democracy," 138.
39. Tony Bennett, "Introduction: Popular Culture and 'the Turn to Gramsci,'" in Tony Bennett, Colin Mercer, and Janet Woollacott, eds., *Popular Culture and Social Relations* (Philadelphia: Open University Press, 1986), xvi.
40. The literature here is voluminous. For a more extended treatment see Apple, *Education and Power*; and Cameron McCarthy and Michael W. Apple, "Race, Class, and Gender in American Educational Research," in Lois Weis, ed., *Class, Race, and Gender in American Education* (Albany: State University Press, 1989).
41. See Apple, *Ideology and Curriculum*; and Linda Christian-Smith, *Becoming a Woman Through Romance* (New York: Routledge, 1991).
42. Luke, *Literacy, Textbooks and Ideology*, 24.
43. Tyson-Bernstein, *A Conspiracy of Good Intentions*, 18.
44. Tony Bennett, "The Politics of the 'Popular' and Popular Culture," 19.

45. Ibid.
46. See Didacus Jules, "Building Democracy," in Michael W. Apple and Linda Christian-Smith, eds., *The Politics of the Textbook* (New York: Routledge, 1991), 259–87.
47. Stuart Hall, "The Toad in the Garden: Thatcherism Among the Theorists," in Cary Nelson and Lawrence Grossberg, eds., *Marxism and the Interpretation of Culture* (Urbana: University of Illinois Press, 1988), 44.
48. Ibid.
49. Allan Bloom, *The Closing of the American Mind* (New York: Simon and Schuster, 1987); and E. D. Hirsch, Jr., *Cultural Literacy* (New York: Houghton Mifflin, 1986).
50. William Bennett, *Our Children and Our Country* (New York: Simon and Schuster, 1988), 9.
51. Ibid., 10.
52. Ibid.
53. Apple, "Redefining Equality."
54. Luke, *Literacy, Textbooks and Ideology*, 29–30. See also Allan Luke, "The Secular Word: Catholic Reconstructions of Dick and Jane," in Apple and Christian-Smith, eds., *The Politics of the Textbook*, 166–90.
55. Lawrence Grossberg and Cary Nelson, "Introduction: The Territory of Marxism," in Nelson and Grossberg, eds., *Marxism and the Interpretation of Culture*, 8.
56. Paulo Freire, *Pedagogy of the Oppressed* (New York: Herder and Herder, 1973).
57. See, for example, Paul Willis, *Learning to Labor* (New York: Columbia University Press, 1981); Angela McRobbie, "Working Class Girls and the Culture of Femininity," in Women's Studies Group, ed., *Women Take Issue* (London: Hutchinson, 1978), 96–108; Robert Everhart, *Reading, Writing and Resistance* (Boston: Routledge and Kegan Paul, 1983); Lois Weis, *Between Two Worlds* (Boston: Routledge and Kegan Paul, 1985); Bonnie Trudell, *Doing Sex Education* (New York: Routledge, in press); and Christian-Smith, *Becoming a Woman Through Romance*.
58. Tania Modleski, "Introduction," in Tania Modleski, ed., *Studies in Entertainment* (Bloomington: Indiana University Press, 1986), xi.
59. See Elizabeth Ellsworth, "Illicit Pleasures: Feminist Spectator and Personal Best," in Roman, Christian-Smith, with Ellsworth, *Becoming Feminine*, 102–19; Elizabeth Ellsworth, "Why Doesn't This Feel Empowering?" *Harvard Educational Review* 59 (August 1989): 297–324; and Christian-Smith, *Becoming a Woman Through Romance*.
60. For an example of powerful and compelling literature for younger students, see the discussion in Joel Taxel, "Reclaiming the Voice of Resistance: The Fiction of Mildred Taylor," in Apple and Christian-Smith, eds., *The Politics of the Textbook*, 111–34.
61. Batsleer et al. *Rewriting English*, 5.
62. This is discussed in more detail in the new preface to the second edition of Apple, *Ideology and Curriculum*.
63. Raymond Williams, *Resources of Hope* (New York: Verso, 1989), 37–38.
64. David Horne, *The Public Culture* (Dover, NH: Pluto Press, 1986), 76.

4

Pedagogy of Love: Embodying Our Humanity

Antonia Darder

> I think that it could be said when I am no longer in this world: "Paulo Freire was a man who lived. He could not understand life and human existence without love and without the search for knowledge. . ."
>
> —Paulo Freire (1993)

Paulo Freire's view on the significance of love to both our pedagogical and political lives remains steadfast and resounding across the landscape of his writings. Freire believed deeply—from the personal to the pedagogical to the political—in the transformative and emancipatory power of love. Freire's radical articulation of love spoke to both a personal and political Eros, grounded in an unwavering faith in the oppressed to generate the political will necessary to transform our lives and the world. In Freire's eyes, to attempt daily engagement with the societal forces that dehumanize and undermine our existence, without the power of love on our side, was like walking like lost sojourners in a vast desert, with insufficient water to complete the crossing. Hence, it is not surprising that Freire (1998) often came back to the notion of an "armed loved—the fighting love of those convinced of the right and the duty to fight, to denounce, and to announce" (Freire, 1998b, p. 42). His is a concept of love not only meant to comfort or assuage the suffering of the oppressed, but also to awaken within us the historical thirst for justice and the political wherewithal to reinvent our world.

Freire's love permeated his existence as a man and an educator. He could be gentle, tender and inspiring, while at the same time, critical, challenging, and strategically unveiling individual or collective follies. As such, Freire's pedagogy of love challenged deeply the false "generosity" of those whose ideologies and practices work to sustain a system of education that transgresses at its very core every emancipatory principle of social justice and democratic life. It was Freire's lucid understanding of love as an untapped political force of consciousness that most drew me to his work and today continues to fuel my commitment to the emancipatory political project he championed throughout his life.

In my academic preparation, never had another educational theorist so fearlessly given the question of love such primacy in his philosophy, pedagogy, or politics. Moreover, he did this *de corazón* (from the heart), without concern for the consequences of mean-spirited critiques that cast him as unsystematic or antiscientific. For a student whose life was mired by the lovelessness of oppression, Freire's (1970) commitment to "the creation of a world in which it will be easier to love" spoke to the suffering of my heart, the weariness of my spirit, and the yearning of my soul. Hence, it is not surprising that I would turn here to Freire's pedagogy of love as a political force, which fundamentally inspired my political and intellectual formation as a critical scholar.

Love as a Political Force

> I have a right to love and to express my love to the world and to use it as a motivational foundation for struggle.
>
> —Paulo Freire (1998a)

Understanding *love as a political force* is essential to understanding Freire's revolutionary vision of consciousness and transformation. The inseparability with which he theorized the political significance of love in the evolution of consciousness and political empowerment is key to our ability to grasp accurately the depth of Freire's meaning. In keeping with Eric Fromm's (1956, 1964) contribution to this question, expressed so formidably in his book *The Art of Loving,* Freire did not see love as a mere sentimental exchange between people, but rather love constitutes an intentional spiritual act of consciousness that emerges and matures through our social and material practices, as we work to live, learn, and labor together. Across Freire's books is found this critical view of love, often glossed over by the very people who most need to comprehend deeply his humanizing intent. Sometimes more directly and other times more subtly, Freire reminded us that a politics of love must serve as the underlying force of any political project that requires us to counter daily with oppression, as we simultaneously seek in its midst new possibilities for transformation.

Freire wrote of the politics of love by engaging with the personal and communal exchanges he considered important to the relationship between teachers and students. In particular, he sought to promote the importance of cultivating greater intimacy between self, others, and the world, in the process of our teaching and learning. Freire (1997) believed that "living with [democracy] and deepening it so it has real meaning in people's everyday lives" (Carnoy, 1987, p. 12) should be a significant political concern of an emancipatory classroom. Here, democracy and the solidarity necessary for its evolution are made possible through a pedagogy fortified by the universal regard for the dignity and equality of all people, no matter their differences or circumstances. Freire's view of love as a dialectical force which simultaneously unites and respects difference, must be imagined as a radical sense of lived kinship, if we are to effectively transform the social and material conditions of inequality and disaffiliation that are the hallmark of capitalism. Freire speaks to a love generated from political grace and born of collective consciousness that emerges from our shared curiosity, creativity, and imagination, giving meaning to both our resistance and counterhegemonic practice.

Through a commitment to love and labor together for a more just world, Freire sincerely believed that relationships of solidarity can be nurtured and political dreams of freedom regenerated. Freire often asserted the notion that we, as human beings, must unite ourselves with the world and others in the process of social and political co-creation—so that through our shared participation in the labor of struggle could impel us toward a deeper sense of ourselves as historical beings. This is also a force that moves us beyond spiritual transcendence, personal-abnegation, or political negations of the dialectic between consciousness and the material. Rather, Freire asserted a love that is born and emerges directly out of our social participation and unwavering political commitment to the transformation of that historical in which we exist as grounded subjects.

Keeping all this in mind, we can better appreciate Freire's concern with the dehumanizing forces so prevalent in hegemonic schooling. He was adamant about the political necessity to unveil authoritarian pedagogies in the classroom, which curtail the pleasure of life and the principle of love, generating in both teachers and students a sense of alienation and estrangement from self and the world. This, in turn, arouses deep anxieties and insecurities that interfere with cultivating and nurturing the political imagination, epistemological curiosity, and the joy of learning necessary to our practice. Freire (1970) wrote in *Pedagogy of the Oppressed* about this historical and systematic disregard for the respect and dignity of students that serves, on one hand, to breed helplessness and disempowerment; while, on the other, it spawns uncritical forms of resistance that can work against the interests of the oppressed. Freire contended that oppression is best served by keeping the oppressed confused and estranged from one another, steeped in sentiments of fatalism and inferiority that blame students for their academic failure and workers for their material misfortunes.

In his conceptualization of love as a motivational force for struggle, Freire linked his pedagogy of love to political values that nurture emancipatory relationships. Some of these include faith and dignity in our relationships with others, social responsibility for our world, participation in the co-construction of knowledge, and solidarity across our differences. Directly and indirectly, Freire touched on the essence of love as inseparable to our labor as educators and democratic citizens of the world. Again, true to Fromm's (1964) adage, Freire embraced the idea that, "One loves that for which one labors, and one labors for that which one loves" (26). This points undeniably to the extent to which Freire, himself, intimately and passionately loved the world—a significant feature of both his pedagogy and personal way of being, whether with children, students, colleagues, family, friends, or simply the many people who crossed his path each day.

Although there are those who summarily issue feminist critiques of Freire's ideas and language to diminish the power of its political influence, it is, ironically, nearly impossible—true to Feminist sensibilities—to separate the political and the personal when engaging Freire's work. Throughout his life, Freire resisted such separation in his own philosophy ideas, political interpretations, and pedagogical praxis. Grounded in an enormous sense of responsibility to use his privilege in the interest of the oppressed, Freire stressed the importance of practicing respect, patience, and faith, if we are to dismantle the structures of domination that alienate and exploit those who exist, overwhelmingly, as slaves of capital, no matter our illusions.

In the process of teaching and learning, it is impossible to express love and respect for students without our willingness to engage them in ways that allow us to know them authentically. This is a form of knowing that demands we transcend our self-absorption and authoritarian fixations, in ways that open us horizontally to know and be known. In many respects, Freire's own capacity for love was an exercise in precisely this humanizing relational dynamic—one that seeks to identify or empathize with the core of another, beyond simply superficial responses or stereotypical distortions. For example, often working class students of color are perceived as being angry; but, rather than to see them beyond preconceptions of anger or to acknowledge that all human beings who are anxious, worried, isolated, fearful, repressed, or suffering can exhibit moments of anger, most teachers generally stop at the surface of the anger and, from there, issue racialized characterizations, devoid of insight into conditions that might inform students of color to express anger or frustration. And, even more disconcerting, seldom do teachers confront their own distortions that cause them to respond defensively and more authoritarian in their response.

Given the manner in which racialized accusations of anger have been so often used to exclude and undermine the voices of teachers, students, parents, and communities of color, it is useful to take a moment here to note that, according to Freire (1998a), "the kind of education that does not recognize the right to express appropriate anger against injustice, against disloyalty, against the negation of love, against exploitation, and against violence fails to see the educational role implicit in the expression of these feelings" (45). He often noted that the right to be angry, just as the right to love, serves as a legitimate motivational foundation for our liberatory struggles; in that just anger can remind us that we are not supposed to live as objects of oppression. In the same light, Freire (1998a) insisted, "my right to be angry presupposes that the historical experience in which I participate tomorrow is not a given, but a challenge and a problem. My just anger is grounded in any indignation in the face of the denial of the right inherent in the very essence of the human condition" (71). Therefore, one of the most important tasks of a pedagogy of love is to create the conditions for students to "engage in the experience of assuming themselves as social, historical, thinking, communicating, transformative, creative persons; dreamers of possible utopias, capable of being angry because of a capacity to love" (45).

This is particularly so, given that many educators are so disconnected from the conditions of "the other" and frightened by their racialized misconceptions to allow themselves to genuinely know their students as vital human beings. Instead, students remain objects to be managed, manipulated, and controlled, in ways that may eventually draw out of them the prescribed answers. As a consequence, the classroom becomes routinized by standards of disembodied expectations removed from the organic responses of student bodies, while teachers conduct themselves "professionally" in ways that distance them from the possibility of expressing authentic human love—beyond the often cliché: "I love all my students!"

However, since students are not objects or bodies static products to be tweaked here and there, Freire knew that learning, like loving, is an act that students must choose freely to practice, through the exercise of their social agency and personal empowerment. With this at the core of his pedagogical sensibilities, Freire also argued that teachers had to avert fixed notions or prescriptions of "the other," for given the changing and evolving nature of our humanity, seldom can we can know our students or even ourselves fully. At best, we can usually know one another only in context and in relation to our shared labor or lived experiences. In fact, it is precisely this unpredictable and dynamic aspect of our humanity that most provides us that rich terrain for cultivating transformative consciousness, in ways that nurture our human complexities and respond to our yearning for freedom.

In his work, Freire (1995) spoke of love for his students, but always in relation to teaching. "When I say to love I mean to love the very process of teaching" (20). In this process of teaching, he reasoned that the forces of love, beauty, and ethics converge to facilitate and enhance a communal experience of learning. Hence, Freire understood his love for students *within* this process of teaching. Of this he wrote,

> It is impossible to think of separating beauty from teaching; beauty from ethics; and the love for students from loving the process through which I must love the student. I love my students not because they are in a room where I am teacher. I love my students to the extent in which I love the very process of being with them.
>
> (p. 20)

In contrast, the banking model of education, with its objectification of students as static vessels to be filled with knowledge, thwarts the establishment of an emancipatory process of learning and, thus, constitutes an act of disrespect and violence. Consequently, this lovelessness undermines our human capacity for solidarity and erodes the beauty of teaching and learning together, across our differences.

Solidarity and Difference

> Our fight against the different discriminations, against any negation of our being, will only lead to victory if we can realize the obvious: unity within diversity.
>
> —Paulo Freire (1997)

Freire argued that the relationship between teaching and loving is fundamental to our pedagogical and political potential, in that only through our courage to love, in the face of difference, is solidarity even a possibility—a solidarity that opens us to know and experience one another, both individually and collectively, within shared moments of tenderness, intellectual uncertainties, doubts, breakthroughs of knowledge, or social anxieties linked to repressed human suffering. In this way, solidarity and difference intertwine to create the social and material space for students to critique oppressive attitudes and practices of their everyday. In an emancipatory classroom, where a shared sense of community prevails, students' critical engagement with the conflicts and contradictions of difference work to sustain the development of critical social consciousness and, thus, bring about conditions that change us all.

Although many educators from subordinate communities dislike the term tolerance, Freire (1995) cast a critical view of tolerance as an important political virtue that is difficult to enact, in that, more often than not, the tolerance-intolerance dialectic is shut down. He explained tolerance as that quality which requires we move outside ourselves. "It is the ability to enjoy difference. It is to learn from the difference. It means not to consider ourselves better than others precisely because they are different from us. When we think about tolerance we immediately think about racism which is the strongest negation of being tolerant; the lowest level of the negation of differences" (21).

In contrast, intolerance thwarts the political rights of oppressed populations to choice and the freedom to be. Furthermore, Freire's critical reading of tolerance does not degenerate into forms of indifference or irresponsibility. Rather, underlying this view is the belief that *love is tolerant.* Herein lies the transformative potential of a genuine solidarity—one not rooted in the negation of difference, but rather in a meaningful reinvention of classroom life and society; where love as a driving pedagogical force consummates the construction of knowledge, through the power of student dialogues founded upon their lived histories. About this relationship between dialogue and love, Freire wrote (1970),

> Dialogue cannot exist . . . in the absence of a profound love for the world and for people. The naming of the world, which is an act of creation and re-creation, is not possible if it is not infused with love. Love is at the same time the foundation of dialogue and dialogue itself . . . Because love is an act of courage, not of fear, love is commitment to others . . . If I do not love the world—if I do not love life—if I do not love people—I cannot enter into dialogue.
>
> (p. 90–91)

It is also within everyday expressions of solidarity and difference that teachers and students come to embrace the powerful dialectic of teacher-student and student-teacher, at the heart of Freire's pedagogy. Through the tension inherent in this process, teachers and students learn to construct knowledge together, discovering a powerful sense of oneness amidst difference and difference even at the core of oneness. For without cultivating this level of shared openness, humility, and compassion (beyond the dictates of the ego), classroom knowledge becomes an object to manipulate and possess, rendering it quickly stagnant, fragmented, and lifeless.

In turn, teachers and students can experience isolation and disconnection, in a perpetual game of sordid competition that offers but fleeting moments of satisfaction within a stagnant consciousness of domination. The utilitarian and individualistic nature of capitalist relations systematically functions within the classroom and the workplace to thwart cultural kinships, communal affiliations, and even familial loyalties, which potentiate the development and deepening of intimacy and solidarity. In the process, students and workers alike become more and more estranged from one another, their labor, and the world around them. In the process, reactionary humanist calls for communities—whether defined by neighborhood, religion, "race", nationality, or class—emerge in the hopes of overcoming a deepening sense of isolation and social abandonment.

For Freire, the enactment of radical love in the classroom, in contrast, seeks to build a democratic field of critical praxis, in which numbing experiences of alienation can be openly named, challenged, and dismantled, creating a place for teachers and students to contend more honestly and effectively with the human differences that exist between us, as we discard reactionary tendencies. This also entails a dialectical acknowledgment that "there is a constant oscillation in the rise and fall of discrimination: one should neither believe in guaranteed progress nor become fatalist about it."[1]

Cultural differences in the classroom are also worthy of discussion here, in that Freire, again, urges us to hold steady within the dialectical tension of differences—differences that can either stimulate greater curiosity, imagination, and questioning or cause dissonance, frustration, and anger when students are not provided substantive opportunities for expression or guidance about the wisdom their cultural knowledge offers the practice of democratic life. Unfortunately, too often hegemonic practices of schooling disrupt processes of democratic awakening, narrowing the field for aliveness, open-mindedness, and solidarity. Accordingly, hegemonic classroom environments deter the expression of decolonizing forms of knowledge, which are derived, more often than not, from the excluded cultural and linguistic sensibilities of students' lived histories and experiences.

It should not be surprising then to discover that one of the greatest challenges that teachers face in our efforts to embody Freire's pedagogy of love is the establishment of cultural and linguistic democracy in the classroom. This is akin to Freire's notion of unity-in-diversity, which is also at the heart of his theorizing about the ethics of difference and democratic life. At the heart of this concept is the recognition that the process of liberation, whether in the classroom or the larger society, can only be enacted through a political vision where neither unity nor difference is sacrificed. This is particularly noteworthy, in that ostensibly Democratic societies tend to exhibit an overwhelming degree of homogeneity and conformity, instilled by banking education. This concept extends onto the realm of the economy, where countries like the U.S., where gross economic disparities are the norm and social mobility, contrary to commonsensical claims, belies the mantra that education ensures personal economic gain.

Of course, the unacknowledged conformity of the classroom and the economy are perpetuated by way of contradictory hegemonic structures and social mechanisms that condition students to think of themselves as solely individual possessors and consumers, with little regard for the common good or sense of responsibility for our communal existence. In conjunction, Freire (1970) spoke to this tendency of capitalism to commodify.

> In their unrestrained eagerness to possess, the oppressors develop the conviction that it is possible for them to transform everything into objects of their purchasing power; hence their strictly materialistic concept of existence. Money is the measure of all things, and profit the primary

> goal. For the oppressors, what is worthwhile is to have more—always more—even at the cost of the oppressed having less or having nothing. For them, *to be is to have* and to be the class of the "haves."
>
> (p. 58)

This possessing consciousness is often reinforced through advertising slogans and differentiating paraphernalia of the marketplace that readily assure consumers that they are, indeed, not only all different, but special. This distorting ideology of the market is embedded in the hidden curriculum of education and the meritocratic culture of elitism and privilege that prevails within schools and the larger social sphere.

This assimilative inclination of the classroom generally remained unaddressed; so that decolonizing forms of knowledge simply cannot surface, in this closed field of banking education. Further, the manufacturing of the insidious belief in the "uniqueness of each individual" by the culture industry functions effectively not only to thwart genuine epistemologies of differences, but also supports policies and practices of what Freire (1970) called *cultural invasion*. Here he referred to "relationships between the invader and invaded [that] are situated at opposite poles. They are relationships of authority. The invader acts, the invaded are under the illusion that they are acting through the action of the other; the invader has his say, the invaded, who are forbidden this, listen to what the invader says" (p. 17).

This relationship continues as an overarching condition even in schools where communities of color desire for their children to experience greater connection with their cultural traditions, primary languages, and histories of survival. The political consequence of hegemonic schooling is the wholesale denial or erasure of communal histories, cultural knowledge, and political self-determination—often replaced with superficial multicultural interventions that do little to respect the dignity or human rights of students, whose histories are indelibly marked by centuries of genocide, slavery, colonization, and economic exploitation.

The increasing tendency to eliminate differences within schools and society is in sync with the hegemonic apparatus of capitalist schooling that once openly drove the Americanization movement in the U.S. and persists in homogenized contortions of neoliberal multiculturalism—where cultural recognition on the surface belies the absence of power. As such, the new politics of assimilation is tied to deceptive notions of "equality" and "fairness," which seem oblivious to the gross accelerating inequality in the distribution of wealth and power—a phenomenon antagonistic to pedagogical expressions of radical love or democratic life. Thus, "in contemporary capitalistic society the meaning of equality now refers to the equality of automatons—human beings who in fact are devoid of their individuality" (Fromm 1964; p. 15). This, in part, is linked to the alienating culture of capitalism, which results in the suppression of cultural differences, on the one hand, and the production of social exclusions, on the other. This phenomenon is well-oriented toward also instilling a false sense of national unity, informed by an entrenched and pervasive culture of U.S. consumerism and militarism.

Commonsense notions of equality and difference in capitalist society function well to persuade consumers into believing that they are, indeed, individuals, while simultaneously they adhere collectively to the dictates of the marketplace. In this way, mass forms of standardization can prevail, while most members of society steeped in the ethers of their "individual uniqueness," seem indifferent. Hence, it is no wonder that there are not more protests and demonstrations waged against wealth inequality or high stakes testing or the current national standardization of the curriculum, which seems to have received little objection, beyond the cost of implementation. In the name of conformity, the construction of knowledge, movement of the body, expression of human feeling, and even the practice of spirituality are miserably routinized and violently hijacked, within traditional classrooms or community institutions that have been charged with the task of public containment of the masses.

In direct opposition, Freire affirmed the revolutionary power of love to enliven our teaching and create the conditions whereby our students experience the meaning and practice of living democracy. Educational practices powered by a radical love also create the conditions where students can critically explore their cultural histories, which can also enhance their individual expression within the classroom. The power behind this pedagogical approach is that it simultaneously breaks barriers that isolate and objectify students, while supporting them to integrate into the heart of classroom life.

The democratizing aspirations of a pedagogy of love are, indeed, far easier to describe on these pages than to practice consistently. This is particularly so, in that it requires teachers to risk vulnerability, when forging democratic relationships with their students, even in the midst of external political struggles that may place pedagogical and curricular constraints upon them. Hence, Freire (1970) considered the practice of revolutionary love in the classroom to constitute *an act of courage and risk,* in that this practice must also be linked to a larger humanizing ethos of education.

Toward a Humanizing Education

> To surmount the situation of oppression, people must first critically recognize its causes, so that through transforming action they can create a new situation, one which makes possible the pursuit of a fuller humanity.
>
> —Paulo Freire (1970)

A pedagogy of love can best be understood as a deeply purposeful educational practice, fueled by an emancipatory political vision that is rooted in what Freire (1970) considered our "true vocation: to be human." Underlying Freire's perspective is a political commitment to a larger humanizing political project of schools and society. This critical conceptualization of humanity encompasses a deeply reflective understanding and political interpretation of the dialectical relationship that exists between our cultural existence as individuals and our political and economic existence as communal beings. Accordingly, Freire understood capitalism as a system of production that denies the humanity of workers, encouraging the wholesale accumulation of material wealth by the few, with little concern for the suffering of those exploited and disempowered in the process. This dynamic is replicated across society, including the policies and practices that inform schools, whether public, charter, or private.

Hence, if educators are to effectively engage the difficulties that students from oppressed communities face, then, this requires that we move beyond solely an individualistic or psychologized understanding of our students and embrace them as both political and communal human beings with enormous potential for not only achieving academically but also with innate potential to transform the concrete conditions that erode their well-being. This requires that we seek answers within the historical realm of economic, social, and political forms, so that we might better understand the structures and political forces that give rise to our humanity, as it currently exists. Accordingly, a humanizing vision of pedagogy nurtures critical consciousness and social agency, in ways that move students away from instrumentalized forms of learning and replaces these with pedagogical activities that ignite both their passion for learning and their creative engagement with the world around them.

The same rich humanizing quality that Freire brought to his writings was also profoundly apparent in his love for life, freedom, and learning; as well as the ways he sought to share the transformative power of this love in his praxis—whether in a small group or a large auditorium of people. Freire consistently expressed a deep sense of joy and love for life, no matter how difficult the conditions or circumstances he had to confront, as an individual or in struggle with others. Again, the political and personal comingle fully here, in that Freire's commitment was consistently expressed as both a personal struggle to be free and a collective struggle for the emancipation of our collective humanity. Similarly, he urged educators to embrace our labor in schools and communities with love and respect for our students, as creators of their own lives and co-creators of the new world to come.

Freire recognized the nature of human beings beyond simply cognitive or mental beings. The sense that we are integral beings encompasses an understanding of our humanity as the combination of our physical, emotional, and spiritual faculties, in addition to the cognitive. Freire cultivated through his world a pedagogy that asks teachers to examine the world beyond the surface of what we often term reality. Instead, He posited a problem posing approach, anchored in dialogue and a radical principle of love, by which teachers and students can come to critically know ourselves and the world. Within this pedagogical practice, Freire sought to contend openly and consistently with the manner in which oppression dehumanizes teachers and students alike. Freire was concerned with the manner in which even well-meaning teachers, through a lack of critical moral leadership, can participate in disabling the heart, minds, and bodies of students—an act that alienates students, forecloses their self-determination, and undermines their political formation. Instead, through a pedagogy that deliberately supports the awakening of critical consciousness, Freire sought to shatter rigid prescriptions of the oppressed and to fight for the restoration of our humanity.

Although some critiqued Freire's ideas as unrealistic or impossible to enact, these critiques are unwarranted. Never did Freire believe that an emancipatory pedagogy or political struggle could magically or instantly transform our consciousness or the world. Instead, he consistently pointed to the hard work required to bring forth any profound change to our lives, the schools in which we teach, and the communities in which we live and labor. What Freire did believe was that through dialogue and relationships of struggle, we could begin to summon the human power and material conditions necessary to reinvent the world around us. He insisted that we could do this through creating new language and new forms of being, which spoke genuinely to democratic possibilities and our existential yearning for freedom. Related to this difficult process, Freire also often warned us of the difficulties we must be prepared to face, in that often at the very moment when structural change is palpable, reactionary backlash can arise, rooted in an extreme and uncompromising negation of democratic possibilities. In direct contrast, Freire's pedagogy of love diametrically opposed such a negation of our humanity, working instead to create the emancipatory conditions necessary for social empowerment through a critical praxis of the body.

The Indispensability of the Body

> It is the human body, young or old, fat or thin, of whatever color, the conscious body that looks at the stars. It is the body that writes. It is the body that speaks. It is the body that fights. It is the body that loves and hates. It is the body that suffers. It is the body that dies. It is the body that lives!
>
> —Paulo Freire (in Freire & Faundez, 1989)

Freire left behind a legacy that speaks passionately to the relationship between love, the body, and knowledge. This encompasses a pedagogical perspective that is fully cognizant about the power of both the discipline of love and the primacy of the body in the construction of knowledge. Freire's pedagogy of love is anchored to an understanding that we are material beings and that the idea of loving, in the pedagogical sense, entails a humanizing ethos of classroom life that supports dialogue and solidarity, as we labor for the common good. As teachers and students participate more fully in the dialogical process of communal learning, the materiality of their bodies also become rightful allies in the formation and expression of collective consciousness. Of this Freire (1983) said, "true education incarnates the permanent search of people together with others for their becoming fully human in the world in which they exist" (96).

Embracing the rightful place of the body in the classroom requires a view of students as integral human beings. It is this integral view that is negated within banking education, where a more complex understanding of the body and its significance to students' intellectual and political formation is absent. Since the epistemological focus is on analytical processes, other important ways of knowing are easily ignored or dismissed. As a result, student voices and other physical expressions of the body that fall outside the mainstream register are systematically silenced or shut down. It is also worth noting that this phenomenon is predicated upon a dominant notion of the individual as a psychological self, whose intelligence and "ego strength" is supposedly gauged by the ability to function, irrespective of external conditions.

As a consequence, educators prepared in the Western paradigm of self seldom possess the political acumen necessary to deflect deficit notions, so that they can engage critically with the larger social inequalities that shape the lives of historically oppressed populations. Accordingly, educators often are taught to place a great deal of attention upon classroom management and control of transgressive expressions of the body seen as disrupting to the pseudo-harmony of the classroom. Common authoritarian responses to student physicality ignore the meaning and intent behind student behavior, converting the body into an object that must acquiesce to the teacher's will or be expelled. In the process, little attention is given to the dialectical relationship that students have with their world—a relationship that for working class students of color requires constant navigation of the minefields of structural oppression perpetuated by racism, poverty, and other forms of social exclusions.

The material conditions and histories of our students are made visible on their bodies. Their histories of survival are witnessed in their skin, their teeth, their hair, their gestures, their speech, and the movement of their arms and legs. As such, bodies are "maps of power and identity" (Haraway 1990, p. 2) that provide meaningful information and powerful insights into the tensions, struggles, and needs students from oppressed communities express in the classroom. Freire (1998) concluded, therefore, that it is insufficient to rely on abstract approaches to learning, where disembodied words and texts are privileged in the construction of knowledge. He argued "words not given body (made flesh) have little or no value" (p. 39) to the process of liberation. His concern here was with the manner in which educational processes of estrangement causes a false dichotomy that alienate students from their world—the only true realm from which liberatory education can emerge.

This requires that teachers and students labor in the flesh. This is to say that our practices of teaching and learning be rooted in the materiality of human existence, as a starting place for critical praxis. Freire (1993) argued that "We learn things about the world by acting and changing the world around us. It is [through] this process of change, of transforming the material world from which we emerged, [where] creation of the cultural and historical world takes place. This transformation of the world [is] done by us while it makes and remakes us" (108). However, he was also clear that there is nothing automatic or natural about this process of social change nor is it a process that can solely rely on calculating logic or cold rationality. Moreover, given the body's sentient quality that overwhelmingly shapes student experiences and responses to the world, just or unjust, their bodies constantly resist or desist, adjust or rebel, rejoice or despair, in the long human quest to be free.

The human body, further, constitutes a significant political terrain from which all emancipatory knowledge must emerge. Without the materiality of the body, our teaching and learning is reduced to a process of abstraction and fragmentation that attempts to falsely render knowledge a neutral and objective phenomenon, absent of history and ideology. Freire recognized that it is the body that provides us the medium for our existence as subjects of history and as politically empowered agents of change. Within the context of gross inequalities, this is particularly salient in that "bodies are also the primary means by which capitalism does its job" (McLaren 1999, p. xiii). We are molded and shaped by the structures, policies and practices of economic domination and social exclusion, which violently insert our bodies into the alienating morass of an intensified global division of labor. In concert with Marx, Freire understood that hegemonic schooling is founded on a pedagogy of estrangement, which like that of estranged labor functions to alienate students from their bodies and the natural world.

Freire (1998a) considered this estrangement of the body akin to "that invisible power of alienating domestication . . . a state of refined estrangement, of the mind's abdication of its own essential self, of a loss of consciousness of the body, of a 'mass production' of the individual, and of conformity" (p. 102). The traditional classroom exists as an arena of domestication, where abstract knowledge and its construction are objectified, along with the students who must acquiesce to its alienating function, limiting rationality, and technocratic instrumentalism. Here, the production of knowledge is neither engaged as historical, collective, or embodied phenomenon. Ignored is the obvious fact that our lives unfold within the vital experiences of the flesh and its sentient capacity. "The flesh, the material aspect of the body, is seen as a hindrance which must be overcome, negated, and transcended" (Beckey, 2000, p. 71). This transcending view sidelines the affective and relational needs of student bodies that must endure, resist, and struggle to become free from the social and material entanglements of a society that imprisons them, both ideologically and corporally.

The historical absence of the body in the classroom is likely due to institutional fears associated with the body's real potential for disruption and subversion. For this reason, a political commitment to counter the disembodiment of our humanity is at the heart of Freire's pedagogy of love. To endure daily confrontations with oppressive forces, for example, Freire (1998a) urged us to "struggle for the material conditions without which our body will suffer from neglect, thus running the risk of becoming frustrated and ineffective, then [we] will no longer be the witness that [we] ought to be, no longer the tenacious fighter who may tire but who never gives up" (95). Yet, missing from educational discourses is precisely this political connection of the body to the critical formation, for both teachers and students. Nevertheless, Freire (1993) embraced the totality of the body in the act of knowing, insisting "It is my entire body that socially knows. I cannot, in the name of exactness and rigor, negate my body, my emotions and my feelings" (1993, p. 105).

Despite Freire's assertion, most teacher preparation programs seldom engage substantively the manner in which students' physical responses can serve as meaningful indications in assessing more accurately their academic needs. No matter the age or grade level, students can experience and express, overtly or covertly, responses of excitement, frustration, joy and despair in the process of their learning. Freire (1998b) considered these emotions as logical human responses, in that "studying is a demanding occupation, in the process of which we will encounter pain, pleasure, victory, defeat, doubt and happiness" (p. 78). When these responses are ignored, pedagogical practices default into domestication, silencing the creativity and imagination rooted in the wisdom of the body.

Thus, as a political and organic entity, the body plays a significant role in making sense of the material conditions and social relations of power that shape our lives. Similarly, as praxis of the body that can support teachers in building a democratic educational practice, where students are not asked to confront themselves and each other as strangers, but rather through the spirit of human kinship and community, from the moment they enter the classroom. True to this view, a pedagogy of love seeks to engage, in the flesh, the embodied histories and knowledges of the oppressed, as well as the repressive circumstances that inhibit their voice, social agency, self-determination, and solidarity. From this liberatory position, Freire (1993) again spoke to the undeniable centrality of the body in the act of knowing the world:

> The importance of the body is indisputable; the body moves, acts, rememorizes, the struggle for its liberation; the body in sum, desires, points out, announces, protests, curves itself, rises, designs and remakes the world . . . and its importance has to do with a certain sensualism . . . contained by the body, even in connection with cognitive ability . . . its absurd to separate the rigorous acts of knowing the world from the [body's] passionate ability to know.
>
> (p. 87)

Unfortunately, and worth repeating, it is the power of this sensualism, with its revolutionary potential to summon dissent and nurture the empowerment of students, that is systematically stripped away from the educational process of hegemonic schooling. In response, Freire's view of the body challenged conservative ideologies of social control historically associated with a Puritanical epistemicide that considers the body as evil, sensual pleasure as sinful, and passions as corrupting to the sanctity of the spirit—all underlying notions reflected in the pedagogical policies and practices today. On this, Freire noted how the sensuality of the body is fettered and confined within schools, discouraged from expression and the freedom to be.

Similarly, the hegemonic tradition of fettered bodies is also product of an educational tradition rooted in the convergence of three dominant paradigms of the West, represented by Socrates, Christianity, and behavioral psychology. In the classical Socratic tradition, the sensual body is quickly subordinated to the mind, while ideas are privileged over the senses (Seidel, 1964). In Christianity, the separation between the body and the soul constitutes the whole relation to learning. In the behaviorist model, the body is transformed into an instrumentalized object to be manipulated and dominated through external stimulus, in the process of learning.

These views of teaching and learning have historically led to pedagogical practices that do violence through an erasure of the body and the annihilation of the flesh in the act of knowing. Accordingly, inequalities are reproduced through class, racialized, gendered, ableist, and heterosexist perceptions and distortions, which are embedded, wittingly or unwittingly, in prevailing attitudes of most well meaning teachers. Implicit here are deficit assumptions and debilitating preconceptions projected upon students seen to be outside the classed, racialized, patriarchal, hetero-normative, abled, or spiritual mainstream. Consequently, students from working class and racialized communities, where the body's spontaneity is given greater primacy and freedom in the act of knowing, are often expected to sacrifice the creative and sensual knowledge of their bodies to an atomized, abstracted, and dispassionate logic of being. Accordingly, the body's sexuality is repressed as an unwelcome intrusion to the regimen of classroom life.

This ill-fated disembodiment begins early in students' academic formation, resulting in a troubling dichotomy between the body and mind in students' reading of the world. Freire (2005) problematized this dichotomy, given the necessity for students to learn how to *read of bodies,* in the course of their political formation.

> Issues of sociability, imagination, feelings, desires, fear, courage, love, hate, raw anger, sexuality, and so on lead us to the need to "read" our bodies as if they were texts, through the interrelations that make-up their whole. There is the need for an interdisciplinary reading of bodies with students, for breaking away from dichotomies, ruptures that are enviable and deforming. (p. 52)

It is worth noting here that Freire's own passionate way of being in the world and the variety of references he made to the "beauty of the body" and "the restlessness of bodies" also bears witness to an appreciation for the sensuality and sexuality of human beings. He insisted that "sexuality has a determining effect on the development of consciousness and reason" (Spring 1994). In *Pedagogy of the Heart,* Freire (1997) commented on the "gradual improvement in performance on the part of the students, as the pedagogy of questioning started to gain ground against the pedagogy of answers, and as issues around the body were addressed in the Sexual Orientation Program" (p. 62)—a program that was in place during his post as Secretary of Education for the city of São Paulo.

Given the significant role of the body in the pedagogical process, the Western epistemological severing of the body in the construction of knowledge interferes dramatically with students' capacities to know themselves, one another, and their world. Repressive views of the body and sexuality within education also serve to negate, overtly or covertly, the cultural knowledges of oppressed cultural populations, whose epistemological view and expression of the body in the cultural process of their knowing may differ substantially from the mainstream's dichotomization of body and consciousness. In the process, this also can render teachers and students alienated and estranged from forms of human suffering that exist outside of the limited scope of the hegemonic lens, whether this is linked to class, gender, ethnicity, sexuality, skin-color, physical constitution, or spiritual beliefs.

With this in mind, it is interesting to note that despite human development theories that affirm we are sexual beings even in the womb, serious engagement with human sexuality is systematically repressed and denied in U.S. classrooms. This is so even at puberty, when students' bodies are experiencing heightened and confusing sensations. Seldom do teachers—many who are not particularly comfortable with their own sexuality—critically engage the question of sexuality, beyond repeated clichés of "raging hormones" in reference to teenage sexuality. In the process, students are not only pedagogically abandoned, but also left at the mercy of the media and corporate pirates that, very deliberately and systematically, prey upon the powerful sensations, emotions, and stirrings of youth. In the culture industry of advertising, for example, teenage bodies are sought after for the exchange value they generate in marketing an adolescent sexuality, which offers a marginal exoticism and ample pleasures to the largely male consumer. Commodification reifies and fixates the complexity of youth bodies and the range of possibilities they might assume, while simultaneously exploiting them as fodder for the marketplace (Giroux, 1998).

Frightened by their own ambivalence and the physicality of student bodies, educational policy makers and educators institute practices that systematically silence physical expression, rigidly limiting any discussion of one of the most significant aspects of our humanity. The message is clear; teachers and students are expected to leave their sexuality, along with all other aspects of their cultural knowledge and lived histories at the door, prior to entering. Yet, despite the difficulties and hardships that such silence portends for many students—isolation and increasing rates of suicide among many LBGTQ youth, for example—schools and teachers, much like the fundamentalist church, function as moralistic agents to police and repress the body's participation, in ways that leave students uninformed about the important role of the body in the struggle for consciousness and liberation.

Yet in spite of major institutional efforts to repress and control the desires, pleasures and mobility of the body within classroom and society, Freire's writings support the view that students seldom surrender their bodies completely or readily acquiesce to authoritarian practices—practices which in themselves provide the impetus for resistance, especially in those students whose dynamic histories are excluded within mainstream education. Instead, Freire (1970) recognized that in their struggle for freedom, those who are repressed, including youth, will "try out forms of rebellious action" (p. 64). As such, many engage in the construction of their own cultural forms of resistance that may or may not always function in their best interest.

However, often, expressions of student resistance are enacted through alterations of the body—be they clothing, hairstyle, posturing, manner of walking, way of speaking, the piercing and tattooing of the body. These actions represent then not only acts of resistance but also alternative ways of experiencing, affirming, and knowing the world, generally perceived by officials as transgressive and disruptive to the social order. In a footnote in *Pedagogy of the Oppressed,* Freire made reference to this phenomenon.

> Young people increasingly view parent and teacher authoritarianism as inimical to their own freedom. For this very reason, they increasingly oppose forms of action which minimize their expressiveness and hinder their self-affirmation. This very positive phenomenon is not accidental. It is actually a symptom of the historical climate . . . For this reason one cannot (unless he [or she] has a personal interest in doing so) see the youth rebellion as a mere example of the traditional differences between generations. Something deeper is involved here. Young people in their rebellion are denouncing and condemning the unjust model of a society of domination. This rebellion with its special dimension, however, is very recent; society continues to be authoritarian in character.
>
> (p. 154)

Such authoritarian views of students are also exacerbated by a "new form of representational politics [that] has emerged in media culture fueled by degrading visual depictions of youth as criminal, sexually decadent, drug crazed, and illiterate. In short, youth are viewed as a growing threat to the public order" (Giroux 1998).[2]

Teachers, whose bodies are similarly restricted, alienated and domesticated by their workplace, are under enormous pressure to follow strict policies and procedures for classroom conduct, instead of employing more creative and humanizing approaches, grounded in the actual needs of their students. Given the impact of disembodied practices, teachers generally experience an uphill battle in meeting standardized mandates, which systematically extricate student bodies from the equation of their learning. Moreover, educators who struggle in this repressive context to implement liberating strategies are often forced to become masters of deception—saying what the principal or district office wishes to hear, while doing behind closed doors what they believe is in the best interest of students. Unfortunately, having to shoulder the physical stress of this duplicity can drive some of the most effective teachers away from their chosen vocation, given the intolerable alienation this engenders. While others, who simply feel defeated or frustrated by the pressure, adopt more authoritarian approaches manipulate or coerce *cooperation,* justifying their decision with contradictory rhetoric about the pragmatic necessity. What cannot be overlooked is that authoritarian practices of the classroom not only "blindfold students and lead them to a domesticated future" (Freire, 1970, p. 79), but also alienate teacher labor as well.

Freire's view of the body is also salient to rethinking university education, where there seems to be little pedagogical tolerance for the emotional needs of adult learners. "Somewhere in the intellectual history of the West there developed the wrongheaded idea that mind and heart are antagonists, that scholarship must be divested of emotion, that spiritual journeys must avoid intellectual concerns" (Lifton, 1990, 29). This tradition sets an expectation that professors and students compartmentalize themselves within the classroom, without serious attention to the manner in which the very essence of university education is often tied to crucial moments of life transition; and even more so for working class students of color who may be the first generation to attend university.

Simultaneously, students are expected to enter their studies or research as objective, distanced, and impartial observers, even when the object of their study may be intimately linked to brutal conditions of human suffering, are a part of their lived histories. Freire (1993) rightly argued that traditional academic expectations of the university affirm "that feelings corrupt research and its findings, the fear of intuition, the categorical negation of emotion and passion, the belief in technicism, [which] ends in convincing many that, the more neutral we are in our actions, the more objective and efficient we will be" (p. 106) in our construction of knowledge. Hence, students are slowly but surely socialized to labor as uncritical, descriptive, "neutral" scholars, dispassionate and alienated from their subject of study. The result is often scholarship conceived epistemologically in a deeply *estranged* way, devoid of the very qualities that comprise our humanity. The unfortunate consequence here is that disembodied knowledge seldom leads teachers and students to grapple critically with deeper moral questions of education, which would undoubtedly challenge social and material relations that sustain human suffering and structural inequalities, in the first place.

Freire (1983) affirmed that we possess *a conscious body,* indispensable to the evolution of critical consciousness. "His or her consciousness, with its 'intentionality' towards the world, is always conscious of something. It is a permanent state of moving towards reality. Hence, the condition of the human being is to be in constant relationship to the world" (p. 146). The dialectical relationships between the body and consciousness, object and subject, students and the world are essential to both a critical understanding of the world and forging actions that can have material consequences on the lives of the oppressed. Similarly, Freire believed that transformation of the social and material structures of oppression could not be undertaken by mere abstraction devoid of action; nor could emancipatory action result devoid of the love that moves us toward social consciousness. For Freire, the greatest emancipatory potential that underlies a pedagogy of love is the integral enactment of our human faculties—body, mind, heart, and spirit—in our pedagogical and political struggles to awaken critical consciousness.

Notes

1. See: interview with Etiene Balibar conducted by Clement Petitjean on April 15, 2014 See: http://www.versobooks.com/blogs/1559-a-racism-without-races
2. See: Giroux, H. (1998) "Teenage Sexuality, Body Politics and the Pedagogy of Display." Available: http://www.henryagiroux.com/online_articles/teenage_sexuality.htm

Suggested Readings for Future Study

Adorno, T. (1987). *Negative Dialectic.* New York: Continuum.

Adorno, T. W., Benjamin, W., Bloch, E., Brecht, B., and Lukacs, G. (1997). *Aesthetics and Politics.* London: Verso Press.

Althusser, L. (1969). *For Marx.* New York: Vintage Books.

Amsler, S., Canaan, J., Cowden, S., Motta, S., and Singh, G. (2010). *Why Critical Pedagogy and Popular Education Matter Today.* Birmingham: Centre for Sociology, Anthropology and Politics, Higher Education Academy.

Ashcroft, B., Griffiths, G., and Tiffin, H. (1995). *Postcolonial Studies Reader.* New York: Routledge.

Au, W. (2011). "Fighting with the Text: Contextualizing and Recontextualizing Freire's Critical Pedagogy." In Apple, M. W., Au, W., and Gandin, L. A. (eds.), *The Routledge International Handbook of Critical Education* (pp. 221–231). New York: Routledge, Taylor & Francis.

Ball, S., ed. (1990). *Foucault and Education: Disciplines and Knowledge.* New York: Routledge.

Bates, T. R. (1975). "Gramsci and the Theory of Hegemony." *Journal of the History of Ideas* XXXVI, April–June.

Benhabib, S. (1986). *Critique, Norm and Utopia: A Study of the Foundations of Critical Theory.* New York: Columbia University Press.

Benhabib, S. (1992). *Situating the Self.* New York: Routledge.

Bennett, T., et al. (1987). *Culture, Ideology and Social Process.* London: Open University Press.

Best, S. and Kellner, D. (1991). *Postmodern Theory: Critical Interrogations.* New York: Guilford Press.

Bhabha, H. (1994). *The Location of Culture.* New York: Routledge.

Bocock, R. (1986). *Hegemony.* London: Tavistock.

Bourdieu, P. (1977a). *Outline of a Theory of Practice.* Cambridge, UK: Cambridge University Press.

Bourdieu, P. (1977b). "Cultural Reproduction and Social Reproduction." In Karabel, J. and Halsey, H. A. (eds.), *Power and Ideology in Education.* New York: Oxford University Press.

Bourdieu, P. and Passeron, J. (1992). *Reproduction in Education, Society and Culture.* London: Sage.

Buck-Morss, S. (1977). *The Origin of Negative Dialectics: Theodore W. Adorno, Walter Benjamin, and the Frankfurt School.* New York: Free Press.

Cherryholmes, C. (1988). *Power and Criticism: Poststructuralist Investigations in Education.* New York: Teachers College Press.

Cole, M. (2008). *Marxism and Educational Theory.* London and New York: Routledge.

Dubiel, H. (1985). *Theory and Politics: Studies in the Development of Critical Theory.* Cambridge, MA: MIT Press.

Eagleton, T. (1991). *Ideology: An Introduction.* New York: Verso.

Fay, B. (1997). *Critical Social Science.* New York: Cornell University Press.

Fischman, G. and McLaren, P. (2005). "Rethinking Critical Pedagogy and the Gramscian and Freirian Legacies." *Cultural Studies/Critical Methodologies,* 5(4), 1–22.

Foucault, M. (1972). *The Archaeology of Knowledge and the Discourse on Language.* New York: Pantheon Books.

Foucault, M. (1979). *Discipline and Punish – the Birth of the Prison.* New York: Vintage Books.

Foucault, M. (1980). *Power/Knowledge: Selected Interviews and Other Writings.* New York: Pantheon Books.

Fromm, E. (1941). *Escape from Freedom.* New York: Avon Books.

Giroux, H. (2011). *On Critical Pedagogy.* New York: Continuum.

Gramsci, A. (1971). *Selections from the Prison Notebooks.* New York: International Publishers.

Gramsci, A., Forgacs, D., and Hobsbawm, E. J. (2000). *The Antonio Gramsci Reader: Selected Writings 1916–1935.* New York: NYU Press.

Gray, A. and McGuigan, J. (1993). *Studying Culture: An Introductory Reader.* London: Edward Arnold.

Greene, M. (1986). "In Search of a Critical Pedagogy." *Harvard Educational Review, 56*(4), 427–441.

Greene, M. (1988). *The Dialectic of Freedom.* New York: Teachers College Press.

Held, D. (1980). *Introduction to Critical Theory: Horkheimer to Habermas.* Berkeley and Los Angeles: University of California Press.

Horkheimer, M. (1972). *Critical Theory: Selected Essays.* New York: Herder & Herder.

Horkheimer, M. (1974). *Critique of Instrumental Reason; Lectures and Essays Since the End of World War II.* New York: Seabury Press.

Horkheimer, M. and Adorno, T. W. (1944). *Dialectic of Enlightenment.* New York: The Continuum Publishing Company.

Hoy, D. C. (1986). *Foucault – A Critical Reader.* Oxford: Blackwell.

Jardine, G. M. (2005). *Foucault & Education.* New York: Peter Lang.

Jay, M. (1973). *The Dialectical Imagination: A History of the Frankfurt School and the Institute of Social Research, 1923–1959.* Boston: Little Brown.

Jay, M. (1984). *Adorno.* Cambridge, MA: Harvard University Press.

Kanpol, B. (1999). *Critical Pedagogy: An Introduction.* Westport, CT: Bergin & Garvey.

Karabel, J. and Halsey, A. H., eds. (1977). *Power and Ideology in Education.* New York: Oxford University Press.

Kellner, D. (1989a). *Critical Theory, Marxism and Modernity.* Cambridge, UK: Polity.

Kellner, D. (1989b). *Critical Theory and Society: A Reader.* New York: Routledge.

Kellner, D. (1997). *Herbert Marcuse and the Crisis of Marxism.* Berkeley: University of California Press.

Kincheloe, J. (2008). *Critical Pedagogy Primer.* New York: Peter Lang Publishing.

Livingstone, D. W., ed. (1987). *Critical Pedagogy and Cultural Power.* New York: Bergin & Garvey Publishers.

Marcus, J. (1984). *Foundations of the Frankfurt School of Social Research.* New Brunswick, NJ: Transaction Books.

Marcuse, H. (1941). *Reason and Revolution: Hegel and the Rise of Social Theory.* London and New York: Oxford University Press.

Marcuse, H. (1966a). *Eros and Civilization: A Philosophical Inquiry into Freud.* Boston: Beacon Press.

Marcuse, H. (1966b). *One Dimensional Man.* Boston: Beacon Press.

Marcuse, H. (1968). *Negations – Essays in Critical Theory.* Boston: Beacon Press.

Marcuse, H. (1969). *An Essay on Liberation.* Boston: Beacon Press.

Marcuse, H. (1972a). *Counter-Revolution and Revolt.* Boston: Beacon Press.

Marcuse, H. (1972b). *Studies in Critical Philosophy.* London: NLB.

Marcuse, H. (1987). *Hegel's Ontology and the Theory of Historicity.* Cambridge, MA: MIT Press.

Marx, K. (1969). *Early Writings.* New York: McGraw Hill.

Mayo, P. (2015). "Antonio Gramsci's Impact on Critical Pedagogy." *Critical Sociology, 41*(7–8), 1121–1136.

Noble, T. (2000). *Social Theory and Social Change.* New York: St. Martin's Press.

Peters, M. (2003). "Critical Pedagogy and the Futures of Critical Theory." In Gur-Ze'ev, I. (ed.), *Critical Theory and Critical Pedagogy Today: Toward a New Critical Language in Education* (pp. 35–48). Haifa, Israel: Faculty of Education, University of Haifa.

Peters, M. and Besley, C. (2006). *Why Foucault? New Directions in Educational Research.* New York: Peter Lang.

Popkewitz, T. (1999). *Critical Theories in Education.* New York: Routledge.

Rasmussen, D., ed. (1996). *The Handbook of Critical Theory.* Oxford: Blackwell.

Rosado, R. (1993). *Culture and Truth: The Remaking of Social Analysis.* Boston: Beacon Press.

Schindler, R. J. (1998). *The Frankfurt School Critique of Capitalist Culture: A Critical Theory for Post-Democratic Society and Its Re-Education.* Aldershot, UK and Brookfield, VT: Ashgate.

Shakouri, N. and Abkenar, H. R. (2012). "Critical Pedagogy: An Ignis Fatuus!" *Journal of Science, 1*(2), 21–25.

Stirk, P. M. R. (2005) *Critical Theory, Politics, and Society: An Introduction.* New York: Continuum International Publishing.

Trifonas, P. P. (2000). *Revolutionary Pedagogies: Cultural Politics, Instituting Education, and the Discourse of Theory.* New York and London: RoutledgeFalmer.

Tripp, D. (1992). "Critical Theory and Educational Research." *Issues In Educational Research, 2*(1), 13–23.

Warren, S. (1984). *The Emergence of Dialectical Theory.* Chicago: University of Chicago Press.

Zygmantas, J. (2009). "Understanding Critical Pedagogy and Its Impact on the Construction of Knowledge." *Acta Paedagogica Vilnensia*, 23, 63–78.

Part Two

Social Class and Education

Introduction to Part Two

The assessment of the U.S. economy with its increasing inequalities has failed to challenge the belief in the power of education and the ability of America's economic machine to create prosperity for all. It is even asserted by some that social class inequality is not inherently wrong as long as "everybody has an opportunity to climb up the ladder" and to achieve the American dream. That is, meritocracy works as long as the ladder has enough rungs to climb. Unfortunately, the delusion that we live in a classless society is perpetuated by teachers and embraced uncritically by most students. Like all component elements of what Antonio Gramsci called *common sense*, much of the everyday discourse of the power of schools to create access to quality jobs and personal fulfillment is considered gospel.

This section on education and social class examines the nature of economic inequalities and the problematic role of a market-driven education policy. Inherent to such an examination is the need to critically interrogate the ways in which macroeconomic trends impact life in schools, as well as create sites of resistance. Critical pedagogical principles encourage educators to reclaim class as both an analytical category and a political toolkit, in order to effectively unpack the idealist assumptions and social implications of schools as the *great equalizer*, in a system driven by the dictates of profit, rather than those of human need.

This points to an urgent need to question whether educational researchers and policy makers are misguided in focusing exclusively on schools as sites of transformation and potential renewal, while ignoring the wider structural sources of social class and inequality. Within a critical pedagogical context, there is a pressing need to breathe new intellectual life into the debate on the possibilities and limits of democratic school reform. Particular attention must be paid to the manner in which contemporary social and cultural transformations and changing class relations impact the life chances of students in and outside of schools.

Such interrogations have significant implications for educational theory, policy, and classroom practice. For example, there is increasing evidence that a correlation exists between social class origin and educational outcomes. Historically, it has been commonsense that quality education will reduce inequality and social class differences. For most Americans, education is heralded as an indisputably "good thing." Parents frequently mortgage their homes and lives, work inhumanely long hours to finance a "good education" for their children, so they will be able to compete in the "new economy." Further, schools are viewed as democratic institutions leading to intergenerational mobility, improved life chances, greater economic opportunities, and fulfillment of the so-called American Dream. Yet, as stated by recent reports by the Economic Policy Institute, worker wages remains stagnant, unemployment is high, and the promise of the American Dream remains elusive for working families.

This recurrent fantasy of the power of education is firmly embedded in American culture. The belief that reforms in education along with improved teaching and school leadership can counter and overcome differentials in school outcomes and student achievement is the driving force in educational policy. These views persist in the face of gross concentrations of wealth and burgeoning class inequality in the U.S. In fact, a Congressional Budget Office report released in 2007 revealed that the gap between wealthy Americans and their fellow citizens has now become a chasm—reaching its widest point since the Roaring Twenties. This gap, according to the report, has actually been widening for nearly three decades. Numerous other studies have reached similar conclusions—despite the tremendous wealth generated by the U.S. economy, the wealth does not reach working families nor those most in need who, thanks to neoliberal policies, have been left without an economic safety net.

Due to a series of inter-linked developments in the 1980s, a paradigm shift rendered inequality, and especially social class, invisible. Research in education reflected this shift, with classroom practice and issues of race, ethnicity, and gender replacing class and inequality—the so-called *death of class*. However, in the midst of stagnant wages, decline in job quality, and unbalanced growth, a return to inequality and class is most timely. In this era of growing inequality—with a drop in real wages, decline in job quality, and unbalanced growth—a reexamination of the popular contention that schools are the miracle panacea capable of solving all our social ills is sorely needed. But to carry this out requires, more than ever, a critical understanding and engagement with the politics of social class and its relationship to the reproduction of inequality within schools and the larger society.

The articles in this section offer, through their diverse interpretive analysis, perspectives of how an unleashed predatory market, driven by global capitalism, shapes the everyday life and culture of schools. For the moment, it should be emphasized that in none of the essays, which follow, is it simply asserted that education does not matter. A major theoretical and conceptual underpinning of the articles is that school-based solutions alone are unlikely to improve the school performance, unless material inequalities are tackled as part of a wider set of public social policies. Thus, America's most distinctive features—inequality and class—matter, in and out of schools. Moreover, the authors examine in broad strokes the different ways in which class and inequality are implicated in the so-called crisis in education. As the reader will discover, these critical theorists use the category of class, or classes, and attach its significance and theoretical ambition in divergent ways; however, the salience of class and traditions of class analysis are embedded in their interrogation of schools.

Summary of Articles

In the first article, "Against Schooling: Education and Social Class," Stanley Aronowitz speaks to the false promise of education, which aims to teach students the world of work. He describes how the structure of schooling embodies and reflects the wider system of class relations. He masterfully debunks the gospel of school reformers—namely, the belief in "education and access." He concludes with a democratic program for the reconstruction of schooling, which includes such reforms as democratizing the curricula and creating spaces of intellectual endeavor, leaving behind the testing mania, and cutting school ties with corporate interests. Aronowitz is fully aware of the difficulty of such a project being successful and the possibility of being viewed as *utopian*. However, as critique, his analysis is essential and timely.

"Social Class and the Hidden Curriculum of Work" comprises an often-overlooked seminal work by the late Jean Anyon. The article stresses the significance of political economy in understanding the sociological underpinnings of schooling in capitalist society. Her methodology encompasses the importance of social class relations and the manner in which these shape school ideology and classroom experience. Anyon argues that the hidden curriculum has major implications for a critical pedagogical theory and practice of work in schools. The research presented here also provides an excellent example of theoretically driven ethnographic research in schools. Anyon also reminds us there is a deeper social meaning to issues and activities of the classroom setting.

Curry Malott's article, "Class Consciousness and Teacher Education: The Socialist Challenge and The Historical Context," speaks to the politics of teacher class-consciousness. Key to his discussion is an understanding of educators as members of the working class and how they are implicated in the process of class formation and capitalist accumulation. As such, he argues that the traditional classroom is designed not in the interest of students and teachers but rather in the interest of capital. In the process, Malott cites the differences and similarities of Karl Marx and Max Weber's concepts of class, concluding that unlike Weber, Marx's relational approach to class far better serves our understanding of the role of schools under capitalism.

The final article, "Confronting Class in the Classroom" by cultural critic bell hooks, utilizes class and class analysis to examine how class is enacted in the classroom. According to hooks, social class remains invisible in educational discourses. She launches a critique of faculty in higher education who legitimate the predatory market by their, conscious or unconscious, refusal to address social class and their tendency to silence working class voices in the classroom. In so doing, hooks highlights the manner in which educators render invisible class and economic inequality.

Questions for Reflection and Dialogue

1. What does "social class" mean? Why does class matter in and out of school?
2. How would you engage with issues of social class in higher education? In elementary school? In middle school? In high school? Describe differences and similarities in your approaches.
3. While all uses of the word "class" in social theory invoke, in one way or another, the problem of understanding systems of economic inequality, different uses of the word are embedded in very different theoretical agendas. How did the authors differ in their use of the concept of class?
4. List and evaluate the arguments for (a) an optimistic, and (b) a pessimistic view of the prospects of democratic renewal, as offered in Stanley Aronowitz's outline for school transformation.
5. In what ways does Jean Anyon engage questions of political economy and schooling?
6. How does Anyon define the hidden curriculum? How does Anyon's notion of hidden curriculum provide a deeper social meaning of classroom life?
7. What does Malott mean by a class-conscious educator? How does this consciousness link to wider contradictions within capitalist schooling?
8. In what ways does Malott contrast the similarities and differences of Weber and Marx's concepts of social class? Why is this significant to a transformative vision of the classroom and society?
9. Why does bell hooks insist that critical educators must create opportunities to engage questions of social class? In what ways can teachers create these spaces for critical engagement in their classrooms?

5

Against Schooling: Education and Social Class

Stanley Aronowitz

> The crisis in American education, on the one hand, announces the bankruptcy of progressive education and, on the other hand, presents a problem of immense difficulty because it has arisen under the conditions and in response to the demands of a mass society.
>
> Hannah Arendt, "Crisis in Education"

At the dawn of the new century no American institution is invested with a greater role to bring the young and their parents into the modernist regime than public schools. The common school is charged with the task of preparing children and youth for their dual responsibilities to the social order: citizenship and, more important, learning to labor. On the one hand, in the older curriculum on the road to citizenship in a democratic, secular society, schools are supposed to transmit the jewels of the Enlightenment, especially literature and science. On the other, students are to be prepared for the work world by means of a loose but definite stress on the redemptive value of work, the importance of family, and, of course, the imperative of love and loyalty to one's country. As to the Enlightenment's concept of citizenship, students are, at least putatively, encouraged to engage in independent, critical thinking.

But the socializing functions of schooling play to the opposite idea: children of the working and professional and middle classes are to be molded to the industrial and technological imperatives of contemporary society. Students learn science and mathematics not as a discourse of liberation from myth and religious superstition but as a series of algorithms, the mastery of which are presumed to improve the student's logical capacities, or with no aim other than fulfilling academic requirements. In most places the social studies do not emphasize the choices between authoritarian and democratic forms of social organization, or democratic values, particularly criticism and renewal, but offer instead bits of information that have little significance for the conduct of life. Perhaps the teaching and learning of world literature where some students are inspired by the power of the story to, in John Dewey's terms, "reconstruct" experience is a partial exception to the rule that for most students school is endured rather than experienced as a series of exciting explorations of self and society.[1]

In the wake of these awesome tasks, fiscal exigency and a changing mission have combined to leave public education in the United States in a chronic state of crisis. For some the main issue is whether schools are failing to transmit the general intellectual culture, even to the most able students. What is at stake in this critique is the fate of America as a global model of civilization, particularly the condition of its democratic institutions and the citizens who are, in the final analysis, responsible for maintaining them. Of course, we may contend that the "global model" is fulfilled by the relentless anti-intellectual bias of schools and by a ruthless regime of the virtual expulsion of the most rebellious students, especially by secondary schools. Hannah Arendt goes so far as to ask whether we "love the world" and our children enough to devise an educational system capable of transmitting to them the salient cultural traditions. Other critics complain that schools are failing to fulfill the promise of equal opportunity for good jobs for working-class students, whether black, Latino, or white. Schools unwittingly reinforce the class bias of schooling by ignoring its content. The two positions, with respect both to their goals and to their implied educational philosophies, may not necessarily be contradictory, but their simultaneous enunciation produces, with exceptions to be discussed below, considerable tension for the American workplace, which has virtually no room for dissent. Individual or collective initiative is not sanctioned by management. The corporate factory, which includes sites of goods and symbolic production alike, is perhaps the nation's most authoritarian institution. But any reasonable concept of democratic citizenship requires an individual who is able to discern knowledge from propaganda, is competent to choose among conflicting claims and programs, and is capable of actively participating in the affairs of the polity. Yet the political system offers few opportunities, beyond the ritual of voting, for active citizen participation.[2]

Even identifying the problem of why and how schools fail has proven to be controversial. For those who define mass education as a form of training for the contemporary workplace, the problem can be traced to the crisis of authority, particularly school authority. That some of the same educational analysts favor a curriculum that stresses critical thinking for a small number of students in a restricted number of sites is consistent with the dominant trends of schooling since the turn of the twenty-first century. In the quest to restore authority, conservative educational policy has forcefully caused schools to abandon, both rhetorically and practically, the so-called child-centered curriculum and pedagogy in favor of measures that not only hold students accountable for passing standardized tests and for a definite quantity of school knowledge—on penalty of being left back from promotion or expelled—but also impose performance-based criteria on administrators and teachers. For example, in New York City the schools chancellor has issued "report cards" to principals and has threatened to fire those whose schools do not meet standards established by high-stakes tests. These tests are the antithesis of critical thought. Their precise object is to evaluate the student's ability to imbibe and regurgitate information and to solve problems according to prescribed algorithms.

On the other side, the progressives—who misread John Dewey's educational philosophy to mean that the past need not be studied too seriously—have offered little resistance to the gradual vocationalizing and dumbing down of the mass education curriculum. In fact, historically they were advocates of making the curriculum less formal, reducing requirements, and, on the basis of a degraded argument that children learn best by "doing," promoting practical, work-oriented programs for high-school students. Curricular deformalization was often justified on interdisciplinary criteria, which resulted in watering down course content and de-emphasizing writing. Most American high-school students, in the affluent as well as the "inner-city" districts, may write short papers that amount to book reviews and autobiographical essays, but most graduate without ever having to perform research and write a paper of considerable length. Moreover, since the late 1960s, in an attempt to make the study of history more "relevant" to students' lives, students have not been required to memorize dates; they may learn the narratives but are often unable to place them in a specific chronological context. Similarly, economics has been eliminated in many schools or is taught as a "unit" of a general social studies course. And if philosophy is taught at all, it is construed in terms of "values clarification," a kind of ethics in which students are assisted to discover and examine their own values.

That after more than a century of universal schooling the relationship between education and class has once more been thrust to the forefront is just one more signal of the crisis in American education. The educational Left, never strong on promoting intellectual knowledge as a substantive demand, clings to one of the crucial precepts of progressive educational philosophy: under the sign of egalitarianism, the idea that class deficits can be overcome by equalizing access to school opportunities without questioning what those opportunities have to do with genuine education. The access question has dominated higher education debates since the early 1970s; even conservatives who favor vouchers and other forms of public funding for private and parochial schools have justified privatizing instruction on access grounds.

The structure of schooling already embodies the class system of society, and, for this reason, the access debate misfires. To gain entrance into schools always entails placement into that system. "Equality of Opportunity" for class mobility is the system's tacit recognition that inequality is normative. In the system of mass education, schools are no longer constituted to transmit the Enlightenment intellectual traditions or the fundamental prerequisites of participatory citizenship, even for a substantial minority. While the acquisition of credentials conferred by schools remains an important prerequisite for many occupations, the conflation of schooling with education is mistaken. Schooling is surely a source of training both by its disciplinary regime and by its credentialing system. But schools do not transmit a "love for the world" or "for our children," as Arendt suggests; contrary to their democratic pretensions, they teach conformity to the social, cultural, and occupational hierarchy. In our contemporary world they are not constituted to foster independent thought, let alone encourage independent action. School knowledge is not the only source of education for students, perhaps not even the most important source. Young people learn, for ill as well as good, from popular culture (especially music), from parents, and, perhaps most important, from their peers. Schools are the stand-in for "society," the aggregation of individuals who, by contract or by coercion, are subject to governing authorities in return for which they may be admitted into the world albeit on the basis of different degrees of reward. To the extent that popular culture, parents, and peers signify solidarity and embody common dreams, they are the worlds of quasi communities that exert more influence on their members.

Access to What?

In the main, the critique of education has been directed to the question of access and its entailments, particularly the idea that greater access presumably opens up the gates to higher learning or to better jobs. Generally speaking, critical education analysis focuses on the degree to which schools are willing and able to open their doors to working-class students, coded in many cities as "black, Asian, and Latino" students, because through the mechanisms of differential access, schools are viewed as, perhaps, the principal reproductive institutions of economically and technologically advanced capitalist societies. With some exceptions, most critics of schooling have paid scant attention to school authority, the conditions for the accumulation of social capital—the intricate network of personal relations that articulate with occupational access—and to cultural capital, the accumulation of the signs, if not the substance, of the kinds of knowledge that are markers of distinction.[3]

The progressives assume that the heart of the class question is whether schooling provides working-class kids equality of opportunity to acquire legitimate knowledge and marketable academic credentials. They have adduced overwhelming evidence that contradicts schooling's reigning doctrine: that despite class, race, or gender hierarchies in the economic and political system, public education provides every individual with the tools to overcome conditions of birth. In reality only about a quarter of people of working-class origin attain professional, technical, and managerial careers through the credentialing system. Many more obtain general diplomas, but as the saying goes, a high-school diploma and $2 gets you a ride on the New York subway. The professional and technical credential implies that students have mastered specialized knowledge and acquired a set of skills associated with the speciality. They find occupational niches, but not at the top of their respective domains. Typically graduating from third-tier, nonresearch colleges and universities, they have not acquired knowledge connected with substantial intellectual work: theory, extensive writing, and independent research. Students leaving these institutions find jobs as line supervisors, computer technicians, teachers, nurses, social workers, and other niches in the social service professions.

A small number may join their better-educated colleagues in getting no-collar jobs, where "no collar"—Andrew Ross's term—designates occupations that afford considerable work autonomy, such as computer design, which, although salaried, cannot be comfortably folded into the conventional division of manual and intellectual labor. That so-called social mobility was a product of the specific conditions of American economic development at a particular time—the first quarter of the twentieth century—and was due, principally, to the absence of an indigenous peasantry during the country's industrial revolution and the forced confinement of millions of blacks to southern agricultural lands, which is conveniently forgotten or ignored by consensus opinion. Nor were the labor shortages provoked by World War II and the subsequent U.S. dominance of world capitalism until 1973 taken into account by the celebrants of mobility. Economic stagnation has afflicted the U.S. economy for more than three decades, and, despite the high-tech bubble of the 1990s, its position has deteriorated in the world market. Yet the mythology of mobility retains a powerful grip on the popular mind. That schooling makes credentials available to anyone regardless of rank or status forms one of the sturdy pillars of American ideology.[4]

In recent years the constitutional and legal assignment to the states and local communities of responsibility for public education has been undermined by what has been termed the "standards" movement that is today the prevailing national educational policy, enforced not so much by federal law—notwithstanding the Bush administration's No Child Left Behind program—as by political and ideological coercion. At the state and district levels the invocation to "tough love" has attained widespread support. We are witnessing the abrogation, both in practice and in rhetoric, of the tradition of social promotion whereby students moved through the system without acquiring academic skills. Having proven unable to provide to most working-class kids the necessary educational experiences that qualify them for academic promotion, the standards movement, more than a decade after its installation, reveals its underlying content: it is the latest means of exclusion, whose success depends on placing the onus for failure to achieve academic credentials on the individual rather than the system. Although state departments of education frequently mandate the teaching of certain subjects and have established standards based on high-stakes tests applicable to all districts, everyone knows that districts with working-class majorities provide neither a curriculum and pedagogy, nor facilities that meet these standards, because, among other problems, they are chronically underfunded. The state aid formulas that, since the advent of conservative policy hegemony, reward those districts whose students perform well on high-stakes tests tend to be unequal. Performance-based aid policies mean that school districts where the affluent live get more than their share; they make up for state budget deficits by raising local property taxes and soliciting annual subventions from parents, measures not affordable by even the top layer of wage workers, or low-level salaried employees. The result is overcrowded classrooms, poor facilities, especially libraries, and underpaid, often poorly prepared teachers, an outcome of financially starved education schools in public universities.

Standards presuppose students' prior possession of cultural capital—an acquisition that almost invariably entails having been reared in a professional or otherwise upper-class family. That, in the main, even the most privileged elementary and secondary schools are ill equipped to compensate for home backgrounds in which reading and writing are virtually absent has become a matter of indifference for school authorities. In this era of social Darwinism, poor school performance is likely to be coded as genetic deficit rather than being ascribed to social policy. Of course, the idea that working-class kids, whatever their gender, race, or ethnic backgrounds, were selected by evolution or by God to perform material rather than immaterial labor is not new; this view is as old as class-divided societies. But in an epoch in which the chances of obtaining a good working-class job have sharply declined, most kids face dire consequences if they don't acquire the skills needed in the world of immaterial labor. Not only are 75 percent assigned to working-class jobs, but in the absence of a shrinking pool of unionized industrial jobs, which often pay more than some professions such as teaching and social work, they must accept low-paying service-sector employment, enter the informal economy, or join the ranks of the chronically unemployed.

The rise of higher education since World War II has been seen by many as a repudiation of academic elitism. Do not the booming higher education enrollments validate the propositions of social mobility and democratic education? Not at all. Rather than constituting a sign of rising qualifications and widening opportunity, burgeoning college and university enrollments signify changing economic and political trends. The scientific and technical nature of our production and service sectors increasingly requires qualified and credentialed workers (it would be a mistake to regard them as identical). Students who would have sought good factory jobs in the past now believe, with reason, they need credentials to qualify for a well-paying job. On the other hand, even as politicians and educators decry social promotion, and most high schools with working-class constituencies remain aging vats, mass higher education is, to a great extent, a holding pen: effectively masking unemployment and underemployment. This may account for its rapid expansion over the last thirty-five years of chronic economic stagnation, deindustrialization, and the proliferation of part-time and temporary jobs, largely in the low-paid service sectors. Consequently, working-class students are able, even encouraged, to enter universities and colleges at the bottom of the academic hierarchy—community colleges but also public four-year colleges—thus fulfilling the formal pledge of equal opportunity for class mobility even as most of these institutions suppress the intellectual content that would fulfill the mobility promise. But grade-point averages, which in the standards era depend as much as the Scholastic Aptitude Test on high-stakes testing, measure the acquired knowledge of students and restrict their access to elite institutions of higher learning, the obligatory training grounds for professional and managerial occupations. Since all credentials are not equal, graduating from third- and fourth-tier institutions does not confer on the successful candidate the prerequisites for entering a leading graduate school—the preparatory institution for professional and managerial occupations, or the most desirable entry-level service jobs that require only a bachelor's degree.

Pierre Bourdieu argues that schools reproduce class relations by reinforcing rather than reducing class-based differential access to social and cultural capital, key markers of class affiliation and mobility. Children of the wealthy, professionals, and the intelligentsia, he argues, always already possess these forms of capital. Far from making possible a rich intellectual education, or providing the chance to affiliate with networks of students and faculty who have handles on better jobs, schooling habituates working-class students, through mechanisms of discipline and punishment, to the bottom rungs of the work world or the academic world by subordinating or expelling them.[5] Poorly prepared for academic work by their primary and secondary schools, and having few alternatives to acquiring some kind of credential, many who stay the course and graduate from high school and third- and fourth-tier college inevitably confront a series of severely limited occupational choices—or none at all. Their life chances are just a cut above those who do not complete high school or college. Their school performances seem to validate what common sense has always suspected: given equal opportunity to attain school knowledge, the cream always rises to the top and those stuck at the bottom must be biologically impaired, victimized by the infamous "culture of poverty" or just plain distracted. That most working-class high-school and college students are obliged to hold full- or part-time jobs in order to stay in school fails to temper this judgment, for as is well known, preconceptions usually trump facts.[6] Nor does the fact that the children of the recent 20 million immigrants from Latin America, Russia, and especially Asia speak their native languages at home, in the neighborhood, and to each other in school evoke more than hand-wringing from educational leaders. In this era of tight school budgets, English as a Second Language funds have been cut or eliminated at every level of schooling.

But Paul Willis insists that working-class kids get working-class jobs by means of their refusal to accept the discipline entailed in curricular mastery and by their rebellion against school authority. Challenging the familiar "socialization" thesis—of which Bourdieu's is perhaps the most sophisticated version, according to which working-class kids "fail" because they are culturally deprived or, in the American critical version, are assaulted by the hidden curriculum and school pedagogy that subsumes kids under the prevailing order—Willis recodes kids' failure as refusal of [school] work, which lands them in the world of factory or low level service work. Willis offers no alternative educational model to schooling: his discovery functions as critique. Indeed, as Willis himself acknowledges, the school remains, in Louis Althusser's famous phrase, the main "ideological state apparatus," but working-class kids are not victims. Implicitly rejecting Richard Sennett and Jonathan Cobb's notion that school failure is a "hidden injury" of class insofar as working-class kids internalize poor school performance as a sign of personal deficit, he argues that most early school leavers are active agents in the production of their own class position. While students' antipathy to school authority is enacted at the site of the school, its origins are the working-class culture from which they spring. Workers do not like bosses, and kids do not like school bosses, the deans and principals, but often as well the teachers, whose main job in the urban centers is to keep order. The source of working-class kids' education is not the school but the shop floor, the places where their parents work, the home, and the neighborhood.[7]

In the past half-century the class question has been inflected by race and gender discrimination, and, in the American way, the "race, gender, class" phrase implies that these domains are ontologically distinct, if not entirely separate. Nor have critics theorized the race and gender question as a class issue, but as an attribute of bioidentities. In fact, in the era of identity politics, for many writers class itself stands alongside race and gender as just another identity. Having made the easy, inaccurate judgment that white students— regardless of their class or gender—stand in a qualitatively different relation to school- related opportunities than blacks, class is often suppressed as a sign of exclusion. In privileging issues of access, not only is the curriculum presupposed, in which case Bourdieu's insistence on the concept of cultural capital is ignored, but also the entire question is elided of whether schooling may be conflated with education. Only rarely do writers examine other forms of education. In both the Marxist and liberal traditions, schooling is presumed to remain—over a vast spectrum of spatial and temporal situations—the theater within which life chances are determined.

Education and Immaterial Labor

Education may be defined as the collective and individual reflection on the totality of life experiences: what we learn from peers, parents (and the socially situated cultures of which they are a part), media, and schools. By reflection I mean the transformation of experience into a multitude of concepts that constitute the abstractions we call "knowledge." Which of the forms of learning predominate are always configured historically. The exclusive focus by theorists and researchers on school knowledges—indeed, the implication that school is the principal site of what we mean by education—reflects the degree to which they have, themselves, internalized the equation of education with school knowledge and its preconditions. The key learning is they (we) have been habituated to a specific regime of intellectual labor that entails a high level of self-discipline, the acquisition of the skills of reading and writing, and the career expectations associated with professionalization.

To say this constitutes the self-reflection by intellectuals—in the broadest sense of the term—of their own relation to schooling. In the age of the decline of critical intelligence and the proliferation of technical intelligence, "intellectual" in its current connotation designates immaterial labor, not traditional intellectual pursuits such as literature, philosophy, and art. Immaterial labor describes those who work not with objects or the administration of things and people, but with ideas, symbols, and signs. Some of the occupations grouped under immaterial labor have an affective dimension. The work demands the complete subordination of brain, emotion, and body to the task while requiring the worker to exercise considerable judgment and imagination in its performance. For example, at sites such as "new economy" private-sector software workplaces; some law firms that deal with questions of intellectual property, public interest, or constitutional and international law; research universities and independent research institutes; and small, innovative design, architectural, and engineering firms, the informality of the labor process, close collaborative relationships among members of task-oriented teams, and the overflow of the space of the shop floor with the spaces of home and play evoke, at times, a high level of exhilaration, even giddiness, among members, and at other times utter exhaustion and burnout because the work invades the dreamwork and prohibits relaxation and genuine attention to partners and children.

To be an immaterial worker means, in the interest of having self-generated work, surrendering much of one's unfettered time. Such workers are obliged to sunder the conventional separation of work and leisure, to adopt the view that time devoted to creative, albeit commodified labor, is actually "free." Or, to be more exact, even play must be engaged in as serious business. For many the golf course, the bar, the weekend at the beach are workplaces, where dreams are shared, plans formulated, and deals are made. Just as time becomes unified around work, so work loses its geographic specificity. As Andrew Ross shows in his path-breaking ethnography of a New York new economy workplace during and after the dot-com boom, the headiness for the pioneers of this new work world was, tacitly, a function of the halcyon period of the computer software industry when everyone felt the sky was no longer the limit.[8] When the economic crunch descended on thousands of workplaces, people were laid off, and those who remained, as well as those who became unemployed, experienced a heavy dose of market reality.

It may be argued that among elite students and institutions, schooling not only prepares immaterial labor by transmitting a bundle of legitimate knowledges; the diligent, academically successful student internalizes the blur between the classroom, play, and home by spending a great deal of time in the library or ostensibly playing at the computer. Thus the price of the promise of autonomy, a situation intrinsic to professional ideology, if not always its practice in the context of bureaucratic and hierarchical corporate systems, is to accept work as a mode of life; one lives to work, rather than the reverse. The hopes and expectations of these strata are formed in the process of schooling; indeed, they have most completely assimilated the ideologies linked to school knowledge and to the credentials conferred by the system. Thus whether professional school people, educational researchers, or not, they tend to evaluate people by the criteria to which they, themselves, were subjected. If the child has not fully embraced work as life, he is consigned to the educational nether land. Even the egalitarians (better read *populists*) accept this regime: their object is to afford those for whom work is a necessary evil entry into the social world, where work is the mission.

The Labor and Radical Movements as Educational Sites

The working-class intellectual as a social type precedes and parallels the emergence of universal public education. At the dawn of the public-school movement in the 1830s, the antebellum labor movement, which consisted largely of literate skilled workers, favored six years of schooling in order to transmit to their children the basics of reading and writing, but opposed compulsory attendance in secondary schools. The reasons were bound up with their congenital suspicion of the state, which they believed never exhibited sympathy for the workers' cause. Although opposed to child labor, the early workers' movements were convinced that the substance of education—literature, history, philosophy—should be supplied by the movement itself. Consequently, in both the oral and the written tradition, workers' organizations often constituted an alternate university to that of public schools. The active program of many workers' and radical movements until World War II consisted largely in education through newspapers, literacy classes for immigrants where the reading materials were drawn from labor and socialist classics, and world literature. These were supplemented by lectures offered by independent scholars who toured the country in the employ of lecture organizations commissioned by the unions and radical organizations.[9]

But the shop floor was also a site of education. Skilled workers were usually literate in their own language and in English, and many were voracious readers and writers. Union and radical newspapers often ran poetry and stories written by workers. Socialist-led unions sponsored educational programs; in the era when the union contract was still a rarity, the union was not so much an agency of contract negotiation and enforcement as an educational, political, and social association. In his autobiography, Samuel Gompers, the founding American Federation of Labor president, remembers his fellow cigar makers hiring a "reader" in the 1870s, who sat at the center of the shop floor and read from literary and historical classics as well as more contemporary works of political and economic analysis such as the writings of Marx and Engels. Reading groups met in the back of a bar, in the union hall, or in the local affiliate of the socialist wing of the nationality federations. Often these groups were ostensibly devoted to preparing immigrants to pass the obligatory language test for citizenship status. But the content of the reading was, in addition to labor and socialist newspapers and magazines, often supplemented by works of fiction by Shakespeare, the great nineteenth-century novelists and poets, and Karl Kautsky. In its anarchist inflection, Peter Kropotkin, Moses Hess, and Michael Bakunin were the required texts.[10]

In New York, Chicago, San Francisco, and other large cities where the Socialist, Anarchist, and Communist movements had considerable membership and a fairly substantial periphery of sympathizers, the parties established adult schools that not only offered courses pertaining to political and ideological knowledge but were vehicles for many working- and middle-class students to gain a general education. Among them, in New York, the socialist-oriented Rand School and the Communist-sponsored Jefferson School (formerly the Workers' School) lasted until the mid-1950s when, because of the decline of a Left intellectual culture among workers as much as the contemporary repressive political environment, they closed. But in their heydays, from the 1920s to the late 1940s, for tens of thousands of working-class people—many of them high-school students and industrial workers—these schools were alternate universities. Many courses concerned history, literature, and philosophy, and, at least at the Jefferson School, students could study art, drama, and music, as could their children. The tradition was revived, briefly, by the 1960s New Left that, in similar sites, sponsored free universities where the term *free* designated not an absence of tuition fees but an ideological and intellectual freedom from either the traditional Left parties or the conventional school system. I participated in organizing New York's Free University and two of its successors. While not affiliated with the labor movement or socialist parties, it successfully attracted more than a thousand mostly young students in each of its semesters and offered a broad range of courses taught by people of divergent intellectual and political orientations, including some free-market libertarians attracted to the school's nonsectarianism.[11]

When I worked in a steel mill in the late 1950s, some of us formed a group that read current literature, labor history, and economics. I discussed books and magazine articles with some of my fellow workers in bars as well as on breaks. Tony Mazzocchi, who was at the same time a worker and union officer of a Long Island local of the Oil, Chemical and Atomic Workers Union, organized a similar group, and I knew of several other cases in which young workers did the same. Some of these groups evolved into rank-and-file caucuses that eventually contested the leadership of their local unions; others were mainly for the self-edification of the participants and had no particular political goals.

But beyond formal programs, the working-class intellectual, although by no means visible in the United States, has been part of shop-floor culture since the industrializing era. In almost every workplace there is a person or persons to whom other workers turn for information about the law, the union contract, contemporary politics, or, equally important, as a source of general education. These individuals may or may not have been schooled, but, until the late 1950s, they rarely had any college education. For schools were not the primary source of their knowledge. They were, and are, largely self-educated. In my own case, having left Brooklyn College after less than a year, I worked in various industrial production jobs. When I worked the midnight shift, I got off at 8:00 a.m., ate breakfast, and spent four hours in the library before going home. Mostly I read American and European history and political economy, particularly the physiocrats, Adam Smith, David Ricardo, John Maynard Keynes, and Joseph Schumpeter. Marx's *Capital* I read in high school, and owned the three volumes.

My friend Russell Rommele, who worked in a nearby mill, was also an autodidact. His father was a first-generation German American brewery worker, with no particular literary interests. But Russell had read a wide range of historical and philosophical works as a high-school student at Saint Benedict's Prep, a Jesuit institution. The priests singled out Russell for the priesthood and mentored him in theology and social theory. The experience radicalized him, and he decided not to answer the call but to enter the industrial working class instead. Like me, he was active in the union and Newark Democratic Party politics. Working as an educator with a local union in the auto industry recently, I have met several active unionists who are intellectuals. The major difference between them and those of my generation is that they are college graduates, although none of them claim to have acquired their love of learning or their analytic perspective from schools. One is a former member of a radical organization; another learned his politics from participation in a shop-based study of a group/union caucus. In both instances, with the demise of their organizational affiliations, they remain habituated to reading, writing, and union activity.

Beneath the radar screen, union–university collaborations sprang up in the 1980s. I was among those who founded the Center for Worker Education at City College. It is a bachelor's degree program, begun for union members and their families, but expanded to other working people as well. Worker education meant, in this case, that the emphasis is not on labor studies in the manner of Cornell, UCLA, University of Minnesota's schools of industrial and labor relations, or the Queens College Labor Resource Center. Instead, City College's center offers a liberal arts and professional curriculum as well as a few courses in labor history. While the educational content is often critical, the intention articulates with the recent focus on credentialism of undergraduate institutions. Similar programs have been in operation for two decades in a collaboration between the large New York municipal employees' District Council 37 and the College of New Rochelle, and the Hospital Workers Union's various arrangements with New York-area colleges that offer upgrading, training, and college courses to thousands of its members.

Parents, Neighborhood, Class, Culture

John Locke observes that, consistent with his rejection of innate ideas, even if conceptions of good and evil are present in divine or civil law, morality is constituted by reference to our parents, relatives, and especially the "club" of peers to which we belong:

> He who imagines commendation and disgrace not to be strong motives to men to accommodate themselves to the opinions and rules of those with whom they converse seems little skilled in the nature or the history of mankind: the greatest part whereof we shall find govern themselves, chiefly, if not solely by this law of *fashion* [emphasis in the original]; and so they do what keeps them in reputation with their company, [with] little regard for the laws of God or the magistrate.[12]

William James puts the matter equally succinctly:

> A man's social self is the recognition which he gets from his mates. We are not only gregarious animals, liking to be in the sight of our fellows, but we have an innate propensity to get ourselves noticed, and noticed favorably, by our kind. No more fiendish punishment could be devised, were such a thing physically possible, than that he should be turned loose in society and remain absolutely unnoticed by all the members thereof.[13]

That the social worlds of peers and family are the chief referents for the formation of the social self, neither philosopher doubted. Each in his own fashion situates the individual in social context, which provides a "common measure of virtue and vice" (Locke) even as they acknowledge the ultimate choice resides with the individual self. These, and not the institutions, even those that have the force of law, are the primary sources of authority.

Hannah Arendt argues that education "by its very nature cannot forego either authority or tradition." Nor can it base itself on the presumption that children share an autonomous existence from adults.[14] Yet schooling ignores the reality of the society of kids at the cost of undermining its own authority. The society of kids is in virtually all classes an alternative and oppositional site of knowledge and of moral valuation. We have already seen how working-class kids get working-class jobs by means of their rebellion against school authority. Since refusal and resistance is a hallmark of that moral order, the few who will not obey the invocation to fail, or to perform indifferently in school, often find themselves marginalized or expelled from the society of kids. While they adopt a rationality that can be justified on eminently practical grounds, the long tradition of rejection of academic culture has proven hard to break, even in the wake of evidence that those working-class jobs to which they were oriented no longer exist. For what is at stake in the resistance of adolescents is their perception that the blandishments of the adult world are vastly inferior to the pleasures of their own. In the first place, the new service economy offers few inducements: wages are low, the job is boring, and the future bleak. And since the schools now openly present themselves as a link in the general system of control, it may appear to some students that cooperation is a form of self-deception.

If not invariably, then in many households parents provide to the young a wealth of knowledges: the family mythologies that feature an uncle or aunt, a grandparent or an absent parent. These are the stories, loosely based on some actual event(s) in which family members have distinguished themselves in various ways that (usually) illustrate a moral virtue or defect, the telling of which constitutes a kind of didactic message. Even when not attached to an overt narrative, parable, or myth, the actions of our parents offer many lessons: How do they deal with adversity? How do they address ordinary, everyday problems? What do they learn from their own trials and tribulations and what do they say to us? What are our parents' attitudes toward money, joblessness, and everyday life disruptions such as sudden, acute illness or accidents? What do they learn from the endless conflicts with their parent(s) over issues of sex, money, and household responsibilities?

The relative weight of parental to peer authority is an empirical question that cannot be decided in advance; what both have in common is their location in everyday life. Parents are likely to be more susceptible to the authority of law and of its magistrates and, in a world of increasing uncertainty, will worry that if their children choose badly, they may be left behind. But the associations with our peers we make in everyday life provide the recognition that we crave, define what is worthy of praise or blame, and confer approbation or disapproval on our decisions. But having made a choice that runs counter to that of "their company" or club, individuals must form or join a new "company" to confer the judgment of virtue on their actions. This company must, of necessity, consist of "peers," the definition of which has proven fungible.

Religion, the law, and, among kids, school authorities face the obstacles erected by the powerful rewards and punishments meted out by the "clubs" to which people are affiliated. At a historical conjunction when—beneath the relentless pressure imposed by capital to transform all labor into wage labor, thereby forcing every adult into the paid labor force—the society of kids increasingly occupies the space of civil society. The neighborhood, once dominated by women and small shopkeepers, has all but disappeared save for the presence of children and youth. As parents toil for endless hours to pay the ever-mounting debts incurred by home ownership, perpetual car and appliance payments, and the costs of health care, kids are increasingly on their own, and this lack of supervision affects their conceptions of education and life.

Some recent studies and teacher observations have discovered a considerable reluctance among black students in elite universities to perform well in school, even among those with professional or managerial family backgrounds. Many seem indifferent to arguments that show that school performance is a central prerequisite to better jobs and higher status in the larger work world. Among the more acute speculations is the conclusion that black students' resistance reflects an anti-intellectual bias and a hesitation, if not refusal, to enter the mainstream corporate world. There are similar attitudes among some relatively affluent white students as well. Although by no means a majority, some students are less enamored by the work world to which they, presumably, have been habituated by school, and especially by the prospect of perpetual work. In the third-tier universities, state and private alike, many students, apparently forced by their parents to enroll, wonder out loud why they are there. Skepticism about schooling still abounds even as they graduate from high school and enroll in postsecondary schools in record numbers. According to one colleague of mine who teaches in a third-tier private university in the New York metropolitan area, many of these mostly suburban students "sleepwalk" through their classes, do not participate in class discussions, and are lucky to get a C grade.[15]

In the working-class neighborhoods—white, black, and Latino—the word is out: given the absence of viable alternatives, you must try to obtain that degree, but this defines the limit of loyalty to the enterprise. Based on testimonies of high-school and community-college teachers, for every student who takes school knowledge seriously there are twenty or more who are timeservers. Most are ill prepared for academic work, and, since the community colleges, four-year state colleges, and "teaching" universities simply lack the resources to provide the means by which such students can improve their school performance, beyond the credential there is little motivation among them to try to get an education.

In some instances, those who break from their club and enter the regime of school knowledge risk being drummed out of a lifetime of relationships with their peers. What has euphemistically been described as "peer pressure" bears, among other moral structures, on the degree to which kids are permitted to cross over the line into the precincts of adult authority. While success in school is not equivalent to squealing on a friend to the cops, or transgressing some sacred moral code of the society of kids, it comes close to committing an act of betrayal. This is comprehensible only if the reader is willing to suspend the prejudice that schooling is tantamount to education and is an unqualified "good," as compared to the presumed evil of school failure, or the decision of the slacker to rebel by refusing to succeed.

To invoke the concept of "class" in either educational debates or any other politically charged discourse generally refers to the white working class. Educational theory and practice treats blacks and Latinos, regardless of their economic positions, as unified categories. That black kids from professional, managerial, and business backgrounds share as much or more with their white counterparts than with working-class blacks is generally ignored by most educational writers, just as in race discourse whites are an undifferentiated racial identity, which refers in slightly different registers to people of African origin and those who migrated from Latin countries of South America and the Caribbean, and are treated as a unified category. The narrowing of the concept of class limits our ability to discern class at all. I want to suggest that, although we must stipulate ethnic, gender, race, and occupational distinction among differentiated strata of wage labor—with the exception of children of salaried professional and technical groups, where the culture of schooling plays a decisive role—class education transcends these distinctions. No doubt there are gradations among the strata that comprise this social formation, but the most privileged professional strata (physicians, attorneys, scientists, professors) and the high-level managers are self-reproducing, not principally through schooling but through social networks. These include private schools, some of which are residential; clubs and associations; and, in suburban public schools, the self-selection of students on the basis of distinctions. Show me a school friendship between the son or daughter of a corporate manager and the child of a janitor or factory worker, and I will show you an anomaly.

Schooling selects a fairly small number of children of the class of wage labor for genuine class mobility. In the first half of the twentieth century, having lost its appeal among middle-class youth, the Catholic Church turned to working-class students as a source of cadre recruitment. In my neighborhood of the East Bronx two close childhood friends, both of Italian background, entered the priesthood. For these sons of construction workers, the Church provided their best chance to escape the hardships and economic uncertainties of manual labor. Another kid became a pharmacist because the local college, Fordham University, offered scholarships. A fourth was among the tiny coterie of students who passed the test for one of the city's special schools, Bronx Science, and became a science teacher. Otherwise, almost everybody else remained a worker or, like my best friend, Kenny, went to prison.

Despite the well-publicized claim that anyone can escape their condition of social and economic birth—a claim reproduced by schools and by the media with numbing regularity—most working-class students, many of whom have some college credits but often do not graduate—end up in low- and middle-level service jobs that do not pay a decent working-class wage. Owing to the steep decline of unionized industrial production jobs, those who enter factories increasingly draw wages substantially below union standards. Those who do graduate find work in computers, although rarely at the professional levels. The relatively low paid become K-12 school teachers and health care professionals, mostly nurses and technicians, or enter the social services field as caseworkers, medical social workers, or nonsupervisory social welfare workers. The question I want to pose is whether these "professional" occupations represent genuine mobility.

During the postwar economic boom that made possible a significant expansion of spending for schools, the social services, and administration of public goods, the public sector workplace became a favored site of black and Latino recruitment, mainly for clerical, maintenance, and entry-level patient care jobs in hospitals and other health care facilities. Within several decades a good number advanced to practical and registered nursing, but not in all sections of the country. As unionization spread to the nonprofit private sector as well as public employment in the 1960s and 1970s, these jobs paid enough to enable many to enjoy what became known as a middle-class living standard, with a measure of job security offered by union security and civil service status. While it is true that "job security" has often been observed in its breach, the traditional deal made by teachers, nurses, and social workers was that they traded higher incomes for job security. But after about 1960, spurred by the resurgent civil rights movement, these "second-level" professionals—white and black—began to see themselves as workers more than professionals: they formed unions, struck for higher pay and shorter hours, and assumed a very unprofessional adversarial stance toward institutional authority. Contracts stipulated higher salaries, definite hours—a sharp departure from professional ideology—and seniority as a basis for layoffs, like any industrial contract, and demanded substantial vacation and sick leave.

Their assertion of working-class values and social position may have been strategic; indeed, it inspired the largest wave of union organizing since the 1930s. But, together with the entrance of huge numbers of women and blacks into the public and quasi-public sector workforces, it was also a symptom of the proletarianization of the second-tier professions. Several decades later, salaried physicians made a similar discovery; they formed unions and struck against high malpractice insurance costs as much as the onerous conditions imposed on their autonomy by health maintenance organizations and government authorities bent on cost containment, often at the physicians' expense. More to the point, the steep rise of public employees' salaries and benefits posed the question of how to maintain services in times of fiscal austerity, which might be due to economic downturn or to probusiness tax policies. The answer has been that the political and public officials told employees that the temporary respite from the classical trade union trade-off was over. All public employees have suffered a relative deterioration in their salaries and benefits. Since the mid-1970s fiscal crises, begun in New York City, they have experienced layoffs for the first time since the Depression. And their unions have been in a concessionary bargaining mode for decades. In the politically and ideologically repressive environment of the last twenty-five years, the class divide has sharpened. Ironically, in the wake of the attacks by legislatures and business against their hard-won gains in the early 1980s, the teachers unions abandoned their militant class posture and reverted to professionalism and a center-right political strategy.

In truth, schools are learning sites, even if only for a handful, of intellectual knowledge. For the most part, they transmit the instrumental logic of credentialism, together with their transformation from institutions of discipline to those of control, especially in working-class districts. Even talented, dedicated teachers have difficulty reaching kids and convincing them that the life of the mind may hold unexpected rewards, though the career implications of critical thought are not apparent. The breakdown of the mission of public schools has produced varied forms of disaffection; if school violence has abated in some places, that does not signify the decline of gangs and other "clubs" that represent the autonomous world of youth. The society of kids is more autonomous because, in contrast to the 1960s, official authorities no longer offer hope; instead, in concert with the doctrine of control, they threaten punishment that includes, but is not necessarily associated with, incarceration. The large number of drug busts of young black and Latino men should not be minimized. With over a million blacks, more than 3 percent of the African American population—most of them young (25 percent of young black men)—within the purview of the criminal justice system, the law may be viewed as a more or less concerted effort to counter by force the power of peers. This may be regarded in the context of the failure of schools. Of course, more than three hundred years ago John Locke knew the limits of the magistrates—indeed, of any adult authority—to overcome the power of the society of kids.[16]

Conclusion

What are the requisite changes that would transform schools from credential mills and institutions of control to sites of education that prepare young people to see themselves as active participants in the world? As my analysis implies, the fundamental condition is to abolish high-stakes tests that dominate the curriculum and subordinate teachers to the role of drillmasters and subject students to stringent controls. By this proposal I do not mean to eliminate the need for evaluative tools. The essay is a fine measure of both writing ability and of the student's grasp of literature, social science, and history. While mathematics, science, and language proficiency do require considerable rote learning, the current curriculum and pedagogy in these fields includes neither a historical account of the changes in scientific and mathematical theory nor a metaconceptual explanation of what the disciplines are about. Nor are courses in language at the secondary level ever concerned with etymological issues, comparative cultural study of semantic differences, and other topics that might relieve the boredom of rote learning by providing depth of understanding. The broader understanding of science in the modern world—its relation to technology, war, and medicine, for example—should surely be integrated into the curriculum; some of these issues appear in the textbooks, but teachers rarely discuss them because they are busy preparing students for the high-stakes tests in which knowledge of the social contexts for science, language, and mathematics is not included.

I agree with Hannah Arendt that education "cannot forgo either authority or tradition." But authority must be earned rather than assumed, and the transmission of tradition needs to be critical rather than worshipful. If teachers were allowed to acknowledge student skepticism to incorporate kids' knowledge into the curriculum by making what they know the object of rigorous study, especially popular music and television, teachers might be treated with greater respect. But there is no point denying the canon; one of the more egregious conditions of subordination is the failure of schools to expose students to the best exemplars, for people who have no cultural capital are thereby condemned to social and political marginality, let alone deprived of some of the genuine pleasures to be derived from encounters with genuine works of art. When the New York City Board of Education (now the Department of Education) mandates that during every semester high-school English classes read a Shakespeare play, and one or two works of nineteenth-century English literature, but afford little or no access to the best Russian novels of the nineteenth century, no opportunities to examine some of the most influential works of Western or Eastern philosophy, and provide no social and historical context for what is learned, tradition is observed in the breach more than in its practice.

Finally, schools should cut their ties to corporate interests and reconstruct the curriculum along the lines of genuine intellectual endeavor. Nor should schools be seen as career conduits, although this function will be difficult to displace: in an era of high economic anxiety, many kids and their parents worry about the future and seek some practical purchase on it. It will take some convincing that their best leg up is to be educated. It is unlikely in the present environment, but possible in some places.

One could elaborate these options; this is only an outline. In order to come close to their fulfillment at least three things are needed. First, we require a conversation concerning the nature and scope of education and the limits of schooling as an educational site. Along with this, theorists and researchers need to link their knowledge of popular culture, culture in the anthropological sense—that is, everyday life—with the politics of education. Teachers who, by their own education, are intellectuals who respect and want to help children obtain a genuine education regardless of their social class are in the forefront of enabling social change and are entrusted with widening students' possibilities in life. For this we need a new regime of teacher education founded on the idea that the educator must be educated well. It would surely entail abolishing the current curricula of most education schools, if not the schools themselves. Teacher training should be embedded in general education, not in "methods," many of which are useless; instruction should include knowledge other than credential and bring the union/movement/organic intellectuals into the classroom. In other words, the classroom should be a window on the world, not a hermetically sealed regime of the imposition of habitus, that is, making the test of academic success equivalent to measuring the degree to which the student has been inculcated with the habit of subordination to school and pedagogic authority.[17] And we need a movement of parents, students, teachers, and labor armed with a political program to force legislatures to adequately fund schooling at the federal, state, and local levels, and boards of education to deauthorize high-stakes tests that currently drive the curriculum and pedagogy.

To outline a program for the reconstruction of schooling does not imply that the chances for its success are good, especially in the current environment. Indeed, almost all current trends oppose the concept of public education as a school of freedom. But if the principle of critique is hope rather than the most rigorous form of nihilism—the suspension of action pending an upsurge from below—we have an obligation to resist but also to suggest alternatives. These will, inevitably, be attacked as Utopian, and, of course, they are. But as many have argued, Utopian thought is the condition for change. Without the "impossible," there is little chance for reform.

Notes

1. John Dewey, *Democracy and Education: An Introduction to the Philosophy of Education* (1916; Glencoe, Ill.: Free Press, 1964).
2. The literature on the limits of democracy in America is vast. For a searing indictment, see the classic critique: Grant McConnell, *Private Power and American Democracy* (New York: Knopf, 1966).
3. Pierre Bourdieu's concepts of cultural and social capital are introduced in Pierre Bourdieu and Jean-Claude Passeron, *Reproduction in Education, Culture, and Society*, trans. Richard Nice (London: Sage, 1977).
4. Andrew Ross, *No-Collar: The Humane Workplace and Its Hidden Costs* (New York: Basic Books, 2003).
5. Bourdieu, *Reproduction*.
6. Aaron V. Cicourel and John I. Kitsuse, *The Educational Decision-Makers* (Indianapolis, Ind.: Bobbs Merrill, 1963). This is one of the most persuasive studies demonstrating the salience of phenomenological investigations of social life. It is a tacit repudiation of the reliance of much of social science, especially sociology and political science, on what people say rather than what they do.
7. The best analysis of the relation of schools to the lives of working-class kids remains Paul Willis, *Learning to Labor: How Working Class Kids Get Working Class Jobs* (New York: Columbia University Press, 1981).
8. Ross, *No-Collar*.
9. Paul C. Mishler, *Raising Reds: The Young Pioneers, Radical Summer Camps, and Communist Political Culture in the United States* (New York: Columbia University Press, 1999).

10. Samuel Gompers, *Seventy Years of Life and Labor: An Autobiography* (New York: E.P. Button, 1925).
11. Marvin Gettleman, "No Varsity Teams: New York's Jefferson School of Social Science, 1943–1956," *Science and Society* (fall 2002), 336–59. My reflections on the Free University and other New Left educational projects may be found in Aronowitz, "When the New Left Was New," in *The Sixties without Apology*, ed. Sohnya Sayres, Anders Stephanson, Stanley Aronowitz, and Fredric Jameson (Minneapolis: University of Minnesota Press, 1984).
12. John Locke, *An Essay concerning Human Understanding* (New York: Dover, 1958), bk. 1, chap. 28, 478.
13. William James, *The Principles of Psychology* (New York: Dover, 1955), 1, 293.
14. Hannah Arendt, "Crisis in Education," *Between Past and Future* (New York: Harcourt, Brace and World, 1961).
15. James H. McWhorter, *Losing the Race: Self-Sabotage in Black America* (New York: Free Press, 2000).
16. Stanley Aronowitz, *False Promises: The Shaping of American Working Class Consciousness*, 2d ed. (Durham, N.C.: Duke University Press, 1992); Henry A. Giroux, *The Abandoned Generation: Democracy beyond the Culture of Fear* (New York: Palgrave, 2003); Stephanie Urso Spina, ed., *Smoke and Mirrors: The Hidden Context of Violence in Schools and Society* (Boulder, Colo.: Rowman and Littlefield, 2001).
17. Bourdieu, *Reproduction.*

6

Social Class and the Hidden Curriculum of Work

Jean Anyon

Scholars in political economy and the sociology of knowledge have recently argued that public schools in complex industrial societies like our own make available different types of educational experience and curriculum knowledge to students in different social classes. Bowles and Gintis (1976), for example, have argued that students from different social class backgrounds are rewarded for classroom behaviors that correspond to personality traits allegedly rewarded in the different occupational strata—the working classes for docility and obedience, the managerial classes for initiative and personal assertiveness. Basil Bernstein (1977), Pierre Bourdieu (Bourdieu and Passeron 1977), and Michael W. Apple (1979), focusing on school knowledge, have argued that knowledge and skills leading to social power and reward (e.g., medical, legal, managerial) are made available to the advantaged social groups but are withheld from the working classes, to whom a more "practical" curriculum is offered (e.g., manual skills, clerical knowledge). While there has been considerable argumentation of these points regarding education in England, France, and North America, there has been little or no attempt to investigate these ideas empirically in elementary or secondary schools and classrooms in this country.[1]

This article offers tentative empirical support (and qualification) of the above arguments by providing illustrative examples of differences in student *work* in classrooms in contrasting social class communities. The examples were gathered as part of an ethnographical study of curricular, pedagogical and pupil evaluation practices in five elementary schools.* The article attempts a theoretical contribution as well, and assesses student work in the light of a theoretical approach to social class analysis. The organization is as follows: the methodology of the ethnographical study is briefly described; a theoretical approach to the definition of social class is offered; income and other characteristics of the parents in each school are provided, and examples from the study that illustrate work tasks and interaction in each school are presented; then the concepts used to define social class are applied to the examples in order to assess the theoretical meaning of classroom events. It will be suggested that there is a "hidden curriculum" in school work that has profound implication for the theory—and consequence—of everyday activity in education.

Methodology

The methods used to gather data were classroom observation; interviews of students, teachers, principals, and district administrative staff; and assessment of curriculum and other materials in each classroom and school. All classroom events to be discussed here involve the fifth grade in each school. All schools but one departmentalize at the fifth grade level. Except for that school where only one fifth grade teacher could be observed, all the fifth grade teachers (that is, two or three) were observed as the children moved from subject to subject. In all schools the art, music, and gym teachers were also observed and interviewed. All teachers in the study were described as "good" or "excellent" by their principals. All except one new teacher had taught for more than four years. The fifth grade in each school was observed by the investigator for ten three-hour periods between September 15, 1978 and June 20, 1979.

Before providing the occupations, incomes, and other relevant social characteristics of the parents of the children in each school, I will offer a theoretical approach to defining social class.

Social Class

One's occupation and income level contribute significantly to one's social class, but they do not define it. Rather, social class is a series of relationships. A person's social class is defined here by the way that person relates to the process in society by which goods, services, and culture are produced.[2] One relates to several aspects of the production process primarily through one's work. One has a relationship to the system of ownership, to other people (at work and in society) and to the content and process of one's own productive activity. One's relationship to all three of these aspects of production determines one's social class; that is, all three relationships are necessary and none is sufficient for determining a person's relation to the process of production in society.

Ownership Relations. In a capitalist society, a person has a relation to the system of private ownership of capital. Capital is usually thought of as being derived from physical property. In this sense capital is property which is used to produce profit, interest, or rent in sufficient quantity so that the result can be used to produce more profit, interest, or rent—that is, more capital. Physical capital may be derived from money, stocks, machines, land, or the labor of workers (whose labor, for instance, may produce products that are sold by others for profit). Capital, however, can also be symbolic. It can be the socially legitimated knowledge of how the production process works, its financial, managerial, technical, or other "secrets." Symbolic capital can also be socially legitimated skills—cognitive (e.g., analytical), linguistic, or technical skills that provide the ability to, say, produce the dominant scientific, artistic, and other culture, or to manage the systems of industrial and cultural production. Skillful application of symbolic capital may yield social and cultural power, and perhaps physical capital as well.

The ownership relation that is definitive for social class is one's relation to physical capital. The first such relationship is that of capitalist. To be a member of the capitalist class in the present-day United States, one must participate in the ownership of the apparatus of production in society. The number of such persons is relatively small: while one person in ten owns some stock, for example, a mere 1.6 percent of the population owns 82.2 percent of *all* stock, and the wealthiest one-fifth owns almost all the rest (see New York Stock Exchange, 1975; Smith and Franklin, 1974; Lampman, 1962).

At the opposite pole of this relationship is the worker. To be in the United States working class a person will not ordinarily own physical capital; to the contrary, his or her work will be wage or salaried labor that is either a *source* of profit (i.e., capital) to others, or that makes it possible for others to *realize* profit. Examples of the latter are white-collar clerical workers in industry and distribution (office and sales) as well as the wage and salaried workers in the institutions of social and economic legitimation and service (e.g., in state education and welfare institutions).[3] According to the criteria to be developed here, the number of persons who presently comprise the working class in the United States is between 50 percent and 60 percent of the population (see also Wright, 1978; Braverman, 1974; Levison, 1974).

In between the defining relationship of capitalist and worker are the middle classes, whose relationship to the process of production is less clear, and whose relationship may indeed exhibit contradictory characteristics. For example, social service employees have a somewhat contradictory relationship to the process of production because, although their income may be at middle-class levels, some characteristics of their work are working-class (e.g. they may have very little control over their work). Analogously, there are persons at the upper income end of the middle class, such as upper-middle-class professionals, who may own quantities of stocks and will therefore share characteristics of the capitalist class. As the next criterion to be discussed makes clear, however, to be a member of the present-day capitalist in the United States, one must also participate in the social *control* of this capital.

Relationships Between People. The second relationship which contributes to one's social class is the relation one has to authority and control at work and in society.[4] One characteristic of most working-class jobs is that there is no built-in mechanism by which the worker can control the content, process, or speed of work. Legitimate decision making is vested in personnel supervisors, in middle or upper management, or, as in an increasing number of white-collar working-class (and most middle-class) jobs, by bureaucratic rule and regulation. For upper-middle-class professional groups there is an increased amount of autonomy regarding work. Moreover, in middle- and upper-middle-class positions there is an increasing chance that one's work will also involve supervising the work of others. A capitalist is defined within these relations of control in an enterprise by having a position which participates in the direct control of the entire enterprise. Capitalists do not directly control workers in physical production and do not directly control ideas in the sphere of cultural production. However, more crucial to control, capitalists make the decisions over how resources are used (e.g., where money is invested) and how profit is allocated.

Relations Between People and Their Work. The third criterion which contributes to a person's social class is the relationship between that person and his or her own productive activity—the type of activity that constitutes his or her work. A working-class job is often characterized by work that is routine and mechanical and that is a small, fragmented part of a larger process with which workers are not usually acquainted. These working-class jobs are usually blue-collar, manual labor. A few skilled jobs such as plumbing and printing are not mechanical, however, and an increasing number of working-class jobs are *white*-collar. These white-collar jobs, such as clerical work, may involve work that necessitates a measure of planning and decision making, but one still has no built-in control over the content. The work of some middle- and most upper-middle-class managerial and professional groups is likely to involve the need for conceptualization and creativity, with many professional jobs demanding one's full creative capacities. Finally, the work that characterizes the capitalist position is that this work is almost entirely a matter of conceptualization (e.g., planning and laying-out) that has as its object management and control of the enterprise.

One's social class, then, is a result of the relationships one has, largely through one's work, to physical capital and its power, to other people at work and in society, and to one's own productive activity. Social class is a lived, developing process. It is not an abstract category, and it is not a fixed, inherited position (although one's family background is, of course, important). Social class is perceived as a complex of social relations that one develops as one grows up—as one acquires and develops certain bodies of knowledge, skills, abilities, and traits, and as one has contact and opportunity in the world.[5] In sum, social class describes relationships which we as adults have developed, may attempt to maintain, and in which we participate every working day. These relationships in a real sense define our material ties to the world. An important concern here is whether these relationships are developing in children in schools within particular social class contexts.

The Sample of Schools

With the above discussion as a theoretical backdrop, the social class designation of each of the five schools will be identified, and the income, occupation, and other relevant available social characteristics of the students and their parents will be described. The first three schools are in a medium-sized city district in northern New Jersey, and the other two are in a nearby New Jersey suburb.

The first two schools I will call *Working-class Schools.* Most of the parents have blue-collar jobs. Less than a third of the fathers are skilled, while the majority are in unskilled or semiskilled jobs. During the period of the study (1978–1979) approximately 15 percent of the fathers were unemployed. The large majority (85 percent) of the families are white. The following occupations are typical: platform, storeroom, and stockroom workers; foundrymen, pipe welders, and boilermakers; semiskilled and unskilled assembly-line operatives; gas station attendants, auto mechanics, maintenance workers, and security guards. Less than 30 percent of the women work, some part-time and some full-time, on assembly lines, in storerooms and stockrooms, as waitresses, barmaids, or sales clerks. Of the fifth grade parents, none of the wives of the skilled workers had jobs. Approximately 15 percent of the families in each school are at or below the federal "poverty" level[6]; most of the rest of the family incomes are at or below $12,000, except some of the skilled workers whose incomes are higher. The incomes of the majority of the families in these two schools (i.e., at or below $12,000) are typical of 38.6 percent of the families in the United States (U.S. Bureau of the Census, 1979, p. 2, table A).

The third school is called the *Middle-class School,* although because of neighborhood residence patterns, the population is a mixture of several social classes. The parents' occupations can be divided into three groups: a small group of blue-collar "rich," who are skilled, well-paid workers such as printers, carpenters, plumbers, and construction workers. The second group is composed of parents in working-class and middle-class white-collar jobs: women in office jobs, technicians, supervisors in industry, and parents employed by the city (such as firemen, policemen, and several of the school's teachers). The third group is composed of occupations such as personnel directors in local firms, accountants, "middle management," and a few small capitalists (owners of shops in the area). The children of several local doctors attend this school. Most family incomes are between $13,000 and $25,000 with a few higher.

This income range is typical of 38.9 percent of the families in the United States (U.S. Bureau of the Census, 1979, p. 2, table A).

The fourth school has a parent population that is at the upper income level of the upper middle class, and is predominantly professional. This school will be called the *Affluent Professional School.* Typical jobs are: cardiologist, interior designer, corporate lawyer or engineer, executive in advertising or television. There are some families who are not as affluent as the majority (e.g., the family of the superintendent of the district's schools, and the one or two families in which the fathers are skilled workers). In addition, a few of the families are more affluent than the majority, and can be classified in the capitalist class (e.g., a partner in a prestigious Wall Street stock brokerage firm). Approximately 90 percent of the children in this school are white. Most family incomes are between $40,000 and $80,000. This income span represents approximately 7 percent of the families in the United States.[7]

In the fifth school the majority of the families belong to the capitalist class. This school will be called the *Executive Elite School* because most of the fathers are top executives, (e.g., presidents and vice presidents) in major U.S.-based multinational corporations—for example, ATT, RCA, City Bank, American Express, U.S. Steel. A sizable group of fathers are top executives in financial firms on Wall Street. There are also a number of fathers who list their occupations as "general counsel" to a particular corporation, and these corporations are also among the large multinationals. Many of the mothers do volunteer work in the Junior League, Junior Fortnightly, or other service groups; some are intricately involved in town politics; and some are themselves in well-paid occupations. There are no minority children in the school. Almost all family incomes are over $100,000 with some in the $500,000 range. The incomes in this school represent less than 1 percent of the families in the United States (see Smith and Franklin, 1974).

Since each of the five schools is only one instance of elementary education in a particular social class context, I will not generalize beyond the sample. However, the examples of school work which follow will suggest characteristics of education in each social setting that appear to have theoretical and social significance and to be worth investigation in a larger number of schools.

Social Class and School Work

There are obvious similarities among United States schools and classrooms. There are school and classroom rules, teachers who ask questions and attempt to exercise control and who give work and homework. There are textbooks and tests. All of these were found in the five schools. Indeed, there were other curricular similarities as well: all schools and fifth grades used the same math book and series (*Mathematics Around Us,* Scott Foresman, 1978); all fifth grades had at least one boxed set of an individualized reading program available in the room (although the variety and amounts of teaching materials in the classrooms increased as the social class of the school population increased); and, all fifth grade language arts curricula included aspects of grammar, punctuation and capitalization.[8]

This section provides examples of work and work-related activities in each school that bear on the categories used to define social class. Thus, examples will be provided concerning students' relation to capital (e.g., as manifest in any symbolic capital that might be acquired through school work); students' relation to persons and types of authority regarding school work; and students' relation to their own productive activity. The section first offers the investigator's interpretation of what school work *is* for children in each setting, and then presents events and interactions that illustrate that assessment.

The Working-class Schools. In the two working-class schools, work is following the steps of a procedure. The procedure is usually mechanical, involving rote behavior and very little decision making or choice. The teachers rarely explain why the work is being assigned, how it might connect to other assignments, or what the idea is that lies behind the procedure or gives it coherence and perhaps meaning or significance. Available textbooks are not always used, and the teachers often prepare their own dittoes or put work examples on the board. Most of the rules regarding work are designations of what the children are to do; the rules are steps to follow. These steps are told to the children by the teachers and often written on the board. The children are usually told to copy the steps as notes. These notes are to be studied. Work is often evaluated not according to whether it is right or wrong, but according to whether the children followed the right steps.

The following examples illustrate these points. In math, when two-digit division was introduced, the teacher in one school gave a four-minute lecture on what the terms are called (i.e., which number is the divisor, dividend, quotient, and remainder). The children were told to copy these names in their notebooks. Then the teacher told them the steps to follow to do the problems, saying, "This is how you do them." The teacher listed the steps on the board, and they appeared several days later as a chart hung in the middle of the front wall: "Divide; Multiply; Subtract; Bring Down." The children often did examples of two-digit division. When the teacher went over the examples with them, he told them for each problem what the procedure was, rarely asking them to conceptualize or explain it themselves: "3 into 22 is 7; do your subtraction and one is left over." During the week that two-digit division was introduced (or at any other time), the investigator did not observe any discussion of the idea of grouping involved in division, any use of manipulables, or any attempt to relate two-digit division to any other mathematical process. Nor was there any attempt to relate the steps to an actual or possible thought process of the children. The observer did not hear the terms dividend, quotient, etc., used again. The math teacher in the other working-class school followed similar procedures regarding two-digit division, and at one point her class seemed confused. She said, "You're confusing yourselves. You're tensing up. Remember, when you do this, it's the same steps over and over again—and that's the way division always is." Several weeks later, after a test, a group of her children "still didn't get it," and she made no attempt to explain the concept of dividing things into groups, or to give them manipulables for their own investigation. Rather, she went over the steps with them again and told them that they "needed more practice."

In other areas of math, work is also carrying out often unexplained, fragmented procedures. For example, one of the teachers led the children through a series of steps to make a one-inch grid on their paper *without* telling them that they were making a one-inch grid, or that it would be used to study scale. She said, "Take your ruler. Put it across the top. Make a mark at every number. Then move your ruler down to the bottom. No, put it across the bottom. Now make a mark on top of every number. Now draw a line from. . . ." At this point a girl said that she had a faster way to do it and the teacher said, "No, you don't; you don't even know what I'm making yet. Do it this way, or it's wrong." After they had made the lines up and down and across, the teacher told them she wanted them to make a figure by connecting some dots and to measure that, using the scale of one inch equals one mile. Then they were to cut it out. She said, "Don't cut until I check it."

In both working-class schools, work in language arts is mechanics of punctuation (commas, periods, question marks, exclamation points), capitalization, and the four kinds of sentences. One teacher explained to me, "Simple punctuation is all they'll ever use." Regarding punctuation, either a teacher or a ditto stated the rules for where, for example, to put commas. The investigator heard no classroom discussion of the aural context of punctuation (which, of course, is what gives each mark its meaning). Nor did the investigator hear any statement or inference that placing a punctuation mark could be a decision-making process, depending, for example, on one's intended meaning. Rather, the children were told to follow the rules. Language arts did not involve creative writing. There were several writing assignments throughout the year, but in each instance the children were given a ditto, and they wrote answers to questions on the sheet. For example, they wrote their "autobiography" by answering such questions as "Where were you born?" "What is your favorite animal?" on a sheet entitled, "All About Me."

In one of the working-class schools the class had a science period several times a week. On the three occasions observed, the children were not called upon to set up experiments or to give explanations for facts or concepts. Rather, on each occasion the teacher told them in his owns words what the book said. The children copied the teacher's sentences from the board. Each day that preceded the day they were to do a science experiment, the teacher told them to copy the directions from the book for the procedure they would carry out the next day, and to study the list at home that night. The day after each experiment, the teacher went over what they had "found" (they did the experiments as a class, and each was actually a class demonstration led by the teacher). Then the teacher wrote what they "found" on the board, and the children copied that in their notebooks. Once or twice a year there are science projects. The project is chosen and assigned by the teacher from a box of three-by-five-inch cards. On the card the teacher has written the question to be answered, the books to use, and how much to write. Explaining the cards to the observer, the teacher said, "It tells them exactly what to do, or they couldn't do it."

Social studies in the working-class schools is also largely mechanical, rote work that was given little explanation or connection to larger contexts. In one school, for example, although there was a book available, social studies work was to copy the teacher's notes from the board. Several times a week for a period of several months, the children copied these notes. The fifth grades in the district were to study U.S. history. The teacher used a booklet she had purchased called "The Fabulous Fifty States." Each day she put information from the booklet in outline form on the board and the children copied it. The type of information did not vary: the name of the state, its abbreviation, state capital, nickname of the state, its main products, main business, and a "Fabulous Fact" (e.g., "Idaho grew 27 billion potatoes in one year. That's enough potatoes for each man, woman and . . ."). As the children finished copying the sentences, the teacher erased them and wrote more. Children would occasionally go to the front to pull down the wall map in order to locate the states they were copying, and the teacher did not dissuade them. But the observer never saw her refer to the map; nor did the observer ever hear her make other than perfunctory remarks concerning the information the children were copying. Occasionally the children colored in a ditto and cut it out to make a stand-up figure (representing, for example, a man roping a cow in the Southwest). These were referred to by the teacher as their social studies "projects."

Rote behavior was often called for in classroom oral work. When going over math and language arts skills sheets, for example, as the teacher asked for the answer to each problem, he fired the questions rapidly, staccato, and the scene reminded the observer of a sergeant drilling recruits: above all, the questions demanded that you stay at attention: "The next one?

What do I put here? . . . Here? Give us the next." Or "How many commas in this sentence? Where do I put them . . . The next one?"

The (four) fifth grade teachers observed in the working-class schools attempted to control classroom time and space by making decisions without consulting the children and without explaining the basis for their decisions. The teacher's control thus often seemed capricious. Teachers, for instance, very often ignored the bells to switch classes—deciding among themselves to keep the children after the period was officially over, to continue with the work, or for disciplinary reasons, or so they (the teachers) could stand in the hall and talk. There were no clocks in the rooms in either school, and the children often asked, "What period is this?" "When do we go to gym?" The children had no access to materials. These were handed out by teachers and closely guarded. Things in the room "belonged" to the teacher: "Bob, bring me my garbage can." The teachers continually gave the children orders. Only three times did the investigator hear a teacher in either working-class school preface a directive with an unsarcastic "please," or "let's" or "would you." Instead, the teachers said, "Shut up," "Shut your mouth," "Open your books," "Throw your *gum* away—if you want to rot your teeth, do it on your *own* time." Teachers made every effort to control the movement of the children, and often shouted, "Why are you out of your *seat*??!!" If the children got permission to leave the room they had to take a written pass with the date and time.

The control that the teachers have is less than they would like. It is a result of constant struggle with the children. The children continually resist the teachers' orders and the work itself. They do not directly challenge the teachers' authority or legitimacy, but they make indirect attempts to sabotage and resist the flow of assignments:

Teacher: I will put some problems on the board. You are to divide.
Child: We got to divide?
Teacher: Yes.
Several children: (Groan) Not again. Mr. B, we done this yesterday.
Child: Do we put the date?
Teacher: Yes. I hope we remember we work in silence. You're supposed to do it on white paper. I'll explain it later.
Child: Somebody broke my pencil. (Crash—a child falls out of his chair.)
Child: (repeats) Mr. B., somebody broke my *pencil!*
Child: Are we going to be here all morning?
(Teacher comes to the observer, shakes his head and grimaces, then smiles.)

The children are successful enough in their struggle against work that there are long periods where they are not asked to *do* any work, but just to sit and be quiet.[9] Very often the work that the teachers assign is "easy," that is, not demanding, and thus receives less resistance. Sometimes a compromise is reached where, although the teachers insist that the children continue to work, there is a constant murmur of talk. The children will be doing arithmetic examples, copying social studies notes, or doing punctuation or other dittoes, and all the while there is muted but spirited conversation—about somebody's broken arm, an afterschool disturbance of the day before, etc. Sometimes the teachers themselves join in the conversation because, as one teacher explained to me, "It's a relief from the routine."

Middle-class School. In the middle-class school, work is getting the right answer. If one accumulates enough right answers one gets a good grade. One must follow the directions in order to get the right answers, but the directions often call for some figuring, some choice, some decision making. For example, the children must often figure out by themselves what the directions ask them to do, and how to get the answer: what do you do first, second, and perhaps third? Answers are usually found in books or by listening to the teacher. Answers are usually words, sentences, numbers, or facts and dates; one writes them on paper, and one should be neat. Answers must be in the right order, and one can not make them up.

The following activities are illustrative. Math involves some choice: one may do two-digit division the long way, or the short way, and there are some math problems that can be done "in your head." When the teacher explains how to do two-digit division, there is recognition that a cognitive process is involved; she gives several ways, and says, "I want to make sure you understand what you're doing—so you get it right"; and, when they go over the homework, she asks the *children* to tell how they did the problem and what answer they got.

In social studies the daily work is to read the assigned pages in the textbook and to answer the teacher's questions. The questions are almost always designed to check on whether the students have read the assignment and understood it: who did so-and-so; what happened after that; when did it happen, where, and sometimes, why did it happen? The answers are in the book and in one's understanding of the book; the teacher's hints when one doesn't know the answer are to "read it again," or to look at the picture or at the rest of the paragraph. One is to search for the answer in the "context," in what is given.

Language arts is "simple grammar, what they need for everyday life." The language arts teacher says, "They should learn to speak properly, to write business letters and thank-you letters, and to understand what nouns and verbs and simple subjects are." Here, as well, the actual work is to choose the right answers, to understand what is given. The teacher often says, "Please read the next sentence and then I'll question you about it." One teacher said in some exasperation to a boy who was fooling around in class, "If you don't know the answers to the questions I ask, then you can't stay in this *class!* (pause) You *never* know the answers to the questions I ask, and it's not fair to me—and certainly not to you!"

Most lessons are based on the textbook. This does not involve a critical perspective on what is given there. For example, a critical perspective in social studies is perceived as dangerous by these teachers because it may lead to controversial topics; the parents might complain. The children, however, are often curious, especially in social studies. Their questions are tolerated, and usually answered perfunctorily. But after a few minutes the teacher will say, "All right, we're not going any farther. Please open your social studies workbook." While the teachers spend a lot of time explaining and expanding on what the textbooks say, there is little attempt to analyze how or why things happen, or to give thought to how pieces of a culture, or, say, a system of numbers or elements of a language fit together or can be analyzed. What has happened in the past, and what exists now may not be equitable or fair, but (shrug) that is the way things are, and one does not confront such matters in school. For example, in social studies after a child is called on to read a passage about the pilgrims, the teacher summarizes the paragraph and then says, "So you can see how strict they were about everything." A child asks, "Why?" "Well, because they felt that if you weren't busy you'd get into trouble." Another child asks, "Is it true that they burned women at the stake?" The teacher says, "Yes, if a woman did anything strange, they hanged them. [sic] What would a woman do, do you think, to make them burn them? [sic] See if you can come up with better answers than my other [social studies] class." Several children offer suggestions, to which the teacher nods but does not comment. Then she says, "OK, good," and calls on the next child to read.

Work tasks do not usually request creativity. Serious attention is rarely given in school work to *how* the children develop or express their own feelings and ideas, either linguistically or in graphic form. On the occasions when creativity or self-expression is requested, it is peripheral to the main activity, or it is "enrichment," or "for fun." During a lesson on what similes are, for example, the teacher explains what they are, puts several on the board, gives some other examples herself, and then asks the children if they can "make some up." She calls on three children who give similes, two of which are actually in the book they have open before them. The teacher does not comment on this, and then asks several others to choose similes from the list of phrases in the book. Several do so correctly, and she says, "Oh *good!* You're picking them out! See how *good* we are?" Their homework is to pick out the rest of the similes from the list.

Creativity is not often requested in social studies and science projects, either. Social studies projects, for example, are given with directions to "find information on your topic," and write it up. The children are not supposed to copy, but to "put it in your own words." Although a number of the projects subsequently went beyond the teacher's direction to find information and had quite expressive covers and inside illustrations, the teacher's evaluative comments had to do with the amount of information, whether they had "copied," and if their work was neat.

The style of control of the three fifth grade teachers observed in this school varied from somewhat easygoing to strict, but in contrast to the working-class schools, the teachers' decisions were usually based on external rules and regulations, for example, on criteria that were known or available to the children. Thus, the teachers always honor the bells for changing classes, and they usually evaluate children's work by what is in the textbooks and answer booklets.

There is little excitement in school work for the children, and the assignments are perceived as having little to do with their interests and feelings. As one child said, what you do is "store facts in your head like cold storage—until you need it later for a test, or your job." Thus, doing well is important because there are thought to be *other* likely rewards: a good job, or college.[10]

Affluent Professional School. In the affluent professional school, work is creative activity carried out independently. The students are continually asked to express and apply ideas and concepts. Work involves individual thought and expressiveness, expansion and illustration of ideas, and choice of appropriate method and material. (The class is not considered an open classroom, and the principal explained that because of the large number of discipline problems in the fifth grade this year they did not departmentalize. The teacher who agreed to take part in the study said she is "more structured" this year than she usually is.) The products of work in this class are often written stories, editorials and essays, or representations of ideas in mural, graph, or craft form. The products of work should not be like everybody else's and should show individuality. They should exhibit good design, and (this is important), they must also fit empirical reality. Moreover, one's work should attempt to interpret or "make sense" of reality. The relatively few rules to be followed regarding work are usually criteria for, or limits on, individual activity. One's product is usually evaluated for the quality of its expression and for the appropriateness of its conception to the task. In many cases one's own satisfaction with the product is an important criterion for its evaluation. When right answers are called for, as in commercial materials like SRA (Science Research Associates) and math, it is important that the children decide on an answer as a result of thinking about the idea involved in what they're being asked to do. Teacher's hints are to "think about it some more."

The following activities are illustrative. The class takes home a sheet requesting each child's parents to fill in the number of cars they have, the number of television sets, refrigerators, games, or rooms in the house, etc. Each child is to figure the average number of a type of possession owned by the fifth grade. Each child must compile the "data" from all the sheets. A calculator is available in the classroom to do the mechanics of finding the average. Some children decide to send sheets to the fourth grade families for comparison. Their work should be "verified" by a classmate before it is handed in.

Each child and his or her family has made a geoboard. The teacher asks the class to get their geoboards from the side cabinet, to take a handful of rubber bands, and then to listen to what she would like them to do. She says, "I would like you to design a figure and then find the perimeter and area. When you have it, check with your neighbor. After you've done that, please transfer it to graph paper and tomorrow I'll ask you to make up a question about it for someone. When you hand it in, please let me know whose it is, and who verified it. Then I have something else for you to do that's really fun. (pause) Find the average number of chocolate chips in three cookies. I'll give you three cookies, and you'll have to *eat* your way through, I'm afraid!" Then she goes around the room and gives help, suggestions, praise, and admonitions that they are getting noisy. They work sitting, or standing up at their desks, at benches in the back, or on the floor. A child hands the teacher his paper and she comments, "I'm not accepting this paper. Do a better design." To another child she says, "That's fantastic! But you'll never find the area. Why don't you draw a figure inside [the big one] and subtract to get the area?"

The school district requires the fifth grades to study ancient civilizations (in particular, Egypt, Athens, and Sumer.) In this classroom, the emphasis is on illustrating and re-creating the culture of the people of ancient times. The following are typical activities: The children made an 8mm film on Egypt, which one of the parents edited. A girl in the class wrote the script, and the class acted it out. They put the sound on themselves. They read stories of those days. They wrote essays and stories depicting the lives of the people and the societal and occupational divisions. They chose from a list of projects, all of which involved graphic representations of ideas: for example, "Make a mural depicting the division of labor in Egyptian society."

Each child wrote and exchanged a letter in hieroglyphics with a fifth grader in another class, and they also exchanged stories they wrote in cuneiform. They made a scroll and singed the edges so it looked authentic. They each chose an occupation and made an Egyptian plaque representing that occupation, simulating the appropriate Egyptian design. They carved their design on a cylinder of wax, pressed the wax into clay, and then baked the clay. Although one girl did not choose an occupation, but carved instead a series of gods and slaves, the teacher said, "That's all right, Amber, it's beautiful." As they were working the teacher said, "Don't cut into your clay until you're satisfied with your design."

Social studies also involves almost daily presentation by the children of some event from the news. The teacher's questions ask the children to expand what they say, to give more details, and to be more specific. Occasionally she adds some remarks to help them see connections between events.

The emphasis on expressing and illustrating ideas in social studies is accompanied in language arts by an emphasis on creative writing. Each child wrote a rhebus story for a first grader whom they had interviewed to see what kind of story the child liked best. They wrote editorials on pending decisions by the school board, and radio plays, some of which were read over the school intercom from the office, and one of which was performed in the auditorium. There is no language arts textbook because, the teacher said, "The principal wants us to be creative." There is not much grammar, but there is punctuation. One morning when the observer arrived the class was doing a punctuation ditto. The teacher later apologized for using the ditto. "It's just for review," she said. "I don't teach punctuation that way. We use their language." The ditto had three unambiguous rules for where to put commas in a sentence. As the teacher was going around to help the children with the ditto, she repeated several times, "Where you put commas depends on how you say the sentence; it depends on the situation and what you want to say." Several weeks later the observer saw another punctuation activity. The teacher had printed a five-paragraph story on an oak tag and then cut it into phrases. She read the whole story to the class from the book, then passed out the phrases. The group had to decide how the phrases could best be put together again. (They arranged the phrases on the floor.) The point was not to replicate the story, although that was not irrelevant, but to "decide what you think the best way is." Punctuation marks on cardboard pieces were then handed out and the children discussed, and then decided, what mark was best at each place they thought one was needed. At the end of each paragraph the teacher asked, "Are you satisfied with the way the paragraphs are now? Read it to yourself and see how it sounds." Then she read the original story again, and they compared the two.

Describing her goals in science to the investigator, the teacher said, "We use ESS (Elementary Science Study). It's very good because it gives a hands-on experience—so they can make *sense* out of it. It doesn't matter whether it [what they find] is right or wrong. I bring them together and there's value in discussing their ideas."

The products of work in this class are often highly valued by the children and the teacher. In fact, this was the only school in which the investigator was not allowed to take original pieces of the children's work for her files. If the work was small enough, however, and was on paper, the investigator could duplicate it on the copying machine in the office.

The teacher's attempt to control the class involves constant negotiation. She does not give direct orders unless she is angry because the children have been too noisy. Normally, she tries to get them to foresee the consequences of their actions and to decide accordingly. For example, lining them up to go see a play written by the sixth graders, she says, "I presume you're lined up by someone with whom you want to sit. I hope you're lined up by someone you won't get in trouble with." The following two dialogues illustrate the process of negotiation between student and teacher.

Teacher: Tom, you're behind in your SRA this marking period.
Tom: So what!
Teacher: Well, last time you had a hard time catching up.
Tom: But I have my [music] lesson at 10:00.
Teacher: Well, that doesn't mean you're going to sit here for twenty minutes.
Tom: Twenty minutes! OK. (He goes to pick out a SRA booklet and chooses one, puts it back, then takes another, and brings it to her.)
Teacher: OK, this is the one you want, right?
Tom: Yes.
Teacher: OK, I'll put tomorrow's date on it so you can take it home tonight or finish it tomorrow if you want.

***

Teacher: (to a child who is wandering around during reading) Kevin, why don't you do *Reading for Concepts?*
Kevin: No, I don't *like Reading for Concepts.*
Teacher: Well, what are you going to do?
Kevin: (pause) I'm going to work on my DAR. (The DAR had sponsored an essay competition on "Life in the American Colonies.")

One of the few rules governing the children's movement is that no more than three children may be out of the room at once. There is a school rule that anyone can go to the library at any time to get a book. In the fifth grade I observed, they sign their name on the chalkboard and leave. There are no passes. Finally, the children have a fair amount of officially sanctioned say over what happens in the class. For example, they often negotiate what work is to be done. If the teacher wants to move on to the next subject, but the children say they are not ready, they want to work on their present projects some more, she very often lets them do it.

Executive Elite School. In the executive elite school, work is developing one's analytical intellectual powers. Children are continually asked to reason through a problem, to produce intellectual products that are both logically sound and of top academic quality. A primary goal of thought is to conceptualize rules by which elements may fit together in systems, and then to apply these rules in solving a problem. School work helps one to achieve, to excel, to prepare for life.

The following are illustrative. The math teacher teaches area and perimeter by having the children derive formulae for each. First she helps them, through discussion at the board, to arrive at $A = W \times L$ as a formula (not *the* formula) for area. After discussing several, she says, "Can anyone make up a formula for perimeter? Can you figure that out yourselves? (pause) Knowing what we know, can we think of a formula?" She works out three children's suggestions at the board, saying to two, "Yes, that's a good one," and then asks the class if they can think of any more. No one volunteers. To prod them, she says, "If you use rules and good reasoning, you get many ways. Chris, can you think up a formula?"

She discusses two-digit division with the children as a decision-making process. Presenting a new type of problem to them, she asks, "What's the *first* decision you'd make if presented with this kind of example? What is the first thing you'd *think*? Craig?" Craig says, "To find my first partial quotient." She responds, "Yes, that would be your first decision. How would you do that?" Craig explains, and then the teacher says, "OK, we'll see how that works for you." The class tries his way. Subsequently, she comments on the merits and shortcomings of several other children's decisions. Later, she tells the investigator that her goals in math are to develop their reasoning and mathematical thinking and that, unfortunately, "there's no *time* for manipulables."

While right answers are important in math, they are not "given" by the book or by the teacher, but may be challenged by the children. Going over some problems in late September the teacher says, "Raise your hand if you do not agree." A child says, "I don't agree with 64." The teacher responds, "OK, there's a question about 64. (to class) Please check it. Owen, they're disagreeing with you. Kristen, they're checking yours." The teacher emphasized this repeatedly during September and October with statements like, "Don't be afraid to say if you disagree. In the last [math] class, somebody disagreed, and they were right. Before you disagree, check yours, and if you still think we're wrong, then we'll check it out." By Thanksgiving, the children did not often speak in terms of right and wrong math problems, but of whether they agreed with the answer that had been given.

There are complicated math mimeos with many word problems. Whenever they go over the examples, they discuss how each child has set up the problem. The children must explain it precisely. On one occasion the teacher said, "I'm more—just as interested in *how* you set up the problem as in what answer you find. If you set up a problem in a good way, the answer is *easy* to find."

Social studies work is most often reading and discussion of concepts and independent research. There are only occasional artistic, expressive, or illustrative projects. Ancient

Athens and Sumer are, rather, societies to analyze. The following questions are typical of those which guide the children's independent research: "What mistakes did Pericles make after the war?" "What mistakes did the citizens of Athens make?" "What are the elements of a civilization?" "How did Greece build an economic empire?" "Compare the way Athens chose its leaders with the way we choose ours." Occasionally the children are asked to make up sample questions for their social studies tests. On an occasion when the investigator was present the social studies teacher rejected a child's question by saying, "That's just fact. If I asked you that question on a test, you'd complain it was just memory! Good questions ask for concepts."

In social studies—but also in reading, science, and health—the teachers initiate classroom discussions of current social issues and problems. These discussions occurred on every one of the investigator's visits, and a teacher told me, "These children's opinions are important—it's important that they learn to reason things through." The classroom discussions always struck the observer as quite realistic and analytical, dealing with concrete social issues like the following: "Why do workers strike?" "Is that right or wrong?" "Why do we have inflation, and what can be done to stop it?" "Why do companies put chemicals in food when the natural ingredients are available?" etc. Usually the children did not have to be prodded to give their opinions. In fact, their statements and the interchanges between them struck the observer as quite sophisticated conceptually and verbally, and well-informed. Occasionally the teachers would prod with statements such as, "Even if you don't know [the answers], if you think logically about it, you can figure it out." And "I'm asking you [these] questions to help you think this through."

Language arts emphasizes language as a complex system, one that should be mastered. The children are asked to diagram sentences of complex grammatical construction, to memorize irregular verb conjugations (he lay, he has lain, etc. . . .), and to use the proper participles, conjunctions, and interjections, in their speech. The teacher (the same one who teaches social studies) told them, "It is not enough to get these right on tests; you must use what you learn [in grammar classes] in your written and oral work. I will grade you on that."

Most writing assignments are either research reports and essays for social studies, or experiment analyses and write-ups for science. There is only an occasional story or other "creative writing" assignment. On the occasion observed by the investigator (the writing of a Halloween story), the points the teacher stressed in preparing the children to write involved the structural aspects of a story rather than the expression of feelings or other ideas. The teacher showed them a filmstrip, "The Seven Parts of a Story," and lectured them on plot development, mood setting, character development, consistency, and the use of a logical or appropriate ending. The stories they subsequently wrote were, in fact, well-structured, but many were also personal and expressive. The teacher's evaluative comments, however, did not refer to the expressiveness or artistry, but were all directed toward whether they had "developed" the story well.

Language arts work also involved a large amount of practice in presentation of the self and in managing situations where the child was expected to be in charge. For example, there was a series of assignments in which each child had to be a "student teacher." The child had to plan a lesson in grammar, outlining, punctuation, or other language arts topic and explain the concept to the class. Each child was to prepare a worksheet or game and a homework assignment as well. After each presentation, the teacher and other children gave a critical appraisal of the "student teacher's" performance. Their criteria were: whether the student spoke clearly; whether the lesson was interesting; whether the student made any mistakes; and whether he or she kept control of the class. On an occasion when a child did not maintain control, the teacher said, "When you're up there, you have authority, and you have to use it. I'll back you up."

The teacher of math and science explained to the observer that she likes the ESS program because "the children can manipulate variables. They generate hypotheses and devise experiments to solve the problem. Then they have to explain what they found."

The executive elite school is the only school where bells do not demarcate the periods of time. The two fifth grade teachers were very strict about changing classes on schedule, however, as specific plans for each session had been made. The teachers attempted to keep tight control over the children during lessons, and the children were sometimes flippant, boisterous, and occasionally rude. However, the children may be brought into line by reminding them that "it is up to you." "You must control yourself," "you are responsible for your work," you must "set your priorities." One teacher told a child, "You are the only driver of your car—and only you can regulate your speed." A new teacher complained to the observer that she had thought "these children" would have more control.

While strict attention to the lesson at hand is required, the teachers make relatively little attempt to regulate the movement of the children at other times. For example, except for the kindergartners, the children in this school do not have to wait for the bell to ring in the morning; they may go to their classroom when they arrive at school. Fifth graders often came early to read, to finish work, or to catch up. After the first two months of school the fifth grade teachers did not line the children up to change classes or to go to gym, etc., but, when the children were ready and quiet, they were told they could go—sometimes without the teachers.

In the classroom, the children could get materials when they needed them and took what they needed from closets and from the teacher's desk. They were in charge of the office at lunchtime. During class they did not have to sign out or ask permission to leave the room; they just got up and left. Because of the pressure to get work done, however, they did not leave the room very often. The teachers were very polite to the children, and the investigator heard no sarcasm, no nasty remarks, and few direct orders. The teachers never called the children "honey," or "dear," but always called them by name. The teachers were expected to be available before school, after school, and for part of their lunch time to provide extra help if needed.

Discussion and Conclusion

One could attempt to identify physical, educational, cultural, and interpersonal characteristics of the environment of each school that might contribute to an empirical explanation of the events and interactions. For example, the investigator could introduce evidence to show that the following *increased* as the social class of the community increased (with the most marked differences occurring between the two districts): increased variety and abundance of teaching materials in the classroom; increased time reported spent by the teachers on preparation; higher social class background and more prestigious educational institutions attended by teachers and administrators; more stringent board of education requirements regarding teaching methods; more frequent and demanding administrative evaluation of teachers; increased teacher support services such as in-service workshops; increased parent expenditure for school equipment over and above district or government funding; higher expectations of student ability on the part of parents, teachers, and administrators; higher expectations and demands regarding student achievement on the part of teachers, parents, and administrators; more positive attitudes on the part of the teachers as to the probable occupational futures of the children; an increase in the children's acceptance of classroom assignments; increased intersubjectivity between students and teachers; and increased cultural congruence between school and community.

All of these—and other—factors may contribute to the character and scope of classroom events. However, what is of primary concern here is not the immediate causes of classroom activity (although these are in themselves quite important). Rather, the concern is to reflect on the deeper social meaning, the wider theoretical significance, of what happens in each social setting. In an attempt to assess the theoretical meaning of the differences among the schools, the work tasks and milieu in each will be discussed in light of the concepts used to define social class.

What potential relationships to the system of ownership of symbolic and physical capital, to authority and control, and to their own productive activity are being developed in children in each school? What economically relevant knowledge, skills, and predispositions are being transmitted in each classroom, and for what future relationship to the system of production are they appropriate? It is of course true that a student's future relationship to the process of production in society is determined by the combined effects of circumstances beyond elementary schooling. However, by examining elementary school activity in its social class context in the light of our theoretical perspective on social class, we can see certain potential relationships already developing. Moreover, in this structure of developing relationships lies theoretical—and social—significance.

The *working-class* children are developing a potential *conflict* relationship with capital. Their present school work is appropriate preparation for future wage labor that is mechanical and routine. Such work, insofar as it denies the human capacities for creativity and planning, is degrading; moreover, when performed in industry, such work is a source of profit to others. This situation produces industrial conflict over wages, working conditions, and control. However, the children in the working-class schools are not learning to be docile and obedient in the face of present or future degrading conditions or financial exploitation. They are developing abilities and skills of resistance. These methods are highly similar to the "slowdown," subtle sabotage and other modes of indirect resistance carried out by adult workers in the shop, on the department store sales floor, and in some offices.[11] As these types of resistance develop in school, they are highly constrained and limited in their ultimate effectiveness. Just as the children's resistance prevents them from learning socially legitimated knowledge and skills in school and is therefore ultimately debilitating, so is this type of resistance ultimately debilitating in industry. Such resistance in industry does not succeed in producing, nor is it intended to produce, fundamental changes in the relationships of exploitation or control. Thus, the methods of resistance that the working-class children are developing in school are only temporarily, and *potentially,* liberating.

In the *middle-class school* the children are developing somewhat different potential relationships to capital, authority, and work. In this school the work tasks and relationships are appropriate for a future relation to capital that is *bureaucratic.* Their school work is appropriate for white-collar working-class and middle-class jobs in the supportive institutions of United States society. In these jobs one does the paperwork, the technical work, the sales and the social service in the private and state bureaucracies. Such work does not usually demand that one be creative, and one is not often rewarded for critical analysis of the system. One is rewarded, rather, for knowing the answers to the questions one is asked, for knowing where or how to find the answers, and for knowing which form, regulation, technique, or procedure is correct. While such work does not usually satisfy human needs for engagement and self-expression, one's salary can be exchanged for objects or activities that attempt to meet these needs.

In the *affluent professional school* the children are developing a potential relationship to capital that is instrumental and expressive and involves substantial negotiation. In their schooling these children are acquiring *symbolic capital:* they are being given the opportunity to develop skills of linguistic, artistic, and scientific expression and creative elaboration of ideas into concrete form. These skills are those needed to produce, for example, culture (e.g., artistic, intellectual, and scientific ideas and other "products"). Their schooling is developing in these children skills necessary to become society's successful artists, intellectuals, legal, scientific, and technical experts and other professionals. The developing relation of the children in this school to their work is creative and relatively autonomous. Although they do not have control over which ideas they develop or express, the creative act in itself affirms and utilizes the human potential for conceptualization and design that is in many cases valued as intrinsically satisfying.

Professional persons in the cultural institutions of society (in, say, academe, publishing, the nonprint media, the arts, and the legal and state bureaucracies) are in an expressive relationship to the system of ownership in society because the ideas and other products of their work are often an important means by which material relationships of society are given ideological (e.g., artistic, intellectual, legal, and scientific) expression. Through the system of laws, for example, the ownership relations of private property are elaborated and legitimated in legal form; through individualistic and meritocratic theories in psychology and sociology, these individualistic economic relations are provided scientific "rationality" and "sense." The relationship to physical capital of those in society who create what counts as the dominant culture or ideology also involves substantial negotiation. The producers of symbolic capital often do not control the socially available physical capital nor the cultural uses to which it is put. They must therefore negotiate for money for their own projects. However, skillful application of one's cultural capital may ultimately lead to social (for example, state) power and to financial reward.

The *executive elite school* gives its children something that none of the other schools does: knowledge of and practice in manipulating the socially legitimated tools of analysis of systems. The children are given the opportunity to learn and to utilize the intellectually and socially prestigious grammatical, mathematical, and other vocabularies and rules by which elements are arranged. They are given the opportunity to use these skills in the analysis of society and in control situations. Such knowledge and skills are a most important kind of *symbolic capital.* They are necessary for control of a production system. The developing relationship of the children in this school to their work affirms and develops in them the human capacities for analysis and planning and helps to prepare them for work in society that would demand these skills. Their schooling is helping them to develop the abilities necessary for ownership and control of physical capital and the means of production in society.

The foregoing analysis of differences in school work in contrasting social class contexts suggests the following conclusion: the "hidden curriculum" of school work is tacit preparation for relating to the process of production in a particular way. Differing curricular, pedagogical, and pupil evaluation practices emphasize different cognitive and behavioral skills in each social setting and thus contribute to the development in the children of certain potential relationships to physical and symbolic capital, to authority, and to the process of work. School experience, in the sample of schools discussed here, differed qualitatively by social class. These differences may not only contribute to the development in the children in each social class of certain types of economically significant relationships and not others, but would thereby help to *reproduce* this system of relations in society. In the contribution to the reproduction of unequal social relations lies a theoretical meaning, and social consequence, of classroom practice.

The identification of different emphases in classrooms in a sample of contrasting social class contexts implies that further research should be conducted in a large number of schools to investigate the types of work tasks and interactions in each, to see if they differ in the ways discussed here, and to see if similar potential relationships are uncovered. Such research could have as a product the further elucidation of complex but not readily apparent connections between everyday activity in schools and classrooms and the unequal structure of economic relationships in which we work and live.

Notes

* The research was funded by Rutgers University Research Council and will be reported in detail elsewhere.

1. But see, in a related vein, Apple and King (1977) and Rist (1973).
2. The definition of social class delineated here is the author's own, but it relies heavily on her interpretation of the work of Eric Olin Wright (1978), Pierre Bourdieu (Bourdieu and Passeron, 1977) and Raymond Williams (1977).
3. For discussion of schools as agencies of social and economic legitimation see Althusser (1971); see also Anyon (1978; 1979).
4. While relationships of control in society will not be discussed here, it can be said that they roughly parallel the relationships of control in the workplace, which will be the focus of this discussion. That is, working-class and many middle-class persons have less control than members of the upper-middle and capitalist classes do, not only over conditions and processes of their work, but over their nonwork lives as well. In addition, it is true that persons from the middle and capitalist classes, rather than workers, are most often those who fill the positions of state and other power in United States society.
5. Occupations may change their relation to the means of production over time, as the expenditure and ownership of capital change, as technology, skills, and the social relations of work change. For example, some jobs which were middle-class, managerial positions in 1900 and which necessitated conceptual laying-out and planning are now working-class and increasingly mechanical: e.g., quality control in industry, clerical work, and computer programming (see Braverman, 1974).
6. The U.S. Bureau of the Census defines "poverty" for a nonfarm family of four as a yearly income of $6,191 a year or less. U.S. Bureau of the Census, *Statistical Abstract of the United States: 1978* (Washington, D.C.: U.S. Government Printing Office, 1978, p. 465, table 754).
7. This figure is an estimate. According to the Bureau of the Census, only 2.6 percent of families in the United States have money income of $50,000 or over. U.S. Bureau of the Census, *Current Population Reports,* series P–60, no. 118, "Money Income in 1977 of Families and Persons in the United States." (Washington, D.C.: U.S. Government Printing Office, 1979, p. 2, table A). For figures on income at these higher levels, see Smith and Franklin (1974).
8. For other similarities alleged to characterize United States classrooms and schools, but which will not be discussed here, see Dreeben (1968), Jackson (1968), and Sarasan (1971).
9. Indeed, strikingly little teaching occurred in either of the working-class schools; this curtailed the amount that the children were taught. Incidentally, it increased the amount of time that had to be spent by the researcher to collect data on teaching style and interaction.
10. A dominant feeling, expressed directly and indirectly by teachers in this school, was boredom with their work. They did, however, in contrast to the working-class schools, almost always carry out lessons during class times.
11. See, for example, discussions in Levison (1974), Aronowitz (1978), and Benson (1978).

References

Althusser, L. Ideology and ideological state apparatuses. In L. Althusser, *Lenin and philosophy and other essays.* Ben Brewster, Trans. New York: Monthly Review Press, 1971.

Anyon, J. Elementary social studies textbooks and legitimating knowledge. *Theory and Research in Social Education,* 1978, *6,* 40–55.

Anyon, J. Ideology and United States history textbooks. *Harvard Educational Review,* 1979, *49,* 361–386.

Apple, M. W. *Ideology and curriculum.* Boston: Routledge and Kegan Paul, 1979.

Apple, M. W., & King, N. What do schools teach? *Curriculum Inquiry,* 1977, *6,* 341–358.

Aronowitz, S. Marx, Braverman, and the logic of capital. *The Insurgent Sociologist,* 1978, *8,* 126–146.

Benson, S. The clerking sisterhood: rationalization and the work culture of saleswomen in American department stores, 1890–1960. *Radical America,* 1978, *12,* 41–55.

Bernstein, B. *Class, codes and control, Vol. 3. Towards a theory of educational transmission,* 2nd ed. London: Routledge and Kegan Paul, 1977.

Bourdieu, P. and Passeron, J. *Reproduction in education, society, and culture.* Beverly Hills, Calif.: Sage, 1977.

Bowles, S. & Gintis, H. *Schooling in capitalist America: educational reform and the contradictions of economic life.* New York: Basic Books, 1976.

Braverman, H. *Labor and monopoly capital: the degradation of work in the twentieth century.* New York: Monthly Review Press, 1974.

Dreeben, R. *On what is learned in school.* Reading, Mass.: Addison-Wesley, 1968.

Jackson, P. *Life in classrooms.* Holt, Rinehart & Winston, 1968.

Lampman, R. J. *The share of top wealth-holders in national wealth, 1922–1956:* A study of the National Bureau of Economic Research. Princeton, N.J.: Princeton University Press, 1962.

Levison, A. *The working-class majority.* New York: Penguin Books, 1974.

New York Stock Exchange. *Census.* New York: New York Stock Exchange, 1975.

Rist, R. C. *The urban school: a factory for failure.* Cambridge, Mass.: MIT Press, 1973.

Sarasan, S. *The culture of school and the problem of change.* Boston: Allyn and Bacon, 1971.

Smith, J. D. and Franklin, S. The concentration of personal wealth, 1922–1969. *American Economic Review,* 1974, *64,* 162–167.

U.S. Bureau of the Census. *Current population reports.* Series P–60, no. 118. Money income in 1977 of families and persons in the United States. Washington, D.C.: U.S. Government Printing Office, 1979.

U.S. Bureau of the Census. *Statistical abstract of the United States: 1978.* Washington, D.C.: U.S. Government Printing Office, 1978.

Williams, R. *Marxism and literature.* New York: Oxford University Press, 1977.

Wright, E. O. *Class, crisis and the state.* London: New Left Books, 1978.

7

Class Consciousness and Teacher Education: The Socialist Challenge and the Historical Context

Curry Stephenson Malott

This essay traces the emergence and decline of class-consciousness within the U.S. as it coincides with the historical developmental of capitalism. I begin this essay in the third period of capital's historical development. Robinson (2008) characterizes this period of the development of global capitalism—the third period—as beginning in the 1870s and marked by the corporate form of capitalism and class struggle, and the subsequent emergence of widespread class-consciousness. As a result, this period is also the beginning of large-scale, compulsory common schooling, which the capitalist class eventually came to understand to be a necessary cost of production needed for social control.

Marx's historical work on the development of capital is crucial here as it laid the foundation for a tradition of revolutionary class-consciousness from Lenin, to Vygotsky, to Freire, respectively. Drawing on these insights regarding class-consciousness, I outline the debilitating tendencies of a Weberian conception of social class in U.S. teacher education programs and beyond situated in the current context of neo-colonialism/neoliberalism, that is, the most current period of global capitalism.

In the final section I expand on the argument for a revolutionary education, not as a prescription, but as a place of departure for the vast diversity of global contexts within the ever-expanding, ever-deepening social universe of capital. Within this context I argue that Joe L. Kincheloe's idea of the epistemological bazaar and his postformal approach to educational psychology are particularly relevant (Malott, 2011a). That is, because the challenges for creating a 21st century global socialism are so intense and immense (see for example, Callinicos, 2010), such a multifaceted, complex approach is needed where anarchists, feminists, critical race theorists, critical postmodernists, animal rights activists, Earth First! eco-pedagogues, critical indigenous sovereignists, orthodox Marxists, neo-Marxists, humanist Marxists, and others, are able to build a genuine challenge and alternative vision and practice to global capitalism. However, this is much easier said than done as many of our differences are fundamental, making it difficult, at times, to find common ground (Malott, 2012). Through this struggle and movement, revolutionary change agents are able to develop, in radical communion and solidarity with others, the ontologically necessary feeling of *relevancy,* having become a genuine contributor/participant/transformer: against the property relations of capitalist production that negate humanity's *species being* (see Kelsh and Hill, 2006, for a discussion on the central significance of property relations within Marx's theory of and against class); against the whitestream settler-state (Grande, 2004); against the monoculturalism of capitalist society (Darder, 2011); these, as I argue below, are all parts of the larger, totalizing, social universe of capital. Again, this Hegelian Marxist position places me in sharp contrast with many people on the Left I consider comrades. The solution to this dilemma is still very much a hotly contested debate.

The Second Industrial Revolution, the Creation of a Working-Class, and the Emergence of Class Consciousness

As suggested above, the *period* of the historical development of capitalism that has had the largest influence on the contemporary era began during the second industrial revolution around 1870. Before this period, in the U.S., the country (acquired from many indigenous Native American nations through unintentional genocide from infectious diseases, intentional genocide through military conquest including the slaughtering of non-combatants such as women, the elderly and children, and biological warfare, and from deceptive legal maneuvers and the breaking of treaty agreements) was largely rural, and land, at least within the white-male settler-state, was relatively evenly distributed. Wealth, as a result, was also not so dramatically unequal (unless you were an enslaved African, indentured European servant, or a member of a displaced Native American nation). However, the ruling class, and therefore the country, *was* capitalist and thus governed by a highly educated, elite ruling class paternalistically overseeing the largely uneducated population.

What led to this period of U.S. capitalist expansion and the co-existence of extreme wealth and poverty—a period American author Mark Twain coined the *Gilded Age* because it looked beautiful from the outside, but was in fact rotten and diseased at the core—is a mix of equally important factors: immigration, urbanization, Westward Expansion, mass schooling, and the advances in science that made the technological innovations a reality. It was during this period that the labor movement emerged and the first real crisis or breakdown in the cycle of capitalist production, called a depression, transpired. At the heart of what influenced the labor movement and caused the depression—the tendency of capital toward over-accumulation—is the same force that has led to the most recent crisis of capital and the flowering of an international anti-capitalist movement (*i.e.,* Occupy Wall Street, the Arab Spring, the Party for Socialism and Liberation USA, the Socialist Workers Party England, the Communist Party of Greece, the Chavistas of Venezuela, the Zapatistas of Mexico, etc.).

***

As we enter our discussion of the second industrial revolution, let us pause for a moment and briefly explain that our discussion here is based on Marx's recognition that the primary difference between the European feudalist system that was *torn asunder* by capitalism is that feudalism is an economic system based on simple reproduction whereas capitalism is a model based on perpetual growth and expansion—two to three percent annual growth for a capitalist economy to be considered *healthy,* somewhat of an oxymoron. From this early history, as Marx and Engels (1848/1972) remind us, the capitalist class has positioned itself as doing workers a favor by liberating them from feudalism. This paternalism continues—a paternalism where the capitalist class advances a discourse that portrays labor as dependent on the generosity and assumed superior intelligence of the bosses to create and provide jobs. It is, therefore, not surprising that the dominant version of history fails to give much importance to the fact that under feudalism the means of production, or the land, is not fully owned by the feudal lords rendering sizable regions in the hands of the peasant class. Under capitalism, these commons, or common lands that peasants supplemented their incomes with under feudalism, are violently abolished and turned into private property controlled by the capitalist class transforming, with deadly force, the peasant classes into a working class.

Challenging the dominant view that portrays the emergence of capitalism as a favor that raised the standard of living for all of humanity, the transition from feudalism, from a Marxist perspective, represents "one of capitalism's first major conflicts with the existing feudal system" driven by "the quest for labor" (Klobby, 1999, p. 13). Making this point in the opening pages of *The Manifesto of the Communist Party* (1848/1978) Marx and Engels note that "the modern bourgeois society that has sprouted from the ruins of feudal society has not done away with class antagonisms. It has but established new classes, new conditions of oppression, new forms of struggle in place of the old ones" (p. 474).

Laying these foundations for the capitalist property relations of production, a series of *enclosure acts,* alluded to above, were passed throughout Europe, making it nearly impossible for people to remain on their ancestral lands. That is, disconnected from the land, and therefore with nothing left to survive on but one's ability to labor, the peasant is forced to relocate to urban areas to sell his or her labor power for a wage far less than the value it produces. No longer in control of one's own creative capacities, the alienated wage slave is born, paving the way for the creation of large reserve pools of labor needed to create competition between workers for a scarcity of jobs as a way to keep wages low and returns or profits high. For example, in *People's History of the United States* Howard Zinn (2003) notes that "between 1860 and 1910, New York grew from 850,000 to 4 million, Chicago from 110,000 to 2 million, Philadelphia from 650,000 to 1 ½ million" (p. 254). Again, the majority of this population explosion was the result of European peasants seeking a means of survival after being disconnected from their traditional European land-bases.

While capitalism is not possible without a large pool of potential workers with no land and thus no means to survive other than their ability to labor, the large-scale manufacturing of the second industrial revolution would not have been possible without particular advances in science and the necessary engineers to put them to work for industry. Summarizing this period of rapid expansion, Foner (2009) notes:

> Between the end of the Civil War and the early twentieth century, the US underwent one of the most rapid economic shifts any country has ever experienced. There were numerous causes . . . Abundant natural resources, a growing supply of labor, an expanding market for manufactured goods, and the availability of capital for investment. In addition, the federal government actively promoted industrial and agricultural development. It granted land to railroad companies to encourage construction, and used the army to remove Indians from Western lands desired by farmers and mining companies.
>
> (pp. 557–558)

At the center of this innovation is arguably the Bessemer process of turning iron into steel, reducing what could be accomplished in an entire day to fifteen minutes (Zinn, 2003). Summarizing this history, which is the history of how steel and oil propelled machines to new heights, Zinn (2003) comments:

> Between the Civil War and 1900, steam and electricity replaced human muscle, iron replaced wood, and steel replaced iron . . . Machines could now drive steel tools. Oil could lubricate machines, light homes, streets and factories. People and goods could move by railroad, propelled

> by steam along steel rails . . . Machines changed farming. Before the Civil War it took 61 hours of labor to produce an acre of wheat. By 1900, it took 3 hours . . . in 1860, 14 million tons of coal were mined; by 1884 it was 100 million tons. More coal meant more steel . . .
>
> (p. 253)

Of particular importance during this time, as alluded to above by Zinn, was the role of not only the increased availability of steel, but the role the railroad played in bringing raw materials, including food, from around the U.S.—the Great Plains and the mid-west in particular—to Eastern centers of manufacturing. The newly created working class, manifested as a population explosion that moved to North American urban centers from Europe, needed new food sources to fuel its labor power that was being exploited in the burgeoning manufacturing centers. It is, therefore, not surprising that investment capitalists moved quickly to profit from this expanding market.

However, this market would not have been as ripe or open as a source of fortune generation without the federal government intervening in the economy on behalf of capitalists. That is, in the 1860s, the federal U.S. government gave millions of acres of stolen Native American land to Union Pacific and Central Pacific railroad companies. The Central Pacific Railroad, for example, "spent $200,000 in Washington on bribes to get 9 million acres of free land and $24 million in bonds, and paid $79 million, an overpayment of $36 million, to a construction company which really was its own" (Zinn, 2003, p. 254). At the same time, the Union Pacific got:

> 12 million acres of free land and 27 million in government bonds. It created the Credit Mobilier company and gave them $94 million for construction when the actual cost was $44 million. Shares were sold cheaply to Congressmen to prevent investigation. This was at the suggestion of Massachusetts Congressman Oaks Ames, a shovel manufacturer and director of Credit Mobilier, who said: 'There is no difficulty in getting men to look after their own property.'
>
> (Zinn, 2003, p. 254)

So much for the common myth that the U.S. Empire was built from the honest, hard work, and ingenuity of the Master Race *free* to excel in a *free* market. Not only were millions of dollars and acres of land given to two major corporations, the cheap labor that built the railroad primarily came from Irish and Chinese immigrants.

One of these profiteers, for example, "Cyrus Holliday, founder of Topeka, Kansas, pushed his Atchison, Topeka & Santa Fe line west to Dodge City. Holliday was determined to tap the growing cattle market by running his railroad nearer to the cattle country of Texas, Colorado, and New Mexico" (Smith, 1984, pp. 97). Consequently, when Kansas Pacific began shipping cattle out of Abilene, Kansas, in 1867 they started with twenty carloads of longhorn the first year. A year later that number rose to 1,000 carloads, and by 1871, it had exploded to 700,000 carloads (Smith, 1984). The working-class tradition of Philly Cheese Steaks in Philadelphia, PA, can be traced back to this time. Of course, the romanticized American hero, the *cowboys*, contrary to Hollywood characterizations, were not the already-Americanized, ruling-class-supporting, white males, toiling in the interests of their own self-direction, but rather tended to come from the most oppressed segments of society, from Irish immigrants, escaped and recently freed African Americans, and Mexican nationals displaced from their homelands as a result of the Mexican-American War, and were therefore low-paid wage earners who, collectively, have played a counter-hegemonic role in the history of labor activism.

Early in this process of industrialization and westward expansion, the federal government invested in universities to fulfill the purpose of making such advancements in the technologies of economic innovation and capitalist expansion (i.e., the railroad). Making this point in their introductory text, *American Education: A History*, Urban and Wagoner (2009) note that the "largest universities . . . were translating [the] latest scientific advances into technology that would support America's new industries" (pp. 274). For example, the Morrill Acts of 1862 and 1890 granted states land for agricultural, mechanical, and military colleges. Similarly, the Hatch Act of 1887 funded agricultural experiment stations for research on farming, animal diseases, and so on (Foner, 2009; Smith, 1984; Urban & Wagoner, 2009). New Mexico State University in Las Cruces, NM is one of the institutions playing a significant role in both agricultural science and military science. So committed to policing the official pro-capitalist purpose of the university, the institution has developed an "NMSU Position on Animals in Research and Emergency Preparedness Plan." The following excerpt is telling:

> An important part of the mission of a land-grant university is to conduct appropriate research to optimize the use of animals in the service of man . . . NMSU defends the right of free speech . . . regarding the use of animals in research . . . however, coercion, intimidation, and unlawful acts will not be allowed . . . Any organization using animals should be prepared for various protests . . . from animal rights' groups . . . Appropriate steps will be taken to limit disruption of NMSU activities.

What this policy alludes to is the interconnectedness between the technologies of capitalist expansion (i.e. military science and agricultural science and engineering) and the technologies of social control (i.e. controlling the ideas of labor through ideological indoctrination as well as physically censoring ideas through policy and police). Economically integrating the North American continent from East to West required not only the methods of social control and other university-inspired technologies and a capitalist worldview informing the railroad and the human labor-power to make it a reality, but also the subjugation of the Plains Indians. Making this connection in *The Rise of Industrial America: A People's History of the Post-Reconstruction Era*, Page Smith (1984) notes that:

> The principle obstacle to peace on the Great Plains was the issue of the railroads bi- and trisecting their hunting grounds. On this issue . . . there could be no compromise. The rails must run their irresistible way through the heart of Indian country.
>
> (p. 89)

Consequently, the discourse of Manifest Destiny, that is, the idea that it was God's will to spread European civilization (i.e., capitalism) from the East coast to the West coast of the U.S. and across the world, became a fundamentally important tool in convincing labor to willingly do the military work of westward expansion. That, and the promise of free land denationalized from Native Americans.

During this period of rapid growth in industrial output, there were virtually no regulations restricting capital's ability to extract surplus value from human labor power. As a result, "by 1890 the richest 1% of Americans received the same total *wealth* as the bottom half of the population and owned more property than the remaining 99%" (Foner, 2009, pp. 567). During this time, the life of the working class consisted of long hours, low wages, no pensions, no compensation for injuries, and the most dangerous working conditions in the industrial world with more than 35,000 deaths a year between 1880 and 1900 (Foner, 2009). In this context, the labor movement was born, first emerging in Philadelphia. The membership of the Knights of Labor exploded during this time. However, this more mainstream or *nativist* (i.e., U.S. born whites) branch of labor had a reputation for being anti-Chinese (Urban & Wagoner, 2009) as they had not been able to overcome their own supremacist indoctrination as white, male Americans. The Industrial Workers of the World, on the other hand, represented a more counter-hegemonic, and thus anti-racist, branch of the revolutionary labor movement (discussed below). What is particularly striking about this early era of labor organizing is its vast militancy and revolutionary fervor. Placing this militancy in a larger context, Marx highlights the inherent savageness of competitive, market capitalism.

Dramatizing the barbarism of capital's insatiable quest for profit and the speed at which the first and second industrial revolutions subsumed the social universe within which they emerged (i.e., the accumulation of surplus value or unpaid labor hours) in *Volume 1* of *Capital: A Critical Analysis of Capitalist Production,* edited by Frederick Engels, Karl Marx (1867/1967), in chapter four, focuses on the length of the working day, which he divides into two components: ". . . the working-time required for the reproduction of the labor-power of the laborer himself" (p. 232) and the amount dedicated to the capitalist class's accumulation of surplus labor. Marx (1867/1967) hones in on the struggle between the capitalist class and the working class's determination for the length of the working day because at the dawn of the second industrial revolution "the capitalist has bought the labor-power at its day-rate" (p. 232). This is significant because when the laborer sells his commodity (i.e., his labor power) on the market to a capitalist, he forfeits control of this commodity (i.e., himself) during the time purchased. If the working day is three times longer than the amount of time needed to reproduce himself, then he or she can protest that they are being robbed of two thirds of the value of their commodity, their own capacity to labor (Marx, 1867/1967).

Because the capitalist is driven by the need to perpetually expand the rate of profit obtained from the purchasing of commodities such as labor power, it is in capital's interest to extend the length of the work day as long as possible. Asking, "what is the length of time during which capital may consume the labor-power whose daily value it buys?" Marx (1867/1967) observes that, "it has been seen that to these questions capital replies: the working-day contains the full 24 hours" (p. 264). As a result, the laborer is "nothing else, his whole life, than labor-power," and all his or her time is, therefore, dedicated to "the self-expansion of capital" leaving no time for "education, intellectual development, for the fulfilling of social functions and for social intercourse, for the free-play of his bodily and mental activity" (Marx, 1867/1967, p. 264) and even for the necessary time to rest and rejuvenate the body for another day's work. The historical development of capitalism, especially during the second industrial revolution, has proven unequivocally, that "capital cares nothing for the length of life of labor-power" (Marx, 1867/1967, p. 265). Communicating this destructive impulse of capital, Marx (1867/1967) summarizes:

> The capitalistic mode of production (essentially the production of surplus value, the absorption of surplus-labor), produces thus, with the extension of the working day, not only the deterioration of human labor-power by robbing it of its normal, moral and physical, conditions of development and function. It produces also the premature exhaustion and death of this labor-power itself. It extends the laborer's time of production during a given period by shortening his actual life-time.
>
> (p. 265)

Marx (1867/1967) reminds us that this impulse toward barbarism has nothing to do with the specific personalities of market profiteers/capitalists. That is, it is not a matter of the "good or ill will of individual capitalists," but rather, "free competition brings out the inherent laws of capitalist production" (p. 270) trumping any generous impulse a human capitalist or CEO may or may not possess. What determines then the length of the normal working day or the rate of exploitation in an hourly wage system is "the result of centuries of struggle between capitalist and laborer" (Marx, 1867/1967, p. 270). The key factor determining the course of history in capitalism is, therefore, class-consciousness.

It was within this context of industrial capitalist barbarism and working-class awakening that Horace Mann set out on a Protestant-inspired crusade for a system of Common Schooling. Mann, working as the Secretary of the Massachusetts Board of Education in the 1840s, saw educating the working class as an effective way to discipline laborers and prevent rebellions and other "crimes." Mann, in fact, wrote reports outlining the merits of educated versus uneducated workers. His primary audience was industrial capitalists from whom he had to gain skeptical approval. Essentially, Mann sought to convince them that a basic or common education was a necessary cost of production more effective in controlling labor than police, that is, physical force. In school, workers would learn "respect for property, for the work ethic, and for the wisdom of the property owners" (Urban & Wagoner, 2009, p. 121). Because of the need to discipline labor and with the emergence of science as a theory of everything, the managers of industry and academics sought to develop a human science as effective at predicting and controlling human behavior as biology and physics were at conquering the natural world. From here, it makes sense why teachers' colleges would open to ensure future teachers were sufficiently trained with the most up-to-date techniques of social control and behaviorist pedagogy. Zinn (2003) accurately describes teachers, managers, engineers, and other constructors and regulators of the system as "loyal buffers against trouble" (p. 263).

These college-educated *middle buffers against trouble* have been vital to the perpetuation of the ruling class because of the cyclical nature of crisis at the heart of the internal laws of accumulation. That is, because capitalism is driven by an insatiable appetite for wealth, the capitalist manager or corporate CEO is forever searching for new ways to reduce the cost of production. The variable cost of labor historically has been one of the areas from which capitalists have sought to cut costs or extract more wealth. As a result, there is a built-in drive that pushes wages down, deeper and deeper, until labor is no longer able to purchase the commodities flooding the market place. At the point when the potential value embedded within commodities is not realized, the cycle of capitalist production breaks down and the system goes into crisis. It is at these moments of increased suffering and hardships within labor that the potential for revolutionary change heightens. Often, it is technological innovation that leads to major reductions in the cost of labor by eliminating the cost of labor.

For example, one of the factors leading to the first major crisis in the globalizing capitalist system of production in the 1890s was the mechanization of harvesting grains, mentioned above. While it took over sixty-one man-hours to produce an acre of wheat, with machines that number was slashed to fewer than three hours. Between 1870 and 1890 the number of farms in the U.S. increased 80% due to the Homestead Act of 1862, which essentially gave millions and millions of acres of Native American lands to European immigrants disconnected from their European ancestral lands as a result of the transition from feudalism to capitalism. However, while mechanization doubled the output of grains, the population grew by only three quarters. Coupled with international competition, grain prices dropped to half the cost of production, leaving thousands of small farmers bankrupt, thus contributing to the emerging crisis and additionally paving the way for the corporate farm (Foner, 2003; Smith, 1984).

Against this context of urban squalor and suffering and rural poverty and displacement, a strong tradition of revolutionary fervor and a spirit of transformation emerged that rocked the capitalist class to their core. The Industrial Workers of the World (IWW) rose and nearly overturned the negative relationship between labor and capital at the heart of capitalism.

We now know that the B of I (later changed to the FBI) waged a secret illegal war against the IWW, arresting leaders on trumped-up charges and costing the organization hundreds of thousands of dollars in legal fees, which effectively bankrupted the IWW. The federal government went as far as bombing buildings and leaving anarchist literature at the crime scene to damage the favorable reputation of the revolutionary-oriented industrial labor movement in the public's eye.

During this era, the Haymarket Massacre happened. That is, on May 4, 1886, the Chicago Police Department opened fire on a crowd of anarchist and socialist labor activist revolutionaries rallying in support of striking union members. Apparently, what started the bloodbath was that an unknown protestor lobbed a dynamite bomb at the police, eight of whom died in the ensuing gunfight, mostly from friendly fire. Consequently, five activists were arrested, charged, and convicted of murder, and were subsequently executed. What is particularly striking about this incident is that the defendants were executed despite the fact that the prosecutor acknowledged that there was no evidence connecting the bombing to any of the defendants. These events, in part, are what have inspired the international day of observing the lives and sacrifices of labor, that is, May Day.

This state-inflicted violence and the tendency to persecute labor only intensified after the first major depression of 1893. During WWI, for example, the creation of a new propaganda machine legitimized this repression, designed as it was to demonize any opposition to capitalism and war as un-American. Supporting this move against labor, the U.S. federal government passed the Alien and Sedition Acts in 1798. The Alien Act was designed to expel foreign radicals from the country while the Sedition Act made illegal "false, scandalous, or malicious" writing against the U.S. (Foner, 2009; Smith, 1984; Zinn, 2003). Drawing on the Sedition Act during WWI, the anti-war movement, which was intimately connected to the labor movement, was criminalized. That is, the IWW and other radical, left revolutionaries had spread the analysis that soldiers were doing nothing more than performing a job designed to benefit the capitalist class at the expense of labor, both in terms of all possible outcomes of the said conflict and in terms of the loss of life or the casualties of war. Protesting war was, therefore, part and parcel of challenging the domination and exploitation of the ruling class. In 1918, for example, socialist presidential candidate and labor leader, Eugene Debs, was arrested and imprisoned for ten years for an anti-war speech in which he challenged the working-class to engage in revolutionary struggle against capitalism and for socialism. This example, to some, may seem like an extreme and rare case, in November of 2011, through the National Defense Authorization Act, which has a budget of more than $662 billion, which overwhelmingly passed legislation bypassing due process for U.S. citizens suspected of being enemy combatants or un-American. Bill Van Auken (2011), writing for the *International Committee of the Fourth International,* connects this recent legislation to the example of Eugene Debs:

> In 1918, the socialist leader Eugene V. Debs was thrown into prison under the draconian Sedition Act for delivering a speech opposing the First World War and calling for the working class to take power and carry out the socialist transformation of society. Even then, however, the government had to try him before a jury. The legislation passed Thursday renders such democratic niceties superfluous. Now such an offense would be punishable by disappearance into a military-run concentration camp.
>
> (para. 12)

This recent increase in state-sanctioned repression can best be understood within the context of growing poverty and an international crisis in the global capitalist system (see below).

After the first crisis (i.e., depression) of 1893, which was partially overcome by the U.S.'s small role in WWI, but was never really resolved, was more or less displaced until the even greater crisis of the Great Depression of 1929. By then, government economic intervention on capital's behalf became more widespread. During the New Deal era, the government put unemployed surplus labor to work building roads, bridges, and schools, that is, the infrastructure that capital needed to expand. While these efforts were able to partially help capital recover to continue exploiting human labor power through accumulation, they were not sufficient by themselves. That is, the shift into a full-scale war-economy during WWII also allowed the American capitalist to survive to exploit and plunder another day. This shift subsidized industrial production, transforming manufacturing from civilian consumer items to death and large-scale warfare machinery. For the capitalist, it is not the commodity's content that matters; it is the rate of return at the end of the business cycle, and death has proven to be one of the most stable and lucrative investments. After all, capitalism, as an ever-expanding system, is driven by an internal need for new markets and, thus, deadly competition (i.e., war) for access to profitable markets and resources.

After WWII, the U.S. emerged as the sole capitalist superpower since many other major industrial production centers in Europe and Japan had been nearly bombed out of existence. The U.S., therefore, experienced a postwar boom in industrial output and growth. However, around the 1970s, most of Europe and Japan had recovered and were thriving centers of industrial output. The post-war Fordist compromise, therefore, became too costly for the U.S. capitalist class and was subsequently abandoned as a sustainable policy. Abandoning Fordism, or the idea that a livable wage will be guaranteed in exchange for the obedience and loyalty of labor, meant, of course, abandoning the American working-class and their wages; these were nearly the highest in the world by the 1970s, and abandoning them triggered a new down-turn or crisis in the cyclical nature of the capital's historical development.

What continued and advanced during the subsequent neoliberal era was capital's policy of military intervention in the so-called Third World in order to ensure that any equitable economic practice, like democratic socialism, was not successful. The U.S., therefore, has a long history of toppling democratically elected governments from Chile to Haiti, to see to it that puppet-dictatorships are in place to discipline labor and guarantee profits flow to the West (Chomsky, 1999). This enabled U.S. corporations to not just reduce the cost of labor a little, but to nearly eliminate it. Transnational trade is trade where centers of production and centers of consumption and management are divided by national borders. The policies that made transnational trade profitable are policies made by organizations such as the World Bank and the International Monetary Fund that eliminated many of the regulations that imposed taxes on corporations moving capital and goods across borders. The North American Free Trade Agreement was one of the most famous of these, as it led to the indigenous Zapatista uprising of central Mexico. More recently, the U.S. has signed a new series of free trade policies with Columbia, South Korea, and Panama, which will lead to further reductions in the middle-class. Understanding how capitalism, under its normal operating conditions, is a form of class warfare and terrorism means seeing how education consistently manipulates the ideas and worldviews held by the population.

We might, therefore, conclude that the current purpose of public schooling—that is, to reproduce the working and middle classes—was forged during the second industrial revolution as Horace Mann saw the rising tide of working-class discontent that threatened the elite class from which he came. Colleges and universities, many of which in the U.S. were founded during this time, embodied a related purpose: that is, advancements in the technologies of social control. In this contemporary context of increasing capitalist indoctrination, Marx's approach to class-consciousness and a serious discussion about a socialist alternative is imperative.

Marx and Class Consciousness

> After Marx the theorization of consciousness became deeply embroiled with the question of revolution.
>
> (Carpenter & Mojab, 2011, p. 125)

It is commonly believed that Marx viewed Hegel's dialectics as a decontexualized, non-materialist form of idealism that fails to challenge concrete reality because it reduces freedom to a mental act. Marxist professor Peter Hudis (2005) argues this belief is fundamentally wrong. In "Marx's Critical Appropriation and Transcendence of Hegel's Theory of Alienation," Hudis (2005) argues that, "Marx does not critique Hegel for failing to deal with reality" (p. 2) but rather is fundamentally influenced by Hegel's deep interest in labor and the alienation that engenders a self-consciousness that is "at home in his other-being as such" (Marx, 1988, p. 158). According to Hudis (2005), one of Marx's primary objections to Hegel was not that he failed to grasp reality, but that he abandons it, concluding that the absolute essence of reality is the Idea belittling the object of the idea as "merely external" (Marx, 1988, p. 167) and thus inferior to the absolute idea or God. Consequently, in abstracting thought from reality, and failing to reunite abstraction to the sensual world, Hegel stops short of the last act:

> The man estranged from himself is also the thinker estranged from his *essence*—that is, from the natural and human essence. His thoughts are therefore fixed mental shapes or ghosts dwelling outside nature and man. Hegel has locked up all these fixed mental forms together in his *Logic*, laying hold of them first as negation—that is, as an *alienation* of *human* thought—and then as the negation of the negation—that is, as a superseding of this alienation, as a *real* expression of human thought. But as even this still takes place within the confines of the estrangement, this negation of the negation is in part the restoring of these fixed forms in their estrangement; in part a stopping-short at the last act—the act of self-reference in alienation—as the true mode of being of these fixed mental forms; and in part, to the extent that this abstraction apprehends itself and experiences an infinite weariness with itself, there makes its appearance in Hegel, in the form of the resolution to recognize *nature* as the essential being and to go over to intuition, the abandonment of abstract thought . . . devoid of eyes, of teeth, of ears, of everything.
>
> (Marx, 1988, pp. 164–165)

Again, we might therefore summarize Marx's central critique of Hegel in the following way: the Hegelian dialectical movement begins with the recognition of an initial negation—the negation of human subjectivity—which stems from the realization that the human is alienated from herself as a result of abstract knowledge; this first negation leads to the conscious or deliberate negation of the cause of the alienation; however, Hegel's negation of the negation, the dialectical movement, ends with the reaffirmation of the alienation from consciousness by positioning the abstract idea as the ultimate essence or truth, rather than nature or the physical objects external to the Idea of it.

Marx's reconfiguration of Hegel's dialectic, therefore, serves as a decisive outline of how we might understand historical change as a collective, all-encompassing, material and ideological development where the economic base of capitalism serves as the primary source of human negation giving way to a complex and contradictory cultural context of false consciousness and critical consciousness (i.e., racism, sexism, homophobia as well as counter-hegemonic, revolutionary social movements with well-established traditions of artistic, musical, discursive, and tactical approaches). For Marx (1988), then, a naturalistic interpretation of the negation of the negation can be expressed as follows: "communism is humanism mediated by itself through the annulment of private property" (p. 161). In other words, not *stopping short* as Marx accuses Hegel of, means abandoning abstract thought (i.e., fixed ideas and categories) or the absolute idea in exchange for a perpetually moving and shifting natural world and the revolutionary implications of negating the property relations of capitalist production, which includes the social universe of capitalist society in its entirety because it is at the root of alienation and human suffering. From this totalizing perspective, it is impossible to separate the historical development of the working classes and the capitalist classes from racial and gender politics and the international relations of competing capitalists from the economic base of the capitalist mode of production—it is the social universe of capital that alienates humanity from itself.

In his summary of the intellectual roots of Marx's historical materialism, Alex Callinicos (2011) argues that for Hegel (1993), contradiction lies at the heart of all change and movement and therefore propels history since all entities embody contradiction. In the opening paragraphs of Hegel's (1993) *Science of Logic,* the German philosopher sets the parameters of this basic contradiction as "pure being and pure nothing are the same" (p. 82) but are also "absolutely distinct." Consequently, they are "inseparable and that each immediately vanishes in its opposite. Their truth is, therefore, this movement of the immediate vanishing of the one in the other: becoming a movement in which both are distinguished, but by a difference which has equally immediately resolved itself" (Hegel, 1993, p. 83). Callinicos (2011) describes this relationship between being and nothing using the example of the acorn and the oak tree. Consider:

> The acorn, in becoming an oak, has itself ceased to be. The oak is different from the acorn. The oak is *not* that acorn. Hegel would say that the oak is the *negation* of the acorn. Yet implicit within the acorn is the potential to become an oak. The acorn contains within itself its own negation, and is thus *contradictory.* It is this contradiction . . . that allows it to grow . . . Hegel then takes this a step further. When something negates itself it turns into its opposite.
>
> (p. 63)

Applied to society, as alluded to above, capitalism is not the end, but a stage in the development of humanity containing within it its own contradiction and thus negation. In capitalism, the central contradiction is the relationship between labor and capital, which simultaneously constitute a larger whole of antagonistically related parts. The two parts dissolve into the other; the more labor toils, the stronger and more powerful capital becomes. But when one breaks free, the other ceases to exist as such. Again, it is labor who suffers under capital as a commodified and thus alienated and exploited being, whose collective negation as labor, a free and non-alienated class for itself, becomes its opposite, not capital, for labor *is* capital, but the opposite of capital, democratic socialism.

Where Hegel abstracted consciousness from the sensual world of suffering and exploitation, Marx reunited knowledge to the body disputing the notion that *truth* only exists in the realm of pure thought unhindered by the sensual experience of the material world. Hegel achieved his abstraction by replacing that which is concrete with the idea of it, discursively transforming that which is finite into the infinite. Summarizing this tendency in Hegel's thought, Marx (1843/1978) notes how he ". . . gives the predicates an independent existence and subsequently transforms them in a mystical fashion into their subjects" (p. 18). The implications of Marx's revision of Hegel is an awareness that it is not only ideas that prevent *men and women* from achieving an assumed *absolute truth* and their subsequent full potential and that the struggle against oppression does not exclusively exist at the level of discourse. Marx and Engels (1932/1996), making this point, comment that the "phrases" Hegelians fight "... are only opposing other phrases, and that they are in no way combating the real existing world when they are merely combating the phrases of this world" (p. 41).

In order to combat *the real existing world*, Marx held that it was necessary to rescue consciousness from the world of Hegelian abstraction and examine its internally related nature in the context of actual material existence, which, for Marx (like Hegel), begins when humans first began to *produce* their own means of subsistence, when they begin to create their own material reality based on their immediate geographical surroundings. What humans are therefore first and foremost is defined by *what* they *produce* and *how* they *produce* it. Hegelian abstraction, while conscious of this historical development, disconnects consciousness from the *material* reality of the labor/capital relationship forever in motion. Summarizing Marx's conceptualization of consciousness, Carpenter and Mojab (2011) note that,

> Marx is entering the German Idealism debate about the relationships between matter and consciousness. He is demonstrating how consciousness is dialectically related to social organization of life and exists in both subjective and objective forms.
>
> (p. 127)

We might therefore note that, for Marx, class-consciousness involves being aware of one's structural/material location within capitalism (Cole, 2011; Kelsh and Hill, 2006; McLaren, 2005). Allman, McLaren, and Rikowski (2005) argue that, "Marx takes great pains to explain that it is not the type of concrete labor one performs that determines one's class position, but rather one's internal/dialectical relation with capital" (p. 145). Reflecting on the place of educators within the social universe of capital as a prelude to an extended discussion of Marx's conceptions of class and class consciousness, Deb Kelsh and Dave Hill (2006) begin by clarifying that the working class/labor consists of all those "who do not own the means of production and are therefore compelled to sell their labor power to survive" (p. 2). In explaining the relationship that education has with capital, Marx conceptualized two kinds of labor, both of which are embodied in all labor: labor that manufactures other commodities or services and labor that produces labor as a commodity (i.e., teachers) (Allman, McLaren and Rikowski, 2005).

Whatever type of work one does, it remains constant that "a central feature of the worker's life under capitalism is alienation, or the removal of one's labor from one's self," (p. 88) as Faith Agostinone-Wilson (2010) reminds us. Making her point in the context of the family, Agostinone-Wilson (2010) quotes Marx (1867/1967) from *Capital, Volume 1*:

> They alienate from him the intellectual potentialities of the labor process in the same proportion as science is incorporated in it as an independent power; they deform the conditions under which he works, subject him during the labor process to the despotism the more hateful for its meanness; they transform his life-time into working time, and drag his wife and child under the juggernaut of capital.
>
> (p. 88)

Again, even pro-capitalist, mainstream economists are beginning to concede that given the current downward spiral of capital, Marx seems to have been correct on many key issues, such as the alienating nature of wage labor. For example, Umair Haque (2011), author of *The New Capitalist Manifesto: Building a Disruptively Better Business*, argues in "Was Marx Right?", which appeared in the Harvard Business Review (September 7, 2011), that while he is a "staunch supporter of capitalism" (p. 1), he acknowledges that there are some relevant insights in Marx's analyses of the dangers of industrial capitalism. Regarding the alienating nature of capitalism Haque (2011) comments:

> As workers were divorced from the output of their labor, Marx claimed, their sense of self-determination dwindled, alienating them from a sense of meaning, purpose, and fulfillment. How's Marx doing on this score? I'd say quite well: even the most self-proclaimed humane modern workplaces, for all their creature comforts, are bastions of bone-crushing tedium and soul-sucking mediocrity, filled with dreary meetings, dismal tasks, and pointless objectives that are well, just a little bit alienating. If sweating over the font in a PowerPoint deck for the mega-leveraged buyout of a line of designer diapers is the portrait of modern "work," then call me—and I'd bet most of you—alienated: disengaged, demoralized, [and] unmotivated.
>
> (p. 2)

Clearly, Haque (2011) is referring here to work typically classified as "middle-class." If the most privileged wage labor is alienating, then we can say with certainty that there are no exceptions or safe-havens within capitalism—it is all, to one degree or another, alienating. The teaching profession as well has become increasingly deskilled and mechanized, although, as outlined above, teaching has always been implicated in the programs and interests of the ruling-class. While it is clear that racial disparities and discrimination are exacerbated during times of crisis, and the continued stagnation of capital is going to have the most devastating consequence for people of color, the creation of jobs within capitalism can only take us to the next crisis. Revolution and a post-capitalist society are our only hope FOR?

I'm risking unnecessary repetition, but I think it is therefore extremely important for teacher education programs to develop within their students a Marxist class-consciousness, as I have argued throughout. More specifically, this Marxist class-consciousness must also be situated in a global context. That is, William I. Robinson (2005), outlining the parameters of a *critical globalization studies,* makes this point, noting that "social arrangements in the early twenty-first century must increasingly be understood—indeed, can only be understood—in the context of global-level structures and processes" (p. 12). However, because not all global thinking and practices are critical (i.e., not all promote progressive or revolutionary transformation), our global class-consciousness must transcend the mainstream global perspective that encourages teacher education students to become technologically savvy and multiculturally sensitive in order to compete in the global market for a shrinking supply of middle-class-paying professional career opportunities. Rather, the global class-consciousness of teacher education programs must be informed by the insight that the increasing poverty in the U.S. is connected to the increasing poverty globally and the neoliberal policies of the World Bank, the International Monetary Fund, and the resulting practices of multinational mega-corporations. This awareness must also be coupled with a dedication to overcome such structural poverty, which requires pushing beyond the limits of reform efforts and abandoning capitalism and a market economy in general.

Again, because labor tends not to be class conscious, working-class workers with middle-class culture and white privilege have a tendency to discriminate or disrespect colleagues of color who do not possess middle-class cultural capital, which implicitly includes whiteness. Consequently, notions of what it means to be articulate are firmly grounded in the cultural capital of middle-class whiteness. Reflecting on her own experiences with middle-class workers as a self-identified working-class woman of color, Antonia Darder (2011) notes that, "middle class liberals . . . seem to love our presence, but are often ambivalent about our participation, particularly when our expressed concerns fall outside of the exceptional notions of the ideal" (pp. 6–7). Essentially, Darder (2011) documents the tendency of white, middle-class colleagues to commodify colleagues of color as either evidence of the existence of meritocracy or as remarkable exceptions to the usual stories of failure. Such dominant social views are unable to situate the experiences and journeys of individuals in a larger historical context of European empire, colonialism, slavery, institutional white privilege, and neoliberal capitalism. This phenomenon can be best understood within the history of whiteness as a mechanism employed by the seventeenth century plantocracy to build a larger base of support for themselves, ensuring the perpetuation of the basic structure of class power. Whiteness has worked brilliantly, in the most devious, deceitful sense, in ensuring the hegemony of capitalism. Consequently, white middle-class workers, embodying the false consciousness that leads them to believe their interests are one and the same as capitalists, manifests itself in the ways Darder (2011) explains above.

It has been documented that middle-class professionals have internalized a capitalist class identity so thoroughly that there is a tendency for them to actively seek to maintain their place of privilege by emerging as the primary supporters of oppressive educational devices, such as testing professionals. Situated in the context of a shrinking middle-class (Pressman, 2007; 2010), these professionals, whom Au (2009) traces back to the emergence of the social efficiency model advanced through Taylorism (see also, Malott, 2010), it is not surprising that "the professional and managerial new middle class not only justify their own existence within educational processes and policies and maintain their own social and economic upward mobility, but they also create the room to align themselves with the interests of neoliberals" (Au, 2009, pp. 58–59). However, Au (2009) makes this argument to challenge the position that the primary driving force behind the neoliberalization of education is the capitalist class. While it is clear enough that middle-class workers independently advocate for their own survival and necessity without external coercion from the capitalist class, a more useful interpretation, in my opinion, would be that this is simply the product of how workers' identities are informed by capitalism and how whiteness is designed to encourage white workers to see that their own interests are one and the same as the capitalist class, especially middle-class workers whose intellectual and managerial labor is significantly less physical than the workers whose work is designed to control and manage. In order to transcend this middle-class indoctrination and the false sense of class position it fosters, what follows are some major points that outline what a class conscious educator might look like in practice.

The Class-Conscious Educator in the Twenty-First Century

Foremost, the class-conscious educator understands that capitalists have traditionally valued the existence of a middle-class because it serves their own interests. For example, Steven Pressman (2007), making the case for the survival of the middle-class and seemingly writing from a global middle-class perspective, argues that, "a large and vibrant middle class is important to every nation. It contributes to economic growth, as well as to social and political stability" (p. 181). Making no mistake about his own alignment with the capitalist class, Pressman (2007) argues that,

> The middle class helps mitigate class warfare. Marx believed that economic history was a class struggle between haves and have-nots, and that the have-nots would eventually band together and overthrow the capitalist system. What Marx missed was that a middle class might arise and serve as a buffer between the poor and the wealthy.
>
> (p. 181)

A class-conscious educator is able to identify the errors in Pressman's (2007) arguments, aware that Marx was intimately conscious of the division of labor and labor's role in self-reproduction, that is, in management's role in policing and enforcing the laws and policies accepted by capital. A class-conscious educator is also aware of the fallacy behind one of the primary reasons that has been put forth for supporting the middle class, which is that "people do care about their relative standing and that relative standing is correlated with subjective assessments of well-being" (p. 181). Educators with a critical point of view are also aware that the middle-class has traditionally served the function of not only racially dividing workers through white privilege, but that the middle-class is needed so the cycle of capitalist production can be completed. That is, without a large pool of active consumers to purchase the commodities made by unknown workers in unknown foreign lands, value realization—the last stage in the cycle before accumulation—would not happen, which leads to over-production and economic crisis, as we are currently experiencing.

Class-conscious education workers also know that the system of mass compulsory education that middle-class workers have designed and supported has always been intended to serve the interests not of pupils or teachers, but of the capitalist class for which students are trained to obediently serve. This helps to explain why the captains of industry, as noted above, supported it since Horace Mann's crusade for mass schooling in the mid-1800s. For example, these educators know that Mann's crusade to educate the masses of peasant immigrants from Ireland, Germany, Italy and other European countries, was successful because the industrial capitalists of the time needed a more regimented and subdued pool of labor power to fuel the booming industrial revolution, so they supported him. Critical educators also understand that the Indian Boarding School Project was an extended government-funded effort designed to both disconnect Native Americans from their ancestral lands by obliterating Native American cultures, customs, economies, and languages, and replacing them with a worldview conducive to industrial capitalism. That is, the effort to *kill the Indian and save the man inside* was an effort to disrupt the Native American systems of cultural and social reproduction by creating consenting low-level wage workers. Industrialist politicians supported the funding of Christian-based schools instead of sending the military to exterminate Native American communities outright because it was deemed less costly; that is, they made not a moral decision but rather one based upon cost-effectiveness. The model of education for African Americans after the Civil War, designed to transform enslaved Africans into law-abiding low-level wage earners, is a history many critically class-conscious educators are also well aware of (Malott, 2008; 2010).

What is more, education workers who are intimately aware of their class position within capitalism understand with precise clarity that they are increasingly used as scapegoats to turn public education dollars over to for-profit management companies eager to cut costs (i.e., lowering teacher wages and/or increasing productivity—longer hours, same pay). Educators who know that high-stakes, standardized exams degrade the control they have over their own labor power and damage the possibility for critical, rigorous thought, are conscious of how their occupation is being increasingly implicated in serving the needs of capital and are thus class conscious.

These class-conscious educators, quite simply, know they are part of the working class, which is why they depend on a wage to survive, that is, because they do not own the means of production and the private property it represents. Critical educators are also conscious of the fact that in North America, the resource-rich land that has fuelled industrial capitalism and enriched not only industrialists, but investment bankers and profiteers in general, for the past three hundred years, was acquired through brutal militarization, violent conquest, and the vast tradition of deception and cultural genocide previously mentioned—a process Marx (1867/1967) referred to as *primitive accumulation.*

Aware of how educators are implicated in this process, Marxist teachers realize that the forceful acquisition of resources is more than just an early stage of industrial capitalism. It is an on-going requirement of capital since human labor power alone is not enough to fuel the ever-expanding model of capitalist accumulation. The value-production process is one that enriches capital and exploits labor in an ever-deepening downward spiral of crisis, since the laws of capital drives capitalists toward perpetual expansion and leads to schemes to drive down the cost of production by neoliberalizing trade laws that enable capitalists to globally drive down wages, reduce environmental regulations, and privatize the commons. Meanwhile, the inevitable resistance against capital by labor is an ever-expanding problem and a concern for capitalists. It, therefore, follows that capital requires a system of social control and reproduction to ensure the ongoing existence of the most important commodity needed for both primitive and wealth accumulation, that is, labor willing to be purchased for both war and commodity/service production. Capital, therefore, needs teachers to be part of the process that indoctrinates students with the fundamentalist worldview that claims capitalism is inevitable and the backbone that makes democracy and civil rights possible. I use the notion of fundamentalism here in the sense of blindly and uncritically accepting universal truths, because there is plenty of evidence that more than suggests capital is anything but inevitable. Educators with class-consciousness understand that their own consent in reproducing labor, ultimately, prevents their own liberation (along with the rest of labor) (Allman, McLaren, and Rikowski, 2005).

Where Marx laid the material foundation for a concrete understanding of consciousness, Lenin, on the other hand, situates the notion of consciousness in terms of developing a "political agenda necessary for revolution" (Carpenter and Mojab, 2011, p. 127). Underscoring this line of reasoning Carpenter and Mojab (2011) elaborate,

> . . . To be "conscious" is to have the kind of consciousness that relates to revolutionary practice. Lenin is moving into the theorization of how to organize thinking and ideas in a revolutionary manner based on the dialectical theorization of Marx.
>
> (p. 127)

From this point of view it is clear that the state of being conscious, for educators and labor in general, refers to a critical, class-consciousness conducive to revolutionary transformation. However, for Lenin (1902/1975), the conscious struggle toward *revolutionary social democracy* or socialism is not likely to emerge within the working-class's spontaneous uprisings and rebellions without outside intervention. Lenin (1902/1975) argues that the experience of being exploited as a wageworker or a peasant by itself is not enough to stimulate a critical awareness of class and its historical development and transformation. Because of the ruling class's use of ideological indoctrination as a form of social control and because the ruling-class's ideology or worldview is far older and more completely developed and entrenched than socialist ideology, the labor movement, when operating independently, has tended toward the reformist tradition of trade unionism, negatively referred to by Lenin (1902/1975) as *economism.*

At the same time, Lenin (1902/1975) acknowledges that it is not only labor who is systematically miseducated. That is, "the entire younger generation of the educated classes has been systematically reared for decades on . . . [the] turn towards bourgeois criticism of all the fundamental ideas of Marxism" (Lenin, 1902/1975, p. 13). Because socialist ideology has been developed by intellectuals, the revolutionary leaders, or the vanguard (those at the front of the class struggle), are most likely to come from internal resistance within the *propertied class,* according to Lenin (1902/1975). Lenin (1902/1975) comes to this conclusion because he is convinced that there are only two ideologies, bourgeois and socialist, therefore rendering the possibility of a "middle course" impossible because "mankind has not created a 'third' ideology" (pp. 28–29). Consequently, "to belittle the socialist ideology in any way, to turn aside from it in the slightest degree means to strengthen bourgeois ideology" (Lenin, 1902/1975, p. 29).

Lenin (1902/1975) discounts the history and legacy of anarchist theory and practice here, thereby setting himself up for critique. By arguing that there are only two ideologies, Lenin (1902/1975) also affirms the Western idea that the world's indigenous peoples are in fact primitive with underdeveloped backgrounds, and thus constitute no non-Western ideologies of their own. Let's set this critique aside and assume there is any legitimacy to the conclusion that socialist leaders will most likely emerge from intellectuals. After all, since the post-WWII years in the U.S. when capital needed a more highly educated and trained working-class to manage and expand the industrial machine, a significant portion of the labor class entered universities. Consequently, thousands upon thousands of workers came into contact with the philosophical traditions of academia. Because higher education has always been designed to serve capital's interests and needs, much of this new middle-class became "loyal buffers against trouble" (Zinn, 2003). However, a sizable segment of this new intelligentsia, coming from the working class rather than from the propertied class, have played an important part in developing Marxist theory through the shifting nature of capital. To say "there can be no talk of an independent ideology formulated by the working masses" (Lenin, 1902/1975, p. 28) is even less true today than it was in 1901.

At the same time, to say that those who rely on a wage to survive are not likely to develop a socialist consciousness on their own, which was Lenin's position, should not be interpreted as a disdain for labor, which has been a common reason to reject both Lenin *and* Marx. The very existence of critical pedagogy and critical theory more generally, from critical race theory to postmodernism, is testament to the need for externally introducing critical analysis and class-consciousness to workers (from teachers and professors to store clerks). However, Lenin, drawing on Marx, rejects eclecticism (i.e., drawing on many theories) because that could only mean moving away from socialist and toward bourgeois ideology. Embracing Joe L. Kincheloe's postformalism, as I have done above and elsewhere (Malott, 2011a), means that we must contribute to socialism and never endorse the reformist drive of bourgeois ideology.

Another common critique of Lenin is that his pedagogy is authoritarian and thus anti-democratic. However, in "The Tasks of the Youth League," Lenin (1920/1975) argues against the mindless banking model of capitalist schooling and makes the case for socialist theory to always be represented in revolutionary practice. While Lenin (1920/1975) supports the revolutionary position that "the old schools" should be done away with, he warns that they do contain some knowledge useful to the building of socialist society, such as the knowledge of agriculture, engineering, and so forth. Unlike the old schools, however, Lenin (1920/1975) argues that these doctrines should be assimilated critically. Summarizing his position and vision of a socialist education, Lenin (1920/1975) notes,

> . . . We must realize that we must replace the old system of instruction, the old cramming and the old drill, with an ability to acquire the sum total of human knowledge, and to acquire it in

> such a way that communism shall not be something to be learned by rote, but something that you yourselves have thought over, something that will embody conclusions inevitable from the standpoint of present-day education.
>
> (p. 666)

Lending legitimacy to this work and legacy of Lenin, in a groundbreaking essay demonstrating how Vygotsky's socially situated interpretive framework is based on Lenin's Marxist conceptualization of the development of class consciousness, Au (2007), in this instance, extends the arguments for Marxism in the twenty-first century. Lenin's interest in a Russian revolution led him to analyze how the working class becomes conscious of their position within capitalism, reflecting upon the St. Petersburg strikes of 1896 as an example of what he called *spontaneity.* These studies led Lenin to acknowledge how spontaneous consciousness and thought can be encouraged and developed into deliberate, revolutionary consciousness. Lenin described examples of spontaneous consciousness, where labor, in acts of *frustration and revenge,* rose up in riots and destroyed the machinery of production. Theorizing this phenomenon, Lenin described it as an emergent class consciousness. The more planned out and organized actions of the working class against capitalists, such as strikes, Lenin described as "the class struggle in embryo" (Lenin quoted in Au, 2007, p. 276). Similarly, Vygotsky theorized the dialectical relationship between "everyday" concepts (i.e. Lenin's spontaneous) and "scientific" concepts (i.e. Lenin's conscious) where the complex interchange between the two, with the assistance of an intervening educator (or revolutionary), could result in purposeful growth and development (Au, 2007, 2009). Evoking Vygotsky's famous methodological construct, the zone of proximal development (ZPD), Au (2007) argues that Lenin's theorization of these two types of consciousness was intended to identify and limit the distance between spontaneous revolt and purposeful revolutionary struggle against the commodification of human labor power and the creation of abstract labor.

Au (2007) stresses the significance of Vygotsky's concept of *conscious awareness* and the ZPD as informing his whole framework. Where Lenin was interested in the working class understanding the whole system in order to transform it, Vygotsky stressed the importance of one being conscious of one's consciousness situated in a larger social context. Following Vygotsky and Lenin's Marxism here, the heart of Paulo Freire's critical pedagogy is the process of becoming conscious of one's own consciousness as one of the first and on-going processes of developing a class consciousness and becoming an active participant in revolutionary movement building (Malott, 2011a). Freire's (2005) reliance on Vygotsky is brought to light in *Teachers as Cultural Workers: Letters to Those Who Dare Teach,* wherein he comments that, "it is undeniably important to read the works of . . . Vygotsky" because he understands "the relationship between reading and writing" as "processes that cannot be separated" and should thus be "organized" by educators "in such a way as to create the perception that they are needed for something" (pp. 43–45) because knowledge is not separate from the social worlds in which it emerges. That "something" Freire refers to, of course, is class-consciousness. That is, reading and writing are important for developing critical lenses and uncovering the ways we are shaped by capitalist schooling, and then recognizing a place of departure for getting to more purposeful, organized, planned out, tactical revolutionary struggle against what Freire calls domestication or indoctrination where workers see their own interests as one and the same, since capitalists lead labor to support their own on-going exploitation and commodification as abstract labor.

Weber and Teacher Education

While Marx's focus on class-consciousness has had a lasting impact on revolutionary education into the twenty-first century, as alluded to above, Marxism's transformative potential has been stunted by the dominance of a Weberian conception of class and the outright ridicule and belittling of Marxist work in general. These trends have been especially severe at the center of contemporary imperialist power—in the United States in particular (Cole, 2011; Hill, McLaren, Cole, and Rikowski, 2002; Kelsh and Hill, 2006; Malott, 2011b; McLaren and Jaramillo, 2010). The most deleterious aspects of the use of Max Weber's sociological conception of class can be summarized as follows:

- In their previously mentioned essay, "The Culturalization of Class and the Occluding of Class Consciousness: The Knowledge Industry in/of Education," Deb Kelsh and Dave Hill (2006) offer an enlightening comparison between Marx and Weber. They begin their investigation, noting that for both writers, "class determination involves property" (p. 5). However, Marx's conception of how property determines class position is based on the realization that those who do not open OWN? property or the means of production are forced out of necessity to sell their labor for a wage while those who do own property live off the profit or surplus value extracted or exploited from labor. Weber, on the other hand, does not connect his theory of property to capital, but to consumption patterns and culture (Kelsh & Hill, 2006).
- We might, therefore, say that unlike Marx's theory of class, Weber's is not relational. That is, Weber does not situate class in the context of one's relation to private property. Making this point, Kelsh and Hill (2006) conclude that, "Weberian-based formulations of class serve the interests of the capitalist class . . . insofar as they erase both the proletariat and the capitalist classes as antagonistic entities unified in the contradictory and exploitative social (property) relations of capitalist production" (p. 6).
- Again, because Weber's theory is not relational, it conceals the antagonistic relationship between the working class and capitalists.
- Weberian conceptions of social class, therefore, present class as a series of disconnected categories determined by one's skills, market appeal, and institutional privilege.
- Failing to grasp the root of inequality under capitalism, Weberian approaches only appear radical because they mention class and *transforming* capital. However, transforming is *not* overthrowing. Consequently, because this model is reformist and not revolutionary, some have argued that it, by default, supports capitalism by creating an opportunity to become more multicultural and equal in its exploitation (Kelsh & Hill, 2006; McLaren & Jaramillo, 2010).
- Social class, for Weber, is therefore not a tool to *explain* one's relationship to capital, but rather a way to *classify* and manage different classes whose *life chances* are determined by *market situation* (Kelsh & Hill, 2006, p. 7).
- The significance here resides in the fact that Weber's theory of class leads to pseudo-radicalism and confusion about what the problem is and what needs to be done to end class oppression and exploitation. Weber's theory can only ever lead to reform when it is revolution that is needed.

Following these insights, it seems reasonable to argue that the major limitation of multicultural foci on white privilege and consumption patterns resides within the fact that they are informed by a Weberian conception of social class, thereby treating capitalism as something to *equalize access to* rather than something to *overcome.* As a result, teacher education students tend not to be challenged to situate white privilege in a larger historical context that demonstrates that even the most privileged "middle-class" ranks of labor would be far better off, psychologically, emotionally, cognitively, and even economically (especially considering the rapid deterioration of this exalted subset of the working class), in a democratic socialist life after capital. In solidifying this analysis, it is necessary to restate the fact that one's class position is not determined by the type of work one does, but rather by one's relationship to capital—if a person must sell labor for a wage to survive, that person is not a capitalist; he or she is part of the working class, even if he or she has white privilege and middle-class consumer culture. The system of institutionalized white privilege was created to maintain the system of class exploitation by convincing poor Europeans that their interests were the same as the capitalists rather than with workers whose identities fell outside the conceptual boundaries of whiteness. It has worked extraordinarily well. However, while the human mind can be conditioned, it is never predetermined or fixed, leading to a complex series of fractures and counter-hegemonies, rendering the hegemonic-building project a never-ending process.

Critically, class-conscious educators know that middle-class privilege and middle-class consumer culture are elaborate schemes designed to ensure the continued support for capitalism by a significant proportion of the working-class. A Weberian conception of social class with its over-emphasis on disconnected categories represents a significant barrier to class-consciousness.

Teacher Education and a Revolutionary Class Consciousness

What Marx's historical analysis of social development is particularly good at, as demonstrated by the likes of Peter McLaren, is revealing the shallowness of socially-acceptable notions of *social justice* in places such as the center of the global capitalist empire, the United States of America. That is, while it is *safe* to speak mildly of social justice, it tends not to be deemed as harmless when the discussion ventures into notions of *economic* justice. Teachers are, therefore, not permitted by democratic institutions to question the economic system in which they live and work (McLaren & Jaramillo, 2007). It is, therefore, not surprising that Weber's conception of social class dominates teacher education, leading, as argued above, to a widespread lack of class-consciousness in classroom teachers, teacher educators, and teacher education students.

Despite the lack of support from democratic institutions, Marxist educators, such as Peter McLaren, Deb Kelsh, Dave Hill, Glenn Rikowski, Ramin Farahmandpur, Antonia Darder, Gregory Martin, Rich Gibson, Faith Agostinone-Wilson, Shahrzad Mojab, the contributors of this volume, and others, have named the destination for humanity in the twenty-first century *democratic socialism* for a post-capitalist society. Mike Cole, for example, notes that while this goal may seem prescriptive, and while there is opportunity for "making concrete suggestions for practice in educational institutions that might move the project forward," "Marxists do not have a blueprint for the future" (pp. 41–44). For these educators, decolonizing education means, paraphrasing McLaren (2005), refusing to ensure the supremacy of international financial capital; troubling the investment and market prerogatives of transnational corporations; and putting corporations under the popular control of the people. Revolutionary education here is informed by a deep understanding that education is always political, and it is of the utmost importance that students be provided the experiences where they can truly imagine a life outside the laws of capital and the social reproduction of abstract labor; where students can debate the shortcomings of past revolutions and tactics; and where educators and students can discuss and experiment with the notion of capacity building where the quest is for social institutions, human relationships and other arrangements that are best suited for human growth and development, enabling us to reach our full potential (McLaren & Jaramillo, 2007). Because of capital's alienating nature, which suppresses human creativity and capacity and leads to psychological health issues and other disorders, a new life-affirming system is needed which may very well be a sort of democratic, post-capitalist socialism.

Challenging students to consider a Marxist-informed analysis of labor situated in a historical and contemporary global context is one of the first steps in engaging them in the process of becoming class conscious and, therefore, a future anti-capitalist educator. This becomes a matter of self-preservation and not a paternalistic gesture, thereby avoiding the pitfalls of Weberian examples of reformist social justice *service* work. Because there are only two ways in which one can be situated in relation to capital—as its creator or its accumulator—there are only two classes in capitalist society. The middle-class is a ruse. Again, a class-conscious educator understands that a false sense of security and belonging and the consumer privileges that have historically accompanied it have seduced the working class into striving to achieve its ranks.

Marxist educators have dedicated a tremendous amount of time and energy over the past twenty years to combat the Weberian plague sapping the revolutionary potential from the educational left, leaving progressive educators unable to locate their own position within capitalism. Through two of his most recent books, Mike Cole (2009; 2011) has made tremendous strides in challenging not only the Weberian mistakes mentioned above, but challenging the false separation of race from class and the retreat from class that has dominated the advent of critical race theory (CRT). Cole's work here has been far more constructive than simply dismissing CRT. Rather, Cole rigorously highlights the many valuable contributions of CRT while challenging its weaknesses regarding Marxist analysis. In the process, Cole (2009, 2011) presents a thoroughly global analysis of capitalism and the hegemonic role that race has traditionally played. Consequently, Cole's socialist alternative is grounded on a vision of a post-capitalist, anti-racist, democratic socialism. Making the case for the possibility of socialism has required Marxists to challenge the idea that capitalism is inevitable. It is, therefore, not surprising that Cole (2011) and many other Marxist educators have been outspoken proponents of President Hugo Chavez of Venezuela and Castro's Cuba because their very existence and their headway toward democratic socialism provides strong evidence against the "inevitability of capitalism" thesis.

While the work of Cole and others reminds us of what is possible by pointing to that which exists, the work of Freud helps labor understand why it suffers so frequently from psychological ailments; this reminds the most privileged workers immersed in middle-class consumer culture that life after capital is a destination not just for the most oppressed or excluded. Again, these insights have been and continue to be of major importance and value to critical pedagogy.

Writing and conducting research in the midst of the Great Depression of 1929, and therefore witnessing, even if he never fully named it as such, the psychological damage of an alienating capitalist system that views the individual, and ultimately the student, as passive receiver of commands and direction, and thus expected to repress fundamental human drives of creativity directly connected to the production and creation of life through the natural employment of ones' own human labor power. Freud (1938/1995) calls his work here, "the theory of repression" (p. 907).

Consequently, we might say that *repression,* in the Freudian sense, is the idea that in a capitalist society, which, by definition, demands obedience in work and other relationships, certain *natural* human drives and desires, such as the creative and free use of language and labor, are subjugated, rendering the individual alienated from self, other, the natural world, and their own labor. As a result, the sources of labor's repression remain buried in the subconscious because the individual is "trying to repress" something to which they "object" (Freud, 1938/1995, p. 190). That is, the realization that to be driven, out of necessity, to sell one's labor power for a wage far less than the value it produces renders one exploited and dehumanized—externally commanded and, therefore, creatively repressed. The worker, therefore, represses this realization and resists any external attempt to bring it to the surface, that is, confronting one's material conditions. Leaving the repressed wage earner a psychological way out of mental, and ultimately material, enslavement, Freud (1938/1995) acknowledges that within the repressed individual, the "psychic mechanism" that allows "suppressed wishes to force their way to realization," despite indoctrination and oppression, "is retained in being and in working order" (p. 256).

For Giroux (2009), "Freud's metapsychology provided an important theoretical foundation for revealing the interplay between the individual and society," and therefore, "the antagonistic character of social reality" (p. 41). The significance of Freud here, argues Giroux (2009), is that he reveals the processes through which "society reproduced its power in and over the individual" (p. 41). Giroux outlines how these insights informed members of Germany's critical Frankfurt School, such as Marcuse and Adorno, around WWII and after, to help them understand how both capitalist and socialist societies operated according to authoritarian principles of governance and enforcement. Frankfurt School scholars argued, in their more liberatory moments, that only through a detailed understanding of how power is reproduced psychologically could it be subverted and transformed. Herbert Marcuse (1964), for example, in *One-Dimensional Man: Studies in the Ideology of Advanced Industrial Society,* observes that, "Freud's fundamental insight that the patient's trouble is rooted in a *general* sickness which cannot be cured by analytic analysis," and the suggestion that "the patient's disease is a protest reaction against the sick world in which he lives" (p. 183) was a ground-breaking insight that paved the way for more contextualized understandings of mental illness.

Again, Freud argued that whenever human desires and drives, such as the creative use of language and labor, are suppressed or subjugated, people suffer, become psychologically and physically ill, and develop disorders. This holds true for segments of the working-class that are the most privileged and, therefore, part of middle-class consumer culture as well as the most exploited and oppressed parts of labor. As the middle-class shrinks, especially the white middle class, and as they increasingly fall victim to the housing market crash that African American and Latino families have been subjected to for far longer, the sense of stability and security of middle-class families suffers, leading to stress, obesity, and a plethora of ailments. Even in times of relative prosperity, the middle-class's satisfaction with life tends not to be significantly higher than workers who are not able to sell their labor power for as high a wage. Other recent studies support this conclusion, finding that the correlation between income and happiness is primarily an unfounded myth (Pressman, 2010).

The call for a democratic socialist future is, therefore, not only a call for a relatively high, constant standard of living globally, but it is a call for the sense of security and peace of mind that comes with knowing one's voice actually has equal weight in the important decisions concerning economics and politics that are currently monopolized by a handful of multinational corporate entities/capitalist governments.

***

While there is widespread consensus among much of the radical left (a small subset within an already marginal left) that capitalism is a deeply flawed and inherently unequal and pathologizing system that must be abolished, there is little agreement about how this might happen. One of the age-old centers of debate, traced back most famously to Marx and his anarchist rival Mikhail Bakunin, is the role of the state in a post-capitalist revolutionary society. Marxists argue that in the transition from capitalism to socialism, the working class must not only take control of the means of production and the schools, but the nation or government as well. The idea is to use the capitalist state to destroy itself as well as to transition out of a market economy.

Anarchists, on the other hand, argue that government itself is an inherently repressive apparatus or tool, and any attempt to take control of it will inevitably lead to the reproduction of some form of oppression. Predictably enough, it is most commonly Stalinism, that inescapable stain that has irrevocably attached itself to the history of Marxism, that anarchist scholarship has focused on as a reason to reject the idea of the possible role of the state in creating real, paradigm-shifting change. That is, Stalinism's history of executing and sentencing peasants to labor prison camps in the name of progress for the Communist Party and educating its citizenry to support uncritically the state and even to sacrifice their lives for it, has led to great skepticism among the world's post-WWII left regarding seizing control of the state and even the means of production as outdated forms of revolutionary practice or pedagogy. Similarly, pro-capitalist forces draw on the 1989 fall of Soviet Communism as evidence against the relevancy of Marx's work.

However, offering a more complex understanding of the failure of the Russian Revolution (as well as Mao's China) in *Why Marx was Right,* Terry Eagleton (2011) begins by reminding his pro-capitalist readers that capitalism "was forged in blood and tears" (p. 12) just as deeply, and perhaps more so, than Stalin's Soviet Union or Mao's Communist China. In other words, while capitalism has worked "some of the time," it has done so, like Stalin and Mao's projects, "at a staggering human cost" (p. 15). Consequently, capitalism has "proved incapable of breeding affluence without creating huge swaths of deprivation alongside it" (Eagleton, 2011, p. 15). Global capitalism, since the second industrial revolution, outlined above, has therefore created a world of elite wealth and widespread poverty. Explaining the global structural reasons behind the failure of the Soviet Union, Eagleton (2011) notes that, "Marx himself never imagined that socialism could be achieved in impoverished conditions" (p. 16). Not only Marx but Lenin and Trotsky, according to Eagleton (2011), were quite aware that:

> You cannot reorganize wealth for the benefit of all if there is precious little wealth to reorganize . . . You cannot abolish social classes in conditions of scarcity, since conflicts over a material surplus too meager to meet everyone's needs will revive them again. . . All you will get is socialized scarcity. If you need to accumulate capital. . .from scratch, then the most effective way of doing so, however brutal, is through the profit motive. Nor did Marxists ever imagine that it was possible to achieve socialism in one country alone. The movement was international or it was nothing. This was a hardheaded materialist claim, not a piously idealist one. If a socialist nation failed to win international support in a world where production was specialized and divided among different nations, it would be unable

> to draw upon the global resources needed to abolish scarcity. . .The outlandish notion of socialism in one country was invented by Stalin in the 1920s, partly as a cynical rationalization of the fact that other nations had been unable to come to the aid of the Soviet Union. It has no warrant in Marx himself.
>
> (pp. 16–17)

Eagleton goes on to point out that global isolation and the resulting poverty are not the only barriers to socialism. That is, he argues that for socialism to emerge, what is required is a highly educated and "politically sophisticated" citizenry with "enlightened liberal traditions and the habit of democracy" (p. 18). Given that much of the world, to one extent or another, has been under colonial rule for the past 500 years (since Columbus washed up on the shores of what is now Haiti and the Dominican Republic in 1492), and, therefore, indoctrinated through capitalist schooling, religion, and/or authoritarian regimes with uncritical dogmatic thinking, the possibility for a global socialist future seems, to an extent, dependent upon the current effectiveness of critical pedagogy challenging the capitalist present.

Consequently, this debate is no longer purely theoretical but now has a complex history of failed states to inform it. British Marxist Alex Callinicos (2010), in *Bonfire of Illusions,* summarizes this debate brilliantly. Making a case for the use of government in working-class, anti-capitalist revolution, Callinicos (2010) argues that the state, since at least the 1930s (the Great Depression of 1929), has played an increasingly interventionist role in the economy, both on behalf of capital, and when labor can demand it, on behalf of workers or the vast majority. Callinicos (2010) then looks to the global South, as it were—that part of the world generally agreed upon by today's left that has been the center of the global anti-capitalist movement since at least the 1990s, and possibly since the end of WWII (Chomsky, 1999)—as especially conscious of the expanding complexity of the global capitalist system and the subsequent necessity of an expansion of state intervention.

This movement has been significant and has led to the nationalization of the hydrocarbon industry in places such as Bolivia under Evo Morales due to his connection to the real demands of the organized, indigenous population that put him in office. However, Callinicos (2010) argues that it has, nevertheless, "often seemed reluctant to see an expansion in the state's economic power" (p. 135). Placing this tendency in context, Callinicos' (2010) insights are instructive: "Behind the suspicion of nationalization lies the memory of the bureaucratic state ownership introduced by Stalinism in the East and social democracy in the West" (p. 135). However, Callinicos (2010) argues that more recently, the theory of "autonomism" has posed the biggest challenge to nationalization because it is based on the belief that "we should forget about the state and try to develop localized alternatives to neoliberalism" (p. 135). While it seems reasonable that some degree of government intervention will likely be necessary in the transition out of capitalism, without the simultaneous anarchist or Indigenous community-building embodied in autonomism, indigeneity, and critical pedagogy more generally, then a truly democratic socialist life after capital will not likely emerge. Consequently, I would agree with Callinicos (2010) that by itself, autonomism is "hopeless" because it is not able to provide a solution to reversing "the privatization of hydrocarbons," for example, which, in Bolivia, was the will of the people. However, I would also argue that nationalization too is hopeless without sufficient autonomous movement work and community building to counter the ways our identities have been shaped by capital. For Callinicos (2010), this debate focuses on the question of who will own particular industries when the people liberate them from corporate control. He (2010) concludes that there is no alternative to nationalization because "the state is a national organization with both the coercive power and political legitimacy to carry through with something as ambitious as the takeover of the hydrocarbon industry" (Callinicos, 2010, p. 135). If this is true, then in the nationalization process, we must never lose sight of our *Anarchist Pedagogies* (Haworth, 2012).

Proceeding cautiously, however, Callinicos (2010) does warn against not repeating "the old mistake of traditional social democracy and identify the existing state as the main agency of progressive social change" (p. 136) because the bureaucratic, hierarchical state will "seek to maintain the domination of capital" even after nationalization. Consequently, "nationalization is not enough" (Callinicos, 2010, p. 136). Offering a framework for a revolutionary pedagogy, Callinicos (2010) explains:

> Indeed, really to break with the logic of capital, any extension of the boundaries of state ownership would have to involve the introduction of forms of democratic self-management through which the workers of the nationalized industry together with the consumers of the products could collectively decide on how it should be run for the common benefit. Seriously addressing this question means breaking another taboo and talking, not just about state ownership, but also about planning.
>
> (pp. 136–7)

From here Callinicos (2010) briefly outlines some of the work being done that attempts to theorize what a possible global life after capital could actually look like in practice as a reason to bring up the issue of planning. For example, Michael Albert's anarchist work on what he has called Participatory Economics or Parecon is outlined. Callinicos (2010) argues that while Albert's work is part of a very important discussion about planning or a planned economy, his proposal still represents a market approach and will nevertheless eventually fall victim to the same kind of austerity measures any competitive capitalist system will always tend toward. What a post-capitalist society will look like, of course, depends on the values and assumptions about human nature and what desired relationships inform it. This, in turn, will depend on how strong or weak the democratic impulse OF? is. A truly post-capitalist society will therefore depend on maximal participation. Critical pedagogy, therefore, still has lots of important work to do assisting people in becoming *conscious of their own consciousness* that has been shaped by the *social* institutions of capitalist *society*, from schools to the mass corporate media.

If nothing else, what I hope to be clear about the complex, enormous task at hand—transcending a market economy and state—is that the challenges posed by creating a socialist alternative demands that the global left embrace all critical tools from anarchists, feminists, critical race theorists, critical postmodernists, animal rights activists, Earth First! eco-pedagogues, critical indigenous sovereignists, orthodox Marxists, neo-Marxists, humanist Marxists, and others. This is no small feat since many of our approaches are theoretically at odds with each other. For example, the call for the democratization of culture and reforming capitalism is theoretically at odds with challenging capitalist property relations, as I argued throughout this chapter. How we might come together despite our many ideological differences will not be easy, especially for those of us who are *academics* with our egos and senses of self-importance and righteousness. The importance of self-reflection is that it raises *consciousness* and thus makes apparent the ways in which we are shaped by schooling.

References

Allman, P., McLaren, P., & Rikowski, G. (2005). After the box people: the labor-capital relation as class constitution and its consequences for Marxist educational theory and human resistance. In P. McLaren (Ed.), *Capitalists and conquerors: A critical pedagogy against empire* (pp. 135–165). New York: Rowman & Littlefield.

Au, W. (2007). Vygotsky and Lenin on learning: The parallel structures of individual and social development. *Science & Society. 71*(3), 273–298.
Au, W. (2009). *Unequal by design: High-stakes testing and the standardization of inequality.* New York: Routledge.
Callinicos, A. (2010). *Bonfire of illusions: The twin crises of the liberal world.* Cambridge, UK: Polity Press.
Callinicos, A. (2011). *The revolutionary ideas of Karl Marx.* Chicago: Haymarket.
Carpenter, S. & Mojab, S. (2011). Adult education and the "matter" of consciousness in Marxist feminism. In P. Jones (Ed.), *Marxism and education: Renewing the dialogue, pedagogy, and culture* (pp. 117–140). New York: Palgrave Macmillan.
Cole, M. (2009). *Critical race theory and education: A Marxist response.* New York: Palgrave Macmillan.
Cole, M. (2011). *Racism and education in the U.K. and the U.S.: Towards a socialist alternative.* New York: Palgrave Macmillan.
Darder, A. (2011). *A dissident voice: Essays on culture, pedagogy, and power.* New York: Peter Lang.
Foner, E. (2009). *Give me liberty! An American history: Vol. 2. From 1865* (2nd Ed.). New York: W.W. Norton & Co.
Freire, P. (2005). *Teachers as cultural workers: Letters to those who dare teach.* Boulder, CO: Westview Press.
Freud, S. (1938/1995). *The basic writings of Sigmund Freud.* (Trans. and edited by A. A. Brill). New York: The Modern Library.
Giroux, H. (2009). Critical theory and educational practice. In A. Darder, M. Baltodano & R. Torres (Eds.). *The critical pedagogy reader* (2nd Ed.). New York: Routledge.
Grande, S. (2004). *Red pedagogy: Native American social and political thought.* New York: Rowman & Littlefield.
Haque, U. (2011, September 7). Was Marx right? *Harvard Business Review.* Retrieved from http://blogs.hbr.org/haque/2011/09/was_marx_right.html
Haworth, R. (2012). *Anarchist pedagogies: Collective actions, theories, and reflections on Education.* Oakland, CA: PM Press.
Hegel, G.W.F. (1993). *Science of Logic* (A.V. Miller, Trans.). Atlantic Highlands, NJ: Humanities Paperback Library.
Hill, D., McLaren, P., Cole, M., & Rikowski, G. (2002). *Marxism against postmodernism in educational theory.* Lanham, MD: Lexington Books.
Hudis, P. (2005). *Marx's critical appropriation and transcendence of Hegel's theory of alienation.* Presented at Brecht Forum, New York City.
Kelsh, D., & Hill, D. (2006). The culturalization of class and the occluding of class consciousness: The knowledge industry in/of education. *Journal for Critical Education Policy Studies. 4*(1). Retrieved from http://www.jceps.com/?pageID=article&articleID=59
Klobby, (1999). *Inequality, power, and development: The task of political sociology.* New York: Humanity Books.
Lenin, V. I. (1901/1975). What is to be done: Burning questions of our movement. In R. C. Tucker (Ed.). *The Lenin anthology.* New York: W.W. Norton & Co.
Lenin, V. I. (1920/1975). The tasks of the youth leagues. In R. C. Tucker (Ed.). *The Lenin anthology.* New York: W.W. Norton & Co.
McLaren, P. (2005). *Capitalists and conquerors: A critical pedagogy against empire.* New York: Rowman & Littlefield.
McLaren, P., & Jaramillo, N. (2007). *Pedagogy and praxis in the age of empire: Towards a new humanism.* New York: Sense.
McLaren, P., & Jaramillo, N. (2010). Not neo-Marxist, not post-Marxist, not Marxian, not autonomous Marxism: Reflections on a revolutionary (Marxist) critical pedagogy. *Cultural Studies Critical Methodologies, 10*(3), 1–12.
McNally, D. (2001). *Bodies of meaning: Studies on language, labor, and liberation.* Albany, NY: State University of New York Press.
Malott, C. (2008). *A call to action: An introduction to education, philosophy and native North America.* New York: Peter Lang.
Malott, C. (2010). *Policy and research in education: A critical pedagogy for educational leadership.* New York: Peter Lang.
Malott, C. (2011a). *Critical pedagogy and cognition: An introduction to a postformal educational psychology.* New York: Springer.
Malott, C. (2011b). Pseudo-Marxism and the reformist retreat from revolution: A critical essay review of *Marx and Education. The Journal for Critical Education Policy Studies. 9*(1). Retrieved from http://www.jceps.com/?pageID=article&articleID=206
Malott, C. (2012). Rethinking educational purpose: The socialist challenge. *Journal For Critical Education Policy Studies. 10*(2), 160–182.
Marcuse, H. (1964). *One dimensional man: Studies in the ideology of advanced industrial society.* Boston: Beacon Press.
Marx, K. (1988). *Economic and philosophic manuscripts of 1844.* Amherst, NY: Prometheus Books.
Marx, K. (1843/1978). Contribution to the critique of Hegel's *Philosophy of Right.* In R. Tucker (Ed.). *The Marx-Engels reader* (2nd Ed.). New York: W.W. Norton & Co.
Marx, K (1844/1978). Contribution to the critique of Hegel's *Philosophy of Right* [Introduction]. In R. Tucker (Ed.). *The Marx-Engels reader* (2nd Ed.). New York: W.W. Norton & Co.
Marx, K (1867/1967). *Capital: A critique of political economy: Vol. 1. The process of capitalist production.* New York: International Publishers.

Marx, K., & Engels, F. (1848/1972). *The manifesto of the Communist Party.* In R. C. Tucker (Ed.). *The Marx-Engels reader* (2nd Ed.), pp. 469–500. New York: W.W. Norton & Co.

Marx, K., & Engels, F. (1932/1996). *The German ideology.* New York: International Publishers.

New Mexico State University (2012). NMSU position on animals in research and emergency preparedness plan. Retrieved from http://www.nmsu.edu/safety/policy-link.htm

Pressman, S. (2007). The decline of the middle class: An international perspective. *Journal of Economic Issues, 41*(1), 181–200.

Pressman, S. (2010). Notes and communications: The middle class throughout the world in the mid-2000s. *Journal of Economic Issues, 41*(1), 181–200.

Robinson, W. I. (2005). What is a critical globalization studies? Intellectual labor and global society. In R. P. Appelbaum & W. I. Robinson (Eds.), *Critical globalization studies.* New York: Routledge.

Robinson, W. I. (2008). *Latin America and global capitalism: A critical globalization perspective.* Baltimore, MD: The Johns Hopkins University Press.

Smith, P. (1984). *The rise of industrial America: A people's history of the post-reconstruction era.* New York: Penguin.

Urban, W., & Wagoner, J. (2009). *American education: A history* (4th Ed.). New York: Routledge.

Van Auken, B. (2011). US senate backs military detention of US citizens. *International Committee of the Fourth International.* Retrieved from http://wsws.org/articles/2011/dec2011/pers-d03.shtml

Zinn, H. (2003). *People's history of the United States: 1492—Present.* New York: Perennial Classics.

8

Confronting Class in the Classroom

bell hooks

Class is rarely talked about in the United States; nowhere is there a more intense silence about the reality of class differences than in educational settings. Significantly, class differences are particularly ignored in classrooms. From grade school on, we are all encouraged to cross the threshold of the classroom believing we are entering a democratic space—a free zone where the desire to study and learn makes us all equal. And even if we enter accepting the reality of class differences, most of us still believe knowledge will be meted out in fair and equal proportions. In those rare cases where it is acknowledged that students and professors do not share the same class backgrounds, the underlying assumption is still that we are all equally committed to getting ahead, to moving up the ladder of success to the top. And even though many of us will not make it to the top, the unspoken understanding is that we will land somewhere in the middle, between top and bottom.

Coming from a nonmaterially privileged background, from the working poor, I entered college acutely aware of class. When I received notice of my acceptance at Stanford University, the first question that was raised in my household was how I would pay for it. My parents understood that I had been awarded scholarships, and allowed to take out loans, but they wanted to know where the money would come from for transportation, clothes, books. Given these concerns, I went to Stanford thinking that class was mainly about materiality. It only took me a short while to understand that class was more than just a question of money, that it shaped values, attitudes, social relations, and the biases that informed the way knowledge would be given and received. These same realizations about class in the academy are expressed again and again by academics from working-class backgrounds in the collection of essays *Strangers in Paradise* edited by Jake Ryan and Charles Sackrey.

During my college years it was tacitly assumed that we all agreed that class should not be talked about, that there would be no critique of the bourgeois class biases shaping and informing pedagogical process (as well as social etiquette) in the classroom. Although no one ever directly stated the rules that would govern our conduct, it was taught by example and reinforced by a system of rewards. As silence and obedience to authority were most rewarded, students learned that this was the appropriate demeanor in the classroom. Loudness, anger, emotional outbursts, and even something as seemingly innocent as unrestrained laughter were deemed unacceptable, vulgar disruptions of classroom social order. These traits were also associated with being a member of the lower classes. If one was not from a privileged class group, adopting a demeanor similar to that of the group could help one to advance. It is still necessary for students to assimilate bourgeois values in order to be deemed acceptable.

Bourgeois values in the classroom create a barrier, blocking the possibility of confrontation and conflict, warding off dissent. Students are often silenced by means of their acceptance of class values that teach them to maintain order at all costs. When the obsession with maintaining order is coupled with the fear of "losing face," of not being thought well of by one's professor and peers, all possibility of constructive dialogue is undermined. Even though students enter the "democratic" classroom believing they have the right to "free speech," most students are not comfortable exercising this right to "free speech." Most students are not comfortable exercising this right—especially if it means they must give voice to thoughts, ideas, feelings that go against the grain, that are unpopular. This censoring process is only one way bourgeois values overdetermine social behavior in the classroom and undermine the democratic exchange of ideas. Writing about his experience in the section of *Strangers in Paradise* entitled "Outsiders," Karl Anderson confessed:

> Power and hierarchy, and not teaching and learning, dominated the graduate school I found myself in. "Knowledge" was one-upmanship, and no one disguised the fact. . . . The one thing I learned absolutely was the inseparability of free speech and free thought. I, as well as some of my peers, were refused the opportunity to speak and sometimes to ask questions deemed "irrelevant" when the instructors didn't wish to discuss or respond to them.

Students who enter the academy unwilling to accept without question the assumptions and values held by privileged classes tend to be silenced, deemed troublemakers.

Conservative discussions of censorship in contemporary university settings often suggest that the absence of constructive dialogue, enforced silencing, takes place as a by-product of progressive efforts to question canonical knowledge, critique relations of domination, or subvert bourgeois class biases. There is little or no discussion of the way in which the attitudes and values of those from materially privileged classes are imposed upon everyone via biased pedagogical strategies. Reflected in choice of subject matter and the manner in which ideas are shared, these biases need never be overtly stated. In his essay Karl Anderson states that silencing is "the most oppressive aspect of middle-class life." He maintains:

> It thrives upon people keeping their mouths shut, unless they are actually endorsing whatever powers exist. The free marketplace of "ideas" that is so beloved of liberals is as much a fantasy as a free marketplace in oil or automobiles; a more harmful fantasy, because it breeds even more hypocrisy and cynicism. Just as teachers can control what is said in their classrooms, most also have ultra-sensitive antennae as to what will be rewarded or punished that is said outside them. And these antennae control them.

Silencing enforced by bourgeois values is sanctioned in the classroom by everyone. Even those professors who embrace the tenets of critical pedagogy (many of whom are white and male) still conduct their classrooms in a manner that only reinforces bourgeois models of decorum. At the same time, the subject matter taught in such classes might reflect professorial awareness of intellectual perspectives that critique domination, that emphasize an understanding of the politics of difference, of race, class, gender, even though classroom dynamics remain conventional, business as usual. When the contemporary feminist movement made its initial presence felt in the academy there was both an ongoing critique of conventional classroom dynamics and an attempt to create alternative pedagogical strategies. However, as feminist scholars endeavored to make Women's Studies a discipline administrators and peers would respect, there was a shift in perspective.

Significantly, feminist classrooms were the first spaces in the university where I encountered any attempt to acknowledge class difference. The focus was usually on the way class differences are structured in the larger society, not on our class position. Yet the focus on gender privilege in patriarchal society often meant that there was a recognition of the ways women were economically disenfranchised and therefore more likely to be poor or working class. Often, the feminist classroom was the only place where students (mostly female) from materially disadvantaged circumstances would speak from that class positionality, acknowledging both the impact of class on our social status as well as critiquing the class biases of feminist thought.

When I first entered university settings I felt estranged from this new environment. Like most of my peers and professors, I initially believed those feelings were there because of differences in racial and cultural background. However, as time passed it was more evident that this estrangement was in part a reflection of class difference. At Stanford, I was often asked by peers and professors if I was there on a scholarship. Underlying this question was the implication that receiving financial aid "diminished" one in some way. It was not just this experience that intensified my awareness of class difference, it was the constant evocation of materially privileged class experience (usually that of the middle class) as a universal norm that not only set those of us from working-class backgrounds apart but effectively excluded those who were not privileged from discussions, from social activities. To avoid feelings of estrangement, students from working-class backgrounds could assimilate into the mainstream, change speech patterns, points of reference, drop any habit that might reveal them to be from a nonmaterially privileged background.

Of course I entered college hoping that a university degree would enhance my class mobility. Yet I thought of this solely in economic terms. Early on I did not realize that class was much more than one's economic standing, that it determined values, standpoint, and interests. It was assumed that any student coming from a poor or working-class background would willingly surrender all values and habits of being associated with this background. Those of us from diverse ethnic/racial backgrounds learned that no aspect of our vernacular culture could be voiced in elite settings. This was especially the case with vernacular language or a first language that was not English. To insist on speaking in any manner that did not conform to privileged class ideals and mannerisms placed one always in the position of interloper.

Demands that individuals from class backgrounds deemed undesirable surrender all vestiges of their past create psychic turmoil. We were encouraged, as many students are today, to betray our class origins. Rewarded if we chose to assimilate, estranged if we chose to maintain those aspects of who we were, some were all too often seen as outsiders. Some of us rebelled by clinging to exaggerated manners and behavior clearly marked as outside the accepted bourgeois norm. During my student years, and now as a professor, I see many students from "undesirable" class backgrounds become unable to complete their studies because the contradictions between the behavior necessary to "make it" in the academy and those that allowed them to be comfortable at home, with their families and friends, are just too great.

Often, African Americans are among those students I teach from poor and working-class backgrounds who are most vocal about issues of class. They express frustration, anger, and sadness about the tensions and stress they experience trying to conform to acceptable white, middle-class behaviors in university settings while retaining the ability to "deal" at home. Sharing strategies for coping from my own experience, I encourage students to reject the notion that they must choose between experiences. They must believe they can inhabit comfortably two different worlds, but they must make each space one of comfort. They must creatively invent ways to cross borders. They must believe in their capacity to alter the bourgeois settings they enter. All too often, students from nonmaterially privileged backgrounds assume a position of passivity—they behave as victims, as though they can only be acted upon against their will. Ultimately, they end up feeling they can only reject or accept the norms imposed upon them. This either/or often sets them up for disappointment and failure.

Those of us in the academy from working-class backgrounds are empowered when we recognize our own agency, our capacity to be active participants in the pedagogical process. This process is not simple or easy: it takes courage to embrace a vision of wholeness of being that does not reinforce the capitalist version that suggests that one must always give something up to gain another. In the introduction to the section of their book titled "Class Mobility and Internalized Conflict," Ryan and Sackrey remind readers that "the academic work process is essentially antagonistic to the working class, and academics for the most part live in a different world of culture, different ways that make it, too, antagonistic to working class life." Yet those of us from working-class backgrounds cannot allow class antagonism to prevent us from gaining knowledge, degrees and enjoying the aspects of higher education that are fulfilling. Class antagonism can be constructively used, not made to reinforce the notion that students and professors from working-class backgrounds are "outsiders" and "interlopers," but to subvert and challenge the existing structure.

When I entered my first Women's Studies classes at Stanford, white professors talked about "women" when they were making the experience of materially privileged white women a norm. It was both a matter of personal and intellectual integrity for me to challenge this biased assumption. By challenging, I refused to be complicit in the erasure of black and/or working-class women of all ethnicities. Personally, that meant I was not able just to sit in class, grooving on the good feminist vibes—that was a loss. The gain was that I was honoring the experience of poor and working-class women in my own family, in that very community that had encouraged and supported me in my efforts to be better educated. Even though my intervention was not wholeheartedly welcomed, it created a context for critical thinking, for dialectical exchange.

Any attempt on the part of individual students to critique the bourgeois biases that shape pedagogical process, particularly as they relate to epistemological perspectives (the points from which information is shared) will, in most cases, no doubt, be viewed as negative and disruptive. Given the presumed radical or liberal nature of early feminist classrooms, it was shocking to me to find those settings were also often closed to different ways of thinking. While it was acceptable to critique patriarchy in that context, it was not acceptable to confront issues of class, especially in ways that were not simply about the evocation of guilt. In general, despite their participation in different disciplines and the diversity of class backgrounds, African American scholars and other nonwhite professors have been no more willing to confront issues of class. Even when it became more acceptable to give at least lip service to the recognition of race, gender, and class, most professors and students just did not feel they were able to address class in anything more than a simplistic way. Certainly, the primary area where there was the possibility of meaningful critique and change was in relation to biased scholarship, work that used the experiences and thoughts of materially privileged people as normative.

In recent years, growing awareness of class differences in progressive academic circles has meant that students and professors committed to critical and feminist pedagogy have the opportunity to make spaces in the academy where class can receive attention. Yet there can be no intervention that challenges the status quo if we are not willing to interrogate the way our presentation of self as well as our pedagogical process is often shaped by middle-class norms. My awareness of class has been continually reinforced by my efforts to remain close to loved ones who remain in materially underprivileged class positions. This has helped me to employ pedagogical strategies that create ruptures in the established order, that promote modes of learning which challenge bourgeois hegemony.

One such strategy has been the emphasis on creating in classrooms learning communities where everyone's voice can be heard, their presence recognized and valued. In the section of *Strangers in Paradise* entitled "Balancing Class Locations," Jane Ellen Wilson shares the way an emphasis on personal voice strengthened her.

> Only by coming to terms with my own past, my own background, and seeing that in the context of the world at large, have I begun to find my true voice and to understand that, since it is my own voice, that no pre-cut niche exists for it; that part of the work to be done is making a place, with others, where my and our voices, can stand clear of the background noise and voice our concerns as part of a larger song.

When those of us in the academy who are working class or from working-class backgrounds share our perspectives, we subvert the tendency to focus only on the thoughts, attitudes, and experiences of those who are materially privileged. Feminist and critical pedagogy are two alternative paradigms for teaching which have really emphasized the issue of coming to voice. That focus emerged as central, precisely because it was so evident that race, sex, and class privilege empower some students more than others, granting "authority" to some voices more than others.

A distinction must be made between a shallow emphasis on coming to voice, which wrongly suggests there can be some democratization of voice wherein everyone's words will be given equal time and be seen as equally valuable (often the model applied in feminist classrooms), and the more complex recognition of the uniqueness of each voice and a willingness to create spaces in the classroom where all voices can be heard because all students are free to speak, knowing their presence will be recognized and valued. This does not mean that anything can be said, no matter how irrelevant to classroom subject matter, and receive attention—or that something meaningful takes place if everyone has equal time to voice an opinion. In the classes I teach, I have students write short paragraphs that they read aloud so that we all have a chance to hear unique perspectives and we are all given an opportunity to pause and listen to one another. Just the physical experience of hearing, of listening intently, to each particular voice strengthens our capacity to learn together. Even though a student may not speak again after this moment, that student's presence has been acknowledged.

Hearing each other's voices, individual thoughts, and sometimes associating these voices with personal experience makes us more acutely aware of each other. That moment of collective participation and dialogue means that students and professor respect—and here I invoke the root meaning of the word, "to look at"—each other, engage in acts of recognition with one another, and do not just talk to the professor. Sharing experiences and confessional narratives in the classroom helps establish communal commitment to learning. These narrative moments usually are the space where the assumption that we share a common class background and perspective is disrupted. While students may be open to the idea that they do not all come from a common class background, they may still expect that the values of materially privileged groups will be the class's norm.

Some students may feel threatened if awareness of class difference leads to changes in the classroom. Today's students all dress alike, wearing clothes from stores such as the Gap and Benetton; this acts to erase the markers of class difference that older generations of students experienced. Young students are more eager to deny the impact of class and class differences in our society. I have found that students from upper- and middle-class backgrounds are disturbed if heated exchange takes place in the classroom. Many of them equate loud talk or interruptions with rude and threatening behavior. Yet those of us from working-class backgrounds may feel that discussion is deeper and richer if it arouses intense responses. In class, students are often disturbed if anyone is interrupted while speaking, even though outside class most of them are not threatened. Few of us are taught to facilitate heated discussions that may include useful interruptions and digressions, but it is often the professor who is most invested in maintaining order in the classroom. Professors cannot empower students to embrace diversities of experience, standpoint, behavior, or style if our training has disempowered us, socialized us to cope effectively only with a single mode of interaction based on middle-class values.

Most progressive professors are more comfortable striving to challenge class biases through the material studied than they are with interrogating how class biases shape conduct in the classroom and transforming their pedagogical process. When I entered my first classroom as a college professor and a feminist, I was deeply afraid of using authority in a way that would perpetuate class elitism and other forms of domination. Fearful that I might abuse power, I falsely pretended that no power difference existed between students and myself. That was a mistake. Yet it was only as I began to interrogate my fear of "power"—the way that fear was related to my own class background where I had so often seen those with class power coerce, abuse, and dominate those without—that I began to understand that power was not itself negative. It depended what one did with it. It was up to me to create ways within my professional power constructively, precisely because I was teaching in institutional structures that affirm it is fine to use power to reinforce and maintain coercive hierarchies.

Fear of losing control in the classroom often leads individual professors to fall into a conventional teaching pattern wherein power is used destructively. It is this fear that leads to collective professorial investment in bourgeois decorum as a means of maintaining a fixed notion of order, of ensuring that the teacher will have absolute authority. Unfortunately, this fear of losing control shapes and informs the professorial pedagogical process to the extent that it acts a barrier preventing any constructive grappling with issues of class.

Sometimes students who want professors to grapple with class differences often simply desire that individuals from less materially privileged backgrounds be given center stage so that an inversion of hierarchical structures takes place, not a disruption. One semester, a number of black female students from working-class backgrounds attended a course I taught on African American women writers. They arrived hoping I would use my professorial power to decenter the voices of privileged white students in nonconstructive ways so that those students would experience what it is like to be an outsider. Some of these black students rigidly resisted attempts to involve the others in an engaged pedagogy where space is created for everyone. Many of the black students feared that learning new terminology or new perspectives would alienate them from familiar social relations. Since these fears are rarely addressed as part of a progressive pedagogical process, students caught in the grip of such anxiety often sit in classes feeling hostile, estranged, refusing to participate. I often face students who think that in my classes they will "naturally" not feel estranged and that part of this feeling of comfort, or being "at home," is that they will not have to work as hard as they do in other classes.

These students are not expecting to find alternative pedagogy in my classes but merely "rest" from the negative tensions they may feel in the majority of other courses. It is my job to address these tensions.

If we can trust the demographics, we must assume that the academy will be full of students from diverse classes, and that more of our students than ever before will be from poor and working-class backgrounds. This change will not be reflected in the class background of professors. In my own experience, I encounter fewer and fewer academics from working-class backgrounds. Our absence is no doubt related to the way class politics and class struggle shapes who will receive graduate degrees in our society. However, constructively confronting issues of class is not simply a task for those of us who came from working-class and poor backgrounds; it is a challenge for all professors. Critiquing the way academic settings are structured to reproduce class hierarchy, Jake Ryan and Charles Sackrey emphasize "that no matter what the politics or ideological stripe of the individual professor, of what the content of his or her teaching, Marxist, anarchist, or nihilist, he or she nonetheless participates in the reproduction of the cultural and class relations of capitalism." Despite this bleak assertion they are willing to acknowledge that "nonconformist intellectuals can, through research and publication, chip away with some success at the conventional orthodoxies, nurture students with comparable ideas and intentions, or find ways to bring some fraction of the resources of the university to the service of the . . . class interests of the workers and others below." Any professor who commits to engaged pedagogy recognizes the importance of constructively confronting issues of class. That means welcoming the opportunity to alter our classroom practices creatively so that the democratic ideal of education for everyone can be realized.

Suggested Readings for Future Study

Anyon, J. (1997). *Ghetto Schooling: A Political Economy of Urban Educational Reform.* New York: Teachers College Press.

Anyon, J. (2005). *Radical Possibilities: Public Policy, Urban Education and a New Social Movement*. New York: Routledge.

Apple, M. (1986). *Teachers and Texts: A Political Economy of Class and Gender Relations in Education.* New York: Routledge & Kegan Paul.

Apple, M. W. (2001). *Educating the "Right" Way: Markets, Standards, God, and Inequality.* New York: RoutledgeFalmer.

Apple, M. (2007). *Late to Class: Social Class and Schooling in the New Economy.* Albany: State University of New York Press.

Archer, L. (2003). *Higher Education and Social Class: Issues of Inclusion and Exclusion.* New York: RoutledgeFalmer.

Aronowitz, S. (2000). *The Knowledge Factory: Dismantling the Corporate University and Creating True Higher Learning.* Boston: Beacon Press.

Aronowitz, S. (2001). *The Last Good Job in America: Work and Education in the New Global Technoculture.* New York: Rowman & Littlefield.

Aronowitz, S. and Cutler, J. (1998). *Post-Work: The Wages of Cybernation.* New York: Routledge.

Ball S. (2006). *Education Policy and Social Class.* New York: Routledge.

Baral, K. C. (2006). "Postcoloniality, Critical Pedagogy, and English Studies in India." *Pedagogy, 6*(3), 475–491.

Bernstein, B. (2003). "Social Class and Pedagogic Practice." In *The Structuring of Pedagogic Discourse, Volume IV: Class, Codes and Control* (pp. 63–93). London: Routledge.

Borg, C. and Mayo, P. (2006). *Learning and Social Difference: Challenges for Public Education and Critical Pedagogy.* Boulder, CO: Paradigm.

Bourdieu, P. (1986). "The Forms of Capital." In Richardson, J. G. (ed.), *Handbook of Theory and Research for the Sociology of Education* (pp. 241–258). New York and London: Greenwood Press.

Bourdieu, P. (1987). "What Makes a Social Class? On The Theoretical and Practical Existence of Groups." *Berkeley Journal of Sociology: A Critical Review, 32*, 1–17.

Bowles, S. and Gintis, H. (1976). *Schooling in Capitalist America.* New York: Basic Books.

Brosio, R. (1994). *A Radical Democratic Critique of Capitalist Education.* New York: Peter Lang.

Brown, A. L. and De Lissovoy, N. (2011). "Economies of Racism: Grounding Education Policy Research in the Complex Dialectic of Race, Class, and Capital." *Journal of Education Policy, 26(*5), 595–619.

Burbules, N. C. and Torres, C. A, (2000). *Globalization and Education: Critical Perspectives.* New York: Routledge.

Carnoy, M. (1994). *Faded Dreams: The Politics and Economics of Race in America.* Cambridge, UK: Cambridge University Press.

Collins, C., Leondar-Wright, B., and Sklar, H. (1999). *Shifting Fortunes: The Perils of the Growing American Wealth Gap.* Boston: United for a Fair Economy.

Evans, A., Evans, R., and Kennedy, W. (1990). *Pedagogies of the Non-Poor.* New York: Orbis Books.

Gee, J. P., Hull, G., and Lankshear, C. (1996). *The New Work Order: Behind the Language of the New Capitalism.* Boulder, CO: Westview.

Greider, W. (1997). *One World Ready or Not: The Manic Logic of Global Capitalism.* New York: Simon & Schuster.

Halsey, A. H., ed. (1997). *Education: Culture, Economy, and Society.* New York: Oxford University Press.

Herman, E. and Chomsky, N. (1988). *Manufacturing Consent: The Political Economy of the Mass Media.* New York: Pantheon Books.

hooks, b. (2000). *Where We Stand: Class Matters.* New York: Routledge.

Jones, J. and Bomer, R. (2006). *Girls, Social Class, and Literacy: What Teachers Can Do to Make a Difference.* Portsmouth, NH: Heinemann.

Kozol, J. (1991). *Savage Inequalities: Children in America's Schools.* New York: Harper Perennial.

Kumar, A. (1997). *Class Issues: Pedagogy, Cultural Studies, and the Public Sphere.* New York: New York University Press.

Larson, J. (2014). *Radical Equality in Education: Starting Over in US Schooling.* New York: Routledge.

Lauder, H. and Hughes, D. (1999). *Trading in Futures: Why Markets in Education Don't Work.* Philadelphia: Open University Press.

Lee, V. (2002). *Inequality at the Starting Gate: Social Background Differences in Achievement as Children Begin School.* Washington, DC: Economic Policy Institute.

Lipman, P. (2011). *The New Political Economy of Urban Education: Neoliberalism, Race, and the Right to the City.* New York: Routledge.

McChesney, R., Wood, E. M., and Foster, J. B., eds. (1998). *Capitalism and the Information Age: The Political Economy of the Global Communication Revolution.* New York: Monthly Review Press.

McLaren, P. (1998). "Revolutionary Pedagogy in Post-Revolutionary Times: Rethinking the Political Economy of Critical Education." *Educational Theory, 48*(4), 431–462.

McLaren, P. (2005). *Capitalist and Conquerors: A Critical Pedagogy Against Empire.* New York: Rowman and Littlefield.

McLaren, P. and Jaramillo, N. (2006). "Critical Pedagogy, Latino/a Education, and the Politics of Class Struggle." *Critical Methodologies,* 6(1), 73–93.

Martin, E. J. and Torres, R. D. (2004). *Savage State: Welfare Capitalism and Inequality.* Lanham, MD: Rowman & Littlefield.

Michales, W. B. (2006). *The Trouble with Diversity: How We Learned to Love Identity and Ignore Inequality.* New York: Metropolitan Books

Milner, A. (1999). *Class.* London: Sage.

Molnar, A. (1996). *Giving Kids the Business: The Commercialization of America's Schools.* Boulder, CO: Westview.

Monahan, T. (2006). "The Surveillance Curriculum: Risk Management and Social Control in the Neoliberal School." In Monahan, T. (ed.), *Surveillance and Security: Technological Politics and Power in Everyday Life* (pp. 109–124). New York: Routledge.

Nelles, W. (2008). "Towards a Critical Pedagogy of Comparative Public Diplomacy: Pseudo-Education, Fear-Mongering and Insecurities in Canadian-American Foreign Policy." *Comparative Education, 44*(3), 333–344.

Newman, K. and Chan, V. T. (2007). *The Missing Class: Portraits of the Near Poor.* Boston: Beacon Press.

Rothstein, R. (2004). *Class and Schools: Using Social, Economic, and Educational Reform to Close the Black-White Achievement Gap.* Washington, DC: Economic Policy Institute.

Sacks, P. (2007). *Tearing Down the Gates: Confronting the Class Divide in American Education.* Berkeley: University of California Press.

Saltman, K. J. (2007a). *Schooling and the POLITICS OF DISASTER.* New York: Routledge.

Saltman, K. J. (2007b). "Schooling in Disaster Capitalism: How the Political Right Is Using Disaster to Privatize Public Schooling." *Teacher Education Quarterly, 34*(2), 131–156.

Saltman, K. J. (2015). "Learning from the Neo-Liberal Movement: Towards a Global Justice Education Movement." *Journal of Educational Administration and History, 47*(3), 315–326.

Sassen, S. (1998). *Globalization and Its Discontent: Essays on the New Mobility of People and Money.* New York: The New York Press.

Smyth, J. (2011). *Critical Pedagogy for Social Justice.* New York: International Continuum Publishing Group.

Spring, J. (2001). *Globalization and Educational Rights.* New York: Lawrence Erlbaum Associates.

Weis, L. (2007). *The Way Class Works: Readings on School, Family, and the Economy.* New York: Routledge.

Weis, L., and Fine, M. (1993). *Beyond Silenced Voices: Class, Race and Gender in United States Schools.* Albany: State University of New York Press.

Willis, P. (1981). *Learning to Labor: How Working Class Kids Get Working Class Jobs.* New York: Columbia University Press.

Wood, E. M. (1995). *Democracy against Capitalism.* New York: Monthly Review Press.

Wood, E. M. (1999). *The Origin of Capitalism.* New York: Monthly Review Press.

Part Three

Racism and Identities

Introduction to Part Three

Over the last several decades, race and ethnicity have been the focus of theoretical debates in the social sciences and educational research. Debates concerning their analytical utility have been the subject of conferences and best-selling books. The academic discourse has focused primarily on how best to untangle the race problematic. Current intellectual concerns in educational research that advance a range of theoretical approaches from post-colonial and post-structural critiques of race and racism reflect broader assumptions that often fail to interrogate the role of capitalism and social class in the reproduction of racialized educational practices.

This so-called analytical "death of class" and its limited explanatory ambition has led to a set of diverse claims about the kind of socioeconomic structures and political and cultural forms that have emerged within schools since the late twentieth century. This is most apparent in the wide proliferation of an eclectic body of critical writings that emerged from the ideas of critical legal scholars. A critical race theory, with its signature idea that "racial power" and "white supremacy" exist as an intractable social phenomenon in U.S. schools, represents a critical educational example of this perspective.

So although there is no biological basis for dividing the human species into groups based on the idea that certain physical traits, such as skin color, are tied to such attributes as intellect and morality, important debates about the utility and significance of race within a critical pedagogical perspective persist. And while "race" may not be a natural category, as asserted by W.E.B. DuBois in 1903, many critical theorists vigorously uphold the notion that "race" has social meaning and therefore should be retained. There are, however, others in the critical tradition that contest the social significance of race and instead argue for the recognition of its historical fabrication and its undeniable connection to economic oppression.

Given the manner in which the commonsensical uses of race have so often permeated and distorted discourses related to communal identities, issues of poverty, the surveillance and assault on black and brown bodies, and even the presidency of Barack Obama, it is impossible to ignore the different ways in which critical educators have struggled to make sense of structural and individual views of racism in U.S. society. The articles included in this section are meant to help illustrate a few of these competing perspectives and shed light on some of the major arguments that inform this contested terrain in critical pedagogy.

Moreover, the essays share a common goal to further develop an oppositional pedagogy of praxis that places anti-racism, social justice, and democracy at the center of teaching and learning in these changing times. This endeavor to untangle the contradictory forces that shape one of the most contested concepts in the social sciences is offered in the spirit of critical collegial exchange and a reminder of the struggle ahead. The authors all place considerable emphasis on the theoretical and conceptual questions put forward in these debates, contributing to the further development of critical pedagogy as an oppositional stronghold in the struggle against racism(s).

Summary of Articles

In "Dancing with Bigotry: The Poisoning of Racial and Ethnic Identities," Lilia Bartolomé and Donaldo Macedo make a specific point of problematizing current discourses of race. Important to this discussion is the assertion that the politics of racism is not only associated with right-wing hate groups but rather is more fundamentally embedded in the structure of U.S. schooling and society. They, moreover, also argue that educators must move beyond the monolithic constructions of race and ethnicity. In this work, Bartolomé and Macedo posit a critical perspective of "cultural broker," which can assist critical educators to better create an important socio-psychological space to support the classroom experience of students from racialized communities. This cultural phenomenon encompasses the need to critically engage questions of language in ways that deconstruct and decode asymmetrical relations of power and meaning within the context of the classroom.

The American Indian question has long been problematic in U.S. scholarly literature, with scant attention to socioeconomic concerns or the cultural histories of the population. Sandy Grande, in "American Indian Geographies of Identity and Power," examines the tension between American Indian epistemology and critical pedagogy. She asserts that critical pedagogical perspectives have failed to acknowledge the unique position of the American Indian population, within the ethno-racial landscape of the United States. She concludes with a critical optimism that a new Red Pedagogy, grounded in critical principles, can emerge from a forthright engagement of the historical and socioeconomic conditions that shape the everyday lives of indigenous populations today. However, Grande rightly insists that this will require a paradigm shift, in which analytical specificity of particular histories and imperial practices imposed on American Indians are made central to critical discussion of indigenous knowledge and pedagogy.

Kevin Lam's article, "Theories of Racism, Asian American Identities and a Materialist Critical Pedagogy," critiques the category of race and the "model minority" myth, moving toward the deconstruction of pan-Asian ethnicity. Similarly, he looks at the implications for a materialist perspective of critical pedagogy. Lam offers a useful discussion of contemporary views of racial theories and politics, since the 1960s in the U.S. Lam also speaks to the limits of identity politics in education, calling for a more substantive political-economic analysis that critiques capitalism within pedagogical discussion of racism and ethnic identities.

In "Decolonizing Schools and Our Mentality: Narratives for Pedagogical Possibilities," Pierre Orelus maintains that the colonial legacy is sustained and reproduced by neoliberal policies. The author incorporates his own personal lived experiences in a high-stakes testing, banking, and market-driven school context to elucidate the legacy of colonialism, the cultural and material conditions of colonized subjects, and the impact of this colonial-based, mis-education on subaltern students. From this analysis of the educational system, emerges the complex dialectic of racism and classism through which Orelus argues for democratic and participatory forms of education that are humanizing, dialectical, and evolutionary, and that assist students in becoming critically informed citizens.

Questions for Reflection and Dialogue

1. Bartolomé and Macedo assert that critical educators must move beyond the monolithic constructions of race and ethnicity. Do you agree or disagree? Why?
2. Why do Bartolomé and Macedo believe that teachers need to become "cultural brokers"? How do they link this phenomenon to the politics of racism and identities within the classroom?
3. What are the limits of the use of race as an analytical category? Discuss the strengths of the concept of racialization as a method of analysis within education.
4. Identify specific acts of racism in education and consider their causes and consequences, using the articles as theoretical points of departure.
5. Assess the contention that American Indians are such a unique ethno-racial population that a paradigm shift in critical pedagogy is necessary, in order to realize a new Red Pedagogy.
6. What educational examples can you identify where it is imperative that educators engage with American Indian geographies of identities, histories, and power? Why is this necessary to a critical pedagogical practice?
7. What does Orelus mean by colonial-based-schools? What are the strengths and weaknesses of this concept with respect to a critical pedagogical approach to engaging racism and identities in education?
8. How does Orelus contend that the colonial legacy is reproduced in schools? And what are the pedagogical implications for students being educated in colonial-based schools systems?
9. What are the similarities and differences in how the articles conceptualize the relationship of race, class, and identity, within the ethno-racial landscape of the United States?

9

Dancing with Bigotry: The Poisoning of Racial and Ethnic Identities

Lilia I. Bartolomé and Donaldo P. Macedo

> I concluded long ago that they found the color of my skin inhibitory. This color seems to operate as a most disagreeable mirror, and a great deal of one's energy is expended in reassuring white Americans that they do not see what they see. . . .
>
> This is utterly futile, of course, since they do see what they see. And what they see is an appallingly oppressive and bloody history known all over the world. What they see is a disastrous, continuing, present condition which menaces them, and for which they bear an inescapable responsibility. But since in the main they seem to lack the energy to change this condition they would not be reminding of it.
>
> — James Baldwin[1]

As James Baldwin so succinctly points out, many White Americans prefer not to be reminded of the "appallingly oppressive and bloody history" of racism that has characterized the very fabric of U.S. society. In fact many, if not most, White Americans from various ethnic backgrounds would feel extremely uncomfortable if the curriculum in schools incorporated an antiracist pedagogy that asked, "mirror, mirror on the wall, is everyone welcome in the hall?"

Sadly, in a good number of halls not everyone is welcome. A report published by the National Association of Black Journalists revealed that 32 percent of African American journalists fear that bringing up issues of race in their articles damages their chances for advancement.[2] This statistic reveals a condition of fear that most likely exists in many forms and many occupations, including teaching. We believe this condition of fear gives rise to a form of censorship that views the aggressive denouncement of racism as worse than the racist act itself.

In this article, we argue that, as the end of the century draws closer, one of the most pressing challenges facing educators in the United States is the specter of an "ethnic and cultural war," which constitutes, in our view, a code phrase that engenders our society's licentiousness toward racism. We use the examples from the mass media, popular culture, and politics to illustrate the larger situations facing educators and how this type of argument is both ignored in much of the academic research and rhetoric, and why taking on the sources of "mass public education" are essential. Academia needs to understand that the popular press and the mass media educate more people about issues regarding ethnicity and race than all other sources of education available to U.S. citizens. By shunning the mass media, educators are missing the obvious: that is, that more public education is done by the media than by teachers, professors, and anyone else. This would serve to further develop the links between the issues discussed so far and education.

Although our article sheds light on the ideological mechanisms that shape and maintain our racist social order, we move our discussion beyond the reductionistic binarism of White versus Black racism. Thus we not only avoid falling prey to a binaristic approach to race analysis, but also differentiate ethnic from racial groups in order to avoid the facile interpretation of these ideological constructs. What is important, we believe, is the development of a critical comprehension of the relationship between the ideological constructs that determine and shape racial and ethnic realities. However, the fragmentation of ethnic and racial realities is part of the social organization of knowledge defined rigidly along disciplinary boundaries, which often results in the study of a single group under the rubric "ethnicity." This fragmentation represents a rupture of ethnic and racial relations, and propagates an ideology that creates and sustains false dichotomies delineated by ethnic or racial disciplinary boundaries. We believe that racism is an ideological construct that interpenetrates both ethnic and racial realities. An analysis of racism isolated from other ideological categories along the lines of ethnicity, class, gender, and culture does little good. Only by a process through which the dominant White ideology is deconstructed can we begin to understand the intimate relationships among the asymmetrical distribution of power and privilege among different ethnic and racial groups, including lower class ethnic Whites. In other words, we need to avoid the lumping of multiple identities into a monolithic entity such as race or ethnicity.

It is important to point out that the analysis of race, ethnicity, or gender as if they were monolithic entities prevents us from understanding that these categories represent interpenetrating realms of a shared dominant ideological foundation. In the case of gender, for example, bell hooks argues that

> sexism, racism, and class exploitation constitute interlocking systems of domination . . . sex, race, and class, and not sex alone, determine the nature of any female's identity status, and circumstance, the degree to which she will or will not be dominated, the extent to which she will have the power to dominate.[3]

The same can be argued for race and ethnicity. As part of a broader struggle to fight oppression of all forms, race and ethnicity need to be understood as ideological constructs that historically have served the purpose of perpetuating racism and as political categories that can function to mobilize resistance against White domination. In the latter case, both racial and ethnic identities take on positive values as they contribute to the struggle for social justice and the eradication of oppression. As ideological constructs, both race and ethnicity are separated from class and gender issues so as to prevent the understanding of the interconnecting relationship hidden in the dominant White ideology.

Part of the deconstruction of dominant White ideology involves understanding how ethnicity and race interpenetrate each other, a concept that Pepi Leistyna refers to as "Racenicity, a process through which the ideological construction of race has a significant impact on ethnicity."[4] We need to move beyond a discourse that views difference as simply aesthetic or as separate categories of analysis. We must link difference to questions of power, where racial categories, among other characteristics, are treated as political categories that do not exist in a power vacuum. These categories exist in relation to one another, mediated always by asymmetrical power relationships. According to Stanley Aronowitz:

> The concept of ethnicity with respect to education expresses two somewhat different characteristics of how issues of inequality are conventionally addressed in the literature. Recently, descriptively, the term has been employed to discuss issues of access and since we have no social scientifically acceptable discourse of class, ethnicity has become the displacement of this largely unacknowledged aspect of educational access and performance.[5]

The challenge for educators is to interrogate the descriptive nature of the discourse on race and ethnicity in order to unveil how the description hides the fact that "ethnicity has become the displacement" of class. Educators need to understand how "cultural differences are purged and social practices are reshaped around a racial identity, [giving rise to] a hierarchy that subcategorizes while devaluing groups of people that are designated 'racial others,' 'ethnics,' 'outsiders.'"[6]

Central to the idea of an ethnic and cultural war is the creation of an ideologically coded language that serves at least two fundamental functions: on the one hand, this language veils the racism that characterizes U.S. society, and on the other hand, it insidiously perpetuates both ethnic and racial stereotypes that devalue identities of resistance and struggle. We argue that, although the present idea of an ethnic and cultural war is characterized by a form of racism at the level of language, it is important to differentiate between language as racism and the experience of racism. For example, former presidential candidate Patrick Buchanan's call for the end of illegal immigration "even if it means putting the National Guard all along the Southern frontier" constitutes a form of racism at the level of language.[7] This language-based racism has had the effect of licensing institutional discrimination, whereby both documented and undocumented immigrants materially experience the loss of their dignity, the denial of their humanity, and, in many cases, outright violence, as witnessed by the recent cruel beatings of a Mexican man and woman by the border patrol. This incident was captured on videotape, and outraged the Latino/Mexicano communities in the United States, as well as in Mexico, leading to a number of demonstrations in Los Angeles. Language such as "border rats," "wetbacks," "aliens," "illegals," "welfare queens," and "non-White hordes" used by the popular press not only dehumanizes other cultural beings, but also serves to justify the violence perpetuated against subordinate groups.

Language as racism is one example of what Pierre Bourdieu refers to as "the hegemony of symbolic violence."[8] As educators, we need to understand fully the interrelationship between symbolic violence produced through language and the essence of the experience of racism. While the two are not mutually exclusive, "language also constitutes and mediates the multiple experiences of identity by both historicizing it and revealing its partiality and incompleteness, its limits are realized in the material nature of experience as it names the body through the specificity of place, space, and history."[9] This is very much in line with John Fiske's notion that "there is a material experience of homelessness . . . but the boundary between the two cannot be drawn sharply. Material conditions are inescapably saturated with culture and, equally, cultural conditions are inescapably experienced as material."[10]

By deconstructing the cultural conditions that give rise to the present violent assault on undocumented immigrants, affirmative action, African Americans, and other racial and ethnic groups, we attempt to single out those ideological factors that enable even highly educated individuals to embrace blindly, for example, conservative radio talk-show host Rush Limbaugh's sexist and racist tirades designed to demonize and dehumanize ethnic and cultural identities other than his own. Some examples are:

> Now I got something for you that's true—1992, Tufts University, Boston. This is 24 years ago or 22 years ago. Three-year study of 5,000 coeds, and they used a benchmark of a bra size of 34 C. They forward that—now wait! It's true. The larger the bra size, the smaller the IQ.
>
> Feminism was established so that unattractive women could have easier access to mainstream society.
>
> There are more American Indians alive today than there were when Columbus arrived or at any other time in history. Does that sound like a record of genocide?
>
> Taxpaying citizens are not being given access to these welfare and health services that they deserve and desire. But if you're an illegal immigrant and cross the border, you get everything you want.[11]

The racism and high level of xenophobia we are witnessing in our society today are not caused by isolated acts by individuals such as Limbaugh or one-time Louisiana gubernatorial candidate David Duke. Rather, these individuals are representatives of an orchestrated effort by segments of the dominant society to wage a war on the poor and on people who, by virtue of their race, ethnicity, language, and class, are reduced at best to half-citizens, and at worst to a national enemy responsible for all the ills afflicting our society. We need to understand the cultural and historical context that gives rise to over twenty million Limbaugh "ditto heads" who tune in to his weekly radio and television programs.

We need also to understand those ideological elements that inform our policymakers and those individuals who shape public opinion by supporting and rewarding Limbaugh's unapologetic demonizing of other cultural subjects. For example, television commentator Ted Koppel considers him "very smart. He does his homework. He is well-informed." Syndicated columnist George Will considers him the "fourth branch of government," and former Secretary of Education William Bennett—the virtue man—describes Limbaugh as "possibly our greatest living American."[12] What remains incomprehensible is why highly educated individuals like Koppel, Will, and Bennett cannot see through Limbaugh's obvious distortions of history and falsification of reality. We posit that the inability to perceive distinctions and falsifications of reality is partly due to the hegemonic forces that promote an acritical education via the fragmentation of bodies of knowledge. Such a process makes it very difficult for students (and the general population) to make connections among historical events so as to gain a more critical understanding of reality. The promotion of an acritical education was evident when David Spritzler, a twelve-year-old student at Boston Latin School, faced disciplinary action for his refusal to recite the Pledge of Allegiance, which he considered "a hypocritical exhortation to patriotism" in that there is not "liberty and justice for all." According to Spritzler, the Pledge is an attempt to unite

> [the] oppressed and oppressors. You have people who drive nice cars, live in nice houses, and don't have to worry about money. Then you have the poor people, living in bad neighborhoods and going to bad schools. Somehow the Pledge makes it seem that everybody's equal when that's not happening. There is no justice for everybody.[13]

Spritzler's teachers' and administrators' inability to see the obvious hypocrisy contained in the Pledge of Allegiance represents what Noam Chomsky calls

> a real sign of deep indoctrination [in] that you can't understand elementary thoughts that any ten year old can understand. That's real indoctrination. So for him [the indoctrinated individual], it's kind of like a theological truth, a truth of received religion.[14]

Against these cruel and racist cultural conditions, we can begin to understand that it is not a coincidence that Patrick Buchanan reiterated in his first presidential campaign platform that his fellow Americans should "wage a cultural revolution in the nineties as sweeping as the political revolution of the eighties."[15] In fact, this cultural revolution is indeed moving forward with rapid speed, from the onslaught on cultural diversity and multicultural education to Patrick Buchanan's call to U.S. national and patriotic sense to build a large wall to keep the "illegals" in Mexico. Some might claim that Patrick Buchanan's vicious attack on immigrants could be interpreted in ways other than racism. If that were the case, how could we explain his unfortunate testament:

> I think God made all people good, but if we had to take a million immigrants in—say Zulus next year or Englishmen—and put them in Virginia, what group would be easier to assimilate and would cause less problems for the people of Virginia?[16]

It is the same U.S. national and patriotic sense that allowed President Clinton not to be outdone by the extreme Right's forcing him to announce in his 1995 State of the Union address that:

> All Americans, not only in the states most heavily affected, but in every place in this country, are rightly disturbed by the large numbers of illegal aliens entering our country. The jobs they hold might otherwise be held by citizens or legal immigrants. The public services they use impose burdens on our taxpayers. That's why our administration has moved aggressively to secure our borders more by hiring a record number of new border guards, by deporting twice as many criminal aliens as ever before, by cracking down on illegal hiring, by barring welfare benefits to illegal aliens.
>
> In the budget I will present to you, we will try to do more to speed the deportation of illegal aliens who are arrested for crimes, to better identify illegal aliens in the workplace as recommended by the commission headed by former Congresswoman Barbara Jordan.[17]

A close analysis of the Republican attack on immigrants and cultural groups and our liberal Democratic president's remarks during his State of the Union address confirm what has been for decades the United States's best-kept secret: there is no critical ideological difference between the Republican and Democratic parties. Ideologically speaking, in the United States we have a one-party system of government represented by two branches with only cosmetic differences, cloaked in the guise of Republicans and Democrats.

We believe that the same racist sentiment enabled President Clinton to abandon the nomination of Lani Guinier to head the Justice Department's Civil Rights Division because she demonstrated in her writings that the working-class poor, African Americans, and members of other minority cultural groups do not have representation in the White male-dominated two-party system and, in fact, that the system, fueled by a capitalist ideology, works aggressively against the interests of these groups. It is again the same racist ideology that is pushing President Clinton to join the chorus calling for an end to affirmative action policies, even though the benefactors of de facto affirmative action through the "good ole boy" networks since the birth of this country have been White males, who continue to dominate all sectors of institutional and economic life in this society. For example, according to employment data on Boston banks from the Equal Employment Opportunity Commission:

> From 1990–1993, the industry added 4,116 jobs. While the percentage of white male officers and managers rose by 10 percent, the percentage of African-American officers and managers dropped by 25 percent. While the percentage of white female clerical workers went up 10 percent, the percentage of African-American clerical workers dropped 15 percent.[18]

"Affirmative action" and "welfare" are also code words that license a form of racism via language that assuages the fear of the White working and middle class as they steadily lose ground to the real "affirmative action and welfare" programs designed to further enrich the upper class and big business:

> When the Fed raises the interest rates, it helps big business at the expense of individual home owners. When politicians resist raising the minimum wage, it helps big business send off the working poor. When politicians want liability caps, they defend Big Oil, Ma Bell and her off-spring and Detroit gas guzzlers over potential victims of defective products and pollution. As the Gingrich revolution slashes school lunches for the poor, corporations get $111 billion in tax breaks, according to Labor secretary Robert Reich.[19]

We also know that even within the context of the present affirmative action policy, the genuine beneficiaries have been White women. Their convenient silence on the present assault on affirmative action makes them complicit with the reproduction of the racist myth that

> black people take jobs from white people . . . [which leads] one to conclude that African-Americans are not considered Americans. White men lose jobs to other white men who do not say, they gave my job to an inferior white man! White male competency is assumed. African-Americans, regardless of achievement, are forever on trial.[20]

In other words, Henry Louis Gates Jr.'s prominence as a scholar did not lessen the racism he had to face at Duke University when he taught there. Cornel West's status as a renowned public intellectual did little for him as he watched nine taxis go by and refuse to pick him up in the streets of New York. bell hooks' eminence as a major feminist scholar does not lessen the pain of racism and sexism she endures; her status as an author of many highly acclaimed feminist books still does not provide her with the access to media and magazines enjoyed by many White feminists. hooks recently pointed out to Naomi Wolf:

> I have written eight feminist books. None of the magazines that have talked about your book, Naomi, have ever talked about my books at all. Now, that's not because there aren't ideas in my books that have universal appeal. It's because the issue that you raised in *The Beauty Myth* is still about beauty. We have to acknowledge that all of us do not have equal access.[21]

hooks's comment denudes the myth created by the anti-affirmative-action discourse that

> pretends that we live in a color-blind society where individuals are treated according to the American ethic [that] has always held that individual effort and achievement are valued and rewarded.[22]

The separation of the individual from the collective consciousness is part of the dominant White ideology's mechanism to fragment reality, which makes it easier for individuals to accept living within the lie that we exist in a raceless and color-blind society.

The real issue behind the present assault on multiculturalism and affirmative action is that we must never fall prey to a pedagogy of big lies.[23] The fundamental challenge for Americans in general, and educators in particular, is to accept Derrick Bell's call for a "continuing quest for new directions in our struggle for racial justice, a struggle we must continue even if . . . racism is an integral, permanent and indestructible component of this society."[24]

Poisoning Racial and Ethnic Identities

Accepting Bell's challenge, we point out that the real issue is not Western civilization versus multiculturalism or affirmative action versus individual effort and merit. Cultural dominance and racism are the hidden issues that inform the pernicious debate on cultural diversity and its ramifications, such as affirmative action. We cannot speak of our American "common culture" and democracy in view of the quasi-apartheid conditions that have relegated American Indians to reservations, created ghettos, and supported the affirmative action of red-lining and Robin Hood policies in reverse. How can we honestly accept the mythical reality of our common culture when its major proponents are simultaneously engaged in a permanent process of putting other cultural identities on trial? A willingness to negate the contributions of subordinated groups can be easily detected in the comments of John Silber, former Boston University president and present Chairman of the Massachusetts State Board of Education, who, during his campaign for governor of Massachusetts in 1990, asked:

> Why has Massachusetts suddenly become so popular for people who are accustomed to living in a tropical climate? Amazing. There has got to be a welfare magnet going on here, and right now I am making a study to find out what that magnet is. Why should Lowell be the Cambodian capital of America?[25]

If John Silber had conducted his study as promised, he would soon realize how he dances with bigotry, since the majority of welfare recipients in Lowell, Massachusetts, are not Cambodians, but White Americans. He would also learn that the Asian community in Lowell represents a real economic force, filling the gaps made by the flight of jobs and capital that have left Lowell struggling with an urban decay like that of other old industrial cities. It is the same dance with bigotry that now informs our politicians in their quest for higher offices, including the presidency.

David Duke, a Republican candidate in the 1990 presidential primaries, minced no words when he stated:

> America is being invaded by hordes of dusty third world peoples, and with each passing hour our economic well-being, cultural heritage, freedom, and racial roots are being battered into oblivion.[26]

He continues his demonization of the "other" cultural and ethnic subjects, stating:

> It's them! They're what's wrong with America! They're taking your job, soaking up your tax dollars, living off food stamps, drinking cheap wine and making babies at our expense.[27]

These racist sentiments are not lost in the proliferation of conservative radio talk shows, like Rush Limbaugh's, whose major purpose is to exacerbate the racist fabric of our society. The agenda of such shows is apparent in a local talk show broadcast in Brockton, Massachusetts, in which a caller remarked:

> Why should we be supporting these bilinguals? We should take care of our own first. The problem with Brockton is the Haitians, the Hispanics, the Cape Verdeans that are ruining our neighborhood.[28]

Although these examples point to racism at the level of language, the relationship between racist statements and the effects on people's lives is direct. For example, while California Governor Pete Wilson and other politicians made speeches using a kind of language that demonized so-called "illegal" immigrants, the actual experience of racism became immeasurably worse with the passage of Proposition 187 in California. In fact, Proposition 187 can be viewed as a precursor in a pattern of assault on subordinated groups that culminated with the passage in November 1996 of Proposition 209, which proposed to end affirmative action in California. The cultural condition that led to the passage of these laws, which were designed to control the flow of illegal immigrants and to end affirmative action in California, has had the effect of licensing institutional discrimination whereby both legal and illegal immigrants materially experience the loss of their dignity, the denial of human citizenship, and, in many cases, outright violent and criminal acts committed by those institutions responsible for implementing the law. According to Human Rights Watch/Americas:

> The politically charged drive to curb illegal immigration may be coming at a serious price: beatings, shootings, rapes and death of aliens at the hand of the US Border Patrol.[29]

As anti-immigrant sentiment grows stronger, the Immigration and Naturalization Service (INS) plans to increase its force from 4,200 to 7,000 by 1998, with few safeguards in place to ensure that the new hires will not continue to increase the human rights abuses perpetrated along the U.S.-Mexican border. As Allyson Collins of Human Rights Watch/Americas notes, the "anti-immigrant sentiment dims the hope of safeguarding aliens as the United States fortifies its border. These are very unpopular victims."[30] Not only is there no guarantee that the INS will protect the rights of human beings who have already been dehumanized as "aliens" or "illegals," but this dehumanizing process has also been met by an unsettling silence, even among liberals. This is not entirely surprising, given the liberals' paradoxical posture with respect to race issues. On the one hand, liberals progressively idealize "principles of liberty, equality, and fraternity [while insisting] upon the moral irrelevance of race. Race is irrelevant, but all is race."[31] On the other hand, some liberals accept the notion of difference and call for ways in which difference is tolerated. For example, there is a rapid growth of textbooks ostensibly designed to teach racial and multicultural tolerance. But, what these texts in fact do is hide the asymmetrical distribution of power and cultural capital through a form of paternalism that promises to the other a dose of tolerance. In other words, since we coexist and must find ways to get along, I will tolerate you. Missing from this posture is the ethical position that calls for mutual respect and even racial and cultural solidarity. As David Goldberg argues, tolerance "presupposes that its object is morally repugnant, that it really needs to be reformed, that is, altered."[32] Accordingly, racial and cultural tolerance practiced by the dominant sectors within U.S. society may view this form of tolerance as a process through which the different "other" is permitted to think, or at least hope, that through this so-called "tolerance," the intolerable features that characterize the different "other" will be eliminated or repressed. Thus, Goldberg is correct in pointing out that

> liberals are moved to overcome the racial differences they tolerate and have been so instrumental in fabricating by diluting them, by bleaching them out through assimilation or integration. The liberal would assume away the difference in otherness, maintaining thereby the dominance of a presumed sameness, the universally imposed similarity in identity. The paradox is perpetrated: the commitment to tolerance turns only on modernity's natural inclination to intolerance; acceptance of otherness presupposes as it at once necessitates delegitimization of the other.[33]

Tolerance for different racial and ethnic groups as proposed by some White liberals not only constitutes a veil behind which they hide their racism, it also puts them in a compromising racial position. While calling for racial tolerance, a paternalistic term, they often maintain the privilege that is complicit with the dominant ideology. In other words, the call for tolerance never questions the asymmetrical power relations that give them their privilege. Thus, many White liberals willingly call and work for cultural tolerance, but are reluctant to confront issues of inequality, power, ethics, race, and ethnicity in a way that could actually lead to social transformation that would make society more democratic and humane, and less racist and discriminatory. This form of racism is readily understood by its victims, as observed by Carol Swain, an African American professor at Princeton University: "White liberals are among the most racist people I know; they're so patronizing towards blacks."[34]

Against this landscape of racism, it becomes difficult to argue that these positions are taken only by fringe individuals such as David Duke. As hard as we may want to stretch the truth, we cannot forget that he has been elected to public office in Louisiana. Nor can we argue that John Silber is on the fringe. He is as mainstream as those Republicans who signed on with the Contract with America, proposing to cut lunch programs for poor children, take away cash assistance to unwed mothers with dependent children, cut fuel assistance to the elderly, abolish the food stamp program, and crack down on illegal immigrants while denying social benefits to legal immigrants. In short, the racism and xenophobia we are witnessing in our society today are not isolated acts of individuals on the fringe.

It is against this mean-spirited and racist backdrop that we analyze the controversy over multiculturalism and the role that language plays in the process. In our analysis we do not discuss the way Puerto Ricans dance Salsa, how Chicanos celebrate *Cinco de Mayo,* or how Haitians believe in Voodooism. Although the knowledge of such cultural traits is useful, we do not think it prepares us to deal with the tensions and contradictions generated by the coexistence of multicultural groups in a racist society. Instead, we argue that multicultural analyses should not be limited to the study of the "other" in a way that makes the White cultural group invisible and beyond study. White invisibility is achieved partly through the very language we use to structure our discourse on race and ethnicity. For example, both Whites and non-White racial and ethnic groups use the linguistic construction "people of color" to designate non-White individuals. The hidden assumption is that White is colorless, a proposition that is semantically impossible. By pointing out that White is also a color, we can begin to interrogate the false assumptions that strip White people of their ethnicity. In fact, a thorough understanding of racial and ethnic realities must begin by reinserting both color and ethnicity into the false discourse of colorless

Whites that contributes to making ethnicity invisible within this concept of Whiteness. In addition, it is not necessarily important for us to understand how cultural differences are structured along specific behavior patterns, but it is important to understand instead the antagonism and tensions engendered by cultural differences that coexist asymmetrically in terms of power relations.

Culture is intertwined with language and represents a sizable dimension of its reality, but language is rarely studied as part of our multicultural understanding. In this country we often take for granted that the study of multiculturalism should be done in English only; in addition, we also rarely question the role of the dominant language in the devaluation of the cultural and ethnic groups under study. Put simply, we understand little how the English language can subordinate and alienate members of the cultures we study through English. We need to understand how English masks the web of ideological manipulation that makes White cultural and ethnic groups invisible and outside the realm of study. Hence, language not only produces cultural and social inequalities, but is also used by the dominant White ideology to distort and falsify realities. Take the proposition "school choice," which creates the illusion that all parents can equally exercise their democratic right to choose the best schools for their children.

The illusion of choice also reinforces the myth that every American can choose where to live and work. However, for a group of African Americans who attempted to implement the court-ordered integration of a public housing complex in Vidor, Texas, the myth soon became a nightmare. Despite their efforts to assimilate quietly, they were subjected for months to Ku Klux Klan threats and racial epithets shouted from passing cars. Unable to endure the unremittingly hostile atmosphere, they decided to leave.

The illusion of choice also creates a pedagogy of entrapment that makes it undemocratic to argue against school choice. Thus school choice becomes part of a discourse that brooks no dissension or argument, for to argue against it is to deny democracy. The hidden curriculum of school choice consists of taking precious resources from poor schools that are on the verge of bankruptcy to support private or well-to-do public schools. For example, at the same time that the Brockton Public Schools in Massachusetts terminated the contract of 120 teachers due to a draconian budget cut, the system shifted approximately $1 million to support middle-class Brockton students who chose to enroll in the more affluent Avon Public Schools nearby. Although the Avon schools benefited greatly from the school choice windfall, they did not welcome equally all students from Brockton. When a Brockton special education student decided to defy his rejection by the Avon schools, the principal stood by the door on the first day of class to prevent this student, accompanied by his parents, from entering the school building. This episode provides a glimpse of possible future behavior by the Avon schools if a large number of Brockton's subordinated students pick an Avon school as their school of choice. The school choice discourse also eclipses the more fundamental issue of educational funding inequity.

Using language as a mirror, we can begin to understand U.S. society's pathological need to demonize the "other" so as to have an enemy to blame for all its ills. During the 1950s, 1960s, and 1970s, we used Communism to represent all the evils that needed to be confronted. This gave rise to a dark chapter in our history that not only threatened the civil liberties guaranteed by our Constitution, but also flirted with the totalitarian impulses of McCarthyism, which differed little from the police states we were denouncing. With the fall of the Berlin Wall, President Bush replaced the Communist threat with the War on

Drugs, a war that is associated mostly with subordinated groups to the extent that they have been framed as a point of reference for the drug problem. This is evident in the disproportionate number of African Americans and Latinos who have been sentenced to jail on drug charges. In fact, the laws that regulate penalties for drug offenses clearly reflect biases against subordinated groups. For example, penalties for possession of cocaine, which is often referred to as a "White drug," are less strict than the penalties given for the possession of the much less expensive cocaine byproduct, "crack," which is more readily found in poor inner-city neighborhoods. The drug war has been used to rationalize the presence of U.S. troops in many Latin American countries, including Columbia, Peru, Bolivia, and Guatemala, to fight and destroy coca fields and drug laboratories. The U.S. government has refused to realize that the only effective way to fight the war on drugs is to decrease demand. In order to decrease demand, we would need a profound social transformation that goes far beyond Nancy Reagan's empty slogan of "Just Say No." Even law enforcement officials and officials of these Latin American countries have admitted that they are losing the drug war. In fact, by focusing only on the elimination of drug production, we ignore the social causes that breed a high demand for drugs. In addition, by focusing on drug production, the government can distract the public from the allegation in the media that the CIA played an important role in introducing drugs in South Los Angeles in order to help finance the Contra War in Nicaragua, while keeping the African American and Latino communities sedated. According to Mary Kimbrough, the owner of an African arts and books store, the CIA-drug link in Los Angeles "fits a historical pattern of racism by the American government . . . designed to keep us in a permanent underclass."[35] In fact, if we look back in history, we soon realize that Kimbrough's statement is not part of a mere conspiracy theory. For instance, Benjamin Franklin, in his autobiography, had no shame when he stated that "indeed if it be the design of Providence to extirpate these savages in order to make room for cultivators of the earth, it seems not improbable that rum may be the appointed means."[36]

Failing, however, to convince society that drugs were the root cause of all societal problems, the Reagan/Bush administrations shifted their attention to another enemy: terrorism. According to Edward Said, a noted scholar and professor at Columbia University:

> The search for a post-Soviet foreign devil has come to rest . . . on Islam. . . . Never mind that most Islamic countries today are too poverty-stricken, tyrannical, and hopelessly inept militarily as well as scientifically to be much of a threat to anyone except their own citizens; and never mind that the most powerful of them—like Saudi Arabia, Egypt, Jordan, and Pakistan—are totally within the U.S. orbit. What matters to "experts" like [Judith] Miller, Samuel Huntington, Martin Kramer, Bernard Lewis, David Pipes, Steven Emerson, and Barry Rubin, plus a whole battery of Israeli academics, is to make sure that the "threat" is kept before our eyes, the better to excoriate Islam for terror, despotism, and violence, while assuring themselves profitable consultancies, frequent TV appearances and book contracts.[37]

This pattern was evident in the Oklahoma bombing, where over one hundred innocent victims died. After "a law enforcement source said that several factors suggested a link, including the size and sophistication of the bomb and the fact that several militant Middle Eastern groups are based in Oklahoma,"[38] the focus of the investigation was mostly on international terrorism, particularly Islamic groups. Interestingly, after Timothy McVeigh and James Nichols, both White Americans, were identified as suspects, the language shifted swiftly from terrorism to militia groups, but the media and the "experts" did not demonize and dehumanize the whole White American culture as they usually do to Arabs. This differential treatment of ethnicities points to the privilege inherent in being White in the U.S. context. The differential treatment was evident in the numerous media analyses that explored what leads angry White men and militia groups to acts of terrorism. Psychological profiles of McVeigh and other militia members became the focus of media coverage, and militia members (mostly White) were given air time to explain their position. In the case of international terrorism, particularly terrorism linked to Islamic movements, this does not occur. It is rare to find the U.S. media discussing how

> more often than not, terrorism is the work of groups, and has its own—if perverse—rationale. Yet this rationale is never mentioned in the discussions of the challenge of terrorism, despite the fact that there is a clear causal connection between U.S. government acts and terrorist retaliation. For example, the United States became a major target of terrorism in the Middle East after the ill conceived 1982 military mission in Lebanon, which made this country a direct participant in the Arab-Israeli dispute.[39]

With the shift in the national media away from Islamic terrorism, we have been given a lasting enemy: so-called illegal immigration. This enemy was readily seized upon by syndicated columnist Richard Estrada, whose own grandfather immigrated to El Paso, Texas, in 1916. Estrada recently declared that "illegal immigration threatens our national security,"[40] substantiating his claim by stating that Americans in Los Angeles cannot find jobs because of immigrants. Therefore, he argued that we need to militarize the border in order to protect the spirit of Proposition 187 and take our country back. Estrada's reference to "taking our country back" means keeping Mexicans from their own land in much the same way as Native Americans have been kept from theirs, for Mexicans inhabited the land until the U.S. government legitimized the expropriation of almost half of Mexico through the Mexican-American War, which it intentionally provoked This expropriation was justified through the idea that *if you fight for it and you win, you deserve the land.* The attempt to reduce war for land expropriation is eloquently captured in Carl Sandburg's poem, "The People, Yes":

> "Get off this estate."
> "What for?"
> "Because it's mine."
> "Where did you get it?"
> "From my father."
> "Where did he get it?"
> "From his father."
>
> "And where did he get it?"
> "He fought for it."
> "Well, I'll fight you for it."[41]

If we critically deconstruct our seemingly democratic society, we begin to understand how the ideological construction of ethnicity and race has played an important role in the reproduction and reinscription of undemocratic structures and power relations along racial, ethnic, cultural, class, and linguistic lines. Thus, it is imperative that we describe and analyze the historical and social conditions of the United States in order to understand how this ideology produces and reproduces inequalities through invisible institutional mechanisms. Central to these hidden mechanisms, language has played a pivotal role in the production and reproduction of distorted realities.

Language and the Construction of Racism

Given the sophisticated use of language in the social construction of the "other" in dehumanizing cultural subjects, we feel that educators need to become "cultural brokers" to help create a psychologically beneficial pedagogical space for all students. Educators also need to make sure that they do not teach a form of literacy that gives learners a lasting experience of subordination. We need to understand that language is the only effective tool for us to deconstruct the web of ideological manipulation that makes the White cultural and ethnic group invisible and outside the realm of study.

Educators, particularly those working with multilingual and multicultural students, need to understand how discourses, according to linguist Oliver Reboul, are very often anchored in

> shock words, terms or expressions produced by themselves, [which,] due to their strong connotations, provoke a reaction no matter what sentence within which they are inserted.[42]

In other words, these terms, expressions, and words have a positive association, almost independent of their meanings. For example, in the present discussion of welfare reform, the word "reform" provokes a positive effect that forces most middle-class White individuals to leave its meaning in different contexts, unexamined. Who in the White-dominated middle class would oppose reforming a welfare system they believe only benefits lazy individuals living off of those who work hard to pay taxes? Who in this segment of the middle class would oppose reforming what Patrick Buchanan characterizes as a "social catastrophe" and as

> Great Society programs not only [responsible] for financial losses but also for the drop in high school test scores, drug problems and "a generation of children and youth with no fathers, no faith and no dreams other than the lure of the streets."[43]

Thus, "welfare reform for the poor" represents a positive shock phrase to the majority of White middle-class individuals, who feel put upon by paying high taxes to, in their view, support lazy individuals who are poor because they do not want to work. When one points out that a higher percentage of their taxes goes to support welfare for the rich, the cry is uniform, immediate, and aggressive: there is no room in the United States for incitement of class warfare. When the call is to reform welfare for the rich, the reaction is as swift as it is disingenuous. By changing the context of welfare reform from the poor to the rich, the shock-word impact changes accordingly, from a positive to a negative effect. Let's examine some positions taken by politicians and policymakers with respect to class warfare:[44]

> Alfonse M. d'Amato, Republican senator from New York, set the tone: "There is something that I think is very dangerous taking place in this nation. Let me tell you what it is. It is class warfare under the theory of 'let's get the rich guy, the richest 1 percent.' So we set them up, target them. Those are the people we are going to get."
>
> William S. Cohen, Republican senator from Maine, put it this way: "We are talking about taxing the rich. Once again, we are engaging in classic class warfare."
>
> Bob Dole, former Republican senator from Kansas: "I do not know how long we can continue that kind of class warfare."
>
> Slade Gordon, Republican senator from Washington: "While reducing the budget deficit may be the most important issue before this Congress, the president and his allies in Congress are offering this country what amounts to class warfare. I object to these higher taxes."
>
> Robert K. Dornan, former Republican representative from California, said: "To sell this program of higher taxes, Clinton and his liberal allies here in the House have turned to the standard liberal theme of class warfare, though they have couched it in terms of 'progressivity,' 'fairness,' and 'equality.' "

> Jim Bunning, Republican representative from Kentucky, labeled the legislation "a historic class warfare scheme."
>
> Gerald B. H. Solomon, Republican representative from New York, observed: "As young Russians cover Marx's statue in Moscow with flippant slogans such as 'workers of the world, forgive me,' America is awash in the Marx-Leninesque rhetoric of class warfare."

These politicians are correct in stating that we have ongoing class warfare in the United States, but it is actually warfare on the middle class and the poor, not on the rich, as they claim. Since the early 1960s, there has been a progressive change in the tax code that enriches the upper class while eroding the economic base of the middle and lower classes.[45] This transfer of wealth from the poor and middle classes to the upper class has created an enormous gap between a small elite and a growing sea of poverty. For example, 2 percent of the U.S. upper class controls 48 percent of the nation's wealth, while 51 percent of African American children live in poverty.[46] Upon close examination of organizations benefiting from the present tax code, we soon realize how the policymakers have insistently waged class warfare that benefits large corporations. For example:

> The Chase Manhattan Corporation, based in New York, is the parent company of Chase Manhattan Bank, the global banking institution. For the years 1991 and 1992, Chase reported income before taxes of $1.5 billion. The company paid $25 million in income tax, which represents a tax rate of 1.7 percent. The official corporate tax rate in those years was 34 percent.
>
> The Ogden Corporation, diversified supplier of aviation, building, and waste management services, reported income before taxes of $217 million. The company paid less than $200,000 in taxes. Given that the rate of $1 being paid for every $1,085 earned by the Ogden corporation, if this were the case for a working class family of four earning $25,000.00 a year, they would be proportionally responsible for paying approximately $25.00 in taxes each year.

While the very rich corporations paid a minuscule percentage of their reported income in taxes, individuals with incomes between $13,000 and $15,000 paid taxes at a rate of 7.2 percent, or four times the Chase rate.[47]

As we can see, the power of ideology is so insidious that the un-analyzed positive association of shock words such as "welfare reform" is often accepted by the very people who are in a position to be adversely affected by such reform. Thus, many working-class White people are misled by the positive illusion of "welfare reform" without realizing that they themselves are, perhaps, one paycheck away from benefiting from the very social safety net they want reformed or destroyed. In an age of institutional downsizing (which is a euphemism for corporate greed and maximization of profit), the economic stability of both the White middle and working classes is fast disappearing, thus creating an even more urgent need to make horizontal the economic oppression that is eating away their once more or less secure economic status. By this, we mean that both the White middle and working classes need a scapegoat in order to blame the Other for their present economic insecurities.

Unfortunately, the same ideology that anchors its discourse on the positive effect of shock words also prevents us from having access to the subtext containing the opposite meaning of the illusory "reality." It is for this reason that conservative politicians who propose welfare reform as a panacea for all the economic ills of our society will not tolerate a counter-response that challenges the false assumption that welfare recipients are the cause of the nation's economic problems. For welfare reform to be equally exercised, it would have to include welfare reform for the rich, who are most responsible for exacerbating the already huge gap between them and the poor. Since discussion concerning welfare reform for the rich is beyond question, the only way to rationalize support for welfare reform is to stay at the level of the positive effect of the shock word that often obfuscates the reality.

As stated earlier, shock words, terms, and expressions do not only produce positive effects. According to Oliver Reboul, they can also "produce by themselves negative effects that disqualify those who use these shock words."[48] Thus, the use of terms such as "welfare for the rich," "oppression," "radical," and "activist" often provokes a negative effect that prevents a thorough analysis of the reality encoded by these terms. In other words, if the word "oppression" is not allowed as part of the debate, there will be no need to identify the "oppressor." An example of this occurred when one of the authors asked a colleague whom he considered politically progressive to read a manuscript of a book he was coauthoring with Paulo Freire. She asked him, a bit irritably, "Why do you and Paulo insist on using this Marxist jargon? Many readers who may enjoy reading Paulo may be put off by the jargon." Macedo calmly explained to her that the equation of Marxism with jargon did not fully capture the richness of Freire's analysis. In fact, his language was the only means through which he could do justice to the complexity of the various concepts dealing with oppression. Macedo asked his colleague to imagine that instead of writing *The Pedagogy of the Oppressed,* Freire had written *The Pedagogy of the Disenfranchised.* The first title utilizes a discourse that conveys the fact that there is an active agent of oppression, whereas the second fails to do so. If there are oppressed, there must be oppressors. What would be the counterpart of disenfranchised? *The Pedagogy of the Disenfranchised* dislodges the agent of the action, leaving in doubt who bears the responsibility for such actions. This leaves the door wide open for blaming the victim for their own disenfranchisement. This example is a clear case in which the object of oppression can be also understood as the subject of oppression. Such language distorts reality. Thus, it is not surprising that most people prefer a discourse of euphemism based on shock words that do not name it.

The dominant discourse uses the presence of taboo words such as "class" and "oppression" to dismiss a counter discourse that challenges the falsification of reality. Thus, to call for welfare reform for the rich is immediately dismissed as "class warfare," a taboo concept not in keeping with the myths that the United States is a classless society. In fact, the ideological power of this myth is so strong that policymakers, the media, and educators can refer to the "working class" being pressured by foreign imports or a "middle class" overburdened by taxes, while simultaneously denying the existence of class differences in the United States. If in fact we live in a classless society, why do we constantly refer to the existence of the working class versus the middle class? What is omitted from the dominant discourse is the existence of the term "upper class." As a substitute, the dominant discourse creates euphemisms such as "rich," "well-to-do," and "affluent." By closing the link between the working, middle, and upper classes, it would be impossible to sustain the myth that we live in a classless society. Therefore, it is important that the dominant discourse suppress the term upper class and, in so doing, deny its existence.

By forbidding the use of the term "upper class," the dominant discourse prevents the public from gaining an understanding of the mechanisms used as obstacles to the development of spaces for dialectal relationships. For example, "radicalism" is a shock word that triggers a negative effect. Those involved in work that is considered by the dominant discourse as "radical" are dismissed as political, and therefore not scientific, and are often prevented from taking part in discussions, particularly if a particular agenda is to maintain the status quo. Similarly, denouncing racism with strong conviction is often considered radical. A preferred position is to acknowledge that racism exists but not to advocate doing anything about it, thus not challenging the very structures that produce racism. In fact, to denounce racism with conviction becomes a worse social crime than the racist acts themselves. In the political sphere, politicians use taboo words to effectively control the population, manufacture consent, and dismiss any challenge presented by a counter discourse. Other taboo shock words such as "socialism," "communism," and "Marxism" have the same effect and are often successfully used for ideological control.

Consider the negative effect of the shock word "migrant." Why do we designate the migration of Latinos to other geographical areas to seek better economic opportunities as "migrants" and, in contrast, call the English migrants who came to Plymouth, Massachusetts, "settlers"? And why do we continue to call the Hispanic community of migrant workers which has been here for centuries "migrant" yet fail to use the same term to categorize the large migration of Massachusetts workers to Florida and elsewhere during the last recession. Clearly, the term is not used to describe the migration of groups of people moving from place to place, but to label and typecast certain Hispanics ethnically and racially, while using this typecast to denigrate and devalue the Hispanic culture. "Migrant" not only relegates the Hispanics labelled in such a manner to a lower status in our society, but it also robs them of their citizenship as human beings who participate and contribute immensely to our society. The following poem was distributed to Republican legislators in California by State Assemblyman William Knight:

Ode to the New California

I come for visit, get treated regal,
So I stay, who care illegal.

Cross the border poor and broke,
Take the bus, see customs bloke.

Welfare say come down no more,
We send cash right to your door.

Welfare checks they make you wealthy,
Medi-Cal it keep you healthy.

By and by, I got plenty money,
Thanks, American working dummy.

Write to friends in mother land,
Tell them come as fast as can.

They come in rags and Chebby trucks,
I buy big house with welfare bucks.

Fourteen families all move in,
Neighbor's patience growing thin.

Finally, white guy moves away,
I buy his house and then I say,

Send for family, they just trash,
But they draw more welfare cash.

Everything is much good,
Soon we own the neighborhood.

We have hobby, it's called "breeding,"
Welfare pay for baby feeding.

Kids need dentist? Wife need pills?
We get free, we got no bills.

We think America damn good place,
Too damn good for white man's race.

If they no like us, they can go,
Got lots of room in Mexico.[49]

When the legislator's Latino caucus complained that the poem was racist, Knight explained without apologizing that he thought the poem was "clever" and "funny,"[50] adding that it was not intended to offend anyone.

In the United States, how can we honestly speak of human freedom in a society that generates and yet ignores ghettos, reservations, human misery, and savage inequalities, and then have the audacity to joke about it? How can we honestly speak of human freedom when the state of California passes Proposition 187, which robs millions of children of their human citizenship? The law proposes to:

1. refuse citizenship to children born on U.S. soil to illegal parents.
2. end the legal requirement that the state provide emergency health care to illegal immigrants.
3. deny public education to children of illegal immigrants.
4. create tamper-proof identification cards for legal immigrants so they can receive benefits.[51]

What becomes clear through our discussion is that our "democracy" remains paralyzed by a historical legacy that has bequeathed to us rampant social inequality along the lines of ethnicity and race.

Conclusion: A Pedagogy of Hope

As cultural brokers, we must have the courage and ethical integrity to denounce any and all attempts to actively dehumanize the very students from whom we make our living as teachers. We need to have the courage and ethical integrity to say to Patrick Buchanan, John Silber, Pete Wilson, and President Clinton that no human being is illegal much less alien. Rather than the "all-out cultural war" called for by Buchanan, what we need is cultural peace. The real challenge for educators is how schools can be brokers in this peace process, or, in other words, how educators can forge cultural unity through diversity.

We conclude by proposing a pedagogy of hope that is informed by tolerance, respect, and solidarity. A pedagogy that rejects the social construction of images that dehumanize the "other"; a pedagogy that points out that in our construction of the other we become intimately tied with that other; a pedagogy that teaches us that by dehumanizing the other we become dehumanized ourselves. In short, we need a pedagogy of hope that guides us toward the critical road of truth, rather than myths and lies, toward reclaiming our dignity and our humanity. A pedagogy of hope will point us toward a world that is more harmonious and more humane, less discriminatory, less dehumanizing, and more just. A pedagogy of hope will reject Patrick Buchanan's and John Silber's policies of hatred, bigotry, and division while celebrating diversity within unity. In other words, a pedagogy of hope points to

> [the] path through which men and women can become conscious about their presence in the world. The way they act and think when they develop all their capacities, taking into consideration their needs, but also the needs and aspirations of others.[52]

A pedagogy of hope will teach us that the social construction of otherness, in its ideological makeup, constitutes the raison d'être for aggression or the nationalization of aggression. In creating the social and cultural separateness that demonizes so-called "illegals," for example, the dominant group creates a distance from them that engenders in the dominant groups an ignorance that borders on stupidification.[53] By creating rigid borders, either by building or maintaining walls between people or nations, we inevitably end up with the same reality where things lose their fluidity while generating more tensions and conflicts.[54]

The creation of otherness not only fosters more ignorance on the part of those in power, but also fails to provide the dominant group with the necessary tools to empathize with the demonized other. The dominant group loses its humanity in its inability to feel bad for discriminating against other human beings. The dominant group's ability to demonize and its inability to empathize with the other points to the inherent demon in those who dehumanize.

A pedagogy of hope will also point out to President Clinton and others that they could learn a great deal from those human beings who, by virtue of their place of birth, race, or ethnicity, have been reduced to the non-status of aliens. As Carlos Fuentes has written:

> People and their cultures perish in isolation, but they are born or reborn in contact with other men and women, with men and women of another culture, another creed, another race. If we do not recognize our humanity in others, we shall not recognize it in ourselves.[55]

In order to fully embrace a humanizing pedagogy, we must go beyond technicism in classroom instruction and engage other fundamental knowledges that are seldom taught to us in our preparation as teachers. These knowledges include, according to Paulo Freire

> The courage to dare, in the full sense of the term, to speak about love without fear of being called ascientific, if not anti-scientific. It is necessary to say, scientifically and not in a pure bla-bla-bla, that we study, we learn, we teach, we know with our entire body. With feelings, with emotions, with desire, with fear, with doubts, with passion and also with critical reasoning. However, critical reasoning alone is not sufficient. It is necessary to dare so that we never dichotomize cognition from the emotional self. It is necessary to dare so we can remain teaching for a long time under conditions that we all know too well, low pay, lack of respect and resisting the risk of falling into cynicism.[56]

It is necessary to dare, to learn to dare, to say no to the bureaucratization of the mind to which we are exposed daily. It is necessary to dare to say that racism is a curable disease. It is necessary to dare to speak of difference as a value and to say that it is possible to find unity in diversity.

Notes

1. James Baldwin, *The Price of the Ticket: Collected Nonfiction 1948–1985* (New York: St. Martin's/MAREK), p. 409.
2. Derrick Z. Jackson, "Muted Voices in the Newsroom," *Boston Globe,* September 2, 1993, p. 15.
3. bell hooks, *Talking Back: Thinking Feminist, Thinking Black* (Boston: South End Press, 1989), p. 22.
4. Pepi Leistyna, "Racenicity: Whitewashing Ethnicity," in *Tongue-Tying Multiculturalism,* ed. Donaldo Macedo (work in progress).

5. Stanley Aronowitz, "Ethnicity and Higher Education in the U.S.," in *Tongue-Typing Multiculturalism,* ed. Donaldo Macedo (work in progress).
6. Leistyna, "Racenicity."
7. Michael Rezendes, "Declaring 'Cultural War': Buchanan Opens '96 Run," *Boston Globe,* March 21, 1995, p. 1.
8. Cited in Henry Giroux, *Border Crossings: Cultural Workers and the Politics of Education* (New York: Routledge, 1992), p. 20.
9. Henry A. Giroux, "Transgression of Difference," in *Culture and Difference: Critical Perspectives on Bicultural Experiences* (Westport, CT: Bergin & Garvey, in press).
10. John Fiske, *Power Plays, Power Works* (London: Verso Press, 1994), p. 13.
11. Steven Randall, Jim Naureckus, and Jeff Cohen, *The Way Things Ought to Be: Rush Limbaugh's Reign of Error* (New York: New Press, 1995), pp. 47–54.
12. Randall et al., *The Way Things Ought to Be,* p. 10.
13. Donaldo Macedo, *Literacies of Power: What Americans Are Not Allowed to Know* (Boulder, CO: Westview Press, 1994), p. 10.
14. C. P. Otero, ed., *Language and Politics,* (New York: Black Rose Books, 1988), p. 681.
15. Cited in Giroux, *Border Crossings,* p. 230.
16. Adam Pertman, "Buchanan Announces Presidential Candidacy," *Boston Globe,* December 15, 1991, p. 13.
17. William Clinton, "Clinton Speech Envisions Local Empowerment," in *Congressional Quarterly,* January 28, 1995, p. 303.
18. Derrick Jackson, "The Assassination of Affirmative Action," *Boston Globe,* March 22, 1995, p. 13.
19. Jackson, "The Assassination," p. 13.
20. Jackson, "The Assassination," p. 13.
21. bell hooks, Gloria Steinem, Urvashi Vaid, and Naomi Wolf, "Let's Get Real About Feminism: The Backlash, the Myths, the Movement," *Ms. Magazine,* September/October 1993, p. 39.
22. Jackson, "The Assassination," p. 13.
23. Donaldo P. Macedo, "Literacy for Stupidification: The Pedagogy of Big Lies," *Harvard Educational Review, 63* (1993), 183–206.
24. Derrick D. Bell, *Faces at the Bottom of the Well: The Permanence of Racism* (New York: Basic Books, 1992), p. xiii.
25. "Horde Invasion," Editorial, *Boston Globe,* January 26, 1990, p. 12.
26. David Nyhan, "David Duke Sent 'em a Scare But Now He Faces the Old Pro," *Boston Globe,* October 24, 1991, p. 13.
27. Nyhan, "David Duke," p. 13.
28. Bill Alex Talk Radio Show, WBET, Brockton, Massachusetts, March 17, 1994.
29. "Trouble on the Mexican Border," *U.S. News and World Report,* April 24, 1995, p. 10.
30. "Trouble," *U.S. News,* p. 10.
31. David T. Goldberg, *Racist Culture* (Oxford, Eng.: Blackwell, 1993), p. 6.
32. Goldberg, *Racist Culture,* p. 7.
33. Goldberg, *Racist Culture,* p. 7.
34. Peter Applebone, "Goals Unmet, Duke Reveals the Perils in Effort to Increase Black Faculty," *New York Times,* September 19, 1993, p. 1.
35. Adam Pertman, "CIA-Drug Link Stories Outrage Blacks in L. A.," *Boston Globe,* October 6, 1996, p. 1.
36. Russell B. Nye, *Autobiography and Other Writings by Benjamin Franklin* (Boston: Houghton Mifflin, 1958), pp. 112–113.
37. Edward W. Said, "A Devil Theory of Islam," *The Nation,* August 12/19, 1996, p. 28.
38. Paul Quinn Judge and Charles Seamot, "Specialists Say the Attack Makes Turning Point in US," *Boston Globe,* April 20, 1995, p. 24.
39. Dimitri, K. Simes, "Using Wisdom to Avert Terrorism," *Boston Globe,* August 8, 1996, p. A21.
40. Richard Estrada, "Immigration: Setting the Context." Paper presented at "In or Out? Immigration and Proposition 187," conference held at Harvard Graduate School of Education, February 15, 1995.
41. Carl Sandburg, *The People, Yes* (New York: Harcourt, Brace & World, 1964), p. 75.
42. Oliver Reboul, *Lenguage e Ideologia* (Mexico City: Fondo de Cultura Economica, 1986), p. 116.
43. Pertman, "Buchanan Announces," p. 1.
44. Donald I. Bartlett and James B. Steele, *America: Who Really Pays the Taxes?* (New York: Simon & Schuster, 1994), p. 93.
45. Robert Kuttner, "The Rewards of Our Labor Are Increasingly Unequal," *Boston Globe,* September 4, 1995, p. 15.
46. Macedo, *Literacies of Power,* pp. 42–43.
47. Macedo, *Literacies of Power,* pp. 144–145.
48. Reboul, *Lenguage e Ideologia,* p. 117.
49. From "I Love America!", a poem distributed in May 1995 to California Legislators by State Assemblyman William J. Knight. Quoted in Dan Morain and Hank Gladstone, "Racist Verse Stirs Up Anger in Assembly," *Los Angeles*

Times, May 19, 1993, p. 3. *The California Journal, 24,* No. 7 (1993), 42–43, included the following abstract concerning this poem:

> GOP Assemblyman Pete Knight of Palmdale CA distributed a poem to Assembly Republicans in May 1993 that may have been the most offensive sliver of verse publicly distributed by a member inside the confines of the state Capitol since the end of WWII. The distribution of the racist poem about illegal Latino immigrants is discussed.

50. Morain and Gladstone, "Racist Verse."
51. Proposition 187 Text approved by California voters on November 8, 1994.
52. Paulo Freire and Frei Betto, *Essa Escola Chamada Vida* (Sao Paulo: Editora Scipione, 1989), p. 32.
53. Macedo, "Literacy for Stupidification," pp. 183–206.
54. Vitor J. Rodrigues, *A Nova Ondem Estupidológica* (Lisbon: Livros Horizonte, 1995), p. 18.
55. Carlos Fuentes, "The Mirror of the Other," *The Nation,* March 30, 1992, p. 411.
56. Paulo Freire, *Teachers as Cultural Workers: Letters to Those Who Dare Teach* (Boulder, CO: Westview Press, in press).

10

American Indian Geographies of Identity and Power: At the Crossroads of Indígena and Mestizaje

Sandy Marie Anglás Grande

> Until Indians resolve for themselves a comfortable modern identity that can be used to energize reservation institutions, radical changes will not be of much assistance.
>
> (Deloria & Lytle, 1984, p. 266)

> Our struggle at the moment is to continue to survive and work toward a time when we can replace the need for being preoccupied with survival with a more responsible and peaceful way of living within communities and with the ever-changing landscape that will ever be our only home.
>
> (Warrior, 1995, p. 126)

Broadly speaking, this article focuses on the intersection between dominant modes of critical pedagogy[1] and American Indian intellectualism.[2] At present, critical theories are often indiscriminately employed to explain the sociopolitical conditions of all marginalized peoples. As a result, many Indigenous scholars view the current liberatory project as simply the latest in a long line of political endeavors that fails to consider American Indians as a unique population.[3] Thus, while critical pedagogy may have propelled mainstream educational theory and practice along the path of social justice, I argue that it has muted and thus marginalized the distinctive concerns of American Indian intellectualism and education. As such, I argue further that the particular history of imperialism enacted upon Indigenous peoples requires a reevaluation of dominant views of democracy and social justice, and of the universal validity of such emancipatory projects—including critical pedagogy. It is not that critical pedagogy is irrelevant to Indigenous peoples, as they clearly experience oppression, but rather that the deep structures of the "pedagogy of oppression" fail to consider American Indians as a categorically different population, virtually incomparable to other minority groups. To assert this is not to advocate any kind of hierarchy of oppression but merely to call attention to the fundamental difference of what it means to be a sovereign and tribal people within the geopolitical confines of the United States.

Previous examinations of the potential for critical theory to inform Indigenous pedagogy (Grande, 1997, 2000) expose significant tensions in their deep theoretical structures. For instance, insofar as critical theorists retain "democracy" as the central struggle concept of liberation, they fail to recognize Indigenous peoples' historical battles to resist absorption into the "democratic imaginary"[4]—and their contemporary struggles to retain tribal sovereignty. In fact, it could be argued that the forces of "democracy" have done more to imperil American Indian nations then they have to sustain them (e.g., the extension of democracy in the form of civil rights and citizenship has acted as a powerful if not lethal colonizing force when imposed on the intricate tribal, clan, and kinship systems of traditional Native communities).

Compounding the tensions between American Indian intellectualism and critical pedagogy is the fact that American Indian scholars have, by and large, resisted engagement with critical theory,[5] and concentrated instead on the production of historical monographs, ethnographic studies, tribally centered curricula, and site-based research. Such a focus stems from the fact that most American Indian scholars feel compelled to address the political urgencies of their own communities, against which engagement in abstract theory appears to be a luxury and privilege of the academic elite. While I recognize the need for practically based research, I argue that the ever-increasing global encroachment on American Indian lands, resources, cultures, and communities points to the equally urgent need to build political coalitions and formulate transcendent theories of liberation. Moreover, while individual tribal needs are in fact great, I believe that, unless the boundaries of coalition are expanded to include non-Indian communities, Indian nations will remain vulnerable to whims of the existing social order.

The combined effect of internal neglect and external resistance to critical pedagogy has pushed American Indian intellectualism to the margins of critical discourse. This reality raises a series of important questions that help form the basis of this discussion:

1. Insofar as critical theory remains disconnected from the work of American Indian scholars, how do its language and epistemic frames serve as homogenizing agents when interfaced with the conceptual and analytical categories persistent within American Indian educational history and intellectualism?
2. How has the resistance of American Indian intellectuals to critical theory contributed to the general lack of analyses on the impact of racism (and, for that matter, other "isms") within American Indian communities?
3. How have the marginalization of critical scholarship and the concomitant fascination with cultural/literary forms of American Indian writing contributed to the preoccupation with parochial questions of identity and authenticity? And, how have these obsessions about identity concealed the social-political realities facing American Indian communities?

While the above questions provide the foundation for a broad discussion of the intersection of critical theory and American Indian intellectualism, I submit that the main source of tension is embedded in their competing notions of identity—one rooted in Western definitions of the civil society and the other in the traditional structures of tribal society.

In terms of identity, critical theorists aim to explode the concretized categories of race, class, gender, and sexuality and to claim the intersections—the borderlands—as the space to create a new culture—*una cultura mestízo*,—in which the only normative standard is hybridity and all subjects are constructed as inherently transgressive.[6] Though American Indian intellectuals support the notion of hybridity, they remain skeptical of the new mestíza as a possible continuation of the colonialist project to fuse Indians into the national model of the democratic citizen. There is, in other words, an undercurrent to the postcolonial lexicon of *mestizaje* that seems to undermine the formation of "a comfortable modern American Indian identity" (Deloria & Lytle, 1984, p. 266). More specifically, I argue that the contemporary pressures of ethnic fraud, corporate commodification, and culture loss render the critical notion of "transgressive" identity highly problematic for Indigenous peoples. As such, the primary argument is that critical efforts to promote mestizaje as the basis of a new cultural democracy does not fully consider Indigenous struggles to sustain the cultural and political integrity of American Indian communities.

That being said, it is important to note that American Indian critical studies are perceived by both Indigenous and non-Indigenous scholars as a "dangerous discourse" equally threatening to the fields of critical pedagogy and American Indian intellectualism.[7] After all, American Indian critical studies would compel "Whitestream" advocates of critical theory to ask how their knowledge and practices may have contributed and remained blind to the continued exploitation of Indigenous peoples. Specifically, it would require a deeper recognition that these are not postcolonial times, that "globalization" is simply the new metaphor for imperialism, and that current constructions of democracy continue to presume the eventual absorption of Indigenous peoples. For American Indian intellectuals, the infusion of critical studies would require a movement away from the safety of unified, essentialized, and idealized constructions of American Indianness toward more complicated readings of American Indian formations of power and identity, particularly those that take into account the existence of internal oppression. Specifically, it would compel American Indian intellectuals to confront the taboo subjects of racism, sexism, and homophobia within American Indian communities.

Ultimately, however, this article is not a call for American Indian scholars to simply join the conversation of critical theorists. Rather, it is an initiation of an Indigenous conversation that can, in turn, engage in dialectical contestation with the dominant modes of critical theory. In this way, I hope that the development of an Indigenous theory of liberation can itself be a politically transformative practice, one that works to transgress tribal divisions and move toward the development of a transcendent theory of American Indian sovereignty and self-determination. With this in mind, my discussion of the central tension between critical pedagogy and American Indian intellectualism unfolds in four parts. Part one examines formations of identity that have emerged from the dominant modes of critical discourse, paying special attention to the notion of transgression, and the construction of mestizaje as a counter-discourse of subjectivity. Part two examines American Indian formations of identity and the external forces that work to threaten these formations, namely ethnic fraud, cultural encroachment, corporate commodification, and culture loss. Part three examines the intersection between American Indian identity and mestizaje, as well as other models of hybridity generated by American Indian and other scholars of color. The article concludes with a call for the development of a new Red Pedagogy,[8] or one that is historically grounded in American Indian intellectualism, politically centered in issues of sovereignty and tribal self-determination, and inspired by the religious and spiritual[9] traditions of American Indian peoples.

Part I. Identity, Subjectivity and Critical Theory: Mestizaje and the New Cultural Democracy

"Critical pedagogy is the term used to describe what emerges when critical theory encounters education" (Kincheloe & Steinberg, 1997, p. 24). Rather than offer prescriptions, critical pedagogy draws from the structural critique of critical theory, extending an analysis of school as a site of reproduction, resistance, and social transformation. It examines the ways that power and domination inform the processes and procedures of schooling and works to expose the sorting and selecting functions of the institution. As it has evolved into its current form(s), critical pedagogy has emerged as both a rhetoric and a social movement. Critical educators continue to advocate an increasingly sophisticated critique of the social, economic, and political barriers to social justice, as well as to crusade for the transformation of schools to reflect the imperatives of democracy.

Critical scholars have, over time, provided a sustained critique of the forces of power and domination and their relation to the pedagogical (Kincheloe & Steinberg, 1997). As defined here, "the pedagogical" refers to the production of identity or the way one learns to see oneself in relation to the world. Identity is thus situated as one of the core struggle concepts of critical pedagogy, where the formation of self serves as the basis for analyses of race, class, gender, and sexuality and their relationship to the questions of democracy, justice, and community.

By positioning identity in the foreground of their theories, critical scholars have fueled as many theories of identity as they have varieties of critical pedagogy. While there are differences between and among these formulations, critical constructions of identity are distinct from both liberal and conservative theories of identity. Such theories are viewed as problematic by critical scholars because of their use of "essentialist" or reductionistic analyses of difference (Kincheloe & Steinberg, 1997; McCarthy & Crichlow, 1993; McLaren, 1997). "Essentialist" analysis refers to the treatment of racial and social groups as if they were stable and homogeneous entities, or as if members of each group possessed "some innate and invariant set of characteristics setting them apart from each other and from 'Whites'" (McCarthy & Crichlow, 1993, p. xviii). Critical scholars argue that essentialism not only undertheorizes race but can also result in a gross misreading of the nature of difference, opening the door for the proliferation of deeply cynical theories of racial superiority, such as Richard Herrnstein and Charles Murray's *The Bell Curve* (1994). While conservatives typically invoke essentialist theories, critical scholars acknowledge that some forms of left-essentialism operate in the contemporary landscape to similarly divisive ends.[10]

In response to the undertheorizing of race by both the Left and the Right, critical theorists advocate a theory of difference that is firmly rooted in the "power-sensitive discourses of power, democracy, social justice and historical memory" (McLaren & Giroux, 1997, p. 17). In so doing, they replace the comparatively static notion of identity as a relatively fixed entity that one embodies with the more fluid concept of subjectivity—an entity that one actively and continually constructs. Subjectivity works to underscore the contingency of identity and the understanding that "individuals consist of a decentered flux of subject positions highly dependent on discourse, social structure, repetition, memory, and affective investment" (McLaren & Giroux, 1997, p. 25). In other words, one's "identity" is historically situated and socially constructed, rather than predetermined by biological or other prima facie indicators.

In addition to calling attention to the relational aspects of identity, the critical notion of subjectivity advances a more complex analysis of cultural and racial identity. It shifts race from a passive product of biological endowment to an active "product of human work" (Said, 1993, p. xix). Critical scholars argue that the rupture of previously rigid racial categories reveals contested spaces or borderlands where cultures collide, creating the space to explore new notions of identity in the resulting contradictions, nuances, and discontinuities they introduce into the terrain of racial identity. Thus, where essentialist scholars examine race, class, gender, and sexuality as discrete categories, critical scholars focus on the spaces of intersection between and among these categories.

The emergence of subjectivity as a socially constructed entity spawned a whole new language about identity. Border cultures, border-crossers, mestíza (Anzaldúa, 1987;

Delgado Bernal, 1998); *Xicanisma* (Castillo, 1995); postcolonial hybridities, cyborg identities (Harraway, 1991); and mestizaje (Darder, Torres, & Gutierrez, 1997; McLaren & Sleeter, 1995; Valle & Torres, 1995) are just some of the emergent concepts formulated to explain and bring language to the experience of multiplicity, relationality, and transgression as they relate to identity. Moreover, critical scholars contend that the development of transgressive subjectivity not only works to resist essentialist constructions of identity but also acts to counter the hegemonic notion of Whiteness as the normative standard for all subjects. Such efforts represent the hope and possibility of critical pedagogy as they seek to construct a critical democracy that includes multiple cultures, languages, and voices. Critical pedagogy thus serves both to challenge the existing sociocultural and economic relations of exploitation and to strengthen collective work toward peace and social justice, thereby creating a more equitable democratic order and, by definition, more equitable educational institutions.

From Mestizaje to Mestíza back to Mestizaje

The critical notion of mestizaje (Darder, Torres, & Gutierrez, 1997; McLaren & Sleeter, 1995; Kincheloe & Steinberg, 1997; Valle & Torres, 1995) is arguably among the most widely embraced models of multisubjectivity. Historically speaking, the counterdiscourse of mestizaje is rooted in the Latin American subjectivity of the *mestízo*—literally, a person of mixed ancestry, especially of American Indian, European, and African backgrounds (Delgado Bernal, 1998). Mestizaje is the Latin American term for cultural ambiguity, representative of "the continent's unfinished business of cultural hybridization" (Valle & Torres, 1995, p. 141). With regard to this history, Latin American scholars Victor Valle and Rodolfo Torres write:

> In Latin America the genetic and cultural dialogue between the descendants of Europe, Africa, Asia, and the hemisphere's indigenous populations has been expressed in discourses reflecting and responding to a host of concrete national circumstances. In some cases, mestizaje has risen to the level of a truly critical counter-discourse of revolutionary aspirations, while at other times it has been co-opted by the state.
>
> (p. 141)

Thus, it could be argued that the political project of mestizaje originated in Latin America, where the cluster of Spanish, Indian, and Afro-Caribbean peoples were ostensibly "fused" through the violence of genocide into the national model of the mestízo.

In the northern hemisphere, Chicana scholar Gloria Anzaldúa's seminal text *Borderlands, la Frontera: The New Mestíza* (1987) reinscribed the cultural terrain with the language and embodiment of mestíza consciousness. Since the book's publication, mestíza has come to embody a new feminist Chicana consciousness that "straddles cultures, races, languages, nations, sexualities, and spiritualities" and the experience of "living with ambivalence while balancing opposing powers" (Delgado Bernal, 1998, p. 561). Anzaldúa (1987) states, "The new mestíza copes by developing a tolerance for contradictions, a tolerance for ambiguity. She learns to be an Indian in Mexican culture [and] to be Mexican from an Anglo point of view" (p. 79). From this base, a variety of Chicana and other border feminisms have emerged, centered on the social histories and epistemologies of women of color.

More recently, the intellectual left, particularly critical scholars, has incorporated the spirit of the Chicana mestíza in its own search for a viable model of subjectivity. It embraces the emergent discourse of mestizaje and its emphasis on the way in which all cultures change in relation to one another as the postcolonial antidote to imperialist notions of racial purity (di Leonardo, 1991). This radically inclusive construct "willfully blurs political, racial, [and] cultural borders in order to better adapt to the world as it is actually constructed" (Valle & Torres, 1995, p. 149) and embodies the mestízo's demonstrated refusal to prefer one language, one national heritage, or one culture at the expense of others. Leading critical scholar Peter McLaren (1997) summarily articulates mestizaje as "the embodiment of a transcultural, transnational subject, a self-reflexive entity capable of rupturing the facile legitimization of 'authentic' national identities through [the] articulation of a subject who is conjunctural, who is a relational part of an ongoing negotiated connection to the larger society, and who is interpolated by multiple subject positionings" (p. 12). In other words, mestizaje crosses all imposed cultural, linguistic, and national borders, refusing all "natural" or transcendent claims that "by definition attempt to escape from any type of historical and normative grounding" (McLaren & Giroux, 1997, p. 117). Ultimately, the critical notion of mestizaje is itself multifunctional, for it signifies a strategic response to the decline of the imperial West, facilitates the decentering of Whiteness, and undermines the myth of the democratic nation-state based on borders and exclusions (Valle & Torres, 1995).

Insofar as the notion of mestizaje disrupts the discourse of jingoistic nationalism, it is indeed crucial to the project of liberation. As McLaren notes, "Educators would do well to consider Gloria Anzaldúa's (1987) project of creating mestizaje theories that create new categories of identity for those left out or pushed out of existing ones" (McLaren, 1997, p. 537). In so doing, however, "care must be taken not to equate hybridity with equality" (McLaren, 1997, p. 46).[11] As Coco Fusco notes, "The postcolonial celebration of hybridity has (too often) been interpreted as the sign that no further concern about the politics of representation and cultural exchange is needed. With ease, we lapse back into the integrationist rhetoric of the 1960's" (Fusco, 1995, p. 46). These words caution us not to lose sight—in the wake of transgressing borders and building postnational coalitions—of the unique challenges presented to particular groups in their distinct struggles for social justice. In taking this admonition seriously, the following discussion moves into an examination of American Indian tribal identity and some of the current pressures facing Indian communities that, I argue, render the notion of mestizaje somewhat problematic. The question remains whether the construction of a transgressive subjectivity-mestizaje—can be reconciled with the pressures of identity appropriation, cultural commodification, culture loss, and, perhaps more importantly, with Indigenous imperatives of self-determination and sovereignty.

Part II. The Formation of Indígena: American Indian Geographies of Power and Identity

Whitestream America has never really understood what it means to be Indian and even less about what it means to be tribal. Such ignorance has deep historical roots and wide political implications of not understanding what it means to be tribal, since the U.S. government determined long ago that to be "tribal" runs deeply counter to the notion of democracy and the proliferation of (individual) civil rights. Throughout the centuries, uncompromising belief in this tenet of democratic order provided the ideological foundation for numerous expurgatory campaigns against Indigenous peoples. The Civilization Act of 1819, the Indian

Removal Act of 1830, the Dawes Allotment Act of 1886, the Indian Citizenship Act of 1924, the Indian Reorganization Act of 1934, and the Indian Civil Rights Act of 1968 are just a few of the legal mechanisms imposed to "further democracy" and concomitantly erode traditional tribal structures.

Although five centuries of continuous contact may have extinguished the traditional societies of the precontact era, modern American Indian communities still resemble traditional societies enough that, "given a choice between Indian society and non-Indian society, most Indians feel comfortable with their own institutions, lands and traditions" (Deloria & Lytle, 1983, p. xii). Despite such significant differences, tribal America remains curiously difficult to articulate. Vine Deloria Jr., one of the preeminent American Indian scholars, has written over eighteen books and one hundred articles defining the political, spiritual, cultural, and intellectual dimensions of American Indian life. His expansive body of work serves as testimony to the difficulty and complexity of defining tribal life and suggests the impossibility of encompassing the multiple dimensions of Indianness in a single article. To do so would not only minimize Deloria's and other scholars' work, but also presume that centuries of ancestral knowledge could be transcribed into a single literary form. Similarly, to tease out, list, name, and assign primacy to a particular subset of defining characteristics of Indianness would not only serve to objectify and over-simplify the diversity of Native cultures, but would also force what is fundamentally traditional, spatial, and interconnected into the modern, temporal, and epistemic frames of Western knowledge. Accordingly, the following is merely a sample of existing legal, prima facie indicators of what it means to be American Indian in U.S. society, rather than some mythic view of a unified Indigenous culture or an objectified view of Indian "identity":

> *Sovereignty vs. Democracy:* American Indians have been engaged in a centuries-long struggle to have what is legally theirs recognized (i.e., land, sovereignty, treaty rights). As such, Indigenous peoples have not, like other marginalized groups, been fighting for inclusion in the democratic imaginary but, rather, for the right to remain distinct, sovereign, and tribal peoples.
>
> *Treaty Rights:* These rights articulate the unique status of Indian tribes as "domestic dependent nations." A dizzying array of tribal, federal, and state laws, policies, and treaties creates a political maze that keeps the legal status of most tribes in a constant state of flux. Treaties are negotiated and renegotiated in a process that typically reduces tribal rights and erodes traditional structures (Deloria & Lytle, 1984; Fixcio, 1998).
>
> *Dual Citizenship:* The Indian Citizenship Act of 1924 extends the rights of full citizenship to American Indians born within the territorial United States, insofar as such status does not infringe upon the rights to tribal and other property. It is a dual citizenship wherein American Indians do not lose civil rights because of their status as tribal members and individual tribal members are not denied tribal rights because of their American citizenship (Deloria & Lytle, 1984).[12]
>
> *Federal Recognition:* Federal law mandates that American Indians prove that they have continued to exist over time as stable, prima facie entities to retain federal recognition as tribes. Acknowledgment of tribal existence by the Department of the Interior is critical, as it is a prerequisite to the protection, services, and benefits of the federal government available to Indian tribes by virtue of their status as tribes. Therefore, a tribe's existence is contingent upon its ability to prove its existence over time, to provide evidence of shared cultural patterns, and to prove "persistence of a named, collective Indian identity" (USD, Bureau of Indian Affairs, n.d., 83.7).
>
> *Economic Dependency:* American Indians continue to exist as nations within a nation wherein the relationship between the U.S. government and Indian tribes is not the fictive "government to government" relationship described in U.S. documents, but, rather, one that positions tribes as fundamentally dependent.[13]

Reservations: Roughly two-thirds of American Indians continue either to live on or to remain significantly tied to their reservations and, as such, remain predominantly "tribally oriented" as opposed to generically Indian (Joe & Miller, 1997).

The aggregate of the above indicators positions American Indians in a wholly unique and paradoxical relationship to the United States. These indicators further illuminate the inherent contradictions of modern American Indian existence and point to the gross insufficiency of models that treat American Indians as simply another ethnic minority group. Moreover, the paradox of having to prove "authenticity" to gain legitimacy as a "recognized" tribe and of simultaneously having to negotiate a postmodern world in which all claims to authenticity and legitimacy are dismissed as essentialist (if not racist) conscripts American Indians to a gravely dangerous and precarious space. This reality of Indian existence not only deeply problematizes various postmodern theories' insistence that we move beyond concretized categories, but also reveals their colonizing impulse.[14]

In addition to the (legal) prima facie indicators of American Indianness, there are external forces that further impede and complicate the landscape of American Indian identity. More specifically, the forces of ethnic fraud, cultural encroachment, and corporate commodification work in tandem to call into question the ostensibly liberatory effects of transgression. Such forces pressure Indian communities to define American Indian subjectivity in stable, prima facie measures. In other words, the forces of colonialism and imperialism deeply problematize the postmodern notion of transgression in terms of its abandonment of totality and its emphasis on pluralism and discontinuity. As Steven Best (1989) points out, where critical scholars rightly deconstruct essentialist and repressive wholes, they fail to see how crippling the valorization of difference, fragmentation, and agnostics can be. For the American Indian community, the "crippling" effects have been significant. In particular, the struggle to define "comfortable modern American Indian identities" becomes deeply complicated, enmeshed in the impossible paradox of having to respond to the growing pluralism within their own communities and thus the need to define more fluid constructions of Indianness, while also recognizing that the pressures of identity appropriation, cultural encroachment, and corporate commodification require more restrictive constructions of Indianness. In order to better understand the significance of this paradox, the forces of ethnic fraud, cultural encroachment, and corporate commodification are discussed in greater detail.

Identity Appropriation

In post-*Dances with Wolves* America, it has become increasingly popular to be American Indian. Joane Nagel, a sociologist and expert in the politics of ethnicity, attests that between 1960 and 1990 the number of Americans reporting "American Indian" as their racial category in the U.S. Census more than tripled. Researchers attribute this growth to the practice of "ethnic switching," where individuals previously identifying themselves as "non-Indian," now claim "Indian" as their racial affiliation. She identifies three factors promoting ethnic switching: changes in federal Indian policy; changes in American ethnic politics; and American Indian political activism (Nagel, 1995). Those seminal changes in federal policy referred to by Nagel are the Indian relocation policies of the 1960s and 1970s that led to the creation of urban Indian populations, and the various land-claims settlement of the 1980s, which also led to increases in certain tribal populations.[15] The changes in ethnic politics emanate from the civil rights and Red Power movements that made American Indian identification "a more attractive ethnic option" (Nagel, 1995, p. 956). According to Nagel, these factors helped to raise American Indian ethnic consciousness and encouraged individuals to claim or reclaim their Native American ancestry.

While she makes strong arguments for the three factors she identifies, Nagel ignores the possibility that part of the resurgence may also be due to increasing incidents of identity appropriation, or *ethnic fraud*. Ethnic fraud is the term used to describe the phenomenon of Whitestream individuals who, in spite of growing up far removed from any discernible American Indian community, claim an Indian identity based on the discovery of residuals of Indian blood in their distant ancestries. There is nothing categorically wrong with "discovering" one's ancestral background, but when such claims are opportunistically used to cash in on scholarships, set-aside programs, and other affirmative economic incentives, it becomes highly problematic. Furthermore, there is evidence that such "new Indians" discard their new-found identities as soon as they no longer serve them. For example, studies conducted at UCLA in 1988–1989 and 1993 reveal that of the enrolled 179 American Indian students, 125 did not or could not provide adequate documentation of their tribal affiliation, and that, on average, less than 15 percent of American Indian students were enrolled in federally recognized tribes (Machamer, 1997). More importantly, a significant number of students chose to identify as American Indian only to relinquish this identification by the time of graduation, suggesting that, economic incentives aside, "new Indians" chose to reclaim their Whiteness (Machamer, 1997). Such practices indicate that it is not only popular but profitable to be "Indian" in postmodern America.

In addition to outright identity fraud, American Indian communities also endure the more superficial but equally problematic phenomena of ethnic "vogueing." The seasonal influx of tour buses, church groups, and do-gooders discharges a veritable wave of Whiteness into reservation communities. Armed with their own constructions of Indianness, Whitestream individuals appropriate and try on various elements of Native culture and, in the name of religion, multiculturalism, environmentalism, and radicalism, voyeuristically tour reservation communities like cultural predators loose in Indian theme parks. During these visits, they acquire the usual assemblage of trinkets and souvenirs, and afterwards exit dysconscious[16] of the fact that their adventures have conscripted Native culture as fashion, Indian as exotic, and the sacred as entertainment. While there is a measure of complicity on the part of some American Indians who sell their culture, the overlay of colonialism situates these practices more as products of lost culture, lost economic vitality, and a lost sense of being than as crass indicators of Indian capitalism.

All told, the practice of identity appropriation is believed to have become so widespread that some American Indian organizations have felt compelled to devise statements and enact policies against its proliferation.[17] Even the federal government has recognized the occurrence and ill effects of ethnic fraud. The Indian Arts and Crafts Act, for example, stipulates that all products must be marketed truthfully regarding the Indian heritage and tribal affiliation of the artist or craftsperson. Though this act does more to protect consumers against the purchase of "fraudulent" merchandise, it also protects American Indian artisans from unfair competition by "fraudulent Indian" profiteers.

While such tactics appear to be reasonable in theory, in practice they require the employment of equally problematic essentialist ideology. In other words, in the same moment that particular groups work to determine who is and who is not Indian, they also define fixed parameters of authenticity, reducing the question of Indianness to quantifiable variables and objectified models of culture. It is also difficult to reconcile such contemporary measures with the historical memory that quantifying Indianness is a remnant of the Dawes Allotment Act (1887),[18] in which the U.S. government first introduced blood quantum policies and tribal rolls, and the knowledge that, regardless of how they are defined, measures of authenticity will conjure the same political divisiveness they always have. Finally, insofar as compliance with ethnic fraud policies requires the formation of an Indian Identity Police,[19] enforcement also becomes a dubious enterprise, inviting increased scrutiny from outside agencies.

Cultural Encroachment

The fact that nearly two-thirds of American Indians remain closely tied to their reservations not only points to the continued significance of land in the formation of American Indian identity, but also suggests that a large portion of the Indian population remains fairly segregated from the rest of the nation. Clearly, "Indian Country" persists as both a metaphorical and literal place, undoubtedly shaping the subjectivities of all those who call it home. In other words, living in a physically circumscribed space where literal borders distinguish "us" from "them" must, by definition, shape American Indian consciousness and emergent views of identity and difference. More specifically, the relationship between American Indian communities and the predominantly White border towns not only shapes the ways Indians perceive and construct Whites, but also significantly influences their own views of American Indian identity.

Thus, although reservations exist as a vestige of forced removal, colonialist domination, and Whitestream greed, they have also come to serve as protective barriers and defensive perimeters between cultural integrity and wholesale assimilation. They also serve to distinguish American Indians as the only peoples with federally recognized land claims, demarcating the borders of the only domestic sovereign nations. Though the power of this domestic-dependent-nation status is continually challenged in federal courts, Indians have retained a significant portion of their plenary powers, such as the right to establish tribal courts, tribal governments, and tribal police forces. Ultimately, however, the notion of self-government remains a bit of a farce, since most tribes remain entrenched in untenable relationships with the U.S. government and most reservation economies can only maintain stability with the infusion of outside capital (Deloria & Lytle, 1984).

The dependency on outside capital generates a subordinating effect, leaving American Indians at the virtual mercy of venture capitalists and Whitestream do-gooders. As a result, most reservation communities are overrun by emissaries of White justice, private entrepreneurs, and New Age liberals seeking to forge lucrative careers from predatory practices. Bivouacked in internal and external compounds, enterprising members of the Whitestream wield power and broker services by day, and by night retreat back into the comforts of their bourgeois border towns. As a result, most of the businessmen, teachers, principals, doctors, and health-care providers in reservation communities are White, and most of the laborers, minimum-wagers, underemployed, and unemployed are American Indian.

In spite of the pressures of cultural encroachment, reservation communities continue to work toward becoming sites of political contestation and empowerment. They are learning to survive the dangers of imperialistic forces by employing both proactive strategies that emphasize education, empowerment, and self-determination, and defensive tactics that protect against unfettered economic and political encroachment. Thus, whatever else reservation borders may or may not signify, they serve as potent geographic filters of all that is non-Indian—literal dividing lines between the real and metaphoric spaces differentiating Indian Country from the rest of Whitestream America.

Corporate Commodification

The forces of both ethnic fraud and cultural encroachment operate to create a climate ripe for the corporate commodification of American Indianness. While this commodification takes many forms, it is perhaps most visible in the marketing of Indian narratives, particularly publishing, in which literary/cultural forms of Indian intellectualism have been historically favored over critical forms.

For instance, Indigenous scholar Elizabeth Cook-Lynn (1998) questions why the same editors and agents who solicit her "life story" also routinely reject her scholarly work. She writes, "While I may have a reasonable understanding why a state-run university press would not want to publish research that has little good to say about America's relationship to tribes, . . . I am at a loss to explain why anyone would be more interested in my life story (which for one thing is quite unremarkable)" (p. 121). The explanation, of course, is that the marketable narrative is that which subscribes to the Whitestream notion of Indian as romantic figure, and not Indian as scholar and social critic. Such a predisposition works to favor not only cultural/literary forms of American Indian intellectualism over critical forms, but also the work of "fraudulent" Indians over that of "legitimate" American Indian scholars. Cook-Lynn (1998) argues that, just as the rights to our land remain in the hands of the Whitestream government, the rights to our stories remain in non-Indian enclaves. Deloria (1998) similarly contends that what passes in the academic world as legitimate scholarship on American Indians is often the product of average scholars (often White) advocating a predetermined anti-Indian agenda[20] and "fraudulent" Indians. That such work has been allowed to corner the market raises the question of who controls access to the intellectual property of American Indian peoples. Deloria himself asks, "Who is it that has made such people as Adolph Hungry Wolf, Jamake Highwater, Joseph Epes Brown, Su Bear, Rolling Thunder, Wallace Black Elk, John Redtail Freesoul, Lynn Andrews, and Dhyani Ywahoo the spokespeople of American Indians?" (p. 79). He responds by naming Whitestream America as both patron and peddler of the Hollywood Indian. He writes, "They [the fraudulent Indians] represent the intense desire of Whites to create in their own minds an Indian they want to believe in" (p. 79).

As such, the market is flooded with tragic stories of lost cultures, intimate narratives of "frontier life," and quasi-historic accounts of the Native Americans' plight. Such stories are told and retold as part of America's dark and distant past, a bygone era of misguided faith where cultural genocide is depicted as an egregious but perhaps unavoidable consequence of the country's manifest destiny toward democracy. While I would never argue that stories depicting the truth of Native peoples' tragic experiences (e.g., Indian boarding schools, the Trail of Tears) do not deserve a central place in the telling of American history, such accounts become problematic in the wider context of Whitestream consumption of Indian history.

Why are these stories the ones most often presented as the prime-time programs in the commodified literary network of Indian history? What is gained by focusing on these particular aspects of White domination and Indian subjugation? I argue that such stories serve several purposes, none of which contributes to the emancipatory project of American Indians. First, by propagating the romantic image of American Indians and concomitantly marginalizing the work of Indigenous intellectuals and social critics, Whitestream publishers maintain control over the epistemic frames that define Indians, and thus over the fund of available knowledge on American Indians. Second, such control is underwritten by the understanding that American Indian intellectualism exists as a threat to the myth of the ever-evolving democratization of Indian–White relations, and to the notion that cultural genocide is a remnant of America's dark and distant past. Third, the often oversimplified accounts of Indian history, framed in good-v.-bad-guy terms, allow the consumer to fault rogue groups of dogmatic missionaries and wayward military officers for the slow but steady erosion of Indigenous life, thereby distancing themselves and mainstream government from the ongoing project of cultural genocide. Finally, the focus on Indian history allows the Whitestream to avoid issues facing American Indians in the twenty-first century. As a result, Indians as a modern people remain invisible, allowing a wide array of distorted myths to flourish as contemporary reality—for example, that all the "real" Indians are extinct, that the surviving Indians are all alcoholic-drug addicts who have forsaken traditional ways to become budding capitalists, gaming entrepreneurs, and casino owners—and find their way into public discourse. At the same time these images are circulated, the intensive, ongoing court battles over land, natural resources, and federal recognition are ignored, fueling the great lie of twenty-first century democracy—that America's "Indian problem" has long been solved.

Discussion

The forces of identity appropriation, cultural encroachment, and corporate commodification pressure American Indian communities to employ essentialist tactics and construct relatively fixed notions of identity, and to render the concepts of fluidity and transgression highly problematic. It is evident from the examples above that the notion of fluid boundaries has never worked to the advantage of Indigenous peoples: federal agencies have invoked the language of fluid or unstable identities as the rationale for dismantling the structures of tribal life and creating greater dependency on the U.S. government; Whitestream America has seized its message to declare open season on Indians, thereby appropriating Native lands, culture, spiritual practices, history, and literature; and Whitestream academics have now employed the language of postmodern fluidity to unwittingly transmute centuries of war between Indigenous peoples and their respective nation-states into a "genetic and cultural dialogue" (Valle & Torres, 1995, p. 141). Thus, in spite of its aspirations to social justice, the notion of a new cultural democracy based on the ideal of mestizaje represents a rather ominous threat to American Indian communities.

In addition, the undercurrent of fluidity and sense of displacedness that permeates, if not defines, mestizaje runs contrary to American Indian sensibilities of connection to place, land, and the Earth itself. Consider, for example, the following statement on the nature of critical subjectivity by Peter McLaren:

> The struggle for critical subjectivity is the struggle to occupy a space of hope—a liminal space, an intimation of the anti-structure, of what lives in the in-between zone of undecidedability—in which one can work toward a praxis of redemption. . . . A sense of atopy has always been with me, a resplendent placelessness, a feeling of living in germinal formlessness. . . . I cannot find words

> to express what this border identity means to me. All I have are what Georges Bastille (1988) calls mots glissants (slippery words).
>
> (1997, pp. 13–14)

McLaren speaks passionately and directly about the crisis of modern society and the need for a "praxis of redemption." As he perceives it, the very possibility of redemption is situated in our willingness not only to accept but to flourish in the "liminal" spaces, border identities, and postcolonial hybridities that are inherent in postmodern life and subjectivity. In fact, McLaren perceives the fostering of a "resplendent placelessness" itself as the gateway to a more just, democratic society.

While American Indian intellectuals also seek to embrace the notion of transcendent subjectivities, they seek a notion of transcendence that remains rooted in historical place and the sacred connection to land. Consider, for example, the following commentary by Deloria (1992) on the centrality of place and land in the construction of American Indian subjectivity:

> Recognizing the sacredness of lands on which previous generations have lived and died is the foundation of all other sentiment. Instead of denying this dimension of our emotional lives, we should be setting aside additional places that have transcendent meaning. Sacred sites that higher spiritual powers have chosen for manifestation enable us to focus our concerns on the specific form of our lives. . . . Sacred places are the foundation of all other beliefs and practices because they represent the presence of the sacred in our lives. They properly inform us that we are not larger than nature and that we have responsibilities to the rest of the natural world that transcend our own personal desires and wishes. This lesson must be learned by each generation.
>
> (pp. 278, 281)

Gross misunderstanding of this connection between American Indian subjectivity and land, and, more importantly, between sovereignty and land has been the source of numerous injustices in Indian country. For instance, I believe there was little understanding on the part of government officials that passage of the Indian Religious Freedom Act (1978) would open a Pandora's box of discord over land, setting up an intractable conflict between property rights and religious freedom. American Indians, on the other hand, viewed the act as an invitation to return to their sacred sites, several of which were on government lands and were being damaged by commercial use. As a result, a flurry of lawsuits alleging mismanagement and destruction of sacred sites was filed by numerous tribes. Similarly, corporations, tourists, and even rock climbers filed suits accusing land managers of unlawfully restricting access to public places by implementing policies that violate the constitutional separation between church and state. All of this is to point out that the critical project of mestizaje continues to operate on the same assumption made by the U.S. government in this instance, that in a democratic society, human subjectivity—and liberation for that matter—is conceived of as inherently rights-based as opposed to land-based.

To be fair, I believe that both American Indian intellectuals and critical theorists share a similar vision—a time, place, and space free of the compulsions of Whitestream, global capitalism and the racism, sexism, classism, and xenophobia it engenders. But where critical scholars ground their vision in Western conceptions of democracy and justice that presume a "liberated" self, American Indian intellectuals ground their vision in conceptions of sovereignty that presume a sacred connection to place and land. Thus, to a large degree, the seemingly liberatory constructs of fluidity, mobility, and transgression are perceived not only as the language of critical subjectivity, but also as part of the fundamental lexicon of Western imperialism. Deloria (1999) writes:

> Although the loss of land must be seen as a political and economic disaster of the first magnitude, the real exile of the tribes occurred with the destruction of ceremonial life (associated with the loss of land) and the failure or inability of white society to offer a sensible and cohesive alternative to the traditions which Indians remembered. People became disoriented with respect to the world in which they lived. They could not practice their old ways, and the new ways which they were expected to learn were in a constant state of change because they were not a cohesive view of the world but simply adjustments which whites were making to the technology they had invented. (p. 247)

In summary, insofar as American Indian identities continue to be defined and shaped in interdependence with place, the transgressive mestizaje functions as a potentially homogenizing force that presumes the continued exile of tribal peoples and their enduring absorption into the American "democratic" Whitestream. The notion of mestizaje as absorption is particularly problematic for the Indigenous peoples of Central and South America, where the myth of the mestizaje (belief that the continent's original cultures and inhabitants no longer exist) has been used for centuries to force the integration of Indigenous communities into the national mestízo model (Van Cott, 1994). According to Rodolfo Stavenhagen (1992), the myth of mestizaje has provided the ideological pretext for numerous South American governmental laws and policies expressly designed to strengthen the nation-state through incorporation of all "non-national" (read "Indigenous") elements into the mainstream. Thus, what Valle and Torres (1995) previously describe as "the continent's unfinished business of cultural hybridization" (p. 141), Indigenous peoples view as the continents' long and bloody battle to absorb their existence into the master narrative of the mestízo.

While critical scholars do construct a very different kind of democratic solidarity that disrupts the sociopolitical and economic hegemony of the dominant culture around a transformed notion of mestizaje (one committed to the destabilization of the isolationist narratives of nationalism and cultural chauvinism), I argue that any liberatory project that does not begin with a clear understanding of the difference of American Indianness will, in the end, work to undermine tribal life. Moreover, there is a potential danger that the ostensibly "new" cultural democracy based upon the radical mestizaje will continue to mute tribal differences and erase distinctive Indian identities. Therefore, as the physical and metaphysical borders of the postmodern world become increasingly fluid, the desire of American Indian communities to protect geographic borders and employ "essentialist" tactics also increases. Though such tactics may be viewed by critical scholars as highly problematic, they are viewed by American Indian intellectuals as a last line of defense against the steady erosion of tribal culture, political sovereignty, Native resources, and Native lands.

The tensions described above indicate the dire need for an Indigenous, revolutionary theory that maintains the distinctiveness of American Indians as tribal peoples of sovereign nations (border patrolling) and also encourages the building of coalitions and political solidarity (border crossing). In contrast to critical scholars McLaren and Kris Gutierrez (1997), who admonish educators to develop a concept of unity and difference as political mobilization rather than cultural authenticity, I urge American Indian intellectuals to develop a language that operates at the crossroads of unity and difference and defines this space in terms of political mobilization and cultural authenticity, thus expressing both the interdependence and distinctiveness of tribal peoples.

Part III. Mestizaje Revisited: Critical Indígena and a New Red Pedagogy

To their credit, Whitestream critical scholars recognize the potential for their own subjectivities and locations of privilege to infiltrate the critical discourse, limiting it in ways they cannot see or anticipate. McLaren (1997) writes, "An individual cannot say he or she has achieved critical pedagogy if he or she stops struggling to attain it. Only sincere discontent and dissatisfaction with the limited effort we exercise in the name of social justice can assure us that we really have the faith in a dialogical commitment to others and otherness" (p. 13). It is perhaps this commitment to self-reflexivity and an ever-evolving pedagogy that represents critical pedagogy's greatest strength. Indeed, critical scholars from other marginalized groups such as Gloria Anzaldúa, Hazel Carby, Antonia Darder, Dolores Delgado Bernal, Kris Gutierrez, bell hooks, Rudy Mattai, Cameron McCarthy, Enrique Murillo, Frances V. Rains, and Sofia Villenas have seized upon its openness, transmuting critical theories to fit their own constructions of culturally relevant praxis. Currently, American Indian scholars are also investigating ways to import the message of critical pedagogy without wholesale adoption of its means. While addressing the impact of racism, sexism, and globalization on American Indian communities, some American Indian intellectuals share underlying principles of mestizaje like reflexivity, hybridity, and multiplicity. However, this notion of a transgressive mestizaje may ultimately undermine American Indian subjectivity. Recognizing the common ground of struggle is an important first step in working to define the ways that critical pedagogy can inform Indigenous praxis.

The following discussion excerpts work by American Indian and other scholars of color who have taken the next step: to define locally and culturally relevant praxis based on a broader critical foundation. I contend that such work represents the possibility and future of both American Indian intellectualism and critical pedagogy.

Voices from the Margin

As might be expected, Latino, Latina, African American, and feminist riffs on Whitestream critical pedagogy speak more directly to the concerns of American Indian intellectuals. In particular, other scholars of color have recognized that the experience of oppression often requires the assertion of hyperauthenticity, and thus have worked to refine critical theorists' hard line against essentialism. For instance, though Chicano scholar Enrique Murillo (1997) rejects the notion of essentialism as a means of recalibrating the balance of power, he employs the term *strategic essentialism* to describe the contradictory experience of many scholars of color caught between the different legitimizing forces of the academy and their own communities. There are times, for example, when scholars of color feel compelled to perform a heightened professional or scholarly identity when seeking legitimacy in the academy, and other times when they feel compelled to perform a hyperauthentic or racialized self to gain or retain legitimacy within their own communities. Murillo's notion of "strategic essentialism" is useful in describing the experience of American Indian intellectuals working to balance the fluidity of the postmodern world with the more stable obligations of their tribal communities. In more concrete terms, this means that, as American Indian scholars work to construct and advocate more complex understandings of American Indian identity, such efforts remain haunted by the knowledge that any failure to continually define and authenticate Indianness in stable and quantifiable terms may result in the loss of everything from school funding to tribal recognition. Within this context, strategic essentialism refers not only to choosing multiple subjectivities where power is located in the self, but also to negotiating between chosen and imposed identities where power continues to be located in the oppressor.

Similar to Murillo's variation on the notion of strategic essentialism, Delgado Bernal (1998) defines a culturally relevant theory of knowledge that brings discussions of power and identity into the realm of epistemology. She argues for a model of identity-based epistemology and develops the notion of "cultural intuition" to validate the centrality of cultural knowledge in the processes of research and in the development of a culture's intellectual history. Specifically, Delgado Bernal employs the notion of cultural intuition to legitimate her unique viewpoint as a Chicana researcher conducting research within the Chicana community.[21] Though similar to Anselm Strauss and Juliet Corbin's concept of "theoretical sensitivity" (1990), Delgado Bernal's paradigm extends the realm of cultural intuition to include collective experience and community memory and to stress the importance of participants' inclusion in the research process, particularly in data analysis. She writes, "While I do not argue for an essentialist notion of who is capable of conducting research with various populations based on personal experiences, I do believe that many Chicana scholars achieve a sense of cultural intuition that is different from other scholars" (p. 567). This insightful articulation of the value and power of cultural intuition brings voice and, more importantly, language to the struggles of Chicano and other scholars of color seeking validation, power, and equity in the domain of academic research. Moreover, the notion of cultural intuition buttresses arguments already made by American Indian scholars on behalf of their own communities; specifically, for the right to speak in their own voices, define their own realities, and develop their own intellectual histories.

Voices from Indian Country

While it is important and beneficial to observe the insights of other critical pedagogies, it is crucial to look to one's own intellectual history and sources of cultural intuition in the development of Indigenous theories and praxis. In this effort, the challenge to American Indian scholars is not merely to "resurrect" these histories and sources of cultural intuition, but to construct meaningful bridges and points of intersection between American Indian intellectualism and Whitestream critical pedagogies.

To this end, while American Indian scholars have, by and large, resisted direct engagement with critical theory, many have begun to theorize their own constructions of Indigenous knowledge and American Indian identity.[22] As a collective effort, such work provides increasingly complex views of American Indian history; of the promise and failures of education; of the struggles for language, agency, and sovereignty; and of the need for political and sociocultural coalitions. Their writings strive to achieve interplay between the past, present, and future, and ride the faultline between continuity, resistance, and possibility.

What follows is a sampling of such works, chosen because of their particular relevance to the topic of American Indian identity and identity formation. The selected scholars differ in their methods and approaches, but they share a thematic undercurrent that includes the interplay of coalition, agency, tradition, and identity; the transformation of curriculum and pedagogy; the retention and reinvigoration of Indigenous languages; the intersection of religion and spirituality; and the quest for sovereignty. While each domain merits extensive discussion, such an effort goes beyond the limits of this work. However, insofar as American Indian "identity" is formulated as an aggregate of the above struggles, they will be discussed interdependently with the understanding that, especially for American Indians, religion/spirituality and sovereignty are inextricably woven into the struggles for identity, education, and language, and vice versa.

The Interplay of Coalition, Agency, and Identity

In the first draft of the final report of the Indian Nations at Risk Task Force, Indigenous scholar and activist Michael Charleston (1994) writes of the importance of coalition and its central role in the development of effective American Indian schools and Indian-centered curricula. Rather than the abstract language of critical pedagogy, however, Charleston invokes the Lakota tradition of the Ghost Dance as a metaphor of the need for healing through community, ceremony, sacrifice, and tradition.[23] He writes:

> The new Ghost Dance calls Native and non-Native peoples to join together and take action. It calls us to be responsible for the future of the people of our tribes. It calls us to protect, revive and restore our cultures, our Native languages, our religions and values. It calls us to heal our people, our families, our tribes, and our societies. It calls for harmony and respect among all relations of creation. It offers a future of co-existence of tribal societies with other American societies . . . indeed domination, oppression, and bigotry are exactly what we are overcoming in the new Ghost Dance as we seek to establish harmony and coexistence of tribes with other societies in the modern world.
>
> (p. 28)

This spirit of coalition reflects the growing desire among American Indians to work together and form alliances with Native and non-Native forces in a mutual quest for American Indian sovereignty and self-determination. Though Charleston's rendition of coalition reflects the spirit of mestizaje—that is, the blurring of political, racial, and cultural borders in the service of social justice—he carefully relegates such coalition to the realm of sociopolitical action. In other words, the new Ghost Dance calls to Indian and non-Indian peoples to take collective action against U.S. policies that continue the project of colonization and cultural genocide. It is thus not a call for the embodiment, in critical-theoretical terms, of a transcultural, transnational subject that calls into question the very notion of authentic identities (McLaren, 1997), but rather a metaphor for collective political action.

This is not to say that Charleston or other American Indian scholars do not support the notion that identity is constructed through multiple, intersecting, and contradictory elements. Rather, they remain wary of constructionist understandings of identity that, in the process of providing a corrective to static notions of culture, ignore the real possibility of culture loss—that is, the real existing threat of cultural genocide of Indigenous peoples. Hale (2000) is worth quoting at length:

> When (cultural) transformation is conflated with loss . . . the collective trauma is obscured and the brute historical fact of ethnocide is softened. The culprits in this erasure are the Indians' . . . enemies, but even more centrally . . . elites who embraced classic nineteenth century liberalism cast in the idiom of mestizáje. A homogeneous and individualized notion of citizenship could not be compatible with the rights of Indian communities whose collective histories and identities stood opposed to the dominant mestizo culture. Just beneath the alluring promises to Indians who would accept these individual rights of citizenship was incomprehension, invisibility, and punishing racism for those who would not.
>
> (p. 269)

Again, though the contemporary critical project of mestizaje is in many ways antithetical to the Latin American one, both projects ignore the "brute historical fact of ethnocide" and the invisibility of Indians within the broader democratic project. In contradistinction to the critical notion of mestizaje, American Indian scholars seek understandings of identity that not only reflect the multiple and contradictory aspects of contemporary experience, but also maintain a sense of American Indians as historically placed, sovereign peoples. For them, sovereignty is not a political ideology but a way of life (Warrior, 1995). As Charleston (1994) writes, "Our tribes are at a very critical point in our history again. We can stand by and wait for our children and grandchildren to be assimilated into mainstream American society as proud ethnic descendants of extinct tribal peoples. . . . Or, we can protect our tribes, as our ancestors did, and ensure a future for our children and grandchildren as tribal people" (p. 28).

Though it may seem from the above that American Indian intellectuals advocate exclusionary rather than coalitionary tactics, impulses toward isolationism need to be understood in the context of unrelenting threats of cultural appropriation and culture loss. Within this context, it is actually remarkable that American Indian tribal communities remain open and working to define the balance between cultural tradition, cultural shift, and cultural transformation.

Identity Formation and American Indian Tradition(s)

Indigenous scholar Devon Mihesuah (1998) examines the notion of "tradition" in the formation of American Indian identity. Acknowledging that, while traditions are important to maintain, they have always been fluid, she writes:

> An Indian who speaks her tribal language and participates in tribal religious ceremonies is often considered traditional, but that term is applicable only within the context of this decade, because chances are she wears jeans, drives a car and watches television—very "untraditional" things to do. Plains Indians who rode horses in the 1860's are considered traditional today, but they were not the same as their traditional ancestors of the early 1500's who had never seen a horse.
> (p. 50)

While contemporary life requires most Indians to negotiate or "transgress" between a multitude of subject positions (i.e., one who is Navajo may also be Catholic, gay, and live in an off-reservation urban center), such movement remains historically embedded and geographically placed. Moreover, the various and competing subjectivities remain tied through memory, ceremony, ritual, and obligation to a traditional identity type that operates not as a measure of authenticity, but rather of cultural continuity and survival. For example, current understanding of a traditional Navajo (Diné) woman is that she lives in a hogan, speaks her language, participates in ceremonies, maintains a subsistence lifestyle, nurtures strong clan and kinship ties, serves as a vast repository of cultural and tribal history, participates in tribal governance, wears long hair wrapped in traditional cotton cloth, dresses in long skirts and velvet blouses, and dons the silver jewelry of her family to reside as matriarch of the clan. Such individuals, along with their male counterparts, are typically held in high esteem and are granted a great deal of respect and social power. While the Diné recognize this identity as only one among many accepted as "authentically" Diné, it forms the essence of their tribal identity, serves as the repository of their ancestral knowledge, and roots them as a historically embedded and geographically placed people.

The struggle for American Indian subjectivity is, in part, a struggle to protect this essence and the right of Indigenous peoples to live in accordance with their traditional ways. In other words, regardless of how any individual American Indian may choose to live his or her life as an Indian person, most experience a deep sense of responsibility and obligation to protect the rights of those choosing to live in the ways of their ancestors. The struggle for identity thus also becomes the struggle to negotiate effectively the line between fetishizing traditional identities and recognizing their importance to the continuation of American Indians as distinctive tribal peoples. Insofar as American Indian traditional identities remain tethered to "traditional" practices (such as ceremony) and such practices remain interconnected with the land, the struggle for identity becomes inextricably linked with political struggles for sovereignty and the ongoing battle against cultural encroachment and capitalist desire to control Native land, resources, traditions, and languages. So, while American Indians join the struggle against the kind of essentialism that recognizes only one way of being, they also work to retain a vast constellation of distinct traditions that serve as the defining characteristics of "traditional" ways of being. As Vine Deloria and Clifford Lytle (1983) note, this allegiance to traditional knowledge has protected American Indians from annihilation or its modern counterpart, categoric absorption into the democratic mainstream.

The Transformation of Curriculum and Pedagogy

There is a growing body of work by Indigenous scholars that examines the intersection between the experiences of formal education and tribal culture. Recently, such work has moved away from comparatively simplistic analyses of "learning style" or curriculum content into deeper examination of the interplay between power, difference, opportunity, and institutional structure (see, for example, Deyhle & Swisher, 1997; Haig-Brown & Archibald, 1996; Hermes, 1998; Lipka, 1994; Pewewardy, 1998). Though such work builds upon the efforts of other scholars of color seeking to define culturally relevant pedagogies (Delpit, 1995; Fordham & Ogbu, 1986; Ladson-Billings, 1995; Trueba, 1988; Watahomigie & McCarty, 1994, for example), American Indian scholars rebuff the undercurrent of democratic inclusion and empowerment that undergirds this work, choosing instead to employ sovereignty as the central struggle in defining relevant praxis.[24]

For example, in her work with Lac Courtie Ojibwe (LCO) reservation schools, Indigenous scholar Mary Hermes (1995, 1998) struggles to define a "culturally based curriculum" where both "culture" and "curriculum" are viewed as fluid, "living" constructs that develop in and through relationship. In her own words, Hermes shifts the research question from "What is the role of culture in knowledge acquisition?" to "What is the role of the school as a site of cultural production?" She argues that research focused on the first question often results in essentialized definitions of culture and the subsequent generation of curricular dichotomies distinguishing "academic" curricula from "cultural" curricula. Instead she seeks answers to the more complicated question, "How can we frame our teaching in an Ojibwe epistemology without representing Ojibwe as a static culture?" (Hermes, 2000). Hermes's question represents a paradigm shift, one that decenters the insertion of a static notion of "culture" into "knowledge" and recenters cultural production as an outcome of the schooling process. In practical terms, such a shift means that community interests not only informed but directed her research methods and outcomes. In her work with Ojibwe schools, she implores educators of American Indian students to recognize culture in the classroom at a deeper level than simply adding content or naming learning styles. She writes:

> I am proposing that we begin to view culture as a complex web of relationships, not just material practices, and enact this in our schools in a way that is central to the curriculum. This could mean, for example, directly teaching tribal history, or simply inviting Elders and community members into the school, regardless of the historical knowledge they bring.
>
> (p. 389)

Although Hermes is clearly committed to defining a liberatory praxis based upon a transformative understanding of Ojibwe identity, a goal reminiscent of critical pedagogies, she remains equally committed to the project of American Indian self-determination and sovereignty. Thus, as she advocates an understanding of identity that reflects the fluidity of mestizaje, she also seeks to define a curriculum that remains grounded in the unfolding relationships of tribalness.

In summary, although the development of culturally relevant pedagogy is an objective shared by many marginalized groups, the goal of such efforts for most non-Indian minorities is to ensure inclusion in the democratic imaginary, while the goal for American Indian scholars and educators is to disrupt and impede absorption into that democracy and continue the struggle to remain distinctive, tribal, and sovereign peoples.

The Retention and Reinvigoration of Indigenous Languages

For many American Indian communities, language retention and renewal efforts signify ground zero in the struggle for American Indian sovereignty. Like other aspects of Indigenous experience, there is no single state or uniform condition of Native languages. Some are vibrant like Quechua, which has over one million speakers, and others, like Passamaquoddy, are threatened with extinction. Although ways of speaking and thinking about language shift and language loss may vary within a single community by age, family, life history, gender, and social role, there is a shared sensibility among American Indian peoples that language is inherently tied to cultural continuity—particularly religious and ceremonial continuity—and therefore remains at the core of American Indian identity formation (Anderson, 1998).

Therefore, while many would eschew the oft-implied and "essentialistic" construction of language fluency as a marker of cultural authenticity, there is virtual consensus among American Indian peoples that language loss is tantamount to cultural eradication. Language, in other words, is viewed as a carrier of culture and culture as a carrier of language so that shifts in one reverberate in the other. As such, most tribes work hard to maintain their language through a variety of means, including school, ceremony, community, and family. However, as the traditional structures of community and family erode under the pressures of Whitestream encroachment, tribal members increasingly look to schools to serve as sites of American Indian cultural production and reproduction.

In this effort, American Indian educators looking to develop a critical language of American Indian selfdetermination and intellectual sovereignty are finding that their own Native languages are replete with metaphors of existence that speak to the lived experience of multiplicity, to the sense of interconnection, and to the understanding that American Indians live not only in relationship with each other, but also with the land. In Quechua, for example, the word for being, person, and Andean person is all the same, *Runa*. This root term has the potential to incorporate the many subcategories of beingness while retaining the same basic reference group, as in *llaqtaruna* (inhabitants of the village) and *qualaruna* (foreigner; literally, naked, peeled). It can be used passively as in *yuyay runa* (one who is knowing or understanding), actively as in *runayáchikk* (that which cultivates a person), or reflexively as in *runaman tukuy* (to complete oneself). Hence, the construct speaks to both the group and the individual and distinguishes in-group from out-group while maintaining the fundamental connection between them. Therefore, it is not a static category or limitation to the sense of Runa as the becoming self (Skar, 1994). Border crossing and the idea of a shifting identity is, thus, neither new nor revolutionary to this Indigenous community, but rather the way of life of Quechua peoples for over five hundred years.

Conclusion

The work outlined above suggests that while American Indian scholars share many of the same concerns as mainstream critical scholars' development of critical agency, construction of political coalition, and transformation through praxis, they reject the construction of the radical mestizaje and work instead to balance their community's needs to both cross and patrol borders of identity and location. They also retain as the central and common goal the perseverance of American Indians as distinctive and sovereign peoples.

Defining that balance is perhaps the quintessential struggle of American Indian peoples today. It is a deeply complicated and contradictory struggle that reflects the colonialist past and portends an uncertain future. In short, American Indians face an identity paradox. At the same time that pressures to respond to internal crises of identity formation—including racism, sexism, and homophobia—require more fluid constructions of Indianness, pressures to respond to external threats to identity formation—cultural encroachment, ethnic fraud, corporate commodification, and culture loss—require more restrictive constructions of Indianness. Hence, as American Indian intellectuals struggle to awaken Indian communities to the "challenges and cultural politics of (their) own ever-burgeoning multiculturalism" (Vizenor, 1999, p. 3), they must also work to ground the ever-changing present in the historical memories of the past while searching for links to an American Indian future.

Though, as I have demonstrated, there is good reason to remain cautious of the constructs that emerge from dominant Whitestream discourses, there is also much to be learned from engagement with such discourse. As Indigenous scholar Robert Allen Warrior (1995) notes, American Indian intellectuals have remained caught in "a death dance of dependence between, on the one hand, abandoning ourselves to the intellectual strategies and categories of white, European thought and, on the other hand, declaring we need nothing outside of ourselves and our cultures in order to understand the world and our place in it" (p. 123). He observes that only when American Indian intellectuals remove themselves from this dichotomy that "much becomes possible" (p. 124).

To this end, I argue that critical scholars need to broaden their own theoretical scopes to consider the different and, at times, competing moral visions of American Indian peoples. Critical engagement with the intellectual histories of Indigenous peoples could only serve to inform discussions of revolutionary theory and praxis. Specifically, such histories call into question the ongoing assumption of conservative and radical ideologies that democracy, as presently constructed in liberal, capitalist terms, presumes the continued absorption or colonization of Indigenous peoples. American Indian scholars also need to enter the critical dialogue and help reimagine the political terrain surrounding identity. They need to create the intellectual space for the struggle for sovereignty and for their efforts to renegotiate the relationship between sovereign American Indian tribal nations and the current democratic order. The challenge to Indigenous scholars is to define the same kind of balance between cultural integrity and critical resistance in their own quest for American Indian intellectual sovereignty. As Warrior (1995) notes, just "as many of the poets find their work continuous with but not circumscribed by Native traditions of story-telling or ceremonial chanting, we can find the work of (critical studies) continuous with Native traditions of deliberation and decision making. Holding these various factors (sovereignty, tradition, community, process and so on) in tension while attempting to understand the role of critics in an American Indian future is of crucial importance" (p. 118).

Ultimately, I am confident that American Indian and non-Indian critical scholars devoted to the remapping of the political project can together define a common ground of struggle and construct an insurgent but poetic moral vision of liberty, sovereignty, and social justice. It is my hope that this discussion will also serve as the foundation for a new critical theory of Indigenous identity and the development of a new Red Pedagogy.

Notes

1. The term *critical pedagogy* will be used interchangeably with *critical theory* to refer to the diverse body of critical educational theories (i.e., postcolonial, feminist, postmodern, multicultural, and Marxist) that advocate an increasingly sophisticated critique of the social, economic, and political barriers to social justice, as well as crusade for the transformation of schools to reflect the imperatives of democracy. The totality of these theories are viewed by critical scholars as the foundation of liberatory discourse and the political project of liberation. *Project* refers to a collectivity of critique and action or solidarity.
2. For the purposes of this article, American Indian intellectualism is distinguished from purely literary or cultural forms of writing, and refers to intellectual activity that engages in substantive critical analysis from an Indigenous perspective.
3. I use the term *American Indians* to refer to the tribal peoples of North America and *Indigenous peoples* as a more inclusive term to relate to global Indigenous peoples.
4. *Democratic imaginary* refers to the notion that democracy is a never-ending project and continuous pursuit—an imagined concept.
5. The comprehensive literature reviews of Robert Allen Warrior (1995), *Tribal Secrets: Recovering American Indian Intellectual Traditions*, and of Donna Deyhle and Karen Swisher (1997), "Research in American Indian and Alaska Native Education: From Assimilation to Self-Determination," provide adequate evidence of the lack of participation of American Indian scholars within the broader field of critical studies.
6. In the critical discourse the notion of transgressive identity takes the postmodern notion of identity as a highly fluid construct with intersections among the perceived stable categories of race, class, ethnicity, sexuality, and gender—a step further by indicating that even within categories there is "transgression" or strategies of resistance that work to destabilize identity. In other words, it is not only that the categories of race, class, gender, and sexuality intersect but also that the categories (e.g., Lesbian, African American, upper class) themselves are highly contested spaces. Moreover, "transgression" is viewed as an inherently subversive and destabilizing construct, where there is constant resistance to any fixed notion of identity.
7. By "dangerous discourse" I mean that American Indian critical studies is viewed in the same spirit that Black feminism was once perceived by Whitestream feminists and African American intellectuals. (Adapting from the feminist notion of "malestream," critical scholar Claude Denis [1997] defines Whitestream as the idea that, while American society is not White in sociodemographic terms, it remains principally and fundamentally structured on the basis of White, Anglo-European experience.)
8. Though Marxist-feminist scholar Teresa Ebert employs the term *Red Pedagogy* to refer to her own work toward revitalizing the Marxist critique in feminist discourse, I use the term as a historical reference to such empowering metaphors as "Red Power" and the "Great Red Road." Moreover, in the spirit of such venerable Indian scholars and activists as Vine Deloria and Winona LaDuke, I reappropriate the signifier *Red* as a contemporary metaphor for the ongoing political project of Indigenous peoples to retain sovereignty and establish self-determination.
9. I wish to be clear that the terms *spiritual* and *spirituality* in this text do not refer to New Age constructions of some mythic pan-Indian spirituality but rather to the historical presence and persistence within Indigenous belief systems of life forces beyond human rationality.

10. For example, various race-centric theories and certain forms of feminism. Joe Kincheloe and Shirley Steinberg (1997) state that "left essentialists tend to focus attention on one form of oppression as elemental, as taking precedence over all modes of subjugation. Certain radical feminists view gender as a central form of oppression, certain ethnic study scholars privilege race, while orthodox Marxists focus on class" (p. 22).
11. Similarly, Cameron McCarthy (1988, 1995), John Ogbu (1978), Chandra Mohanty (1989), and Henry Giroux (1992)—among others—caution against equating hybridity with equality.
12. The very "protection" typically proffered by citizenship rights (i.e., civil liberties) has often worked to erode traditional structures of tribal life, sometimes pitting Indian against Indian and tribe against tribe. For a more complete discussion of the difference between that which is civic and that which is tribal, see Vine Deloria and Clifford Lytle's *The Nations Within: The Past and Future of American Indian Sovereignty*, or Claude Denis's *We Are Not You: First Nations and Canadian Modernity*.
13. As presently constructed, tribal governments retain many powers of nations, some powers greater than those of states, and some governing powers greater than local non-Indian municipalities (Deloria & Lytle, 1984). In spite of their "sovereign" status, Indian tribes currently rely on the federal government for their operating funds, for the right to interpret and renegotiate their own treaty rights, and for access to the natural resources on their own reservations.
14. By "colonizing impulse" I mean the inherent perhaps unconscious impulse to include or conscript Indigenous (tribal) people into the "democratic project."
15. For example, in Maine, with the setting of land claims in the 1970s Carter administration, many people of varying Indian blood quantums "returned" to the reservation since they had a place to call home. The same thing has happened with the Pequot in Connecticut.
16. Joyce King (1991) defines *dysconcious racism* as an uncritical habit of mind; a form of racism that tacitly accepts White norms and privileges. She contends that such unintended racism does not reflect the absence of consciousness, but rather an impaired or distorted way of thinking about race.
17. For example, in response to the growing phenomenon of "ethnic fraud," the Association of American Indian and Alaska Native Professors has issued a position statement urging colleges and universities to follow specific guidelines in their considerations of admissions, scholarships, and hiring practices. Those guidelines are as follows: 1) Require documentation of enrollment in a state or federally recognized nation/tribe, with preference given to those who meet this criterion; 2) Establish a case-by-case review process for those unable to meet the first criterion; 3) Include American Indian/Alaska Native faculty in the selection process; 4) Require a statement from the applicant that demonstrates past and future commitment to American Indian/Alaska Native concerns; 5) Require higher education administrators to attend workshops on tribal sovereignty and meet with local tribal officials, and 6) Advertise vacancies at all levels on a broad scale and in tribal publications. Contrary to the backlash that this statement received, the association does not promote "policing," nor do they employ exclusionary tactics within their own organization, instead relying on self-disclosure.
18. The Dawes Allotment Act (1887) authorized the president of the United States to allot any reservation according to the following formula: 1) To each head of family, one quarter section; 2) To each single person over 18, one-eighth section; 3) To each orphan under eighteen, one-eighth section; 4) To each other single person under eighteen, born prior to the date of the order, one-sixteenth section (Deloria & Lytle, 1983). In order to allot the land, however, government officials required an efficient method by which to determine who was a "legitimate" member of a given community, which resulted in the beginning of widespread use of tribal rolls and blood-quantum policies.
19. The term *Indian Identity Police* is used by M. Annette Jaimes Guerrero (1996).
20. Deloria (1998) includes among such scholars James Clifton, Sam Gill, Elisabeth Tooker, Alice Kehoe, Richard deMille, and Stephen Farca.
21. Dolores Delgado Bernal (1998) identifies four sources of cultural intuition that together provide the epistemological framework for her analysis of Chicana experience: personal experience, knowledge of existing (academic) literature, professional experience, and the analytical research process itself.
22. See, for example, Elizabeth Cook-Lynn (1998), Michael Charleston (1994, 1998); Vine Deloria (1992, 1998); M. Annette Jaimes Guererro (1996); Mary Hermes (1998); K. Tsianina Lomawaima (1994); Devon Mihesuah (1998); Frances Rains (1998, 1999); Karen Swisher (1998); Gerald Vizenor (1999); Robert Warrior (1995).
23. The Ghost Dance was started in 1890 by Chief Big Foot and his band of Lakota as a means of declaring that the Creator would prevent the total destruction of Native people, alleviate their suffering, and return the people to pre-war days of happiness.
24. The Freirean notion of praxis is best understood as action and reflection upon the world in order to change it or simply as intentional action.

References

Anderson, J. (1998). Ethnolinguistic dimensions of northern Arapaho language shift. *Anthropological Linguistics, 40*(1), 43–108.

Anzaldúa, G. (1987). *Borderlands, la frontera: The new mestíza*. San Francisco: Aunt Lute Books.

Best, S. (1989). Jameson totality and post-structuralist critique: In D. Kellener (Ed.), *Postmodernism/Jameson/critique* (pp. 233–368). Washington, DC: Maisonneuve.

Castillo, A. (1995). *Massacre of dreamers: Essays on Xicanisma*. New York: Plume.

Charleston, G.M. (1994). Toward true native education: A treaty of 1992 (Final Report of the Indian Nations at Risk Task Force, draft 3). *Journal of American Indian Education, 33*(2), 7–56.

Cook-Lynn, E. (1998). American Indian intellectualism and the new Indian story. In D.A. Mihesuah (Ed.), *Natives and academics: Researching and writing about American Indians* (pp. 111–138), Lincoln: University of Nebraska Press.

Darder, A., Torres, R., & Gutiérrez, H. (Eds.). (1997). *Latinos and education: A critical reader*. New York: Routledge.

Delgado Bernal, D. (1998). Using a Chicana feminist epistemology in educational research. *Harvard Educational Review, 68*, 555–582.

Deloria, V. (1992). *God is Red: A Native view of religion*. Golden, CO: North American Press.

Deloria, V., Jr. (1998). Comfortable fictions and the struggles for turf: An essay review of *The invented Indian: Cultural fictions and government policies*. In D.A. Mihesuah (Ed.), *Natives and academics: Researching and writing about American Indians* (pp. 65–83). Lincoln: University of Nebraska Press.

Deloria, V., Jr. (1999). *For this land: Writings on religion in America*. New York: Routledge.

Deloria, V., Jr., & Lytle, C. (1983). *American Indians, American justice*. Austin: University of Texas Press.

Deloria, V., Jr., & Lytle, C. (1984). *The nations within: The past and future of American Indian sovereignty*. Austin: University of Texas Press.

Delpit, L. (1995). *Other people's children; Cultural conflicts in the classroom*. New York: New Press.

Denis, C. (1997). *We are not you*. Toronto: Broadview.

Deyhle, R., & Swisher, K. (1997). Research in American Indian and Alaskan Native education: From assimilation to self-determination. In *Review of Research in Education* (pp. 113–183). Washington, DC: American Educational Research Association.

di Leonardo, M. (1991). *Gender at the crossroads of knowledge: Feminist anthropology in the postmodernist era*. Berkeley: University of California Press.

Fixcio, D.L. (1998). *The invasion of Indian country in the twentieth century: American capitalism and tribal natural resources*. Niwot: University Press of Colorado.

Fordham, S., & Ogbu, J. (1986). Black students and the burden of "acting White." *Urban Review, 18*, 176–203.

Fusco, C. (1995). *English is broken here: Notes on the cultural fusion in the Americas*. New York: New Press.

Giroux, H. (1992). *Border crossings: Cultural workers and the politics of education*. New York: Routledge.

Grande, S. (1997). *Critical multicultural education and the modern project: An exploratory analysis*. Unpublished doctoral dissertation, Kent State University.

Grande, S. (2000). American Indian identity and intellectualism: The quest for a new Red pedagogy. *Journal of Qualitative Studies in Education, 13*, 373–354.

Guerrero, M.A.J. (1996). Academic apartheid: American Indian studies and "multiculturalism." In A. Gordon & C. Newfield (Eds.), *Mapping multiculturalism* (pp. 49–63). Minneapolis: University of Minnesota Press.

Haig-Brown, C., & Archibald, J. (1996). Transforming First Nations research with respect and power. *International Journal of Qualitative Studies in Education, 9*, 245–267.

Hale, C.R. (2000). Book review of *To die in this way: Nicaraguan Indians and the myth of mestizaje 1880–1965. American Society for Ethnohistory, 47*, 268–271.

Harraway, D.J. (1991). *Simians, cyborgs, and women*. New York: Routledge.

Hermes, M. (1995). *Making culture, making curriculum: Teaching through meanings and identities at an American Indian tribal school*. Unpublished doctoral dissertation, University of Wisconsin-Madison.

Hermes, M. (1998). Research methods as a situated response: Towards a First Nation's methodology. *International Journal of Qualitative Studies in Education, 11*, 155–168.

Hermes, M. (2000). The scientific method, Nintendo, and eagle feathers: Rethinking the meaning of "culture based" curriculum at an Ojibwe tribal school. *International Journal of Qualitative Studies in Education, 13*, 387–400.

Herrnstein, R.J., & Murray, C. (1994). *The bell curve: Intelligence and class structure in American life*. New York: Free Press.

Joe, J.R., & Miller, D.L. (1997). Cultural survival and contemporary American Indian women in the city. In C.J. Cohen (Ed.), *Indigenous women transforming politics: An alternative reader* (pp. 137–150). New York: New York University Press.

Kincheloe, J., & Steinberg, S. (1997). *Changing multiculturalism*. Bristol, PA: Open University Press.

King, J. (1991). Dysconcious racism: Ideology, identity and the miseducation of teachers. *Journal of New Education, 60*, 133–146.

Ladson-Billings, G. (1995). "But that's just good teaching!" The case for culturally relevant pedagogy. *Theory Into Practice, 34*, 159–165.

Lipka, J. (1994). Language, power, and pedagogy: Whose school is it? *Peabody Journal of Education, 69*, 71–93.

Lomawaima, K.T. (1994). *They called it prairie light: The story of Chilocco Indian school*. Lincoln: University of Nebraska Press.

Machamer, A.M. (1997). Ethnic fraud in the university: Serious implications for American Indian education. *Native Bruin, 2*, 1–2.

McCarthy, C. (1988). Rethinking liberal and radical perspectives on racial inequality in schooling: Making the case for nonsynchrony. *Harvard Educational Review, 58*, 265–269.

McCarthy, C. (1995). The problem with origins: Race and the contrapuntal nature of the educational experience. In P. McLaren & C. Sleeter (Eds.), *Multicultural education, critical pedagogy and the politics of difference* (pp. 245–268). Albany: State University of New York Press.

McCarthy, C., & Crichlow, W. (1993). *Race and identity and representation in education.* New York: Routledge.

McLaren, P. (Ed.). (1997). *Revolutionary multiculturalism: Pedagogies of dissent for the new millennium.* Boulder, CO: Westview Press.

McLaren, P., & Giroux, H. (1997). Writing from the margins: Geographies of identity, pedagogy and power. In P. McLaren (Ed.), *Revolutionary multiculturalism: Pedagogies of dissent for the new millennium* (pp. 16–41). Boulder, CO: Westview Press.

McLaren, P., & Gutierrez, K. (1997). Global politics and local antagonists: Research and practice as dissent and possibility. In P. McLaren (Ed.), *Revolutionary multiculturalism: Pedagogy of dissent for the new millennium*, (pp. 192–222) Boulder, CO: Westview Press.

McLaren, P., & Sleeter, C. (Eds.). (1995). *Multicultural education, critical pedagogy, and the politics of difference.* Albany: State University of New York Press.

Mihesuah, D. (1998). *Natives and academics: Researching and writing about American Indians.* Lincoln: University of Nebraska Press.

Mohanty, C. (1989). On race and violence: Challenges for liberal education in the 1990s. *Cultural Critique*, 14, 179–208.

Murillo, E.G. (1997, April). *Research under cultural assault: Mojado ethnography.* Paper presented at the annual meeting of the American Educational Studies Association, San Diego.

Nagel, J. (1995). American Indian ethnic renewal: Politics and the resurgence of identity. *American Sociological Review, 60*, 947–965.

Ogbu, J. (1978). *Minority education and caste: The American system in cross-cultural perspective.* New York: Academic Press.

Pewewardy, C. (1998). Fluff and feathers: Treatment of American Indians in the literature and the classroom. *Equity and Excellence in Education, 31*, 69–76.

Rains, F.V. (1998). Is the benign really harmless? Deconstructing some "benign" manifestations of operationalized White privilege. In J. Kincheloe, S.R. Steinberg, & R.E. Chennault (Eds.), *White reign: Deploying Whiteness in America* (pp. 77–101). New York: St. Martin's Press.

Rains, F.V. (1999). Indigenous knowledge, historical amnesia and intellectual authority: Deconstructing hegemony and the social and political implications of the curricular other. In L.M. Semeli & J. Kincheloe (Eds.), *What is Indigenous knowledge? Voices from the academy* (pp. 317–332). New York: Falmer Press.

Said, E. (1985). Orientalism reconsidered. *Race and Class, 26*, 1–15.

Said, E. (1993). *Culture and Imperialism.* New York: Knopf.

Skar, S.L. (1994). *Lives together—worlds apart: Quechua colonization in jungle and city.* New York: Scandinavian University Press.

Stavenhagen, R. (1992). Challenging the nation-state in Latin America. *Journal of International Affairs, 34*, 421–441.

Strauss, A., & Corbin, J. (1990). *Basics of qualitative research: Grounded theory procedures and techniques.* Newbury Park, CA: Sage.

Swisher, K. (1998). Why Indian people should write about Indian education. In D.A. Mihesuah (Ed.), *Natives and academics: Researching and writing about American Indians* (pp. 190–199). Omaha: University of Nebraska Press.

Trueba, E. (1988). Culturally based explanation of minority students' academic achievement. *Minority Achievement, 19*, 270–287.

USD, Bureau of Indian Affairs, 209 manual 8, 83.7. Mandatory Criteria for Federal Recognition. 44 U.S.C. 3501 (et seq.) n.d.

Valle, V., & Torres, R. (1995). The idea of mestizaje and the "race" problematic: Racialized media discourse in a post-Fordist landscape. In A. Darder (Ed.), *Culture and difference: Critical perspectives on the bi-cultural experience in the United States* (pp. 139–153). Westport: Bergin & Garvey.

Van Cott, D.L. (1994). *Indigenous peoples and democracy in Latin America.* New York: St. Martin's Press.

Vizenor, G. (1999). *Postindian conversations.* Lincoln: University of Nebraska Press.

Warrior, R.A. (1995). *Tribal secrets: Recovering American Indian intellectual traditions.* Minneapolis: University of Minnesota Press.

Watahomigie, J., & McCarty, T.L. (1994). Bilingual/bicultural education at Peach Springs: A Hualapai way of schooling. *Peabody Journal of Education, 69*, 26–42.

11

Theories of Racism, Asian American Identities, and a Materialist Critical Pedagogy

Kevin D. Lam

Introduction

Historically, the development of U.S. capitalism and the American *citizen* have been defined "against" the Asian *immigrant* (though not limited to Asians), legally, economically, and culturally (Lowe, 1996, p. 4). Hence, the racialization of Asians in the U.S. must be framed historically and contextually. "Asia," "Asians," and "Asian Americans" have always been on contested and tenuous terrain in their relationship with the U.S. nation-state. According to Lowe, Asia has emerged as a particularly complicated "double front of threat and encroachment" for the United States (p. 5). On the one hand, some Asian countries have become rivals to U.S. imperial domination within the global economy; and on the other hand, Asian American subjects are still a necessary racialized labor force (intellectual, manual, and otherwise) within the domestic political economy. By all means, immigration exclusion acts, naturalization laws, and education policies and practices continue to be used to regulate Asian bodies, but how these bodies are racialized has varied historically and contextually.

Asian Americans as the U.S. nation-state's "model minority" can also be traced back to the 1850s when the Chinese were "obedient" and "satisfactory" workers in the gold mines and the railroads of California, and the "model" Japanese, Chinese, Filipino, and Korean workers labored in the sugar-cane plantations in Hawai'i (Chan, 1991; Takaki, 1989). But the model minority thesis that we have come to know in the popular imagination first arose in the late 1950s, by sociologists attempting to explain the low levels of juvenile delinquency among Chinese and Japanese Americans (Omatsu, 1994, p. 63). The myth remained a social science construct until the 1960s—when it was used again by conservative political commentators to pit Asian Americans' "respect for the law" against African Americans' involvement with the black power and civil rights movements. In this sense, Asian Americans were racialized as the "good race" and African Americans the "bad race." Asian Americans were "good" subjects who represented hope, possibility, and academic excellence for other historically marginalized groups in capitalist America. This rhetoric helped to generate much resentment towards Asians in the U.S at a time of social and political fervor. The intent was to take focus away from the issues at hand—state-sanctioned racism and class inequalities.

In this paper, I examine the problematic of "race" as a central unit of analysis. I engage theories of race and racism—with the expressed focus on the influential work of U.S. scholars

Michael Omi and Howard Winant and British sociologist Robert Miles. I engage Miles's notion of racialization—which re-emphasizes the multiple forms of racism and specificities of oppression that impact historically oppressed populations in the U.S. I critique "race relations" sociology because it essentially reproduces a black/white dichotomy. In my attempt to ground the conversation, I examine "Asian American" identities and the ways in which they have been racialized in the U.S. I discuss the implications for a materialist critical pedagogy.

Literature Review

Omi and Winant's *Racial Formation in the United States* (1986/1994) has been critical to the discussion of race and racism in the U.S. Undoubtedly, they have left a mark on progressive scholars and theorists alike, including those on the educational left. They examine the legal genealogy of Asian Americans (and other racialized populations) in what they call "racial formation." They define "racial formation" as the "socio-historical process by which racial categories are created, inhabited, transformed, and destroyed" (1994, p. 55). They argue for a theory of racial formation by proposing a process of historically situated projects in which "humans and social structures are represented and organized" (p. 56). As Omi and Winant indicate, "race" is both a matter of social structure and cultural representation for U.S. national groups like African Americans, Latinos, Native Americans, and Asian Americans. They state that too often, attempts to understand "race" and "racial inequality" simply as a social structural phenomenon, for example, are unable to account for the origins, patterning, and transformation of racial difference (1994, p. 56).

Omi and Winant's critique of mainstream approaches to racial theory and politics is useful in understanding racialized formation since the 1960s in the U.S. I agree with their distinction that racialized, rather than "racial" categories are socially constructed, transformed, and then destroyed. In addition, they continue to problematize the temptation to think of "race" as something fixed, concrete, and objective or to see the concept just as an ideological construction. However, there are limitations to their theoretical and political approach. As they critique the notion of "race" as neither "concrete" nor merely a "construction," they continue to reify the concept of "race" by stating that it "signifies and symbolizes social conflicts and interests by referring to different types of human bodies" (p. 55). In other words, while Omi and Winant (1994) point out that selection of particular human features for purposes of racial signification is always and necessarily a social and historical process, they reify social relations by concluding that all human beings belong to a "race" (e.g., Asian American race, Latino race, et cetera).

Limitations of "Race"

The fact of the matter is that "race" has its limits because it is simultaneously geographical and historical. Furthermore, the focus on "racial" identity as the basis for political mobilization has led to serious analytical problems. Scholars often continue to use the concept without critically engaging the construct itself. "Obviousness," as Miles (1993) indicates, is "a condition which depends upon the location of the observer and the set of concepts employed to conceive and interpret the object" (p. 3).

According to Miles (1989), "race" is a social construction of reality "imagined" rather than based on biological reality (p. 71). Its commonsense usage speaks volumes for its practicality but not its specific utility. The fact that we are selectively choosing physical characteristics indicates that this is by no means a natural category. Miles (1987) notes that the processes and representations of "race" have a history: signification and representation have been used in Europe the last centuries to categorize human beings. When somatic and phenotypical characteristics were not convenient, religion and nationality were used as a way to demarcate populations. The creation of the "Other" was based on the signification of human biological characteristics and socially constructed mental capacities. Furthermore, to simply focus on "race" is problematic due to the "abstraction" of cultural differentiations and the failure to identify class divisions within distinct groups.

Miles's Notion of Racialization: Conceptually Detaching "Race" from Racism

Miles (1982, 1989, 1993, 2003) notes that the notion of "race" first appeared in the English language in the 17th century. However, it did not become prominent until the scientific movements in the late 18th century Europe and North America (p. 69). Miles (1989) posits that the contemporary theoretical framework of racism was first used to identify Nazi Germany's notion of Aryan superiority and Jewish inferiority. As a result, racism came to refer strictly and exclusively to "race." What Miles vehemently attempts to do is break the conceptual link between the notion of "race" with that of racism as a way to distinguish the analytical use of racism. The word "race" is used to label groups on the sole basis of phenotypical features. There is no scientific justification to simply distinguish "races" based on select phenotypical characteristics that vary widely from height, to weight, length of arms and legs, hair, skin color, and so on. The idea of "race" is employed as the result of a "process of signification" that are attributed with meaning and thereby used to organize and sort out populations.

The notion of racialization has been widely used and understood in different ways. Fanon (1963) was one of the first to use the concept in discussing the difficulties facing decolonized intellectuals in Africa when constructing a cultural future (Miles & Brown, 2003, p. 99). Banton (1977) uses racialization to refer more formally to the use of "race" to "structure" people's perceptions of the world's population. Miles and Brown (2003) note that Banton's usage of the concept was limited due to its scientific theories of topology for categorizing populations (p. 100). Some scholars during the 1980s distinguished between "practical" and "ideological" racialization. The former refers to the formation of "racial" groups and the latter refer to the idea of "race" in discourse. U.S. scholars like Omi and Winant (1994) use the concept to "signify the extension of racial meaning to a previously racially unclassified relationship, social practices or group . . . racialization is an ideological process, a historically specific one" (Miles & Brown, 2003, p. 100). For Miles, the concept is synonymous with racialized categorization.

In an attempt to contextualize Miles's deconstruction of "race" and the move to racialization, Ngin and Torres (2001) suggest that the language of "race" and "race relations" should be carefully analyzed without reifying it. This is done so by some scholars who consciously place the term "race" in quotation marks to distinguish its use from any biological implications. These scholars mention that until recently, discourse on African Americans, Latinos, Native Americans, and Asian Americans were largely based on phenotypical characteristics. These physical makers were used as a mechanism to exclude and exploit racialized groups. For Miles (1993), concepts of racialization, racism, and exclusionary practice identify specific means of disrupting the capitalist mode of production. This allows us to "stress consistently and rigorously the role of human agency even within particular historical and material circumstances and to recognize the specificity of particular forms of oppression" (p. 52). In other words, Miles's notion of racialization, in not reifying "races" of human being, does not homogenize the experiences of different "races."

Towards a Marxist Project of Theorizing Racism

Omi and Winant (1994) argue that "radical" theories of racism, while critical of the existing "racial" order, cannot appreciate the uniqueness of "race" in the U.S. (p. 3). They claim that these radical theories simply fail to address specific U.S. conditions due to the fact that movements and intellectual traditions outside of the U.S. have influenced them. The left, as Omi and Winant (1994) would have us believe, have "succumbed" to romantic illusions. Even more significant, they state that there are little theoretical and analytical efforts to "counter" the right (p. viii). It might be true, but it is also clear that there is much analysis done by Miles and other scholars working from a particular strand of Marxist analysis. This "racism" paradigm, which surfaced in the 1970s and was rearticulated most nobly by Miles (1982), is critiqued by scholars in the U.S. and abroad. This approach, according to "race" scholars, reduces "race" to ethnicity. It neglects to see the "continuing organization" of social inequality and oppression along "racial" lines (Omi & Winant, 1994, p. 70). The political and intellectual discussion of reducing "race" to ethnicity has many people up in arms because for them, it advocates a "colorblind" discourse.

It is assumed that the elimination of "race" as an analytical category would lead to a "colorblind" discourse. This is not what Miles and other scholars (including myself) are arguing. For this reason, there is much resistance to the deconstruction of "race" due to the fear of de-legitimating the historical movements that are grounded in "race." Instead, the intent is to argue that skin color is not an inherent characteristic, but in fact, a product of signification. For example, human beings "identify" skin color to mark or symbolize other phenomena in a historical context in which other signification occurs: "Collective identities are produced and social inequalities are structured when people include and exclude people through the signification of skin color" (Darder & Torres, 2004, p. 41). Thus, it is important to understand the signification of skin color and to understand how it is produced and reproduced, given different historical contexts. In order for us to address structural inequalities, there has to be a shift from "race" to a plural conceptualization of racism. In so doing, we can interrogate the different meanings attributed to racialized groups.

The strongest case for retention of "race" as an analytical concept has much to do with how victims of racism have taken on this term as a way to resist their political and economic subordinations. This retention of "race" has many consequences because of its lack of analytical rigor. The idea of "race" was closely associated with the idea of "black" in the U.S. and Britain (Miles, 1993; Hall, 1996). In fact, one can argue that the notion of "race" struggle is synonymous with the "black" struggle. However, the use of "black" as a means of political mobilization "embodies" a specific rather than a universal tradition of resistance—a resistance that focuses solely on the colonial domination of African subjects (Miles, 1993, p. 3). The attempt to generalize the "black" struggle to all colonized subjects, whose lives are influence by racism, "disavows" the specific cultural and historical origin of non-African people. The analysis of racism in the U.S. (and Britain) with a "race" perspective, radical or otherwise is misleading because the idea of "race" is highly ideological. The political economy of migration perspective, proposed forcefully by Miles (1982, 1989, 1993, and 2003), Darder and Torres (1999, 2004), and others is a major theoretical break from Marxist theory of "race relations," prevalent in much of the Marxist writings in the U.S. academy.

Gilroy (1989, 2000) (who has since shifted his position along the lines of Miles's critique) and other "race" scholars argue that a Marxist analysis of capitalism based on historical stances of 19th century Europe is inadequate. While both Gilroy and Sivanandan (1983) distance themselves from the Eurocentric Marxist tradition (largely because of its presumed inability to deal with "race"), Sivanandan has reclaimed Marxism in order to contextualize "race" relative to class, while Gilroy rejects Marxism in order to establish the absolute autonomy of "race" apart from class (Miles, 1993, p. 43). This important distinction reminds us that neither Marxism nor the black radical tradition is monolithic, but in fact, has very diverse conflicting and contradictory positions.

Hence, the task for scholars working from a political economy of migration perspective is not to create a Marxist theory of "race" that is more "valid" than conservative or liberal theories. The task at hand is to deconstruct the notion of "race" and detach it from the concept of racism. Skeptics reiterate that Marx's theoretical and historical analysis on the mode of production has limited analytical value because examples are specific to the nature of capitalist development in Britain and Europe in general. This type of analysis presumes that it would be best to articulate the notion of "race" in a place like the U.S. where there is a long history of slavery. On the contrary, Miles (1982) has convincingly argued that the totalizing nature of capitalism does not recognize the color or national line. In the following section, I discuss the ways in which "Asian American" identities have been negotiated, maneuvered, and used. I examine the racialization of Asian Americans historically and the impact (and consequences) it has on our theorizing of "race," "race relations," and identity politics in the U.S.

The Racialization of Asian Americans

Omatsu (1994) notes the Asian American radical/liberationist movement coincided not with civil rights, but the black power movement and that Malcolm X, rather than Martin Luther King Jr., was the leading influence. The struggle for many Asian American scholars and activists was not based so much on "racial" pride but to reclaim larger political and economic struggles of past generations. Due to the prominence of the black/white paradigm, Asian Americans and other racialized groups were left out of the theoretical and political discussion because they were neither black nor white. The black/white paradigm deemed the histories and issues of Asian Americans as insignificant or secondary in the existing U.S. hierarchy of racialized oppression. Suffice it to say, Italian Marxist philosopher Antonio Gramsci's *war of position* contends that Asian Americans had to situate themselves as a "racial" group for social, cultural, political, economic, and educational purposes (Hoare & Smith, 1971; Lam, 2009). Due to discriminatory practices against U.S. Asians, the desire to create a pan-Asian coalition was a necessary political tool for the sustenance and survival of the group.

The inclusion of Asian Americans in the "people as color" paradigm is a precarious and tenuous one at best. Given that Asian Americans are categorically labeled as the "model minority" and have "honorary white" status, it is sometimes difficult for other racialized groups (who might not be aware of the histories and struggles of Asians in the U.S.) to conceive them as "legitimate" people of color. "Whites" also perceive them as not as "legitimate" because historically they have not "suffered as much," in relation to say, African Americans. I have no intention of "showing" or arguing that Asian Americans have "suffered enough" to qualify them as "people of color" or an "oppressed" group. My intent here is to show the limitations of a "people of color" analysis because it still falls into a black/white paradigm. It does not take into account the different political and ideological perspectives or class locations of individuals from different groups. In engaging the discourse, I am not taking away from its historical and political significance in the continued attempt to create solidarity across ethnic and class lines. Asian Americans and their *war of maneuver* speak to how complicated identity politics can get, as they negotiate the murky waters of "race relations." The analysis on racism must go beyond what "white" people say and do to "black" people. However, this is not to suggest that white-on-black racism is not significant.

A Critique of the Model Minority Myth

According to Omatsu (1994), the widespread acceptance of the model minority thesis was not just a result of the growing number of Asians in the U.S. or the increasing attention from mainstream institutions, but in fact, coincided with the rise of the New Right and the corporate offensive on the poor (p. 63). Omatsu correctly notes that the model minority myth has been critiqued politically, but not ideologically. It is critical that we do not leave out this important dimension. I would also like to stress a materialist dimension in my critique of the myth for Asian American subjects.

It is fundamental to understand the myth in the context of material conditions in U.S. society at different historical junctures. The racialization of Asian Americans has much to do with the economic and political imperatives of the U.S. with the Asian country of origin. Asian Americans as "obedient," "docile," and "apolitical" bodies are also used to perpetuate and reproduce certain colonial relationships in the domestic sphere. In particular, the neo-conservative movements of the early 1980s played an important role in redefining the language of civil rights and creating a "moral vision" of capitalism. It clearly constituted a campaign to "restore" trust in capitalism and those values associated with the rhetoric of "free enterprise." It was a return to a "celebration of values, an emphasis on hard work and self-reliance, a respect for authority, and an attack on prevailing civil rights thinking associated with the African American community" (Omatsu, 1994, p. 63). Asian Americans, in this instance, were used to symbolize the resurrection of capitalist values. The images of hard-working Asian American petit bourgeois class and immigrant merchants laboring in our inner-cities and over-achieving students excelling in the classrooms reinforce the long-held meritocratic belief that if you work hard and do not complain, the system will reward you regardless of ethnicity or class location.

Describing Asian Americans as "model minority" continues to obfuscate the diverse and complex experiences of Asians in the U.S. Instead of recognizing difference, Asian Americans are lumped into a "race." By "painting" Asian Americans as a homogeneous group, the model minority myth "erases ethnic, cultural, social-class, gender, language, sexual, generational, achievement, and other differences (Lee, 1996, p. 6). The imposition of categorical labeling on a "race" suggests that all Asians are "successful" in the face of racism, in the classrooms, at the office, restaurant, cleaner, liquor store, or doughnut shop. In any case, the myth denies the rates of poverty, illiteracy, and high dropout rates in Asian American communities, especially from Southeast Asian American students (U.S. Commission on Civil Rights, 1992).

Situating Asian American experiences in relation to political economy, migration, diaspora, and critical pedagogical approaches (Freire, 1970/2001; McLaren, 2007; Darder, 2012) help us begin to comprehend the complex nature of this racialized population.

There are ideological and material implications to which we must tend. The "model minority" myth as a hegemonic device tells us that we need to engage in more substantive analyses of the racialization of Asian Americans (and other populations) and challenge the presupposition of "race" as a commonsense notion. Gramsci's notion of *hegemony* is a concept referring to a particular form of dominance in which the ruling class legitimates its position and secures the acceptance, if not outright support, of those below them (Hoare & Smith, 1971). In this instance, Asian Americans have "consented" to their label as the "model minority." This is not to suggest that there is no resistance or agency. In fact, Asian American scholars and activists have critiqued this stereotype from its inception. Regardless, the myth has great adhesive value, for it still plays a prominent role in our thinking and analysis of and about Asians in the U.S.

The minority model stereotype as a hegemonic device maintains the dominance of elites in a racialized hierarchy by diverting attention away from racialized inequality and by "setting standards for how minorities should behave" (Lee, 1996, p. 6). Asian Americans as the "model minority" captured the U.S. imagination when the *U.S. News and World Report* published an article in 1966 "lauding" Chinese Americans as a "success" in the midst political upheavals. As the article states, "At a time when it is being proposed that hundreds of billions be spent to uplift Negroes and other minorities, the nation's 300,000 Chinese Americans are moving ahead on their own-with no help from anyone ("Success Story," p. 73). The article also presented Chinese Americans as "good citizens" and Chinatowns across the U.S. as "safe" places. Asian American writer and activist Frank Chin (1990) articulates in his writings the notion of a "racist love" for Asian Americans, and paradoxically, a "racist hate" for African Americans and other marginalized groups in their relationship to the nation-state. Chin's naming gives context to the positionality of racialized populations in U.S. society and how they have always been strategically used against each other.

Asian American Pan-ethnicity

Nguyen (2002) states that the Asian American body politic has been mostly concerned with *demographic* heterogeneity and not necessarily *ideological* heterogeneity (p. 6). Ideological heterogeneity should not to be mistaken for class heterogeneity, which most Asian American scholars and activists are willing to acknowledge. Nguyen points out that the Asian American intellectual class "betrays" their own ideological rigidity when they are not willing to read for ideological heterogeneity (p. 7). The Asian American movement, the subsequent development of Asian American Studies programs has attempted, though with limited success, to unify diverse Asian ethnicities into one political, cultural, and historic bloc. Along with intellectuals, Asian American capitalists and unabashed pan-ethnic "entrepreneurs" have transformed perceptions of Asian America (Nguyen, 2000).

The racialization of Asian Americans, especially before the 1960s, forced Asians in the U.S. to frequently practice "ethnic dis-identification." This is the act of distancing one's group from another group so as to not be mistaken for and suffer the blame for the presumed misdeeds of a particular group (Espiritu, 1992, p. 20). Given the imperial wars between their mother countries and Japan, ethnic dis-identification was most evident during the Second

World War when Chinese, Koreans, and Filipinos distanced themselves from Japanese Americans. Chinese, Filipinos, and Koreans wore "ethnic" clothing and identification buttons to differentiate themselves from Japan and Japanese Americans, seen as "the enemy race" at the time. These identification buttons would explicitly state the hatred and animosity Chinese, Koreans, and Filipinos had for Japan, and thus, Japanese Americans. During the Cold War era, the Chinese were racialized as the "enemy race," and Japanese Americans were seen in a "positive" light. One can certainly argue that Muslim and Arab Americans are similarly racialized as such today. This also attests to the pervasive problem of "racial" lumping historically and contemporarily.

The black power and civil rights movements in the U.S. and the anti-colonial national liberation movements in Asia had a profound impact on the political consciousness of Asian American educators, scholars, and activists. Influenced by these broader political, economic, and educational struggles, Americans of Asian ancestry worked in solidarity to "denounce racist institutional structures, demand new or unattended rights, and assert their cultural and racial distinctiveness" (Espiritu, 1992, p. 25). However, this does not explain why a pan-Asian identity or consciousness did not develop until the 1960s. Given the nature of Asian exclusion acts and naturalization policies, a pan-Asian identity prior to the 1960s was not feasible because the U.S. Asian population was predominantly foreign-born and they did not share a common language. In addition, demographic and residential segregation, with its history grounded in the segregated Chinatown and Manila-town ghettos or the farming enclaves in many parts of the West Coast, made it difficult for the creation an "Asian American" consciousness.

There is also a class dimension to the development of pan-Asian identity, coined first by college activists. The term was later extended by professional and community spokespersons to lobby for the "welfare" of *all* Asians (Espiritu, 1992, p. 35). The term was (and still is) embraced by university students, professionals, artists, and political activists—most of who came from the middle-class. Pan-Asian consciousness "thrived" on college campuses and in urban settings; however, it made very little impact on Asian ethnic enclaves. Here lies the concern of scholars and activists *theorizing* as Asian Americans but also recognizing the limitations (and even dangers) of a pan-Asian identity. The pan-Asian structure has continued to be a source of friction and mistrust, with less "dominant" groups feeling "shortchanged and excluded" (Espiritu, 1992, p. 51). The influx of Asian immigrants after 1965 and "tightening" of public funding sources further deepened ethnic and class inequalities amongst Asians.

Due to the material implications of the "Asian American" designation, certain groups have made (successful and unsuccessful) attempts to break away from the category. This is largely because their needs are neither met nor addressed under auspicious labeling. Leonardo (2000) looks at the identity of Filipino Americans and their continued struggles with the "Asian American" category. Filipino Americans have adopted new labels like "Pacific Islanders" to signify their desire to shift in association with the category. Unlike most other Asian groups, Filipinos have had a profound Spanish influence due to the colonization of the Philippines by Spain. Some would argue that Filipino identity in the U.S. may perhaps be more linked to "Hispanic" than "Asian." This is the result of some previous cultural commonalities like language, but more so their own responses to the Asian American political climate.

The insistence on pan-ethnicity has and continues to do much harm in obfuscating problems of educational achievement, unemployment and underemployment, unequal reward (i.e., "glass ceiling"), occupational segregation, under-presentation, and most important, class polarization in Asian American communities. The U.S. Census (2002) substantiates this argument. The average yearly income during a three-year period (2000–2002) for "Asians" was $54,999, about $10,000 more than "whites," $25,000 more than "blacks," and $21,000 more than "Hispanics." As Kitano and Daniels (1998) point out, this homogenizing mechanism does not reflect the high rate of poverty among Asian Americans refugees: 26 percent for Vietnamese, 35 percent for Laotians, 43 percent for Cambodians, and 64 percent for Hmong (San Juan, 2002, p. 101). This data does not speak to the historical particularities of different Asian groups and their relationship to U.S. hegemony. Moreover, Ngin and Torres (2001) argue that theorizing Asian American (and Latino) identities and ethnicities can best be understood within the changing U.S. political economy and international division of labor.

The aforementioned statistics clearly show that the Asian American population is not a monolithic socioeconomic group. In fact, it is increasingly differentiated along class lines. The postwar removal of "racial" barriers in the economic sector did in fact increase the number of educated and professional Asians in the U.S. Espiritu and Ong (1994) posit that the preference for highly educated labor in immigration legislation further widened the economic/achievement gap, thereby reinforcing class inequalities in Asian American communities (p. 298). This is most apparent with migration policies: Asian professional class entered the country through occupational categories whereas mostly working-class Asians were allowed entry through family reunification categories.

Espiritu and Ong's (1994) concern is not with "class variations within any given Asian population, but rather with systematic variations in the class distribution among Asian populations" (309). In understanding differences in historical development, migration patterns and contemporary conditions of different groups, we begin to see why Asian American groups have had very different class profiles. As a result, there are inter-ethnic conflicts and tensions that existed within Asian American communities. This speaks to the reproduction of power and control of resources by certain ethnic groups. Lopez and Espiritu (1990) have argued that the relative success of Asian American pan-ethnicity has largely been due to the influence of a sizeable middle and professional class (Espiritu & Ong, p. 314). However, I agree with Espiritu and Ong (1994) in saying that there is a heavy price to pay for the "relative success" of coalition building among Asian American groups, a price that is sometimes too big for some.

Implications for a Materialist Critical Pedagogy

As we move well into the 21th century, perhaps the price is too heavy to pay for a political bloc based on "race" and traditional notions of "race relations." Given dramatic demographic and economic changes (especially in the U.S. metropoles) for Asian Americans and other historically marginalized populations and the desire to fundamentally understand difference, I am calling for a return to class struggle—grounded in political economy of racism and migration. This call is more urgent and timely than ever—especially for critical scholars and educators interested in a materialist critical pedagogy.

Due to the utility of "race" as the central unit of analysis, it is not surprising that the theories, practices, and policies that have informed social science and education-based analyses of marginalized populations during the last few decades are deeply rooted in identity politics (Darder & Torres, 2004). A political economy-inspired class analysis and a critique of capitalism are noticeably missing from much of the historical and contemporary analysis of racialized groups. In addition, most scholars doing work on African Americans, Latinos, Asian Americans, and other subordinated groups are unwilling to engage class divisions and their contradictions within and between these diverse racialized populations. This neglect of class analysis is often carried out with an effort to sustain a political base that was first developed during the civil rights movements in the 1960s.

When class is mentioned, it is done so through the all-too-familiar references to the "race, class, and gender" intersection of oppressions. As a result, it reinforces the idea that class should be treated as one of many equally valued components of analysis. The fact of the matter is that class and "race" are concepts of different sociological order. Darder and Torres (2004) make this important distinction by positing that class and "race" do not occupy the same analytical space and "thereby cannot constitute explanatory alternatives to one another . . . class is a material space, even within the mainstream definition that links the concept to occupation, income status, and educational attainment—all of which reflect the materiality of class, though without analytical specificity" (p. 128). In effect, it places "race" in the middle of the discussion and moves the analysis of class to the background.

Despite the fact that "race" and gender invariably intersect and interact with class, they are not co-primary (McLaren & Jaramillo, 2006, p. 79). In agreement with McLaren and Jaramillo (2006), I also conceptualize class struggle as one in a series of social antagonisms, but argue that class most often "sustains" the conditions that produce and reproduce the other antagonisms (p. 79). This is not to say that we can reduce racism and sexism to class. These antagonisms are indeed dialectical in its nature. However, class struggle as the primary antagonism helps shape and forms the particularities of other social antagonisms like racism, ethnocentrism, gender, et cetera. Class exploitation as a topic of discussion, not surprisingly, is hardly explored in schools of education and teacher education programs (McLaren & Jaramillo, p. 79) when speaking of income and educational stratification. It is often linked (in very limited way) to distribution of resources and opportunities.

Malott (2014) makes the distinction between a Weberian-informed conception of class that is prominent in critical pedagogy and multicultural education (the aforementioned schools of education and teacher education programs are sites of such work) versus a Marxian analysis (134). He states, taking critical insights from Kelsh and Hill (2006), that for both Weber and Marx, class determination does indeed involves property; however, Marx's conception of how property determines class position is based on the

> Realization that those who do not own property or the means of production are forced out of necessity to sell their labor for a wage while those who own property live off the profit or surplus value extracted or exploited from labor.
>
> (p. 134)

Marx's conception of class is inextricably linked to capital while Weber's notion is connected to consumption patterns and culture (Kelsh & Hill, 2006; Malott, 2014). To further substantiate this distinction, Kelsh and Hill (2006) make clear that "Weberian-based formulations of class served the interests of the capitalist class . . . insofar as they erase both the proletariat and the capitalist classes as antagonistic entities unified in the contradictory and exploitative social relation of capitalist production" (Kelsh & Hill in Malott, 2014, p. 135). As Malott speaks to these insights to understand white privilege and consumption patterns in his formation as a Marxist scholar, I use it to discuss the utility (or rather limitations) of "race" and questions of identity politics that continue to be *the* theoretical driving force in our understanding of racialized populations and education in the U.S.

In their conceptual interrogation of critical race theory (CRT), Darder and Torres (2004) are concerned that CRT, in using "race" as the central unit of analysis, does not carefully undertake a systematic discussion of class and, more important, a substantive critique of capitalism (99). In contending with questions of "race" and institutional power, references are made to "class" and/or "capitalism." However, the lack of serious engagement by critical race theorists with these issues is a shortcoming. Their efforts in analyzing socioeconomic interests grounded in law and education are "generally vague and under-theorized" (99). Due to under-theorizing, critical race theory fails to provide an in-depth analysis of capitalist social relations in our efforts to understand social, educational, and economic inequalities. Ambiguous concepts like "white supremacy" and "institutional racism" used by critical race theorists are, according to Miles, problematic due to the tendency toward conceptual inflation (99). Their intent is not to dismiss the important body of work in CRT. However, there is a clear analytical distinction in the political and intellectual project of CRT scholars and those of racism—grounded in political economy.

In their incisive article, "Class Dismissed? Historical materialism and the politics of 'difference,'" Scatamburlo-D'Annibale and McLaren (2006) note their political and intellectual trajectory for a materialist critical pedagogy:

> There is no doubt that post-Marxism has advanced our knowledge of the hidden trajectories of power within the processes of representation and that it remains useful in adumbrating the formation of subjectivity and its expressive dimensions as well as complementing our understandings of the relationships between 'difference,' language, and cultural configurations. However, post-Marxists have been woefully remiss in addressing the constitution of class formations and the machinations of capitalist social organizations.
>
> (p. 142)

Undoubtedly, the desire to take up 'post-al' frameworks and culture-based analyses, in lieu of political economy, has been a major concern for critical scholars and educators working within the materialist tradition. The emphasis on difference and representational politics is done so in ways that minimized, and in some instances, devoid of the *political* and *economic* aspects of difference (Scatamburlo-D'Annibale and McLaren, 2006, p. 142).

As I have made clear throughout this paper, my interrogation of "race," "race relations" paradigm, and the politics of identity are done so in my (our collective) desire to theoretically and politically advance the conversation—a conversation that is very necessary at this moment in time. It is at this moment in time, where capitalism as a totalizing force, has a stranglehold on the majority of the world's population. Here in the U.S., the ever-widening gap between the rich and the poor continue to grow. In engaging this discourse, it is not my intent to take away from the social, cultural, and historical significance of said social movements—grounded in the blood, sweat, and tears (and sometimes lives) of our comrades of the last few decades. In fact, I am indebted to these liberation struggles in the U.S. (and around the world). What I am hoping to do (as a site of analysis and point of departure) is to offer something critical, something personal, and hopefully something useful—as an organic Asian American intellectual, U.S. ethnic studies scholar, critical pedagogue, but foremost—a political refugee and working-class subject (products of both U.S. imperialism and capitalism). To be sure, capitalism as *the* totalizing force the world has ever known does not see the color line, national line, or the identity line.

References

Banton, M. (1977). *The idea of race.* London: Tavistock.

Chan, S. (1991). *Asian Americans: An interpretive history.* New York: Twayne Publishers.

Chin, F. (1990). Come all ye Asian American writers of the real and the fake. In K. Ono (Ed.), *A companion to Asian American studies* (pp. 83–90). Malden, MA: Blackwell Publishing.

Darder, A. (2012). *Culture and Power in the Classroom.* Boulder, CO: Paradigm Press.

Darder, A. & Torres, R. (1999). Shattering the 'race' lens: Toward a critical theory of racism. In R. Tai & M. Kenyatta (Eds.), *Critical ethnicity: Countering the waves of identity politics* (pp. 73–192). New York: Rowman & Littlefield.

Darder, A. & Torres, R. (2004). *After race: Racism after multiculturalism.* New York: New York University Press.

Espiritu, Y.L. (1992). *Asian American panethnicity.* Philadelphia: Temple University Press.

Espiritu, Y.L. & Ong, P. (1994). Class constraints on racial solidarity among Asian Americans. In Ong, P., E. Bonacich & L. Cheng (Eds.) *The new Asian immigration in Los Angeles and global restructuring* (pp. 296–321). Philadelphia: Temple University Press.

Fanon, F. (1963). *The wretched of the earth.* New York: Grove Press.

Freire, P. (1970/2001). *Pedagogy of the oppressed.* New York: Continuum.

Gilroy, P. (1989). *'There ain't no black in the union jack'* Chicago: University of Chicago Press.

Gilroy, P. (2000). *Against race: Imaging political culture beyond the color line.* Cambridge: Harvard University Press.

Hall, S. (1996). What is this 'black' in black popular culture? In D. Morley & K.H. Chen (Eds.), *Stuart Hall: Critical dialogues in cultural* studies (pp. 465–475). London: Routledge.

Kelsh, D. & Hill, D. (2006). The culturalization of class and the occluding of class consciousness: The knowledge industry in/of education. *Journal for Critical Education Policy Studies.* 4(1). http://www.jceps.com/index.php?pageID=home&issueID=7

Kitano, H. & Daniels, R. (1998). *Asian Americans: Emerging minorities.* Englewoods Cliffs, NJ: Prentice Hall.

Lam, K.D. (2009). *Reppin' 4 life: The formation and racialization of Vietnamese American youth gangs in Southern California* (Unpublished doctoral dissertation). University of Illinois, Urbana Champaign, Illinois.

Lee, S. J. (1996). *Unraveling the "model minority" stereotype.* New York: Teachers College Press.

Leonardo, Z. (2000). Betwixt and between: An introduction to the politics of identity. In C. Tejeda, C. Martinez, & Z. Leonardo (Eds.), *Chartering the new terrains of Chicana(o)/Latina/o education* (pp. 107–129). Cresskill, NJ: Hampton Press, Inc.

Leonardo, Z. (2005). *Critical Pedagogy and Race.* Malden, MA: Blackwell.

Lopez, D. & Espiritu, Y.L. (1990). Panethnicity in the United States: A theoretical framework. *Ethnic and Racial Studies,* Vol.13, 198–224.

Lopez-Garza, M. & Diaz, D.R. (2001). *Asian and Latino immigrants in a restructuring economy: The metamorphosis of Southern California.* Palo Alto, CA: Stanford University Press.

Lowe, L. (1996). *Immigrant acts: On Asian American cultural politics.* Durham, NC: Duke University Press.

Malott, C.S. (2014). Coming to critical pedagogy: A Marxist autobiography in the history of higher education. *Journal for Critical Education Policy Studies.* 12(1). http://www.jceps.com/index.php?pageID=home&issueID=25

McLaren, P. (2007). *Life in Schools.* New York: Pearson.

McLaren, P. & Jaramillo, N. (2006). Critical pedagogy, Latino/a education, and the politics of class struggle. *Cultural Studies/Critical Methodologies,* Vol.6, No.1, 73–93.

Miles, R. (1982). *Racism and migrant labour.* London: Routledge.

Miles, R. (1989). *Racism.* London: Routledge.

Miles, R. (1993). *Racism after 'race relations'* London: Routledge.

Miles, R. & Brown, M. (2003). *Racism.* London: Routledge.

Ngin, C. & Torres, R. (2001). Racialized metropolis: Theorizing Asian American and Latino identities and ethnicities in Southern California. In M. Lopez-Garza & D.R. Diaz, *Asian and Latino immigrants in a restructuring economy* (pp. 368–390). Palo Alto, CA: Stanford University Press.

Nguyen, V. (2002). *Race and resistance: Literature and politics in Asian America.* Oxford, England: Oxford University Press.

Omatsu, G. (1994). The 'four prisons' and the movements of liberation: Asian American activism from the 1960s to the 1990s. In K. Aguilar-San Juan, *State of Asian America: Activism and resistance in the 1990s* (pp. 19–69). Boston: South End Press.

Omi, M. & Winant, H. (1986/1994). *Racial formation in the United States: From the 1960s to the 1990s.* New York: Routledge.

San Juan, E. (2002). *Racism and cultural studies: Critiques of multiculturalist ideology and the politics of difference.* Durham, NC: Duke University Press.

Scatamburlo-D'Annibale & McLaren, P. (2005). Class dismissed? Historical materialism and the politics of 'difference.' In Z. Leonardo (Ed.), *Critical pedagogy and Race* (pp. 141–157). Malden, MA: Blackwell.

Sivanandan, A. (1983). Challenging racism: Strategies in the 80s'. *Race and Class,* Vol. 25, No.2, 1–12.
Takaki, R. (1989). *Strangers from a different shore.* New York: William Morrow.
Tejeda, C., Martinez, C. & Leonardo, Z. (2000). *Charting new terrains of Chicana(o)/Latina(o)education.* Cresskill, NJ: Hampton Press.
United States Census Bureau, *Annual income statistics* (2002).
United States Commission on Civil Rights (2002).
United States World News & Report (1966, 26 December). Success story of one minority group in the U.S.

12

Decolonizing Schools and Our Mentality: Narratives for Pedagogical Possibilities from a Former High School Teacher and Colonized Subject

Pierre Orelus

For many critical educators, colonialism is still at work; its legacy continues to shape the practices of many institutions, such as schools, governments, churches, workplaces, and the mass media (Fanon, 1965; Kempf & Dei, 2006; Wa Thiong'o, 1986). Colonialism has been implemented through different educational, socio-economic, and political policies that have had a negative impact on the school system of many countries, particularly formerly colonized countries, as well as those that are currently occupied (Author, 2007; Dei, 2009; Loomba, 2002; Nkruma, 1965). The educational, socio-economic, political, and cultural disaster that colonialism has engendered may not be as obvious as neoliberalism, for example, partly because those in power have used the corporate media to gain the consent of people, including the poor, leading them to believe that they have benefited from global capitalism and the *free market.*

However, those who have presence of mind and are thus able to critically reflect on their direct experience with neocolonialism know this system mostly works for those who have created it (Fanon, 1963, 1965; Loomba, 2002; Wa Thiong'o, 1986; Young, 2006). In light of this view, I draw on personal and professional experiences teaching and being educated in a colonial-based, capitalist test-driven school system to examine the ways and the degree to which the legacy of colonialism continues to impact the learning, the subjectivity, and cultural and material conditions of colonial subjects, including linguistically and culturally diverse students. In the section that follows, I critically reflect on and examine my mis-education in a colonial-based school system. I go further to articulate what a democratic and participatory form of education should look like in a classroom context, arguing that this form of education aims at preparing students to become well-educated and informed critical citizens.

My Mis-education in a Colonial-Based School System: A Critical Self-reflection

As a high school student, who was educated in a school system that mimicked and followed the rules and teaching codes of the French colonial model of education, I was taught to believe that knowledge is something that is transferred mechanically from teachers to pupils. I was not allowed to challenge and engage in a dialogue with my teachers and peers during class.

Instead, I was expected to sit, listen, and copy what the teachers wrote on the board. I was also expected to memorize and regurgitate back to my teachers what I "learned." Needless to say, the teaching procedure involved rote behavior, and most of my teachers failed to create space where I could use what I "learned" and linked it to real life situations beyond the classroom's walls and the collapsing fences that encircled the school building. I was not encouraged to make decisions on my own, to be a creative and an independent thinker, and to be a problem solver. While there was ample room in my classrooms for plenty meaningless activities, there was little room for teacher-student and student-student interactions.

As a prime example, I had to follow whatever my teachers assigned to me. My work was evaluated based on how well I followed what teachers did in class. I was mostly tested on what I was expected to copy in my notebooks even though my teacher's explanation was often unclear. I felt that poor thinking, writing, and reading skills that I acquired could only prepare me for routine and menial types of jobs in the real world. Freire (1993) in the *Pedagogy of the Oppressed* eloquently synthesizes this oppressive style of the education that I received. Freire summarizes it in these terms:

> the teacher teaches and the students are taught;
> the teacher knows everything and the students know nothing;
> the teacher thinks and the students are taught about;
> the teacher talks and the students listen-meekly;
> the teacher disciplines and the students are disciplined;
> the teacher chooses and enforces his choice, and the students comply;
> the teacher acts and the students have the illusion of acting through the action of the teacher;
> the teacher chooses the program content, and the students (who are not consulted) adapt to it;
> the teacher confuses the authority of knowledge with his or her own professional authority, which she and he sets in opposition to the freedom of the students;
> the teacher is the Subject of the learning process, while the pupils are mere objects.
>
> (p. 54)

Similarly, in *Cries from the Corridor* McLaren (1980) describes the horrible and anti-democratic conditions in which poor urban school students are expected to learn. McLaren argues these students often have to memorize and regurgitate to teachers what they "learn" via rote teaching and learning mechanisms. Those who manage to do so are usually considered the best students. At some point during my high school and college years, I was perceived like one of these students, for I managed to regurgitate to my teachers what I was taught in my classes. It was not until I came across and read avidly a book called *Emile Ou de L'education* written by a French writer named Jean Jacques Rousseau that I realized I was being mis-educated. Specifically, thanks to this book, I was finally able to draw the conclusion that the form of education that I was receiving from my teachers was essentially domesticating my mind. The overarching argument Rousseau (1966) makes in *Emile Ou de L'education* is that pupils should be allowed to learn at their own pace and should not be expected to engage in any learning endeavor that is abstract and meaningless to their life. Education in this sense is conceived as a self-discovery learning process where pupils explore their learning without any forcible control of a teacher. Kneller (1964) captures Rousseau's philosophy of education and states:

> [Rousseau] stated that it was useless to expect a child to indulge abstract intellectual pursuits until he had reached the age of reason. Instead, a child should learn the things that he is capable

> of understanding through personal discovery. Followers of Rousseau urged teachers to connect what the child learned in school with what he would experience at home in his community, that is, to connect education and life.
>
> (pp. 104–105)

Although later in my learning curves I partially rejected Rousseau's view on education, at that time I found his radical philosophy of education refreshing and inspiring, especially after being mis-educated by almost all my high school and college teachers. I later refuted some of Rousseau's view on education because I felt and still feel that it is essentially a laissez-faire learning style that he consciously or unconsciously promoted through his book, which is worth reading nonetheless. Unlike Rousseau, I believe that if students are to learn, they need to be clearly guided and challenged by their teachers, although there are people who manage to learn on their own. However, even the so-called autodidacts do not construct knowledge alone. They do so collectively with others, whether it be in school settings or other settings.

Furthermore, before I became familiar with the scholarly work of the Russian philosopher Bakhtin (1986), the American educator John Dewey (1997), and the Brazilian educator Paulo Freire (1993) who believe in co-construction of knowledge, my learning experience had already taught me that knowledge is constructed collectively. In other words, I already knew before being introduced to the work of these theorists that knowledge is not something that is automatically passed on from a teacher, who is believed to know everything, to a student, who does not know much or, worse yet, does not know anything.

Centuries before Dewey, Freire, Plato and Socrates already illustrated for us that knowledge is dialectically constructed through dialogue between teachers and students, and/or mentors and mentees. Plato (1992) demonstrated in *the Republic* that through open dialogue, a mentee learns from his/her mentor and vice versa. The dialogue in which he and Socrates engaged is a case in point. By creating space for a genuine dialogue between him and his mentee, Plato, Socrates does not merely guide, teach, and challenge Plato, but he also learns from him. Although one might think that he is playing the role of a master, by dialoguing with his mentee, Plato, Socrates learns from him in the process. In my view, teachers' philosophy of education and teaching practices should reflect the dialogical learning relationship that Socrates and Plato established between themselves as teacher and pupil. In other words, as Kneller (1964) argues:

> The Socratic method is the ideal mode of education, since by it the student learns what he personally asserts to be true. The teacher-pupil relationship becomes intimate and personal. The teacher persuades the student to think by questioning him about his beliefs, by setting before him other beliefs and thus forcing him to probe the workings of his own mind. In this way the student accepts the truth, but only because it is true for him.
>
> (p. 70)

My Evolving Philosophy of Education and Teaching

My philosophy of education is grand yet simple. I believe that teachers first and foremost ought to be aware of what they are teaching students to become. In other words, before engaging in the act of teaching, they need to ask themselves questions such as: Am I going to teach my students a set of fragmented knowledge and how to regurgitate it to people as tangible evidence that they are "smart" and prepared to meet certain academic, intellectual, and professional expectations, and fit certain social norms? Am I going to help them develop critical thinking skills to dismantle this set of fragmented knowledge and reconstruct it based on their prior knowledge, lived experience, imagination, and own understanding of it? Am I going to encourage my students to take intelligent risks informed by their intellectual curiosity and personal interests? Or am I going to censure their learning by expecting them to open up their mind and fill it up with a pre-packaged information and knowledge that I prepare for and impose on them? Am I going to encourage them to interrogate that information and knowledge and to figure out what piece of it they can relate to their interests and goals? Am I going to single them out in my class for daring to question what I teach them and for disagreeing with my teaching approach and philosophy of education?

More importantly, am I going to be willing to engage in a dialogue with them to find out more about their previous learning experience, different approaches of teaching and philosophy of education, and be open to learn from them new ideas about learning and teaching? Or am I going to be continuously stuck in my comfort teaching zone expecting my students to passively receive and repeat like parrots the knowledge that I pass on to them? Am I going to cultivate the intellectual and moral courage, the respect for human intelligence, and self awareness so I am prepared to treat my students as intellectual beings who have the innate ability to think critically, reflect actively, decide for themselves, and with whom I can deconstruct knowledge while, at the same time, constructing new ones in the process?

Teachers guided by a progressive philosophy of education help students develop creative and critical thinking skills to continuously question their own learning, which should always be in the making. These teachers assume a responsible task to help their students understand that education is not how about many theories they "learn" through rote memorization. Rather, it is about challenging students to interrogate, constantly search, and figure out how these theories come into being; how they can connect them to their interest, intellectual needs, and life; and how they can use these theories to effect social change. Teachers who teach students to become critical and independent thinkers also take on a gigantic teaching task to help their students develop sociopolitical, cultural, and historical awareness and consciousness to challenge social norms, instead of preparing them to become mere docile adapters to these norms. Equally crucial, progressive educators are the ones who urge students to discover their own path through continuous search and exploration of novel ideas while providing them with genuine support and mentorship.

What students are expected to learn in school is meaningless to the extent they are not able to read their own meaning into it, that is, linking their own experience and interests to it. Students study and learn best when the relevance of what they study or are expected to learn is made clear to them or, better yet, when they themselves see its relevance to their intellectual interests, needs, or curiosity. Stated otherwise, something is meaningful to students so long they feel they can connect it to their own real-life situations and those of others.

Since their real life situations might change as they go through higher stages in their academic and intellectual journey, students ought to be encouraged and helped by their teachers to cultivate intellectual flexibility and openness to try novel ideas, deconstruct prior ones, construct new ones, and take on new challenges. Their teachers ought to help them develop intellectual awareness so that they understand that the knowledge they acquire, as a result of personal intellectual search and interaction with their teachers and peers, is not a fixed entity. Simply stated, they need to fully comprehend that knowledge is not like a beautiful piece of art they buy at an art studio, take it home, hang on the wall in their living room, and leave it there. Rather, knowledge is acquired through social, cultural, and historical transactions with people and exposure to varying sources of literature. While knowledge should be highly appreciated and valued, it needs to be continuously expanded on, re-examined, questioned, and constantly put to tests.

As noted earlier, students should not be expected to develop all these critical skills on their own. They ought to receive assistance and guidance from their teachers. However, in order for all this to be a reality, educators need to make a conscious effort to reach out to and know their students, which can only be possible through genuine dialogical relationships. Knowing their students will enable educators to have a sound understanding of their learning styles, their cultural, linguistic, and historical repertoires, their prior knowledge, and how to help them build on that knowledge. Building on students' various repertoires and prior knowledge facilitates the learning process of students and the teaching practices of teachers and most importantly validates students' identities while strengthening their confidence and self-esteem.

Equally important, teachers have a professional and moral obligation to find ways to make the school curriculum accessible and meaningful to students whose backgrounds might not match with the content of this curriculum. In other words, since education is the essence of life but not the means and the end to it, therefore in order for students to be able to relate what they learn in school to their lived experience, school materials should be based on real life circumstances, but not on abstract ideas. To this end, it is critically important that students and teachers collectively question how school materials and curricula are selected and developed; what shapes them and where they come from. It is equally imperative that they interrogate which voices are being represented in these written curricula, as occupied and colonized students' voices often are not represented in the learning materials they are often required to use in class.

Since "the curriculum is often seen as the driving force for instructional practice, the framework within which day-to-day decisions are made" (Auerbach, 1995, p. 15), should not school materials, such as textbooks and school curricula, then emerge from students' world and lived experience? In other words, should not school curricula student-centered to allow space students' active participation and interaction with other students and teachers? As Auerbach (1995) maintained, when teachers "start from the students to the curriculum rather from the curriculum to the students" (p. 16) students are able to arrive to construct their own knowledge and act upon it.

Drawing on Auerbach's contention above, I argue that in order to understand what fundamentally causes the mis-education of students, it is educationally vital that one looks closely at what is going on in the classroom in terms of how teachers teach, interact with, construct or fail to construct knowledge with students. I am not implying here that the mis-education of students should be placed on teachers' shoulders alone because such an argument will take off responsibilities of the school system, policy makers and the government, and overlook other factors, such as the negative effects of the legacy of western colonialism and neoliberal education policies have had on the learning of students, particularly linguistically and culturally diverse students, and teaching practices of teachers, especially urban school teachers. However, teachers' teaching practices, attitude towards, level of trust in students, and level of investment in the learning of each student need to be taken into consideration, for arguably these factors play a crucial role in students' academic achievement.

Lessons Learned

As a social justice educator, it took me a long time before I finally understood the vital role a culturally relevant and meaningful curriculum plays in student learning. It also took me a long time to understand how crucial it is to know first and foremost my students and use their prior knowledge as a building block in order to help them achieve academically. I come to that understanding through my personal schooling experience; the contact with the great works of Dewey (1997), Vygotsky (1978), and Freire (1993); the acquisition of various teaching methods and theories in multicultural education articulated by Nieto & Bode (2011) and Sleeter (2005); and through constant self-questioning on what kind of teacher I want to become and how I would teach my students to become what they want to be.

Before I became a teacher, I questioned myself as to whether I had the human understanding and political and cultural awareness to teach effectively. I also wondered if I had a strong enough sense of social justice, responsibility, and commitment to begin this long journey. This was when the immensity of the teaching profession seemed really challenging to me, for I knew whatever I taught my students in the classroom would impact their lives. These puzzling questions were left unanswered until I started teaching culturally and linguistically diverse students from poor working class background. Working with these students made me realize that I could not teach them these subjects without considering their cultural background and identity, which constitute an integral part of their learning process.

My Experience Teaching Linguistically and Culturally Diverse Students

I taught minority students in the most marginalized high school in Boston, Massachusetts. This experience helped me better understand how racial and social inequality impacts the learning and academic growth of poor minority students and poor White students. This high school was underfunded, so many caring and dedicated teachers had to teach their poor students of color and Whites under horrible working conditions. For example, school materials were scarce, consequently many of my colleagues and I had to use our own money to buy school supplies. Worse yet, many of us were forced to leave our teaching jobs because of budget cuts. I was one of the teachers who were laid off. I question why schools in poor neighborhood serving poor children of color and poor Whites are always the first ones to drastically suffer from state and federal budget cuts. Shouldn't these schools be the least affected by these cuts?

I was fortunate to be hired as a bilingual reading and ESL (English as a second language) teacher at a high school located in Boston, Massachusetts. This experience has shaped my teaching experience and philosophy. I remember the intensity of inner fear that I experienced when I first became a high school teacher, especially during my first year. Though my Master's degree provided me with the necessary critical and analytical tools to look at the world with a critical eye, I did not feel that it prepared me to teach. Consequently, during my first year as a teacher I experienced much fear that nearly paralyzed me. I incessantly questioned myself if it was ethical to dare teach students, especially marginalized groups of students, as I did not feel adequately prepare to do so. Suddenly, this type of self-questioning led me to reflect on many ill-prepared teachers that I had in high school and even in college. I did not learn much from them. Hence, I did not want to reproduce what was done to me: being mis-educated by poorly prepared teachers.

However, I was and am still sure that I have much love and passion for teaching and, more importantly, for co-constructing knowledge with students. Such passion and love enabled me as a first year teacher to make the effort to find enough humility in myself to reach out to colleagues, especially those who had extensive teaching experience. Some of these colleagues tremendously helped me by sharing with me teaching material resources, while others served as my mentor.

For example, during my first and second year as a high school teacher, I asked two of my colleagues, who were like mentors to me, if I could go to their classrooms and observe how they taught. They both happily honored my request. They also came to observe my class while teaching. They gave me constructive feedback on my teaching methods. In fact, one of them invited me to come to his class during recess, so that he could share with me some of his teaching methods and strategies, which I experimented in my reading and ESL. These two colleagues were very kind, friendly, and welcoming, and showed genuine concern for their students who were from poor working class background and living in marginalized neighborhoods. However, I would soon be disappointed by one of them who made a value judgment about one of his students. He said that his student, who apparently was not doing well in his class due to a temporary language barrier and cultural shock, should drop out of high school and go learn how to be a mechanic because he did not think that this student was college materials. His judgment suggested that he had very low expectations for this student.

As a teacher I felt hurt. It was sad to hear such a harmful comment from a colleague for whom I had much respect and to whom I was and am still grateful for his mentorship when I needed it the most. At first, I wondered whether I should distance myself from him because of his insensitive comment, which is, in my view, a deficit view about his student. Because my colleague was white and middle class and this student was black from a poor working class background, the idea of him being possibly racist and classist inevitably crossed my mind. I challenged such a thought, however, asking myself: Could a teacher like my colleague, who said that he cared for his students, be racist and classist? I am still puzzled by this question, to which I have not yet found an answer.

Reflecting on the example of my former high school colleague, I felt that by remaining silent I was in complicity with my colleague's dehumanizing way of looking at his student's potential. I regret not having taken a stand for this student by challenging my colleague's comment. In my mind, by choosing to not challenge him I thought I was trying to be tolerant and respectful to him as a dear colleague and a mentor.

Now reflecting back on this professional experience as an educator, I have come to the conclusion that teachers who are biased and lack political and cultural awareness can negatively affect students' self worth and the course of their learning. In other words, a teacher can psychologically and educationally break his or her students in small pieces, especially those working in schools that are colonial-based and corporate driven. Echoing Freire, I argue that my colleague's comment about this student suggests that he did not have a humanizing approach of education. Freire and Betto (1985) states, "A humanizing education is the path through which men and women can become conscious about their presence in the world. The way they act and think when they develop all of their capacities, taking into consideration their needs, but also the needs and aspirations of others" (pp. 14–15).

The majority of the students who attended this high school were African Americans and Cape Verdeans from poor working-class backgrounds. During my three years teaching at the high school, teachers were pressured to teach to the test. Students, including my bilingual students, were taking tests almost every two months regardless of their limited English skills. I constantly had to administer tests to my students. I was required to use a scripted curriculum to teach my students how to read. The curriculum required giving my students a pre-test on Mondays and a post-test on Fridays. These tests were supposedly designed to help my students build on their vocabulary words. This curriculum did not allow me enough space to engage my students in sufficient critical literacy activity. Despite my opposition to these tests, I had to administer them to my bilingual students, including those who just arrived in the United States and could barely read, write, and speak English. In fact, in my class there were many students who did not receive formal education in their first language. For this category of students, taking these tests was much more painful.

When I was not under the surveillance of my supervisor and the school's assistant principals, who came to my class whenever they wished, I engaged my students in activities that I thought would be meaningful to their lives. For example, I knew that what I taught had to matter to them, therefore I incorporated in my lesson plans thoughts and ideas generated from their classroom group discussions. Writing exercises and class discussions were usually generated from the questions that I encouraged them to ask about their family, living conditions at home and in their neighborhood, and the socio-economic and political realities that they were facing in their daily lives. The concerns they expressed and questions they asked in class about these factors were part of the classroom experience. For example, my students were always eager to talk about their culture and experience as immigrants. Thus, to make what I taught in the classroom meaningful to them, I produced a unit about culture and immigration. They wrote short essays in which they compared their culture with American culture and talked about their experience as immigrants living in the United States. Repeatedly, I was amazed to see that all of my students were actively engaged in the class discussion and activities.

As a result of this experience, I have learned that teachers have an obligation to find ways to teach their students what is practical and relevant to their lives. From this experience, I have concluded that it is crucial that the school system has well-trained educators who are capable of effectively teaching students necessary writing, reading, and critical thinking skills so they are prepared to face multiple challenges in the real world. Teaching students of various ethnic, cultural, linguistic, and social class backgrounds has made me fully aware that students need full support and encouragement from their teachers to preserve their cultural heritage and identity. This might help them connect with the past, make sense of the present, and prepare them for the future.

Conclusion

It is hoped that my narratives in this essay about my learning and teaching experiences in a neocolonial, capitalist, test-driven school system would not discourage the reader from believing that educators, especially those who believe in social justice, can play the role of agents of social change by helping their students develop a language of hope to believe that the creation of a better school system and society is possible. It is also hoped that these narratives would not dissuade the reader that there are educators who have helped students develop a language of critique, which has enabled many to counter the negative consequences of the colonial legacy on their learning. Even though the neocolonial context of countries whose school systems continue to be affected by the colonial legacy entrenched in the capitalist system, many progressive teachers have risked their jobs to ensure that we have a democratic school system where students are treated fairly and are given the opportunities to fulfill their potential irrespective of their backgrounds. This is what has given hope to many teachers, parents, and students. We need to build on this hope for a better future where all students will have the opportunity to attend well-resourced schools and receive high-quality education regardless of their cultural, linguistic, social class, and racial backgrounds.

References

Auerbach, E. R. (1995). The politics of the ESL classroom: Issues of power in pedagogical choices. In J. W. Tollefson (Ed.), *Power and inequality in language education* (pp. 1–18). Cambridge, MA: Cambridge University Press.
Dei, G.J.S. (2009). "Afterword. The Anti-Colonial Theory and the Questions of Survival and Responsibility," In Arlo Kempf (Ed.). *Breaching the Colonial Contract: Anti-Colonialism in the US and Canada.* New York: Springer Press.
Dewey, J. (1997). *Democracy and education.* New York: Free Press.
Fanon, F. (1965). *A dying colonialism.* New York: Grove Press.
Fanon, F. (1963). *The wretched of the earth.* New York: Grove Press.
Freire, P. (1993). *Pedagogy of the oppressed.* Trans. M. Ramos. New York: Continuum. Originally published in 1970.
Kempf, A., & Dei, S. (2006). Anti-colonial historiography: Interrogating colonial education. In G. J. Sefa & A. Kempf (Eds.), *Anti-colonialism and education: The politics of resistance.* Rotterdam/Taipei: Sense Publishers.
Kneller, F. G. (1964). *Introduction to the philosophy of education.* New York: John Wiley & Sons.
Loomba, A. (2002). *Colonialism/Postcolonialism: The new critical idiom.* New York: Routledge.
McLaren, P. (1980). *Cries from the Corridor.* London: Methuen.
Nkruma, K. (1965). *Neo-colonialism: The last stage of imperialism.* London, Heinemann.
Nieto, S. & Bode, P. (2011). *Affirming diversity: The Sociopolitical Context of Multicultural Education.* Boston, MA: Allyn & Bacon.
Orelus, P.W. (2007). *Education under occupation: The heavy price of living in a neocolonized and globalized world.* Rotterdam, The Netherlands: Sense.
Plato (2008). *The Republic* (Trans. Robin Waterfield). New York: Oxford University Press.
Rousseau, J. J. (1966). *Emile Ou de L'education.* Paris: Garnier-Flammarion.
Sleeter, C. E. (Ed.) (2005). *Un-standardizing curriculum: Multicultural teaching in the standardized-based classroom.* Routledge: New York.
Vygotsky, L. (1978). *Mind in society.* Cambridge, MA: Harvard University Press.
Wa Thiong'o. (1986). *Decolonizing the Mind: The Politics of Language in African Literature.* London: James Currey.
Young, R. (2006). *Postcolonialism: An historical introduction.* Malden, Mass: Blackwell Publishing.

Suggested Readings for Future Study

Alexander, B. K., Anderson, G. L., and Gallegos, B. P. (2004). *Performance Theories in Education: Power, Pedagogy, and the Politics of Identity.* Mahwah, NJ: L. Erlbaum Associates.

Anderson, J. D. and Watkins, W. H. (2005). *Black Protest Thought and Education.* New York: Peter Lang.

Annamma, S. A., Connor, D., and Ferri, B. (2013). "Dis/Ability Critical Race Studies (DisCrit): Theorizing at the Intersections of Race and Dis/Ability." *Race, Ethnicity and Education, 16*(1), 1–31.

Anzaldúa, G. (1987). *Borderlands/La Frontera: The New Mestiza.* San Francisco: Spinster/Aunt Lute.

Bekerman, Z. and Zembylas, M. (2012). *Teaching Contested Narratives: Identity, Memory and Reconciliation in Peace Education and Beyond.* Cambridge, New York, Melbourne, Madrid, Cape Town, Singapore, São Paulo, Delhi, Tokyo, Mexico City: Cambridge University Press.

Bell, D. (1992). *Faces at the Bottom of the Well: The Permanence of Racism.* New York: Basic Books.

Bernard-Carreño, R. (2009). "The Critical Pedagogy of Black Studies." *Journal of Pan African Studies, 2*(10), 261d–275.

Clark, S., ed. (1992). *Malcolm X: The Final Speeches, February 1965.* New York: Pathfinder.

Cox, O. (1948). *Caste, Class and Race.* New York: Modern Reader.

Darder, A. (1995). *Culture and Difference.* Westport, CT: Bergin & Garvey.

Darder, A. and Torres, R. (1996). *The Latino Studies Reader: Culture, Economy and Politics.* Boston: Blackwell.

Darder, A. and Torres, R. D. (2004). *After Race: Racism after Multiculturalism.* New York: New York University Press.

Darder, A. and Torres, R. (2013). *Latinos and Education: A Critical Reader.* New York: Routledge.

Dent, G. (1992). *Black Popular Culture.* Seattle: Bay Press.

Dixson, A. D. and Rousseau C. K., eds. (2006). *Critical Race Theory in Education: All God's Children Got a Song.* New York: Routledge.

DuBois, W. E. B. (1903). *The Souls of Black Folk.* New York: Gramercy.

Dyer, R. (1993). *The Matter of Images: Essays on Representations.* New York: Routledge.

Epstein, I. (1989). "Critical Pedagogy and Chinese Education." *Journal of Curricular Theorizing, 9*(2), 69–98.

Fanon, F. (1967). *Black Skin, White Masks.* New York: Grove Press.

Ferguson, R., Gever, M., Minh-ha, T., and West, C. (1990). *Out There: Marginalization and Contemporary Cultures.* Cambridge, MA: MIT Press.

Fredrickson, G. M. (2003). *Racism: A Short History.* Princeton, NJ: Princeton University Press.

Gallegos, B., Villenas, S., and Braybo, B. (2003). *Indigenous Education in the Americas. A Special Issue of Educational Studies.* Mahwah, NJ: Lawrence Erlbaum.

Gates, H. L., Jr. (1992). *Loose Canons: Notes on the Culture Wars.* New York: Oxford University Press.

Gillborn, D. (2008). *Conspiracy? Racism and Education.* New York: Routledge.

Gilroy, P. (1993). *Black Atlantic: Modernity and Double Consciousness.* Cambridge, MA: Harvard University Press.

Giroux, H. (1992). *Border Crossings.* New York: Routledge.

Giroux, H. (1993). *Living Dangerously: Multiculturalism and the Politics of Difference.* New York: Peter Lang.

Giroux, H. and McLaren, P., eds. (1994). *Between Borders: Pedagogy and the Politics of Cultural Study.* New York: Routledge.

Goldberg, D. T. (1994). *Multiculturalism: A Critical Reader.* Oxford: Blackwell.

Gordon, A. and Newfield, C. (1996). *Mapping Multiculturalism.* Minneapolis: University of Minnesota Press.

Grande, S. (2000). "American Indian Identity and Intellectualism: The Quest for a New Red Pedagogy." *Qualitative Studies in Education, 13,* 415–426.

Grande, S. (2004). *Red Pedagogy: Native American Social and Political Thought.* New York: Rowman & Littlefield.

Gutierrez, R. (2004). "Internal Colonialism: An American Theory of Race." *DuBois Review, 1*(2), 281–295.

Hauptman, L. (1995). *Tribes and Tribulations: Misconceptions about American Indians and Their Histories.* Albuquerque: University of New Mexico Press.

Haymes, S. (1995). *Race, Culture and the City: Pedagogy for Black Urban Struggle.* Albany, NY: SUNY Press.

hooks, b. (1992). *Black Looks: Race and Representation*. Boston: South End Press.

hooks, b. and West, C. (1991). *Breaking Bread: Insurgent Black Intellectual Life*. Boston: South End.

Johansen, B. (1998). *Debating Democracy: Native American Legacy of Freedom*. Santa Fe, NM: Clear Light.

Kameda, A. (1995). "Sexism and Gender Stereotyping in Schools." In Fujimura-Fanselow, K. and Kameda, A. (eds.), *Japanese Women: New Feminist Perspectives on the Past, Present, and Future* (pp. 107–124). New York: The Feminist Press.

Karim, M. and Solomos J., eds. (2005). *Racialization: Studies in Theory and Practice*. Oxford: Oxford University Press.

Kashope Wright, H. (2012). "Is This an African I See Before Me? Black African Identity and the Politics of (Western, Academic) Knowledge." In Kashope Wright, H. and Abdi, A. A. (eds.), *The Dialectic of African Education and Western Discourses*. New York: Peter Lang.

Kehily, M. J. (2002). *Sexuality, Gender and Schooling: Shifting Agendas in Social Learning*. New York: Routledge.

Kelley, R. (1997). *Yo' Mama's DisFUNKtional! Fighting the Culture Wars in Urban America*. Boston: Beacon.

Keohane, N., et al. (1982). *Feminist Theory: A Critique of Ideology*. Chicago: University of Chicago Press.

Kubota, R. and Lin, A. (2009). *Race, Culture, and Identities in Second Language Education: Introduction to Research and Practice*. London: Routledge.

Kumashiro, K. (2002). *Troubling Education: Queer Activism and Anti-Oppressive Pedagogy*. New York: RoutledgeFalmer.

Labidi, I. (2010). "Arab Education Going Medieval: Sanitizing Western Representation in Arab Schools." *Journal for Critical Education Policy Studies, 8*(2), 195–221.

Ladson-Billings, G. and Tate, W. F. (1995) "Toward a Critical Race Theory of Education." *Teachers College Record, 97*, 47–68.

Lam, K. D. (2015). "Theories of Racism, Asian American Identities, and a Materialist Critical Pedagogy." *Journal of Critical Education Policy Studies, 13*, 83–102.

Lancaster, R. and Di Leonardo, M., eds. (1997). *The Gender Sexuality Reader*. New York: Routledge.

Lather, P. (1995). "Post-Critical Pedagogies: A Feminist Reading." In McLaren, P. (ed.), *Postmodernism, Post-Colonialism and Pedagogy*. Albert Park, Australia: James Nicholas Publishers.

Leistyna, P. (1999). *Presence of Mind: Education and the Politics of Deception*. Boulder, CO: Westview.

Leonardo, Z. (2005). *Critical Pedagogy and Race*. New York: Blackwell Publishers.

Liggett, T. (2007). "The Alchemy of Identity: The Role of White Racial Identity in the Teaching and Pedagogy of New ESOL Teachers." In Mantero, M. (ed.), *Identity and Second Language Learning: Culture, Inquiry, and Dialogic Activity in Educational Contexts* (pp. 45 –69). Charlotte, NC: Information Age Publishing.

McCarthy, C. (1997). *The Uses of Culture: Education and the Limits of Ethnic Affiliation*. New York: Routledge.

McCarthy, C. and Crichlow, W., eds. (1993). *Race, Identity and Representations in Education*. New York: Routledge.

McLaren, P. (1995). *Critical Pedagogy and Predatory Culture: Oppositional Politics in a Postmodern Era*. New York: Bergin & Garvey.

McLaren, P. (1997). *Revolutionary Multiculturalism: Pedagogies of Dissent for the New Millennium*. Boulder, CO: Westview.

Memmi, A. (1991). *The Colonizer and the Colonized*. Boston: Beacon.

Miles, R. (1993). *Racism after 'Race' Relations*. London: Routledge.

Monk, R. (1994). *Taking Sides: Clashing Views on Controversial Issues in Race and Ethnicity*. Guilford, CN: The Dushkin Publishing Group.

Morrison, T. (1992). *Playing in the Dark: Whiteness and the Literary Imagination*. Cambridge, MA: Harvard University Press.

Nandi, M. (2005). "Pedagogy by the Oppressed: Negotiating Power and Identity in the White Academy." *Women and Performance: A Journal of Feminist Theory, 15*, 127–140.

Ngũgĩ, W. T'O. (1986). *Decolonizing the Mind: The Politics of Language in African Literature*. Oxford: James Currey & Heinemann.

Noguera, P. A. (2008). *The Trouble with Black Boys: And Other Reflections on Race, Equity, and the Future of Public Education*. New York: Jossey-Bass.

Olsen, L. (1997). *Made in America: Immigrant Students in Our Public Schools*. New York: The New Press.

Omi, M. and Winant, H. (1994). *Racial Formation in the United States*. New York: Routledge.

Paredes-Canilao, N. (2007). "Engendering Asian Critical Pedagogies." Proceedings of the Redesigning Pedagogy: Culture, Knowledge and Understanding Conference.

Parker, L., Deyhle, D., and Villenas, S. (1999). *Race Is—Race Isn't: Critical Race Theory and Qualitative Studies in Education*. Boulder, CO: Westview.

Pisani, M. (2012). "Addressing the 'Citizenship Assumption' in Critical Pedagogy: Exploring the Case of Rejected Female Sub-Saharan African Asylum Seekers in Malta." *Power and Education, 4*(2), 185–195.

Rossatto, C. A., Allen, R. L., and Pruyn, M. (2006). *Reinventing Critical Pedagogy: Widening the Circle of Anti-Oppression*. Lanham, MD: Rowman & Littlefield.

Said, E. (1993). *Culture and Imperialism*. New York: Knopf.

Salaita, S. (2006). *Anti-Arab Racism in the USA: Where It Comes from and What It Means for Politics Today*. London: Pluto Press.

Schulz, S. (2007). "Inside the Contract Zone: White Teachers in the Anangu Pitjantjatjara Yankunytjatjara Landa." *International Education Journal, 8*(2), 270–283.

Sleeter, C. E. and McLaren, P. L. (1999). *Multicultural Education, Critical Pedagogy, and the Politics of Difference.* Albany, NY: State University of New York Press.

Smith, G. H. (1999). "Reform of the New Zealand Education System and Responses by the Indigenous Maori of New Zealand." *Journal of Educational Studies, 21*, 60–72.

Smith, L. T. (2005). "On Tricky Ground Researching the Native in the Age of Uncertainty." In Denzin, N. K. and Lincoln, Y. S. (eds.), *The Sage Handbook of Qualitative Research* (3rd ed., pp. 85–108). Thousand Oaks, CA: Sage.

Stanton-Salazar, R. (2001). *Manufacturing Hope and Despair: The School and Kin Support Networks of US-Mexican Youth.* New York: Teachers College.

Steinberg, S. (2007). *Race Relations: A Critique.* Stanford, CA: Stanford University Press.

Tai, R. and Kenyatta, M., eds. (1999). *Critical Ethnicity: Countering the Waves of Identity Politics.* Lanham, MD: Rowman and Littlefield.

Takaki, R. (1990). *Iron Cages: Race and Culture in 19th Century America.* New York: Oxford University Press.

Takezawa, Y. (1995). *Breaking the Silence: Redress and Japanese American Ethnicity.* New York: Cornell University Press.

Torres, R. and Hamamoto, D., eds. (1997). *New American Destinies: A Reader in Contemporary Asian and Latino Immigration.* New York: Routledge.

Torres, R., Miron, L., and Inda, J. X. (1999). *Race, Identity and Citizenship: A Reader.* Boston, Blackwell.

Valenzuela, A. (1999). *Subtractive Schooling: U.S.-Mexican Youth and the Politics of Caring.* Albany, NY: SUNY Press.

Ventura, M. (2012). "Between Intercultural and Critical Pedagogy: The Subtle Exclusion of Immigrant Students." *Intercultural Education, 23*(6), 555–565.

Viola, M. (2009). "The Filipinization of Critical Pedagogy: Widening the Scope of Critical Educational Theory." *Journal for Critical Education Policy Studies, 7*, 1–28.

Viola, M. (2014). "Toward a Filipino Critical Pedagogy: Exposure Programs to the Philippines and the Politicization of Melissa Roxas." *Journal of Asian American Studies, 17*, 1–30.

Wacquant, L. (2008). *Urban Outcasts: A Comparative Sociology of Advanced Marginality.* Cambridge, UK: Polity Press.

Watkins, W. H. (2001). *The White Architects of Black Education: Ideology and Power in America, 1865–1954.* New York: Teachers College Press.

Watkins, W. H., Lewis, J. H., and Chou, V. (2000). *Race and Education: The Roles of History and Society in Educating African American Students.* New York: Allyn & Bacon.

West, C. (1993). *Race Matters.* Boston: Beacon.

Winant, H. (1994). *Racial Conditions.* Minneapolis, MN: University of Minnesota Press.

Woodson, C. G. (2007). *The Mis-Education of the Negro.* San Diego, CA: Book Tree Publisher.

Young, I. (1990). *Justice and the Politics of Difference.* Princeton, NJ: Princeton University Press.

Part Four

Gender, Sexuality, and Schooling

Introduction to Part Four

In the late 1980s, formidable feminist critiques charged critical pedagogical scholars with both analytical neglect in their engagement of asymmetrical gender relations and deficiency in their classroom practice of empowerment. In response, a flurry of critical pedagogical writings emerged that spoke to feminist questions of gender and sexuality in important and meaningful ways. Feminist critical scholars and educators sought to interrogate the missing discourse of power and privilege, associated with the deep patriarchal tenets of Western philosophical thought that, they contended, undergird critical theoretical discourses. Namely, feminist views challenged masculine notions of technocratic rationality, instrumentalism, efficiency, objectivity, and a privileging of the intellectual domain in the production of knowledge—values considered to permeate the hierarchical structures and pedagogical relationships within schools and society.

In place of these staunchly masculine conceptions of knowledge production and social relations, critical feminist educators have called for a pedagogy that unapologetically centers the voices and lived experiences associated with issues of gender inequalities and heterosexual domination. This entails the creation of counter-hegemonic classroom spaces in which students can name their world, while they simultaneously grapple with commonsense notions of gender and sexuality. Linked to this pedagogical intent is the ability of educators to affirm and enable a multiplicity of lived histories, diverse voices, and personal narratives, through creating the conditions for consistent dialogical interaction.

As such, the principle of critical dialogue is imperative in efforts to deconstruct mainstream ideologies associated with social inequalities and exclusions, which can lead students to initiate emancipatory possibilities that integrate the personal, political, and pedagogical. As such, critical feminist educators encourage students to contend rigorously with diverse ways of thinking, feeling, and being, as they undertake the arduous task of challenging the recalcitrant institutional sexism that undermines their humanity and self-determination. In conjunction with efforts to question the larger oppressive conditions of society, a critical feminist approach vigorously affirms the importance of recognizing and nurturing students in negotiating multiple identities and experiences of cultural hybridity. Many feminist educators contend that this is best accomplished through a fluid pedagogy that embraces ambiguities, contradictions, and uncertainties, as an essential feature of democratic life.

Foremost to a feminist understanding of schooling is an acknowledgment that gendered attitudes, practices, and language are inextricably linked to the hierarchical structure of gender relations, which are not biologically defined, but rather naturalized within social relationships that authorize dominant formations of gender and sexuality. Hence, from our arrival into the world, hegemonic and universal notions of gender and sexuality constrain and oppress, systematically silencing alternative ways of being human—rendering moral and commonsense the subordination of women and the enactment of compulsory heterosexuality.

In a similar vein, a queer pedagogy has sought to critique and challenge the silencing of sexual identities, by derailing the plethora of false notions and mistaken beliefs about sexualities—notions and beliefs heavily driven by the hegemony of an essentialized heterosexual identity. This pedagogical approach, in concert with feminist ideals, highlights the significance of critically contending with the politics of gender roles and sexual identities, the pedagogical negation of eroticism, and the homophobic underpinnings of the classroom curriculum. By openly exploring such issues within the classroom, teachers and students can grapple with the impact of repressive notions of sexuality, in context to social relations and the production of knowledge.

For example, openly countering classroom practices in which the sexualities of lesbian, gay, bisexual, transgendered, and queer students (LGBTQ) are silenced and undermined by the representation of heterosexual dominance is imperative of any pedagogy which claims an emancipatory vision of a genuinely pluralistic society. Such a commitment, indeed, requires the courage to transgress the structures of silence that often persist even when students' sexualities are maligned and denigrated, and they are subjected to brutal bullying and harassment within the classroom, the community, and often even at home. Significant to note here is the manner in which the silence of educators regarding diverse sexualities not only silences LGBTQ students, but also reinscribes a homophobic morality that renders taboo diverse sexual desires and inhibits the exercise of freedom.

Hence, a critical queer pedagogy summons teachers to enter the danger zones of transgressive knowledge and risky possibilities, in the name of social justice and human rights. This also carries the expectation that educators begin with an interrogation of their personal beliefs and values associated with gender and sexual formations. To effectively challenge and transform gendered and sexual inequalities produced in schools, teachers must develop a critical understanding of sexual orientation and the suppressed histories, knowledge, and cultural communities of LGBTQ students, whose lives are shaped by the anxieties of repression and resistance to their sexual location at the margins. Hence, critical educators must openly contend with the struggles of lesbian, gay, bisexual, and queer students, who are often marked by a society where "hate speech" is sanctioned and license is given to bully, torment, and endanger those who are deemed outside the heterosexual norm. There is no question then that the degree of powerlessness experienced by many of these students is particularly pervasive during adolescence, given the highly homophobic nature of educational institutions.

Summary of Articles

Kathleen Weiler's essay, "Feminist Analysis of Gender and Schooling," introduces the reader to notions of gender, schooling, and sexuality with a review of the major feminist approaches to education. Her work examines some of the problematic assumptions of traditional and liberal perspectives of gender oppression. Weiler also looks at feminist research of the 1970s and '80s conducted in response to the all-male-oriented research of the correspondence movement. Following the tradition of other exponents of critical pedagogy, Weiler exposes the weaknesses of correspondence theories, in an effort to address, in a comprehensive manner, how both gender and race are at work in the classroom. In particular, she engages the concept of counter-hegemony, as conceptualized by Gramsci, and its utility to an emancipatory feminist pedagogy. Weiler argues that, through providing an analysis of resistance, gender, race, and social class, critical pedagogy can provide a theoretical framework for the transcendence of limitations found in earlier feminist discourses.

In "Sexuality, Schooling and the Adolescent Female: Still Missing After All These Years," Michelle Fine and Sara McClelland reengage with Fine's thoughtful analysis that effectively integrates feminist concerns within a critical pedagogical perspective. Here the authors examine the federal promotion of curricula advocating abstinence only until marriage in public schools and expose the hypocrisy at work in the politics of sex education—a politics that functions to suppress an ever-present (but hidden) discourse of desire among female adolescents Their findings, moreover, highlight the fact that national policies have an uneven impact on young people and disproportionately burden girls, youth of color, teens with disabilities, and lesbian/gay/bisexual/transgender youth. The article also provides research guidelines to encourage researchers, policymakers, and advocates as they collect data on, develop curricula for, and change the contexts in which young people are educated about sexuality and health.

A critical Black feminist perspective serves as the theoretical lens for Rochelle Brock's "Recovering from 'Yo Mama Is So Stupid': (En)gendering a Critical Paradigm on Black Feminist Theory and Pedagogy." Brock critically engages the ritualized verbal insult game of "the dozens" to unveil the manner in which historically this practice has been linked to Black female devaluation. Through the creative methodological device of imagining a dialogue with Oshun, the African goddess of love, Brock critically deconstructs the historical and cultural significance of the dozens. By so doing, she offers both a language of critique and a pedagogical tool to assist students to interrogate more deeply their understanding of commonsensical cultural practices and their impact on Black women.

In "LGBTQ Inclusions as an Outcome of Critical Pedagogy," Michelle Page engages with the manner in which students who identify as lesbian, gay, bisexual, transgender, or queer find themselves at greater personal and academic risk than their heterosexual peers. Beyond experiencing the school context as a debilitating academic and social environment, Page argues that the absence of LGBTQ representations in the curriculum further isolate and alienate these students from their peers. Through a thoughtful discussion of multiple strands of classroom instruction, Page demonstrates how teachers can utilize a critical pedagogy to create challenging, safe, and inclusive educational experiences for both sexual minority and other students, in ways that counter the homophobic tendencies of the traditional classroom.

Questions for Reflection and Dialogue

1. Describe the historical development of feminist approaches to schooling and education.
2. What are the major distinctions between liberal, radical, and socialist feminisms?
3. What are the shortcomings of reproduction theory in explaining gender oppression and human agency?
4. What do Fine and McClelland mean by "thick desire"? In what ways can this framework help teachers to create enabling conditions that support young people in understanding themselves as sexual beings, capable of pleasure and of contending with issues that surround their sexuality?

5. What research guidelines do Fine and McClelland provide to encourage researchers, policymakers, and advocates as they collect data on, develop curricula for, and work to change the contexts in which young people are educated about sexuality and health?
6. In what ways might Brock's critical analysis of the dozens as a cultural phenomenon extend to other cultural practices that can result in the devaluation of Black women and women in other cultural communities?
7. In what ways are the conditions of lesbian, gay, bisexual, transgendered, and queer students different from those of heterosexual students?
8. Why does Page conclude that teachers and teacher education must move beyond a notion of LGBTQ inclusion that only looks at the content of curriculum?
9. What are useful instructional approaches that educators can employ in the classroom to engage with issues related to the sexuality of their students? How can they help to prevent the harassment or bullying of LGBTQ students by classmates?

13

Feminist Analysis of Gender and Schooling

Kathleen Weiler

Much of the work that has been done to date on the relationship of women and schooling has emerged from liberal feminist analyses of schools. Such work has focused on sex stereotyping and bias. Theorists working from this perspective have outlined and exposed the sexual bias in curricular materials and school practices. Their focus has been on the reform of both texts and practices and on state policies toward education. Both classroom ethnographies and analyses of textbooks have emerged from this tradition.[2]

This liberal feminist work has been extremely important in documenting the biases and distortions of texts and the sexism that underlies such practices as course and career counseling for girls and boys. But it also has significant shortcomings in its narrow focus on texts and institutional structures. It has tended to ignore the depth of sexism in power relationships and the relationship of gender and class. Because this approach fails to place schools and schooling in the context of a wider social and economic analysis, it does not analyze the constraints under which the process of schooling actually takes place. Moreover, the liberal approach omits any class analysis and thus ignores not only differences between middle-class and working-class girls and women, but ignores the oppression and exploitation of working-class boys as well. As Arnot comments:

> This literature does not search too deeply into the class basis or the inequality of opportunity which boys suffer . . . The implication then appears to be that girls should match the class differentials of educational achievement and access to occupations which boys experience. Equality of opportunity in this context therefore appears to mean similar class-based inequalities of opportunity for both men and women. Or, one could say, equal oppression.
>
> (Arnot, 1982, p. 68)

While the strength of the liberal perspective lies in its documentation of gender discrimination and the analysis of specific sexist texts and practices, its lack of social or economic analysis limits its ability to explain the origins of these practices or the ways in which other structures of power and control affect what goes on within schools. Its lack of class analysis leads to a blurring of what actually happens in schools as individuals are described only in terms of their gender and are not viewed in terms of their class or race location as well.

In the liberal feminist studies of sex-role stereotyping, there has been an implicit assumption that changes of texts and practices will lead to changes in social relationships and that girls and boys will then be equal within capitalist society. Implicit in this view is the concept that sexism exists within the realm of ideas, and that if those ideas are changed, then social relationships will also change. Such a view ignores the constraints of the material world and the various forms of power and privilege that work together in a complex and mutually reinforced process to make up social reality as we know it. It also ignores the complexity of consciousness and the existence of ideology and culture. Thus while liberal feminist critiques of sex-role stereotyping in school texts and descriptions of classroom practices have been very useful, they are of limited analytic value in investigating the complexity of the social construction of gender in the intersection of school, family, and work.

In this chapter, I examine the work of feminists influenced by socialist feminism and by critical educational theory who have investigated the relationship of schooling and gender. This critical feminist educational theory begins with certain assumptions that distinguish it from liberal feminist studies. The first assumption is that schooling is deeply connected to the class structure and economic system of capitalism; thus one focus of this work is on the relationship of women's schooling and women's work. The second assumption, again derived from more general socialist feminist theory, is that capitalism and patriarchy are related and mutually reinforcing of one another. In other words, both men and women exist in interconnected and overlapping relationships of gender and class—and, as feminists of color have increasingly emphasized, of race as well.

These theorists share the difficulties of other socialist-feminist theorists who attempt to fuse Marxism and feminism. They are deeply influenced by traditional Marxist theory, and want to apply that theory to the situation of women. But Marx and Engels were primarily concerned with the mode of production and relationships of production in class and not in gender terms. For Marx and Engels as well as for later Marxist theorists, women's oppression was subsumed within their class position and was analyzed through examining the demands of capital. Socialist-feminist theorists have argued that this traditional Marxist analysis is inadequate to reveal the nature of women's experience and oppression (Jagger, 1983; Hartsock, 1983; Eisenstein, 1979). As Kuhn and Wolpe comment, "much marxist analysis, in subsuming women to the general categories of that problematic—class relations, labour process, the state, and so on—fails to confront the specificity of women's oppression" (Kuhn and Wolpe, 1978, p. 8). This theoretical debate, what Hartmann has called "the unhappy marriage of socialism and feminism," is complex and still being worked out. The immediate task for socialist feminists is to create a synthesis of these two lines of analysis, to create a theory that can relate what Rubin has called "the sex/gender system" and the economic system through an analysis of the sexual division of labor and an understanding of the intersection of these two forms of power (Barrett, 1980; Eisenstein, 1979; Rubin, 1975). As Hartmann puts it:

> Both marxist analysis, particularly its historical and materialist method, and feminist analysis, especially the identification of patriarchy as a social and historical structure, must be drawn upon if we are to understand the development of western capitalist societies and the predicament of women within them.
>
> (Hartmann, 1981, p. 191)

These arguments are complex and as yet incomplete. The historical development of socialist feminism itself has recently come under scrutiny and the question of its future development is hardly clear (Barrett, 1980; Ehrenreich, 1984; Rowbotham, Segal and Wainwright, 1981; Tax, 1984). But while the relationship between socialism and feminism, capitalism and patriarchy is filled with tension, as Ehrenreich writes, a socialist and feminist perspective is still needed:

> Socialist—or perhaps here I should say Marxist—because a Marxist way of thinking, at its best, helps us understand the cutting edge of change, the blind driving force of capital, the

> dislocations, innovations, and global reshufflings. Feminist because feminism offers our best insight into that which is most ancient and intractable about our common situation: the gulf that divides the species by gender and, tragically, divides us all from nature and that which is most human in our nature.
>
> (1984, p. 57)

This study of feminist teachers is grounded in this complex and developing tradition of socialist feminist theory. But I have also been influenced by a variety of feminist theorists who have concerned themselves with the relationship of gender and schooling and who have approached these questions from less clearly defined theoretical perspectives.

In discussing ongoing feminist work on the relationship of gender and schooling, I have identified the same two perspectives that I use in discussing critical educational theory in general: theories of social and cultural reproduction and theories of cultural production and resistance. But I want to make clear at the outset of this discussion that this division is in certain ways artificial and should not be taken as connoting a rigid separation of these theorists into competing schools of thought. What I have identified in their work are tendencies, a concern with certain problems, a way of defining what is significant or causal in looking at the relationship of gender and schooling. What I think we can see here is what Althusser calls the "problematique" of theory—that is, the underlying questions that define what is significant and therefore what is to be investigated. I feel this distinction between those concerned with social and cultural reproduction and those concerned with cultural production and resistance is a valid one. But in a field of inquiry as new and fluid as this one, in which feminist scholars are in the process of generating theory, there will be a blurring and shifting of perspectives as the theorists themselves develop and refine their own concerns.[3]

The earliest of these investigations into gender and school from a critical feminist perspective can be found in what I have called feminist reproduction theory. Feminist reproduction theory is concerned with the ways in which schools function to reproduce gender divisions and oppression. In response to this emphasis on reproduction, a smaller but growing body of work has emerged which employs the concepts of resistance and cultural production to look at the lived experience of girls in schools. Most recently, the concept of counter-hegemony has been raised as a way of approaching the politically conscious work of teachers. These theoretical traditions focus on different moments in the experience of girls and women in schools, and as I have emphasized, it should be kept in mind that these categories are a kind of heuristic device, and that the individual theorists themselves may be engaged in their own process of growth and reconceptualization. But trying to clarify and identify their underlying theoretical assumptions can be of help to all of us as we attempt to generate theory and focus our own research.

Feminist Reproduction Theory

Although socialist feminist theory has developed rapidly in the last decade, work that explicitly addresses the role of schools in reproducing gender oppression has been somewhat limited. The most significant work has emerged in England, and has been influenced by the work of both new sociologists of education and Marxist theorists who have focused on the role of schools as ideological state apparatuses. While these feminist reproduction theorists take somewhat different approaches, they all share a common belief in the power of material historical analysis and a focus on the relationship of class and gender. Basic to their approach is the view that women's oppression in the paid workforce and in domestic work is reproduced through what happens in the schools. Thus statistical analyses of women's inferior position in the economy are tied to sexist texts and discriminatory practices in schools. Official state educational policies are examined for their overt and hidden assumptions about women and their "proper" role in the economy. The major focus of this approach is on the connection between sexist practices in the schools and women's oppression in society as a whole.

Feminist reproduction theorists are deeply influenced by traditional Marxist analysis and have been primarily concerned with social reproduction—that is, the reproduction of relationships to and control over economic production and work.[4] These theorists are concerned with the nature of women's work, both within the public sphere and within the domestic or private sphere. Thus the focus of their analysis is on the class-based nature of women's experiences in schools and the ways in which the experience of schooling reproduces gender oppression. But they also emphasize the differences between middle-class and working-class experience of gender. For them, what are being reproduced are not simply "men" and "women," but working-class or bourgeois men and women who have particular relationships to one another and to production which are the result of their class as well as their gender. As Arnot comments, this approach reveals "the diversity of class experience and the nature of class hegemony in education" (Arnot, 1982, p. 69).

The debate about the relationship of gender and class underlies the work of all of these feminist reproduction theorists who concern themselves with schooling. While they recognize the "specificity" of women's oppression and often speak of patriarchal as opposed to class oppression, they remain committed to the primacy of production. Because of the centrality of this sphere of material life and production in their thought, feminist reproduction theorists see the relationship between gender as an ideology and women's role in production as fundamental to any analysis of women and schooling. Thus for them, work, both paid and unpaid, becomes the central focus of analysis. Since they are concerned with the role of schooling in the reproduction of existing society, they focus on the way schools work ideologically to prepare girls to accept their role as low paid or unpaid workers in capitalism.

Several socialist feminist analyses of reproduction and schooling are also deeply influenced by the work of Althusser. This is particularly true of the work of Michelle Barrett. An Althusserian perspective in this case implies an emphasis on the "relative autonomy" of schools as sites of ideological reproduction. The most obvious difficulty of using an Althusserian approach for an analysis of gender is that Althusser is concerned with the category of class, not gender, and there is some question whether it is fruitful or even possible to substitute "gender" for "class" in this analysis. However, Althusser's insistence that ideological apparatuses are "relatively autonomous" from the economic sphere appears to provide the means to raise questions of gender and patriarchal practices apart from, although not unrelated to, questions of class and capitalist practices. Barrett recognizes the complexity of this issue and argues that the method of analysis must include an analysis of gender *within* specific class structures (1980). While feminist theorists of schooling influenced by Althusser provide a more complex view of the role of schools in relation to women's oppression in capitalism, they remain focused on the question of how this oppression is reproduced and, like Althusser, argue at a very abstract level of analysis that leaves little room for human agency or resistance. While a view of schools as ideological state apparatuses "relatively autonomous" from the economic base provides room for the contradictions and disjunctions evident in schools, it still remains within a paradigm of reproduction. The strengths and weaknesses of feminist reproduction theory may be clarified if we look at the work of several representative theorists.

AnnMarie Wolpe was one of the earliest socialist feminists to address the role of gender in schooling. Her work includes both a critique of official government statements on education and a critique of earlier work on sexism in schools for its lack of economic or social analysis. One of the strongest parts of Wolpe's argument is her attack on what she calls "stratification" theories, which look at women's position as the result of innate psychological differences such as lack of aggression, excessive anxiety, or orientation toward "intrinsic" rewards such as nurturing relationships (1978, p. 306). Wolpe argues that such interpretations fail to recognize the powerful forces of the capitalist economy with its need for unpaid domestic work and a reserve army of labor.

Wolpe reveals in detail the ideological assumptions about the role of women in society which underlie the official British Norwood (1943), Crowther (1959), and Newsom (1963) reports and the later unofficial Conservative Green and Black papers (1977). Wolpe shows clearly the acceptance of the role of women as wives and mothers doing unpaid work in the home and the failure to recognize either that women *do* work in paid jobs or that the paid work that they do is in low-paying and dead-end jobs. Thus by failing to recognize the reality of women's actual work as paid workers and by encouraging girls to see their own work (both paid and unpaid) as insignificant, Wolpe argues that these reports perpetuated and helped to reproduce existing inequality. She argues that in influencing school policies, these reports have played a vital ideological role in reproducing the oppression and subordination of women in the economy.

This kind of analysis is valuable since it points to the connection between hegemonic ideological views (in the consciousness of the groups—primarily men—who wrote these reports) and actual educational policy and practices as they are carried out in the schools. But what Wolpe does not address is precisely *how* these assumptions and views are put into practice in the schools or how students and teachers have accepted, incorporated, or resisted them. This is not to discredit or discount Wolpe's analysis, but to point to the limitations inherent in a view of ideology as the uncontested imposition of a view of reality or set of values. Wolpe's tendency to depict the imposition of ideology as a relatively smooth and almost mechanical process is the result of her focus on reproduction at a very abstract level of economic and structural analysis. It is Wolpe's reliance on reproduction and her failure to address the question of human agency that ultimately limits her work. While she criticizes stratification theories of education for their failure to provide any economic analysis of the role of schooling, she accepts without much criticism social reproduction theories of education. As she says:

> I want to consider the educational system first, as a mechanism of *reproduction* of "agents" in the sense that it operates, more or less successfully, to qualify them both "technically" and ideologically; and second, as a mediating agency in the *allocation* of agents into the division of labour.
> (Wolpe, 1978, p. 313)

Since Wolpe is concerned with women and women's oppression, the use of this reproduction paradigm ultimately leads her to depict schools as the means of reproducing women who will accept their role as workers in both paid and unpaid work. The ideology of the school is seen as important in justifying this role both for those who control the educational system and for the girls and women in the schools.

Wolpe's approach shares the limitations and shortcomings of all social reproduction theory, in that it fails to address individual consciousness or the possibilities of resistance, but it also fails to address forms of women's oppression other than those of work. Wolpe later qualifies her early, rather functionalist, view by referring to the "relative autonomy" of schools. Following Althusser, she sees schools as mediating between students and the demands of capital. This "relative autonomy" recognizes the contradictions involved in the relationship between the economic base and the schools. Nonetheless, Wolpe's central concern remains the reproduction of women in relation to work. Thus, Wolpe's analysis has no place for sexuality, human needs, the historical and class-based forms of resistance of women, or the contradictory role of schooling for girls in a system of patriarchy. Ultimately Wolpe's work is valuable in pointing out the need to locate women's oppression and women's experience in schooling within a larger social structure and in making central the role of work in women's lives, but at the same time her work is frustrating in its tendency toward a mechanical form of reproduction theory.

Another early influential feminist analysis of schooling was Rosemary Deem's *Women and Schooling* (1978). In this general overview, Deem combines quantitative information about the percentage of girls in various courses, the numbers of girls taking and passing exams, and the percentage of women in various teaching and administrative jobs. She also writes from the general perspective of social reproduction, arguing that the schools are central to the process of maintaining and reproducing the existing sexual division of labor. This underlying paradigm of social reproduction leads Deem to emphasize the significance of work and the role of schooling in preparing women for certain kinds of work. Thus she emphasizes the domestic nature of working-class girls' curriculum, with its assumption that women's primary work will be unpaid labor in the home. She also points to the small number of girls in mathematics and science, and shows how that in turn excludes women from certain university courses and later technological and professional jobs. Deem points out that the schools do not create this division, but that they reinforce the present arrangement of society through their acceptance of the status quo in both class and gender terms:

> Education does not create the sexual division of labour, nor the kinds of work available in the labour market, nor the class relationships of society, but it rarely does anything to undermine them.
> (Deem, 1978, p. 20)

Deem emphasizes that schools, in their expectations of boys and girls and in their authority structures (so heavily dominated by men in positions of power and authority), transmit different cultures to boys and to girls, and that the "choices" made by students in school reproduce the existing sexual division of labor.

One of the strengths of Deem's analysis is her emphasis on the continuity of women's work as mothers in the family and as teachers in the primary schools. As she makes clear, the role of women in doing the unpaid labor of nurturing, feeding, and caring for the material needs of children is not the reflection of some innate "women's nature," but is part of the existing social division of labor in capitalism. This arrangement may not be inevitable in capitalist societies, but in the present organization of capitalism, it is central to the reproduction of the work force. Thus Deem argues that there is a continuum between the rearing and socialization of children within the family, where the primary work is done by mothers, and the socialization that takes place in the early years of schooling, with the work done by women teachers.[5] Deem's grounding in social reproduction theory leads her to reject views of women's nurturing role as either "natural" or the "fault" of women. As she emphasizes, it is the structural organization of capitalist societies that leads to this division of labor and the resulting personal and psychological traits assumed to be natural to men and women. She criticizes the view that women teachers are inadequate because of their feminine qualities or their roles within their own families:

> Furthermore, there is the implicit assumption (in criticizing women teachers) that all these factors are the fault of women and are not attributable to their relationship with men in the sexual

> division of labour, or to the manner in which capitalist societies organize and reward productive and non-productive work.
>
> (Deem, 1978, p. 116)

This emphasis on the existing division of capitalist societies in gender as well as class terms is one of the strongest elements in Deem's work, since it leads her to see the experiences and struggles of women teachers in the context of larger social dynamics.

Although Deem's book provides a valuable overview of the relationship of women and schooling, its strength—a recognition of the role of schools in reproducing an unequal gender and class system—is at the same time a limitation. Like Wolpe, Deem fails to deal adequately with ideology and the way in which women teachers and students exist within a structure of socially influenced needs and desires—an ideological world of male hegemony, in Arnot's phrase. Moreover, she ignores the struggles and resistance of both teachers and students to this hegemony. While her work is useful in providing specific evidence of discriminatory patterns, the picture it gives of this process is one sided. Again, what is needed here is an examination of the way in which these meanings and forms of power are negotiated and worked out in the actual lived reality of teachers and students in schools.

An interesting analysis of women's schooling from a similar perspective but in the United States context is provided by the recent work of Kelly and Nihlen (1982). Like many other socialist feminists, Kelly and Nihlen argue that an emphasis on paid work as the only meaningful form of work ignores the significance of domestic unpaid labor—a domain that has been defined as "women's sphere" in advanced capitalist societies like the United States. They argue that the ideological assumption that this work is the responsibility (and natural province) of women profoundly shapes women's working lives, making certain jobs "unnatural" for women because of the difficulties involved in doing both paid and unpaid work. Moreover, the assumption that certain characteristics are natural to women —such as nurturance, caring, sensitivity, etc.—leads women into certain jobs and not others. Kelly and Nihlen consider the evidence that links schools to this division of labor, but unlike some of the earlier writers who focus on reproduction, they also raise the question of the extent to which students "do in fact become what the messages of the schools would have them become" (Kelly and Nihlen, 1982, p. 174). Thus, while they work from the perspective of reproduction theory, seeking to delineate the reproductive role of schools in the creation of the sexual division of labor, they also begin to question the adequacy of that perspective in addressing the realities of women's experience in schools.

In looking at the relationship of schooling and women's work, Kelly and Nihlen focus on several areas of schooling. They look first at authority patterns and staffing. Using available statistics and data, they show clearly the unequal representation of women in positions of authority and status and note the *decline* of women in higher paying and higher status jobs since the 1950s. They also examine the formal curriculum, and, citing the numerous studies of curriculum and texts that exist, particularly in the 1970s, show again the sex-stereotyping prevalent in curricular material at both the primary and secondary levels. They then examine the ways in which knowledge is distributed in the classroom itself and in the social relationships of schooling. As they point out, this area is least researched; we know the least about the ways in which girls and boys are treated by male and female teachers. But the studies that do exist point to discrimination and stereotyped expectations based not only on gender, but on race and class as well. Thus working-class girls of color receive the least attention and have the lowest expectations from teachers. On the other hand, there is evidence that teachers tend to prefer white middle-class girls to black working-class boys, for example.

The most interesting part of Kelly and Nihlen's discussion is the final section on the possible resistance of girls. As they make clear, girls do continue to higher education (although disproportionally to two-year colleges as opposed to more elite public and private four-year colleges) despite the ideological message of the school curriculum that their place is at home doing domestic work. As Kelly and Nihlen point out, women do not accept the ideological message of the school unproblematically. Instead, they obviously "negotiate" that knowledge in light of their own emotional, intellectual and material needs:

> While the above suggests that women may not necessarily incorporate all "school knowledge" it should not be taken by any means to deny what school knowledge in fact is or its attempted transmission in the classroom. Rather, it is to point out that within the classroom sets of knowledge renegotiation and/or active filtering occurs that may counter what the schools consider legitimate. How this renegotiation occurs we do not know, yet there is ample evidence to suggest its existence.
> (Kelly and Nihlen, 1982, p. 175)

Kelly and Nihlen's work is valuable in pointing to the weaknesses of the reproduction paradigm and in calling for an examination of the ways in which girls appropriate or reject school knowledge about the roles of women in paid and domestic work. They point to evidence that girls do not unproblematically accept the vision of sexual identity transmitted to them through the social relationships, authority patterns, and curriculum of the schools. However, despite their valuable work in recognizing the need to take into account resistance in looking at girls in schools, Kelly and Nihlen's work has certain limitations. First, I think, is their failure to apply or develop the concept of resistance to account for contradictory relationships to schooling on the part of both students and teachers. And second, they are still tied to a theory of work and work value that does not address the sexuality and power in the relationships of men and women which are extremely important in school settings, as in all socially constructed gender relationships.

Certainly the most sophisticated and fully developed theoretical work in the socialist feminist sociology of education can be found in the work of Madeleine Arnot. A sociologist of education versed in the theories of Bernstein and Bourdieu, Arnot has developed a critique of their work and an analysis of traditional reproduction theory from a feminist perspective. Her work combines a thorough knowledge of both reproduction and resistance theory. Her use of these difficult and sometimes contradictory traditions provides a complex analysis of the relationship of gender, class, and schooling. As Arnot defines her own position: "I do not believe that one can disassociate the ideological forms of masculinity and femininity, in their historical specificity, from either the material basis of patriarchy or from the class structure" (1980, p. 60). Underlying all of her work is the central understanding that social relationships are always in process and are constructed by individual human beings within a web of power and material constraints.

While Arnot has been influenced by reproduction theory and is sympathetic to a materialist analysis, she is critical of feminist reproduction theory for its failure to deal with the question of resistance and the contested nature of the construction of both class and gender identities. Arnot argues that socialist feminist social reproduction theorists, like social reproduction theorists in general, project too total a vision of domination and oppression. In some of these accounts, girls are turned into women through the effects of schooling in a mechanical process in which their humanity and consciousness are simply ignored. Thus Arnot suggests replacing the concept of reproduction with Gramsci's concept of hegemony. As she says:

> By putting the concept of hegemony, rather than "reproduction" at the fore of an analysis of class and gender, it is less easy in research to forget the *active* nature of the learning process, the

> existence of dialectical relations, power struggles, and points of conflict, the range of alternative practices which may exist inside, or exist outside and be brought into the school.
>
> (1982, p. 66)

In seeking a way to address questions of cultural production, Arnot looks back to the work of Bernstein and Bourdieu. While Arnot criticizes their work for their failure to address gender, she is also deeply influenced by this work, particularly that of Bernstein and his theories of the framing and transmission of knowledge. She uses his concept of a code to suggest that "one can develop a theory of gender codes which is class based and which can expose the structural and interactional features of gender reproduction and conflict in families, in schools and in work places" (1982, p. 80). What this focus on gender codes would allow us, Arnot argues, is to remain conscious of the different moments and crossing structures of power which are negotiated by individuals in social settings. Thus she emphasizes that girls negotiate and construct their own gendered identities through different definitions of what it means to be a woman from their families, their peers, the school, the media, etc., and that this involves both contradictions and conflict. Arnot argues that feminist educational theorists, by emphasizing hegemony, the existence of competing codes of meaning and the continual *process* of social relationships, will be able to unravel the complexities of the effects of both capitalism and patriarchy on individual lives without falling into the mechanical functionalism of reproduction theory or the atheoretical stance of liberal theory.

The work of Arnot and Kelly and Nihlen draws attention to the need to take into account agency and the production of meaning on the part of girls and women in schools. It also reiterates the basic argument of Barrett and other socialist feminists that we must try to understand the construction of gender within specific historical and social sites. While this project is only beginning, the basis for this investigation can be found in the work of feminists who have turned to the lived experience of girls and women in school. The most developed of this work has come from feminists using the concept of resistance to investigate the lived reality of working-class girls in and out of schools. But other work is in process and emerging that considers the lives and work of women teachers as well as students. This new work builds upon the earlier reproduction studies, but its basic focus is quite different. It is to this work that I now want to turn.

Feminist Resistance and Cultural Production Theory

As we have seen, feminist reproduction theory has emphasized the ways in which schooling *reproduces* existing gender inequalities. This work has focused on the ideological function of texts and classroom practices in reinforcing patriarchal hegemony. And because much of this work is grounded in traditional Marxist class analysis, it has also focused on the connection between schooling and women's work in the paid work force. I have argued that the limitation of this approach lies in its failure to consider human beings as agents who are able to contest and redefine the ideological messages they receive in schools. It is a much too mechanistic and all-encompassing view of social reality. In response to these limitations, some feminists have begun to examine girls' and women's experiences in schools from the perspective of resistance and cultural production theories.

While traditionally the concept of resistance has been used to describe public counter-school or antisocial actions, there is an emerging view that this definition is inadequate to explain or understand the lives of girls or women. Some feminist theorists argue that resistance has different meanings for boys and for girls and that girls' resistance can only be understood in relation to both gender and class position (Connell et al., 1982; Davies, 1983; Kessler et al., 1985). These theorists insist that women as well as men can resist domination and oppression and they as well as men negotiate social forces and possibilities in an attempt to meet their own needs. This is the same dialectic between human needs and human will that we see in other critical studies. Women, as well as men, are enmeshed in social relationships and ideological, as well as material, webs of meaning and power. But because they are oppressed by sexism as well as class, the form of their resistance will be different from that of men. Moreover, schooling may have a different meaning for them than it has for boys of their same class or race. As Gaskell comments:

> . . . schools, operating in their traditional function, do not simply reproduce sex-stereotypes or confirm girls in subordinate positions. Certainly they do that much of the time. But they have also long been a vehicle for women who wish to construct their own intellectual lives and careers.
> (1985, p. 35)

Girls and women with different race and class subjectivities will have different experiences in schools. Both their resistance and their "reading" of the ideological messages of schools will differ in specific school settings. And of course girls of different class and race subjectivities will be met with varying expectations on the part of white and black, male and female teachers, depending on these teachers' own views of what is gender appropriate. By adding the categories of race and class to that of gender, we can begin to reveal the diversity and complexity of girls' and women's experiences in schools.

Some of the most important work addressing the experiences of working-class girls in schools has come from feminist sociologists of education who have studied groups of antisocial or antischool girls. The work of these theorists has emerged from a wider sociological investigation of youth subcultures as the site of working-class resistance to the hegemonic ideology of capitalism. Much of this research has come from the Centre for Contemporary Cultural Studies at the University of Birmingham in England and the feminist research group there has engaged in a number of valuable projects and critiques (Women's Study Group, 1978). While these feminist sociologists have worked closely with the male sociologists using this perspective, they have also generated sharp criticisms of this male-focused work. In particular, feminist sociologists interested in the question of working-class girls' resistance have been both influenced by and critical of the work of Willis. Willis's study of working-class boys, *Learning to Labour*, made an immediate impact on critical educational theory, and particularly on critical ethnographic studies of schools. However, despite its originality and richness, it shared the weakness of earlier studies in its exclusive examination of the public subcultures of young men. This exclusive interest in men and a subsequent (sometimes subtle, and sometimes not) definition of male counter-culture as working-class culture evoked a feminist response, both in the form of critiques of Willis and also in the sociological investigation of working-class girls' experiences and subcultures on the part of feminist sociologists (McRobbie, 1980; Acker, 1981).

The feminist critique of Willis centers around two general points. First is the fundamental question of the reliability of descriptions of working-class culture by male sociologists. The question raised here is whether Willis has given weight to certain aspects of that culture because of his own ideological valuing of male actions. That is, does Willis, in common with other male sociologists, "see" male activities and spheres as significant, but remain "blind" to the significance of female spheres. This criticism follows the line of argument of feminist anthropologists who have critiqued male anthropologists for their own form of male ethnocentrism (Reiter, 1975).

The second feminist criticism of Willis's work highlights his failure to address the sexist oppression inherent in male working-class culture. As McRobbie puts it:

> Shopfloor culture may have developed a toughness and resilience to deal with the brutality of capitalist productive relations, but these same "values" can be used internally . . . They can also be used, and often are, against women and girls in the form of both wife and girlfriend battering. A fully *sexed* notion of working class culture would have to consider such features more centrally.
> (McRobbie, 1980, p. 41)

Thus a failure to recognize the oppressive sexism of male subcultures and an acceptance of the absence of girls in these subcultures are clearly interrelated. In fact, of course, the boys' own sexism reproduces the role of girls in working-class culture as oppressed and subordinate.

While these relationships may in some sense reflect a logic of capitalism, it is not the ideology or state policies of capitalism that directly pressures these working-class girls, but rather the immediate and oppressive sexism of working-class boys. As we will see, feminists argue that the moral failure to condemn or even to see the sexism of male subcultures leads in turn to a failure to understand the full dynamics of working-class culture and life.

In response to this feminist critique of Willis and other male work on boys' public subcultures, feminists have turned to an examination of girls' antisocial and counter-school groups. While studies of girls' subcultures are still relatively few in comparison to studies of boys', McRobbie, Fuller and others in England, and Thomas in Australia have contributed ethnographic studies that raise new questions about the intersection of gender, race, and class in the lives of working-class girls.

Studies of white working-class girls have been undertaken by McRobbie and her associates at the Centre for Contemporary Cultural Studies in England and by Thomas in Australia. These studies have been deeply influenced by the cultural production theories of Willis and others at the CCCS and provide an alternative approach to similar problems. McRobbie worked with a group of 14–16 year-old-girls at a Birmingham youth club for six months, while Thomas studied two groups of antischool or antiacademic girls—one group in a middle-class and one in a working-class school—for an academic year. In both cases, there was a clear and stated recognition that the experiences and actions of girls could not be explained solely through an analysis of class, but that, as McRobbie put it, "their culture would be linked to and partly determined by, although not mechanically so, the material position occupied by the girls in society" (1978, p. 97). Thus, unlike comparable studies of male subcultures, McRobbie and Thomas begin with an awareness of the dual oppression of working-class girls through both capitalism and patriarchy. And in looking at the gender-specific nature of their oppression and their resistance, they focus on the private, domestic world of sexuality and the family as well as the public world of the street and paid work.

Both McRobbie and Thomas studied girls who rejected the values of school and official state institutions. In both cases, these girls rejected school values of propriety and behavior. They challenged dominant views of what a "proper girl" should be like by asserting the values of their own sexuality in sites where that sexuality was deemed inappropriate. Both McRobbie and Thomas emphasize the ways in which these girls use sexuality as opposition to the authority of the school or to middle-class definitions of femininity. As McRobbie comments:

> One way in which girls combat the class-based and oppressive features of the school is to assert their "femaleness," to introduce into the classroom their physical maturity in such a way as to

> force the teachers to take notice. A class instinct then finds expression at the level of jettisoning the official ideology for girls in the school (neatness, diligence, appliance, femininity, passivity, etc.) and replacing it with a *more* feminine, even sexual one.
>
> (1978, p. 104)

Thomas found that counterculture girls in opposition to school authority vacillated between aggressive defiance and an assertive and sometimes coy sexuality, particularly toward younger men teachers (Thomas, 1980, p. 148). What these girls appear to be doing, then, is using their sexuality as an act of resistance to accepted norms of female behavior. They take what society tells them is their most significant characteristic and exaggerate it as an assertion of their own individuality. Thus their aggressive use of sexuality becomes a form of power. This use of sexuality, however, is particularly true of working-class girls, and only in the context of situations defined by school or state authorities. Thomas found that antischool middle-class girls were much more likely to be immersed in the ideology of romance, and to view marriage as a way out of the boring and irrelevant world of school and the dead-end world of work (Thomas, 1980, p. 152). And working-class girls, although they would flaunt their sexuality in such sites as schools, were in fact very cautious in entering into sexual relationships, since they were very much aware of the dangers of becoming labeled "loose" in the context of their own working-class culture.

This attitude toward sexuality among working-class girls is supported by Wilson's study of "delinquent" or "semi-delinquent" girls in a northern England working-class community (Wilson, 1978). She found that girls categorized themselves into three groups based on sexual activity—virgins, one-man girls, and lays. Most of the girls categorized themselves as one-man girls, which meant they engaged in sex, but with an ideology of romance and the intention of marriage. For them, marriage seemed the only possible future. Thomas points out that in the groups of antischool girls she studied, working-class girls, although committed to marriage and in particular to motherhood, had far fewer illusions about what married life would be like. Middle-class girls, on the other hand, were immersed in an ideology of heterosexual romance (Thomas, 1980, p. 152). In fact, for working-class girls with no education and no skills, marriage is virtually an economic necessity. Thus what the girls have to oppose to the dominant-class culture and ideology of the school and the state is the assertion of their own exploited and submissive role in working-class culture. Just as Willis's lads emphasize their masculinity as manual workers and thus end up in dead-end and exploited unskilled jobs, so these girls emphasize their femininity in a traditional sense and end up exploited both in their unpaid labor in the home as well as in the marginal and low paying jobs they can get as waged workers. As Thomas comments:

> In this way, counter-school youth subcultures serve to reproduce working-class culture in the new generation; by providing a vehicle for the expression of opposition to the school's central academic purpose, they help to ensure the perpetuation of a voluntary labouring class under capitalism.
>
> (1980, p. 131)

In the case of girls, this reproduction is achieved not only through the conflict of class cultures, but within the context of patriarchal definitions of sexuality and exploitative sexual relationships that *appear* to provide girls with their only source of personal power.

Feminists have argued that a definition of working-class culture that only considers the public world of paid labor and public sites such as the pub or the street corner in fact ignores the domestic world of unpaid labor, sexuality, and childcare that is found in the private world of the family. They call for studies of girls and women that can reveal the ways in which their lives reflect the forces of production and reproduction and the ways in which they experience the social world and negotiate within it. Such studies should reveal the ways in which women's lives also reflect and are shaped by the forces of production and reproduction in different configurations but just as powerfully as men's. In this way, a more complete picture of working-class culture and of the process that Willis calls cultural production would be illuminated. Such studies would approach both public and private sites, definitions of work that include both waged and nonwaged work, and an analysis of sexuality and deep human needs as they are mediated in all aspects of class culture, for both men and women.

In order to understand the totality of working-class life both for men and women it is necessary to realize that culture is produced in *both* public and private sites and that social relationships, the production of culture, and the values given to both work and individual experience are profoundly influenced by both capitalism and patriarchy in both sites. This is not to argue that the public and private are unrelated. Quite the contrary. They are deeply related and intertwined as they make up a whole cultural world. But because boys and girls, men and women, are associated in sometimes very rigid ways with one sphere or the other, they work out individual and collective cultural responses that are quite different, though at the same time complementary. The central argument here is that to ignore the cultural world of women is to distort any understanding of the *totality* of working-class culture or resistance. A focus solely on the public male world of waged work and public oppositional culture is inadequate to come to grips with the ways in which the logics of both capitalism and patriarchy structure the individual experiences of working-class men and women and their common class culture as well as their separate men's and women's cultures.

The emphasis on the production of meaning and culture in public and private sites is, I think, instructive when we turn back to the question of schooling and the nature of the resistance of girls to the school. As both McRobbie and Thomas make clear, while the official ideology of schooling for girls sometimes reinforces the messages of working-class culture, at other times it is in opposition to that culture. But the working-class girls studied by McRobbie and Thomas fall back on an exaggerated form of the definitions of gender from wider working-class culture (as well as the ideological messages of the dominant culture as expressed in advertisements and the media). Their resistance thus simply embeds them more deeply in the culture of domination and submission, of double work, both waged and nonwaged.

The concept of resistance is used by McRobbie and Thomas to address the complexity of class and gender experience of working-class girls. But that concept is also useful in examining the nature of race and its relation to gender and class. The work of Fuller is particularly interesting in raising questions about the nature and implications of girls' resistance. Fuller studied groups of Afro-Caribbean, Indo-Pakistani, and white British girls in a London comprehensive school (Fuller, 1980; 1983). By making the category of race central to her work, she brings the realities of racism and the need to consider racial identity as well as gender and class position into her work in a fundamental way.[6]

Thus the question of cultural production and resistance takes on a more complex meaning, since these girls have to negotiate structures of what Amos and Parmar have called "triple oppression" (Amos and Parmar, 1981). Fuller explores the strategies these girls of color employ to try to gain some control over their lives. She points to three areas of control that emerged from her observation and interviews with these girls: "Firstly, their being controlled by others in and out of school; secondly, their wish for control for themselves at some time in the future; and lastly (and perhaps paradoxically) their need to exercise forms of self-control and resentment now in order to achieve self-determination later" (1983, p. 127). While Fuller has been influenced by the work of Willis and male sociological theorists of resistance, her work is more concerned with the ways in which girls, both individually and collectively, make sense of and try to negotiate oppressive social relationships and structures in order to gain more control over their own lives.

Fuller's work calls into question certain qualities of the concept of resistance that are relatively unquestioned in work that has focused on counter-school girls' subcultures. Basic to Fuller's analysis is the idea that critical understanding (what Willis would call "penetration") and the formation of an oppositional subcultural view of society is not necessarily tied to public antiauthority and counter-school groups. Instead, she argues in the case of black British girls in particular that they can combine a critical view of schools with an ability to manipulate and succeed within the school system of examinations and certification. She sees these girls' ability to combine two apparently contradictory perspectives as the result of their own social identities as black girls in a racist and sexist society. In their negotiation of these double or triple forms of oppression, the girls create complex responses. As Fuller points out:

> Indeed in regard to many aspects of their current and likely future lives some of the fifth-year girls were markedly *more* critical and politically sophisticated than most of the boys. Yet in terms of overt "symptoms" within the school the girls' opposition to what was actually and what in the future they thought was likely to be happening to them, did not come across as obviously oppositional or troublesome in the terms that others describe "troublesome" male pupils.
>
> (1983 p. 125)

Thus while the black girls were conscious of the racism and sexism they faced, they did not express that criticism as opposition to the school and the system of certification that the school represented. Instead, they overtly conformed to school mores (although in a way that was often on the edge of overt rejection of the rules) and more specifically saw the school as the means to resist the sexism of black British culture and the racism of white British culture. As Fuller puts it:

> I would suggest that in concentrating on pupils rather than on opposition we can get away from seeing pupils' cultural criticism as residing solely or even mainly in overt resistance to schooling. It may be that girls are too busy resisting other aspects of their life for resistance to schooling to have a high priority for them.
>
> (1983, p. 140)

Fuller argues that black girls saw the obtaining of academic qualifications as an assertion of their own sense of competence and intelligence that was denied them in black culture as girls. In her interviews, Fuller cites the girls' consciousness of and rejection of the sexist and sometimes sexually violent attitudes of black boys. In the face of this they asserted their own toughness and, in particular, their ability to work for wages and thus have a basis for their own identity and autonomy. They were also conscious of the double standard within their own families in which they were expected to do unpaid domestic work while their brothers were allowed and even expected to be out of the house. The success of black girls in state schools caused resentment among black boys, who saw this as a challenge to accepted women's roles. Here is Marcia, a black fifteen-year-old girl:

> I've always got my head in a book. I don't think they like it because they [black boys] are always commenting on it and they say, "You won't get anywhere," and sometimes I think they don't want me to learn or something like that, you know, but I spoke to my mum about it, and she said I shouldn't listen and I should keep working hard.
>
> (Fuller, 1983, p. 131)

This is not to argue that the sexism these black girls face is unique to black culture, or that they are not equally or more affected by racism. Fuller argues that it is in fact the conjunction of these two forms of oppression along with their assertion of their value as girls and as blacks that gives them the anger and power to resist dominant definitions of themselves and to assert their own control over their futures by taking control of the educational system of certification and examinations:

> The conjunction of all these—their positive identity as black but knowledge of racial discrimination in Britain, their positive identity as female but belief that both in Britain and in the Caribbean women were often accorded less than their due status—meant that the girls were angry at the foreclosing of options available to them as blacks and as women.
>
> (Fuller, 1980, p. 57)

Fuller's work raises important issues not only for the study of resistance and cultural production, but also about the nature of subcultures in general. First of all, the combination of critical consciousness and an apparent acceptance of the official ideology of school success needs to be examined. Fuller argues that these girls have achieved a certain "penetration" of the ideology of certification, in that they consciously intend to use school examinations to gain some control over their lives. However, this might also be viewed as a form of individual accommodation to existing social conditions rather than a collective cultural pattern that can be called resistance. I think the question that is not addressed in Fuller's work concerns the nature of class in capitalist societies. By positing only race and gender as relationships of oppression, Fuller's black girls fail to critique the nature of work in class society and thus in one sense oppose one relationship of oppression to another in just the way Willis's lads do. That is, just as the lads use racial and sexual domination to assert themselves and thus obscure their own class oppression and the nature of the work that they will do, so these black girls use "success" in school and an acceptance of the dominant definitions of work in capitalism to oppose the racism and sexism they experience in both black and white culture. The individual manipulation of school and certification may allow them to oppose oppressive aspects of their own lives, but without a more political and public expression, it may be more individual accommodation than collective resistance.

The other question raised by Fuller's work is about the nature of subcultures in general. Because, as we have seen, girls are usually excluded from the public arena of the street, the subcultural groups they form are private and exist in the domestic sphere of the home or in friendship groups among girls. While the black boys in the school in which Fuller worked joined a wider Rastafarian culture and adopted the style and clothes of that subculture, the girls were excluded. Thus what Fuller calls a subculture in fact was based on a kind of common understanding and attitude toward both whites and boys and an assertion of a common pride in being black and female. While this common understanding was very significant as the girls struggled to assert their own autonomy and to gain some measure of control over their lives, it did not have the weight of more public male subcultures. What Fuller does not address is the need for a more public and politically conscious assertion of black women's identity and strength that could be the basis for more organized resistance. As Amos and Parmar state:

> Existing political organizations cannot always incorporate all these struggles and although we feel that as black women we should organize with other black people against the racism in this society, and as part of the working class we should organize around the issues of work and non-work, and as women we should organize with other women, as black women we also need

> to organize separately around the issues that are particular to our experience as black women, experiences which come out of the triple oppression we face.
>
> (Amos and Parmar, 1981, p. 146)

Resistance is an important concept in looking at the lives of girls and women in schools, because it highlights their ability as human agents to make meaning and to act in social situations as well as to be acted upon. However, resistance must be used with some caution and careful definition if it is to help us understand social processes. We can see some of the difficulties involved in the use of the term resistance in Anyon's work on girls in fifth-grade classrooms. Anyon's research rests on a more general and shallow study of the cultural life of younger girls. She studied one hundred students in five different schools and depended on one seemingly quite structured interview with each child. Anyon's data is rather weak in comparison with the work of Fuller, McRobbie, and Thomas, but she does raise similar issues in her theoretical discussion. Like the cultural production theorists, Anyon questions the view of ideology as complete and uncontested. Instead, she argues that girls and women do not passively accept the dominant ideology of sexism, but rather negotiate ideology and needs. She argues that "gender development involves not so much passive imprinting as active response to social contradictions" (Anyon, 1984, p. 26).

Like Fuller, Anyon questions the depiction of resistance as solely found in public anti-social or counter-school actions. Instead, and following Genovese in his work on black slavery, she argues that women employ a "simultaneous process of accommodation and resistance" in their negotiation of social relationships. However, the line between accommodation and resistance is somewhat blurred in Anyon's discussion and it is not always clear when exaggerated feminine behavior or acquiescence to school authority can be viewed as accommodation or resistance. What is lacking in this work is a more rigorous discussion of what resistance might mean in complex and overlapping relationships of domination and oppression. Because Anyon does not locate the girls she interviews in a more complete social world, she is left with a description of attitudes or actions in school and must interpret them outside of a social totality. In this use, terms like resistance and accommodation become convenient categories into which observed behavior or beliefs can be slotted. Anyon's work is frustrating in this regard. Consider, for example her analysis of this incident in one of the working-class fifth-grade classrooms she observed:

> She told me that she wanted to be a veterinarian, and that she did not want to work in a factory like her mother did. I watched her persist at her desk to do her school work as the teacher screamed at the other children and gave confusing directions, and as belligerent boys roamed the classroom. Thus, I interpret her hard work not only as an accommodation to expectations that she do what is demanded in school, but also that through this accommodation she can resist both present and future social discomfort.
>
> (Anyon, 1984, p. 41)

There is something in this picture of a hostile school world ("screaming" teacher, "belligerent" boys) and the obedient, hardworking girl that smooths over the complexity of the competing forms of social power that this girl (not to mention the teacher and boys) negotiates in order to make sense of the world and to try to assert herself. I think the problem here rests ultimately in the lack of depth in our understanding of this girl, the school, the class and gender ideology that is embodied in the texts and social relationships of the school and among school children and in the dynamics of the girl's own family. In this case, the terms accommodation and resistance feel like empty generalities that can, in fact, be applied to any social action.

Anyon does make some valuable points about the need to make "resistance" cultural and public if it is to serve as the basis for social change. Like McRobbie, McCabe, and Garber, Anyon points out that individual resistance to sexism and the negotiation of existing concepts of femininity lead to an acceptance of the status quo: "While accommodation and resistance as modes of daily activity provide most females with ways of negotiating individually felt social conflict or oppression, this individual activity of everyday life remains just that: individual, fragmented, and isolated from group effort" (Anyon, 1984, p. 45). It has been argued that the failure of girls and women to participate in public antisocial groups and activities is the result of a certain psychological tendency to turn opposition and anger inward in private, self-destructive activities (Cloward and Piven, 1979). However, it may be that girls and women resist dominant and oppressive patriarchal values and relationships, though in different ways from men. But the question for women is how the human ability to create meaning and resist an imposed ideology can be turned to praxis and social transformation.

The work of Gaskell (1985) and Kessler, Ashenden, Connell, and Dowsett (1985) develops the question of women's relationships to schooling by examining the activities and choices of girls and women in particular school settings. Both of these studies argue that schools are contradictory sites for girls and women and, despite the existence of sexist texts and practices, provide the possibility of resistance to male hegemony on the part of both students and teachers. Kessler et al. argue:

> Yet the central fact, perhaps the most important point our interviews have demonstrated, is that the complex of gender inequality and patriarchal ideology is not a smoothly functioning machine. It is a mass of tensions, contradictions, and complexities that always have the potential for change.
>
> (1985, p. 47)

By looking at girls and women teachers in both a working-class public school and an elite private school, Kessler et al. show the need to analyze power relations and the intersection of family and school in each particular site. They argue that we need to understand the intersection of the family, the workplace, and the state in terms of sexual ideology and structural constraints on girls and women. Thus the struggles of elite girls will be quite different from those of working-class women teachers. To ignore class and racial difference in studying gender is to distort both the realities of their experience and the possibilities for resistance in each site.

Gaskell argues along similar lines. In studying working-class girls' course choices, Gaskell argues that girls were not simply "reproduced" by male hegemony, but that they made choices according to what their own understanding of the world was like:

> They knew, for their own good reasons, what the world was like, and their experience acted as a filter through which any new message was tested, confirmed, rejected, challenged, and reinterpreted. Changing their minds would have meant changing the world they experienced, not simply convincing them of a new set of ideals around equality of opportunity and the desirability of a different world.
>
> (1985, p. 58)

Gaskell emphasizes the need to hear the girls' own stories. She argues that reproduction theories that view women as simply the creation of male hegemony or sexist institutions obscure and fail to see the realities of women's strengths and agency.

> There is . . . a tradition in feminist scholarship that has emphasized that women's consciousness is not simply an internalization of male forms but contains its own alternative interpretations, commitments and connections . . . The relation between women's consciousness and man's

> world is complex and involves accommodation, resistance, and self-imposed and externally imposed silences. Correspondence does not account for their relationship.
>
> (1985, p. 58)

These studies point out and analyze oppressive practices and ideology, but at the same time insist that the schooling of girls is a complex process that contains contradictions and points of resistance which must be analyzed in each particular historical instance.

Throughout the feminist studies of resistance and cultural production certain themes are illuminated. First is the assertion that all people have the capacity to make meaning of their lives and to resist oppression. This is expressed in Giroux's remark that "inherent in a radical notion of resistance is an expressed hope, an element of transcendence" (1983, p. 108). Second, that that capacity to resist and to understand is limited and influenced by class, race, and gender position. People will use the means at hand, the power that they can employ to meet their needs and assert their humanity. This is clear in the work of Fuller, Gaskell, and Kessler, Ashenden, Connell, and Dowsett. Third, as is clear from the work of Willis, McRobbie, and Thomas in particular, the various "solutions" sought by people embedded in sexist, racist, and classist society can lead in fact to deeper forms of domination and the oppression of others. Willis's lads "partially penetrate" the logic of capitalism, but that rejection leads them to a rejection of mental work and to the celebration of a masculinity defined by sexism and racism. McRobbie's and Thomas's girls' rejection of school ideology leads them to a definition of their own sexuality that leads back to the oppressive sexism of working-class culture. And Fuller's girls, in succeeding in school and gaining certification, assert their abilities and value as black women, but accept the logic of work in capitalism. For women, who are so often excluded from the public sphere, the question of whether resistance can lead to change if it is only expressed in individual critique or private opposition is a very real one. And this leads back to the schools. Can schools become a possible "public sphere" for the encouragement of resistance and the building of a critical counter-hegemony for girls?

Feminist Teaching as Counter-Hegemony

I have argued that the concept of resistance has been used as a heuristic device to explore the possibilities of human agency. But various theorists have argued that we need to expand our view of agency to include not only resistance in the form of various kinds of opposition to oppressive beliefs and practices, but also to include more critical and politicized work in the form of organized and conscious collective oppositional actions. This kind of opposition has been called counter-hegemony. By this is meant the creation of a self-conscious analysis of a situation and the development of collective practices and organization that can oppose the hegemony of the existing order and begin to build the base for a new understanding and transformation of society. Feminist counter-hegemonic teaching has been developed and refined at the university level in a variety of women's studies programs (Bunch and Pollack, 1983; Spanier, Bloom and Boroviak, 1984). In these programs both feminist theory and methods have been developed to provide a counter-hegemonic vision and critique (Bunch, 1983; Schniedewind, 1983). Teaching in public schools, although more profoundly bounded by institutional constraints, also contains the possibility of transformative work. This does not imply that this work will be achieved without enormous and sometimes overpowering opposition. As Freire says, critical teaching in dominant institutions means that teachers are constantly living a contradiction. But possibilities for critical work exist within that very contradiction. It is vital that teachers recognize not only the structural constraints under which they work, but also the potential inherent in teaching for transformative and political work. As Connell comments:

> The doctrine that tells teachers the schools are captive to capitalism and exhorts them to get on with the revolution outside, could not be more mistaken; it is teachers' work as teachers that is central to the remaking of the social patterns investing education.
>
> (1985, p. 4)

If the work of critical teachers can be viewed as counter-hegemonic work, the latent and unarticulated resistance of students can in turn become the focus of critical teaching. As Giroux points out, "the concept of resistance highlights the need for classroom teachers to decipher how modes of cultural production displayed by subordinate groups can be analyzed to reveal both their limits and their possibilities for enabling critical thinking, analytic discourse, and new modes of intellectual appropriation" (1983, p. 111). Thus the ability of students to resist and the forms of subcultural resistance become the focus of critical teaching, which can be part of the creation of a counterhegemony.

As several feminist educational theorists have argued, the schools can provide the site for feminist teachers to raise issues of sexism and gender oppression. Kelly and Nihlen, for example, mention the potential significance of the women's movement in legitimating an alternative vision of gender. As they comment, "It well may be—and more research is needed—that the presence of a woman's movement provides a means of making resistance 'count' and sets the tenor for the renegotiation of knowledge within the classroom" (1982, p. 176). McRobbie and Garber have argued along the same lines that the school can be a progressive force if it can serve as a site for feminist teachers to introduce the ideas of the women's movement to girls and to open up a discussion of the structural limitations and oppression they face (McRobbie, 1978, p. 102). Kessler et al. argue the need to "democratize the curriculum by reorganizing knowledge to advantage the disadvantaged; and to mobilize support for democratization of the schools in relation to gender, as much as other structures of power" (1985, p. 46).

This view of teaching as critical work leads us to see the resistance of students as an important basis for the building of a counter-hegemony, as teachers and students together struggle to understand the forces acting upon their lives. Many feminists have argued that feminist teaching can contribute to the building of this alternative vision of social reality and morality (Hartsock, 1979; Lather, 1984). The outline of this kind of argument can be found in the work of Lather (1984). Lather's work has focused on the impact of feminism and women's studies courses on the education of teachers. She has argued that while male critical educational theorists speak of the need for critical teaching, they have overlooked the power of feminism to challenge the status quo through the creation of women's studies courses and critiques of sexist texts and practices. Looking back to Gramsci for a theoretical perspective to understand the work of feminist teachers, she argues that his call for a progressive social group who can create what he calls a new historical bloc can be found in the women's movement.

> Adopting gender as a basic analytic tool will enable critical theory to see what is right under its nose: the possibilities for fundamental social changes that open up when we put women at the center of our transformation.
>
> (Lather, 1984, p. 52)

In Gramsci's view, revolutionary theory had to be grounded in the struggles of everyday life. Lather argues that feminist theory and the women's movement are grounded in precisely these struggles to make the personal political. A critical, materialist feminism could illuminate these relationships of personal and public and begin to create a new politics that would be truly revolutionary. Lather applies the Gramscian concept of counter-hegemony to this feminist work. She emphasizes the difference between counter-hegemony and the more commonly used term of *resistance. Resistance* is "usually informal, disorganized, and apolitical," but *counter-hegemony* implies a more critical theoretical understanding and is expressed in organized and active political opposition. As Lather defines it:

> The task of counter-hegemonic groups is the development of counter-institutions, ideologies, and cultures that provide an ethical alternative to the dominant hegemony, a lived experience of how the world can be different.
>
> (1984, p. 55)

While the starting point of counter-hegemonic work is the world of students, both their oppression and their opposition, it must move beyond that point to provide more democratic relationships, an alternative value system and a critique of existing society.[7]

While feminist teaching has focused on gender oppression, we need to remember that feminists in teaching and outside of it tend to be middle class and white. Thus although they share with working-class girls the common oppression of being female in a patriarchal and sexist society, they are divided from them by class and, in the case of girls of color, by race as well. Nonetheless, the work of conscious feminists *is* important in building counter-hegemony; schools can be sites for critical teaching and work in specific sites and under certain conditions. What we need to do is to be very clear about the specific meanings of class, race, and gender for people in differing relationships of control and power in a society dominated by capitalism, racism, and patriarchy. We need to locate ourselves in these complex webs of relationships and then attempt to act at whatever sites we find ourselves, in ways that will encourage both resistance to oppression and the building of a counter-hegemony through critical understanding.

Notes

1. See Jagger (1983) for the clearest and most accessible discussion of the differences among radical feminism, liberal feminism, and socialist feminism in terms of feminist theory in general.
2. Significant examples of this approach are Frazier and Sadker (1973); Levy (1974); Chetwynd and Harnett (1978); Byrne (1978); and Delamont (1980). See Acker (1982) for an overview of various feminist approaches to the question of the relationship of gender and schooling from the perspective of the early 1980s, particularly with reference to British studies.
3. Feminist inquiry into the relation of gender and schooling has continued in recent British works which have addressed the existence of sex bias in schools and have begun to focus on potential strategies to redress those practices from a variety of theoretical perspectives. *Girl-friendly schooling* (1985), a selection of papers from the 1984 conference on girl-friendly schooling, provides both studies of sexist practices and discussions of feminist intervention and policy suggestions. Weiner's *Just a bunch of girls* (1985) contributes a valuable perspective on race that has been missing from most accounts. Mahony's *Schools for the boys* (1985) presents a powerful indictment of co-education from a radical feminist perspective. Like Walkerdine (1981) Mahony raises significant questions about the nature of male sexual power and privilege that have not been adequately addressed in either liberal or socialist feminist studies.
4. Representative theorists in this tradition are Barrett (1980); David (1980); Deem (1978; 1980); Kelly and Nihlen (1982); and Wolpe (1978; 1981).
5. As Mannicom has shown, this shared nurturing role of mothers and primary teachers does not necessarily lead to mutual understanding and cooperation between mothers and primary teachers, even though sexist assumptions about the "natural" nurturing qualities of women are at work in both instances (Mannicom, 1984).
6. See also the recent articles by Brak and Mihas (1985), Foster (1985) and Riley (1985).

7. Examples of curriculum and teaching can be found that begin to bring together feminist and critical thinking. For example, a group of radical teachers at the Group School in Cambridge, Mass. created various curricula with working-class girls. This work has been published as *Changing learning, changing lives* (Gates, Klaw, and Steinberg, 1979). These teachers used the life experiences of working-class girls to draw out themes of race, class, and gender for critical analysis. Schniedewind and Davidson have provided a feminist curriculum for public schools in *Open minds to equality* (1983). McRobbie and her associate Trisha McCabe have published *Feminism for girls*, directed at both students and teachers and youth workers. McRobbie and McCabe raise questions of the transmission of images and values through the media and texts, both in school and outside of school. Articles in this collection critique such areas as the depiction of girls in the literature curriculum, the nature of secretarial work, and the overt and hidden meanings of *Jackie*, the British equivalent of *Seventeen*. In providing analyses and critiques of sites and texts that make up the cultural world of teenage girls, McRobbie and McCabe hope to provide these girls with the kind of critical vision that will lead them to see their experiences critically as socially created and thus open to resistance and change.

References

Acker, Sandra. No-woman's land: British sociology of education 1960–1979. *The Sociological Review* (1981) 29, 1.

Amos, Valerie and Parmar, Pratibha. Resistances and responses: The experiences of black girls in Britain. In Angela McRobbie and Trisha McCabe, eds., *Feminism for girls*. London and Boston: Routledge and Kegan Paul, 1981.

Anyon, Jean. Intersections of gender and class: Accommodation and resistance by working class and affluent females to contradictory sex-role ideologies. *Journal of Education* (1984) 166, 1, 25–48.

Arnot, Madeleine. Male hegemony, social class and women's education. *Journal of Education* (1982) 164, 1, 64–89.

Barrett, Michele. *Women's oppression today*. London: Virago Press, 1980.

Bunch, Charlotte. Not by degrees: Feminist theory and education. In Charlotte Bunch and Sandra Pollack, eds. *Learning our way*. Trumansburg, N.Y.: Crossing Press, 1983.

Bunch, Charlotte and Pollack, Sandra, eds. *Learning our way*. Trumansburg, N.Y.: Crossing Press. 1983.

Cloward, Richard and Piven, Frances Fox. Hidden protest: The channeling of female innovation and resistance. *Signs* (1979) 4, 4, 651–669.

Connell, R. W. *Teachers' work*. London: George Allen and Unwin, 1985.

Connell, R. W., Dowsett, G. W., Kessler, S., and Ashenden, D. J. *Making the difference*. Boston: Allen and Unwin, 1982.

Davies, Lynn. Gender, resistance and power. In Stephen Walker and Len Barton, eds. *Gender class and education*. Lewes, Sussex: The Falmer Press, 1983.

Deem, Rosemary. *Women and schooling*. London and Boston: Routledge and Kegan Paul, 1978.

——. ed. *Schooling for women's work*. London and Boston: Routledge and Kegan Paul, 1980.

Ehrenreich, Barbara. Life without father: Reconsidering socialist-feminist theory. *Socialist Review* (Jan.–Feb., 1984) 73, 48–58.

Eisenstein, Zillah. ed. *Capitalist patriarchy and the case for socialist feminism*. New York and London: Monthly Review Press, 1979.

——, Qualified criticism, critical qualifications. In Jane Purvis and Margaret Hales. *Achievement and inequality in education*. London: Routledge and Kegan Paul, 1983.

Fuller, Mary. Black girls in a London comprehensive school. In Rosemary Deem, ed. *Schooling for women's work*. London and Boston: Routledge and Kegan Paul, 1980.

——. Qualified criticism, critical qualifications. In Jane Purvis and Margaret Hales. *Achievement and inequality in education*. London: Routledge and Kegan Paul, 1983.

Gaskell, Jane. Course enrollment in the high school: The perspective of working class females. *Sociology of Education* (1985) 58, 1, 48–59.

Giroux, Henry. *Theory, resistance, and education*. South Hadley, Mass.: Bergin and Garvey, 1983.

Hartsock, Nancy. Feminist theory and the development of revolutionary strategy. In Zillah Eisenstein, ed. *Capitalist patriarchy and the case for socialist feminism*. London and New York: Monthly Review Press, 1979.

Hartsock, Nancy. *Money, Sex, and Power: Toward a Feminist Historical Materialism*. New York: Longman, 1983.

Hartmann, Heidi. The unhappy marriage of socialism and feminism. In Lydia Sargent, ed. *Women and Revolution*. Boston: South End Press, 1981.

Jagger, Alison. *Feminist theory and human nature*. Sussex: Harvester Press, 1983.

Kelly, Gayle and Nihlen, Ann. Schooling and the reproduction of patriarchy: Unequal workloads, unequal rewards. In Michael Apple, ed. *Cultural and economic reproduction in education*. London and Boston: Routledge and Kegan Paul, 1982.

Kessler, S., Ashenden, R., Connell, R., and Dowsett, G. Gender relations in secondary schooling. *Sociology of Education* (1985) 58, 1, 34–48.

Kuhn, Annette and Wolpe, AnnMarie, eds. *Feminism and materialism.* London and Boston: Routledge and Kegan Paul, 1978.

Lather, Patti. Critical theory, curricular transformation and feminist mainstreaming. *Journal of Education* (1984) 166, 1, 49–62.

McRobbie, Angela. Working class girls and the culture of femininity. In Centre for Contemporary Cultural Studies Women's Group. *Women take issue.* London: Hutchison, 1978.

——. Settling accounts with subcultures, *Screen Education* (1980) 34, 37–51.

Reiter, Rayna, ed. *Toward an anthropology of women.* New York and London: Monthly Review Press, 1975.

Rowbotham, Sheila, Segal, Lynne, and Wainwright, Hilary. *Beyond the fragments: Feminism and the making of socialism.* Boston: Alyson Publications, 1981.

Rubin, Gayle. The traffic in women: Notes on the political economy of sex. In Rayna Reiter, ed. *Toward an anthropology of women.* New York and London: Monthly Review Press, 1975.

Schniedewind, Nancy. Feminist values: Guidelines for teaching methodology in women's studies. In Charlotte Bunch and Sandra Pollack, eds. *Learning our way: Essays in feminist education.* Trumansburg, N.Y.: Crossing Press, 1983.

Spanier, Bonnie, Bloom, Alex, and Boroviak, Darlene. *Toward a balanced curriculum.* Cambridge, Mass.: Schenkman Publishing Company, 1984.

Tax, Meredith. Learning how to bake. *Socialist Review* (Jan.–Feb. 1984) 73, 36–41.

Thomas, Claire. Girls and counter-school culture. *Melbourne Working Papers.* Melbourne, 1980.

Wilson, Deirdre. Sexual codes and conduct: A study of teenage girls. In Carol Smart and Barry Smart, eds. *Women, sexuality and social control.* London and Boston: Routledge and Kegan Paul, 1978.

Wolpe, AnnMarie. Education and the sexual division of labour. In Annette Kuhn and AnnMarie Wolpe, eds. *Feminism and materialism.* Boston and London: Routledge and Kegan Paul, 1978.

Women's Study Group. *Women take issue.* London: CCCS/Hutchison, 1978.

14

Sexuality Education and Desire: Still Missing After All These Years

Michelle Fine and Sara I. McClelland

Michelle Fine's (1988) article "Sexuality, Schooling, and Adolescent Females: The Missing Discourse of Desire" was published in the *Harvard Educational Review* almost twenty years ago. In that essay, Fine questioned the ways in which schools taught young people about sexuality. She argued that schools, by positioning young women primarily as potential victims of male sexual aggression, seriously compromised young women and men's development of sexual subjectivities. The capacity of young women to be sexually educated—to engage, negotiate, or resist—was hobbled by schools' refusal to deliver comprehensive sexuality education. The power of this argument lay in naming the relationship between the absence of sexuality education on desire and the presence of sexual risk:

> The absence of a discourse of desire, combined with the lack of analysis of the language of victimization, may actually retard the development of sexual subjectivity and responsibility in students. Those most "at risk" of victimization through pregnancy, disease, violence, or harassment—all female students, low-income females in particular, and non-heterosexual males—are those most likely to be victimized by the absence of critical conversation in public schools. . . . Public schools constitute a sphere in which young women could be offered access to a language and experience of empowerment. . . . "Well educated" young women could breathe life into positions of social critique and experience entitlement rather than victimization; autonomy rather than terror.
> (pp. 49–50)

Educated as neither desiring subjects seeking pleasure nor potentially abused subjects who could fight back, young women were denied knowledge and skills, and left to their own (and others') devices in a sea of pleasures and dangers. Even before Fine's article, but especially in the two decades since, feminist scholars, educators, and activists have voiced concern about the missing discourse of female desire (see Rose, 2003; Snitow, Stansell, & Thompson, 1983; Tolman, 2002; Vance, 1993).

Today we continue to worry. Our worries, however, stretch to include the severe and unevenly distributed educational and health consequences of the federal education campaign promoting abstinence only until marriage (AOUM). This educational crusade has been unleashed through public institutions and laws advocating the virtues of abstinence, the dangers of unmarried sex, and the promised safety of heterosexual marriage.

This article focuses on sexuality education through the window of the federally funded AOUM movement. Using federal abstinence guidelines, interviews with sexuality educators, visits to abstinence-only conferences, conversations with youth in schools, and evaluations of abstinence curricula, we critically analyze the history of AOUM policies and the consequences of AOUM for distinct groups of young women living and desiring at the embodied intersections of gender, sexuality, race, ethnicity, class, and disability. We draw from a larger project we have undertaken that focuses on the role the courts, schools, and states play in infringing on young women's sexuality via parental consent mandates, AOUM curricula, and emergency contraception battles (see Fine & McClelland, in press). The sexual subjectivity of young women remains our focus in this discussion because their bodies bear the consequences of limited sexuality education and are the site where progressive educational and health policies can have significant effect.

Contemporary Analysis of Sexuality Education

Adolescent desires develop within the context of global and national politics, ideologies, community life, religious practices, and popular culture; in family living rooms, on the Internet and on MTV; in bedrooms, cars, and alleys (Douglas, 1966; Foucault, 1988; Phillips, 2000). We situate our analysis of adolescent sexuality education within a human rights framework, allied with struggles over reproductive rights, political economy, health care, education and prison reform, structural and personal violence (see Correa, 1994; Correa & Petchesky, 1994; Impett, Schooler, & Tolman, in press; Luttrell, 2002; Nussbaum, 2003; Petchesky, 2005; Roberts, 2002; Sen, George, & Ostlin, 2002; Sen, 1994; Tolman, Striepe, & Harmon, 2003; Zavella, 2003).[1]

We understand further that while all young people, by virtue of age, depend on the state and develop under state regulations, the adverse consequences of state policies that curtail education and health are not equally distributed. In fact, national policies concerning sexuality fall unevenly on girls, poor and working-class youth, teens with disabilities, Black and Latino adolescents, and lesbian/gay/bisexual and transgender youth.

By considering national sexuality education policy and young women's access to contraception and abortion, it is fair to say that young women's sexuality has become a designated "dense transfer point for relations of power" (Foucault, 1990, p. 103). We focus here on young women's sexual encounters with the state—through law, policy, and public institutions—as "the best hidden things in the social body" (p. 118). Young women's sexual relations with the state offer a window onto the intimate implications of neo-liberalism and fundamentalism.

While early seeds of the abstinence movement can be traced back to the 1981 Adolescent Family Life Act (AFLA), and followed up fifteen years later by the Personal Responsibility and Work Opportunity Reconciliation Act signed into law by President Clinton in 1996, the contemporary AOUM campaign marks a moment when social policy, ideology, and educational practice are being aligned for abstinence, for heterosexual marriage, and against critical education about power, desires, or dangers. Put differently, in the language of Antonio Gramsci, today we witness varied public institutions deployed in a "passive revolution" for abstinence:

> The category of "passive revolution" . . . qualify[ies] the most usual form of hegemony of the bourgeoisie involving a model of articulation whose aim is to neutralize the other social force . . . enlarging the state whereby the interests of the dominant class are articulated with the needs, desires, interests of subordinated groups.
>
> (Gramsci, 1971, as cited in Mouffe, 1979, p. 192)

This process accelerates, Jovchelovitch (2001) argues, when arenas for public conversation close, when spaces for dissent are infiltrated by surveillance or threats, and when the "fizz of dialogue" flattens.

We believe we are on the cusp of such a moment in public education, as the argument for abstinence only until marriage is beginning to assert a kind of natural cultural authority, in schools and out. The fizz of dialogue is being censored in many classrooms and beyond, with serious educational and health consequence for young women—for some more than others, but indeed for us all.

Thick Desire

This article picks up where we left off in 1988. Almost twenty years later, for better or worse, the discourse of adolescent desire is no longer missing (Harris, 2005). It has been splashed all over MTV, thoroughly commodified by the market, and repetitively performed in popular culture. A caricature of desire itself is now displayed loudly, as it remains simultaneously silent (Burns & Torre, 2005; Harris, 2005; Tolman, 1994, 2002, 2006). A telling piece of evidence that demonstrates how fully young women have taken on the performance of desire is the startling statistic that the number of teens having breast implants nearly quadrupled from 2,872 in 2002 to 11,326 in 2003 (Albert et al., 2005).

Today we can "google" for information about the average young woman's age of "sexual debut," if she used a condom, got pregnant, the number of partners she had, if she aborted or gave birth, and what the baby weighed. However, we don't know if she enjoyed it, wanted it, or if she was violently coerced. Little has actually been heard from young women who desire pleasure, an education, freedom from violence, a future, intimacy, an abortion, safe and affordable child care for their babies, or health care for their mothers. There is almost nothing heard from the young women who are most often tossed aside by state, family, church, and school—those who are lesbian, gay, bisexual, queer, or questioning (LGBTQQ),[2] immigrant and undocumented youth, and young women with disabilities. While these marginalized young people may yearn for quality education, health care, economic well being, and healthy sexual lives, day to day they attend under-funded schools, contend with high-stakes testing, endure heightened police surveillance, are seduced by military recruitment promises, and are surrounded by fundamentalist ideologies working to reconstitute their public school classrooms and penetrate courts and state legislatures (Fine, Burns, Payne, & Torre, 2004).

The past two decades have seen a radical growth curve of neo-liberal reform. Throughout this period, the very public policies and institutions designed to facilitate the healthy development of young people—particularly Black, Latino, and Native American youth, those living in poverty, and/or recently immigrated to the United States—have been severely compromised.

Thus, as a friendly amendment to the 1988 essay—and with the wisdom of hindsight and living in a different global politic—we offer educators and researchers a historic revision to the missing discourse of desire. We offer instead a framework of *thick desire,* arguing that young people are entitled to a broad range of desires for meaningful intellectual, political, and social engagement, the possibility of financial independence, sexual and reproductive freedom, protection from racialized and sexualized violence, and a way to imagine living in the future tense (Appadurai, 2001, 2004; Nussbaum, 2003). We understand that young women's thick desires require a set of publicly funded enabling conditions, in which teen women have opportunities to: (a) develop intellectually, emotionally, economically, and culturally; (b) imagine themselves as sexual beings capable of pleasure and cautious about danger without carrying the undue burden of social, medical, and reproductive consequences;

(c) have access to information and health-care resources; (d) be protected from structural and intimate violence and abuse; and (e) rely on a public safety net of resources to support youth, families, and community.

A framework of thick desire situates sexual well being within structural contexts that enable economic, educational, social, and psychological health. In this essay, we seek to understand how laws, public policies, and institutions today both nourish and threaten young women's sense of economic, social, and sexual possibility (Appadurai, 2004; Nussbaum, 2003).

In the remainder of this article, we examine various public contexts in which thick desire grows or is extinguished—public education, juvenile justice, and sexuality policies. In these contexts, we illuminate specific embodied intersections where young women live, varied by race, ethnicity, class, disability, sexuality, family arrangements, and even geography (Crenshaw, 1995). By examining the changes in sex education policy over the past two decades, and the effects on distinct groups of young women, we can see that enabling conditions for thick desire ossify as *public assistance* and are replaced with *punishing morality* as neoliberalism and fundamentalism frame public educational policy.

Developmental Contexts for Thick Desire: Public Institutions and "Private" Choices

Neo-liberalism marks the government's shift to the Right, whereby public responsibility for social well being has been evacuated by the state and replaced with private resources, or more often, not replaced at all. Personal needs have been exiled from the public sphere, sent out to the marketplace or back into the family (Luker, 2006). At the same time that the state walks away, it leaves behind a moralizing ideology about bad "personal choices" enacted by those who transgress (see Fine & McClelland, in press, for a discussion of moralizing discourses regarding reproductive freedoms). During the past twenty years, the social contract with poor and working-class Americans has been severed. The wealth gap between elites and the poor has swelled (Reich, 2002). College tuition rates have risen while financial aid in the form of need-based scholarship has declined (Burd, 2006, p. 3). During this era, quality and insured health care, even for the middle class, has moved increasingly out of reach (Starr, 2004). Many teens have made seemingly bad "choices" in this era.

Young women's bodies and desires take intimate shape in responding to and contesting public policy shifts (Brown, 2003; Srinivasan, 2004). In order to document the tangled enmeshment of public policy and adolescent female sexuality, we select two public policies which severely disable young people's material and social resources. The proliferation of high-stakes testing and juvenile incarceration remind us how personal choices and outcomes are not "natural," nor are they entirely personal. While differential educational, criminal justice, and reproductive outcomes by race and class are typically cast as (ir)responsible private choices, we bind these outcomes to deliberate public policy decisions (Geronimus, 1997).

Unequal Schooling Opportunities

A number of public policies, including fiscal inequity, unequal distribution of certified educators, high-stakes testing, retreat from bilingual education, and affirmative action, have colluded to produce a grossly uneven landscape of public education; what Jonathan Kozol has called the "shame of the nation" (2005). To take just one policy and unravel its consequences, let's consider the well-documented relationship of high-stakes exit examinations and the associated rise in Black and Latino dropout rates. Here we bear witness to the harsh consequences of a public policy seemingly remote from sexual and reproductive outcomes (Anyon, 2005; Sullivan et al., 2005).

Policymakers claim that the implementation of high-stakes exit exams leads to improved performance and increased achievement. Yet cross-state studies reveal that as these tests are implemented, dropout/push out rates of English-language learners and minority students rise and the achievement gap widens (see Allensworth, 2004; Haney, 2000; McNeil, 2005; Sullivan et al., 2005; Valenzuela, 2004). Amrein and Berliner (2002) map the geography of high-stakes exit examinations and find that African American, Latino, English-language learners, and immigrant students are disproportionately required to pass high-stakes tests in order to graduate from high school and disproportionately fail. The widespread reliance on high-stakes exit exams has unleashed an increase in what is now called "diploma penalty," denying more and more youth their diplomas (Haney, 2000; Orfield, Losen, Wald, & Swanson, 2004).

Students who drop out/are pushed out of high school earn less, are more likely to be sick, have higher mortality rates, are more likely to be incarcerated, be on public assistance, get pregnant, bear a second child, and/or give birth to a low-birth-weight infant than those who graduate (Fine, 1991; Luttrell, 2002; Freudenberg & Ruglis, 2006; Reichman, 2005). In fact, 38 percent of teen women who left school prior to graduation had a subsequent pregnancy and birth while still a teen, compared to 11 percent of young women who did not (Kaufman, Alt, & Chapman, 2004; Manlove, 1998). This pattern is even more dramatic for young women with disabilities. The National Longitudinal Transition Study (2005) reported that learning disabled students who drop out of high school are five times more likely to bear a child within two years than those who graduate (p. 5). The correlation of drop out and teen pregnancy is particularly high for young women with mental retardation. Academic failure and leaving school prior to graduation are strong predictors of early pregnancy (Rousso, 2001).

Across diverse groups of teens, every year of education has economic, health, and reproductive benefits. Young adults who graduate from college are far more likely to vote and pay taxes, and are three times less likely to have an "unintended" pregnancy than those who drop out of high school (Finer & Henshaw, 2006). High dropout rates are costly for individuals, families, communities, and the fabric of our nation; they are most deeply etched into the backs of students attending under-funded schools, living in poverty, and facing racism. While 70 percent of all U.S. students graduate from high school with a regular diploma, this is true for only 51.6 percent of Blacks, 55.6 percent of Latinos, and 47.4 percent of Native Americans ("Diplomas count," 2006). This single policy move of high stakes testing, enacted presumably in an effort to leave no child behind, bears significant economic, criminal justice, and reproductive consequences (see Lipman, 2005; Orfield et al., 2004).

Unequal Placement in Juvenile Detention Facilities

In the very same communities where drop out rates are rising we see another public policy avalanche: the aggressive criminalization and incarceration of juveniles. Within a political economy hostile to non-college graduates, these two policy initiatives tragically short circuit the developmental possibilities for poor and working class youth of color (Richie, 1996; U.S. Department of Justice, 1999, p. 2).

The 1999 Census of Juveniles in Corrections showed a 43 percent increase in youth involved with the criminal justice system since 1991 (Sickmund, 2004, p. 4). This increase is accounted for by young people who are disproportionately minority, under-educated, and female. While Black juveniles constitute 15 percent of the U.S. population aged ten to seventeen, they account for 45 percent of delinquency cases involving detention, 40 percent of those placed in residential placement, and 46 percent of cases judicially waived to criminal court (Hsia, Bridges, & McHale, 2004). From 60 to 80 percent of juveniles and young adults in prison have neither a high school diploma nor a G.E.D. (see Fine et al., 2001).

Analyzing these data over time reveals a significant rise in arrest rates for teen women. From 1980 to 2002, female juveniles arrested for aggravated assault rose by 99 percent (compared to a 14 percent increase for boys); 258 percent for simple assault (compared to a 99 percent increase for boys); 125 percent for a weapons charge (compared to a 7 percent increase for boys); and 42 percent for drug offenses (Office of Juvenile Justice and Delinquency Prevention [OJJDP], 2004; Sickmund, 2004). Once in the system, racial disparities within gender accumulate: a full 70 percent of cases involving White girls but only 30 percent involving Black girls are dismissed (Poe-Yamagata & Jones, 2000), with Black girls far more likely to be waived into adult facilities (Bloom, Park, & Covington, 2001; Schoen et al., 1997). Girls constitute 60 percent of those teens arrested as runaways. They are far more likely than boys to be subsequently placed in care or detained for minor offenses, public disturbances, truancy, and status offences; almost three times as likely to be detained for parole and probation violations, and yet far less likely to recidivate based on a new crime (Miller & White, 2004; Schaffner, 2002, 2004).

Since the 1980s, criminal detention for young women has come to represent our national response to racialized and classed educational inequities (Kozol, 2005), family abuse, adolescent mental health, and drug problems (Richie, 1996, 2000, 2001). Just over 61 percent of young women in juvenile facilities report having a history of physical abuse, and 54.3 percent have experienced sexual abuse (American Correctional Association, 1990; see also, Brown, Miller, & Maguin, 1999; Brown & Taverner, 2001; Chesney-Lind & Okamoto, 2001; Simkins, Hirsch, & Horvat, 2003; Simkins & Katz, 2002). As a form of social control on girls, and disproportionately on Black and Latino girls, juvenile detention fails to remedy the original problems and serves instead to criminalize and diminish the educational, economic, and health outcomes of young women.

Roberts (1997) has documented a long history of reproductive racism, juxtaposing the innocence of White childhood with the guilt of Black childhood. "The powerful Western images of childhood innocence do not seem to benefit Black children. Black children are born guilty. The new bio-underclass constitutes nothing but a menace to society—criminals, crack heads, and welfare cheats waiting to happen" (p. 21). Roberts argues that presumptions of guilt linger in the bodies of poor youth of color. For evidence of this sentiment, we need look no further than former Secretary of Education William Bennett (1993), author of *The Book of Virtues*, who commented recently on the radio:

> If you wanted to reduce crime . . . if that were your sole purpose, you could abort every Black baby in this country and your crime rate would go down. This would be an impossible, ridiculous and morally reprehensible thing to do . . . but the crime rate would go down.
>
> (CNN, 2005)

Symbolic violence (Bourdieu & Passeron, 1977) combines with structural and intimate violence to escort young Black (and Latina, Native, poor, and working class) women out of their schools and homes, toward the streets, and into juvenile facilities. The absence of educational, health, sexual, and reproductive resources before they enter (and once they are in) these facilities only makes it more likely that they will return, next time perhaps infected with a sexually transmitted disease, perhaps with a baby who will, in all likelihood, have to be put in foster care.

Adolescent sexual well-being sits within a broad politic of homeland insecurity: high-stakes testing, aggressive incarceration of youth of color, and the evaporation of medical benefits for millions (Starr, 2004). Private acts are never wholly private; intimate choices are always profoundly social. In the midst of these parallel public policies, the press for abstinence-only education reveals just how far, and for whom, social policies can harm and then punish private lives. In this contentious political context, the campaign for abstinence in schools and communities may seem trivial, an ideological nuisance, but at its core it is a further violation of human rights and a betrayal of our next generation, which is desperately in need of knowledge, conversation, and resources to negotiate the delicious and treacherous terrain of sexuality in the twenty-first century.

Abstinence Only Until Marriage

A Brief History

Understanding the policy contexts in which young women try to carve out meaningful lives, we turn now to a brief history of the abstinence only until marriage (AOUM) movement to expose yet another layer of public life with which young people must contend as they stitch together sexual lives.

The 1981 passage of the Adolescent Family Life Act marked the first federal law expressly funding sex education "to promote self-discipline and other prudent approaches" (Adolescent Family Life Act, 42 U.S.C. § 300z [1982 & Supp. III 1985], as cited in Kelly, 2005). In 1996, with the Congressional passage of the Personal Responsibility and Work Opportunity Reconciliation Act, AOUM education funds gained an additional funding source through the approval of Title V of the Social Security Act. Under Title V, the U.S. Department of Health and Human Services (DHHS) allocates $50 million annually in federal funds to the states. Since 1982, when funding was first earmarked for AOUM education, over one billion dollars has been spent through federally sponsored programs (including AFLA, Title V, and CBAE; *Sexuality Information and Education Council of the U.S. [SIECUS]*, 2004c). For the 2007 budget, President Bush advocated for and was granted $204 million in AOUM funding and, according to the U.S. Office of Management and Budget (2006), the federal budget "supports increasing funding for abstinence-only education programs to $270 million by 2009."

Virtually all of the growth in funding since 2001 has come from the Community Based Abstinence Education (CBAE) program (Santelli et al., 2006a; SIECUS, 2004c). CBAE funding is typically granted to community and local organizations, but states are eligible to apply, and many states use this funding stream to bolster their existing AOUM school programming that rely on federal Title V monies (SIECUS, 2004a). Programs funded under CBAE are explicitly restricted from providing young people information about contraception or safer-sex practices—this includes organizations that might use nonfederal funds to do so (Santelli et al., 2006a; see SIECUS, 2004a, for description of federal AOUM funding streams). In early 2006, the U.S. DHHS issued a request for proposals, anticipating spending $24 million on approximately fifty programs at an average of $425,000 for five years (U.S. Department of Health and Human Services [U.S. DHHS], 2006). Faith-based organizations were encouraged to apply.

All federally funded abstinence programming must adhere to the following series of principles, called "A to H." According to Section 510(b) of Title V of the Social Security Act (U.S. DHHS, 2003, p. 14), the term "abstinence education" means an educational or motivational program that

a. has the exclusive purpose of teaching the social, psychological, and health gains to be realized by abstaining from sexuality activity;
b. teaches abstinence from sexual activity outside marriage as the expected standard for all school-age children;
c. teaches that abstinence from sexual activity is the only certain way to avoid out-of-wedlock pregnancy, sexually transmitted diseases, and other associated health problems;
d. teaches that a mutually faithful monogamous relationship in the context of marriage is the expected standard of sexual activity;
e. teaches that sexual activity outside marriage is likely to have harmful psychological and physical effects;
f. teaches that bearing children out-of-wedlock is likely to have harmful consequences for the child, the child's parents, and society;
g. teaches young people how to reject sexual advances and how alcohol and drug use increase vulnerability to sexual advances;
h. teaches the importance of attaining self-sufficiency before engaging in sexual activity.

The eight central tenets of AOUM education impose a strict set of criteria on educators who are looking to educate young people about their sexuality. The "A to H" points are designed to discourage teenage sexual behavior and, ultimately, to reduce rates of teenage pregnancy and sexually transmitted diseases. At the same time, however, they also introduce ideological intrusions that are not merely about reducing sexual behavior, but also instruct young people to adopt very specific normative relationships to their sexuality. There is, notably, the "expected standard" that sexual activity occurs only within the context of marriage, a move that places not only teenage sexual behavior but the sexual choices made by people of all ages and all sexual orientations outside the limits of appropriate behavior. Furthermore, the eight central tenets of AOUM suggest a direct and (im)moral route from nonmarital sex to disease and social problems. Insisting that young people be instructed that "sexual activity outside of the context of marriage is likely to have harmful psychological and physical effects" and that "bearing children out of wedlock is likely to have harmful consequences for the child, the child's parents, and society" does not lodge sexuality education in a foundation of information and support for a healthy adult sexuality. Instead, it lodges sexuality education in fear and shame, firmly burying discussions of desire and pleasure.

The promise of federal dollars often pushes the schools and communities in impoverished areas into accepting these curricular restrictions in order to fill funding gaps. Students who are most in need of education and health care—poor urban and rural students—are thereby the most likely to be mis-educated through these curricula (see SIECUS, 2004a for state-level data on the distribution of AOUM funds). The distribution of AOUM curricula favors communities with high levels of teen sexual activity and teen pregnancy and, importantly, imposes religious and moralizing curricula more strongly on youth who have already been sexual and who most need information about how to avoid pregnancy and sexually transmitted diseases. These are the very communities already plagued by increased drop out/push out rates and juvenile incarceration. For example, in 2006, Massachusetts governor Mitt Romney's administration shifted federal AOUM funding from an emphasis on media campaigns to classroom programming that was specifically aimed at students ages twelve to fourteen in schools in Black and Hispanic communities throughout the state (Helman, 2005). This example reflects the trend toward State-sponsored distribution of religious fundamentalism in communities where state policies threaten educational and health outcomes for youth.

Marriage Legislation and Promotion

In addition to the federal monies devoted to AOUM programming, other relevant policy shifts have focused state energies and funding on encouraging men and women to marry if they have a child together. The 1996 Personal Responsibility and Work Opportunity Reconciliation Act established a financial incentive to reduce out-of-wedlock childbearing. It authorized $100 million in annual bonus payments to the five states that achieved the largest reduction in out-of-wedlock births among welfare and non-welfare teens and adults and reduced abortion rates among that population to less than the 1995 level in their state. In 2000, four new measures were created for the High-Performance Bonus, including a measure of family formation and stability. The marriage bonus is awarded to a state that can demonstrate an increase in the percent of children who reside in married couple families (Ooms, 2001).

According to the U.S. Department of Health and Human Services (2003), federal funding is meant to enable states to "focus on those groups most likely to bear children out-of-wedlock" (p. 14). Federal policies that promote marriage through interventions like the Personal Responsibility Act punish poor single mothers for not choosing to marry. This type of monetary and institutional enforcement of marriage negates their right to form intimate associations on their own terms (Mink, 2002; see also Levin-Epstein, 2005, for a discussion of marriage promotion policies). By targeting communities with high rates of children born outside marriage, federal marriage policies not only dictate who receives funding, but also place blame for societal woes on those individuals who are most denied enabling conditions for thick desire (see Karney, 2006, for discussion of attitudes about premarital sex among various groups).

What Is Taught in Schools: The Chill

To give some sense of how federal policies move into classrooms, it is useful to note for example, that New York State received $9,346,650 in federal funding for AOUM programs in 2004 (SIECUS, 2004a). While this is just one state, it exemplifies the national trend at both the federal and state levels to allocate funds for exclusively teaching abstinence-only to young people. It is estimated that 33 percent of all public schools now offer AOUM curricula (Planned Parenthood, 2005a). Since 1988, the number of sex education teachers who teach AOUM has grown tenfold, from 2 percent to 23 percent (Santelli et al., 2006a). As abstinence funding and education spread across the nation, the net of teen activities considered in violation of abstinence regulations stretches as well. In 2006, the federal guidelines for funding AOUM education underwent substantial revisions (see U.S. DHHS, 2006). The new guidelines explicitly endorse the U.S. government's support of abstinence. However, instead of encouraging adolescents to avoid sexual intercourse, the new definition casts a much wider net of proscribed activity: "Sexual activity refers to any type of genital contact or sexual stimulation between two persons including, but not limited to sexual intercourse" (pg. 5). Apparently in responding to criticism that abstinence previously had not been adequately defined (Santelli, Ott, Lyon, Rogers, & Summers, 2006b), this updated version creeps into the territory of all things "stimulating." This broad definition of abstinence removes any possibility for sex education curricula to mention how teens might engage in non-intercourse behaviors, even in an effort to remain "technically" abstinent.

These guidelines set up an impenetrable wall between youth and adults, reducing the likelihood that conversations will occur between young people and educators, health-care practitioners, and youth workers. The loss of these conversations puts young people's health at risk (see Fine & McClelland, in press, for discussion of how a lack of supportive adults affects adolescent reproductive freedoms). Again, we can see that the costs of constricted talk are quite severe for some groups of youth. Consider, for instance, Harilyn Rousso's (2001) finding that young women with physical and sensory disabilities are far less likely than their nondisabled peers to receive any kind of sexuality education and are far less likely to talk to their mothers, friends, or teachers about sexuality and reproduction. Combine this with the finding that disabled youth are almost twice as likely to report sexual abuse as are nondisabled children, with estimates that 39 percent to 68 percent of disabled girls and 16 percent to 30 percent of disabled boys are sexually abused before the age of eighteen (Rousso, 2001). Looking at the cumulative effect of parents who are particularly overprotective of young women with disabilities and special education programs that are typically under-equipped to take up sexuality education, we see that

> the consequences of inadequate sex education may be more severe for students with disabilities who have less access to informal sources of sex education such as peers, casual observation, written materials, and the media.
>
> (p. 38)

With disproportionate histories of abuse and little in the way of home or peer guidance around sexuality, students with disabilities make clear the need for more information although they receive less.

The 2006 federal guidelines regarding AOUM education funding cut off any discussion of how teenagers might develop healthy sexual behaviors for present or future relations. In the name of protection, the teenage sexual body has been sent underground with little information and almost no protection.

A Closer Look at the AOUM Content

In 2004, a systematic review of the abstinence-only curricula was commissioned by U.S. Representative Henry A. Waxman, ranking minority member of the Committee on Government Reform (2004), to evaluate the scientific and medical accuracy of thirteen of the most commonly used of these curricula. Reviewers found that two-thirds of the programs contained basic scientific errors (e.g., warnings that sweat and tears are risk factors for HIV transmission; see p. 219); relied on curricula that distorted information about the effectiveness of contraceptives (e.g., claims that condoms fail approximately 31 percent of the time; see p. 91); blurred religion and science (e.g., presenting as fact that life begins with conception; see p. 23); and reinforced stereotypes about girls and boys as scientific facts (see Brown, 2005).

Many curricula for AOUM programs link nonmarital sex with disease and possible death (see Kempner, 2001, for further discussion). Researchers have noted that these curricula often include scare tactics such as the video titled *No Second Chance*, in which a student asks a school nurse, "What if I want to have sex before I get married?" to which the nurse replies, "Well, I guess you'll just have to be prepared to die" (as cited in Levine, 2002). The national AOUM program Family Accountability Communicating Teen Sexuality (FACTS) instructs students that "there is no such thing as 'safe' or 'safer' premarital sex. There are always risks associated with it, even dangerous, life-threatening ones" (Fuller, McLaughlin, & Asato, 2000, as cited in Kempner, 2001, p. 19). Young people are being instructed continually to believe sexual activity is dangerous to their health.

The Press for Heterosexual Marriage

In the AOUM curriculum, not only is teen sexuality always bad, but heterosexual marriage is always good. In fact, marriage is presented as the only context for safe sex. The pro-marriage language of the AOUM curricula was strengthened in 2005, when programs once designed to discourage "*premature* sexual activity" and to encourage "abstinence" were redesigned to discourage "*premarital* sexuality activity" and encourage "abstinence only until marriage" decisions (Dailard, 2005). The framework for AOUM funding demanded that abstinence curricula define marriage as "a legal union between one man and one woman as a husband and wife, and the word 'spouse' refers only to a person of the opposite sex" (U.S. DHHS, 2006). In addition, funding restrictions required that having sex within marriage be presented as the only way for teens to avoid getting STDs and related health problems. Heterosexual marriage was presented as the answer to safe sex even as same-sex marriage was fought by many of these same abstinence advocates.

In this push for heterosexual marriage, we see a telling instance where the chance to educate teens about the potential dangers inherent in early (and any) marriage gets lost. The little research that exists on teen marriage has found that young marriages often have high levels of violence. Young mothers who marry are more likely to have a second child shortly after the first than those who do not, and teenage women who marry and then divorce have worse economic outcomes than teenage mothers who never marry (Seiler, 2002). Teen marriage significantly reduces the likelihood that a woman, especially a young mother, will return to school. A study of African American teenage mothers found that 56.4 percent returned to school within six months of having a baby if they did not marry, compared to 14.9 percent of those who did marry (Seiler, 2002). In AOUM instruction, these problems of heterosexual marriage are sidelined, the risks of contracting sexually transmitted diseases, including HIV within marriage, are ignored, and the issue of same-sex marriage is silenced.

Homophobic Violence and Harassment

For lesbian, gay, bisexual, transgender, queer, and questioning (LGBTQQ) youth, the AOUM curriculum not only fails to address their very real educational needs and concerns, but, more significantly, it colludes in the homophobic harassment already present in public school settings. More than one-third of LGBTQQ students report hearing homophobic remarks from teachers or school staff, and nearly 40 percent indicated that no one intervened when homophobic comments were made (Brown & Taverner, 2001). While this kind of harassment certainly preceded the introduction of AOUM curriculum (and AOUM doesn't cause this kind of harassment), the curriculum fails to challenge the heterosexual normativity in schools. Because the abstinence model is predicated on waiting until marriage for sexual expression, and marriage is not an option for these youth, the AOUM curricula not only denies LGBTQQ youth legitimacy, but it also asks them to hold aside (and silence) significant pieces of their identities in order to participate in the *moral* community of students (Opotow, 1990) who deserve sexuality education. This is particularly true when the conversation turns to misinformation about same sex practices, the presumed failures of condoms, and the much repeated claim that sex inside marriage is the only form of healthy sexuality.

A Question of Accountability: Educational and Health Consequences

Given the fact that the aim of AOUM policies is to protect the health of young people, one would assume that this instruction would be joined by an ambitious evaluation of the health and sexual outcomes of those youth who are exposed to AOUM curricula. This has not been the case. Instead, concern for adolescent health has been set aside and replaced with a simple evaluation focus on whether or not students endorse beliefs about abstinence and marriage. This can be seen in the guidelines produced by the U.S. DHHS. In 2005, programs that received federal AOUM funding were required to include demonstrable outcomes, such as a reduction in STDs and pregnancies among adolescents (U.S. DHHS, 2005). By 2006, the U.S. DHHS stepped away from using behavioral and health outcomes as a way of judging a program's success and replaced these with the requirement that programs demonstrate that they "create an environment within communities that supports teen decisions to postpone sexual activity until marriage" (U.S. DHHS, 2006). This shift is important as it marks a distinct lack of accountability for education and health behaviors on the part of AOUM programs (see McClelland & Fine, in press, for further discussion of the evaluation of AOUM programs).

That these programs are no longer required to improve young people's health in order to be considered successful is worrisome in light of empirical data about how abstinence education actually affects adolescent (and later, adult) sexual health. These include how long youth remain abstinent, what choices they make when they decide to have sex (including sexual behaviors and contraception use), and the long-term consequences of learning exclusively about the dangers of sexuality.

One way to measure the question of what choices young people make when they decide to engage in sexual activity is to measure STD rates after young people take "virginity pledges," an exercise that exists within some AOUM programming. Bearman and Brückner (2001) found that "pledgers" typically delayed their first heterosexual intercourse an average of eighteen months later than nonpledgers. In a follow up, however, Brückner and Bearman (2005) found that 88 percent of the middle and high school students who had sworn to abstain did, in fact, have premarital sex—and, importantly, often had unprotected sex. Pledgers were 30 percent less likely than nonpledgers to use contraception once they became sexually active, and also less likely to use condoms and seek medical testing and treatment.

Other adolescent health researchers have studied the "user-failure" rates for abstinence; in other words, the numbers of youth who promise to be abstinent until marriage, but in fact do have premarital sex. By studying teens that abstained for a period of time, Haignere and her colleagues (Haignere, Gold, & McDanel, 1999) found that abstinence education had a user-failure rate between 26 percent and 86 percent. This rate is higher than the condom user-failure rate, which is between 12 percent and 70 percent. These findings highlight the temporary quality of virginity pledges and the nonsustainability of intentions to abstain. This finding would not be cause for alarm, except for the fact that these youth who have been instructed using AOUM curricula and who have pledged to remain abstinent are becoming sexually active with no information about how to do so successfully and safely.

These young people are being educated to mistrust condoms and contraception, to feel shame about their premarital sexuality, and to remain silent about their own sexual development. By insisting that a pledge of abstinence is enough to guarantee subsequent sexual decision-making—by condemning premarital sexual activity, contraception, and condoms—educators, policymakers, and families are placing young people at risk. Even adults who want young people to remain abstinent until marriage recognize that it is unlikely they will do so. For example, in a recent national poll, of those parents who stated that they thought girls should wait until they are married to have sexual intercourse, 89 percent said they thought that most girls will have intercourse earlier [than that] (National Public Radio et al., 2004, p. 19).

Research has repeatedly shown that students in comprehensive sexuality education classes—those that teach various strategies to reduce pregnancy and disease, and to pursue healthy sexual development—do not engage in sexual activity more often or earlier than those in AOUM classes; they do, however, use contraception and practice safer sex more consistently when they become sexually active (Kirby, 1997, 1999, 2000, 2001). Kirby (1997) found that "the weight of the evidence indicates that these abstinence programs do not delay the onset of intercourse" (p. 25). Kirby also found evidence that programs that address both abstinence and contraception resulted in better sexual health outcomes for young people.

As a significant adjunct to comprehensive sexuality education, there has been an important school-based health center (SBHC) movement underway since the 1970s that has positively affected adolescent health outcomes. From 1988 to 2001, the number of SBHCs has grown from 120 to almost 1,400 in forty-five states. SBHCs aim to provide comprehensive, accessible, and quality health services in culturally sensitive contexts for youth lacking insurance and/or access to medical care. Reduction in the misuse of emergency rooms and an increase in medical and mental health services have been well documented (Schlitt et al., 2000). A quasi-experimental evaluation of condom distribution programs found that school-based access to condoms does not increase rates of sexual activity, but does heighten the use of condoms by students who are sexually active (Guttmacher et al., 1997). Moving educational and health resources to schools does not appear to increase sexual activity, but does contribute to a sense of sexual responsibility.

It is clear that sexuality education must serve all youth with information, support, and resources that allow young people to make informed decisions about their bodies and their sexual health. As you will see from what follows, young people desperately need and deserve far more information, sustained and safe conversations with peers and adults, and more sophisticated critical skills to negotiate the pleasures and dangers of their quite active—and often uninformed—sexual lives.

Sex in Numbers

We turn now to the epidemiological data on teen sexuality, trying to understand how sexual and reproductive health outcomes distribute across youth. But first, a warning about how to read sexuality statistics. The statistics that follow tell us something about what young women are doing with their bodies, but they do not tell us about sexual subjectivities (Horne & Zimmer-Gembeck, 2006)—that is, if these activities were wanted or enjoyed by these young women. When we see high rates of STDs and pregnancy among teenage girls, *whom* do we imagine (Wyatt, 1994)? Do we imagine a girl we consider a desirous subject, a victim, or both? And what of her access to a quality high school, college, health insurance, a place to call home? Have we learned whether her school district was adequately financed with certified educators? Was she able to attend a high school that offered her a sense of cultural belonging, a chance to enquire, a strong curriculum of advanced mathematics, science, writing, and informed college counseling? Has her community received more resources devoted to policing and criminal justice than education, more military recruiters than sexuality educators? Was she taught about masturbation, LGBTQQ sexualities, abortion, pleasures, and dangers? Could she confide in anyone about her stepfather, uncle, disability-related caretaker, or mother abusing her? How many sick or dependent relatives was she caring for because the state didn't?

In the end, what do statistics on sexual behaviors tell us about the presence, absence, or subversion of enabling conditions for thick desire? More importantly, what do they obscure about a girl's access to health-care, insurance, the quality of her school, or the wide variation of sexual histories within her racial group? As we turn now to the seductive details of teen sexuality—rates, types, and consequences—we hope that the reader will ingest these numbers critically, always imagining real young women developing real bodies at vibrant intersections, affected by distant international and federal policies, local institutions, communities, complex intimate relations, and itchy, unformed, and still developing desires for a better tomorrow.

Teen Heterosexual Sex and Pregnancy

The Centers for Disease Control and Prevention (CDC) report that more than one-third of fifteen to seventeen year-old males (36 percent) and females (39 percent) have had vaginal intercourse; almost one-third have given oral sex (28 percent of males and 30 percent of females); and more have received oral sex (40 percent of males and 38 percent of females). Adolescent females are about twice as likely to report same-sex sexual contact as males (Mosher, Chandra, and Jones, 2005, p. 9).

International comparisons are critical because they allow us to consider what these numbers reveal about adolescent life in the U.S. Teens in the U.S., on average, begin having heterosexual intercourse at 17.4 years of age; the average age is 18 in France, 17.4 in Germany, and 17.7 in the Netherlands (Feijoo, 2001). Yet young women in the United States are *nine* times more likely to become pregnant than young women in the Netherlands. The U.S. teen pregnancy rate is almost twice that of Great Britain, four times that of France and Germany, and more than ten times that of Japan. National context matters—intimately.

Despite these international comparisons, by 2000, U.S. teen pregnancy rates had dropped to an all-time low for White, Black, and Latina women (CDC, 2005; National Campaign to Prevent Teen Pregnancy, 2005). Teen birth rates also dipped from 89.1 for every 1,000 young women in 1960 to 41.7 in 2003; 18.3 teen births per 1,000 for Asian Americans; 28.5 for Whites; 68.3 for African Americans and 83.4 for Latinas (Kaiser Family Foundation, 2004). Santelli and colleagues (2004) have suggested that the recent decline in pregnancy rates can be attributed to a combination of decreased sexual experience and increased use of contraception.

Condoms, Contraception, and Abortions

Using our 1988 benchmark to track progress, we can see that young women's risk of pregnancy has declined by 21 percent from 1991 to 2003, largely because of improvements in contraceptive use among White and Black teens. In 1991, in a sample of surveyed high school girls, 22 percent used the pill only and 35 percent condoms only. By 2003, 14 percent used the pill and 49.3 percent used condoms (Santelli, Morrow, Anderson, & Lindberg, 2006c).

What looks like good "individual" news seems a bit more complex "relationally" in our ethnographic conversations with diverse groups of high school students in the New York metropolitan area, where we got an earful about the gendered politics of negotiating condom use:

Michelle: So, for those young people who do engage in sex, do they use condoms?
Young men: Sometimes, yeah, not always.
John: Really, I like it raw.
Michelle: Do you worry about pregnancy or disease, HIV?
Kevin: Yeah, we got SuperAids in this town.
Lawrence: Nah. . . Magic Johnson's OK—if you got money you don't get AIDS, they got medicines, but for the rest of us, it will kill you in three weeks.
Michelle: Can young women carry condoms and pull them out as needed?
Marcos: No way, I wouldn't trust the girls to do that. They would stick pin holes in the condoms.
Two young women: *(appearing shocked)* Why would we do that?
Steve: To get the baby, then you think he'll stick around.
Michelle (after viewing a bag that the teacher displayed of more than twelve forms of contraception, all to be used by/inserted into young women): So what if there were a pill for young men. You can have an erection, ejaculation, just no sperm. Would you use it?
(Half of the students say "yes" while the other half give other responses.)
Young men: No way, I'm not putting anything into my body. Could kill you. Could make you sterile.
(Two young women roll their eyes.)

In this conversation we heard young men who were worried about HIV/AIDS but who still preferred to have sex "raw." In another setting, we heard that many "guys where I live" considered "protection is for soft n—gers." We heard young men and women agree that with access to enough money, a person could avoid dying from AIDS, like Magic Johnson, but those without money were likely to die within three weeks. In another school, the young men worried aloud that their partners may not be clean: "I make sure she carries Baby Wipes and uses them before we get involved." Young men were clear that they didn't want to insert chemicals or barriers into their bodies, as young women rolled their eyes and detailed the labors, risks, and burdens of assuming sole responsibility for protection.

Across our conversations with youth, however, young men and women agreed that conversations like these were desperately needed in order to dispel the myths and layers of misinformation that are already part of how young people learn about sex. Referring to the 2003 opinion issued by the Kansas attorney general (see Kline & Nohe, 2003), we asked, "What would happen if adults—teachers, nurses, counselors—had to report to the State, any sexual activity by anyone sixteen or younger?" After the gasps, one young woman gathered up the courage to whisper, "I couldn't live in a world like that. Who could I talk to? I would have no one." The critical role of caring and supportive adults, for conversation and information, was repeated across schools, across gender, across race, ethnic, and class lines.

In one of the schools, our conversation turned to the question of abortion. The discomfort in the room was palpable; we could feel the strong resistance to acknowledging abortions in this low-income, predominantly African American and immigrant community.

Michelle: So, do people in this school talk about how you can get an abortion if you need or want one?
Teacher: Not so much in this community. They don't really get abortions here.
Students: We don't talk about it that much.

Most of the young people (and their educators) knew much about the pregnancies and births in their community, but not about the abortions. We sent them the local statistics to contradict the shared sense that "they don't really get abortions here." When we look at the rates at which young women are terminating their pregnancies (Table 1), it is clear that there is a silent yet highly regular process that young women are engaging in—privately, maybe with a friend or relative, perhaps with shame, perhaps with a sense of relief, but likely imagining themselves to be the only young women in their community having an abortion. Table 1 summarizes the data on teen women's pregnancies, births, and abortions. The statistics come from the Guttmacher Institute, one of the most reliable resources for health indicators for young women.

Table 1 also displays the differential rates by which White, African American, and Latina teens experience pregnancy and abortions. For example, Latinas get pregnant close to three times the rate of White girls, and African Americans at rates more than three times those of Whites. Table 2 is more nuanced in terms of use of birth control. It shows that while all three groups rely on condoms more than other methods, White girls are the group most likely to use the pill (which requires access to a health-care provider, a prescription, and some way to pay for contraception), African Americans are more likely to use condoms, and Latinas are more likely to rely on withdrawal or no method at all.

Table 1 U.S. Teen Pregnancies, Births, and Abortions Per Thousand Women Ages Fifteen to Seventeen

	Pregnancies	*Births*	*Abortions*
White	31.0	19.4	11.6
African-American	103.2	62.6	40.6
Latina	88.2	66.3	21.9

Source: Frost, Jones, Woog, Singh, & Darroch (2001, p. 7)

Table 2 Percent of Birth Control Methods by Race, Sexually Active Women Ages Fifteen to Seventeen

	Pill	*Condoms*	*Withdrawal*	*No Method*
White	18.9	44.0	11.5	12.3
African-American	5.6	57.3	10.6	12.1
Latina	4.9	45.2	16.3	19.8

Source: Santelli et al. (2004)

Simply put, the consequences of unequal knowledge about, access to, and use of affordable contraception, health care, and education are unevenly distributed by race, ethnicity, and class. While these data are too often framed as good or bad, moral or immoral, reproductive choices or cultural differences, we highlight the fact that choices are never made independent of history and politics, both outside and within communities. Laws concerning young women are some of the most powerful (and relatively unseen) structural factors that exist. Looking at these data that enumerate the consequences of sexual activity, it is clear that young women of different ethnicities in the same nation, state, or even community may be living within very different social, political, and economic structures; it is not simply a matter of their making individual choices about their sexuality. The gendered, raced, and classed burden of teen sexuality is neither natural nor merely a question of biological destiny or culture. A full 82 percent of pregnant teens ages fifteen to nineteen reported that their pregnancies were unintended (Finer & Henshaw, 2006). And yet teen women are viewed as being at fault, or at least responsible, by laws governing reproductive choices. This is even more startling given the prevalence of sexual coercion that young women experience. Twelve percent of girls in grades 9–12 reported having been physically forced to have sexual intercourse when they didn't want to (CDC, 2004, p. 39).

The issues of unintended pregnancies and coercion are of course not a problem for teens alone. The Guttmacher Institute reported that 49 percent of all pregnancies in the United States are unintended. Unintended pregnancy rates are substantially higher for women ages fifteen to forty who are living in poverty (58 percent unintended birth rate for the poorest women compared to 11 percent for the wealthiest) and those without a high school diploma (Finer & Henshaw, 2006). Of all unintended pregnancies, 48 percent end in abortion, as do 40 percent of unintended teen pregnancies.

Once young women find that they are pregnant, the state does little to enable her to make a "choice." For indigent women, the absence of Medicaid funding for abortion severely limits their access to abortion. As of 2006, only seventeen states use public funds to pay for abortions for some poor women; four states cover the costs voluntarily, and thirteen do so under a court order (Guttmacher Institute, 2006a). Only about 13 percent of all abortions in the United States are paid for with public funds (Henshaw and Finer, 2003).

For women under eighteen, an additional obstacle to reproductive choice concerns parental consent for notification of their abortion, which has become nearly standard. As of June 2006, thirty-four states require some parental involvement in a minor's decision to have an abortion (Guttmacher Institute, 2006b). Placing serious constraints on minors seeking an abortion, these laws are designed to place familial and institutional barriers between young women and their right to a legal abortion. While the laws are regularly described as providing support to minors, in practice they only make the option of abortion less available and usually delay the procedure, putting girls' health (and potentially the fetus' health) increasingly at risk (Bitler & Zavodny, 2001; Ellertson, 1997; Griffin-Carlson & Schwanenflugel, 1998; Henshaw & Kost, 1992). To be clear, it is important to know that most young women already involve their mothers or a close relative in decisions about sexuality and reproduction. Even in states with no parental involvement laws, 66 percent of the young women report that they voluntarily involved at least one parent (Henshaw & Kost, 1992). Other estimates are that from 50 to 61 percent of all pregnant teens involved their parent(s) in their decisionmaking to remain pregnant or abort (Guttmacher Institute, 2005). For younger teens, age fourteen and below, 90 percent indicated that at least one parent knew, and that most parents supported their daughters' actions (Henshaw & Kost, 1992). African American teens are in fact more likely to discuss sexuality with their mothers than other groups; even those who sought judicial bypasses did so after telling their mothers about the pregnancy (Blum, Resnick, & Stark, 1990).

While involving families may be a form of support for some young women, there is a group of young women who do not have a parent or guardian to whom they can safely turn; many of these women have been sexually or physically abused at home (Schoen, Davis, & Collins, 1997). Henshaw and Kost (1992) found that of those who can't or won't tell parents about their pregnancy, 30 percent indicated they had experienced violence in their families, 30 percent feared more violence, and 18 percent feared pressure to leave home. Parental consent laws limit teen access to reproductive conversation and choice for precisely the young women most in need of supportive adults. And so too does geography.

Eighty-six percent of counties in the United States have no abortion provider, which means that 32 percent of women of reproductive age must travel out of their home county to obtain a legal abortion (Henshaw, 1998). While many factors undoubtedly influence a young woman's decision to have an abortion, variations in access, legal limitations, and Medicaid funding dramatically affect state rates of teenage pregnancies that end in abortion, ranging from 60 percent in New Jersey and 50 percent in New York, Massachusetts, and Washington, D.C., to the dramatically lower rates of 13 percent in Utah and Kentucky (Alan Guttmacher Institute, 2004).

If young women are expected to carry the burden of unwanted pregnancies or of abortion, why do they have to do so silently? According to the CDC report on "abortion surveillance" (Strauss et al., 2004), which reflects state-reported abortions only and does not include procedures performed by private physicians, 18 to 19 percent of all abortions are performed on teens. This is not a trivial matter that should be ignored in sexuality curricula.

Sexually Transmitted Diseases

Evidence on venereal disease is also critical to a full understanding of the consequences of sexual behavior. In 2003, women age 13 to 19 accounted for half of the HIV cases in their age group. This number demonstrates the growing impact of HIV on women, and young women in particular. As a comparison, women age 20 to 24 accounted for only 37 percent of the HIV cases in their age group. Again, these numbers fall unevenly across ethnicities and most seriously affect women of color (for further discussion of HIV/AIDS data, see Kates & Carbaugh, 2006). Girls age ten to fourteen and fifteen to nineteen are more than six times more likely than their male peers to contract chlamydia, and those age fifteen to nineteen are almost three times more likely to contract gonorrhea, with the incidence of both conditions substantially higher for African American teens age fifteen to nineteen than Whites (Advocates for Youth, 2005). Young people most at risk for pregnancy and sexually transmitted diseases are also more likely to experience medical indigence, rely on publicly funded health care, and report lower rates of physician contact (Fuligni & Hardway, 2004; Office of Women's Health, 1998).

The wretched combination of rising drop out/push out rates, expansion of the criminal justice system into communities of color, and uninsured health care (Nussbaum, 2003) bodes poorly for young women's sexual health and reproductive freedom. As these young people are denied access to "enabling contexts"[3] for social and sexual development, we see, as Brown (2003) has described, how neo-liberalism operates such that "the state leads and controls subjects without being responsible for them." With the introduction and growth of funding and programming for AOUM curriculum in schools, many of these young women are taught to just say no—with no attention to the contexts in which they live, the institutions they inhabit, or the families in which they reside. When we read these statistics on sexual outcomes, we may blame (or pity) the young women themselves, either way camouflaging their (dis)abling contexts (Geronimus & Thompson, 2004). The cleverness of neo-liberalism lies in the strategic maneuver by which "subjects are controlled through their freedom . . . and neo-liberalism's moralization of the consequences of this freedom" (Brown, 2003). The state slips gently off the hook as the young woman stands alone, holding the consequences and the blame.

Taking Positions

Two groups have distinct reactions to the material about teen sexuality and health outcomes presented above. Both agree that young people should be healthy and free of sexual coercion and that abstinence is a reasonable choice for adolescents. Both are anxious to reduce unintended pregnancies, STD rates, and all forms of sexual coercion. Where these two groups part ways lies in how they view young people's, and especially young women's, sexuality. One group—which includes most parents and educators (Dailard, 2001; Darroch, Landry, & Singh, 2000)—is committed to providing detailed information to young people about their bodies in order to encourage young women and men to make decisions that are driven by their own experience of sexual agency, desire, and an informed consideration of sexual dangers.

In fact, a national poll undertaken by National Public Radio, the Kaiser Family Foundation, and the John F. Kennedy School of Government (2004) found that 90 percent of parents of junior and senior high school students believed it was very or somewhat important to have sexuality education as part of the school curriculum, while 7 percent of parents did not want sex education to be taught in school at all (p. 5). Sixty-seven percent of parents of junior and senior high school students stated that federal government funding "should be used to fund more comprehensive sex education programs that include information on how to obtain and use condoms and other contraceptives," instead of funding programs that have "abstaining from sexual activity" as their only purpose (p. 7). People in this group argue that healthy sex lives are developed through comprehensive sexuality education, trusting relationships with adults and peers, and sufficient emotional and medical support in the form of contraceptives, access to abortion and child care, and protection against STDs. Healthy sexual lives require serious education and ongoing conversation about how to pursue pleasure, understand consequences, and protect against violence and coercion (see Tolman, 2002, 2006).

Another small but quite powerful and well-funded group sees the statistics on teen pregnancy, abortions, and STDs as evidence that sexual activity is inherently dangerous for young people. They believe that sexual health can be found only in adult, married, heterosexual relations. Against teen sexuality and for heterosexual marriage, this second group advocates for teaching sexual abstinence only until marriage. They maintain that if sexual behaviors are successfully halted—not discouraged—the dangerous aspects of sexuality will be avoided. As one abstinence advocate declared recently, "We don't tell them to smoke a little! We say 'Don't smoke!' " (Golden, 2005). Assumptions about the need to control sexual urges undergird this line of argument, as you can hear in the words of Claude Allen, the former assistant to the president for domestic policy, who justified the need for

AOUM education as an obligation of the state: "If the choice is between self-restraint and self-destruction, the government can't be neutral. The government has to speak. We need to encourage self-denial, self-restraint. They need to control their impulses" (Allen, 2005).

AOUM advocates argue that by teaching abstinence-only, social problems such as teen pregnancy, STDs, or family violence will be avoided because it is the act of sex that is seen as inherently injurious—both to the teen and to the social fabric (see Santelli et al., 2006a, for discussion). If all sexual activity were to cease prior to marriage, AOUM advocates argue those problems that stem from sex (STDs, psychological problems, etc.) would also cease. AOUM advocates argue that media, readily available contraception, and poor parenting encourage teen sex and that these circumstances cause family violence, incarceration, etc.

Disagreeing with this argument is not simply a matter of believing in different moral or family values. It is a matter of seeing the causal chain of events in a wholly different order and insisting that the implications for the policies be more fully considered. Instead of holding the act of unmarried teen sex—defined largely by the penetration of a woman by a man—responsible for causing social and psychological problems, advocates for comprehensive sexuality education place the genesis of social problems not in the act of teen sex, but in the uneven social contexts in which teens develop and sex occurs (see Advocates for Youth, n.d., for further discussion of the differences between comprehensive sexuality education and AOUM education).

Those advocating comprehensive sexuality education maintain that AOUM education requires an unrealistic expectation of sexual behavior; enforces gender rules that inhibit development of female desire; targets Black and Latino youth and reaffirms stereotypes about race and sexual promiscuity; takes money away from other public services, such as schools and clinics; inscribes and enforces a heterosexual marriage model (bringing in the family values rhetoric through the back door); sidelines LGBTQQ teens; censors teachers; undermines school-based conversations about sexuality and health clinic resources; and, ultimately, places blame for social ills on young women who are asked to bear the brunt of all subsequent social problems if they engage in sexual activity, either because they wanted to, were forced to, or felt compelled to for reasons other than their own sexual desire.

Indeed, abstinence models fail to provide adequate information for youth in general, but some are protected from the fall out. A thick desire framework begs the question of gender-, race-, and class-based consequences of AOUM, revealing that those who have insurance, confidential relationships with medical practitioners, and strong community supports may be able to endure the abstinence models and compensate if things go awry. For those lacking in material and social resources, these outcomes become publicly known and, as a result, only certain groups of youth become publicly known as "failures." Thus, abstinence models place a disparate burden on girls, youth of poverty, teens with disabilities, sexually abused young people, and LGBTQQ youth.

Sexual Surveillance: Implications for Educators

Despite the press for AOUM, many teachers and health-care practitioners continue to teach the comprehensive sexuality curriculum, always with an opt-out provision for families that choose for their child to not participate in the class (for a discussion of the history of comprehensive sex education, see Goldfarb, 2005; Kirby, Alter, & Scales, 1979). Those who persist in teaching comprehensive sexuality education, however, report experiencing a "chill" on what they can and can't teach, despite parents' desire for comprehensive sexuality education. For example, more than nine in ten teachers believe that students should be taught about contraception, but one in four are prohibited from doing so (Darroch et al., 2000). At the school level, there are policies in place that enforce these silences within the classroom; 35 percent of public school districts require that abstinence be taught as the only option for unmarried people, and either prohibit the discussion of contraception or limit discussion to its ineffectiveness (Guttmacher Institute, 2002). There are regional differences as well: Over half of the districts in the South have an abstinence-only policy, compared with 20 percent of districts in the Northeast (Landry, Kaeser, & Richards, 1999). This chill of censorship in the classroom extends to the specifics of what is taught. For example, only 21 percent of junior high teachers reported that they taught the correct use of condoms in 2000; only 14 percent of U.S. school districts discuss abortion and sexual orientation (Kelly, 2005). Some school boards, like those in Franklin County, North Carolina, have ordered that chapters be sliced out of health books if they reveal more than what the abstinence-only state law permits (Kelly, 2005). In Lynchburg, Virginia, school board members refused to approve a high school science text until the illustration of a vagina was covered or cut out (Texas Citizens for Science, 2004).

Beyond censorship, a kind of sexual vigilantism has been unleashed by public school administrators, particularly in low-income schools and poorer communities. In 2004, the principal of a New York City middle school accused a group of thirteen and fourteen year-old girls of skipping school to attend a hooky party. The girls (not the boys) were suspended until they would submit to HIV, STD, and pregnancy tests, and the young women were required to turn the results over to the school (see New York Civil Liberties Union [NYCLU], 2004). In California, a high school principal called the mother of a young lesbian student to tell her about a series of "run-ins [the student had] with the principal . . . over her hugging, kissing, and holding hands with her girlfriend." The student was not only counseled to leave her school, but her privacy rights were administratively violated as the principal "outed" her to her mother (Lewin, 2005, p. A21). The Gay-Straight Alliance Network has sued a number of districts, on behalf of students' right to safety and freedom from harassment.

There have been reports in other communities of significant pressure on young women seeking contraceptive and pregnancy services to tell their parents about receiving these services. This pressure to inform parents about students' reproductive choices has also extended to those who help the young women, even when a young woman has refused to include her parents in her health care and reproductive decisions. The Reproductive Rights Project at the NYCLU (2004) gathered a number of complaints from social workers, guidance counselors, and school personnel who were being required by administrators to contact parents about a student's pregnancy. Students' right to privacy and educators' professionalism are being undermined.

Dissent and Resistance

Historically and today, there have been waves of resistance against the AOUM movement, launched by human rights groups, educators, feminists, lawyers, parents, youth, and healthcare providers throughout the nation and globally. Despite a relentless and well-funded assault from the Right, over the past twenty years we have seen waves of a broad-based commitment to deep and comprehensive sexuality education by youth, educators, community members, and feminist lawyers. Thus, we consider this political moment to be an "interval," as Brown would argue,

> a way of . . . telling the present's story differently. . . . Many of us experience the present as terribly closed. I think the opening that we have to cultivate is a kind of affective and intellectual [and we would add *pedagogical*] opening to political possibility that would help us read the present differently.
>
> (Brown, Colegate, Dalton, Rayner, & Thill, 2006, p. 37)

To see ourselves in an interval, rather than a political stranglehold, we offer a few images here of what these acts of resistance look like and the impact they are having. In the spirit of democratic access to education and public health, many are arguing for comprehensive sexuality education. In response to the well-funded and chilling campaign launched at the state and federal levels, in 2005, Representative Barbara Lee (D-CA) and Senator Frank Lautenberg (D-NJ) introduced the Responsible Education about Life (REAL) Act in Congress (H.R. 2553 and S. 368). Formerly known as the Family Life Education Act, REAL would allocate $206 million federal dollars to states for medically accurate, age appropriate, comprehensive sex education in schools, including information about both abstinence and contraception (U.S. House of Representatives, 2005; U.S. Senate, 2005). This legislation spells out a few important differences that would be included in federal sexuality education requirements: for example, these curricula must "not teach or promote religion," stress "the value of abstinence while not ignoring those young people who have had or are having sexual intercourse," and insist that information "about the health benefits and side effects of all contraceptives and barrier methods" be provided to young people (Boonstra, 2002, p. 3). To date, over one hundred organizations, including the American Medical Association, American Public Health Association, and the American Psychological Association, have come out publicly in support of this legislation (p. 2).

Moving from the national to the local level, we see communities organizing to resist the pressures and strings that come with federal funding. In Texas, scientists and educators have joined to create a website (http://www.texscience.org) where they can post informed protests against textbook censorship in their communities. The Colorado Council of Black Nurses returned $16,000 in abstinence-only funding because they believed that the dollars interfered with responsible health education (Planned Parenthood, 2005b). Due to the organization and protests of adolescent health advocates and a group of high school students, the Board of Education of the Chicago Public Schools voted in 2006 to require its schools to offer comprehensive sexual education in grades 6–12, including information about contraception (Mendell, 2006). Finally, youth and youth advocates have created a series of websites for and by young women and young men, addressing questions of pleasure, danger, sexuality, and health for young people seeking information.[4]

Finally, there are a number of comprehensive sexuality education resources available for use in and outside of school settings (Bay-Cheng, 2003; Brick & Taverner, 2003; Brown & Taverner, 2001; Mabray & LaBauve, 2002; Mackler, 1999; SIECUS, 1998, 2004b; Taverner & Montfort, 2005). Community-based organizations, the Unitarian Church, and other groups serving youth have stepped up to the challenge and offered courses, seminars, and workshops on healthy sexual development (Unitarian Universalist Association, 2006a, 2006b). Rich sex education curricula remain available through SIECUS (2004b, 2005). In the face of a massive policy onslaught, there are seeds of resistance and mobilization in every sector of the nation.

It is important to note, further, that there is a curious history within the White House and the executive branch of strategic advocacy for pleasure and sexual health. Interestingly, over time, a number of African American members of the cabinet have challenged the abstinence-only campaign. Each was summarily punished thereafter. For example, in 1994 Surgeon General Jocelyn Elders commented that, "[masturbation] is an alternative. Now teenagers know that they're not going to go blind, they're not going to go crazy. Hair's not going to grow on their hands. We need to just stop lying to our children" (Elders & Chanoff, 1996, p. 14). Elders was forced to resign her position soon thereafter. Years later, official talk against condoms was challenged when Colin Powell advocated for condom use on MTV and his comments were quickly retracted by the White House (Purdum, 2002). Echoes of these challenges were heard when Surgeon General David Satcher, also African American, ran into trouble with the Bush administration after publishing his extremely bold and comprehensive report, *The Surgeon General's Call to Action to Promote Sexual Health and Responsible Sexual Behavior* in 2001. The administration quickly distanced itself from the report.

Medical and public health organizations, educators, and government bodies are mobilizing across disciplines and professions to resist the trend toward censoring educators, suppressing science, and silencing young people's sexuality. In 2006, John Santelli and colleagues from Indiana University, George Washington University, the American College of Preventive Medicine, Mt. Sinai School of Medicine, and Human Rights Watch reviewed current federal policy and evaluations of abstinence education, including approaches to program evaluation (Santelli et al., 2006a). In their report, they framed the exclusive reliance on AOUM programs and policies as a human rights violation that

> appears to be undermining more comprehensive sexuality education and other government-sponsored programs. We believe that abstinence-only education programs, as defined by federal funding requirements, are morally problematic, by withholding information and promoting questionable and inaccurate opinions. Abstinence-only programs threaten fundamental human rights to health, information, and life.
>
> (p. 1)

Conclusion: Theorizing Thick Desire and Fantasizing Critical Sexuality Research

Thick desire places sexual activity for all people, regardless of age or gender, within a larger context of social and interpersonal structures that enable a person to engage in the political act of wanting. Wanting can be interpreted in any number of ways, but it necessarily positions a young person as feeling entitled to that which comes in the future. It includes wanting to have unhindered access to structural and institutional supports, such as education, health care, and protection from coercion. With wanting securely in place and thick desire as an organizing frame, it is possible to theorize about young women's sexual and reproductive freedoms not merely from a perspective of minimal loss, but from a perspective that sees them as entitled to desire in all of its forms; entitled to publicly funded enabling conditions across racial, ethnic, class, sexual, geographic, and disability lines.

This essay has interrogated two kinds of desire: the unbridled desire of the state and the religious Right to re-create public education in their own image, and the thick desire of youth to create lives filled with educational and economic opportunity, free of violence, and protected by knowledge of and resources for sexual and reproductive health. We have documented the geographic spread of the religious Right in terms of policy incursions into many of the "private" sites where young women and men seek assistance, resources, and support for healthy sexual development. And yet, more importantly, we want to leave the reader with a sense of how we might educate and research with the recognition that young minds, souls, and bodies *desire* broadly, in areas that are economic, educational, health-minded, and, indeed, sexual. That is, young people carry thick desires for a tomorrow of meaning, hoping for rich enabling contexts where they can feed these desires in conversation with peers and elders (Chavkin & Chesler, 2005; Diamond, 2000; Levine, 2002; Lipman, 2005; Rose, 2003; Santelli et al., 2006a; Tolman, 2006).

To elaborate on a vision for critical sexuality studies, we argue that youth sexuality be theorized about and studied inside a stew of desires for opportunity, community, pleasure, and protection from coercion and danger. Adolescents need good schools, health-care, and freedom from violence (structural, institutional, family, and intimate) in order to develop healthy sexual subjectivities. Given this frame, sexuality and reproductive struggles must be linked to fights for equity in school finance, civil/queer/feminist/disability rights, health care, school and prison reform, affirmative action, and access to higher education. Economic, social, and corporeal struggles must be linked through the bodies, imaginations, dreams, and demands of young women and men.

Further, comprehensive sexuality education and youth development must help young women and men navigate across the dialectics of danger and pleasure. Risk cannot be severed from pleasure. They are braided, parasitic, nested inside one another. An exclusive focus on risk not only alienates, but also distorts the complexity of human relations and sexual desire. Therefore, it is naïve to educate for pleasure without attending to risk; but more perverse to imagine that teaching only about risk will transform human behavior.

We have also tried to advance, theoretically and methodologically, a framework for thinking through how state policy penetrates bodies at embodied intersections. We have tried to model how gender intersects with race, ethnicity, class, sexuality, disability, geography, and institutional biographies, and to document the disparate impact state laws, public policy, and educational practice have on differentially situated young bodies. Whether researchers rely on hierarchical linear modeling or sophisticated narrative analysis or both; whether we study youth in privileged communities or in long-neglected neighborhoods; whether we conduct life histories or delve into the statistical archives of seemingly unrelated public institutions like schools, prisons, and health clinics—this article is a call to recognize, study, and document how broadly and deeply state policies slice into the seemingly private lives of very differently situated youth, most particularly those with no private safety net.

Turning now to the question of sexuality education, we repeat the words of young people we met from various communities, ranging from those in extreme poverty to those more middle class. When we asked, "What do you need in the way of sexuality education?" young people were clear: "More conversations like this, where we're asked what we think, what we want to know." And yet, according to one of the speakers at the Network for Family Life Education conference in New Jersey in 2005, such pedagogical contexts are unfortunately growing extinct: "In sexuality education, talk is becoming a four-letter word" (Rodriguez, 2005).

We are tempted, of course, to argue that the era of comprehensive sexuality education is over in public schools, that educators and youth workers would be better off creating safe spaces for this kind of talk outside of schools, in local community centers, churches, synagogues, mosques, LGBTQQ community centers, health clinics, the YMCA, and the Girl Scouts. While we believe all of this should happen, we are more sure than ever that we cannot abandon schools—the place where all children and youth are required to attend, and attend together; the place where intellectual, political, and personal possibilities are inspired; where democracy, inquiry, and human rights are supposed to be fundamental.

Turning then to schools, we recognize that young people spend 30 percent of their day in classrooms; they are one of the most important places for talk, learning, and building skills. The evidence gathered here and confirmed in conversations with educators and youth, suggests that schools and school-based health clinics (see Geierstanger & Amaral, 2005) are precisely the places where young people can be engaged in safe, critical talk about bodies, sexuality, relationships, violence, contraception, abortion, disability rights, LGBTQQ struggles, gender equality, and sexuality as a human right. In language arts, history, science, math, and in courses on the visual and performing arts, young people can learn the skills of critical inquiry and democratic engagement, the power of dissent and action on one's own behalf and for a larger political project. Young people need to develop skills for finding key pieces of information and resources; building trusting relations with peers, adults, and professionals; speaking publicly for social justice (see Rogow & Haberland, 2005).

Though we take the question of *skill* seriously, we are concerned that the definition of skill within AOUM policies has atrophied. Skills to express political and sexual agency are just the kind of muscles young people need to develop in order to undertake critical analysis, trusting conversation, and help-seeking, and finally, to negotiate risk and pursue pleasure. Having skills merely to say no does not help young people make tough decisions, but instead simply drains decision-making from them and places them in the hands of more powerful others—the state, the media, advertisements, a partner, abuser, or predator. The echoes of lost skill reverberate for a lifetime in the student—we see the loss when a student is afraid to speak to a teacher or health practitioner or pharmacist about contraception or an STD; when he feels afraid to use a condom because he learned it will probably fail; when she finds herself not knowing that she is entitled to pleasure or to resist aggression; when she or he tries to find an identity as a lesbian, gay man, or transgendered person in a sea of "silver rings" (see Alwyn, 2004 for description of the "Silver Ring Thing," a Christian abstinence group which encourages the use of silver rings to signify young people's pledges of abstinence until marriage) and promises of sexual bliss in the confines of marriage.

One young woman in a high school focus group explained to us, "I do not want to have sex until I am married. So I don't really need these conversations." Later in the group she spoke again, a bit less calm and detached, "But, when I am ready, where will I learn about contraception or even about what might feel good for me? Where will I learn about sexuality after high school? Will it magically happen when I marry?" Denied sexuality education, she will likely lack the knowledge, sense of entitlement, and skills to find out in the future what she doesn't know but needs to.

It is important to note that sexuality education is the *only* academic content area that is taught as if the knowledge gained in the classroom is meant to exclusively serve the young person's present situation. In an editorial in the journal *Contraception,* a group of physicians and medical researchers wrote, "School is intended to prepare young people with skills they need for the future. There is no controversy about good math education even though few teens have a compelling need for algebra in their daily lives" (Stewart, Shields, & Hwang, 2004, p. 345). A national commitment to abstinence only until marriage casts a wide net that will ensnare us all; it creeps into our imaginations and into our beds by prescribing a constricted form of sexual expression for young people, as well as adults, leaving clouds of shame, guilt, ignorance, and silence where knowledge, skills, and safe conversation should grow.

We introduced the concept of thick desire in this discussion, and we hope to make it a lens through which to conceptualize and evaluate youth-based education and social policies across public institutions. Instead of merely documenting risk and loss, we call for policies and research that recognize how macro-structures, public institutions, practices, and relationships affect "personal decisions," particularly for those without private supports and buffers. Thick desire is offered as a framework to move us away from mourning the "missing discourse of desire" and on to demanding more publicly subsidized educational, social, legal, economic, and health care supports for young people as they develop complex social and sexual biographies in adolescence and beyond. It is a way of evaluating policies, both local and global. Thick desire is meant to be a tool to see what is missing *and* to say what needs to be in place.

In this spirit, we invite educators, youth organizers, policy analysts, community activists, YMCA directors, health clinic professionals, and youth to create a surge of information and conversation about sexuality, power, and justice. Researchers, educators, community workers, lawyers, youth, and progressive clergy can come together to demand that thick desire be the benchmark—a progressive form of accountability—for measuring the extent to which a community supports full youth development (for an example, see the Forum for Youth Investment, http://www.forumforyouthinvestment.org). Campaigns and research projects for healthy youth development can be launched in schools, community centers, libraries, clinics, afterschool programs, and on the Internet, in which conversations about desire, danger, power, and bodies can be reclaimed as spaces for doubt, giggles, honesty, negotiation, struggle, pleasure, pain, and information. Young people are dying for good conversation about sexuality, and are dying without it.

Notes

1. Structural violence is a form of violence that occurs when individuals are systematically denied rights, resources, and opportunities. Institutionalized racism, sexism, and ageism are examples of structural violence.
2. We use LGBTQQ throughout this article to acknowledge the wide range of sexualities that do not necessarily manifest in same-sex sexual activities, but in how people choose to identify themselves. There is a 'queer' identity that is separate from lesbian, gay, bi, and transgender. Queer is a self-defined identity that encompasses people that may not be engaging in same-sex sexual activity, but may nevertheless be marginalized for nontraditional gender or sexual choices, and people who challenge the very use of sexual/gender/sexuality categories.
3. Correa and Petchesky (1994) define enabling contexts as those conditions and resources that aid in supporting individuals and groups.
4. For examples of websites, see the following: http://www.Scarleteen.com, "sex positive sex education"; http://www.sxetc.org, "a web site by teens for teens"; http://www.MySistahs.org, "by and for young women of color"; and http://gURL.com, "an online community and content site for teenage girls."

References

Advocates for Youth. (2005). *Youth of color: At disproportionate risk of negative sexual health outcomes.* Washington, DC: Author.

Advocates for Youth. (n.d.). *Sex education programs: Definitions and point by point comparison.* Washington, DC: Author. Retrieved July 31, 2006, from http://www.advocatesforyouth.org/rrr/definitions.htm

Alan Guttmacher Institute. (2004). *U.S. teen pregnancy rates.* New York: Author.

Albert, B., Lippman, L., Franzetta, K., Ikramullah, E., Dombrowski Keith, J., Shwalb, R., et al. (2005). *Freeze frame: A snapshot of American teens.* Washington, DC: National Campaign to Prevent Teen Pregnancy.

Allen, C. (2005, November 3). *Untitled.* Paper presented at the conference of the Department of Health and Human Services, Strengthening Abstinence Education Programs through Scientific Evaluation. Baltimore, MD, USA.

Allensworth, E. (2004). Graduation and drop-out rates after implementation of high stakes testing in Chicago's elementary schools. In G. Orfield (Ed.), *Dropouts in America: Confronting the graduation rate crisis* (pp. 157–205). Cambridge, MA: Harvard Education Press.

Alwyn, R. (2004, January 22). The power of the ring thing. *BBC News.* Retrieved August 9, 2006, from http://news.bbc.co.uk/2/hi/programmes/this_world/3419693.stm

American Correctional Association. (1990). *The female offender: What does the future hold?* Washington, DC: St. Mary's Press.

Amrein, A., & Berliner, D. (2002). *The impact of high-stakes tests on student academic performance: An analysis of NAEP results in states with high-stakes tests and ACT, SAT, and AP test results in states with high school graduation exams.* Tempe: Arizona State University. Retrieved February 2, 2006, from http://www.asu.edu/educ/epsl/EPRU/documents/EPSL-0211-126-EPRU-exec.pdf

Anyon, J. (2005). *Radical possibilities: Public policy, urban education, and a new social movement.* New York: Routledge.

Appadurai, A. (2001, July). New logics of violence. *Seminar,* #503. Retrieved July 31, 2006, from http://www.india-seminar.com/2001/503/503%20arjun%20apadurai.htm

Appadurai, A. (2004). The capacity to aspire: Culture and the terms of recognition. In V. Rao & M. Walton (Eds.), *Culture and public action* (pp. 59–84). New York: Russell Sage Foundation.

Bay-Cheng, L. (2003). The trouble of teen sex: The construction of adolescent sexuality through school based sexuality education. *Sex Education, 3*(1), 61–74.

Bearman, P., & Brückner, H. (2001). Promising the future: Virginity pledges and the transition to first intercourse. *American Journal of Sociology, 206,* 859–912.

Bennett, W. (1993). *The book of virtues: A treasury of great moral stories.* New York: Simon & Schuster.

Bitler, M., & Zavodny, M. (2001). The effect of abortion restrictions on the timing of abortions. *Journal of Health Economics, 20,* 1011–1032.

Bloom, B., Park, R., & Covington, S. (2001, November). *Effective responsive interventions in juvenile justice.* Paper presented at the annual meeting of American Society of Criminology, Atlanta.

Blum, R. W., Resnick, M. D., & Stark, T. (1990). Factors associated with the use of court bypass by minors to obtain abortions. *Family Planning Perspectives, 22,* 158–160.

Boonstra, H., (2002). Legislators craft alternative vision of sex education to counter abstinence-only drive. *The Guttmacher Report on Public Policy, 5* (2), 1–3. Retrieved July 31, 2006, from http://www.guttmacher.org/pubs/tgr/05/2/gr050201.pdf

Bourdieu, P., & Passeron, J. (1977). *Reproduction in education, society and culture.* London: Sage.

Brick, P., & Taverner, B. (2003). *Educating about abortion.* New York: Planned Parenthood.

Brown, A., Miller, B., & Maguin, E. (1999). Prevalence and severity of lifetime physical and sexual victimization among incarcerated women. *International Journal of Law and Psychiatry, 22,* 301–322.

Brown, S. (2005, September 21). *Untitled.* Letter to Commissioner Peter McWalters, Rhode Island Department of Education. Retrieved July 31, 2006, from http://www.riaclu.org/documents/sex_ed_letter.pdf

Brown, S., & Taverner, W. (2001). *Streetwise to sex-wise: Sexuality education for high risk youth.* New York: Planned Parenthood.

Brown, W. (2003). Neoliberalism and the end of liberal democracy. *Theory and Event, 7* (1). Retrieved July 31, 2006, from http://muse.jhu.edu/journals/theory_and_event/v007/7.1brown.html

Brown, W., Colegate, C., Dalton, J., Rayner, T., & Thill, C. (2006, January). Learning to love again: An interview with Wendy Brown. *Contretemps, 6,* 41. Retrieved July 31, 2006, from http://www.usyd.edu.au/contretemps/6January2006/brown.pdf

Brückner, H., & Bearman, P. (2005). After the promise: The STD consequences of adolescent virginity pledges. *Journal of Adolescent Health, 36,* 271–278. Retrieved July 31, 2006, from http://www.iserp.columbia.edu/people/downloads/after_the_promise.pdf

Burd, S. (2006, June 9). Working class students feel the pinch. *Chronicle of Higher Education,* p. 3.

Burns, A., & Torre, M. E. (2005). Revolutionary sexualities. *Feminism & Psychology, 15*(10), 21–26.

Centers for Disease Control and Prevention. (2004, May 21). Youth risk behavior surveillance—United States, 2003. *Morbidity and Mortality Weekly Report, 53,* SS-02. Retrieved July 31, 2006, from www.cdc.gov/mmwr/PDF/SS/SS5302.pdf

Center for Disease Control. (2005, February 4). QuickStats: Pregnancy, birth and abortion rates for teenagers aged 15–17—United States, 1976–2003, *Morbidity and Mortality Weekly Report, 54* (4), p. 100. Retrieved July 31, 2006, from http://www.cdc.gov/mmwr/preview/mmwrhtml/mm5404a6.htm

Chavkin, W., & Chesler, E. (2005). *Where human rights begin.* New Brunswick: Rutgers University Press.

Chesney-Lind, M., & Okamoto, S. (2001). Gender matters: Patterns in girls' delinquency and gender responsive programming. *Journal of Forensic Psychology Practice, 1*(3), 1–28.

CNN. (2005, September 30). *Bennett under fire for remarks on blacks, crime.* CNN.com Retrieved July 31, 2006, from http://www.cnn.com/2005/POLITICS/09/30/bennett.comments/

Committee on Government Reform, Minority Staff, Special Investigations Division. (2004, December). *The content of federally-funded abstinence-only education programs.* Washington, DC: United States House of Representatives. Retrieved July 31, 2006, from http://reform.democrats.house.gov/Documents/20041201102153-50247.pdf

Correa, S. (1994). *Population and reproductive rights.* London: Zed Books.

Correa, S., & Petchesky, R. (1994). Reproductive and sexual rights: A feminist perspective. In G. Sen, A. Germain, & L. Chen (Eds.), *Population policy reconsidered: Health, empowerment and rights (Harvard series on population and international health* (pp. 107–126). Cambridge, MA: Harvard University Press.

Crenshaw, K. (1995). Mapping the margins: Intersectionality, identity politics, and violence against women of colour. In K. Crenshaw, N. Gotanda, G. Peller, & K. Thomas (Eds.), *Critical race theory: The key writings that formed the movement* (pp. 357–383). New York: New Press.

Dailard, C. (2001, October). Community health centers and family planning: What we know. *The Guttmacher Report on Public Policy, 4* (5). Retrieved July 31, 2006, from http://www.guttmacher.org/pubs/tgr/04/5/gr040506.html

Dailard, C. (2005, November). Administration tightens rules for abstinence education grants. *The Guttmacher Report, 8* (4), p. 13. Retrieved July 31, 2006, from http://www.guttmacher.org/pubs/tgr/08/4/gr080413.html

Darroch, J. E., Landry, D. J., & Singh, S. (2000). Changing emphases in sexuality education in U.S. public secondary schools, 1988–1999, *Family Planning Perspectives, 32,* 204–211 & 265.

Diamond, L. (2000). Sexual identity, attractions and behavior among young sexual-minority women over a 2-year period. *Developmental Psychology, 36,* 241–250.

Diplomas count: An essential guide to graduation policy and rates. (2006, June 22). *Education Week,* pp. 25, 41S.

Douglas, M. (1966). *Purity and danger: An analysis of conceptions of pollution and taboo.* New York: Routledge.

Elders, J., & Chanoff, D. (1996). *From sharecropper's daughter to surgeon general.* New York: William Morrow.

Ellertson, C. (1997). Mandatory parental involvement in minors' abortions: Effects of the laws in Minnesota, Missouri, and Indiana. *American Journal of Public Health, 87,* 1367–1374.

Feijoo, A. N. (2001). *Adolescent sexual health in Europe and the U.S.: Why the difference?* (2nd ed.). Washington, DC: Advocates for Youth.

Fine, M. (1988). Sexuality, schooling, and adolescent females: The missing discourse of desire. *Harvard Educational Review, 58*(1), 29–51.

Fine, M. (1991). *Framing dropouts.* Albany: State University of New York Press.

Fine, M., Torre, M. E., Boudin, K., Bowen, I., Clark, J., Hylton, D., et al. (2001). *Changing minds: The impact of college in a maximum security prison.* Montclair, NJ: Ronald Ridgeway, Inc. Retrieved July 31, 2006, from http://www.changingminds.ws

Fine, M., Burns, A., Payne, Y., & Torre, M. (2004). Civics lessons: The color and class of betrayal. *Teachers College Record, 106,* 2193–2223.

Fine, M., & McClelland, S. I. (in press). The politics of teen women's desire: Public policy and the adolescent female body. *Emory Law Journal.*

Finer, L. B. & Henshaw, S. K. (2006, June). Disparities in rates of unintended pregnancy in the United States, 1994 and 2001. *Perspectives on Sexual and Reproductive Health, 38*(2), 90–96.

Foucault, M. (1979). *Discipline and punish: The birth of the prison.* New York: Vintage Books.

Foucault, M. (1988). *Politics, philosophy and culture.* London: Routledge.

Foucault, M. (1990). *The history of sexuality, vol. 1,* (Robert Hurley, Trans.) London: Penguin. (Original work published 1976)

Freudenberg, N., & Ruglis, J. (2006). *Redefining high school dropout as a public health issue: A call to action.* Manuscript submitted for publication.

Frost, J. K., Jones, R. K., Woog, V., Singh, S., & Darroch, J. E. (2001, November). *Teenage sexual and reproductive behavior in developed countries: Country report for the United States. Occasional Report No. 8.* New York: Alan Guttmacher Institute.

Fuligni, A. J., & Hardway, C. (2004, Summer). Preparing diverse adolescents for the transition to adulthood. *Children of immigrant families, 14,* (2), 99–119. Retrieved August 11, 2006, from http://www.futureofchildren.org/usr_doc/fulignihardway.pdf

Geierstanger, S. P., & Amaral, G. (2005). *School-based health centers and academic performance: What's the intersection? April 2004 Meeting Proceedings.* Washington, DC: National Assembly on School-Based Health-Care. Retrieved June 30, 2006, from http://www.nasbhc.org/EQ/Academic_Outcomes.pdf

Geronimus, A. T. (1997, Fall). Teen childbearing and personal responsibility: An alternative view. *Political Science Quarterly, 112* (3), 405–430.

Geronimus, A. T., & Thompson, J. P. (2004). To denigrate, ignore, or disrupt: The health impact of policy-induced breakdown of urban African American communities of support. *Du Bois Review, 1,*247–279.

Golden, A. (2005, November 3). *Introductory comments of strengthening abstinence education programs through scientific evaluation.* Presented at the conference of the Department of Health and Human Services. Baltimore.

Goldfarb, E. (2005). What is comprehensive sexuality education really all about? Perceptions of students enrolled in an undergraduate human sexuality course. *American Journal of Sexuality Education, 1*(1), 85–100.

Griffin-Carlson, M. S., & Schwanenflugel, P. J. (1998). Adolescent abortion and parental notification: Evidence for the importance of family functioning. *Journal of Child Psychology & Psychiatry & Allied Disciplines, 39,* 543–553.

Guttmacher Institute. (2002). *Sexuality education. Facts in brief.* New York: Author. Retrieved July 31, 2006, from http://www.guttmacher.org/pubs/fb_sex_ed02.pdf

Guttmacher Institute. (2005, May). *Facts on induced abortion in the United States.* New York: Author. Retrieved July 31, 2006, from http://www.agi-usa.org/pubs/fb_induced_abortion.html

Guttmacher Institute. (2006a, April). *State funding of abortion under Medicaid. State policies in brief.* New York: Author. Retrieved July 31, 2006, from http://www.guttmacher.org/statecenter/spibs/spib_SFAM.pdf

Guttmacher Institute. (2006b, June). *Parental involvement in minors' abortions. State policies in brief.* New York: Author. Retrieved July 31, 2006, from http://www.guttmacher.org/statecenter/spibs/spib_PIMA.pdf

Guttmacher, S., Lieberman, L., Ward, D., Freudenberg, N., Radosh, A., & Des Jarlais, D. (1997, September). Condom availability in New York City public high schools: Relationships to condom use and sexual behaviors. *American Journal of Public Health, 87,*1427–1433.

Haignere, C. S., Gold, R., & McDanel, H. J. (1999). Adolescent abstinence and condom use: Are we sure we are really teaching what is safe? *Health Education & Behavior, 26*(1), 43–54.

Haney, W. (2000). The myth of the Texas miracle in education. *Education Policy Archives, 8*(41), 1.

Harris, A. (2005). Discourses of desire as governmentality: Young women, sexuality and the significance of safe spaces. *Feminism and Psychology, 15,* 39–43.

Helman, S. (2005, December 21). State to push abstinence in schools. *The Boston Globe.* Retrieved July 31, 2006, from http://www.boston.com/news/local/articles/2005/12/21/state_to_push_abstinence_in_schools

Henshaw, S. K. (1998). Abortion incidence and services in the United States. *Family Planning Perspectives, 30,*263–270.

Henshaw, S. K., & Kost, K. (1992). Parental involvement in minors' abortion decisions. *Family Planning Perspectives, 24,* 5.

Henshaw, S. K., & Finer, L. B. (2003). The accessibility of abortion services in the United States, 2001. *Perspectives on Sexual and Reproductive Health, 35*(1), 16–24.

Horne, S., & Zimmer-Gembeck, M. J. (2006). The female sexual subjectivity inventory: Development and validation of a multidimensional inventory for late adolescents and emerging adults. *Psychology of Women Quarterly, 30,*125–138.

Hsia, H., Bridges, G. S., & McHale, R. (2004, September). *Disproportionate minority confinement: 2002 update.* Washington, D.C.: Office of Juvenile Justice and Delinquency Prevention, Department of Justice. Retrieved July 31, 2006, from http://www.ncjrs.gov/pdffiles1/ojjdp/201240.pdf

Impett, E., Schooler, D., & Tolman, D. (in press). To be seen and not heard: Femininity ideology and adolescent girls' sexual health. *Archives of Sexual Behavior.*

Jovchelovitch, S. (2001). Social representations, public life and social construction. In K. Deaux & G. Philogene (Eds.), *Representations of the Social* (pp. 165–182). London: Blackwell.

Kaiser Family Foundation (2004). *Kaiser state facts.* Menlo Park, CA: Author. Retrieved June 21, 2006, from http://www.statehealthfacts.kff.org/cgi-bin/healthfacts.cgi

Karney, B. (2006, January 28). *How lay theories about marriage differ according to income: Evidence from survey research.* Paper presented at the Annual Meeting for the Society for Personality and Social Psychology, Palm Springs, CA, USA.

Kates, J., & Carbaugh, A. (2006, February). *HIV/AIDS policy fact sheet.* Menlo Park, CA: Kaiser Family Foundation. Retrieved July 31, 2006, from http://www.kff.org/hivaids/upload/6092-03.pdf

Kaufman, P., Alt, M.N., & Chapman, C. (2004). *Dropout rates in the United States: 2001 (NCES 2005-046). U.S. Department of Education. National Center for Education Statistics.* Washington, DC: U.S. Government Printing Office.

Kelly, K. (2005, October 17). Just don't do it. *U.S. News and World Report,* pp. 44–51.

Kempner, M. E. (2001). *Toward a sexually healthy America: Abstinence only until marriage programs that try to keep our youth "scared chaste."* New York: Sexuality Information & Education Council of the United States.

Kirby, D., Alter, J., & Scales, P. (1979). *An analysis of U.S. sex education programs and evaluation methods.* Atlanta, GA: Center for Disease Control, Bureau of Health Education.

Kirby, D. (1997). *No easy answers: Research findings on programs to reduce teen pregnancy.* Washington, D.C.: The National Campaign to Prevent Teen Pregnancy.

Kirby, D. (1999). Sexuality and sex education at home and school. *Adolescent Medicine: State of the Art Reviews, 10,*195–209.

Kirby, D. (2000, July). *Effective approaches to reducing adolescent unprotected sex, pregnancy, and childbearing.* Washington DC: Report to the Surgeon General.

Kirby, D. (2001). *Emerging answers: Research findings on programs to reduce teen pregnancy.* Washington DC: National Campaign to Prevent Pregnancy.

Kline, P., & Nohe, C. (2003, June 18). *Kansas Attorney General opinion no. 2003-17, 2003 WL 21492493.* Letter to the Honorable Mark S. Gilstrap. Retrieved July 31, 2006, from http://www.kscourts.org/ksag/opinions/2003/2003-017.htm

Kozol, J. (2005). *The shame of the nation.* New York: Crowne.

Landry D. J., Kaeser, L., & Richards, C. L. (1999). Abstinence promotion and the provision of information about contraception in public school district sexuality education policies. *Family Planning Perspectives, 31,*280–286.

Levin-Epstein, J. (2005, March). *To have and to hold: Congressional vows on marriage and sex.* Washington, D.C.: Center for Law and Social Policy.

Levine, J. (2002). *Harmful to minors.* Minneapolis: University of Minnesota Press.

Lewin, T. (December 2, 2005). Openly gay student's lawsuit over privacy will proceed. *New York Times,* p. A21.

Lipman, P. (2005). Educational ethnography and the politics of globalization, war and resistance. *Anthropology and Education Quarterly, 36,*315–328.

Luker, K. (2006). *When sex goes to school: Warring views on sex – and sex education – since the sixties.* New York: W.W. Norton.

Luttrell, W. (2002). *Pregnant bodies, fertile minds.* New York: Routledge.

Mabray, D., & LaBauve, B. (2002). A multidimensional approach to sexual education. *Sex Education, 2*(1), 31–44.

Mackler, C. (1999, August/September). Sex ed: How do we score? *Ms. Magazine,* pp. 67–73.

Manlove, J. (1998). The influence of high school dropout and school disengagement on the risk of school age pregnancy. *Journal of Research on Adolescents, 8,* 187–220.

Maynard, R. A., Trenholm, C., Devaney, B., Johnson, A., Clark, M. A., Homrighausen, J., et al. (2005, June). *First-year impacts of four Title V, section 510 abstinence education programs.* Princeton, NJ: Mathematica Policy Research.

McClelland, S. I., & Fine, M. (in press). Embedded science: The production of consensus in evaluation of abstinence-only curricula. *Qualitative Inquiry.*

McNeil, L. (2005). Faking equity: High-stakes testing and the education of Latino youth. In A. Valenzuela (Ed.), *Leaving children behind: How "Texas style" accountability fails Latino youth* (pp. 57–112). Albany: State University of New York Press.

Mendell, D. (2006, April 27). Sex ed to cover birth control: Abstinence will be city classes' focus. *Chicago Tribune.* Retrieved April 27, 2006, from http://www.chicagotribune.com/news/local/chicago/chi-0604270023apr27,1,2262647.story

Miller, J., & White, N. (2004). Situational effects of gender inequality of girls' participation in violence. In C. Alder & A. Worrall (Eds.), *Girls' Violence* (pp. 167–187). Albany: State University of New York Press.

Mink, G. (2002). From welfare to wedlock: Marriage promotion and poor mothers' inequality. *The Good Society, 11*(3), 68–73.

Mosher, W. D., Chandra, A., & Jones, J. (2005, September 15). *Sexual behavior and selected health measures: Men and women 15–44 years of age, United States, 2002. Advance Data From Vital and Health Statistics.* Atlanta: Centers for Disease Control and Prevention. Retrieved July 31, 2006, from http://www.cdc.gov/nchs/data/ad/ad362.pdf

Mouffe, C. (1979). *Gramsci and Marxist theory.* London: Routledge.

National Campaign to Prevent Teen Pregnancy. (2005, April 13). *Declining teen birth rates contribute to improvements in child well-being in all states.* Washington, DC: Author. Retrieved March 8, 2006, from http://www.teenpregnancy.org/whycare/pdf/National_Press_Release.pdf

National Longitudinal Transition Study. (2005, November). *Facts from NLTS2: High school completion by youths with disabilities.* Washington, DC: U.S. Department of Education. Retrieved July 31, 2006, from http://ies.ed.gov/ncser/pubs/doc/NLTS2_selfdeterm_11_23_05.pdf

National Public Radio, Kaiser Family Foundation, & Harvard University (2004, January). *Sex education in America: General public/parents survey.* Menlo Park, CA: Kaiser Family Foundation. Retrieved July 31, 2006, from http://www.npr.org/programs/morning/features/2004/jan/kaiserpoll/publicfinal.pdf

New York Civil Liberties Union. (2004). *The reproductive rights project: 2004 in review.* New York: Author. Retrieved July 31, 2006, from http://www.nyclu.org/rrp_annualreport_2004.html

Nussbaum, M. (2003). Women's education: A global challenge. *Signs: Journal of Women in Culture and Society, 29,*325–355.

Office of Juvenile Justice and Delinquency Prevention. (2004, September). Victims of violent juvenile crime. *Juvenile Justice Bulletin.* Retrieved July 31, 2006, from http://www.ncjrs.gov/html/ojjdp/201628/contents.html

Office of Women's Health. (1998). *Women of color health data book: Adolescents to seniors.* Bethesda, MD: National Institutes of Health.

Ooms, T. (2001, May 22). *Testimony of Theodora Ooms.* House Committee on Ways and Means, Subcommittee on Human Resources. Washington, DC. Retrieved March 8, 2006, from http://www.smartmarriages.com/ooms.testimony.html

Opotow, S. (1990). Moral exclusion and injustice. *Journal of Social Issues, 46* (1), 1–20.

Orfield, G., Losen, D., Wald, J., & Swanson, C. (2004, March 11) *Losing our future: How minority youth are being left behind by the graduation rate crisis.* Cambridge, MA: The Civil Rights Project at Harvard University, The Urban Institute, Advocates for Children of New York, The Civil Society Institute. Retrieved July 31, 2006, from http://www.civilrightsproject.harvard.edu/research/dropouts/LosingOurFuture.pdf

Petchesky, R. P. (2005). *Global prescriptions.* London: Zed Books.

Phillips, L. (2000). *Flirting with danger.* New York: New York University Press.

Planned Parenthood Federation of America, Inc. (2005a, January). *Abstinence-only "sex" education.* New York: Author. Retrieved March 8, 2006, from http://www.plannedparenthood.org/pp2/portal/medicalinfo/teensexualhealth/fact-abstinence-education.xml

Planned Parenthood Federation of America, Inc. (2005b). *The war on women: A pernicious web. A chronology of attacks on reproductive rights. Planned Parenthood report on the administration and congress.* New York: Author. Retrieved July 31, 2006, from http://www.plannedparenthood.org/pp2/portal/files/portal/medicalinfo/femalesexualhealth/report_waronwomen-chronology.pdf

Poe-Yamagata, E., & Jones, M. (2000). *And justice for some: Differential treatment of minority youth in the justice system.* Washington, DC: Building Blocks for Youth.

Purdum, T. S. (2002, February 15). With candor, Powell charms global MTV audience. *New York Times,* p. A4.

Reich, R. B. (2002). *I'll be short: Essentials for a decent working society.* Boston: Beacon Press.

Reichman, N. (2005, Spring). Low birth weight and school readiness. *School readiness: Closing the racial and ethnic gaps, 15*(1), 91–116.

Richie, B. E. (1996). *Compelled to crime: The gender entrapment of battered, black women.* New York: Routledge.

Richie, B. E. (2000). A black feminist reflection on the antiviolence movement. *Signs: Journal of Women in Culture and Society, 25,*1133–1137.

Richie, B. E. (2001). Challenges incarcerated women face as they return to their communities: Findings from life history interviews. *Crime and Delinquency, 47,*368–389.

Roberts, D. (1997). *Killing the black body.* New York: Vintage.

Roberts, D. (2002). *Shattered bonds: The color of child welfare.* New York: Basic Books.

Rodriguez, M. (2005). *Talking to Teens.* Presented at the conference of the Network for Family Life Education. New Brunswick, NJ.

Rogow, D., & Haberland, N. (2005, November). Sexuality and relationships education: Toward a social studies approach. *Sex Education, 5,* 333–344.

Rose, T. (2003). *Longing to tell.* New York: Farrar, Straus, Giroux.

Rousso, H. (2001). *Strong, proud sisters: Girls and young women with disabilities.* Washington, DC: Center for Women Policy Studies.

Satcher, D. (2001, July 9). *The surgeon general's call to action to promote sexual health and responsible sexual behavior.* Washington, DC: U. S. Department of Health and Human Services. Retrieved March 8, 2006, from http://www.surgeongeneral.gov/library/sexualhealth/call.pdf

Santelli, J. S., Abma, J., Ventura, S., Lindberg, L., Morrow, B., Anderson, J.E., et al. (2004). Can changes in sexual behaviors among high school students explain the decline in teen pregnancy rates in the 1990s? *The Journal of Adolescent Health, 35*(2), 86.

Santelli, J. S., Ott, M., Lyon, M., Rogers, J., Summers, D., & Schleifer, R. (2006a). Abstinence and abstinence-only education: A review of U.S. policies and programs. *Journal of Adolescent Health, 38,* 72–81.

Santelli, J. S., Ott, M., Lyon, M., Rogers, J., & Summers, D. (2006b). Abstinence-only education policies and programs: A position paper of the society for adolescent medicine. *Journal of Adolescent Health, 38,* 83–87.

Santelli, J. S., Morrow, B., Anderson, J., & Lindberg, L. (2006c, June). Contraceptive use and pregnancy risk among U.S. high school students, 1991–2003. *Perspectives on Sexual and Reproductive Health, 38,*106–111.

Schaffner, L. (2002). An age of reason: Paradoxes in the U.S. legal construction of adulthood. *The International Journal of Children's Rights, 10,* 201–232.

Schaffner, L. (2004). Capturing girls' experiences of "community violence" in the United States. In C. Alder & A. Worrall (Eds.), *Girls' Violence* (pp. 105–129). Albany: State University of New York Press.

Schlitt, J., Santelli, J., Juszczak, L. Brindis, C., Nystrom, R., Klein, J., Kaplan, D., & Seibou, M. D. (2000). Creating access to care: School-based health care census 1998–1999. Washington, DC: National Assembly on School-Based Health Care.

Schoen, C., Davis, K., Collins, K. S., Greenberg, L., Des Roches, C., & Abrams, M. (1997, November). *The commonwealth fund survey of the health of adolescent girls.* New York: Commonwealth Fund.

Seiler, N. (2002, April). *Is teen marriage a solution?* Washington, DC: Center for Law and Social Policy.

Sen, G. (1994). Reproduction: The feminist challenge to social policy. In G. Sen & R.C. Snow (Eds.), *Power and decision: The social control of reproduction* (pp. 5–18). Boston: Harvard School of Public Health.

Sen, G., George, A., & Ostlin, P. (Eds.) (2002). *Engendering international health: The challenge of equity.* Cambridge, MA: MIT Press.

Sexuality Information and Education Council of the U.S. (SIECUS). (1998). *Filling the gaps: hard to teach topics in sexuality education.* Washington, DC: Author. Retrieved March 8, 2006, from http://www.siecus.org/pubs/filling_the_gaps.pdf

Sexuality Information and Education Council of the U.S. (SIECUS). (2004a). *State profiles (2004): A portrait of sexuality education and abstinence only until marriage programs in the States.* Washington, DC: Author. Retrieved July 31, 2006, from http://www.siecus.org/policy/states/

Sexuality Information and Education Council of the U.S. (SIECUS). (2004b). *National guidelines task force: Guidelines for comprehensive sexuality education* (3rd ed.). Washington, DC: Author. Retrieved from March 8, 2006, from http://www.siecus.org/pubs/guidelines/guidelines.pdf

Sexuality Information and Education Council of the U.S. (SIECUS). (2004c). *Federal spending for abstinence only until marriage programs (1982–2006).* Washington, DC: Author. Retrieved July 31, 2006, from http://www.siecus.org/policy/states/2004/federal-Graph.html

Sexuality Information and Education Council of the U.S. (SIECUS). (2005, September 26). *How medical inaccuracies, fear, and shame in federally funded abstinence only until marriage programs put our youth at risk.* Washington, DC: Author. Retrieved March 8, 2006, from http://www.siecus.org/media/press/press0114.html

Sickmund, M. (2004, June). *Juveniles in corrections. Juvenile offenders and victims: National report series.* Washington, DC: U.S. Department of Justice. Retrieved from http://www.ncjrs.gov/pdffiles1/ojjdp/202885.pdf

Simkins, S. B., & Katz, S. (2002). Criminalizing abused girls. *Violence Against Women, 8,* 1474–1999.

Simkins, S. B., Hirsch, A. E., & Horvat, E. M. (2003). The school to prison pipeline for girls: The role of physical and sexual abuse. *The dropout problem.* Cambridge, MA: Harvard Civil Rights Project. Retrieved August 4, 2006, from http://www.civilrightsproject.harvard.edu/research/pipeline03/Hirsch.pdf

Snitow, A., Stansell, C., & Thompson, S. (1983). *Powers of desire: The politics of sexuality.* New York: Monthly Review Press.

Srinivasan, B. (2004). Religious fundamentalism, community disintegration and violence against women: All issues are women's issues. *Socialism and Democracy, 18*(1), 135–149.

Starr, P. (2004, October 1). Health-care's big choice. *The American Prospect: Online Edition.* Retrieved August 4, 2006, from http://www.prospect.org/web/page.ww?section=root&name=ViewPrint&articleId=8541

Stewart, F. H., Shields, W. C. & Hwang, A. C. (2004, May). Faulty assumptions, harmful consequences: Coming to terms with adolescent sexuality. *Contraception, 69 (5),* 345–346. Retrieved August 4, 2006, from http://www.arhp.org/files/journaleditorialmay2004.pdf

Strauss, L. T., Herndon, J., Chang, J., Parker, W. Y., Bowens, S. V., Zane, S. B., et al. (2004, November 26). Abortion surveillance – United States, 2001. *Weekly Report, 53,* (SS09), 1–32. Retrieved August 4, 2006, from http://www.cdc.gov/mmwr/preview/mmwrhtml/ss5309a1.htm

Sullivan, P., Yeager, M., Chudowsky, Kober, N., O'Brien, E., & Gayler, K. (2005, August). *2005 state high school exit exams, states try harder, but gaps persist.* Washington, DC: Center on Education Policy. Retrieved August 4, 2006, from http://www.ctredpol.org/highschoolexit/reportAug2005/hseeAug2005.pdf

Taverner, B., & Montfort, S. (2005). *Making sense of abstinence: Lessons for comprehensive sex education.* Morristown, NJ: Planned Parenthood.

Texas Citizens for Science. (2004). *Texas adopted censored, inadequate and danger health education textbooks in 2004.* Midland, TX: Author. Retrieved March 8, 2006, from http://www.texscience.org

Tolman, D. L. (1994). Doing desire: Adolescent girls' struggles for/with sexuality. *Gender and Society, 8,* 324–342.

Tolman, D. L. (2002). *Dilemmas of desire.* Cambridge, MA: Harvard University Press.

Tolman, D. L., Striepe, M., & Harmon, P. (2003). Gender matters: Constructing a model of adolescent sexual health. *The Journal of Sex Research, 40*(1), 4–12.

Tolman, D. L. (2006). In a different position: Conceptualizing female adolescent sexuality development within compulsory heterosexuality. In L. Diamond (Ed.), *New directions in child and adolescent development: Positive female adolescent sexuality, 112* (pp. 71–89). San Francisco: Jossey-Bass.

Unitarian Universalist Association (2006a). *Our whole lives: Sexuality education for grades 4–6.* Boston, MA: Author. Retrieved June 21, 2006, from http://www.uua.org/owl/4-6.html

Unitarian Universalist Association (2006b). *Our whole lives (OWL).* Boston: Author. Retrieved June 21, 2006, from http://www.uua.org/owl/what.html

U.S. Department of Health and Human Services. (2003). *Understanding Title V of the Social Security Act: A guide to the provisions of the federal maternal and child health block grants.* Rockville, MD: The Maternal and Child Health Bureau. Retrieved August 4, 2006, from http://www.dph.state.ct.us/BCH/Family%20Health/cyshcn/understandingtitlev.pdf

U.S. Department of Health and Human Services. (2005). *Family and youth services bureau: Administration on children, youth, and families; Community-based abstinence education program. Funding opportunity number HHS-2005-ACF-ACYF-AE-0099.* Rockville, MD: Author.

U.S. Department of Health and Human Services. (2006). *Family and youth services bureau: Administration on children, youth, and families; Community-based abstinence education program. Request for proposals. Funding opportunity number: HHS-2006-ACF-ACYF-AE-0099.* Rockville, MD: Author. Retrieved August 4, 2006, from http://www.acf.hhs.gov/grants/pdf/HHS-2006-ACF-ACYF-AE-0099.pdf

U.S. Department of Justice. (1999, December). *Minorities in the juvenile justice system. 1999 National Report Series.* Washington, DC: Office of Juvenile Justice and Delinquency Prevention. Retrieved August 4, 2006, from http://www.ncjrs.gov/pdffiles1/ojjdp/179007.pdf

U.S. House of Representatives. (2005, February 10). *H.R. 2553. 109th Congress, 1st session.* Washington, DC: Author. Retrieved August 4, 2006, from http://www.advocatesforyouth.org/real_hr2553.pdf

U.S. Office of Management and Budget. (August 4, 2006). *Health and human services: Enhancing the faith-based and community initiative.* Washington, DC: Author. Retrieved August 4, 2006, from http://www.whitehouse.gov/omb/budget/fy2007/hhs.html

U.S. Senate. (2005, February 10). *S. 368. 109th Congress, 1st session.* Washington, DC: Author. Retrieved August 4, 2006, from http://www.advocatesforyouth.org/real_s368.pdf

Valenzuela, A. (2004). Introduction: The accountability debate in Texas: Continuing the conversation. In A. Valenzuela (Ed.), *Leaving children behind: How "Texas style" accountability fails Latino youth* (pp. 1–26). Albany: State University of New York Press.

Vance, C. (1993). *Pleasure and danger: Exploring female sexuality.* New York: Harper Collins.

Wyatt, G. E. (1994). The sociocultural relevance of sex research. *American Psychologist, 49,*748–754.

Zavella, P. (2003). Talkin' sex: Chicanas and Mexicanas theorize about silences and sexual pleasures. In G.F. Arredondo, A. Hurtado, N. Klahn, O. Najera-Ramirez, & P. Zavella (Eds.), *Chicana feminisms: A critical reader* (pp. 228–253). Chapel Hill, NC: Duke University Press.

The authors would like to thank Susan Buckley, Donna Cangelosi, Eva Goldfarb, Thea and Bailey Jackson, Evelyn Shalom, Nancy Walker-Hunter, Susie Wilson, Bethany Rogers, Bernadette Anand, and Debbie Rogow for the their thoughtful feedback on earlier drafts. The authors would also like to thank Radhika Rao and Jacy Ippolito for their editorial support and the Leslie Glass Foundation for its generous support of this research.

15

Recovering From "Yo Mama Is So Stupid": (En)gendering a Critical Paradigm on Black Feminist Theory and Pedagogy

Rochelle Brock

Introduction

Writing is an extension of my soul. I string letters together to make words and words to craft sentences, and sentences to create an intricate dance into theory and my truth. In my dance, self and text become one. The movement of the words pushes life into the text, which is where the text finds the freedom to 'reinscribe experience' and bring 'newly discovered meanings to the [my] reader' (Denzin 1998, 322). When we structure our writing in ways that lay itself bare, we create a world of unforeseen possibilities where previous meanings morph into something new and unique (Brock 2005; Denzin and Lincoln 1998; Richardson 1998). I continuously aim for three-dimensional writing where words do not sit motionless and flat on the page but instead are filled with all of the emotions I experience when writing; the words take on a life of their own; they lead where I need to go. In this way, I unearth the meaning and purpose of what I am writing through the actual act of writing. Writing is personal. I find joy and sadness in writing. I become one with the words, and those words mirror whatever angst or intellectual breakthroughs I experience.

The personal method of writing has been discussed by many qualitative researchers (Brock 1999, 2005; Denzin and Lincoln 1998; Fine 1998; Kincheloe 2005; Richardson 1998). I take what I need from them; play with their theories, extracting those pieces that fit my purpose, always attempting to develop what is unique to me. I learn and teach best through dialog with others and importantly dialog with self. I have to creatively articulate the internal struggle that is central to my thought process. I have to write my truth, and my truth is the demystification that happens through dialog. My purpose is to experiment with the traditional format of academic writing as I deconstruct a cultural phenomenon within the African American community by considering it as a pedagogical activity for higher education. The current emphasis on standards and testing (Cavanagh 2005; Sternberg 2006) makes it too easy to set aside the socio-emotional and cognitive dimensions of education where 'real' learning and transformation occur. I take pieces of the real and the imagined and marry them into a story concerned with redirecting the boundaries about how I discuss and analyze *the dozens.* In my writing I create an 'other world', one in which the fluidity of past and present coalesces in the creation of a new present. Denzin and Lincoln (1998, 322) state that:

> [i]n writing, the writer creates the world. He or she fills it with real and fictional people. Their problems and their crisis are brought to life. Their lives gone out of control are vividly described. Their lives, suddenly illuminated with new meanings and new transformation of self, are depicted.

My purpose in this article is to analyze the dozens as a pedagogical site using Black feminist theory. Black feminist theory reconceptualizes all dimensions of the dialectic of oppression and activism of and by Black women, which forces me to see the misogyny inherent in the game. Black feminist theory gives voice to my analysis of the dozens because it allows me to use a specific way of knowing and experiencing the world from a Black woman's perspective as I study a Black cultural phenomenon. The epistemology of Black feminist theory utilizes those criteria important to me as a Black woman – dialog, experiential understanding, criticality and putting Black woman at the center of the discussion. It is especially useful in the study of the dozens because it has the ability to reinterpret what has already been done through new theoretical frameworks by beginning with the assumption that Black women's knowledge has been subjugated/suppressed and that Black women have the right and responsibility to reclaim, discover and reinterpret that which affects their reality. Moving toward this reinterpretation requires an epistemology centered in Black feminist theory. A Black feminist epistemology aims to raise the political consciousness of people with an Afrocentric worldview, placing them at the center of their own reality. In addition, a Black feminist epistemology challenges patriarchal structures and gender inequalities. I do not need to theorize about Black women using an epistemology that attempts to deny our humanity or existence. Instead, I choose to work within epistemological assumptions grounded in my history as a Black woman. I choose to learn from the all-too-often ignored and silenced theories of Black women regarding how we know and experience our world. Working within a Black feminist epistemological framework provides the space to challenge ontological questions of existence and being. How do I understand my realities as an objectified other? Where do I fight the battle for my selfhood? Where is my fight/struggle as a teacher, a scholar, a guide in the journey I take with my students? What can I learn from the historical exploitation of my sisters, and how does this knowledge influence/shape my pedagogy? These are all ontological questions asked as I search for a new way to understand the dozens from a pedagogical place.

The Dozens

Known by many names[1] – rapping, signifying, giving rag, making mock, giving fatigue, capping, snaps and mother-rhyming – the dozens most often consist of references 'to alleged or incestuous activities of the opponent's mother, grandmother, daughters, sisters, wife, or other female relatives' (Foster 1986, 215). 'Yo mama is so stupid' represents a cornerstone of the joking game known as 'the dozens'. The dozens are a ritualized verbal game of insults that involve 'taunts and curses [which] are used to circumvent the point' (1986, 215). Take a listen:

> I hate to talk about your mother, she's a good old soul; she's got a leather-lined pussy and a brass asshole. Man tell your mama to stop coming around my house all the time. I'm tired of fucking

> her, and I think you should know that it ain't no accident you look like me. I fucked your mama for a solid hour. Baby came out screaming. Black Power.

Initially the topic of the dozens began for me when 'yo mama is so stupid' jokes were sent out on the Black Graduate Student listserv. Representing a cornerstone of 'the dozens', the jokes angered my womanist sensibilities, thereby forcing me to jot a quick reply. I made it short and simple, yet academic; ending with 'let's remember that the "dozens" began on the slave block as families were torn apart and think before we take part in our own subjugation'. Damn I was angry and determined to speak out against the misogyny and the continued devaluations of Black women that were part of the jokes. I also understood the power of words in the jokes that were supposedly benign. Anger becomes positive when you work within it so that it leads to an understanding of what initially caused the anger. When you allow anger to make you impotent, stop you from moving forward, then it is negative. But when the anger becomes a force that propels you into motion then go with it!

To this end, I received several pieces of electronic mail that exemplified this point. In particular, two of the responses were from Black male graduate students expressing their opinions on the jokes as well as my reaction to them. The first response, although seemingly naive, posited, 'Life is only as serious as you let it *not* be!' He seemed to postulate that life (here referring to the jokes) would only hurt me if I gave it the power to do so. Thus life's existential nature effectively reduced the underlying power and history the jokes possessed to construct and perpetrate Black female devaluation, to the level of non-effect. This comment was followed by a more detailed one stating, 'Some of it (the yo mama jokes) was definitely a mild form of self-hate. However, other parts were just fun between kids being kids.' After reading that message, I immediately called a sister-friend and together we questioned: What is *mild* self-hate? How can a person hate a small part of themselves and not hate the entire self? If the mild self-hate is just kids being kids, where does the hate go when those kids become adults?

These questions were the geneses of my need to critically deconstruct this game. My feelings about the jokes were visceral, but as an intellectual how could I epistemologically understand my reaction? I needed to tear apart the jokes and understand where my anger came from, and why for others the jokes were harmless. Was I being too sensitive? Where was the disconnect between what I heard and what others heard? I knew that deconstructing the dozens from a critical perspective would allow me to: (1) analyze the root philosophies germane to its emergence and sustainability; (2) understand the relation of the dozens to the societal structures in the African American community; (3) scrutinize the forms of patriarchy and misogyny within the dozens; and (4) examine the impact of this patriarchy on the concepts of Black womanhood. Important to answering these questions as a teacher and a teacher educator, I needed to place my search within a pedagogical framework utilizing a critical theory.

Although I love and crave intellectual debate, the listserv argument was one-sided – patriarchal – and the scholar in me insisted on reframing how we looked at and talked about the dozens. I felt in my bones that it was misogynistic, and I knew there was a relationship between the devaluation of Black womanhood and the dozens. Perhaps not causal but definitely parallel, I saw the online discussion as one of those 'teachable moments' that we educators are constantly looking for. The dichotomy between my view and the view of others regarding the dozens was based on our opposing ideological lens. My job became to figure out how to analyze the dozens from a critical place so that I could support my visceral reaction. The most understandable way I found to do this was to look at how I would teach a critical analysis of the dozens to my students.

Often times, the ideological forces that anchor our decision-making processes remain hidden from consciousness. My goal is to ensure that these forces are made visible and that students understand the political and economic structures of domination and oppression and develop tools for change. Through a *Pedagogy of Wholeness* (Brock 1999), a greater understanding of those qualities important in a transformative education and teaching is possible. When pedagogy is transformative, students stop thinking of themselves in individualistic terms and instead as part of a community, realizing their freedom cannot come at the expense of the freedom of all people. They understand the historical connection between struggle and survival and then work to create a self-defined standpoint. A sociopolitical transformation allows a life transformation for the student to happen.

Ultimately students, especially those who are disenfranchised, understand the social, political and economic obstacles they are facing and have the tools to succeed in spite of those obstacles. When students are provided with the tools to analyze their everyday life through the lens of race, class and gender oppression they are able to think critically and to deconstruct the world. Sociopolitical transformation allows students to think politically and see the connections between thought and action because they have the criticality to understand historical occurrences. This understanding enables them to demystify the injustices of the world. Importantly, students possess the knowledge to interrogate those societal structures working against them, how they can combat the structures, and the form that fight will take.

A 'pedagogy of wholeness' affords a teacher the space to create a unique way of teaching and learning because it is not concerned with the traditional modalities of instruction. Instead a teacher utilizes whatever means they can because when we afford students the opportunity to use their constructive imagination (Bartlett 1928) they are able to grapple with intricate issues. According to Bartlett (1928, 85), in constructive imagination:

> [t]he material dealt with is not simply accepted or interpreted, but is taken as a problem and a challenge; and thus it is used and changed. Dominance is the essential temperamental characteristic of the genuine constructive imagination. It gathers its own material wherever it can, often searching wide fields; and what it gathers it shapes.

When I combine the three-dimensional writing discussed earlier with my understanding of constructed imagination, I accept the freedom to create whatever reality is needed. My reality is a constructed conversation (Brock 1999) between Oshun, the African goddess of love, and me. A constructed conversation methodology opens the space for dialog, a central epistemological tenet of Black feminist theory. According to Hill-Collins (1991, 212), 'A primary epistemological assumption underlying the use of dialogue in assessing knowledge claims is that connectedness rather than separation is an essential component of the knowledge validation process.' The connectedness dialog brings forth is reified (for me) when I use Oshun as my conduit to truth. She is my African past and my African American present. The dichotomy I love about Oshun is that she is both omniscient and questioning; at times she leads me to where I need to go in my thinking, and at other times I am the teacher providing her with my insights. Writing is typically experienced as a solitary act. Instead I call forth Oshun and together what was once solitary becomes a conversation between compañeras.

What follows is a glimpse into my created reality. In writing and conceptualizing this reality, I combine the factual with fiction. The theories and history are factual. The argument on the listserv that first brought up the topic of the dozens was real. The dream occurred just as I described it, and the frustration I was feeling prior to the dream was real. I wrap these facts in my conversation with Oshun, the entity that can feel and know those things that are difficult for me to touch. Please join my conversations with my innermost self as I bring to life the words that will engage the reader to participate in my struggle to articulate a feminist pedagogy as I deconstruct the dozens in a new way.

Making the Subconscious Conscious: My Dream

When our mind is at rest we can at times see what has remained hidden from the conscious. For me a dream about my mother opened up a new way of thinking.

Rochelle: Oshun, do you dream?

Oshun: I am what you are; I do what you need me to do. Dreams are like a vessel into that which we cannot always name.

Rochelle: Not so long ago I had a dream. Prior to falling asleep all I could feel was the angst of being a Black woman living in a world hell-bent on silencing me at every turn. It was all making me so very, very tired and exhausted both emotionally and physically. Well, one night I laid in bed debating whether I should simply pull the covers over my head, block out the world, hide from reality, and try to find my private dreamland or be brave, roll out of bed, and face life (and by extension my computer) armed and ready for battle. Since both my mind and body were tired, doing battle seemed less interesting, as well as less do-able, than finding that magic happy place where all is right with the world.

Oshun: At times there are events in our lives that provide the impetus for us to search for such a place.

Rochelle: Yes. We may find that place either in music, food, drugs, or countless other vices. Since I am too cheap to buy much music, too vain to overeat, and too fearful of addiction to do drugs, I did the next best thing – I slept. More succinctly, I slept while temporarily hiding from the world of academia and all that identity forced me to deal with.

Stressed, upset, confused, alone, scared, tossing and turning, crying and screaming against the night, I fell asleep in the fetal position on my tiny sofa and dreamt about my mother. I reached back in my mind for a time and place different from where I now was; my childhood bedroom became where I re-remembered a different time. Although in my dream I was the age I am now, everyone else was younger. I saw myself brushing my little sister's hair when the phone rang. Answering it I heard my mother's voice but that was impossible – she was dead. I screamed into the receiver, 'You're dead, you're dead!' Calmly she replied, 'No, I am not. They lied to you.' I next saw myself in a hallway, running and there she was before me, looking younger and happier than when I had last seen her in the hospital as she waited to die. Always one to be stylish, mom was wearing a peach linen pantsuit embroidered around the collar with her hair pulled back in a bun. *Funny that I dream about my mother and remember vividly what she was wearing.* Again I screamed at her that she was dead; she could not be standing in front of me. Again she calmly told me that she was not dead, that I had been lied to, and she was here standing before me. I don't remember anything about my dream after that, although I feel it lasted much longer. I do remember that when I woke, peace was my blanket, wrapping me in a cocoon of tranquility. The angst that I experienced prior to falling asleep, if not completely gone, was at least manageable.

Oshun: Your mother appearing to you in a dream was anything but fortuitous. The forces of empowerment and disempowerment, which construct a Black woman's reality, are extremely varied, which of course makes it that much more difficult to understand. At the time you were teaching a class on the African American woman and therefore consumed with attempting to understand those aspects of Black female identity formation that proved both functional and dysfunctional. Your mother reminded you of several things. First and most importantly you were not alone; spiritually, she was by your side. Second, she reminded you on a personal level of the effects of Black women's devaluation. As a child and as an adult you saw your mother mentally beaten down because of her Black femaleness and how her mental fatigue framed her whole existence. You said earlier that you were in a quandary about writing this article as well as your purpose in the academy – see, as a Black woman in this society you are constantly having to do battle to prove your worth. You of course know this, but you were only dealing with it on a theoretical and historical level – you thought you could depersonalize by removing yourself and therefore be able to deal with it. But we can never completely remove ourselves and this is what was causing your angst, your questioning of self.

Rochelle: And I should know better, but I thought it would be easier if I could objectively study Black women. I see now (or I remembered) that as Black women we cannot remove ourselves from the study of us. The personal told me that what my mom's life was and what she could not make it become were affected in so many ways, because she did not have the strength to overcome the assaults on her humanity. My Black mother, sisters, aunts, and sister-friends were beautiful and strong and caring and smart and wise and not what society keeps trying to make them out to be. I knew what I needed and began to rethink how to look at and understand jokes that use Black women as the vehicle to laughter.

Once I accepted and begin to work with my anger and disappointment I started to see everything from a much deeper place. It always surprises and saddens me when I experience foolishness from folks who should know better. After the original exchange of yo mama jokes, messages born with wings flew across the listserv, at times slamming my Black female self in the face. The exchanges were angry, sarcastic, and superficial. Although I knew my exasperation with the jokes was justified, it took several days before I was finally able to step back from my original anger and disappointment, so that I might conceptualize the yo mama jokes and their place in the historical devaluation of Black womanhood. I began to realize that within the exchange of views, the animosity cast light on a larger chasm not only between Black men and women, but also between Black people. Our placement within the 'web of reality' was distinctly different and at times oppositional (J. Kincheloe, pers. comm., 16 October 1996). Consequently, disparate views on 'yo mama' become understandable. With this understanding I began to ponder what I believed to be critical questions regarding 'yo mama'.

Once I put my feelings aside long enough to think beyond the anger and disappointment I was able to allow myself to begin to intellectually delve into a historical analysis of the evolution of the dozens which led me to inquire: What does the role of women as the object of assault in the dozens tell us about the place of Black women in the community? How does it reflect and extend the way Black women are shaped by patriarchal power structures? Placing these questions within a Black feminist pedagogical context presented the challenge of how not to dismiss the dozens in their entirety but to reframe their function when analyzed from a critical perspective. As we begin to unearth our subjugated knowledge we are naturally led to ask difficult and sometimes painful questions. I think about my mother and the ways in which a White, patriarchal, racist society thwarted her consciousness. I remember my dream, and my mom's words, 'You've been lied to.' Realizing the lie she spoke of was not about her death but about the misinformation I had been fed my entire life as a Black woman. But the key was to go past the personal and see how the myths and untruths relate to the whole of my existence. The teacher in me needed to ask, how do these various lies undermine the self-concept of African American women, and, importantly, how can this knowledge inform a pedagogy of Black female liberation?

Oshun: I believe you first have to accept or at least understand the conceptual power that is within the jokes. The dozens are powerful weapons because they use 'those aspects of the social order that are unacceptable in any other context, i.e., incest, passive homosexuality, cowardice, taboos and personal defects' (Foster 1986, 216). In opposition to the 'it's only humor' responses that I received via electronic mail, Abrahams states that: 'The art of joking gives a license which permits a restructuring of the world in terms of whatever logic asserts itself' (Abrahams 1972, 229). Jokes are not benign but carry with them nuggets of perceived truth.

Rochelle: Yes, that's what I'm trying to get at. Considered a cultural right by some, the dozens have always been an important aspect of the cultural capital of African American adolescent males. Seen as a 'unique cultural phenomenon' and 'distinctive mode of oppression', the dozens cut across social and class boundaries (Majors and Mancini 1992). For many African Americans, both male and female, the dozens like a cultural heirloom has been passed down from generation to generation. Inasmuch as education seeks to transmit or transfer various copi of information, the dozens represent a major educational legacy in the lives of African Americans. But still I continued to get grief about it all. For some people my basic assumptions concerning the importance of playin' the dozens were simplistic at first glance.

Oshun: Meaning?

Rochelle: I constantly heard that the dozens is a game; it's funny, innocent, and I should stop being such a feminist. I also constantly received the rhetoric regarding the importance of signifying in Black culture. But I see it differently. First, the dozens is a cultural norm that has outlived its usefulness. Second, the dozens has a negative impact on both Black male and female perceptions of Black women.

Oshun: Are they a reflection of or a reaction to?

Rochelle: Good question. I think they are both. Although the dozens are by no means the only way Black females suffer devaluation at the hands of racist, sexist society, I do believe that they play an important role. I also maintain that a knowledge of the dozens as a cultural phenomenon can serve as a tool in developing a critical pedagogy for African American students. By viewing the dozens through the lens of race, class, and gender and from a Black feminist perspective which acknowledges patriarchy, that which has been viewed as humor or verbal agility can instead be seen as misogynistic and a serious assault on Black women. Accordingly, an analytical dissection of the structures which originally acted as the conduit for the production of the dozens can be used as a basis for an understanding of Black social thought. In order to establish the connection between the dozens and the historic devaluation of Black women it is first necessary to lay a foundation for the study of the dozens. Because I refuse to place myself in one specific camp of thought, I need to use the pieces of various camps that will help me understand and explain the dozens.

The dozens, in some form, originated in West Africa, came to America during enslavement and was transformed and used to help Black men maintain their 'cool' in the face of a cruel and inhumane system. Following enslavement the dozens continued to be played in various sectors of the Black community, eventually becoming canonized which is why (in my opinion) the email argument turned mean at various points. Despite the accepted patriarchal analysis of the benefits of the dozens (a means to manhood, verbal agility, etc.), viewing the game through the lens of Black feminist theory shows its inherent misogyny. Rather than 'business as usual' we deconstruct and search for the whys of the dozens by problematizing our beliefs and assumptions. We ask about its necessity, and we raise questions regarding its affect on Black female devaluation. Importantly we don't run from the answers, even if those answers go against the grain. Ultimately, as an educator we place it all within a pedagogical framework that will engender in our students the ability to read the world and then know what to do with their new awareness.

The Theory: Black Feminism

Rochelle: Often when research is done on Black women, especially research that examines historical moments in Black women's existence, these women's voices are silenced, or they are portrayed as objects within their own history. It makes sense that I can and should use Black feminist theory in the analysis of the dozens. Black feminist theory understands the nexus of race, class, and gender as controlling forces in Black women's struggles.

Black feminist theory creates the space, as well as the language of critique, that allows us to negotiate between and within theory and knowledge as we search for understanding (Hill-Collins 1991). An understanding of the dozens, their formation, their effects on Black women's image, and the form of resistance Black women enact against negative characterizations has to occur in large part through the use of a theory which articulates the perspective of Black women and acts as a channel for a long denied voice. Negative images of African American women, fabricated in part by the dozens, can best be understood within an ideological framework which produces an understanding of the connection between ideology, stereotypes, and African American women.

Black feminist theory furnishes the space for voice and a self-defined Black woman's standpoint by challenging prevailing approaches to studying oppressed groups (Hill-Collins 1991). The notion exists that the oppressed identify with the powerful and are seen as less human and intellectual and therefore less capable of interpreting or articulating their own oppression. Specifically, Black women's histories have been discussed and analyzed (often incorrectly or at least incompletely and second-hand) by White and Black men, as well as White women who have too often ignored the influence of race, class and gender on the experiences of Black women.

To begin my deconstruction of the dozens I place Black feminist theory in a pedagogy of wholeness, which then allows students to 'read' a popular culture phenomenon through the lens of race, class, and gender (Brock 2005). Students can do a critical analysis from a Black woman's perspective looking at the intersection of race, class, and gender and the historical significance of a Black woman's reality. They are able to deconstruct everyday, seemingly innocent practices and provide an analysis grounded in Black feminist theory.

You know, what really irritates me is that the history of African Americans begins neither in America nor with slavery. When historians or sociologists attempt to produce theories regarding an occurrence in African American culture they either begin their analysis from an ahistorical perspective or insist that all African traits were lost during the centuries of enslavement. Therefore, a casual or causal relationship does not exist. We know that scholarship has substantiated that the slave community maintained and transformed many aspects of African culture – ranging from religion to language to family structure and beyond (Bennett 1988; Herskovits 1958; Raboteau 1978). When I utilize a pedagogy of wholeness or way of knowing, I begin with a historical analysis of the subject under study. For this reason, a scrutiny of the dozens needs to begin with an examination of its occurrence in Africa.

Oshun: Home, sweet home.

Mother-Rhyming in Africa

Rochelle: Leading my students to think outside the confines of what they know is always challenging. So much misinformation on Africans and slavery has been fed to us that first we must be on the same page before we deconstruct the present usage of the dozens. I began by contextualizing the connections between Africans in Africa and Africans in the US in an attempt to remove the 'us' and 'them' way of seeing. The lesson is not simply on Africa or on the slave community in the US but a weaving together of the two.

Oshun: I shed an ocean of tears when our homeland was robbed. I remember the majority of my brothers and sisters were taken from West Africa and came primarily from the area drained by the Senegal, Gambia, Volta, Niger, and Congo Rivers (Meier and Rudwick 1976). The African ethnic groups of the Moor, Serere, Taureg, Wolof, Mandingo, Akan, Ewe, Yoruba, Dogan, lbo, Hausa-Fulani, Angolo, Namib, Ashante, Susu, Baule, Vai, Awikam, Fante, Ga, Seke, Gabon, and Efik became merchandise in the European slave trade and comprised a major part of the African American community (Asante and Mattson 1992). Beginning in Europe, slave ships traveled to Africa where they captured Africans, and sailed to the West Indies where Africans were physically and psychologically broken and trained for enslavement, and then transported to the North and South American mainland. It is among these ethnic groups and ports of the slave trade that we begin our search for the dozens.

Mother-rhyming is the name we used for a dozens-like game back home in West Africa. During my travels, I saw the game played among Ashanti, Gikuku, Yoruba, Efi, Dogan, and some Bantu tribes (Abrahams 1972; Perclay, Monteria, and Dweck 1994). And in the Bantu Wagogo I know that men and boys freely used verbal sexual abuse about grandparents and especially mothers in spoken combat (Rigby 1968). Among the Gusi, close friends exchanged pornographic references about the other's mother and alleged that he would be prepared for incestuous relations with her (Abrahams 1972).

Rochelle: Once we establish the documented use of mother rhyming in specific parts of West Africa we turn to the game elsewhere. I want students to trace the game along the same path used to forcibly bring Africans to US America.

Oshun: The first stop in the slave triangle was the West Indies, which also has a tradition of mother rhyming. Abrahams (1972) has done extensive ethnographic work on the ritualized verbal tradition in several West Indian communities. Plymouth, Tobago, a fishing community, permits mother-rhyming but severely restricts the practice. Abrahams further states that in Nevis, British Leeward Islands the focus of mother-rhyming is on feminine and older people. It's obvious that a version of your dozens has been practiced in West Africa and the West Indies.

Rochelle: Don't call them *my* dozens.

Oshun: As I was saying, mother rhyming and the dozens are in some way kin to one another. Despite what some say, I know that enslaved Africans did not magically forget all that they knew in Africa and that the connection between our African ancestors and African Americans is a strong one. Africans remembered and brought with them to America words and phrases from their native languages that naturally influenced various cultures and behavioral patterns in the 'new' world. The influence of West Africa on African American culture can especially be seen in the West African language of Wolof, which is spoken between the rivers Senegal and Gambia and was the first African language that Europeans came into contact with. Its impact on slave language was considerable since many of the last slaves came from this area. I know that I hear a variety of English words or phrases that illustrate the African influence on African American speech and behavior.

Rochelle: While researching the connections between African and African American culture, I discovered a book by Dalby (1972, 183) called *The African Elements in American English,* where the usage of 'mother' insults in Wolof and Black American English is referenced:

> *mother, yo mama, as a term of severe abuse, or as a term of jocular abuse between friends (incl. use in explicit insults, e.g., mother-fucker). Note similar but less frequent use of father. Cf. use of 'your mother' (less frequently 'your' father) as a term of severe abuse, or as a term of jocular abuse between friends, is in many West African languages, incl. use in explicit insults, literally 'mother-fucker', etc. (esp. in Wolof).

Dalby noted that the impact of Wolof on American English reflects the fact that it is spoken on the stretch of African coastline nearest to the United States. I suspect that forced immigration from this area may have been high at the very end of slavery, since slaveships seeking to make secret runs from Africa to the southern states would have taken the shortest route.

Oshun: Did I ever share with you that I was onboard the Clothilde when it arrived in America in 1859?

Rochelle: No you didn't. But you know what is really interesting is that 1859 was not that long ago, and if we use 30 years as a conservative estimate of the number of years in a generation then the last ship landed a mere four generations ago. And it makes perfect sense to me when African scholars state that 'black Americans [can] look toward a specific area of Africa for a major part of their cultural and linguistic heritage' (Asante and Mattson 1992, 176).

A variation of the dozens was practiced in parts of West Africa. Although in my research I read information on who can joke with whom in various West African tribes, I found little work on how and why they joke. Clearly, it's difficult at this point in my knowledge base to know how widespread the mother-rhyming tradition was in Africa, and how it differs from that in the African American community. What I do know is that joking and mother-rhyming played an important part in the informal verbal traditions in Africa.

African American culture, like African culture, is an oral culture rich with storytelling and verbal repartee (Abrahams 1972). In both cultures the power of words is well respected. Understanding the connection of Africa to African Americans, W.E.B. DuBois was the first person to suggest that the culture of African Americans had been substantially influenced by the cultures of Africa (Meier and Rudwick 1976). Asante and Mattson (1992) state that the first and second generations of Africans in America remember or were told about Africa. These Africans knew the names of rivers, towns, and mountains, and they had at their disposal the rituals, ceremonies, dances, and music of their respective ethnic communities. Although the home they knew was no longer, enslaved Africans used what was remembered from a time in the past to respond to and deal with slavery. I believe it was the physical and psychological dislocation of Africans that served as the impetus in the creation of the dozens.

Oshun: Its creation? What about mother-rhyming in Africa?

Rochelle: Although a form of the dozens was practiced in West Africa it necessarily transformed as the lives of enslaved Africans changed. Life was different in the US than it had been in Africa, so it is logical that although mother-rhyming was practiced, its justification was different in the New World. I mean even the name changed to the dozens.[2]

Oshun: Once your students have analyzed the linguistic and cultural connections between Africa and America, they can begin to critically study the dozens in the slave community. I see how you guide students to contextualize the study and also utilize their critical thinking to draw connections.

The Dozens in the New World

Rochelle: I place the study of slavery in its historical context by showing the students the mental and physical scope of enslavement.

Oshun: How?

Rochelle: By giving the students facts. The European slave trade took place between the middle of the fifteenth century and the middle of the nineteenth century and was the largest forced migration in the history of the world. The estimated removal of Africans from their continent ranged between 20 and 50 million (Asante and Mattson 1992). Since complete records of the actual number don't exist, this figure is based on those Africans who actually survived the long, tormenting journey across the middle passage and arrived in America. The first American slave ship, the Rainbow, set sail in 1645 and as I have already said in 1859 the last slaver, the Clothilde, brought Africans to Mobile, Alabama (Asante and Mattson 1992). Enslavement of Africans lasted close to 400 years and is generally considered one of the cruelest chapters in world history (Bennett 1988).

You were there. Tell me about slave communities.

Oshun: The atrocities committed against enslaved Africans were of the mind, body, and spirit, with the goal of complete acquiescence. As much as possible, I tried to cushion my people from the harshness of their new life, which was no easy task. Systematically deprived of every right of personhood, I saw enslaved Africans struggle to survive in their new home – the plantation. See, the slave community was separate from – while at the same time in response to – the structure of White power and domination, and it was organized into various institutions which provided patterns of behavior for maintaining standards, dealing with the slave master, inducting new members into the group, and expressing the soul and style of the people (Bennett 1988).

Creating a community that could act as a cushion against the assault of a cruel system was as necessary for the slave as with any oppressed people. I see these institutions as paramount for survival on the plantation. If a man, woman, or child, regardless of age or health, committed an infraction of one of the many rules, a severe beating would most likely occur. The most common offense was impudence which according to Fredrick Douglass:

> might mean almost anything, or nothing at all, just according to the caprice of the master or overseer at the moment. But, whatever it is, or is not, if it gets the name 'impudence,' the party charged with it is sure of a flogging. This offense may be committed in various ways; in the tone of an answer; in answering at all; in not answering; in the expression of the countenance; in the motion of the head; in the gait, manner and bearing of the slave.
>
> (quoted in Bennett 1988, 94)

We had to be 'crafty' in order to survive. Expressing any form of emotion was paramount to punishment, so slaves mastered the skill of removing themselves mentally from a situation, becoming adept at developing methods by which they could mask their true feelings. Rather playing the buffoon, the happy-singing slave, pretending ignorance of the infraction, using simple utterances in response to a command, or a host of other survival techniques, enslaved Africans developed various modes of survival. For male slaves the dozens was one of these forms.

Rochelle: For my students, I continuously draw the connections between Africans in West Africa and Africans/African Americans in the United States. For instance, we know that a form of mother-rhyming existed in various West African tribes and these tribes, especially Wolof, were the direct ancestors of the slave community. Slaves were sold between plantations that existed in various locales, and therefore the slave culture did not remain in an enclave.

A transformed version of the mother-rhyming that was prevalent in West African cultures became part of the new slave community. For Africans in the New World, mother-rhyming became a 'song of survival', which offset the pain of not being able to express their true feelings in front of their masters (Perclay, Monteria, and Dweck 1994). In her autobiography Ossie Guffy (1971, 48) recalls her grandfather describing the dozens:

> When I was coming up I heard about that game, only I heard about it the way it used to be, and I heard how it started and why it started. It was a game slaves used to play, only they wasn't just playing for fun. They was playing to teach themselves and their sons how to stay alive. The whole idea was to learn to take whatever the master said to you without answering back or hitting him, 'cause that was the way the slave had to be so he could go on living.

Rochelle: The game afforded a skill that allowed male slaves to endure an unendurable system. Can you imagine the necessity of such a game for male slaves in that it taught them how to maintain and control their anger and frustration?

Oshun: Question. If the dozens were the vehicle to teach male slaves endurance, what did the female slaves use? I mean, enslavement was just as harsh on them so what did they do?

Rochelle: Good question. This becomes a perfect time to allow my students to creatively imagine what strategies female slaves developed. I ask students to take this part of the discussion in two opposite directions. First they brainstorm possible strategies and I let them be as *out there* with those strategies as they want. The second step is to see which of their brainstormed strategies they can tie into the various class readings. In both cases I always get some pretty interesting strategies and an extremely rich discussion.

The Dozens and African American Women

> Nealee started out but she couldn't or wouldn't make it. She was being driven to the west African coast for sale when she became ill and refused to walk another step. Mungo Park, who was one of the last persons to see Nealee, said she was put on an ass but the ass was so very unruly, that no sort of treatment could induce him to proceed with his load and as Nealee made no exertion to prevent herself from falling, she was quickly thrown off, and had one of her legs much bruised. Every attempt to carry her forward being thus found ineffectual, the general cry of the coffel [slave caravan] was, kang-tegi, kang-tegi, 'cut her throat, cut her throat' an operation I did not wish to see performed, and therefore marched onwards with the foremost of the coffel. I had not walked above a mile when one of Kara's [the leader] domestic slaves came to me, with poor Nealee's garment upon the end of his bow and exclaimed, 'Nealee affeeleeta' (Nealee is lost). I asked him whether the Slattees had given him the garment as a reward for cutting her throat, he replied that Kara and the schoolmaster would not consent to that measure, but had left her on there at where undoubtedly she soon perished, and was probably devoured by wild beast.
>
> (Bennett 1988, 30)

Oshun: I remember. I held Nealee close to me as she took her last breath and was set free.

Rochelle: Perhaps Nealee knew what was in store for her as an African woman in US America. On some level while walking in that coffel she pictured the sexual abuse she would receive as the property of an inhumane society. Maybe she saw the battle her granddaughters and great-granddaughters would have to wage as African American women just to receive the rights and privileges shown to White women. Could it be that she foresaw Zora Neale Hurston (1978, 29) writing 300 years later that the, 'Nigger woman is de mule of de world', and therefore refused to ride that mule into bondage? Nealee must have known the system of degradation that was imminent, inasmuch as it eventually came to pass for African women in America. Oh yes, even a brother from the macho 60s wrote that: 'It has been the Negro woman, more than anyone else, who has borne the constant agonies of racial barbarity in America, from the very first day she was bought in chains to this soil' (Hernton 1965, 10).

The sexual offenses against slave women by White men have been well documented (Giddings [1992]1995; Hill-Collins 1991; hooks 1993). There existed an economic necessity for slavery and therefore the proliferation of slaves. The fact that slave women were used for breeding is well known, as is the knowledge that sexual relations, whether voluntary or involuntary, occurred between slave women and their masters. In fact another theory on the origins of the name dozens states that the term may have in fact been meant to represent the (opponent's) mother as being one of the dozens of women available to the sexual whims of her master (Majors and Mancini 1992; Perclay, Monteria, and Dweck 1994).

Remember the need to question the world as we discussed earlier? Well here is where it becomes extremely important for students. They have to question women's place in the dozens and if they stop at the first question then they feel the 'Wrath of Rochelle'. Were women used because of their sacred place in the community (Foster 1986; Grier and Price 1968, 1971; Perclay, Monteria, and Dweck 1994) or because of a more intricately woven connection between the abuse slave women suffered and the resulting pathology these abuses developed in men? Although it has been asserted by many historians that the slave system in the US serves as a useful trajectory to describe the particular form of oppression that African American women experienced (Giddings [1992]1995; Hill-Collins 1991; hooks 1993; Jordan 1992), scholars writing about the dozens have not connected its usage of women as objects of insults with this devaluation. Instead, the dozens have mainly been viewed from a patriarchal framework.

For example, Majors and Mancini (1992) state that young males are often brought closer to the needs and feelings of their mothers because of their father's absence and inability to provide for the family. Because African American boys are constantly exposed to the problems and sacrifices of their mother's attempt to raise a family, they may become unexpectedly sensitive, protective, and empathetic toward their mother and other women. Based on this sense of protection, mothers and women are used in the dozens as the ultimate hurtful insult. In this same vein, Foster believes that the dozens requires Black boys to put aside a mother's special sanctification. According to Foster (1986, 219), 'The natural inclination to defend a mother's honor must be suppressed as young black males move to their world of men where love of a mother is perverted in the medium of wit.' Clearly, according to the aforementioned authors, Black women are objectified, vilified, and dehumanized in a man's attempt at independence. Ain't that some shit?

Oshun: Okay we have discussed and attempted to outline a theoretical framework for the study of the dozens in the African American community. So how do you frame the conversation with your students? How do you explain what makes the dozens of enslavement different than or distinct from the dozens of today?

Rochelle: As a class we analyze several things. An important question in understanding the affective consequences of the dozens is an in-depth analysis of the contextual ideology of society as the game has been historically practiced. How has the ideology undergirding the dozens changed? Within this analysis we can begin to understand the spirit of the game as it relates to the continued devaluation of Black women. Of course ideology not only supports but also constructs our views, beliefs, feelings and opinions on lived reality. Consequently, Asante and Atwater state that, '[H]ierchal discourse which seeks to maintain its hierarchal position is supported by ideology. Without the ideological context, the discourse is vacuous, empty, a hollow form without power' (1986, 170). Through ideology the social justification underlying jokes remains hidden, or at the very least mystified. Klump and Hollihan observed:

> Ritual is not only the essential process of reaffirming a piety, but also the process of a rebirth through which ideology may be changed. Whether an event precipitates a conservative ritual reaffirming an old ideology or a new ideology depends on the rhetoric surrounding it.
>
> (quoted in Gresson 1995, 175)

I struggle to get my students to understand that the hegemonic nature of humor allows racist, patriarchal, misogynist jokes to be viewed as an innocuous, funny bit of non-factual information, never allowing for the space to exist for a form of feminist critique. Instead, we are forewarned to believe only that the dozens have always been a cultural necessity aimed at initiating Black men into a racist society. Gresson (1995, 176) maintains that a critical form of collusion operates in racist joking and by extension patriarchal misogynist jokes in the form of the dozens: 'The shared stance that no continuity exists between the public and personal domains . . . is precisely this shared stance of nonrelationship that sustains both objective (public) and subjective (private) actions of racism.'

Oshun: That all sounds smart and necessary, but what do you really mean?

Rochelle: We play detective and seek answers to unknown questions. The class analyzes every aspect of joking – the how and why of the jokes. We ask what makes the jokes hurtful to others. Why is the sexuality of women used as a means of insult instead of that of men? We look at how the jokes might have been used in West Africa,[3] how we know they were reported to have been used during slavery and how they are used today and then we layer in the historical realities of the women during those various times and places.

Next we place our epistemological assumptions into a Black feminist frame of reference. It's important that we discuss and understand the application of a study of the dozens to a pedagogy of liberation and empowerment of Black females. To be empowered is to recreate the definition of the *other*, and redefining the other is a goal of a Black feminist epistemology. This definition is one that comes from Black women themselves, instead of being placed on them. Black feminist epistemology offers two significant contributions toward understanding self and designing a pedagogy of empowerment. First, a Black feminist epistemology fosters a fundamental paradigmatic shift in how we think about oppression. By embracing a paradigm of race, class, and gender as interlocking systems of oppression, a Black feminist epistemology reconceptualizes the social relations of domination and resistance. Second, a Black feminist epistemology addresses ways of assessing 'truth' and reality of Black women. Empowerment is manifested in the individual when they are able to define their reality and name their truth.

Oshun: Do they 'get it'? I mean your students.

Rochelle: Sometimes they do. Even though they may call me 'the angry Black woman', they understand the various levels of the all-consuming nature of negativity that surrounds Black women. The knowledge that an Afriwomanist epistemology engenders allows us to understand the effects of controlling images of Black women (hooks 1993). Once gained, students view everything in their world with an eye of critique – jokes, videos, movies, television, etc. They begin to see the pervasive nature of the negative images of Black women in movies, in magazines, on television, on billboards, on the news and in the paper and understand how some Black women acquiesce to those images, believing them real.

Instead our dominant knowledge of self provides us with the needed strength and wisdom to get rid of and subvert the stereotypes and controlling images, causing them to lose their control to define. I also make sure they understand this is no easy task. Remember my own angst at being silenced that led to my dream? We can all fall victim to the place society attempts to put us, so it is all that more important to find ways out.

Oshun: Yes and redefining our knowledge begets empowerment, which forces a reconceptualization of the power relations that control and define our society. African American women have been victimized by race, gender, and class oppression, but portraying Black women as passive, unfortunate recipients of racial and sexual abuse denies the legacy of resistance and struggle which has always been a part of Black women's lives. Similarly, presenting African American women solely as heroic figures who easily engage in resisting oppression on all fronts minimizes the very real cost of oppression and can foster the perception that Black women need no help because we can 'take it'.

When I tell students that it was a Black woman that initially sent the jokes on the listserv they begin to see how ideology can *blind* us to seeing how we can become part of our own oppression. We must develop a true grounded history of the role of Black women in America. Accept and be proud of the truth but also accept what we have done and are doing that hurts us!

Rochelle: Understanding how a Black feminist consciousness leads to activism and the determination to fight for social justice is important for especially students to understand. The dynamics between consciousness and activism have the goal that the world is not someplace where we must be tolerated or that we want or have to find some quiet corner and hide away. Instead, we look at the world as something, given the right tools, we can change. With agency we gain the ability to act on and change our world/environment, always remembering that while we want and strive for individual empowerment, only collective action can effectively generate lasting social transformation of political and economic institutions. This knowledge gives students the responsibility to 'do something', become an agent for change. I constantly tell my students that with knowledge comes responsibility to change the world. Important to a pedagogy of wholeness and which I have not discussed yet is the social justice aspect. The new way of reading the world is not frivolous – we learn new ways of thinking and seeing so that we can make the changes in our society that need to be made – so that we can address the problems that need to be addressed.

The deconstruction of the ideologies undergirding the dozens affords a new paradigm and a Black woman's pedagogy. Once controlling images are understood by students, they can begin to see these images in music videos, television commercials, advertisements and importantly a ritualized verbal game of insults, which make obvious and overt references 'to alleged or incestuous activities of the opponent's mother, grandmother, daughters, sisters, wife, or other female relatives' (Foster 1986, 215). We can proclaim to the spirit of Nealee, and all the Black women since that within us lies the power to resist and change that which does not make us stronger.

Oshun: You go girl!

Notes

1. The most common names I found in my research that are also the most fitting, are the dozens and mother rhyming (Foster 1986). For purposes of distinction, mother-rhyming will be used when referring to the 'game' in West Africa and the West Indies. The term 'dozens' will be used when referring to the game in the African American community.
2. One theory on the genesis of the name states that the term 'dozens' originated in slavery where after the middle passage, scurvy ravaged many of the slaves and the 12 most 'damaged' Africans were sold at a bargain rate – the dirty dozen. Supposedly, the only thing more degrading than slavery was to be part of the dirty dozen and degrading a person's mother was to make them 'feel as low as one of the dirty dozen' (Perclay, Monteria, and Dweck 1994, 8).
3. In answering this question I ask my students to utilize Bartlett's (1928) constructed imagination since short of a time machine and without specific primary source research we must instead each use the information at hand and then 'wonder'.

References

Abrahams, R.D. 1972. Joking: The training of the man of words in talking broad. In *Rappin' and stylin' out: Communication in urban Black America,* ed. T. Kochman, 215–41. Urbana, IL: University of Illinois Press.

Asante, M.K., and D. Atwater. 1986. The rhetorical condition as symbolic structure in discourse. *Communication Quarterly* 34, no. 2: 170–7.

Asante, M.K., and M.T. Mattson. 1992. *Historical and cultural atlas of African Americans.* New York: Macmillan.

Bartlett, F.E. 1928. Types of imagination. *Journal of Philosophical Studies* 3: 78–85.

Bennett, L., Jr. 1988. *Before the Mayflower: A history of Black America.* 6th ed. New York: Penguin Books.

Brock, R. 1999. Theorizing away the pain: Hyphenating the space between the personal and the pedagogical. Unpublished doctoral diss., Pennsylvania State University.

Brock, R. 2005. *Sista talk: The personal and the pedagogical.* New York: Peter Lang.

Cavanagh, S. 2005. Lawmakers ratchet up graduation requirements. *Education Week* 25, no. 2: 30.

Dalby, D. 1972. The African element in American English. In *Rappin' and stylin' out: Communication in urban Black America,* ed. T. Kochman, 170–88. Urbana, IL: University of Illinois Press.

Denzin, N.K. 1998. The art and politics of interpretation. In *Collecting and interpreting qualitative materials,* ed. N.K. Denzin and Y.S. Lincoln, 313–44. Thousand Oaks, CA: Sage.

Denzin, N.K., and Y.S. Lincoln. 1998. Entering the field of qualitative research. In *Strategies of qualitative inquiry,* ed. N.K. Denzin and Y.S. Lincoln, 1–34. Thousand Oaks, CA: Sage.

Fine, M. 1998. Working in the hyphens: Reinventing self and other in qualitative research. In *The landscape of qualitative research,* ed. N.K. Denzin and Y.S. Lincoln, 130–55. Thousand Oaks, CA: Sage.

Foster, H.L. 1986. *Ribbin', jivin', and playin' the dozens: The persistent dilemma in our schools.* Boston, MA: Ballinger.

Giddings, P. [1992]1995. The last taboo. In *Words of fire: An anthology of African American feminist thought,* ed. B. Guy-Sheftall, 414–28. New York: The New York Press.

Gresson, A.D. 1995. *The recovery of race in America.* Minneapolis, MN: University of Minnesota Press.

Grier, W.H., and M.C. Price. 1968. *Black rage.* New York: Basic Books.

Grier, W.H., and M.C. Price. 1971. *The Jesus bag.* New York: McGraw-Hill.

Guffy, O. 1971. *The autobiography of a Black woman by Ossie Guffy as told to Gerda Lerner.* 1st ed. New York: Norton.

Hernton, C.C. 1965. *Sex and racism in America.* New York: Grove Press.

Herskovits, M. 1958. *The myth of the Negro past.* Boston, MA: Beacon Press.

Hill-Collins, P. 1991. *Black feminist thought: Knowledge, consciousness and the politics of empowerment.* New York: Routledge.

hooks, b. 1993. *Sisters of the yam: Black women and self-recovery.* Boston, MA: South End Press.

Hurston, Z.N. 1978. *Their eyes were watching God.* Urbana, IL: University of Illinois Press.

Jordan, J. 1992. *Technical difficulties: African-American notes on the state of the union.* New York: Pantheon Books.

Kincheloe, J. 2005. Describing the bricolage: Conceptualizing a new rigor in qualitative research. *Qualitative Inquiry* 11, no. 3: 323–50.

Majors, R., and J.B. Mancini. 1992. *Cool pose: The dilemmas of black manhood in America.* New York: Lexington Books.

Meier, A., and E. Rudwick. 1976. *From plantation to ghetto.* 3rd ed. New York: Hill & Wang.

Perclay, J., I. Monteria, and S. Dweck. 1994. *Snaps: If ugliness were bricks your mother would be a housing project . . . and more than 450 other snaps, caps, and insults for playing the dozens.* New York: Quill William Morrow.

Raboteau, A.J. 1978. *Slave religion: The 'invisible institution' in the antebellum south.* Oxford/London: Oxford University Press.

Richardson, L. 1998. Writing: A method of inquiry. In *Collecting and interpreting qualitative materials,* ed. N.K. Denzin and Y.S. Lincoln, 345–71. Thousand Oaks, CA: Sage.

Rigby, P. 1968. Joking relationships, kin categories and clanship among the Gogo. *Africa* 38, no. 2: 133–54.

Sternberg, B.J. 2006. Real improvement for real students: Test smarter, serve better. *Harvard Educational Review* 76, no. 4: 557–63.

16

LGBTQ Inclusion as an Outcome of Critical Pedagogy

Michelle L. Page

Perspective and Purpose

Principles of critical pedagogy and critical multicultural education (which includes attention to sexual orientation and gender identity) embrace transforming curriculum, increasing educational equity, and preparing students to live in a diverse society (Banks, 2008; Darder, Baltodano, & Torres, 2003; Mayo, 2010). Critical multiculturalism also demands a change in how educators understand knowledge, difference, and action, envisioning a redefinition of school knowledge from the heterogeneous perspectives and identities of disadvantaged groups. This theory asks that educators avoid either minimizing or universalizing difference, or emphasizing or exoticizing otherness. Both critical pedagogy and critical multicultural education require a reorientation from an ethnocentric perspective to a consideration of diverse, contradictory, and marginalized (or silenced) interpretations. Such perspectives call for the acknowledgement of power and privilege and the ways they operate to reproduce inequity. Asymmetrical power relationships are established and maintained through obscuring and mythicizing social phenomena and keeping oppressed groups anesthetized and passive (Freire, 1997). "The dominant class secures hegemony—the consent of the dominated—by supplying the symbols, representation, and practices of social life in such a way that the basis of social authority and the unequal relations of power and privilege remain hidden" (McLaren, 2003, pp. 76–77). Schools often serve as sites of hegemonic control, reproducing inequitable outcomes.

Yet, schools and classrooms can also function as sites of resistance (McLaren, 2003, p. 78). Teachers and students can unveil power structures and discourses in order to question them. If educators view the curriculum as a place of conflict and struggle, we can use it for empowerment, "the process by which students learn to question and selectively appropriate those aspects of the dominant culture that will provide them with the basis for defining and transforming, rather than merely serving, the wider social order" (p. 89). According to critical values, teachers, teacher educators, and researchers should challenge social and structural inequity and commit ourselves to carrying our critique into transformative action.

Unfortunately, practices based on principles of equity, inclusion, and transformative action are not implemented effectively where K-12 students who identify as lesbian, gay, bisexual, or transgender (LGBT)[1] are concerned. Sexual minority students feel less safe, less engaged, less respected, and less valued in schools than do their heterosexual peers (Kosciw et al., 2012; Lecesne, 2012; Robinson & Espelage, 2011). The National School Climate Survey (NSCS) reports that LGBT students still commonly experience a negative school environment (Kosciw et al., 2014). A negative school environment not only affects students' attitudes toward school but also impacts students' academic achievement and goals. According to the NSCS report, LGBT students who experienced harassment had lower grade point averages and were more than twice as likely to report that they did not intend to pursue post-secondary education (Kosciw et al., 2012, p. xv). Lower educational achievement and aspirations, in turn, can influence students' future wealth, stability, and economic, social, and political power.

Recently, fueled in part by these findings as well as by publicized youth suicides, bullying has been in the national spotlight. While victimization of youth is an important issue, there is evidence to suggest that bullying alone may not fully account for the psychological and educational risks experienced by LGBTQ students. In a recent study, Robinson and Espelage (2012) found that "although victimization does explain a portion of the LGBTQ–heterosexual risk disparities, substantial differences persist even when the differences in victimization are taken into account" (p. 309). They continue to say that schools and educators must attend to stigmatizing messages through implementing other means of addressing school climate than just anti-bullying policies.

Such findings suggest that other approaches to creating a positive school environment for LGBTQ students, such as implementing LGBTQ-inclusive curriculum, are imperative. Studies find that few students (<17%) have experienced inclusive curriculum (Kosciw et al., 2012; Blackburn and Buckley, 2005). In schools where students *do* report usage of an inclusive curriculum, LGBT students experience a safer school environment, less absenteeism, a feeling of more connection to their schools, and greater acceptance from their peers (GLSEN, 2011). Other studies have reported positive impacts of inclusive curriculum, including a greater perception of safety (Toomey et al.; 2012, Russell et al., 2006; O'Shaughnessey et al., 2004) and reduced homophobia (Knotts & Gregorio, 2011).

Perhaps more important than the functionality of inclusive curriculum is the fact that curriculum is tied to power. The curriculum demonstrates whose stories deserve to be told and who deserves to be represented—and most often, LGBTQ youth are not represented (Cart & Jenkins, 2006; Curwood et al., 2009; McLean, 1997). "There is a loud silence in curricula that indicates to all students that there are some people in the school who do not deserve to be spoken about and that even some interested in protecting sexual minority youth appear willing to use a community agreement on civil silence as protection" (Mayo, 2009, p. 267). Discourses in schools normalize invisibility of sexual minority youth and thus perpetuate dehumanizing bias against them. "Official silence makes schools hostile places for sexual minority youth and any youth perceived to be a sexual minority" (Mayo, 2009, p. 268).

Questions

Research highlights the need for teachers to support LGBTQ students through structures, policies, and equitable practices in addition to addressing bullying (Kosciw et al., 2012; Robinson & Espelage, 2011, 2012). Educators must adopt broader understandings of LGBTQ-inclusive environments. Pre-service and in-service teachers can benefit from seeing examples of inclusion in action. I sought out an English/Language Arts teacher who regularly integrated LGBTQ texts in her courses as a focus for a case study in order to provide such a portrait. The questions explored in this case study were: How does one English/Language Arts teacher integrate LGBTQ curriculum in the classroom? What are the elements of her practice that make her practice inclusive (or not)? How did inclusion occur? In what ways were LGBTQ people and themes included in the classroom and curriculum?

While the study began as an investigation of curriculum and how students were included or excluded in the classroom, as I analyzed data I found that this case study also provided an example of an evolving critical pedagogy. Therefore, I also asked "What elements of critical pedagogy were most prominent in the teacher's practice?" since the teacher's engagement in inclusive education seemed to reflect core concepts and practices of critical pedagogy. Scholars point out that critical pedagogy can be seen as deeply theoretical, in need of living strategies to carry out its theoretical and conceptual goals (Darder, Baltodano, & Torres 2003; Ellsworth 1989). This case study provides a model not only for LGBTQ-inclusive practice but also a portrait of critical pedagogy in action.

The case teacher, Ms. Lanza[2], spoke frequently and explicitly of power, equity, and democracy; therefore, I have chosen to focus on critical pedagogy as the primary construct. Critical pedagogy, however, serves as a philosophical support for approaches such as queer pedagogy and critical multicultural education. Like critical pedagogy, queer pedagogy decenters dominant power discourses and makes visible marginalized voices and experiences, as it encourages oppositional and resistant teaching (Britzman, 1995; Bryson & de Castell, 1993). Thus, this case might provide insights into an enacted queer pedagogy as well as critical pedagogy.

Methods and Data Sources

I explored these questions and topics by studying the focal teacher's curriculum, pedagogical practices, and students' perspectives. In order to understand the complex and multifaceted nature of teaching and learning in this context, I utilized ethnographic methods of participant-observation and qualitative interviews to collect and analyze data (Atkinson & Hammersley, 1994; Creswell, 1998). The classroom teacher participated in one semi-structured interview of approximately two hours and four unstructured interviews that varied in duration from 30 to 90 minutes. In addition, numerous other informal conversations and interactions were captured in field notes. Students in the teacher's classes also participated in a semi-structured interview of approximately 45 minutes. Students were given the option to participate in focus groups or to engage in individual interviews. A total of 22 students participated in interviews, while other additional student perspectives were included in field notes.

I was immersed in the research site full time for at least 10 days twice during the school year in order to gather information about the school community beyond the classroom. In addition to interviews, I gathered data in the form of field notes resulting from participant-observation of three instructional units, and I collected and analyzed documents and artifacts (such as student work samples and photographs). I used an inductive, recursive coding technique (Miles & Huberman, 1994), reading data multiple times and applying a coding system to identify emerging themes (Seidman, 1998). At every reading, themes were further refined and confirmed from other data sources. Utilizing multiple data sources, as advocated by Lincoln and Guba (1985) and Patton (1990), as well as discussing and verifying emerging themes with the research participant (the classroom teacher), helped to establish trustworthiness.

The context of the study was a small secondary school (grades 9–12) of approximately 150 students, located in a community of about 40,000 residents, which is often described as "metropolitan adjacent" in the Upper Midwest United States. Woodland Hills Senior High is highly diverse in terms of race and approximately 85% of the students are eligible for free or reduced lunch. The school primarily serves students who have had personal difficulties that impacted their performance in other high schools—for example, students who were expelled, incarcerated, homeless; dealt with substance abuse; or faced other issues. Though the school identified itself as an alternative school, it followed the same curriculum as the other schools in the district and met the same state and district standards. The classroom teacher is female, White Italian-American, in her early 30s, and has approximately ten years of teaching experience. She self-identifies as a straight ally to the LGBTQ community. Approximately 17% of Ms. Lanza's students openly identified as LGBTQ, and every student who focused on this topic in interviews or informal conversation informed me that her classroom was known as a safe space for all students.

Ms. Lanza divided her time between teaching three courses and two class periods of instructional coach duties. The three courses she taught (and I observed) were a "reading intervention"-focused grade 10 English class, Read 180 (a course which used the Scholastic Read 180 program to assist struggling readers), and a senior English elective course focused on essential questions about art and literature. During my time in Ms. Lanza's classes, I observed readers' workshops, a unit on Sherlock Holmes (which also integrated study of censorship and academic freedom), a unit on nonfiction text related to illness and epidemics, and a unit about banned, censored, and challenged books.

Findings and Themes

At the heart of this study is concern over the school experiences of sexual minority students. The case study teacher displayed several attitudes and behaviors that, taken together, created a safe yet challenging educational space for all, but particularly for LGBTQ students. This section will detail the elements of Ms. Lanza's classroom that signaled inclusion and safety to sexual minority students. Then, the ways in which critical pedagogy played out and supported curricular and pedagogical inclusion of LGBTQ students and themes are discussed.

Elements of Inclusion

The district's senior high curriculum is comprised of sets of texts that have been approved by a curriculum team as meeting the themes of the curriculum and meeting the state standards. Individual instructors choose texts to teach from these collections. Ms. Lanza's choices included as many LGBTQ characters, storylines, and issues as possible within the approved curriculum. She also made the curriculum more inclusive and multicultural by encouraging LGBTQ texts for student choice reading in readers' workshops, and by utilizing some of these texts in whole-class readings. The school does not have a school library; the only texts available to students come from Ms. Lanza's classroom library that she has created. Her collection is multicultural and includes a large number of texts featuring LGBTQ characters and storylines, thus signaling inclusion to her diverse array of students and demonstrating Ms. Lanza's commitment to equitable representation of diverse groups.

Ms. Lanza utilized several other techniques to include marginalized groups in her curriculum. She taught units on academic freedom and censorship wherein she skillfully and sensitively engaged students with questions of LGBTQ curricular inclusion, discussions of racism, and questions of privilege. In addition, student identities were honored through the building of a learning community in which members supported each other and understood the need to eliminate slurs and discriminatory speech. Through questioning, inclusion of students' choices in the curriculum, and attention to experiences and issues in students' worlds, the definition of what could be known was expanded and transformed (McLaren, 2003).

Though there were multiple "curricular layers" present in the classroom—units on academic freedom and censorship, focuses on gender and gender identity in non-fiction articles, the use of whole-class readings that included LGBTQ characters or issues—LGBTQ literature featured most prominently in Ms. Lanza's reader workshops. Students enthusiastically reported reading works such as *Hard Love, Killing Mr. Griffin,* and *The Perks of Being a Wallflower* during their choice reading time. While these LGBTQ texts were the most often cited in interviews, many other texts were read by students, including choices like *Ask the Passengers* and *Rainbow Boys.* Ms. Lanza had a clearly articulated philosophy when working with curriculum selection at both the district level and for her individual courses. At the district level, she helped to shift the focus to be a more student-centered one; she attempted to serve as a proxy for student voices in the process:

> . . . But we really kind of hashed through [book selection]. . .and this was kind of an uncomfortable conversation, but [I kept saying] 'Let's pick books that address contemporary issues that are facing young people now.' Because I think that so many times the students are not the main part of the equation when we make these instructional decisions, because you've got adults at the table reading young adult lit, and reacting to it as adults would react to it.

Ms. Lanza believed that if the curriculum was student-centered it would need to include texts that addressed real world issues and themes relevant to students' experiences—and some adults being uncomfortable with those texts came with the territory. Drawing on students' lives and experiences in curriculum choices was empowering, making LGBTQ students and experiences visible.

Elements of Critical Pedagogy

I assert that though the multiple approaches Ms. Lanza utilized were effective (as judged by improvement in test scores and by students' responses), they were enhanced by the philosophies and practices of critical pedagogy which permeated everything she did. Ms. Lanza's multifaceted approach illustrated critical pedagogy in action. This is helpful, as critical pedagogy carries with it a diverse range of meanings and practices that are ever contested and evolving. As such, it is not a mechanistic series of steps to be followed (Darder, Baltodano, & Torres, 2003). This complexity can challenge pre-service and in-service teachers who ask, "How do we DO critical pedagogy?" Portraits such as this are not meant to provide a prescriptive formula to "doing" critical pedagogy but to provide a means of concretizing the abstract and spurring reflection on individual practice, as educators seek how they can "do" critical pedagogy within their own contexts and positionalities.

Though I observed several dimensions of critical pedagogy in action (such as enacting a loving community, centering student voice, and using critical literacy practices), here I will focus primarily on equity and power (empowerment) and dialogue.

Empowerment: Equity and power. Ms. Lanza cited equity as the core of her philosophy of education. Though she considered herself an ardent advocate for the LGBTQ community, her focus was on equity for all and justice for those who were marginalized, not solely on converting homophobic students or boosting self-esteem of LGBTQ students (Britzman, 1995). She frequently discussed fairness and equity of opportunity for students and also often referred to structural inequity in her interviews. She was deeply aware of how societal structures, asymmetrical power relationships, and imbalances of resource distribution affected students' educations and their lives. She saw how inequities in society based on income level, sexual orientation, gender, and race marginalized and disempowered her students. One example of her understanding and critique emerged in her initial interview. She said,

> I think that there's a huge disparity in [our community]. I think we've got the diversity piece; people are really working on [that], because we're seeing the community change [to] being a big hub for recent immigrants from Western Africa and Sudan . . . I think that [the community is] more ready to deal with that because it's a visible change in the district . . . [W]e're not talking as much about [the fact that] . . . there's a huge disparity wealth-wise in our community. We've got a huge population of students who are homeless, or who are bouncing from motel to motel to a friend's couch, and I don't think people are as aware of what the new face of homelessness looks like, because we think of homeless as the people who live under the bridge by the [river] . . . but there's a huge population of these kids who don't have a place to stay. . .[O]n the other end you've got a huge community of people who are very, very wealthy because of the corporations and the businesses . . . And so what does that mean for our students, and what is the role of school in all that, and what do we want our [school] community to look like.

An equity lens filtered the teacher's actions in and out of the classroom. For example, Ms. Lanza commented how her students experience poverty and inequity:

> Isn't it interesting that 85% of our kids who end up here are low-income students who get free and reduced lunch? What does that say about . . . all of these things set up against them that are not equal? What does that say about how the district views these kids?

The students who were filtered out of the other high schools in the region (whether intentionally or unintentionally) were primarily low income students and/or students of color and/or LGBTQ students. Ms. Lanza and her students were very aware of Woodland Hills being seen by other students and teachers as a devalued school attended by devalued students. The differential status of the students at various schools was experienced painfully when Ms. Lanza's students were regularly not invited to district-wide activities—until the assembly on drug use was held and her students were encouraged to attend.

Not only was Ms. Lanza aware of the factors that affected her students' lives outside of school, but she also worked to help colleagues reflect on this. At Woodland Hills Senior High, the faculty and administration made the decision not to assign homework. The school understood that students do not all have the same advantages or access to resources. Ms. Lanza commented on this policy:

> We read so much research when we made that decision to go homework-free . . . because kids are like, "Well, I have to work from 3:30 to 9:30 to support a family that I'm taking care of." We have students who are the mom for six other kids, you know? And so, they don't have the time to do homework. It's not that they don't want to do it, it's that . . . it's an older worldview, to think that every kid is gonna leave school and go home and have a snack and a desk, and a quiet place to work, and a mom who's gonna be like, "You need to do your homework." They don't have that, and so we're not gonna do them any favors by sending them home with seventy problems.

Ms. Lanza saw that school structures and practices (such as homework) set up students for success or failure, which ultimately marginalizes or empowers youth. She saw problems not only as individual but systemic (Lankshear & McLaren, 1993; McLaren, 2003), whether those issues be related to class, sexuality, race, or things like struggling in school. As the problems were systemic, they called for systemic "solutions" such as the school-wide homework policy. Ms. Lanza saw the homework policy particularly benefitting low income students and sexual minority students, as a large number of her students were homeless and LGBTQ students were disproportionately represented in this population.

Other examples of understanding problems as rooted in individual and institutional systems of power are Ms. Lanza's political activism (she was very active in the fight to defeat a bill banning same-sex marriage) and her willingness to address school culture. She described how the school has been challenged by its students and faculty to support LGBTQ persons:

> We bust a lot of same-sex PDA [public displays of affection] in the hallway. . .I remember there was one instance where there were girls making out in the stairwell, and I [told them to stop] . . . And they were like, "You're a homophobe!" Part of me wanted to say, "Obviously you're talking to the wrong lady!" Because it was the first time anyone has ever said that to me, but I get that . . . maybe as a student people have responded to you that way, and so it's less about me and more about what their experiences are . . . And so I had to say, really genuinely, "Why would you think that?" and talk it through with them . . . So with teachers, I brought that up at the staff meeting, and we really talked through, are we calling heterosexual students on [PDA] as much as we are calling the same-sex-partnered students on it? Because if we aren't, then that's something we need to take into consideration . . . It's an opportunity to take stock, and to just take a step back and look instead of reacting defensively and saying, "I am not!", but to say, "This is indicative of something in their experience", so it's just a gut check. Let's step back, let's take a look, and if we can honestly say it's all equal, then great! Um, but maybe we can't, maybe they're experiencing something that we need to know about. It's not about me, it's about the whole situation.

The idea of equity and fairness was not only interpersonal to Ms. Lanza in terms of treating all students well, but was institutional as she and her colleagues explored their policies and the ways fairness was or was not experienced by students in their school. Equity was not assumed by Ms. Lanza; rather, she continually questioned how she and her colleagues could create more fair and supportive policies and practices for the students. In this small way, Ms. Lanza began to question the practices and policies of the school (McLaren, 2003) and also challenge a deeply embedded heterosexism which permeates schools.

Ms. Lanza practiced empowering students through equitable advocacy and policy action on many levels. For instance, in an interview, one transgender student told the story about how when he first came to the school he immediately noticed how Ms. Lanza integrated LGBTQ experiences in terms of the texts they read in class. He also noticed how she created space for all students at the table during instruction. This led the student to share his experiences with Ms. Lanza and ask her to help him navigate how to handle his transgender identity within the school, which had policies about using students' legal names on records. The policy led school officials to use the student's former, non-preferred name in all interactions, which made the student uncomfortable. Not only did Ms. Lanza go discuss this student's dilemma with the office and ask that the staff use the student's preferred name, but she began an exploration of the value of the policy with the administration to see if the school could be structurally more inclusive of transgender students.

Empowerment: Literacy. Ms. Lanza believed literacy could empower students (Delpit, 1995); therefore, she endeavored to help students to be competent and critical readers and thinkers and not just consumers of texts. She stated:

> I want them to be proficient readers and proficient writers when they leave us, because I owe it to them to make sure that they can do that. Because if you can't, you're at a disadvantage. And so I think we're seeing that [high priority], because we have 70% of our kids proficient in reading [up from 25%], because we really have decided, 'This matters to them. And it's really important.' And we've done that through aligning with the standards and with high expectations for them. So, we gotta make sure it happens. It affects their lives. Will they only be equipped to make [minimum wage] at McDonald's or will they be able to do something different with their lives? Will they question or will they be drones?

Though critical literacy explores how human subjectivity is transformed through literacy, it also acknowledges the social, economic, and political power that can be exercised through literacy (Luke & Freebody, 1997).

Ms. Lanza recognized that if she and the schools failed to help students become literate citizens, students would simply be channeled into a lower echelon of society. Her low income students would have little chance of social mobility as adults. They would not be able to advocate for themselves or for anyone else. In other words, Ms. Lanza recognized that the school (and she) played a role in social reproduction (Apple, 1995; McLaren, 2003). She saw that schools prepare students for positions in society and it was important for her students to be able to defy low expectations. Ms. Lanza understood that if students were seen as victims or saw themselves as victims that "they lose sight not only of their strength to resist but of the possibility that they can intervene and change the perspective of those in power" (hooks, 2003, p. 74).

Empowerment: Pedagogy. Ms. Lanza enacted critical pedagogy by focusing on issues of power as related to gender, class, race, socioeconomic status, culture, and sexuality in her teaching. Examples were sprinkled throughout nearly all of her lessons. Ms. Lanza discussed one upcoming lesson like this:

> I think that the books. . .and the texts that we choose, really link into that [power, justice, culture, gender]. . .And so, we even do that with the nonfiction stuff we pick. . .We do "Article of the Week" every Friday in [English 10]. . .and the one that we're gonna be doing this Friday is about the young girl in Pakistan who was attacked because she wanted to go to school. So, we pick different things that have different ideas in them, to promote that. So what does it mean to want to go to school against all odds, and what does that mean about your gender, or what does that mean about, you know, equal access? Who benefits from her going or not going to school? What does that mean about how power functions? How is the story told? What is the impact of that? Is there something comparable happening in our community or in your life? [We dig] through that.

During the unit on *A Study in Scarlet,* a Sherlock Holmes story, Ms. Lanza guided the discussion about the book in ways that helped engage students in critical explorations. For example, the killer in the book has a long back story related to being Mormon and the mistreatment of the woman he loved by the Mormon leadership. Ms. Lanza used this aspect of the novel to discuss with the class the notion of prejudice, the idea of how context influences perception, the role of gender in the occurrences of the story, abuse of power, and the cycle of abuse. When discussing prejudice, the students took the conversation in the direction of who experiences prejudice today. They engaged deeply with how sexual minority people and people of color are framed in our society.

In another lesson with a different set of students, the teacher described historical instances of censorship and also displayed images of contemporary book-burnings. Related to the historical incidents, she asked, "If you're having a war with someone, why would a library be a target?" In small groups, the students talked about how taking away the library takes away the people's culture. "It takes away your history," one student said. "It's a way to control you." In these lessons, students not only learned about censorship but about how institutions and cultural forms (texts) serve to control knowledge and engage in social production and reproduction.

Students took these lessons about power and control to heart. In focus groups, the students continued to discuss who has the authority to choose books and they expressed adamant opposition to censoring or challenging books, particularly ones that were not part of the core curriculum:

Michaela: Well, the book that I'm reading for first hour . . . is *The Perks of Being a Wallflower* . . . but I think it's being banned because it talks about underage kids partying, and one of his friends is gay . . . A lot of the stuff he says, I can relate to it so much . . . I don't see why they would wanna take that away from people to be able to read it, 'cause I'm a firm believer that when I find a book, it's like fate for me, 'cause then I'll read it and it teaches me something about myself, or it opens me more in my mind to figure myself out. So if you take that away from people, it's like taking away their chance to find themselves from other people's literature or work. That's just messed up to me. That's controlling my mind.

Jack: Yeah, 'cause you know that Patrick is gay, but you can still see that he's a good person. Like, it's not gonna turn everybody gay if you read that book. They still have really good messages for people to take away from it.

The students used their lessons from Ms. Lanza's class to question school and societal structures and to reflect on representation. They appreciated the variety of representations in literature that they encountered in Ms. Lanza's classroom and expressed uniformly positive views toward LGBTQ literature. Additionally, they saw reading and writing as powerful. The critical literacy skills modeled by Ms. Lanza helped students to analyze rhetoric and understand how language was used as a tool of power. As one student reported,

> You see how people's opinions are affected by the commercials and marketing and stuff. I'm learning more ways to say things so that maybe things will change. I mean, that's what politicians do, right? Talk a lot? You just have to talk the right way to make things happen.

Ms. Lanza understood the importance of learning language so that students could be armed in the struggle to improve the world (Delpit, 1995; Freire, 1998). She consistently articulated her desire to help students to improve their own lives, their communities, and the world. She saw this as the end goal of education—an expression of *phronesis,* the idea that "actions and knowledge must be directed at eliminating pain, oppression, and inequality, and at promoting justice and freedom" (McLaren, 2003, p. 85).

Dialogue. One of my pre-service teachers asked Ms. Lanza about her philosophy of teaching. The response was simple: "Everything's a conversation." She considered all aspects of teaching to be dialogic in some fashion and she enacted the principle of dialogue by various means. She had taken to heart the idea that "conversation is the central location of pedagogy for the democratic educator" (hooks, 2003, p. 44).

In Ms. Lanza's classes, dialogue occurred throughout instruction. For example, students responded to texts in multiple ways via speaking and writing. It was important to Ms. Lanza to always engage students in discussion and dialogue so that students could process texts and ideas. One way in which she evoked dialogue and helped students learn was to allow all perspectives to be present in the class—she did not have unilateral rules about what opinions could be expressed when responding to literature. Rather, she always challenged students to discuss why they held a perspective or why a text or comment might be compelling or offensive or inaccurate. Students were constantly engaged in conversations about how to make their communities more just and more inclusive.

One example occurred during the day's opening journal assignment. Ms. Lanza had asked students to write about the five things they thought teens should read about. The students shared their examples with each other, which included such responses as politics, dropping out of school, violence, drugs and alcohol, sex and relationships, friendships, and self-respect. Ms. Lanza said, "A lot of people in the community might be concerned about teens reading about sex or drugs or sexuality. So why is it important that teens read about that stuff?" Students animatedly discussed why adults want to control teenagers and the importance of love and relationships. During this conversation, the students and Ms. Lanza consistently included all kinds of love and relationships:

Taz: I think it's important to have books about sex and love because we [teenagers] are human, too! I think everybody wants to be loved. But it's scary, too. Like when you're first starting to hook up with somebody . . .

Jaycee: My sister's gay and it's even scarier—you don't know if the person you like is gay or straight sometimes. She asked a girl out once . . . and then the chick . . . said she was gonna kick her ass!

Ms. Lanza: That does sound scary. What did . . .

Jaycee: Yeah, she wasn't so scared about, like, getting beat or anything but just sad that this girl didn't like her and maybe really hated her because of being gay.

Ms. Lanza: Why do you think that books about sex and love would make a difference?

Laura: Maybe if that girl knew some gay people she, like, wouldn't freak out.

Taz: Maybe J's sis needs a book on gaydar! 'Ten Steps to Figuring out Who's Gay.'

Jaycee: I don't get why it matters if you're gay or straight or whatever. If people could just be who they are it would be so much better. Like, why do you have to pop off when someone likes you? That's stupid.

Ms. Lanza: So reading stories about all sorts of relationships might be helpful in figuring out how to establish those relationships?

Troy: But we already got that fake-ass stuff [delivers movie lines in falsetto]. We don't need no more Romeo and Juliet. If you're gonna make us read that crap you gotta keep it real!

Love and relationships weren't framed only as heterosexual in discussions in Ms. Lanza's class. Because the classroom was a safe space for dialogue in general and students' voices were valued, they were free to express themselves about topics that might be challenging, like sex and sexuality.

Because throughout her courses Ms. Lanza focused on equity and inclusion related to race, income, and religion in addition to sexual orientation and gender (in other words, focused on equity across the board), students were receptive and open to classroom readings and activities related to gender identity and sexual orientation; they did not see these as extraordinary or as the teacher having a "hidden agenda." Focusing on LGBTQ topics was not a "special event" in the classroom (Britzman, 1995, p. 151) but were just a normal part of the conversation. Not only did this openness allow for all sorts of dialogue, but it created spaces for LGBTQ issues in particular. Ms. Lanza expressed her views on having open linguistic spaces, saying:

> There's a fairly clear expectation that, especially when we have conversations like this [about equity, sexual orientation, race, etc.], that it's cool to say whatever you think. Because I think that sometimes . . . the kids are uncomfortable to wade through their understandings, because . . . the flip can happen where, if you're a kid who honestly feels conflicted about whether or not we should be talking to children about homosexuality because of what your belief system is [you get shut down] . . . it feels like they should be allowed to talk through those things, and think about them, instead of other kids shutting them down and saying, 'That's hateful, you're a bigot, blah blah blah.' . . . It's just as totalitarian to shut down the conversation, you know, quote-unquote 'for the good'—it's at least not productive, I think, in terms of learning. They're not going to really process whatever the issue is that they're thinking about and they won't feel welcome or free in the classroom.

Ms. Lanza enacted this philosophy of open dialogue in her classroom not only during discussions of big issues but also in responding to students' off-the-cuff statements. On the rare occasion when a student would say something like "That's so gay," Ms. Lanza did not simply say that this was unacceptable and shut down communication. Rather, she would say to the student something like, "I don't think that's what you mean—what are you really trying to say?" or "Tell me more about why you think that" or "I think you're looking for a different word than the one you used." Then, privately, Ms. Lanza would have a conversation with the student where she would pose a series of questions to help the student come to the understanding of why this comment was unacceptable (because it is hurtful, inaccurate, reinforced homophobia, etc.) and the student comprehended that statements like these were not allowed in class for reasons other than because "the teacher said so." Ms. Lanza consistently would work through issues with students dialogically rather than authoritatively.

Through class discussion and classroom management/discipline practices, Ms. Lanza opened dialogue rather than shutting it down. Like Ellsworth (1989) and Blackburn (2003), Ms. Lanza recognized that there may be a sort of backlash in dialogue. Discourses that are intended to be liberating or which appear to be equitable may instead re-establish existing (or inscribe new) forms of oppression. Ms. Lanza was aware of this possibility and prepared to combat it. She attempted to avoid recreating her own totalitarian "regime" in her classroom but rather to create "good hegemony." As McLaren (2003) writes,

> Not all prevailing values are oppressive. Critical educators, too, would like to secure hegemony for their own ideas. The challenge for teachers is to recognize and attempt to transform those undemocratic and oppressive features of hegemonic control that often structure everyday classroom existence in ways not readily apparent.
>
> (p. 78)

Another manifestation of hegemonic control in schools is the curriculum. The formal curriculum, fundamentally, is a conversation or dialogue among professional discourse communities. Teachers have power; they are mediators of formal knowledge and individual students in classrooms (Darder, 2002; Shor, 1992) and they are also mediators of the formal curriculum. Ms. Lanza recognized that while teachers are leaders in their own classrooms, to inform broader learning outcomes, foci, and professional conversations, she needed to collaborate with her colleagues and be a leader in the district. She did this by being an instructional coach and by serving on curriculum development teams. While Ms. Lanza was initially recruited for one review team, she later volunteered for two others. She said:

> I was lucky enough to be on the ninth grade, eleventh grade, and twelfth grade alignment teams that re-wrote the curriculum. . .I found myself having to fight for the books. . .It got pretty outrageous. People were getting so mad that they would have to get up and leave the room and then come back. . .and I don't know if that happens in other subject areas or if it's just the English people. Like, I don't know if physics teachers get real wound up about, like, "This is how we're gonna attach molecules!" But, it may happen. . .

Ms. Lanza used her own personal and professional agency to empower students by including works related to students' lives (McLaren, 2003). She attempted to alter the curricular ideologies in place and integrate diverse perspectives into the core curriculum rather than treat them as add-ons or nonessential (Lankshear & McLaren, 1993; Winans, 2006). She recognized that if students are not known, not represented, not engaged, they are silent and invisible; they are oppressed (Lankshear & McLaren, 1993).

Discussion

Often, when teachers and teacher educators think about LGBTQ inclusion, we think about curriculum, the "stuff" we teach. While the curriculum is one important piece of creating an inclusive schooling experience, we must think about more than the topics or texts that are integrated. Exposure to LGBTQ texts without critical analysis is simply additive curriculum (rather than knowledge transformation) (Banks, 2008; Winans, 2006). Lankshear and McLaren (1993) remind us that "tokenism does not constitute recognition" (p. 20). Exposure alone does not adequately challenge heteronormativity (Schieble, 2012). However, LGBTQ texts must be present if they are to be a part of a critical pedagogy which engages marginalized students, as in Ms. Lanza's classroom.

Ms. Lanza successfully garnered the trust of her building administrator, her students, and parents and guardians. In part, this was because of the demonstrated academic achievement of the students. Ms. Lanza's instruction was standards-based and helped students achieve academically while still using equity and inclusion as an umbrella for her practice. Students' grades were high and the school's scores on reading tests dramatically increased under her leadership. This led colleagues and families to have faith in the instructor as a teacher. Ms. Lanza blended academic efficacy with equity, saying, "The standards really tell us what to do for the most part, but we get to decide the how. And I choose to address the standards through essential questions of equity and justice." In this way, Ms. Lanza attempted to appropriate the discourses and ideologies of schooling (standards) and to use them, resist them, or subvert them.

The case study demonstrates that just choosing the "right" texts is not equivalent to engaging in inclusive practice. Though it was powerful that LGBTQ-inclusive texts were studied in the classroom, this was not the sum of Ms. Lanza's practice. She habitually enacted dialogic practice wherein she eroded heteronormative discourse in her classroom, school, and curriculum. Likewise, inclusive and critical pedagogy is not simply a collection of the "right" teaching strategies or practices, nor is there any singular exemplar or set of steps in how to implement a critical pedagogy. Rather, many elements combined to form such practice: committing to equity, modeling dialogic and democratic practice, integrating notions of power and privilege in instruction, having an activist mentality and questioning the status quo, attending to student achievement for the purpose of offsetting asymmetrical power relationships, helping students develop critical thinking skills, and having a deep care for students and community. Ms. Lanza understood her work as interpersonal and individual, but she also understood the importance of structures and institutions. She impacted policy, comprehended social inequity, and understood the effects of power and privilege on her own practice and on her students' lives. In particular, she dramatically affected policies related to sexual minority inclusion in her school. Further, she understood the value of the context in which she taught and saw herself as part of an educational team. She was willing to take risks to impact her students' educations and schooling experiences for the better.

In examining the case of Ms. Lanza, several recommendations as well as questions for future study emerge. First, critical practices are key to helping students "read the word and read the world" (Freire, 1987). Teachers must be equipped with understandings of the theories and practices related to critical pedagogy. Continued study of how to implement these practices is important, including accounts of model lessons from multiple subject areas and grade levels.

Fundamentally, Ms. Lanza had a driving philosophy and disposition that embraced equity and inclusion at the core. Not only did she have a belief in equity, but she had a commitment to it. This commitment led her to keep increasing her knowledge about social issues, her students, her community, pedagogy, and literature. Though Ms. Lanza did not name it as such, her practices and discussions indicate an effort to enact a critical pedagogy. The question arises, then, of how one's educational philosophies and dispositions develop and how they can be impacted or changed. This question has implications for professional relationships, professional development, teacher preparation practices and programs, and teacher recruitment and retention strategies. How do teacher educators incite pre-service and in-service teachers to "do" critical pedagogy? What role do teacher preparation programs play? What are the implications for curriculum? For recruitment? Perhaps modeling critical pedagogy in practice and presenting portraits and case studies such as this one can serve as catalysts to action, change, and hope.

Conclusion

This study provides a portrait of critical practice centered on equity that enhanced LGBTQ inclusion. Such portraits are rare in the literature (particularly related to K-12 settings) and can be extremely helpful in supporting in-service and pre-service teachers as they seek to transform the curriculum and functions of schooling and affect students' lives in impactful ways. In this case, the classroom teacher utilized a layered pedagogical approach built upon dialogue and empowerment, with the goal of providing her students a critical and inclusive educational experience. Many more such portraits of inclusive critical education need to be disseminated so that instructors of various subject areas and grade levels have models to inspire thinking, reflection, and transformation in their own practice. It can be challenging in this era of standardization and testing to envision how one can meet the multiple demands of standards and test preparation while still embracing equity, inclusion, and justice. Even in contemporary American society, which seems more open to LGBTQ people and issues, it is challenging to address sexual orientation in schools. Many teachers are fearful of engaging with this topic and providing curriculum that represents sexual minority students (Page, 2014), but this case study provides one demonstration of critical and inclusive education. This model is not a road map but rather a representation that may incite the sociological imagination, allowing teachers to envision what can be. Simply adding LGBTQ texts may not be enough to transform schooling for LGBTQ students, but engaging a robust, layered, critical approach to education that incorporates many strands can be transformative.

References

Apple, M. (1995). *Education and power.* London: Routledge.

Atkinson, P. & Hammersley, M. (1994). Ethnography and participant observation. In N. K. Denzin & Y. S. Lincoln (Eds.), *Handbook of qualitative research* (pp. 248–261). Thousand Oaks, CA: Sage Publications.

Banks, J. A. (2008). *An introduction to multicultural education* (4th ed). Boston: Pearson Education.

Blackburn, M. (2003). Exploring literacy performances and power dynamics at the Loft: "Queer youth reading the world and the word." *Research in the Teaching of English, 37*(4), 467–490.

Blackburn, M. & Buckley, J. F. (2005). Teaching queer-inclusive English Language Arts. *Journal of Adolescent & Adult Literacy, 49*(3), 202–212.

Britzman, D. (1995). Is there a queer pedagogy? Or, stop reading straight. *Educational Theory, 45*(2), 151–165.

Bryson, M. & de Castell, S. (1993). Queer pedagogy: Praxis makes im/perfect. *Canadian Journal of Education, 18*(3), 285–305.

Cart, M. & Jenkins, C. (2006). *The heart has its reasons: Young adult literature with gay/lesbian/queer content, 1969–2004.* Lanham, MD: Scarecrow Press.

Creswell, J. W. (1998). *Qualitative inquiry and research design: Choosing among five traditions.* Thousand Oaks, CA: Sage Publications.

Curwood, J. S., Schliesman, M., & Horning, K. (2009). Fight for your right: Censorship, selection, and LGBTQ literature. *English Journal, 98*(4), 37–43.

Darder, A. (2002). *Reinventing Paulo Freire: A pedagogy of love.* Boulder, CO: Westview Press.

Darder, A., Baltodano, M. & Torres, R. D. (Eds.) (2003). *The critical pedagogy reader.* New York: RoutledgeFalmer.

Delpit, L. (1995). *Other people's children.* New York: The New Press.

Ellsworth, E. (1989). Why doesn't this feel empowering?: Working through the repressive myths of critical pedagogy. *Harvard Educational Review, 59*(3), 297–324.

Freire, P. (1997/1970). *Pedagogy of the* oppressed. New York: Continuum Publishing Company.

Freire, P. (1987). The importance of the act of reading. In P. Freire & D. Macedo (Eds.), *Literacy: Reading the word and the world* (pp. 29–36). Westport, CT: Bergin & Garvey.

Freire, P. (1998). *Teachers as cultural workers: Letters to those who dare to teach.* Boulder, CO: Westview.

GLSEN (2011). *Teaching respect: LGBT-Inclusive curriculum and school climate (Research Brief).* New York: GLSEN.

hooks, b. (2003). *Teaching community: A pedagogy of hope.* New York: Routledge.

Knotts, G., & Gregorio, D. (2011). Confronting homophobia at school: High school students and the Gay Men's Chorus of Los Angeles. *Journal of LGBT Youth, 8*(1), 66–83.

Kosciw, J. G., Gretak, E. A., Palmer, N. A., & Boesen, M. J. (2014). *The 2013 National School Climate Survey: The experiences of lesbian, gay, bisexual and transgender youth in our nation's schools.* New York: GLSEN.

Lankshear, C. & McLaren, P. L. (Eds.) (1993). *Critical literacy: Politics, praxis, and the postmodern.* Albany, NY: State University of New York.

Lecesne, J. (2012). Aliens among us: Exploring identity and identities in young adult literature. *The ALAN Review, 39*(2), 74–78.

Lincoln, Y. S., & Guba, E. G. (1985). *Naturalistic inquiry.* Beverly Hills, CA: Sage.

Luke, A. & Freebody, P. (1997). Critical literacy and the question of normativity: An introduction. In S. Muspratt, A. Luke & P. Freebody (Eds.), *Constructing critical literacies: Teaching and learning textual practice* (pp. 1–18). Sydney, Australia: Allen and Unwin.

Mayo, C. (2009). The tolerance that dare not speak its name. In A. Darder, M. Baltodano, & R.D. Torres (Eds.), *The critical pedagogy reader* (2nd ed., pp. 262–273). New York: Routledge.

Mayo, C. (2010). Queer lessons: Sexual and gender minorities in multicultural education. In J. Banks & C. M. Banks (Eds.), *Multicultural education: Issues and perspectives* (pp. 209–227). Hoboken, NJ: John Wiley & Sons.

McLaren, P. (2003). Critical pedagogy: A look at the major concepts. In A. Darder, M. Baltodano, & R.D. Torres (Eds.), *The critical pedagogy reader* (pp. 69–96). New York: RoutledgeFalmer.

McLean, M. M. (1997). Out of the closet and onto the bookshelves: Images of gays and lesbians in young adult literature. In T. Rogers & A. Soter (Eds.), *Reading across cultures: Teaching literature in a diverse society* (pp. 178–198). New York: Teachers College Press.

Miles, M. B. & Huberman, A. M. (1994). *An expanded sourcebook: Qualitative data analysis.* (2nd ed.). Thousand Oaks, CA: Sage.

O'Shaughnessy, M., Russell, S., Heck, K., Calhoun, C., & Laub, C. (2004). *Safe space to learn: Consequences of harassment based on actual or perceived sexual orientation and gender non-conformity and steps for making schools safer.* San Francisco, CA: California Safe Schools Coalition.

Page, M. L. (2014, April). English/Language Arts Teachers' Comfort and Awareness Levels Related to LGBT-Inclusive Literature and Curriculum. Paper presented at the Annual Meeting of the American Educational Research Association, Philadelphia, PA.

Patton, M. Q. (1990). *Qualitative evaluation methods* (2nd ed.). Beverly Hills, CA: Sage.

Robinson, J. P. & Espelage, D. L. (2011). Inequities in educational and psychological outcomes between LGBTQ and straight students in middle and high school. *Educational Researcher 40,* 315–330.

Robinson, J. P. & Espelage, D. (2012). Bullying explains only part of the LGBTQ-heterosexual risk disparities: Implications for policy and practice. *Educational Researcher, 41*(8), 309–319.

Russell, S. T., Kostroski, O., McGuire, J. K., Laub, C., & Manke, E. (2006). *LGBT issues in the curriculum promotes school safety* (California Safe Schools Coalition Research Brief No. 4). San Francisco: California Safe Schools Coalition.

Schieble, M. (2012). A critical discourse analysis of teachers' views on LGBT literature. *Discourse: Studies in the Cultural Politics of Education, 33*(2), 207–222.

Seidman, I. (1998). *Interviewing as qualitative research: A guide for researchers in Education and the Social Sciences.* New York: Teachers College Press.

Shor, I. (1992). *Empowering education.* Chicago: University of Chicago Press.

Winans, A. E. (2006). Queering pedagogy in the English classroom: Engaging with the places where thinking stops. *Pedagogy: Critical Approaches to Teaching Literature, Language, Composition, and Culture, 6*(1), 103–122.

Notes

1. I will use multiple labels in this paper. The National School Climate Survey utilizes "LGBT" as a label in its reports; when discussing this document or citing research using the same label, I, too, will use "LGBT." However, in other cases when talking about students' identities I will use the slightly more expansive "LGBTQ", which includes "queer" or "questioning" or the term "sexual minority" to capture the underrepresented nature of the group.
2. All names of people and places are pseudonyms.

Suggested Readings for Future Study

Abdo, N. (2002). *Women and the Politics of Military Confrontation: Palestinian and Israeli Gendered Narratives of Dislocation*. New York and Oxford: Berghahn.

Abelove, H., Barale, M., and Halperin, D. (1993). *Lesbian and Gay Studies Reader*. New York: Routledge.

Anzaldúa, G., ed. (1990). *Haciendo Caras: Creative and Critical Perspectives by Feminists of Color.* San Francisco: Aunt Lute Books.

Azzarito, L. and Solmon, M. (2006). "A Feminist Poststructuralist View on Student Bodies in Physical Education: Sites of Compliance, Resistance, and Transformation." *Journal of Teaching Physical Education, 25*, 200–225.

Beasley, C. (2005). *Gender and Sexuality: Critical Theories, Critical Thinkers.* Thousand Oaks, CA: Sage.

de Beauvoir, Simone. (1953). *The Second Sex.* New York: Vintage Books.

Berry, T. R. (2010). "Engaged Pedagogy and Critical Race Feminism." *Educational Foundations, 24*(3), 19–26.

Boler, M. (2004). *Democratic Dialogue in Education: Troubling Speech, Disturbing Silence.* New York: Peter Lang.

Boler, M. (2007). *Feeling Power: Emotions and Education*. New York: Taylor & Francis.

Butler, J. (1990). *Gender Trouble: Feminism and the Subversion of Identity*. New York: Routledge.

Butler, J. and Scott, J. (1992). *Feminists Theorize the Political.* New York: Routledge.

Chang, Y. K. (2005). "Through Queer Eyes: Critical Educational Ethnography in Queer Studies." *The Review of Education, Pedagogy, and Cultural Students, 27*, 171–208.

Christou, M. and Puigvert, L. (2011). "The Role of 'Other Women' in Current Educational Transformations." *International Studies in Sociology of Education, 21*(1), 77–90.

Clinnin, K. (2013). "Critical Essay-Playing with Masculinity: Gender Bending in Second Life." *Technoculture: An Online Journal of Technology in Society.*

Cruz, C. (2011). "LGBTQ Street Youth Talk Back: A Meditation on Resistance and Witnessing." *International Journal of Qualitative Studies in Education, 24*(5), 547–558.

Delgado Bernal, D., Elenes, C. A., Godinez, F. E., and Villenas, S. (2006). *Chicana/Latina Education in Everyday Life: Feminista Perspectives on Pedagogy and Epistemology*. Albany, NY: SUNY Press.

Ellsworth, E. (1989). "Why Doesn't This Feel Empowering? Working Through the Repressive Myths of Critical Pedagogy." *Harvard Educational Review, 59*(3), 297–324.

Fagan, G. H. (1991). "Local Struggles: Women in the Home and Critical Feminist Pedagogy in Ireland." *Journal of Education, 173*, 65–75.

Fields, J. and Tolman, D. L. (2006). "Risky Business: Sexuality Education and Research in U.S. Schools." *Sexuality Research and Social Policy, 3*(4), 63–76.

Fischman, G. (2000). *Imagining Teachers: Rethinking Gender Dynamics in Teacher Education.* Lanham, MD: Rowman and Littlefield.

Forrest, S. (2006). "Straight Talking: Challenges in Teaching and Learning about Sexuality and Homophobia in Schools." In Cole, M. (ed.), *Education, Equality and Human Rights: Issues of Gender, 'Race', Sexuality, Disability and Social Class* (pp. 111–133). London: Routledge.

Frankenstein, M. (1990). "Incorporating Race, Gender, and Class Issues into a Critical Mathematical Literacy Curriculum." *Journal of Negro Education, 59*, 336–347.

Fuss, D. (1991). *Inside/Outside: Lesbian Theories, Gay Theories*. New York: Routledge.

Garcia, A., ed. (1997). *Chicana Feminist Thought*. New York: Routledge.

Gore, J. (1993). *The Struggle for Pedagogies: Critical and Feminist Discourses as Regimes of Truth.* New York: Routledge.

Gore, J. (1998). "On the Limits to Empowerment through Critical and Feminist Pedagogies." In Carlson, D. and Apple, M. W. (eds.), *From Power, Knowledge, and Pedagogy: The Meaning of Democratic Education in Unsettling Times* (pp. 271–288). Boulder, CO: Westview Press.

Giroux, H., ed. (1991). *Postmodernism, Feminism, and Cultural Politics.* Albany, NY: SUNY Press.

Grace, A. P. and Benson, F. J. (2000). "Using Autobiographical Queer Life Narratives of Teachers to Connect Personal, Political and Pedagogical Spaces." *International Journal of Inclusive Education, 4*(2), 89–109.

Gregoriou, Z. (1998) *Learning Performances of Dislocation, Receptivity and Hybridity in Women's Utopian Writing.* Urbana-Champaign: University of Illinois at Urbana-Champaign.

Grumet, M. (1988). *Bitter Milk.* Cambridge, MA: University of Massachusetts Press.

Guillaumin, C. (1995). *Racism, Sexism, Power and Ideology.* London: Routledge.

Hernandez, A. (1987). *Pedagogy, Democracy, and Feminism: Rethinking the Public Sphere.* Albany, NY: SUNY Press.

Hill, R. J. (1995). "Gay Discourse in Adult Education: A Critical Review." *Adult Education Quarterly, 45*(3), 142–158.

Hill, R. J. (1996). "Learning to Transgress: A Social-Historical Conspectus of the American Gay Lifeworld as a Site of Struggle and Resistance." *Studies in the Education of Adults, 28*(2), 253–279.

hooks, b. (1990). *Yearning: Race, Gender and Cultural Politics.* Boston: South End Press.

hooks, b. (1999). *Talking Back: Thinking Feminist, Thinking Black.* Boston: South End Press.

hooks, b. and Shapiro, E. P. (2000). *Feminist Theory: From Margin to Center.* Boston: South End Press.

Irvine, J. (1994). *Sexual Cultures and the Construction of Adolescent Identity.* Philadelphia: Temple University Press.

James, P. (1999). "Masculinities under Reconstruction: Classroom Pedagogy and Cultural Change." *Gender and Education, 11*(4), 395–412.

Jones, K. T. and Brazo, C. (2014). "Cultivating a Community of Truth through Critical Pedagogy when Faced with Resistance: Teaching My Gender Students How to 'Ride the Bus'." *International Journal for Innovation Education and Research, 2*(03), 43–55.

Kumashiro, K. (2002). *Troubling Education: Queer Activism and Anti-Oppressive Pedagogy.* New York: RoutledgeFalmer.

Letts, W., IV, and Sears, T. (1999). *Queering Elementary Education: Advancing the Dialogue about Sexuality and Schooling.* Lanham, MD: Rowman and Littlefield.

Lewis, M. (1992). "Interrupting Patriarchy: Politics, Resistance and Transformation in the Feminist Classroom." in Luke, C., *Feminisms and Critical Pedagogy.* New York: Routledge.

Lewis, M. (1993). *Without a Word: Teaching Beyond Women's Silence.* New York: Routledge.

Liasidou, A. (2012). "Inclusive Education and Critical Pedagogy at the Intersections of Disability, Race, Gender and Class." *Journal for Critical Education Policy Studies, 10,* 168–184.

Luke, C. (1996). "Feminist Pedagogy Theory: Reflections on Power and Authority." *Educational Theory, 46,* 283–302.

Luke, C. and Gore, J. (1992). *Feminisms and Critical Pedagogy.* New York: Routledge.

Luker, K. (1997). *Dubious Conceptions: The Politics of Teenage Pregnancy.* Cambridge, MA: Harvard University Press.

Lundberg, A. and Werner, A. (2012). "The Pedagogy of Gender Studies: Between Experience-Based Learning and Scholarly Dialogue." In Lundberg, A. and Werner, A. (eds.), *Gender Studies Education and Pedagogy* (pp. 5–7). Gothenburg: Swedish Secretariat for Gender Research.

Lutrell, W. (2003). *Pregnant Bodies, Fertile Minds: Gender, Race, and the Schooling of Pregnant Teens.* New York: Routledge.

Lynch, K., Grummel, B., and Devine, D. (2012). *New Managerialism in Education: Commercialization, Carelessness and Gender.* New York and London: Palgrave-Macmillan.

Macdonald, A. and Sanchez-Casal, S. (2002). *Twenty-First Century Feminist Classrooms: Pedagogies of Identity and Difference.* New York: Palgrave Macmillan.

McRobbie, A. (1991). *Feminism and Youth Culture: From Jackie to Just Seventeen.* London: Macmillan.

Maher, F. (1999). "Progressive Education and Feminist Pedagogies: Issues in Gender, Power, and Authority." *Teachers College Record, 101*(1) (Fall), 35–39.

Mason, G. (2001). *The Spectacle of Violence: Homophobia, Gender and Knowledge.* New York: Routledge.

Mayo, C. (2004). "The Tolerance that Dare Not Speak Its Name." In Boler, M. (ed.), *Democratic Dialogue in Education: Troubling Speech, Disturbing Silence* (pp. 33–47). New York: Peter Lang.

Mayo, C. (2007). *Disputing the Subject of Sex: Sexuality and Public School Controversies.* Lanham, MD: Rowman and Littlefield.

Meyer, E. J. (2008). "A Feminist Reframing of Bullying and Harassment: Transforming Schools through Critical Pedagogy." *McGill Journal of Education, 1*(1), 33–48.

Mignolo, W. D. and Tlostanova, M. V. (2006). "Theorizing from the Borders: Shifting to Geo- and Body-Politics of Knowledge." *European Journal of Social Theory, 9*(2), 205–221.

Minh-ha, T. (1989). *Woman Native Other: Writing Postcoloniality and Feminism.* Bloomington: Indiana University Press.

Mohanty, C., Russo, A., and Torres, L. (1991). *Third World Women and the Politics of Feminism.* Bloomington: Indiana University Press.

Ng, R., Staton, P., and Scane, J. (1995). *Anti-Racism, Feminism, and Critical Approaches to Education.* Westport, CN: Bergin & Garvey.

Parmeter, S., Reti, I., Hart, E. L., and Rosa, M. E. (1988). *The Lesbian in Front of the Classroom: Writings by Lesbian Teachers.* Santa Cruz, CA: HerBooks.

Perumal, J. (2007). *Identity, Diversity and Teaching for Social Justice.* New York: Peter Lang.

Pillow, W. (2004). *Unfit Subjects: Educational Policy and the Teen Mother.* New York: Routledge.

Pinar, W. (1988). *Queer Theory in Education*. New York: Lawrence Erlbaum.
Puigvert, L. (2008). "Breaking the Silence: The Struggle against Gender Violence in Universities." *International Journal of Critical Pedagogy, 1*, 1–6.
Rasmussen, M. L., Rofes, E., and Talburt, S. (2004). *Youth and Sexualities: Pleasure, Subversion, and Insubordination In and Out of Schools*. London: Palgrave McMillan.
Rhoads, R. (1994). *Coming Out in College: The Struggle for a Queer Identity.* Westport, CN: Bergin & Garvey.
Rosaldo, M. and Lamphere, L., eds. (1974). *Women, Culture, and Society.* Stanford, CA: Stanford University Press.
Sanjakdar, F., Allen, L., Rasmussen, M. L., Quinlivan, K., Brömdal, A., and Aspin, C. (2015). "In Search of Critical Pedagogy in Sexuality Education: Visions, Imaginations, and Paradoxes." *Review of Education, Pedagogy, and Cultural Studies, 37*(1), 53–70.
Segal, L. (1997). "Sexualities." In Woodward, K. (ed.), *Identity and Difference* (pp. 183–238). London: Sage.
Shapiro, S. (1999). *Pedagogy and the Politics of the Body: A Critical Praxis*. New York and London: Garland Publishing.
Simon, R. I. (1992). *Teaching against the Grain: Texts for a Pedagogy of Possibility.* New York: Bergin & Garvey.
Stromquist, N. (2004). "The Educational Nature of Feminist Action." In G. Foley (ed.), *Dimensions of Adult Learning: Adult Education and Training in a Global Era.* Sydney: Allen & Unwin; Berkshire, UK: Open University Press-McGraw Hill.
Sudbury, J. (1998). *Other Kinds of Dreams.* New York: Routledge.
Talburt, S. and Steinberg, S. (2000). *Thinking Queer: Sexuality, Culture, and Education* (*Counterpoints: Studies in the Postmodern Theory of Education*, vol. 118). New York: Peter Lang.
Thomas, M. and Rugambwa, A. (2011). "Equity, Power, and Capabilities: Constructions of Gender in a Tanzanian Secondary School." *The John Hopkins University Press, 23*(3), 153–175.
Thompson, J. (1983). *Learning Liberation: Women's Response to Men's Education.* London: Croom Helm.
Thompson, J. (2000). *Women, Class, and Education*. London: Routledge.
Tierney, W. G. (1997). *Academic Outlaws: Queer Theory and Cultural Studies in the Academy.* Thousand Oaks, CA: Sage.
Tisdell, E. J. (1993). "Feminism and Adult Learning: Power, Pedagogy, and Praxis." In Merriam, S. B. (ed.), *An Update on Adult Learning Theory* (pp. 91–103). San Francisco: Jossey-Bass Publishers.
Tisdell, E. J. (1998). "Poststructural Feminist Pedagogies: The Possibilities and Limitations of Feminist Emancipatory Adult Learning Theory and Practice." *Adult Education Quarterly, 48*, 139–156.
Tisdell, E. J. (2000). "Feminist Pedagogies." In Hayes, E. and Flannery, D. D. (eds.), *Women as Learners: The Significance of Gender in Adult Learning* (pp. 155–183). San Francisco: Jossey-Bass.
Trujillo, C. (1998). *Living Chicana Theory*. Berkeley, CA: Third Woman Press.
Unks, G., ed. (1995). *The Gay Teen. Educational Practice and Theory for Lesbian, Gay and Bisexual Adolescents*. New York: Routledge.
Valadez, G. and Elsbree, A. (2005). "Queer Coyotes: Transforming Education to Be More Accepting, Affirming, and Supportive of Queer Individuals." *Journal of Latinos and Education, 4*(3), 171–192.
Vavrus, M. (2008). "Sexuality, Schooling, and Teacher Identity Formation: A Critical Pedagogy for Teacher Education." *Teaching and Teacher Education, 25*(3), 383–390.
Wallace, M. (1990). *Invisibility Blues: From Pop to Theory*. New York: Routledge.
Warren, K., ed. (1997). *Ecofeminism: Women, Culture, Nature*. Bloomington: Indiana University Press.
Weedon, C. (1987). *Feminist Practice and Poststructuralist Theory*. Oxford: Blackwell.
Weeks, B. (1995). "The Body and Sexuality." In Hall, S., Held, D., Hubert, D., and Thompson, K. (eds.), *Modernity: An Introduction to Modern Societies* (pp. 363–388). Cambridge, UK: Polity.
Weiler, K. (1994). "Freire and a Feminist Pedagogy of Difference." In McLaren, P. L. and Lankshear, C. (eds.). *Politics of Liberation: Paths from Freire* (pp. 12–40). New York: Routledge.
Weiler, K. (1998). *Women Teaching for Change: Gender, Class and Power*. South Hadley, MA: Bergin & Garvey.
Weiler, K. (2001). *Feminist Engagements: Reading, Resisting, and Reinventing Male Theorists in Education and Cultural Studies*. New York: Routledge.
Weis, L. and Fine, M. (2005). *Beyond Silenced Voices: Class, Race, and Gender in United State Schools*. Albany, NY: SUNY Press.
Welton, D. (1998). *Body and Flesh*. Boston: Blackwell.

Part Five

Critical Literacies

Introduction to Part Five

In concert with Paulo Freire's integrated vision of language literacy and pedagogy, critical literacy does not constitute a subfield or a different approach to literacy, but, rather, is one of the major pillars of critical pedagogy. For Freire, an emancipatory education is founded on an evolving capacity to read the world critically and effectively problematize the asymmetrical relations of power, which structurally reproduce inequalities and social exclusions within schools and society. Moreover, the tradition of emancipatory education is firmly rooted in the teaching and learning of literacy and orality in its multiple forms, as vehicles for the development of conscientization.

Given the eminently political nature of education, literacy cannot simply be reduced to the mastery of decoding and encoding skills, or to the neutral and technical teaching of language symbols, in that language and power are pivotal to understanding the politics of critical literacies in schools. As such, critical literacies can be understood as the vehicles through which critical pedagogy is implemented and enacted, including biliteracies and media literacies. These all encompass a pedagogical process of teaching and learning, by which students and teachers interrogate the world, unmask ideological and hegemonic discourses, and frame their actions, in the interest of the larger struggle for social justice. As such, teachers and students together deconstruct and demystify the curriculum, challenging the fragmentation, instrumentalism, and absolute nature of official knowledge. This is actualized, in part, through the use of a political economic framework that helps to unveil how education serves the interests of the marketplace.

Media literacy too has received increasing attention in the last two decades, as greater classroom emphasis continues to be placed on the use of different forms of visual media. Moreover, the link between literacy, media, and popular culture has also played a significant role in the manner in which critical educators have theorized the images and messages that students are exposed to out in the world as consumers of media. Much of the critical pedagogical focus has been directed toward assisting students to develop critical media literacy skills in order to counter stereotypes and debilitating images that can negatively impact their lives and communities. In addition, critical media literacy along with popular culture also encompasses important pedagogical efforts to create empowering spaces, where youth can create images that support their cultural evolution as historical subjects of their own lives and transformative participants in their communities and the world.

Accordingly, the articles included in this section are informed by a critical pedagogical view of literacies and media literacy. Exposed is the value-laden, political nature of education that informs the teaching of literacy in schools. Fundamental to this understanding of schooling is awareness that the teaching of literacy, the media, and popular culture can all function as mechanisms to perpetuate asymmetries of power and privilege in the larger society or as emancipatory opportunities for a transformative vision of education and society. Proposed here is a liberatory vision of literacy in its different manifestations, intrinsically linked to the diverse identities, languages, and cultural meanings that students bring to the classroom and that they enact in their everyday lives.

True to this intent, the articles examine a variety of key questions, related to the teaching of literacy. How is literacy taught? What are teachers' expectations and interactions with students? What is the goal of literacy? What kind of curriculum is being used in the classroom? How is student experience incorporated? How conducive for learning is the classroom environment? How are issues of power addressed? What is the hierarchy of diverse knowledge and languages at work in the classroom? What are the assumptions, stereotypes, and ideologies that teachers bring to their teaching? What are the messages that young people receive about themselves from the media? In sum, the authors address the cultural politics that undergird traditional notions of literacy—extending our political understanding of literacy and its significance to education and society.

Summary of Articles

"In Critical Literacy: Bringing Theory to Praxis," Elizabeth Bishop argues for an activist approach to critical literacy in both theory and praxis. Given this approach, Bishop traces the historical and contemporary foundations of critical literacy, situated within a political and ideological battlefield. She does this by providing a comprehensive overview of the seminal literature by scholars who have informed multiple and alternative critical literacies. She offers examples and limitations of critical literacy projects in schools, with hopes of deepening the understanding of youth organizing and activism outside of schools, as a democratic and emancipatory form of educating alongside youth—revealing the powerful impact of learning how to read the word and the world.

In his article, "Teaching How to Read the World and Change It," Robert Peterson explains how the teaching of the world and the word happens. This article provides an excellent example of how critical pedagogy is enacted in the classroom, even under the heavy constraints of a powerful conservative movement in schools. Peterson's account offers a variety of practical applications, from thematic teaching—or generative themes as Freire calls them—to experiential learning for second language students. He provides excellent examples of how to teach using a problem posing pedagogy and how to use dialogue and conscientization, as a vehicle for the development of voice and participation within a middle-school classroom.

The article by Bettina Love, "Oh, They're Sending a Bad Message," reveals the ways in which Hip Hop critical literacy/pedagogy challenges dominant educational and Eurocentric discourses of schooling and society. As an empowering critical pedagogical tool, Hip Hop literacies expose the misleading constructions of Black masculinity that glamorize crime, sex, and violence in the media. This ethnographic journey situated within the context of the Dirty South leads Love to examine the ways in which three African American males read Hip Hop and their world, using counter-narratives that challenge the racist messages and stereotypical archetypes of Black males found embedded within popular culture and media. Love suggests that these *bad messages* and hegemonic notions of Blackness can be best challenged and resisted through critical dialogues that serve to foster critical consciousness.

Ernest Morrell examines important questions of youth literacy development in his article "Toward a Critical Pedagogy of Popular Culture: Literacy Development Among Urban Youth." Morrell contends that popular culture can assist youth to deconstruct dominant narratives and, in so doing, engage more effectively with hegemonic school practices, in an effort to forge a more inclusive society. Morrell provides examples for critical literacy educators drawing from his personal experiences teaching hip-hop culture, popular film, and media literacy in ways that allow students to learn, interpret, and deconstruct literary texts and, by so doing, develop their own cultural meanings in ways that support critical consciousness.

In "Reconstructing Technoliteracy," Richard Kahn and Douglas Kellner provide a critical examination into the meanings of technology and literacy and provide insight into what sort of knowledge and skills technoliteracy brings to expanding our understanding of literacy in schools and the world. Kahn and Kellner summarize broad trajectories of development in hegemonic programs of contemporary technoliteracy from their arguable origins as "computer literacy" in the *A Nation at Risk* report of 1983 up to the present call for integration of technology across the curriculum and the standards-based approach, as exemplified by the No Child Left Behind Act of 2001 and 2004's U.S. National Educational Technology Plan. In so doing, they reveal how this approach has been tacitly challenged at the global institutional level and theorize how this might link to a democratic project of revisioning education through multiple literacies.

Questions for Reflection and Dialogue

1. Why do critical pedagogical theorists contend that literacy is a political act? What implication does this have for teaching literacy?
2. What classroom suggestions does Robert Peterson offer to counterbalance the debilitating impact of teacher-proof reading programs?
3. How does Peterson incorporate dialogue, reflection, political action, and critical literacy in his middle school teaching?
4. What are the implications of dominant literacy approaches to the cultural formation and education of working-class students from racialized communities?
5. In what ways does Love conclude that rap messages contribute to the ways that youth construct their racial and gendered identities? What contribution does this make to the education of black male youth?
6. According to Morrell, what contributes to the failure of urban youth to develop "academic" literacy skills? In what ways can critical pedagogical approaches in schools and communities support urban youth in the development of critical literacy skills?
7. What role can critical literacy play in the context of youth organizing, both in and out of the school context?
8. What do Kahn and Kellner mean by reconstructing technoliteracy more broadly? What recommendations do they provide for new critical pedagogies that can inform and be informed by multiple technoliteracies? How can teachers integrate these in their classrooms?

17

Critical Literacy: Bringing Theory to Praxis

Elizabeth Bishop

Literacy is a political battleground. As a writer, I approach literacy learning as an activist educator and a cultural studies researcher. To expand the discourse of activist explorations into literacy, this article discusses critical literacy research with the aim of contextualizing out-of-school youth organizing as a potent learning space for critical literacy praxis. To determine what theoretical frameworks, taxonomies and modes of inquiry offered the most potential to successfully execute further study around literacy learning with activist youth, I read widely across the literature on literacy inside and outside of schools. From a survey of the literature across literacy and youth organizing, there are important connections but only limited research on the exercise of critically literate practices in the development of youth as social justice activists (Blackburn & Clark, 2008).

Critical literacy theory and pedagogy is operationalized through understanding and critically engaging with the material economy of the present. Anderson and Irvine (1993) presented an early conceptual platform that looked at critical literacy through cultural studies, writing:

> The importance of critical literacy being grounded pedagogically in a politics of difference offers learners, regardless of their particular classed, raced, or gendered subjectivities, opportunities to become 'border crossers.' Critical literacy, then, is learning to read and write as part of the process of becoming conscious of one's experience as historically constructed within specific power relations.
>
> (p. 82)

Youth organizers engage in an activist model of citizenship through grassroots organizing, partnering with other community organizers and conducting research with a focus on social responsibility. This method of social inquiry as activism, where individuals organize for education and justice (Morrell, 2008) posits the space for the construction of sociopolitical and activist identities in youth that support literate practice. The skills exercised when participatory in such projects include working with others to building consensus through collaborative decision-making, interpreting public problems and taking action—while promoting youth efficacy (O'Donoghue & Kirshner, 2008).

The skills involved in youth activist and organizing pursuits support the construction of sociopolitical activist identities through learning processes focused on social action. Such organizing frequently involved youth-led decisions to engage topics of identity politics and challenge the stereotypes of youth, particularly the negative representations of young women, youth of color, queer youth, and other marginalized groups (Ginwright, 2010).

This work is aligned, as I demonstrate below, with many traditions in the history of critical literacy—operationalized in both theory and praxis.

Defining Critical Literacy to Become Critically Literate

> In addressing critical literacy we are concerned with the extent to which, and the ways in which, actual and possible social practices and conceptions of reading and writing enable human subjects to understand and engage the politics of daily life in the quest for a more truly democratic social order . . . referring to critical literacy only where concerted efforts are being made to understand and practice reading and writing in ways that enhance the quest for democratic emancipation.
>
> (Lankshear & McLaren, 1993, p. xix)

Critical literacy is built on exploring personal, sociopolitical, economic and intellectual border identities. It dictates a politics of location where learners are positioned to operate as "border crossers" (Anderson & Irvine, 1993). It is also grounded in the ethical imperative to examine the contradictions in society between the meaning of freedom, the demands of social justice, the obligations of citizenship and the structured silence that permeates incidences of suffering in everyday life. It is a kind of literacy about structures, structural violence, and power systems. Critical literacy uses texts and print skills in ways that enable students to examine the politics of daily life within contemporary society with a view to understanding what it means to locate and actively seek out contradictions within modes of life, theories, and substantive intellectual positions.

It is important to maintain deferral in defining critical literacy. Since the 1990s, critical literacy theorists have outlined emancipatory theories of learning (Freire & Macedo, 1987) that addressed the complex relations of language and power through social critique, advocacy, and cultural transformation (Knoblauch & Brannon, 1993). Educational researchers discuss critical literacy as a theory of social practice, as the negotiation of and the creation of meaning for social justice (Greene, 2008). While there is no single model of critical literacy (as there is no single model of youth organizing), the emphasis on Freire's (1970) action-reflection cycle of "praxis" has offered participants a concept through which to construct meanings that support their literacy for civic engagement (Lankshear & McLaren, 1993).

Tracing the History of Critical Literacy Theory

Much of the earliest scholarship on critical literacy is grounded in Freirian pedagogy. In 1987, Freire and Macedo published their expansive volume on literacy and critical pedagogy. In it, they argued that those who are critically literate can not only understand how meaning is socially constructed within texts, but can also come to understand the political and economic contexts in which those texts were created and embedded (Freire & Macedo, 1987). While Freire and Macedo were perhaps the first to initiate a dialogue around the idea of critical literacy in their collection, it was not until 1993 that Lankshear and McLaren issued what was to become the seminal text devoted to the topic. In it, they stated that literacy is more complex than the traditionally defined skills of reading and writing. Rather, they argued that such a traditional definition of literacy is ideologically aligned with particular postures of normative sociopolitical consciousness that are inherently exploitative. By contrast, critical literacy emphasized the social construction of reading, writing and text production within political contexts of inequitable economic, cultural, political, and institutional structures. Lankshear and McLaren argued for critically reflective teaching and research agendas in the tradition of Street (1984), focused on both the forms that literate skills take as social practices and the uses to which those skills are employed.

Lankshear and McLaren made a strong distinction between critical literacy and Hirsch's (1988) "cultural literacy," the latter of which dictated a particular corpus of knowledge young people were expected to know to be appropriately informed Americans. Critical literacy seriously challenged this notion of propriety and warned against such a "colonization of culture" (Lankshear & McLaren, 1993, p. 17). The authors argued that critical literacy is an approach to teaching and learning committed to exploring how and why particular social and cultural groups of persons occupy unequal political positions of access to social structures. Rather than promoting any particular reading of any particular group, critical literacy seeks to interrogate the historical and contemporaneous privileging of and exclusion of groups of people and ideas from mainstream narratives. Throughout their volume, there is a lingering concern for doing critical literacy without falling into a "colonizing logic" or other forms of theoretical imperialism.

The authors did identify three forms of educational practice that critical literacy can take on, varying by their commitment to inquiry and action: liberal education, pluralism, and transformative praxis. Liberal education here means an approach to disciplinary knowledge where intellectual freedom exists and where disparate interpretations are considered, but inevitably contradiction is avoided and rational argumentation wins out. In pluralism, there is an emphasis on reading to evaluate principles that support a loose conception of tolerance. Tolerance here is aligned with a notion of diversity that is grounded on benevolence toward those who are not mainstream (and in the process maintains the mainstream). Against these approaches, the authors forwarded "transformative praxis" as that which takes the radical potential of critical literacy into direct emancipatory action in the world. Praxis is here defined through the Freirian (1970) process of naming the conditions of oppression and struggling collectively with others in a cycle of action-reflection-action against such oppression. Lankshear and McLaren argued that a guiding principle behind the processes of transformative critical literacy praxis involves an analysis "attempting to understand how agents working within established structures of power participate in the social construction of literacies, revealing their political implications" (p. 7).

Critical literacy praxis, which Lankshear and McLaren also called "political and social literacies," involves textual studies that are analyzed at the discursive level in which the texts were created and in which they are sustained. While the authors understood that this move might lead to such literacies being seen as "potentially subversive," they forwarded a key distinction centering on the difference between political indoctrination and the development of a critical consciousness—or what Freire (1970) called "conscientization." They argued that even when students are introduced to texts that might be considered "reactionary," a critical literacy approach involves working with them "to understand the nature and implications of the ideologies on parade; and in doing so engage students in reflection upon their own ideological investments" (p. 8). This purpose and direction of critical literacy is important because it illuminates the difference between the moralistic position taking of indoctrination and an ethical approach to reading through a critical consciousness that neither moralizes nor normalizes.

In the early 1990s, McLaren and Lankshear were some of the more radical scholars writing on the topic of critical literacy. Around the same time, Apple (1992) published an essay on "the text and cultural politics" which examined the social legitimation of certain knowledge in schools. Making the argument that "no curriculum is neutral" and that the selection and organization of curricular information is necessarily an ideological process, Apple argued that schools, teachers, and students must study the constructed nature of knowledge about institutions and experiences (whose history and knowledge is included in and replicated by curricular texts and operational contexts) in order to reflectively determine if the school functions as a democratic institution and/or as a site of social control.

Illuminating this struggle in their collection on critical teaching and literacy, Knoblauch and Brannon (1993) outlined four approaches to critical teaching and the idea of literacy learning which spanned: functional literacy and the rhetoric of objectivism; interpretive literacy and the politics of nostalgia; expressivism as a literacy for personal growth; and critical literacy. Of these four central approaches, the authors argued that only critical literacy offered the complexity of a sociopolitical framework which foregrounded the study of "the relationships of language and power with practical knowledge of how to use language for advocacy, social critique, and cultural transformation" (Knoblauch & Brannon, 1993, p. 152). This made critical literacy distinct amongst a variety of approaches to literacy learning that claimed to address the sociocultural while remaining intentionally distant from the political.

Across their collection, Knoblauch and Brannon echoed Street's (1984) concern that the tyranny of academic literacies can serve to socially reproduce dominant ideologies (racism, sexism, classism, homophobia, xenophobia) that perpetuate forms of injustice. Writing that same year, scholars ranging from Hull (1993) to Comber (1993) were beginning to study the implications for critical literacy learning in schools. Comber (2001) later argued that one of the best ways to approach critical literacy is to begin with multiple sources and opposing views to interrogate their construction by specific individuals with particular (always political) goals.

At the turn of the millennium, just before the 2001 re-authorization of the Elementary and Secondary Education Act (ESEA) as the controversial No Child Left Behind Act (NCLB), Janks (2000) posited four possible orientations for future approaches to critical literacy education based on different perspectives on the relationship between language and power: (a) to understand how language maintains social and political forms of domination; (b) to provide access to dominant forms of language without compromising the integrity of non-dominant forms; (c) to promote a diversity which requires attention to the way that uses of language create social identities; and (d) to bring a design perspective that emphasizes the need to use and select from a wide range of available cultural sign systems. Although frequently taken in isolation, Janks argued that it is through the interdependence of these approaches that learners can most fully engage theories and pedagogies of critical literacy.

Contemporary Examples of Critical Literacy Research

Where and how is critical literacy most fully realized? Recent scholarship on critical literacy reified the emphasis on a type of "reading the world" through understanding the social and historical factors influencing social justices and injustices. Across the last decade of research, five overlapping components have been consistently articulated as "core principles" for cycles of critical literacy (Comber & Simpson, 2001), frequently conceived of as the "transformative elements" in critical literacy pedagogy (Lewison, Flint & Van Sluys, 2002). I have synthesized these concepts from across the literature as: (a) mobilizing learners as social actors with knowledge and skills to disrupt the commonplace; (b) conducting research, analysis and interrogation of multiple viewpoints on an issue; (c) identifying issues focused on sociopolitical realities in the context of the lives of the learners; (d) designing and undertaking actions focused on social justice outside of the classroom; and (e) reflecting upon actions taken and creating vision(s) for future project(s). This taxonomy of critical literacy outlines five tenets that researchers, educators and youth have used across the literature to define their own projects on their own terms.

The major emphasis across various critical literacy projects has been a naming of and a willingness to reflect upon the role that language and texts play in the construction of the self and the social. Provenzo (2005) called it an activist practice to ask questions that critically interrogate, interpret and contextualize the ways in which people can be empowered and disempowered. He argued that all learners should ask questions about who speaks in a culture, who defines literacy and whose knowledge is included in the creation and definition of curricula in learning communities.

In practice, researchers and educators have articulated and studied critical literacy in a host of different ways. Petrone and Gibney (2005) drew on the work of critical literacy theorists to articulate a "democratic pedagogy" in American literature classrooms where students investigate and transform their worlds through an inquiry-based examination of culture and society, to consider what is present, what is missing, and what is possible. For Petrone and Gibney, this approach to teaching literature and intertextuality is about "foregrounding historical, cultural, and social issues" in the interest of supporting the development of critical citizens who seek to expand the possibilities of democratic public life (p. 36). They argued that the English Language Arts curriculum should provide a space for students to deepen their traditional literacy skills while becoming critical and skilled "consumers, producers, and distributors of texts and information" (p. 39).

Singer's (2006) text on "writing and reading to change the world" offered a series of stories of justice told through collaborative writing practices. Using examples inside of schools, Singer studied students writing about stories of injustice, finding an audience and collaborators while writing themselves into activism. In Singer's study, the youth studied models of expository essays about activists while reading Philip Hoose's (2001) text about the influence of youth throughout the history of the social justice movement in the United States. Writing "toward change," the students were asked: "what does your activist story teach about movement toward making positive social change?" (Singer, 2006, p. 97). As the students selected and executed their culminating projects on issues of activism, Singer noted that the participants became "consumed with the world outside of the school," becoming experts in activism as well as experts in research literacy (Singer, 2006, p. 112).

That same year, Borsheim and Petrone (2006) published a study about "teaching the research paper for local action" in which they framed classroom-based learning through a consideration of how students engage in critical literacies through the consumption, production, and distribution of texts. As classroom teachers, the authors introduced a research paper unit that focused on social action locally to provide students with an opportunity to critically investigate their contexts and respond through the production of texts promoting positive social change. Echoing Freire and Macedo (1987), they called for individuals to make "meaningful" observations about their contexts – in this case, their schools. Individually, students were asked to follow a research cycle that followed five steps: (a) develop community-based topics to learn more about them or seek to change them; (b) conduct primary as well as secondary research, including interviews, observations, and surveys; (c) write a traditional academic research paper; (d) produce a "real" research text (e.g. documentary, newspaper article, etc.); and (e) distribute their text to real audiences to help raise awareness about or change some aspect of their school or community (Borsheim & Petrone, 2006, p. 79). The authors spoke of the commitment, curiosity, and motivation necessary for students to see themselves as researchers who can exact "real" change in their school or community context.

One interesting finding to emerge from this study was that students reported the research project process was a positive experience that filled the void of traditional research papers in school (lack of voice, purpose, or audience). By identifying issues and constructing research rooted in their everyday lives, the youth remained engaged in a literate process of contextualized inquiry and research. Students secured interviews with executives and political figures in their community, and reported feeling like "real citizens" (p. 82). Borsheim and Petrone also wrote that many positive results were unanticipated, such as shifts in "attitudes, ownership, community involvement, and oral and written communication" (p. 82). There is much to explore here in relation to the relevance of the unanticipated, including a continued interrogation of the definitions of citizenship.

More recently, Phelps (2010) argued that there are uses in applying critical literacy to the non-fiction study of cultural and ideological diversity, focusing particularly on learning about Islam in America. Phelps demonstrated how critical literacy is used to debunk stereotypical and harmful representations by introducing sociopolitical dimensions. By acknowledging that the ideological foundations of knowledge, culture, and identity are always political, Phelps argued that a critical literacy lens helps to reveal the social functions of texts in positioning individuals and groups of people (p. 191). Echoing the distinctions between critical teaching and critical literacy, Phelps replicated Cervetti, Pardales and Damico (2001)'s model of critical literacy that disrupted the commonplace to focus on sociopolitical issues, to develop more nuanced views on complex contemporary topics and take action to promote social justice. Citing the work of Leland, Harste, Ociepka, Lewison and Vasquez (1999), Phelps argued that "doing critical literacy" in classrooms involves guiding learners to ask certain kinds of questions when engaging with any texts, such as: what is the purpose of the text? How does the text try to position the reader? How does the text construct reality? Whose interests are or are not served by the ideas in the text? What worldviews are or are not represented?

Limitations to Critical Literacy Projects in Schools

In search of practical applications of critical literacy, Behrman (2006) conducted a review of the research on classroom practices that support critical literacy. Attempting to identify and locate teaching and learning strategies consistent with critical literacy, Behrman cited an immediate problem: critical literacy is frequently described in the research literature as a theory with practical implication rather than an instructional method. Arguably, it is both and neither. While Behrman argued that such conceptions lack consistent application, he acknowledged that critical literacy authors such as Luke (2000) have intentionally resisted the development of any narrow methodology that claimed to formulaically enact critical literacy (while nevertheless replicating certain approaches).

Citing the democratizing values of bringing critical literacy from theory into practice, Behrman catalogued a list of common practices, articulated in six broad categories for critical literacy learning tasks: (a) reading supplementary texts; (b) reading multiple texts; (c) reading from a resistant perspective; (d) producing counter-texts; (e) conducting student-choice research projects; and (f) taking social action. Noting that the "social action" projects can produce unsatisfactory results despite the best intentions, Behrman found that the goals of critical literacy (detailed through an emphasis on democratization and social justice in the classroom) are not reflected in the hierarchical relations through which the classroom traditionally functions. As such, he argued that no pedagogy that presumes a hierarchical relationship can support the development of critical literacy learning.

In her foreword to Lankshear and McLaren's (1993) critical text, Maxine Greene called for a pedagogy that emphasized personal and social transformation beyond mere identification with dominant social codes. At that time, Greene contended that the postmodern emphasis on discourse, textuality, difference, and the structures of power should promote action-oriented dialogues around problems of oppression, equality, and justice. Yet time and again, postmodern scholars and their critics alike have articulated the tragic fault of critical literacy, naming the context of formal schooling as a limitation hindering social action. Although not always true, the overwhelming obstacle to critical literacy in schools has been the failure to put principle to practice, to fully enact models of critical literacy learning through activist actions in authentic spaces that extend outside of the classroom.

Since its entrance into educational theoretical parlance, critical literacy (like its relative critical theory) has been displaced and dislocated. It has been dismissed as being anything from too pedagogically loose of a model to too politically activist of a model (Freesmith, 2006; Luke & Dooley, 2007). As early as 1999, critical literacy scholars Comber and Nixon (1999) noted that literacy practices inside schools primarily function to sustain dominant cultural norms and ideologies. Even Borsheim and Petrone (2006) acknowledged that, "because of the nature of critical research, students are likely to ask questions that some people prefer they not ask about topics that some people prefer they not address" (p. 82). The focus on reflection and the examination of immediate context and internal constructions proved to be the most threatening aspect of critical literacy learning. Even when students considered sociopolitical, cultural, and ideological issues that could lead to possible action steps, they frequently did not take action if they were not explicitly supported to do so (Phelps, 2010).

While critical literacy has historically been theorized within classroom spaces (Comber & Simpson, 2001; McDaniel, 2006) and researched as a conceptualization of particular operations of curricula inside schools, the central purpose and function of critical literacy praxis had been articulated as an assessment of texts in order to understand, uncover, and/or alter relationships of power and domination both inside and outside of formal educational contexts (Freire & Macedo, 1987; Hull, 1993; Morrell, 2004). Yet, despite being theorized as an emancipatory theory of learning, researchers have consistently demonstrated that critical literacy is limited when attempting to take social action to redress political inequities and injustices within the context of school-based literacy curricula. This limitation is both systemic and diffuse, and points directly to the question: where can critical literacy learning be authentically exercised?

In 2007, Blackburn and Clark published their collection on "literacy research for political action and social change." In it, they identified the need to take critical reading and text production outside of the classroom and into activist spaces with youth to engage their immediate needs for social change through political action that is not regulated by school-based interests. The authors argued that future literacy research must engage methodologies that foreground the immediate needs of participants, particularly focused on tackling the connections between the local and the global in literacy research for political action. They contended that such research creates kinetic connections beyond the local through a focus on the social practice of collaborative, collective engagement with the texts and context of activism.

Lessons on the Actionable Elements of Critical Literacy Praxis

The limitations to conducting critical literacy in classrooms have numerous implications. For some educators and youth, the lack of support to enact "social action" projects out of classroom-based curricula results in either a reticence to engage in such work, or a fear of the implications for doing so extra-institutionally. Even in conversation with some researchers, it is easy to trace a sense of defeat in conducting deep critical literacy work to examine social and political injustices and inequities. For many, such outlooks are valid and confirmed by experience. Yet as researchers, we overlook the important question of context when assessing where to engage critical literacy praxis.

Lankshear and McLaren argued two decades ago that in order to continue conducting critical literacy research, scholars need to conduct research that: has historical function; approaches the process of becoming literate as more than simply becoming rational; takes an oppositional stance toward privileged groups; seeks means toward political empowerment; supports multiple literacies; and counters the essentialization of difference. The authors argued that the most serious issues confronting literacy researchers was to create and participate in studies that accounted for the subjectivity of individuals while maintaining a fight for social justice:

> We must maintain recognition of the materiality of the sign as a product of social forces and relations of power, as a lived embodiment of both oppression and possibility, subordination and emancipation; in the final analysis, we must reject any notion of the human subject which seals itself off from its own history, its own link to the community of multiple selves which surrounds it, its narratives of freedom; to construct a truly critical literacy, we need to make despair less salutary and economic, social, racial, and gender equality politically conceivable and pedagogically possible.
>
> (Lankshear & McLaren, 1993, p. 415)

Arguably one of the most prominent contemporary critical literacy scholars, Ernest Morrell foregrounded his early work (2004) in a cultural studies epistemology where the historical, social, economic, and cultural contexts of urban youth are ethnographically explored. He approached critical literacy with an emphasis on situated learning (Morrell, 2004). Here, learning is defined as changing participation in relevant sociocultural activity over a period of time as one is apprenticed into activist practice.

Across his corpus, Morrell frequently posits critical literacy as a "critical theory of literacy" overtly aimed at social and political change (2004, 2007, 2008). Morrell's 2004 study apprenticing youth as critical researchers of popular culture was designed around core components of critical literacy work with youth that would "capture literacy events that demonstrate academic mastery and critical consciousness" (p. 8). At that time, Morrell (2004) designated the tenets of critical literacy as:

> The ability to challenge existing power relations in texts and to produce new texts that delegitimize these relations; a consciousness of the relationship between the dominant culture's use of language, literacy and social injustice; the ability not only to read words but to read the world into and onto texts and recognize the correlation between the word and the world; and the ability to create political texts that inspire transformative action and conscious reflection.
>
> (p. 57)

Morrell's research frequently focused on the ways in which young people come to know and adhere to socially sanctioned ways of speaking and acting without being subsumed into oppressive relations. Morrell argued in his 2004 critical ethnography that the urban literacy classroom is an ideal context for critical literacy learning that engages students personally and as citizens actively transforming their sociopolitical world. The findings of the 2004 study demonstrated that critical literacy projects could produce proficiency in academic and other literacies, where student-researchers began to value popular cultural knowledge as well as academic content while developing their skills with the tools of investigation, inquiry, analysis and text production. His project demonstrates the need for the further study of organizing projects geared toward engaging youth as "critical citizens" through critical literacy.

In Blackburn and Clark's (2007) collection, Morrell (2007) discussed critical literacy and popular culture in urban education "toward a pedagogy of access and dissent." In that chapter, he contended that engaging in critical literacy involves the consumption, production, and distribution of print and new media texts by, with, and on behalf of marginalized populations in the interests of naming, exposing, and destabilizing power relations while promoting individual freedom and expression. Citing Hull (1993), Morrell (2007) argued that critical literacy is the ability to not only read and write, but also to assess textual relationships between power and domination.

The classroom-based limitation yet lingers here amidst an actionable optimism. Beck (2005) wrote in search of a "place" for critical literacy in schools. Locating critical literacy as a movement drawn out of a cultural studies tradition aimed at transforming social inequity, Beck warned against placing issues of power and difference at the foreground of classroom conversations. Connected as it is to the attitude of questioning the social, political, and economic conditions under which texts were constructed, Beck wrote that critical literacy learning involves students examining the reproduction of inequality and injustice, while gaining a critical consciousness to participate in and transform their social worlds. Studying the use of critical literacy learning practices in an all-male maximum-security facility in Canada, Beck concluded that it is not a good idea to teach critical literacy in settings where silence is encouraged, such as prisons and schools.

Approaching Critical Literacy Through Youth Organizing

Janks (2000) defined critical literacy as multiple, as skill and social practice that is both embodied and shifting. She argued that there is an on-going socio-historical imperative for critical literacy learning that positions identity investment and the constitution of subjectivities within complex, multimodal, inter-textual social spaces. She highlighted this notion of critical literacy as both a shifting skill set and embodied social practices that function through the interdependent negotiation of pedagogical domination, diversity, access and design.

Such negotiations are central when considering the constraints to critical literacy inside of schools based on structural and institutional limitations. The tension between school-based literacy acquisition and critical language awareness (Dozier, Johnston & Rogers, 2006) points toward the need to create and support out-of-school spaces for the development of critical literacy practices that counteract the normalization of inequity and the privileging of academic literacy. Doing so supports learners to engage alternative literacies as powerful everyday practices that generate critical social thought and action. This is not to say that literacy skills cannot be developed. Rather, this points to the questions that I have raised throughout: where, when and under what conditions can critical literacy learning be more fully realized for young people?

As if in answer to the challenge of conducting critical literacy learning inside school spaces, the field of youth organizing emerged over the past decade as an exemplar alternative space for critical literacy to be enacted outside of schools (Ginwright, 2010). These spaces support youth engagement in activism as a process, making social and political change in many ways that align to the working conception of critical literacy praxis that has been outlined throughout this chapter. Specifically, taking critical reading and text production outside of school and into activist spaces with youth engages their immediate needs (Blackburn & Clark, 2007).

The theories and practices of critical literacy are prevalent throughout the literature on youth organizing although the taxonomy has not been overtly named in the research. Youth organizing is a relatively new field of research, a hybrid space that is activist in content and that actively resists co-optation. Obviously, youth community organizing and social activism have a long history well before either concept was even considered a "field" for study. In brief, the contemporary study of youth organizing is an extension of positive youth development, situated in the crux between traditional youth development, youth leadership and community organizing (Ginwright, 2010). The study of youth organizing and activism emerged out of the field of youth development, built on a foundation of an analysis of power and inequity. In organizing programs, such processes are learned through the practice and acquisition of skills necessary to pursue policy and social change, from lobbying and campaigning to taking direct action (Torres-Fleming, Valdes & Pillai, 2010).

As a context for critical education, youth organizing projects take on critical literacy through four central components: (a) youth identify community issues for thematic investigation; (b) they participate in and conduct social movement history and political education workshops; (c) community organizing and media trainings; and (d) campaign development, outreach, action and reflection. However, what is not yet well defined are the literacy-related skills and outcomes of this community-based work.

Defining the parameters of critical literacy is intentionally challenging—and is thus well suited for the task of understanding the dynamic learning models of urban youth organizing without dictating the parameters for future projects. Emerging from these insights, as well as from an ethical and political commitment to democratic and emancipatory forms of educating alongside youth, it is imperative for critical literacy researchers to foreground the language of activist learning as political and historical. By focusing on instantiations of critical literacy praxis that demonstrate critical consciousness, inter-subjective re-imaginings and articulations of becoming, youth organizing is an ideal frontier for enacting positive social change work with young people. In the process, the deep skills of critical literacy can be honored, supported, expanded and re-visioned to allow deep individual and collective development. More research is needed to understand the function and operation of critical literacy in the context of organizing, such that supports powerful learning beyond school walls.

References

Anderson, G. L., & Irvine, P. (1993). Informing critical literacy with ethnography. In. C. Lankshear & P. L. McLaren, (Eds.) *Critical literacy: Politics, praxis, and the postmodern* (pp. 81–104). Albany, NY: SUNY Press.

Apple, M. (1992). The text and cultural politics. *Educational Researcher,* 5, 4–11.

Beck, A. S. (2005). A place for critical literacy. *Journal of Adolescent and Adult Literacy, 48*(5), February 2005, 392–400.

Behrman, E. H. (2006). Teaching about language, power, and text: A review of classroom practices that support critical literacy. *Journal of Adolescent and Adult Literacy, 49*(6), March 2006, 490–498.

Blackburn, M. V. & Clark, C.T. (2007). *Literacy research for political action and social change.* New York: Peter Lang.

Borsheim, C., & Petrone, R. (2006). Teaching the research paper for local action. *The English Journal, 95*(4), 78–83.

Cervetti, G., Pardales, M., & Damico, J. (2001). A tale of differences: Comparing the traditions, perspectives, and educational goals of critical reading and critical literacy. *Reading Online, 4*(4).

Comber, B. (1993). *Classroom explorations in critical literacy.* The Australian Journal of Language and Literacy, 16(1), 73–83.

Comber, B., & Nixon, H. (1999) Literacy education as a site for social justice: what do our practices do? In C. Edelsky (Ed.), *Making justice our project: Teachers working toward critical whole language practice* (pp. 316–351). Urbana, Illinois: National Council of Teachers of English.

Comber, B. (2001). Negotiating critical literacies. *School Talk 6*(3), 1–2.

Comber, B., & Simpson, A. (2001). (Eds.) *Negotiating critical literacies in classrooms.* New Jersey: Lawrence Erlbaum.

Dozier, C., Johnston P., & Rogers, R. (2006). *Critical literacy/critical teaching: Tools for preparing responsive teachers.* New York: Teachers College Press.

Freesmith, D. (2006). The politics of the English curriculum: Ideology in the campaign against critical literacy in The Australian. *English in Australia, 41*(1), 25–30.

Freire, P. (1970). *Pedagogy of the oppressed.* New York: Herder & Herder.

Freire, P. & Macedo, D. (1987). *Literacy: Reading the word and the world.* South Hadley, MA: Bergin & Garve.

Ginwright, S. (2010). *Building a pipeline for justice: Understanding youth organizing and the leadership pipeline.* Occasional Paper Series, no. 10. New York: Funder's Collaborative on Youth Organizing.

Greene, S., ed. (2008). *Literacy as a civil right: Reclaiming social justice in literacy teaching and learning.* New York: Peter Lang.

Hirsch, E.D. (1988). *Cultural literacy: What every American needs to know.* New York: Vintage.

Hoose, P. (2001) *It's our world, too! Young people who are making a difference.* New York: Farrar, Straus and Giroux.

Hull, G. (1993). Critical literacy and beyond: Lessons learned from students and workers in a vocational program and on the job. *Anthropology and Education Quarterly, 24*(4), 308–317.

Janks, H. (2000). Domination, access, diversity, and design: A synthesis for critical literacy education. *Educational Review,* 52, 175–186.

Knoblauch, C. H. & Brannon, L. (1993). *Critical teaching and the idea of literacy.* Heinemann: Portsmouth, NH.

Lankshear, C. & McLaren, P., eds. (1993). *Critical literacy: Radical and postmodernist perspectives.* Albany, NY: SUNY Press.

Lankshear, C. (1994). Critical literacy (Occasional Paper No. 3). Belconnen, Australian Capital Territory: Australian Curriculum Studies Association.

Leland, C., Harste, J., Ociepka, A., Lewison, M., & Vasquez, V. (1999). Exploring critical literacy: You can hear a pin drop. *Language Arts, 77*(1), 70–78.

Lewison, M., Flint, A.S., & Van Sluys, K. (2002). Taking on critical literacy: The journey of newcomers and novices. *Language Arts 79*(5), 382–392.

Luke, A. (2000). Critical literacy in Australia: A matter of context and standpoint. *Journal of Adolescent & Adult Literacy, 43*(5), 448–461.

Luke, A. & Dooley, K. (2007). Critical literacy and second language In E. Hinkel (Ed.), *Handbook of Research in Second Language Teaching and Learning* (Vol II). New York: Routledge.

McDaniel, C. (2006). *Critical literacy: A way of thinking, a way of life.* New York: Peter Lang.

Morrell, E. (2004). *Becoming critical researchers: Literacy and empowerment for urban youth.* New York: Peter Lang.

Morrell, E. (2007). Critical literacy and popular culture in urban education: Toward a pedagogy of access and dissent. In C. Clark and M. Blackburn (Eds.). *Working With/in the Local: New Directions in Literacy Research for Political Action.* New York: Peter Lang.

Morrell, E. (2008). *Critical literacy and urban youth: Pedagogies of access, dissent, and liberation.* New York: Taylor & Francis.

O'Donoghue, J. & Kirshner, B. (2008). Engaging urban youth in civic practice: Community-based youth organizations as alternative sites for democratic education. In Bixby, J. S. & Pace, J. L., eds. *Educating democratic citizens in troubled times: Qualitative studies of current efforts.* (pp. 227–251). Albany, NY: SUNY Press.

Petrone, R. & Gibney, R. (2005). The power to speak and listen: Democratic pedagogies for American Literature Classrooms. *The English Journal. 94*(5), 35–39.

Phelps, S. (2010). Critical literacy: Using nonfiction to learn about Islam. *Journal of Adolescent and Adult Literacy, 54*(3), pp. 190–198.

Provenzo, Jr., E.F. (2005). *Critical literacy: What every educated American ought to know.* Boulder, CO: Paradigm Publishing.

Singer, J. (2006). *Stirring up justice: Writing & reading to change the world.* Portsmouth, HH: Heinemann.

Street, B. (1984). *Literacy in Theory and Practice.* Cambridge: Cambridge University Press.

18

Teaching How to Read the World and Change It: Critical Pedagogy in the Intermediate Grades

Robert E. Peterson

Introduction

Monday morning a child brings a stray dog into the classroom.

The traditional teacher sees that it is removed immediately.

The progressive teacher builds on the students' interest; perhaps measures and weighs the animal with the children, has the children draw and write about the dog, and eventually calls the humane society.

The Freirian teacher does what the progressive teacher does but more. She asks questions, using the dog as the object of reflection. "Why are there so many stray dogs in our neighborhood?" "Why are there more here than in the rich suburbs?" "Why do people have dogs?" "Why doesn't the city allocate enough money to clean up after the dogs and care for the strays?" While accepting stray animals into a classroom isn't the bellwether mark of an elementary Freirian teacher, engaging children in reflective dialogue on topics of their interest is.

Not surprisingly, the classroom of an elementary teacher applying a Freirian method is markedly different than that of a traditional teacher. What perhaps is not as expected is that a Freirian approach also differs significantly from the methods of many progressive teachers, that is, those who organize their classes in child-centered and holistic ways.

Going to public school in the 1960s I became a proponent of progressive education as a student, but it was only when I read Freire as a junior in high school, that I realized education could be more than just "relevant" and "student-centered." However, the political reality of being a high school student activist in the late 1960s and early 1970s made me doubt the likelihood of a Freirian method being used in the public schools.

It wasn't until a decade later, that I came back to Freire and reexamined his applicability to the public school setting. I was on the other side of the teacher's desk, now looking at things as an educator rather than a student. I had traveled to Nicaragua and observed the week-long celebration that concluded the National Literacy Campaign in August of 1980, and the experience convinced me that I should look again at Freire's work. I knew that the conditions of teaching and learning in the United States differed greatly from those encountered by Freire in the Third World, and yet I felt that the essence of Freire's approach would be appropriate for an urban school setting.

Throughout the 1980s, I worked on applying Freire's ideas in my fourth and fifth grade bilingual inner-city classrooms. My approach contrasted sharply with the numerous "educational reforms" being tried elsewhere. These mainstream proposals were often state and system mandates; their goal was to "teacher-proof" the curricula through the use of basal reader programs, direct instruction, the methods of Madeline Hunter and an expansion of standardized testing (Fairtest, 1988; Gibboney, 1988; Levine, 1988). Under the banners of "back to the basics" and "improving student achievement" these efforts further reinforced and strengthened what Freire calls the "banking" method of education, whereby the teacher puts periodic deposits of knowledge into the students' heads. Such classrooms are very teacher- and text-centered. Little discussion and reflection take place. While the relevance of a banking-type approach appears to go counter to what recent research on literacy suggests (Calkins, 1983; Goodman 1986; Goodman, Smith, Meredith, & Goodman, 1987; Graves, 1983; Smith 1985) this model continues to be the most prevalent method in public school classrooms. Goodlad (1984), for example, found that not even 1 percent of the instructional time in high schools was devoted to discussion that "required some kind of open response involving reasoning or perhaps an opinion from students." As he notes, "the extraordinary degree of student passivity stands out" (p. 229).

Freire posits a dialogic "problem posing" method of education as an alternative. Here, teachers and students both become actors in figuring out the world through a process of mutual communication. In the banking method of education the teacher and the curricular texts have the "right answers" which the students are expected to regurgitate periodically onto criterion referenced tests. However in Freire's model, questions and not answers are the core of the curriculum; open-ended questions prod students to critically analyze their social situation and encourage them to ultimately work towards changing it.

To apply Freire's approach in the elementary classroom one has to have a perspective about the learners and learning which runs counter to the dominant educational ideology. A Freirian approach relies on the experience of the students and implies a respect and use of the students' culture, language, and dialect. It values dialogue and reflection over lecture and repetition. It means constructing a classroom in which students have the maximum amount of power that is legally permitted and that they can socially handle. It means challenging the students to reflect on the social nature of knowledge and the curriculum, to get them to think about why they think and act the way they do.

Ultimately a Freirian approach means moving beyond thought and words to action. This is done on the one hand by teachers themselves modeling social responsibility and critical engagement in community and global issues. On the other hand it means constructing with the students an atmosphere in the classroom and the school where students feel secure and confident enough to interrogate their own realities, see them in a different light, and act on their developing convictions to change their own social reality. In order to do all this, the teachers themselves have to go through a transformative process, breaking the ideological chains of their own formal education, of past training, and the inertia of habit of past teaching.

Teaching Organically

Freire uses generative words and themes in his teaching, words that invoke passion and feeling among his students. In North American jargon this is sometimes called a "language experience" approach for it utilizes students' own language and experiences as the basis of instruction. An example from European literature and from the experience of a New Zealand teacher illustrate the significance of this approach.

In Bertolt Brecht's (1978) famous play *The Mother*, which takes place during the 1905 revolution in Czarist Russia, the mother and a metal worker go to ask a professor to teach them to read and write. The professor, begrudgingly and condescendingly, agrees and proceeds to write two words on a slate board: "Branch" and "nest." The two workers immediately become frustrated by the irrelevance of the situation and demand to know how to spell "worker," "class struggle," and "exploitation." Not clear as to why his initial words were inappropriate, the professor obligingly changes his plans. And, thus, through the power of their own words, the workers learn how to read and write rapidly.

In her work with Maori children in New Zealand, Sylvia Ashton-Warner (1965) developed an educational approach very similar to that of Freire. She understood that the failure of the Aborigine children in New Zealand schools was mainly due to their cultural clash with the Anglicized system. She drew on the interests and experience of her students, within the context of the culture they brought to school. Her use of "organic vocabulary" to teach reading, spelling, and writing was based on the belief that words significant to the learner would motivate the learner into learning. As she explained:

> Pleasant words won't do. Respectable words won't do. They must be words organically tied up, organically born from the dynamic life itself. They must be words that are already part of the child's being.
>
> (1965, p. 33)

The proof of her method was in the students themselves. While it took four months for them to learn words like "come, look, and," in four minutes they could learn words like "police, bulldog, knife, cry, yell, fight, Daddy, Mummy, ghost, kiss, and frightened."

The meaningfulness of these words stands in sharp contrast to the first words taught to many children in urban school settings in the United States. One widely used basal company chose eight words as the primary starting point for reading: "red, yellow, blue, girl, boy, the, a, has." In fact, an entire kindergarten workbook is devoted to the word "the." The Commission on Reading of the National Council of Teachers of English (1988) documents how basal reading programs control vocabulary and syntax to such an extent as to make the initial exposure to reading irrelevant and boring to most children.

Children's learning should be centered in their own experience, language, and culture. For this to happen, the classroom environment should be "language rich," allowing the children to develop their language and thinking abilities in as natural a setting as possible. This applies equally to first and second language learning (Krashen & Terrell, 1983; Goodman, 1986). A generative theme approach fosters the development of such an environment.

Practical Application

A generative theme is an issue or topic that catches the interest of students in such a way that discussion, study, and project work can be built around it. Themes may come from an incident in a particular student's life, a problem in the community, or an idea that a student latched onto from the media, the news, or a classroom activity. Writing, reading, talking, acting, and reflecting are the key ways through which generative themes develop. I start the year with a unit on the child's own family and background—placing their birthdates on the class timeline. The second day we place their parents' dates on the timeline, the third, their grandparents. We put pins in a world map indicating the places of birth. I ask them to talk to their parents or other family members and collect at least one story, joke, or memory from their family and either write it down or prepare to tell it orally.

The first day of school I also have the students in my class write a book. Inspired by Ashton-Warner's (1965) continual construction of books based on her children's writings and drawings, I do the same. Quality is not important on the first day. I want to show students that we can write, draw, and accomplish things they would not have dreamed of. We choose a topic or topics together, write, draw, and put the unedited papers into a plastic theme binder creating an instant book. This action of collaboratively producing a book based on the students' own experiences provides both a model of what can be accomplished the rest of the year and a benchmark upon which the teacher and the students can judge growth in their abilities. "If we can accomplish this in only one day by working together," I tell my students, "just imagine what we can do in an entire year!"

Throughout the year I use the "writing process" approach (Graves 1983, Calkins, 1986) which focuses on production of student generated and meaningful themes. Students write for a purpose, whether it is for publication, a pen pal or display. We publish in the school newsletter, the city newspaper, children's magazines,[1] or our own books. Never have I seen students think so much about a piece of writing than when they know it is to be published.

The most ambitious writing we do is for the publication of our own books. Usually this is in the form of anthologies of students' prose, poetry, and drawings—*Kid Power, Colors Laugh, Splashing in Action* are the titles of a few that we have produced. I especially encourage writings on the students' own communities and families (Wigginton, 1989). At times children have written entire booklets—legends, adventures, autobiographies—that they may give to a parent or sibling as a gift for a birthday or holiday. These booklets validate the children's lives, give them self-confidence in their ability to do projects, help focus reflection on our common field trips and areas of study, provide an inspiration to write and a motivation to read. They are also useful for me, not only as the basis for future writing lessons, but because I learn more about my students and their communities.

Generative themes can be discovered and reflected upon not only through writing in the classroom but through a variety of other language and performance arts activities. Mime, drama, role playing, reading aloud from their own writings, chants, and oral story telling allow students to describe and reflect on their world while improving their basic first language and second language abilities.

Even when standardized curricula must be used, a teacher can utilize the life experiences of their students. For example, if by state law or local decree a teacher must use a basal reader, approaches can be taken that downplay its segmented skills orientation. A student could: Write or tell about what would happen if she were to take the main character home for dinner; write a letter to the main character comparing the student's life to that of the main characters; or write a version of the story that draws on some comparable situation in their school community. Teachers can also supplement basals by having students read quality children's literature in decent anthologies[2] or in whole books. My experience has shown that if children shelve the basal a few times a week and instead read classroom sets of entire novels, they are more likely to think longer and more deeply about a piece of literature and how it relates to their lives.

But there are some problems with this organic style of teaching. Given class oppression in our society, poor children usually have a narrower range of experiences than those from more affluent homes. This does not mean they are culturally or experientially deprived—as spending the summer in Mexico or the Mississippi delta or even playing in the back alleys of one of our big cities can be a rich experience. Their culture and experience is just different than that of many teachers; it is also in discordance with the texts of the dominant curricula. I believe though that we should stretch what is organic in the children's lives by taking them out into the world and by bringing the world into the classroom (Searle, 1977). Field trips, speakers, movies, and current events studies are obvious ways to do this.

Poetry and music can also bring the world into the classroom. For example, Langston Hughes' poems "Colored Child at the Carnival" or "The Ballad of the Landlord," speak to the experience of many African-Americans and poor people and spark critical discussions. I have had similar success with songs such as "Harriet Tubman" and "I Cried" sung by Holly Near, "Lives in the Balance" and "Lawless Avenue" by Jackson Browne, "Sambo Lando" sung by Inti Illimani, "El Pueblo Unido Jamas Sera Vencido" by Quilapayun. Whenever I use poems or songs I reproduce the words so that each student can follow along and keep a copy.

As we delve deeper into the nature of students' experiences in urban America, new problems with the application of Freire's theory confront us. Freire (1970) assumes that what will most inspire the learner is discussion and reflection on his or her own experiences, particularly his or her own oppression. In my eyes, many children in urban America are oppressed by a few key institutions: school, family, and community.

For an elementary teacher to apply Freire by focusing on such oppression raises difficult problems. The degree to which a teacher can "deviate" from the standard curriculum depends on a number of factors—the amount of peer and parental support, the political situation in the school and district, and the sophistication and maturity of the particular group of students, to name a few. But there is deviation and there is deviation. To study the Plains Indians instead of the Pilgrims is one thing. To help students become aware and critical about how they are being oppressed in society can be quite another. I have found two ways to approach this problem. First is to deal with power relationships and "oppression" within my own classroom. The second way is to bring the world into the classroom, so that children start reflecting on their own lives. I will first explain the latter.

One year I showed my students the video *The Wrath of Grapes* (United Farm Workers, 1987) about the current grape boycott and followed it up with a field trip to see Cesar Chavez speak at the local technical college. All sorts of good things came out of this activity, but the most interesting was that on the Monday after our trip my students came to school and the first thing they yelled was "Mr. Peterson, Sixth Street is on strike."

"What?" I replied.

"Sixth and National Ave. is on strike!"

Now the streets in Milwaukee have a lot of pot holes after the long winter but I had never heard of a street being on strike. What had in fact occurred was a strike by workers at a local factory. Later that week during art period I took six students armed with a tape recorder over to the company so they could interview the workers. I believe they learned more during their half-hour interview than they had in years of social studies lessons. We debriefed in the teachers' lounge. When we were reviewing the reason for the strike—a wage cut from $7.00 down to $4.00—Cecilia said rather unemotionally, "That's more money than my mom makes now." We examined where each of the children's parents worked and if they were in a union. "Grievance" became a spelling word the next week and pretty soon there seemed to be grievances about all sorts of things in the children's lives. By bringing the world into the classroom they were better able to reflect upon their own lives.

But as I enlarge the world in which my students operate through sharing of such experiences, always tying issues to and building upon the students' own realities, I habitually confront another problem. The "generative themes" of many media-saturated children often seem to have more to do with life on the cathode ray tube than life in our community.

During writing workshop or group discussions I sometimes feel I am in another world of professional wrestlers, super heros, and video games. The average child watches television six hours a day and in one year sees 800 war toy commercials, 250 episodes of war cartoons; the violent commercials and episodes being the equivalent of 22 days of school (Liebert & Sprafkin, 1988).[3]

One consequence of this television addiction is physical atrophy, but the deadening of the child's imagination and the imposition of a violent, consumerist ideology are other results that have a direct effect on a "generative theme"-based classroom. When my kids moan about the President their solution is to kill him. A child doesn't like gangs—solve the problem by machine gunning them down or by sending them to the electric chair. There is no simple or short-term solution to this problem, and certainly a single classroom teacher is not going to solve this problem alone. I challenge these ideas through dialogue attempting to get children to think about why they think the way they do (which I explain in more detail in the section on critiquing curriculum and the media). I take what I hear and try to rework it from a different angle—codify it to use Freire's term—and bring it up again in the future in the context of other curricular areas.

In a generative theme-oriented classroom, the tendency is often to try to cover too much too fast. My most successful experiences have been when I've had the class concentrate on one thing in depth. The concept of "less is more" (Coalition of Essential Schools, 1984) applies equally well to a single classroom as it does to an entire school curricula. I have ensured this by using a variety of methods: a word for the day, a quotation of the week, a short poem, a graphic, a cartoon, story, or news article.

When I have a special word for the day it often relates to a topic the children have been discussing or studying. I or one of the students present it in both English and Spanish, explain its epistemology, teach the others how to sign it in American Sign Language, discuss its significance and use it as a "password" as we move through the day's activities. Sometimes the word comes from the conversations I hear, or from a topic of interest that we have discussed in our studies. The focus on one word, particularly in a bilingual setting, helps students become aware of language in a metacognitive sense. Through word webbing or semantic mapping I help connect this word again to the life experiences of the students.

Regardless of whether it's a word, a scripted dialogue, a story, or a discussion which serves to organize classroom dialogue, the focus of instruction and locus of control is learner- rather than teacher-centered. The essence of an organic theme-based approach thus lies in the connections it builds between the topic at hand, the students' lives and broader world around them (Ellwood, 1989).

The Empowerment of Students

Since students have so few rights, they rarely develop responsibility. By fifth grade I get children who are so damaged by society that they are only able to behave if they are given no rights—even going to the pencil sharpener without having to ask permission is too much for some to handle. This irresponsibility is rooted in the teacher-centered and textbook-driven curriculum which serves to disempower children. Because students are denied rights and kept from decision making throughout their school life and subjected to tedious worksheets and boring curriculum, school life prevents them from developing the responsibility and self-discipline necessary to be independent thinkers and actors in our society.[4] Freire (1970) maintains that through this subjugation students become *objects* acted upon by the authoritarian school system and society. He argues, instead, for a pedagogical process of dialogue, reflection, dramatization, and interaction, whereby students move towards being *subjects* capable of understanding the world and their social context, and ultimately engaging in activity based on this new understanding. Again, the realization of students as subjects is not always easily attained.

I want my students to take responsibility for their own learning, but when I begin to encourage this many see it as license to goof off. Shor and Freire (1987) speak of the need to develop transitionary models and activities to train people to be more responsible. In making the transition to empower students, one must therefore be prepared for a sometimes enormous struggle.

The first step in this transition is to enhance the students' self-esteem and reduce the anxiety level. This is done through creating an overall positive atmosphere in the classroom and by planning very specific activities which stress self-awareness, respect, and cooperation. Activities like those suggested by Canfield and Wells (1976), Prutzman, Stern, Burger, and Bodenhamer (1988), and Schniedewind (1987) help students become more aware of their own attitudes about themselves and others while developing skills of listening, speaking, and cooperating.

I have children interview each other at the beginning of the year and report on it to the whole class. This shows them that they should take each other seriously and it practices public speaking and careful listening. I play circle games involving drama, storytelling, and physical activity as well as small group activities which stress brainstorming, problem solving, and creative writing and dramatics. Instead of segregating affective education activities off into an afternoon corner of the curriculum I try as much as possible to integrate group process and self-esteem-building activities into the curriculum as a whole. No matter where such activities are during the day, however, I have found that I need to model, role play, and teach many of these social skills. I model something, involve a small group of students with me doing the activity in front of the class, then have another small group do it again in front without my participation. Finally, after a short discussion with the whole class everyone becomes involved in the activity. Later, it is important for the class to discuss both the content and the process of the activity, with both strengths and shortcomings being highlighted. Modeling and discussing with students how to manage their time and to stay organized—from one's desk to one's three-ring binder—are also very powerful tools for the development of independence and high self-esteem.

Finally, I have found that I can reach even more students by linking my attempts at developing self-confidence and responsibility to history. For example, each year I make sure to focus for a while on the fact that in our nation's past females were not allowed to attend many schools, not allowed to speak at political meetings or vote. Through role play, storytelling, discussion, and project work about the past, some students are inspired to take a stronger and more self-conscious role in the classroom.

Beyond the building of self-esteem, students need to be involved with establishing and periodically reviewing the rules and curriculum of the classroom. Students' ability to do this depends on several factors including their maturity and previous schooling experience. At the beginning of the year, I carefully plan lessons which give students a taste of what it would mean to have a large say over what happens in the class. At the same time I am quick to restrict student decision making at the first signs that students are using the increased power as a license to goof off. As I restrict it, I go through a long process of explanation: discussion, role playing, and a lessening of the restrictions. After several cycles of this process, students usually become better able to take on increased responsibility and freedom. Sometimes such restrictions must be done on an individual level. For example, if the desks are arranged in clusters, those students who demonstrate they are capable of sitting close to their classmates and yet still listen to class discussions are permitted to stay in the clusters, while those who are disruptive have as a logical consequence their desk being placed in a "row."

Empowerment does not mean "giving" someone their freedom. Nor does it mean creating a type of surface "empowerment" in which one gives the students the impression that they are "equal" to the teacher. The challenge for the teacher who believes in student empowerment is to create an environment which is both stimulating and flexible in which students can exercise increasing levels of power while regularly reflecting upon and evaluating the new learner–teacher relationship.

One element of this environment is class organization. We arrange our classroom according to our needs: rows for presentations, a circle of chairs for large group discussion, and clusters of desks for small group discussion and work.

For class meetings, for instance, desks are pushed to the walls and the chairs are placed in a big circle. Such meetings form the basis of democraticizing the classroom (Glasser, 1969, 1986; Schmuck & Schmuck, 1983) through discussions, voting, and class problem solving. At the beginning of each school year, I chair the meetings but eventually the students take over. One person takes notes each session into a spiral notebook that we keep hung on the wall. I have a special rock which is passed from person to person so we know whose turn it is to speak. The first part of the year is often spent just improving our listening skills so that we can have an interactive dialogue instead of a series of monologues. I do this through modeling what a good listener does and playing listening games, such as having each person repeat one thing or the main idea of the person who spoke immediately before them prior to them speaking.

I start the class meetings with a circle game and then pass the rock and let people state the concern or problem they would like to discuss. I note these and then decide what will be discussed that day, usually starting off with a smaller, solvable problem and then moving into the hot and heavy ones. We use a five-step plan:

1. What is the problem?
2. Are you sure about it?
3. What can we do about it?
4. Try it.
5. How did it work?

Through this five-step process, students begin to work collectively, reflecting upon the problem and together seeking solutions. While many of the problems poor and minority children and communities face cannot be easily or immediately "solved" a "problem-posing" pedagogy can encourage a questioning of why things are the way they are and the identification of actions, no matter how small, to begin to address them. Inherent is a recognition of the "complexity and time needed for solutions with individuals and communities" (Wallerstein & Bernstein, 1988).

A Dialogical Instructional Method

If "student empowerment" is going to be meaningful, students not only need to be involved in some of the problem-solving and posing practices outlined above, but teachers must fundamentally change their methods. Education should not be viewed as the transmission of knowledge by trained technicians, but rather as an interactive process through which problems are posed and answers collaboratively sought. Dewey (1916) felt similarly and spoke of a conception of instruction for knowledge as opposed to instruction for habit. Like Freire, he saw education as an interactive process based on the history, experience, and culture of the student. Dewey said a mechanic taught mechanically would not be able to solve a new problem that might arise, but one taught to understand the whole machine and machines in general would be able to adapt to the new situation. The difference between Dewey and Freire is in part defined by the kinds of activities they advocate as ways for students to gain knowledge. Dewey took a deliberate apolitical stance. The practical educational activities he advocated usually involved students transforming the natural world, that is, gardening or laboratory experiments. Freire, on the other hand, defines practical education activities as critical discussion and collective action aimed at solving political and social problems.

The centerpiece of Freire's method, and what distinguishes it so sharply from the dominant practices in classrooms of most of North America, is its emphasis on dialogue. *Dialogue*, as Freire defines it, is not just permissive talk, but *conversation with a focus and a purpose*. Dialogue shows that the object of study is not the exclusive property of the teacher; knowledge is not produced somewhere in textbook offices and then transferred to the student. By discussion and extensive use of open-ended questioning by the teacher, students begin to think about the object or topic under study. Freire (Shor & Freire, 1987) is not opposed to lectures per se and in fact suggests the use of a variety of formats in the classroom. Since factual knowledge is the foundation upon which many discussions and opinions should be based, short lectures are sometimes important even at the elementary level. However, with the recent trend towards direct instruction, teachers too often demonstrate an overreliance on lecture to convey knowledge, even though only a small amount of such information is retained.

To initiate dialogue, I may use a motivating drawing, photo, cartoon, poem, written dialogue, oral story, or piece of prose. These dialogue "triggers" are useful for full classroom or small group discussions. Wallerstein and Bernstein (1988) have used a simple acronym "SHOWED" as a way to help students systematically respond to such a trigger.

S what do you *S*ee?
H what's *H*appening to your feelings?
O relate it to your *O*wn lives
W *W*hy do we face these problems?
E
D what can we *D*o about it?

The students are encouraged to use this format to help facilitate their dialogue. It helps to direct students away from spontaneous conversation to a progression that moves from personal reactions to social analysis to consideration of action. A few examples from my class serve to illustrate this process.

One year as my class played at recess, a student slipped and fell on a broken bottle, putting a ghastly wound into the back of her thigh—over 50 stitches. After the police and ambulance had carried her off on a stretcher, we tearfully retreated back into the safety of our classroom and I thought, "What the heck should I do now?" I sent two kids out to retrieve the guilty piece of glass. We put the piece in an open box and passed it around. The rest of the afternoon we discussed everything from the high school students who share our playground, to the bottle manufacturing companies who have prevented the Wisconsin state legislature from passing a bottle deposit law. One of my students, Fernando Valadez, put his thoughts to poetry:

Pig Pen
Nobody likes to live
in the pigpen of broken bottles,
muddy papers and squished cans.
In our neighborhood of
lonely streets, messy parks,
dirty alleys and dangerous playgrounds
you might get hurt like a friend
of mine who got a big cut on the back
of her leg when she was running
by the swings and fell on some glass.
The ambulance came
and took her away.
Who's going to take the junk
away?

At times the triggers I use are more explicitly value-laden and often cut across the curricula integrating language arts, history, and other subject areas. Some of the best dialogue in my class has come from discussions following the reading of poems or short historical pieces. Will Fisher's poem, for instance, helped initiate discussion of history and justice. The context is ice cream cones and mud, one that a child can relate to and understand:

A Command to Drive Horse Recklessly

The first warm day in May, a line of common folk in front of the Dairy Queen shop. A carriage dashes by, spraying mud. Women curse and shake their fists. Two men rush after the carriage. It has been stopped by a traffic light. The men angrily threaten the coachman. Clutching his fifty-cent cone, a child catches up and, ignoring the others, flings the cone through the open window into the face of the nobleperson.

Utilizing the "SHOWED" question format with this simple poem has enabled my students to discuss a wide variety of topics ranging from racial and class discrimination, inflation, splashing each other on the playground, to the invention of traffic lights and cars.

Critique the Curriculum and Society

There is more to Freire than generative themes of the learners' lives and a dialogic style. He speaks of the need to illuminate reality to the student, as opposed to the standard curriculum which obscures reality. Freire (1985) suggests that the "question is a different relationship to knowledge and society and that the only way to truly understand the curriculum of the classroom is to go beyond its walls into the society."

In most schools, facts are presented as value-free. Conceptual analysis—to the degree it exists—does not make contact with the real world. History is presented as a series of non-related sequential facts. Scientific "truths" are presented without historical context with little regard to the ramifications such matters have on the learners' environment or global ecology. Students are expected to learn—usually memorize and occasionally "discover"—such facts without regard to the values or interests which inform such perspectives (Shor, 1980, 1987).

As stated previously, teachers should help students draw connections between their own lives, communities, and environment. But we must also *help them reflect upon why they think the way they do; to discover that knowledge is socially constructed, that truth is relative not only to time and place but to class, race, and gender interests as well.* Students need to know that what they have before them in their textbooks, in the newspapers, or on the television is not always true. We should thus engage our students in thinking about the validity of texts (Bigelow, 1989). In fact, this is one of the few uses I have found for them in my classroom.

The third-grade basal reader, *Golden Secrets* (Scott Foresman, 1980), for example, has a story on inventions. The anonymous author states that the traffic light was invented by an anonymous policeman. Actually it was invented by the African-American scientist Garrett A. Morgan. I give my students a short piece on Morgan that is from a black history book (Adams, 1969) and we compare and question. Some of my classes decided to write to Scott Foresman and complain.

The problem with textbooks is also what they omit (Council on Interracial Books for Children, 1977a). The Silver Burdett Social Studies Series, *The World and Its People* (Helmus, Arnsdorff, Toppin, & Pounds, 1984), used in over two-thirds of the nation's school districts, has a 502-page reader on U.S. History. Only five paragraphs of this text mention unions and working-class struggle, only one labor leader, Samuel Gompers, is mentioned and most of the text is written in the passive voice. "Why?" I ask the students, as I provide interesting stories and we role-play the history of working-class struggle in our country. I connect this to local history, like the several-day general strike for the eight-hour day in 1886 which ended with the massacre of seven people including a 13-year-old boy. I have the students survey their parents and neighbors as to knowledge of this strike and other important events in our community's history and then we reflect on why people do not know such things. We recreate such history through readers' theater, role plays, simulations, dramas, and special projects.

Similarly, a Heath science text book (Barufaldi, Ladd, & Moses, 1981) has a short biography on an African-American scientist Charles Drew, who pioneered blood transfusions and plasma research. Omitted is the fact that Dr. Drew died after a car accident in the south when a southern hospital refused to treat him and give him a blood transfusion because of his skin color.

One example that I particularly like to use in my bilingual class is the story of Sequoyah and the Cherokees. Most history books mention Sequoyah's creation of the alphabet and the Trail of Tears, but few mention that the Cherokee nation had a bilingual weekly newspaper and a bilingual school system with over 200 of their own schools including a normal school—that is, until the early 1900s when the federal government stepped in and disbanded it.[5] I tell the children this story of the Cherokees and say, "Let's see what the history books and encyclopedias say." Usually there are gross omissions and we proceed to discuss why and what impact these omissions have on how we view the world. I ask, "Why didn't the government want the Cherokees to maintain their language?" This is a crucial question in my classroom since, by fifth grade, many of the students have already developed negative attitudes toward their native Spanish language.

There are many stories from the untold history of the oppressed that expose the social nature of knowledge and nurture civic courage and a sense of social justice. I find the history of Shea's Rebellion and the Seminole Wars particularly worthwhile because not only was there a struggle for a just cause but a key ingredient was unity among nationalities, a persistent problem in our nation's history.

Another important way to deal with the socially constructed nature of knowledge is to directly deal with racist and sexist stereotypes.[6] Around Thanksgiving time I show my students the filmstrip, *Unlearning "Indian" Stereotypes* (Council on Interracial Books for Children, 1977b). It is narrated by Native American children who visit a public library and become outraged at the various stereotypes of Indians in the books.

One year after viewing the filmstrip the students seemed particularly outraged at what they had learned. They came the next day talking about how their siblings in first grade had come home with construction paper headdresses with feathers. "That's a stereotype," the students proudly proclaimed. "What did you do about it?" I responded. "I ripped it up." "I slugged him," came the chorus of responses. As we continued the discussion, I asked why their brothers and sisters had the objects and interrogated them as to how children learn about such things. Finally they decided there were more productive things they could do. They first scoured the school library for books with stereotypes but since they found few, they decided to investigate their sibling's first grade room and look for stereotypes there. They wrote a letter to the teacher asking permission and then went in armed with clipboards, paper, and pens. Results were a picture of an Indian next to the letter "I" in the alphabet strip on the wall. They came back and decided they wanted to teach the first graders about stereotypes. I was skeptical but agreed and after much rehearsal they entered the first grade classroom to give their lesson—rather unsuccessfully I am afraid. But, they reflected on it and later Paco Resendez and Faviola Alvarez wrote in our school newspaper:

> We have been studying stereotypes on Native Americans. What is a stereotype? It's when somebody says something that's not true about another group of people. For example, it is a stereotype if you think all Indians wear feathers or say "HOW!" Or if you think that all girls are delicate. Why? Because some girls are strong.

Another way to show students that knowledge is socially constructed is to get different newspaper or magazine articles about the same subject, from different points of view. Subscribe to newspapers from another country, like *La Barricada*, or use excerpts from papers such as *The Nation, In These Times, Food and Justice*, or the *Guardian* to contrast the reporting from the established press. Or videotape a children's cartoon or tape record lyrics of a popular tune and then watch or play it, analyze it as a class, and draw out its values. I watch for outrageous stories or advertisements in the paper—these can be real thought provokers—or invite in guests who will shock the students out of their complacency. I also use posters, quotations, and maps.

I place a "poster of the week" on a special moveable bulletin board on my classroom wall. By using dramatic, historical, and/or controversial posters I encourage writing, discussion, and critique.[7] I also use a quotation of the week—in English, Spanish, or both. I begin the year providing the quotations myself, but as time passes children offer ones that they have found or created. Some quotations in particular, lend themselves to comparison, analysis and critique:

> When the missionaries first came to Africa they had bibles and we had the land. They said, "Let us pray." We closed our eyes. When we opened them we had the bibles and they had the land.
> (Bishop Desmond Tutu, Nobel Peace Prize Recipient)

Pointing out the biases in maps is also particularly thought provoking. The Mercator projection map, for example, places the equator two-thirds of the way down and depicts Europe as larger than South America although the area of the latter is approximately (6.9 million square miles) double that of Europe (3.8). The newly created Peters Projection may correct this. Another map challenges the conception that Argentina is on the bottom and North America is on top, by reversing the North and South Poles. Such media invokes considerable dialogue and thinking, including who makes maps, why they are the way they are, and how maps shape our thinking about the world.[8]

Teaching Social Responsibility

As students develop the interest and ability to discuss and reflect on their lives, communities, and the broader world, questions inevitably arise as to how people change the world. This concern and interest in social change can be encouraged by consciously fostering what Giroux (1985) calls "civic courage": stimulating "their passions, imaginations, and intellects so that they will be moved to challenge the social, political and economic forces that weigh so heavily upon their lives" (p. 201). In other words, students should be encouraged to act *as if* they were living in a democracy.

One way this can be done is through class meetings and positive reinforcement of socially responsible actions in the classroom. In other words, the first way to build social responsibility is to try to democratize and humanize the educational setting. In my classroom, for example, there is a small quartz rock which is given to the student who has helped someone else. At the beginning of each day, the student who had been awarded for her or his social responsibility the day before chooses the next recipient.

The central theme in my classroom is that the quest for social justice is a neverending struggle in our nation and world; that the vast majority of people have benefited by this struggle; that we must understand this struggle; and that we must make decisions about whether to be involved in it. The academic content areas can be woven around this theme. In reading poetry and literature to children, social issues can be emphasized through books that specifically empower children (Peterson, 1987). Contemporary struggles can be highlighted through curricular materials and readings on Central America, apartheid, and on racism at home.[9] And pictures of real people who have worked for social justice can help children see these struggles as human. In my classroom there is a gallery of freedom fighters, the "luchadores por la justicia" or strugglers for justice that we have studied in social studies and current events. The large portraits—some commercially purchased and others drawn by the children—serve as reminders that women and men of all races have made important contributions to society and serve as keys to unlock our past discussions and studies about people and their struggles. A few years ago one of my students reflected on Cesar Chavez in this way:

> Cesar Chavez is a good man. He is very famous but he is poor. I thought that if people are famous they have to be rich. But this man is poor because he has a group of people and the money he earns he gives to them.

In most curricula, struggle is omitted and conflict forgotten. History is not of social movements or eras but rather the succession of rulers from the earliest Egyptian pharaohs to the most recent presidential administration. It has been fragmented, distorted, and rewritten. With our common history of struggle denied us, the past rewritten, the rulers of our society find the present much easier to manipulate. When Nixon said, "History will absolve our roles in Vietnam," he knew what he was talking about, for corporate textbook companies continue to write and rewrite our history—at least for the immediate future.

In contrast, Freire points to the positive role of struggle in history. He calls conflict the "midwife of real consciousness" and says it should be the focus of learning (Freire, 1970). The cynic might say that with all the conflict in our schools our students must be of very high consciousness. The key point here is to reflect on and critique conflict, in our daily lives, classrooms, and communities, as well as in history.[10]

Focusing on societal conflict—both historic and contemporary—is not only highly motivating and educational but also helps children, even the very young, to analyze and evaluate different points of view and express opinions as to what they think is just. The study of conflicts can be integrated into social studies units, for example, personal conflicts like Fredrick Douglass's struggle to learn to read; historic conflicts like the wars to take the land from American Indians, slave rebellions, worker strikes, bus boycotts, civil rights marches, antiwar movements; and contemporary conflicts like the United Farm Worker grape boycott, the war in El Salvador, apartheid, the antitoxin "Not in My Back Yard Movement." In my classroom, each conflict studied and any other historical event encountered in the normal course of our school day, is recorded on a 3 × 5 file card with a word description and the date. This card is hung on the class time line which circles three sides of the room. This process provides students with a visual representation of time, history, and sequence while fostering the understanding that everything is interrelated.

Historical conflict is best understood through engaging students in participatory activities. Often I will read or tell a story about a conflict and have children role-play parts of it either during or after the story. Occasionally such stories lead to small group or whole class drama presentations. I also use readers theater, that is, scripted plays written so that no acting needs to take place.[11] Sometimes I also encourage students to draw a conflict either together as a mural on large sheets of paper for display or separately for publication.

In addition, each student builds a people's textbook—a three-ring binder in which they put alternative materials. There are sections for geography, history, science, songs, poetry, and quotations. One year after *Rethinking Schools* printed an article on an important Milwaukee event of 1854 when 5,000 people stormed the county jail to free a runaway slave the students used the information to write their own bilingual book about the historic incident. By examining local history in which European Americans fought alongside African-Americans for the abolition of slavery, my students began to understand that social responsibility in a race-divided society means working together on issues that might not necessarily be deemed as in one's immediate self-interest.[12]

Freire takes liberating education even one step further—to action or praxis. He believes learners should use their newfound analysis to transform the world. In the school setting transforming-type activities depend on the nature of the group of students, the community, and the school system, and the courage and seniority of the teacher. My students have gone with me to marches that protested police brutality, demanded that King's birthday be made a national holiday, asked that Congress not fund the Contras, and requested nuclear disarmament. Two of my students testified before the City Council, asking that a Jobs with Peace referendum be placed on the ballot. In another instance, the students went to observe the court proceedings in the case of a police killing of an African-American man. Obviously teachers need to be involved in the community in order to know what's happening and what possibilities exist for involvement of children.

Projects that are less overtly political can also stimulate critical thinking: Joining Amnesty International as a class and adopting a political prisoner, adopting a section of beach on a lake or river and keeping it clean, interviewing people involved in a local strike or community struggle, raising money for earthquake or famine relief, writing letters to governmental representatives, having such representatives or social activists visit the classroom, or corresponding with children in other parts of the USA, Puerto Rico, the USSR, El Salvador and Mozambique.[13] Discussion, writing, and critical reflection on these activities, however, are crucial so these are not to be just "interesting" field trips or projects.

One year we studied the underground railroad as part of the fifth grade U.S. history curriculum. We also studied the second underground railroad, the sanctuary movement. I invited a speaker to my class who had lived in El Salvador for several years. He showed slides of the people. My children at first laughed at the distended bellies of the starving Salvadoran children, but their chuckles turned to horror and then anger as they began to understand that U.S. bombs are being dropped on these children. The class meeting after the presentation was quite informative. The kids asked "Why?" Why was the U.S. government doing this? Why did Reagan do it?" We asked them "Why do you think?" "Because Reagan supports the rich," said one. "Yeah," agreed the others. But others were still not satisfied. "Why? Why does he support the rich?" Finally the speaker responded. "Because it is the job of the president in this country to support the rich." Paco's hand shot up. "If that's the case," he argued, "what about Kennedy?" The bell rang before the speaker could answer. As I drove him home he said the discussion was better than many he had had on university campuses.

In a group meeting the following day the children decided to write letters to our representatives and the President on the issue. The next day one boy, Michael, came in and said, "Mr. Peterson, we have to send weapons down to Central America or else the Russians will take over and no one will believe in God anymore." I said, "Michael, you've been talking to your mom . . . Great. Keep it up. We'll talk about that later." But that day we didn't get to it and as he left I gave him some *Food First* leaflets about hunger in Central America being the real enemy and asked him to read them with his mom. The following day he did not show up for school—I was a bit concerned. The day after he was back and we talked in detail about the various perspectives on Nicaragua, El Salvador, the USSR and the United States of America. The children decided that even if the Sandinistas received money and weapons from aliens from Saturn they had that right because all they wanted to do was run their own country.

A week later at a group meeting, Emma announced that we had to discuss the letters we wrote to the President. "They won't do any good," she lamented, "I bet he just tore them up." She then proposed we go on a field trip to Washington DC to meet the President in person and that I, the teacher, finance it. I politely declined. At that point there was what Freire (Shor & Freire 1987) would call an inductive moment—when the students are stalled and need direction—I said that sometimes people protested in Washington DC but often people protested right here in Milwaukee, as the Pledge of Resistance was doing regularly. The kids immediately said they wanted to go, and before I knew it I was sending home letters to the parents explaining that although it was not part of the official curriculum, if they consented, I would supervise a public bus trip after school up to the Federal Building to protest U.S. aid to the contras. I bought tag board and markers from the local bookstore careful not to use the school's supplies. Half the class—12 children—brought back signed notes. The next Monday the students stayed after school and made their signs. At first they asked me what they should say, but I responded that if they were going on a protest march they had better know what they were protesting. They could make the signs themselves. They did. Their signs included:

Let them run their land!
Support the Poor! Not the "freedom fighters." They're the Rich.
Help Central America Don't Kill Them

Give the Nicaraguans their Freedom
Let Nicaragua Live!
Give Nicaragua Some Food Instead of Weapons
We want Freedom and Peace
Stop spending money to make bombs.

When they were finished making their signs we walked two blocks to the public bus stop and during a steady drizzle headed downtown to the Federal Building. They were the only Hispanics at the march of 150 people and were welcomed with open arms. We walked, marched, chanted, and finally went home wet and exhausted.

The next day we had a panel discussion and the kids talked and listened like they were on top of the world. Paula Martinez wrote about it later in our magazine, *Kid Power*:

> On a rainy Tuesday in April some of the students from our class went to protest against the contras. The people in Central America are poor and being bombed on their heads. When we went protesting it was raining and it seemed like the contras were bombing us. A week before we had visitor, Jim Harney. He had been to El Salvador. He talked to our class about what was going on in El Salvador. He said it was terrible. A lot of people are dying. He showed us slides of El Salvador and told us its bad to be there. He hoped that our government will give them food and money and not bombs.

Michael, the boy who had come back from home concerned about the Russians and God did not go to the march. He said he had to babysit his little brother. Parent conferences were a week later and I was a bit apprehensive to see his mother—a socially mobile Puerto Rican studying to become a nurse. She walked into the room, sat down and said, "Mr Peterson, I want to thank you. Michael has become interested in everything. He watches the news, he talks to me about what's going on, he knows more about things than me sometime. I don't know what you did. But thanks." As our conversation progressed it was clear her conservative political views on Central America had not changed, but our differences were secondary, because what was central to both of us was that her son had started to read the world.

Notes

1. Publications which accept children's writings include: *Children's Album*, PO Box 6086, Concord, CA 94524 ($10/year); *Rethinking Schools*, 1001 E. Keefe Ave., Milwaukee, WI 53212 ($10/year); *Stone Soup*, PO Box 83, Santa Cruz, CA 95063 ($17.50/year); *Reflections*, Box 368, Ducan Falls, OH 43734 ($3/year); *The McGuffy Writer*, 400A McGuffey Hall, Miami University, Oxford, OH 45056 ($3/year); *Chart Your Course*, PO Box 6448, Mobile, AL, 36660 ($20/year); *Creative Kids*, PO Box 637, 100 Pine Ave., Holmes, PA 19043 ($10/year.); *A Young Author's Guide to Publishing* lists submission guidelines for children's magazines; send $2.50 to Dr. Nicholas Spennato, Delaware County Reading Council, 6th and Olive St., Media, PA 19063.
2. One excellent anthology is called *Embers: Stories for a Changing World* edited by Meyers, Banfield, and Colon J. (1983) distributed by the Council on Interracial Books for Children, 1841 Broadway, New York, NY, 10023. For a bibliography of children's books that have young people as protagonists who are working for social justice see Peterson (1987). Books to empower young people. *Rethinking Schools*, Vol. 1, No. 3, pp. 9–10, available from *Rethinking Schools*, 1001 E., Keefe Ave., Milwaukee, WI 53212.
3. Marie Winn (1987) offers some innovative ideas to both parents and teachers to help children kick the television habit, including plans for classroom and school wide television turnoff campaigns.
4. This generalization ignores the class, race, and gender factors which profoundly affect school structure and student self-esteem. For example, Wodtke (1986) found discrepancies between instructional approaches received by suburban kindergarten and those in poor, working-class settings. The suburban kindergartens tended to encourage children to participate in show-and-tell and speak in front of the class, while the predominantly poor and working-class kindergartens rarely utilized such activities, instead relying more heavily on worksheets and drill because of the pressures to cover standardized curriculum and the emphasis put on direct instruction. This differentiated approach tends to inculcate certain habits and outlooks in children based on class and race factors.

5. In 1838, the United States government forced the Cherokee people and other southeastern tribes to abandon their land in Georgia and move to Oklahoma. The Indians suffered such hardships along the way that the path they followed became known as the Trail of Tears. For more information on the bilingual education system established by the Cherokees see Payne (1984) and Weinberg (1977).
6. The recognition of the importance of dealing with racism among children leads some educators (ALTARF, 1984) to argue that multicultural education is limited if not accompanied by an anti-racist component.
7. High-quality, politically progressive posters can be found through a number of outlets. Particularly good sources are the Syracuse Cultural Worker, Box 6367, Syracuse, NY 13217 and Northern Sun Merchandising, 2916 E. Lake St., Minneapolis, MN 55406. A source for excellent posters of Native American leaders is the Perfection Form Company, Logan, Iowa and for women posters contact: TABS, 438 Fourth St., Brooklyn, NY 11215 (718) 788–3478.
8. The Peters Projection Map can be ordered from Friendship Press, PO Box 37844, Cincinnati, Ohio 45237. The Turnabout map is distributed by Laguna Sales, Inc., 7040 Via Valverde, San Jose, CA 95135.
9. I collect and weave into our class curricula parts of progressive curricula such as *Winning "Justice for All"* (Racism & Sexism Resource Center, 1981), *Open Minds to Equality* (Schniedewind & Davidson, 1983) *Food First Curriculum* (Rubin, 1984), *Cooperative Learning, Cooperative Lives* (Schniedewind, 1987), and a variety of curriculum on contemporary issues such as Central America (contact Network of Educators' Committees on Central America, PO Box 43509, Washington DC 20010–9509. 202–667–2618); apartheid (Bigelow, 1985); U.S. labor struggles (Bigelow & Diamond, 1988); women (contact National Women's History Project, PO Box 316 Santa Rosa CA 95402 (707)526–5974; peace (contact the Wilmington College Peace Resource Center, Pyle Center Box 1183, Willmington, OH 45177; and racism (see the "Unlearning Stereotypes" filmstrips and guides from the CIBC, 1977b, 1982a, 1982b).
10. Simulating classroom and interpersonal conflict through trigger cartoons, scripted dialogues, and role plays helps students to develop the skills and responsibility to analyze and resolve their own interpersonal problems. In classroom conflict, such reflection helps children understand the purposes behind the "misbehavior" and allows them to develop strategies and skills to diffuse and mediate such conflict. For a theoretical and practical approach to helping children understand the reasons for misbehavior see Dreikurs, Grunwald, and Pepper (1982) and for additional ways to mediate conflict see Prutzman et al. (1988), Schniedewind (1987), and the curriculum produced by teachers and administrators in NYC Community School District 15 in collaboration with the New York Chapter of Educators for Social Responsibility (New York City Board of Education, 1988).
11. Dozens of high-quality reader theaters which deal with a host of conflicts in the history of labor, women, and racial minorities are available from Stevens and Shea, Dept. S, PO Box 794, Stockton, CA 95201.
12. The pamphlet *Joshua Glover: The freeing of a runaway slave in Milwaukee—La liberación de un esclavo fugitivo en Milwaukee* is available from Communicate! Rural Route 2, Pulaski, WI 54162.
13. One such telecommunications linkup is De Orilla a Orilla (from Shore to Shore) which can be contacted by writing to Dennis Sayers, De Orilla a Orilla, N.E. MRC, University of Massachusetts, 250 Stuart St., Rm 1105, Boston, MA 02116. Additional information about communication linkups can be obtained from the book, *School Links International: A New Approach to Primary School Linking Around the World*, by Rex Deddis and Cherry Mares (1988), published by the Avon County Council, Tidy Britain Group Schools Research Project.

References

Adams, R. (1969). *Great Negroes: Past and present.* Chicago: Afro-Am Publishing Co.

All London Teachers Against Racism and Fascism (ALTARF). (1984). *Challenging racism.* Nottingham, UK: Russell Press. Available from ALTARF, Room 216, Panther House, 38 Mount Pleasant, London WCIX OAP.

Ashton-Warner, S. (1965). *Teacher.* New York: Simon and Schuster.

Barufaldi, J., Ladd, G., & Moses, A. (1981). *Heath Science.* Lexington, MA: D.C. Heath.

Bigelow, W. (1985). *Strangers in their own land: A curriculum guide to South Africa.* New York: Africa World Press.

Bigelow, W. (1989, October/November). Discovering Columbus: Re-reading the past. *Rethinking Schools*, 4(1), 1, 12–13.

Bigelow, W., & Diamond, N. (1988). *The power in our hands: A curriculum on the history of work and workers in the United States.* New York: Monthly Review Press.

Brecht, B. (1978). *The mother.* New York: Grove Press.

Calkins, L. (1983). *Lessons from a child.* Portsmouth, NH: Heinemann.

Calkins, L. (1986). *The art of teaching writing.* Portsmouth, NH: Heinemann.

Canfield, J., & Wells, H. (1976). *100 ways to enhance self-concept in the classroom: A handbook for teachers and parents.* Englewood Cliffs, NJ: Prentice-Hall.

Coalition of Essential Schools. (1984). *Prospectus: 1984–1994.* Providence, RI: Brown University.

Commission on Reading by the National Council of Teachers of English. (1988). *Report card on basal readers.* Katonah, NY: Richard C. Owen.

Council on Interracial Books for Children (CIBC). (1977a). *Stereotypes, distortions and omissions in U.S. history textbooks.* New York: Racism and Sexism Resource Center for Educators.

Council on Interracial Books for Children. (1977b). *Unlearning "Indian" stereotypes.* New York: Racism and Sexism Resource Center for Educators.

Council on Interracial Books for Children. (1982a). *Unlearning Chicano and Puerto Rican stereotypes.* New York: Racism and Sexism Resource Center for Educators.

Council on Interracial Books for Children. (1982b). *Unlearning Asian American stereotypes.* New York: Racism and Sexism Resource Center for Educators.

Dewey, J. (1916). *Democracy and education.* New York: MacMillan.

Dreikurs, R. Grunwald, B., & Pepper, F. (1982). *Maintaining sanity in the classroom.* New York: Harper & Row.

Ellwood, C. (1989). Making connections: Challenges we face, *Rethinking Schools*, 3(3), 1, 12–13.

Fairtest (National Center for Fair and Open Testing). (1988). *Fallout from the testing explosion: How 100 million standardized exams undermine equity and excellence in American's public schools.* Available from P.O. Box 1272, Harvard Square Station, Cambridge MA 02238.

Freire, P. (1970). *Pedagogy of the oppressed.* New York: Seabury.

Freire, P. (1985). *The politics of education.* South Hadley, MA: Bergin & Garvey.

Gibboney, R. A. (1988). Madeline Hunter's teaching machine. *Rethinking Schools*, 2(3), 10–11.

Giroux, H. (1985). *Theory and resistance in education.* South Hadley, MA: Bergin and Garvey.

Glasser, W. (1969). *Schools without failure.* New York: Harper & Row.

Glasser, W. (1986). *Control theory in the classroom.* New York: Harper & Row.

Goodlad, J. (1984). *A place called school: Prospects for the future.* New York: McGraw-Hill.

Goodman, K. (1986). *What's whole in whole language?* Richmond Hill, Ontario; Canada Scholastic TAB. (Distributed in the United States by Heinemann.)

Goodman, K., Smith, E. B., Meredith, R., & Goodman, Y. (1987). *Language and thinking in school: A whole language curriculum.* New York: Richard C. Owen.

Graves, D. H. (1983). *Writing: Teachers and children at work.* Portsmouth, NH: Heinemann.

Helmus, T., Arnsdorf, V., Toppin, E., & Pounds, N. (1984). *The United States and its neighbors.* Atlanta: Silver Burdett Co.

Krashen, S., & Terrell, T. (1983). *The natural approach: Language acquisition in the classroom.* Hayward, CA: Alemany Press.

Levine, D. (1988). Outcome based education: Grand design or blueprint for failure? *Rethinking Schools*, 2(2), 1, 12–13.

Liebert, R., & Sprafkin, J. (1988). *The early window: Effects of television on children and youth.* New York: Pergamon Press.

Meyers, R., Banfield, B., & Colon, J. (Eds.). (1983). *Embers: Stories for a changing world.* Old Westbury, NY: The Feminist Press.

New York City Board of Education. (1988). *Resolving conflict creatively: A draft teaching guide for grades Kindergarten through six.* New York: Board of Education.

Payne, C. (1984). Multicultural education and racism in American schools. *Theory into Practice*, 33 (2), 124–131.

Peterson, R. (1987). Books to empower young people. *Rethinking Schools*, 1(3), 9–10.

Prutzman, P., Stern, L., Burger, M. L., & Bodenhamer, G. (1988). *The friendly classroom for a small planet: A handbook on creative approaches to living and problem solving for children.* Philadelphia, PA: New Society Publishers.

Racism & Sexism Resource Center. (1981). *Winning justice for all: A supplementary curriculum unit on sexism and racism, stereotyping and discrimination.* New York: Council on Interracial Books for Children.

Rubin, L. (1984). *Food first curriculum.* San Francisco: Food First.

Schmuck P. A., & Schmuck, R. A. (1983). *Group process in the classroom.* Dubuque, IA: Wm. C. Brown Company.

Schniedewind, N. (1987). *Cooperative learning, cooperative lives: A sourcebook of learning activities for building a peaceful world.* Somerville, MA: Circle Press.

Schniedewind, N., & Davidson, E. (1983). *Open minds to equality: A sourcebook of learning activities to promote race, sex, class, and age equity.* Englewood Cliffs, NJ: Prentice-Hall.

Scott, Foresman & Co. (1981). *Scott Foresman reading.* New York.

Searle, C. (1977). *The world in a classroom.* London: Writers and Readers Publishing Cooperative.

Shor, I. (1980). *Critical teaching and everyday life.* Boston: South End Press.

Shor, I. (1987). *Freire for the classroom: A sourcebook for liberatory teaching.* Portsmouth, NH: Heinemann.

Shor, I., & Freire, P. (1987). *A pedagogy for liberation: Dialogues on transforming education.* South Hadley, MA: Bergin and Garvey.

Smith, F. (1985). *Reading without nonsense.* New York: Teachers College Press.

United Farm Workers. (1987). *The wrath of grapes* (video). Keene, CA: The United Farm Workers.

Wallerstein, N., & Bernstein, E. (1988). Empowerment education: Freire's ideas adapted to health education. *Health Education Quarterly*, 15 (4), 379–394.

Weinberg, M. (1977). *A chance to learn: The history of race and education in the United States.* New York: Cambridge University Press.

Wigginton, E. (1989). Foxfire grows up. *Harvard Educational Review*, 59 (1), 24–49.

Winn, M. (1987). *Unplugging the plug-in drug.* New York: Penguin.

Wodtke, K. (1986). Inequality at Age Five? *Rethinking Schools*, 1 (1), 7.

19

"Oh, They're Sending a Bad Message": Black Males Resisting & Challenging Eurocentric Notions of Blackness Within Hip Hop & the Mass Media Through Critical Pedagogy

Bettina Love

Many of Hip Hop's strongest critics stress that Hip Hop is "holding Blacks back" intellectually, financially, and socially (McWhorter, 2003). In 2007, cultural critic Michelle Malkin denounced Hip Hop music and culture as "cultural pollution" (*New York Post*). What these critics ignore is that these mainstream and popular diatribes surrounding Hip Hop are constructed around a Eurocentric psyche and imagination of Black masculinity (West, 2001). Archetypes of Black males as hypersexual, violent, misogynistic, and materialistic inform Hip Hop's construction of Black masculinity. However, popular treatments of Hip Hop consistently fail to interrogate the commodification and exploitation of Hip Hop, while youth of color are labeled nihilistic and destructive (Kilson, 2003; McWhorter, 2003). Thus, there is much debate surrounding Hip Hop as a cultural and musical art form, which is why many educators ignore Hip Hop as an empowering pedagogical tool (Petchauer, 2009). Much of Hip Hop is (mis)represented by corporate America as dangerous popular Black expression that is inconstant with American values (Rose, 1991). Although Hip Hop music and culture is emblazoned by pillorying images and rhetoric of social pathology (Mahiri & Conner, 2003), Neal (2005) reminds us, "just because black men are under siege in White America, it doesn't mean that they don't exhibit behaviors that do real damage to others, particularly within black communities" (p. 152). Neal's position is critical to understanding the plight of Black males because it takes in to account how the media creates and maintains Hip Hop for the White imagination and the real life implications of Hip Hop's co-opted narratives of glamorized violence, crime, and sex. However, the ways in which Hip Hop influences youth, especially Black males, needs to be unpacked: the standard tropes of Black males as rebellious and hypersexual persist, even as Hip Hop scholarship illuminates the prophetic educational potential of Hip Hop as a form of critical pedagogy (Ginwright, 2004; Hill, 2009; Love, 2012). Thus, to state simply that Black males are learning how to cope with society's injustices by listening to explicit rap lyrics and mimicking the attitudes and aggressive posture of male rappers is misleading and irresponsible. In opposition to that theory, the purpose of this article is to demystify Black males as "cultural dopes" (Hall, 1981, p. 59) and illustrate that Black males are resisting and challenging Eurocentric, hegemonic notions of Blackness found in Hip Hop and the mass media through critical pedagogy outside of the normal school walls. The article aims to: (1) demonstrate how Black males are deconstructing rap to expose racial stereotyping within society and the media; (2) explore how Black males are debunking monolithic notions of Black masculinity; and (3) investigate youths' knowledge-making processes outside the walls of their schools.

Power: Hip Hop Critical Pedagogy in & out of Schools

There is a burgeoning body of Hip Hop scholarship centered on Hip Hop music and culture that can be divided into three strands: (1) Hip Hop critical pedagogy that positions Hip Hop to the center of formal and informal school curricula; (2) the meaning making processes and fluid identity work of Hip Hop; and (3) the historical, textual, and social commentary of Hip Hop (Petchauer, 2009). No matter the strand, Hip Hop scholarship is a direct derivative of Hip Hop itself—rebellious, bold, and resilient, while challenging education's dominant middle-class, Eurocentric discourse (Williams, 2009). Hip Hop critical pedagogy is rooted in the principles of culturally responsive teaching (Gay, 2000; Ladson-Billings, 1994), critical pedagogical frameworks (Freire, 2000; Kincheloe, 2008; Shor, 1987), and cultural modeling methods (Lee, 1995) because Hip Hop critical pedagogy positions the culture, social context, learning styles, and experiences of students to the center of the curricula (Petchauer, 2009). Hip Hop critical pedagogy encourages youth to engage in thoughtful discourse and meaningful classroom work that critiques society and its fixed representations of what is considered normal and what is deemed "the other."

A popular stand of Hip Hop critical pedagogy is Hip Hop critical literacy. The crux of Hip Hop critical literacy emphasizes the notion that students engage in literacy practices beyond school walls or normal school settings (community centers, night schools, after school enrichment programs) and that literacy incorporates students ways of "behaving, interacting, valuing, thinking, believing, speaking, and often reading and writing" (Gee, 1996, p. vii). Hip Hop critical literacy researchers and practitioners draw on the critical literacy work of Freire and Macedo (1987) to empower individuals to read the word and the world. Freire and Macedo (1987) contend,

> Reading the world always precedes reading the word, and reading the word implies continually reading the world. Reading the word is not merely preceded by reading the world, but by a certain form of writing it or rewriting it, that is of transforming it by means of conscious, practical work. Words should be laden with the meaning of the people's existential experience, and not the teacher's experience.
>
> (p. 36)

Hip Hop critical literacy scholarship (Alim, 2004; Duncan-Andrade & Morrell, 2005; Ginwright, 2004; Hill, 2006, 2009, Morrell & Duncan-Andrade, 2002) rests on "problem-posing" (Freire, 2000) student-teacher dialogue in order to deconstruct dominant narratives, which can lead students to resist Hip Hop's more pugnacious messages, create counter-narratives, and take social action. According to Morrell and Duncan-Andrade (2002) it is imperative that young people "understand the difference between reality and the media's various representations of reality" (p. 2). The work of Hill (2006) who taught a Hip Hop Literature class to a group of high school students attending an evening education program in Philadelphia illuminates how students interpret Hip Hop, media, and society in response to their daily lives. Hill describes his Hip Hop Lit class as a Hip Hop centered English literature course. The course was designed not only to teach students literary interpretations, creative writing, rhyme scheme, and personification, but also to create a space where "the literacy practices of the hip hop community are moved from the margins to the center of the curriculum" (Hill, 2006, p. 24). For one particular class lesson, Hill chose Jay-Z's song "A Ballad for the Fallen Soldier" to help the students reflect on the complicated issues of post 9/11 race relations in the U.S. After reading "Ballad" many of the students compared Al Qaeda's attack on the World Trade Center to the civic terror that plagues neighborhoods of people of color before and after 9/11. Students expressed a keen insight to the moral and ethical contradictions of U.S. policy towards people of color and public outcry for solidarity post 9/11. Jay-Z's words, "Crack was Anthrax back then, back when Police was Al Qaeda to Black men," inspired students to interrogate America's treatment of people of color and how Blacks have felt "unsafe, unprotected, subject to random violence, and hatred" (West, 2004, p. 20) for centuries as Africans and African Americans. The most salient illumination gained from this one particular lesson, even though there are many, for the current research is that African American students in Hill's class through Hip Hop pedagogy started to unpack how people of color have been mistreated and labeled criminals, when in reality Blacks have been the victims of police brutality, racial profiling, and racist mandatory drug sentencing laws. Hill's lesson is one way that Hip Hop critical literacy can engage students in critical analysis that challenges reproductive cycles of oppression by fostering a classroom discussion that is grounded in students' lived culture. According to Williams (2009), "Hip Hop culture is the lens through which many students today seek meaning, acceptance, and belonging, which in turn, posits Hip Hop as one of the most important, but underutilized cultural lenses that teachers can employ for the development of critical consciousness" (p. 2). Hip Hop critical pedagogy, at its core, is a vehicle for teaching not only critical consciousness, but also a social justice agenda centered on democratic education aimed at helping students of color multidimensionally conceptualize oppression in an effort to gain political and social equality (Collins, 2000; Crenshaw, 1991).

Studies similar to Hill's are emerging at a brisk rate. These studies are all aimed at dismantling Hip Hop's mainstream persona as too provocative for classrooms and introducing Hip Hop as an educational tool for analysis and the development of counter-narratives (Alim, 2004; Emdin, 2010; Hill, 2009; Leard & Lashua, 2006; Low, 2011; Williams, 2009). The aforementioned scholarship rests on the work of Morrell and Duncan-Andrade (2002), who outlined a framework for teaching media and culture studies to urban youth in ways that promoted academic and critical literacies. Morrell and Duncan-Andrade's Hip-Hop project, structured by the tenets of "problem-posing" and "culturally affirming pedagogy" (Ladson-Billings, 1994), empowered youth by examining the media's contrived depiction of urban youth. Morrell and Duncan-Andrade contended that many rappers see themselves as educators with a message that critically examines their community. The researchers argued that Hip Hop could serve as a "bridge between the streets and the classroom to promote empowerment and activism within the students social and communal spaces" (p. 92).

Another strand of Hip Hop scholarship that grounds this work are studies that focus on how youth understand, read, and interrupt the text of Hip Hop to form identities (Dimitriadis, 2001; Clay, 2003; Love, 2011, 2012; Richardson, 2006, 2007). An exemplary example of how Black males make meaning of Hip Hop music and culture to inform their lives is the work of Dimitriadis (2001, 2003). Researching youth and Hip Hop through anthropological perspectives that recognize the ways in which youth construct meaning in their communities, Dimitriadis (2003) examined how Black males in urban America used popular texts to "construct, sustain, and maintain notions of self, history, and community through popular culture" (p. 6). To contextualize urban youth and how they construct meaning of their complex lives, Dimitriadis invites his readers in to the lives of two best friends, Tony (17) and Rufus (18), to explore how Black males consume Hip Hop and form kinship roots. Tony and

Rufus' family roots, entrenched in Southern traditions, became a primary tool in the way they constructed meaning of Hip Hop and popular texts. Hip Hop nurtured Tony and Rufus' sense of community and family. Tony and Rufus bonded to their families and their neighborhood through the rap lyrics of Southern rappers because they felt out of place at times as Southerners living in the Midwest. The work of Dimitriadis affirms how two Black males read rap; however, youth's interpretations of Hip Hop, regardless of race, are unpredictable because of youths' personal, educational, and communal differences. Simply put, youth's reading of rap is unique and individualized, but there are some evident commonalties.

The ways in which youth read Hip Hop while reading the world is complex, especially for youth hailing from marginalized backgrounds, but a fundamental aspect of interacting with popular culture is critiquing it and at times resisting its messages. Therefore, youth, regardless of social constructs, intuitively resist aspects of popular culture that exploit and degrade them. A fundamental part of consuming popular culture is resisting popular culture. However, this space of critique is complex, as youth contest, confer and simultaneously yield to popular culture. For instance, Richardson (2007) explored the ways in which Black women negotiated stereotypical images located in rap videos. She found that young Black women resisted, negotiated and succumbed to the racist stereotypes embedded in rap music and culture. Through her research, Richardson discovered that African American females have complex and fluid "language, literacy and knowledge-making capacity" as they participate in Hip Hop music and culture and read the world in which they live (p. 789). Richardson (2007) also expanded the definition of Hip Hop literacies to refer to "ways in which people who are socialized into hip hop discourse manipulate as well as read language, gestures, images, material possessions, and people to position themselves against or within discourse in order to advance and protect themselves" (p. 792). This study attempts to embody Richardson's inclusive definition of Hip Hop literacies by analyzing how three African American males read Hip Hop and the racist messages embedded within popular culture. These three young men, all from working class homes, have a unique cultural background as Southerners living in a city with a distinctive racial and sociopolitical history, newly dubbed as the colloquial "home of Hip Hop."

The Dirty South

Atlanta, Georgia is what many refer to as a "chocolate city," where Black folks outnumber the White population. However, racism and inequity are prevalent in Atlanta. This paradoxical dynamic is not surprising in a city heavily populated by Black folks with Black leadership, but based on a provocative past of segregation, forced desegregation, and the permanence of racism. But in the face of racism and color lines of elitism, Atlanta has held on to what Sarig (2007) calls the "genesis of rap": Southern-flavored Hip Hop deeply rooted in Black Southern traditions. Sarig (2007) argues that rap music was born in the South because Atlanta's special marque of Southern rap style is grounded in the sounds that came before rap: West African storytellers (griots), spoken word, slave songs coded in metaphors and euphemisms, spirituals, the African drum, bebop, call and response, blues, jazz, funk, rhythm and blues, soul, rock and roll, and Civil Rights freedom songs all inform Southern rap (Sarig, 2007). Thus, Atlanta's fusion of Southern-flavored Hip Hop is a melodic improvisation of various types of African and African American inspired music mixed with ubiquitous experiences of being young, urban, and Black. However, instead of Black youth in Atlanta, primarily Black males, being celebrated for their ingenuity and resourcefulness because they created an ingenious billion dollar sound, they are socially constructed as anti-intellectual, hyper-sexual, nihilistic, and violent. Atlanta's officials in 2007 considered banning baggy pants; Atlanta public schools have a zero-tolerance policy that leads to the "increasing confinement and incarceration of youthful offenders" (Polakow, 2000, p. 1). Recent dominant discourse surrounding youth, especially Blacks males of color in Atlanta, criminalize Black males as perpetrators of violent acts influenced by the same Hip Hop music and culture that has made corporate America billions in yearly revenue. By utilizing a Hip Hop literacy framework, rooted in critical pedagogy, this study seeks to understand Black males' knowledge-making abilities and everyday commonsense interpretations at a local community center in Atlanta, GA. The three males that comprise this study attended the center's afterschool program.

Community Context & Methods

Hope Community Center (HCC) is a non-profit organization whose mission was to build a sense of community within a neighborhood that was undergoing extreme levels of gentrification. It was evident by the center's population makeup that many of the students who were attending HCC were the last faces of color within the neighborhood. The cornerstone of HCC was the after-school program, which provided academic and social enrichment programs for school-age children at no cost. The youth examined within this study were among those enrolled in this after-school program. During the school year, the participating students attended the center daily, where they received homework assistance, one-on-one tutoring and monthly field trips intended to broaden their exposure to higher education, the arts and sports. I limit the information that I disclose about HCC because I am revealing the city and state of my research site. While disclosing the location of my research is uncommon in qualitative research and is risky, the location is important to understanding the lived experiences of the young men in the study.

The methodological framework that informed the research project was ethnography. Ethnography focuses on how people make meaning of their culture and beliefs in their everyday lives. Furthermore, ethnography does not place limitations on the boundaries of data collection, time at the research site, or the scope of questioning. In order to understand the complexity of HCC youth as they engaged with rap music, I spent 16 months at HCC researching the ways in which youth read and understood rap music. By the end of study, I had spent a year and a half at the community center as a researcher. Data collection started in November 2006 and ended March 2008. I visited the site every week, two to three times a week, for roughly 3 hours per day, not including weekend programs.

The findings presented within this article are part of my dissertation. Many of the individual interviews lasted 30–40 minutes. Group interviews were much longer in time, lasting an hour or more, depending on the group dynamics. I interviewed the students from August 2007 until March 2008. I chose to interview the youth during this time because of their availability. During the summer, the students participated in various field-trips and sport camps, which made it difficult to interview the youth on a consistent basis. Therefore, I decided that when school started in August 2007, and the students had a defined routine and schedule, I then would begin interviews. For the first 8 months at the center, I merely observed the youth and conducted informal interviews. The entire study is comprised of nine students: six young ladies and three young men. However, for the purpose of this article, I will only report the findings from the three males. Although there were over 40 students who attended

HCC regularly, a number of those students were in elementary school. The nine Black students that comprised this research study were the older students of the center, ages 13–17 years old. At that particular time in my research trajectory, I was particularly interested in understanding how middle and high school students consume and construct identities as they engage with Hip Hop music and culture.

Negotiating Access and the Researcher's Role

In the summer of 2005, before I even began the research project at HCC, I was a summer camp counselor and girls' basketball coach at the community center. Still in my second year as a doctoral student, I was thinking about investigating alternative spaces of learning and how youth understand and construct identities through rap music. However, I was apprehensive about conducting my dissertation research at HCC because I was grappling with issues of objectivity (at this time in my life I thought being objective was possible), my ethical responsibility to the center and the youth, and, more generally, positions of power. After the summer camp ended, the director of the center asked me to work at HCC full-time during the school year. Once I had the chance to get to know the students and hear their thoughts on Hip Hop, race, issues of class, sexism and schooling, I knew that I had found my research site. At the end of the school year of 2006, I resigned. I began my work at the center as a researcher five months later in November of 2006. My resignation allowed me a few months to think through my new role at the center as a researcher "working the hyphen" (Fine, 1994). She defines "working the hyphen" as a way in which "researchers probe how we are in relation with the context we study and with our informants, understanding that we are all multiple in those relations . . . to see how these 'relations between' get us 'better' data" (p. 72). My multiple roles – staff member, volunteer, tutor, and researcher – shaped my research as I entered HCC as an "embodied knowledge-producing agent" (Dimitriadis, 2001, p. 578) with insider and outsider status. Furthermore, throughout the research process I was constantly negotiating my multiple roles, identities and power positions at the center with youth, parents and former coworkers.

Research Questions, Data Collection & Analysis

The study's main inquiry focused on how youth at HCC construct identities through rap music in their everyday lives. The following additional questions also guided my research:

1. How do youth understand the images presented in rap music and rap videos?
2. How do rap's messages contribute to youth's construction of race and gender identities?
3. How does rap music shape youth's lived experiences?

Interviews were the primary source of data. The interviews consisted of semi-structured and unstructured open-ended questions. I constructed many of the interview questions on an ongoing basis because they pertained to each student's experiences with rap music. I also conducted group interviews, which I found to be quite helpful as the participants spoke candidly with their peers about issues and experiences. In all, I conducted 8 individual interviews and 3 group interviews with both Reggie and Dave, and 4 individual interviews and 2 group interviews with Darrell. After the interview process, I utilized the "open coding" method to analyze my data. While coding, I wrote countless memos reflecting on the substantive issues and summarizing my observer comments. These memos served as the analysis foundation as I began to ask myself analytic questions to create themes grounded first in my codes and then in the literature.

Darrell, Dave & Reggie

Darrell was a young man who exuded personality. Darrell stood about 6 feet tall, wore thick glasses that were often crooked on his face and was a self-proclaimed ladies man. Darrell spoke with a charming Southern drawl. Darrell was a breath of fresh air. He was always smiling and talking to anybody who would listen. When I asked Darrell if he would like to participate he said, "Ya, I know a lot about the rap and street game." I then asked him what he knew. He replied, "I will tell you a thing or two" as he smiled and laughed. I instantly handed Darrell two permission forms, one for his parents and one for him. The next day I asked Darrell about the permission slips. He said, "Ya, I have it, it's in my pocket . . . you want it . . . you thought I was going to forget, huh." He was right; I did think he was going to forget. Actually, he was the only teen to bring the form back the next day. I did not meet Darrell's parents, but I learned through conversation that Darrell lived with his mother.

Dave was the highest achieving male at the center academically. Dave excelled in school with a grade point average of 3.6. Dave was tall and slim and had a smile that lit up a room. Dave was always smiling. He had a comedic sensibility and was always doing something to get a laugh. The timing of his jokes were thought out and delivered in a manner that made everyone around him laugh. He was a likeable young man. Dave lived with his mother, stepfather, younger sister, and brother.

Reggie was the athlete out of the boys that attended the center. He was tall with broad shoulders and a face that could sell any sports drink. Reggie received all the attention from the girls at the center; nevertheless, he was humble and had a boyish charm about him. His sport of choice was football, and he idolized Peyton Manning. Reggie wanted to be a quarterback in the National Football League (NFL). Reggie lived with his mother, father, and his younger siblings.

Findings

Not All Black People . . .

Through critical dialogue aimed at discovering how they made meaning of Hip Hop and popular culture's embedded racism, the youth insightfully recognized and articulated, without hesitation, the racial issues surrounding rap music that connected to broader issues facing the Black urban community. For instance, when the young men were asked how they thought the media represented people of color they responded with keen criticism:

> They try to say all black people eat chicken, and macaroni and cheese, corn-bread. Talk about collard greens, all black people eat collard greens. That's what people think. They think just cause a lot of us do it, that all of us do it. That's what I'm trying to say.
>
> (Dave, Interview, 12/07)

> Oh, they're sending a bad message to kids and about Blacks.
>
> (Reggie, Interview, 11/07)

Both young men understood that the media is a contrived space built on the stereotypes of Blacks. Dave was alerted to the racial trope that Blacks are monolithic and all eat the same food. Dave was deconstructing elements of what Hill Collins (2004) calls the "new racism," which is the mass media heavily relying on racial tropes to justify racism. Darrell added, "They see us people on TV, that all the black people be doing is fighting" (Darrell, Interview, 10/07). Reggie echoed Darrell's images of violent behavior by Blacks on television: "Like they think whatever you show them. If you show them violence, they gonna think you're violent" (Reggie, Interview, 10/07). Here Reggie is speaking of how negative stereotypes impact his daily life as a young Black man. Reggie feels he is labeled violent by society because of how Black males are portrayed in the media. There exists a substantial amount of research that examines the disparities in how the media depicts both Whites and Blacks that validates the teens' statements (Oliver & Shapiro, 1997). Watkins (2006) argued that "blacks are underrepresented in many areas of the mass media [and] they are overrepresented in television sports broadcasts and crime and violence portrayals" (p. 2). As I engaged with these three males individually through interviews focused on how race was constructed and represented within Hip Hop music and culture, and the media in general, the issue of class became apparent as well.

> Like you know in Africa is right now, they got TVs and stuff. They show you like old movies of Africa, so you're gonna think that they don't have anything. I used to think that, too.
>
> (Dave, Interview, 1/08)

> If you look on TV, all white people are rich.
>
> (Reggie, Interview, 10/07)

Dave's insightful statement illuminates how the media repackages and obscures representations of Africa to African American youth. The teens' remarks about the racism embedded in mass media are the teens' reality and experiences as they watch television with a critical eye. It is important to keep in mind that youth construct identities at the intersections of school and society. Therefore, what society tells them about their race and class is a site of education, which they are verbally resisting through their attempt to debunk racist stereotypes of Black males. Dave and Reggie frequently discussed techniques they used so they would not be labeled "bad," violent, or unintelligent. In a group interview with Dave and Reggie, they explained how individuals stereotyped them, and how they codeswitched to counter negative assumptions. Dave stated, "You come from Atlanta, like Bankhead [urban neighborhood in Atlanta], or something, they think you act crazy. That represents only one person . . . Like when I tell them we're from Bankhead you can tell them [White people], but show your good side" (Dave, Interview, 10/07). Dave was also a high achieving student who was motivated by racism and the stereotype that Atlanta Blacks are "crazy." (Dave, 10/07). Reggie's sentiments echoed Dave's when he stated, "They think we crazy, but I know how to act when I am around them [White people]." Richardson (2002) suggested, "Codeswitching is also a valuable resource since each language represents a way of knowing and expressing the world. Style/ codeswitching allows Black people to move between worldviews" (p. 691). Reggie and Dave rejected the notion that they had to perform a particular way because they are Black youth. When faced with racism they debunked monolithic notions of Blackness and dispelled myths about being young, Black, male and urban.

Real Talk

During the study, the police arrested Atlanta-based rapper T.I. (Clifford Joseph Harris, Jr.) on federal gun charges, and the courts sentenced him to house arrest until his court date.

Many of the students referred to T.I. as an example of poor decision-making and a negative role model for youth. Prior to his arrest, T.I. was a local hero. However, the teens expressed disappointment in T.I. and his gangster image.

> That's not the only way they gone get their money but that's how they want to make themselves be a gangster, you know, and their self be hard Like T.I, I don't like him no more cause you know he made himself as a gangster.
>
> (Reggie, Interview, 1/08)

> Nothing wrong with being, I mean yeah, ain't nothing wrong with being soft. T.I. has to be hard.
>
> (Reggie, Interview, 1/08)

T.I. is just one example of a large group of rappers who dramatize and romanticize selling drugs and being a gangster. Reggie understood T.I.'s rapper image as a façade and a means to sell records in his above recorded statement. Reggie implied that T.I.'s gangster image is a ploy to sell records. Reggie questioned the authenticity of T.I.'s pugnacious image. The fact that many of the teens questioned T.I.'s image and reasons for making records showed they were aware of and concerned with the messages of his music. Reggie did not applaud T.I.'s fall from greatness through criminal activity. Reggie also thought rappers were "stupid" because they do not understand their racial, social, and economic position, which makes them a target for racial profiling. Reggie questioned whether rappers understand their visibility to the police. He stated,

> They [rappers] stupid, you know, the police gonna be looking at you like yeah, he might do it for real because he rap, so they're going to be doing background checks and all that junk up on you trying to catch you and put you in jail.
>
> (Reggie, Interview, 10/07)

Reggie's comments make it apparent that the youth have the ability to negotiate not only rap, but also social issues around the music and urban life. Reggie claimed that police purposefully target rappers for incarceration, which indicated that he was aware of racial profiling and the xenophobic ideology of the criminal justice system (Wacquant, 2005). Wacquant argued that society has "a generalized fear of blacks in public space" (p. 21). The teens without hesitation challenged dominant public discourse surrounding youth of color as they consumed Hip Hop and popular culture without adopting the messages and values of the music in their everyday lives. As I will discuss next, the male teens' semi-transitive consciousness allowed them to resist some of rap's more negative message on a personal cognitive level, but the hegemonic ideologies that they felt assiduously worked to prevent a shift in dominant public discourse impeded them from taking action. These youth were well-mannered, intelligent and respectful young men, who consumed rap and mass media for pleasure, yet they struggled to take action and reach Freire's highest level of consciousness because they conceptualized racism within Hip Hop and mass media as permanent.

That's Just How It Is: Semi-transitive & Critical Consciousness

Although the young men displayed intellectual rigor when analyzing issues of racism and classism in Hip Hop and the media, as well as critiquing rappers' authenticity because of their inherent connection to capitalism, they did not feel as though they could change and challenge the narrative surrounding people of color. These young men were striving to be critically conscious individuals who recognized that there is a problem embedded within society that needs to be addressed to create a more just and equitable world (Kincheloe, 2008; Shor & Freire, 1987). However, the idea of possessing what Freire (2000) calls *conscientization,* or critical consciousness, cannot manifest without critical dialogue, which in turn can lead to action, as individuals are empowered to challenge marginalizing social contexts, ideologies, organizations, experiences, policies, and discourses (Williams, 2009). Yet, there are tensions and levels of resistance as individuals strive for critical consciousness. For instance, hegemony can stifle critical consciousness through systemic strategies to keep consciousness underdeveloped. McLaren (1994) defined hegemony as "a struggle in which the powerful win the consent of those who are oppressed . . . Within the hegemonic process, established meanings are often laundered of contradiction, contestation, and ambiguity" (p. 183). The space of popular culture is ripe for the complex layered manipulation of hegemony because, according to Hall (1981), "Popular culture is one of the sites where this struggle for and against culture of the powerful is engaged . . . It is an arena of consent and resistance. It is partly where hegemony arises, and where it is secured" (p. 65). Hill Collins (2004) argues that popular culture corresponding with mass media and global technologies provides a cunning mechanism for disseminating hegemonic ideologies. As argued by Richardson (2007),

> Commercial rap videos provide a hefty dissemination of hegemonic images of black youth culture throughout the world. These images are decontextualized from their roots in slavery and its legacy of racial rule, and are repackaged by mass media and popular culture, helping to reproduce the hegemonic ideologies and replicate social inequality.
>
> (p. 791)

This is why Freire (2000) argues that there are three levels of consciousness: intransitive, semi-transitive, and critical. Boyles (2005) explained that intransitive "means noncritical (in)action" (p. 220). Semi-transitive consciousness beings are "individuals who see the world as changeable (Boyles, p. 220), but they are reluctant to do anything about it. The last form of consciousness is critical consciousness. Critically conscious individuals recognize that there is a problem embedded within society that needs to be addressed through dialogue and action and attempt to rectify societal inadequacies.

In the case of Darrell, Dave and Reggie, these teens managed to resist some of rap and popular culture's explicit racist representations of people of color. However, they believed these same messages within rap and the media were permanent; thus, they felt defeated by just the mere thought of taking action and challenging dominant discourse. For example, the teens thought resisting rap in the form of action was pointless, they understood that something needed to be done, but were reluctant to do so. All three males told me that there was nothing that they could do to change the music or mass media because racism was an unyielding element of the music and television shows they consumed. When I asked Dave why he thought television show creators depicted Blacks as criminals or all of Africa as an exotic and primal continent he told me in a matter of fact manner, "that's just how it is" (10/07). I was taken aback by his response because typically Dave is outspoken with sharp critiques of racial inequalities. When I asked Dave what he meant by his latter statement he said, "Man, they do what they do." When I asked Dave who the "they" were he said, "I don't know." When I asked Darrell the same question he stated, "That's just how is it, Coach T" (10/07). Both young men framed the stereotypes of Black identity disseminated by the mass media and Hip Hop as core narratives of the media's discourse at-large. Dave and Darrell are utilizing a critical race theory (CRT) lens to examine Hip Hop and mass media. Bell perceived America's racial legacy as "permanent and indestructible" (Bell, 1992, p. x). CRT scholars view race and racism as vital parts of American society deeply embedded within America's ethos (Bell, 1992). These young men do as well. All three of these young men possessed the ability and knowledge making skills to achieve Freire's highest level of critical consciousness, but were stifled at semi-transitive consciousness because they viewed racism as a fixed aspect of their daily lives as young Black men.

Implications for Educational Policy

The findings of this study call for action: critical dialogues aimed at fostering critical consciousness so that it becomes a fundamental aspect of all students' educational experience. Classrooms are needed where students learn and develop theoretical or pedagogical frameworks that challenge the status quo within the media and society at-large. One example of a pedagogical lens that could assist students in reaching Freire's highest level of critical consciousness is critical media literacy. Kellner and Share (2006) argued that implementing critical media literacy is not an option in today's multimedia world and an educational system driven by standardized high stakes testing. The implementation of critical media literacy is necessary to empower students "to create their own messages that can challenge media texts and narratives" (p. 60). Lewis and Jhally (1998) stated that, "the goal of media literacy is to help people become sophisticated citizens rather than sophisticated consumers" (p. 109). Lewis and Jhally's definition of media literacy moves individuals to a greater sense of democracy as people challenge "scripted and defined" (p. 109) narratives about all groups of people. Going one-step further, critical media literacy is a "multiperspectival approach addressing issues of gender, race, class, and power" (Kellner & Share, p. 59). One of the primary goals of critical media literacy is to create counter representations or alternative perspectives of the media (Love, 2011). Critical media literacy provides students, particularly Black males with a framework and space to challenge, debunk and find ways to take action against the media's attack on Black masculinity. According to Collins (2005), Black masculinity is pitted in narrow terms, in that, "manhood matches up to the White normality/Black deviancy framework that accompanies racism" (p. 187). However, Black males need a space to speak back to debasing narratives within the media and create new narratives that represent their experiences. Dave, Reggie and Darrell needed a framework to interrogate rap and feel empowered doing so. They also needed a safe space where both teachers and students could openly critique rap and still locate the beauty, joy and artistic genius that is Hip Hop. These three young men were engaging in critical dialogues that could have been the spark to action, but without community programs and schools aimed at promoting world views that ask students to think in critically consciousness ways, they are left to imagine a world where racism is constant and change is elusive.

References

Alim, S, H. (2004). *You know my steez: An ethnographic and sociolinguistic study of styleshifting in black American speech community.* Durham, NC: Duke University Press.

Bell, D. (1992). Faces at the bottom of the well. New York: Basic.

Boyles, D. (Ed.). (2005). *Schools or markets? Commercialism, privatization, and school business partnerships.* Mahwah, N.J.: Lawrence Erlbaum Associates.

Clay, A. (2003). Keepin' it real: Black youth, hip-hop culture, and Black identity. *American Behavioral Scientist, 46*(10), 1346–1358.

Dimitriadis, G. (2001). *Performing identity/performing culture: hip hop as text, pedagogy, and lived practice.* New York, NY: Peter Lang.

Dimitriadis, G. (2003). *Friendship, cliques, and gangs: Young black men coming of age in urban America.* New York: Teachers College Press.

Emdin, C. (2010). *Urban science education for hip-hop generation.* New York, NY: Sense Publishers.

Freire, P. & Macedo, D. (1987). *Literacy: Reading the word and the world.* South Hadley, MA: Bergin & Garvey.

Freire, P. (2000). *Pedagogy of the oppressed* (30th anniversary ed.). New York: Continuum.

Gay, G. (2000). *Culturally responsive teaching: Theory, research, and practice.* New York: Teacher College Press.

Gee, J. P. (1996). *Social linguistics and literacies: Ideology in discourses.* London: Taylor and Francis.

Ginwright, S. (2004). *Black in school. Afrocentric reform, urban youth, and the promise of hip-hop culture.* New York: Teachers College Press.

Giroux, H. (1996). *Fugitive cultures: Race, violence, and youth.* New York. Routledge.

Hall, S. (1981). Notes on deconstructing the popular. *People's History and Socialist Theory,* 233–269.

Hill Collins, P. (2000). *Black feminist thought: knowledge, consciousness, and the politics of empowerment* (2nd ed.). New York, NY: Routledge.

Hill, M. L. (2006). Using Jay-Z to reflect on post-9/11 race relations. *English Journal, 96*(2), 23–27.

Hill, M.L. (2009). *Beats, rhymes, and classroom life.* New York, New York: Teachers College Press.

Kincheloe, J. L (2008). *Critical pedagogy primer.* New York: Peter Lang.

Ladson-Billings, G. (1994). *The dreamkeepers: Successful teachers of African American children.* San Francisco: Jossey-Bass.

Leard, D. W., & Lashua, B. (2006). Popular media, critical pedagogy, and inner city youth. *Canadian Journal of Education, 29*(1), 244.

Lee, C. (1995). The use of signifying as a scaffold for literary interpretation. *Journal of Black Psychology, 21*(4), 357–381.

Love, B. L. (2011). Where are the White girls? A qualitative analysis of how six African American girls made meaning of their sexuality, race and gender through the lens of rap. In D. Carlson & D. Roseboro (Eds.), *The sexuality curriculum: Youth culture, popular culture, and progressive sexuality education* (pp. 122–135). New York: Peter Lang Publishing

Love, B. (2012). *Hip hop's li'l sistas speak: Negotiating identities and politics in the new south.* New York: Peter Lang Publishing.

Low, B. (2011). *Slam school: Learning through conflict in the hop-hop and spoken word classroom.* Stanford, CA: Stanford University Press.

Mahiri, J., & Conner, E. (2003). Black youth violence has a bad rap. *Journal of Social Issues,* 59(1), 121–140.

McLaren, P. (1994). *Life in schools. An introduction to critical pedagogy in the foundations of education.* Addison Wesley Longman, Inc.

McWhorter, J. H. (2003). What's holding blacks back?. *City Journal, 2*(1), 24–32.

Morrell, E., & Duncan-Andrade, J. M. R. (2002). Promoting academic literacy with urban youth through engaging hip-hop culture. *English Journal, 91*(6), 88–92.

Neal, M. A. (2006). *New Black man.* New York: Routledge.

Oliver, M. L., & Shapiro T. M. (1997). *Black wealth/White wealth: A new perspective on racial inequality.* Routledge.

Petchauer, E. (2009). Framing and reviewing hip-hop educational research. *Review of Educational Research,* (79)2, 946–978.

Polakow, V. (Ed.). (2000). *The public assault on American's children: Poverty, violence, and juvenile injustice.* New York, NY: Teachers College Press.

Rose, T. (1991). "Fear of a black plant": Rap music and black cultural politics in the 1990s. *Journal of Negro Education,* (60)3, 276–290.

Rose, T. (2008). *The hip hop wars.* Basic Civitas Books.

Richardson, E. (2006). *Hiphop literacies.* New York: Routledge.

Richardson, E. (2007). "She workin' it like foreal": Critical literacy and discourse practices of African American females in the age of hip hop. *Discourse and Society,* 18, 789–809.

Sarig, R. (2007). *Third coast: Outkast, Timbaland, and how hip hop became a southern thing.* Cambridge, MA: Da Capo Press.

Shor, I. (1987). *Critical teaching and everyday life.* Chicago, IL: University of Chicago Press.

Wacquant, L. J. D. (2005). *Urban outcasts: Stigma and division in the black American ghetto and the French urban periphery.* New York, NY: Routledge.

West, C. (2001). *Race matters.* Boston, MA: Beacon Press.

Williams, A. D. (2009). The critical cultural cypher: Remaking Paulo Freire's cultural circles using hip hop culture. *The International Journal of Critical Pedagogy, 2(1), 1–29.*

20

Toward a Critical Pedagogy of Popular Culture: Literacy Development Among Urban Youth

Ernest Morrell

Finding effective ways to teach today's student population is perhaps the greatest challenge facing literacy educators in the United States. As classrooms become increasingly diverse, educators struggle to find curricula and pedagogical strategies that are inclusive and affirmative yet facilitate the development of academic and critical literacies. Unfortunately, much of the multicultural education literature—with its limited conception of culture as a racial or ethnic identity—offers little to help teachers attempting to make connections and create learning communities in multiethnic urban classrooms (McCarthy, 1998). New approaches, such as the critical teaching of popular culture, can help students acquire and develop the literacies needed to navigate "new-century" schools. Popular culture can help students deconstruct dominant narratives and contend with oppressive practices in hopes of achieving a more egalitarian and inclusive society.

New Literacy Studies and Popular Culture

New Literacy theorists argue that social context and cultural diversity significantly affect the literacy process. Often, the failure of urban students to develop "academic" literacy skills stems not from a lack of intelligence but from the inaccessibility of the school curriculum to students who are not in the "dominant" or "mainstream" culture. These theorists believe that such students are literate but that their literacies have little connection with the dominant literacies promoted in public schools (New London Group, 1996; Street, 1995). Educators of new-century schools, these theorists argue, need to examine nonschool literacy practices to find connections between local literacies and the dominant, academic literacies. Mahiri (1998), for example, found strong connections between urban youth's literacy practices with popular culture and the types of literacies required in schools. Mahiri's work suggested that the critical teaching of popular culture is one way to make connections that are relevant to all students in diverse urban classrooms.

Academic literacy, for the purposes of this column, refers to those forms of engaging with, producing, and talking about texts that have currency in primary, secondary, and postsecondary education (Harris & Hodges, 1995; Street, 1995; Venezky, Wagner, & Ciliberti, 1990). Critical literacy, on the other hand, is defined as the ability not only to read and write, but also to assess texts in order to understand the relationships between power and domination that underlie and inform those texts (Hull, 1993). The critically literate can understand the socially constructed meaning embedded in texts as well as the political and economic contexts in which texts are embedded. Ultimately, critical literacy can lead to an emancipated worldview and even transformational social action (Freire, 1970; Hull, 1993; McLaren, 1989; UNESCO, 1975).

As I situate literacy learning in the critical study of popular culture, it is important to define the terms *culture* and *popular culture.* Williams (1995) suggested that culture is one of the most complex terms in the English language. Critiquing sociologists, anthropologists, and "cultural" critics who examine only single components of culture, Williams (1998, p. 48) articulated the following three components of culture that are essential to any thorough analysis of the subject.

1. The *ideal* component of culture is a state or process of human perfection in terms of absolute or universal values.
2. The *documentary* component of culture is the body of intellectual and imaginative work in which human thought and experience are recorded.
3. The *social* component of culture is a description of a particular way of life that expresses certain meanings and values not only in art and learning, but also in institutions and ordinary behavior.

Each of Williams's components are represented in this analysis of the critical pedagogy of popular culture. In the *ideal* sense, I analyze popular culture as it relates to the expression of universal human values, namely the desire and struggle for freedom from tyranny and oppression. I also *document* and analyze elements of the body of intellectual and imaginative work that popular culture comprises, such as hip-hop music, film, and texts produced by mainstream media. Finally, I examine popular culture as the everyday *social* experience of marginalized students as they confront, make sense of, and contend with social institutions such as schools, the mass media, corporations, and governments.

My definition of popular culture was inspired by cultural and critical theorists (e.g., Adorno & Horkheimer, 1999; Docker, 1994; Hall, 1998; McCarthy, 1998; Storey, 1998; Williams, 1995, 1998). These theorists saw popular culture as a site of struggle between the subordinate and the dominant groups in society. Popular culture, they argued, is not an imposed mass culture or a people's culture, it is more a terrain of exchange between the two. The texts and practices of popular culture move within what Gramsci (1971) called a compromise equilibrium. Those who look at popular culture from this perspective see it as a terrain of ideological struggle expressed through music, film, mass media artifacts, language, customs, and values. For the critical educator, then, popular culture provides a logical connection between lived experiences and the school culture for urban youth.

The arguments for incorporating popular culture into traditional curricula are quite compelling and have generated much excitement, along with much confusion and anxiety, among urban educators. In my experiences as a teacher and teacher educator, I have met countless colleagues who verbally support incorporating popular culture, yet feel unprepared and daunted by the project. Much of the reticence and confusion surrounding the inclusion of popular culture stems from a lack of understanding. Given its roots and ethos, any investigation of popular culture must emanate from and serve the interests of members of marginalized groups. That is, any pedagogy of popular culture has to be a critical pedagogy where students and teachers learn from and with one another while engaging in authentic dialogue that is centered on the experiences of urban youth as participants in and creators of popular culture (Freire, 1970; Giroux, 1997; hooks, 1994; McLaren, 1989).

The Practice

I want to illustrate how the critical teaching of popular culture can produce powerful academic and social results with urban youth. I draw from data collected during the eight years that I taught urban teens in the San Francisco Bay area and southern California, USA. I focus on a few particular manifestations of popular culture (i.e., hip-hop, film, and mass media) around which I prepared classroom units. I include classroom unit descriptions and vignettes where appropriate.

Teaching Hip-Hop Culture

It can be argued that hip-hop music is the representative voice of urban youth because the genre was created by and for urban youth (George, 1998; Rose, 1994). In addition to acting as voices in the urban community, many rappers consider themselves educators and see at least a portion of their mission as raising the consciousness of their communities. The raising of critical consciousness in people who have been oppressed is the first step in helping them to obtain critical literacy (Freire, 1970). The influence of rap as a voice of resistance for urban youth proliferates through artists who endeavor to bring an accurate yet critical depiction of the urban situation to a hip-hop generation.

Given the social, cultural, and academic relevance of hip-hop music, a colleague and I designed a classroom unit that incorporated hip-hop music and culture into a traditional high school senior English poetry unit. We began the unit with an overview of poetry in general, attempting to redefine poetry and the poet's role. We emphasized the importance of understanding the historical period in which a poem was written in order to come to a deep interpretation. In the introductory lecture, we laid out all of the historical and literary periods that would be covered in the unit (e.g., the Elizabethan age, the Puritan Revolution in England, the Civil War, and the Post–Industrial Revolution in the United States). We placed hip-hop music and the Post–Industrial Revolution right alongside other historical and literary periods so that students could use a period and genre of poetry they were familiar with as a lens to examine the other literary works. We also wanted to encourage our students to re-evaluate how they view elements of their popular culture.

The second major portion of the unit was the group presentation of a poem and a rap song. The groups were asked to prepare a justifiable interpretation of their poem and song with relation to their specific historical and literary periods and to analyze the links between the two. After a week of preparation, each group was given a class period to present its work and have its arguments critiqued by peers. In addition to the group presentations, students were asked to complete an anthology of 10 poems, 5 of which would be presented at a poetry reading. Finally, students were asked to write a five- to seven-page critical essay on a song of their choice.

The students generated quality interpretations and made interesting connections between the canonical poems and the rap songs. They were also inspired to create their own critical poems to serve as celebration and social commentary. Their critical investigations of popular texts brought about oral and written critiques similar to those required by college preparatory English classrooms. The students moved beyond critical reading of literary texts to become cultural producers themselves, creating and presenting poems that provided critical social commentary and encouraged action for social justice. The unit adhered to critical pedagogy because it was situated in the experiences of the students, called for critical dialogue and a critical engagement of the text, and related the texts to larger social and political issues.

Teaching Popular Film

The National Council of Teachers of English and International Reading Association Standards for the English Language Arts (1996) mentions popular film and television as visual texts worthy of study in K–12 classrooms in this landmark statement:

> Being literate in contemporary society means being active, critical, and creative users not only of print and spoken language but also of the visual language of film and television .... Teaching students how to interpret and create visual texts . . . is another essential component of the English language arts curriculum. Visual communication is part of the fabric of contemporary life.
>
> (p. 5)

The notion of films as visual texts worthy of academic study has been growing within the postsecondary academy for some time. The critical film studies field has grown in prominence, and there are now academics who use critical theory to study film at nearly every major university in the U.S. These recent developments point to the legitimacy of popular films as academic texts worthy of critical interrogation by urban educators and their students.

In my classrooms, I created units in which students were able to use their visual literacies and experiences with popular film to learn, interpret, and deconstruct literary texts. This analysis focuses on two classroom units that incorporated popular film with the traditional curriculum to make meaningful connections with canonical texts and to promote the development of academic and critical literacies. The first unit began with *The Godfather* trilogy (Coppola, 1972, 1974, 1993) and incorporated Homer's *The Odyssey.* Another unit joined Richard Wright's (1989) *Native Son* with the film *A Time to Kill* (Schumaker, 1996).

During the units, the students watched the films in class while reading the accompanying texts at home. They would take notes on the film, and we would discuss each segment of the movie in class. On a typical day, there might be 30 minutes of film watching and 25 minutes of critical discussion. During the films, the corresponding books were introduced, and students discussed similarities and differences between characters in the film and the books and people in their own lives. For instance, while watching *The Godfather* and reading *The Odyssey,* students discussed the portrayal of heroes in Western epics and Western society. They compared Homer's Odysseus to Coppola's Michael Corleone. They also looked to their own society for examples of heroes. While watching *A Time to Kill,* the students discussed justice in the context of the lives of Wright's Bigger Thomas and Schumaker's Carl Lee Hailey, and they examined their own school for examples of injustice. Ultimately, one class decided to devote the last six weeks of school to creating a magazine that depicted the injustices they experienced as students at an underresourced urban school.

By combining popular film with canonical texts, the students were able to hone their critical and analytical skills and use them in interpretations. They were also able to understand the connection between literature, popular culture, and their everyday lives. Further, they were able to translate their analyses into quality oral debates and expository pieces. The *A Time to Kill* and *Native Son* unit traditionally concluded with a mock trial, while *The Odyssey* and *The Godfather* unit ended with a formal debate. As with the hip-hop unit, classroom activities laid the groundwork for more traditional academic work while fostering student activism.

Teaching Television and Media

While working with urban youth in Los Angeles, I helped coordinate a series of research seminars that brought high school students to the local university for several weeks during the summer. These teens were apprenticed as critical researchers to study the access urban youth had to public spaces and social institutions. During one such seminar, we found ourselves studying these issues while the Democratic National Convention was taking place in the city. One student research team decided to study access to corporate media and the corporate media's portrayal of urban youth. The students read literature relating to critical media literacy and the sociology of education, designed a study, conducted interviews, analyzed countless hours of news coverage, and performed a content analysis of major U.S. daily newspapers.

As I followed these teens through their research process, I noticed that they were able to meaningfully draw upon personal experiences during the reading of texts concerning critical media literacy or during interviews they conducted with members of the mainstream media (Kellner, 1995). Motivated and empowered by the prospect of addressing a real problem in their community, the students learned the tools of research, read difficult texts, and produced their own text of high academic merit.

The Politics and Possibilities

Much of the excitement about popular culture in the United States is tempered by the recent focus, at the state and national levels, on standardized tests as the sole evaluators of academic merit and skill. I believe that critical-literacy educators should envision teaching popular culture as compatible with the current educational climate and, at the same time, as culturally and socially relevant (Ladson-Billings, 1994). Critical-literacy educators in urban schools should not avoid standards debates or apologize to colleagues and parents about innovative curricula and pedagogies that can teach the skills students need to be successful in school. Educators need to conduct classroom-based research on innovative practices and participate in policy debates at every level of schooling. They also need to participate in conversations about alternative forms of assessment that are more compatible with recent developments in literacy studies and inclusive of students' nonschool literacy practices—such as those associated with participation in popular culture. Critical teachers and teacher educators can use classroom-based research to prove that there are ways to meet the challenges the new century offers and turn them into opportunities to connect to the worlds of students, to promote academic achievement, and to prepare students for critical citizenship in a multicultural democracy.

References

Adorno, T., & Horkheimer, M. (1999). The culture industry: Enlightenment as mass deception. In S. During (Ed.), *The cultural studies reader* (pp. 31–41). New York: Routledge.

Barton, D., & Hamilton, M. (1998). *Local literacies: Reading and writing in one community.* New York: Routledge.

Coppola, F.F. (Director). (1972, 1974, 1993). *The Godfather I, II,* and *III* [Motion pictures]. United States: Paramount Pictures.

Delpit, L. (1988). The silenced dialogue: Power and pedagogy in educating other people's children. *Harvard Educational Review, 58,* 280–298.

Docker, J. (1994). *Postmodernism and popular culture: A cultural history.* New York: Cambridge University Press.

Freire, P. (1970). *Pedagogy of the oppressed.* New York: Continuum.

Freire, P., & Macedo, D. (1987). *Reading the word and the world.* Westport, CT: Bergin & Garvey.

George, N. (1998). *Hiphopamerica.* New York: Penguin.

Giroux, H.A. (1997). *Pedagogy and the politics of hope.* Boulder, CO: Westview.

Gramsci, A. (1971). *Selections from prison notebooks.* London: New Left Books.

Hall, S. (1998). Notes on deconstructing the popular. In J. Storey (Ed.), *Cultural theory and popular culture: A reader* (pp. 442–453). Athens, GA: University of Georgia Press.

Harris, T.L., & Hodges, R.E. (Eds.). (1995). *The literacy dictionary: The vocabulary of reading and writing.* Newark, DE: International Reading Association.

Homer. (1998). *The Odyssey.* New York: Noonday Press.

hooks, b. (1994). *Teaching to transgress: Education as the practice of freedom.* New York: Routledge.

Hull, G. (1993). Critical literacy and beyond: Lessons learned from students and workers in a vocational program and on the job. *Anthropology and Education Quarterly, 24,* 308–317.

Kellner, D. (1995). *Media culture: Cultural studies, identity and politics between the modern and postmodern.* New York: Routledge.

Ladson-Billings, G. (1994). *The dreamkeepers: Successful teachers of African American children.* San Francisco: Jossey-Bass.

Mahiri, J. (1998). *Shooting for excellence: African American and youth culture in new century schools.* New York: Teachers College Press.

McCarthy, C. (1998). *The uses of culture: Education and the limits of ethnic affiliation.* New York: Routledge.

McLaren, P. (1989). *Life in schools: An introduction to critical pedagogy in the foundations of education.* New York: Longman.

National Council of Teachers of English and International Reading Association. (1996). *Standards for the English language arts.* Urbana, IL, & Newark, DE: Authors.

New London Group. (1996). A pedagogy of multiliteracies: Designing social futures. *Harvard Educational Review, 66,* 60–92.

Rose, T. (1994). *Black noise: Rap music and black culture in contemporary America.* Middletown, CT: Wesleyan University Press.

Schumaker, J. (Director). (1996). *A time to kill* [Motion picture]. United States: Warner Brothers.

Storey, J. (1998). *An introduction to cultural theory and popular culture.* Athens, GA: University of Georgia Press.

Street, B.V. (1995). *Literacy in theory and practice.* Cambridge, England: Cambridge University Press.

UNESCO. (1975). *Final report for international symposium for literacy.* Persepolis, Iran: Author.

Venezky, R.L., Wagner, D.A., & Ciliberti, B.S. (Eds.). (1990). *Toward defining literacy.* Newark, DE: International Reading Association.

Williams, R. (1995). *The sociology of culture.* Chicago: University of Chicago Press.

Williams, R. (1998). The analysis of culture. In J. Storey (Ed.), *Cultural theory and popular culture: A reader* (pp. 48–56). Athens, GA: University of Georgia Press.

Wright, R. (1989). *Native son.* New York: HarperPerennial.

21

Reconstructing Technoliteracy: A Multiple Literacies Approach

Richard Kahn and Douglas Kellner

> The great advance of electrical science in the last generation was closely associated, as effect and as cause, with the application of electric agencies to means of communication, transportation, lighting of cities and houses, and more economical production of goods. These are social ends, moreover, and if they are too closely associated with notions of private profit, it is not because of anything in them, but because they have been deflected to private uses: a fact which puts upon the school the responsibility of restoring their connection in the mind of the coming generation, with public scientific and social interests.
>
> — John Dewey (1916)

The ongoing debate about the nature and benefits of technoliteracy is without a doubt one of the most hotly contested topics in education today. Alongside their related analyses and recommendations, the last two decades have seen a variety of state and corporate stake holders, academic disciplinary factions, cultural interests, and social organizations ranging from the local to the global weigh in with competing definitions of "technological literacy." Whereas utopian notions such as Marshall McLuhan's "global village" (1964) and H.G. Wells's "world brain" (1938) imagined a technological world of growing unity in diversity, ours is perhaps better characterized as the highly complex and socio-politically stratified global culture of media spectacle[1] and the ever-developing mega-technics of a worldwide information (Castells 1996), cum technocapitalist infotainment society (Kellner 2003a: 11–15). As such, there is presently little reason to expect general agreement as regards what types of knowledge are entailed by technoliteracy, what sorts of practices might most greatly inform it, or even as to what institutional formations technoliteracy can best serve and be served by in kind. Further, despite the many divergent and conflicting views about techno-literacy that presently exist, it is only relatively recently that existing debates have begun to be challenged and informed by oppositional movements based on race, class, gender, anti-imperialism, and the ecological well-being of all. As these varying movements begin to ask their own questions about the ever-dovetailing realms of technology and the construction of a globalized culture, political realm, and economy, we may well yet see technoliteracy at once become more multiple in one sense, even as it becomes more and more singularly important for all in another.[2]

Much has been written that describes the history of the concept of "technological literacy" (Petrina 2000; Selfe 2000; Jenkins 1997; Waetjen 1993; Lewis and Gagel 1992; Dyrenfurth 1991; Todd 1991; Hayden 1989) and, as noted, a literature attempting to chart emancipatory technoliteracies has begun to emerge over the last decade (Kellner 2004, 2003c, 1998;

Lankshear & Snyder 2000; Petrina 2000; Luke 1997; Bromley & Apple, 1998; Ó Tuathail & McCormack 1998; Burbules & Callister 1996; McLaren, Hammer, Sholle & Reilly, 1995). We do not seek to reinvent the wheel here or reproduce yet another account of the same. Yet, considering that tremendous variance exists in the published definitions of technoliteracy, it will prove fruitful to begin with a brief examination of the meanings that "technology" and "literacy" have received towards achieving with more precision exactly what sort of knowledge and skills "technoliteracy" hails.

From this, we will seek to summarize the broad trajectories of development in hegemonic programs of contemporary technoliteracy from their arguable origins as "computer literacy" in the United States' *A Nation at Risk* report of 1983, through the Clinton years and the economic boom of information-communication technologies (ICTs) in the 1990s, up to the present call for integration of technology across the curriculum and the standards-based approach of the *No Child Left Behind Act of 2001* and 2004's U.S. *National Educational Technology Plan.* Agreeing with Petrina (2000), that such development is largely the construction of a neutralized version of technoliteracy which bolsters a conservative politics of ideological "competitive supremacy," we will show how this has been tacitly challenged at the global institutional level through the United Nations' Project 2000+.

In following, we analyze how these contestations link up with the oppositional democratic project for the re-visioning of education through multiple literacies. Finally, in closing, we think about what it will mean to reconstruct "technoliteracies" in light of our discussion, as we propose that a major goal will be to involve people in the large-scale movements to actively transform mainstream understandings, policies, and practices of technoliteracy through the politicization of the hegemonic norms that currently pervade social terrains.

Technology, Literacy, Technoliteracy: Definitions

> "Technological literacy is a term of little meaning and many meanings."
>
> — R.D. Todd (1991)

Upon first consideration, seeking a suitable definition of "technology" itself appears to be overly technical. Surely, in discussions concerning technology, it is rare indeed that people need to pause so as to ask for a clarification of the term. In a given context, if it is suggested that technology is either causing problems or alleviating them, people generally know what sort of thing is due for blame or praise.

Yet, the popular meaning of "technology" is problematically insufficient in at least two ways. First, it narrowly equivocates technological artifacts with "high-tech," such as those scientific machines used in medical and biotechnology, modern industrial apparatuses, and digital components like computers, ICTs, and other electronic media. This reductive view fails to recognize, for instance, that indigenous artifacts are themselves technologies in their own right, as well as other cultural objects that may once have represented the leading-edge of technological inventiveness during previous historical eras, such as books, hand tools, or even clothing. Secondly, popular conceptions of technology today make the additional error of construing technology as being merely object-oriented, identifying it as only the sort of machined products that arise through industry. In fact, from the first, technology has always meant far more; and this is reflected in recent definitions of technology as "a seamless web or network combining artifacts, people, organizations, cultural meanings and knowledge" (Wajcman 2004: 106) or that which "comprises the entire system of people and organizations, knowledge, processes, and devices that go into creating and operating technological artifacts, as well as the artifacts themselves" (Pearson & Young 2002).

These broader definitions of technology are supported by the important insights of John Dewey. For Dewey, technology is central to humanity and girds human inquiry in its totality (Hickman 2001). In his view, technology is evidenced in all manner of creative experience and problem-solving. It should extend beyond the sciences proper, as it encompasses not only the arts and humanities, but the professions, and the practices of our everyday lives. In this account, technology is inherently political and historical and in Dewey's philosophy it is strongly tethered to notions of democracy and education, which are considered technologies that intend social progress and greater freedom for the future.

Dewey's view is hardly naïve, but it is unabashedly optimistic and hopeful that it is within the nature of humanity that people may be sufficiently educated so as to be able to understand the problems which they face and, thusly, that people can experimentally produce and deploy a wide range of technologies so as to solve those problems accordingly. While we agree strongly with the spirit of Dewey, we also recognize that the present age is potentially beset by the unprecedented problem of globalized technological oppressions in many forms.

To this end, we additionally seek to highlight the insights of radical social critic and technology theorist Ivan Illich (Kahn & Kellner *forthcoming*). Specifically, Illich's notion of "tools" mirrors the broad humanistic understanding of technology outlined so far, while it additionally distinguishes "rationally designed devices, be they artifacts or rules, codes or operators ... from other things such as food or implements, which in a given culture are not deemed to be subject to rationalization" (Illich 1973: 22). Consequently, Illich polemicizes for "tools for conviviality," which are technologies mindfully rationed to work within the balances of both cultural and natural limits. In our view, technology so defined will prove useful for a 21st century technoliteracy challenged to meet the demands of a sustainable and ecumenical world.

"Literacy" is another concept, often used by educators and policy makers, but in a variety of ways and for a broad array of purposes. In its initial form, basic literacy equated to vocational proficiency with language and numbers such that individuals could function at work and in society. Thus, even at the start of the 20th century, literacy largely meant the ability to write one's name and decode popular print-based texts, with the additional goal of written self-expression only emerging over the following decades. Street (1984) identifies these attributes as typical of an autonomous model of literacy that is politically conservative in that it is primarily economistic, individualistic, and is driven by a deficit theory of learning. On the other hand, Street characterizes ideological models of literacy as prefiguring positive notions of collective empowerment, social context, the encoding and decoding of non-print-based and print-based texts, as well as a progressive commitment to critical thinking-oriented skills.

In our conception, "literacy" is not a singular set of abilities but is multiple and comprises gaining competencies involved in effectively using socially constructed forms of communication and representation. Learning literacies requires attaining competencies in practices and in contexts that are governed by rules and conventions and we see literacies as being necessarily socially constructed in educational and cultural practices involving various institutional discourses and pedagogies. Against the autonomous view that posits literacy as static, we see literacies as continuously evolving and shifting in response to social and cultural changes, as well as the interests of the elites who control hegemonic institutions. Further, it is a crucial part of the literacy process that people come to understand hegemonic codes as "hegemonic." Thus, our conception of literacy follows Freire and Macedo (1987) in conceiving literacy as tethered to issues of power. As they note, literacy is a cultural politics that "promotes democratic and emancipatory change" (viii) and it should be interpreted widely as the ability to engage in a variety of forms of problem-posing and dialectical analyses of self and society.

Based on our definitions of "technology" and "literacy" it should be obvious that, holistically conceived, literacies are themselves technologies of a sort—meta-inquiry processes that serve to facilitate and regulate technological systems. In this respect, to speak of "technoliteracies" may seem inherently tautological. On the other hand, however, it also helps to highlight the constructed and potentially reconstructive nature of literacies, as well as the educative, social, and political nature of technologies. Further, more than ever, we need philosophical reflection on the ends and purposes of education and on what we are doing and trying to achieve in our educational practices and institutions. Such would be a technoliteracy in its deepest sense.

Less philosophically, we see contemporary technoliteracies as involved with the need to comprehend and make use of proliferating high-technologies, and the political economy that drives them, towards furthering radical democratic understandings and transformations of our worlds. In a world inexorably undergoing processes of globalization and technological transformation, we cannot advocate a policy of clean hands and purity, in which people shield themselves from new technologies and their transnational proliferation.[3] Instead, technoliteracies must be deployed and promoted that allow for popular interventions into the ongoing (often anti-democratic) economic and technological revolutions taking place, thereby potentially deflecting these forces for progressive ends like social justice and ecological well-being.

In this, technoliteracies encompass the computer, information, critical media, and multimedia literacies presently theorized under the concept "multiliteracies" (Cope & Kalantzis 2000; Luke 2000, 1997; Rassool 1999; New London Group 1996). But whereas multiliteracies theory often remains focused upon digital technologies, with an implicit thrust towards providing new media job skills for the Internet age, we seek to explicitly highlight the social and cultural appropriateness of technologies and provide a critique of the new media economy as technocapitalist (Best & Kellner 2001; Kellner 1989), while acknowledging its progressive potentials. Thus, we draw upon the language of "multiple literacies" (Lonsdale & McCurry 2004; Kellner 2000) to augment a critical theory of technoliteracies as will be expounded upon later.

Functional and Market-based Technoliteracy: United States

> From being a Nation at Risk we might now be more accurately described as a Nation on the Move. As these encouraging trends develop and expand over the next decade, facilitated and supported by our ongoing investment in educational technology . . . we may be well on our way to a new golden age in American education.
>
> — U.S. Department of Education (2004)

The very fledging Internet, then known as the ARPANET due to its development as a research project of U.S. Defense Advanced Research Projects Agency (DARPA), was still a year away when the *Phi Delta Kappan* published the following utopian call for a computer-centric technoliteracy:

> Just as books freed serious students from the tyranny of overly simple methods of oral recitation, so computers can free students from the drudgery of doing exactly similar tasks unadjusted and

> untailored to their individual needs. As in the case of other parts of our society, our new and wondrous technology is there for beneficial use. It is our problem to learn how to use it well.
>
> (Suppes: 423)

However, it was mainly not until *A Nation at Risk* (1983) that literacy in computers was popularly cited as particularly crucial for education.

The report resurrected a critique of American schools made during the Cold War era that sufficient emphases (specifically in science and technology) were lacking in curriculum for U.S. students to compete in the global marketplace of the future, as it prognosticated the coming of a high-tech "information age." Occurring in the midst of the first great boom of personal computers (PCs), *A Nation at Risk* recommended primarily for the creation of a half-year class in computer science that would:

> equip graduates to: (a) understand the computer as an information, computation, and communication device; (b) use the computer in the study of the other Basics and for personal and work-related purposes; and (c) understand the world of computers, electronics, and related technologies.
>
> (National Commission on Excellence in Education 1983)

While *A Nation at Risk* declared that experts were then unable to classify "technological literacy" in unambiguous terms, the document clearly argues for such literacy to be understood in more functional understandings of computer (Aronowitz 1985; Apple 1992) and information (Plotnick 1999) literacy. Technology, such as the computer, was to be seen for the novel skill sets it afforded and professional discourse began to hype the "new vocationalism" in which the needs of industry were identified as educational priorities (Grubb 1996). Surveying this development, Stephen Petrina (2000) concludes, "By the mid-1980s in the US, technology education and technological literacy had been defined through the capitalist interests of private corporations and the state" (183) and Besser (1983) underscores the degree to which this period was foundational in constructing education as a marketplace.

The 1990's saw the salience and, to some degree, the consequences of such reasoning as the World Wide Web came into being and the burgeoning Internet created an electronic frontier "Dot-Com" economic boom via its commercialization in a range of personal computing hardware and software. In the age of Microsoft and America Online, computer and information skills were indeed increasingly highly necessary. Al Gore's "data highway" of the 1970s had grown an order of magnitude to become the "information superhighway" of the Clinton presidency and the plan for a "Global Information Infrastructure" was being promoted as "a metaphor for democracy itself" (Gore 1994) as social and technological transformation ignited globally under the pressures of the "new economy" (Kelly 1998).

By the decade's end, technological literacy was clearly a challenge that could be ignored only at one's peril. Yet, in keeping with the logic of the 1980's, such literacy was again narrowly conceived in largely functional terms as "meaning computer skills and the ability to use computers and other technology to improve learning, productivity, and performance" (U.S. Department of Education 1996). Specifically, the Department located the challenge as training for the future which should take place in schools, thereby taking the host of issues raised by the information revolution out of the public sphere proper and reducing them to standardized technical and vocational competencies for which children and youth should be trained. Further, technological literacy, conceived as "the new basic" (U.S. Department of Education 1996) skill, became the buzz word that signified a policy program for saturating schools with computer technology as well as training for teachers and students both.

Thereby, it not only guaranteed a marketplace for American ICT companies to sell their technology, but it created entirely new spheres for the extension of professional development, as teachers and administrators began to be held accountable for properly infusing computer technology into curricula.

Come the time of the Bush administration's second term, the U.S. National Education Technology Plan quoted approvingly from a high schooler who remarked, "we have technology in our blood" (U.S. Department of Education 2004: 4), and the effects of two decades worth of debate and policy on technoliteracy was thus hailed as both a resounding technocratic success and a continuing pressure upon educational institutions to innovate up to the standards of the times.[4] Interestingly, however, the Plan itself moved away from the language of technological literacy and returned to the more specific term "computer literacy" (13). Still, in its overarching gesture to the *No Child Left Behind Act of 2001*, which had called for technology to be infused across the curriculum—meaning the use of multimedia computers and the Internet across the arts and sciences—and for every student to be "technologically literate by the time the student finishes the eighth grade, regardless of the student's race, ethnicity, gender, family income, geographic location, or disability" (U.S. Congress 2001), the United States demonstrated its ongoing commitment to delimit "technological literacy" in the functional and economistic terms of computer-based competencies.[5]

Technoliteracy for Sustainable Development: United Nations

> Who benefits, who loses? Who pays? What are the social, environmental, personal, or other consequences of following, or not following, a particular course of action? What alternative courses of action are available? These questions are not always, and perhaps only rarely, going to yield agreed answers, but addressing them is arguably fundamental to any educational program that claims to advance technological literacy for all.
>
> — Edgar W. Jenkins (1997)

In order to chart trajectories in technoliteracy at the international level, we now turn to a brief examination of the United Nations' Project 2000+: Scientific and Technological Literacy for All. In 1993, UNESCO and eleven major international agencies launched Project 2000+ in order to prepare citizens worldwide to understand, deliberate on, and implement strategies in their everyday lives concerning "a variety of societal problems that deal with issues such as population, health, nutrition and environment, as well as sustainable development at local, national, and international levels" (Holbrook, et al. 2000: 1). The project's mission underscores the degree to which the United Nations conceives of technological literacy as a social and community-building practice, as opposed to an individual economic aptitude. Further, in contradistinction to the functional computer literacy movements found in the United States context, the U.N.'s goal of "scientific and technological literacy" (STL) for all should be seen as connected to affective-order precedents such as the "public understanding of science" (Royal Society 1985) and "science-technology-society" (Power 1987) movements.

Though directly inspired by the social development focus of 1990's World Declaration on Education, Project 2000+ also draws in large part from the Rio Declaration on Environment and Development agreed upon at the 1992 Earth Summit (UNESCO 1999). While the Rio Declaration itself contains ample language focused upon the economic and other developmental rights enjoyed by states, such notions of development were articulated as inseparable from the equally important goals of "environmental protection" and the conservation, protection, and restoration of "the health and integrity of the Earth's ecosystem" (United Nations 1992). "Sustainable development," defined as "development that meets the needs of the present without compromising the ability of future generations to meet their own needs" (Brundtland 1987), cannot be properly separated from radical critiques of ecologically damaging political economy and other social behavior. Yet, neither can it be separated from the ability of people everywhere to gain access and understanding of the information that can help to promote sustainability.

UNESCO does not make ICTs a centerpiece of STL projects, however. Of course, a major reason that UNESCO downplays an emphasis upon computer-related technology in its approach to technoliteracy is because the great majority of the illiterate populations it seeks to serve are to be found in the relatively poor and un-modernized regions of Latin America, Africa, and Asia, where an ICT focus would have less relevance at present. A more comprehensive reason, however, is that the United Nations has specifically adopted a non-functional commitment to literacy, conceiving of it as multiple literacies "which are diverse, have many dimensions, and are learned in different ways" (Lonsdale and McCurry 2004: 5). STL, then, calls for understandings and deployments of appropriate technology—the simplest and most sustainable technological means which can meet a given end—as part of a commitment to literacy for social justice and human dignity. This is far different than in the United States, where technoliteracy has generally been reduced to a program of skills and fluency in ICTs.

Still, it would be incorrect to conclude that the United Nations is anti-computer. In fact, the institution is strongly committed to utilizing ICTs as part of its literacy and development campaigns worldwide (Wagner and Kozma 2003; Jegede 2002) whenever appropriate. But as it is also conscious of the ability of new technologies to exacerbate divides between rich and poor, male and female, and North and South, the United Nations promotes "understanding of the nature of, and need for, scientific and technological literacy in relation to local culture and values" (UNESCO 1999) and believes that Scientific and Technological Literacy is best exhibited when it is embedded in prevailing traditions and cultures and meets people's real needs (Rassool 1999). Consequently, while the United Nations finds that technoliteracy is a universal goal of mounting importance due to global technological transformation, STL programs require that various individuals, cultural groups, and states will formulate the questions through which they gain literacy differently and for diverse reasons (Holbrook 2000).

Oppositional Technoliteracy: Towards Critical Multiple Literacies

> Technical and scientific training need not be inimical to humanistic education as long as science and technology in the revolutionary society are at the service of permanent liberation, of humanization.
>
> — Paulo Freire (1972)

As we have seen, technoliteracy should be seen as a site of struggle, as a contested terrain used by the Left, Right, and Center of different nations to promote their own interests, and so those interested in social and ecological justice should look to define and institute their own oppositional forms. Dominant corporate and state powers, as well as conservative and rightist groups, have been making serious use of high-technologies and education to advance their agendas. In the political battles of the future, then, educators (along with citizens everywhere) will need to devise ways to produce and use these technologies to advance a critical oppositional pedagogy that serves the interests of the oppressed. Therefore, in addition to more traditional literacies such as the print literacies of reading and writing[6], as well as other non-digital new literacies (Lankshear and Knobel 2000), we argue that robustly critical forms of media, computer, and multimedia literacies need to be developed as subsets of a larger project of multiple technoliteracies that furthers the ethical reconstruction of technology, literacy, and society in an era of technological revolution.

Critical Media Literacies

With the emergence of a global media culture, technoliteracy is arguably more important than ever, as media essentially are technologies. Recently cultural studies and critical pedagogy have begun to teach us to recognize the ubiquity of media culture in contemporary society, the growing trends toward multicultural education, and the need for a media literacy that addresses the issue of multicultural and social difference (Kellner 1998). Additionally, there is an expanding recognition that media representations help construct our images and understanding of the world and that education must meet the dual challenges of teaching media literacy in a multicultural society and of sensitizing students and publics to the inequities and injustices of a society based on gender, race, and class inequalities and discrimination. Also, critical studies have pointed out the role of mainstream media in exacerbating or diminishing these inequalities, as well as the ways that media education and the production of alternative media can help create a healthy multiculturalism of diversity and strengthened democracy. While significant gains have been made, continual technological change means that those involved in theorizing and practicing media literacy confront some of the most serious difficulties and problems that face us as educators and citizens today.

It should be noted that media culture is itself a form of pedagogy that teaches proper and improper behavior, gender roles, values, and knowledge of the world (Kellner 1995a; b). Yet, people are often not aware that they are being educated and constructed by media culture, as its pedagogy is frequently invisible and subliminal. This situation calls for critical approaches that make us aware of how media construct meanings, influence and educate audiences, and impose their messages and values. A media-literate person, then, is skillful in analyzing media codes and conventions, able to criticize stereotypes, values, and ideologies, and competent to interpret the multiple meanings and messages generated by media texts. Thus, media literacy helps people to use media intelligently, to discriminate and evaluate media content, to critically dissect media forms, and to investigate media effects and uses (see Kellner, 1995a; b).

Traditional literacy approaches attempted to "inoculate" people against the effects of media addiction and manipulation by cultivating high cultured book literacy and by denigrating dominant forms of media and computer culture (see Postman 1985; 1992). In contrast, the media literacy movement attempts to teach students to read, analyze, and decode media texts, in a fashion parallel to the advancement of print literacy. Critical media literacy, as outlined here, goes further still in its call for the analysis of media culture as technologies of social production and struggle, thereby teaching students to be critical of media representations and discourses, as it stresses the importance of learning to use media technologies as modes of self-expression and social activism wherever appropriate (Kellner 1995a).

Developing critical media literacy and pedagogy also involves perceiving how media like film or video can also be used positively to teach a wide range of topics, like multicultural understanding and education. If, for example, multicultural education is to champion genuine diversity and expand the curriculum, it is important both for groups excluded from mainstream education to learn about their own heritage and for dominant groups to explore the experiences and voices of minority and excluded groups. Thus, media literacy can promote a more multicultural technoliteracy, conceived as understanding and engaging the heterogeneity of cultures and subcultures that constitute an increasingly global and multicultural world (Courts 1998; Weil 1998).

Critical media literacy not only teaches students to learn from media, to resist media manipulation, and to use media materials in constructive ways, but it is also concerned with developing skills that will help create good citizens and make them more motivated and competent participants in social life. Critical media literacy can be connected with the project of radical democracy as it is concerned to develop technologies that will enhance democratization and participation. In this respect, critical media literacy takes a comprehensive approach that teaches critical attitudes and provides experimental use of media as technologies of social communication and change (Hammer 1995). The technologies of communication are becoming more and more accessible to young people and ordinary citizens, and can be used to promote education, democratic self-expression, and social progress. Technologies that could help produce the end of participatory democracy, by transforming politics into media spectacles and the battle of images, and by turning spectators into cultural zombies, could also be used to help invigorate democratic debate and participation (Kellner 1990; 2003b).

Critical Computer Literacies

To fully participate in a high-tech and global society, people should cultivate new forms of computer literacy in ways that go beyond standard technical notions. Critical computer literacy involves learning how to use computer technologies to do research and gather information, to perceive computer culture as a contested terrain containing texts, spectacles, games, and interactive multimedia, as well as interrogation of the political economy, cultural bias, and environmental effects of computer-related technologies (Park and Pellow 2004; Grossman 2004; Plepys 2002; Heinonen, Jokinen, and Kaivo-oja 2001; Bowers 2000).

The emergent cybercultures can be seen as a discursive and political location in which students, teachers, and citizens can all intervene, engaging in discussion groups and collaborative research projects, creating websites, producing innovative multimedia for cultural dissemination, and cultivating novel modes of social interaction and learning. Computers can thereby enable people to actively participate in the production of culture, ranging from dialogue and debate on public issues to the creation and expression of their own cultural forms. Thus, computers and the Internet can provide opportunities for multiple voices, alternative online communities, and enhanced political activism (Kahn & Kellner 2003). However, to take part in this culture requires multiple forms of technoliteracy.

For not only are accelerated skills of print literacy necessary, which are often restricted to the growing elite of students who are privileged to attend adequate and superior public and private schools, but in fact it demands a critical information literacy as well. Such literacy would require learning how to distinguish between good and bad information, identifying what Burbules & Callister (2000) identify as misinformation, malinformation, messed-up information, and mostly useless information. In this sense, information literacy is closely connected with education itself, with learning where information is found, how to produce knowledge and understanding, and how to critically evaluate and interpret information sources and material. It also raises profound questions of power and knowledge, concerning the definitions of high and low-status knowledge, who gets to produce and valorize various modes of information, whose ideas get circulated and discussed, and whose get marginalized.

Critical Multimedia Literacies

With an ever-developing multimedia cyberculture, beyond popular film and television culture, visual literacy takes on increased importance. On the whole, computer screens are more graphic, multisensory, and interactive than conventional print fields, something that disconcerted many of us when first confronted with the new environments. Icons, windows, mouses, and the various clicking, linking, and interaction involved in computer-mediated hypertext dictate new competencies and a dramatic expansion of literacy within the context of skills.

Visuality is obviously crucial, compelling users to perceptively scrutinize visual fields, perceive and interact with icons and graphics, and use technical devices like a mouse to access the desired material and field. But tactility is also important, as individuals must learn navigational skills of how to proceed from one field and screen to another, how to negotiate hypertexts and links, and how to move from one program to another if one operates, as most now do, in a window-based computer environment. Further, as voice and sound enter multimedia culture, refined hearing also becomes part of the aesthetics and pedagogies of an expanded technoliteracy that should allow for multiple methods of learning (Gardner 1983).

Contemporary multimedia environments necessitate a diversity of types of multisemiotic and multimodal interactions, involving interfacing with word and print material and often images, graphics, as well as audio and video material (Hammer and Kellner 2001). As technological convergence develops apace, individuals will need to combine the skills of critical media literacy with traditional print literacy and new forms of multiple literacies to access, navigate, and participate in multimediated reality. Reading and interpreting print was the appropriate mode of literacy for an age in which the primary source of information was books and tabloids, while critical multimedia literacy entails reading and interpreting a plethora of discourse, images, spectacle, narratives, and the forms and genres of global media culture. Thus, technoliteracy in this conception involves the ability to engage effectively in modes of multimedia communication that include print, speech, visuality, tactility, and sound, within a hybrid field that combines these forms, all of which incorporate skills of interpretation and critique.

Reconstructing Technoliteracy

> We are, indeed, designers of our social futures.
>
> — New London Group (1996)

Adequately meeting the challenge issued by the concept of technoliteracy raises questions about the design and reconstruction of technology itself. As Andrew Feenberg has long argued (1991, 1995, 1999), democratizing technology often requires its reconstruction and re-visioning by individuals. "Hackers" have redesigned technological systems, notably starting the largely anti-capitalist Open Source and Free Software movements, and indeed much of the Internet itself has been the result of individuals contributing collective knowledge and making improvements that aid various educational, political, and cultural projects.

Of course, there are corporate and technical constraints in that dominant programs and machines impose their rules and abilities upon users, but part of re-visioning technoliteracy requires the very perception and transformation of those limits. Technoliteracy must help teach people to become more ethical producers, as well as consumers, and thus it can help to redesign and reconstruct modern technology towards making it more applicable to people's needs and not just their manufactured desires.

Crucially, alternative technoliteracies must become reflective and critical, aware of the educational, social, and political assumptions involved in the restructuring of education, technology, and society currently under way. In response to the excessive hype concerning new technologies and education, it is important to maintain the critical dimension and to reflect upon the nature and effects of emergent technologies and the pedagogies developed as a response to their challenge. Many advocates of new technologies, however, eschew critique for a more purely affirmative agenda.

For instance, after an excellent discussion of new modes of literacy and the need to rethink education, Gunther Kress argues that we must move from critique to design, beyond a negative deconstruction to more positive construction (1997). But rather than following such modern logic of either/or, critical pedagogues should pursue the logic of both/and, perceiving design and critique, deconstruction and reconstruction, as complementary and supplementary rather than as antithetical choices. Certainly, we need to design alternative pedagogies and curricula for the future, as well as developing improved social and cultural relations, but we need also to criticize misuse, inappropriate use, over-inflated claims, and exclusions and oppressions involved in the introduction of ICTs into education. Moreover, the critical dimension is more than ever necessary as we attempt to develop contemporary approaches to technoliteracy, and design more emancipatory and democratizing technologies. In this process, we must be critically vigilant, practicing critique and self-criticism, putting in question our assumptions, discourses, and practices, as we seek to develop technoliteracies and pedagogies of resistance (Kellner 2003a).

In sum, people should be helped to advance the multiple technoliteracies that will allow them to understand, critique, and transform the oppressive social and cultural conditions in which they live, as they become ecologically-informed, ethical, and transformative subjects as opposed to objects of technological domination and manipulation. This requires producing multiple oppositional literacies for critical thinking, reflection, and the capacity to engage in the creation of discourse, cultural artifacts, and political action amidst widespread technological revolution. Further, as active and engaged subjects arise through social interactions with others, a notion of convivial technologies must come to be a part of the kinds of technoliteracy that a radical reconstruction of education now seeks to cultivate.

We cannot stress it enough: the project of reconstructing technoliteracy must take different forms in different contexts. In almost every cultural and social situation, however, a literacy of critique should be enhanced so that citizens can name the technological system, describe and grasp the technological changes occurring as defining features of the new global order, and learn to experimentally engage in critical and oppositional practices in the interests of democratization and progressive transformation. As part of a truly multicultural order, we need to encourage the growth and flourishing of numerous standpoints (Harding 2004) on technoliteracy, looking out for and legitimizing counter-hegemonic needs, values, and understandings. Such would be to propound multiple technoliteracies "from below" as opposed to the largely functional, economistic, and technocratic technoliteracy "from above" that is favored by many industries and states. Thereby, projects for technoliteracies can allow reconstructive opportunities for a better world to be forged out of the present age of unfolding crisis.

Notes

1. On the concept of "media spectacle" see Kellner (2005, 2003a); it builds upon Guy Debord's notion of the "society of the spectacle," which describes a media and consumer society organized around the production and consumption of images, commodities, and staged events and defines those phenomena of media culture that embody contemporary society's basic values, serve to initiate individuals into its way of life, and dramatize its controversies and struggles, as well as its modes of conflict resolution.
2. The idea that different forms of knowledge (e.g.; different types of questions which in turn beget different answers) are produced as an oppressed group begins to achieve a collective identity vis-à-vis the social, cultural, and political issues of the day is a central insight of the critical theory known as feminist standpoint theory (Harding 2004). It can be argued that this idea girds critical theory in general, and a radical formulation can be seen in Marcuse (1965), as well as in the works of Marx and Engels proper as Sandra Harding points out.
3. Though, stressing the social and cultural specificity of technologies, neither are we calling for the universal adoption of high-technologies, nor do we link them essentially to progress as necessary stages of development. On the other hand, we urge caution against technophobic attitudes, as we favor a dialectical view of technology and society.
4. A definition of "technocracy" is offered by Kovel (1983: 9) as being the social order where "the logic of the machine settles into the spirit of the master. There it dresses itself up as 'value-free' technical reasoning."
5. In 2002, the International Technology Education Association issued its *Standards for Technological Literacy: Content for the Study of Technology,* which intends to be definitive for the field. To be fair, at least 8 of its 20 standards evoke the possibility of affective components that move beyond the functional, market-based approaches chronicled here. However, as Petrina (2000: 186) notes, the Director of the Technology for All Americans project involved in creating the standards declared that they were "the vital link to enhance America's global competitiveness in the future" and so their vocational and economic concerns must be considered central.
6. We resist that technoliteracy outmodes print literacy. Indeed, in the emergent information-communication technology environment, traditional print literacy takes on increasing importance in the computer-mediated cyberworld as people need to critically scrutinize tremendous amounts of information, putting increasing emphasis on developing reading and writing abilities. Theories of secondary illiteracy, in which new media modes contribute to the complete or partial loss of existing print literacy skills due to lack of practice, demonstrates that new technologies cannot be counted upon to deliver print literacy of their own accord.

Bibliography

Apple, Michael. (1992). "Is New Technology Part of the Solution or Part of the Problem in Education." John Beynon and Hughie Mackay (eds.), *Technological Literacy and the Curriculum.* London: The Falmer Press, 105–124.

Aronowitz, Stanley. (1985). "Why Should Johnny Read?" *The Village Voice Literary Supplement,* (May).

Besser, Howard. (1993). "Education as Marketplace." In R. Muffoletto and N. Knupfer. *Computers in education: Social, historical, and political perspectives.* New Jersey: Hampton Press.

Best, Steven and D. Kellner. (2001). *The Postmodern Adventure: Science, Technology, and Cultural Studies at the Third Millennium.* New York and London: Guilford Press and Routledge.

Bowers, C. A. (2000). Let Them Eat Data: How Computers Affect Education, Cultural Diversity, and the Prospects of Ecological Sustainability. Athens, GA: University of Georgia Press.

Brundtland, G. H., et al. (1987). Our Common Future: Report of the World Commission on Environment and Development. Oxford: Oxford University Press.

Burbules, N. and Callister, T. (1996). "Knowledge at the crossroads." *Educational Theory.* Vol. 46(1): 23–34.

———. (2000). *Watch IT: the risks and promises of information technology.* Boulder: Westview Press.

Bromley, H. and M. Apple (eds.). (1998). Education/Technology/Power: Educational Computing as Social Practice. Albany, NY: State University of New York Press.

Castells, Manuel. (1996). The Information Age: Economy, Society and Culture Vol.I: The Rise of the Network Society. Cambridge: MA. Blackwell Publishers.

Cope, B., & Kalantzis, M. (eds.). (2000). *Multiliteracies: Literacy learning and the design of social futures.* New York: Routledge.

Coppola, N. W. (1999). "Greening the technological curriculum: A model for environmental literacy." *Journal of Technology Studies.* Vol. 25(2): 39–46.

Courts, Patrick L.(1998). *Multicultural Literacies: dialect, discourses, and diversity.* New York: Peter Lang.

Dewey, John. (1916). *Democracy and education: An introduction to the philosophy of education.* Carbondale and Edwardsville: Southern Illinois University Press.

Dyrenfurth, M. J. (1991). "Technological literacy synthesized." In M. J. Dyrenfurth & M. R. Kozak (eds.), *Technological literacy.* Peoria, IL: Glencoe, McGraw-Hill: 138–186.

Feenberg, Andrew. (1991). *Critical Theory of Technology.* New York: Oxford University Press.
———. (1995). *Alternative Modernity.* Berkeley: University of California Press.
———. (1999). *Questioning Technology.* New York and London: Routledge.
Freire, Paulo. (1972). *Pedagogy of the Oppressed.* New York: Herder & Herder.
Freire, Paulo and D. Macedo. (1987). *Literacy: Reading the Word and the World.* Westport, CT: Bergin & Garvey.
Gardner, Howard. (1983). *Frames of Mind.* New York: Basic Books Inc.
Gore, Albert. (1994). "Remarks Prepared for Delivery." Speech at the International Telecommunications Union (Buenos Aires:). Online at: http://263.aka.org.cn/Magazine/Aka4/gorestalk.html.
Grossman, Elizabeth. (2004). "High-tech Wasteland." *Orion.* July/August. Online at: http://www.oriononline.org/pages/om/04-4om/Grossman.html.
Grubb, W. N. (1996). "The new vocationalism - What it is, what it could be." *Phi Delta Kappan, 77*(8): 535–546.
Hammer, Rhonda. (1995). "Strategies for Media Literacy." In Peter McLaren, R. Hammer, D. Sholle and S. Reilly. *Rethinking Media Literacy: a critical pedagogy of representation.* New York: Peter Lang: 225–235.
Hammer, Rhonda & D. Kellner. (2001). "Multimedia pedagogy and multicultural education for the new millennium." *Current Issues in Education.* Vol. 4(2). Online at: http://cie.ed.asu.edu/volume4/number2/.
Harding, Sandra (ed.). (2004). *The Feminist Standpoint Theory Reader: Intellectual and Political Controversies.* New York and London: Routledge.
Hayden, M. (1989). "What is technological literacy?" *Bulletin of Science, Technology and Society.* Vol. *119*: 220–233, STS Press.
Heinonen, S., Jokinen, P. and Kaivo-oja, J. (2001). "The ecological transparency of the information society." *Futures.* Vol. 33: 319–337.
Hickman, Larry. (2001). *Philosophical Tools for Technological Culture.* Bloomington: Indiana University Press.
Holbrook, Jack, A. Mukherjee and V.S. Varma. (eds.) (2000). *Scientific and Technological Literacy for All.* UNESCO and International Council of Associations for Science Education. Delhi, India: Center for Science Education and Communication.
Illich, Ivan. (1973). *Tools for Conviviality.* New York: Harper and Row.
Jegede, Olugbemiro. (2002). "An Integrated ICT-Support for ODL in Nigeria: The Vision, the Mission and the Journey so Far." Paper prepared for the LEARNTEC-UNESCO 2002 Global Forum on Learning Technology. Karlsruhe, Germany.
Jenkins, Edgar W. (1997). "Technological Literacy: Concepts and Constructs." *Journal of Technology Studies. Vol.* 23(1).
Kahn, Richard and D. Kellner. (2003). "Internet Subcultures and Oppositional Politics." David Muggleton (ed.), *The Post-Subcultures Reader.* London: Berg Publishers.
———. (2005). "Oppositional Politics and the Internet: A Critical/Reconstructive Approach." *Cultural Politics,* Vol. 1, No. 1. Berg Publishers.
———. (*forthcoming*). "Paulo Freire and Ivan Illich: Technology, Politics, and the Reconstruction of Education." C. Torres (ed.) *Paulo Freire and the Possible Dream.* Urbana, IL: University of Illinois Press.
Kelly, K. (1998). *New Rules for the New Economy.* Fourth Estate, London.
Kellner, Douglas. (1989). *Critical Theory, Marxism and Modernity.* Baltimore, MD: Johns Hopkins University Press.
———. (1995). Media Culture: Identity and Politics Between the Modern and the Postmodern. New York, NY: Routledge.
———. (1998). "Multiple Literacies and Critical Pedagogy in a Multicultural Society." *Educational Theory,* 48: 103–122.
———. (2000). "Globalization and New Social Movements: Lessons for Critical Theory and Pedagogy." Nick Burbules and C.A. Torres (eds.), *Globalization and Education: Critical Perspectives.* New York: Routledge.
———. (2002). "Theorizing Globalization." *Sociological Theory* (November), 20:3, 285–305.
———. (2003a). *Media Spectacle.* London and New York: Routledge.
———. (2003b). *From 9/11 to Terror War: The Dangers of the Bush Legacy.* Lanham, MD: Rowman & Littlefield.
———. (2003c). "Toward a Critical Theory of Education." *Democracy & Nature,* vol. 9, no. 1. Taylor and Francis: 51–64.
———. (2004). "Technological Transformation, Multiple Literacies, and the Re-visioning of Education." *E-Learning.* Volume 1, Number 1.
———. (2005). *Media Spectacle And The Crisis Of Democracy: Terrorism, War, And Election Battles.* Boulder, CO: Paradigm Publishers.
Kovel, Joel. (1983). "Theses on Technocracy." *Telos.* No. 54 (Winter).
Kress, Gunther. (1997). "Visual and Verbal Modes of Representation in Electronically Mediated Communication: the potentials of new forms of text." In I. Snyder (Ed.) *Page to Screen: taking literacy into the electronic era.* Sydney, Australia: Allen & Unwin: 53–79.
Lankshear, C. and M. Knobel. (2000). "Mapping postmodern literacies: A preliminary chart." *The Journal of Literacy and Technology.* Vol.1, No.1, Fall. Online at: http://www.literacyandtechnology.org/v1n1/lk.html.
Lankshear, C. and I. Snyder. (2000). *Teachers and Technoliteracy: Managing Literacy, Technology and Learning in Schools.* Sydney, Australia: Allen & Unwin.
Lewis, T. & C. Gagel. (1992). "Technological literacy: A critical analysis." *Journal of Curriculum Studies.* Vol. 24(2).
Lonsdale, Michele and D. McCurry. (2004). *Literacy in the New Millennium.* Adelaide, Australia: NCVER.
Luke, Carmen. (1997). *Technological Literacy.* Melbourne: National Languages & Literacy Institute. Adult Literacy Network.

———. (2000). "Cyber-schooling and Technological Change: Multiliteracies for New Times" in *Multiliteracies: Literacy, Learning, and the Design of Social Futures.* B. Cope and M. Kalantzis (eds.), Australia: Macmillan, 69–105.

Luke, Allan and C. Luke. (2002). "Adolescence Lost/Childhood Regained: On Early Intervention and the Emergence of the Techno-Subject." *Journal of Early Childhood Literacy,* Vol 1 (1): 91–120.

Marcuse, Herbert. (1965). "Repressive Tolerance." in: Robert Paul Wolff, Barrington Moore, jr., and Herbert Marcuse, *A Critique of Pure Tolerance* (Boston: Beacon Press, 1969), pp. 95–137.

McLaren, Peter, R. Hammer, D. Sholle, and S. Reilly. (1995). *Rethinking Media Literacy: a critical pedagogy of representation.* New York: Peter Lang.

McLuhan, Marshall. (1964). *Understanding Media: The Extensions of Man.* New York: Signet Books.

National Commission on Excellence in Education. (1983). *A Nation at Risk: The Imperative for Educational Reform.* Washington, DC.

National Telecommunications & Information Administration. (2002). *A Nation Online: How Americans are Expanding Their Use of the Internet.* Online at: http://www.ntia.doc.gov/ntiahome/dn/nationonline_020502.htm.

New London Group. (1996). "A Pedagogy of Multiliteracies: designing social futures." *Harvard Educational Review.* Vol. 66: 60–92.

Park, Lisa Sun-Hee and David N. Pellow. (2004). "Racial formation, environmental racism, and the emergence of Silicon Valley." *Ethnicities.* Vol. 4(3): 403–424.

Pearson, Greg and A. Thomas Young. (2002). *Technically Speaking: Why All Americans Need to Know More About Technology.* National Academies Press.

Petrina, S. (2000). "The Politics of Technological Literacy." *International Journal of Technology and Design Education* 10, no. 2: 181–206.

Plepys, Andrius. (2002). "The grey side of ICT." *Environmental Impact Assessment Review.* Vol. 22: 509–23.

Plotnick, E. (1999). Information literacy. ERIC Clearinghouse on Information and Technology, Syracuse University. ED-427777.

Postman, Neil. (1985). *Amusing Ourselves to Death.* New York: Viking-Penguin.

———. (1992). Technopolis: the surrender of culture to technology. New York: Random House.

Power, C. (1987). "Science and technology towards informed citizenship." *Castme Journal.* Vol. 7, 3: 5–18.

Rassool, N. (1999). Literacy for sustainable development in the age of information. London, UK: Multilingual Matters Ltd.

Royal Society. (1985). *The public understanding of science.* London: Royal Society.

Selfe, Cynthia L. (1999). *Technology and Literacy in the Twenty-First Century: The Importance of Paying Attention.* Carbondale, IL: Southern Illinois University Press.

Street, Brian. (1984). *Literacy in theory and practice.* Cambridge, UK: Cambridge University Press.

Suppes, Patrick. (1968). "Computer Technology and the Future of Education." *Phi Delta Kappan.* April: 420–23.

Todd, R. D. (1991). "The natures and challenges of technological literacy." In M. J. Dyrenfurth & M. R. Kozak (eds.) *Technological literacy.* Peoria, IL: Glencoe, McGraw-Hill: 10–27.

Trend, David. (2001). *Welcome to Cyberschool: Education at the Crossroads in the Information Age.* Lanham, Md: Rowman & Littlefield.

United Nations. (1992). *Report of the United Nations Conference on Environment and Development.* Rio de Janeiro, Brazil.

UNESCO. (1994). *The Project 2000+ declaration: The way forward.* Paris, France.

———. (1999). *Science and Technology Education: Philosophy of Project 2000+.* The Association for Science Education. Paris, France.

U.S. Congress. (2001). *No Child Left Behind Act of 2001.* Public Law 107–110. Washington, DC.

U.S. Department of Education. (1996). *Getting America's Students Ready for the 21st Century — Meeting the Technology Literacy Challenge, A Report to the Nation on Technology and Education.* National Education Technology Plan. Washington, D.C.

———. (2004). *Toward a New Golden Age in American Education: How the Internet, the Law, and Today's Students are Revolutionizing Expectations.* National Education Technology Plan. Washington, D.C.

Waetjen, W. (1993). "Technological Literacy Reconsidered." *Journal of Technology Education.* Vol. 4, No. 2.

Wagner, Dan and R. Kozma. (2003). "New Technologies for Literacy and Adult Education: A Global Perspective." Paper for NCAL/OECD International Roundtable. Philadelphia, PN. Online at: http://www.literacy.org/ICTconf/PhilaRT_wagner_kozma_final.pdf.

Wajcman, Judy. (2004). *Technofeminism.* Malden, MA: Polity Press.

Weil, Danny K. (1998). *Toward a Critical Multicultural Literacy.* New York: Peter Lang.

Wells, H.G. (1938). *World Brain.* New York, Doubleday.

Suggested Readings for Future Study

Akom, A. A. (2009). "Critical Hip Hop Pedagogy as a Form of Liberatory Praxis." *Equity and Excellence in Education, 42*(1), 52–66.

Alford, J. (2001). "Learning Language and Critical Literacy: Adolescent ESL students." *Journal of Adolescent & Adult Literacy, 45*(3), 238–242.

Ávila, J. and Pandya, J. Z. (2013). *Critical Digital Literacies as Social Praxis: Intersections and Challenges* (vol. 54). New York: Peter Lang Publishing Inc.

Bartolomé, L. (1998). *The Misteaching of Academic Discourses: The Politics of Language in the classroom.* Boulder, CO: Westview.

Biggs-El, C. (2012). "Spreading the Indigenous Gospel of Rap Music and Spoken Word Poetry: Critical Pedagogy in the Public Sphere as a Stratagem of Empowerment and Critique." *Western Journal of Black Studies, 36*(2), 161–168.

Bizell, P. (1992). *Academic Discourse and Critical Consciousness.* Pittsburgh, PN: University of Pittsburgh Press.

Cadiero-Kaplan, K. (2002). "Literacy Ideologies: Critically Engaging the Language Arts Curriculum." *Language Arts Journal, 79*(5), 372–392.

Cameron, D. (1990). *The Feminist Critique of Language: A Reader.* New York: Routledge.

Chomsky, N. (1977). *Language and Responsibility.* New York: Pantheon.

Courts, P. (1991). *Literacy and Empowerment.* Westport, CT: Bergin & Garvey.

Crawford, J. (1992). *Hold Your Tongue: Bilingualism and the Politics of "English only."* New York: Addison-Wesley.

Crawford-Lange, Linda M. (1981). "Redirecting Foreign Language Curricula: Paulo Freire's Contribution." *Foreign Language Annals, 14*, 257–273.

Crookes, Graham. (1993). "Action Research for SL Teachers—Going beyond Teacher Research." *Applied Linguistics 14*(2), 130–144.

Cummins, J. (1996). *Negotiating Identities: Education for Empowerment in a Diverse Society.* Ontario, CA: California Association for Bilingual Educators.

Davis, K. (1995). "Qualitative Theory and Methods in Applied Linguistics Research." *TESOL Quarterly, 29*(3), 427–453.

Delpit, L. (1990). "Language Diversity and Learning." In Hynds, S. and Rubin, D. (eds.), *Perspectives on Talk and Learning* (pp. 247–266). Urbana, IL: National Council of Teachers of English.

Delpit, L. (1995). *Other Peoples' Children: Cultural Conflict in the Classroom.* New York: The New Press.

Diaz-Soto, L. (1997). *Language, Culture and Power.* Albany, NY: SUNY Press.

Duncan-Andrade, J. M. R. (2007). "Urban Youth and the Counter-Narration of Inequality." *Transforming Anthropology, 15*(1), 26–37.

Fairclough, N. (1995). *Critical Discourse Analysis: The Critical Study of Language.* New York: Longman.

Frederickson, J. and Ada, A., eds. (1995). *Reclaiming Our Voices: Bilingual Education, Critical Pedagogy and Praxis.* Ontario: California Association for Bilingual Education.

Freire, P. and Macedo, D. (1987). *Literacy, Reading the Word and the World.* South Hadley, MA: Bergin & Garvey.

Fowler, R., Hodge, B., Kress, G., and Trew, T. (1979). *Language and Control.* Boston: Routledge.

Gallego, M. and Hollingsworth, S., eds. (2000). *What Counts as Literacy: Challenging the School Standard.* New York: Teachers College.

Gee, J. (1992). *The Social Mind: Language, Ideology and Social Practice.* Westport: Bergin & Garvey.

Giroux, H. (2005). "Literacy, Critical Pedagogy and Empowerment." In *Schooling and the Struggle for Public Life: Democracy's Promise and Education's Challenge* (pp. 147–172). Boulder, CO: Paradigm Publishers.

Hill, M. L. (2009). "Wounded Healing: Forming a Storytelling Community in Hip-Hop Lit." *Teachers College Record, 111*(1), 248–293.

Janks, H. (2010). *Literacy and Power.* New York: Routledge.

Johnson, E. and Vasudevan, L. (2012). "Seeing and Hearing Students' Lived and Embodied Critical Literacy Practices." *Theory Into Practice, 51*(1), 34–41.

Kellner, D. and Kim, G. (2009). "YouTube, Critical Pedagogy, and Media Activism: An Articulation." In Hammer, R. and Kellner, D. (eds.), *Media/Cultural Studies: Critical Approaches* (pp. 615–636). New York: Peter Lang.

Larson, K. R. (2014). "Critical Pedagogy(ies) for ELT in Indonesia." *TEFLIN Journal, 25*, 122–138.

Lewison, M., Flint, A. S., and Van Sluys, K. (2002). "Taking on Critical Literacy: The Journey of Newcomers and Novices." *Language Arts, 79*(5), 382–392.

Luke, A. (2014). "Defining Critical Literacy." In Pandya, J. Z. and Ávila, J. (eds.), *Moving Critical Literacies Forward* (pp. 20–32). New York: Routledge.

Luna, C., Botelho, M. J., Fontaine, D., French, K., Iverson, K., and Matos, N. (2004). "Making the Road by Walking and Talking: Critical Literacy and/as Professional Development in a Teacher Inquiry Group." *Teacher Education Quarterly, 31*(1), 67–80.

McCarty, T. L. (2002). *A Place to Be Navajo: Rough Rock and the Struggle for Self Determination in Indigenous Schooling.* Mahwah, NJ: Lawrence Erlbaum.

Macedo, D. (1994). *Literacies of Power.* Boulder, CO: Westview.

Malott, C. (2011). *Critical Pedagogy and Cognition: An Introduction to a Postformal Educational Psychology.* New York: Springer.

Mayo, P. (2004). "Critical Literacy, Praxis and Emancipatory Politics." *In Liberating Praxis: Paulo Freire's Legacy for Radical Education and Politics.* Westport, CT: Praeger Publishers.

Mitchell, C. and Weiler, K. (1991). *Rewriting Literacy.* New York: Bergin & Garvey.

Morrell, E. and Duncan-Andrade, J. M. R. (2002). "Promoting Academic Literacy with Urban Youth through Engaging Hip-Hop Culture." *English Journal, 91*(6), 88.

Nettle, D. and Romaine, S. (2000). *Vanishing Voices: The Extinction of the World's Languages.* New York: Oxford University Press.

Norton, B. and Toohey, K. (2004). *Critical Pedagogies and Language Learning.* New York: Cambridge University Press.

Pirbhai-Illich, F. (2010). "Aboriginal Students Engaging and Struggling with Critical Multiliteracies." *Journal of Adolescent & Adult Literacy, 54*(4), 257–266.

Pruyn, M. (1999). *Discourse Wars in Gotham-West: A Latino Immigrant Urban Tale of Resistance and Agency.* Boulder, CO: Westview.

Riasati, M. J. and Mollaei, F. (2012). "Critical Pedagogy and Language Learning." *International Journal of Humanities and Social Science, 2*(21), 223–229.

Schoorman, D. (2006). "The Politics of 'Literacy' and 'Justice': A Critical Analysis of an Immigrant Teenager's Murder Case and Its Implications for Literacy Educators." *International Journal of Learning, 12*(10), 319–326.

Shannon, P. (1989). *Broken Promises: Reading Instruction in Twentieth-Century America.* South Hadley, MA: Bergin & Garvey.

Shor, I. (1999). "What Is Critical Literacy?" In Shor, I. and Pari, C. (eds.), *Critical Literacy in Action: Writing Words, Changing Worlds* (pp. 1–31). Portsmouth, NH: Heinemann.

Skutnabb-Kangas, T. (2000). *Linguistic Genocide in Education or Worldwide Diversity and Human Rights?* Mahwah, NJ: Lawrence Erlbaum.

Smith, A. and Hull, G. (2013). "Critical Literacies and Social Media: Fostering Ethical Engagement with Global Youth." In Ávila, J. and Pandya, J. Z. (eds.), *Critical Digital Literacies as Social Praxis: Intersections and Challenges* (pp. 63–84). New York: Peter Lang.

Talbot, M. (1998). *Language and Gender: An Introduction.* New York: Polity Press.

Tinson, C. M. and McBride, C. R. E. C. (2013). "Introduction to Special Issue: Hip Hop, Critical Pedagogy, and Radical Education in a Time of Crisis." *Radical Teacher, 97*, 1–9.

Torres, M. N. and Mercado, M. (2006). "The Need for Critical Media Literacy in Teacher Education Core Curriculum." *Educational Studies, 38(3)*, 260–282.

Vasquez, V. M. (2004). *Negotiating Critical Literacies with Young Children.* Mahwah, NJ: Lawrence Erlbaum Associates.

Vasquez, V., Tate, S., and Harste, J. (2013). *Negotiating Critical Literacies with Teachers: Theoretical Foundations and Pedagogical Resources for Pre-Service and In-Service Contexts.* New York: Routledge.

Xu, S. (2007). "Critical Literacy Practices in Teaching and Learning." *New England Reading Association Journal, 43*(2), 12–22.

Part Six

Critical Pedagogy and the Classroom

Introduction to Part Six

The current conservative educational climate in the United States is reflected in the violent imposition of high-stakes testing and test-prep curriculum in schools across the nation. These practices resoundingly echo the "banking" approach to education at the center of Freire's critique of traditional schooling. Accountability measures, standardized curriculum, and instrumentalized teaching approaches have all worked to strip education of its democratic ideals and transformative potential. Neoliberal educational policies have effectively derailed the development of critical abilities among poor and working class students, by aligning the school curriculum with the imperatives of a grossly stratified labor market. Rather than creating educational opportunities, as advocates claim, the conservative privatization agenda imposes teaching regimes that deskill teachers, corrupt classroom practice, and reduce learning to rote memorization—all factors that contribute to poor academic achievement.

The consequence of such neoliberalism is the intensification of a deeply stratified society, where wealthier students are guaranteed opportunities at the top, while the majority of poor and working class students are educated to enter the vast pool of low skilled, poorly paid workers, at the bottom. This phenomenon persists despite neoliberal rhetoric to the contrary, for it fails to address fundamentally the most significant reason why children are left behind—namely, rampant economic inequalities. When the quality of education is reduced to test scores and credentials, emancipatory classroom practices that support the development of voice, participation, and community self-determination easily slip by the wayside. In place of open democratic exchange and pedagogical vitality, teachers face mounds of paperwork, teacher-proof curriculum, low teacher morale, increased surveillance, and the unbridled corporate colonization of every aspect of schooling.

This constitutes the contemporary arena in which educators struggle to keep alive the principles of a critical pedagogical practice. These teachers often seek both a clear understanding of the institutional dynamics at work, as well as classroom strategies to help them enact their commitment to democratic schooling. The articles in the section capture three important facets of classroom life. These include an analysis of the detrimental effect of testing policies on schools, the examination of the silencing of disability in K–16 education, and an effective revisiting of Freire's *Pedagogy of the Oppressed,* to glean strategies for transforming the insidious and alienating conditions at work in schools today.

Summary of Articles

Herbert Kohl, in "I Won't Learn From You! Thoughts on the Role of Assent in Learning," discusses the intellectual and social challenge of not-learning and the dissolution of culture.

A key concept discussed here is the manner in which teachers must learn to distinguish non-learning from failure, respecting the conditions tied to the rejection of schooling among poor and oppressed communities. Using concrete examples of student struggles in the classroom and his own critical responses to their rejection of learning, Kohl weaves a grounded understanding of the manner in which critical dialogue with students can work to create classroom environments where teaching and learning is tied to a communal process of knowledge production that transforms the destructive authoritarian dynamic of a banking pedagogy, so teachers and students learn from one another about racism, class, and other forms of social and material inequality. Kohl insists, however, that in order to do so effectively requires educators concede that for many students not-learning is a sane and direct confrontation with the oppressive conditions of schooling they face daily.

"A Feminist Reframing of Bullying and Harassment: Transforming Schools Through Critical Pedagogy" touches on what has become a frequently discussed pedagogical issue within schools across the country. By applying a critical feminist lens to patterns of verbal and psychological harassment among students, Elizabeth Meyer strives to radically reformulate our existing understanding of bully behavior among high school students. The intent here is to consider ways in which critical educators may better understand the causes of (hetero) sexist, transphobic, and homophobic behaviors. Meyer contends that with a more complex understanding of power relations, teachers, teacher educators, and educational leadership scholars can integrate critical approaches to help them transform the oppressive cultures of schools.

In "Redirecting the Teacher's Gaze: Teacher Education, Youth Surveillance and the School-to-Prison Pipeline," John Raible and Jason Irizarry argue that there is an under-examined relationship between the policing of youth of color in schools and their over-representation in the prison industrial complex. The authors critically examine the role of teacher education in contributing to the criminalization of certain youth in urban communities and the resulting school-to-prison pipeline crisis that leads too many students from the schoolhouse to the jailhouse. They note that teacher preparation programs overemphasize surveillance practices in their interactions with youth of color. They assert that it is this disciplinary gaze of schooling that has led to an increase in police and metal detectors, the incarceration of 2.1 million persons in the United States, and the extreme over representation of minority groups in the penal system. Raible and Irizarry link this debilitating phenomenon to several conditions, including a still overwhelmingly heterogeneous teaching force, with 85 percent of teachers in the U.S. being white females; the lack of teacher ability to connect with or understand the diverse student body; high attrition rates of teachers in urban centers; and the inability of the teaching force to understand and question educational policies that negatively impact students.

In Robert Anderson's "Teaching (with) Disability: Pedagogies of Lived Experience," he calls into question the lack of examination of "disability" as an identity in critical disciplines such as gender studies and race studies. Disabilities, without the current social construction, are impairments that change the relationship between the human body and the physical world. Anderson further argues for the need to include the body politics and lived experiences of disabled teachers in the learning experience, due to nearly one in five of individuals in the United States having a disability. Reframing the knowledge about individuals living with disabilities in school can contribute to the appreciation of differences as well as a more understanding world for those living with disabilities. Anderson adopts Bhabha's (1988) concept of the *Third Space,* which transforms the classroom into a Freirean centered educational site, questioning commonsensical knowledge, and engaging students in the process of creating knowledge. This vision of disability studies is crucial to critical pedagogies in that it centers the experiences of students with disabilities.

Questions for Reflection and Dialogue

1. How does Herbert Kohl define the notion of not-learning? What are the reasons he attributes to this response from students?
2. What do teachers need to understand when students refuse to learn? What are some effective interactions that can serve to support the assent of learning in the lives of students from poor and oppressed communities?
3. What are the long-term effects of gendered harassment on students' lives?
4. How does the over surveillance of youth of color impact their self-image and relationship to both their education and experiences with law enforcement?
5. More specifically, how can alternative disciplinary policies possibly impact the prison industrial complex? What might these alternatives look like within schools?
6. What are ways in which critical pedagogical approaches in the classroom can deter the current phenomenon of the school-to-prison pipeline?
7. How might teachers apply Anderson's vision of body politics and the lived experiences of disabled students in their classroom practices? How might you integrate this view in your personal life?
8. What kinds of changes would have to be made in public schools in order to implement an emancipatory vision of disability?

22

I Won't Learn From You! Thoughts on the Role of Assent in Learning

Herbert Kohl

Years ago, one of my fifth-grade students told me that his grandfather Wilfredo wouldn't learn to speak English. He said that no matter how hard you tried to teach him, he ignored whatever words you tried to teach and forced you to speak to him in Spanish. When I got to know his grandfather I asked, in Spanish, whether I could teach him English and he told me unambiguously that he did not want to learn. He was frightened, he said, that his grandchildren would never learn Spanish if he gave in like the rest of the adults and spoke English with the children. Then, he said, they would not know who they were. At the end of our conversation he repeated adamantly that nothing could make him learn to speak English, that families and cultures could not survive if the children lost their parents' language, and, finally, that learning what others wanted you to learn can sometimes destroy you.

I discussed Wilfredo's reflections with several friends, and they interpreted his remarks as a cover-up of either his own fear of trying to learn English or his failure to do so. These explanations, however, show a lack of respect for Wilfredo's ability to judge what is appropriate learning for himself and his grandchildren. By attributing failure to Wilfredo and refusing to acknowledge the loss his family would experience through not knowing Spanish, they turned a cultural problem into a personal psychological problem: they turned willed refusal to learn into failure to learn.

I've thought a lot about Wilfredo's conscious refusal to learn English and have great sympathy for his decision. I grew up in a partially bilingual family and in a house shared by my parents, born in New York City, and grandparents, born in the Yiddish-speaking Polish part of the Jewish settlements in East Europe called the Pale, and know what it is like to face the problem of not-learning and the dissolution of culture. In addition I have encountered willed not-learning throughout my 30 years of teaching, and believe that such not-learning is often and disastrously mistaken for failure to learn or the inability to learn.

Learning how to not-learn is an intellectual and social challenge; sometimes you have to work very hard at it. It consists of an active, often ingenious, willful rejection of even the most compassionate and well-designed teaching. It subverts attempts at remediation as much as it rejects learning in the first place. It was through insight into my own not-learning that I began to understand the inner world of students who chose to not-learn what I wanted to teach. Over the years I've come to side with them in their refusal to be molded by a hostile society and have come to look upon not-learning as positive and healthy in many situations.

Not-learning tends to take place when someone has to deal with unavoidable challenges to her or his personal and family loyalties, integrity, and identity. In such situations, there are forced choices and no apparent middle ground. To agree to learn from a stranger who does not respect your integrity causes a major loss of self. The only alternative is to not-learn and reject their world.

In the course of my teaching career, I have seen children choose to not-learn many different skills, ideas, attitudes, opinions, and values. At first I confused not-learning with failing. When I had youngsters in my classes who were substantially "behind" in reading I assumed that they had failed to learn how to read. Therefore I looked for the sources of their failure in the reading programs they were exposed to, in their relationships with teachers and other adults in authority, in the social and economic conditions of their lives. I assumed that something went wrong when they faced a written text: that either they made errors they didn't know how to correct, or were the victims of bad teaching. Other causes of failure I searched for were mismatches between the students' language and the language of the schools, or between the students' experiences and the kind of experience presupposed by their teachers or the reading texts.

In all of these cases I assumed that my students had failed at something they had tried to do. Sometimes I was correct, and then it was easy to figure out a strategy to help them avoid old errors and learn, free of failure. But there were many cases I came upon where obviously intelligent students were beyond success or failure when it came to reading or other school-related learning. They had consciously placed themselves outside the entire system that was trying to coerce or seduce them into learning and spent all of their time and energy in the classroom devising ways of not-learning and short-circuiting the business of learning altogether. They were engaged in a struggle of wills with authority, and what seemed to be at stake for them was nothing less than their pride and integrity. Most of them did not believe they were failures or inferior to students who succeeded on the school's terms, and it was easy to distinguish them from the wounded self-effacing students who wanted to learn and had not been able to do so.

Barry's Not-Learning

I remember one student, Barry, who was in one of my combined kindergarten / first-grade classes in Berkeley in the 1970s. He had been held back in the first grade by his previous teacher for being uncooperative, defiant, and "not ready for the demands of second grade." He was sent to my class because it was multi-age graded, and the principal hoped I could get him to catch up and go on with other students his age by the end of the year. Barry was confident and cocky but not rude. From his comments in class it was clear that he was quite sensitive and intelligent. The other students in the class respected him as the best fighter and athlete in class, and as a skilled and funny story teller.

During the first week of school one of the students mentioned to me that their last year's teacher was afraid of Barry. I've seen a number of cases where white teachers treat very young African American boys as if they were 17, over six feet tall, addicted to drugs, and menacing. Barry was a victim of that manifestation of racism. He evidently was given the run of the school the previous year – was allowed to wander around the halls at will, refuse participation in group activities, and avoid any semblance of academic work. Consequently he fell behind and was not promoted from first to second grade.

The first time I asked Barry to sit down and read with me he threw a temper tantrum and called me all kinds of names. We never got near a book. I had to relate to his behavior, not his reading. There was no way for me to discover the level of his skills or his knowledge of how reading works. I tried to get him to read a few more times and watched his responses to me very carefully. His tantrums were clearly manufactured on the spot. They were a strategy of not-reading. He never got close enough to a book to have failed to learn how to read.

The year before, this response had the effect he wanted. He was let alone and as a bonus gained status in the eyes of the other children as someone teachers feared. Not-reading, as tragic as it might become in his future, was very successful for him as a kindergartner. My job as a teacher was to get him to feel more empowered doing reading than practicing his active not-learning to read.

I developed a strategy of empowerment for Barry and didn't even bother with thinking about remediation. I was convinced he could learn to read perfectly well if he assented to learn how to read. The strategy was simple and involved a calculated risk. I decided to force him to read with me and then make it appear to other members of the class that he read so well that his past resistance was just a game he controlled. The goal was to have him show me up in class, as if his past failure was a joke he was playing on us all, and display to the entire class reading ability he didn't know he had.

I prepared myself for a bit of drama. One Monday afternoon I asked Barry to come read with me. Naturally all of the other students stopped whatever they were doing and waited for the show. They wanted to see if Barry would be able to not-read one more time. He looked at me, then turned around and walked away. I picked up a book and went over to him. Then I gently but firmly sat him down in a chair and sat down myself. Before he could throw the inevitable tantrum I opened the book and said, "Here's the page you have to read, it says, 'This is a bug. This is a jug. This is a bug in the jug.' Now read it to me." He started to squirm and put his hands over his eyes. Only I could see a sly grin forming a he snuck a look at the book. I had given him the answers, told him exactly what he had do to show me and the rest of the class that he knew how to read all along. It was his decision: to go on playing his not-learning game or accept my face-saving gift and open up the possibility of learning to read. I offered him the possibility of entering into a teaching/learning relationship with me without forcing him to give up any of his status and fortunately he accepted the gift. He mumbled "This is a bug, this is a jug. This is a bug in a jug," then tossed the book on the floor, and, turning to one of the other children, said defiantly, "See, I told you I already know how to read."

This ritual battle was repeated all week and into the next, subsiding slowly as he felt that the game was no longer necessary and that he was figuring out the relationship of letter to sounds, words and meaning. After a while reading became just another one of the things that Barry did in class. I never did any remedial teaching or treated him as a failed reader. In fact, I was able to reach him by acknowledging his choice to not-learn and by tricking him out of it. However, if he had refused assent, there is no way I could have forced him to learn to read. That was a very important lesson to me. It helped me understand the essential role will and free choice play in learning and taught me the importance of considering people's stance towards learning in the larger context of the choices they make as they create lives and identities for themselves.

Over the years I've known many youngsters who chose to actively not-learn what school, society, or their families tried to teach them. Not all of them were potential victims of their own choices to not-learn. For some, not-learning was a strategy that made it possible for them to function on the margins of society instead of falling into madness or total despair.

It helped them build a small safe world in which their feelings of being rejected by family and society could be softened. Not-learning played a positive role and enabled them to take control of their lives and get through difficult times.

The Struggles of Akmir

Akmir, a young African American man I had the privilege of knowing for the last three years of his life, was wiser than I was, and struggled to learn and maintain his culture and learn his roots despite a racist school system that he was required to attend. In school he was a passionate not-learner. I remember him telling me of spending a semester in a junior high school social studies class not merely not-learning the subject but actively trying to destroy the teacher's and text book's credibility. Akmir had joined a militant separatist group that was an offshoot of the Nation of Islam. They believed that they were among the 7% of African Americans who understood the truth that the white man was a devil and had to be ruthlessly rooted out and destroyed. One of their goals was purifying Harlem of all whites.

Akmir's experiences with whites did very little to refute the 7%ers' analysis. That opinion accurately applied to one of Akmir's high school history teachers who believed that his students, who were all African American and Puerto Rican, were stupid, lazy, and not capable of understanding complex ideas. He talked to the class in a condescending way, addressing them as "you" as in, "You people don't know how to hold a job," and "You people have never learned to adopt American values and that's why you can't compete in the marketplace."

Most of the students were content to not-learn what he taught by playing dumb. A few actually learned what he taught and believed that they were stupid and incapable of productive lives. Akmir and one friend, Thomas X, were actively defiant. They not only refused to learn what he taught, but tried to take over the class and change the curriculum into an attack on white racism. Whenever he talked about American values, for example, they would point out that slavery was an American value according to the Constitution, and try to demonstrate that racism, not lack of intelligence or ability, was the root of black failure and poverty. The teacher tried to shut them up, referred them to the guidance counselor, sent them to the principal, and, in every way but answering their challenges, tried to silence them. Nothing worked, since Akmir and Thomas X refused to accept the validity of school authority and preached to the principal and the counselors the same line they preached in class. After one semester of bitter struggle within the school, both Akmir and Thomas X were transferred to a special school for students with discipline problems who had no criminal records. These were schools for youngsters who had mastered strategies of not-learning and infuriated school authorities but had done nothing wrong. They were created to segregate teachers who were failing their students from their angry victims, within an already racially segregated system.

I didn't know Akmir until three years after he left high school. He had passed all of his classes, but his diploma had been withheld from him for "citizenship" reasons. The principal and guidance counselor decided that he wasn't a loyal American, since he raised questions which they interpreted as anti-American. They decided that he didn't deserve to graduate because of this attitude and decreed that he had to take and pass a course in citizenship sometime during the two years after his class graduated in order to receive the diploma he had earned by passing all the required courses. They also told him that they would decide what work or school experience could count as a citizenship class sometime in the future.

Akmir told them what he thought of them before leaving the school for what he believed was the last time.

At the time (it was 1965) I was a graduate student at Teachers College, Columbia University, and Betty Rawls, another graduate student, and I were teaching a class in psychology for a group of high-school-aged students who were older brothers and sisters of former students of mine from Harlem. Brenda Jackson, one of the students, brought Akmir to class one day. They were a bit late, and when they arrived the class was discussing whether Freudian ideas applied to teenagers growing up in Harlem. The discussion was quite lively, but when Brenda and Akmir came into the room, everyone fell silent. Brenda sat down, but Akmir remained standing and looked straight at me. I noticed how strong he looked, both physically and mentally.

Since everyone else in the room remained silent, I talked about my understanding of Freud and brought up some questions I had about some main Freudian concepts. After about five minutes Akmir took a few steps towards the front of the room and said, quietly but fiercely, "That's white man's psychology."

I didn't disagree, and suggested he go into his reasons for making that statement. He said there was no point in doing it for a white man, and I told him he was wrong, adding that though Freud was a white man, he also was a bourgeois Viennese Jew who grew up in the late 1800s and it was unclear whether his ideas were adequate to account for the psychology of non-Jews, of working class people, of women, and of young people in the 1960s as well as of blacks.

He pushed aside my comments and began a harangue on racism, injustice, and the Wilderness of North America, which was the way Black Muslims referred to the United States. I got angry and told him that the class was voluntary, that he could leave if he wanted to, but that we were there to learn together, and I wasn't bullshitting about wanting to know his ideas. Any intelligent position could be presented, defended, argued, but learning couldn't take place without respect for everybody's voice.

The students anxiously glanced back and forth from Akmir to me. I rested my case and he smiled and said, "Well, maybe we should start with ego psychology and see what ego means for white people and for black people." I agreed and we entered into that discussion.

After class Akmir came up and introduced himself. I told him that his questions and challenges were just what the class needed and invited him to join us. Betty and I usually assigned material to be read for each class, but most of the students didn't get around to reading it so we began each class summarizing the issues we intended to discuss. Akmir read everything, studied it thoroughly and came to class prepared to argue. He read all of the material aggressively, looking for sentences or phrases that indicated or could be interpreted to imply racism, ranging from uses of the words "black" or "dark" to signify evil to sophisticated arguments that implied the superiority of Western culture. For a few sessions the class was dominated by his questioning our texts. At first I thought it was a game meant to provoke me, but it soon became clear that that was an egotistic response on my part. Akmir was hunting down American English for insinuations of racism and trying to purify the language. He had learned some of these techniques from the Black Muslims and 7%ers who were very skillful in hunting out claims of European pureness and African primitivity, and who understood that when sophisticated Westerners were contrasted with unsophisticated peoples of color, racism was afoot.

I learned from Akmir's analyses how I too fell into sloppy, racist linguistic habits and came to take his criticisms seriously. I tried to read texts from his point of view and pick out the phrases and thoughts that he might find offensive. In some cases it made reading some familiar material very uncomfortable. I had thought of having the class analyze Conrad's *The Heart of Darkness* from a psychoanalytic point of view, but decided to abandon that exercise because, on rereading it with Akmir's sensitivities in mind, the explicit and offensive racism at the heart of the story appalled me. I knew before that the story could be interpreted as racist, but had always felt that that was just a secondary, unfortunate aspect of an extraordinary piece of writing. This time, though the quality of the writing wasn't diminished by my new reading, the story had become repugnant to me. The racism became the primary characteristic of the writing, not a secondary one that could be understood and explained away in light of Conrad's cultural background and historical situation. And I understood that I shouldn't teach *The Heart of Darkness* unless I was to deal explicitly with the text's racism and condemn Conrad.

Last year, more than 20 years after this incident, I read an essay by the Nigerian novelist Chinua Achebe entitled, "An Image of Africa: Racism in Conrad's *Heart of Darkness*" (in *Hopes and Impediments,* Doubleday 1989, pp. 1–20) that confirmed my analysis of the Conrad story. In the essay, Achebe, after making his case against Conrad, states quite unambiguously, "The point of my observations should be quite clear by now, namely that Joseph Conrad was a thoroughgoing racist. That this simple truth is glossed over in criticisms of his work is due to the fact that white racism against Africa is such a normal way of thinking that its manifestations go completely unremarked." (page 11)

The Lessons of San Antonio

Over the years I've come to believe that many of the young people who fail in our schools do so for the same reasons Akmir did and use many of the same strategies he adopted. I remember visiting some teacher friends in San Antonio, Texas, about 15 years ago. I was there trying to help in their struggles to eliminate anti-Latino racism in the public schools in the barrios. There were very few Latino teachers and no Latino administrators in barrio schools in the parts of San Antonio where my friends worked. Many of the administrators were Anglo, retired military personnel from the San Antonio air force base who had hostile, imperialist attitudes towards the children they taught and the communities they served. I was asked by a community group, as an outsider and as an Anglo myself, to visit a number of classrooms and participate in some workshops discussing the specific ways in which racism functioned in their schools.

In one junior high I was invited to observe a history class by a teacher who admitted that he needed help with this particular group of students, all of whom were Latino. The teacher gave me a copy of his textbook, and I sat in the back of the room and followed the lesson for the day, which was entitled, "The first people to settle Texas." The teacher asked for someone to volunteer to read and no one responded. Most of the students were slumped down in their desks and none of them looked directly at the teacher. Some gazed off into space, others exchanged glimpses and grimaces. The teacher didn't ask for attention and started to read the text himself. It went something like, "The first people to settle Texas arrived from New England and the South in. . . ." Two boys in the back put their hands in their eyes, there were a few giggles and some murmuring. One hand shot up and that student blurted out, "What are we, animals or something?" The teacher's response was, "What does that have to do with the text?" Then he decided to abandon the lesson, introduced me as a visiting teacher who would substitute for the rest of the period and left the room.

I don't know if he planned to do that all along and set me up to fail with the students just as he did, or if his anger at being observed overcame him and he decided to dump the whole thing on me. Whatever the motivation, he left the room, and I was there with the students. I went up front and reread the sentence from the book and asked the class to raise their hands if they believed what I had just read. A few of them became alert, though they looked at me suspiciously as I continued, "This is lies, nonsense. In fact, I think the textbook is racist and an insult to everyone in this room." Everyone woke up and the same student who had asked the teacher about animal life turned to me and asked, "You mean that?" I said I did, and then he interrupted and said, "Well, there's more than that book that's racist around here." . . . I decided to continue on and said I didn't know their teacher but that I had run into more than one racist who was teaching and ought to be thrown out by the students and their parents. I added that it was obvious that the textbook was racist, it was there for everyone to read, but wondered how they detected racism in their teachers. The class launched into a serious and sophisticated discussion of the way in which racism manifests itself in their everyday lives at school. And they described the stance they took in order to resist that racism and yet not be thrown out of school. It amounted to nothing less than full-blown and cooperative not-learning. They accepted the failing grades it produced in exchange for the passive defense of their personal and cultural integrity. This was a class of school failures, and perhaps, I believed then and still believe, the repository for the positive leadership and intelligence of their generation.

In rethinking my teaching experience in the light of not-learning, I realize that many youngsters who ask impertinent questions, listen to their teachers in order to contradict them, and do not take homework or tests seriously are practiced not-learners. The quieter not-learners sit sullenly in class daydreaming and shutting out the sound of their teacher's voice. They sometimes fall off their chairs or throw things across the room or resort to other strategies of disruption. Some push things so far that they get put in special classes or thrown out of school. . . . On that level, no failure is possible, since there has been no attempt to learn. It is common to consider such students dumb or psychologically disturbed. Conscious, willed refusal of schooling for political or cultural reasons is not acknowledged as an appropriate response to oppressive education. Since students have no way to legitimately criticize the schooling they are subjected to or the people they are required to learn from, resistance and rebellion are stigmatized. The system's problem becomes the victim's problem.

However, not-learning is a healthy though frequently dysfunctional response to racism, sexism, and other forms of bias. In times of social movements for justice, such refusal is often turned to more positive mass protest and demonstration, and the development of alternative learning situations. For example, during the 1960s in New York, students who maintained their integrity and consciously refused the racist teachings of their segregated schools became leaders in the school boycotts and teachers of reading and African American history in Freedom schools.

Until we learn to distinguish not-learning from failure and respect the truth behind this massive rejection of schooling by students from poor and oppressed communities, it will not be possible to solve the major problems of education in the United States today. Risk-taking is at the heart of teaching well. That means that teachers will have to not-learn the ways of loyalty to the system and to speak out for, as the traditional African-American song goes, the concept that everyone has a right to the tree of life. We must give up looking at resistant students as failures and turn a critical eye towards this wealthy society and the schools that it supports.

No amount of educational research, no development of techniques or materials, no special programs or compensatory services, no restructuring or retraining of teachers will make any fundamental difference until we concede that for many students, the only sane alternative to not-learning is the acknowledgement and direct confrontation of oppression—social, sexual, and economic—both in school and in society. Education built on accepting that hard truth about our society can break through not-learning and lead students and teachers together, not to the solution of problems but to direct intelligent engagement in the struggles that might lead to solutions.

23

A Feminist Reframing of Bullying and Harassment: Transforming Schools Through Critical Pedagogy

Elizabeth J. Meyer

The problem of gendered harassment in North American schools is persistent, prevalent, and commonly misunderstood. Many schools have been trying to combat violence and harassing behaviours by implementing blanket bullying policies that do little to address the underlying issues of the school climate and culture that allow these behaviours to persist (Shariff, 2003; Soutter & McKenzie, 2000; Walton, 2004). The long term impact on individuals targeted for harassment is well-documented and severe: lower academic performance, absenteeism, drug and alcohol abuse, and suicidal behaviours have all been linked to schoolyard bullying (Bond, Carlin, Thomas, Rubin, & Patton, 2001; Rigby & Slee, 1999; Sharp, 1995). Students who are targets of sexual and homophobic harassment have been identified as being at even greater risk for these harmful behaviours and leaving school (California Safe Schools Coalition, 2004; Kosciw & Diaz, 2006; Reis & Saewyc, 1999; Williams, Connolly, Pepler, & Craig, 2005).

This article reviews research on the negative impact of gendered harassment in North American schools, and provides a critical feminist framework to help educators better understand possible roots of these behaviours. By placing the gendered dimensions of behaviours commonly viewed as bullying at the centre of this analysis, I make explicit how gendered hierarchies get taught and reinforced in schools. Finally, I introduce critical and anti-oppressive pedagogies as philosophical approaches that disrupt and challenge the reproduction of dominant heteronormative gender roles in schools. This transformative and liberatory approach to learning can help educators to read their environments and act consistently and proactively towards student behaviours and school cultures with a view to creating more inclusive and equitable learning environments for all.

What is Gendered Harassment?

Gendered harassment is a term used to describe any behaviour that acts to assert the boundaries of traditional gender norms: heterosexual masculinity and femininity. It is related to, but different from, bullying. Bullying is defined as behaviour that repeatedly and over time intentionally inflicts injury on another individual (Olweus, 1993), whereas harassment includes biased behaviours that have a negative impact on the target or the environment (Land, 2003). Forms of gendered harassment include (hetero)sexual harassment, homophobic harassment, and harassment for gender non-conformity (or transphobic harassment). I link these three forms of harassment because the impact of the harassers' behaviour is linked to norm-setting and policing the performance of traditional (heterosexual) gender roles (Larkin, 1994; Martino, 1995; Martino & Pallotta-Chiarolli, 2003; Renold, 2002; Smith & Smith, 1998; Stein, 1995). Although physical bullying is often the most obvious form addressed in schools, verbal bullying and harassment are also prevalent and often ignored, even though they have been found to be quite damaging to students as well. Hoover and Juul (1993) found in their study on bullying that repeated verbal attacks by peers are as devastating as infrequent cases of physical abuse (p. 27). Most bullying policies and interventions are not designed to get at the more persistent and insidious forms of harassment that occur in schools. Canadian researcher Gerald Walton observes that bullying and zero-tolerance policies, "do not consider the cultural and societal antecedents of violence in schools. Neither do these programs consider *psychological* violence" (2004, p. 29). While I do not wish to ignore the painful experiences that victims of physical harassment and violence endure, this article will address the emotional violence caused by the more insidious and often ignored issue of gendered harassment that is verbal and psychological in nature

Understanding the Scope of the Problem

I began investigating this problem as a result of my experience as a high school teacher in the U.S. observing the hostile climate that existed for gay, lesbian, bisexual, and transgender (glbt) students in my school. During my first year of teaching, I observed a very bright and athletic student – a leader in the school – dissolve into depression, drug use, and absenteeism as a result of how her friends were treating her. She had fallen in love with a young woman she had met that summer, and her classmates made sure she felt their disapproval. In addition to being excluded from her peer group, she was verbally harassed on a regular basis. This change in her school experience was enough to send a previously strong and confident young woman into a downward spiral of self-doubt and dangerous behaviour. As a young teacher who wanted to support this student, I felt frustrated and angry by what the other teachers allowed to happen in their presence at the school.

As I investigated this problem further, I learned that although glbt youth are commonly targeted for harassment, they are not the only ones suffering from the homophobic and heterosexist climate of schools. Any student whose behaviour is perceived as different in some way can be isolated and harassed using anti-gay insults (O'Conor, 1995; Renold, 2002; Rofes, 1995; Smith & Smith, 1998), and any student who wishes to assert and defend his/her place in the heteronormative social order of the school must engage in heterosexualised discourse that includes various forms of gendered harassment (Duncan, 1999; Martino & Berrill, 2003; Renold, 2003).

Students who are harassed in their schools have been found to be more likely to skip school, abuse drugs and alcohol, and have a higher rate of suicidal ideation (Bagley, Bolitho, & Bertrand, 1997; Irving & Parker-Jenkins, 1995; Rigby & Slee, 1999; Sharp, 1995;

Slee, 1995). Most of these students perceive school as a dangerous place, and that causes significant damage to their level of engagement in the school community. One group of students that is regularly targeted in schools is glbt youth (California Safe Schools Coalition, 2004; Kosciw & Diaz, 2006; Reis, 1999; Reis & Saewyc, 1999).

In a national phone survey of U.S. youth, the National Mental Health Association (2002) found that 50% of respondents reported that students who were gay would be bullied most or all of the time. In another U.S. survey, 91% of glbt students reported hearing homophobic remarks in school frequently or often (GLSEN, 2001). What is disturbing about this trend is not only its prevalence, but the lack of effective intervention to stop this problem. In the Gay, Lesbian, and Straight Education Network (GLSEN) 2001 School Climate Survey, 83% of glbt youth said that their teachers rarely or never intervene when hearing homophobic remarks (GLSEN, 2001). In a more recent study in California, students were asked how often they heard biased remarks (sex, sexual orientation, gender expression, religion, race, disability), and how often teachers intervened. The two forms of verbal harassment which students reported hearing the most were based on sexual orientation and gender presentation. These were also the two forms that students reported teachers were least likely to interrupt (California Safe Schools Coalition, 2004).

These studies indicate that educators are not adequately intervening in these forms of harassment. This inaction on the part of educators teaches students that the institution of the school – and by extension, society as a whole – condones such activity. By teaching students that gendered harassment is tolerated, schools effectively support the discriminatory attitudes that cause it in the first place. As democratic institutions in a diverse and changing society, schools must teach about the causes of such harmful attitudes and work to reduce the impact of them on their students. In so doing, we will more effectively work to reduce prejudice and violence in schools. I will now address each of these forms of harassment in-depth to understand them more fully: homophobic harassment, harassment for gender non-conformity (or transphobic harassment), and (hetero)sexual harassment.

Homophobic Harassment

Homophobic harassment is any behaviour, covert or overt, that reinforces negative attitudes towards gay, lesbian, and bisexual people. The most common form of this harassment is verbal in nature and includes the use of anti-gay language as an insult (e.g., "that's so gay" "don't be such a fag"), anti-gay jokes, and behaviours that intend to make fun of gays and lesbians (such as affecting the speech and walk of a stereotypically effeminate gay man to get a laugh). The prevalence of this discourse in schools allows homophobic attitudes to develop and grow as students learn that this language is tacitly condoned by educators who fail to intervene when it is used. As George Smith (1998) explains in his article, *The Ideology of "FAG,"*

> The local practices of the ideology of "fag" are never penalized or publicly condemned. Explicitly homophobic ridicule in sports contexts goes unremarked. Effective toleration of the ideology of "fag" among students and teachers condemns gay students to the isolation of "passing" or ostracism and sometimes to a life of hell in school.
>
> (p. 332)

The isolation and vulnerability experienced by these students is exacerbated by the refusal of teachers and administrators to intervene on their behalf. Many students' experiences support Smith's assertion. In the Human Rights Watch (Bochenek & Brown, 2001) study, *Hatred in the Hallways,* several students spoke of similar experiences:

> Nothing was done by the administration. A guy screamed "queer" down the hall in front of the principal's office, but nothing happened to him. The teachers – yeah, the teachers could have seen what was going on. Nothing happened.
>
> (p. 39)

> One day in the parking lot outside his school, six students surrounded [Dylan]. One threw a lasso around his neck, saying, "Let's tie the faggot to the back of the truck." He escaped from his tormentors and ran inside the school. Finding one of the vice-principals, he tried to tell her what had just happened to him. "I was still hysterical," he said, "I was trying to explain, but I was stumbling over my words. She laughed." The school took no action to discipline Dylan's harassers. Instead, school officials told him not to discuss his sexual orientation with other students. After the lasso incident, the harassment and violence intensified. "I was living in the disciplinary office because other harassment was going on. Everyone knew," he said. "It gave permission for a whole new level of physical stuff to occur."
>
> (p. 1)

These stories are not exceptional. In GLSEN's National School Climate Survey (2001), 84% of glbt youth report being verbally harassed in school and 64.3% report feeling unsafe. These students are also targets for school graffiti, vandalism, and ostracism that often leave them at high risk for depression, dropping out, and suicide (California Safe Schools Coalition, 2004; GLSEN, 2001; Reis & Saewyc, 1999). On a more positive note, these students report less harassment and increased feelings of school safety when a teacher intervenes sometimes or often to stop name-calling (California Safe Schools Coalition, 2004).

Students who are perceived to be gender non-conforming are also frequently targeted in schools. Harassment for behaviour that transcends narrow gender norms is one often lumped together with homophobic harassment, but it is important to investigate each separately so as not to further confuse existing misconceptions of gender identity and expression with sexual orientation.

Harassment for Gender Non-Conformity or Transphobic Harassment

Harassment for gender non-conforming behaviours is under researched, but important to understand. According to the California Safe Schools study, 27% of all students (n=230,000) report being harassed for gender non-conformity (2004). Due to prevalent stereotypes of gay men and lesbian women who transgress traditional gender norms, people whose behaviour challenges popular notions of masculinity and femininity are often perceived to be gay themselves. This is a dangerous assumption to make, as it mistakenly conflates the concepts of sexual orientation and gender identity. Many adults also engage in this flawed logic due to their misunderstanding of gender and sexual orientation. However sex, gender identity, and sexual orientation are each distinct and may be expressed in a variety of ways.[1] For example, although many biological females *(sex)* identify as heterosexual *(sexual orientation)* women *(gender identity)*, that does not mean that is the only possible combination of orientations and identities. By allowing students to engage in this way of thinking and behaving, schools reinforce traditional notions of heterosexual masculinity and femininity that effectively reduce educational opportunities for all students.

Research has demonstrated that more rigid adherence to traditional sex roles correlates with more negative attitudes and violent behaviours towards homosexuals (Bufkin, 1999; Whitley, 2001). When boys disengage from the arts and girls avoid appearing too athletic, it is often the result of teasing and "harmless" jokes. The threat of being perceived as a "sissy" or a "tomboy" and the resulting homophobic backlash does limit the ways in which students participate in school life. Martino & Pallotta-Chiarolli (2003) describe an interview with a student who was harassed for his interest in art:

> On his way to school one morning a group of boys at the back of the bus from one of the local high schools started calling him names. Initially, he was targeted as an "art boy" because he was carrying an art file. But the harassment escalated and they began calling him "fag boy."
>
> (p. 52)

Unfortunately, our society's tendency to devalue qualities associated with femininity make this gender performance much harder on nonconforming boys than on nonconforming girls. Schools tend to place a higher value on strength, competitiveness, aggressiveness, and being tough: qualities generally viewed to be masculine. Whereas being creative, caring, good at school, and quiet are often considered to be feminine qualities and are viewed by many as signs of weakness – particularly in boys. In their study on masculinities in Australian schools, Martino & Pallotta-Chiarolli (2003) found that "many boys said that while they were able to perform the techniques of literacy ('I can read'), performing an 'appropriate' masculinity often prevented or deterred them from displaying their literacy abilities ('I can't read')" (p. 246). They also discuss how this plays out in physical education: "physically demanding activities such as dance and gymnastics, where both men and women excel, are not as esteemed as those sports which serve to provide an arena for the expression of traditional forms of hegemonic masculinity" (Lingard and Douglas, 1999, cited in Martino & Pallotta-Chiarolli, 2003, p. 254). It is not surprising, then, that bullying studies report that "typical victims are described as physically weak, and they tended to be timid, anxious, sensitive and shy. . . . In contrast, bullies were physically strong, aggressive, and impulsive, and had a strong need to dominate others" (Hoover & Juul, 1993, p. 26).

It is difficult to effectively intervene to stop bullying when the qualities that bullies embody are the ones that are most valued by many and demonstrate a power that is esteemed in a patriarchal society. Hegemonic masculinity (Connell, 1995), the embodiment of the dominant, tough, competitive, athletic male, is the standard of behaviour in schools and any variation tends to be punished by the peer group (Robinson, 2005; Stoudt, 2006). Though many researchers understand bullying as anti-social behavior, the fact that bullies usually hold social power and get what they want out of such activity shows that they have learned to assert their strength in ways that benefit them. As Walton argues, understanding bullying as anti-social behaviour, "is a misconceptualization because it affords dominance and social status and is often rewarded and supported by other children. It may not be nice, but it is, nevertheless, very social" (2004, p. 33).

The social constructs of ideal masculinity and femininity are at the core of much bullying behaviour. As a result of this, students report that schools are safer for gender non-conforming girls (California Safe Schools Coalition, 2004). The pressure on boys to conform to traditional notions of masculinity is great and the risk of being perceived as gay is an effective threat in policing the boundaries of acceptable behavior. One male student described its impact on his life,

> When I was in elementary school, I did a lot of ballet. I was at the National Ballet School one summer. And that sort of stigma (laugh) which I never thought was a stigma, or could be a stigma, but which became a stigma, followed me into high school. And that was followed with comments continually – "fag," you know, "fag." I think that was actually . . . one of the reasons why I eventually gave up ballet was just because of the constant harassment, and also pursuing other interests. But I think that was at the back of my mind a lot of the time with the harassment, and realizing that they're right. That's what I was. I knew that that's what I was.
>
> (Smith, 1998, p. 322)

When students are limited from developing their strengths because of the climate of the school, then the educational system has failed.

In order to assert their heterosexual masculinity, many boys engage in overt forms of heterosexualised behaviours, as this is seen as the best way to avoid being called gay. One gay student gave the following example:

> You know when all the guys would be making girl jokes, you'd have to go along with them, as much as you tried not to, you still had to chuckle here and there to not raise suspicion. . . . very frequently, jokingly, some students would say to other students – when they didn't necessarily conform to all the jokes and the way of thinking of women students – they'd say, "what, you're not gay, are you?"
>
> (Smith, 1998, p. 324)

The student feels obliged to participate in the (hetero)sexual harassment of his female peers in order to protect himself from being the target of homophobic harassment. The pressure to participate in these oppressive practices works in multiple ways to assert the power of hegemonic masculinity: it engages additional participants in the sexual harassment of females and labels those who choose not to participate as gay. This pressure to conform to ideals of hegemonic masculinity is at the core of most gendered harassment. This example leads us to the third area of gendered harassment: (hetero)sexual harassment.

(Hetero)sexual Harassment

Sexual harassment in schools has been the subject of research and public discourse since the early 1990's (Corbett, Gentry, & Pearson, 1993; Larkin, 1994; Louis Harris & Associates, 1993; Stein, 1992). In spite of this, it is still prevalent. Verbal harassment is the most common form of sexual harassment reported by students, and female students experience more frequent and more severe forms of sexual harassment than males (Lee, Croninger, Linn, & Chen, 1996). Terms such as *bitch, baby, chick,* and *fucking broad,* are commonly used in schools by male students as ways to assert masculinity by degrading female peers (Larkin,

1994, p. 268). Another common way for males to perform their masculinity is to engage in heterosexual discourse by sexually objectifying female peers and discussing sexual acts they would like to engage in or have already engaged in (Duncan, 1999; Eder, 1997; Larkin, 1994; Stein, 2002). This is often done near the female students, but is not always directed at them, thus creating a space where women are targeted and objectified with no outlet for response or complaint of tangible harm. This activity creates a hostile climate for most students (Stein, 1995; Wood, 1987) is generally not stopped by teachers, and sometimes is encouraged by their tacit participation. Students reported that male teachers might, "laugh along with the guys" (Larkin, 1994, p. 270) or support the comments and even blame the victim, as demonstrated in the following incident:

> I took a photography class, and the majority of the class was boys. . . . One day I was in the room alone and one of the boys came in. When I went to leave he grabbed me and threw me down and grabbed my breast. I felt I was helpless but I punched him and he ran out. The teacher (who was a man) came in and yelled at me. When I tried to explain why I had hit him the teacher told me I deserved it because I wore short skirts. I was sent to the principal and I had to serve detention. I didn't want to tell the principal because I feared he would do the same and tell me it was my fault. I felt so alone. Everyday I had to go to class and face it. No girl should have to be uncomfortable because of what she wears or how she acts.
>
> (Stein, 1995, p. 4)

Teachers can exacerbate situations by reinforcing the behavior of the offending students. In this case, not only did the teacher not intervene in the sexual harassment, but he added to it by commenting on her attire and stating that she "deserved it." With teachers role modeling and reinforcing such behaviours, it is clear that a new approach to preventing sexual harassment in schools is needed.

Although sexual harassment, by definition, is sexual in nature, I have included it as a form of gendered harassment due to its roots: the public performance of traditional heterosexual gender roles. In its most commonly understood form, sexual harassment is that of a male towards a female and ranges from comments, gestures, leers or "invitations" of a sexual nature to physical touching, grabbing, rubbing, and violent assault such as rape. I will continue to focus here on the more subtle and insidious behaviours, where the harassers assert their gender role through acts of domination and humiliation, since physically violent and intrusive acts are ones that get a response from school authorities regardless of motive or context.

Although females are most commonly targeted, it is important to acknowledge that men can also be victims of sexual harassment, much of it from other men and usually homophobic in nature. Young women may also be implicated in such behaviours, and it is most commonly exhibited as verbal insults directed towards other females as a result of competition for boyfriends or friendship groups (Duncan, 2004).

Sexual harassment has been described as the way patriarchy works: men continuing to assert their power over women. Though this is a useful place to begin, it is important to stretch our understanding of this problem to include how valorized forms of traditionally masculine behaviours are allowed to be practiced and performed over the devalued forms of traditional notions of femininity. These gender roles are constructed within a heterosexual matrix (Butler, 1990) that only allows for a single dominant form of compulsory heterosexuality (Rich, 1978/1993). As long as these attitudes and behaviours continue to go unchallenged, schools will continue to be sites where youths are harassed out of an education. In order to prevent this from continuing, we must learn effective strategies for intervention that will help educators create schools where such discriminatory behaviours will be replaced by more inclusive and radical notions of respect, equality, and understanding. The next section will explore potential strategies for educators to employ to transform the behaviours and qualities are endorsed and valued in schools.

Why Critical and Anti-Oppressive Pedagogy?

In this seminal work, *Pedagogy of the Oppressed,* Paulo Freire outlined the framework for what has become the field of critical pedagogy (Freire, 1970/1993). This book has influenced the work of scholars and educators who seek to transform learning while making explicit the dominant power structures that influence how knowledge is produced. Freire's work focused on the process of consciousness-raising with people who had been marginalized in order to empower them and create more positive educational experiences and social outcomes. Applying this approach to learning can help reduce gendered harassment and create safer school environments for all students by making explicit gendered hierarchies in schools and exploring multiple ways of undoing the heterosexist patriarchal structures that allow them to persist. Teacher education and school leadership programs that are infused with critical and anti-oppressive pedagogy can provide the knowledge and the tools necessary to help teachers and administrators reduce these behaviours.

While physical acts of violence are difficult for schools to ignore, the daily acts of psychological violence that persist teach lasting lessons that impact students' lives in ways that many teachers and administrators fail to acknowledge. In order to change this second order curriculum (Kincheloe, 2005), the entire culture of the school must shift. In order for this shift to be successful, all stakeholders in the community must be involved in the process, including students, families, and teachers. The onus is on administrators and school boards to create the conditions for this level of community engagement to occur. Even though, "all students can be silenced to some extent by top-down, memory-based classroom arrangements," Kincheloe argues that, "marginalized students . . . [often experience] anger, depression, and anxiety" as a result of these practices (p. 24). As a result, a critical pedagogy must be applied in our schools to change the types of lessons students are internalizing.

An anti-oppressive approach to education informed by critical pedagogy is one that is central to confronting and transforming these power dynamics in schools, and the best way to help schools embrace such an approach is to start with teacher education and leadership programs. We must better prepare educators to critically examine the power structures of the school and the community so that they may act as role models and provide their students with the language and the tools to confront the inequalities (re)produced within that system.

The concept of anti-oppressive teacher education grounded in critical pedagogy requires that educators be taught about privilege and oppression and how these factors influence the kind of education different students receive. In his book, *Troubling Education: Queer activism and antioppressive pedagogy,* Kevin Kumashiro explores four different conceptions of anti-oppressive education: education for the Other, education about the

Other, education that is critical of privileging and othering, and education that changes students and society (Kumashiro, 2002). Here I will advocate for the fourth conception as the best approach to preparing educators to change gendered harassment in schools. This approach assumes that oppression is "produced by discourse, and in particular, is produced when certain discourses (especially ways of thinking that privilege certain identities and marginalize others) are cited over and over. Such citational processes serve to reproduce these hierarchies and their harmful effects in society" (Kumashiro, 2002, p. 50). By helping teachers and administrators understand how systems of oppression are perpetuated by language and behaviour in schools, we can work more effectively to transform our understandings of the dominant gender stereotypes students mobilize to hurt their peers.

An anti-oppressive pedagogy is not limited to understanding how jokes and teasing hurt students. It also challenges the banking style of education, in which students are viewed as empty vessels for teachers to fill with information that supports dominant power structures (Freire, 1970/1993). Kumashiro explains that many disciplines perpetuate oppressive knowledges, by presenting only the dominant culture's point of view in a history textbook, or by teaching science as purely objective and never questioning how it has been used to validate only certain ways of understanding the world. By excluding the experiences and cultural contributions of women, non-Western thinkers, glbt people, and racialized peoples, educators teach that power and knowledge is only valid when it comes from the white, western, heterosexual, male perspective. Kumashiro asserts: "we need to acknowledge that the desire to continue teaching the disciplines as they have traditionally been taught is a desire to maintain the privilege of certain identities, worldviews, and social relations" (p. 58). When fully enacted, anti-oppressive pedagogies can help students learn in new and exciting ways and create a school culture that allows room for multiple gender identities and expressions and sexual orientations.

A critical transformation of school culture can start by ending name-calling and related forms of verbal harassment. The simplest step that teachers can take is to make a public and consistent stand against any kind of name-calling and related verbal harassment. This shows students that they can expect to be treated fairly and no hurtful or discriminatory language is acceptable. An example of an approach that a critical educator can take is to "stop and educate" in situations where oppressive language has been used. In addition to setting the standards for acceptable language in the classroom, it is important for educators to provide information about why certain names are especially hurtful due to their biased meanings. If students only learn that it is punishable to call someone "gay" or a "dyke," then they may internalize the message that being gay or gender nonconforming is something shameful or bad. Helping students learn to interrogate daily discourses, to explore the historical specificity of certain terminologies, and to understand how language is used to control identities and behaviours will offer them a different way of seeing the world.

Teacher education programs can help new teachers reflect on their educational experiences and what perspectives they bring into their classrooms. Kincheloe defines critical teacher education as one that "problematizes knowledge" and that can offer students the space to challenge, debate, and analyze assumptions and normative knowledges (2005, p. 102). It can also offer future teachers effective tools by using innovative curricular materials, discussing concepts such as hegemony and patriarchy, and providing interactive class activities that allow students to practice critiquing normative classroom practices and ideas. For example, student teachers have told me that they are afraid that they will get in trouble for talking about gay issues in class. Providing student teachers a safe environment in which to practice these discussions and experience a model of a critical classroom is important so that they can experience this form of learning and develop confidence in their abilities to teach from a standpoint that can often cause discomfort and disrupt familiar knowledges.

Educational leadership programs and coursework must also model critical, anti-oppressive approaches to school leadership. Programs should consider how these philosophies influence a principal's approach to leadership. A principal's philosophy is a powerful influence on the culture of the school: what accomplishments get celebrated, what learning is rewarded, whose knowledge is valued, and who advances professionally (Dinham, Cairney, Craigie, & Wilson, 1995; Riehl, 2000; Ryan, 2003). These are the strategies that school leaders use to communicate to teachers, staff, and students which behaviours and achievements are to be emulated and which are to be avoided. School administrators need to create an environment where anti-oppressive educators are supported and teachers are encouraged to recognize and value alternative knowledges and diverse student accomplishments.

Conclusion

My experiences as a classroom teacher are what led me to pursue a deeper understanding of this phenomenon in schools. The frustration I felt at the inaction of my colleagues led me to study the factors that influence how teachers understand and respond to gendered harassment in schools. The findings from my dissertation research on this subject have focused my attention on teacher education and school leadership programs and the potential for critical and anti-oppressive pedagogies to transform what knowledges and worldviews are taught (Meyer, 2007a; Meyer, 2007 in press).

Students who are targets for gendered harassment tend to suffer silently and internalize the harmful messages embedded in the insults and jokes that permeate many school cultures. The focus on bullying and physical aggression has brought into perspective some important concerns, but has also obscured others. By using vague terms such as bullying and name calling, scholars and educators avoid examining the underlying power dynamics that such behaviours build and reinforce. When policies and interventions don't name and explore systems of power and privilege, they effectively reinforce the status quo. Educators must understand that when insults and jokes are used to marginalize groups, the damage goes beyond the harm to individual students. These discourses normalize the hegemony of white, male, heterosexual, middle-class, able-bodied values and leave many students feeling hurt, excluded, and limited in their chances for educational success (Meyer, 2007b).

It is essential for teachers to learn to examine critically the impacts of gendered harassment in schools and to develop tools to work against it. By enacting a critical anti-oppressive pedagogy in teacher education and school leadership programs, we can better equip professionals to transform such oppressive discourses in schools. Until the hegemonic masculine values that privilege power, individual strength, and competition are challenged, most interventions will be temporary band-aid solutions and the negative cycles of violence and oppression will continue. By examining bullying and harassment together, and explicitly addressing the underlying homophobia, transphobia, and (hetero)sexism, we will be able to create more systemic approaches to addressing violence in schools and help educators understand how to change the culture of their schools by transforming sexist, transphobic, and homophobic practices, policies, procedures, and curricula.

Note

1. See Butler (1990, 2004) for a more in-depth explanation of these concepts and their differences.

References

Bagley, C., Bolitho, F., & Bertrand, L. (1997). Sexual assault in school, mental health and suicidal behaviours in adolescent women in Canada. *Adolescence, 32*(126), 361–366.

Bochenek, M., & Brown, A. W. (2001). *Hatred in the hallways: Violence and discrimination against lesbian, gay, bisexual, and transgender students in U.S. schools*: Human Rights Watch.

Bond, L., Carlin, J. B., Thomas, L., Rubin, K., & Patton, G. (2001). Does bullying cause emotional problems? A prospective study of young teenagers. *BMJ: British Medical Journal, 323*(7311), 480–484.

Bufkin, J. L. (1999). Bias crime as gendered behavior. *Social Justice, 26*(1), 155–176.

Butler, J. (1990). *Gender Trouble.* New York: Routledge Falmer.

California Safe Schools Coalition. (2004). *Consequences of harassment based on actual or perceived sexual orientation and gender non-conformity and steps for making schools safer.* Davis: University of California.

Connell, R. W. (1995). *Masculinities.* Sydney: Allen and Unwin.

Corbett, K., Gentry, C. A., & Pearson, W. J. (1993). Sexual harassment in high school. *Youth & Society, 25*(1), 93–103.

Dinham, S., Cairney, T., Craigie, D., & Wilson, S. (1995). School climate and leadership: Research into three secondary schools. *Journal of Educational Administration, 33*(4), 36–59.

Duncan, N. (1999). *Sexual bullying: Gender conflict and pupil culture in secondary schools.* London: Routledge.

Duncan, N. (2004). It's important to be nice, but it's nicer to be important: Girls, popularity and sexual competition. *Sex Education, 4*(2), 137–152.

Eder, D. (1997). Sexual aggression within the school culture. In B. Bank & P. M. Hall (Eds.), *Gender, equity, and schooling* (pp. 93–112). London: Garland Publishing.

Freire, P. (1970/1993). *Pedagogy of the oppressed.* New York: Continuum.

GLSEN. (2001). *The national school climate survey: Lesbian, gay, bisexual and transgender youth and their experiences in schools.* New York, NY: The Gay, Lesbian, and Straight Education Network.

Hoover, J. H., & Juul, K. (1993). Bullying in Europe and the United States. *Journal of Emotional and Behavioral Problems, 2*(1), 25–29.

Irving, B. A., & Parker-Jenkins, M. (1995). Tackling truancy: An examination of persistent non-attendance amongst disaffected school pupils and positive support strategies. *Cambridge Journal of Education, 25*(2), 225–235.

Kincheloe, J. (2005). *Critical pedagogy.* New York: Peter Lang.

Kosciw, J., & Diaz, E. (2006). *The 2005 national school climate survey: The experiences of lesbian, gay, bisexual and transgender youth in our nation's schools.* New York: Gay, Lesbian, and Straight Education Network.

Kumashiro, K. (2002). *Troubling education: Queer activism and antioppressive pedagogy.* New York: Routledge Falmer.

Land, D. (2003). Teasing apart secondary students' conceptualizations of peer teasing, bullying and sexual harassment *School Psychology International, 24*(2), 147–165.

Larkin, J. (1994). Walking through walls: The sexual harassment of high school girls. *Gender and Education, 6*(3), 263–280.

Lee, V., Croninger, R. G., Linn, E., & Chen, Z. (1996). The culture of sexual harassment in secondary schools. *American Educational Research Journal, 33*(2), 383–417.

Louis Harris & Associates. (1993). *Hostile hallways: The AAUW survey on sexual harassment in America's schools.* Washington, DC: American Association of University Women.

Martino, W. (1995). 'Cool boys', 'party animals', 'squids' and 'poofters': Interrogating the dynamics and politics of adolescent masculinities in school. *British Journal of Sociology of Education, 22*(2), 239–263.

Martino, W., & Berrill, D. (2003). Boys, schooling and masculinities: Interrogating the 'Right' way to educate boys. *Educational Review, 55*(2), 99–117.

Martino, W., & Pallotta-Chiarolli, M. (2003). *So what's a boy? Addressing issues of masculinity and schooling.* Buckingham: Open University Press.

Meyer, E. (2007a) *Gendered harassment in secondary schools: Understanding teachers' perceptions of and responses to the problem.* Unpublished doctoral dissertation. McGill University, Montreal, QC.

Meyer, E. (2007b, April 9–13) *Bullying and harassment in secondary schools: A critical feminist analysis of the gaps, overlaps and implications from a decade of research.* Paper presented at the Annual meeting of the American Educational Research Association, Chicago, IL.

Meyer, E. (2007, in press). Gendered harassment in high school: Understanding teachers' (non) interventions. *Gender and Education.*

National Mental Health Association. (2002). *"What does gay mean?" Teen survey executive summary.* Alexandria, VA: National Mental Health Association.

O'Conor, A. (1995). Who gets called queer in school? Lesbian, gay, and bisexual teenagers, homophobia, and high school. In G. Unks (Ed.), *The gay teen: Educational practice and theory for lesbian, gay, and bisexual adolescents* (pp. 95–104). New York: Routledge.

Olweus, D. (1993). *Bullying at school: What we know and what we can do.* Oxford: Blackwell.

Reis, B. (1999). *They don't even know me: Understanding anti-gay harassment and violence in schools.* Seattle: Safe Schools Coalition of Washington.

Reis, B., & Saewyc, E. (1999). *83,000 Youth: Selected findings of eight population-based studies.* Seattle: Safe Schools Coalition of Washington.

Renold, E. (2002). Presumed innocence – (Hetero)sexual, heterosexist and homophobic harassment among primary school girls and boys *Childhood – A global journal of child research, 9*(4), 415–434.

Renold, E. (2003). 'If you don't kiss me you're dumped': Boys, boyfriends and heterosexualised masculinities in the primary school. *Educational Review, 55*(2), 179–194.

Rich, A. (1978/1993). Compulsory heterosexuality and lesbian existence. In H. Abelove, D. Halperin & M. A. Barale (Eds.), *The lesbian and gay studies reader* (pp. 227–254). New York: Routledge.

Riehl, C. J. (2000). The principal's role in creating inclusive schools for diverse students: A review of normative, empirical, and critical literature on the practice of educational administration. *Review of Educational Research, 70*(1), 55–81.

Rigby, K., & Slee, P. (1999). Suicidal ideation among adolescent school children, involvement in bully-victim problems, and perceived social support. *Suicide and Life-Threatening Behavior, 29*(2), 119–130.

Robinson, K. H. (2005). Reinforcing hegemonic masculinities through sexual harassment: issues of identity, power and popularity in secondary schools. *Gender and Education, 17*(1), 19–37.

Rofes, E. (1995). Making our schools safe for sissies. In G. Unks (Ed.), *The gay teen: Educational practice and theory for lesbian, gay, and bisexual adolescents* (pp. 79–84). New York: Routledge.

Ryan, J. (2003). Educational administrators' perceptions of racism in diverse school contexts. *Race Ethnicity and Education, 6*(2), 145–164.

Shariff, S. (2003). *A system on trial: Educational, ethical, and legally defensible approaches to handling bullying.* Unpublished Doctoral dissertation, Simon Fraser University, Burnaby, BC.

Sharp, S. (1995). How much does bullying hurt? The effects of bullying on the personal wellbeing and educational progress of secondary aged students. *Educational & Child Psychology, 12*(2), 81–88.

Slee, P. (1995). Bullying: Health concerns of Australian secondary school students. *International Journal of Adolescence & Youth, 5*(4), 215–224.

Smith, G. W., & Smith, D., Ed. (1998). The ideology of "fag": The school experience of gay students. *Sociological Quarterly, 39*(2), 309–335.

Soutter, A., & McKenzie, A. (2000). The use and effects of anti-bullying and anti-harassment policies in Australian schools. *School Psychology International, 21*(1), 96–105.

Stein, N. (1992). Bitter lessons for all: Sexual harassment in schools. In J. T. Sears (Ed.), *Sexuality and the curriculum: The politics and practices of sexuality education (Critical issues in curriculum)* (pp. 10–123). New York: Teachers College Press.

Stein, N. (1995). Sexual harassment in school: The public performance of gendered violence. *Harvard Educational Review, 65*(2), 145–162.

Stein, N. (2002). Bullying as sexual harassment in elementary schools. In *The Jossey-Bass reader on gender in education* (pp. 409–429). San Francisco: Jossey-Bass.

Stoudt, B. G. (2006). "You're either in or you're out": School violence, peer discipline, and the (re)production of hegemonic masculinity. *Men And Masculinities, 8*(3), 273–287.

Walton, G. (2004). Bullying and homophobia in Canadian schools: The politics of policies, programs, and educational leadership. *Journal of Gay and Lesbian Issues in Education, 1*(4), 23–36.

Whitley, B. E., Jr. (2001). Gender-role variables and attitudes toward homosexuality. *Sex Roles, 45*(11/12), 691–721.
Williams, T., Connolly, J., Pepler, D., & Craig, W. (2005). Peer victimization, social support, and psychosocial adjustment of sexual minority adolescents. *Journal of Youth and Adolescence, 34*(5), 471–482.
Wood, J. (1987). Groping towards sexism: Boys' sex talk. In M. Arnot & G. Weiner (Eds.), *Gender under scrutiny: New inquiries in education* (pp. 187–230). London: Hutchinson Education.

24

Redirecting the Teacher's Gaze: Teacher Education, Youth Surveillance and the School-To-Prison Pipeline

John Raible and Jason G. Irizarry

> It seems to me that whether the prisoners get an extra chocolate bar on Christmas . . . is not the real political issue. What we have to denounce is not so much the "human" side of life in prison but rather their real social function—that is, to serve as the instrument that creates a criminal milieu that the ruling classes can control
>
> (Michel Foucault interviewed by Roger-Pol Droit, 1975)

Deciding exactly what social roles the young should be encouraged to play remains highly contested in the socio-political context of education. Particularly in the American context, social institutions such as child welfare, juvenile justice, and schooling—and by extension, the field of teacher education—reflect the unfinished ideological struggles between social and political forces that advocate competing visions of democracy and the related agendas of state agencies that enable different futures for particular children. Although our practise as teacher educators lies in the United States, we can point to certain eerie parallels in other industrialized nations, particularly in societies with similar histories of settlement by European colonial powers and subsequent patterns of widespread immigration. While our concern for the burgeoning problem of incarcerated youth stems from our positions as critical researchers working in the field of multicultural teacher education as it is practiced in the United States, we believe that teacher educators who work in other contexts can benefit from—and contribute to—the perspective advanced here.

As we shall argue, we have found an under-examined link between the surveillance role played by many teachers in public schools and the over-representation of youth of colour in the U.S. penal system. We surmise that similar links can be made in other societies with visible minority populations. For example, Aboriginal or First Nations people in Canada account for only 4% of that country's population but comprise almost one-quarter of the population in provincial/territorial custody (Landry & Sinha, 2008). Similarly, according to the Australian Bureau of Statistics (2009), the imprisonment rate for indigenous Australians is 14 times higher than that of non-indigenous prisoners (Australian Bureau of Statistics, 2009). Given similar social dynamics between majority and minority populations across the globe and the historic uses of schooling to manage minority populations (see Spring, 2004), our colleagues outside the U.S. should be able to contribute research that uncovers the connections between schooling in their own societies and the over-representation of minority and immigrant populations in the penal system in their local contexts.

Teaching Teachers to Resist Youth Surveillance

This article addresses one of the profound contradictions in teacher education that results in conflicting goals for educators who work with the young. It asks: How do we prepare future teachers to interrogate their inherited professional roles in the ongoing surveillance, management, and disciplining of youth? How does teacher education move students to care about youth who belong to socio-economic and racial subgroups that have been deemed problematic and "undesirable?" How can teachers resist the urge to collude with the institutional processes that help to create the criminal milieu as described by Foucault in the opening quotation?

To begin to answer these questions, we critically examine the role of teacher education in exacerbating what has come to be known in the U.S. as the school-to-prison pipeline, that combination of personal and institutional failures that leads too many students on a trajectory from the schoolhouse to the jailhouse (Brown, 2007). We begin by addressing ways in which teachers are encouraged, most recently in the name of accountability, to become principally agents of surveillance and behaviour management. We also explore the potential for teacher education to serve as a site of resistance to heightened surveillance, particularly of youth from dominated, marginalized communities, and possibilities for providing a counter-narrative to the "expectation of incarceration" (Meiners, 2007) for youth that have been effectively written off as problem children. In raising these questions about our field, we aim to redirect the gaze of educators away from a simplistic concern for "deviant" youth (and their management) as the problem, to a more comprehensive understanding that accounts for the intersections between state institutions, including schools, prisons, and colleges of education, and the discourses that create certain views and understandings of the roles of teachers and students. Finally, we call for renewed attention to our collective professional responsibility to promote social justice in and through education.

The Disciplinary Gaze as School Tradition

As alluded to in our opening quote from Foucault (1975), we wonder about the frequently unmentioned yet powerful collusion of teachers with a broad system of youth surveillance and regulation. How might teachers more effectively resist pressures to label, discipline, and, as we shall argue, eventually contribute to the process of criminalizing certain segments of school-age populations, namely students from poor communities of colour? In recent years, we have become concerned by shifts in popular views of children and youth in general. In our view, the growing presence of police and metal detectors in U.S. schools, and increasing reliance on medication to manage student behaviour, suggest that the experience of school, and indeed of childhood itself, may now be understood in radically different ways compared to during previous generations.

Given the growing pressures for accountability that influence the daily work of teachers and administrators, which scholars have linked to recent economic trends towards privatization and globalization and the ideology of neoliberalism (Giroux, 2000; Lipman, 2003; Sleeter 2007), our view is that teacher educators must attend more explicitly to the intersections of these issues in our work in K-12 schools and in colleges of education. Alongside teacher educators, pre-service teachers (i.e., those who are currently training to become teachers) must be encouraged to clarify their understanding of the socio-political context of their work and the political nature of the roles they will soon take on while they fashion identities as novice teachers within an increasingly regulated and punitive system of youth-serving agencies that includes schools, law enforcement, the courts, and prisons. We believe that a critical orientation to social justice can facilitate the process of consciousness-raising and role clarification for pre-service teachers and teacher educators alike, thereby improving the chances for future teachers to connect more meaningfully with their students.

It is clear that teachers play a significant role, for better or worse, in the sorting and labelling of young people once they enter school. As Meiners (2007) documents in her recent research, disciplinary action, assessment techniques, pedagogy, and other school practices and policies all too often set in motion a series of actions that "function to normalize an 'expectation' of incarceration" for growing numbers of youth (p. 31). In the United States, the cumulative impact of current practices of surveillance that place children at risk for exclusion from school is nothing short of alarming. According to the National Centre for Educational Statistics (NCES, 2003) school officials meted out 3 million suspensions and approximately 1000 expulsions during the 2002–2003 academic year alone. When students disengage from (or are pushed out of) school, many are set up for failure in other ways. Increasingly, youth advocates, educators, prison activists, and others are calling attention to the escalating rates of suspension and disengagement from school in terms of a trajectory that effectively moves students from school to prison.

The discourse generated from research on the school-to-prison pipeline provides a way of framing the larger issues that result in the failure of schools to meet the needs of poor students from dominated communities. Wald and Losen (2003b) aptly describe the metaphor of the pipeline as the intersection of major American institutions that wield enormous power over the life chances of the young, namely education and the criminal justice system. In our view, the current preoccupation of school officials on behaviour management and regulation reflects an age-old tension between *disciplining* and *educating* the young, dating as far back as the Enlightenment. The ways in which schools staffed by ostensibly well-intentioned teachers come to support, to actively participate in, and hopefully to ultimately reject such a system of punishment and regulation is the focus of our analysis.

As Foucault (1977) famously observed, social control has been influenced by the model of the panopticon in prominent social institutions, including in schools, mental hospitals, and prisons. Foucault described the panopticon, based on Jeremy Bentham's 19th century ideas for prison reform, as a central tower around which prison cells would be organized, allowing for ongoing surveillance of prisoners at all times. Key to the panoptic model was the idea that the guards would remain hidden, so that prisoners would never know when they were being watched. In theory, panoptic surveillance becomes highly effective because the prisoners thus guarded—and the non-incarcerated masses that witness from the sidelines—begin to police themselves.

Surveillance and regulation, rather than punishment alone, became normalized throughout western societies as the exercise of power progressed from reliance on brute torture and physical punishment (e.g., public hangings and beheadings) during what Foucault (1975) called the "culture of spectacle" to a more "carcercal culture" through which criminals were incarcerated, disciplined, and potentially, even rehabilitated. The implications of the move towards surveillance and behaviour management meant, in Foucault's view, political profit for ruling elites through the criminalization of certain segments of the populace, "political profit in that the more criminals there are, the more readily the population will accept police controls" (p. 26). Importantly for Foucault, the panoptic gaze and its emphasis on regulation influenced multiple emerging social institutions, including prisons and schools.

Educational researchers in recent years have taken up Foucault's interest in power and disciplinary practices, and have written about the role of surveillance and behaviour management in public education. For example, Noguera (2003) draws on social reproduction theory to remind us of the traditional functions of schools under the system of American capitalism, which he describes succinctly as three-fold: (1) to sort students and determine "who will lead and manage corporations and government, and who will be led and managed by those in charge;" (2) to socialize children into the "values and norms that are regarded as central to civil society and the social order"; and (3) to "operate as institutions of social control . . . as surrogate parents" (p. 344). Noguera underscores how present-day students' experience of school can vary profoundly, depending on their socio-economic and racial status. Such variations can be observed in the approaches to school discipline used with students from diverse backgrounds. According to Noguera, in the differential education designed for students *not* tracked to become mangers, schools

> contribute to the marginalization of such students, often pushing them out of school altogether, while ignoring the issues that actually cause the problematic behaviour. Schools also punish the neediest children because in many schools there is a fixation with behaviour management and social control that outweighs and overrides all other priorities and goals.
>
> (p. 342)

Noguera's analysis begins to connect the dots between discipline practices in modern-day schools, teachers' surveillance of youthful behaviour, and the increased chances for involvement with the criminal justice system for students who refuse to conform to school norms and who subvert the official agenda of conformity, accountability, and control.

From Surveillance to Incarceration

As of 2002, the USA—which prides itself on serving as the alleged beacon of liberty for the free world—incarcerated 2.1 million members of its population, by far the highest rate of incarceration of any nation on the planet (Bohrman & Murakawa, 2005, p. 112). Families in poor urban communities—especially among African Americans and Latinos—bear the brunt of the spreading grip of the prison-industrial complex. Over the last two decades, observers of the "new penology" have documented the ideological "shift from rehabilitation and reform to incapacitation and mass warehousing of surplus populations" (Feeley & Simon, 1992; cited in Sudbury. J. [ed.], 2005, p. xvi). In our view, this represents the latest phase of Foucault's carceral culture. Others have noted with concern the unforgiving, punitive assault that specifically targets "dangerous" working class minority children (Lipman, 2003) as "public enemies" in need of containment (Meiners, 2007), positioning minority youth of colour particularly as what we refer to as "undesirables."

The origins of the governing elites' antipathy towards racialized undesirable populations have been articulated recently for teacher educators by Noguera (2003), who draws from the insights of sociologist Wacquant (2000). In Wacquant's analysis, lingering hostility towards undesirables can be traced to the quandary faced by ruling elites over the fate of African Americans once the institution of slavery ended. Wacquant has argued "that in the current period, the melding of ghetto and prison through various carceral strategies is the latest method devised for achieving these longstanding objectives" (p. 15), namely of creating and maintaining a pool of exploitable, cheap labour, on the one hand, and on the other, of curtailing growing demands for black inclusion in the rights and privileges of citizenship.

This history of ambivalence, if not outright hostility, towards a socially undesirable but economically useful population for American capitalism grounds our view that certain populations have come to be represented as threatening, and therefore in need of increasingly stringent degrees of social control. In the case of African Americans, once slavery was abolished and the economic justification for the presence of huge masses of Africans vanished, the problem for governing elites became what to do with (and how to manage) the surplus population. Based on his analysis of the status of African Americans, Wacquant argues that African Americans now occupy "the first prison society of history" (p. 121), which represents the fourth phase of the U.S. social order, following from the first phase of slavery (from 1619 to 1865, respectively the year of the first importation of Africans to the end of the Civil War), through the Jim Crow era of legal segregation (1865–1965), to the third phase of the urban hyperghettos (1914–1968).

Similarly Latinos, who, combined with African Americans, account for one-quarter of the U. S. population and more than three-quarters of incarcerated persons in American prisons, have experienced similar phases of repression throughout history. For example, inter-country relations in the western hemisphere have been characterized by American domination, including genocide, territorial encroachment, and colonization in Mexico and Puerto Rico (Acuña, 2000; Fernández, 1996). Moreover, there exists a historic legacy of rounding up and removing Latinos from the USA. One million Mexican Americans were deported during the 1930s, blamed in the American popular imagination for the misery of the Great Depression (Cockcroft, 1996; Durand, Massey, & Zenteno, 2001; Kanellos & Esteva-Fabregat, 1994). More recent manifestations of anti-Latino sentiment are evident in the proposal to construct an imposing two thousand mile wall (euphemistically referred to as a "fence") along the USA—Mexican border. The presence of military personnel and private militia along the American southern border ostensibly prevents admission or reentry for so-called "illegals" and others while restrictions at the northern border with Canada are significantly more lax. Importantly, containment—including the use of detention and incarceration—have always been used to control dominated communities labelled as undesirable, whether they are African American and Latino, or American Indians who were historically relegated to reservations, and Asian Americans, as evident in the case of the internment camps for Japanese Americans during the Second World War (Spring, 2004; Takaki, 1993; Zinn, 1995).

It is worth remembering, too, how education has historically played a prominent role in various responses to the social problem thus defined. While space constraints do not permit a detailed examination of the contentious history of schooling for African Americans and Latinos, suffice it to say that education has been championed as the liberator and equalizer for communities of colour, at the same time that it has been used as the mechanism for their assimilation and social control, depending in large measure on *who* controlled the schools set up for the descendants of slaves, colonized communities, and immigrants (Spring, 2004).

Moreover, we note that students and their families are not merely passive victims of processes of control done to them by others; dominated communities of colour have always attempted to resist, subvert, reform, and in some cases take over those processes and institutions which impact the conditions of their lives and their chances for survival (Spring, 2004). These counter-moves against social control reverberate in contemporary classrooms and, in our view, should also be taken up in teacher education programs if teachers are to address effectively the real lives of students; hence, our call for increased attention to issues of social justice in teacher education.

Confronting the School-To-Prison Pipeline

As teacher educators, we share with other educational researchers an interest in issues that link minority youth and schooling, such as gaps (i.e., in achievement and opportunity) and drop-out rates, sorting and "tracking" students by their perceived ability, and the over-representation in special education classes of youth from poor and dominated communities. Nevertheless, our view of youth has expanded to consider the fate of school drop-outs once they leave school, and even more importantly, what happens to them *during* their trajectories away from school participation while still in attendance or at least on the official school enrolment rosters.

In May 2003, the Civil Rights Project at Harvard University convened a conference for researchers and youth advocates on the School-to-Prison Pipeline (see Wald & Losen, 2003a). One finding from that conference indicated that "racial disparity in school discipline and achievement mirrors racially disproportionate minority confinement" in the larger society. Our interest as researchers in the school-to-prison pipeline arises from our drive to understand our own complicity, as teachers and teacher educators, in positioning certain students on previously unexamined trajectories. We are confronted with such questions as: What roles do we play, perhaps inadvertently, in the school-to-prison pipeline? How might we as teachers transform those roles to take up work that more actively counters negative student trajectories? What do teacher educators need to understand in order to cultivate an awareness of and commitment to interrupting pipeline dynamics among pre-service teachers? How can the field of teacher education advance counter-narratives that resist the criminalization of youth from dominated communities? How might we more clearly connect the stark parallels between the over-representation of students of colour in special education classes, school discipline cases, the child welfare system (e.g., in foster care and other out-of-home placements), juvenile justice cases that result in detention, and the ultimate confinement of imprisonment?

As Wald and Losen (2003b) have pointed out, the same punitive mentality that results in the over-representation of youth of colour who land in trouble at school extends to the juvenile justice system. African American youth are six times more likely to be confined than white youth for the same offence; Latino youth, more than three times (p. 10). Beginning in the 1990s, nearly all (i.e., forty-five of the fifty) American states passed laws to make it easier to try minors as adults. According to Wald and Losen, between 1983 and 1997, four out of five youth confined to detention or correctional facilities were minority youth (ibid.). In our view, the growing reliance on zero-tolerance approaches to discipline (i.e., no second chances for youth offenders) translates into diminishing adult understanding of and patience for the mistakes and unwise choices made by the young. The combination of the racism that sustains a view of certain segments of the populace as undesirable, combined with adult ageism towards youth in general coalesces in collective fears that target youth of colour in particular.

The 2005 report of the Children's Defence Fund on "Dismantling the Cradle to Prison Pipeline" identified three major risk indicators that set poor young Americans on the trajectory to incarceration: (1) early involvement in the child welfare system, (2) educational failure, and (3) involvement with the juvenile justice system (Murray, 2005). By linking the treatment of minority youth to recent concerns in the U.S. over increased efforts towards racial profiling (the practise of targeting visible minorities for scrutiny by police or security officials at airports), Meiners (2007) flags the complicity of schools in facilitating the transition of certain students into the school-to-prison pipeline:

> Clearly, the grotesque over-representation of youth of colour caught up in school discipline policies and in the category of special education illustrates that educators and educational institutions are not exempt from a kind of "racial profiling" endemic to our police systems. Rather, racialized surveillance *prefigures* the practices undertaken by police, customs, and other punitive institutions, and I argue that the establishment of these practices in schools functions to seemingly launch, for individuals caught in these punitive practices and for those who participate and observe, the processes of racial profiling.
>
> (p. 41)

Without question, schools play a significant role among an array of adult interventions into the dire circumstances facing youth in the USA. The contradiction is that such well-intentioned interventions too often exacerbate the problems faced by youth rather than provide solutions. For example, in their study of the intersections between high-poverty high American schools and the juvenile justice system, Balfanz, Spiridakis, Neild, and Legters (2003) documented ways in which youth-serving institutions frequently work at cross purposes. Ironically, in an era of cutbacks in social services for those most in need, rather than easing their transition to productive and responsible adulthood, "incarceration . . . has become America's social programme for troubled youths" (Murray, 2005).

The Role of Teacher Education in the School-To-Prison Pipeline

The links between schools and the prison-industrial complex are becoming increasingly clear. Thus far escaping the inquiry of many educational researchers is the role that teacher education plays in legitimating and reifying the school-to-prison pipeline. Although there are positive aspects of teacher education that do effectively prepare teachers to serve poor students and students of colour, there are three detrimental aspects that, from our perspective, contribute directly to the school-to-prison pipeline: the lack of student diversity in U.S. teacher education programmes; the over-emphasis on classroom management and control, particularly when it comes to urban youth of colour; and the superficial treatment of issues of diversity within American teacher education.

As the American school-aged population has become more racially, ethnically, and linguistically diverse, the population of pre-service teachers enrolled in traditional teacher preparation programmes has become increasingly monocultural and monolingual. Currently, 85% of all teacher candidates in the USA are white women, and the composition of teacher education programmes can best be characterized by an "overwhelming presence of whiteness" (Sleeter, 2001). Moreover, the majority of pre-service teachers comes from suburban communities and from middle or upper middle-class families (Chizhik, 2003). As a result, pre-service teachers are often disconnected from and unfamiliar with the sociocultural realities of the urban poor. We do not argue that white, middle-class, female identities are a problem per se. However, research suggests that many women in U.S. colleges enact and actively try to preserve identities as "good girls" (Galman, 2006; Holland & Eisenhart, 1992), which often revolve around conforming to traditional Western gender norms that maintain the status quo, as opposed to challenging injustice and oppression based on age, race, gender, or social class. Despite the highly politicized nature of schooling, American teacher education programmes have continued to primarily attract conformist "good girls." At the same time, they have created curricula and experiences that, for the most part, reinforce mainstream identities while failing to help students to develop more critical stances regarding education, particularly for populations that have been traditionally underserved by schools. Moreover, U.S. teacher education has done relatively little to help these pre-service candidates become more critical consumers of educational policies (i.e. high stakes testing or scripted "teacher-proof" curricula) that impact their work in classrooms. This is not to say that men or women of colour in teacher education programmes are necessarily more critical or make better teachers. Nor do we deny that everyone in the academy, regardless of background, has been socialized to perform racialised and gendered identities in ways that tend to reinforce unequal power relations. However, it is imperative that teacher education as a field addresses the intersections of race, gender and class, and how these are manifested and reproduced in schools of education. "Good" girls (and boys, too) in pre-service programmes need encouragement to interrogate conformity to dominant oppressive norms, and to understand, if not identify with, students often represented as "bad," that is, as dangerous, deviant, and undesirable.

Pre-service teachers often enter higher education with preconceived notions about poor students of colour; teacher education, for the most part, does little to change those limited perceptions. In fact, there is evidence to suggest that field experiences and coursework devoid of a systematic analysis of race and class may do more to reinforce stereotypes than to challenge them (Melnick & Zeichner 1995; Vavrus, 2002). Commenting on the influence of teacher education on pre-service teachers, Banks (2006) notes,

> Educational reform is impeded by the misconceptions and lack of knowledge about ethnic and racial groups that teachers learn in the wider society. Much of the popular knowledge that teachers acquire is either reinforced or is not challenged by the mainstream knowledge they acquire in their undergraduate university education and in teacher education programs. Educators often accept mainstream knowledge and resist other knowledge forms because it reinforces the social, economic, and political arrangements that they perceive as beneficial (C.E. Sleeter, personal communication, 2003). The assumptions and values that underlie mainstream academic knowledge are often unexamined in the school, college, and university curriculum.
>
> (p. 769)

When unchallenged, these dominant "good" identities allow teachers to continue to see themselves as the norm and construct student diversity as a problem (Achinstein & Barrett, 2004), thus resulting in the hyper-surveillance of poor, deviant students of colour that can lead to school exclusion, and, as data have demonstrated, set them on the pathway to prison.

A major emphasis within the literature regarding teacher education for diversity in the USA has been to prepare teachers to more effectively educate students of colour (Dilworth, 1992; Grant and Sleeter, 1999; Ladson-Billings, 1994; Vavrus, 2002). As teacher educators who lead courses that address issues of diversity, we (the authors) have struggled in our own work with the challenges posed by helping pre-service teachers who are often disconnected from, and unaware of, the socio-cultural realities of communities of colour, and who, at times, appear resistant to acknowledging the roles they play in perpetuating, let alone combating, oppression. Nevertheless, we have through our teaching and research encountered rare individuals, particularly white women, who perform their identities in ways that allow them to meaningfully connect with, learn from, and teach people of colour from dominated communities (see Raible & Irizarry, 2007).

At the same time, we advocate for teacher education programmes to more accurately mirror the demographic characteristics of American society at large and the school-aged population in particular. If the national cohort of pre-service teachers and teacher educators were to more accurately reflect U.S. society's demographics, approximately one in four individuals participating in teacher education programmes would be people of colour, and one in five would come from a home where a language other than English is spoken. While it is important to educate all pre-service teachers to develop the knowledge, skills, and dispositions to work effectively with students of colour, we believe that teacher education would be significantly enhanced if, paraphrasing the words of former U.S. Secretary of Education Richard Riley, "our teachers looked more like America" (Riley, 1998). That is, given the increasing diversity among public school students in the USA and the shortage of teachers of colour and multilingual teachers, it behoves our profession to pursue diversity within its ranks with a renewed sense of urgency and vigour.

The ability of teacher education to prepare educators to improve the school experiences and outcomes for students of colour is predicated partly on its ability to recruit and prepare a more diverse cadre of teachers. At the same time, it is imperative that we recruit individuals from a variety of backgrounds who have connections to individuals and communities of colour. We call for the recruitment of pre-service teachers who demonstrate a vested interest in restructuring schools so that they can become spaces where students and teachers engage in a process of liberation, as opposed to the reification of hegemony. Today's students need teachers—from all backgrounds—who understand the dire stakes involved in liberating communities from rigid domination and state control. We emphatically do not argue for only minority teachers for minority students. Instead, we call for teacher education programmes to better prepare *all* teachers to participate in community struggles for self-determination and survival, for family preservation rather than separation of families (for instance, through detention and foster care), in direct opposition to the prison-industrial complex by deliberately interrupting the school-to-prison pipeline.

Second, as a consequence of soaring teacher attrition rates in urban districts, city schools in the United States tend to have a disproportionately high percentage of novice teachers, and are more likely to feel the adverse impacts associated with the national teacher shortage (Howard, 2003; Ingersoll, 2001). Research conducted in the 1980s in the area of new teacher development posited that many novice teachers cited classroom discipline as their most pressing concern (Veenman, 1984). Approximately a quarter of a century later, novice teachers continue to cite classroom management as their greatest weakness (Wang, Odell, & Schwille, 2008). Recent literature suggests that teachers' struggles with classroom management may in fact be a result of problems with curriculum and pedagogy and the challenge to engage learners of diverse backgrounds (Feiman-Nemser, 2003). This perceived need to gain control of the classroom may be exacerbated by the presumption among many teachers in impoverished schools that urban contexts tend to be more violent, chaotic, and dangerous places in which to work.

Representations of communities of colour as inherently problematic are often reinforced in teacher education programmes through formal experiences, such as coursework and internships in actual classrooms. In our own work with pre-service teachers, we have become aware of instances where faculty and mentoring teachers have warned pre-service teachers of the potential dangers that may await them in urban schools. For example, on several occasions, students in our programmes have reported receiving negative messages from faculty prior to entering their urban field placement sites to "travel in groups," "leave by 3:00" and to "protect your belongings." Pre-service students may enter diverse settings with an array of unexamined stereotypes, for which they then seek—and often find—validation, failing to acknowledge the more hopeful counter-narratives that also exist in these settings. Thus, many field placement experiences may do more to reinforce stereotypes about racialised others than to improve teachers' ability to work in cross-cultural contexts (Sleeter, 2001).

We assert that the day to day struggles of teachers to effectively work with students of colour in urban settings are constrained under a framework that reflects an official discourse of accountability, and are further compromised by teachers' inabilities to reconcile egalitarian notions of schooling (e.g., schools as the great equalizer) with actual institutional structures that reflect a legacy of racism, classism, ageism, and other forms of oppression that impact their work. For example, many pre-service teachers articulate an intellectual appreciation and respect for diversity, yet still refer to members of diverse cultural groups as culturally deficient or inferior. Gaertner and Dovidio (1986) refer to this phenomenon as aversive racism. Quite simply, aversive racists firmly believe they do not discriminate against others on the basis of race while simultaneously unconsciously bearing feelings of uneasiness towards people of colour. Moreover, aversive racists often adopt ideologies that "justif[y] group inequalities [and] reinforce group hierarchy," thus "producing and justifying discriminatory behaviour" (p. 619). This is particularly troublesome because, since pre-service teachers may uncritically believe that the proverbial playing field is level, they may fail to implicate themselves in their own ineffectiveness in the classroom. Additionally, there may be no incentive for pre-service teachers to change their beliefs or practise without carefully guided and facilitated opportunities for critical reflection.

In sum, because comprehensive, anti-racist multicultural education is marginalized within teacher education programmes, often taking the form of an individual course that is disconnected from internship experiences, and because multicultural education is rarely infused throughout the curriculum (Vavrus, 2002), there is as yet untapped potential for teacher education programmes to do much more to transform teachers' ideologies and pedagogy in meaningful ways (Ladson-Billings, 1999). Too many teachers leave colleges of education ill-prepared to meet the challenges of successfully promoting the academic, linguistic, and personal growth of students from diverse backgrounds. Under-prepared teachers may in fact do more harm than good, particularly by adopting uncritically the roles and practise of surveillance and behaviour management that bolster the school-to-prison pipeline dynamic.

Tapping the Potential for a More Critical Teacher Education

As they are currently constructed, teacher education programmes do little to prepare teachers to respond to the educational crisis that results in the school-to-prison pipeline. The crisis, of course, is bigger than the pipeline. In fact, from a Foucauldian perspective as noted earlier, colleges of education often prepare teachers to become agents of state-sponsored youth surveillance and managers of deviant behaviour, which effectively shapes the educational experiences of students, especially poor students of colour, in ways that may serve to push them away from engagement with school. Nevertheless, we hold onto hope that schools can become sites of anti-racist resistance where critical pedagogy moves from rhetoric to practise, resulting in the establishment of multiracial and intergenerational coalitions for social justice based on genuinely caring relationships between teachers and students. Given the far-reaching influence that educators potentially can have on future generations, teacher education potentially has a significant role to play in this transformation of schooling. Key to activating this potential is a commitment to developing a more comprehensive analysis of the role of race, gender, and other differences within the field, and how these dynamics play out in the intersections between institutions such as education, law, child welfare, and the juvenile justice system.

Turning again to the work of Meiners (2007), whose insights illuminate the connections between race and gender in schools, we find support for our view concerning the twin tasks for teacher education. The first addresses the dwindling number of teachers of colour in the field, and the need to recruit pre-service students from the very communities from which urban public school students come. The second is developing a comprehensive approach to expanding the ranks of pre-service students currently predominating in the field (namely, white women), so that more teachers come to self-identify as allies in the struggle against racism, and make explicit connections between the work of teaching and ongoing community struggles for social justice.

Regarding the latter task, the multicultural education and racial identity development of white educators have been written about extensively in recent years. Nevertheless, the work of Meiners (2007) is once again pertinent to the present discussion. Meiners draws on the racial contract theory of philosopher Mills (1997) to suggest ways in which educators might interrogate race in order to develop clarity about their subjectivity as teachers who happen to be white:

> The racial contract constructs . . . an *epistemology of ignorance*, or a deliberate scaffolding to protect white folks from a material awareness of the flawed institutions, discourses, and laws created by white supremacy.
>
> (p. 95)

Meiners describes how the epistemology of ignorance results in what she calls white cognitive impairment that prevents whites "from knowing the effects of white supremacy they themselves have constructed" (p. 95). Exposing the links between race and gender, Meiners suggests that teacher education can also deconstruct its basic gendered construction, i.e., the "good girl" identities of many teachers. She argues that

> shifting the foundational idea of the concept of the teacher, drawing on other archetypes not the lady, and highlighting teachers and educators whose work, identity, and definitions of teaching radically expose the sexual and racial foundation in education, is one possibility. The field can take responsibility for initiating change to actively challenge the archetype that is currently shaping the profession, and to work to recruit new bodies into the profession.
>
> (p. 53)

Our interest in the multicultural identity development of pre-service teachers reflects one of the field's primary aims, namely to prepare educators to work effectively in 21st century classrooms. The population of students in the USA has become increasingly more diverse in the past few decades. More than 40% of children enrolled in K-12 schools are students of colour, and one in every 5 students comes from a home where a language other than English is spoken (National Centre for Education Statistics, 2007). It is therefore crucial for pre-service teachers to become aware of issues of diversity *before* they enter their multicultural classrooms. For example, addressing the disparities in disciplinary actions taken against students of colour, Banks et al. (2005) maintain that teacher education must help pre-service teachers grapple with the inequities they will inevitably face in schools:

> If we are to create schools where all students have opportunities to learn, teachers must know how to be alert for these kinds of disparities and aware of how to provide classroom environments that are both physically and psychologically safe for all students.
>
> (p. 242)

Again, teacher education programmes must facilitate the development of critical consciousness, with particular regard to multicultural issues such as race, gender, and class among pre-service teachers.

As American society has grown more diverse, the impact of the school-to-prison pipeline has become far-reaching, if not staggering. Between 1980 and 2000, the national inmate population quadrupled, while more than 700 new prisons were built (Bureau of Justice Statistics, 2004). The link between schools and prisons becomes more pronounced upon examination of data regarding the educational attainment of current inmates. Approximately three-quarters of state prison inmates, 60 percent of federal inmates, and almost seven out of every ten inmates in jail have not completed high school (Alliance for Excellent Education, 2006). While it would be inaccurate to assume that all high school drop-outs will commit crimes, it is fair to conclude that, of the people who receive convictions and serve time in prison, the overwhelming majority will not have received an adequate education. Many observers have noted a direct correlation between educational failure and participation in the penal system. As such, with the alarmingly high drop-out rates among students of colour, it is no surprise that there are now more than three African Americans in jail for everyone in college (U.S. Census Bureau, 2007). The ratio for Latinos is similarly high, at 2.7:1, while the rate for white students is, not surprisingly, inverted, with more than three white Americans in college for everyone serving time in prison (U.S. Census Bureau, 2007).

Conclusion

As critical teacher educators working in the United States context, we aim to encourage more pre-service students to effectively connect with, and forge bonds of solidarity with, poor students of colour in order to counter the dynamics that result in widespread school failure, which, as we have argued, too often results in incarceration. An explicitly anti-racist orientation among teachers can be cultivated through the transracialisation of teacher identities (Raible & Irizarry, 2007). Transracialisation may enhance the multicultural development of individual teacher identities. Yet it is important to bear in mind that transracialisation only occurs when close relationships between individuals of different races enables genuine relationships of caring to unfold over time (Raible, 2005).

The related development of what Banks et al. (2005) refer to as socio-cultural consciousness can also facilitate closer connections between teachers and students from diverse backgrounds. Teachers who develop socio-cultural consciousness understand that the life-experiences of students (and teachers) can profoundly influence their worldviews, which are understood as anything but universal. Banks and his colleagues argue further that teachers not stop merely at greater awareness, but take responsibility for working actively as agents of change within schools:

> Teachers need to be aware of how the formal and informal systems of the school operate to construct opportunity and how to participate in school-level change processes that call attention to organisational needs and help develop a supportive culture school-wide.
>
> (p. 255)

We remain hopeful about the potential for genuine intercultural connectedness to emerge when teachers demonstrate care and respect for students and their lives and concerns beyond the walls of the classroom. We bear in mind the implications of a recent study that found school connectedness, "defined as a student's feeling part of and cared for at school," to be linked with lower levels of substance use, violence, suicide attempts, pregnancy, and emotional distress among young people (cited in Wald & Losen, 2003a, p. 12). We view such connectedness as crucial for success in education, and we seek to help pre-service teachers to value connectedness, and to cultivate strategies that foster mutually enriching teacher-student bonds.

We invite teachers, both pre-service and in the field, along with other teacher educators, to rethink their connections to (or disconnections from) urban poor students and their communities. Teachers can be encouraged to meet students on their own turf, and to see them as partners in the educative process, rather than as passive recipients of charity and good intentions. It is simply too easy for educators to fall in step uncritically with the ideologies and social practices that feed into the school-to-prison pipeline. For this reason, critical consciousness about our personal roles in larger institutional structures becomes vital to the ongoing struggle for social justice and democracy. In light of persistent racism and its effects in schools during the present era of accountability, our work focuses on how we collectively (i.e., educators, youth, and their families) might effectively develop cross-cultural, intergenerational, anti-racist alliances, in schools, and within and between communities. This, we have come to believe, is absolutely necessary in order to turn present nightmares into more hopeful futures.

Although it has been estimated that African American boys today have a one in three chance of going to jail before they attain thirty years of age, we refuse to abandon these and other minority youth to such a pessimistic foregone conclusion. Given the dire implications of the "cradle-to-prison pipeline" (Edelman, 2007) of which the school phase is but one (although hardly insignificant) link, we anticipate that more and more educators and families will of necessity find ways to work together to counter this dangerous trend. If schools are to become sites of transformational resistance, teacher education can and must insist on personal introspection and critical analysis as key elements of effective programmes. Moreover, teachers must learn to redirect their gaze from the hyper-surveillance of poor students of colour that results in viewing them problematically, and begin to see the ways in which institutional structures can either facilitate their oppression or support their liberation.

References

Achinstein, B., & Barrett, A. (2004). (Re)Framing classroom contexts: how new teachers and mentors view diverse learners and the challenges of practice. *Teachers College Record, 106*(4), 716–746.

Acuña, R. (2000). *Occupied America: A history of Chicanos* (4th ed.). New York: Harper & Row.

Alliance for Excellent Education. (2006). *Saving futures, saving dollars: The impact of education on crime reduction and earnings.* Washington, DC: Alliance for Excellent Education.

Australian Bureau of Statistics (2009). *Prisoners in Australia 2009.* Report. June 30, 2009. Canberra, Australia.

Balfanz, R., Spiridakis, K., Neild, R. C., & Legters, N. (2003). High poverty secondary schools and the juvenile justice system: how neither helps the other and how that could change. *New Directions for Youth Development, 99,* 71–89.

Banks, J., Cochran-Smith, M., Moll, L., Richert, A., Zeichner, K., LePage, P., et al. (2005). Teaching diverse learners. In L. Darling-Hammond, L., & J. Bransford (Eds.), *Preparing teachers for a changing world: What teachers should learn and be able to do* (pp. 232–274). San Francisco: Jossey-Bass.

Banks, J. (2006). Researching race, culture and difference: epistemological challenges and possibilities. In J. L. Green, G. Camili, & P. B. Elmore (Eds.), *Handbook of complementary methods in education research* (pp. 786–789). Mahwah, NJ: Lawrence Erlbaum Associates.

Bohrman, R., & Murakawa, N. (2005). Remaking big government: Immigration and crime control in the United States. In J. Sudbury (Ed.), *Global lockdown: Race, gender, and the prison-industrial complex* (pp. 112). New York: Routledge.

Brown, T. M. (2007). Lost and turned out: Academic, social and emotional experiences of students excluded from school. *Urban Education, 42*(5), 432–455.

Bureau of Justice Statistics. (2004). *Bureau of justice statistics, prisoners in 2003.* Washington, DC: Paige M. Harrison & Allen J. Beck.

Chizhik, E. W. (2003). Reflecting on the challenges of preparing suburban teachers for urban schools. *Education and Urban Society, 35*(4), 443–461.

Cockcroft, J. (1996). *Latinos in the making of the United States: The hispanic experience in the Americas.* New York: Franklin Watts.

Dilworth, M. E. (Ed.). (1992). *Diversity in teacher education: New expectations.* San Francisco: Jossey-Bass.

Durand, J., Massey, D. S., & Zenteno, R. M. (2001). Mexican immigration to the United States: continuities and changes. *Latin American Research Review, 36*(1), 107–127.

Edelman, M. W. (2007). The cradle to prison pipeline: an American health crisis. *Preventing Chronic Disease, July, 4*(3), A43, Published online June 15, 2007.

Feeley, M., & Simon, J. (1992). The new penology: notes on the emerging strategy of corrections and its implications. *Criminology, 30*(4). Cited in J. Sudbury (Ed.) (2005), *Global lockdown: Race, gender, and the prison–industrial complex.* New York: Routledge, p. xvi.

Feiman-Nemser, S. (2003). What new teachers need to learn. *Educational Leadership, 60*(8), 25–30.

Fernández, R. (1996). *The disenchanted island: Puerto Rico and the United States in the twentieth century.* Westport, Connecticut: Praeger.

Foucault, M. (1975). On the role of prisons. Interview by Roger-Pol Droit. http://www.nytimes.com/books/00/12/17/specials/foucault-prisons.html. Accessed 07.02.08, p. 26.

Foucault, M. (1977). *Discipline and punish: The birth of the prison.* New York: Vintage.

Gaertner, S. L., & Dovidio, J. F. (1986). The aversive form of racism. In J. F. Dovidio, & S. L. Gaertner (Eds.), *Prejudice, discrimination, and racism* (pp. 61–89). Orlando, FL: Academic Press.

Galman, S. (2006). "Rich white girls": developing critical identities in teacher education and novice teaching settings. *International Journal of Learning, 13*(3), 47–55.

Giroux, H. (2000). Postmodern education and disposable youth. In P. P. Trifonas (Ed.), *Revolutionary pedagogies: Cultural politics, instituting education, and the discourse of theory* (pp. 174–195). New York: Routledge.

Grant, C. A., & Sleeter, C. E. (1999). *Making choices for multicultural education: five approaches to race, class, and gender.* New York: Merrill.

Holland, D., & Eisenhart, M. (1992). *Educated in romance: Women, achievement and college culture.* Chicago, IL: University of Chicago Press.

Howard, T. (2003). Who receives the short end of the shortage? Implications of the U.S. teacher shortage on urban schools. *Journal of Curriculum and Supervision, 18*(2), 142–160.

Ingersoll, R. M. (2001). Teacher turnover and teacher shortages: an organizational analysis. *American Educational Research Journal, 38*(3), 499–534.

Kanellos, N., & Esteva-Fabregat, C. (Eds.). (1994). *Handbook of hispanic cultures in the United States.* Houston, Texas: Arte Publico Press and Madrid, Spain: Instituto de Cooperacion Iberoamericana.

Ladson-Billings, G. (1994). Who will teach our children? Preparing teachers to successfully teach African American students. In E. Hollins, J. King, & W. C. Hayman (Eds.), *Teaching diverse populations: Formulating a knowledge base* (pp. 129–142). Albany: State University of New York Press.

Ladson-Billings, G. (1999). Preparing teachers for diverse student populations: a critical race theory perspective. *Review of Research in Education, 24*(21), 211–247.

Landry, L., & Sinha, M. (2008). Adult correctional services in Canada, 2005/2006. *Statistics Canada – Catalogue, 28*(6), 1–26.

Lipman, P. (2003). Cracking down: Chicago school policy and the regulation of black and Latino youth. In K. Saltman, & D. Gabbard (Eds.), *Education as enforcement: The militarization and corporatization of schools* (pp. 81–101). New York: Routledge Falmer.

Meiners, E. (2007). *Right to be hostile: Schools, prisons, and the making of public enemies.* New York: Routledge.

Melnick, S. L., & Zeichner, K. M. (1995). *Teacher education for cultural diversity: Enhancing the capacity of teacher education institutions to address diversity issues.* 116 Erickson Hall, Michigan State University, East Lansing, MI 48824-1034: National Center for Research on Teacher Learning.

Mills, C. (1997). *The racial contract.* Ithaca, NY: Cornell University Press.

Murray, M. (2005). *The cradle to prison pipeline crisis.* Poverty and Race Research Action Council. http://wwwprrac.org/full_textphp?text_id=1043&item_id=9518&newsletter_id=82&header=Education. Accessed 18.12.07.

National Center for Education Statistics. (2003). Suspension and expulsions of public elementary and secondary school students, by state, sex and percent of enrollment: 2000. http://nces.ed.gov/programs/digest/d03/tables/dt147.asp. Retrieved 10.03.08.

National Center for Education Statistics. (2007). *The condition of education, 2007.* Washington, DC: U.S. Department of Education.

Noguera, P. (Autumn 2003). Schools, prisons, and social implications of punishment: Rethinking disciplinary practices. *Theory Into Practice, 42*(4).

Raible, J. (2005) *Sharing the spotlight: The non-adopted siblings of transracial adoptees.* Doctoral thesis, University of Massachusetts, Amherst.

Raible, J., & Irizarry, J. G. (2007). Transracialized selves and the emergence of post-white teacher identities. *Race, Ethnicity and Education, 10*(2), 177–198.

Riley, R. W. (1998). Our teachers should be excellent, and they should look like America. *Education and Urban Society, 31*(1), 18–29.

Sleeter, C. (2007). Vice President's invited address: equity, democracy and neoliberal assaults on teacher education. In: *Paper presented at American Educational Research Association Conference, Chicago, IL.*

Sleeter, C. E. (2001). Preparing teachers for culturally diverse schools: research and the overwhelming presence of whiteness. *Journal of Teacher Education, 52*(2), 94–106.

Spring, J. (2004). *Deculturalization and the struggle for equality: A brief history of the education of dominated cultures in the United States.* New York: McGraw-Hill.

Takaki, R. (1993). *A different mirror: A history of multiculturalism in America.* Boston, MA: Little, Brown.

U.S. Census Bureau (2007). Press release. Census bureau releases new data on residents of adult correctional facilities, nursing homes and other group quarters: Annual data also paint diverse portrait of nation's race, ethnic and ancestry groups. September 27, 2007.

Vavrus, M. (2002). *Transforming the multicultural education of teachers.* New York: Teachers College Press.

Veenman, S. (1984). The perceived problems of beginning teachers. *Review of Educational Research, 19*(3), 143–178.

Wacquant, L. (2000). Deadly symbiosis: when ghetto and prison meet and mesh. *Punishment and Society, 3*(1), 95–134.

Wang, J., Odell, S., & Schwille, S. (2008). Effects of teacher induction on beginning teachers' teaching: a critical review of the literature. *Journal of Teacher Education, 59*(2), 132–152.

Wald, J., & Losen, D. (Eds.). (Fall 2003a). Deconstructing the school-to-prison pipeline. *New Directions in Youth Development: Theory, Practice, Research, 99.*

Wald, J., & Losen, D. (Fall 2003b). Defining and redirecting the school-to-prison pipeline. *New Directions for Youth Development: Theory, Practice, Research, 99.*

Zinn, H. (1995). *A people's history of the United States 1492–present.* New York: Harper Perennial.

25

Teaching (with) Disability: Pedagogies of Lived Experience

Robert C. Anderson

"If a fish were an anthropologist, the last thing it would discover would be water." This saying, widely attributed to Margaret Mead, illuminates the irony of cultural conditioning. In teaching about disability, the first step means becoming aware of one's own body—and the bodies of others in the room. The body is everywhere in social life, texts, and public discourse. We just have trouble seeing it, because we are so immersed in our own skin.

Serious consideration of disability in the major social theories is a relatively new development. Feminism, critical race, and queer studies have rigorously grappled with issues of embodiment and social justice. These perspectives greatly enhance pedagogy and learning. However, the embodied experience of disability has not been a traditional topic for pedagogy and praxis. People with disabilities still fight for a place at the table in academe.

The disability perspective promises new insights for critical pedagogy. Disability is not just another specialty with concerns loosely related to other minorities. The experience of disability is relevant to all marginalized groups—*for all groups have people with disabilities in them.* The persistent irony is that the experiences of people with disabilities have been noticeably absent from critical discourse *within* these groups. Indeed, people with disabilities are the world's largest multicultural minority. This essay presents a means for considering disability in educational practice, and identifies points of discovery for future critical research. Specifically, it considers the intersections of experience and pedagogy that professors with disabilities bring to the classroom.

Disability as Pedagogy, Story and Lived Experience

Narrating with Stories, Interrogating with Experience

Nineteen percent of the U.S. population has a disability. Worldwide, this figure tops 500 million people (World Health Organization, 1999). With all the bodies in academe, one wonders why more of them aren't people with disabilities. Teachers with disabilities are particularly under-represented (only 3.6%, according to the U.S. Department of Education, 2004). For those of us in education, this issue is indeed relevant: most of us will experience disability at some time—if only through the aging process. Chances are high that any teacher or faculty member will become impaired in some way if one teaches long enough.

Pedagogy is about knowing and performing what you know. Reflexive pedagogy considers what one knows, how one performs it, and its implications for others. Pedagogy is also shaped by our life experiences. Teachers with disabilities offer knowledge through their bodies and experiences that isn't usually part of the curriculum. Disabled teachers embody pedagogies of justice, interdependence, and respect for differences. Teaching (with) disability reveals spaces in education that often get silenced. Who decides which stories are worth being told?

Experiencing Disability, Teaching Justice

The 2004 case of a Chicago professor has implications for all who teach, since disability may occur at any time in the life cycle—particularly for teachers with high workloads. Jacqueline Haas, a chemistry professor at Kennedy-King College, experienced a brain aneurysm in 1989 that diminished her mobility, vision, and muscular strength. However, she remained able to fulfill all of her teaching and university responsibilities. Haas returned to work and resumed those duties, receiving high commendations from her department chair and exemplary course evaluations from students for her teaching. However, she had to work much longer hours to prepare for classes, meetings, and particularly the extensive requirements of her tenure project. The university refused her accommodation requests as too expensive and unreasonable.

Lack of accommodations left Haas in a precarious situation, one she found both demeaning and inconsiderate—even though the college abided by its own policies. Haas decided to provide her own power wheelchair, an expensive purchase that she kept in her office building. At times, Haas still had to drag herself upstairs "because of a frequently inoperative elevator" to reach her office and classrooms. She also had to "urinate in a basket inside the chemistry storeroom because there was no restroom on the floor where she taught" (Goldman 2004).

Implications

Haas' case illustrates the complexities faced by teachers with disabilities. Their lives and stories help create a robust learning environment. Professors such as Dr. Haas encounter not only policies but attitudes alongside the daily lived realities of their impairments. Granted, schools are ramping up their policies and practices on disability. But ramps are not enough. I speak not only of bricks and mortar but also of relationships, stories of experience, even theory. Academe has limited experience in teaching disability, and teachers *with* disabilities are noticeably absent on campuses. People with disabilities call structures into question both with their bodies and their voices. Disabled bodies disrupt 'normal' educational settings: enter guide dogs, sign language interpreters, and motorized wheelchairs. Teaching strategies must be examined. How may these 'bodies of possibility' interrogate and transform educational spaces?

Disabled Bodies, Identity Politics and the Learning Environment

"PEOPLE WITH DISABILITIES: THEY ARE YOU." By offering this personalized observation, Davis (2002, 1) locates the human experience of disability as an embodied and universal one. Insights for pedagogy emerge when we consider disability as a valuable source of lived experiences, rather than see disabled bodies as 'something to be accommodated.' When disabled and nondisabled people engage each other, these experiences have the capacity to transform the educational environment.

There is a garish beauty about the body. The body is always speaking—telling us to eat, to make love, to breathe, to defecate. We enjoy the body's appealing features, listen to its language, and benefit emotionally from the companionship of other bodies—for then we are not alone. Under "ordinary" circumstances, we downplay the body. Still, the body remains the primary site for lived experience. Everything that is learned must pass through one of its senses, and interacting with the world requires the body's mediation. We are keenly dependent on our embodiment, yet we do not always bring that awareness to the foreground—particularly in the classroom. People with disabilities are almost always foregrounded by their bodies in some form or fashion. hooks reminded educators that "once we start talking in the classroom about the body and about how we live in our bodies, we're automatically challenging the way power has orchestrated itself in that particular institutionalized space" (1994, 136–137).

Theoretical Tensions about Disability, Impairment and Difference

hooks' observation illustrates how disability challenges us to reconsider embodiment in academic theories and classroom spaces. Contemporary theories often characterize embodiment as the performance of social meanings.[1] By deconstructing those meanings, social theories expose the oppressive force of (ab)normalization. However, disability and impairment pose theoretical dilemmas that have not been fully addressed in contemporary theory. For example, social theorists often cite Judith Butler's work, but disability scholars seldom employed her work until 1999 (Samuels 2002). This is perhaps because Butler's notion of performativity[2] does not translate well in terms of impairment. One may perform "disability" socially through encounters with disabling structures. However, one does not perform the experience of impairment in quite the same way as gender, sexuality or race. We may deconstruct how society stigmatizes those of us who are blind or have quadriplegia, yet we will still not see or walk.

Disability scholars express concern about "approaches to cultural construction of 'the body' that . . . deny or ignore bodily experience in favor of fascination with bodily representations" (Wendell 1996, 44). Disability Studies emerged as scholars noted how critical race and gender studies did not consider the human experience of disability. If a group's stories aren't told, they don't really have a place in that learning community. Justice-minded learning communities also need to interact with people as these stories are told. Despite being the largest multicultural minority in the world, "one would never know this to be the case by looking at the literature on minorities" (Davis 1997, 1). Disability studies is a relatively new discipline, yet (like people with disabilities) has only recently been recognized as a lens to interrogate social practices.

Difference Reframed

Some scholars reconceptualize difference to question how people with disabilities are oppressed (Erevelles 2005). Reconceptualizing difference exposes how *power* harnesses culture to shape the way people see themselves and each other. For example, the children of oil barons and peanut farmers perceive their lives differently, yet one is not inherently better or worse than the other. Re-imagining difference does not remove impairments, but resists how society disables people who have them. Paraphrasing Stuart Hall's comments on race and ethnicity, the end of disablement in society requires that we reconceive the way we do politics and education (Hall 1992).

Difference springs from what is considered "normal" in a given culture. Laws such as the Americans with Disabilities Act are no exception: legal definitions of disability are based on the medical model. Medicine classifies disabilities based on the diagnosis of defects. Yet difference and defect are not synonymous. To re-frame difference in relation to disability, Garland-Thomson suggested:

> As a category of analysis, disability provides fresh ways of thinking about the complexity of embodied identity . . . . Seldom do we see disability presented as an integral part of one's embodiment, character, life, and way of relating to the world. Even less often do we see disability presented as part of the spectrum of human variation, the particularization of individual bodies.
> (2005, 1559/1568)

Garland-Thomson identifies the concept of human variation as one of feminist disability studies' "most fully developed critical strategies" (1567). Interpreting impairment as *human variation* allows consideration in theories where the disabled body has been forced to enter through the back door. When people with impairments resist "disablement," they create new expressions of their embodied differences (McRuer 2004, 51). Differences shape one's identity and personal experiences but society need not cast them as disabling. These implications are relevant to all educators—not just those with disabilities—because "of all the ways of becoming 'other' in our society, disability is the only one that can happen to anyone, in an instant, transforming that person's life and identity" (King 1993, 75).

Disability in the Classroom: Pedagogy and Shared Learning

> Does a disabled body harbor a particular and valuable pedagogy? Are professors merely 'talking heads,' or do our bodies speak as well, and, if so, what do they say in the classroom, and how are they heard?
> —Rod Michalko, " 'I've Got a Blind Prof': The Place of Blindness in the Academy"

> Teaching was always what I had done best. Being disabled was always what I had done—not best, but just done.
> —Brenda Brueggemann, "An Enabling Pedagogy"

The experiences of faculty with disabilities are vital for critically interrogating educational practice. In this section, I relate disability to the shared experience of teaching and learning. Shared learning is a collaboration between people, where all are learners and teachers alike. Each person impacts and is impacted by the others. Shared learning creates an environment where students learn how to accommodate and appreciate each other's differences. This has promising implications for people with disabilities. Shared learning transforms the multiple demands of student diversity into an asset "by capitalizing on the multiple, socio-cultural perspectives that can be experienced when students from diverse backgrounds are placed in heterogeneously-formed cooperative learning groups" (Cuseo 1996, 24). Bresler (2004) called this phenomenon "embodied teaching and learning." Personal encounters engage the minds and bodies of people in the classroom.

In *The Teacher's Body,* Freedman and Holmes note the link between pedagogy, bodies, and learning. They described the "unexpected teaching opportunities" that emerge when we "discard the fiction that the teacher has no body":

> Bodies dominate the room and seem to justify its existence . . . . When students think the teacher's body is clearly marked by ethnicity, race, disability, size, gender, sexuality, illness, age, pregnancy, class, linguistic and geographic origins . . . both the mode and content of education can change.
> (2003, 7)

The authors address several levels of engagement with "the body." First, teacher and students engage each other around culturally defined meanings and values about difference. These differences have histories surrounded by forces of power (Foucault 1980). Second, these differences refer to, but are not fully separate from, the fleshly bodies that people inhabit. Where disability and impairment are concerned, both of these levels are at play:

> We are dis-abled. We live with particular social and physical struggles that are partly consequences of the conditions of our bodies and partly consequences of the structures and expectations of our societies, but they are struggles which only people with bodies like ours experience.
> (Wendell 1996, 117)

Teachers with disabilities have occasion to study disability and pedagogy together. The experience of disability has a generative impact on shared teaching and learning. That is, dynamic encounters shape what happens in the classroom. These encounters may happen when the professor's impairment is obvious or when one chooses to self-disclose. Such opportunities reinforce interdependence between disabled and non-disabled learners.

"Body" refers to several surfaces of encounter that impact what happens in the classroom, each with different meanings. Van Manen (1990) suggested that pedagogy fosters meaning-making by connecting doing and being. Richard Radtke, an oceanographer who is paralyzed from the neck down, shared the personal and social aspects of his life as a teacher: "although I cannot move, there are many ways I can teach using my body . . . . We used my body as one of our teaching tools" in trips to ocean destinations and The Great Wall of China (2003, 91). These influences have an enabling impact on those who teach and learn:

> But here, in the blind leading the blind, lies a powerful enabling metaphor. Disability can create knowledge, open doors wider, build ramps to awareness that we all essentially have in us anyway. This happens when any *body* leads anybody.
> (Brueggemann 2001, 800)

Most of what happens in the classroom is traditionally associated with the intellect. Some hold that "erotics" is part of what energizes teaching and learning: passion to learn and engage others in learning. Peters (2004) contends that bodies and minds arouse (awaken) each other. As the number of teachers with disabilities increases, education will benefit from the wisdom imparted by their historically "disqualified knowledges" (Foucault 1980, 82).

Whether one is disabled or nondisabled, introducing one's body into the classroom requires a deepened level of reflexivity. This journey negotiates personal and vulnerable spaces. The teacher with a body marked as different (disabled, gay, pregnant) is keenly aware of embodiment in the classroom. Unlocking these moments creates "the potential for an intensely ethical classroom encounter" (Freedman and Holmes 2003, 12). Negotiating these spaces offers opportunities for dialogue that have been seldom explored in traditional pedagogies. People with disabilities challenge our notions of what a classroom should look and feel like:

> It might look different because some of the people envisioned would be operating wheelchairs, or wearing diapers, or using computers to communicate, or getting nourishment through feeding tubes. It might feel different because it could entail listening to people who use digitized voice, or communicating with someone through an interpreter, or walking more leisurely down the street to keep pace with companions whose gait is slow, or reconsidering the flow of lesson plans to accommodate students who process information differently.
>
> (Gabel 2002, 187)

The concerns of many teachers and faculty members with disabilities are remarkably aligned with those of critical pedagogy.

Disability and Critical Pedagogy

"Critical pedagogy" refers to a constellation of educational theories, teaching, and learning practices that raise critical consciousness about oppressive social conditions. Critical pedagogy aims to reconfigure the "traditional" teacher-student relationship. Rather than the teacher being a vessel that pours out knowledge, students and teachers alike learn by sharing experiences through meaningful dialogue. Critical pedagogy emerged from the work of Paulo Freire, Henry Giroux, Peter McLaren, and Michael Apple. Feminist, critical race, postcolonial, and queer studies have extended reflexive teaching practices even further. However, there has been limited consideration of disability in critical pedagogy. This omission is puzzling given critical pedagogy's commitment to disrupt oppressive practices in the classroom and society at large.

The place to remedy these concerns begins in educational spaces. Classrooms are unique places to explore how meanings, bodies, and histories converge. For example, Brueggemann "made *Abilities in America* the title of an otherwise subjectless freshman composition course . . . because I think we can read race, class, sexuality, and a whole host of other American-as-apple-pie cultural-academic concerns through the lens of disability" (2002, 326). Erevelles (2005) encourages her students to share their experiences of disability, race, gender, and sexuality. Unspoken attitudes about difference are aired and addressed. Teachers can also help nondisabled students find points of connection with disabled peers without slipping into pity responses. These approaches help students to understand how campus practices impact the lives of people with disabilities. People are then better able to relate with disabled peers.

Pedagogical encounters also provide a space for questioning how society transforms an impairment into a disability (Davis 2002). For example, *what is it that disability policies actually address?* Students may consider the politics, ethics, and implications of how disability is regulated on their campus. They learn to question policies that affect their disabled classmates or teachers. This approach transforms students into reflexive practitioners. They learn that creative leaders think in action, not from the page, and certainly not from the status quo.

Many teachers with disabilities ride the intersections of theory and practice because they "live with critical pedagogy while acknowledging the dilemmas and constraints of the material world" (Gabel 2002, 196). They have the opportunity to create ethical learning spaces charged with a critical consciousness of disability. Teachers with disabilities engage the *political* by living with inaccessible buildings, attitudes, and policies. Colliding with these structures impacts personal experience: the self confronts social disablement *with* one's impairment. Teachers with disabilities live out a highly personal and embodied politics of resistance while serving as a guide to students in the classroom.

Incorporating embodied pedagogies for the classroom should be done with careful and intentional consideration. This mode of pedagogy reflects a degree of personal authenticity that promotes deepening levels of trust and exploration among the learners. Entering this ethical space often requires that the teacher "set the stage" for a period of time before leading classroom discussions in this direction.

Exposure to disability inquiry and culture broadens a school's capacity for inclusion. In effect, all participants (students, faculty, and staff) have opportunities for more enhanced learning experiences—about the world, people with disabilities, and themselves. Infusing disability education into the curriculum is a process that creates content learning with contextual applications. It creates affective awareness of human experience beyond content.

Bodies of Possibility: Toward an Enabling Pedagogical Environment

"How do we make the historically invisible, visible?" Ann Firor Scott asks this question in her exposition of why people "see some things and not others" (1984, 19). She noted the wisdom of critiquing social and educational practices, particularly if the experiences of certain people are being overlooked. Her observations are well suited for educators who express genuine interest to introduce enabling pedagogies into the classroom. Brueggemann frames these ethical spaces:

> Standing in front of a new class, each and every time, I feel the burden of representation. Somewhere in the briefing over course policies, the obligatory run through the syllabus, the remarks on key texts and assignments, and the stumble over reading a roster of names I might struggle to pronounce . . . somewhere in there I need to tell them that I'm Deaf. . . . At this point, they are definitely paying attention now.
>
> (2001, 318–319)

Brueggemann further illustrates the intersections of experience and pedagogy that professors with disabilities bring to the classroom. She infuses critical insight about disability into the curriculum environment. Students and teacher alike encounter disability not as an abstract issue but as a living document. In Deweyan terms, learners encounter places to learn and care about others. People make an "organic connection between education and experience" (1939, p. 12).

Transforming Classrooms: The "Third Space"

"Third space" describes a pedagogical environment for dialogue that may not be equal for all, but it gives teachers and students a means to grapple with concepts not studied elsewhere. *Third space* is a term borrowed from postcolonial studies. Bhabha describes this space as one where "we will find those words with which we can speak of Ourselves and Others" (1988, 209). Conversations about disability connect to other marginalized spaces on campuses. The perspectives of teachers with disabilities speak to issues that surround the concerns of people "categorized" as queer, raced, gendered, and Other. This space was not even imaginable for these groups until the last few decades. Dialogue in the classroom is incomplete without meaningful engagement between diverse cultural groups. This engagement needs to occur in every corner of the educational environment. To enable these learning spaces, Wilson and Lewiecki-Wilson suggest:

> A third-space classroom is thus admittedly a political contestation and a remaking of subjectivity, but it must preserve a process that is dynamic and open, encouraging the transformation of knowledge including those of the teacher and the academy as well as those of the students.
> (2002, 306)

Where should educational content about disability appear in the curriculum? Garland-Thomson argued that "it should be an integrated part of all the courses we design, just as many of us have begun to consider race, gender, and class issues as fundamental aspects of all disciplines and subject of inquiry" (1995, 16). In this sense, disability is presented (and hopefully understood) as a common human experience. Nondisabled educators may engage disability issues more actively by including a "negotiated curriculum" in their courses. From a list of topics, the class can choose readings about embodiment and disability during the semester. This exercise can be done with any course. Including topics about disability offers new possibilities to learn and explore the body as a site of knowledge and wisdom.

Teachers with disabilities offer talents and contributions like other scholars. With increasing numbers of disabled students, there will likely be future increases in the number of educators with disabilities as those students seek teaching positions. This cohort effect will make its own impact on policies and classrooms alike. Colleges and universities are wise to proactively hire faculty with disabilities and build campus access into their long range plans, rather than waiting for this cohort effect to emerge.

Conclusion

The disabled human body is one of the last "body frontiers" to be addressed in education. This reality is quite paradoxical since "disabled people are everywhere and nowhere at the same time" (Stuart 2000, 169). Disabled bodies disrupt educational environments. This disruption is perceived as a threat, and finances are often cited. More disruption is needed (this said with the most optimistic and hopeful of intentions). More stories must be told by people with disabilities *inside* pedagogical spaces. Teachers with disabilities offer "bodies of possibility" that interrogate and transform the spaces of academe.

Notes

1. Post-structural theory influences how a number of social critical theories now treat embodiment. Judith Butler's work on the performance of social roles has made a particular impact on how 'the body' is perceived in social theory.
2. Performativity is Butler's way of describing how social identities and roles are performed.

References

Bhabha, Homi. (1988). The Commitment to Theory. *New Formations,* 5(Summer), 5–23.

Bresler, Liora. (2004). *Knowing Bodies, Moving Minds: Towards Embodied Teaching and Learning.* Dordrecht, The Netherlands: Kluwer Academic Publications.

Brueggemann, Brenda Jo. (2001). An Enabling Pedagogy: Meditations on Writing and Disability. *Journal of Advanced Composition,* 21(Fall), 791–820.

———. (2002). An Enabling Pedagogy. In S. L. Snyder, B. J. Brueggemann, & R. Garland-Thomson (Eds.), *Disability Studies: Enabling the Humanities.* New York: The Modern Language Association of America.

Cuseo, Joseph B. (1996). *Cooperative Learning: A Pedagogy for Addressing Contemporary Challenges and Critical Issues in Higher Education.* Stillwater, OK: New Forums Press.

Davis, Lennard J. (ed.) (1997). *The Disability Studies Reader.* New York: Routledge.

———. (2002). *Bending Over Backwards: Disability, Dismodernism, and Other Difficult Positions.* New York: New York University Press.

Dewey, J. F. (1939). *Experience and Education.* New York: The Macmillan Company.

Erevelles, Nirmala. (2005). Rewriting Critical Pedagogy from the Periphery: Materiality, Disability and the Politics of Schooling. In S. Gabel. (Ed.), *Disability Studies in Education: Readings in Theory and Method.* New York: Peter Lang.

Foucault, Michel. (1980). *Power/knowledge: Selected Interviews and Other Writings, 1972–1977.* Trans. C. Gordon, L. Marshall, J. Mepham, & K. Soper. 1972. Reprint, New York: Pantheon.

Freedman, Diane P. and Holmes, Martha S. (2003). *The Teacher's Body: Embodiment, Authority, and Identity in the Academy.* Albany, NY: State University of New York Press.

Gabel, Susan. (2002). Some Conceptual Problems with Critical Pedagogy. *Curriculum Inquiry, 32,* 177–201.

Garland-Thomson, Rosemarie. (1995). Integrating Disability Studies into the Existing Curriculum: The Example of "Women and Literature" at Howard University. *Radical Teacher, 47*(October), 15–21.

———. (2005). Feminist Disability Studies. *Signs: The Journal of Women in Culture and Society, 30,* 1557–1587.

Goldman, C. D. (2004). Colleges Can Provide Equality in Tenure Programs. *Section 504 Compliance Handbook 312* (November), 5–6. Washington, DC: Thompson Publishing Group.

Hall, Stuart. (1992). New Ethnicities. In J. Donald & A. Rattansi (Eds.), *Race, Culture and Difference.* Thousand Oaks, CA: Sage Publications.

hooks, bell. (1994). *Teaching to Transgress: Education as the Practice of Freedom.* New York: Routledge Press.

King, Ynestra. (1993). The Other Body. *Ms, 3,* 72–75.

McRuer, Robert. (2004). Composing Bodies; or, De-Composition: Queer Theory, Disability Studies, and Alternative Corporealities. *Journal of Advanced Composition, 24,* 47–78.

Michalko, Rod. (2003). "I've Got a Blind Prof": The Place of Blindness in the Academy. In D. Freedman & M. S. Holmes (Eds.), *The Teacher's Body: Embodiment, Authority, and Identity in the Academy.* Albany, NY: State University of New York Press.

Peters, Michael. (2004). Education and the Philosophy of the Body: Bodies of Knowledge and Knowledges of the Body. In L. Bresler (Ed.), *Knowing Bodies, Moving Minds: Towards Embodied Teaching and Learning.* Dordrecht, The Netherlands: Kluwer Academic Publications.

Radtke, Richard with James Skouge. (2003). My Body, Myself: A Quadriplegic's Perception of and Approach to Teaching. In D. Freedman & M. S. Holmes (Eds.), *The Teacher's Body: Embodiment, Authority, and Identity in the Academy.* New York: State University of New York Press.

Samuels, Ellen. (2002). Critical Divides: Judith Butler's Body Theory and the Question of Disability. *National Women's Studies Association Journal, 14,* 58–76.

Scott, Ann Firor. (1984). On Seeing and Not Seeing: A Case of Historical Invisibility. *The Journal of American History, 71*(June), 7–21.

Stuart, Elizabeth. (2000). Disruptive Bodies: Disability, Embodiment and Sexuality. In L. Isherwood (Ed.), *The Good News of the Body: Sexual Theology and Feminism* New York: New York University Press.

United States Department of Education. 2004, October. *National Survey of Postsecondary Faculty (NSOPF), 1999.* National Center for Education Statistics. (NCES Report Nos. 2002-151 and 2001-01). Project Officer: Zimbler, L. J. Washington, DC: Author.

Van Manen, M. (1990). *Researching Lived Experience: Human Science for an Action Sensitive Pedagogy.* New York: State University of New York Press.

Wendell, Susan. (1996). *The Rejected Body: Feminist Reflections on Disability.* New York: Routledge.

Wilson, James C. and Cynthia Lewiecki-Wilson. (2002). Constructing a Third Space: Disability Studies, the Teaching of English, and Institutional Transformation. In S. L. Snyder, B. J. Brueggemann, & R. Garland-Thomson (Eds.), *Disability Studies: Enabling the Humanities* New York: The Modern Language Association of America.

World Health Organization. (1999). *World Health Report 1999.* (NLM # WA 540.1). Geneva, Switzerland: Author.

Suggested Readings for Future Study

Acosta, C. (2007). "Developing Critical Consciousness: Resistance Literature in a Raza Studies Classroom." *English Journal*, 97(2), 36–42.
Ainsa, P. (2011). "Critical Pedagogy towards a Sociomoral Classroom." *Journal of Instructional Psychology*, *38*(2), 84–92.
Akbari, R. (2008). "Transforming Lives: Introducing Critical Pedagogy into ELT Classrooms." *ELT Journal*, *62*(3), 276–283.
Alvarez, Z., Calvete, M., and Sarasa, M. C. (2012). "Integrating Critical Pedagogy Theory and Practice: Classroom Experiences in Argentinean EFL Teacher Education." *Journal for Educators, Teachers and Trainers*, *3*, 60–70.
Alverman, D. E., Moon, J. S., and Hagwood, M. C. (1999). *Popular Culture in the Classroom: Teaching and Researching Critical Media Literacy*. Newark, DE: International Reading Association.
Anyon, J. (1981). "Social Class and School Knowledge." *Curriculum Inquiry*, *11*(1), 3–42.
Apple, M. W. (1993). *Official Knowledge: Democratic Education in a Conservative Age*. New York: Routledge.
Apple, M. and Christian-Smith, L. K., eds. (1991). *The Politics of the Textbook*. New York: Routledge.
Arriaza, G. (2003). "Schools, Social Capital and Children of Color." *Race, Ethnicity and Education*, *6*(1), 71–93.
Artiles, A. J. and Trent, S. C. (1994). "Overrepresentation of Minority Students in Special Education: A Continuing Debate." *The Journal of Special Education*, *27*(4), 410–437.
Baker, C. (2006). *Foundations of Bilingual Education and Bilingualism*. Buffalo, NY: Multilingual Matters.
Bartolomé, L. (1998). *The Misteaching of Academic Discourses: The Politics of Language in the Classroom*. Boulder, CO: Westview Press.
Bartolomé, L. (2003). "Beyond the Methods Fetish: Toward a Humanizing Pedagogy." In Darder, A., Baltodano, M., and Torres, R. (eds.), *The Critical Pedagogy Reader*. New York: RoutledgeFalmer.
Batini, F., Mayo, P. and Surian, A. (2014). *Lorenzo Milani, the School of Barbiana and the Struggle for Social Justice*. Frankfurt, Vienna, New York: Peter Lang.
Baynton, D. (2001). "Disability and the Justification of Inequality in American History." In Longmore, P. and Umansky, L. (eds.), *The New Disability History: American Perspectives* (pp. 33–57). New York: New York University Press.
Berliner, D. C. and Biddle, B. J. (1995). *The Manufactured Crisis: Myths, Fraud, and the Attack on America's Public Schools*. Cambridge, MA: Perseus Books.
Beyer, L. and Apple, M. (1998). *The Curriculum: Problems, Politics and Possibilities*. Albany, NY: SUNY Press.
Borg, C. and Mayo, P. (2006). *Learning and Social Difference. Challenges for Public Education and Critical Pedagogy*. Boulder, CO: Paradigm.
Bourdieu, P. and Passeron, J. C. (1977). *Reproduction in Education, Society, and Culture*. Beverly Hills, CA: Sage.
Bowles, S. and Gintis, H. (1976). *Schooling in Capitalist America*. New York: Basic Books.
Buhler, S., Settee, P., and Styvendale, N. V. (2014). "Teaching and Learning about Justice through Wahkohtowin." *Annual Review of Interdisciplinary Justice*, *4*, 182–210.
Chomsky, N. and Robichaud, A. (2014). "Standardized Testing as an Assault on Humanism and Critical Thinking in Education." *Radical Pedagogy*, *11*, 3.
Comer, J. P. (2004). *Leave No Child Behind*. New Haven, CT: Yale University Press.
Connolly, B. (2013). "Theorising Creative Critical Pedagogy: The Art of Politicized Agency." *Rizoma freireano*, *14*, 1–15.
Cummins, J. (1983). "Bilingualism and Special Education: Program and Pedagogical Issues." *Learning Disabilities Quarterly*, *6*, 373–386.
D'Ambrosio, U. (1999). "Literacy, Matheracy, and Technocracy: A Trivium for Today." *Mathematical Thinking and Learning*, *1*(2), 131–153.
Dance, L. J. (2002). *Tough Fronts: The Impact of Street Culture on Schooling*. New York: Routledge.
Darder, A. (2011). *A Dissident Voice: Essays on Culture, Pedagogy, and Power*. New York: Peter Lang.

Davis, L. J. (1995). *Enforcing Normalcy: Disability, Deafness and the Body*. London: Verso.

Davis, L. J. (1997). *The Disability Studies Reader*. New York: Routledge.

De Alba, A. (1999). "Curriculum and Society: Rethinking the Link." *International Review of Education, 45*(5/6), 479–490.

Dewey, J. (1916). *Democracy and Education: An Introduction to the Philosophy of Education*. New York: Macmillan.

Ditchburn, G. M. (2012). "The Australian Curriculum: Finding the Hidden Narrative?" *Critical Studies in Education, 53*(3), 347–360.

Duncan-Andrade, J. and Morrell, E. (2008). *The Art of Critical Pedagogy: Possibilities for Moving from Theory to Practice in Urban Schools*. New York: Peter Lang.

Erevelles, N. (2000). "Educating Unruly Bodies: Critical Pedagogy, Disability Studies, and the Politics of Schooling." *Educational Theory, 50*(1), 25–47.

Espinoza-Herold, M. (2003). *Issues in Latino Education: Race, School, Culture and the Politics of Academic Success*. Boston: Pearson Education Group.

Fine, M. (1991). *Framing Dropouts: Notes on the Politics of an Urban Public High School*. Albany, NY: SUNY.

FitzSimmons, R. and Uusiautti, S. (2013). "Critical Revolutionary Pedagogy Spiced by Pedagogical Love." *Journal for Critical Education Policy Studies, 11*(3), 230–243.

Flecha, R. (2000). *Sharing Words—Theory and Practice of Dialogic Learning*. Lanham, MD: Rowman & Littlefield.

Foster, M. (1997). *Black Teachers on Teaching*. New York: New Press.

Gabel, S., ed. (2005). *Disability Studies in Education: Readings in Theory and Method*. New York: Peter Lang.

Gleeson, B. (1999). *Geographies of Disability*. London and New York: Routledge.

Guilherme, M. (2006). "Is There a Role for Critical Pedagogy in Language/Culture Studies? An Interview with Henry A. Giroux." *Language and Intercultural Communication, 6*(2), 163–175.

Gutierrez, F. and Prado, C. (1999). *Ecopedagogia e Cidadania Planetaria* (*Ecopedagogy and Planetary Citizenship*). São Paulo, Brazil: Cortez.

Gutstein, E. (2003). "Teaching and Learning Mathematics for Social Justice in an Urban, Latino School." *Journal for Research in Mathematics Education, 34*(1), 37–73.

Gutstein, E. (2006). *Reading and Writing the World with Mathematics: Toward a Pedagogy for Social Justice*. New York: Routledge.

Hall, H. R. (2015). "Food for Thought: Using Critical Pedagogy in Mentoring African American Adolescent Males." *Black Scholar, 45*(3), 39–53.

Hinchey, P. (2004). *Becoming a Critical Educator: Defining a Classroom Identity, Designing a Critical Pedagogy*. New York: P. Lang.

Irvine, J. J. (1990). *Black Students and School Failure: Policies, Practices, and Prescriptions*. New York: Praeger.

Katz, L. (2014). "Teachers' Reflections on Critical Pedagogy in the Classroom." *InterActions: UCLA Journal of Education and Information Studies, 10*(2), 1–19.

Kaufmann, J. J. (2010). "The Practice of Dialogue in Critical Pedagogy." *Adult Education Quarterly, 60*(5), 456–476.

Kozol, J. (1991). *Savage Inequalities: Children in America's Schools*. New York: Crown.

Leistyna, P., Woodrum, A., and Sherblom, S. A., eds. (1996). *Breaking Free: The Transformative Power of Critical Pedagogy*. Cambridge, MA: Harvard Education Press.

McInerney, P. (2009). "Toward a Critical Pedagogy of Engagement for Alienated Youth: Insights from Freire and School-Based Research." *Critical Studies in Education, 50*, 23–35.

McInerney, P., Smyth, J., and Down, B. (2011). "'Coming to a Place Near You?' The Politics and Possibilities of a Critical Pedagogy of Place-Based Education." *Asia-Pacific Journal of Teacher Education, 39*(1), 3–16.

McKinney, C. (2005). "A Balancing Act: Ethical Dilemmas of Democratic Teaching within Critical Pedagogy." *Educational Action Research, 13*(3), 375–391.

McLaren, P. (1989). *Life in Schools: An Introduction to Critical Pedagogy in the Foundations of Education*. New York: Longman.

MacLeod, J. (1995). *Ain't No Makin' it: Aspirations and Attainment in a Low-Income Neighborhood*. Boulder, CO: Westview.

McNeil, L. (2009). "Standardization, Defensive Teaching, and the Problems of Control." In Darder, A., Baltodano, M., and Torres, R. (eds.), *The Critical Pedagogy Reader* (2nd ed.) (pp. 384–396). New York: Routledge.

Moschkovich, J. "A Situated and Sociocultural Perspective on Bilingual Mathematics Learners." *Mathematical Thinking and Learning* 4(2–3), 189–212.

Oakes, J. (1985). *Keeping Track: How Schools Structure Inequality*. New Haven, CT: Yale University Press.

Olsen, L. (1997). *Made in America: Immigrant Students in Our Public Schools*. New York: The New Press.

Perry, T., Steele, C., and Hilliard, A. G. (2003). *Young, Gifted and Black: Promoting High Achievement among African-American Students*. Boston: Beacon Press.

Portelli, J. P (1993). "Exposing the Hidden Curriculum." *The Journal of Curriculum Studies, 25*(4), 343–358.

Rodriguez, A. (2014). "A Critical Pedagogy for STEM Education." In Bencze, L. and Alsop, S. (eds.), *Activist Science and Technology Education* (pp. 55–66). New York: Springer.

Ryoo, J. J., Crawford, J., Moreno, D., and McLaren, P. (2009). "Critical Spiritual Pedagogy: Reclaiming Humanity through a Pedagogy of Integrity, Community, and Love." *Power and Education, 1*(1), 132–146.

Sarroub, L. K. and Quadros, S. (2015). "Critical Pedagogy in Classroom Discourse." In Bigelow, M. and Ennser-Kananen, J. (eds.), *Handbook of Educational Linguistics* (pp. 252–260). New York: Routledge.

Schneider, S. (2006). "Freedom Schooling: Stokely Carmichael and Critical Rhetorical. Education." *College Composition and Communication, 58*(1), 46–69.

Seltzer-Kelly, D. (2009). "Adventures in Critical Pedagogy: A Lesson in US History." *Teacher Education Quarterly*, (Winter), 149–162.

Skrtic, T., ed. (1995). *Disability and Democracy: Reconstructing [Special] Education for Postmodernity.* New York: Teachers College Press.

Stinson, D., Bidwell, C., and Powell, G. (2012). "Critical Pedagogy and Teaching Mathematics for Social Justice." *International Journal of Critical Pedagogy*, *4*(1), 76–94.

Stovall, D. (2006). "We Can Relate: Hip-Hop Culture, Critical Pedagogy, and the Secondary Classroom." *Urban Education*, *41*(6), 585–602.

Sultana, R. G. (1995). "A Uniting Europe, a Dividing Education? Eurocentrism and the Curriculum." *International Studies in Sociology of Education*, *5*(2), 115–144.

Sultana, R. G., ed. (1997). *Inside/Outside Schools: Towards a Critical Sociology of Education in Malta.* San Gwann, Malta: PEG Publications.

Ware, L. (2001). "Writing, Identity, and the Other: Dare We Do Disability Studies?" *Journal of Teacher Education, 52*(2), 107–123.

Part Seven

Critical Pedagogy and Teacher Education

Introduction to Part Seven

Schools are one of the primary social institutions at work in the reproduction of social inequalities, while simultaneously portraying a humanist vision of their redemptive and transformative power. In light of the impact of schools on students' lives and futures, critical pedagogy identifies teacher education as one of the key ideological state apparatuses implicated in the production and transmission of capitalist values and the hegemonic procurement of consent. Teacher education is also the space in which classroom educators are socialized and initiated into pedagogical attitudes and practices that support the power asymmetries of the larger society.

The struggle for social justice and school transformation, then, must engage the politics of teacher education as a primary site of contestation, in the forging of a school culture that functions in the interest of disenfranchised populations. As such, much of the work within teacher education entails the struggle over the meaning and practice of democracy. More specifically, this includes the role of teachers as ideological agents at the service of a corporatized world, or as transformative intellectuals committed to a liberatory ethos of schooling. The notion of teachers as intellectuals with its focus on teaching and its democratically inspired possibilities has been at the forefront of proposals posited by progressive educators in the last century.

In concert with this tradition, critical pedagogy proposes a new arrangement of power relations in teacher preparation, to facilitate the formation of teachers as cultural workers preoccupied with the formation of critical citizenship and civic engagement. In contrast to the guiding neoliberal vision of schools as engines for the global economy, critical pedagogy proposes an emancipatory formation of teachers—one that socializes teachers through a language of critique and possibility, through which they can begin to sidestep the transmission of hegemonic values. This speaks to a teacher education project grounded upon liberatory ideals and teacher preparation as an important form of "cultural politics," where issues of power, economics, history, culture, language, and pedagogy are all employed to both confront and transform historical oppressions associated with public schooling in America.

Summary of Articles

Through a poetic disruption and analysis, Maxine Greene in "Teaching as Possibility: A Light in Dark Times" tackles the daunting conditions that the schooling system produces in an effort to kindle the light of the teacher's imagination to push against impossibility and toward believing what should be or might be possible. By so doing, teaching as possibility under dark times is a call for an emancipatory and empowering process in which teachers encourage youth to name, reflect, imagine, and act. Moreover, Greene points out that even though the light may be uncertain and flickering at times, teachers as intellectuals possess the capacity through their lives and work to make their light shine, in all sorts of conditions.

Joe Kincheloe uncovers the contempt for teacher education and pedagogy in "The Knowledges of Teacher Education: Developing a Critical Complex Epistemology." He examines the complexities of the pedagogical process and the intricacies of teacher education through the conceptualization of a critical complex teacher education. In a climate where teacher education is subject to reform efforts and possible destruction, Kincheloe makes the case for the empowerment of teachers, teacher educators, and teacher education students as scholars, researchers, and intellectuals. Through an understanding of multiple epistemologies, he reveals that a critical complex teacher education involves recognizing various types of knowledges of education such as experiential, empirical, normative, critical, ontological, and reflective-synthetic domains. Kincheloe argues that teachers as researchers can bring together these various educational knowledges with research, which in turn serves to empower and unveil the unjust structures of hegemonic schooling. It also challenges teachers to overcome positivist tendencies that devalue and discredit their integrity as intellectuals capable of pedagogical rigor.

Employing Paulo Freire's concept of radical love, Ty-Ron Douglas and Christine Nganga in "What's Radical Love Got to Do With It: Navigating Identity, Pedagogy, and Positionality in Pre-Service Education," draw upon their experiences teaching pre-service teachers to explore how they have enacted radical love in the classroom. As international scholars of color, the authors situate themselves and their multiple, complex identities within the sphere of their work as teacher educators. Both authors provide intimate accounts of their efforts to engage their *teaching as an act of love* not in the sentimental, affectionate sense, but rather in the profound, Freirean sense. They reveal that as a critical pedagogical approach, embedding radical love into teaching constitutes an act of courage, a commitment to dialogue, and an embrace of the various and complex epistemologies that both students and teachers hold based on their lived experiences.

In "Power, Politics, and Critical Race Pedagogy: A Critical Race Analysis of Black Male Teachers' Pedagogy," Marvin Lynn and Michael E. Jennings examine the development of critical pedagogy and the scholarship on Black teachers through a detailed analysis and critique of the discourse that informs these two realms. The authors chart the scholarship on Black teachers through the lenses of Black feminism/womanism and critical race theory/pedagogy. Their engagement with the under-theorization of teaching by African American male teachers provides valuable contributions, particularly with respect to developing and practicing critical pedagogical awareness with students suffering under violent conditions. As the authors argue, moreover, that an understanding and recognition of historical and contemporary African American philosophers and teachers is vital to theorizing pedagogies of resistance.

Questions for Reflection and Dialogue

1. Identify the hidden discourse of teacher preparation programs, centered on accountability schemes, testing, standardization, and teacher-proof curricula.
2. How does teaching as possibility impact your understanding of teacher education and the potential role of critical pedagogy, in the preparation of future teachers?

3. What roles does an understanding of epistemologies play in teacher education?
4. What does the concept of radical love represent for teacher education? How might teachers enact radical love in the classroom given their context and positionality?
5. Describe the links between critical pedagogy and the scholarship on Black teachers. What implications does this have for teacher education and the schooling of culturally diverse students?
6. What role might teacher education play in supporting the practice of democracy?

26

Teaching as Possibility: A Light in Dark Times

Maxine Greene

Borrowing from a bitter poem by Bertolt Brecht, Hannah Arendt entitled a book of essays, *Men in Dark Times* (1968). The poem, "To Posterity," she explained, spoke of the horrors taking place in the early days of Nazi rule in Germany and of the absence of outrage. Things were covered up, she wrote, by "highly efficient talk and double talk;" and she stressed how important it always is to have a space in which light can be shed on what is happening and what is being said. Granted, our times may not be marked by the kinds of monstrosities associated with the Nazis; but dark times are no rarity, even in American history. In the darkest moments, she wrote, we still "have the right to expect some illumination . . . and such illumination may well come less from theories and concepts than from the uncertain, flickering, and often weak light that some men and women, in their lives and their works, will kindle under all circumstances . . ." (p. ix). I view our times as shadowed by violations and erosions taking place around us: the harm being done to children; the eating away of social support systems; the "savage inequalities" in our schools; the spread of violence; the intergroup hatreds; the power of media; the undermining of arts in the lives of the young. And then I think of the "light that some men and women will kindle under almost all circumstances," and that makes me ponder (and sometimes wonder at) the work that is and might be done by teachers at this problematic moment in our history.

There is doubt, unquestionably, within and outside the schools; and there is dread. The poet Adrienne Rich has written some remarkable poetry about the different kinds of dread experienced by different people. When asked how, in the face of this, she could maintain such an affirmative attitude, she said, "If poetry is forced by the conditions in which it is created to speak of dread and of bitter, bitter conditions, by its very nature, poetry speaks to something different. That's why poetry can bring together those parts of us which exist in dread and those which have the surviving sense of a possible happiness, collectivity, community, a loss of isolation" (Moyers, 1995, p. 342).

Arendt and Rich, each in her distinctive voice, are speaking of the capacity of human beings to reach beyond themselves to what they believe should be, might be in some space they bring into being among and between themselves. The two remind us (by speaking of an uncertain light and of something different) of what it signifies to imagine not what is necessarily probable or predictable, but what may be conceived as possible. All of those who have parented children or taught the young may resonate to this on some level, particularly when they recall the diverse, often unexpected shapes of children's growing and becoming. Many may find a truth in Emily Dickinson's saying that "The Possible's slow fuse is lit/ By the Imagination" (1960, pp. 688–689). Imagination, after all, allows people to think of things as if they could be otherwise; it is the capacity that allows a looking through the windows of the actual towards alternative realities.

It is obvious enough that arguments for the values and possibilities of teaching acts (no matter how enlightened) within the presently existing system cannot be expressed through poetry, even as it is clear that the notion of "teaching as possibility" cannot simply be asserted and left to do persuasive work. The contexts have to be held in mind, as does what strikes many of us as a backward leaning, inhumane tendency in our society today. For all the apparent resurgence of Deweyan progressive thinking in the school renewal movement, parent bodies and community representatives in many places are explicitly at odds with what they believe is being proposed. They respond more readily to the media-sustained talk of standards and technology than they do to the idea of multiple patterns of being and knowing, to a regard for cultural differences, to an attentiveness when it comes to voices never listened to before.

Teachers who are consciously and reflectively choosing themselves as participants in school renewal are being challenged to clarify their beliefs and (more and more often) to defend their practices. If the discourse they are developing can be infused with the kinds of metaphor that reorient ordinary common-sense thinking, if they can break through more often what John Dewey called "the crust of conventionalized and routine consciousness" (1954, p. 183) when attention is turned to the school, neighborhood or district discussions may be moved beyond the customary and the self-regarding. If the fears and suffering of local people, some of them feeling themselves to be ignorant and powerless, can be taken into account, what Paulo Freire called a "pedagogy of hope" might even take form (1995), and dialogue of a different sort might take the place of the language of prescription or complaint or demand. If teachers can begin to think of themselves as among those able to kindle the light Arendt described or among those willing to confront the dread and keep alive the sense of "a possible happiness," they might find themselves revisioning their life projects, existing proactively in the world.

Paying heed to the repetitive drumbeat of current concerns—for professional development, standard-setting, authentic assessment, an enriched knowledge base, technological expertise, teachers cannot but occasionally ask themselves "to what end?". There are, of course, the official announcements and prescriptions. There are presumably obvious "goods" linked to each statement of an educational goal. Most often, we realize, the benefits of reform are linked to the nation's welfare, or to market expansion, or to technological dominance in a competitive world. Suppose, however, we were to summon up an articulation of purpose suggested by Rich's "possible happiness, collectivity, community, a loss of isolation." The words imply a reaching out for individual fulfillment among others, in (perhaps) the kind of community in the making John Dewey called democracy. They are, to a degree, abstract, metaphorical; but, speaking indirectly as they do, they respond to some of the evident lacks in our society, to the spaces where people feel solitary and abandoned, to domains of felt powerlessness.

If our purposes were to be framed in such a fashion, they would not exclude the multiple-literacies and the diverse modes of understanding young persons need if they are to act knowledgeably and reflectively within the frameworks of their lived lives. Situatedness; vantage point; the construction of meanings: all can and must be held in mind if teachers are to treat their students with regard, if they are to release them to learn how to learn. Their questions will differ, as their perspectives will differ, along with their memories and their dreams. But if teachers cannot enable them to resist the humdrum, the routine, or what

Dewey called the "anesthetic" (1931, p. 40), they will be in danger of miseducative behavior, ending in cul-de-sacs rather than in openings. If situations cannot be created that enable the young to deal with feelings of being manipulated by outside forces, there will be far too little sense of agency among them. Without a sense of agency, young people are unlikely to pose significant questions, the existentially rooted questions in which learning begins. Indeed, it is difficult to picture learner-centered classrooms if students' lived situations are not brought alive, if dread and desire are not both given play. There is too much of a temptation otherwise to concentrate on training rather than teaching, to focus on skills for the work place rather than any "possible happiness" or any real consciousness of self. Drawn to comply, to march in more or less contented lockstep (sneakered, baseball capped, T-shirted), familiar with the same media-derived referents, many youngsters will tacitly agree to enter a community of the competent, to live lives according to "what is." There are, of course, young persons in the inner cities, the ones lashed by "savage inequalities" (Kozol, 1993), the ones whose very schools are made sick by the social problems the young bring in from without (O'Connor, 1996). Here, more frequently than not, are the real tests of "teaching as possibility" in the face of what looks like an impossible social reality at a time when few adults seem to care. There are examples, in Mike Rose's work on "possible lives," for instance, where he expresses his belief that "a defining characteristic of good teaching is a tendency to push on the existing order of things" (1995, p. 428).

In Toni Morrison's *The Bluest Eye,* the child Claudia is explaining her hatred of Shirley Temple dolls, to her the very exemplars of a world of objects, a world in which people yearn for possessions, above all, including white china dolls for Black children. "I did not know why I destroyed those dolls," writes Claudia. "But I did know that nobody ever asked me what I wanted for Christmas. Had any adult with the power to fulfill my desires taken me seriously and asked me what I wanted, they would have known that I did not want anything to own, or to possess any object. I wanted rather to feel something on Christmas day. The real question would have been, 'Dear Claudia, what experience would you like on Christmas?' I could have spoken up, 'I want to sit on the low stool in Big Mama's kitchen with my lap full of lilacs and listen to Big Papa play his violin for me alone.' The lowness of the stool made for my body, the security and warmth of Big Mama's kitchen, the smell of the lilacs, the sound of the music, and, since it would be good to have all of my senses engaged, the taste of a peach, perhaps, afterward" (1972, p. 21). This cannot be attributed to teaching; but it is a "push on the existing order of things"; and it may hold clues to what good teaching can be. Claudia is cared for harshly by her mother; but she is confident of her concern and of her love. She is, at least at that young age, able to resist the existing order of consumable and ownable things and to tap into some deeper need for what she calls "experience." Perhaps this cannot be taught but Claudia's seems to be an insight that underlies the insistences of the culture, that has to do with being sensually alive and within a loving world.

This is not a purely fictional phenomenon. Too many teachers, by now, have read their students' journals and stories and poems; they have exposed themselves to many kinds of dread and many kinds of desire. Much of the suffering, much of the deprivation is due, quite obviously, to economic and social injustices; but there is a sense in which imagination and desire can feed the recognition of the need to transform and, perhaps, the passion to change. To have that sense is to be able to listen to what Wallace Stevens calls "the man with the blue guitar" who "does not play things as they are" (1964, p. 165). Imagination alters the vision of the way things are; it opens spaces in experience where projects can be devised, the kinds of projects that may bring things closer to what ought to be. Without such a capacity, even young people may resemble the inhabitants of the town of Oran Albert Camus described at the start of *The Plague,* "where everyone is bored and devotes himself to cultivating habits." The point is made that you can get through the day without trouble once you have formed habits. In some other places, the narrator says, "People have now and then an inkling of something different" (1948, p. 4). They have had an intimation, and that is so much to the good. He did not necessarily mean an intimation of the end of the plague and a return to normal life. He meant, perhaps, an intimation of mortality, of injustice that has to be struggled against, of silences that have to be acknowledged and at once overcome.

For us, that may imply a recognition, not solely of the human condition, but of the contradictions in what we think of as a democratic society. Even to think about bringing about significant changes within the school is to contest on many levels the behaviorist, stratifying tendencies that still mark the culture as it impinges on the school. To encourage the young to develop visions of what might be and then, against those visions recognize how much is lacking and what it may be to strike against all sorts of easy platitudes that obscure the turmoil of change. Most of us realize that, only when we envisage a better social order, do we find the present one in many ways unendurable and stir ourselves to repair. The sight and description of the new schools at the present time—the Coalition schools, the Charter schools, the New Vision Schools—make it uniquely possible to identify what is wrong with the traditional schools. All we need to do is to take heed of what can happen when a junior high school girl, caught in an overcrowded city school, visits one of the new theme schools. Abruptly, she may notice what is lacking in her own school: a brightly decorated classroom, small groups and family circles, a breaking through of the forty-five minute class period. Without witnessing a better state of things, she could not have realized what was lacking, what was wrong.

Sometimes, introduced to a reflective or a learning community, someone will become aware of the dearth of understanding in her/his own domain, of the blocks to knowing and to questioning. Sometimes, a teacher or a relative or a friend may pay heed, as does the singer Shug Avery in *The Color Purple* (Walker, 1982). She suggests to Miss Celie a way of being without "that old white man" in her head, actually a way of becoming free. Celie writes: "Trying to chase that old white man out of my head. I been so busy thinking bout him I never truly notice nothing God make. Not a blade of corn (how it do that?) not the color purple (where it come from?) Not the little wild flowers. Nothing." (p. 25). She, too, made aware of alternatives, can discover that "she feels like a fool" because of what she was never enabled to notice and about which she had never asked.

Inklings and intimations, of course, are not sufficient, as the townspeople in Oran discovered when they organized sanitary squads to fight the plague, "since they knew it was the only thing to do" (p. 120). Imagination is what imparts a conscious quality to experience and the realization that things do not repeat themselves, that experience should not be expected to be uniform or frictionless. Imagination, moreover, is enriched and stimulated through live encounters with others, through exposure to diverse vantage points and unfamiliar ways of looking at the world. Imagination should not, however, as Dewey warned, be permitted to run loose so that it merely builds "castles in the air" and lets "them be a substitute for an actual achievement which involves the pains of thought" (1916, p. 404). Yes, there are distinctive moments made possible by the poetic imagination; but the social and ethical imagination is concerned for using ideas and aspirations to reorganize the environment or the lived situation.

Paulo Freire had this in mind when he wrote about the shaping of a critical discourse that showed adult learners "the lovelier world to which they aspired was being announced, somehow anticipated, in their imagination. It was not a matter of idealism. Imagination and conjecture about a different world than the one of oppression are as necessary to the praxis of historical 'subjects' (agents in the process of transforming reality as it necessarily belongs to human toil that the worker or artisan first have in his or her head a design a 'conjecture,' of what he or she is about to make" (1994, p. 39). Freire believes that democratic education requires enabling ordinary people to develop their own language, derived from their readings of their own social realities, their own namings, their own anticipations of a better state of things. We might return to the present use of story-telling, especially contextualized story-telling, by means of which young people explore the influences of social life on their becoming, of race and gender and ethnic membership, of traditions, of the stories told to them.

Dialogue can arise from story telling in a shared classroom space; and out of dialogue and conjecture can come the making of projects also shared. They may be as simple and concrete as polling the neighborhood mothers on immunization of their babies, as rehabilitating rooms somewhere for homeless classmates, as volunteering for a tutoring program, as organizing street dances or a marching band. There is considerable talk these days of how fair societies may be nurtured in families, schools, work places, and congregations. Modern democracies, says Michael Sandel (1996), can be nourished close to home, in settings where people experience and act upon accepted responsibility. One of his examples is of the civil rights movement, which actually began in small black Baptist churches in the South and extended from there to a national movement. We might be reminded also of Vaclav Havel writing from prison a decade ago. He found hope in small student movements, ecological movements, peace movements, because he believed that "human communality" begins in a "renaissance of elementary human relationships which new projects can at the very most only mediate" (1989, p. 371). This may well ascribe new importance to the school and to teachers willing to foster the values Havel talked about: "love, charity, sympathy, tolerance, understanding, self-control, solidarity, friendship, feelings of belonging, the acceptance of concrete responsibility for those close to one"—all with an eye on the social formations that decide the fate of the world. Freire, also thinking of how to move beyond the small community, the local, spoke about "the invention of citizenship," clearly with imagination in mind once again (p. 39).

The processes of speaking, writing, and reading must be attended to; there must be reflectiveness with regard to the languages in use—the language of images, of technology, of ordinary communication grounded in everyday life. The current interest in narrative and in the landscapes on which people's stories take shape is enabling many learners to explore their own idioms, to create projects by means of which they can identify themselves. To do that is inevitably to take the social setting into account, the social situation without which no self can come to be. We might recall Edward Said saying that no one is purely one thing, that "labels like Indian, or woman, or Muslim, or American are not more than starting points, which if followed into actual experience for only a moment are quickly left behind" (1991, p. 336). We need to listen to other echoes in the garden, he reminds us, to attend to the continuity of old traditions as well as to the connections only now being disclosed. Both require a consciousness of location, an awareness of both contemporaries and predecessors.

We are realizing how much the negotiation of identity today has to do with connectedness and membership; and the notion of participant membership has to feed into our conceptions of democratic citizenship. Visions of public spaces may open, if we allow them to, spaces where all kinds of persons can come together in collaborative concern for what is lacking or what is wrong, what needs to be improved or repaired. The greatest obstacle in the way, as Hannah Arendt saw it, is "thoughtlessness—the heedless recklessness or hopeless confusion or complacent repetition of truths which have become trivial and empty . . ."

(1958, p. 5). Clearly, this has pedagogical implications, as did Dewey's warning about a "social pathology" standing in the way of inquiry into social conditions. "It manifests itself in a thousand ways," he wrote, "in querulousness, in impotent drifting, in uneasy snatching at distractions, in idealization of the long established, in a facile optimism assumed as a cloak, in glorification of things 'as they are' . . ." (1954, p. 170). Again, there is the implied demand for attention to a "blue guitar," even as persons are asked to think about their own thinking, their own denials, their own ends in view. Both Dewey and Arendt paid attention to the problem of impersonality and to the empty sociability taking over from community. Both spoke of business, consumerism, and (in time) of bureaucracy. Action and the sense of agency were crucial for both; their writings urged readers to appear before one another, to allow something to take shape between them, a space where diverse beings could reach towards possibility.

Both knew that dialogue and communication were focal and, when conceivable, face-to-face communication, with persons addressing one another as who, not what they were. It was the lack of authentic communication, Dewey wrote, that led to the "eclipse of the public." He pointed out that Americans had at hand "the physical tools of communication as never before, but the thoughts and aspirations congruent with them are not communicated and therefore are not common. Without such communication, the public will remain shadowy and formless, seeking spasmodically for itself, but seizing and holding its shadow rather than its substance" (1954, p. 142). Writing seventy years ago, Dewey may have anticipated the predicaments of a computerized society with a public transmuted into audience or listeners interested in consumption of ideas as well as goods. He might not have been surprised by the crotchety, of insulting telephone calls to the talk shows by the prayerful heaves at evangelists' meetings, the shouts at rock concerts, the hoots and screams at football games. Certainly, people are entitled to make all sorts of sounds, to express themselves in multiple ways; but when the "thoughts and aspirations" Dewey sought are subsumed under noise and sound bytes, teachers are challenged to pay heed.

Classroom preoccupations with efficacy or technical efficiency or even "world-class standards" will not solve the problem of communication or the "eclipse of the public." Nor will they suffice when it comes to consideration of the arts of practice, much less the arts and mystery of being human. The things covered up by "highly efficient talk and double talk" (Arendt, 1968, p. viii) still call for many kinds of illumination. Teachers may well be among the few in a position to kindle the light that might illuminate the spaces of discourse and events in which young newcomers have some day to find their ways. Dewey wrote that "democracy is a name for a life of free and enriching communion. It had its seer in Walt Whitman" (1954, p. 184). Whitman's "Song of Myself" comes insistently to mind, with its call for liberation and for equity! "Unscrew the locks from the doors!", he wrote. "Unscrew the doors themselves from their jambs!/ Whoever degrades another degrades me,/ And whatever is done or said returns at last to me./ Through me the afflatus surging and surging, through me the current and index./ I speak the pass-word primeval, I give the sign of democracy,/ By God! I will accept nothing which all cannot have their counterpart of on the same terms" (1931, p. 53). Dewey knew this was not a definition of democracy, nor a series of slogans nor a sermon nor a lesson in political science. The function of art "has always been," he said, "to break through the conventionalized and routine consciousness." Art is what touches "the deeper levels of life," and when they are touched "they spring up as desire and thought. This process is art." And then: "Artists have always been the real purveyors of the news, for it is not the outward happening in itself which is new, but the kindling by it of emotion, perception and appreciation" (p. 184).

It must be noted that Dewey affirmed the uses of the arts in the midst of a study of the public, and he spoke about the "deeper levels of life" at the end of the chapter called "Search for the Great Community." Not only was he emphasizing the place of art experiences in moving persons beyond what was fixed and stale and taken for granted. He was suggesting once again the importance of informing the state of social affairs with knowledge, intelligence, and the kinds of connections—past and present—that compose the fabric of what we have come to call the common world. Teachers, often troubled by charges of imposition of white, western culture upon young people arriving from different worlds, are often at a loss when it comes to providing the kinds of shared cultural referents that help weave networks of relationship. There was a time when the Scriptures offered something in common, or the orations of statesmen like Thomas Jefferson and Abraham Lincoln, or certain plays of Shakespeare, or folktales or (beginning in the 19th century) fictions capturing aspects of the American experience at sea, in the woods on the rivers, on the open roads. It is said today that television shows have replaced such common cultural holdings: "David Letterman", "The Today Show," and "Saturday Night Live" shape the culture's conversation, and the "deeper levels of life" are rolled over or ignored.

Teachers concerned about illumination and possibility know well that there is some profound sense in which a curriculum in the making is very much a part of a community in the making. Many are aware of the call on the part of hitherto marginal groups—ethnic minorities, women, gays and lesbians—for an inclusion of their own traditions in what is sometimes thought of as the "core" of intellectual and artistic life. For all the dissonances and uneasiness, there is a demand for a kind of historical consciousness on the part of diverse persons within and outside of their associations. That signifies a recognition that the past is like a stream in which all of us in our distinctiveness and diversity participate every time we try to understand. There are, of course, thousands of silenced voices still; there are thousands of beings striving for visibility; there are thousands of interpretations still to be made, thousands of questions to be posed.

The common world we are trying to create may be thought of as a fabric of interpretations of many texts, many images, many sounds. We might think of interpreted experiences with such texts taking the place of a tradition in the old sense of canonical objectivity. When Hannah Arendt wrote about a common world (1958), she put her stress on the innumerable perspectives through which that common world perceives itself and for which a common denominator can never be devised. In a classroom, this would mean acknowledgment of and recognition of the different biographical histories that affect the shaping of perspectives. More than in previous times, teachers are asked to confront and honor the differences even as they work for a free and responsible acceptance of the norms marking whatever community is in the making: concrete responsibility for one another; respect for the rights of others; solidarity; regard for reflective habits of thought. At once, there are the ways of thinking and seeing that enable various young persons to decode and interpret what is made available: the ability to distinguish among the discourses in use, to have regard for evidence and experience, to be critically conscious of what is read and heard, to construct meanings in the diverse domains of their lives. "Be it grand or slender," said Toni Morrison in her Nobel Address, "burrowing, blasting or refusing to sanctify; whether it laughs out loud or is a cry without an alphabet, the choice word or the chosen silence, unmolested language surges toward knowledge, not its destruction. But who does not know of literature banned because it is interrogative; discredited because it is critical; erased because alternate? And how many are outraged by the thought of a self-ravaged tongue? Word-work is sublime because it is generative; it makes meaning that secures our difference, our human difference—the way in which we are like no other life. We die. That may be the meaning of life. But we do language. That may be the measure of our lives" (March/April 1996, p. 11). This should apply to all the young, whoever they are, if—like Whitman and Morrison as well—we refuse at last to withhold recognition, to degrade or to exclude.

Michael Fischer, an ethnologist also concerned for connectedness, writes about the importance of the present tendency to encourage participation of readers themselves in the production of meaning. The conscious effort to move readers to respond to incompleteness and make connections becomes, he suggests, an ethical device attempting to activate in readers a "desire for communitas with others, while preserving rather than effacing differences" (1986, p. 233). We might visualize interpretive encounters with Hawthorne's Hester Prynne daring to engage in speculative thought while living on the verge of the wilderness; Melville's Bartleby who "preferred not to," compared with "a piece of wreckage in the mid Atlantic": Edith Wharton's Lily Bart, caught like a cog in the wheel of a material society. Or we might think of the narrator of Ellison's *Invisible Man* saying he has "whipped it all except the mind, the mind. And the mind that has conceived a plan of living must never lose sight of the chaos against which that pattern was conceived." Or the chaos due to nameless pollution and the falsifications of the media in De Lillo's *White Noise,* or Doctorow's cities with their denials and their cover-ups and their violations of children. Or Tillie Olsen's narrator standing behind her ironing board, hoping only that her daughter will be more than a dress beneath the iron. And so many other voices, Hispanic and Asian and Native American, all activating questions whose answers create no "common denominator," but which make each text deeper, richer, more expansive, yes, and more replete with mystery.

That, in part, suggests what is meant by teaching as possibility in dark and constraining times. It is a matter of awakening and empowering today's young people to name, to reflect, to imagine, and to act with more and more concrete responsibility in an increasingly multifarious world. At once, it is a matter of enabling them to remain in touch with dread and desire, with the smell of lilacs and the taste of a peach. The light may be uncertain and flickering; but teachers in their lives and works have the remarkable capacity to make it shine in all sorts of corners and, perhaps, to move newcomers to join with others and transform. Muriel Rukeyser has written:

> Darkness arrives
> splitting the mind open.
> Something again
> Is beginning to be born.
> A dance is dancing me.
> I wake in the dark.
> *(1994, p. 284)*

She offers a metaphor and a watchword. It may help us light the fuse.

References

Arendt, H. (1968) *Men in Dark Times.* New York: Harcourt Brace (Harvest Books).
Arendt, H. (1958) *The Human Condition.* Chicago: Chicago University Press.
Camus, A. (1948) *The Plague.* New York: Alfred A. Knopf.
Dewey, J. (1931) *Art as Experience.* New York: Minton, Balch, & Co.
Dewey, J. (1954) *The Public and Its Problems.* Athens, O.: The Swallow Press.

Dickinson, E. (1960) "The Gleam of an Heroic act," in T.H. Johnson, Ed. *The Complete Poems.* Boston: Little Brown.
Fischer, M.M.J. (1986) "Ethnicity and the Arts of Memory," in J. Clifford and G.E. Marcus, *Writing Culture.* Berkeley: University of California Press.
Freire, P. (1994) *Pedagogy of Hope.* New York: Continuum.
Havel, V. (1989) *Letters to Olga.* New York: Henry Holt.
Kozol, J. (1991) *Savage Inequalities.* New York: Crown Publishers.
Morrison, T. (1970) *The Bluest Eye.* New York: Washington Square Press/Pocket Books.
Morrison, T. (1996) "The 1993 Nobel Prize Lecture: Honors in Stockholm," in *Humanities* March/April 1996, Vol. 17, No. 1.
Moyers, B. (1995) *The Language of Life.* New York: Doubleday.
O'Connor, S. (1996) *Will My Name Be Shouted Out?* New York: Simon and Schuster.
Rose, M. (1995) *Possible Lives: The Promise of Public Education.* Wilmington, MA: Houghton Mifflin.
Rukeyser, M. (1994) *Muriel Rukeyser Reader.* New York: W. W. Norton and Co Inc.
Said, E. (1991) *Musical Elaborations.* New York: Columbia University Press.
Sandel, M. (1996) *Democracy's Discontent: America in Search of Public Philosophy.* Cambridge, MA: Belknap Press.
Stevens, W. (1937) *The Man with the Blue Guitar.* New York: Alfred A Knopf.
Walker, A. (1982) *The Color Purple.* New York: Harcourt Brace Jovanovich.

27

The Knowledges of Teacher Education: Developing a Critical Complex Epistemology

Joe L. Kincheloe

The first decade of the twenty-first century is an exciting and frightening time for supporters of a rigorous, practical, socially just, and democratic teacher education. It is a time of dangerous efforts to destroy teacher education and of brilliant attempts to reform it. A sense of urgency permeates discussions of the topic, as studies indicate that presently there is a need for more teachers in a shorter timeframe than ever before in U.S. history. About 1,025 teacher education programs graduate around 100,000 new teachers annually. The problem is that over the next few years 2 million teachers are needed in U.S. elementary and secondary schools. Many analysts argue that the problem will be solved by lowering standards for teacher certification or simply doing away with the certification process and admitting any one who breathes regularly into the teaching ranks (U.S. Department of Education, 1998). Such capitulation to short-term needs would be tragic.

I wish I had a dollar for every time someone in higher education or the professions reacted condescendingly upon learning that the individual with whom they were conversing was a professor of teacher education or pedagogy. Understanding the history of teacher education, one is provided with plenty of reasons to look at the domain askance—but not any more than other elements of higher/professional education. Too often the condescension toward teacher education and teacher educators is harbored for all the wrong reasons. Contempt for teacher education and pedagogy emanates not from knowledge of their historical failures but from a generic devaluing of the art and science of teaching as an unnecessary contrivance. "As long as one knows her subject matter," the clichéd argument goes, "she doesn't need anything else to teach." Anyone who makes such an assertion should be mandated to teach the fourth grade for six weeks. Such a crash immersion may induce a reconsideration of the platitude, as the complexity of doing such a job well becomes apparent.

Indeed, the complexity of the pedagogical process and the intricacies of a rigorous teacher education are central concerns of this article. What is a critical complex teacher education? What types of knowledges should professional educators possess? In a climate as hostile as the first decade of the twenty-first century the ability of teacher educators to articulate a case for particular knowledges is not merely important, it may just be a survival skill. In its devaluation, pedagogy has been rendered invisible in many higher educational settings. Teacher educators, teachers, and teacher education students must not only understand the complexity of good teaching, but stand ready to make this known to political leaders and the general population. If we are not successful in such a political effort, we will witness the death of the scholarly conception of teacher education to the degree it now exists. While such articulations of teacher education are not dominant, many scholarly, rigorous, and democratic teacher education programs exist and produce excellent teachers. At the same time in countless mediocre programs great teacher educators ply their trade in unfavorable conditions, turning out good teachers despite the circumstances.

The Critical Complex Vision: Teachers as Scholars and Policy Makers

The vision on which this essay is grounded involves the empowerment of teachers in an era where teacher professionalism is under assault. I want universities to produce rigorously educated teachers with an awareness of the complexities of educational practice and an understanding of and commitment to a socially just, democratic notion of schooling. Only with a solid foundation in various mainstream and alternative canons of knowledge can they begin to make wise judgments and informed choices about curriculum development and classroom practice. In this context they can craft a teacher persona that enables them to diagnose individual and collective needs of their students and connect them to their pedagogical strategies and goals. It is naïve and dangerous to think that teachers can become the rigorous professionals envisioned here without a conceptual understanding of contemporary and past societies and the socio-cultural, political, and economic forces that have shaped them. Such knowledges are essential in the process of both understanding and connecting the cultural landscape of the twenty-first century to questions of educational purpose and practice (Bruner, 1997; Ferreira & Alexandre, 2000; Horn & Kincheloe, 2001; McGuire, 1996; McNeil, 2000).

Few seem to understand the demands of high-quality teaching of a critical democratic variety in the twenty-first century. After listening, for example, to former mayor of New York, Rudolph Guiliani and other high ranking city officials chastise and degrade New York City teachers over the last decade, I understand the anger and cynicism these teachers harbor as they open their classroom doors to start the day. The emotional complexity of their lives haunts me as I engage them in rigorous graduate school analyses of the various knowledges demanded by the critical complex vision. "Why learn this," they sometimes ask me, "when the system won't let us apply it in our deskilled classrooms?" This is a tough question. I struggle for the right words, for inspirational words to let them know the value of the vision. Literally, there is little hope for educational reform if they do not gain detailed insight into:

- the context in which education takes place;
- the historical forces that have shaped the purposes of schooling;
- the ways dominant power uses schools for anti-democratic ideological self interest;
- how all of this relates to the effort to develop a democratic, transformative pedagogy;
- the specific ways all of these knowledges relate to transformative classroom teaching in general and to their particular curricular domain in particular.

Only with these and similar insights and skills can teachers build rigorous communities of practice (Edwards, 2000) that empower them to develop more compelling ways of teaching and conceptualizing pedagogy. And just as importantly, in these communities of practice they can mobilize the political power to educate the public about the nature of a rigorous, democratic education and the types of resources and citizen action that are necessary to making it a reality. Given the political context of the twenty-first century with its "reeducated" public and corporatized information environment, the friends of democracy and education have no other choice. Thus, critical complex teaching involves teachers as knowledge producers, knowledge workers who pursue their own intellectual development. At the same time such teachers work together in their communities of practice to sophisticate both the profession's and the public's appreciation of what it means to be an educated person. They ask how schools can work to ensure that students from all possible backgrounds achieve this goal (Bereiter, 2002; Horn, 2000; Smyth, 2001; Steinberg, 2001). In this context, such educators engage the public in developing more sophisticated responses to questions such as:

- What does it mean "to know" something?
- What is involved in the process of understanding?
- What are the moral responsibilities of understanding?
- What does it mean to act on one's knowledge and understanding in the world?
- How do we assess when individuals have engaged these processes in a rigorous way?

Teachers as scholars demand respect as they engage diverse groups in these and other questions about education in a democratic society. They alert individuals to the demands of democratic citizenship that require the lifelong pursuit of learning. In such a context no teacher, no concerned citizen is ever fully educated; they are always "in process," waiting for the next learning experience. As they claim and occupy such an important socio-political role, critical complex teachers dismantle the Berlin wall that separates educational policy from practice. Those who make educational policy almost never engage in classroom practice. These policy makers, especially in the recent standards reforms, have in many cases completely disregarded the expertise and concerns of classroom teachers and imposed the most specific modes of instructional practice on them (Elmore, 1997; Schubert, 1998). This type of imposition is unacceptable. Teachers in a democratic society have to play a role in the formulation of professional practice, educating the public, and educational policymaking.

Categorizing the Multiple Forms of Pedagogical Knowledge: Developing a Meta-Epistemological Perspective

We are asking teachers and teacher education students to gain complex understandings not previously demanded of educational practitioners. What follows is a delineation of the types of knowledges required in a critical complex teacher education. This delineation is conceptually wrapped in what might be called a meta-epistemological package that grounds many of the categories of knowledges teachers need to know. A meta-epistemological perspective is a central understanding in a critical complex conception of teacher professionalism (Strom, 2000). Simply put, such an insight helps us approach the contested concept of a "knowledge base for education." In our meta-epistemological construction, the educational knowledge base involves the recognition of different types of knowledges of education including but not limited to empirical, experiential, normative, critical, ontological, and reflective-synthetic domains.

Such an assertion challenges more traditional and technical forms of teacher education that conceptualized teaching as a set of skills—not a body of knowledges. Thus, in the framework promoted here, teaching before it is anything else is epistemological—a concept that wreaks havoc in the pedagogical world. As an epistemological dynamic, teaching, as

Hugh Munby and Tom Russell (1996) contend, "depends on, is grounded in, and constitutes knowledge" (p. 75). If the teaching profession doesn't grasp and embrace this understanding, as well as the different types of knowledge associated with teaching and the diverse ways they are taught and learned, teacher education will continue to be epistemologically bankrupt and viewed as a Philistine vocation. In the meta-epistemological domain critical complex teacher educators avoid this Philistinism by analyzing the epistemological and other types of tacit assumptions embedded in and shaping particular articulations of practice.

Empirical Knowledge about Education

Empirical knowledge comes from research based on data derived from sense data/observations of various aspects of education. Throughout my scholarship I have expressed reservations about the positivist version of empirical knowledge and its uses—but not about the concept of empirical knowledge itself. A critical complex teacher education demands more sophisticated forms of sense observational knowledges of education. A thicker, more complex, more textured, self-conscious form of empirical knowledge takes into account the situatedness of the researcher and the researched—where they are standing or are placed in the social, cultural, historical, philosophical, economic, political, and psychological web of reality. Such insight respects the complexity of the interpretive dimension of empirical knowledge production.

A critical complex empiricism understands that there may be many interpretations of the observations made and the data collected, that different researchers depending on their relative situatedness may see very different phenomena in a study of the same classroom. Power dynamics such as ideological orientation, discursive embeddedness, disciplinary experience, ad infinitum may shape the research lenses of various researchers in diverse and even contradictory ways (Kincheloe, 2003). Once we understand these dynamics we can never be naïve researchers again. Empirical knowledge about education enters into an even more complex realm when educators ask what it tells them about practice. Since such knowledge has such a complex interaction with and multidimensional relationship to practice, there will always be diverse articulations of its practical implications. Too many teacher educators have not understood these dynamics.

A critical complex empiricism understands that knowledge about humans and their social practices is fragmented, diverse, and always constructed by human beings coming from different contexts. Such a form of knowledge does not lend itself to propositional statements—i.e., final truths. Indeed, a critical complex empirical knowledge does not seek validation by reference to universal truths. Rather it remains somewhat elusive, resistant to the trap of stable and consistent meaning. The way it is understood will always involve the interaction between our general conceptions of it and its relationship with ever-changing contexts. Thus, our conception of empirical knowledge is more dialectical than propositional. Simply put, there is not one single answer to any research question and no one question is superior to all others. Particular empirical descriptions will always conflict with others, tensions between accounts will persist, and alternative perspectives will continue to struggle for acceptance. As Elvis might have put it: "Man, you better believe this stuff is complicated."

The technical rationality of positivism failed to heed Elvis's warning. In this articulation of the empirical project there was nothing too complex about educational knowledge production and its role in teacher education: researchers defined educational problems and solved them by rigorous fidelity to the scientific method. These solutions were passed along to practitioners who put them into practice. A critical complex empiricism avoids this technical rationality and the certainty that accompanies it. It never prescribes precise content and validated instructional techniques for teachers' use. In the critical complex perspective there is no certain knowledge about:

- what subject matter to teach;
- the proper way to develop a curriculum;
- the correct understanding of students;
- the right way to teach.

(Center for Policy Research in Education (CPRE), 1995; Pozzuto, Angell & Pierpont, 2000; Report of Undergraduate Teacher Education Program, 1997)

The relationship between such knowledge and practice in its complexity is always open to discussion and interpretation.

In this discussion a critical complex empiricism refuses to undermine other types of educational knowledges and exclude them from the process. For example, the experiential knowledge teachers derive from teaching is deemed very important in this context. Traditional positivist perspectives created a chasm between empirical knowledge and experience, as they excluded teachers from the knowledge production dimension of the profession. The concept of great teachers as virtuosos who produce brilliant pieces of pedagogical performance/knowledge was alien to the positivist conception of empirical knowledge about education. In a positivist context teachers were expected to follow empirical imperatives, not to produce masterpieces (Britzman, 1991; Horn, 2000; Segall, 2002). If teachers don't belong at the conference table of knowledge production in education, then the table deserves to be dismantled.

Critical, complex empirical knowledge about education avoids the positivist tendency to represent itself as a distinct, autonomous object—a thing-in-itself. Here critical, complex knowledge always acknowledges the contexts of its production and interpretation. Valuing the relationships that connect various knowledges, researchers in the complex domain ask how education experience is constructed and educational meaning is made (Cannella & Kincheloe, 2002; Day, 1996; Denzin & Lincoln, 2000). In such explorations they walk through a star gate into a more pragmatic dimension of empirical research. Understanding the contexts of knowledge production and the nature of its relation to practice, critical complex educational researchers study the half-life of their data in terms of its implementation. How could it be used to improve education? How is educational improvement defined? Did it promote professional awareness? How does professional relate to practice? Within such analyses, reflections, and inquiries a new dawn breaks for the role of empirical knowledge in education.

Normative Knowledge about Education

Normative knowledge concerns "what should be" in relation to moral and ethical issues about education. What constitutes moral and ethical behavior on the part of teacher educators and teachers? How do we develop a vision of practice that will empower educators to embrace these behaviors without fear of reprisals? Such questions began the theoretical work necessary to the development of a democratic, egalitarian sense of educational purpose. Such normative knowledge is central to the effort to establish just and rigorous colleges/schools/departments of education and schools of various kinds. Such knowledge is not produced arbitrarily but in relation to particular social visions, power relations, and cultural/historical contexts. With these concerns in mind we ask questions about the nature of education, the role of schools in a democratic society, and the philosophical issues raised in this process.

The "critical" in our critical complex teacher education is directly related to normative knowledge. Critical theorists such as Max Horkheimer, Theodor Adorno, and Herbert Marcuse directly addressed this normative dimension when they wrote about the concept of "eminent critique." Moral and ethical action, they argued, cannot take place until one can envision a more desirable state of affairs, alternatives to injustice. In this context, they argued, any domain of study is ethically required to examine not only "what is" but also "what could be"—the notion of eminence. In critical pedagogy—the educational articulation of critical theory buoyed by the work of feminist theorists and Brazilian educator, Paulo Freire—advocates have confronted the positivistic, decontextualized, and depoliticized education often found in mainstream teacher education and higher education in general, and elementary and secondary schools on normative grounds. These institutions, critical analysts maintain, have often failed to develop an ethical vision for the pedagogical process in a democratic society.

From the critical complex perspective developed in this essay, educational rigor and social justice cannot be ethically separated. Questions of oppression and empowerment are always implicated in visions of scholarship. When positivistic schools, for example are set up to serve the needs of individuals abstracted form their social, cultural, political, and economic context, the privileged will be rewarded and the marginalized punished. Thus, the critical perspective develops a language of critique to expose the way contemporary democratic societies maintain disparate social relations and in turn how these relationships shape pedagogy. The complex part of the critical complex equation insists that these dynamics are even more complicated than originally understood and that advocates of critical pedagogy must be consistently vigilant about their own oppressive tendencies. In this complex normative context they must always be reflective about modes of oppression growing up around their own relationship to issues of race, class, gender, sexuality, religion, geographic place, etc.

As critical professionals develop these modes of normative knowledge, they begin to understand how ethical concerns are often hidden in everyday life and professional practice. They observe such masking processes at work in many cultural sites, in many colleges of education, and in secondary and elementary schools. In this cloaking process educators are induced to accept the organizational structure and daily operations of schools as if they could be no other way. This hidden normative curriculum moves critical complex teacher educators to be concerned with positivist forms of educational knowledge production and the role it plays in this great denial of the moral and ethical dimensions of pedagogy. Moved by this concern criticalists argue that all of the other educational knowledges must be produced in close connection to normative knowledges.

Empirical knowledge produced outside of such normative concerns takes on the pseudo-neutrality of positivism that promotes an unexamined normative agenda even as it claims it does not. Moreover, as we clarify the distinctions between normative knowledge and empirical knowledge, we begin to realize that positivistic requests for empirical proof of what are normative questions are epistemologically naïve and misguided. One cannot "prove" a normative statement about educational purpose or professional ethics (Aronowitz, 1988; Fischer, 1998; Giroux, 1997; Goodlad, 1994; Hinchey, 1998). No study empirically proves the inadequacy of an educational purpose—this is a different form of knowledge. Teacher educators concerned with social justice and democracy have been confronted with such epistemological inconsistencies for decades. In my own work around issues of social justice in teacher education I have often been asked by colleagues to provide empirical evidence of the validity of such concerns. From the perspective of such educators, there was only one form of professional knowledge about education—empirical. If pedagogical insights could not be empirically proved or disproved, then they were relegated to the epistemological junk heap.

All educational programs and curricula are built on a foundation of normative knowledge—even if such knowledge is hidden or even not fully understood. This is what is so often not understood in teacher education and in schooling. Thus, a key dimension of the work of teacher education is to bring these norms, these ethical and moral assumptions, these visions to the light of day so they can be analyzed and discussed. Because many in teacher education have not conceptualized and talked about normative knowledge, those operating within a positivist culture of neutrality often view this analytical process with great discomfort. When we discuss concepts such as a political vision undergirding teaching, this often is heard as a "politicization of education." More attention to normative types of knowledge can sometimes clear up these misunderstandings.

When one claims neutrality and promotes a view of education that doesn't attend to effects of human suffering, exploitation, and oppression in relation to the teaching act, a serious contradiction arises. By failing to address such issues one has taken a distinct moral position. Such orientations in the analysis of normative knowledge are revealed and problematized. Indeed, critical complex educators consider it an ethical duty to disclose their normative perspectives, to admit their value structures, and to help students understand how such allegiances affect their teaching. Critical complex teacher education openly embraces democratic values, a vision of race, class, gender, and sexual equality, and the necessity of exposing the effects of power in shaping individual identity and educational purpose. This is not an act of politicization of education; education has always been politicized. Critical complex teacher educators are attempting to understand and act ethically in light of such politicization.

Critical Knowledge about Education

Critical knowledge is closely associated with normative knowledge, as it focuses on the political/power-related aspects of teacher education and teaching. In the context of critical knowledge the charges of politicization heard in the normative domain grow louder and often more strident. Critical complex teacher educators maintain that it is impossible to conceptualize curricula outside of a sociopolitical context. No matter what form they take all curricula bear the imprint of power. When teacher education students are induced to study the curriculum outside of such horizons, they are being deceived by a claim of neutrality concerning the production of knowledge. The culture of positivism defines the curriculum as a body of agreed-upon knowledges being systematically passed along to students as an ever evolving, but neutral, instructional process.

Critical complex teacher educators know too much to be seduced by the sirens of political neutrality. As a deliberate process, the curriculum is always a formal transmission of particular aspects of a culture's knowledge. Do we teach women's and African-American history in eleventh grade social studies? Do we read Toni Morrison and Alice Walker in twelfth grade literature? In colleges of education do we teach the history of Horace Mann's crusade for public education from a political economic perspective? These are all sociopolitical questions—this means they involve power and its influence. In this context critical complex teacher educators understand the need to build a teacher education that infuses this critical knowledge into all phases of professional education. As this takes place, teacher education students gain a far more rigorous and nuanced understanding of why education exists in its present form.

Teacher educators don't have to look very far to uncover critical knowledges in education, the exercise of power in shaping "the way things are." Colleges of education, themselves, are implicated in power relations shaped by interest-driven legislative intervention in academic life. Responding to the needs of business and corporate leaders, legislators often impose policies that presuppose a view of an educational profession that acts in the power interests of managerial elites. Appreciating such dynamics, critical complex teacher educators ground their curriculum on the notion that the socio-educational world has been constructed by dominant power and thus can be reconstructed by human action and savvy political organization. Thus, critical complex teacher educators inject a literacy of power into their professional education curriculum. Such an orientation studies critical knowledges such as hegemony, ideology, discursive power, regulatory power, disciplinary power, etc.

With these critical knowledges critical complex teacher educators gain greater familiarity with diverse cultural expressions and the ways teacher education and schooling brush against them. As researchers and knowledge workers they develop the analytical ability to expose the insidious ways dominant cultural inscriptions in educational contexts marginalize culturally diverse and lower socio-economic class groups. Thinking in terms of race, class, and gender differences, critical complex practitioners survey their classes for patterns developing along these lines. The critical respect for diversity allows such teachers the ability to conceptualize multiple perspectives on issues such as intelligence, student ability, evaluation, community needs, and educational justice. Such perspectives allow for the acceptance of a diversity of expressions that exposes the fingerprints of power, in the process bringing more parents and students to the negotiating table of educational purpose.

Appreciating that all knowledges about education, all disciplinary knowledges are produced in discourses of power, critical complex teacher education understands there is no neutral ground. Imbued with such critical knowledges, they see through positivistic technical rationality and its claim that objective researchers produce educational knowledge and theory which is then applied to neutral sites of practice. In the technical rational context the assumption of ideological innocence on the part of researchers and educational policy-makers leads to unproblematized hierarchical assumptions between the educated and the uneducated. Wearing the badge of neutrality such hierarchies can quickly mutate into schooling as a neo-White Man's Burden where educational missionaries attempt to deliver the civilizing "gospel" of European high culture to the poor and/or "off-white" masses.

Ontological Knowledge in Education

There is nothing new in asserting that the ways one teaches, the pedagogical purposes one pursues is directly connected to the way teachers see themselves. At the same time, the ways teachers come to see themselves as learners, in particular the ways they conceptualize what they need to learn, where they need to learn it, and how the process should take place shape their teacher persona (CPRE, 1995). Such a persona cannot be separated from the various forms of knowledge delineated here and the larger notion of "professional awareness." Too infrequently are teachers in university, student teaching, or in-service professional education encouraged to confront why they think as they do about themselves as teachers—especially in relationship to the social, cultural, political, economic, and historical world around them. Teacher education provides little insight into the forces that shape identity and consciousness. Becoming educated, becoming a critical complex practitioner necessitates personal transformation.

With such dynamics in mind, critical complex teachers are asked to confront their relationship to some long-term historical trends rarely discussed in the contemporary public conversation. Critical complex teacher educators maintain these trends hold profound implications for the development of both professional awareness and a teacher persona. In my own case the understanding of my personal historicization in light of five centuries of European colonialism from the fifteenth to the twentieth century—and new forms of economic, geo-political, cultural, and educational colonialism picking up steam in the contemporary era—is essential knowledge. Indeed, everyone in the contemporary U.S. is shaped by this knowledge in some way whether or not they are conscious of it. We cannot contemplate our professional awareness without reference to these last five hundred and some years and their effects. I was born in 1950, in the middle of the post-colonial rebellion against this half millennium of colonial violence emerging in Africa, Asia, Latin America, and throughout the indigenous world.

While anti-colonial activity continues into the twenty-first century, such discontent reached its apex in the U.S. in the 1960s and early 1970s finding expression in the civil rights, women's, anti-Vietnam war, gay rights, and other liberation movements. By the mid-1970s a conservative counter-reaction was taking shape with the goals of "recovering" what was perceived to be lost in these movements. Thus, the politics, cultural wars, and educational debates, policies, and practices of the last three decades cannot be understood outside of these efforts to "recover" white supremacy, patriarchy, class privilege, heterosexual "normality," Christian dominance, and the European intellectual canon. I must decide where I stand in relation to such profound yet muffled historical processes. I cannot conceptualize my teacher persona outside of them. They are the defining macro-concerns of our time, as every topic is refracted through their lenses. Any view of education, any curriculum development, any professional education conceived outside of their framework ends up becoming a form of ideological mystification. Once we turn our analysis to the examination of ontological knowledges vis-à-vis such historical processes, we set the teacher "self" in question. As self-images, inherited dogmas, and absolute beliefs are interrogated, teachers begin to see themselves in relation to the world around them. They perceive the school as a piece of a larger mosaic. With such a conceptual matrix, teachers start to see an inseparable relationship between thinking and acting, as the boundary between feeling and logic begins to fade from the map of teacher thinking—a map redrawn by the cartography of teacher education and its ontological knowledges. In such an ontological context, teachers derive the motivation to produce their own knowledge. If teachers hold power to produce their own knowledges, then they are empowered to reconstruct their own consciousness. The top-down tyranny of expert-produced interpretations of tradition and its oppressive power can be subverted and our futures can be reinvented along the lines of a critical complex system of meaning making.

If positivism prevails and successfully excludes ontological, normative, and critical knowledges from professional education, teaching will too often remain a technical act. These issues of self-production will be removed from the consciousness of prospective teachers, as they memorize the generic theories and the fragments of the "knowledge base." Relegated to a static state of being, teachers in the technicist paradigm are conceived as a unit of production of an assembly line—historically abstracted selves located outside of a wider social context. Standards reforms that decontextualize students in this manner are molded by the dynamics of history and social structure (Kincheloe & Weil, 2001). Identity is never complete and always subject to modification in relation to prevailing ideologies, discourses, and knowledges. Critical complex teacher education encourages desocialization via ideological disembedding. Critical complex professional education coursework and practicum experiences focus on the ways in which the values of power-driven, information-saturated hyperreality of the twenty-first century shape the consciousness of both students and teachers (Apple, 1999; Britzman, 1991; Carson, 1997; Gordon, 2001; Macedo, 1994; Malewski, 2001; Soto, 2000). The rigorous study of cultural and historical context alerts prospective teachers to the ways dominant myths, behavior, and language shape their view of the teacher's role without conscious filtering.

Experiential Knowledge about Education

Obviously, there are experiential knowledges of education. Educators need knowledges about practice; teacher educators need to take these knowledges seriously and place them neither above nor below other forms of knowledges about education. Knowledges about practice are inherently problematic, however, because the nature of what constitutes practice is profoundly complex. There are many different forms of educational practice:

- classroom teaching;
- teacher leadership involving areas of curriculum and instruction;
- educational administration;
- educational policy making;
- teacher education;
- knowledge production in education;
- political activism.

The point here is that there are many types of educational practice—these are just a few. Yet too often in teaching and teacher education the only type of practice signified by the term involves classroom teaching. We have to be very careful about this type of reductionism as we work to develop and put into practice a critical complex teacher education.

Thus, the model of teacher education advocated here recognizes that not only are there numerous forms of practice but that all of them are complex. Donald Schon (1995) has used the term, "indeterminate zones of practice" to signify the uncertainty, complexity, uniqueness, and contested nature of any practice. The positivistic epistemology of the contemporary university often is incapable of coping with the complexity of practice, as it applies scientific theories to practical situations. Instead, Schon promotes a practice grounded on reflection-in-action. Here practitioners engage in conscious thinking and analysis while "in practice." They have no choice, they have to do this Schon argues, because each situation a practitioner encounters is unique. This demands a rigor that falls outside the boundaries of positivistic technical rationality and its reductionistic rule following. As one technicist teacher educator put it: "Look to the overhead projector, class; here are the five steps to writing on the chalkboard:

- always keep chalk longer than two inches readily available in the chalk tray;
- before writing adjust shades to minimize glare on board;
- hold the chalk at a 45 degree angle relative to the board;
- write letters at least five inches tall;
- dust hands before leaving the board so not to wipe them inadvertently on clothing."

I actually endured this lesson in an undergraduate teacher education class in 1971. I am still trying to recover.

Thus, our meta-epistemological understanding reasserts itself here in the context of experiential knowledge. From such a perspective the knowledge derived from practice about education is shaped by an epistemology significantly different from the one shaping propositional empirical knowledge. Such a position undermines the technically rational notion that teacher education researchers should continue to produce positivist empirical knowledge about educational practice until they can tell teachers how to do it correctly (Hatton & Smith, 1995; Munby & Russell, 1996). Experiential knowledge in the critical complex paradigm is rooted in action and informed by a subtle interaction with the empirical, normative, critical, ontological, and reflective-synthetic knowledges. There is no way to specify these interactions and routinize practice accordingly. Professional practice is always marked by surprises. Such interruption forces the practitioner to restructure her understanding of the situation. Critical complex practitioners learn to improvise and develop new ways of dealing with the new circumstances, new modes of action.

A new teaching situation, for example, may be created by a particular student's behavior or by a reprimand by the principal. How do I address the needs that are moving the student to be so violent? How do I work with the principal productively when she holds views of educational purpose so different from my own? Schon (1995) contends that such reflection-in-action brings the medium of words to the action orientation of practice. And this is the context in which experiential knowledge begins to come into its own as one of many knowledges related to education. Valuing this knowledge—not as the only important form of knowledge—brings practitioners to the negotiating table as respected participants in the professional conversation. With practitioners at the table no longer will education be subjected to mandated "expert-produced systems" with rules and scripts for teachers to follow (Capra, 1996; Goodson, 1999; Schon, 1983, 1987, 1995).

In this context it is important to note that a critical complex teacher education values experiential knowledge about teaching. Because of its value and because of teacher education students' concern with obtaining such knowledge, it may be wise to begin teacher education in school settings. In this context teacher education students could be directed to take note of and analyze the experiential knowledges they encounter. A critical complex teacher education is dedicated to making sure that experiential knowledge is not deemed second class information about education. Given its importance and student concern with obtaining it, beginning teacher education with school experience with experiential knowledge may be desirable. Such a positioning would challenge the debasement of experiential knowledge, while helping students deconstruct the positivist view that we can only do after being told what to do. This epistemological assumption must be challenged before a critical complex teacher education can get students to analyze the diverse forms of knowledge involved in becoming a professional educator. In this context critical complex teacher educators listen carefully to the experiential knowledge of teachers and other types of educational practitioners. We must be sensitive to not only the value of such knowledge but the ways it is obtained, altered, and sophisticated in lived contexts. Understanding these features of experiential knowledge, we are better prepared to teach it and integrate it with the other forms of educational knowledge (Kincheloe, 2001; Munby & Hutchinson, 1998; Munby & Russell, 1996; Quinn, 2001).

Reflective-Synthetic Knowledge about Education

Acknowledging our debt to Schon's notion of the reflective practitioner, a critical complex teacher education includes a reflective-synthetic form of educational knowledge. Since our purpose is not to indoctrinate practitioners to operate in a particular manner but to think about practice in more sophisticated ways, a central dimension of teacher education involves reflecting on and examining all of these knowledges in relation to one another. A reflective-synthetic knowledge of education involves developing a way of thinking about the professional role in light of a body of knowledges, principles, purposes, and experiences. In this process educators work to devise ways of using these various knowledges to perform our jobs in more informed, practical, ethical, democratic, politically just, self-aware, and purposeful ways. At the same time they work to expose the assumptions about knowledge embedded in various conceptions of practice and in the officially approved educational information they encounter.

In the reflective-synthetic context the practitioners' purpose is not to commit various knowledges to memory or to learn the right answers. Instead, teachers and other practitioners work studiously to avoid generic forms of educational knowledge applicable in all situations. Neither does their reflection on and synthesis of all the knowledges we have described reduce the uncertainty of the profession. The recognition of such uncertainty and complexity elicits humility, an understanding that all teachers and teacher educators agonize over the confusing nature of everyday practice. To do otherwise would involve a reductionistic retreat to the dishonesty of positivism's veil of certainty. In the reflective-synthetic domain practitioners learn they cannot separate their knowledges from the context in which they are generated. Thus, they study their own usage of such knowledges and the schemas they develop in this process.

In the reflective-synthetic domain, teacher educators engage teacher education students and teachers in an examination of not only the contexts in which teaching has taken place but the various forces and cultural knowledges shaping everyone involved with the teaching act. How do cultural knowledges of educational purpose connected with racialized and class-inscribed definitions of what it means to be an "educated person" shape the pedagogical act? How do folk knowledges about the nature of children and the ways they must be treated insert themselves into pedagogy? How do craft knowledges of the proper role of the teacher shape practice? How does the larger depoliticization of American culture shape teachers', parents', and the public's view of the political role of schools in a democratic society? How does the public's view of the "ideal teacher" influence who chooses education as a career path? How do all of these dynamics intersect to shape education in the U.S. writ large, as well as the individual lives of teachers and students?

All teacher educators, educational leaders, and friends of democratic education must make sure that all teachers have the time and opportunity to cultivate such reflective-synthetic knowledges. Such knowledges help them come to terms with their early concerns with survival skills and move to a more sophisticated understanding of the diverse factors that shape teaching and the broad contexts that must be accounted for as pedagogy proceeds. When positivism reduces teacher education to training in methods of transferring knowledge in light of the demands of standards, a teacher possessing reflective-synthetic skills knows that such teacher education has already embraced many political assumptions about knowing. Synthesizing a variety of the educational knowledges we have studied, such teachers begin to put together the complex ways these political assumptions shape the purposes of schools, the image of the "good teacher," the validated knowledge about "best practices" they are provided, and the ways they are evaluated. In this synthetic context they know that the way particular knowledges are transmitted reflects a variety of value positions and hidden assumptions.

In this context, critical complex teachers use their insights to connect their students to these understandings. Such teachers get to know their students and help their students know them by producing a form of authentic dialogue. With their students, they analyze and reflect on classroom conversations (How do we talk to one another?), the nature of classroom learning (What do we call knowledge?), curriculum decisions (What do we need to know?), and assessment (Is what we are doing working?). In this conversation with students they ask how the macro-level decisions about larger educational, political, and moral issues shape these everyday classroom dynamics. When thinking advances and the dialogues grow in sophistication, students come to reflect on the socio-political, moral, and epistemological dimensions of their school experiences. When this happens, a new level of learning has been reached.

The concept of teachers as researchers becomes extremely important in critical complex practice (Kincheloe, 2003). If teachers and eventually students are to be able to engage in these types of exercises, they must become researchers of educational contexts. Bringing the various educational knowledges together with research skills, all parties are empowered to reveal the deep structures that shape school activities. In this process they develop a reflexive awareness that allows them to discern the ways that teacher and student perception is shaped by the socio-educational context with its accompanying linguistic codes, cultural signs, and tacit views of the world. This reflexive awareness, this stepping back from the world as we are accustomed to seeing it, requires that the prospective teachers construct their perceptions of the world anew. For teachers this reconstruction of perception is not conducted in a random way but in a manner that undermines the forms of teacher thinking that the culture makes appear natural. Reflexively aware teacher researchers ask where their own ways of seeing come from, in the process clarifying their own meaning systems as they reconstruct the role of the practitioner. The ultimate justification for such reflective research activity is practitioner and student empowerment. In this context teachers gain the skills to overcome the positivist tendency to discredit their integrity as capable, reflexively aware, self-directed professionals (Carson & Sumara, 1997; Diamond & Mullin, 1999; Hatton & Smith, 1995; McLaren, 2000; Wesson & Weaver, 2001). An awareness of these knowledges can elicit productive analyses, conversations, and actions that lead to new forms of pedagogical and intellectual rigor.

References

Apple, M. (1999). Power, Meaning, and Identity: Essays in Critical Educational Studies. New York: Peter Lang.

Aronowitz, S. (1988). Science as Power: Discourse and Ideology in Modern Society. Minneapolis, MN: University of Minnesota Press.

Bereiter, C. (2002). Education and the Mind in the Knowledge Age, Mahwah, NJ: Lawrence Erlbaum Associates.

Britzman, D. (1991). Practice Makes Practice: A Critical Study of Learning to Teach. Albany, NY: State University of New York Press.

Bruner, J. (1997). The Culture of Education. Cambridge, MA: Harvard University Press.

Cannella, G. & Kincheloe, J. (2002). Kidworld: Childhood Studies, Global Perspectives, and Education. New York: Peter Lang.

Capra, F. (1996). The Web of Life: A New Scientific Understanding of Living Systems. New York: Anchor Books.

Carson, T. (1997). Reflection and Its Resistances: Teacher Education as Living Practice. In T. Carson & D. Sumara (Eds.). Action Research as a Living Practice. New York: Peter Lang.

Carson, T. & Sumara, D. (1997). Action Research as a Living Practice. New York: Peter Lang.

Center for Policy Research (CPRE) (1995). Dimensions of Capacity. Available at: <http://www.ed.gov/pubs/CPRE/rb18/rb18b.html>

Day, R. (1996). LIS, Method, and Postmodern Science. Journal of Education for Library and Information Science, 37(4), pp. 317–25.

Denzin, N. & Lincoln, Y. (2000). Introduction: The Discipline and Practice of Qualitative Research. In N. Denzin & Y. Lincoln (Eds.). Handbook of Qualitative Research (2nd edition). Thousand Oaks, CA: Sage.

Diamond, P. & Mullin, C. (Ed.) (1999). The Postmodern Educator: Arts-Based Inquiries and Teacher Development. New York: Peter Lang.

Edwards, A. (2000). Researching Pedagogy: A Sociocultural Agenda. Inaugural Lecture: University of Birmingham.

Elmore, R. (1997). Education Policy and Practice in the Aftermath of TIMSS. Available at: http://www.enc.org/TIMSS/addtools/pubs/symp/cd163/cd163.htm

Ferreira, M. & Alexandre, F. (2000). Education for Citizenship: The Challenge of Teacher Education in Postmodernity. Available at: http://www.ioe.ac.uk./ccs/conference2000/papers/epsd/ferreiraandalexandre.html

Fischer, F. (1998). Beyond Empiricism: Policy Inquiry in Postpositivist Perspective. Policy Studies Journal, 26(1), pp. 129–46.

Giroux, H. (1997). Pedagogy and the Politics of Hope: Theory, Culture, and Schooling. Boulder, CO: Westview.

Goodlad, J. (1994). Educational Renewal: Better Teachers, Better Schools. San Francisco: Jossey-Bass.

Goodson, I. (1999). The Educational Researcher as Public Intellectual. British Educational Research Journal, 25(3), pp. 277–97.

Gordon, M. (2001). Philosophical Analysis and Standards—Philosophical and Analytical Standards. In J. Kincheloe & D. Weil (Eds.). Standards and Schooling in the United States: An Encyclopedia, 3 vols. Santa Barbara, CA: ABC-CLIO.

Hatton, N. & Smith, D. (1995). Reflection in Education: Toward Definition and Implementation. Available at: http://www2.edfac.usyd.edu.au/LocalResource/study1/hattonart.html

Hinchey, P. (1998). Finding Freedom in the Classroom: A Practical Introduction to Critical Theory. New York: Peter Lang.

Horn, R. (2000). Teacher Talk: A Post-formal Inquiry into Education Change. New York: Peter Lang.

Horn, R. & Kincheloe, J. (Eds.) (2001). American Standards: Quality Education in a Complex World. New York: Peter Lang.

Kincheloe, J. (2001). Getting Beyond the Facts: Teaching Social Studies/Social Science in the Twenty-First Century (2nd edition). New York: Peter Lang.

Kincheloe, J. (2003). Teachers as Researchers: Qualitative Paths to Empowerment. New York: Falmer.

Kincheloe, J. & Weil, D. (Eds.) (2001). Standards and schooling in the United States: An Encyclopedia. 3 vols. Santa Barbara, CA, ABC-Clio.

McLaren, P. (2000). Che Guevara, Paulo Freire, and the Pedagogy of Revolution. Lanham, MD: Rowan & Littlefield.

Macedo, D. (1994). Literacies of Power: What Americans Are Not Allowed to Know. Boulder, CO: Westview Press.

Malewski, E. (2001). Administration—Administrative Leadership and Public Consciousness: Discourse Matters in the Struggle for New Standards. In J. Kincheloe & D. Weil (Eds.). Standards and Schooling in the United States: An Encyclopedia, 3 vols. Santa Barbara, CA: ABC-CLIO.

McGuire, M. (1996). Teacher Education: Some Current Challenges. Social Education, 60(2), pp. 89–94.

McNeil, L. (2000). Contradictions of School Reform: Educational Costs of Standardized Testing, New York: Routledge.

Munby, H. & Hutchinson, N. (1998). Using Experience to Prepare Teachers for Inclusive Classrooms: Teacher Education and the Epistemology of Practice. Teacher Education and Special Education, 21(2), pp. 75–82.

Munby, H. & Russell, T. (1996). Theory Follows Practice in Learning to Teach and in Research on Teaching. Paper Presented to American Educational Research Association: New York.

Pozzuto, R., Angell, G. & Pierpont, J. (2000). Power and Knowledge in Social Work. Available at: http://www.arcaf.net/social_work_proceedings/ftp_files5/pozzuto3.pdf

Quinn, M. (2001). Going Out, Not Knowing Whither: Education, the Upward Journey, and the Faith of Reason. New York: Peter Lang.

Report of the Undergraduate Teacher Education Program Design Team (University of Missouri-Columbia) (1997). Available at: http://www.cos.missouri.edu/syllabi/report.html

Schön, D. (1983). The Reflective Practitioner: How Professionals Think in Action. New York: Basic Books.

Schön, D. (1987). Educating the Reflective Practitioner. San Francisco: Jossey-Bass.

Schön, D. (1995). The New Scholarship Requires a New Epistemology. Change, 27(6), p. 9.

Schubert, W. (1998). Toward Constructivist Teacher Education for Elementary Schools in the Twenty-first Century: A Framework for Decision-Making. Available at: <my.netian.com/~yhhknue/coned19.htm>

Segall, A. (2002). Disturbing Practice: Reading Teacher Education as Text. New York: Peter Lang.
Smyth, J. (2001). Critical Politics of Teachers' Work. New York: Peter Lang.
Soto, L. (Ed.) (2000). The Politics of Early Childhood Education. New York: Peter Lang.
Steinberg, S. (Ed.) (2001). Multi/Intercultural Conversations. New York: Peter Lang.
Strom, S. (2000). Knowledge Base for Teaching. Available at: http://www.ericsp.org/pages/digests/knowledge_base.html
U.S. Department of Education (1998). Improving Teacher Preparation. Available at: http://www.ed.gov/pubs/prompractice/title.html
Wesson, L. & Weaver, J. (2001). Administration—Educational Standards: Using the Lens of Postmodern Thinking to Examine the Role of the School Administrator. In J. Kincheloe & D. Weil (Eds.). Standards and Schooling in the United States: An Encyclopedia, 3 vols. Santa Barbara, CA: ABC-CLIO.

28

What's Radical Love Got To Do With It: Navigating Identity, Pedagogy, and Positionality in Pre-Service Education

Ty-Ron Douglas and Christine Nganga

Critiques of teacher preparation and leadership programs have suggested that it is not enough to expose prospective teachers and school leaders to "best" practices of teaching linguistically, culturally, and ethnically diverse students. The need to develop the attitudes, knowledge, skills and dispositions necessary among pre-service educators for them to be competent to teach and lead a diverse student population has remained a major policy issue in U.S. teacher education (Horsford, Grosland, & Gunn; Milner, 2003; Zeichner & Liston, 1990). In a quest to continue the commitment to social justice and equity in public schools, there is still a lot that remains to be done pertaining to developing effective teachers who are culturally competent and critically conscious. The student population in U.S. schools continues to become increasingly different in background from the background of their teachers. Key researchers have broken ground in this area through their various perspectives on the issue of educating pre-service teachers and leaders—Gloria Ladson-Billings (1995) on culturally relevant pedagogy, Geneva Gay (2000) on culturally responsive teaching, Brooks and Miles (2010) and Horsford, Grosland, and Gunn (2011) on culturally relevant leadership, Kenneth Zeichner (1983) on traditions of reform in teacher education and Christine Sleeter (2001) on preparing mainly white preservice teachers to teach diverse students. Their work has been influential in enhancing the knowledge of policy, theory, and practice in educating students effectively and highlighting what still needs to be done.

However Bartolomé (1994), Giroux (2005), and Wilson, Douglas, and Nganga (2013), among others, point out that the debate about improving minority academic achievement has often been reduced to a technical issue in policy texts and in preparation programs. Bartolomé (1994) further explains that the academic underachievement of minority students is often explained as a result of a lack of "cognitively, culturally, and/or linguistically appropriate teaching methods and educational programs" while "the solution to the problem of academic underachievement tends to be constructed in primarily methodological and mechanistic terms dislodged from the sociocultural reality that shapes it" (pp. 173–174). Further, the question of how teachers and leaders should be educated cannot be explored without taking into consideration the role of teacher education and leadership preparation programs in maintaining or transforming the institutional arrangements of schools and understanding the complex social, political, and economic patterns that are linked to schooling (Brunner, Hammel, & Miller, 2010; Sloan, 2009; Zeichner, 1983, 1993). In this regard, as scholars and educators of pre-service teachers and school leaders, we wish to extend this conversation using a critical pedagogical lens and specifically Paulo Freire's concept of *radical love* to interrogate our ways of teaching and opening up spaces for dialogue towards educating pre-service teachers and leaders who are critically conscious. Preparing to teach and lead a culturally and linguistically diverse student body warrants that educators examine their own values and assumptions about working with students who are different from them. Indeed, teacher educators such as Sleeter (2001) acknowledge that the cultural gap between students in the schools and the educators who teach and lead them continues to grow. Statistics confirm this cultural gap with the teaching work force being over 80% white (NCES, 2009). One's ideological posture informs and often times unconsciously colors the perceptions of teachers who work with diverse students (Bartolomé, 2004). Hence, it is important for pre-service teachers and those in leadership preparation programs from dominant cultures to have avenues in university classrooms where they can process issues pertaining to cultural differences, their uncertainties, and assumptions that they may have about the students they will teach and lead.

An important aspect of preparing teachers and leaders who are critically conscious is integrating and interrogating the positionalities of those who work with pre-service teachers and school leaders. In turn, the process of interrogating our positionalities as educators also allows us to incorporate pedagogies that offer pre-service teachers and school leaders an opportunity to interrogate who they are as future teachers of diverse student populations. In this paper, we therefore use Paulo Freire's concept of radical love to explore the similarities and disjunctures in our pedagogy and positionalities as international scholars of color. Specifically, we draw from our experiences teaching undergraduate and graduate pre-service teachers, and school leaders. The purpose of this paper is twofold—to discuss how our positionalities impact the practice of our teaching and to explore ways in which we enact radical love in our classrooms.

Defining *epistemology* and *positionality* is a necessary endeavor in this essay, and so for the purposes of linguistic transparency and authorial catharsis, we acknowledge and accept that there are embedded complexities and challenges to amalgamating our voices, positionalities, and epistemologies into a coherent co-written manuscript. We persist with this highly nuanced project, rift with its own complexities, because of our commitments to social justice and anti-oppressive teaching. We embrace Dillard's (2003) admonition that "epistemology (how we know reality) is not a monolithic body, but is instead the ways in which reality is a deeply cultured knowing that arises from and embodies the habits, wisdom, and patterns of its contexts of origin" (p. 155). Said another way, one's epistemology is a highly nuanced filter that is constructed from an amalgamation of the social, political, and historical dynamics of lived experience. How we know reality is not a streamlined process that leads to a static end. Instead, much like one's positionality, the process of knowing shifts and morphs as variables and contexts change. In this light, we find Villaverde's (2008) definition of positionality to be powerful and apropos for this essay because it explicitly reveals the intersections between identities, epistemology, and positionality. Villaverde (2008) describes positionality as "how one is situated through the intersection of power and the politics of gender, race, class, sexuality, ethnicity, culture, language, and other social factors" (p. 10). Moreover, we seek to account for the complexity and diversity that inform our identities, our practices as educators in teacher-education classrooms, and our roles as researchers/scholar-practitioners who embrace elements of critical pedagogy and radical love in our praxis.

Pedagogy not oppression. There is a false assumption that pedagogy and teaching are necessarily synonymous. There are many teaching practices and ideologies that are not pedagogical in the Freirian sense, and these distinctions must be made explicit, through critical reflection, thoughtful interrogation, and conscientious inquiry if we are to honor the intent of Freire's (1970) manifesto, *Pedagogy of the Oppressed,* and more importantly, become critical agents of anti-oppressive education as a political project. Sadly, pre-service teachers and school leaders are given far too few opportunities to reflect on, inquire about, and interrogate who they are as human beings, developing pedagogues, and critical agents/ facilitators of anti-oppressive 21st century classrooms and schools. This is not to suggest that there is a neat and unified approach to critical or anti-oppressive pedagogy. Our position is quite the opposite, in fact. Teachers who honor and embrace the Freirian tradition of pedagogy do not simply acknowledge and adjust to the messiness concomitant with critical reflection, thoughtful interrogation, and conscientious inquiry. Instead, these pedagogues are intentional about elucidating (and even creating) the inherent tensions, while respecting the "liminal spaces" (Villaverde, 2008) that members of the learning community will need to see the intersections between power, oppression, and pedagogy, *identify* their complicity in the status quo, and *embrace* their responsibility to act. Villaverde (2008) reminds us that "[t]here is no set way or process for pedagogy; it is ever evolving, organic, and dynamic" (p. 135). What is clear is that one's pedagogy (and leadership, for that matter) cannot be disassociated from power differentials and oppression, for and across individuals and institutions. Still, defining or describing *pedagogy* as the positionality of the teacher or leader in relation to these dynamics alone falls short of Freire's philosophy of education. Aronowitz (1993) declares that, the term he (Freire) employs to summarize his approach to education, 'pedagogy' is often interpreted as a 'teaching' method rather than a philosophy or a social theory. Few who invoke his name make the distinction. To be sure, neither does *The Oxford English Dictionary* (p. 8). Macedo (2000) makes this distinction clear in describing pedagogy in his introduction to *30th Anniversary Edition of Pedagogy of the Oppressed,* where he points out that "education is inherently directive and must always be transformative" (p. 25). Macedo (2000) asserts that educators must understand that education is never neutral, even "as they engage in a social construction of not seeing" (pp. 24–25). For Villaverde (2008), "pedagogy sits at the intersection of understanding the systems of oppression, one's location within these, and one's agency in negotiating such experiences" (pp. 128–129). This broader conceptualization of pedagogy is vital to this analysis, because it lays the groundwork for understanding how revolutionary ideologies like critical pedagogy/ theory (of which Freire is often credited as the founder), engaged pedagogy (hooks, 1994), and even post-structural pedagogy are embodied in and operationalized within the context of *radical love* (as a pedagogical strategy/ approach). In the following section, we further explore critical pedagogy, radical love, and teacher identity in order to situate our own positionalities and praxis as teacher-educators who are committed to anti-oppressive, transformative pedagogy.

Critical Pedagogy

Critical pedagogy is an approach to education that involves liberation. Freire's work has been pertinent in furthering a critical pedagogical approach to education (Freire 1970, 1992, 2005). Other 20th century thinkers that have furthered this approach include McLaren (1999) and Bartlett (2005). Darder (1991) describes *critical pedagogy* as an

> educational approach rooted in the tradition of critical theory. Critical educators perceive their primary function as emancipatory and their primary purpose as commitment to creating the

> conditions for students to learn skills, knowledge, and modes of inquiry that will allow them to examine critically the role that society has played in their self-formation.
>
> (p. xvii)

In this respect, critical pedagogy is highly contextual and is neither a "recipe" nor a "method" (Darder, 1991). Villaverde (2008) offers this poignant description:

> Critical pedagogy aims to develop and nurture critical consciousness to address larger political struggles and transformations in dealing with rampant oppressive social conditions. It works from Paulo Freire's critique on the banking concept of education to chart new pedagogical experiences, carefully mining popular culture for a wide range of learning possibilities. A transformative pedagogy is made possible by the close investigation of margins and center (that is, of power) and through the cultivation of critical consciousness, praxis, and engagement of the self as a public change agent.
>
> (p. 129)

Further, Kincheloe (2008) asserts, "proponents of critical pedagogy understand that every dimension of schooling and every form of educational practice are politically contested spaces" (p. 2). The culture of schooling is not a neutral culture where every child naturally finds a sense of belonging. Teachers have to intentionally carry a disposition in their practice that enacts an inviting space for all students, including those who have been traditionally marginalized (Douglas & Peck, 2013).

Said differently, a critical pedagogical approach to education values learning experiences as an avenue for bringing forth social change by engaging in criticisms of capitalism, inequity, injustice, and other social ills that plague institutions and the larger society. Critique is never disassociated from the learners' responsibility to reflect on how they may be complicit in and beneficiaries of inequitable systems and disproportionate power relations. Critique is not an end in and of itself. It is only as effective as the learners' capacity to both question and ground their ideologies and those of the wider community within larger geo-political, socio-historical, and cultural constructs. Therefore, teachers who engage in critical pedagogical approaches are always informed about current issues pertaining to injustices and intentional about contextualizing and connecting these issues to the past. Critical pedagogy is a larger filter that undergirds conceptualizations of *radical love* which we discuss below.

Radical Love

Trying to establish a unified and universally accepted definition of love is an exercise in futility. And we will make no such attempt, since we respect that there are many interpretations of what love is and isn't based on various social, cultural, and spiritual traditions. Instead, for the sake of grounding our discussion of Freire's notion of *radical love* and our descriptions of how we mobilize his conceptualization in our own praxis, we believe it is necessary to acknowledge various understandings of *love. The New American Webster Handy College Dictionary* defines love as "affection for another person; an object of affection, a sweetheart; any strong liking or affection; (in games) a score of zero." Cunningham (2004) delineates between what she sees as "false love" and "real love" to suggest that: "*real* love involves radical action. . . . When we choose real love, we refuse to work within the system. We don't play by The Rules. In real love, we choose to speak not in the language of competition and violence, but in that of cooperation and compassion. The language of real love is simple and straightforward. It begins with self-acceptance. Once we begin to remove the superficial measures of beauty, success, and what's considered 'good and normal' from our lives, we start to move towards accepting people in all their flawed glory . . . Real love can be as simple as a glass of water" (p. 37). Darder (2002) embraces a similar philosophy by asserting that love can be an anti-oppressive force used to resist exploitation.

Not surprisingly, there is disagreement among scholars on the various *types* of love as historically framed by Greek philosophers. While Helm (2005) asserts that there are three brands of *love* that are traditionally attributed to the Greek philosophical tradition, Lewis (1960) asserts that there are actually four types of love: *eros* ("romance"); *philia* (friendship); *storge* ("affection"); and *agape* ("unconditional love"). While Helm (2005) and Lewis (1960) disagree on the validity of *storge,* and the distinctions between the various brands of love are not always clear, there appears to be more consensus on the connections between *agape love* and spiritual traditions. For example, Ryoo, Crawford, Moreno, and McLaren (2009) "privilege" *agape love* as the most appropriate 'brand' for framing their conceptualization of *critical spiritual pedagogy.* Lewis (1960) contends that *agape love* is the brand of love that is described in 1 Corinthians 13, which is also described as the *love chapter.* Christian biblical tradition affirms that "love is patient, love is kind. It does not envy, it does not boast, it is not proud. It is not easily angered, it keeps no record of wrongs. Love does not delight in evil but rejoices in the truth. It always protects, always trusts, always hopes, always perseveres. Love never fails" (1 Corinthians 13: 4 – 8, NIV). 1 John 4: 18 suggests that "perfect love casteth out all fear." In this biblical text, there's the suggestion that the opposite of love is not hate but fear. While both hooks (2003) and Hanh (1993) suggest that fear is an impediment of love, hooks is intentional about highlighting the interconnectedness of spirituality, education, and love. Similarly, Hanh (1993) declares that "[t]he usual way to generate force is to create anger, desire, and fear. But these are dangerous sources of energy because they are blind, whereas the force of love springs from awareness, and does not destroy its own aims" (p. 84). These theoretical conceptualizations have interesting connections to Freire's understanding of *love,* and more specifically, *radical love.*

Freire's notion of love is not entirely dissimilar from the perspectives of many popular traditions. In fact, he asserts that "love is an act of courage, *not fear*. . . . a commitment to others. . . . [and] to the cause of liberation" (1970, p. 78). Equally significant is the centrality of dialogue to Freire's conceptualization of love, and by extension, the relevance of language and its inherent power. Freire (1993) declares:

> Dialogue cannot exist . . . in the absence of a profound love for the world and for people. The naming of the world, which is an act of creation and re-creation, is not possible if it is not infused with love. Love is at the same time the foundation of dialogue and dialogue itself.
>
> (p. 89)

It is on this foundation that Freire's conceptualization of *radical love* stands. For Freire, radical love requires a commitment to dialogue and the capacity to take risks for the benefit of those we teach and ourselves. One of the risks we must take as pedagogues is to relinquish oppressive practices in the classroom, such as *the banking system of education,* in which students are treated like empty receptacles. In place of trying to *fill* students with knowledge, *radical love* demands that we utilize dialogue as a means of subverting dominant positionalities, since [love] "cannot exist in a relation of domination" (Freire, 1993, p. 89). In this respect, Freire's conceptualization of dialogue is far more demanding than surface conversations: "Founding itself upon *love, humility,* and *faith,* dialogue becomes a horizontal relationship of which *mutual trust* between the dialoguers is the logical consequence" (Freire, 1993, p. 91, emphasis added). This is a high calling that seems diametrically opposed to traditional conceptions of schooling and common conceptualizations that many new and experienced teachers hold in the classroom. Freire's (1993) questioning in this regard is profound and worthy of extended consideration:

> How can I dialogue if I always project ignorance onto others and never perceive my own? How can I dialogue if I regard myself as a case apart from others—mere 'its' in whom I cannot recognize other 'I's'? How can I dialogue if I consider myself a member of the in-group of 'pure' men, the owners of truth and knowledge, for whom all non-members are 'these people' or the 'the great unwashed'? How can I dialogue if I start from the premise that naming the world is the task of an elite. . .? How can I dialogue if I am close to—and offended by—the contribution of others? How can I dialogue if I am afraid of being displaced, the mere possibility causing me torment and weakness? Self-sufficiency is incompatible with dialogue. . ..At the point of encounter there are neither utter ignoramuses nor perfect sages; there are only people who are attempting, together, to learn more than they now know.
>
> (p. 90)

In many respects, Freire's questioning above is the antithesis of traditional conceptualizations of what it means to teach. For one thing, far too few pre-service educators were/are challenged to reflect on these questions prior to entering the sacred space of the classroom. Without doubt, Freire (1970) would assert that this reality exists for the same reason that problem-posing education is unpopular in many schools: "[it] does not and cannot serve the interests of the oppressor. No oppressive order could permit the oppressed to begin to question: Why?" (p. 86). Notably, undergirding dialogue is an active *hope* and a commitment to *critical thinking* that is never disassociated from fearless action—all of which are always more potent than "false love, false humility, and feeble faith" (pp. 91–92). For those who claim or seek to educate, Freire's emphasis on communication, critical thinking, and dialogue as hallmarks of true education demand that radical love is extricated from the realm of the ephemeral so that our daily, horizontal interactions with humanity—in our classrooms and beyond—become the barometer by which we judge our praxis.

A profound love for humanity, coupled with a love for our subject matter and the power of ideas, must be present in order to teach—since teaching requires a love for the people and a love for the world (Darder, 2002; Freire, 1993, 1998). In fact, Freire staunchly believed that "teaching is an act of love" (Darder, 2002). McLaren (2000) described this love as "the oxygen of revolution, nourishing the blood . . . [and] spirit of struggle" (as cited in Darder, 2002, p. 148). As teachers of future educators and proponents of *radical love,* we recognize that we must equip our students with tools that they can use to liberate themselves from forms of ignorance and oppressive practices in order to embrace and enact "a revolutionary pedagogy" (Darder, 2002, p. 148) in their own classrooms. Radical love, as a theorization that privileges the voices and perspectives of marginalized voices and non-dominant positionalities/ perspectives, allows us to recast power differences in our classrooms, even as it provides tools for dialogue, action, and hope.

Teacher Identity

In exploring our teaching through the concept of *radical love* we offer a space where educators have a better understanding of the "self" they bring to the classroom in addition to the historic, social, cultural and political forces that have played a role in how they perceive themselves as future teachers and leaders. Scholars who explore *teacher identity* have mainly explored the concept within the framework of professional and personal aspects of teaching, such as effectiveness and commitment in teaching, subject matter expertise, student relationships and collegial relationships, dispositions, values and beliefs towards teaching (Day, 2002; Day & Kington, 2008; Walkington, 2005). Additionally, even for those who explore teacher identity among pre-service teachers, such as Danielewicz (2001) and Olsen (2009) who utilize a holistic view of how teacher education programs impact the teacher-self that is emerging, their work—though significant—does not focus on the social, historical and political factors that shape the ideological stances of teachers. Specifically, how those ideologies are linked to issues of power and privilege is not made explicit. We wish to incorporate the sociopolitical factors that impact teacher identity and thus the perspectives they bring to the classroom about teaching and leading diverse learners. We acknowledge that identity markers such as race, ethnicity, class or gender are not static but fluid. In this regard, Cochran-Smith (1995) contends that it is crucial for educators to understand their identity with this kind of examination, beginning with investigating our own histories as educators—"our own cultural, racial, and linguistic backgrounds and our own experiences as raced, classed, and gendered children, parents, and teachers in the world" (p. 500). For this reason, there is need for educators in teacher education and leadership programs to incorporate the socio-cultural and political dimensions of identity to the professional and personal aspects to helping pre-service teachers and leaders understand who they are and how the self impacts their practice.

The works of Florio-Ruane with de Tar (2001) and Cooper (2007) are particularly useful in linking the personal-professional dimensions of teacher identity with the socio-cultural and political dimensions in helping pre-service teachers understand how who they are impacts how they teach. Florio-Ruane focuses on the dialectical relationship between the teacher and the diverse student body that preservice teachers will teach by using autobiographies of authors of diverse backgrounds, with the aim that "in their conversational responses to those writers and texts, teachers can awaken to their own experiences of their culture, especially those that influence their work as educators" (Florio-Ruane & de Tar, 2001, p. xxvi–xxvii). In his review of Florio-Ruane's text, Sloan (2004) adds that "while reading such texts by teachers is a way for them to learn about lived experiences of persons whose backgrounds are different from their own, the real power of such texts lies in their potential to foster reflexivity about teachers' own cultural identities" (p. 119). Indeed, Florio-Ruane and de Tar point out that conversations of such texts need to go beyond comfortable narratives of self and society in order to unsettle conventional notions of culture. Embracing an identity that entails teaching for diversity then requires the act of interrogating other people's experiences against the backdrop of one's own.

While Florio-Ruane and de Tar (2001) privilege cultural texts as the avenue through which identity work happens among pre-service teachers, Cooper (2007) places significance on community-based learning as an avenue for pre-service teachers to locate their professional selves by correcting misconceptions about culturally and linguistically diverse students. Through incorporating a series of activities in her course such as writing one's own autobiography and "walking a mile in another's shoes," Cooper noticed a shift in pre-service teachers' views and beliefs about the students they teach, as well as their families and the communities in which they live begin. The "connected sequential activities" they embark on allows them to learn "(a) who they are, (b) who they want to appear to be, and (c) who they are but do not want others to see" (Cooper, 2007, p. 253). In so doing, pre-service teachers critically examine their ideologies about teaching diverse learners. Thus, developing a professional identity is not just a matter of examining "who am I as a teacher," but additionally "who am I as a teacher of diverse learners?" This is an important component of identity work among pre-service teachers that has heavily influenced how we think about our teaching and scholarship.

Interrogating Our Positionalities and Epistemologies

In order to evaluate how we navigate our identities, pedagogies, and positionalities (as well as those of our students) in our work as educators, it is necessary to make the connections between these concepts explicit. We see our positionalities and pedagogy as two interrelated concepts that are grounded in and outgrowths of various elements of personal, cultural, and community identity. Despite the many scholars who have commented on the social constructedness of the concepts of race, class, and gender (Dillard, 2003; Douglas, 2012; Fine, Weis, Weseen, & Wong, 2000; Gresson, 2008; hooks, 2000; Johnson, 2006; Omi & Winant, 1986; Schwalbe, 2005), there appears to be a reluctance in scholarly discourse to consistently interrogate the impact of socially constructed knowledge and "patterns of epistemology" (Dillard, 2003). As a result of this reluctance, many people also fail to see the social constructedness and constructive (or destructive, depending on one's positionality) powers of research (Dillard, 2003) and pedagogy. In this respect, post-formal thinking is significant in expanding the narrow conceptualizations of intelligence in order to uncover how particular communities (usually non-white, poor, and feminine) have been excluded and marginalized (Kincheloe & Steinberg, 1993). Much like critical pedagogy, "post-formal thinking works to get behind the curtain of ostensible normality," and post-formal thinkers/ teachers "work to create situations that bring hidden assumptions to our attention and make the tacit visible" (Kincheloe & Steinberg, 1993, p. 306). For example, critical pedagogues/ post-formal thinkers challenge how research has been used historically to *scientifically prove* the inferiority of minority groups (Dodson, 2007; Kincheloe & Steinberg, 1993; Kincheloe, Steinberg, & Gresson III, 1996). Critical pedagogues not only acknowledge how teachers have used their positionalities and classroom powers to reinforce oppressive paradigms in the minds, hearts, and report cards of students; additionally, through their praxis, they work against systems of domination for the good of all students.

Research and pedagogy are shaped by people, social contexts, and institutional forces, even as they also shape people (and perceptions of people), social contexts, and institutional forces. Ladson-Billings (2000) hints at the multiple ways in which knowledge construction and research intersect by reminding us that "epistemology is more than a 'way of knowing.' An epistemology is a 'system of knowing' that has both an internal logic and external validity" (p. 257). Moreover, as pedagogues and researchers, we inform others (and ourselves), as we stand on and speak from the (mis)understandings and (mis)interpretations of our own positionalities, our own identities, and our research. In the subsequent sections, we seek to account for the complexity and diversity of identity and positionality in our own experiences as scholar-practitioners, recognizing that there are distinct similarities and differences in who we are and how we teach.

Learning to Teach and Teaching to Learn: Christine's Reflection

Naming who I am as an educator and scholar is problematic. One of the reasons is because I believe that identity (whether as an educator or as a person) is fluid, multiple and dependent upon social, political, historical and cultural forces. I have been acted upon as I act upon these forces in the multiple worlds that I have lived and continue to live in. I do believe as Taylor, Tisdell and Hanley (2000) affirm that my positionality and that of the students impact the classroom dynamics and how we construct knowledge in this shared space. Though I may be perceived to have some level of power as the instructor, I am also aware that my ethnicity (coming from a different country of origin) warrants questioning regarding my capacity to understand and analyze issues of diversity and difference in foreign soil, in this case a U.S. university classroom. I also realize that how I am positioned by my students may be different from how I position myself. My ways of knowing what I know and how I utilize that knowledge is culturally nuanced by my background that has been impacted by having studied in an educational system that still bears the markers of Britain as Kenya is a former colony. I am also aware that I may be (and often have been) viewed by students and professionals in the academy as a "native informant" who knows everything about Africa and may speak for Africans in an academic space. I therefore wrestle with my teaching within and between the intersections of who I think I am and who I am perceived to be. In this regard, Freire's concept of radical love offers me a footstool on which to stand as I enact my teaching. I accept his call to take risks in the classroom, and embrace the courage to teach (Palmer, 1998) while creating spaces of dialogue (even uncomfortable conversations).

In seeking to teach as an act of love, I conceptualize that kind of love as one that critically challenges the way we think and act by denying being a part of a dehumanizing education even when the system constantly beckons educators to be such, but instead embrace a liberatory educational practice as Freire admonishes. Indeed, love is the basis of education that seeks justice and equality for all (Kincheloe, 2008).

I embrace a love for humanity, for the students I teach, for self, and for others. I cannot have the courage to teach if I do not care enough for my students and the larger humanity whom they will impact. I understand that this is not an easy task. I must guard myself against the inflictions of fear and intimidation as an upcoming scholar-practitioner who seeks not only to unsettle issues of power and privilege within U.S. schools but to help my students understand the global world that we live in— that one nation's decisions impacts other nations as well. I therefore stretch the dismantling of issues of power and privilege in my classroom not only to reach U.S. classrooms but also to sensitize students to an awareness that we live in an interconnected world and to examine how the U.S. utilizes its international space to consider how issues such as economic trends, social ills, impacts other nations including developing nations.

I am a firm believer in co-constructing knowledge in the classroom. However, I am also aware that the ways of knowing and what we know that we bring into the classroom are sometimes problematic, especially when layered with oppressive notions, deficit thinking, and "I am better than you" attitudes. Therefore, for me embracing a pedagogy of radical love also includes helping students to analyze the roots of their knowledge basis and often times offering tools to garden different roots for what they come to believe and know about themselves, society, and the students they will teach. Hence a humanizing education must embrace a "deeply reflective interpretation of the dialectical relationship between our cultural existence as individuals and our political and economic existence as social beings" (Darder, 2009, p. 568). I am committed to this way of educating, knowing and being.

Enacting Radical Love in the Classroom

Over the course of my doctoral work, I taught a course called *Diverse Learners* to preservice and alternative licensure teachers and a similar course as faculty to school leaders in preparation. This course was designed to provide students with a broad base of knowledge and skills that will facilitate their effectiveness in meeting the needs of diverse learners through appropriate instructional, curricular, and behavioral strategies. Students also explored diversity with respect to race, ethnicity, socioeconomic class, language, gender and exceptionalities. The majority of the students were white and came from varying socioeconomic backgrounds. I was cognizant of the complexities of teaching in a university classroom where none of the voices are silenced even when those voices are not of the majority. I concur with Montecinos (2004) who points out that instructors in teacher education programs should not simply be concerned about training white teachers to teach diverse learners. Pre-service students of color can also benefit from such courses by validating the cultural knowledge they bring and helping them translate it into a libratory pedagogy. Additionally, students from poor and working class backgrounds need to affirm their own agency even as they sometimes "express frustration, anger and sadness about the tensions they experience in trying to conform to acceptable white middle class behaviors in university settings" (hooks, 1994, p. 182). Teaching in a classroom within such complexities is not an easy venture. However, even within such complexities and tensions, I found three interrelated aspects of enacting a pedagogy of radical love that helps me to remain true to what I believe about teaching and learning and to offer pre-service teachers a classroom space where they could have the freedom and the safety to examine who they were as well as the knowledge they bring about teaching culturally, ethnically and linguistically different populations. These were building community, creating dialogic spaces, and critical reflective practice.

Building community. Building community among students is a beginning point in creating a space for enacting radical love in the classroom. Palmer (1998) with whom I concur, believes that teaching, learning, and knowing happens through a communal web of relationships. Creating a sense of community in the classroom helps the instructor to step away from the banking method of education that Freire strongly reproves of. In teaching within a community, students are regarded as a "reservoir of knowledge" and the teacher's role varies from "facilitator to co-learner" (Palmer, 1998, p. 116). Indeed, Freire believes that students and teachers simultaneously carry both embodiments. Building community helps every student to feel valued and like their experiences matter even when they are different from the majority. Second, it is also a forum to understand that the realities of lived experiences are varied both for the pre-service teachers and for the future students they will teach. It is within community that students and teachers can have authentic dialogue and that education becomes a process of inquiry in which students and the instructors are all engaged in the process of co-constructing knowledge.

Creating Dialogic Spaces. Teacher education classrooms need to be spaces where students can question

> the omissions and tensions that exist between the master narratives and the hegemonic discourses that make up the official curriculum and the self representations of subordinated groups as they might appear in 'forgotten' or erased histories, histories, texts, memories, experiences and community narratives.
>
> (Giroux, 2005, p. 25)

Such spaces can either be in traditional classroom spaces, through electronic media, and in large or small groups. Offering students multiple spaces for dialogue has proved to be functional and constructive. For students who are less forthcoming in larger settings, they seem to find their voice in smaller groups. Additionally, online discussion groups provide forums where students can dialogue about the course material using directed prompts when they do not meet in traditional classrooms. Second, when students respond to one another through online discussions, they are able to see how their assumptions continue to be challenged from the beginning of the course to the end. Respect for all is required in these discussions. This kind of dialogue "requires an intense faith in human kind to make and remake, to create and re-create, faith in their vocation to be more fully human" (Freire, 1970, p. 90).

Critical Reflective Practice. Critical reflection among pre-service educators is crucial in helping them uncover biases, assumptions and beliefs about teaching students who are culturally, ethnically and linguistically different (Howard, 2003; Miller, 2003). As an avenue to uncover their biases, beliefs and assumptions about each aspect of diversity, students respond to prompts taken from the course readings and materials. In this regard, it is important to expose pre-service educators to course materials that offer them the opportunity to understand aspects of systemic inequalities in schools and societies as well as what they can do as teachers and leaders in their classrooms, schools, and communities. Critical reflective practice in this way helps them to situate their beliefs with the current literature on aspects of diversity and to subsequently build on their own future practice in teaching and leadership.

Building community, creating dialogic spaces, and critical reflective practice cannot be treated as isolated elements of enacting the concept of radical love. Each of them enhances the others. When students feel a sense of belonging in a learning community, their uncertainties do not become barriers to learning as they discover how to challenge reductionistic notions of schooling and education.

Pedagogue as Border Crosser: Ty's Reflection on Positionality

As a Christian, Black (African Bermudian/American), heterosexual man, I recognize that it is a privilege and responsibility to be in the academy at this time. I believe that my unique background affords me the opportunity to transcend cultural borders as an educator, researcher and scholar. Still, I recognize that I can be viewed with some degree of suspicion and distrust by those who hold different views, particularly if these views have been influenced by distasteful experiences with institutions and individuals who utilize similar labels to the ones that reflect elements of my positionality. For instance, as a Christian, I recognize that more people have been killed in the name of God than any other name; as a Black man, I also understand that despite the accomplishments of inspirational Black men like President Obama and Dr. King, Black men are still, by in large, expected to emulate the characteristics espoused by the media—criminals, athletes, and dead-beats (Gause, 2008). The image of men as egotistical, unfaithful brutes, in addition to the changing roles of men, both influence my role as an educator and researcher because they influence how I know reality; moreover, my epistemology has been shaped by socio-cultural practices and norms in Bermuda and the United States that espouse particular brands of Black masculinity. As a Black Bermudian/American male who has been afforded the opportunity to prepare educators in the United States, I am both an insider and an outsider on multiple levels—a border crosser. Still, my positionality encompasses more than my ethnic background and national affiliations.

Naming how my beliefs as a Seventh-day Adventist Christian inform and intersect with my work as a scholar-practitioner is a necessary step if I am to honestly account for my subjectivity in the classroom and define my positionality. By drawing on what some would describe as primitive Biblical principles, in one sense my positionality as a Seventh-day Adventist reflects traditional Christianity; yet, in another sense, it is far from traditional in that it espouses teachings that are no longer common in traditional or mainstream Christianity. For example, unlike many who reduce Christianity to a religion of New Testament teachings, my perspective encompasses the whole Bible as the standard for truth, hope, and wisdom in ways that many nominal Christians no longer acknowledge or accept—this includes adherence to all of the Ten Commandments. Drawing from the work of Peshkin (1988), I have determined that all of my "I"s are undergirded by my primary researcher positionality as a *non-traditional Christian intellectual.* I have determined that my other (more specific) "I"s include, but are not limited to: the non-traditional Christian Intellectual/ Witness I; the Husband and Father I; the Family/People Centered I; the Black Masculinity I; the African Bermudian/American I; the Ethnic and International Difference I; the Border Crossing I; the Questioning of the Establishment/Authority/Status Quo I; the Respectfully Rebellious I; and the Critically Hopeful I. All of these lenses intersect to impact my gaze and role as an educator, researcher and scholar.

Wrestling with radical love. I continue to wrestle with Freire's notion of *radical love.* I question whether the term radical love is even appropriate to use to describe our daily human interactions. My discomfort is rooted in the belief that *love* is one of the most abused concepts in the human experience. I believe the capacity to love, radically or otherwise, is a gift from God. More than that, I believe that God is love (1 John 4: 8). In fact, my initial thoughts upon hearing the term *radical love* used in an academic setting raced to reflections of Christ hanging on a cross for the sake of humans who would reject Him. In this context, Freire's notion is not radical or loving enough, I thought. Certainly, Freire wasn't asking me to give my life for someone else. . .or was he? My questioning of whether the term radical love was/is an appropriate describer for our daily human interactions is rooted in my belief that much of what we do as humans is actually rooted in selfishness and fear, rather than love. In spite of my initial discomfort, I began to conceptualize what *radical love* could look like in the classroom. Recognizing and respecting that individuals embrace various spiritual and existential positions, I wondered how this notion of *radical love* could be reeled in from its perch and operationalized so that it is not reduced to lofty, overstated language.

As I reflected on what I see as radical love personified—Christ's sacrifice for humanity, I was reminded that He did not simply offer Himself as *the* sacrifice; in addition, He lived a life *of* sacrifice. His life was not merely about moments. His life was devoted to ministry. Biblical record suggests that Jesus engaged in a (radical) pedagogy that challenged the religious leaders of His day and is a far cry from nominal Christianity today, where the tangible needs and pain of human beings seem to be obscured by mere church attendance, emblems on a chain, and sermonic overtures. In this context, dialogue has been replaced with dogmatism, passion for the destitute has been usurped by prejudice, and love has been kidnapped by lip-service on one extreme and legalism on the other. Sadly, some of the most damaging and divisive language runs off the lips of people who would self-identify as Christians. This pattern is typified by the disturbing billboard posted by a *Christian* minister in Kansas after the election of Barak Obama: "America, we have a Muslim president. This is a sin against the Lord." Certainly, the abuse of God and religion has caused many to echo the words of Mahatma Gandhi: "I like your Christ, I do not like your Christians. Your Christians are so unlike your Christ." In this light, I realized that the challenge to operationalize *radical love* is a personal one: I reflected on my praxis. Pedagogically speaking, I thought about what sacrificing my life for my students looks like. Ultimately, I sought a balanced interpretation of *radical love* as a pedagogical imperative for all educators, understanding and respecting that there are a variety of life philosophies, spiritual traditions, existential allegiances, and belief systems that inform how we think, feel, act, and teach: some choose to eschew any notion of faith; others aim to live a life of faith; and still others operate on a continuum somewhere in-between. For Freire (1970), faith in humanity (along with an abiding trust and hope) is critical to our capacity for dialogue.

Radical Love, Radical Pedagogy

Teaching a course for undergraduate pre-service teachers on the "institution of education" and similar graduate courses for school leaders has allowed me to enact *radical love,* engage in radical pedagogy, and reflect on my positionality and responsibility as an educator. As I engaged in these processes, I was encouraged by the work of scholars like Freire (1970), Dillard (2000), West (1982, 1993), Dantley (2005), and hooks (1994), who (in their own ways) name how spirituality undergirds who they are and the risks they take for the sake of the educational advancement of their students. Even now, as an emerging scholar who sees spirituality as central to my work in the academy, I can relate to the "spiritual crisis" and tensions Cozart (2010) experienced as a result of her "belief that spirituality was a separate layer of marginalization, separate from race and gender. . .[which caused her to act] as if spirituality was a third consciousness, rather than part of my merging double-consciousness into a better truer self" (p. 253). Like Cozart, I have no desire to live, teach or lead from such an oppressive paradigm, even as I embrace the inherent risks that emerge anytime one names her/his positionality. I understand and embrace these risks, knowing that, at times, it feels easier and safer to discuss issues of race, class, gender, and sexuality in the academy than it does to dialogue about issues of spirituality. Clearly, there are a number of reasons that can account for this reality, including the tendency and tensions created by the conflation of spirituality with religion and religious experiences (Cozart, 2010; Dantley, 2005; Douglas & Peck, 2013), respect for separation of church and state legislation, and the personal nature of spirituality. Frankly, to encourage dialogue and investigation around issues of spirituality is risqué – radical even. To be clear, I feel the tension now as I attempt to articulate some of the strategies I utilize in my classroom. Still, I draw strength from my commitment to my students and my praxis, understanding that, there is an aspect of our vocation that is sacred

> . . . our work is not merely to share information but to share in the intellectual and spiritual growth of our students. To teach in a manner that respects and cares for the souls of our students is essential if we are to provide the necessary conditions where learning can most deeply and intimately begin.
>
> (hooks, 1994, p. 13)

More than that, I teach, lead, and live by the mantra that "perfect love casteth out all fear" (1 John 4: 18) or in the words of Freire (1970), "love is an act of courage, not fear. . . . a commitment to others. . . . [and] to the cause of liberation" (p. 78).

Going beyond 'middle people.' Many of my students have expressed their discomfort and fear of discussing topics like religion/ spirituality in their other course experiences. Colleagues who embrace various religious/ spiritual traditions have expressed similar sentiments to me. Having taught in somewhat conservative communities, including areas in the Bible-belt, I understand that many of my students enter my classroom with prior knowledge and experiences with some form of religion. Ironically, this topic is rarely broached within the context of their identities as educators and individuals who wrestle with their beliefs.

In my classroom, I emphasize the importance of dialogue, recognizing that it is a means through which transformation can begin, relationships are developed, and mutual respect is forged. I also emphasize the importance of reading and researching primary documents for ourselves. For example, we discuss how religion—particularly Christianity in the U.S.—has been abused and used as a means of oppression and domination. My students are usually astounded by what they learn about Christopher Columbus and his disturbing exploits in the name of God (Loewen, 2007). As students try to reconcile the purpose for and means by which they will teach their students about Columbus (in light of their new knowledge), they are also challenged with the reality that most school textbooks herald Christopher Columbus as a brilliant hero. These revelations and discussions often propel students to declare: "what else haven't we been told and why have these truths been kept from us?" Through various exercises and activities, I challenge students to research and consider contemporary manifestations of these dynamics, particularly as it relates to textbooks. In this context, spiritual/biblical texts are textbooks. Students are encouraged to bypass the "middle people" (my gender-sensitive adaption of "the middle men")—i.e. teachers, pastors, rabbis, bishops, priests—in order to engage in their own study of primary and secondary documents. Students are encouraged to dialogue with the documents in whatever manner they deem appropriate: listening, responding, contesting, interrogating, meditating, and praying are options that some students utilize to dialogue with the documents. I give no parameters for how students should engage in this research, except that they look at the documents for themselves and allow their previously held perspectives to be challenged. For me, this is not a sneaky evangelistic strategy. This is about encouraging future teachers to develop the agency to challenge paradigms and institutions, understanding that the schoolhouse is not the only *institution of education* (Douglas, in press; Douglas & Peck, 2013; Khalifa, Dunbar, & Douglas, 2013).

Students often research common assumptions that are grounded in historical, political, and religious traditions: for example, students are often amazed when they uncover that the history of Sunday observance as the Sabbath is rooted in the dictates of Emperor Constantine and the Roman Catholic Church, rather than the Bible. Other students challenge the history and validity of the Bible, and discussions about whether there are actually lost books of the Bible or who actually wrote the Bible become platforms for deeper dialogue and inquiry into power, language, positionality, and institutions (of education). We also reflect on how racism is institutionally perpetuated in religious settings today; for example, we challenge what Black church/ White church dichotomies reveal about humanity and the Christian church. We question children's literature that portrays angels as exclusively White and male. We look at gender roles—in particular, the oppression of women in some biblical cartoon portrayals. We also interrogate the assumption that America is a Christian nation. These activities push students to reflect on their individual and collective identities, their positionalities, and the implications these dynamics have for their praxis.

Fear factor. When students first walk into my classroom, I sense that they bring with them many fears. Some are afraid to fail; some are afraid to talk; some are afraid to sound obtuse, while others seem to be afraid of each other. . .or at least afraid to talk to each other; then there are those who appear to be afraid of me, in the sense that I am the one who supposedly holds the power. As an instructor who hasn't forgotten what it feels like to be a student, I have come to know many of these fears all too well. As I help my students unpack these dynamics throughout the semester, it also becomes clear that most of these pre-service teachers and leaders are also afraid of not being in *control* of their students or the learning process. For many of these future teachers and leaders, to be publically challenged by a student or to not know the *correct answer* to a student's question is an unpardonable sin. For me, *radical love* demands that I challenge these fears and help them to relinquish the belief that they can actually control the learning process or the learning spaces that function beyond the walls of their classrooms.

Learning from community-based pedagogical spaces. Teachers, administrators, and policy makers continue to ignore the impact of non-school based educative locales on students. Community-based pedagogical spaces are "non-school based locales, institutions, forces, or methods that have been/ are utilized for educational purposes," such as the media, music, churches, barbershops, hair salons, sports clubs/fields, and theaters (Douglas, in press; Douglas & Gause, 2009; Douglas & Peck, 2013). Drawing on the tradition of historical scholarship and the works of Freire (1970) and Cremin (1970, 1980, 1988), scholars who embrace the breadth of what it means to educate, I utilize a community-based pedagogical space assignment to encourage students to talk to people and learn from spaces outside of traditional classrooms. Pre-service teachers and leaders are challenged to consider where and how learning takes place. Much like educators fear losing control in their classrooms or not knowing a correct answer, there also seems to be a fear of acknowledging or embracing the educative power of spaces outside of the schoolhouse. As an act of radical love, this is a fear that I try to dismantle and challenge in my work with pre-service teachers.

As I challenge my students to face the fear and contradictions of lived experiences inside and outside of the classroom, I simultaneously challenge them to reflect on the risks that will be necessary if they are to share a sense of hope through their pedagogy and leadership. The outcomes of these processes are not always fully apparent to me. I often remind my students that *the process is more important than the product; in fact, the process is the product.* Often, the fruits of the process are readily apparent in students who exit the course more committed to a social justice agenda. Ultimately though, this process-based approach is rooted in the hope and faith that I have in my students to continue the inquiry process that is promoted in my class. Where the journey leads them is beyond my influence and jurisdiction. My responsibility is to give them tools and opportunities to challenge oppressive systems and ideals. It's a process that I continue to engage in personally. Even as I participate in and name particular positionalities, systems and ideologies, my position as a non-traditional Christian intellectual is not a passive one: I am willing to name and challenge "injustice anywhere," recognizing that it is always "a threat to justice everywhere" (King, 1963, p. 1854).

Conclusion: Radical Love as Process and Product

Enacting radical love in our classrooms has become a way to take risks in having conversations about the socio-cultural dynamics imbedded in our positionalities, our identities as instructors, and the positionalities and identities of our students. It is an approach in our teaching that helps us to stay true to the ideals of critical pedagogical approaches, while still modeling a more humanizing way of teaching and learning for our students. As leaders of pre-service teachers, we believe that: *having a position* is expected; *knowing* your position is important; *naming* one's positions is vital, but *critically reflecting* on how your *havings, knowings,* and *namings* may impact your interactions with students is the difference between preparing to teach/lead and preparing to be an anti-oppressive pedagogue and leader who will radically love all students.

References

Aronowitz, S. (1992). *The politics of identity: Class, culture and social movements.* New York: Routledge.

Bartolomé, L. (1994). Beyond the methods fetish: Toward a humanizing pedagogy, *Harvard Educational Review,* 64(2), 173–194.

Bartolomé, L. (2004). Critical pedagogy and teacher education: Radicalizing prospective teachers. Teacher Education Quarterly, 31(1), 97–122.

Brooks, J. S., & Miles, M. T. (2010). Educational leadership and the shaping of school culture: Classic concepts and cutting-edge possibilities. In S. Douglass Horsford (Ed.), *New possibilities in educational leadership: Exploring social, political, and community contexts and meaning* (pp. 7–28). New York: Peter Lang.

Brunner, C. C., Hammel, K., & Miller, M. D. (2010). Transforming leadership preparation for social justice: Dissatisfaction, inspiration, and rebirth—an exemplar. In S. Douglass Horsford (Ed.), *New possibilities in educational leadership: Exploring social, political, and community contexts and meaning* (pp. 261–277). New York: Peter Lang.

Cochran-Smith, M. (1995). Color blindness and basket making are not the answers: Confronting the dilemmas of race, culture, and language diversity in teacher education. *American Educational Research Journal,* 32(3), 493–522.

Cooper, J. (2007). Strengthening the case of community-based learning in teacher education. *Journal of Teacher Education,* 58(3), 245–255.

Cozart, S. C. (2010). When the spirit shows up: An autoethnography of spiritual reconciliation with the academy. *Educational Studies,* 46(2), 250–269.

Cunningham, V. (2004). Radical love. *Off Our Backs.* May-June, 36–37.

Dantley, M. E. (2005). African American spirituality and Cornell West's notions of prophetic pragmatism: Restructuring educational leadership in American urban schools. *Educational Administration Quarterly,* 41, 651–674.

Darder, A. (1991). *Culture and power in the classroom: A critical foundation of bicultural education.* New York, NY: Bergin & Havery.

Darder, A. (2002). *Reinventing Paulo Freire: A pedagogy of love.* Boulder, Colorado: Westview.

Darder, A. (2009). Teaching as an act of love: Reflections on Paulo Freire and his contribution to our lives and our work. In A. Darder, M. P. Baltodano & R. D. Torres (Eds.), *The critical pedagogy reader* (pp. 567–578). New York, NY: Routledge.

Day, C. (2002). School reforms and transitions in teacher professionalism and identity, *International Journal of Educational Research,* 37, 677–692.

Day, C. & Kington, A. (2008). Identity, well-being and effectiveness: The emotional contexts of teaching. *Pedagogy, Culture and Society,* 16(1), 7–23.

Dillard, C. B. (2003). Cut to heal, not to bleed: A response to Handel Wright's "An endarkened feminist epistemology?" Identity, difference and the politics of representation in educational research. *Qualitative Studies in Education,* 16(2), 227–232.

Dodson, J. E. (2007). Conceptualizations and research of African American family life in the United States. In H.P. McAdoo (Ed.), *Black families* (4th ed., pp. 51–68). Thousand Oaks: Sage.

Douglas, T.M.O. (2012). Resisting idol worship at HBCUs: The malignity of materialism, Western masculinity, and spiritual malefaction. *The Urban Review,* 44(3): 378–400.

Douglas, T. M. O., & Peck, C. M. (2013). Education by any means necessary: An historical exploration of community-based pedagogical spaces for peoples of African descent. *Educational Studies,* 49(1), 67–91.

Douglas, T.M.O. (in press). Conflicting Messages, Complex Leadership: A Critical Examination of the Influence of Sports Clubs and Neighborhoods in Leading Black Bermudian Males. Journal manuscript. *Planning & Changing.*

Fine, M., Weis, L., Weseen, S., & Wong, L. (2000). For whom? Qualitative research, representations, and social responsibilities. In N. K. Denzin & Y. S. Lincoln (eds.), *Handbook of qualitative research* (2nd ed.) (pp. 107–131). Thousand Oaks, CA: Sage Publications, Inc.

Freire, P. (1970). *Pedagogy of the oppressed.* New York: Continuum.

Freire, P. (1993). *Pedagogy of the city.* New York: Continuum.

Freire, P. (1998). *Teachers as cultural workers.* Boulder, CO: Westview Press.

Florio-Ruane, S. with de Tar, J. (2001). *Teacher education and the cultural imagination: Autobiography, conversation and narrative.* Mahweh, NJ: Lawrence Erlbaum.

Gause, C.P. (2008). *Integration matters: Navigating identity, culture, and resistance.* Peter Lang Publishing.

Giroux, H. A. (2005). *Border crossings* (2nd ed.). New York: Routledge.

Gresson, A. D. III. (2008). *Race and education primer.* New York: Peter Lang.

Hanh, T. N. (1993). *Love in action: Writings on nonviolent social change.* Berkeley, CA: Parallax Press.

Helm, B. (Ed.) (2005). Stanford Encyclopedia of Philosophy. http://plato.stanford.edu/entries/love/.

hooks, b. (1994). *Teaching to transgress: Education as the practice of freedom.* New York, NY: Routledge.

hooks, b. (2000). *Where we stand: Class matters.* New York: Routledge.

Howard, T. (2003). Culturally relevant pedagogy: Ingredients for critical teacher reflection, *Theory into Practice,* 42(3), 195–202.

Horsford, S., Grosland, T., & Gunn, K. M. (2011). *Pedagogy of the personal and professional: Toward a framework for culturally relevant leadership,* 21, 582–606.

Johnson, A. G. (2006). *Privilege, power, and difference* (2nd ed.). Boston: McGraw Hill.

Khalifa, M., Dunbar, C., & Douglas, T. M. O. (2013). Derrick Bell, CRT and educational leadership 1995-present. *Race, Ethnicity, and Education,* 16(4), 489–513.

Kincheloe, J. (2008). *Critical pedagogy* (2nd ed.). New York, NY: Peter Lang Publishing Inc.

Kincheloe, J. L., & Steinberg, S. R. (1993). A tentative description of post-formal thinking: The critical confrontation with cognitive theory. *Harvard Educational Review.* 63, 296–320.

Kincheloe, J. L., Steinberg, S. R., & Gresson III, A. D. (1996). *Measured lies.* New York: St. Martin's Press.

King, M. L. (1963). *Letter from Birmingham jail.* In H. L. Gates Jr. & N. Y. McKay (Eds.), *The Norton Anthology: African American Literature* (pp. 1854–1866). New York: W. W. Norton & Company.

Ladson-Billings, G. (1995). Toward a theory of culturally relevant pedagogy. *American Educational Research Journal.* 32(93), 465–491.

Lewis, C. S. (1960). *The four loves.* Ireland: Harvest Books.

Loewen, J. W. (2007). *Lies my teacher told me: Everything your American history textbook got wrong.* New York: Touchstone.

McLaren, P. (2000). *Che Guevara: Paulo Freire and the pedagogy of revolution.* New York: Rowman & Littlefield.

Milner, H. R. (2000) Reflection, racial competence, and critical pedagogy: How do we prepare pre-service teachers to pose tough questions? *Race Ethnicity and Education,* 6(2), 193–208.

Montecinos, C. (2004). Paradoxes in multicultural teacher education research: students of color positioned as objects while ignored as subjects. *International Journal of Qualitative Studies in Education,* 17(2), 167–181.

Omi, M., & Winant, H. (1986). *Racial formation in the United States: From the 1960s to the 1980s.* New York: Routledge.

Palmer, P. (1998). *The courage to teach: The inner landscape of a teachers life.* San Francisco, CA: Jossey-Bass.

Peshkin, A. (1988). In search of subjectivity – One's own. *Educational Researcher,* 17(7), 17–21.

Ryoo, J. J., Crawford, J., Moreno, D. & McLaren, P. (2009). Critical spiritual pedagogy: Reclaiming humanity through a pedagogy of integrity, community, and love. *Power and Education,* 1(1), 132–146.

Schwalbe, M. (2005). *The sociologically examined life: Pieces of the conversation.* Boston: McGraw Hill.

Sleeter, C. (2001). Preparing teachers for culturally diverse schools: Research and the overwhelming presence of whiteness. *Journal of Teacher Education,* 52(2), 94–106.

Sloan, K. (2009). Dialoguing towards a racialized identity: A necessary first step in politics of recognition. In P. M. Jenlink & F. H. Townes (Eds.). *The struggle for identity in today's schools: Cultural recognition in a time of increasing diversity* (pp. 30–48). Lanham, MD: Rowman & Littlefield.

Taylor, E., Tisdell, J. E. & Hanley, S.M. The role of teaching for critical consciousness: Implications for Adult Education. Retrieved August 5, 2008 from http://www.edst.educ.ubc.ca/aerc/2000/tayloreetal1-final.PDF.

Villaverde, L. (2008). *Feminist primer.* New York: Peter Lang.

Walkington, J. (2005). Becoming a teacher: encouraging development of teacher identity through reflective practice. *Asia-Pacific Journal of Teacher Education,* 33(1), 53–64.

West, C. (1982). *Prophecy deliverance: An Afro-American revolutionary Christianity.* Philadelphia: Westminster Press.

West, C. (1993). *Race matters.* Boston: Beacon.

Wilson, C. M., Douglas, T. M. O., & Nganga, C. (2013). Starting with African American success: A strengths-based approach to transformative educational leadership. In L.C. Tillman & J. J. Scheurich (Eds.), *Handbook of research on educational leadership for diversity and equity.* (pp. 111–133). New York, N.Y.: Routledge/Taylor and Francis.

Zeichner, K. M. (1983). Alternative paradigms of teacher education. *Journal of Teacher Education,* 34(3), 3–9.

Zeichner, K. (1993). *Educating teachers for cultural diversity* (Special Report). East Lansing, MI: National Center for Research on Teacher Learning.

Zeichner, K., & Liston, D. (1990). Traditions of reform in U.S. teacher education. *Journal of Teacher Education,* 41(2), 3–20.

29

Power, Politics, and Critical Race Pedagogy: A Critical Race Analysis of Black Male Teachers' Pedagogy

Marvin Lynn and Michael E. Jennings

Introduction

In this article, we discuss two important areas of study in the research on African-American education: the development of critical pedagogy and the emerging scholarship on Black teachers. In particular, we conduct an analysis and critique of critical pedagogy and then we examine how Black feminist thought and critical race theory have been used as frameworks to examine the work of politically conscious teachers of African descent.

There have been numerous critiques of critical pedagogy as a discourse that theoretically gives shape to the practices, beliefs and dispositions of teachers who foster social criticism in their classrooms. There is also an existing literature that discusses the specific practices of Black teachers. However, there are few studies that have explicitly examined the links between critical pedagogy and the scholarship on Black teachers. When referring to 'the scholarship on Black teachers' we are referring to the entire body of studies – past and present – that describes and typifies the experiences, beliefs, characteristics and practices of Black teachers in the US and abroad.[1]

While scholars who conduct research on Black teachers have often been explicit about the influence of critical theory (Foster 1992; Ladson-Billings 1994) in their work, critical theorists have not been as willing to admit how their work has, in turn, been influenced by the ongoing scholarship on Black teachers. Specifically, explorations of how Black teachers prepare Black children (and others) to become highly literate and culturally competent social critics (Lynn 2004), has been overlooked by contemporary critical theorists.

We problematize this issue in several ways. First we explore what we believe to be the 'true roots' of critical pedagogy. The discussion is further supported and augmented by examples of the work of 'critical pedagogues in practice' who happen to be African-American male teachers. As we will explain later, these men theorize and employ many of the strategies that are commonly accepted as part of the critical pedagogical discourse. Of prime importance however, is an understanding that these teachers also differ in significant ways from other socially conscious teachers who are represented in the work of researchers such as Weiler (1988) and Kanpol (1992). These differences, as we explain, are explored and discussed, to some extent, in the works of Foster (1997), Henry (1998), Irvine (2004), Ladson-Billings

(1994) and others who explore the unique contributions of Black teachers. However, as we will show, African-American male teachers offer a unique contribution to teaching that is under-theorized and must be explored further.

We begin by providing a brief overview of critical pedagogy and its theoretical and historical foundations. Next, we review some of the more recent empirical examinations of Black teachers' work and show how these areas of study cohere by cross-referencing illustrative themes. Lastly, these themes are used to explore the work of two African-American critical pedagogues who have taught in urban schools. As is consistent with previous studies, we find that these critical pedagogues teach in ways that reflect the tenets of critical pedagogy as well as those issues addressed in the scholarship on Black teachers. Furthermore, we conclude by showing how their work is in line with these ways of thinking and discuss implications for further research and policy.

Origins of Critical Pedagogy Within Critical Theory

> Critical theory seeks to understand the origins and operation of repressive social structures. Critical theory is the critique of domination. It seeks to focus on a world becoming less free, to cast doubt on claims of technological scientific rationality, and then to imply that present configurations do not have to be as they are.
>
> (Gordon 1995, 190)

Not only do critical theorists attempt to discover why oppressive structures exist and offer criticisms of their effects; they also explore the ways in which we can transform our society.[2] In this sense, critical theory is not simply a critique of social structures, but an analysis of power relations. Such questions as: 'What constitutes power?' and: 'Who holds it?' and: 'In what ways is power utilized to benefit those already in power?' are central to critical theory. These theoretical underpinnings of critical theory provide the foundation for our contemporary understanding of critical pedagogy. In a recent article (Jennings and Lynn 2006), we explored the connection between critical pedagogy and critical theory and discussed the influence of decades of theorizing about the relationship between society's educational structures and their relationship to the socio-cultural positions of individuals in society. In short, critical pedagogy echoes critical theory by calling for a re-examination of the links between knowledge and power and how power in particular is constituted and maintained through educational institutions.

Critical Pedagogy in the US

Many contemporary educational theorists have adopted a highly interdisciplinary approach to the study of critical pedagogy. This contemporary critical pedagogy (as conceived in the academy) is often viewed as an idea largely grounded in the research of scholars such as Henry Giroux, Peter McLaren, Stanley Aronowitz, Michele Fine, Michael Apple and numerous others. The term 'critical pedagogy' was in fact first used in text by Henry Giroux in 1983 (Darder, Baltodano and Torres 2003). The approach to critical pedagogy taken by Giroux is of special importance because of the primacy of his contributions to educational theory and research throughout the shifting intellectual and historical scenes of the past thirty years (Morrow and Torres 1995).

Giroux has displayed a strong interest in sociology and critical thinking. His work followed the research of Bowles and Gintis (1976) who strongly argued that schools were closely linked to the industrial order through their reproduction of inequality in society (Giroux 1983). McLaren (1989), Aronowitz (1981), Kanpol (1991), Kincheloe and other key thinkers also subscribed to this school of thought. This ideology was in stark contrast to many other educational theorists who believed school primarily provided a means by which students could gain power and status in American society (Cubberley 1919; Cremin 1961).

Collectively, these theorists challenged such assumptions by emphasizing schools as sites that embody the elements of both domination and liberation. By doing so, schools became contested spaces rather than simple sites for reproducing dominant ideology. This view of critical pedagogy rejected the idea that individuals were passive beings whose fate was subservient to the dominant powers of society. Instead, they combined a focus on domination and oppression with an examination of how individuals exercise agency to counter such forces. The resulting critical pedagogy required both a critique of society (particularly in relation to issues of power) and an attempt to develop the 'critical abilities' of students and teachers so they might work towards the positive transformation of society (deMarrais and LeCompte 1999). Central to this ideal was a focus on teaching/learning practices that are 'intended to interrupt particular historical, situated systems of oppression' (Lather 1991, 121). For critical pedagogues in the US, this means fostering a view of both students and teachers as 'transformative intellectuals' who engage in critical dialogues that view classrooms as sites where they can challenge basic assumptions about the relationship between power and knowledge (deMarrais and LeCompte 1999).

Critical pedagogues were also interested in the links between structure and agency. In examining this link, they paid particular attention to the role of human beings as both reproducers and producers of culture who could actively resist oppression through pedagogical work. In short, critical pedagogues:

1. Question the links between knowledge and power.
2. Recognize the dialectical nature of oppression as a dehumanizing force that requires some level of 'participation' from their students.
3. Believe that dialogue and reflection are key ways to empower students in the classroom.
4. View their students as 'producers' of knowledge with the ability to transform oppressive social and cultural structures.

These four tenets will be instrumental to helping us establish a view of critical pedagogy 'from the bottom'.

While critical pedagogy has been a key discourse on emancipation in US classrooms, it has been critiqued widely (Ellsworth 1989; Gordon 1995; Gore 1990; Lather 1991; Hytten 1998; Jennings 1999; Jennings and Lynn 2006; Lynn 2004; McCarthy and Apple 1988; Murillo 1999). These critiques suggest that critical pedagogues have minimized or ignored the reality that oppressed groups in America have produced 'critical' ways of knowing and learning that have been transformed into practice by oppressed people themselves (Jennings 1999). Perhaps even more importantly, critics suggest that specific examples of 'critical theory in practice' can be found in diverse social and philosophical movements worldwide (Leonard 1990, xv) and that this knowledge has not been sufficiently attended to by critical theorists who believe that the classroom can be both a site of liberation and oppression (Gordon 1995; Jennings and Lynn 2006). The research on Black teachers illustrates this clearly.

Black Education Research and Black Feminist/Womanist Teachers

African-American scholars and educators have explored the differences between 'schooling' as a process of hegemonic control of African-American self-determination and 'education' as a liberatory process of obtaining and utilizing community-sanctioned forms of knowledge in order to improve society (Shujaa 1994). Knowledge of this distinction is important for a more complete understanding of the socio-cultural context and uneven power dynamics that have shaped the African-American educational experience (Jennings and Lynn 2006). Schooling is a formal process that takes place within institutions that are directly (or indirectly) linked to the state (Aronowitz and Giroux 1994). This process is 'intended to perpetuate and maintain the society's existing power relations and the institutional structures that support those arrangements' (Shujaa 1994, 15). In contrast, education is a broader and often less formalized process (often taking place outside of formalized educational institutions) that represents a 'collectively produced set of experiences organized around issues and concerns that allow for a critical understanding of everyday oppression as well as the dynamics involved in constructing alternative political cultures' (Aronowitz and Giroux 1994, 127).

This is not to say that schooling and education (or schools and non-schools) are mutually exclusive in their existence and goals. It is possible for the two to overlap. There are certain aspects of schooling that can serve the common interests of an entire society regardless of the particular 'position' (as related to race, class, gender, etc.) of any given individual or group in that society (Shujaa 1994). However, these commonalities are often overshadowed by the fact that the common mutual benefits of schooling and education are contextualized within a particular set of experiences shaped by the race and class distinctions of American society. For African-Americans, these experiences speak closely to how issues of race, identity, and resistance are negotiated in America. Despite this realization, it must be understood that the formalized learning process engendered within schools is an important component for analyzing and understanding critical pedagogy. However, limiting this analysis to the formal structures of schooling has left other educational venues un-examined and under-theorized (Jennings 1999).

A careful review and analysis of the research on Black teachers in the US and abroad reveals that Black teachers use their classrooms as spaces to: (1) question the links between knowledge and power; (2) encourage their students to become active agents of social and cultural transformation through their participation in civic and community-based organizing and activism; (3) strategically use dialogue as a means to 'dig out knowledge' (Ladson-Billings 1994) and incite their students to act on their own behalf as agents of democracy and freedom; and (4) illustrate the ways in which they value their students as 'producers of culture' by using their contextually and regionally specific cultural/linguistic knowledge as a means to inform, and create curriculum in the classroom (Foster 1990, 1991, 1993, 1994, 1995a, b, 1997). Research on Black teachers has been informed by multiple theoretical viewpoints including critical theory (Casey 1993; Henry 1998), multicultural education (Ladson-Billings 1994, 1995; Lynn in press), Black feminism/womanist thought

(Beauboeuf-Lafontant 2002, 2005; Dixson 2003; Johnson 1999; Henry 1990, 1992, 1998), critical race theory (Lynn 1999; Jennings and Lynn 2006; Morris 2001) and Afrocentricity (King 1991; Lee 1992). Of special note is research in the critical race and womanist/Black feminist traditions, which draws from critical pedagogy in significant ways. Black feminism/womanism with its outwardly political stance against racism, sexism and classism closely resembles both critical pedagogy and critical race pedagogy in significant ways. We will explore this concept further in the next section.

Black feminist and womanist[3] research raises 'questions about how Black women teachers' consciousness and understandings at the intersections of race, class, gender, and culture contribute to and shape their pedagogical practice' (Henry 1998, 3). In other words, womanist research on teaching explores how Black women's multiple identities and their understanding of that identity influences their pedagogies.[4] Their pedagogies also reflect intersectional identities that call attention to racist, sexist and elitist schooling practices in fundamentally transformative ways (Beauboeuf-Lafontant 2005). Womanist teachers, according to Henry (1998) 'work toward the cultural, political, educational, and spiritual survival of Black children' (3) and embody many of the beliefs and principles discussed in critical pedagogy. First, they employ 'oppositional' political, social and educational standpoints. They offer criticisms of inequities in the broader society and participate in efforts to organize movements against forms of political and economic tyranny that disenfranchises Black communities. So, while they speak from an authoritative Black woman's standpoint and take up strong positions against sexism in their communities, their ultimate goal is ensure the survival of all Black children. Henry's womanist teachers also have strong beliefs about the use of culturally appropriate practices for Black students living in Canada. They are critical of teaching methods that purport to be progressive while ignoring the cultural realities of African descended students. In that sense, they vehemently oppose methods and practices that they believe are harmful to Black children irrespective of their intent. Their pedagogical practices are tied to their political beliefs about the need for Black Canadians to foster freedom from the political and pedagogical constraints that confine them.

Womanist teachers are also activists who participate in, critique, resist and work to transform the political process in many different ways. According to Beauboeuf-Lafontant, they 'locate themselves in the traditions of female activism' and embrace the notion of 'politicized mothering' as a form of caring activism (2005, 440). Expounding on the notion of politicized mothering, one teacher in her study of African-American womanist teachers commented:

> Blacks have *always* escaped from the plantation, returned to help others get Freedom. Escape from the community, the ghetto, what, *return* and help those that will get out... I see my *role* to step back and help those that *will* come out. [Original author's emphasis.]
>
> (Beauboeuf-Lafontant 2005, 440)

In this way, the act of mothering is not only a deep expression of caring, it is deeply political act; one that is part of one's responsibility as a member of the African-American community (Casey 1993). Mothering becomes a key method through which womanist teachers not only provide safety and security to children in need of love and protection but it is a key way in which they ensure the survival of the community. Dixson, in her study of Black feminist teachers (see our previous endnote regarding Collins' 1996 article 'What's in a name?'), argues that 'African women teacher's [community-based] political activities are part of a broader conception of pedagogy' (2003, 219). In other words, activism is teaching and teaching constitutes an 'act of love' (Darder 1998). African-American women teachers don't love simply for the sake of loving they also tie their love to their personal and political commitments. This combination of the political and personal is a hallmark of Black feminist research and theory (Collins 1991). In other words, the act of 'othermothering' could be described as a form of 'politically relevant teaching' (Beauboeuf-Lafontant 1999); she argues that 'because of the political understanding of education held by these educators, their actions are sensitive to and supportive of the antiracism and anti-oppression struggles of students of color generally' (704). In other words, it is these teachers' understanding of the political crises faced by the African community that drives their work. In short, Black Feminist and/or womanist teachers see teaching as a deeply political act; one that is ultimately about community transformation.

Within the context of American education, the mothering done by Black teachers helps to affirm the multiple identities of their students as part of the process of ensuring the survival of the African-American community. Their teaching is shaped and influenced by their own experiences with race, gender and class subjugation. Their indignation about social inequality is fueled by their very personal experiences with hegemony and domination. This indignation fuels their political work in and out of the classroom. They often work beyond the four walls of the classroom to include activist work in progressive community-based political organizations. This may also include aggressive forms of resistance to school structures and policies that unnecessarily hurt African-American children (Henry 1998). In summary, African-American women who are driven by a Black feminist or womanist ethic embody the previously discussed four essential qualities endemic to critical pedagogues in a multitude of ways.

First, these teachers engage in a broad questioning of the links between knowledge and power. Not only do they ask questions about who holds the key to knowledge and why, but they ask important questions about the political purposes and functions of certain forms of knowledge. Even more important, they attempt to situate knowledge within its historical context and connect it to their students' lives recognizing the extent to which African descended students are indeed 'producers of culture'. Second, these teachers also recognize the extent to which oppression is dialectical in nature and requires some participation from the oppressed. They work to foster a critical consciousness in their students about race, class and gender oppression so that students do not remain complicit in their dehumanization. Third, Black feminist or womanist educators believe in the power of dialogue as a liberating force in the classroom. However, they do not 'give up' their authority in the classroom in order to facilitate their students' freedom. They are deeply critical of classroom practices that promote freedom without providing students with the proper guidance. Lastly, Black feminist and womanist teachers view their students as producers of knowledge who possess the ability to transform oppressive social and cultural structures. These teachers often model this behavior through the cultural act of 'talkin' and testifyin'' as a form of pedagogy. This act often involves elements of storytelling and narrative that utilizes African linguistic styles such as Ebonics or Jamaican patois. Many Black feminist/womanist teachers see this as a culturally appropriate way to help raise students' consciousness about their own development as well as the development of their communities. Students participate in this form of pedagogy by 'talking back' in their own language through the sharing of their own stories and drawing relationships between their stories and those of others (Ladson-Billings and Henry 1992; Henry 1998).

They illustrate of critical pedagogues are strongly evident in the work of Black feminist/womanist teachers. These characteristics illustrate the integral connection between these teachers and the communities they have come from as well as the communities in which they teach. Their love for and commitment to these communities often extends from the personal relationships they have with their students and the commitments they have to the broader Black community. Next, we will explore the pedagogy of African-American male teachers – whom we identify as critical race pedagogues – that embody both similar and different characteristics.

Positioning Our Positionalities

Black feminist and womanist research has served as a guiding framework for critical race research on teaching.[5] This research has expressed a commitment to social change and utilized critical methodologies as lens through which to enact that social change. Henry's expression of her agenda is a key example. She expresses solidarity with and a sense of political commitment towards other Black women who choose to struggle against what hooks (1998) refers to as a White supremacist patriarchy. The question we must ask ourselves is: what does it mean to be a Black man struggling against similar systems of dehumanization and oppression? How can Black men challenge systems of race, gender and class domination while articulating and perhaps re-articulating their subjectivities as dominated people who also have the power to dominate? How do we 'sing our sacred song' (Lee 1990) in a land that positions us as anti-intellectual, oversexed, violent, misogynistic, and emotionally distant and cold? How do we overcome even Afrocentric representations of Black masculinity that can sometimes present us as homophobic and one-dimensional? Is it possible to challenge the notion that caring is essentially a feminine quality and that men who care about children are pedophiles or perhaps simply less masculine than 'real men' who leave the task of teaching to women (Sargent 2001)?

In what ways does critical race theory provide possibilities for engaging these questions? Like Black feminist thought, critical race theory (CRT) centralizes the Black subject as both narrator and subject. However, CRT removes feminist/womanist paradigms from the central focus of analysis and permits a re-focusing on the unique positionality of African-American male teachers. This positionality embodies a duality that stems from the position of African-American males as both privileged males in a patriarchal society and as racialized 'others' in a society that historically supports the maintenance of racial oppression.

CRT as a Critical Theoretical Guidepost

CRT as a critique of racism in law and society emerged as a race-based critique growing from the National Critical Legal Studies conferences that took place at the Harvard and UC-Berkeley Law Schools in the early to mid 1980s (Crenshaw et al. 1995; Lawrence 2002). This group of law professors and students began to question the objective rationalist nature of the law and the process of adjudication in US courts. They criticized the way in which the real effects of the law served to privilege the wealthy and powerful in the US while having a deleterious impact on the rights of the poor to use the courts as a means of redress. Out of this evolving critique of the role of law in society, a second strand of critical scholarship emerged through the writings of Derrick Bell, Mari Matsuda, Richard Delgado, Angela Harris, and Kimberle Crenshaw. These scholars argued that the critical legal studies movement did not go far enough in challenging the specific racialized nature of the law and its impact on persons of color. These young legal scholars of color, many of whom eventually became the architects of critical race theory as a political scholarly movement, made several distinct claims that gave shape and emphasis to their arguments:

1. Racism has been a normal daily fact of life in society and the ideology and assumptions of racism are ingrained in the political and legal structures as to be almost unrecognizable. Legal racial designations have complex, historical and socially constructed meanings that insure the location of political superiority of racially marginalized groups.
2. As a form of oppositional scholarship, CRT challenges the experience of White European Americans as the normative standard; CRT grounds its conceptual framework in the distinctive contextual experiences of people of color and racial oppression through the use of literary narrative knowledge and storytelling to challenge the existing social construction of race.
3. CRT attacks liberalism and the inherent belief in the law to create an equitable just society. CRT advocates have pointed out the legal racial irony and liberal contradiction of the frustrating legal pace of meaningful reform that has eliminated blatant hateful expressions of racism, yet, has kept intact exclusionary relations of power as exemplified by the legal conservative backlash of the courts, legislative bodies, voters, etc., against special rights for racially marginalized groups (Bell 1988; Crenshaw et al. 1995; Delgado 1987; Matsuda et al. 1993).

As CRT has evolved, it has begun to take up new discourses and offer new challenges to legal doctrine in American jurisprudence. Critical race feminism, for example, has emerged as an area of study with respect to women of color and their connection to the law and public policy's impact on their lives as women, both in the US and in an international context of race, gender and nationality (Berry and Mizelle 2004; Wing 2000). In particular, critical race feminism examines the impact of that law on women of color in terms of a more interactive and intersecting gender/race/social class analysis. Critical race feminism calls on women to form coalitions with artists and activists in local communities to push for change that will benefit women of color and their families in local contexts.

Critical race scholars in education have worked over the past decade to explore the theoretical and methodological significance of CRT and its role in as well as its links to education theory and practice. CRT literature that examines teaching looks at the practices and beliefs of teachers in K-12 classrooms. They have used CRT as a means through which to explore the experiences of teachers and students of color in US classrooms. They have also used the knowledge that teachers of color of possess to construct 'critical race pedagogies' that construct a critique of racism in education while also putting forth some ideas about how to address race and racism in the classroom. In general, critical race studies of teaching and teacher education call attention to racist classroom practices that not only marginalize students of color but they address the ways in which local and national policies impact teaching in America's diverse classrooms. They ask important questions such as: 'How does racism shape and influence how teachers interact with minority youth?' and: 'How can a critical interrogation and understanding of race and racism transform our classroom practices?' Hence, the development of a critical race pedagogy is a way of addressing inequalities in classrooms as well as providing some information about the best way to move forward in order to transform our classrooms into places where minority students might thrive.

Framing the Study

Studying the work of teachers (and African-American teachers in particular) has been a continuing challenge to educational researchers. This challenge is especially evident in studying the complex and multi-layered (Weiner 1993) dynamics that teachers face both in and out of the classroom. For researchers of African-American teachers this has been made even more problematic due to their exclusion from many historical records and the resulting lack of research related to their own experiences (Foster 1997). Foster (1997) quotes Margaret Meade in asserting that teachers are still viewed almost exclusively as White, middle-class women in the popular imagination. Making this challenge more difficult is the fact that teachers work within dynamic school environments that contain students, administrators and other educators. Thus research related to the work of teachers invites a broad range of research methodologies that can be instituted to illuminate particular phenomena in the context of teachers' experiences. This particular study seeks to examine the knowledge and dispositions of African-American teachers. Specifically, this study asks, 'What is unique about the pedagogy of African-American teachers, especially as related to African-American students?'

To fully explore this question, a methodology based primarily on acquiring, analyzing and interpreting narrative data was sought. Direct contact with a purposeful sample of African-American teachers was utilized to create access points that would facilitate an understanding of the daily lives of African-American teachers. In meeting these teachers and pursuing knowledge about their pedagogy and their relationship to the school community we encouraged individual teachers to 'tell' their own stories but also remained cognizant of our place as co-constructors of the narratives that unfolded. Our purpose in seeking the teachers' narratives extended beyond a mere recording and analyzing of information and instead amounted to what Dixon, Chapman and Hill (2005) have described as a 'search for goodness'. This search is a methodological hallmark of 'portraiture', a narrative methodology developed by Sara Lawrence-Lightfoot in her ongoing in-depth studies of education in socio-cultural context (1983, 1997, 1995). The notion of searching for goodness informs our move as researchers to go beyond the traditional emphasis on pathology that has been a hallmark of research surrounding the African-American experience in educational institutions (Dixon et al. 2005; Lawrence-Lightfoot 1983, 1997). Despite this, our work with African-American teachers differs from portraiture in that it is framed by the more explicitly political context of critical race theory.

In our study of African-American male teachers, critical race theory is utilized as a lens to develop a set of counter narratives that challenge prevailing ideas about African-American educators. This methodological approach utilizes aspects of portraiture framed by critical race theory that informs social context allowing for a more nuanced understanding of the experiences of African-American teachers. It also provides further insight regarding the pedagogies that have been shaped by these teachers' experiences. Solorzano and Yosso (2005) have extensively explored the concept of 'critical race methodology' and its importance as an analytical framework for educational research. In developing this line of inquiry, Solorzano and Yosso (2005) distinguish critical race methodologies from '. . . deficit informed research that silences and distorts' (23) the unique experiences and epistemologies of people of color. Tillman (2002) adds to this discourse by specifically discussing the importance of culturally sensitive research in the African-American community and points to research on Black teachers and students as prime examples for a culturally sensitive research framework. It is within such a framework that we have undertaken our examination of African-American teachers and how their narratives reveal a critical pedagogy of resistance that seeks to challenge hegemonic structures in the African-American educational experience.

The Study

This study of the work and lives of Black urban schoolteachers was conducted during the 1999–2000 school year. Across the nation, the majority of Black teachers taught in large urban school districts where the majority of students were Black (Frederick. D. Patterson Research Institute 1997). This was also true for California. Black teachers constituted nearly 16% of Los Angeles Unified School District's teacher population during the 1998–1999 school year (Los Angeles Unified School ITD 1998). The study was conducted in a small working class African-American community nestled at the northern edge of South Central Los Angeles; a community that has traditionally been home to the area's African-American population.[6] The community was called *Strivers Point* because it had developed a reputation over the years for being the site of political and social action for African-Americans in Los Angeles. As visits were conducted in the community over a period of nearly two years, it was found that people in the community were always 'striving' to make the community and the city a better place for those who were the most disenfranchised. All of the schools in the study could be considered 'Black schools' because more than 75% of the students in each school were Black. In both cases, the majority of teachers (65% or more) were also Black. In addition, the majority of students in these schools were also eligible for free and reduced lunch. One of the schools, Strivers Point Middle School was nestled in the midst of this community. South Central High was located outside of the official community boundaries but it was the school most often attended by children who graduated from Strivers Point Middle School. Two teachers, one from each school, participated in this study. See Table 1.

Each teacher was chosen on the basis of several criteria. First, they were to be working as full-time classroom teachers. Second, since past research on Black teachers often illuminated these teachers' commitment to making certain that African-American children could attain academic success while instilling in them a critique of inequality and thirst for social change (Henry 1998; Ladson-Billings 1994), it was important to find teachers who met this criteria. In other words, the goal was to find teachers who were committed to helping children develop a critical consciousness while attaining academic success. It was also important to find teachers who not only had a love of teaching but a love of African-American children. In order to do this, we constructed a short interview protocol and conducted a formal classroom observation as a means to determine whether or not teachers were 'culturally relevant' in their socio-pedagogical[7] thought and actions (Ladson-Billings 1994). For example, Ladson-Billings (1994) compares the traits of culturally

Table 1 Study participants

Name	*Age*	*Subject/grade*	*Years of experience*
Mr Teranishi	34	Seventh and eighth grade English, math	7 years
Mr Green	54	Accounting	10 years

relevant teachers to assimilationist teachers. Culturally relevant teachers see themselves as part of the community in which they teach; assimilationist teachers do not. Culturally relevant teachers believe in African-American students and have high expectations for them. Assimilationist teachers, on the other hand, promote deficit-based thinking about the ability of African-American students to achieve. Black male teachers, who agreed and were available to participate in the study, were asked questions about their identity and the minority achievement gap. Teachers who expressed a commitment to the community in which they taught and had a strong belief in the potential of African-American students to succeed, were further considered for participation in the study. On the other hand, teachers who indicated a lack of faith in their students' ability to achieve academically were not considered further. Third, the final candidates were selected based on their overall contribution to a diverse pool of candidates who would vary in terms of subject area, grade level, age and years of experience. The portraits provide a description and analysis of the practices of two Black male teachers equally committed to the preservation and advancement of the African-American community.

Portraits of Critical Race Pedagogy in Context

In this section, we present brief portraits of two Black male teachers – one from the middle school and another from the high school. In general, the portraits address their entree into teaching, their views on pedagogy, and offer an illustration of their pedagogical practice. The portraits illustrate poignant examples of what might traditionally be considered 'good teaching'. Both of the teachers, through their work and their ideas, expressed a commitment to African-American children in working class and poor communities. As the portraits will illustrate, each teacher expressed their commitment in different ways.

Leon Teranishi: Seventh Grade Math Teacher, Strivers Point Middle School

Leon began teaching seventh grade at Brett Harte Middle School in the mid 1990s. After six years, he felt dehumanized and emasculated. Here, he describes in detail what happened:

> They had me misplaced. They had me teaching ESL. All my credentials and all my expertise, I should have been in mathematics. I would teach sixth, seventh and eighth grade. I would teach four bilingual classes to English. I would teach classes, all Latino. And, so, I felt like I was their packhorse for years. They'll write you up for stupid things. I get pulled out of my classroom to see my roll book – no warning, nothing. They violated my union contract. Most males left.

Not only was he teaching in the wrong subject areas, but he was teaching several different grade levels. More than that, when he spoke up about it, they punished him by writing him up and demanding that he meet them on short notice. As I, the lead author, sat across from him in this slightly disheveled second floor classroom, I remembered my own struggles with school administrators. As this conversation drew to a close, I reminded him that I – in fact – experienced the same thing. 'Something's got to be done about that, brother', he said with a sense of urgency. 'I know, I know', I uttered in response. We walked out of the classroom with the sad recognition that public schools were, in some ways, hostile territory for Black men who were committed to improving the lives of African-American children. While I knew this was true at an intellectual level, I was deeply saddened by this news, however. After all the difficulties he faced in school, as a child, why should he be forced to endure such hardship as a working professional in the same schools? Mr Teranishi talked about a challenging childhood where he transferred from one school after the other because he was continuously attacked by gang members. He also suffered abuse at the hand of an alcoholic father. After six years of strained relationships and 'write-ups' at Brett Harte Elementary, he left the school in search of more hospitable environs.

After leaving this school, he began working as a substitute. A year later, he ended up at Strivers Point Middle School where he taught seventh grade math at the time of the study. When we met, he had been teaching there for almost two years. Although he was happy with his position at Strivers Point, conditions are less than optimal. Leon did not have a classroom of his own. Because he was new, he shared a classroom with two other teachers, both of whom are Black men. Yet, and still, he viewed his administrators as 'fair and committed to the intellectual development of the students'. In short, Leon did not outwardly express outrage at having to travel to three different classrooms; one of which was located in a different building entirely. Instead, he adapted. He rolled around a suitcase on wheels that allowed him to carry his books and personal belongings from one location to another without the frustration of having to carry everything. Perhaps this adaptation was a form of survival. I could not be certain. What was certain was that he shared these classrooms with two other Black men teachers. This meant that not one but three Black men in the school were forced to share their classrooms with others. I did not investigate the extent to which this phenomenon was particular to Black men or if it was more widespread. At any rate, Leon and I spent a good deal of time in the hallways as he moved from one destination to the next one.

As I walked from classroom to classroom with him, we often talked about the crisis in urban education or the problems experienced by Black boys in the US. It was during those times that he began to express his disappointment in a system that was failing our children. Often, when he talked about issues of poverty and racism, his disposition changed from that of a happy-go-lucky young man who smiled at everyone to that of someone who was quite angry about the state of affairs for Black America. These enriching conversations helped me to better understand the sense of urgency that he brought to his teaching practice.

In various sessions I observed, I found that while the subject was formally mathematics, his students were often given a lesson in social justice. In one session, he gave students a relevant example regarding the extent to which they must support and 'check their facts'. 'They want facts. In the South, Black boys were lynched. They pulled boys out of the river. It was a common practice. I must encourage you to understand the history'. Here, he is making a point about how Blacks could not prove that the boys had been lynched until they could get the financial support to have the bodies exhumed from the water. This, according to Leon, is what provided the proof that these atrocities had occurred. The only way to provide proof was to keep a running record of the number of lynchings that had occurred over a period of several years. In conclusion, he states 'I want you to use mathematics to learn how to get your facts together'. Not only did he provide them with a lesson about the importance of 'checking their work' and 'knowing their math facts', he taught them about the severity of Jim Crow racism in the South. Although it was apparent that Black men were being killed at alarming rates, Black communities were still forced to bear the burden of proof when trying to prove that such atrocities had actually occurred. Black people then had to find ways in which to support claims of racism through the consistent documentation of events that led up to 'lynchings' or other more serious acts of violence against the community. Such documentation eventually led to the creation of laws that outlawed such heinous crimes, he pointed out. While teaching Black children to 'check their work' and 'support their suppositions with fact' is, in and of itself, a valuable tool, he situated the discussion within an historical analysis of Black domination in a racist society. One must do the same in mathematics, he argued.

In addition to providing students with important historical knowledge about the ability of African-Americans to utilize their observation and analysis skills to support claims of racial injustice, he also provides them with concrete examples of the way in which mathematical concepts are often utilized in everyday life. In the next session, he asked students to consider the dubious ways in which numerical data are tossed about in the media:

> You see, you have to know your numbers. I heard a report the other day that said that the joblessness rate in the country had gone down. I knew that that didn't make sense because there's a large percentage of people in my community who are unemployed. The numbers don't add up. 50% of African-American males do not have jobs, yet they say the jobless rate is down.

In the previous example, he warned students that they should critically examine the ways in which numbers get utilized in an unjust society. For example, 'lower rates of joblessness' as professed by the White media do not necessarily translate into greater prosperity for the majority of African-Americans, particularly African-American males. Students were asked to examine such issues by becoming social archeologists who explore in greater detail that which was presented to them as truth. In that sense, he implored them to be critical of taken-for-granted notions in society (Freire 1970). His commitment to raising the children's social consciousness about the uses and abuses of mathematics was not overshadowed by his willingness to be responsive to the emotional needs of his students.

In another session, I watched as he began his class: 'This is what we're going to do. I'm gonna write 15 problems. You must copy it down in 3 minutes'. Without the benefit of an adequate supply of mathematics textbooks, he was forced have children copy math problems on paper. He wrote the same problems on the board. I took a seat in the back of the room. As he monitored the students, he noticed that one of his students was upset. He then asked the student, a Black boy, to step outside of the room: 'What's the problem? You're teary-eyed and you look upset'. The boy breaks down and begins to talk sadly about something that had occurred just prior to entering Teranishi's class. Before asking him to rejoin the class, he tried to reassure the student that his situation would improve and that he would provide whatever support deemed necessary. The boy calmed down, took his seat and immediately began actively participating in class.

The student seemed to be very pleased that Mr Teranishi had taken the time to talk to him instead of demanding that he 'suck it up' or 'get with the program'. His demonstration of caring saved the day for this young man. As I sat there that day, I was stunned because I, for one, never noticed that the student was not in a good mood. More than likely, the student would have sulked quietly as Leon attempted to illuminate some important connection between math and life. For most teachers, this would have been acceptable. Leon chose instead to respond compassionately to the emotional needs of a Black male student who was visibly saddened by an experience he had just prior to coming to class. By doing so, he not only acknowledged the boy's emotions as real and worth attention, he helped to create better conditions for learning. Perhaps Leon's response to this student has much to do with his own experiences as a child whose emotional needs were unmet. Perhaps the educational neglect he experienced makes him more sensitive to the needs of others in need of a similar kind of support.

A Portrait of Mr Green, Accounting Teacher at South Central High School

> I wasn't sure at that point what I was going to do. But I had been in Junior Achievement, volunteering my time with them. So in 1990, a teacher was here, suggested that I really consider teaching. So, young Black children really kind'a took hold of me and before I knew it, the teacher had convinced me. She went on sabbatical and convinced me to take over the classes every day. And, you know, one year passed, two years passed when I started to take classes, and some how . . . I only intended to stay a couple of years. Now, it's been eight or nine years here.

Like some of the other men in the study, Mr Green was encouraged by an older Black woman educator to consider teaching full-time. Teaching was supposed to provide him with a much-needed one to two-year hiatus from the taxing world of business. Instead, it 'took hold' of him and he has not been able to leave. Because he came to the schools after having lived in the community as a high-profile business leader for many years, he approached the district differently. Here, he explained:

> I went to the superintendent of the schools and I said: 'I would like to come and teach'. When I was in business, I gave schools in this district an awful lot of money. So, what you could do for me is let me come and teach economics a couple days a week and that would be OK. I had to go take a test and I had to take these classes. I wasn't really up for all that.

Needless to say, his clout and his superior educational background got him nowhere with the district administration – even though knew some of them personally. When he began teaching at South Central he had to work for several years with emergency credential until he completed the requirements. This, of course, meant that he had to take exams and classes, complete portfolios and do student teaching like everyone else. To him, much of this training was useless. It did not provide him with the skills needed for competently teaching economics and accounting at an urban school in the middle of South Central! According to him, it simply legitimized him as one of the few 'certified' teachers in a school where a large number of teachers lacked the proper credentials.

Because Mr Green's classes were advanced in nature, the majority of his students were juniors and seniors who took the class as an elective. For the most part, he taught students how to start their own businesses by teaching basic economic and accounting principles. In addition to that, students learned how to manage budgets for personal and business purposes. They also learned how to design a marketing strategy and execute it. Students worked in teams to create a business concept and then worked throughout the semester to concretize their ideas. Students become so engaged in this activity, that they often spend a great deal of time outside of class perfecting the marketing strategies and business plans. On several occasions, I observed students – most of them Black males – sitting in Mr Green's room during lunch periods discussing the various ways in which to improve their mock corporations. In this sense, the connection to 'the real world of work' as Mr Green always says, became apparent. As these examples illustrate 'work experience' was not simply a code word for vocational education, it imbibed in students an 'entrepreneurial spirit'. They saw themselves as people with the potential to successfully create, market and maintain corporations that impacted the lives of their community. Sometimes, these mock corporations turned into reality. One earlier class started a business designed for the purposes of collecting and disseminating food to the needy. Housed at South Central High School, the successful business was 'owned and operated' by students.

In addition to engendering in students a sense that they could and would be the authors of their own fate, his courses provided students with an opportunity to reflect on the ways in which they utilized money in their own lives. One of his students, a 16-year-old African-American female student who lived by herself in her own apartment, used the skills gained from the class to help her budget her very limited finances. His extremely honest and subsequently emotionally charged class sessions often addressed these issues.

In a number of class sessions, he talked with students about 'opportunity costs'. An 'opportunity cost is the value of the next best thing given up', according to Mr Green. In other words, he was trying to get the students to apply a basic business principle of considering the impact that one's spending can have on his or her 'opportunities' to buy or have access to other valuable resources. Mr Green turned the conversation away from financial budgetary issues and begins to focus on life: 'When you watch TV, are there any opportunity costs?' A student responds, 'Studying'. At that point, the class gets into a debate about whether or not watching TV necessarily forces one to give up studying. One student exclaims: 'You can do your homework and watch TV. I always do that'. The conversation moved on: 'It's the same thing with making yo' college choices. If you become a manager at a fast food corporation, you might be doing that for the rest of your life because you don't have a college education'. The students became actively engaged in the practice of applying the theory presented in class to their own lives. Even more important, they considered how the specific choices they made as teens could affect their entire lives. Among the many lessons that needed to be learned by teenagers, this one was key. Green makes the example even more concrete:

> Suppose you could make \$8.50 an hour coming out of high school? My nephew makes \$10 an hour. He just had a baby. His girlfriend lives with him. They add up the pay. \$1600 is his monthly. He takes home about \$1120. They subtract rent. \$620 left.

Before he could finish the scenario, the students began to engage in a vigorous argument about how much one should pay for food. He tried to convince them that one should pay at least \$100 for food. The polyphonic screed mounted to a fever pitch. 'Hold it! Hold it! Do you really want toilet paper from the 99¢ store?' Mr Green retorted. He got their attention. He then talked with them about all the necessary costs involved in managing a household. They attempted to figure out ways to cut costs along the way. 'You could eat at your mother's house', a student suggests. It is, at this point, that the students begin to realize how difficult it would be to live on a very limited amount of resources. While some still attempt to argue that Green's notions regarding what is necessary to manage a household are beyond reach, many of them seem to be thinking very differently about this issue. The most vociferous grow quieter as he begins to explain the importance of considering the 'opportunity costs' involved in making various decisions that will affect their lives for years to come. The conversation continued in another session.

Having felt frustrated by the remarks made by students in previous sessions regarding their lack of understanding or even concern about tending to 'opportunity costs' he began to talk to the class about values. 'Crystal is pregnant. She says she bought shoes instead of school supplies and NOT diapers!' he said with a hint of indignation. The students laughed loudly. He continued: 'Some of the other students come and they are dressed and they ask me for a pencil. Our values lead us to make a decision about what's important'. He gave examples of how college can, in fact, be beneficial for a host of reasons. He also pointed out that college without direction could lead one toward financial ruin. Again, students provided counterexamples: 'I know people who never went to college and they make a lot of money'. Instead of disagreeing with the student, he added more weight to the comment by saying, 'Yes. Bill Gates dropped out of college after the first year. He is very successful'. He then went on to tell that it is still true that: 'A high school diploma doesn't give you a lot of weight'. He provided them with examples of students in his various classes that, for one reason or another, opted not to vigorously pursue their educational goals. Again, trying to push the envelope, he says: 'The reality is sometimes different from what you think! One of the things you don't wanna do is be surprised about how much it will take to live'. They begin to respond. In jest, a student says: 'Go on welfare'. This time, he pushed back: 'You're dependent on MY tax dollars to pay for your lifestyle!' A number of students began arguing with him. After the class ends, some of them stand in the front of the room and argued with Mr Green in an attempt to get him to see their point of view. Others rushed as they continue their conversations about what it would cost to live in a one-bedroom apartment as opposed to a two-bedroom or buy generic as opposed to name-brand products. As they hastily moved about, I walked over to a very despondent Mr Green who began to tell me how disappointed he is with the mindset of the students. I reminded him that I found his class discussion invigorating because I enjoyed watching Black children get fired up about the realities of life. While I was excited about their enthusiasm about the issues, I was also very privately concerned about what sounded like 'conservative capitalist rhetoric' on the part of Mr Green. I asked him about this. He said that African-Americans should 'learn how to operate in the current system'. This view coincided with a notion regarding the pervasiveness of culture of poverty among his students. This, I decided, was symptomatic of an ever widening gulf between the poor and the middle classes (Bell 1992a; Freire 1993). Had his '$100,000 a year' income and his Ivy League degrees put a considerable degree of distance between him and his students? I never resolved this question because while he, at times, subscribed to cultural deprivation theories, he seemed absolutely committed to improving education for students at South Central High School.

What was most compelling about Richard's professional life was his level of involvement in school change efforts. Having studied other Black male teachers who were ignored and rarely noticed except when they did something exceptionally good or exceptionally bad, it was a nice change. Richard was recognized and respected by his colleagues. At the time of the study, he was head of the committee that approved of the school's budget for the fiscal year. South Central, designated as one of the 'Super 8' poorest high schools in the city, was part of school reform strategy referred which requires that they reorganized in such a way as to increase the level of decision-making among faculty. The budget committee, which consists of both teachers and administrators at the school, is one such organization. Because of his financial expertise, he had been given the responsibilities of leading this group. I watched once as he engaged in a very tense conversation regarding his reasons for not approving a budget that 'was not in the best interest of the students'. To that extent, he was willing to risk his professional livelihood in order to make certain that students were going to receive the best education possible. Even more important, he spent a great deal of time negotiating business relationships with nearby companies in an effort to get them to come to South Central High School to hire students. part-time and in the summers. Not only did he want them to hire students, he wanted them to provide on-the-job training for students interested in business management. Many days, he was absolutely exhausted from all of the hard work inside and outside of the classroom. 'I could really use some help in here', he would often lament. Watching him perspire one day, I said 'Do you regret leaving the business world for this?' Assuming, he would immediately respond affirmatively, I was somewhat taken aback when he shouted: 'Oh, no! Not for one minute!'

African-American Male Teachers' Critical Race Pedagogy

Drawing from Children's Lives

As both Mr Leon Teranishi and Mr Richard Green illustrated, they use their student's lives as texts through which to build curriculum in the classroom context. Mr Teranishi situated his math instruction within the Black experience in the US and helps his students understand how math can be used to improve their lives. He also used his classroom as a platform to discuss important equity concerns in the broader society. Mr Green used his classroom as a way to help his students learn the fundamentals of budgeting. For him, it was important for African-American children to learn this skill if they were going to lead fulfilling lives. He was deeply concerned about the financial state of the community – with African-Americans, as whole, having either too few resources or not knowing how to properly utilize those they have in order to build community wealth. While he did not experience immediate success with his students, he did awaken their minds and their spirits to a major problem in our community. In addition, students were excited about using numbers as a way to construct their own lives. They were no longer passive observers but active participants in the making of their own lives. Even more important, rather than shut down conversations by providing boring lectures about the importance of financial solvency, he allowed the students to engage in serious debates with him and each other about the best approaches to living. These spirited discussions forced students to think seriously about the directions of their own lives and whether their career goals were in line with their desired lifestyle choices. It was, in many, regards an awakening for some students who were headed in the wrong the direction. He didn't know it, but he was probably saving lives.

Developing and Practicing a Pedagogical Sensitivity

Black male teachers committed to the development of Black youth expressed a profound belief in the notion that one has to be sensitive to the particular needs of Black students who live in economically depressed communities where violence is a regular occurrence. Describing what happens after his students have witnessed a fatal shooting or some other violent act, Leon talks specifically about how teachers must begin to respond to students who are living in traumatic situations:

> [Sometimes], they come to school traumatized. How can you teach that child? I don't see a psychological team coming into South Central when there's a shooting. I've taught in South Central for seven years, and I have witnessed shootings. No one showed up. So, sometimes when the students act out, I have to take my time and ask them what's going on. Not talk at 'em. Talk to 'em and see if we can come to some type of agreement to where, okay, take some time out to work this out.

Not only does this urban schoolteacher begin the process of getting us to rethink how we respond to children living in violent worlds, he is also critical of a system that ignores the psychological trauma of African-American children. As we have witnessed fatal shootings at White middle class high schools all over the nation, we have also had the privilege of watching teams of counselors, psychiatrists, and psychologists rush in to 'ease the pain' of grieving White students. In response, he asks the important question 'Why don't they come here?' As I spent time in the halls of Strivers Point Middle School, I learned that the school did not have a counselor who could address the emotional needs of students. To that extent, the responsibility became that of the teacher. As Leon suggested, this calls for teachers to have a more nuanced and balanced understanding of Black student misbehavior. In his view, their 'acting out' often stems from the emotional distress that comes from living under the constant threat of violence. While teachers typically interpret any misbehavior as a 'threat' to their authority, he suggested that teachers try to work 'with' students to understand the problems with which their students are faced and then agree on some mutual terms of communication. In other words, Leon is promoting a form of pedagogical sensitivity and understanding that considers the specific emotional needs of the individual student. For Richard, developing this sensitivity means that one must make wholehearted attempts to 'understand their students' and 'respect their points of view'. This sensitivity leads to a good deal of understanding regarding the ways in which to pedagogically meet the needs of students. This sensitivity and understanding, in turn, begets a kind of mutual respect between teacher and student. This, they argue, is essential to teaching effectively. While sensitivity to children's emotional needs is important, an understanding of their living conditions and a healthy respect for their humanity and individuality is key to effective practice in urban schools, it must also be an integral part of one's teaching practice.

Why They Teach: A Compassion for African-American Children and a Commitment to Community

'I teach 'cause I keep seeing me'. Leon explained as he recounted his experience as a child growing up in a gang-infested community in South Central Los Angeles. For him and others, the experience with race and class oppression had created a degree of 'empathetic regard' for others similarly situated. He elaborated:

> Maybe it quiets some of the pain in my soul about bad experiences I've had. And, maybe, just maybe, I can help someone. When your souls hurt and your mind and emotions are hurting, sometimes it's hard to study.

His experiences, as tragic as they might have been, prepared him in a special way to be able to deal with the particular needs of his students – many of whom lived in the midst of on-going violence and hopelessness. The commitment to teach in urban schools in the community was a 'way of being able to have some significant impact on our future as a community'. Green elaborated on this point when he said:

> I realized that there are very few African-American men who are willing to make that leap in our community given the challenges of what you can earn in terms of income as well as the challenges of dealing with youth and young people. You have to kind'a have a commitment to stay and work with them [because] our ability to learn the language of business and economics relates to our ability to rise up from the ranks of the disenfranchised and into an area of prosperity for our community.

In this way, his expertise as an Ivy League-educated former businessman with skills in applied economics becomes directly tied, in his view, to the economic well being of the African-American community.

Conclusion

> A critical race pedagogy challenges the traditional claims that the educational system and its institutions make toward objectivity, meritocracy, color-blindness, race neutrality, and equal opportunity. Critical race educators argue that these traditional claims act as a camouflage for the self-interest, power, and privilege of dominant groups in US society.
>
> (Solorzano and Yosso 2005, 598)

As we have shown, the pedagogical practices of African-American male teachers who express a compassion for Black children and a commitment to the African-American community are reminiscent of the pedagogies practices and beliefs of Black feminist/womanist educators and critical pedagogues. Embedded within these teachers' analyses of schooling and society are critiques of racist relations in the broader society. Their critical race analysis of the conditions of the African-American community lead them to construct both pedagogies of dissent and affirmation. Teranishi's pedagogy of affirmation is both political and personal. He politicizes his teaching while attending to the socio-emotional needs of students. Through their pedagogies of affirmation, both men provided safe spaces for African-American male students in their classrooms. These students felt safe to voice their concerns, express their desires, and contemplate the larger questions of life. As avid dissenters, they voiced concerns about policies both locally and nationally that endangered the livelihood of African-Americans. Green's constructs a pedagogy of dissent that rejects racist beliefs about the ability of African-Americans to lead productive lives that are based on healthy knowledge about budgeting. These notions also affirm his students because it helps them make better decisions about their futures. Mr Teranishi actively participated in national organizations that were connected to the African-American reparations movement. Mr Green was an active participant in school-based committees that would affect the lives of his students. As the portrait illustrated, his often a vociferous opponent of zero tolerance policies that actively sought to further marginalize his students. A critical race pedagogy, in this sense, is as much about dissent as it is about affirmation. Teachers who affirm the culture of their students and fail to oppose unequal school policies or speak out against unfair social policies illustrate a kind of passiveness that is necessary for a White supremacist patriarchy to thrive. While it often complicates the lives of those who are engaged in it, resistance is key to social change. Teachers who resist structures of domination model this important quality for students. Equally important, we recognize that teachers dissent but don't affirm their students cannot successfully teach African-American students. In this way, a critical race pedagogy must attend to the relational aspects of teaching since the building of relationships is essential to effective practice.

One of the things we find consistent throughout the narratives of Black feminist/womanist and critical race teachers is an insistence on using their classrooms as a space to promote community healing. Leon's arresting statement: 'When I see them, I see me', helps capture the essence of the notion of racial uplift and community empowerment that is tied to their work. Mr Green defines this in very real terms when he suggests that helping African-American children develop expertise as entrepreneurs could go a long way toward re-building and transforming the African-American community. In this sense, critical race pedagogies are grounded in based on a vision of healthy and whole community. The work of critical race pedagogues help to make this vision into a reality. As we surveyed the literature on African-American education, we have these themes to be present in the work of African-American educators and intellectuals throughout history.

Charting the Critical Race Tradition Among African-American Educators

African-American thinkers like W.E.B. DuBois, Ida B. Wells, Anna Julia Cooper and Carter G. Woodson led principled scholarly struggles against the systematic dehumanization of African-Americans (Gordon 1995; Ladson-Billings 2001). As a result, they theorized about the nature of the conditions for people who were racially and culturally subjugated. The pedagogies of resistance theorized by African-American researchers and practiced by

African-American educators and activist African-American thinkers such as W.E.B. DuBois, Carter G. Woodson, and Alexander Crummell expressed critical ideas in relation to the state of African-American education in the late nineteenth and early twentieth century (Watkins 1996). These thinkers were part of an important intellectual tradition that emphasized education and reform tradition, however they are rarely viewed as part of the historical legacy of critical pedagogy (Watkins 1996). The African-American intellectuals of the early twentieth century developed a scholarly/intellectual tradition that was different from their White counterparts. White social scientists were approaching their research through the development of academic disciplines that emphasized the compartmentalization of knowledge (Ross 1991). African-American social scientists were often trained in specific subject areas but developed a generalist scholarship based on their desire to critically examine the African-American experience in the US (Watkins 1996). While mainstream (i.e., 'White') educational theorists became more focused on specific educational movements (Kliebard, 1987 cited in Watkins 1996), African-American educational theorists established themselves through a more general focus on sociological inquiry (Watkins 1996). Watkins (1994) and Shujaa (1994) both point out that the schooling and education of African-Americans has been heavily shaped by the complex interplay of power and politics in American society. Marginalized groups within the US have created and maintained institutions and ideologies that represent powerful critiques of society's dominant paradigms. As discussed previously, this study of pedagogy conceived and conducted from the margins represents the possibility of a critical paradigm that has been envisioned and practiced by African-Americans for many years has gone largely unexplored by mainstream educational researchers (Watkins 1996).

Notes

1. We will not attempt to address all studies on Black teachers. Rather our mission to focus on more recent research based on empirical examinations of Black teachers' beliefs, their teaching practices and their personal lives as they relate to the schooling of African-American children.
2. For more detailed analyses of critical theory and its relationship to Critical Pedagogy, see Peter McLaren's 'Life in schools' (1998).
3. In this article, we do not make a clear distinction between Black feminist and womanist thought. In fact, we use the two concepts interchangeably. In a seminal article that addresses the questions of the differences between the concepts of womanism and Black feminism (see Collins 1996). She argues that while both terms operate from slight different historical standpoints, they essentially support Black women's right to self-determination. In the final analysis, she suggests that we should be spending less time playing the name game and more time trying to understand how to frame and transform racism, sexism and classism.
4. According to Murrell (2002), 'instruction and pedagogy are by no means synonymous . . . Pedagogy . . . includes teachers' awareness of their own culturally mediated values and biases, as well as an understanding of how success and failure are rooted in larger societal and institutional structures' (xxiii).
5. In a 1999 article, Lynn argued that Black feminist/womanist research on teaching was, in some way, an inappropriate tool for analyzing the experiences of both men and women in schools. Michael Awkward (1995) has illustrated that men can use feminism as a lens for exploring important questions around race and gender.
6. The research was conducted by the lead author.
7. The term socio-pedagogical refers to the nexus between teachers' beliefs on teaching and society.

References

Awkward, M. 1995. *Negotiating difference: Race, gender and the politics of positionality.* Chicago, IL: University of Chicago Press.

Beauboeuf-Lafontant, T. 1999. A movement against and beyond boundaries: Politically relevant teaching among African-American teachers. *Teachers College Record* 100, no. 4: 702–23.

Bell, D. 1992. *Faces at the bottom of the well: The permanence of racism.* New York: Basic Books.

Bell, D. 1995. The racism is permanent thesis: Courageous revelations or unconscious denial of racial genocide. *Capital University Law Review* 22: 571–8.

Berry, T.R., and N.D. Mizelle. 2006. *From oppression to grace: Women of color and their dilemmas in the academy.* Sterling, Va: Stylus Pub.

Bowles, S., and H. Gintis. 1976. *Schooling in capitalist America.* London: Routledge and Kegan Paul.

Bennett, K., and M. LeCompte. 1999. *The way schools work: A sociological analysis of education.* New York: Longman.

Casey, K. 1993. *I answer with my life: Life histories of women teachers working for social change.* New York: Routledge.

Collins, P.H. 1991. *Black feminist thought: Knowledge, consciousness, and the politics of empowerment.* New York: Routledge.

Collins, P.H. 1996. What's in a name? Womanism, Black Feminism, and beyond. *The Black Scholar* 26, no. 1: 9–17.

Cremin, L. 1961. The *transformation of the school: Progressivism in American education, 1876–1957.* New York: Knopf.

Crenshaw, K., Gotanda, N., Peller, G., and K. Thomas. (eds). 1995. *Critical Race Theory: Key writings that formed the movement.* New York: New Press.

Cubberley, E.P. 1919. *Public education in the United States.* Boston, MA: Houghton Mifflin.

Darder, A. 1993. How does the culture of the teacher shape the experience of Latino students?: The unexamined question in critical pedagogy. In *Handbook of Schooling in Urban America,* ed. W.S. Rothstein. Westport, CT: Greenwood Press.

Darder, A. 1998. Teaching as an act of love: Reflections on Paulo Freire and his contributions to our lives and our work. In *Reclaiming our voices.* Los Angeles, CA: California Association for Bilingual Education.

Delgado, R. (Ed.). 1995. *Critical race theory: The cutting edge.* Philadelphia, PA: Temple University Press.

Dixon, A.D., Chapman, T. and D. Hill. 2005. Research as an aesthetic process: Extending the portraiture methodology. *Qualitative Inquiry* 11, no. 1: 16–26.

DeMarrais, K.B. and M. LeCompte. (1999). *The way schools work* (3rd Edition). New York: Allyn & Bacon.

Ellsworth, E. 1989. Why doesn't this feel empowering? The repressive myths of critical pedagogy. *Harvard Educational Review.*

Foster, M. 1990. The politics of race through the eyes of African-American teachers. *Journal of Education* 172, no. 3: 123–41.

Foster, M. 1991. 'Just got to find a way': Case studies of the lives and practice of exemplary Black high school teachers. In *Readings on equal education: Qualitative investigations in schools and schooling (Vol.11),* ed. M. Foster, 273–309. New York: AMS Press.

Foster, M. 1993. Urban African-American teachers' views of organizational change: Speculations on the experiences of exemplary teachers. *Equity and Excellence in Education* 26, no. 3: 16–24.

Foster, M. 1994. Effective Black teachers: A literature review. In *Teaching diverse populations: Formulating a knowledge base,* ed. E.R. Hollins, J.E. King, and W.C. Hayman, 225–41. Albany, NY: State University of New York Press.

Foster, M. 1995a. African American teachers and culturally relevant pedagogy. In *Handbook of research on multicultural education,* ed. J. Banks and C.A. McGee Banks, 570–581. New York: Macmillan.

Foster, M. 1997. *Black teachers on teaching.* New York: The New Press.

Frederick D. Patterson Research Institute. 1997. *The African-American education data book.* Fairfax, VA: Frederick D. Patterson Research Institute.

Freire, P. 1970. *Pedagogy of the oppressed.* New York: Herder and Herder.

Giroux, H. 1983. *Theory and resistance in education: A pedagogy for the opposition.* South Hadley, MA: Bergin and Garvey.

Giroux, H. 1997. *Pedagogy and the politics of hope: Theory, culture, and schooling.* Boulder, CO: Westview.

Giroux, H., and P. McLaren. 1994. *Between borders: Pedagogy and the politics of cultural studies.* New York: Routledge.

Gordon, B. M. 1995. *Knowledge construction, competing critical theories, and education.* In *Handbook of research on multicultural education,* ed. J. Banks and C.A. McGee Banks, 570–81. New York: MacMillan Publishing.

Gore, J. 1990. What can we do for you! What *can* we do for you? Struggling over empowerment in critical and feminist pedagogy. *Educational Foundations* 4, no. 3: 5–26.

Gramsci, A. 1971. *Selections from the prison notebooks.* New York: International.

Henry, A. 1998. *Taking back Control: African Canadian women teachers' lives and practice.* Albany, NY: SUNY Press.

Hytten, K. 1998. Post-critical ethnography: Research as a pedagogical encounter. Paper presented at the annual meeting of the Philosophy in Education Society.

Irvine, J.J. 2002. *In search of wholeness: African-American teachers and their culturally specific classroom practice.* New York: Palgrave Macmillan.

Jennings, M. 1999. Social theory and transformation in the pedagogy of Dr Huey P. Newton: A nativist reclamation of the critical ethnographic project. *Educational Foundations* 13, no. 1: 77–94.

Jennings, M. 2000. Learning to live our lives: Case studies of critical pedagogy in the African-American experience. *Dissertation Abstracts International* 61, no. 7: 2654. (UMI No. AAT 9979455.)

Jennings, M., and M. Lynn. 2006. The house that race built: Toward a critical race analysis of critical pedagogy. *Educational Foundations* 19, nos. 3–4:.

Kanpol, B. 1992. *Towards a theory and practice of teacher cultural politics.* Norwood, NJ: Ablex.

King, J. E. 1991. Unfinished Business: Black student's alienation and Black teachers' pedagogy. In *Readings on equal education: Qualitative investigations in schools and schooling,* ed. M. Foster. New York: AMS Press.

Ladson-Billings, G. 1994. *The dreamkeepers: Successful teachers of African-American children.* San Francisco, CA: Jossey Bass.

Lather, P. 1991. Post-critical pedagogies: A feminist reading. In *Feminisms and critical pedagogy,* ed. C. Luke, and J. Gore, 120–37. New York: Routledge.

Lawrence, C. 1991. The Word and the river: Pedagogy as scholarship and struggle. *Southern California Law Review* 65: 2231–98.

Lawrence-Lightfoot, S. 1983. *The good high school: Portraits of character and culture.* New York: Basic Books.

Lawrence-Lightfoot, S. 2005. Reflections on portraiture: A dialogue between art and science. *Qualitative Inquiry* 11, no. 1: 3–15.

Lawrence-Lightfoot, S., and J.H. Davis. 1997. *The art and science of portraiture.* San Francisco, CA: Jossey-Bass.

Lee, C.D. 1990. How shall we sing our sacred song in a strange Land? The dilemma of a double consciousness and the complexities of an African-Centered pedagogy. *Journal of Education* 172, no. 2: 45–61.

Lee, C.D. 1992. Profile of an independent Black institution: African-centered education at work. *Journal of Negro Education* 61, no. 2: 160–77.

Leistyna, P., et al. 1996. *Breaking free: The transformative power of critical pedagogy.* Reprint series No. 27. Cambridge, MA: Harvard Educational Review.

Leistyna, P. 1999. *Presences of mind: Education and the politics of deception.* Boulder, CO: Westview.

Leonard, S. 1990. *Critical theory in political practice.* Princeton, NJ: Princeton University Press.

Lightfoot, S.L. 1995. *I've known rivers: Lives of loss and liberation.* New York, N.Y.: Penguin Books.

Lynn, M. 1999. Toward a critical race pedagogy: A research note. *Urban Education* 33, no. 5: 606–26.

Lynn, M. 2002. Critical race theory and the lives of Black male teachers in the Los Angeles Public Schools. *Equity and Excellence in Education* 35, no. 2: 119–30.

Lynn, M. 2004. Inserting the race into critical pedagogy: An analysis of race-based epistemologies. *The Journal of Educational Philosophy and Theory* 37, no. 2: 153–65.

Lynn, M., Bacon, J.N., Totten, T.L., Bridges, T.L., and M.L. Jennings. In press. Examining teacher beliefs about African American males in a low performing high school: the impact on African American males. *Teachers College Record* 112, no. 1.

Matsuda, M., Lawrence, C., Delgado, R. and K. Crenshaw. 1993. *Words that wound: Critical Race Theory, assaultive speech, and the first amendment.* Boulder, CO: Westview.

McCarthy, C., and M. Apple. 1988. Race, class, and gender in American educational research: Towards a nonsynchronous parallelist approach. *Perspectives in Education* 4, no. 2: 67–9.

McLaren, P. 1989. *Life in Schools: an introduction to critical pedagogy in the foundations of education.* New York: Longman.

Morris, J.E. 2001. Forgotten voices of Black educators: Critical race perspectives on the implementation of a desegregation plan. *Educational Policy* 15, no. 4: 575–600.

Morrow, R.A., and C.A. Torres. 1995. *Social theory and education: A critique of theories of social and cultural reproduction.* Albany, NY: SUNY Press.

Murrell, P.C. 2001. *The community teacher: A new framework for effective urban teaching.* New York: Teachers College Press.

Murillo, E. 1999. Mojado crossings along neoliberal borderlands. *Educational Foundations* 13, no. 1: 7–30.

Sargent, P. 2001. *Real men or real teachers?: Contradictions in the lives of men elementary school teachers.* Harriman, Tenn: Men's Studies Press.

Shujaa, M. (Ed.) 1994. *Too much schooling, too little education: A paradox of Black life in White societies.* Baltimore, MD: Africa World Press.

Solorzano, D.G., and T.J. Yosso. 2002. Critical Race Methodology: Counter-storytelling as an analytical framework for education research. *Qualitative Inquiry* 8: 23–44.

Tillman, L.C. 2002. Culturally sensitive research approaches: An African-American perspective. *Educational Researcher: a Publication of the American Educational Research Association* 31, no. 9: 3.

Solorzano, D., and T. Yosso. 2005. Critical race methodology: Counter-storytelling as an analytical framework for education research. *Qualitative Inquiry* 8, no. 1: 23–44.

Weiler, K. 1988. *Women teaching for change.* South Hadley, MA: Bergin and Garvey Publishers.

Weiner, L. 1993. *Preparing teachers for urban schools: Lessons from thirty years of school reform.* New York: Teachers College Press.

Wing, A. K. 2000. *Global critical race feminism: An international reader. Critical America.* New York: New York University Press.

Suggested Readings for Future Study

Ayers, W. (2004). "Where We Might Begin with Teaching." In Burant, T., Christensen, L., Dawson Salas, K., and Walters, S. (eds.), *Rethinking Schools, The New Teacher Book: Finding Purpose, Balance, and Hope During Your First Years in the Classroom* (pp. 20–25). Milwaukee, WI: Rethinking Schools Publications.

Bartolomé, L. (2004). "Critical Pedagogy and Teacher Education: Radicalizing Prospective Teachers." *Teacher Education Quarterly, 31*(1), 97–122.

Bercaw, L. A. and Stooksberry, L. M. (2004). "Teacher Education, Critical Pedagogy, and Standards: An Exploration of Theory and Practice" [Electronic Version]. *Essays in Education, 12.*

Beyer, L. E. (1989). "Reconceptualizing Teacher Preparation: Institutions and Ideologies." *Journal of Teacher Education, 40*, 22–26.

Beyer, L. E. and Zeichner, K. (1987). "Teacher Education in Cultural Context: Beyond Reproduction." In Popkewitz, T. S. (ed.), *Critical Studies in Teacher Education.* Philadelphia: The Falmer Press.

Brown, K. D. (2012). "Trouble on My Mind: Toward a Framework of Humanizing Critical Sociocultural Knowledge for Teaching and Teacher Education." *Race Ethnicity and Education, 16*(3), 316–338.

Cárdenas, R. (2009). "Tendencias Globales y Locales en la Formación de Docentes de Lenguas Extranjeras" [Global and Local Tendencies in Foreign Language Teachers' Formation]. *Íkala, Revista de Lenguaje y Cultura, 14*(22), 71–106.

Carr, W. and Kennis, S. (1986). *Becoming Critical: Education Knowledge and Action Research.* New York: Routledge.

Claus, J. (1999). "You Can't Avoid the Politics: Lessons for Teacher Education from a Case Study of Teacher-Initiated Tracking Reform." In *Journal of Teacher Education, 50*(1), 5–16.

Cochran-Smith, M. (2001). "Sticks, Stones, and Ideology: The Discourse of Reform in Teacher Education." *Educational Researcher, 30*(8), 3–15.

Cochran-Smith, M. (2005). "Studying Teacher Education. What We Know and Need to Know." *Journal of Teacher Education, 56*, 301–306.

Cochran-Smith, M. and Lytle, S. L., eds. (1993). *Inside/Outside: Teacher Research and Knowledge.* New York: Teachers College.

Darling-Hammond, L. (2006). "Constructing 21st-Century Teacher Education." *Journal of Teacher Education, 57*(3), 300–314.

Denzin, N. K. (2003). *Performance Ethnography: Critical Pedagogy and the Politics of Culture.* London: Sage.

Ellsworth, E. (1997). *Teaching Positions: Difference, Pedagogy and the Power of Address.* New York: Teachers College Press.

Finn, P. J. and Finn, M. E. (2007). *Teacher Education with an Attitude: Preparing Teachers to Educate Working-Class Students in Their Collective Self-Interest.* Albany, NY: SUNY Press.

Freire, P. (2005). *Teachers as Cultural Workers: Letters to Those Who Dare Teach.* Boulder, CO: Westview Press.

Han, K. T., Madhuri, M., and Scull, W. R. (2015). "Two Sides of the Same Coin: Preservice Teachers' Dispositions towards Critical Pedagogy and Social Justice Concerns in Rural and Urban Teacher Education Contexts." *The Urban Review, 47*(4), 1–31.

Harman, R. (2007). "Critical Teacher Education in Urban Contexts: Discursive Dance of a Middle School Teacher." *Language and Education, 21*(1), 31–45.

Helmer, K. (2014). "Disruptive Practices: Enacting Critical Pedagogy through Meditation, Community Building, and Explorative Spaces in a Graduate Course for Pre-Service Teachers." *Journal of Classroom Interaction, 49*(2), 33–40.

hooks, b. (1994). *Teaching to Transgress: Education as the Practice of Freedom.* New York: Routledge.

Kanpol, B. (1998). "Critical Pedagogy for Beginning Teachers: The Movement from Despair to Hope." *Online Journal of Critical Pedagogy, 2*(1).

Keesing-Styles, L. (2003). "The Relationship between Critical Pedagogy and Assessment in Teacher Education." *Radical Pedagogy, 5*(1), 1–20.

Kincheloe, J. (1993). *Toward a Critical Politics of Teacher Thinking: Mapping the Postmodern.* Westport, CT: Bergin and Garvey.

Kincheloe, J. (2003). *Teachers as Researchers: Qualitative Inquiry as a Path to Empowerment.* New York: RoutledgeFalmer.

Kincheloe, J., Slattery, P., and Steinberg, S. R. (2000). *Contextualizing Teaching: Introduction to Education and Educational Foundations.* New York: Longman.

Kincheloe, J., Bursztyn, A., and Steinberg, S. R. (2004). *Teaching Teachers: Building a Quality School of Urban Education.* New York: Peter Lang.

King, J. E. (2005). *Black Education: A Transformative Research and Action Agenda for the New Century.* New York: Lawrence Erlbaum.

Ladson-Billings, G. (2000). "Fighting for Our Lives: Preparing Teachers to Teach African American Students." *Journal of Teacher Education, 51*(3), 206–214.

Lam, K. D. (2015). "Teaching for Liberation: Critical Reflections in Teacher Education." *Multicultural Perspectives, 17*(3), 157–162.

Leistyna, P., Lavandez, M., and Nelson, T. G. (2004). "Critical Pedagogy: Revitalizing and Democratizing Teacher Education." *Teacher Education Quarterly, 31*(1), 3–15.

Lipman, P. (2003). *High Stakes Education: Inequality, Globalization, and Urban School Reform.* Oxford: RoutledgeFalmer.

McKenna, B. (2012). "Medical Education under Siege: Critical Pedagogy, Primary Care, and the Making of 'Slave Doctors'." *International Journal of Critical Pedagogy, 4*(1), 95–117.

Mayo, J. B. (2013). "Critical Pedagogy Enacted in the Gay–Straight Alliance: New Possibilities for a Third Space in Teacher Development." *Educational Researcher, 42*(5), 266–275.

Morrell, E. and Collatos, A. M. (2002). "Toward a Critical Teacher Education: High School Student Sociologists as Teacher Educators." *Social Justice, 29*(4), 60–71.

Ollis, T. (2012). *A Critical Pedagogy of Embodied Education: Learning to Become an Activist.* New York: Palgrave Macmillan.

Pereira, F. (2013). "Concepts, Policies and Practices of Teacher Education: An Analysis of Studies on Teacher Education in Portugal." *Journal of Education for Teaching: International Research and Pedagogy, 39*(5), 474–491.

Poetter, T. (2004). *Critical Perspectives on the Curriculum of Teacher Education.* Lanham, MD: University Press of America.

Popkewitz, T. S. (1987). *Critical Studies in Teacher Education: Its Folklore, Theory and Practice.* New York: Falmer Press.

Ragoonaden, K. (2015). "Self-Study of Teacher Education Practices and Critical Pedagogy: The Fifth Moment in a Teacher Educator's Journey." *Studying Teacher Education: Journal of Self-Study of Teacher Education Practices, 11*(1), 81–95.

Torres, M. N. and Mercado, M. D. (2007). "The Need for Critical Media Literacy in Teacher Education Core Curricula." In Macedo, D. and Steinberg, S. (eds.), *Media Literacy: A Reader* (pp. 538–558). New York: Peter Lang.

Vavrus, M. (2009). "Sexuality, Schooling, and Teacher Identity Formation: A Critical Pedagogy for Teacher Education." *Teaching and Teacher Education, 25*(3), 383–390.

Wink, J. (2004). *Critical Pedagogy: Notes from the Real World.* New York: Allyn & Bacon.

Zeichner, K. M. (1996). "Teachers as Reflective Practitioners and the Democratization of School Reform." In Zeichner, K. M., Melnik, S. and Gomez, M. L. (eds.), *Current of Reforms in Preservice Teacher Education.* New York: College Press.

Zeichner, K. M. (1999). "The New Scholarship in Teacher Education." *Educational Researcher, 28*(9), 4–15.

Part Eight

Education, Democracy, and Capitalist Society

Introduction to Part Eight

As we contend with the ascendancy of Donald Trump to the presidency, our minds are being bombarded daily with fear and increasing economic insecurity that inspire images of brutality and turmoil, while thin promises of normalcy dangle alongside the plunder and greed of a fierce globalized economy. Since our last edition the so-called 1 percent has only grown richer and the gap between rich and poor wider. This spectacle has been capriciously reproduced and publicly enacted through the most powerful hegemonic force of our time—a mass media muzzled and controlled by the corporate elite. In the midst of increasing job insecurity, immigrant bashing, and the privatization of public welfare resources, the U.S. population has been forced to contend with the deleterious impact of two major national tragedies and the mendacity of the Bush administration's foreign policy.

During the first decade of the twenty-first century, the nation underwent three historically defining moments. September 11, 2001 (9/11) signaled the first suicide terrorist attack on the U.S. mainland. On March 20, 2003 war was declared on Iraq, as an orchestrated retaliation tied to the War on Terrorism. And, in late August 2005, New Orleans experienced massive destruction at the hands of Hurricane Katrina—not only one of the most intense, but the costliest hurricane on record in the country's history. There are those who would deem these three disasters—one political, one "natural," and one military—as direct or indirect consequences of internationalized neoliberal policies—namely, poverty, racism, ecological devastation, and the massive ideological corruption of the corporatized media. These three were immediately followed by a strictly man-made financial disaster—the mortgage debacle of 2007, which resulted in one of the biggest historical losses of wealth to Black and Latino working families.

These historical tragedies—along with military torture in Abu Ghraib and Guantanamo; the Patriot Act and its intensification of public surveillance during the George W. Bush administration; the Halliburton, Enron and Blackwater scandals of the last decade; numerous national crises tied to unemployment, child poverty, health care, education, immigration, housing, and youth incarceration; and the culture industry's promotion of unchecked consumerism—and most recently the urban unrest and police killings of black youth have all deeply influenced our view of the world, whether we are conscious of this or not.

In the wake of these conditions, critical educators are left to contend with the crushing blow of media distortions and misrepresentations on our critical faculties and political sensibilities. In the hope of dislodging adherence to uncritical acceptance reinforced by the power of the airwaves, there is the need to cultivate pedagogical conditions beyond the classroom, where alternative readings of the world can emerge through community praxis. This summons the pedagogical power of people's lives and community traditions to the formation of an organic critical literacy—a literacy that can counter the impact of blind patriotism or mindless accumulation that obscure critical readings of the world.

To gain a better understanding of the impact of economic and political conditions on prevailing social views, it is useful to also examine the manner in which the current ecological crisis is unquestionably linked to the destructive structural conditions savagely proliferated around the globe. This is so, whether examining relationships between profit-generated pollution and devastating changes in weather patterns, or the justification of prisoner abuse and the infringement of civil rights, or the use of mass scale technology in the fabrication of hegemonic consent and the repression of political dissent. Moreover, in all these instances, the break with our synergetic existence with nature and all organic life potentially leaves us estranged and disaffected. Inherent, here, is a need to counter the potential narcissistic indifference to the suffering of *the Other*, by laying the groundwork for establishing the community solidarity and universal kinship, in and out of schools, necessary to forging a larger struggle for social justice, human rights, and democratic life.

This emancipatory feature of solidarity and kinship within communities is an often-overlooked legacy of Freire's work to critical pedagogy—a feature that grounded much of his early approach to the development of literacy. Much of the impetus, in fact, for his groundbreaking treatise, *Pedagogy of the Oppressed*, was actually not his work in the formal classroom, but rather his pedagogical relationships within poor rural communities of Brazil, where illiterate men, women, and their children lived and labored. It should then come as no surprise that critical pedagogy is conceived as a living and organic pedagogy, one that by definition extends beyond the classroom walls. This is particularly important in keeping with a dialectical understanding of knowledge as dialectically tied to the larger social order and shaped by historical events, changing economic conditions, technological advances, and shifting political landscapes.

With this in mind, an emancipatory pedagogy, rooted in a praxis of reflection, dialogue, and action, can be enacted wherever subordinate populations struggle to affirm, challenge, resist, and transform the dehumanizing conditions of their existence. Anchored in a solid commitment to a vision of social justice and human rights, many critical educators, cultural workers, and community activists integrate critical pedagogy in alternative spaces, such as adult education, community organizing, youth cultural arts programs, health care initiatives, worker education, and independent media programming. Within these community spaces, an array of untold possibilities can emerge as children, youth, and adults create opportunities together to grapple with meaningful issues and identify solutions that make sense in their world. Such efforts assist us to unveil the deep hegemonic impact of public institutions, the mainstream media, public surveillance, and unbridled consumerism, so that we might counter the forces of domination and exploitation and meet the challenge of creating an ecologically harmonious and life-affirming future.

Summary of Articles

Richard A. Brosio's thoughtful and insightful article "The Continuing Conflicts Between Capitalism and Democracy: Ramification for Schooling-Education" builds on the earlier work of Sam Bowles, Henry Levin, Francis Piven, and late historian Michael Katz to critique the contradictory nature of capitalist schooling in the U.S. An important feature of his overall critique is his claim that Marx's critique of political economy remains relevant in the twenty-first century. One of the main features of this article is Brosio's critique of profound changes that occurred in Central and Eastern Europe in the 1980s, particularly what was once called the Soviet Union and its former satellites and the so-called momentary victory of Western liberal capitalism. This critique is followed by larger discussion of the limits of this so-called victory in which Brosio lays out the incompatibility of capitalism and democracy and the contradictory imperatives it poses for schooling under capitalism. In the final analysis, Brosio provides the reader a political and economic context for understanding limits and possibilities of a critical pedagogy in schools in a capitalist society.

In Pauline Lipman's article, "Beyond Accountability," she maintains that the invasive politics of the accountability and standardization movement is ravaging public schools, by pushing out teachers committed to an emancipatory education. Lipman insists that the mandates of NCLB have robbed public education of the democratic possibilities that Dewey envisioned at an earlier time. She contends that the politics of globalization have entered school life and appropriated its discourses. So, *equity* has now become *meritocracy*; while *knowledge* has been converted to *rational information and efficiency*. Along the same lines, *equal opportunity* has been reduced to *tracking; access* defined by the *needs of labor*; and *literacy* has been reduced to *functional skills*, necessary for menial employment. Lipman further argues that "good schools" has become NCLB's euphemism for colonial education, where social control and accountability, as surveillance, impose a "stratified knowledge for a stratified society." However, despite these dismal conditions, Lipman offers concrete examples of counter-hegemonic education and inspiring school practices.

In "Creating a Pedagogy in Common," Noah De Lissovoy, Alex Means, and Kenneth Saltman offer a new vision for a critical pedagogy in school settings and most importantly a pedagogy that is linked to a broader struggle for democratic rights—a liberatory education. The authors outline three pedagogical approaches to a critical education and pedagogical praxis: Rupture, Project, and Conversation. All three approaches are organically connected in ways that empower student and teacher and challenge the neoliberal foundations of contemporary education. The writers stress the importance of going beyond narrow policy prescriptions, albeit policy is important, to rethinking the ideological underpinnings of the decision-making processes of a new school movement. They conclude that such a movement will take activists beyond the schools to reimagine a new social and democratic social order.

In his foundational article, "Broadening the Circle of Critical Pedagogy," Wayne Ross provides us with an interrogation of critical pedagogy, beginning with the unequivocal statement that "there is no single ideological perspective that defines critical pedagogy" despite common assertions. Ross's overall aim is to offer a more inclusive and operational definition of critical pedagogy. That is, according to Ross, the origins of critical pedagogy have their roots in diverse traditions of critical thought. He cites the importance of philosopher John Dewey's work informing the foundations of critical pedagogy. In particular, that education is not a neutral process—it's a political act. Another important influence of Dewey is the concept of democracy that is much more than government—it extends into participatory democracy and human emancipation. This according to Ross has important implications for schooling under capitalism. Ross goes on to discuss the role of dialectics and critical pedagogy. That is, to understand the world in terms of interconnections and tensions, given that critical pedagogies are epistemologically grounded in a dialectical approach that engages with the lived experiences of students and the materiality of the world.

Questions for Reflection and Dialogue

1. What features of Marx's critique of political economy are still relevant today? Explain why these are important to education.
2. What are the hidden values and ideas that inform the accountability and standardization movement? What are its implications for the future of public education?

3. In what ways is the neoliberal discourse of accountability and standardization reforms propelled by globalization? Explain.
4. Education is not value free or neutral but a political process/act. According to the readings in this section, what does this statement mean? And in what ways is this perspective significant to democratic education?
5. De Lissovoy, Means, and Saltman use the terms "the commons," "global commons," and "a new commons." What does "commons" mean here and how are these notions contrasted in the article?
6. Why is the idea of the commons useful to critical pedagogical efforts in schools and society?
7. What are the strengths and weaknesses of so-called policy reforms to address the structural problems of schools under the current social order?
8. Do activists need to explore more than just school-based policy prescriptions to address the problems of the so-called education crisis? Why?
9. How does Ross link the questions of democratic education to the dialectical approach of critical pedagogy? How does a dialectical approach to knowledge production differ from a banking approach?

30

The Continuing Conflicts Between Capitalism and Democracy: Ramifications for Schooling-Education

Richard A. Brosio

Introduction

This analysis seeks to explain a model which posits the contradictory character of capitalist and democratic imperatives within countries like the United States. Although this work depends primarily upon concepts, historical occurrences, and examples from the society within which the present writer lives, the model is intended to be relevant to other advanced, late capitalist societies, which are also characterized by constitutional restraints, broad suffrage, traditions of popular/mass involvement in public life, etc. This explanatory model is offered as preferable to liberal ones which do not take the reality of capitalism's awesome power seriously enough, and have over-emphasized the autonomy, and good intentions, of the central government. Furthermore, the model being presented in this work is superior to reductionist, orthodox Marxist ones which have been committed to portraying the central government, or State, as merely the executive committee of the whole bourgeoisie.

As Antonio Gramsci, et al., has taught us, capitalist hegemony in advanced capitalist countries must be fought for, and maintained within the context of constitutional, and even *de jure,* democratic political systems. The State must be answerable to the capitalist imperative which seeks a continuation and reproduction of favorable work relations, profit accumulation, etc.; and to the democratic-egalitarian imperative which privileges outcomes favorable to personal rights over property. This study features the ideas of Martin Carnoy, Henry Levin, Samuel Bowles, Herbert Gintis, Michael B. Katz, Frances Piven, Richard Cloward, Michael Apple, et al. Special emphasis is placed upon the consequences which the competing, or conflicting imperative model has for schooling-education. This emphasis is not only logical because the public school, like the State, is a contested terrain, but also attributable to the fact that the present writer's location is within the higher education community which is charged with analyzing teaching and learning. The interpretation of the ideas referred to is, obviously, my own. The continuing relevance of Marx's overall insight into social, economic, political, education, and other problems is a given within the work you have before you.

It is the author's view that capitalism is incompatible with authentic democracy, as it is understood in the contemporary, industrialized world. The present need to emphasize this incompatibility is especially poignant and necessary, because of the triumphant claims made by persons within the West, "free world", and by pro-capitalists wherever they may be found, as a result of the recent events in Central and Eastern Europe. Those who have superficially, erroneously, and misleadingly equated formal democratic rights with the complex realities and requirements of an authentically participatory, democratic society must not be allowed to preempt the interpretation(s) of the momentously important events which are occurring in the former Soviet Bloc. Fortunately, discourses exist, within countries and/or societies enjoying certain democratic rights and securities, and these arguments have maintained that the power of capital prevented the conversion of *de jure* democratic rights into *de facto* ones. The collapse of the centralized, command economies and their authoritarian, one-party systems may properly be applauded by democrats; however, it must be made clear that the attempt to include the newly freed peoples of the Warsaw Pact into the world capitalist system could result in new forms of flawed democracies. This is not to claim that problems in Poland will be the same as in Britain, or that Rumania can blindly follow theoretical insights and political strategies from Italy. However, it is important for us to realize that democrats have been involved in a long and bitter (mostly defensive) struggle against the priorities, power and hegemony of capital, even within *de jure* constitutional, and representative-democratic systems. Let us turn to a description and analysis of some specific arguments which have been occurring in the wake of the collapse of Soviet power, before proceeding to the actual conflicting imperatives model. It is clear that readers of this study could find analogies to the specific arguments about to be featured in part (1) from their own societies and/or countries.

(1)

During this historical period which features such profound changes in Central and Eastern Europe, it is necessary to evaluate carefully what is actually occurring – and what is not. Relatedly, it is of utmost importance for persons living in the United States, where the mainstream media has trumpeted the alleged oneness of capitalism and democracy, to evaluate especially carefully this old claim by the political right. How will the momentous events which are occurring the former Soviet Bloc affect those of us who have held that authentic democracy – and education for democratic empowerment – must necessarily struggle against the hegemony of capitalism?

It could be argued that all too many Americans have been interpreting the momentous occurrences in Central and Eastern Europe with a good deal of myopia, self-righteousness, and self-congratulation. All too many Western academicians and politicians saw the Soviet system as the very antithesis of what they believe to be a "universally valid model of liberal democracy and free-market capitalism with Judeo-Christian underpinnings."[1] As the events in the former Soviet Bloc unfold we see the analysis of Jeanne Kirkpatrick, et al. come undone; although there has occurred no *mea culpa* so far. Her rightist distinction between "their totalitarianism" and "our authoritarianism" has not been convincing to critical thinkers who do not already share her assumptions. Many rightists in the United States, and elsewhere, have turned a blind eye to the persistence of savage human rights violations within client states in Latin America, and in other parts of the world. Partisan wishes are being taken for historical realities, as we are told that there is no alternative to the ultimate triumph of political pluralism, liberalism, market capitalism, and "Americanism". As Arno Mayer has written, "it takes an uncommon hubris to prescribe a frail Western European and Northern American formula, conditioned by particular historical circumstances, not only for Eastern Europe but also for much of the Third World . . . history is not about to end or travel down a unilinear ... road. Instead, it will ... follow a sinuous and contested path mined with the promises and perils of violent eruptions".[2]

Francis Fukuyama, who is the deputy director of the American State Department's policy planning staff, wrote "The End of History," which was published in the neo-conservative *The National Interest* during the summer of 1989. Fukuyama begins by celebrating the triumph of "Western liberal democracy" but one can see early on that his definition of it is highly problematic, and certainly rightist-oriented. In fact, it sounds like "liberal democracy" is a stalking horse for capitalism. According to Fukuyama, the triumph of "liberal democracy" extends beyond "high politics and can be seen also in the ineluctable [inescapable, in a determinist sense] spread of consumerist Western culture in such diverse contexts as ... clothing stores opened in Moscow, the Beethoven piped into Japanese department stores, and the rock music enjoyed ... in Prague, Rangoon, and Tehran."[3] His essentialist position becomes clear when he writes that post-history will not feature art nor philosophy, but instead, only the continuous "caretaking of the museum of history".

E. P. Thompson claims that Fukuyama's position is absurd, as well as historically inaccurate. There have been, and are, many alternatives to centralized statism. Thompson suggests that there is a social democratic alternative, an emerging "green" position, various models of workers' control, small-scale autonomous and cooperative units, and "many more". New forms of intelligent improvisation will be required for the twenty-first century, and these will surely be characterized by public and private components. In order to solve the very real problems of ecological disaster, growth at the expense of the poor, and insuring the continuation of human history we will have to employ the "fullest repertory of forms" – and this includes communities, neighborhoods, and families.

Certainly, the "unrestrained market economy" is inadequate as a solution to the global problems facing civilized men and women. For Thompson, who sees socialism as an extension and broadening of participatory democracy, "the most viable future may well be a kind of socialism, although of a green and individualistic kind, with strong antistate resistances."[4] Gavan McCormack has said that only "the most adversarial logic" could reduce the problems of the East Bloc to the victory of capitalism. In fact, as we know, "free market" advocates have not always felt comfortable with, nor seen the necessity for, democracy – or even constitutional restraint. Chile under Pinochet comes readily to mind, as do the "Four Tigers" of East Asia: South Korea, Taiwan, Singapore, and Hong Kong. Noam Chomsky has pointed out that "as for democratic forms, at best they are limited under the constraints imposed by private command of resources and investment decisions . . ."[5] McCormack makes another important criticism of Fukuyama, and other smug celebrators of victory in the Cold War, when he points out the extraordinary conceit inherent in the claim that "all that has really mattered to the world has been the struggle between the two military superpowers."[6] Chomsky, and others, have repeatedly asserted that the United States has intervened into the domestic affairs of nations which have tried to democratize their relationships while seeking to establish a modicum of equity, in terms of access, education, income, medical care, etc. – and that this intervention against popular forces has been advertised as anti-Soviet activity. According to Chomsky, the United States governments have manifested "extreme hostility to democracy unless power remains securely in the hands of business, oligarchy and military elements that respect U.S. priorities."[7]

In the studied opinions of many critical observers during the momentous occurrences in the former Soviet Bloc, it is highly naive, as well as irresponsible, to assume that "untrammeled marketization" will guarantee the future development of political freedom in Central and Eastern Europe. The experiences had by Latin Americans make clear that the intended generation, or exacerbation, of massive inequalities which are the inevitable results of "untrammeled marketization" tend to destabilize the foundations of political democracy. According to Geoffrey Eley, if the rhetoric of "freedom" by the right continues to be used mostly as a club to beat upon discredited statism, then the promise of democracy in the East, and West, will remain unrealized. Will Western aid for the former Soviet Bloc become a vehicle for the expansion of capital markets? Will the economic fate of Europe beyond the Elbe be mostly dependent upon Western capitalism's decision-making? Eley thinks that it is of crucial importance who exercises power in Western Europe. "The best chance for a strengthening of democratic decision making inside the EC [Common Market] during the 1990s, and therefore . . . a more equitable integration of the Eastern Countries, would be a strengthening of the left in the national governments."[8]

Daniel Singer has said that there are many reasons for the people in the former Soviet Bloc to look at us with envy – and they aren't all economic. However, those of us who live in the West know about the problems which are chronic and systemic within our societies.

> We know the spuriousness of that equality that makes it illegal for both the Baron de Rothschild and the *clochard* [vagrant] to sleep under the bridges of Paris. We know the sham of an electoral system that pretends that a Rupert Murdoch . . . has no more clout than Tom, Dick or Harry. We know that the Rockefellers stay in power even when they lose office . . . we are aware that handing over our sovereignty at regular intervals to representatives elected by the people – or rather imposed upon them by the power of money with the help of the media – is not the best way to gain mastery over our lives as producers and citizens.[9]

"Bourgeois democracy" was spoken of with contempt by persons on the left, not because they thought the freedoms which had been achieved were unimportant, but "because they wanted to expand the social content of those freedoms in order to give real meaning to such grand terms as liberty and equality . . ."[10] Flora Lewis has clarified what the events of 1989–90 in the former Soviet Bloc really mean. A system which has been stripped of its power to command may now develop in a manner yet to be decided upon – but almost surely not in the way Fukuyama and other contemporary pro-capitalist Panglosses have suggested. There have occurred profound changes in the world near this bloody century's end; however, there has been no pure triumph for American-style capitalism – nor for Western-style liberalism. The next round of competition will include an analysis of the weaknesses and injustices of a society where monopoly capitalism has long frustrated the realization of democratic hopes. Lewis writes that we don't have enough laurels to rest on. "The scourge of drugs should suggest much more than inadequate law enforcement . . . It has to mean that there is something . . . our society is failing to provide in its basic promise of community. We are producing . . . youths with inferior education . . . homeless who live on park benches and streets in the midst of empty buildings where they cannot afford space . . . We too have to deliver."[11]

Grzegorz Boguta, who is co-founder and director of Poland's premier underground publishing house, has explained that under the severe economic medicine proposed for Poland the very underground culture which helped topple his country's Soviet-backed, communist regime is itself in trouble. The draconian economic formula for Poland's hoped-for recovery has included components of Reaganism and Thatcherism. The standard of living for many Poles has plummeted. Poland seems to be opening itself to capitalist investment, while unruly workers are pressured to go along.[12] As Boguta has taught us, the price of paper has increased so dramatically that reading material is too costly to produce. "Books in Poland are on their way to becoming as expensive as books in the West, while our [the majority of Poles] salaries aren't anywhere near those in the West."[13] Ironically, "we regained our democracy. But now what the censor forbade is forbidden by price."[14]

As it becomes increasingly possible for dialogue to occur among Europeans, and with persons around the world, we can continue to learn from each other. The problems involved in trying to build an authentically democratic society, and democratic educational system-process, will continue to be difficult. The specifics of those difficulties will be addressed most effectively by those who are involved in the struggles within their own sites and terrains.

The crises and opportunities which confront all of us as this century nears its end can be framed in a variety of ways. It has been my choice to view the crises and opportunities through the lenses provided for by the discourse featuring the continued incompatibility of capitalism and authentic, participatory democracy. This discourse has long been of great importance within societies which feature both capitalism, and some democratic forms and achievements; however, it takes on added importance as a result of the momentary fluidity of the situation in the former Soviet sphere. The momentary, seeming victory of Western, liberal capitalism is of great importance, not only for the Soviet Union and its former satellites, but for nations within the countries which are called "underdeveloped". Part (2) of this paper provides a specific version of a larger discussion which should be taking place in many places, and by a multitude of persons, around the world at this time.

(2)

The conceptual model which explains most clearly the theoretical work of these theorists who are convinced of the incompatibility of capitalism and democracy can be described as follows. This model emphasizes schooling-education as a contested site, and it enables us to see the schools – especially public ones – as functionally answerable to the awesomely powerful economy under capitalist aegis, but also influenced by demands made by working people, minorities, people of color, women, etc. This susceptibility to different and conflicting imperatives situates the schools within dynamic and dialectical relationships within the larger society comprised of other contested sites. If capitalism and participatory democracy were compatible, as rightists (and many liberals) have claimed, there would be no need for having developed a theoretical, explanatory model which is empirically grounded in historical events – events which validate the reality and necessity for struggle. It has been theorized that public schools in the United States, and elsewhere, are Janus-faced (having two contrasting aspects) because they are answerable to the imperatives of (1) capitalism, and (2) democracy, and/or egalitarianism. These contradictory imperatives create problems for public schools in other "developed" countries, as well, whose governmental forms are basically democratic, and whose social policies are committed to broad participation – while their economic systems are still dominated by capitalism. The capitalist economic imperative requests that the schools produce competent, willing workers; whereas, the democratic-egalitarian imperative requests that public education develop critical, well-rounded, citizen-workers who are committed to complex roles beyond work – and who may use their critical skills to analyze capitalist work relations, and command of the economy. The public school's role can be understood most clearly if it is seen as occupying a contested site where two, historically powerful and contradictory, imperatives clash. Seeing the school as a contested site, in the continuing battle between capital and democracy, allows us to connect with Gramsci, et al., who have argued that the formally constitutional State is itself a contested site. When the schools are studied relationally to the dynamics of the larger host society, the analysis has the advantage of not being simplistic or parochial.

Martin Carnoy and Henry Levin have sought to explain in their *Schooling and Work in the Democratic State,* (1985) how the public school can be (1) an institution which reproduces the hierarchical and unequal class relations characteristic of capitalism, and (2) an institution which is fairer, more democratic and equal than the workplace to which students are eventually bound. Capitalist hegemony works, but only imperfectly. The relationship between work and education is dialectical. According to Carnoy and Levin, "caught up in the larger conflicts inherent in a capitalist economy and liberal capitalist State. . . . The school is essential to the accumulation of capital and the reproduction of the dominant capitalist relations of production, and it is valued . . . as a means of greater participation in economic and political life."[15] The public school does respond to the requirements of unequal hierarchies which are inherent to capitalist work relations, so educators must select and sort for highly unfair work slots; however, the school responds to democratic values and expectations associated with equality of access to citizen rights and opportunities. This battle occurs because, "the very nature of capitalism and democracy creates internal incompatibilities and conflicts in institutions."[16] It is well known that different historical periods have been characterized by comparative strengths and weaknesses with regard to the conflicting imperatives; although it is the position of this writer that the strength of capitalism has been greater, in almost every case, than its democratic opponent. Because capitalism is unfair to the majority of persons' hopes for equity, security, and democratic voice (although it is riotously productive of useful, and not so useful, consumer goods) a class conflict model becomes useful to our analysis. Class, and other forms of conflict, are continuously occurring because those who are the losers in the capitalist economy, and attendant social, political, cultural, and educational institutions, have learned to use the freedoms afforded by the liberal constitutional State – which has become increasingly democratic in *de jure* terms – to redress grievances caused by the undemocratic, hierarchical nature of capitalism.

Even though the public school in the United States has responded historically to the democratic imperative, it is well known that from the beginning of secondary schooling, very different things happened to the students who were included under one, comprehensive roof. Michael Katz has argued that the basic structure of American education was set in circa 1880, and that it has not changed fundamentally since then. The fundamental characteristics of the system were, and are, "universal, tax-supported, free, compulsory, bureaucratic, racist, and class-biased."[17] It is clear that when working class kids were directed into vocational tracks and classes, they met with an anti-union bias. Furthermore, the newly developing "Scientific" testing movement in the late nineteenth and early twentieth centuries was able to "objectively" classify the sons and daughters of the working class, immigrants, poor, and people of color as lacking and unworthy. Colin Greer has said that the United States "has a public school system designed to preserve . . . [a] contradiction – by institutionalizing the rhetoric of change to preserve social stasis . . . In fact, the public school stands as an instrument of the conservative strategy for defusing movements for social change which seriously challenge the established order . . ."[18] When we use the Janus-faced model to explain various forms of answerability to the conflicting imperatives, we must remember that an authentically radical left has had little influence, let alone power, in the United States.

Even when the official American left has been somewhat successful in its attempt to ameliorate the most brutal aspects of a market (Darwinian) distribution of goods, services, access, etc., the reaction from the right has been withering in its intensity. Katz has written, "I expect . . . that any serious effort to equip poor children as effective competitors for the well-to-do will meet enormous, and probably successful resistance."[19] The fierce, and momentarily successful, reaction mounted by capital, and its allies, during the time since Katz wrote those lines attests to the accuracy of his insight. It is obvious that the reaction mounted by capital, and the right, has not been limited to the United States. Although there are many and varied lyrics which are specific to the various countries within the capitalist world system, it could be demonstrated empirically that the melody is known to students of school and society around the globe. The growing power of transnational capitalism, which is obviously supported by the central governments of the strongest capitalist nations, has been able to bring pressure to bear on most "superstructural" institutions so that they are more compliant with the needs of capitalist development and reproduction. The specific lyrics which are all compatible with the overall, dominant melody is beyond the scope of this work. The school's role as reproducer of capitalist relations of production and class stratification is tempered by occasional periods of effective popular democratic counterweight. Without this action, the capitalist imperative upon the schools is nearly preemptive.

As a result of real, and/or perceived, gains made by the left throughout American society during the 1960s (and since the New Deal), the forces of rightist reaction have mounted a counterattack in order to roll back and "chill" the democratic imperative. The flurry of activities within the American educational community during the 1980s can be seen as an attempt by capital, and its followers, to get the public school back into sync with the newly developing requirements. As I have said elsewhere, because the current crisis of global monopoly capitalism has been primarily responsible for the present economic sea changes, the educational reforms proposed and enacted have corresponded to the economic crisis as defined by capital and "its conscious or seemingly unaware allies and minions." Had the present economic crisis been defined by other social classes, groups, and alliances – those using other discourses – then the pressure on the educational system would be different from what we have experienced.[20]

Michael Apple has said, "There has been a remarkable offensive – one combining big business and finance, and conservative and religious groups – aimed at delegitimating democratic discourse and restoring 'authority' . . . In education . . . what is also at stake are the conditions under which teachers will labor, the kinds of knowledge our children will learn, and ultimately whether we will have an educated citizenry that can raise the ethical and political questions so necessary to keep democracy a vital living force or instead a quiescent population more interested in personal gain than the social good."[21] It would be interesting to compare the constitutive parts of rightist "offences" within the various countries which make up the capitalist inner core. The similarities between Thatcher's programs in Britain, and Reagan's in the United States, are well-known; whereas one has to do research in order to learn of comparable happenings in Italy, France, Canada, Australia, New Zealand, etc. Obviously the persons in those countries *are* knowledgeable about events in their recent, national past.

In the U. S., the rightist counterattack began as early as the Nixon administration. As we know, the first of several chilling recessions reintroduced many Americans to hard times in the 1970s. Furthermore, and relatedly, "in schooling, the Nixon program included a vast national plan called 'career education'. Curriculum was tilted in the direction of work discipline and job training. Perhaps this would cool the ardor of youth. If not, careerism was followed in the mid-1970s by a 'Literacy Crisis' and a 'back-to-basics' movement. Perhaps those programs would put some noses to the grindstone."[22] We have come to understand that on educational sites conservative reaction intervenes against the possibilities of a more equitable, egalitarian, and democratic distribution of wealth, power, and access. The restoration has generally meant redistribution from the bottom and middle to the top. It is clear that rightist, restoration discourse has chosen words and dichotomies such as "equality versus equality"; furthermore, this reactionary movement poses as the defender of "high standards" and especially of "excellence". Many critics on the left believe that the words used in the reaction, whose purpose it is to restore and strengthen capitalist hegemony, are words which camouflage the real intention, which is to restore hierarchy, bossism, and domination by the powerful over subaltern groups. The reactionary discourse, which we have heard increasingly since 1970, poses as a universal one, instead of a self-conscious, and class-conscious attempt to roll back real, and alleged, gains made by popular and democratic groups.

Francis Fox Piven and Richard A. Cloward have provided us with an exceptionally clear analysis of what is at stake during the recent rightist attempt to strengthen capitalist hegemony. Speaking of the Reagan administration's efforts to reverse policies which allowed ordinary citizens to force the State to protect them in the irrational and predatory marketplace, Piven and Cloward point out accurately that capital and its allies have attempted to seize the ideological ground which enables them to claim that politics and the market, or economy, are separate. One could argue plausibly that neither the protest culture of the 1960s, nor the attempted rightist reaction since the first Nixon administration, have been successful at bringing stability to, or acceptance of, a system which is based upon contradictory imperatives, viz. capitalism and democracy. The popular forces, during the 1960s and since, have not been able to muster the power to make the economy answerable to democratic and egalitarian imperatives. As a result of the left's attempt, and failure, a powerful rightist coalition made up of the National Rifle Association, chief executive officers, religious zealots, frightened lower middle class persons concerned with loss of status, racists, sexists, militarists, elitist professors and intellectuals, etc. has arisen. This rightist coalition has been forced to operate within a system where it is difficult to act like fellow rightists in other countries where constitutional safeguards and democratic traditions are either weak or absent. The distinct possibility that the Reagan-Bush administration acted illegally in its arming of the "Contras" is beyond the scope of this analysis.

As Gramsci has taught us, the constitutional, democratic State must be answerable to its many constituents, in order to preserve its legitimacy, but it is difficult to deny that in the last analysis it "tilts" toward favoring and representing capital, along with its myriad interests. It is true that superstructural institutions, like the schools, are able to exercise some autonomy vis-a-vis the substructure. The pressures emanating from those who control, and most greatly benefit from, capital are mediated through complex institutions and actions before they have an impact upon the majority of persons – but these pressures affect us mightily day after day. In fact, as Henri Lebvre has said, capitalist hegemony has "colonized the everyday". Men, women, and kids do resist the blandishments and power of capitalism while in school, factories, offices, neighborhoods, etc.; however, they seldom resist on terrain, or under circumstances, which are favorable to democratic and egalitarian outcomes. More often than not, the resistance is unsuccessful. One is often haunted by the fear that popular gains have been won mainly because a rich, expansive capitalism could afford to give concessions, and that the so-called democratic imperative would be seriously weakened – as it has been since 1970, and especially during the 1980s – when capital felt the pinch and began to reveal the iron fist formerly concealed under the velvet glove.

Bowles and Gintis's *Democracy and Capitalism* was published in 1986, and it is to their interpretation of the conflict between the capitalist and democratic imperatives that we turn. In spite of the term democratic capitalism, Bowles and Gintis argue that the two are not complementary; in fact, they represent profoundly different rules which regulate the development of persons and societies. Capitalism is characterized by the preeminence of economic privilege which is based upon property rights; whereas, democracy champions the priorities of liberty and accountability which are based upon the exercise of personal rights.[23] The incompatibility of the two imperatives, or organizing principles, is described this way by Bowles and Gintis: "no capitalist society may reasonably be called democratic in the . . . sense of securing personal liberty or rendering the exercise of power socially accountable."[24] One of the main theses of *Democracy and Capitalism* is that "democracy" has been used as window-dressing, or ornamentally, in capitalist societies. The "places" where things really get decided have not been democratic at all. "Representative government, civil liberties, and due process have, at best, curbed the more glaring excesses . . . of unaccountable power while often obscuring and strengthening underlying forms of privilege and domination."[25]

Social change in liberal capitalist societies is explained by Bowles and Gintis as the result primarily of the interaction and conflict between the "expansionary logics" of personal vs. property rights. In fact, their mid-1980's analysis states that the full extension of personal rights has posed the most fundamental challenge to capitalism, within its liberal context. According to Bowles and Gintis, in the United States, it has been the liberal, not socialist, discourse which has been the greatest threat to capitalist hegemony. The failure of the socialist discourse, and socialist politics, in the United States is a fact; however, an analysis of how this occurred is not central to my argument here. Their view of the liberal discourse is one which sees its historical evolution in such a way that allows its present concerns to be deemed radical. The fulfillment of the liberal emphasis on freedom becomes, in time, a critique and politics, which comprise a form of the democratic imperative threatening capitalist hegemony.[26]

Bowles and Gintis are convinced that the tension between property rights and personal rights has existed for a very long time within liberal republicanism, and they point to the classic Putney debates as a landmark. The officers were property-oriented, and the most famous of them, Ireton, worried that if all were given the vote without references to property, "'why may not those men vote against all property . . .'"[27] The soldiers, on the other hand, stressed personhood. The Leveller leader, Rainboro, argued that the chief end of government is to preserve persons, as well as estates. "Rainboro could find nothing in the law of God or of nature saying that 'a Lord should choose 20 Burgesses, and a Gentleman but two or a poor man should choose none.'"[28] Perhaps the most famous quote to have come down to us from the Putney Debates states Rainboro's personal rights position best, "'I think that the poorest he that is in England hath a life to live as the greatest he; and therefore . . . every man that has to live under a government ought first by his own consent to put himself under that government.'"[29] It must be pointed out here that the development of liberal republican, and even democratic governments throughout the West did not include the full possibility of a threat to property privileges which the seventeenth century Debates already made explicit. E. J. Hobsbawm has pointed out that during the reign of Louis Philippe in France, a distinction was made between the "legal country" and the "real country". According to Hobsbawm, "from the moment when the 'real country' began to penetrate the political enclosure of the 'legal' or 'political' country defended by the fortifications of property and educational qualifications for voting . . . the social order was at risk."[30] Those whose power came from property worried increasingly that the appearance of the masses upon the political stage – armed with the franchise – would mean the end of privileged power. As Hobsbawm has written about the great fear among the privileged and powerful persons of nineteenth century,

> What would happen in politics when the masses of the people . . . unable to understand the . . . logic of Adam Smith's free market, controlled the political fate of states? They would, as likely as not, pursue a road which led to that social revolution whose brief reappearance in 1871 has so terrified the respectable. In its ancient insurrectional form, revolution might no longer be imminent, but was it not concealed beyond any major extension of the franchise beyond the ranks of the propertied and educated? Would this not, as . . . Lord Salisbury feared in 1866, inevitably lead to communism?[31]

It is important to remember that Marx is properly considered a radical democrat. There has long been an assumption, if not a belief, that ordinary (non-pejorative connotation) men and women would make a radically different society from the bourgeois/capitalist one they suffered under, once they achieved the power of political participation. The story of this century is of how democratic power has been blunted in terms of its revolutionary potential.

Bowles and Gintis think that the dominant (in some Western, capitalist countries) liberal tradition or discourse can be forged into a powerful tool of democratic mobilization which can "burst the bonds" of that discourse itself. They see the discourse and project of socialism as historic means through which to secure an extended conception of liberty and popular sovereignty. More specifically they assert,

> Our insistence on the priority of the terms "democracy" and its constituent elements – "popular sovereignty" and liberty – over more traditional economic phrases in the socialist Lexicon . . . thus expresses our conception of the political nature of economic concerns, not their unimportance . . . Our choice of terms reflect a recognition of both the hegemony of liberal discourse as the virtually exclusive medium of political communication in the advanced capitalist nations and the profoundly contradictory, malleable, and potentially radical nature of this discourse. No less important, the privileged status of democracy in our discourse reflects our central moral commitment and political project: to the creation of a new social order in which people . . . and communities – are more nearly the authors of their own individual and collective histories.[32]

Whether Bowles and Gintis's allegiance to their version of the liberal discourse will allow the radical transformation they apparently seek is not obvious to many students of liberalism as a tradition, because of its historic subservience to property and capital. Within educational scholarship one has only to look at Clarence Karier's essay, "Liberal Ideology and the Quest for Orderly change",[33] or the position of Western Marxists[34] to understand that many on the left see liberalism, and liberals, as instinctively turning to the right whenever their interests – and the interests of property and capital – are threatened. Perhaps the following passage from *Schooling in Capitalist America* (1976) can be incorporated into Bowles and Gintis's later (1986) version of liberal discourse, or it may be that this proposed democratization is too radical for real liberalism.

> An educational system can be egalitarian and liberating only when it prepares youth for fully democratic participation in social life and an equal claim to the fruits of economic activity. In the United States, democratic forms in the electoral sphere of political life are paralleled by highly dictatorial forms in the economic sphere. Thus we believe that the key to reform is the democratization of economic relationships: social ownership, democratic and participatory control of the production process by workers, equal sharing of socially necessary labor by all, and progressive equalization of incomes and destruction of hierarchical economic relationships. This is, of course, socialism, conceived of as an extension of democracy from the narrowly political to the economic realm.[35]

If Bowles and Gintis's ideas/program were translated into reality, it is clear that the balance between the conflicting imperatives would be altered profoundly in democracy's favor.

As has already been noted, it is open to question for many, whether liberalism can be translated into the kind of radical democracy which Bowles and Gintis espouse. It is clear from reading their *Democracy and Capitalism* (1986) that the authors view the further expansion of capitalist property relations as inimical to – and at the expense of – democratic institutions. The seeming rush to privatize within the erstwhile Soviet Bloc would not be supported by Bowles and Gintis. Their view is that "democracy can only survive by expanding to cover areas of social life now dominated by prerogatives of capitalist property."[36] The expansion of the preferred discourse of rights over property is dependent upon the ability of organized men and women, who must learn to take advantage of the juridical reality of democratic forms and procedures within systems which are both capitalist and democratic. However, as the lead editorial (Review of the Month) called "Dangers of Democracy," in the journal *Monthly Review* has argued, Gavril Popov, the recently elected mayor of Moscow, has warned that too much democracy "seriously threatens the reconstruction being attempted in Eastern Europe . . ."[37] Popov is afraid that too much democracy in the Soviet Union will prevent the establishment of inequalities, based upon the development of private property. Similar to the American *Federalist Papers* of the eighteenth century, Popov seeks to base society upon inequality and property, but with an ironic difference: "the [American] founding fathers [of the U. S. Constitution] were spokesmen for existing ruling classes. Gavril Popov is a spokesman for classes based on a property system that does not yet exist."[38] The recent developments in Poland, especially the election of Walesa to the presidency in December 1990, provides an analogous development in that country.

At the conclusion of both *Schooling in Capitalist America* and *Democracy and Capitalism,* Bowles and Gintis assert that it is up to organized, historical actors to act upon their understanding of the realities and issues of our time in order to tip the balance – or current imbalance – in favor of egalitarianism, and the enhancement of personal rights, over property, in general. It has been the strategy of the right to prevent popular forces from seeing issues clearly – including their own authentic self-interest – so that they will be unable to use their, potentially, greater electoral strength to dominate the political process, the political economy, and the State itself. It is to Bowles and Gintis's credit, as well as to much of the contemporary democratic left, that they give greater attention to exploitation which is racially, ethnically, and gender based than has been the case when class was privileged, almost to the exclusion of other categories. Unfortunately, these different categories of exploitation have reflected divisions among victims, and may have helped make it more difficult to construct a unifying umbrella, under which coalitions could be formed, in order to contest the main citadels of non-democratic power in advanced capitalist societies. For Bowles and Gintis, and many other persons on the contemporary left, the promise of democracy includes the expansion of personal rights, which means holding property rights and State power accountable. This "postliberal" democracy proposes "novel forms of social power independent of the state; namely democratically accountable, chartered freedoms in community and work . . . Democracy is necessarily a relationship among free people, and economic dependency no less than personal bondage is the antithesis of freedom."[39]

Conclusion

This analysis has sought to explain a model which posits the contradictory character of capitalist and democratic imperatives within advanced capitalist countries, that also feature constitutional safeguards, democratic procedures, broad suffrage, and commitments to some forms of rough equity. It has been this writer's position that monopoly capitalism and authentic democracy are incompatible. Furthermore, the power of the capitalist imperative is much greater than the democratic one. Relatedly, it was emphasized that at an historical time marking the coming-apart of State socialism in the former Soviet Bloc it is of great importance to combat the political right's attempts to equate capitalism with democracy. It has been suggested that a rich tradition exists within countries which have developed the conflicting imperatives model(s), and its adherents have clearly demonstrated that *de facto* democracy can be, and has been, stymied by the awesome power of capitalism. There is no lesson to be taught by the West's experience; however, a stating of the fact that *de jure* democracy is not the same as authentic, participatory, *de facto* democracy seems justifiable. George S. Counts wrote in 1932 that, "unless the democratic tradition is able to organize and conduct a successful attack on the economic system, its complete destruction is inevitable. If democracy is to survive, it must seek new economic foundations."[40] This warning is still relevant today.

Notes

1. Mayer, Arno J. (April 9, 1990) "Europe After the Great Thaw," *The Nation* 250, 14:488.
2. Ibid., 492.
3. Fukuyama, Francis (Summer 1989) "The End of History?" *The National Interest* 16:3.
4. Thompson, E. P. (January 29, 1990) "History Turns on A New Hinge," *The Nation* 250, 4:120.
5. Chomsky, Noam (January 29, 1990) "The Dawn, So Far, Is in the East," *The Nation* 250, 4:133.
6. McCormack, Gavan (May 1990) "Capitalism Triumphant? The Evidence From 'Number One' (Japan)," *Monthly Review* 42, 1:4.
7. Chomsky, N. "Dawn in the East," 133.
8. Morris, Ellen (June 1990) "Europe 1999: The Process and the Prospect," piece of the analysis by Geoffrey Eley, *Michigan Today* 22, 3:6.
9. Singer, Daniel (May 1, 1990) "New Days That Shake the World," *The Nation* 248, 17:594.
10. Ibid., 594.
11. Lewis, Flora (August 6, 1989) "The Society Race," *The New York Times* Op-Ed section, 21.
12. Wiener, Jon (June 25, 1990) "Capitalist Shock Therapy: The Plan in Poland," *The Nation* 250, 25:892.
13. "Talk of the Town," *The New Yorker* 66, 1 (February 19, 1990): 33.
14. Ibid., 34.
15. Carnoy, Martin and Levin, Henry (1985) *Schooling and Work in The Democratic State,* Stanford, CA: Stanford University Press, 4.
16. Ibid., 4–5.
17. Katz, Michael B. (1975) *Class, Bureaucracy, and Schools,* Expanded Edition, New York: Praeger Publishers, XVIII.
18. Greer, Colin (1972) *The Great School Legend: A Revisionist Interpretation of American Public Education,* New York: Basic Books, Inc., Publishers, 59.
19. Katz, M.B. *Class, Bureaucracy and Schools,* 152.
20. Brosio, Richard A. (Fall 1987) "The Present Economic Sea Changes and the Corresponding Consequences for Education," *Educational Foundations* 3:31.
21. Apple, Michael W. (1986) from Series editor's introduction, in Ira Shor, *Culture Wars: School and Society in the Conservative Restoration 1969–1984,* Boston: Routledge & Kegan Paul, X.
22. Shor, *Culture Wars,* 3–4.
23. Bowles, Samuel and Gintis, Herbert (1986) *Democracy and Capitalism,* New York: Basic Books, Inc., Publishers, 3.
24. Ibid., 3.
25. Ibid, 4–5.

26. Brosio, Richard A. (1989) "Response to Worsfold," in *Philosophy of Education 1988,* Proceedings of the Forty-fourth Annual Meeting of the Philosophy of Education Society (Normal, IL: Philosophy of Education Society), 72, and passim.
27. Mason, A. T. and Leach, R. H. (1959) *In Quest of Freedom: American Political Thought and Practice,* Eaglewood Cliffs, NJ: Prentice-Hall, Inc., 8.
28. Ibid., 7.
29. Bowles and Gintis, *Democracy and Capitalism,* 28.
30. Hobsbawm, E. J. (1987) *The Age of Empire 1875–1914,* New York: Pantheon Books, 85.
31. Ibid., 85.
32. Bowles and Gintis, *Democracy and Capitalism,* 209.
33. See: Karier, Clarence J. (1973) "Liberal Ideology and the Quest for Orderly Change," in *Roots of the Crises: American Education in the Twentieth Century,* eds. Clarence J. Karier, et al., Chicago: Rand McNally & Company, 84–107.
34. See: (1) Palmiro Togliatti, *Lectures on Fascism,* New York: International Publishers, 1976, (2) An interview by Eric Hobsbawm with Giorgio Napolitano, in *The Italian Road to Socialism,* Westport, CT: Lawrence Hill & Company, 1977, and (3) the corpus of Antonio Gramsci's work.
35. Bowles, S. and Gintis, H. (1976) *Schooling in Capitalist America,* New York: Basic Books, Inc., Publishers, 14.
36. Bowles and Gintis, *Democracy and Capitalism,* 211.
37. The Editors, (1990) "Danger of Democracy," *Monthly Review* 42, 7:1.
38. Ibid., 7.
39. Bowles and Gintis, *Democracy and Education,* 177.
40. Counts, George S. (1932) *Dare the School Build a New Social Order?* New York: The John Day Company, 45.

31

Beyond Accountability: Toward Schools that Create New People for a New Way of Life

Pauline Lipman

In February 2003, I was having dinner with several friends, all Chicago Public Schools (CPS) teachers. As I looked around the table, I saw stress etched into everyone's face. One friend, who teaches sixth grade, described going to the opera for the first time and being shocked at her own lack of analytical keenness. "And that's something I'm really good at, literary analysis." With all the constant monitoring and test preparation, she said, she just has no time to think. "I want to do those creative things in the classroom, but there's just no space. What happened to the intellectual excitement? I feel like I'm operating on a low 6th grade level." Another teacher talked about feeling schizophrenic. She is active in Teachers for Social Justice, but in her school she finds herself doing things against her beliefs in order to manage a situation in which the pressures of accountability are worse than ever and the social stress on kids rebounds on the classroom. A new high school teacher, also a social activist, with two master's degrees, said, "If it's going to be like this, more mandates every day and no time, I don't think I can do this job for more than three or four years. And this is what I want to do." These are some of the most thoughtful, committed, critically minded teachers I know.

January 2003: At a meeting of CPS students and teachers, a student at one of the city's regular high schools (I'll call him Manuel) described his school. It is so overcrowded they are on double shifts. There are forty kids in a class, and his math class shares a classroom with an English class. It is hard to concentrate on math with the English teacher right next to him. There are lockers for only one third of the students, and the students are not allowed to wear coats and backpacks in school (CPS discipline policy). It is winter, so lots of kids just do not go to school because they do not have lockers. He missed school for two weeks in the fall for this reason. Finally he found a friend who let him share his locker. There are three kids and all their stuff is in one narrow locker. Half of his chemistry lab is roped off because there is a big hole in the floor. Some of his teachers are not teaching in their subject area, and the curriculum provides no space for his voice; nor is it relevant to the serious issues he and his friend grappled with in their lives. Manuel is a senior, and he has been bombarded by military recruiters promising him training, job skills, free college tuition. That is the only recruitment he has seen. He has received no college counseling and does not think he has a future in college. There are few true college prep classes in his high school except for the small, selective IB program. Manuel is a leader of a citywide student activist organization.

These stories capture a slice of life in Chicago's mostly nonselective public schools eight years after the introduction of a regime of accountability that, in many respects, has become national policy with George W. Bush's *No Child Left Behind* (NCLB) (2001). NCLB crystallizes neoliberal, business-oriented education policy.[1] Business rhetoric of efficiency, accountability, and performance standards and the redefinition of education to serve the labor market have become the common vocabulary of educational policies across the United States, and increasingly, globally. Chicago embodies this agenda in action, with its high stakes testing and penalties for failure and its differentiated schools (a variant on neoliberal school choice). Under NCLB, every school district and every school will be measured, driven, and sanctioned or rewarded on the basis of its students' performance on standardized tests. Test-driven, standardized teaching is one product of this agenda, except in selective or high-scoring schools that negotiate or are exempted from it.[2] In practice, having served as a stalking horse for NCLB, Chicago is now ironically circumscribed by it even as some officials talk about new teaching initiatives. In a NCLB world of state regulation, deviation from this agenda has become even more difficult. In my last interview with Ms. Grimes, Westview's principal, she defined the power of the national policy context: "If they're not able to master what's on that Iowa, I don't care what other things you're taught. Looking at it from what Bush is looking for, you're not taught. You are a failing school" (January 2001). What we can learn from accountability, centralized regulation, standardization, and differentiated schools in Chicago has implications for what is meant to be the national norm.

Chicago has a specific history and the school district has its own particularities. And the four schools in this study have their own institutional characters, micropolitics, and histories. What happens behind their brick facades is only partially determined by dominant policies. Moreover, my research is just a brief look at each school. I do not suggest that Chicago and these four schools are representative of U.S. schools or urban school systems. Yet I have attempted, through an overview of CPS policies and an examination of how they play out in four different contexts, to tell stories not told about a hegemonic national education agenda. Thus I hope to say something of what might be expected in other contexts, particularly in relation to issues of educational and social equity, the agency of adults and children, the valuing of cultures and languages, and possibilities for making schools places where children develop tools to critique authorized knowledge and challenge social injustice. In this chapter I summarize some main insights from the school case studies and analysis of districtwide policies and their implications in relation to processes of globalization. I counterpose this emphasis with an outline for an alternative educational agenda and three powerful examples of doing education very differently. These examples challenge hegemonic discourses about education by showing that teachers, administrators, students, and families can create schools and school systems that prepare children to be empowered subjects and critical actors for social change. These examples also concretize the strategic role of education in reconstructing the state and challenging neoliberal hegemony. I conclude by commenting on what these policies mean in a post-9/11 world and possibilities for linking education change with emerging, critically conscious social movements.

Lessons from Chicago

I have argued that the regime of accountability supports processes of economic and social dualization linked to globalization. Education policies concretely and symbolically produce a highly segmented and economically polarized labor force and the reconstitution of urban space as the cultural and material province of real estate developers, corporate headquarters, and the new urban gentry. Accountability language, practices, social relations, and ways of valuing and thinking constitute a discourse of social discipline and subjugation that is highly racialized. They legitimate and produce the regulation and control of youth of color and support the eviction and criminalization of communities of color. In this section, I review these arguments and draw out their implications in the present political context.

Changing the Discourse of, and about, Education

Aligned with a broad social agenda that is retrenching on every social gain wrung from the state in the post-World War II era, neoliberal education discourses shift responsibility for inequality produced by the state onto parents, students, schools, communities, and teachers. Chicago's policies bring these discourses to life. *Equity* ("ending the injustice of social promotion," "holding all students to the same high standards," expanding "a variety of education opportunities") is tied to *individual responsibility* (students who progress are those who "work hard"; failure is publicly penalized through grade retention, assignment to remedial high schools, and school probation). *Technical rationality and efficiency* (educational processes are standardized, centrally prescribed and scripted, and subject to accounting measures) are substituted for the complex ethical and social processes and goals of education. This is lived through test-prep drills, educational triage, and semi-scripted curricula. *Business metaphors* of quality control, accountability, and standards replace any notion of democratic participation in education as a public good in a democratic society. The purpose of education is redefined to develop the skills and dispositions necessary for the labor market of a post-Fordist, globalized capitalism.

The four case studies demonstrate the power of the dominant policy agenda to change educational discourse at the level of the classroom and school. In all four schools, to varying degrees, accountability redefined what it means to be a "good school" in technical and narrowly instrumental terms (Ball, 1997a). The practices induced by accountability and centralized regulation created and exacerbated contradictions between substantive long-term projects to change teaching and learning and short-term accountability-driven goals. This process was illustrated by dropping rich mathematics curricula at Grover and Brewer; undermining a budding process of collective, critical reflection at Brewer; channeling Westview teachers' commitment to their students into raising test scores; and chipping away at Farley teachers' sense of professional efficacy.

In this discourse, teachers who were "good" according to multidimensional and complicated criteria, including those constructed by families and communities, became less so. Teachers recognized for their commitment to children and the community, their determination to help students become people who could "read" and "write" the world (Freire & Macedo, 1987), and their defense of children's language and home culture were ultimately judged by a single, instrumental measure. Students, as well as teachers, with all their varied talents and challenges, were reduced to a test score. And schools, as well as their communities, in all their complexity—their failings, inadequacies, strong points, superb and weak teachers, ethical commitments to collective uplift, their energy, demoralization, courage, potential, and setbacks—were blended, homogenized, and reduced to a stanine score and a narrow business model of "success" or "failure." In the process, brilliant spots in the schools were rubbed out rather than cultivated and extended. A few uncommitted and unprepared teachers were driven out, and others were upgraded to standardized teaching. Instead of inducing schools to develop their curricular and pedagogical strengths, accountability policies promoted or reinforced a narrow focus on specific skills and on test-taking techniques. Instead of supporting and extending the strengths of culturally relevant, critical teachers at

Grover and Brewer, the policies drove them out or forced them to accommodate. Even when accountability exposed weaknesses, such as racial disparities in achievement at Farley, the policies did little to help address them and may have reinforced conservatism, out of fear of not drawing attention to issues of race. Despite a vocabulary of excellence that clothes school accountability, this is a discourse that produces mediocrity, conservatism, and narrowly instrumental conceptions of people, learning, and the purposes of education. The policies are given life through social practices in specific contexts. The four schools provide a glimpse of how the "ethical retooling of the public sector to emphasize excellence, effectiveness and quality that can be measured" (Ball, 1990, p. 259) is actually *lived* inside the discourses of accountability in schools.

Reproducing and Extending Inequality

I have also demonstrated that Chicago's education policies reproduce existing educational and social inequalities and create new ones. In the name of "choice" of educational "opportunities," Chicago has superimposed new forms of educational tracking on an already tracked system. This differentiated system illustrates the strategic relationship between new forms of educational tracking and the production of a stratified labor force for the new economy. Carlson's (1997) outline of this trend is remarkably close to Chicago's policies: The academic track is becoming more differentiated from other tracks and more spatially separate through magnet and specialty schools and separate academic programs within schools, thus stripping academic track students from the general high school. These selective programs, employing more constructivist and "higher-order-thinking" curricula, as well as advanced course offerings, prepare students to be knowledge producers in the new economy. The new vocationalism of Education-to-Career Academies creates a closer link between applied vocationalism and academics. At the same time, general high schools provide the new basic literacies (i.e., better than eighth grade reading and math skills and compliant and amiable social dispositions) that correspond to the skills required for the large number of low-skill, low-wage service jobs. Because of the fairly low level of these skills and the emphasis on test-driven practices, the new functional literacies are not conducive to critical literacy. As a whole this system constructs new "selective mechanisms within a system that claims inclusivity" (Ozga, 2000, p. 104). As I have argued, this stratified education produces identities for a stratified labor force, stratified city, and stratified society. Gee, Hull, and Lankshear (1996) point to the social logic of these policies in the context of the capitalist informational economy:

> "Education reform" in terms of ensuring quality schools for everyone is deeply paradoxical, because if everyone were educated there would be no servants. The new capitalism is in danger of producing and reproducing an even steeper pyramid than the old capitalism did. And, just as in the old capitalism, it will need institutions—like schools, first and foremost—to reproduce that social structure.
>
> (p. 47)

At the school level, although accountability has pushed some schools, such as Grover, to focus more on curriculum coordination and planning of instruction, my data suggest that it reinforces, even extends inequalities. I observed Farley, a high-scoring multiracial, mixed-class school, to be much less oriented to test-prep than the other three schools that served low-income and working-class African American and Latino/a children. There is virtually no evidence in the data from Grover, Westview, and Brewer that accountability policies helped them develop rich literacies, rigorous curriculum, or challenging intellectual experiences for students. The new policies also created a schism between the professional culture of these three schools, which became more regulated, and that of Farley, whose teachers were able to maintain some independent professional judgment. Particularly at Grover, probation and the school's array of external supervisors promoted technical and routinized approaches to improving instruction, deskilling teachers rather than enriching their thinking and knowledge. Accountability undermined the collective self-study at Brewer and practices and orientations that promoted bilingualism and biculturalism. It worked against critical literacy practices and drove out some of the strongest teachers at Brewer and Grover.

In short, the technical and routinized practices promoted by accountability policies have not helped Grover, Brewer, and Westview acquire the strengths of Farley's rich culture of literacy. Nor have they helped teachers to develop the professional competencies and independent professional judgment of some Farley teachers. These strengths are important elements to ensure that all children have access to an intellectually rigorous and multi-faceted literacy curriculum. If anything, accountability has made them more routinized and pushed out teachers who embodied this professional culture making these schools less like Farley. (See McNeil, 2000; Valenzuela, 1999, for similar findings.) However, the other important issue is that accountability-as-surveillance is likely to promote conservatism in high-scoring schools, reinforcing existing tendencies to avoid controversy and in-depth analysis of politically charged issues of race, culture, educational disparities, as well as critical pedagogies. Taking up these issues is a central challenge, but it is made even more difficult in a coercive climate in which public attention might produce closer monitoring and thus pressures to conform to the dominant agenda.

Education for Social Control

The Chicago example demonstrates how accountability and centralized regulation of schools constitute a regime of social control. This is a system that robs principals, teachers, students, and communities of agency. Through accountability the state shifts responsibility for "success" and "improvement" to the school but gives it less control over its evaluation and less room to maneuver. As a Grover teacher said, "You really don't have too much power or say-so in what goes on." The four schools illustrate concretely how regulation of teaching through direct external oversight, standards, and assessment by high stakes tests strips teachers of opportunities for professional and ethical judgment, further eroding whatever agency teachers, principals, and communities have in relation to their schools. As a result of mandated curricula, imposed standards, and the exigencies of preparing for standardized tests, teachers and communities are losing control of knowledge, to the extent they ever had any. This trend was reflected in the thirteen weeks of test preparation at Westview, the instructional routines dictated by Grover's probation partner, the pressure to teach children English at the expense of their Spanish at Brewer, and the curricular compromises pressed on Farley teachers.

This is a complex set of issues because some teachers need more content and pedagogical knowledge, and in its absence, routines and semiscripted curricula fill this gap, as they did for teaching interns at Grover. But no middle-class school would be likely to accept these technical fixes as a substitute for thoughtful pedagogical decisions. Nor is this an acceptable substitute for the pedagogical judgment, sociopolitical knowledge, and cultural sensitivity of teaching that is culturally and politically relevant to students and their communities. Moreover, imposed standardization negates the contested nature of what should constitute common knowledge (Apple, 1996, 2001; Bohn & Sleeter, 2000) and of what constitutes a good school and good teaching (e.g., Darder, 1995; Delpit, 1988; Ladson-Billings, 1994).

In the schools I studied, teachers faced a moral crisis as they were, to paraphrase one teacher, forced to compromise their beliefs. The public display of individual and school failure and the meting out of punishment by the state remind students, teachers, and communities that they have little power, that they are all "on probation" or in danger of being put there. Accountability becomes a totalizing system that infiltrates all aspects of school life and demands that each level of authority, each classroom, each school, and each grade level capitulate more or less, even if a given class or school is not immediately threatened with sanctions. This process is undergirded by a logic of inevitability. "There will always be tests, each grade needs to prepare students to be tested at the next grade, and if we don't comply, we too may be under tighter surveillance"—so goes the refrain. However, this system is deployed differentially. In the four schools in this study there was a continuum of enforcement, from near-total supervision of Grover to relative flexibility at Farley. This mirrors citywide patterns of race and class differentiation as revealed by the pattern of schools on probation—all enrolling predominantly low-income African Americans or Latinos/as. Thus, although everyone is swallowed up in this system, the accrued race and class advantages of some schools versus others mean that there are different constraints and that policies are "read" and accommodated differently in different contexts with different consequences for human agency.

Accountability works as a panoptic system of surveillance that teaches people to comply and to press others into compliance. This works, in part, because "deficiency" is made visible, individual, easily measured, and highly stigmatized within a hierarchical system of authority and supervision. By holding individuals all along the line—students, teachers, parents—responsible for their own "failure," the system and culture of accountability encourage both self-blame (as with Brewer students who failed the eighth grade ITBS) and passing on of the blame to others in a pecking order that originates in the CPS central office and ends at the student's and teacher's desk and parent's living room. This individualization of blame reinforces race-, ethnicity-, and class-based ideologies of deficient "others."

The four case studies illustrate that accountability, centralized regulation, and differentiated schools are (collectively) a system of social discipline that works through everyday practices in schools to shape student and teacher identities. The policies create actual material conditions—military discipline, routines of Direct Instruction, classroom language of accountability, unending test preparation, privileging of English over students' home language, challenging intellectual discussions, International Baccalaureate programs of study—"that construct the truth of who we are" (Ferguson, 2000, p. 59). Within this continuum, routinized, basic skills and highly regulated and assimilationist practices—delivered without critique—produce docile subjectivities:

> These are forms of power that are realized and reproduced through social interaction within the everyday life of institutions. They play upon the insecurities of the discipline subject. . . . They do not so much bear down upon but take shape within the practices of the institution itself and construct individuals and their social relations through direct interaction.
>
> (Ball, 1997b, p. 261)

Education Policy as a Racialized System of Regulation

Although all Chicago public schools are subject to surveillance and control by the state, patterns of racial subjugation are clear. Schools in low-income neighborhoods of color are the least in charge of their own destiny. (This is clear from the demographics of schools on probation and is illustrated by the differential regulation of the four schools in this study.) These are schools where both students and teachers are disciplined by the routines and frameworks of standardized tests and external supervision. As Ms. Dupree, a Grover teacher, said: “I don’t think their [CPS leaders] children are going through this. And they need to realize that these are human beings. And what kind of effects are you having on the students?” (March 2000). School accountability is not a policy of public engagement in the improvement of schooling. Without any real public discussion or participation of teachers, school administrators, students, and parents, powerful city and school officials have held up these schools in Black and Latino/a neighborhoods, and by implication, their communities, as examples of failure, dictated what will happen in their schools; and undermined Local School Councils. As these policies are “rolled out” nationally, through state accountability systems under *No Child Left Behind*, this trend has serious implications for African Americans and Latinos/as, who are most likely to attend schools with low test scores and thus are most likely to be subject to a model of education as social regulation.

This is a form of colonial education governed by powerful (primarily white) outsiders. It signals that the communities affected have neither the knowledge nor the right to debate and act together with educators to improve their children’s education. At Grover and Brewer this process also drove out some of the most committed, critical, and culturally relevant teachers. The loss of these teachers and the consolidation of a technical, instrumental version of education disarm African American and Latino/a students, particularly in a context of growing economic polarization, racial repression, and marginalization. Ladson-Billings’s argument (1994) is important here:

> Parents, teachers, and neighbors need to help arm African American children with the knowledge, skills, and attitude needed to struggle successfully against oppression. These, more than test scores, more than high grade point averages, are the critical features of education for African Americans. If students are to be equipped to struggle against racism, they need excellent skills from the basics of reading, writing, and math, to understanding history, thinking critically, solving problems, and making decisions; they must go beyond merely filling in test sheet bubbles with Number 2 pencils.
>
> (pp. 139–40)

Accountability is also a highly racialized discourse of deficits. The separation of “good” and “bad” schools, of “failing” and “successful” students, that is accomplished through the testing, sorting, and ordering processes of standardized tests, distribution of stanine scores, retention of students, and determination of probation lists constructs categories of functionality and dysfunctionality, normalcy and deviance. In this sense, the test is, in Foucault’s language, “a ritual of power.” It embodies the power of the state to sort and define students and schools, creating and reinforcing oppressive power relations (Carlson, 1997) of race and class. “Failing” schools and “failing” students (and by implication, “failing” communities), most African American and Latino/a, are measured against the “success” of schools that are generally more white, more middle-class. Low-income schools of color that are defined as relatively successful in this scheme (Brewer is an example) are marked as exceptions, models of functionality in a sea of dysfunctional “others,” much as the military high schools demarcate disciplined youth from undisciplined “others.” Policies that regulate and punish especially African American, and to some extent Latino/a, students and schools also contribute to the pathologizing of African American and Latino/a communities. In this way, education policy contributes to the construction of consciousness about race in the city and justifies the containment and eviction of African American and Latino/a communities.

Education Policy and Global Transformations

Education policy in Chicago is strategically linked to the restructured economy, urban development and gentrification, transnational migrations, and the politics of race, ethnicity, and racial exclusion in the city. The social, economic, spatial, and cultural changes in Chicago are both products of and responses to transformations in the global economy since the 1970s. The contradictions and tensions of globalization play out on the streets of the city. Here we see a new urban geography—sweeping contrasts of wealth and poverty, centrality and marginality, blatant corporate and financial power, and growing masses of people of color and immigrants whose labor is essential but whose presence (language, culture, place-making practices, and demands for justice) is unwelcome. These tensions and contradictions also play out in the city's public schools. The story of urban education policy today is embedded in this larger narrative of globalization with its social and economic polarization, urban displacement and exclusion, and the salience of race and ethnicity as well as class. The significance of Chicago's education policies lies in their intersection with these economic, political, and cultural processes.

When we say education policy is another front in the struggle over the direction of globalization (Lipman, 2002), this is not a rhetorical flourish but a statement about material and cultural survival and space for agency and transformation. The policy regime I have described is producing stratified knowledge, skills, dispositions, and identities for a deeply stratified society. Under the rubric of standards, the policies impose standardization and enforce language and cultural assimilation to mold the children of the increasingly linguistically and culturally diverse workforce into a more malleable and governable source of future labor. This is a system that treats people as a means to an end. The "economizing of education" and the discourse of accounting reduce people to potential sources of capital accumulation, manipulators of knowledge for global economic expansion, or providers of the services and accessories of leisure and pleasure for the rich. Students are reduced to test scores, future slots in the labor market, prison numbers, and possible cannon fodder in military conquests. Teachers are reduced to technicians and supervisors in the education assembly line—"objects" rather than "subjects" of history. This system is fundamentally about the negation of human agency, despite the good intentions of individuals at all levels.

The nature of this regime is to produce the docile subjectivities necessary for the maintenance of a world of nearly unfathomable contrasts of wealth and poverty. As Gee, Hull, and Lankshear point out, this is a world "in which a small number of countries and a small number of people within them will benefit substantively from the new capitalism, while a large number of others will be progressively worse off and exploited" (1996, p. 44). Such a polarized world requires the sort of domestication of critical thought and agency that is integral to the regime of accountability and discourses of high stakes testing and centralized regulation of schooling. It also requires intensified policing, nationally and locally, as well as internationally. The militarization of schooling and regimentation, policing, and criminalization of youth of color become increasingly useful as some African American and Latino/a communities, and especially the youth, are becoming a "fourth world" inside the United States. Again, Gee, Hull and Lankshear (1996): "[I]t has become possible for vast tracts of humanity to be dismissed now as simply having nothing of relevance to contribute to the new world economy" (p. 149). These are key targets of social control.

As global economic processes make gentrification "the cutting edge of urban change" (Smith, 1996, p. 8), education policies become a material force supporting the displacement of working-class and low-income communities, the transformation of others into urban ethnic theme parks, and the consolidation of the city as a space of corporate culture, middle-class stability, and whiteness. This is what Neal Smith calls the "class conquest" of the city. New forms of selectivity within and among schools are an important quality of life factor in attracting the high-paid knowledge workers central to globalization and the global city.

At the other end of the spectrum, specialized schooling, such as military schools, that discipline and regulate African Americans and some other people of color also mark them as requiring special forms of social control. This is particularly significant in the context of the global city, with its simultaneous dependence on low-paid labor of people of color, exclusion of those superfluous to the labor force, and need to recruit high-paid, primarily white knowledge workers who want to appropriate the city—neatly boulevarded, gated, and skyscrapered—as their own. Although the racialized policing of youth is nothing new, this has become a vastly expanded social policy and practice as the economy excludes whole sectors and as transnational migrations create a more diverse population of youth. The criminalization of some is related to the assimilation of others as part of the process of differentiated racialization. Schools are central to this process. The ideological force of these policies is deeply implicated in struggles over representation and power in increasingly racially and ethnically diverse urban contexts.

Toward an Alternative Educational Agenda

There is good reason why people back tough measures to ensure that when their children are sent to school, they are taught. That these policies resonate with families and communities is a measure of the persistent and urgent need to act immediately and decisively to address the abysmal material and intellectual conditions in too many urban schools. Support for accountability also reflects the absence of a viable alternative that grasps this urgency *and* makes a liberatory agenda concrete. In schools, as well as in the broader public, there is an absence of counterhegemonic discourses that capture the gravity of the current situation in urban schools and press for rich intellectual experiences, cultural and social relevance, democratic participation, and critical thought. More equitable, humane, and liberatory schooling can only grow out of a rich dialogue that includes the multiple perspectives of committed educators and students, families, and communities about what is in the best interest of their children (Delpit, 1988). Specifically, this requires the broad participation and cultural resources of the diverse racially, ethnically, and economically marginalized communities most failed by public schools in the United States. A central problem in Chicago is that city and school officials have captured the common sense about school reform. There an absence of public debate and there is no public forum for fundamentally different perspectives. Moreover, some of the best, most committed teachers who might provide leadership in a more democratic process at the school level, whose practices might be the basis for a liberatory educational program, are being driven out by the current policies.

In part, neoliberal education programs and the drive to accountability and standardization have won out because they have captured the national, even international conversation about education as the only alternative for the "failure" of public schooling. Their hegemonic project has succeeded in redefining education as job preparation, learning as standardized skills and information, educational quality as measurable by test scores, and teaching as the technical delivery of that which is centrally mandated and tested. By defining the problem of education as standards and accountability they have made simply irrelevant any talk about humanity, difference, democracy, culture, thinking, personal meaning, ethical deliberation, intellectual rigor, social responsibility, and joy in education. Challenging the dominant discourse and posing alternative frameworks are strategic aspects of reversing the present direction. Parents, students, and committed teachers—especially those in the communities most affected—can provide a new language of critique and possibility that is grounded in their own knowledge, experiences, and commitments. Critics of current policies need to work together with them, and their perspectives need to be injected into discussions about education. The power of such a participatory process is illustrated by the development of Citizen Schools in Brazil, which I discuss in this chapter.

In the spirit of dialogue, I have suggested (Lipman, 2002) several premises of an alternative agenda. First, all students need an education that is intellectually rich and rigorous and that instills a sense of personal, cultural, and social agency. Students need both the knowledge and skills traditionally associated with academic excellence and a curriculum that is meaningfully related to their lives. They need an education that teaches them to think critically about knowledge and social institutions and locate their own history and cultural identity within broader contexts. Students need an education that instills a sense of hope and possibility that they can make a difference in their own family, school, and community and in the broader national and global community while it prepares them for multiple life choices.

Second, a commitment to educate all students requires the deployment of significant resources. This point almost seems a hollow joke at a moment when the U.S. government spends billions of tax dollars on global military domination and corporate enrichment while there are cutbacks in education funding. But what is needed is nothing short of a massive reconstruction and renewal project. Without new intellectual, cultural, material, and ideological resources, urban schools cannot overcome long-standing problems rooted in racism and a history of neglect. In most urban schools, if not most school systems, there is a compelling need to reduce class size substantially; to provide consistent high-quality professional development and time for teachers to plan and reflect in order to transform the nature of teaching, learning, and assessment; to recruit and retain expert committed teachers in schools in the poorest communities; to provide up-to-date science labs, current and well-stocked school libraries, arts and foreign language programs, state of the art and well-run computer labs. The failure to marshal these resources leads to blaming of communities and democratic policy itself for educational failure. This was the case in Chicago when business leaders and political officials declared that Local School Councils were not "working." Failure due to lack of resources provides a justification for the state to impose controls (Apple, 1991) to overcome the "failed policies of the past," as in Chicago, or to privatize public education, as in Philadelphia. In a period of retrenchment of social benefits at home and squandering of billions in military conquest abroad, the lack of political will for such an investment is self-evident. With huge local and state budget deficits, the necessity to reprioritize federal funding for education is obvious. Although reversing historical inequities requires reciprocal responsibility and participation of educators, students, parents, school leaders, and policy makers, political officials should be held accountable to ensure necessary resources. Obviously, this is a question of political priorities, and will require a social movement to enforce the reallocation of resources from militarism and support of corporate profit to these human needs.

Third, transforming urban schools entails a protracted cultural campaign directed against deficit notions about the potential of low-income children and children of color (Lipman, 1998). Changing entrenched discourses of "ability" and of children and communities as "problems" is obviously complex, long-term, and multifaceted. Clearly it requires the active involvement of parents and children as well as committed educators of children of color and others. The work of urban educators has provided a wealth of knowledge about rich, culturally relevant, critical pedagogies. The beginning process of collective reflection about some of these issues at Brewer hints at possibilities for examining assumptions and ideologies at the school level, as do more developed and systematic programs of preparing teachers to teach in diverse classrooms (e.g., Cochran-Smith, 1995; Ladson-Billings, 2001). There is also a substantial body of research that outlines pedagogical theories that build on the experience, language, and cultural identity of students as a basis for learning and that support the development of critical consciousness and the agency of students of color in particular (e.g., Cummins, 1996; Darder, 1995; Delpit, 1988; Ladson-Billings, 1994).

Finally, the state of urban education is deeply embedded in the state of cities and national and global economic and social priorities. Although much needs to be done in schools, putting the onus on them overlooks the impact of the social-economic context. Although much can be done by committed, culturally relevant, critical educators, the state of education at schools like Grover and Westview cannot be separated from the reality of life in deeply impoverished neighborhoods. Nor can it be addressed without addressing the documented history of inequality and racism that has permeated public schooling in the United States, and urban education in particular. Thus, any serious effort to transform public schools ultimately can only succeed as part of a larger local and global social struggle for material redistribution and cultural recognition (Fraser, 1997).

Policy Borrowing from Below—Three Strategic Models of Counter Hegemonic Education

One effect of globalization has been rapid international policy borrowing among states (Blackmore, 2000). As I noted earlier, this policy borrowing *from above* is reflected in the convergence of neoliberal education policies in Western Europe, the United States, New Zealand, and elsewhere, and in the role of the World Bank in setting educational standards to promote market-driven economies in "developing countries" (Jones, 2000). But as globalization strives to bend all nations, all peoples, all economic sectors and organizations of civil society to the discipline of international capital, the ensuing economic and cultural dislocations and generalized immiseration have given rise to new solidarities and links between disparate social movements across the globe. This is globalization from below. The dialogue among social movements, embodied in the World Social Forum, provides a model of policy borrowing *from below* (Coates, 2002). Examples of counterhegemonic practices drawn from disparate social contexts can deepen our understanding of how to proceed in a period in which discourses of inevitability preach every day that there is no alternative to the existing social order. Here I want to discuss three quite different, but theoretically linked examples and what we might learn from them.

The first are the Citizen Schools being created by the Workers Party Municipal Government in Porto Alegre, Brazil. In a powerful chapter, Luís Armando Gandin and Michael Apple (2003) describe ways in which these schools concretely challenge neoliberal conceptions of education and their role in the struggle for radical democracy in Brazil. My summary is drawn from their discussion, Gandin's research (2002), and my own investigation in Porto Alegre. The Citizen Schools Project was initiated by the Workers Party not only to create better schools for those students who have been excluded from education in Brazil, particularly the children of the *favelas* (the most impoverished neighborhoods), but also to initiate a pedagogical project in radical democracy. Gandin and Apple outline three aspects of this unfolding project. One, the schools respond to the historical exclusion, failure, and dropping out of poor students by reorganizing the structure of schooling to eliminate the mechanisms that have contributed to the problem in the past. New "cycles of formation" challenge notions of "failure" by assigning students to classes with children of their own age while providing a challenging environment in which they can fill in gaps in their development. Two, the schools reconstitute official knowledge by centering the curriculum on interdisciplinary "thematic complexes" grounded in the central issues facing the favela community. The new epistemological perspective is meant to ensure that students learn Brazilian "high culture," *but through new perspectives* grounded in their sociopolitical reality. A stated goal of the new curriculum is to move the culture and history of Afro-Brazilians to the center to openly challenge racism, a central issue in Brazilian society and a principal form of oppression.[3] Three, Citizen Schools are run by councils of teachers, school staff, parents, students, and one member of the school administration. The responsibility of the council to define the aims and direction of the school, allocate economic resources, and ensure implementation makes them schools of democratic participation and collective governance in their own right. The community power and democracy of these councils are redefining neoliberal notions of accountability, reframing it as collective responsibility to ensure that the school serves the community. These three aspects of the project are captured in the idea of democratization of access, knowledge, and management (Gandin, 2002).

While the schools are attempting to productively address the very serious issues of educational exclusion, most important, their goal is to generate a new way of thinking about society as a whole and who should run it. Gandin and Apple report that the schools—their structure, curriculum, and governance—are part of the creation of a movement that "contains as a real social process, the origins of a new way of life" (p. 196). The Citizen Schools provide a powerful example that education projects can be part of a conscious strategy to challenge dominant discourses about schooling and citizenship. Gandin and Apple (2003) emphasize this point:

> . . . there is a constant struggle to legitimize the experience of the Citizen School, to make it socially visible, to pose the discussion over education in terms other than those of neoliberalism, to pull education from the technical economistic realm favored by neoliberal assumptions and to push it to a more politicized one that has as its basic concern the role of education in social emancipation. (p. 200)

The democratic participatory experiences of creating and running the schools redefine the relationship of communities to schools and of communities to the state. "They develop the collective capacities among people to enable them to continue to engage in the democratic administration and control of their lives" (p. 195). By reconstructing school knowledge to draw on the experiences of the community and developing the democratic leadership of the councils, Citizen Schools are also attempting to transform the "separation between the ones who 'know' and . . . ones who 'don't know' " (p. 211).

The Citizen School Project clarifies strategic relationships between educational change and the protracted process of concretely transforming society. This is an important theoretical foundation for conceptualizing education reform and its relationship to a larger liberatory social project. The schools embody reforms that build up democratic participation, reconceptualize school knowledge around the perspectives and experiences of the oppressed, and create conditions for poor and marginalized people to see themselves as people with the capacity to run society and experiences in doing so. Although the actual practice is fraught with challenges, this framework is a powerful lens through which to assess the liberatory potential of specific educational policy agendas. It provides an orientation for both the process and the content of policies that move in a liberatory direction. The Citizen Schools also challenge neoliberal educational frameworks by rearticulating elements of the dominant agenda to a liberatory educational framework. This insight helps us think about the ways in which neoliberalism articulates equity to accountability, for example, and how we might rearticulate it to a democratic agenda. In short, the Citizen Schools give us new tools to think and act in the field of education in more strategic ways in the context of neoliberalism.

The second example is the Rethinking Schools project anchored in the Milwaukee-based teacher journal *Rethinking Schools*. Since 1986 the editors of *Rethinking Schools*, most of them teachers, have provided a space for educators to read about social justice curriculum in action as well as educational issues from a critical, antiracist perspective. Articles about teaching, from kindergarten through high school, demonstrate that teachers can develop pedagogies that help children grapple with issues of racism, sexism, homophobia, social inequality, destruction of the environment, globalization, war, militarism, repressive discipline, community disinvestment, and more. The power of this journal is that it presents the writing of real teachers going against the grain in real schools, working under real ideological and material constraints. The classrooms they describe provide concrete examples of what critical, antiracist, participatory education looks like. They make possibility tangible, concretely challenging discourses of inevitability and disempowerment. Taken as a whole and over time, the journal constructs a counterhegemonic educational discourse grounded in critical social praxis. *Rethinking Schools* books on topics of curriculum and classroom practice (*Rethinking Our Classrooms*, 1994, 2001), *Rethinking Columbus* (Bigelow & Peterson, 1998), *The Real Ebonics Debate* (Perry & Delpit, 1998), *Reading, Writing, and Rising Up* (Christensen, 2000), and *Rethinking Globalization* (Bigelow & Peterson, 2002, among others), provide a powerful knowledge base for teaching that is grounded in critical social theory, thus directly challenging neoliberal assumptions of teachers as technicians.

These publications and the Rethinking Schools critical listserv are nodes of a national network of critical educational praxis. They establish a community across distance, a center at a time when discourse of inevitability drives out all notions that there are others who also dare to think and act differently. A central insight from the Rethinking Schools project is the strategic importance of social justice teachers' creating public spaces for dialogue and presentation of theoretically grounded alternative practices. These concrete models of practice are an important aspect of building up schools and classrooms that instantiate a counternarrative about schooling, ideologically and practically.

The third example is the practice of culturally relevant, liberatory teachers of African American students. Since the late 1980s, an important body of literature by African American scholars (e.g., Delpit, 1988, 1992b; Foster, 1997; Irvine, 1991; King, 1991; Ladson-Billings, 1994, 2001) has made visible the practices of teachers who draw on the culture of African American students to promote their academic competence and sociopolitical awareness. From studies of the practices of these teachers and the history of Black education in the United States, these scholars have constructed an ensemble of theories of culturally relevant, culturally responsive, emancipatory education for African American students. Drawing on students' African American cultural frame of reference, teachers who are the subjects and collaborators in these studies link literacy with students' social identities. Academic success is connected with developing tools to resist racism and oppression and with social analysis of community issues such as homelessness and global issues such as the Gulf War. Students are encouraged to see themselves as African American intellectual leaders. These theories have made their way into some teacher education programs, into scholarly journals, and onto the programs of national education conferences and have become a fashionable part of conversations among educational researchers. Yet, teaching remains largely color-blind (i.e., white-centered) and disconnected from the sociopolitical realities and psychic experiences of children of color, and the practice of liberatory education for African American students is disconnected from the discourse about education as a whole, including some critical discourse. Yet, these practices and the historically grounded philosophy underpinning them constitute a powerful counterhegemonic discourse.

In an extended essay on African American education, Teresa Perry (2003) explains the philosophy of African American education as "freedom for literacy and literacy for freedom" (see also Murrell, 1997). Perry argues that this philosophy is grounded in African Americans' existential necessity to assert their humanness, their very existence as intellectual beings, in a white supremacist context that historically negated Black intellectual capacity as a central tenet. Literacy from this perspective is a means of personal and collective emancipation and is essential to develop leadership for liberation:

> Read and write yourself into freedom! Read and write to assert your identity as human! Read and write yourself into history! Read and write as an act of resistance, as a political act, for racial uplift, so you can lead your people well in the struggle for liberation!
>
> (p. 19)

Thus education is inherently an act of resistance, a political act, and a collective responsibility (see also Anderson, 1988).

I see this philosophy at work in the practices of eight culturally relevant teachers in Ladson-Billings's study (1994) who ground teaching in students' cultural identity, are connected with the students' community, and aim to foster their students' intellectual leadership and critical consciousness about their role in fighting injustice. Despite the restrictive public school settings in which they work, they deliberately go against the grain because they understand education as political. This philosophy is also at work in the narratives of Black teachers (Foster, 1997) who describe challenging racism as central to their work. An Oakland teacher, Carrie Secret (Miner, 1997), exemplifies pedagogy rooted in the centrality of culture and the intersection of culture and power. Secret's culturally responsive classroom foregrounds African American intellectual and creative production and the power of Ebonics as a literary language while developing students' linguistic and cultural competence in the dominant code.

As did Black schools during segregation as described by Perry (2003) and Delpit (1992a), these pedagogies create spaces of resistance, organized to counter the myth of Black inferiority. Perry describes segregated Black schools as " 'figured universes'—or more precisely counterhegemonic figured communities" (p. 91) where African Americans forged a collective identity as literate and achieving people. I would argue that the present-day examples of culturally relevant, liberatory pedagogy fit this description and stand as examples of a fundamentally subversive notion of education for African American students—one we can draw upon in general. Not just academic, education in these classrooms is described as social, cultural, and political—directly counter to the narrow test-driven, technical notions of neoliberal accountability oriented schooling. As a whole, this pedagogical discourse challenges the education-for-work agenda that dominates discussions of education and education reform, particularly for "low-achieving" students of color. This is a praxis that rearticulates equity (framed as test scores in the dominant accountability discourse) to its roots in liberation. Although localized and operating sometimes behind closed doors and in narrow spaces, it is like the Brazilian Citizen Schools that work to transform consciousness about one's subject position in society. In this sense, the practices of culturally relevant emancipatory teachers and the philosophy they embody are challenging the dominant discourse about education and are resources with which concretely to demonstrate a liberatory vision of education. Along with the other two, this is an example of an educational project that can concretize an alternative way of thinking about and doing education that embodies liberatory social processes and specifically challenges the dominant discourse.

Education Policy in a Post-9/11, Preemptive-War Era

When we sort through all the nuances, differences, and complexities, the essence of educational accountability, centralized regulation, policing of youth of color, and standards is the imposition of the authority of the state on the work and consciousness of adults and children in schools. I have argued throughout that the new authoritarianism is both material and ideological, disciplining bodies and minds. In some respects it is hardly new at all. The neoliberal project of recent decades has been the steady erosion of the social welfare functions of the state and expansion of its policing functions. The responsibility of the state to educate children and provide educators and communities with the necessary resources to do so has fully morphed into the role of overseer, judge, and dispenser of rewards and punishments—as well as subcontractor to corporations and supplier for the armed services. But education policies that legislate the policing of schools and schooling take on new and ominous implications in a post-September 11 present of militarism and repression at home and war abroad. School policies that teach people to be docile subjects and that undermine critical thought, imposing a reign of surveillance, coercion, and intimidation, are magnified when we look at them through the lens of the U.S. Patriot Act, Total Information Awareness, legalized merger of the spying functions of the Central Intelligence Agency (CIA) with the domestic "investigation" functions of the Federal Bureau of Investigation (FBI), proposals to recruit ordinary people to spy on their neighbors, unlimited secret detention without civil liberties of several thousand people, racial profiling as national policy, and an orgy of jingoistic patriotism in what passes for the nightly newscast. This new political landscape justifies the criminalization and surveillance that have been a fact of life for some communities of color in the United States and extends it to everyone, targeting specific immigrant groups in particular.

The state's repressive response to September 11 and the Bush doctrine of preemptive war have ushered in, at mind boggling speed, the retrenchment of basic civil liberties. We are living in a dangerous historical moment when state repression is openly being bartered for supposed security from enemies within and without—in fact, the majority of the world's people. As I write this, the devastation wrought by the war against Iraq and threats of other U.S. military aggressions loom as a monstrous storm cloud on our global horizon, school districts all around announce they are forced to lay off teachers and eliminate programs, CPS has announced 15 percent budget cuts, and high school students have walked out of their classes in protest at these deeply interrelated disasters. A historical dialectic is beginning to unfold. A nascent social movement is building as the full ideological and material force of the state and the avaricious goals of transnational capital bear down on us.

Adjusting our lenses to align dual images of authoritarianism in the schools and in the streets puts in focus the political implications of education policies that impose a tight regulatory and surveillance regime. They have dangerous implications for the suppression of critical thought and agency just when we need them most. Despite the truism that there are multiple, potent pedagogical sites beyond schools, schools remain important ideological institutions and spaces for the construction of identities. What we need most right now are "problem posing pedagogies" (Freire, 1970/1994) that help students question and investigate questions such as, Why did September 11 happen? Why does so much of the world hate "us"? What is the history of the Middle East and U.S. involvement in it? How can the United States change its actions in the world to address the resentments so many peoples feel toward its policies? What is the relationship between U.S. militarism and racism in the U.S.?

Instead, accountability policies expand the state's function to police knowledge and educational practices and intensify the repression of critical thought and action. High stakes tests (with all their accoutrements) take on a whole new meaning as "rituals of power" in the present context when docile subjectivities serve not only new labor force demands and global city images but the politics of state repression. Education policies that sort students and schools into neat, simplified opposites of "failures" and "successes" also promote a kind of binary thinking that serves the new official discourse of "good" and "evil" countries, nationalities, and people. Policies that obscure the richly textured strengths and weaknesses of schools, teachers, students, and communities not only erase the possibility of addressing in complex ways the process of educational improvement and transformation. They impose definitions of winners and losers and teach us to identify quickly and absolutely those who are deviant and must be controlled.

The containment and policing of communities of color take on new dimensions in this political context. Black and Latino/a communities that have faced repression all along are now more vulnerable as national security legitimates police raids and singling out of individuals based solely on nationality. Just at the moment when racial profiling had begun to be subjected to national scrutiny and critique, the state's response to 9/11 made it official policy. At the same moment, in a sinister reversal, African Americans and Latinos/as are expected to join in the demonization of people of Arab descent and certain immigrant groups. And in a zero-tolerance world, zero-tolerance discipline policies in schools fit a new common sense of militarism and repression to crack down on dangerous "others." Intense surveillance in urban schools becomes one more part of a commonsense national agenda that allows the state to monitor every facet of private life in the name of national security. If the merger of the military and public schools might have been problematic for some before 9/11, it is now national policy writ large. A provision of No Child Left Behind gives military recruiters access to all high school juniors and seniors. We can be sure that those being recruited are not primarily at the select magnet schools. They are the graduates of general high schools in Chicago and elsewhere, mainly African American and Latino/a youth, eighteen-year-olds whose substandard education and subzero options make them prime candidates for what has been called an unofficial "poverty draft." Indeed the general high school may truly be a "military prep track" as U.S. plans for global military domination require expansion of the military ranks.

Education Change and Social Movements

What is to be done? One source of insight is the history of school reforms since the 1950s that pressed for equity and justice. Desegregation struggles, campaigns by African American communities and others for community control of schools, challenges to the Eurocentric and male-centric curriculum, and demands for bilingual education, equal education for children with disabilities, and equal funding for school programs for girls and women—all were born of, and sustained by, broad social justice movements. The educational demands they proposed were concrete expressions of these social movements and at the same time helped to build and extend them. At a moment when accountability has become a new regime of truth, the history of these movements provides an important counterdiscourse and an alternative perspective on the role of democratic participation and activism in shaping social policy. Although only partially successful in achieving their aims, these movements linked education reforms to wider social change and challenged existing power relations. This relationship was captured by African American parents in Chicago in their 1968 call for an education organizing conference titled "Judgment Day for Racism in West Side Schools" (Danns, 2002).

This is a language that names the political nature of education. Its challenges a system that treats people as a means to an end. There are kernels of organized resistance in Chicago Public Schools today. In fall 2002, twelve teachers at Curie High School refused to give the high stakes Chicago Academic Standards Exam; actions of "The Curie 12" and their support from others around the city led the district to drop the test. The Youth First *Youth Summit*, also in fall 2002, and subsequent public actions have injected the voice of several hundred high school youth into school policies affecting their lives. The high school student walk out against war on Iraq in March 2003 demonstrated heightened political consciousness. An alternative assessment proposal developed by a coalition of local school councils and school reform groups (LSC Summit, 2000) introduced an element of debate to the heretofore narrow discourse of high stakes tests in Chicago.

The three counter-hegemonic education projects that I describe above were born of social movements and the participation of educators in those movements. Educational projects grounded in critical social theories and democratic participation (especially by those who have been most marginalized) help make the emancipatory visions of social movements concrete. Culturally relevant, critical, democratic education can help develop "new people" and new social organization to challenge the existing social order. In the recent past, appeals (including my own, Lipman, 1998) to link education change with social and economic reconstruction have been largely rhetorical in the context of fragmented and largely quiescent social movements. But that may be changing. As globalization increasingly divides the world into a small number of super-rich countries and people on one side and literally billions of increasingly impoverished and dislocated people on the other, it is sowing the seeds of its own destruction. There are new solidarities manifested in a worldwide antiglobalization movement that is perhaps most sharply reflected in the diverse social movements that make up the Porto Alegre World Social Forum and its agenda of "globalization from the bottom": economic, social, and cultural justice and opposition to neoliberalism, war, and militarism (see Coates, 2002). The true face of the "neoliberal miracle" in economically developing countries is being exposed in the intensified exploitation of workers, displacement of peasants and small farmers, destruction of the environment, growing national debt, and regulation by transnational lending institutions. Voters in Latin America are rejecting these policies from Brazil to Bolivia to Venezuela, another sign of the times. This is coupled with a massive worldwide showing of opposition to the U.S.-U.K. war on Iraq. From a historical perspective, the world significance of these gathering social forces as a counter to the global hegemony of transnational capital and U.S. militarism should not be underestimated.

As the effects of globalization have also come home to roost in low-wage jobs, lack of health care and retirement security, a crisis in affordable housing, and homelessness they have begun to awaken the U.S. labor movement and infuse it with the energy of immigrant and women workers in new alliances with African American and white workers. The slogan *Si Se Puede* heard from Chicago's hotel workers signals the rumblings of a new labor militance fortified by new Asian, Latino/a, African, Arab, and Eastern European voices. As I write, the Bush doctrine of preemptive, unilateral military action has begun to give rise to an antiwar, antimilitarization movement with a scope not seen since the Vietnam era. Today's activists are beginning to make critical connections between militarism abroad and racism, economic crisis, labor exploitation, and lack of high-quality education, housing, and health care at home.

These connections bear seeds of a significant new, socially conscious movement in education. It is also quite transparent that those who will fight on the front lines in the U.S. military are overwhelmingly African American and Latino/a, products of the general high schools and the military prep tracks. There is a new hopefulness in a socially conscious, hip hop generation represented by Chicago's Youth First Campaign (September 2002) that says: "We are the generation who asks the question: *Why?* Why do things have to be the way they are? We *challenge the system* by organizing *direct action* to gain respect and have our *opinions heard*, so that we can *make change!*"

Notes

1. This agenda has a long history, going back to the free market proposals of Milton Friedman (1962), Chubb and Moe's (1990) argument for the introduction of market forces and school choice, *A Nation at Risk* (National Commission, 1983), and the business-centered reforms advocated under President Reagan.
2. New York's Board of Education mandated a standard curriculum for all its 1,291 schools but then exempted 208, five-sixths of which are in middle- or upper-income neighborhoods (Hoff, 2003).
3. Racism is deeply entrenched in Brazilian society and in schooling, but one hopeful development is the initiative of the municipal education department (SMED) racial justice working group to make racism visible through the Citizen Schools (personal communications, SMED official, July 2003).

References

Anderson, J.D. (1988). *The education of blacks in the South, 1860–1935.* Chapel Hill: University of North Carolina Press.

Apple, M.W. (1991) Conservative agendas and progressive possibilities: Understanding the wider politics of curriculum and teaching. *Education and Urban Society, 23*(3), 279–291.

Apple, M.W. (1996). *Cultural politics and education.* New York: Teachers College Press.

Apple, M.W. (2001). *Educating the "Right way."* New York: Routledge.

Apple, M.W. et al. (2003). *The state and the politics of knowledge.* New York: Routledge.

Ball, S.J. (1990). *Politics and policy making in education.* London: Routledge.

Ball, S.J. (1997a). Good school/bad school: Paradox and fabrication. *British Journal of Sociology of Education, 18*(3), 317–336.

Ball, S.J. (1997b). Policy sociology and critical social research: A personal review of recent education policy and policy research. *British Educational Research Journal, 23*, 257–274.

Bigelow, B., & Peterson, B. (Eds.). (1998). *Rethinking Columbus: The next 500 years.* Milwaukee: Rethinking Schools.

Bigelow, B., & Peterson, B. (Eds.). (2002). *Rethinking globalization: Teaching for justice in an unjust world.* Milwaukee: Rethinking Schools.

Blackmore, J. (2000). Warning signals or dangerous opportunities? Globalization, gender, and educational policy shifts. *Education Theory, 50*(4), 467–486.

Bohn, A.P., & Sleeter, C.E. (2000). Multicultural education and the standards movement. *Phi Delta Kappan, 82*(2), 156–159.

Carlson, D. (1997). *Making progress: Education and culture in new times*. New York: Teachers College Press.

Christensen, L. (2000). *Reading, writing, and rising up: Teaching about social justice and the power of the written word*, Milwaukee: Rethinking Schools.

Chubb, J.M. & Moe, T.E. (1990). *Politics, markets, and America's schools*. Washington, D.C.: Brookings Institution.

Coates, K. (Ed.). (2002). A better world is possible. *The Spokesman, 74.*

Cochran-Smith, M. (1995). Uncertain allies: Understanding the boundaries of race and teaching. *Harvard Educational Review, 65*(4), 541–570.

Cummins, J. (1996). *Negotiating identities: Education for empowerment in a diverse society*. Ontario, CA: California Association for Bilingual Education.

Darder, A. (1995). Buscando America: The contribution of critical Latino educators to the academic development and empowerment of Latino students in the U.S. In C.E. Sleeter & P.L. McLaren (Eds.), *Multicultural education, critical pedagogy, and the politics of difference* (pp. 319–348). Albany, NY: SUNY Press.

Delpit, L. (1988). The silenced dialogue: Power and pedagogy in educating other people's children. *Harvard Educational Review, 58*, 280–298.

Delpit, L.D. (1992a). Acquisition of literate discourse: Bowing before the master? *Theory into Practice, 31*, 296–302.

Delpit, L.D. (1992b). Education in a multicultural society: Our future's greatest challenge. *Journal of Negro Education, 61*, 237–249.

Ferguson, A.A. (2000). *Bad boys: Public schools in the making of Black masculinity*. Ann Arbor: University of Michigan Press.

Foster, M. (1997). *Black teachers on teaching*. New York: New Press.

Fraser, N. (1997). *Justice interruptus: Critical reflections on the "postsocialist" condition*. New York: Routledge.

Freire, P. (1970/94). *Pedagogy of the oppressed* (Trans. M.B. Ramos). New York: Continuum.

Freire, R. & Macedo, D. (1987). *Literacy: Reading the word and the world*. Westport, CT: Bergin & Garvey.

Friedman, M. (1962). *Capitalism and Freedom*. Chicago: University of Chicago Press.

Gandin, L.A. (2002). *Democratizing access, governance, and knowledge: The struggle for educational alternatives in Porto Alegre, Brazil*. Unpublished doctoral dissertation, University of Wisconsin, Madison.

Gandin, L.A., & Apple, M.W. (2003). Educating the state, democratizing knowledge: The Citizen School Project in Porto Alegre, Brazil. In M.W. Apple, *The state and the politics of knowledge* (pp. 193–219). New York: Routledge.

Gee, J.P., Hull, G., & Lankshear, C. (1996). *The new work order: Behind the language of the new capitalism*. Boulder, CO: Westview Press.

Hoff, D.J. (2003, March 9). Complaints pour in over NYC curriculum exemptions. *Education Week*. Retrieved March 14, 2003, from http://www.edweek.org

Irvine, J.J. (1991). *Black students and school failure: Policies, practices, and prescriptions*. New York: Praeger.

Jones, P.W. (2000). Globalization and internationalism: Democratic prospects for world education. In N.P. Stromquist & K. Monkman (Eds.), *Globalization and education*. Lanham, MD: Rowman & Littlefield.

King, J.E. (1991). Unfinished business: Black student alienation and Black teachers' emancipatory pedagogy. In M. Foster (Ed.), *Readings in equal education: Qualitative investigations into schools and schooling* (Vol. 11, pp. 245–271). New York: AMS Press.

Ladson-Billings, G. (1994). *Dreamkeepers: Successful teachers of African American students*. San Francisco: Jossey Bass.

Ladson-Billings, G. (2001). *Crossing over to Canaan: The journey of new teachers in diverse classrooms*. San Francisco: Jossey Bass.

Lipman, P. (1998). *Race, class, and power in school restructuring*. Albany: State University of New York Press.

Lipman, P. (2002). Making the global city, making inequality. Political economy and cultural politics of Chicago school policy. *American Educational Research Journal, 39*(2), 379–419.

LSC Summit. (2000). *The new ERA plan*. Chicago: Author. Contact: Parents United for Responsible Education. Retrieved October 21, 2000 from http://www.pureparents.org

McNeil, L.M. (2000). *Contradictions of school reform: Educational costs of standardized testing*. New York: Routledge.

Miner, B. (1997, Fall). Embracing Ebonics and teaching standard English: An interview with Oakland teacher Carrie Secret. *Rethinking Schools, 12*(1), 18–19, 34.

Murrell, P.C., Jr. (1997). Digging again the family wells: A Freirian literacy framework for emancipatory pedagogy for African American children. In P. Freire (Ed.), *Mentoring the mentor: A critical dialogue with Paulo Freire* (pp. 19–58). New York: Peter Lang.

National Commission on Excellence in Education (1983). *A nation at risk: The imperative for educational reform*. Washington, DC: Government Printing Office.

Ozga, J. (2000). *Policy research in educational settings*. Buckingham, England: Open University Press.

Perry, T. (2003). Up from the parched earth: Toward a theory of African American achievement. In T. Perry, C. Steele, & A. Hilliard III (Eds.), *Young, gifted and Black: Promoting high achievement among African-American students* (pp. 1–108). Boston: Beacon Press..

Perry, T., & Delpit, L. (Eds.), (1998). *The real Ebonics debate: Power, language and the education of African-American children*. Boston: Beacon Press.

Rethinking Columbus (2001). Milwaukee: Rethinking Schools.
Rethinking our classrooms (Vol. 1) (1994). Milwaukee: Rethinking Schools.
Rethinking our classrooms (Vol. 2) (2001). Milwaukee: Rethinking Schools.
Smith, N. (1996). *The new urban frontier: Gentrification and the revanchist city.* New York: Routledge.
Valenzuela, A. (1999). *Subtractive schooling: U.S. Mexican youth and the politics of caring.* Albany: State University of New York Press.

32

Creating a Pedagogy in Common: Excerpt From "Toward a New Common School Movement"

Noah De Lissovoy, Alex Means, and Kenneth Saltman

From the natural world to the social world, the commons appear everywhere in peril. The all-encompassing drive for profit and endless commodification is despoiling the shared basis of life on the planet, and as a set of global crises widen and deepen, demands for authentic democracy and community become the minimal demands for the survival of humanity. Any adequate effort to overcome these challenges will have to start from the premise of our belongingness, globally, to each other. This fundamental social condition of interrelation and entanglement sets the parameters for any meaningful global community. What we refer to as a new common school movement is the form of education that sets its sights on the development and democratization of this condition.

Like the commons, the very idea of democratic education is everywhere under assault. Within public schooling, this takes the form of for-profit educational management, charters, vouchers, standardization of curriculum, high-stakes testing and the integration of corporate managerialism into the fabric of teacher education, educational leadership, and schools themselves. We suggest that engagement with the notion of the global commons opens a different space for reimagining public schooling outside of the false choice between either market imperatives or state domination, and instead locates questions of educational value and organization within the principles of human equality and global commonality. We don't merely need to defend public schooling; we need to remake it for a genuinely democratic society beyond failure of neoliberal capitalism. We believe that engagement with the theory and practice of the global commons provides a set of creative and ethical referents suitable to this task.

The Struggle Over the Global Commons

When land, labor, and other social and natural resources necessary to sustain life are held and valued as collective property they can be said to form a commons. As Nobel economist Elinor Ostrum has detailed, communities have historically developed ingenious strategies for governing access and usage of common property resources in order to maintain their collective value and benefit over time.[1]

Commons cannot be separated from the notion of enclosure, which signals efforts to transfer aspects of the commons from collective management for common benefit to private ownership for private gain. At the end of the first volume of *Capital,* Marx extended the perspectives of Adam Smith who, in his *Wealth of Nations,* described the enclosure of the commons in feudal Europe as a form of *original* or *primitive accumulation.* Whereas Smith argued that this was largely a peaceful historical passage, Marx detailed how the enclosures constituted a form of theft and violence that made the original development of capitalism possible.

Building on Marx's observations, historians like Peter Linebaugh have detailed how the forces of primitive accumulation and the enclosures of the commons in feudal Europe gave birth to modem economic, legal, administrative, and military systems of sovereignty that have operated to legitimate European colonial and imperial domination over the world's land and people.[2] Silvia Federici has also highlighted how women have always been central to this story. From the European witch-hunts to the current neoconservative "war on women," women's bodies and their labor have been longstanding historical targets of enclosure and control.[3]

As a system defined by endless growth, capitalism is prone to crisis and stagnation. Therefore it must continually incorporate new territories, markets, and laborers into its orbit in order to expand and thrive. In relation to the commons, this underscores the idea that capitalism must periodically convert shared social resources that have previously existed outside its domain into sources of private property and profit. This process of enclosure has reemerged on a planetary scale since the onset of neoliberal globalization in the 1980s and 1990s.

The philosopher Slavoj Zizek argues that there are four central antagonisms in the contemporary enclosure of the commons - 'the commons of nature as the substance of our life, the problem of our biogenetic commons, the problem of our cultural commons ('intellectual property'), and, last but not least, the problem of the commons as the universal space of humanity from which no one should be excluded'.[4] Increasingly, as global capitalism faces new constraints to profitable expansion, produces surplus populations globally, and pursues the endless commodification and exploitation of the planetary bios, all of humanity potentially becomes excluded 'bare life'.

Crucially, efforts to enclose the commons have always been defined by extensive contestation. So it is with the new global enclosures. Whether it is the privatization of public water in Bolivia, the displacement of tens of millions of indigenous people from the land in rural India to make way for transnational mining companies and agribusinesses like Monsanto, or efforts to defund and further privatize secondary and higher education in Santiago, Chicago, or Montreal - the new enclosures have been met by extensive opposition from commoners seeking to retain democratic control over common resources for collective benefit.

The Enclosure of Public Schooling in the United States

Schooling is a key site in present struggles over the commons as it represents a shared resource of democratic potentiality. At all levels of the educational endeavor, neoliberal policy architectures have sought to convert public schooling into a marketplace, to subordinate educational value to economic value, and to open all facets of education to profit making and corporate control. This has only intensified in the post-2008 period of economic decline and generalized social insecurity and austerity.

In the United States, educational enclosure has been lubricated by the strategic devaluation of the public educational system. Since 2008 and the onset of economic crisis, states have laid off hundreds of thousands of teachers and staff, cut back curriculum and extracurricular programs, expanded class sizes, shortened school days and weeks, and even closed many schools altogether. For example, Illinois has cut $152 million, New York $1.3 billion, Pennsylvania $422 million, Washington $1 billion, and Arizona $560 million in yearly funding to k-12 schools, early childhood education, and child development services.[5] This has paved the way for closing public schools in economically devastated communities and creating networks of charter, contract, and for-profit schools. The strategic devaluation of the public sector presents business with opportunities to institute draconian reforms that enable the transfer of public resources like schools from the public trust to private interests. In the wake of Hurricane Katrina, for instance, market reformers presented the storm as a "golden opportunity" to "clean the slate" and to privatize the historically neglected New Orleans public schools.[6] Similarly in Michigan, a state devastated by deindustrialization and the financialization of the economy, 80% of its rapidly expanding base of charter schools is now run for-profit.

The vanguard of the educational enclosure movement includes venture philanthropists, Wall Street financiers, hedge fund managers, opportunistic politicians from both major political parties, and corporate CEOs. This alliance has used the altruistic language of educational reform and equity to garner support for privatization. In 2007 there was $78 billion in venture capital invested in US educational startups. In 2011, it had reached a staggering $452 billion.[7] Wall Street has projected that in just the K-12 online learning market alone, profits are expected to soar 43% by 2015 as states are being coerced into lifting the cap on cyber-charter schools allowing public money that would be going to public schools to instead go to deregulated online learning mills.[8] Major Wall Street firms like Goldman Sachs and Merrill Lynch have dived into for-profit education alongside major hedge funds and wealth management groups all clamoring for a piece of the $600 billion estimated to be at stake each year in the educational marketplace.

These financial and corporate interests are seeking to capitalize not only through private management of schools, but also directly on processes of teaching and learning. This is the underlying reality driving the proliferation of corporate contracts for educational technology services, standardized curriculum programs, scripted lessons, value-added assessments for teachers, big data surveillance systems in education, and incessant high-stakes testing embodied in the new "common core" curriculum. Efforts to "teacher proof" education vastly extend the scope of profiteering and repressive bureaucratic authority in schools. This disables the capacity of educators to connect broader issues of public concern such as child poverty and homelessness, neighborhood instability and unemployment, institutional racism and mass incarceration, and the destruction of the environment to learning and thus to possibilities for social change. Instead learning is reduced to a set of anti-intellectual procedural skills that enclose the imaginative and democratic potential of educational experience.

Toward a Common Vision for Schooling

What is important to understand here is that neoliberal schooling represents not merely better or worse school reform - adjusting pedagogical methods, tweaking the curriculum, on so on. We argue that it is crucially about redistributing control over social life and as such is part of a much broader trend - the enclosure of the global commons. It is this struggle, we believe, that is underway in schools in the present. The question is whether we will continue to suffer the distorted and truncated forms of community that mainstream educational policy and practice impose on us, or whether we will fight against the limits of the neoliberal imagination to realize authentically democratic forms of teaching and learning.

The task ahead is to imagine pedagogical practices, curriculum, and school organization that enact the global commons. What path should teachers and students take together with communities in recovering control over the work of teaching and learning? How can the struggle against neoliberal school reform not simply demand limits on testing and a cessation to privatization in all its guises but also demand that public education be the basis for reimagining a truly democratic society? To begin, it is important to note that a new common school movement has an inevitably hopeful dimension to it. The common can be built and expanded, and it can never be fully enclosed because there are parts of human experience that cannot be turned into property and have to be held in common. Compassion, ideas, social relationships, and the planet itself must be held in common. In what follows we provide a series of broad proposals for orienting a new common school movement. To speak of the commons is to speak of a struggle over universal claims on the future. If we consider neoliberal schooling in terms of the commons, we can ask the question of how to formulate a response that recognizes the need for alternative school reform and also how such reform might provide a basis for a new commonwealth open to all.

Four Proposals for a New Common School Movement

Commoning Public Control

A first proposal for a new common school movement is the project of commoning public authority and control. This involves becoming clear on how public control differs from private control. Privatization enables for-profit educational companies to skim public tax money that would otherwise be reinvested in educational services and transfer it to investor profits. These profits take concrete form in the limousines, private jets, and mansions that public tax money provides to rich investors. These profits also take symbolic form as they are used to hire public relations firms to influence parents, communities, and other investors to have faith in educational privatization and the corporation. This is a parasitical financial relationship that maximizes the potential profit for investors while cutting educational services (the expansion of primary and secondary online cyber-charter schools is the best example). This has tended to result in antiunionism, the reduction of education to the most measurable and replicable forms, assaults on teacher autonomy, and so on.

There is no evidence that the siphoning of public wealth to capitalists has improved public education. Moreover, such redistribution shifts collective control over the processes of teaching and learning to private educational management operators. It captures educational labor and channels it toward profit making for owners in the short term and future exploitable labor relations in the long term. Last, despite claims to efficiency and innovation, neoliberal school reforms have only added to dysfunctional bureaucracy through the top-down management of decision-making. Demands for an end to privatization and for a reinvigoration of public education should thus be combined with a path toward opening up greater flexibility, autonomy, and democracy in the public system in order to spur progressive innovation, enrichment, and democratic creativity.

Commoning Public Finance

A second proposal for a new common school movement would be to rethink school finance as a common as opposed to a private matter. In a financial sense, the history of the US public system has been privatized since its inception in that public funding has been tied to local property taxes and local real estate wealth. We might call this the original privatization of the public school system. The task of expanding a commons in public school finance involves countering both the original privatization of real estate and taxes and the more recent neoliberal privatizations. One initial solution to countering these trends is extremely simple. It would involve the United States following other industrialized nations and putting in place a federal system that ensures funding equity for all public schools and students. Importantly, schools and communities ravaged by poverty and historical neglect require more investment than others. This requires progressive distribution not equal distribution.

Commoning Educational Labor and Governance

A third proposal for a new common school movement would involve expanding common teacher and common administrator labor within a framework of common governance. As we have stated above, part of what is wrong with educational privatization is that it involves expropriating from the educational process part of the educational resources to generate profits for owners and investors. This setup not only replicates the private sector workforce but results in the devaluation of the teacher's labor and in deteriorating working conditions for teachers. It has also been part of an expansion of corporate culture into educational policy that seeks to downwardly distribute "accountability" while upwardly distributing rewards.

A crucial aim of working in common must be to establish participatory democratic governance over public educational institutions. This must involve ending the divide between teachers and administrators and schools and communities. Teachers must have professional autonomy at the same time that schools must be made transparent and open to the community. To put it differently, educational leadership ought to be primarily teacher leadership that is embedded within a framework of collective governance and community decision-making. The existing educational leadership establishment and district management justifies itself through the discourses of measurable accountability and disciplinary threat. To rethink accountability means the measure of educational progress should no longer be testing and standardized matrices, which are really just a performance of efficacy. Instead, accountability in common is realized through the extent to which schooling furthers and reflects public values and interests - that is, collective benefit, shared democratic forms of control, and improvements in communities. A new common school movement would facilitate public schooling by actually strengthening the public through the professional autonomy of teachers in a system of common values and shared responsibility.

Commoning Collective Livelihoods

A fourth proposal for a new common school movement is that it must be connected to reclaiming a public commons that can ensure social as well as economic justice. At the core of this proposal is the need to create a new social compact that would include the right to dignified work and a guaranteed basic income; the right to a decent and affordable home; the right to medical and health care; the right to protection against economic dislocation, old age, and sickness; and the right to a free, equitable, and enriching public education. Reviving, renewing, reimagining, and agitating for such a commitment to public rights and protections would provide a foundation for ameliorating some of the most immediate and pressing issues facing working people and marginalized populations across the United States. In the long term, they could provide an educational and organizational basis for radical democratic alternatives to present economic and political arrangements.

Current global enclosures of culture, land, and labor are enacting a future of deepening inequality, human insecurity, and environmental catastrophe. Our current historical moment thus demands a broader conversation that can connect education and the imagination to radical democratic alternatives to capitalism. The commons of the school includes not just the commons of the building but also more importantly the common labor of teaching and learning. The most important task ahead is to rethink the relationship between the common labor of teaching and learning and the common labor people do throughout all institutions of the society. This is an educational as well as a cultural challenge. To reproduce the capitalist labor force students have to learn to accept their places in the hierarchy. This is a matter of teaching values wrapped in capitalist ideology that appear as natural and uncontestable. Critical education teaches alternative values, social relations, and identifications that are contrary to those of schooling for capitalist reproduction - critical rather than dogmatic, egalitarian rather than hierarchical, collective rather than individualizing, emancipatory rather than exploitative.

A new common school movement must establish fundamentally new ways of learning and thinking in relation to our global commonality and our shared fate. This necessarily means rethinking curriculum, teaching and learning in ways that recover the radical impulse of the progressive and critical tradition and that push beyond this tradition as well. We imagine this global horizon as pedagogy in common. In what follows, we elaborate on how a new common school movement must make pedagogy in common central to the reconstruction of schooling.

Toward a Pedagogy in Common

A new common school movement must be able to envision new forms of pedagogy and curriculum, both in school settings and in the context of struggles for democracy, at the same time that it critiques the landscape of politics and policy. Teaching is a fundamental moment in the becoming of selves, understandings, and relationships. A liberatory education, what we call here a pedagogy in common, foregrounds the commons as a site of both contestation and social production. We believe education can become a powerful force for the production of alternative forms of community and enactment of the global commons. In this way, rather than radical hope confronting a deadening reality, an emergent emancipatory reality (the collective production of the common) confronts power's own desperate hope: to cling to the impossible limits of the given.

We propose here three figures or modes of pedagogy and praxis in common:

1. *Rupture.* Contemporary scripted curriculum, test preparation, and classroom management regimes demand that teachers do more than endorse a set of values; they

must also act as the effective instrument of schooling as procedure. In this way, neoliberal education aims to reconstruct not only beliefs but even subjectivity itself - for both teachers and students. The push-out phenomenon, in which "low-performing" students are encouraged to quit for the sake of raising test scores, the school-to-prison pipeline, and the racist coding of students of color as irremediable convert education into a process of violation. In this context, the first task of the teacher is to refuse to act as the agent of injury. Rupture, in this case, means a difficult turn away from given habits and procedures. For instance, the accountability regime: Should teachers work around the edges, and make the best of the space that is left to them outside of testing and test preparation, or should they undertake a more radical break? In our view, ultimately teachers will need to refuse to participate in the scripting of pedagogy as simple preparation for assessment.

2. *Project.* The emphasis on projects in teaching is a familiar progressive educational idea. However, progressive project-oriented approaches generally fail to explore the underlying political assumptions that set the terms for teaching. By contrast, a radical thinking of pedagogy as project involves the production of new teaching and learning subjects - and new subjects of democracy. We should reframe our sense of the projective in pedagogy - highlighting this category as a radical opening up of the possibilities of politics and subjectivity, within a shared responsibility to the commons. In a pedagogy in common teaching and learning construct new political and agentic communities. The recent struggle over the ethnic studies program in the Tucson, Arizona, schools illustrates the reaction provoked by community-based and projective pedagogy. In an active rather than a reactive stance, the Raza Studies program in Tucson aimed to create an affirming, critical, and rigorous educational space for Latina/o students. Nevertheless, its delinking from dominant frameworks was portrayed by white officials as an attack.
3. *Conversation.* The notion of conversation, understood in a militantly democratic frame, can be useful in constructing a pedagogy in common. Conversation can suggest a superficial exchange of opinions. But it can also be understood in a different way: as a collaborative investigation of reality, and as a mobilization of collective imagination against power. In this sense, conversation can be thought of as a polycentric dialogue that seeks to awaken the outrage and creativity of a community. Challenging the theory/practice binary, this model proposes a model in which these poles partly overlap. Thus, conversations on the terrain of cultural politics can affect the parameters of struggles on the ground, and on the other hand material struggles can crucially impact the framing of political narratives. For instance, the 2012 strike by Chicago teachers succeeded in stalling the corporatist attack on working conditions for educators in the city. At the same time, it was a crucial intervention on the terrain of political discourse and discussions of the labor movement, as the union demonstrated its strength, its concern for students, and its commitment to public schools.

Globalization, the Common, and Curriculum

Understanding the itinerary of the common that we have described - from the historical moment of enclosure to the contemporary horizon of the global - has important implications for the curriculum as well, especially where this means not simply the manifest content of education, but also the ideological and epistemological foundations of this content. In the first place, being sensitive to the emergence of the condition of transnationalism implies an unraveling of national identifications that anchor student and teacher subjectivities, and which are painstakingly constructed through the experience of schooling - in the U.S. case, in the rituals of the pledge of allegiance, the celebrations of the so-called "founding fathers", and in the often perfunctory gestures of multicultural inclusion. This means a political project of alliance, and an intellectual project of discovering the purposes that determine shared, and different, situations. Progressive approaches neglect the conceptual and political unraveling of the authority and autonomy of the so-called "center" that is implied by a global perspective. The allegiance to U.S. exceptionalism that is mandatory in public discourse, and in education as well, is an expression of the defensiveness that characterizes a declining global hegemon. Within a pedagogy in common, it is a discourse we should crucially contest.

In addition, in contrast to the retrospective orientation of John Dewey's *reconstructionism,* which sought to reorder and improve existing knowledge and social relationships, our curricular approach involves a forward-looking *constructionism* that is motivated by the emergency of responding to the crises of neoliberal globalization. The focus of curriculum within such an approach is less to initiate students into the understandings and practices of society, and more to provoke them to the discovery of the knowledge and society of the future. This approach does not just respect but even depends upon the autonomy and intelligence of students.

There are several important practical implications here. First, teachers can create space in their classrooms for the investigation of emerging forms of alternative and youth cultures and movements, as they are lived in and out of school. For instance, not just hip-hop - the favorite case - but also the global diaspora of *rock en español* recodes and transnationalizes working class culture. Likewise, as youth begin to participate in efforts to reclaim public space for a new urban cultural and ecological commons - as they have begun to do in many inner city community gardens - they can be helped to investigate the connections between these efforts and international ones to defend collective space and resources from appropriation and privatization. In addition, the history of the "market," so touted in the popular media, can be retold from the standpoint of the victims of enclosure. And in response to official and reductionistic forms of teaching and learning, the senses of the global common that we have described suggest site-specific investigations of local *educational* conditions in relationship to larger contexts. For instance, in order to explore the way that administrative rationality and privatization efforts come together in neoliberal social policy, teachers can foreground (as crucial examples) the pervasive accountability regimes that they themselves confront along with their students. Rather than simply trying to elude these constraints, teachers and students might systematically investigate their origins, meanings, and effects.

Politics should be a process of teaching and learning, rather than a static system of ideas. In other words, if we want to build a new and more democratic global society, the point is not to produce a blueprint that we then simply execute, but rather to begin a collective and organic process in which the social body teaches itself a new way of being. Progressive pedagogies emphasize the *experimental* character of education, on the basis of which the teacher creates the parameters within which the intelligence of students can investigate the world. But our sense of experimentation today should be broader, extending to the collective investigation and practice, by teachers and students together, of *new* democratic values, norms, and practices - ones which do not reside at the core of existing society, but rather press against it from the outside, as premonitions of a different order of collective life.

Steps Forward: Organization and Action

In contrast to those who advocate a guerilla tactics of subversion, we believe that an organized movement is necessary - which seeks not just to evade the status quo but to challenge it directly and to construct alternatives that can replace it. This implies that a new common school movement will need to think of ways to occupy and reorganize - on a collective and system-wide scale - the infrastructure of public schooling, and to do so on the basis of the distributed leadership of the community. Below we suggest some key organizational principles for such a movement.

1. Educational advocacy and activism currently aim to influence the crafting of legislation or the implementation of policy. By contrast, we argue that a new common school movement should struggle as much for new decision-making processes as for the specific content of policy or curriculum. Such a movement should depend on the power of people involved in schools - students, parents, teachers, community members - rather than on the good will of elites. The time has come to move from discontent to action, and this shift should be coordinated among communities. Such a shift is already beginning to take place. New groups have formed to resist excessive testing of students. Alliances of parents and teachers exist in many locations to challenge the corporate schooling agenda - as expressed in the closure of neighborhood schools, the proliferation of charters, and gentrification. In addition, many university-based projects and protests have developed, which challenge the commodification of knowledge and the mortgaging of students' futures. Connecting this work to K-12 campaigns can reveal more fully the corporatization of education within capitalism's "knowledge economy" while also building bridges between differently affected communities.
2. For a movement to transform education to move forward, there has to be a forum for dialogue. Collective discussion and debate that occurs across communities already begins the pedagogical process in itself and suggests models for formal approaches to pedagogy that might be instituted in schools. A useful precedent is the Zapatista encuentro: a popular, non-hierarchical gathering of diverse communities and organizations focused on advancing discussion around a particular issue. A series of large-scale, community-based meetings, taking place at first outside the schools, could bring together parents, students, teachers, scholars, and activists. The question of curriculum and instruction ought to be opened at a basic level in these encuentros: Recognizing the colonial determination of what counts as knowledge within the traditional disciplines, what do we think - *starting from scratch* - students ought to learn, and what do we think learning is? Diverse communities have crucial knowledges and ways of knowing that should be centered within a new common school movement. A radical dialogue needs to move through these basic questions, engaging regular folks in producing what would be no less than a contemporary radical-popular philosophy of education.
3. Ideologically, an important part of neoliberalism is its foreclosure of alternatives - the sense it gives that there are no other options. This twisted "realism" is not new to capitalism, but neoliberalism seeks to make good on this old promise: to subsume social life entirely and to make the market the sole model and measure for doing and being. In this way, accountability in education, and neoliberalism more generally, works as a kind of fantasy, as Zizek describes, that *structures reality* for subjects, whether or not they "believe" in it. A common school movement needs to introduce

> a break in this fantasy. One tactic that would be useful is the *curricular strike.* In the curricular strike, teachers refuse (for a set period) to follow the official curriculum, and instead implement projects and conversations not already given by the standards but instead answerable to the goals set by the community and the imagination of the educator. If these strikes are successful in building courage and resistance, in a further step educators and community members might undertake *school occupations,* understood not in the sense of the Occupy movement but rather in the sense of the Argentine worker occupations of abandoned factories: that is, as a process of appropriation in which those already at work at a site restart it and redirect it through a collective and democratic process. In the school occupation, teaching and learning would be not be stopped but rather reimagined.

Starting from the interventions just described, a larger movement might then be built, within and beyond schools, as part of a broader reconstruction of society against neoliberalism and capitalism itself. What distinguishes the organizing effort that we describe, and gives it a special energy, is its focus on basic educational meanings and purposes. We often lapse into an easy dialectic in which schools are characterized as, alternately, sites of domination or sites of emancipation. While it is true that schools have been sites in which oppressed and marginalized groups have struggled for a limited degree of access and inclusion, at the same time schooling has been largely determined - in the past and in the present - by the imperative of class-racial domination. The public in the public schools that we argue should be defended is not quite an existing reality of the common, but rather the site itself of struggle: That is, the *public* should be defended as the privileged territory for the opening of a movement that would need to *invent* democracy, *against* a system of schooling that has historically parodied and persecuted it.

Notes

1. Elinor Ostrum, *Governing the Commons: The Evolution of Institutions for Collective Action* Cambridge: Cambridge University Press, 1990.
2. Peter Linebaugh, *The Magna Carta Manifesto* Berkeley: University of California Press, 2008.
3. Silvia Federici, *Caliban and the Witch: Women, The Body, and Primitive Accumulation* Brooklyn: Autonomedia, 2009.
4. Slavoj Zizek, *Demanding the Impossible* New York: Verso, 2013.
5. Jeff Bryant, "Starving America's schools" (2011). National Education Association.
6. Kenneth J. Saltman, *Capitalizing on Disaster: Taking and Breaking Public Schools* Boulder: Paradigm Publishers, "Chapter 1: Silver Linings and Golden Opportunities".
7. Harper's Index, Harper's Magazine (April 2012).
8. Lee Fang, "How Online Learning Companies Bought America's Schools" The Nation, (December 2011).

33

Broadening the Circle of Critical Pedagogy

E. Wayne Ross

Critical pedagogy is understood (and misunderstood) in myriad ways. Most often associated with Paulo Freire's (1970) problem-posing approach in opposition to the traditional banking method of education, it is also closely connected with neo-Marxist, critical theory-based analyses of education, schooling, and society. Despite popular perception, and the conceptualizations of critical pedagogy by some of its most well-known proponents, there is no single ideological perspective or particular social movement that defines critical pedagogy.

The dominant conceptualizations of critical pedagogy are unnecessarily narrow, both politically and philosophically. As a result, a pedagogical approach that is undeniably powerful has been undermined and its impact blunted. Critical pedagogy has become less a process of students investigating the world and constructing personally meaningful understandings that aid them in the struggle to overcome oppression and achieve freedom and more akin to an *a priori* set of beliefs about the world presented as maps to be followed. In other words, critical pedagogy has met the enemy and he is us, or at least includes us. If critical pedagogy, as a process of education, is to achieve its aims it cannot exempt itself from the same uprooting and examination of its own underlying assumptions, pronouncements, clichés, and received wisdom.

My aim here is to broaden the circle of critical pedagogy. I will illustrate how we might increase its uptake by teachers and its effects on individuals, schools, and society by adopting a less orthodox conception of what it means to practice critical pedagogy.

Broadening the Circle Philosophically

Critical pedagogy did not evolve from a single philosophical source and its core aims and methods can be tied to a variety of philosophical traditions.

Freire and Dewey

The core idea of critical pedagogy is to submit received understandings to critical analysis with the aim of increasing human knowledge and freedom. Ira Shor offers the most straightforward description of critical pedagogy:

> Habits of thought, reading, writing, and speaking which go beneath surface meaning, first impressions, dominant myths, official pronouncements, traditional clichés, received wisdom,

> and mere opinions, to understand the deep meaning, root causes, social context, ideology, and personal consequences of any action, event, object, process, organization, experience, text, subject matter, policy, mass media, or discourse.
>
> (Shor, 1992, p. 129)

Now consider philosopher John Dewey's description of "reflective" thinking.

> Active, persistent, and careful consideration of any belief or supposed form of knowledge in the light of the grounds that support and the further conclusions to which it tends . . .
>
> (p. 8)

While Dewey's philosophy falls outside the realm we know as critical theory, there is significant commonality between these two approaches to understanding and knowing the world. Critical pedagogy is a tool to expose and deconstruct cultural hegemony, the idea that the ruling elite manipulates social mores so that their view becomes the dominant worldview. While Dewey did not use the term hegemony, he recognized the problem and constructed his conception of education in response to it. In *Democracy and Education* (1916) Dewey wrote

> . . . the word education means just a process of leading or bringing up. When we have the outcome of the process in mind, we speak of education as shaping, forming, molding activity—that is, a shaping into the standard form of social activity. . . .The required beliefs cannot be hammered in; the needed attitudes cannot be plastered on. But the particular medium in which an individual exists leads him to see and feel one thing rather than another; it leads him to have certain plans in order that he may act successfully with others; it strengthens some beliefs and weakens others as a condition of winning the approval of others. Thus it gradually produces in him a certain system of behavior, a certain disposition of action.
>
> (Chapter 2, paras. 1–2)

Dewey and Freire share the idea that education is not a neutral process. Dewey's *Democracy and Education* (1916) opens with a discussion of the way in which all societies use education as a means of social control by which adults consciously shape the dispositions of children. He goes on to argue that education as a social process and function has no definite meaning until we define the kind of society we have in mind. In other words, there is no "scientifically objective" answer to the question of the purposes of education, because those purposes are not things that can be discovered. Similarly, Freire (1970; 1974) described education as either an instrument that is used to integrate people into the logic of the present system and bring about conformity to it, or it becomes "the practice of freedom," that is the means by which people deal critically and creatively with reality and discover how to participate in the transformation of their world.

Dewey's radical reconceptualization of democracy has much to offer critical pedagogy (Bernstein, 2010). His notion of democracy cannot be found in the electoral democracies of capitalism. For Dewey, the primary responsibility of democratic citizens is concern with the development of shared interests that lead to sensitivity about repercussions of their actions on others. Dewey characterized democracy as a force that breaks down barriers that separate people and creates community. The more porous the boundaries of social groups the more they welcome participation from all individuals, and as the varied groupings enjoy multiple and flexible relations, society moves closer to fulfilling the democratic ideal.

From a Deweyan perspective, democracy is not merely a form of government nor is it an end in itself; it is the means by which people discover, extend, and manifest human nature and human rights. For Dewey, democracy has three roots: free individual existence;

solidarity with others; and choice of work and other forms of participation in society. The aim of democratic education and thus a democratic society is the production of free human beings associated with one another on terms of equality.

For me, there is an easy connection to be made between Dewey and the more traditional roots of critical pedagogy in Freire's work. Additionally, I see threads in these Deweyan roots of democracy that are in sync with at least some strains of anarchist thought, particularly opposition to authority and hierarchical organization in human relations and mutual aid and respect. Dewey was not an anarchist; far from it. But, as Noam Chomsky (2000; Ross, 2014) has pointed out, Dewey's conceptualization of democracy and democratic education can be understood as supportive of social anarchist principles (something I come back to later). While Dewey's democratically informed education philosophy is quite familiar to folks in education, it has largely been influential only conceptually; its radical potential remains, in almost every respect, unrealized in schools and society and that is a challenge for critical pedagogues.

Dialectics and Critical Pedagogy

From Shor's defining of critical pedagogy we can see reality is more than appearances and focusing exclusively on appearances—on the evidence that strikes us immediately and directly—can be misleading. Basing an understanding of ourselves and our world on what we see, hear, or touch in our immediate surroundings can lead us to conclusions that are distorted or false.

> Understanding anything in our everyday experience requires that we know something about how it arose and developed and how it fits into the larger context or system of which it is a part. Just recognizing this, however, is not enough.... After all, few would deny that everything in the world is changing and interacting at some pace and in one way or another, that history and systemic connections belong to the real world. The difficulty has always been how to think adequately about them, how not to distort them and how to give them the attention and weight that they deserve.
>
> (Ollman, 1993, p. 11)

Dialectics, Ollman explains, is an attempt to resolve this difficulty by expanding the notion of "anything" to include (as aspects of what is) both the process by which it has become that thing and the broader interactive context in which it is found. Dialectics restructures thinking about reality by replacing the commonsense notion of "thing," as something that has a history and has external connections to other things, with notions of "process" (which contains its history and possible futures) and "relation" (which contains as part of what it is its ties with other relations). Or, as Sciabarra puts it, dialectics is the "art of context-keeping":

> It counsels us to study the object of our inquiry from a variety of perspectives and levels of generality, so as to gain a more comprehensive picture of it. That study often requires that we grasp the object in terms of the larger system within which it is situated, as well as its development across time. Because human beings are not omniscient, because none of us can see the "whole" as if from a "synoptic" godlike perspective, it is only through selective abstraction that we are able to piece together a more integrated understanding of the phenomenon before us—an understanding of its antecedent conditions, interrelationships, and tendencies.
>
> (2005, para. 8)

Abstraction is like using camera lenses with different focal lengths: a zoom lens to bring a distant object into focus (what is the history of this?) or using a wide-angle lens to capture more of a scene (what is the social context of the issue now?) This raises important questions: Where does one start and what does one look for? The traditional approach to inquiry starts with small parts and attempts to establish connections with other parts leading to an understanding of the larger whole. Beginning with the whole, the system, or as much as we understand of it, and then inquiring into the part or parts of it to see how it fits and functions leads to a fuller understanding of the whole.

For example, many people of various political persuasions have pointed out the paradox of the growing wealth of the few and the increasing poverty of the many, as well as connections between the interests of corporations and the actions of governments and of being powerless and poor. As Ollman (1993) points out, despite awareness of these relations, most people do not take such observations seriously. Lacking a theory to make sense of what they are seeing, people don't know what importance to give it; forget what they have just seen, or exorcise the contradictions by labeling them a paradox. The problem is that the socialization we undergo (in and out of school) encourages us to focus on the particulars of our circumstances and to ignore interconnections. Thus, we miss the patterns that emerge from relations. Social studies education plays an important role in reinforcing this tendency. The social sciences break up human knowledge into various disciplines (history, anthropology, sociology, geography, etc.), each with its own distinctive language and ways of knowing, which encourages concentrating on bits and pieces of human experience. What existed before is usually taken as given and unchanging. As a result, political and economic upheavals (such as the revolutions of 1789, 1848, 1917, and 1989) are treated as anomalous events with discrete explanations.

Dialectical thinking, on the other hand, is an effort to understand the world in terms of interconnections—the ties among things as they are right now, their own preconditions, and future possibilities. The dialectical method takes change as the given and treats apparent stability as that which needs to be explained (and provides specialized concepts and frameworks to explain it). Dialectical thinking is an approach to understanding the world that requires not only a lot of facts that are usually hidden from view, but a more interconnected grasp of the facts we already know.

Dialectics is a core method of critical pedagogy. And while dialectics has been called "Marx's method" it should be noted that most of Marx's dialectic evolved from Georg Wilhelm Friedrich Hegel, who systematized a way of thinking that goes back to the ancient Greeks, Aristotle's *Topics*. Additionally, non-Marxist thinkers like Alfred North Whitehead and British Idealist F. H. Bradley developed their own versions of dialectics, while Chris Matthew Sciabarra and John F. Welsh (2007) put dialects to use in the service of libertarian social theory. And as Sciabarra (2005) writes:

> What makes a dialectical approach into a *radical* approach is that the task of going to the root of a social problem, seeking to understand it and resolve it, often requires that we make transparent the relationships among social problems. Understanding the complexities at work within any given society is a prerequisite for changing it. It is simply mistaken to believe that Marx and Marxists have had a monopoly on this type of analysis. It is also mistaken to believe that this emphasis on grasping the full context is, somehow, a vestige of Marxism.

Priestcraft and Critical Pedagogy

Like mainstream liberal educators who believe in the culturally redemptive power of schooling, critical pedagogy has an educational messiah complex that too often turns critical educators into priests, whose aim is to mediate the everyday life of students and teachers. Too often critical pedagogy is conceptualized from above.

Paulo Freire is undoubtedly the key figure in the development of critical pedagogy. His focus on consciousness, critique, utopian vision (the need for imagining a better future before it can be achieved), the critical role of education for social justice, and the necessity of leadership unified with the people, should be seen as fundamental guidelines for movements for social change. Yet as Gibson (2007) points out, there are problems with Freire's work and he and his work have been reified in uncritical praise by prominent academics surrounding his work in the English-speaking world.

> As an icon, Freire indeed became a commodity. His work was purchased, rarely as a whole, but in selective pieces, which could further the career of an academic, propel the interests of a corporation or a state-capitalist "revolutionary" party. Many of his enthusiasts called his work "eclectic," and let it go at that. But Freire called himself a contradictory man. His politics were often seemingly at odds.
>
> (p. 180)

Gibson's analysis reveals two Freires. The Marxist Freire urged the analysis of labor and production, but was unable to resolve the incongruity of human liberation and capitalism's demand for inequality in order to motivate national economic development. The Catholic-humanist-postmodern Freire denied the centrality of class and focused on deconstructing culture and language. In both cases, Freire relied on the ethics of the educator-leader to mediate the tensions between middle-class teachers and profoundly exploited students.

It is impossible to imagine critical pedagogy without the profound contributions of Freire (e.g., his emphasis on the pivotal role of ideas as a material force, his critical method of analysis, his determination to engage in concrete social practice, his democratic and ethical pedagogy, and his insistence on non-hierarchical leadership), however, being true to his legacy requires us to critically re-examine his work and what it means for us today; avoiding reification of his texts; taking care not to strip them of their politics or overlook the contradictions to be found there.

There is no place for evangelists in critical pedagogy because the aim is not to convert people to *a priori* assumptions, beliefs, or knowledge. At the heart of Freire's interactive approach to education, and often overlooked or ignored, is observation, experience, and judgment (as opposed to knowledge that proceeds just from theoretical deduction).

Humans tend to construct beliefs based upon insufficient knowledge and understanding, then cling to them, rejecting evidence to the contrary, as a result, there is no place for "believers" in critical pedagogy. Critical pedagogy as a process rejects prejudices or prejudgements, that is, thought or belief that accepts superficial appearances. Tradition, instruction, and imitation all depend on authority in some form. A critical pedagogy thrives on scepticism, doubt, analysis, radical inquiry, thus no priests are necessary because the point is for people to think for themselves. Whether the promise of critical consciousness and liberation from oppression can be achieved by Freire's theoretical stance or his "see-judge-act" system of interactive education is an empirical question.

The Individual, Institutions, Social Change, and Critical Pedagogy

Critical pedagogy as a practice has been critiqued both internally and externally. For example, McLaren laments "the domestication of critical pedagogy," that is critical pedagogy efforts that have been accommodated to mainstream liberal humanism and progressivism and "marked by flirtation with but never full commitment to revolutionary praxis" (2000, p. 98). Identifying postmodernism and poststructuralism as the heart of this problem, McLaren quotes Carl Boggs to make his point:

> In politics as in the cultural and intellectual realm, a postmodern fascination with indeterminacy, ambiguity, and chaos easily supports a drift toward cynicism and passivity; the subject becomes powerless to change either itself or society. Further the pretentious, jargon-filled and often indecipherable discourse of postmodernism reinforces the most faddish tendencies in academia. Endless (and often pointless) attempts to deconstruct texts and narrative readily become a façade behind which professional scholars justify their own retreat from political commitment . . . the extreme postmodern assault on macro institutions severs the connections between critique and action.
>
> (1997, p. 767)

On the other hand postmodernist Elizabeth Ellsworth (1989) critiques the critical pedagogy literature as highly abstract, utopian, and out of touch with the everyday practice of teachers. Ellsworth maintains that the discourse of critical pedagogy gives rise to repressive myths that perpetuate relations of domination where "objects, nature, and 'Others' are seen to be known or ultimately knowable, in the sense of being 'defined, delineated, captured, understood, explained, and diagnosed' at a level of determination never accorded to the 'knower' herself or himself" (p. 321). In response to critical pedagogy Ellsworth offers her preferred version of classroom practice as a kind of communication across difference that is represented in this statement:

> If you can talk to me in ways that show you understand that your knowledge of me, the world, and 'the Right thing to do' will always be partial, interested, and potentially oppressive to others, and if I can do the same, then we can work together on shaping and reshaping alliances for constructing circumstances in which students of difference can thrive.
>
> (p. 324)

In this argument I tend to agree with McLaren (see, for example, Hill, McLaren, Cole, Rikowski, 2002; Ross & Gibson, 2007), but Ellsworth's critique identifies an important blind spot within critical pedagogy regarding the individual, the personal, and identity.

In his excellent history of the free school movement of the 1960s, Ron Miller (2002) reassesses and revives the legacy of John Holt. Holt was not a scholar or a theorist, but rather a moralist and reformer, a thinker described as a social ecologist and constructive postmodernist, who became closely associated with the deschooling and homeschooling movements in North America.

As Miller points out, Holt, like John Dewey, was not an ideologue and endorsed no "-ism." Holt warned against the quest for ideological purity and "over-abstractness." He advocated an organic worldview, "an appreciation for the living, dynamic, evolving, interacting, and responsive nature of reality" (Miller, p. 83). Holt held several fundamental principles that should be taken seriously by critical educators:

- the dignity and value of human existence and faith in the human capacity to learn;
- concern for freedom and belief that it was being seriously eroded by the impersonality of large organizations and the forms of surveillance and control practiced in social institutions, particularly schools;
- opposing centralized political and economic power that rests on scientific-technological management of natural and human resources;

- the driving concern for the need of each person to find a meaningful, fulfilling sense of identity in a mass society that makes this difficult.

(Miller, p. 83)

Holt "sought a thorough renewal of culture that would be as concerned with personal wholeness and authenticity as with social justice" (Miller, p. 85). In the tradition of Thoreau, he saw himself as a "decentralist" who "leaned in the direction of anarchism," he "did not so much seek to reform social institutions as to circumvent and thus deflate them" (Miller, p. 85). Holt was primarily concerned about human growth and learning, but he focused on the relationship between social institutions and human development. His emphasis on the personal dimension of social reality addresses a blind spot within critical pedagogy, which too often privileges the institutional analysis at the expense of existential authenticity, that is the individual person's concern that his or her life is meaningful and fulfilling. Holt described his deepest interest as, "how can we adults work to create a more decent, humane, conserving, peaceful, just, etc. community, nation, world, and how can we make it possible for children to join us in this work?" (Miller, p. 86).

> Holt emphasized the connection between the social and the individual, between the political and the existential. Human beings could not grow whole in a fragmented or violent culture, but at the same time a decent culture would only emerge when people personally experienced meaning and fulfillment.
>
> (Miller, p. 86)

Miller argues that what distinguishes Holt's position from "progressive" critiques was his insistence that reform of social institutions alone was not sufficient for cultural renewal. For Holt, the source of violence, racism, and exploitation was not in institutions as such, but in the psychological reality people experience as they live in society. The implication for critical pedagogy is that its focus on institutional transformation has neglected the existential dimension of meaning, too often ignoring personal desire for belonging, community, and moral commitment.

To be clear, neither Holt nor I am advocating a perspective that is merely personal or individualistic. Holt was very aware of political forces and expressed his concern that the worship of progress and growth was inevitably leading to fascism. In his 1970 book, *What Do I Do Monday?* Holt suggests that alienation bred by authoritarian education could "prepare the ground for some naïve American brand of Fascism, which now seems uncomfortably close." Miller quotes a letter Holt wrote to Paul Goodman, in 1970:

> I keep looking for and hoping to find evidence that [Americans] are not as callous and greedy and cruel and envious as I fear they are, and I keep getting disappointed. . . . What scares me is the amount of Fascism in people's spirit. It is the government that so many of our fellow citizens would get if they could that scares me—and I fear we are moving in that direction.
>
> (p. 89)

Unfortunately, Holt was prescient about politics in the United States, as well as about institutional, particularly school, reform, as an effective path for social change. In 1971, Holt wrote in *New Schools Exchange Newsletter,*

> I do not believe that any movement for educational reform that addresses itself exclusively or even primarily to the problems or needs of children can progress very far. In short, in a society that is absurd, unworkable, wasteful, destructive, coercive, monopolistic, and generally anti-human, we could never have good education, no matter what kind of schools the powers that

> be permit, because it is not the educators or the schools but the whole society and the quality of life in it that really educate.... More and more it seems to me, and this is a reversal of what I felt not long ago, that it makes very little sense to talk about education *for* social change, as if education was or could be a kind of getting ready. The best and perhaps only education for social change is action to bring about that change.... There cannot be little worlds fit for children in a world not fit for anyone else.
>
> (Quoted in Miller, 2002, p. 90)

In his 1972 book, *Freedom and Beyond,* Holt grappled with the key concepts of critical pedagogy: social justice, racism, poverty, and class conflict, arguing, as Miller points out, that schools were contributing to these problems rather than helping to solve them. Unlike the social reconstructionists of mid-20th century (e.g., Counts, 1932), Holt came to see schools (even democratic free schools) not as potential sources for recreation of the social order, but rather obstacles to be overcome in the pursuit of social change. He wondered whether "we are trying to salve our consciences by asking our children to do what we can't and don't want to do" (1972, p. 232).

Holt concluded that schools "tend to take learning out of its living context and turn it into an abstraction, a commodity" (Miller, p. 95). Or as he once said, "I'm enough of an anarchist to feel that things are improved in general when they are improved in their particulars." And this is the principle that addresses, at least in part, the concerns Ellsworth famously raised in her critique of critical pedagogy.

The question becomes how can we create a better balance between the abstraction (a focus on the general nature of things) and authenticity (a focus on the particulars) within critical pedagogy. Holt argued that attempting to change society through schools was an evasion of personal responsibility because authentic meaning cannot be cultivated en masse. "People don't change their ideas, much less their lives, because someone comes along with a clever argument to show that they're wrong" (Holt, 1981, p. 66). So, critical educators are left with a conundrum.

The Future of Critical Pedagogy

Foucault argued that practicing criticism is a matter of making facile gestures difficult and his definition of critique has much in common with Shor's definition of critical pedagogy.

> A critique is not a matter of saying that things are not right as they are. It is a matter of pointing out on what kinds of assumptions, what kinds of familiar, unchallenged, unconsidered modes of thought the practices that we accept rest.... Criticism is a matter of flushing out that thought and trying to change it: to show that things are not as self-evident as one believed, to see what is accepted as self-evident will no longer be accepted as such.
>
> (1988, pp. 154–155)

Critical pedagogy continues to evolve and it is up to us, as critical educators, to continually engage in self-critique and pedagogical renovation.

People who talk about transformational learning or educational revolution without referring explicitly to everyday life, without understanding what is subversive about learning, and love, and what is positive in the refusal of constraints, are trapped in a net of received ideas, the common-nonsense and false reality of technocrats (or worse).

Schools are alluring contradictions, harboring possibilities for liberation, emancipation, and social progress, but, as fundamentally authoritarian and hierarchical institutions, they produce myriad oppressive and inequitable by-products. The challenge, perhaps impossibility, is discovering ways in which schools can contribute to positive liberty. That is a society where individuals have the power and resources to realize and fulfill their own potential, free from the obstacles of classism, racism, sexism, and other inequalities encouraged by capitalism and its educational systems as well as the influence of the state and religious ideologies. A society where people have agency and capacity to make their own free choices and act independently based on reason, not authority, tradition, or dogma.

Education, as a whole, really is a critical knowledge of everyday life. Genuine community and genuine dialogue can exist only when each person has access to a direct experience of reality, when everyone has at his or her disposal the practical and intellectual means needed to solve problems. The question is not to determine what the students *are* at present, but rather what they *can become,* for only then is it possible to grasp what in truth they *already are.* (And the same applies to us, as critical educators.)

Studying how people (and things) change is the heart of social understanding and critical pedagogy. For me, perhaps the most compelling element of critical pedagogy is that active investigation of social and educational issues contributes to change. As Mao Zedong (1937) said,

> If you want to know the taste of a pear, you must change the pear by eating it yourself. If you want to know the theory and methods of revolution, you must take part in revolution. All genuine knowledge originates in direct experience.

Mao's position on the role of experience in learning is remarkably similar to those of John Dewey. Both of these philosophers, although poles apart ideologically, share what has been described as an activist conception of human beings, that is the view that people create themselves on the basis of their own self-interpretations. Although, as Marx points out, while people make their own history, they do not make it as they please, but under circumstances existing already, given and transmitted from the past.

Reduced to its most basic elements, critical pedagogy should seek to create conditions in which students (and educators) can develop personally meaningful understandings of the world and recognize they have agency to act on the world, to make change.

Critical pedagogy is not about showing life to people, but bringing them to life. The aim is not getting students to listen to convincing lectures by experts, but getting them to speak for themselves in order to achieve, or at least strive toward an equal degree of participation and a better future.

References

Bernstein, R. J. (2010). Dewey's vision of radical democracy. In M. Cochran, *The Cambridge companion to Dewey* (pp. 288–308). Cambridge, UK: America's Cambridge University Press.

Boggs, C. (1997). The great retreat: Decline of the public sphere in late twentieth century America. *Theory and Society, 26,* 741–780.

Chomsky, N., & Macedo, D. P. (2000). *Chomsky on miseducation.* Lanham, MD: Rowman & Littlefield.

Counts, G. S. (1932). *Dare the school build a new social order?* New York: John Day Company.

Dewey, J. (1916). *Democracy and education.* New York: Macmillan. Retrieved from http://xroads.virginia.edu/~HYPER2/dewey/ch02.html

Dewey, J. (1933). *How we think.* Lexington, MA: Heath.

Ellsworth, E. (1989). Why doesn't this feel empowering? Working through the repressive myths of critical pedagogy. *Harvard Educational Review, 59*(3), 297–324.

Foucault, M. (1988). Practicing criticism. In L. D. Kritzman (Ed.), *Politics, Philosophy, Culture: Interviews and Other Writings 1977–1984.* New York: Routledge.

Freire, P. (1970). *Pedagogy of the oppressed.* New York: Continuum.
Freire, P. (1974). *Education for critical consciousness.* New York: Continuum.
Freire, P. (1985). Reading the world and reading the word: An interview with Paulo Freire. *Language Arts, 62*(1), 15–21.
Gibson, R. (2007). Paulo Freire and revolutionary pedagogy for social justice. In E. W. Ross & R. Gibson (Eds.), *Neoliberalism and education reform* (pp. 177–215). Cresskill, NJ: Hampton Press.
Hill, D., McLaren, P., Cole, M., & Rikowski, G. (Eds.). (2002). *Marxism against postmodernism in educational theory.* Lanham, MD: Lexington Books.
Holt, J. (1981). *Teach your own.* New York: Dell.
Holt, J. (1995). *Freedom and beyond.* Portsmouth, NH: Boynton/Cook. (Originally published in 1972).
Holt, J. (1995). *What do I do Monday?* Portsmouth, NH: Boynton/Cook. (Originally published in 1970).
McLaren, P. (2000). *Che Guevara, Paulo Freire, and the pedagogy of revolution.* Lanham, MD: Rowman & Littlefield.
Miller, R. (2002). *Free schools, free people: Education and democracy after the 1960s.* Albany State University of New York Press.
Ollman, B. (1999). *Dance of the dialectic.* New York: Routledge.
Ross, E. W., & Gibson, G. (Eds.). (2007). *Neoliberalism and education reform.* Cresskill, NJ: Hampton Press.
Ross, E. W. (2014). Noam Chomsky. In D. C. Phillips (Ed.), *Encyclopedia of educational theory and philosophy* (pp. 126–127). Thousand Oaks, CA: Sage.
Sciabarra, C. M. (2005, September 1). Dialectics and liberty: A defense of dialectical method in the service of a libertarian social theory. *The Freeman.* Retrieved from http://fee.org/freeman/detail/dialectics-and-liberty
Shor, I. (1992). *Empowering education: Critical teaching for social change.* Chicago: University of Chicago Press.
Welsh, J. F. (2007). *After multiculturalism: The politics of race and dialectics of liberty.* Lanham, MD: Lexington Books.

Suggested Readings for Future Study

Allman, P. (2001). *Revolutionary Social Transformation: Democratic Hopes, Politic Possibilities and Critical Education.* Westport, CT: Bergin & Garvey.

Allman, P. (2010). *Critical Education against Global Capitalism: Karl Marx and Revolutionary Critical Education.* Rotterdam, The Netherlands: Sense Publishers.

Anyon, J. (2005). *Radical Possibilities: Public Policy, Urban Education, and a New Social Movement.* New York: Routledge.

Apple, M. (1993). "The Politics of Official Knowledge: Does a National Curriculum Make Sense?" *Teachers College Record, 95*(2), Winter, 222–241.

Apple, M. (1996). *Cultural Politics and Education.* New York and London: Teachers College, Columbia University.

Apple, M. (2000a). *Official Knowledge, Democratic Education in a Conservative Age.* New York: Routledge.

Apple, M. (2000b). "The Shock of the Real—Critical Pedagogies and Rightist Reconstruction." In Trifonas, P. (ed.), *Revolutionary Pedagogies* (pp. 225–250). New York, London: RoutledgeFalmer.

Apple, M. (2011). "Democratic Education in Neoliberal and Neoconservative Times." *International Studies in Sociology of Education, 21*(1), 21–31.

Araujo Freire, A. and Macedo, D. (1998). *The Paulo Freire Reader.* New York: Continuum.

Aronowitz, S. and Giroux, H. (1985). *Education under Siege.* South Hadley, MA: Bergin & Garvey.

Ayers, W. (1998). *Teaching for Social Justice: A Democracy and Education Reader.* New York: New Press.

Ayers, W. (2004). *Teaching the Personal and the Political: Essays on Hope and Justice.* New York: Teachers College Press.

Bagdikian, B. (2004). *The New Media Monopoly.* Boston: Beacon.

Barbules, N. (1992). *Dialogue in Teaching: Theory and Practice.* New York: Teachers College Press.

Boal, A. (1998). *Legislative Theatre: Using Performance to Make Politics.* New York: Routledge.

Boler, M. (2004). *Democratic Dialogue in Education: Troubling Speech, Disturbing Silence.* New York: Peter Lang.

Borg, C., Buttiegieg, J., and Mayo, P. (2002). *Gramsci and Education.* Lanham, MD: Rowman & Littlefield.

Borg, C. and Mayo, P. (2005). "Challenges for Critical Pedagogy: A Southern European Perspective." *Cultural Studies/Critical Methodologies, 6,* 143–154.

Boykoff, J. (2006). *The Suppression of Dissent.* New York: Routledge.

Buckingham, D. (2003a). *Media Education: Literacy, Learning and Contemporary Culture.* Malden, MA: Blackwell.

Buckingham, D. (2003b). "Media Education and the End of the Critical Consumer." *Harvard Educational Review, 73*(3), 309–328.

Butsch, R. (2007). *Media and Public Spheres.* New York: Palgrave Macmillan.

Canaan, J. E. (2002). "Theorizing Pedagogic Practices in the Contexts of Marketization and of September 11, 2001, and Its Aftermath." *Anthropology & Education Quarterly, 33*(3), 368–382.

Carlson, D. and Apple, M. W. (1998). *Power, Knowledge, and Pedagogy: The Meaning of Democratic Education in Unsettling Times.* Boulder, CO: Westview Press.

Carr, W. (1995). *For Education: Towards Critical Educational Inquiry.* Bristol, UK: Open University Press.

Carr, W. and Harnett, A. (1996). *Education and the Struggle for Democracy: The Politics of Educational Ideas.* Bristol, UK: Open University Press.

Carty, V. and Onyett, J. (2006). "Protest, Cyberactivism and New Social Movements: The Reemergence of the Peace Movement Post 9/11." *Social Movement Studies, 5*(3), 229–249.

Chilcoat, G. W. and Ligon, J. A. (1999). "Helping to Make Democracy a Living Reality: The Curriculum Conference of the Mississippi Freedom Schools." *Journal of Curriculum and Supervision, 15,* 43–68.

Cho, S. (2010). "Politics of Critical Pedagogy and New Social Movements." *Educational Philosophy and Theory, 42*(3), 310–325.

Chomsky, N. (2000). *Chomsky on Miseducation.* Lanham, MD: Rowman & Littlefield Publishers.

Chun, C. W. (2014). "Reflexivity and Critical Language Education at Occupy L.A." In Clark, J. B. and Dervin, F. (eds.), *Reflexivity in Language and Education: Rethinking Multilingualism and Interculturality* (pp. 172–192). London: Routledge.

Cole, M. (2006). *Education, Equality and Human Rights: Issues of Gender, 'Race', Sexuality, Disability and Social Class.* London: Routledge.

Conway, J. (2006). *Praxis and Politics: Knowledge Production in Social Movements.* New York: Routledge.

Coyer, K. (2005). "If It Leads It Bleeds: The Participatory Newsmaking of the Independent Media Centre." In de Jong, W., Shaw, M., and Stammers, N. (eds.), *Global Activism, Global Media* (pp. 165–178). Ann Arbor, MI: Pluto.

Darder, A. (1991). *Culture and Power in the Classroom.* Westport, CT: Bergin & Garvey.

Darder, A. (2002). *Reinventing Paulo Freire: A Pedagogy of Love.* Boulder, CO: Westview.

Darder, A. (2012). *Culture and Power in the Classroom: Educational Foundations for the Schooling of Bicultural Students.* Boulder, CO: Paradigm Publishers.

Darder, A. (2015). *Freire and Education.* New York: Routledge.

Davidson, H. S. (1995). *Schooling in a "Total Institution": Critical Perspectives on Prison Education.* Westport, CT: Bergin & Garvey.

de Jong, W., Shaw, M., and Stammers, N., eds. (2005). *Global Activism, Global Media.* Ann Arbor, MI: Pluto.

De Lissovoy, N. (2008). *Power, Crisis and Education for Liberation: Rethinking Critical Pedagogy.* New York: Palgrave Macmillan.

Dewey, J. (1916). *Democracy and Education.* New York: The Free Press.

Dolby, N. (2003). Popular Culture and Democratic Practice. *Harvard Educational Review, 73*(3), 258–284.

Dolby, N. and Rizvi, F. (2007). *Youth Moves: Identities and Education in Global Perspective.* New York: Routledge.

Downing, J. (2001). *Radical Media: Rebellious Communication and Social Movements.* Thousand Oaks, CA: Sage.

Duncan-Andrade, J. M. R. (2009). "Note to Educators: Hope Required When Growing Roses in Concrete." *Harvard Educational Review, 79*, 181–194.

Edu-Factory Collective (2009). *Toward a Global Autonomous University: Cognitive Labor, the Production of Knowledge, and Exodus from the Education Factory.* New York: Autonomedia.

Edwards, D. B. (2010). "Critical Pedagogy and Democratic Education: Possibilities for Cross-Pollination." *The Urban Review, 42*(3), 221–242.

Fischman, G., et al., eds. (2005). *Critical Theories, Radical Pedagogies, and Global Conflicts.* Lanham, MD: Rowman and Littlefield Publishers.

Fletcher, S. (2000). *Education and Emancipation Theory and Practice in a New Constellation.* New York: Teachers College Press.

Flores, J. (2012). "Jail Pedagogy: Liberatory Education inside a California Juvenile Detention Facility." *Journal of Education for Students Placed at Risk, 17*(4), 286–300.

Forester, J. (1985). *Critical Theory and Public Life.* Cambridge, MA: MIT Press.

Forester, J. (1993). *Critical Theory, Public Policy and Planning Practice: Toward a Critical Pragmatism.* New York: SUNY Press.

Frechette, J. D. (2002). *Developing Media Literacy in Cyberspace: Pedagogy and Critical Learning for the Twenty-First Century Classroom.* Westport, CT: Greenwood.

Freire, P. (1973). *Education for Critical Consciousness.* New York: Continuum.

Freire, P. (1985). *The Politics of Education.* South Hadley, MA: Bergin & Garvey.

Freire, P. (1993). *Pedagogy of the City.* New York: Continuum.

Freire, P. (1994). *Pedagogy of the Oppressed* (Anniversary Edition). New York: Continuum.

Freire, P. (1996). *Pedagogy of Hope.* New York: Continuum.

Freire, P. (1997). *Pedagogy of the Heart.* New York: Continuum.

Freire, P. (1998). *Pedagogy of Freedom: Ethics, Democracy, and Civic Courage.* Lanham: Rowman and Littlefield.

Freire, P. (2004). "Television Literacy." In *Pedagogy of Indignation* (pp. 87–95). Boulder, CO: Paradigm.

Freire, P. and Faundez, A. (1989). *Learning to Question: A Pedagogy of Liberation.* New York: Continuum.

Gabbard, D., ed. (2008). *Knowledge and Power in the Global Economy: The Effects of School Reform in Neoliberal/Neoconservative Age.* New York: Lawrence Erlbaum.

Gadotti, M. (1994). *Reading Paulo Freire: His life and Work.* Albany, NY: SUNY Press.

Garrido, M. and Halavais, A. (2003). "Mapping Networks of Support for the Zapatista Movement: Applying Social-Networks Analysis to Study Contemporary Social Movements." In McCaughey, M. and Ayers, M. (eds.), *Cyberactivism: Online Activism in Theory and Practice* (pp. 165–184). New York: Routledge.

Gatimu, M. W. (2009). "Rationale for Critical Pedagogy of Decolonization: Kenya as a Unit of Analysis." *Journal for Critical Education Policy Studies, 7*(2), 67–97.

Gezgin, U. B., Inal, K., and Hill, D., eds. (2014). *The Gezi Revolt: People's Revolutionary Resistance against Neoliberal Capitalism in Turkey.* Brighton: Institute for Education Policy Studies.

Gilmore, R. (2007). *Golden Gulag: Prisons, Surplus, Crisis, and Opposition in Globalizing California.* Berkeley: University of California Press.

Giroux, H. (1981). *Ideology, Culture and the Process of Schooling*. Philadelphia: Temple University Press.

Giroux, H. (1983). *Theory and Resistance in Education*. South Hadley, MA: Bergin & Garvey.

Giroux, H. (1988a). *Schooling and the Struggle for Public Life: Critical Pedagogy in the Modern Age*. Minneapolis, MN: University of Minnesota Press.

Giroux, H. (1988b). *Teachers as Intellectuals: Toward a Critical Pedagogy of Learning*. South Hadley, MA: Bergin & Garvey.

Giroux, H. (1989). *Popular Culture: Schooling and Everyday life*. Westport, CT: Bergin & Garvey.

Giroux, H. (1994). *Disturbing Pleasures: Learning Popular Culture*. New York: Routledge.

Giroux, H. (1997). *Pedagogy and the Politics of Hope: Theory, Culture and Schooling*. Boulder, CO: Westview.

Giroux, H. (2001). *The Mouse that Roared: Disney and the End of Innocence*. Lanham: Rowman and Littlefield.

Giroux, H. (2005) *Against the New Authoritarianism: Politics after Abu Ghraib*. Winnepeg, MB: Arbeiter Ring Publishing.

Giroux, H. (2006a). "Breaking into the Movies: Film as Cultural Politics." In *America on the Edge: Henry Giroux on Politics, Culture, and Education* (pp. 117–128). New York: Palgrave Macmillan.

Giroux, H. (2006b). *America on the Edge: Henry Giroux on Politics, Culture, and Education*. New York: Palgrave Macmillan.

Giroux, H. (2007). *The University in Chains: Confronting the Military-Industrial-Academic Complex*. Boulder, CO: Paradigm Publishers.

Giroux, H. and McLaren, P. (1989). *Critical Pedagogy, the State and Cultural Struggle*. Albany: State University of New York Press.

Gitlin, A. (1994). *Power and Method: Political Activism and Educational Research*. New York: Routledge.

Goodman, J. (1992). *Elementary Schooling for Critical Democracy*. Albany: State University of New York Press.

Goodman, S. (2003). *Teaching Youth Media: A Critical Guide to Literacy, Video Production, and Social Change*. New York: Teachers College.

Greene, M. (2000). *Releasing the Imagination: Essays on Education, the Arts and Social Change*. New York: Jossey-Bass.

Gur-Ze'ev, I. (1998). "Towards a Nonrepressive Critical Pedagogy." *Educational Theory, 48*, 463–486.

Halleck, D. (2002). *Hand-Held Visions: The Impossible Possibilities of Community Media*. New York: Fordham University.

Herman, E. and Chomsky, N. (2002). *Manufacturing Consent: The Political Economy of the Mass Media* (2nd ed.). New York: Pantheon.

Holst, J. (2002). *Social Movements, Civil Society, and Radical Adult Education*. Westport, CT: Bergin & Garvey.

Holst, J. (2006). "Paulo Freire in Chile, 1964–1969: Pedagogy of the Oppressed in Its Sociopolitical Economic Context." *Harvard Educational Review*, 76(2), 243–270.

Holtz, H. and Associates (1988). *Education and the American Dream: Conservative, Liberals and Radical Debate the Future of Education*. South Hadley, MA: Bergin & Garvey.

hooks, b. (1994). *Outlaw Culture: Resisting Representations*. New York: Routledge.

Horton, M. (2003). "What Is Liberating Education?" In Jacobs, D. (ed.). *The Myles Horton Reader* (pp. 184–189). Knoxville, TN: University of Tennessee.

Inglis, F. and Carr, W. (2004). *Education and the Good Society*. London: Palgrave MacMillan.

Kanpol, B. (1994). *Critical Pedagogy—An Introduction*. Westport, CT: Bergin & Garvey.

Kellner, D. (2001). *Media and Cultural Studies: Keyworks*. Malden, MA: Blackwell.

Kellner, D. (2005). *Media Spectacle and the Crisis of Democracy: Terrorism, War, and Election Battles*. Boulder, CO: Paradigm.

Kelly, E. (1995). *Education, Democracy and Public Knowledge*. Boulder, CO: Westview Press.

Kemal, I. and Akkaymak, G., eds. (2012). *Neoliberal Transformation of Education in Turkey: Political and Ideological Analysis of Educational Reforms in the Age of the AKP*. New York and London: Palgrave-Macmillan.

Kid, D. (2003). "Indymedia.org: A New Communications Commons." In McCaughey, M. and Ayers, M. (eds.), *Cyberactivism: Online Activism in Theory and Practice* (pp. 47–69). New York: Routledge.

Kincheloe, J. (1998). *How Do We Tell the Workers?: The Socioeconomic Foundations of Work*. Boulder, CO: Westview.

Kincheloe, J. (2004). *The Critical Pedagogy Primer*. New York: Peter Lang.

Kincheloe, J. and Steinberg, J., eds. (1995). *Thirteen Questions: Reframing Education's Conversation*. New York: Peter Lang Publishers.

Kincheloe, J. L. and Steinberg, S. R. (2004). *The Miseducation of the West: How Schools and the Media Distort Our Understanding of the Islamic World*. Westport, CT: Praeger Publishers.

Kirylo, J. (2013). *A Critical Pedagogy of Resistance: 34 Pedagogues We Need to Know*. Rotterdam: Sense Publishers.

Kohl, H. (1998). *The Discipline of Hope: Learning from a Lifetime of Teaching*. New York: The New Press.

Kozol, J. (1991). *Savage Inequalities—Children in America's Schools*. New York: Harper Perennial.

Kozol, J. (2001). *Ordinary Resurrections: Children in the Years of Hope*. New York: HarperCollins Publishers.

Kozol, J. and Merrow, J. (2001). *Choosing Excellence*. Lanham, MD: Scarecrow Press, Inc.

Kumar, R. (2016). *Neoliberalism, Critical Pedagogy and Education*. New York: Routledge.

Kumashiro, K. K. (2000). "Toward a Theory of Anti-Oppressive Education." *Review of Educational Research, 70*(1), 25–53.

Landri, P. (2009). "Temporary Eclipse of Bureaucracy. The Circulation of School Autonomy in Italy." *Italian Journal of Sociology of Education, 3*, 76–93.

Lankshear, C. and Knobel, M. (2005). "Paulo Freire and Digital Youth in Marginal Spaces." In *Critical Theories, Radical Pedagogies, and Global Conflicts* (pp. 293–306). Lanham, MD: Rowman and Littlefield.

Lankshear, C. and Knobel, M. (2006). *New Literacies: Everyday Practices and Classroom Learning.* Berkshire, UK: Open University.

Ledwith, M. (2001). "Community Work as Critical Pedagogy: Re-Envisioning Freire and Gramsci." *Community Development Journal, 36,* 171–182.

Ledwith, M. (2005). *Community Development: A Critical Approach.* Cambridge, UK: The Policy Press.

Leistyna, P. (1999). *Presence of Mind: Education and the Politics of Deception.* Boulder, CO: Westview Press.

Leistyna, P. and Alper, L. (2007). "Critical Media Literacy for the Twenty-First Century." In Macedo, D. and Steinberg, S. (eds.), *Media Literacy: A Reader* (pp. 54–78). New York: Peter Lang.

Leistyna, P., Woodrum, A., and Sherblom, S., eds. (1996). *Breaking Free: The Transformative Power of Critical Pedagogy.* Cambridge, MA: Harvard Educational Review.

Livingstone, D., ed. (1987). *Critical Pedagogy and Cultural Power.* South Hadley, MA: Bergin & Garvey.

Logue, J. (2008). "Mississippi Freedom Schools' Radical Conception of Pedagogy, Citizenship and Power." *Ohio Valley Philosophy of Education Society, 39,* 57–65.

Macedo, D. and Steinberg, S., eds. (2007). *Media Literacy: A Reader.* New York: Peter Lang.

Magendzo, A. (2005). "Pedagogy of Human Rights Education: A Latin American Perspective." *Intercultural Education, 16(2),* 137–143. doi: 10.1080/14675980500133549

Malott, C. (2010). *Policy and Research in Education: A Critical Pedagogy for Educational Leadership.* New York: Peter Lang.

Malott, C. S. and Porfilio, B., eds. (2011). *Critical Pedagogy in the Twenty-First Century: A New Generation of Scholars.* Charlotte, NC: Information Age.

Marino, D. (1997). *Wild Garden: Art, Education, and the Culture of Resistance.* Toronto, ON: Between the Lines Production.

Mayo, P. (2013a). "Museums as Sites of Critical Pedagogical Practice." *Review of Education, Pedagogy, and Cultural Studies, 35*(2), 144–153.

Mayo, P. (2013b). "Italian Signposts for a Sociologically and Critically Engaged Pedagogy. Don Lorenzo Milani (1923–1967) and the Schools of San Donato and Barbiana Revisited." *British Journal of Sociology of Education,* 1–18. doi: 10.1080/01425692.2013.848781

McChesney, R. (2000). *Rich Media, Poor Democracy: Communication Politics in Dubious Times.* New York: New York Press.

McChesney, R. (2004). *The Problem of the Media: U.S. Communication Politics in the Twenty-First Century.* New York: Monthly Review.

McCullagh, C. (2002). *Media Power.* New York: Palgrave.

McDonnell, L., Timpane, P. M., and Benjamin, R., eds. (2000). *Rediscovering the Democratic Purposes of Education.* Lawrence: University Press of Kansas.

McLaren, P. (1986). *Schooling as Ritual Performance.* London: Routledge and Kegan Paul.

McLaren, P. (1989). *Life in Schools: An Introduction to Critical Pedagogy and the Foundations of Education.* New York: Longman.

McLaren, P. (1995). *Critical Pedagogy and Predatory Culture.* New York: Routledge.

McLaren, P. (1997). *Revolutionary Multiculturalism: Pedagogies of Dissent for the New Millennium.* Boulder, CO: Westview.

McLaren, P. (2000). *Che Guevara, Paulo Freire, and the Pedagogy of Revolution.* Lanham, Boulder, New York, Oxford: Rowman & Littlefield Publishers, Inc.

McLaren, P. (2001). *Revolutionary Social Transformation: Democratic Hopes, Political Possibilities and Critical Education.* Westport, CT: Greenwood Publishing.

McLaren, P. (2005). *Capitalists and Conquerors: A Critical Pedagogy against Empire.* New York: Rowman & Littlefield.

McLaren, P. and Lankshear, C. (1994). *Politics of Liberation: Paths from Freire.* New York: Routledge.

McLaren, P. and Giarelli, J. (1995) *Critical Theory and Educational Research.* Albany, NY: SUNY Press.

McLaren, P. and Farahmandpur, R. (2001). "Teaching against Globalization and the New Imperialism: Toward a Revolutionary Pedagogy." *Journal of Teacher Education, 52,* 136–150.

McLaren, P. and Kincheloe, J. (2007). *Critical Pedagogy: Where Are We Now?* New York: Peter Lang.

Merideth E. (1994). "Critical Pedagogy and Its Application to Health Education: A Critical Appraisal of the Casa en Casa Model." *Health Education & Behavior, 21*(3), 355–367.

Monzó, L. D. (2014). "A Critical Pedagogy for Democracy: Confronting Higher Education's Neoliberal Agenda with a Critical Latina Feminist Episteme." *Journal for Critical Education Policy Studies, 12*(1), 73–100.

Monzó, L. and McLaren, P. (2014). "Critical Pedagogy and the Decolonial Option: Challenges to the Inevitability of Capitalism." *Policy Futures in Education, 12*(4), 513–525.

Morrell, E. (2002). "Toward a Critical Pedagogy of Popular Culture: Literacy Development among Urban Youth." *Journal of Adolescent & Adult Literacy, 46*(1), 72–77.

Morrow, R. and Torres, C. A. (2002). *Reading Freire and Habermas: Critical Pedagogy and Transformative Social Change.* New York: Teachers College Press.

Nikolakaki, M. (2011). "Critical Pedagogy and Democracy: Cultivating the Democratic Ethos." *Journal for Critical Education Policy Studies, 9,* 48–70.

Nikolakaki, M. (2012a). "Building a Society of Solidarity through Critical Pedagogy: Group Teaching as a Social and Democratic Tool." *Journal for Critical Education Policy Studies, 10*(2), 392–417.

Nikolakaki, M. (2012b). "Critical Pedagogy in the New Dark Ages: Challenges and Possibilities: An Introduction." In Nikolakaki, M (ed.), *Critical Pedagogy in the New Dark Ages: Challenges and Possibilities*. New York, Berne, Vienna, Brussels, Oxford and Frankfurt: Peter Lang.

Nuryatno, M. A. (2005). "In Search of Paulo Freire's Reception in Indonesia." *Convergence, 38*, 50–68.

Nyerere, J. K. (1968). *Freedom and Socialism*. Oxford: Oxford University Press.

Oaks, J., Rogers, J., and Lipton, M. (2006). *Learning Power: Organizing for Education and Justice*. New York: Teachers College Press.

O'Cadiz, M., Wong, P., and Torres, C. (1998). *Education and Democracy: Paulo Freire, Social Movements and Educational Reform in Sao Paulo*. Boulder, CO: Westview.

Oldenski, T. (1997). *Liberation Theology and Critical Pedagogy in Today's Catholic Schools: Social Justice in Action*. New York: Routledge.

Pannu, R. S. (1996). "Neoliberal Project of Globalization: Prospects for Democratisation of Education." *Alberta Journal of Educational Research, XL11*(2), 87–101.

Papastephanou, M. (2009). *Educated Fear and Educated Hope: Utopia, Dystopia and the Plasticity of Humanity*. Rotterdam, Taipei and Boston: Sense Publishers.

Papastephanou, M., Christou, M., and Gregoriou, Z. (2013). "Globalisation, the Challenge of Educational Synchronisation and Teacher Education." *Globalization, Societies and Education, 11*(1), 61–68.

Paraskeva, Joao, M. (2011). *Conflicts in Curriculum Theory. Challenging Hegemonic Epistemicides*. New York: Palgrave.

Puett, T. (2005). "On Transforming the World: Critical Pedagogy for Interfaith Education." *Cross Currents, 55*(2), (Summer), 264–73.

Puigvert, L. and Santacruz, I. (2006). "La Transformación de Centros Educativos en Comunidades de Aprendizaje: Calidad para Todas y Todos" (The Transformation of Education Centres into Communities of Learning: Quality for All, Women and Men). *Revista de Educación, 339*, 169–176.

Purpel, D. (1989). *The Moral and Spiritual Crisis in Education: A Curriculum for Justice and Compassion in Education*. South Hadley, MA: Bergin & Garvey.

Rodney, W. (1973). *How Europe Underdeveloped Africa*. London and Dar Es Salaam: Bogle-L'Ouverture Publications.

Rosa, R. and Rosa, J. (2015) *Capitalism's Educational Catastrophe*. New York: Peter Lang.

Santos, B. de Sousa (1995). *Toward a New Common Sense: Law, Science and Politics in the Paradigmatic Transition*. Nova Iorque: Routledge.

Santos, B. de Sousa (2002). *Toward a New Legal Common Sense. Law, Globalization, and Emancipation*. Londres: Butterworths.

Santos, B. de Sousa (2006). *The Rise of the Global Left: The World Social Forum and Beyond*. Londres: Zed Books.

Santos, B. de Sousa (2014). *Epistemologies of the South. Justice against Epistemicide*. Boulder/Londres: Paradigm Publishers.

Schoorman, D., Acosta, M., Sena, R., and Baxley, T. (2012). "Critical Pedagogy in HIV-AIDS Education for a Maya Immigrant Community." *Multicultural Perspectives, 14*(4), 194–200.

Schugurensky, D. (2002). "Transformative Learning and Transformative Politics. The Pedagogical Dimension of Participatory Democracy and Social Action." In O'Sullivan, E., Morrell, A., and O'Connor, M. (eds.), *Expanding the Boundaries of Transformative Learning*. New York: Palgrave.

Shiva, V. (2003). "The Living Democracy Movement: Alternatives to the Bankruptcy of Globalization." In Fisher, W. and Ponniah, T. (eds.), *Another World Is Possible. Popular Alternatives to Globalization at the World Social Forum* (pp. 115–124). London: Zed Books; Nova Scotia: Fernwood Publishers; Malaysia: SIRD; South Africa: David Philip.

Shor, I. (1980). *Critical Teaching and Everyday Life*. Boston: South End Press.

Shor, I. (1992). *Empowering Education: Critical Teaching for Social Change*. Chicago: University of Chicago Press.

Shor, I. and Freire, P. (1987). *A Pedagogy for Liberation: Dialogues on Transforming Education*. South Hadley, MA: Bergin & Garvey.

Silwadi, N. and Mayo, P. (2014). "Education under Siege in Palestine. Insights from Freire." *Holy Land Studies, 13*(1), 71–87.

Simon, R. (1992). *Teaching against the Grain: A Pedagogy of Possibility*. New York: Bergin and Garvey.

Steinberg, S. R. (1997). *Kinderculture: The Corporate Construction of Childhood*. Boulder, CO: Westview.

Steiner, S. (1999). *Freireian Pedagogy, Praxis, and Possibilities: Projects for the New Millennium*. Oxford: RoutledgeFalmer.

Stevenson, N. (2010). "Critical Pedagogy, Democracy and Capitalism." *Review of Education, Pedagogy, and Cultural Studies, 32*, 66–92.

Strech, D. (2010). *A New Social Contract in a Latin American Context*. London and New York: Palgrave-Macmillan.

Subedi, B., ed. (2010). *Critical Global Perspectives: Rethinking Knowledge about Global Societies*. Charlotte, NC: Information Age Publishing, Inc.

Sullivan, E. (1990). *Critical Psychology and Pedagogy: Interpretation of the Personal World*. New York: Bergin & Garvey.

Sünker, H. (1997). *Education and Fascism: Political Formation and Social Education in German National Socialism*. London and New York: Routledge.

Sünker, H. (2006). "Globalization, Democratic Education (Bildung), Educating for Democracy." *Journal of International Association for the Advancement of Curriculum Studies, 3*(2), 16–30.

Tierney, W. (1993). *Building Communities of Difference: Higher Education in the Twenty-First Century*. Westport, CT: Bergin & Garvey.

Tisdell, E. and Thompson, M. (2007). *Popular Culture and Entertainment Media in Adult Education.* San Francisco: Jossey-Bass.

Torres, C. A. (ed.) (2000). *Challenges of Urban Education.* Albany, NY: SUNY Press.

Trend, D. (2003). "Merchants of Death: Media Violence and American Empire." *Harvard Educational Review, 73*(3), 285–307.

Ty, R. (2011). "Social Injustice, Human Rights-Based Education and Citizens' Direct Action to Promote Social Transformation in the Philippines." *Education, Citizenship and Social Justice, 6*(3), 205–221.

Veuglers, W. (2007). "Creating Critical-Democratic Citizenship Education: Empowering Humanity and Democracy in Dutch Education." *Compare, 37*, 105–119.

Vigilante, A. and Vittoria, P. (2011). *Pedagogie della Liberazione. Freire, Boal, Capitini, Dolci* (Pedagogies of Liberation: Freire, Boal, Capitini, Dolci). Foggia: Edizioni del Rosone.

Wiggins, N. (2011). "Critical Pedagogy and Popular Education: Towards a Unity of Theory and Practice." *Studies in the Education of Adults, 43*, 34–49.

Willhauck, S. (2009). "Crossing Pedagogical Borders in the Yucatan Peninsula." *Teaching Theology and Religion, 12*(3), 222–232.

Afterword: The War Against Teachers as Public Intellectuals

Henry A. Giroux

A little learning is a dangerous thing.

Alexander Pope

Right-wing fundamentalists and corporate ideologues are not just waging a war against the rights of unions, workers, students, women, the disabled, low-income groups and poor minorities, but also against those public spheres that provide a vocabulary for connecting values, desires, identities, social relations and institutions to the discourse of social responsibility, ethics and democracy, if not thinking itself. Neoliberalism, or unbridled free-market fundamentalism, employs modes of governance, discipline and regulation that are totalizing in their insistence that all aspects of social life be determined, shaped and weighted through market-driven measures.[2] Neoliberalism is not merely an economic doctrine that prioritizes buying and selling, makes the supermarket and mall the temples of public life and defines the obligations of citizenship in strictly consumerist terms. It is also a mode of pedagogy and set of social arrangements that uses education to win consent, produce consumer-based notions of agency and militarize reason in the service of war, profits, power and violence while simultaneously instrumentalizing all forms of knowledge.

The increasing militarization of reason and growing expansion of forms of militarized discipline are most visible in policies currently promoted by wealthy conservative foundations such as the Heritage Foundation and the American Enterprise Institute, along with the high-profile presence and advocacy of corporate reform spokespersons such as Joel Klein and Michelle Rhee and billionaire financers such as Michael Milken.[3] As Ken Saltman, Diane Ravitch, Alex Means and others have pointed out, wealthy billionaires such as Bill Gates are financing educational reforms that promote privatization, de-professionalization, online classes and high-stakes testing, while at the same time impugning the character and autonomy of teachers and the unions that support them.[4] Consequently, public school teachers have become the new class of government-dependent moochers and the disparaged culture of Wall Street has emerged as the only model or resource from which to develop theories of educational leadership and reform.[5] The same people who gave us the economic recession of 2008, lost billions in corrupt trading practices and sold fraudulent mortgages to millions of homeowners have ironically become sources of wisdom and insight regarding how young people should be educated.

Attesting to the fact that political culture has become an adjunct of the culture of finance, politicians at the state and federal levels, irrespective of their political affiliation, advocate reforms that amount to selling off or giving away public schools to the apostles of casino capitalism.[6] More importantly, the hysterical fury now being waged by the new educational reformists against public education exhibits no interest in modes of education that invest in an "educated public for the culture of the present and future."[7] On the contrary, their relevance and power can be measured by the speed with which any notion of civic responsibilities is evaded.

What these individuals and institutions all share is an utter disregard for public values, critical thinking and any notion of education as a moral and political practice.[8] The wealthy hedge fund managers, think tank operatives and increasingly corrupt corporate CEOs are panicked by the possibility that teachers and public schools might provide the conditions for the cultivation of an informed and critical citizenry capable of actively and critically participating in the governance of a democratic society. In the name of educational reform, reason is gutted of its critical potential and reduced to a deadening pedagogy of memorization, teaching to the test and classroom practices that celebrate mindless repetition and conformity. Rather than embraced as central to what it means to be an engaged and thoughtful citizen, the capacity for critical thinking, imagining and reflection are derided as crucial pedagogical values necessary for "both the health of democracy and to the creation of a decent world culture and a robust type of global citizenship."[9]

This is clear by virtue of the fact that testing and punishing have become the two most influential forces that now shape American public education. As Stanley Aronowitz points out,

> Numerous studies have shown the tendency of public schooling to dumb down the curriculum and impose punitive testing algorithms on teachers and students alike. Whether intended or not, we live in an era when the traditional concepts of liberal education and popular critical thinking are under assault. Neo-liberals of the center, no less than those of the right, are equally committed to the reduction of education to a mean-spirited regime of keeping its subjects' noses to the grindstone. As the post-war "prosperity," which offered limited opportunities to some from the lower orders to gain a measure of mobility fades into memory, the chief function of schools is repression.[10]

Instead of talking about the relationship between schools and democracy, the new educational reformers call for the disinvestment in public schools, the militarization of school culture, the commodification of knowledge and the privatizing of both the learning process and the spaces in which it takes place. The crusade for privatizing is now advanced with a vengeance by the corporate elite, a crusade designed to place the control of public schools and other public spheres in the alleged reliable hands of the apostles of casino capitalism.[11] Budgets are now balanced on the backs of teachers and students while the wealthy get tax reductions and the promise of gentrification and private schools.[12] In the name of austerity, schools are defunded so as to fail and provide an excuse to be turned over to the privatizing advocates of free-market fundamentalism. In this discourse, free-market reform refuses to imagine public education as the provision of the public good and social right and reduces education to meet the immediate needs of the economy.

For those schools and students that are considered excess, the assault on reason is matched by the enactment of a militaristic culture of security, policing and containment, particularly in urban schools.[13] Low-income and poor minority students now attend schools that have more security guards than teachers and are educated to believe that there is no distinction between prison culture and the culture of schooling.[14] The underlying theme that connects the current attack on reason and the militarizing of social relations is that education is both a Petri dish for producing individuals who are wedded to the logic of the market and consumerism and a sorting machine for ushering largely poor black and brown youth into the criminal justice system. There is no language among these various political positions for defending public schools as a vital social institution and public good. Public education, in this view, no longer benefits the entire society but only individuals and, rather than being defined as a public good, is redefined as a private right.

Within this atomistic, highly individualizing script, shared struggles and bonds of solidarity are viewed as either dangerous or pathological. Power relations disappear and there is no room for understanding how corporate power and civic values rub up against each other in ways that are detrimental to the promise of a robust democracy and an emancipatory mode of schooling. In fact, in this discourse, corporate power is used to undermine any vestige of the civic good and cover up the detrimental influence of its anti-democratic pressures. It gets worse. A pedagogy of management and conformity does more than simply repress the analytical skills and knowledge necessary for students to learn the practice of freedom and assume the role of critical agents, it also reinforces deeply authoritarian lessons while reproducing deep inequities in the educational opportunities that different students acquire. As Sara Robinson points out,

> In the conservative model, critical thinking is horrifically dangerous, because it teaches kids to reject the assessment of external authorities in favor of their own judgment—a habit of mind that invites opposition and rebellion. This is why, for much of Western history, critical thinking skills have only been taught to the elite students— the ones headed for the professions, who will be entrusted with managing society on behalf of the aristocracy. (The aristocrats, of course, are sending their kids to private schools, where they will receive a classical education that teaches them everything they'll need to know to remain in charge.) Our public schools, unfortunately, have replicated a class stratification on this front that's been in place since the Renaissance.[15]

As powerful as this utterly reactionary and right-wing educational reform movement might be, educators are far from willingly accepting the role of deskilled technicians groomed to service the needs of finance capital and produce students who are happy consumers and unquestioning future workers. Public school teachers have mobilized in Wisconsin and a number of other states where public schools, educators and other public servants are under attack. They have been collectively energized in pushing back the corporate and religious fundamentalist visions of public education, and they are slowly mobilizing into a larger social movement to defend both their role as engaged intellectuals and schooling as a public good. In refusing to be fit for domestication, many teachers are committed to fulfilling the civic purpose of public education through a new understanding of the relationship between democracy and schooling, learning and social change. In the interest of expanding this struggle, educators need a new vocabulary for not only defining schools as democratic public spheres, students as informed and critically engaged citizens, but also teachers as public intellectuals. In what follows, I want to focus on this issue as one important register of individual and collective struggle for teachers. At stake here is the presupposition that a critical consciousness is not only necessary for producing good teachers, but also enables individual teachers to see their classroom struggles as part of a much broader social, political and economic landscape.

Unlike many past educational reform movements, the present call for educational change presents both a threat and a challenge to public school teachers that appear unprecedented. The threat comes in the form of a series of educational reforms that display little confidence in the ability of public school teachers to provide intellectual and moral leadership for our youth. For instance, many recommendations that have emerged in the current debate across the world either ignore the role teachers play in preparing learners to be active and critical citizens or they suggest reforms that ignore the intelligence, judgment and experience that teachers might offer in such a debate. At the same time, the current conservative reform movement aggressively disinvests in public schooling so as to eliminate the literal spaces and resources necessary for schools to work successfully.

Where teachers do enter the debate, they are objects of educational reforms that reduce them to the status of high-level technicians carrying out dictates and objectives decided by experts far removed from the everyday realities of classroom life. Or they are reduced to the status of commercial salespersons selling knowledge, skills and values that have less to do with education than with training students for low-wage jobs in a global marketplace. Or, even worse, they are reduced to security officers employed largely to discipline, contain, and all too often, turn students who commit infractions over to the police and the criminal justice system.[16] Not only do students not count in this mode of schooling, teachers are also stripped of their dignity and capacities when it comes to critically examining the nature and process of educational reform.

While the political and ideological climate does not look favorable for the teachers at the moment, it does offer them the challenge to join a public debate with their critics, as well as the opportunity to engage in a much needed self-critique regarding the nature and purpose of schooling, classroom teaching and the relationship between education and social change. Similarly, the debate provides teachers with the opportunity to organize collectively to improve the conditions under which they work and to demonstrate to the public the central role that teachers must play in any viable attempt to reform the public schools.

In order for teachers and others to engage in such a debate, it is necessary that theoretical perspectives be developed that redefine the nature of the current educational crisis while simultaneously providing the basis for an alternative view of teacher work. In short, this means recognizing that the current crisis in education cannot be separated from the rise and pernicious influence of neoliberal capitalism and market driven power relations, both of which work in the interest of disempowering teachers, dismantling teacher unions and privatizing public schools. At the very least, such recognition will have to come to grips with a growing loss of power among teachers around the basic conditions of their work, but also with a changing public perception of their role as reflective practitioners.

I want to make a small theoretical contribution to this debate and the challenge it calls forth by examining two major problems that need to be addressed in the interest of improving the quality of "teacher work," which includes all the clerical tasks and extra assignments as well as classroom instruction. First, I think it is imperative to examine the ideological and material forces that have contributed to what I want to call the deskilling and commodification of teacher work; that is, the tendency to reduce teachers to the status of specialized technicians within the school bureaucracy, whose function then becomes one of the managing and implementing curricular programs rather than developing or critically appropriating curricula to fit specific pedagogical concerns and the particular needs of students. Second, there is a need to defend schools as institutions essential to maintaining and developing a critical democracy and also to defending teachers as public intellectuals who combine scholarly reflection and practice in the service of educating students to be thoughtful, active citizens.

Devaluing and Deskilling Teacher Work

One of the major threats facing prospective and existing teachers within the public schools is the increasing development of instrumental and corporate ideologies that emphasize a technocratic approach to both teacher preparation and classroom pedagogy. At the core of the current emphasis on the instrumental and pragmatic factors in school life are a number of important pedagogical assumptions. These include: a call for the separation of conception from execution; the standardization of school knowledge in the interest of managing and controlling it, the increased call for standardized testing, and the devaluation of critical, intellectual work on the part of teachers and students for the primacy of practical considerations. In this view, teaching is reduced to training and concepts are substituted by methods. Teaching in this view is reduced to a set of strategies and skills and becomes synonymous with a method or technique. Instead of learning to raise questions about the principles underlying different classroom methods, research techniques and theories of education, teachers are often preoccupied with learning the "how to," with what works or with mastering the best way to teach a given body of knowledge.

What is ignored in this retrograde view is any understanding of pedagogy as a moral and political practice that functions as a deliberate attempt to influence how and what knowledge, values and identities are produced with particular sets of classroom social relations. What is purposely derided in conservative notions of teaching and learning is a view of pedagogy, which in the most critical sense, illuminates the relationship among knowledge, authority and power and draws attention to questions concerning who has control over the conditions for the production of knowledge. Pedagogy in this sense addresses and connects ethics, politics, power and knowledge within practices that allow for generating multiple solidarities, narratives and vocabularies as part of a broader democratic project. As Chandra Mohanty insists, pedagogy is not only about the act of knowing, but also about how knowledge is related to the power of self-definition, understanding one's relationship to others and one's understanding and connection to the larger world.[17] In the end, pedagogy is not, as many conservatives argue, about immersing young people in predefined and isolated bits of information, but about the issue of agency and how it can be developed in the interest of deepening and expanding the meaning and purpose of democratization and the formative cultures that make it possible.

Technocratic and instrumental rationalities are also at work within the teaching field itself, and they play an increasing role in reducing teacher autonomy with respect to the development and planning of curricula and the judging and implementation of classroom instruction. In the past, this took the form of what has been called "teacher-proof" curriculum packages. The underlying rationale in many of these packages viewed teacher work as simply the carrying out of predetermined content and instructional procedures. The method and aim of such packages was to legitimate what might be called "market-driven management pedagogies." That knowledge is broken down into discrete parts, standardized for easier management and consumption and measured through predefined forms of assessment. Curricular approaches of this sort are management pedagogies because the central questions regarding teaching and learning are reduced to the problems of management, regulation and control. While such curricula are far from absent in many schools, they have been replaced by modes of classroom instruction geared to a pedagogy of repression defined through the rubric of accountability. This approach works to discipline both the body and mind in the interest of training students to perform well in high-stakes testing schemes. It defines quality teaching through reductive mathematical models.[18]

Pedagogy as an intellectual, moral and political practice is now based on "measurements of value derived from market competition."[19] Mathematical utility has now replaced critical dialogue, debate, risk-taking, the power of imaginative leaps and learning for the sake of learning. A crude instrumental rationality now governs the form and content of curricula, and where content has the potential to open up the possibility of critical thinking, it is quickly shut down. This is a pedagogy that has led to the abandonment of democratic impulses, analytic thinking and social responsibility. It is also a pedagogy that infantilizes both teachers and students. For instance, the Texas GOP built into its platform the banning of critical thinking.[20] Not too long ago, the Florida legislature passed a law claiming that history had to be taught simply as a ledger of facts, banning any attempt at what can loosely be called interpretation.

The soft underlying theoretical assumption that guides this type of pedagogy is that the behavior of teachers needs to be controlled and made consistent and predictable across different schools and student populations. The more hidden and hard assumption at work here is that teachers cannot be intellectuals, cannot think imaginatively and cannot engage in forms of pedagogy that might enable students to think differently, critically or more imaginatively. The deskilling of teachers, the reduction of reason to a form of instrumental rationality, and the disinvestment in education as a public good is also evident on a global level in policies produced by the World Bank that impose on countries forms of privatization and standardized curricula that undermine the potential for critical inquiry and engaged citizenship. Learning in this instance is depoliticized, prioritized as a method and often reduced to teaching low-level skills, disciplinary-imposed behaviors and corporate values. Neoliberal disciplinary measures now function to limit students to the private orbits in which they experience their lives while restricting the power of teachers to teach students to think rationally, judge wisely and be able to connect private troubles to broader public considerations.

Public schools have become an object of disdain, and teachers labor under educational reforms that separate conception from execution, theory from practice, and pedagogy from moral and social considerations. As content is devalued, history erased and the economic, racial and social inequities intensified, public schools increasingly are hijacked by corporate and religious fundamentalists. The effect is not only to deskill teachers, to remove them from the processes of deliberation and reflection, but also to routinize the nature of learning and classroom pedagogy. Needless to say, the principles underlying corporate pedagogies are at odds with the premise that teachers should be actively involved in producing curricular materials suited to the cultural and social contexts in which they teach.

More specifically, the narrowing of curricular choices to a back-to-basics format and the introduction of lock-step, time-on-task pedagogies operate from the theoretically erroneous assumption that all students can learn from the same materials, classroom instructional techniques and modes of evaluation. The notion that students come from different histories and embody different experiences, linguistic practices, cultures and talents is strategically ignored within the logic and accountability of management pedagogy theory. At the same time, the school increasingly is modeled as a factory, prison or both. Curiosity is replaced by monotony, and learning withers under the weight of dead time.

Teachers as Public Intellectuals

In what follows, I want to argue that one way to rethink and restructure the nature of teacher work is to view teachers as public intellectuals. The category of intellectual is helpful in a number of ways. First, it provides a theoretical basis for examining teacher work as a form of intellectual labor, as opposed to defining it in purely instrumental or technical terms. Second, it clarifies the kinds of ideological and practical conditions necessary for teachers to function as intellectuals. Third, it helps to make clear the role teachers play in producing and legitimating various political, economic and social interests through the pedagogies they endorse and utilize.

By viewing teachers as public intellectuals, we can illuminate the important idea that all human activity involves some form of thinking. No activity, regardless of how routinized it might become, can be abstracted from the functioning of the mind in some capacity. This is a crucial issue, because by arguing that the use of the mind is a general part of all human activity we dignify the human capacity for integrating thinking and practice, and in doing so highlight the core of what it means to view teachers as reflective practitioners. Within this discourse, teachers can be seen not merely as "performers professionally equipped to realize effectively any goals that may be set for them. Rather [they should] be viewed as free men and women with a special dedication to the values of the intellect and the enhancement of the critical powers of the young."[21]

Viewing teachers as public intellectuals also provides a strong theoretical critique of technocratic and instrumental ideologies underlying educational theories that separate the conceptualization, planning and design of curricula from the processes of implementation and execution. It is important to stress that teachers must take active responsibility for raising serious questions about what they teach, how they are to teach and what the larger goals are for which they are striving. This means that they must take a responsible role in shaping the purposes and conditions of schooling. Such a task is impossible within a division of labor in which teachers have little influence over the conceptual and economic conditions of their work. This point has a normative and political dimension that seems especially relevant for teachers. If we believe that the role of teaching cannot be reduced to merely training in the practical skills but involves, instead, the education of a class of engaged and public intellectuals vital to the development of a free society, then the category of intellectual becomes a way of linking the purpose of teacher education, public schooling and in-service training to the principles necessary for developing a democratic order and society. Recognizing teachers as engaged and public intellectuals means that educators should never be reduced to technicians, just as education should never be reduced to training. Instead, pedagogy should be rooted in the practice of freedom—in those ethical and political formations that expand democratic underpinnings and principles of both the self and the broader social order.

I have argued that by viewing teachers as intellectuals we can begin to rethink and reform the traditions and conditions that have prevented teachers from assuming their full potential as active, reflective scholars and practitioners. I believe that it is important not only to view teachers as public intellectuals, but also to contextualize in political and normative terms the concrete social functions that teachers have both to their work and to the dominant society.

A starting point for interrogating the social function of teachers as public intellectuals is to view schools as economic, cultural and social sites that are inextricably tied to the issues of politics, power and control. This means that schools do more than pass on in an objective fashion a common set of values and knowledge. On the contrary, schools are places that represent forms of knowledge, language practices, social relations and values that are particular selections and exclusions from the wider culture. As such, schools serve to introduce and legitimate particular forms of social life. Rather than being objective institutions removed from the dynamics of politics and power, schools actually are contested spheres that embody and express struggles over what forms of authority, types of knowledge, forms of moral regulation and versions of the past and future should be legitimated and transmitted to students.

Schools are always political because they both produce particular kinds of agents, desires and social relations and they legitimate particular notions of the past, present and future.

The struggle is most visible in the demands, for example, of right-wing religious groups currently trying to inject creationism in the schools, institute school prayer, remove certain books from school libraries and include certain forms of religious teachings in the curricula. Of course, different demands are made by feminists, ecologists, minorities, and other interest groups who believe that the schools should teach women's studies, courses on the environment or black history. In short, schools are not neutral sites, and teachers cannot assume the posture of being neutral either.

Central to the category of public intellectual is the necessity of making the pedagogical more political and the political more pedagogical. Making the pedagogical more political means inserting schooling directly into the political sphere by arguing that schooling represents both a struggle to define meaning and a struggle over agency and power relations. Within this perspective, critical reflection and action become part of a fundamental social project to help students develop a deep and abiding faith in the struggle to overcome economic, political and social injustices, and to further humanize themselves as part of this struggle. In this case, knowledge and power are inextricably linked to the presupposition that to choose life, to recognize the necessity of improving its democratic and qualitative character for all people, is to understand the preconditions necessary to struggle for it. Teaching must be seen as a political, civic and ethical practice precisely because it is directive, that is, an intervention that takes up the ethical responsibility of recognizing, as Paulo Freire points out, that human life is conditioned but not determined.

A critical pedagogical practice does not transfer knowledge but create the possibilities for its production, analysis and use. Without succumbing to a kind of rigid dogmatism, teachers should provide the pedagogical conditions for students to bear witness to history, their own actions and the mechanisms that drive the larger social order so that they can imagine the inseparable connection between the human condition and the ethical basis of our existence. Educators have a responsibility for educating students in ways that allow them to hold power accountable, learn how to govern and develop a responsibility to others and a respect for civic life. The key here is to recognize that being a public intellectual is no excuse for being dogmatic. While it is crucial to recognize that education has a critical function, the teachers' task is not to mold students but to encourage human agency, to provide the conditions for students to be self-determining and to struggle for a society that is both autonomous and democratic.

Making the political more pedagogical means treating students as critical agents; making knowledge problematic and open to debate; engaging in critical and thoughtful dialogue; and making the case for a qualitatively better world for all people. In part, this suggests that teachers as public intellectuals take seriously the need to give students an active voice in their learning experiences. It also means developing a critical vernacular that is attentive to problems experienced at the level of everyday life, particularly as they are related to pedagogical experiences connected to classroom practice. As such, the pedagogical starting point for such intellectuals is not the isolated student removed from the historical and cultural forces that bear down on their lives but individuals in their various cultural, class, racial and historical contexts, along with the particularity of their diverse problems, hopes and dreams.

As public intellectuals, teachers should develop a discourse that unites the language of critique with the language of possibility. In this instance, educators not only recognize the need to act on the world, to connect reading the word with reading the world, but also make clear that it is within their power individually and collectively to do so. In taking up this project, they should work under conditions that allow them to speak out against economic, political and social injustices both within and outside of schools. At the same time, they should work to create the conditions that give students the opportunity to become critical and engaged citizens who have the knowledge and courage to struggle in order to make desolation and cynicism unconvincing and hope practical. Hope in this case is neither a call to social engineering nor an excuse to overlook the difficult conditions that shape both schools and the larger social order. On the contrary, it is the precondition for providing those languages and values that point the way to a more democratic and just world. As Judith Butler has argued, there is more hope in the world when we can question common sense assumptions and believe that what we know is directly related to our ability to help change the world around us, though it is far from the only condition necessary for such change.[22] Hope provides the basis for dignifying our labor as intellectuals; it offers up critical knowledge linked to democratic social change, and allows teachers and students to recognize ambivalence and uncertainty as fundamental dimensions of learning. As Ernst Bloch insists, hope is "not yet in the sense of a possibility; that it could be there if we could only do something for it."[23] Hope offers the possibility of thinking beyond the given—and lays open a pedagogical terrain in which teachers and students can engage in critique, dialogue and an open-ended struggle for justice. As difficult as this task may seem to educators, if not to a larger public, it is a struggle worth waging. To deny educators the opportunity to assume the role of public intellectuals is to prevent teachers from gaining control over the conditions of the work, denying them the right to "push at the frontiers, to worry the edges of the human imagination, to conjure beauty from the most unexpected things, to find magic in places where others never thought to look,"[24] and to model what it means for intellectuals to exhibit civic courage by giving education a central role in constructing a world that is more just, equitable and democratic in dark times.

What role might public school teachers play as public intellectuals in light of the brutal killings at Sandy Hook Elementary School? In the most immediate sense, they can raise their collective voices against the educational influence of a larger culture and spectacle of violence and the power of the gun lobby to flood the country with deadly weapons. They can show how this culture of violence is only one part of a broader and all-embracing militarized culture of war, arms industry and a Darwinian survival of the fittest ethic, more characteristic of an authoritarian society than a democracy. They can mobilize young people to both stand up for teachers, students and public schools by advocating for policies that invest in schools rather than in the military-industrial complex and its massive and expensive weapons of death. They can educate young people and a larger public to support gun regulation and the democratization of the culture industries that now trade in violence as a form of entertainment; they can speak out against the educational, political and economic conditions in which violence has become a sport in America—one of the most valuable practices and assets of the national entertainment state. The violent screen culture of video games, extreme sports, violent Hollywood films, television dramas and other cultural productions do not just produce entertainment, they are mainly teaching machines that instruct children into a sadistic culture in which killing is all right, violence is fun and masculinity is defined increasingly through its propensity to make celebrities out of killers. This is a culture that serves as a recruiting tool for the military, makes military force rather than democratic idealism the highest national ideal and war the most important organizing principle of society.

Public school teachers can join with parents, churches, synagogues, Mosques and other individuals and institutions to address the larger socioeconomic and ideological values and practices that legitimize a hyper-masculinity fueled by the death-dealing assumption that war and a primitive tribalism make men, irrespective of the violence they promote against women, gays, students and people with disabilities. America is obsessed with violence and death, and this fixation not only provides profits for Hollywood, the defense industries and the weapons industries, it also reproduces a culture of war and cruelty that has become central to America's national identity—one that is as shameful as it is deadly to its children and others. The war on public school teachers and children has reached its tragic apogee with the brutal and incomprehensible killing of the young children in Sandy Hook. What kind of country has the United States become in its willingness allow this endless barrage of symbolic and material violence to continue? Why has violence become the most powerful mediating force shaping social relations in the United States? Why do we allow a government to use drones to kill young children abroad? Why do we allow the right-wing media and the mainstream press to constantly denigrate both teachers and young people? Why are the lives of young people one of our lowest national priorities? Why do we denigrate public servants such as teachers, who educate, nurture and safeguard young people? What kind of country betrays its teachers and denigrates public education? How does the violence against teachers and students destroy the connective tissue that makes the shared bonds of trust, compassion and justice possible not only in our schools but also in a democracy?

Notes

1. Adam Bessie, "Public Teachers: America's New 'Welfare Queens'" *Truthout* (March 6, 2011). For a list such humiliations, see VetGrl, "Here are your Parasites and Terrorists, M*therf*ckers," *Daily Kos* (December 15, 2012). Online: http://www.dailykos.com/story/2012/12/15/1170268/-Here-are-your-parasites-and-terrorists-m-therf-ckers
2. Manfred B. Steger and Ravi K. Roy, *Neoliberalism: A Very Short Introduction* (Oxford University Press, 2010); Henry A. Giroux, *Against the Terror of Neoliberalism* (Boulder: Paradigm Press, 2008); David Harvey, *A Brief History of Neoliberalism* (New York: Oxford University Press, 2005).
3. Diane Ravitch, "The People Behind the Lawmakers Out to Destroy Public Education: A Primer: What You Need to Know about ALEC," *CommonDreams* (May 2, 2012).
4. See Henry A. Giroux, *Education and the Struggle for Public Values* (Boulder: Paradigm, 2012); Ken Saltman, *The Failure of Corporate School Reform* (New York: Palgrave, 2012); Diane Ravitch, *The Death and Life of the Great American School System* (New York: Basic Books, 2011); Alex Means, *Schooling in the Age of Austerity* (New York: Palgrave, 2013).
5. In the corruption of Wall Street, see, for example, Jeff Madrick, *Age of Greed: The Triumph of Finance and the Decline of America, 1970 to the Present* (New York: Vintage, 2011); Charles Ferguson, *Predator Nation* (New York: Crown Business, 2012); Henry A. Giroux, *Zombie Politics in the Age of Casino Capitalism* (New York: Peter Lang, 2010).
6. I am not just talking about right-wing Republicans but also about the Obama administration policy on education, which has reproduced the worst dimensions of the former Bush administration's policies on educational reform, which are as reactionary as they are detrimental to the quality, if not future, of public education in the United States.
7. Mustafha Marruchi, "The Value of Literature as a Public Institution," *College Literature* 33: 4 (Fall 2006), p. 176.
8. Sara Robinson, "How the Conservative Worldview Quashes Critical Thinking—And What That Means for Our Kids' Future," *AlterNet* (May 20, 2012). Online: http://www.alternet.org/education/155469/how_the_conservative_world view_quashes_critical_thinking_--_and_what_that_means_for_our_kids%27_future?page=entire.
9. Martha C. Nussbaum, "Education for Profit, Education for Freedom," *Liberal Education* (Summer 2009), p. 6. Also see, Martha C. Nussbaum, *Not for Profit: Why Democracy Needs the Humanities* (Princeton, NJ: Princeton University Press, 2010).
10. Stanley Aronowitz, "Paulo Freire's Pedagogy: Not Mainly a Teaching Method," in Robert Lake and Tricia Kress, *Paulo Freire's Intellectual Roots: Toward Historicity in Praxis* (New York: Continuum, 2012).
11. Noam Chomsky, "The Assault on Public Education," *TruthOut* (April 4, 2012).
12. Les Leopold, "Hey Dad, Why Does this Country Protect Billionaires, and Not Teachers?" *AlterNet* (May 5, 2010).
13. Ken Saltman and David A. Gabbard (eds.), *Education as Enforcement: The Militarization and Corporatization of Schools*, 2nd edition (New York: Routledge, 2010); David A. Gabbard and E. Wayne Ross (eds.), *Education Under the Security State (Defending Public Schools)* (New York: Teachers College Press, 2008).
14. Henry Giroux, *Youth in a Suspect Society: Democracy or Disposability* (New York: Palgrave, 2009).
15. Ibid., Robinson, "How the Conservative Worldview Quashes Critical Thinking—And What That Means for Our Kids' Future."
16. There is a great deal of literature written about zero-tolerance policies. For a brilliant academic discussion, see Christopher Robbins, *Expelling Hope: The Assault on Youth and the Militarization of Schooling* (New York: SUNY

Press, 2009); Julianne Hing, "The Shocking Details of a Mississippi School-to-Prison Pipeline," *Truthout* (December 3, 2012); Donna Lierberman, "Schoolhouse to Courthouse," *The New York Times* (December 8, 2012).

17. Chandra Mohanty, "On Race and Voice: Challenges for Liberal Education in the 1990s," *Cultural Critique* (Winter 1989–1990), p. 192.
18. See, for example, Sam Dillon, "Formula to Grade Teachers' Skill Gains in Use, and Critics," *New York Times* (August 31, 2010), p. A1.
19. Michael Collins, "Universities Need Reform—But the Market is Not the Answer," *openDemocracy* (November 23, 2010).
20. Danny Weil, "Texas GOP Declares: 'No More Teaching of "Critical Thinking Skills" in Texas Public Schools'" *Truthout* (July 7, 2012).
21. Israel Scheffler, *Reason and Teaching* (New York: Routledge, 1973), p. 92.
22. Cited in Gary Olson and Lynn Worsham, "Changing the Subject: Judith Butler's Politics of Radical Resignification," *JAC* 20:4 (200), p. 765.
23. Ernst Bloch, "Something's Missing: A Discussion Between Ernst Bloch and Theodor W. Adorno on the Contradictions of Utopian Longing," in Ernst Bloch, *The Utopian Function of Art and Literature: Selected Essays* (Cambridge, MA: MIT Press, 1988), p. 3.
24. Arundhati Roy, *Power Politics* (Cambridge: South End Press, 2001), p. 1.

Permissions

Giroux, Henry A. "Critical Theory and Educational Practice" in *Theory and Resistance in Education* by Henry A. Giroux, pp. 7–41. Copyright © 1983 by Bergin & Garvey. Reproduced with permission of Greenwood Publishing Group, Inc., Westport, CT.

McLaren, Peter, "Critical Pedagogy: A Look at the Major Concepts" from Peter McLaren, *Life in Schools: An Introduction to Critical Pedagogy in the Foundations of Education.* Published by Allyn and Bacon, Boston, MA. © 1989 by Pearson Education. Reprinted by permission of the publisher.

Apple, Michael W. "Cultural Politics and the Text" from *Official Knowledge: Democratic Education in a Conservative Age,* by Michael W. Apple. New York: Routledge, 1999, pp. 42–60. Reprinted with permission of Routledge, a member of Taylor & Francis Books.

Darder, Antonia. "Pedagogy of Love: Embodying Our Humanity" from *Reinventing Paulo Freire: A Pedagogy of Love,* by Antonia Darder. Boulder, CO: Westview Press, 2002, pp. 32–48. Reprinted with permission from Westview Press, a member of the Perseus Book Group

Aronowitz, Stanley, "Against Schooling: Education and Social Class" in *Social Text,* vol. 22, Summer 2004. pp. 13–35. © 2004, Duke University Press. All rights reserved. Used by permission of the publisher.

Anyon, Jean. "Social Class and the Hidden Curriculum of Work" in *Journal of Education,* vol. 162.1, Winter 1980. pp. 67–92. © 1980, Trustees of Boston University. All rights reserved. Used by permission of the publisher.

Malott, Curry Stephenson. "Class Consciousness and Teacher Education: The Socialist Challenge and the Historical Context" in *Cultural Logic: An Electronic Journal of Marxist Theory and Practice,* "Special Issue: Education for Revolution," edited by E. Wayne Ross & Rich Gibson, Special Issue. © 2013, Cultural Logic. All rights reserved. Used by permission of the publisher.

hooks, bell, "Confronting Class in the Classroom" from *Teaching to Transgress* by bell hooks. © 1994. pp 177–190. Reprinted with permission from Routledge, a member of Taylor & Francis Books.

Bartolomé, Lilia I. and Donaldo P. Macedo. "Dancing with Bigotry: The Poisoning of Racial and Ethnic Identities" in *Harvard Educational Review,* vol. 67.2, Summer 1997. pp. 222–246. © 1997, the President and Fellows of Harvard College. All rights reserved. Used by permission of the publisher.

Grande, Sandy Marie Anglás. "American Indian Geographies of Identity and Power: At the Crossroads of Indigena and Mestizaje" in *Harvard Educational Review,* vol. 70.4, Winter 2000. pp. 467–498. © 2000, the President and Fellows of Harvard College. All rights reserved. Used by permission of the publisher.

Lam, Kevin D. "Theories of Racism, Asian American Identities, and a Materialist Critical Pedagogy" in Journal for Critical Education Policy Studies, vol. 13.1, Jun 2015. pp. 83–102. © 2015, Institute for Education Policy Studies. All rights reserved. Used by permission of the publisher.

Orelus, Pierre. "Decolonizing Schools and Our Mentality: Narratives for Pedagogical Possibilities" in *Excellence in Education Journal,* vol. 2.1, Spring 2013. pp. 4–22. © 2013 Excellence in Education Journal. All rights reserved. Used by permission of the publisher.

Weiler, Kathleen. "Feminist Analysis of Gender and Schooling" in *Women Teaching for Change: Gender, Class and Power* by Kathleen Weiler, pp. 27–56. Copyright © 1988 by Bergin & Garvey. Reproduced with permission of Greenwood Publishing Group, Inc., Westport, CT.

Fine, Michelle and Sarah I. McClelland. "Sexuality Education and Desire: Still Missing After All These Years" in *Harvard Educational Review,* vol. 76.3, Fall 2006. pp. 297–338. © 2006, the President and Fellows of Harvard College. All rights reserved. Used by permission of the publisher.

Brock, Rochelle. "Recovering from 'Yo Mama Is So Stupid': (En)gendering a Critical Paradigm on Black Feminist Theory and Pedagogy" in *International Journal of Qualitative Studies in Education*, vol. 24.3, May–June 2011. pp. 379–396. © 2011 Taylor & Francis. Reprinted with permission from Routledge, a member of Taylor & Francis Books.

Page, Michelle L. "LGBTQ Inclusion as an Outcome of Critical Pedagogy" in *International Journal of Critical Pedagogy,* vol. 7.1, 2016 pp. 115–142. © 2016, the International Journal of Critical Pedagogy. All rights reserved. Used by permission of the publisher.

Bishop, Elizabeth. "Critical Literacy: Bringing Theory to Praxis" in *Journal of Curriculum Theorizing,* vol. 30.1, 2014 pp. 51–63. © 2014, Foundation for Curriculum Theory. All rights reserved. Used by permission of the publisher.

Peterson, Robert E., "Teaching How to Read the World and Change It" in *Literacy as Praxis: Culture, Language, and Pedagogy* edited by C. Walsh, pp. 156–182. Copyright © 1990 by Ablex. Reproduced with permission of Greenwood Publishing Group, Inc., Westport, CT.

Love, Bettina. "Oh, They're Sending a Bad Message" in *International Journal of Critical Pedagogy,* vol. 4.3, 2013 pp. 24–39. © 2016, the International Journal of Critical Pedagogy. All rights reserved. Used by permission of the publisher.

Morrell, Ernest. "Toward a Critical Pedagogy of Popular Culture: Literacy Development among Urban Youth" in *Journal of Adolescent & Adult Literacy,* vol. 46.1, September 2002. pp. 72–77. © 2002 International Reading Association. All rights reserved. Used by permission of the publisher.

Kahn, Richard and Douglas Kellner. "Reconstructing Technoliteracy: A Multiple Literacies Approach" in *E-Learning,* vol. 2.3 2005 pp. 238–251. This chapter appears with permission of the publisher ELearning © 2005. All rights reserved.

Kohl, Herbert. "I Won't Learn From You! Thoughts on the Role of Assent in Learning" in *Rethinking Schools* vol. 7.1 Autumn 1992. © 1992 Rethinking Schools. All rights reserved. Used by permission of the publisher.

Meyer, Elizabeth J. "A Feminist Reframing of Bullying and Harassment: Transforming Schools Through Critical Pedagogy" in *McGill Journal of Education* vol. 43.1 Winter 2008. pp. 33–48. © 2008 McGill University Faculty of Education. All rights reserved. Reprinted with permission.

Raible, John and Jason G. Irizarry. "Redirecting the Teacher's Gaze: Teacher Education, Youth Surveillance and the School-To-Prison Pipeline" in *Teaching and Teacher Education*, vol. 26, February 2010. pp. 1196–1203. © 2010 Elsevier Ltd. All rights reserved. Reprinted with permission.

Anderson, Robert C. "Teaching (with) Disability: Pedagogies of Lived Experience" in *Review of Education, Pedagogy, and Cultural Studies*, vol. 28.3–4, pp. 367–379. © 2006 Taylor & Francis. Reprinted with permission from Routledge, a member of Taylor & Francis Books.

Greene, Maxine "Teaching as Possibility: A Light in Dark Times" from *The Journal of Pedagogy, Pluralism & Practice*, Issue 1, vol.1: Spring 1997, pp. 1–11. A Publication of Lesley College, Cambridge, MA. Reprinted with permission.

Kincheloe, Joe L. "The Knowledges of Teacher Education: Developing a Critical Complex Epistemology" in *Teacher Education Quarterly*, Winter 2004, pp. 49–66. © 2004 the California Council on Teacher Education. All rights reserved. Used by permission of the publisher.

Douglas, Ty-Ron and Christine Nganga. "What's Radical Love Got To Do With It: Navigating Identity, Pedagogy, and Positionality in Pre-Service Education" in *International Journal of Critical Pedagogy*, vol. 5.1, 2013 pp. 58–82. © 2013, the International Journal of Critical Pedagogy. All rights reserved. Used by permission of the publisher.

Lynn, Marvin and Michael E. Jennings. "Power, Politics, and Critical Race Pedagogy: A Critical Race Analysis of Black Male Teachers' Pedagogy" in *Race Ethnicity and Education*, vol. 12.2, pp. 173–196. © 2009 Taylor & Francis. Reprinted with permission from Routledge, a member of Taylor & Francis Books.

Brosio, Richard A. "The Continuing Conflicts Between Capitalism and Democracy: Ramifications for Schooling-Education" in *Educational Philosophy and Theory*, vol. 23.2, pp. 30–45. © 1991 Taylor & Francis. Reprinted with permission from Routledge, a member of Taylor & Francis Books.

Lipman, Pauline, "Beyond Accountability: Toward Schools that Create New People for a New Way of Life" in *High Stakes Education: Inequality, Globalization, and Urban School Reform.* © 2004. pp 169–192. Reprinted with permission from Routledge, a member of Taylor & Francis Books.

De Lissovoy, Noah, Alex Means, and Kenneth Saltman. "Creating a Pedagogy in Common" from *Toward a New Common School Movement.* Paradigm Publishers, 2014. Reprinted with permission.

Ross, E. Wayne. "Broadening the Circle of Critical Pedagogy" from *Working for Social Justice Inside and Outside the Classroom.* Peter Lang, 2015. Reprinted with permission.

Index

Note: 'N' after a page number indicates a note.